THE OXFORD HANDBOOK OF
SWISS POLITICS

THE OXFORD HANDBOOK OF

SWISS POLITICS

Edited by
PATRICK EMMENEGGER,
FLAVIA FOSSATI, SILJA HÄUSERMANN,
YANNIS PAPADOPOULOS, PASCAL SCIARINI,
and
ADRIAN VATTER

OXFORD
UNIVERSITY PRESS

Great Clarendon Street, Oxford, OX2 6DP,
United Kingdom

Oxford University Press is a department of the University of Oxford.
It furthers the University's objective of excellence in research, scholarship,
and education by publishing worldwide. Oxford is a registered trade mark of
Oxford University Press in the UK and in certain other countries

© Oxford University Press 2024

The moral rights of the authors have been asserted

First Edition published in 2024

All rights reserved. No part of this publication may be reproduced, stored in
a retrieval system, or transmitted, in any form or by any means, without the
prior permission in writing of Oxford University Press, or as expressly permitted
by law, by licence or under terms agreed with the appropriate reprographics
rights organization. Enquiries concerning reproduction outside the scope of the
above should be sent to the Rights Department, Oxford University Press, at the
address above

You must not circulate this work in any other form
and you must impose this same condition on any acquirer

Published in the United States of America by Oxford University Press
198 Madison Avenue, New York, NY 10016, United States of America

British Library Cataloguing in Publication Data

Data available

Library of Congress Control Number: 2023937250

ISBN 978–0–19–287178–7

DOI: 10.1093/oxfordhb/9780192871787.001.0001

Printed and bound by
CPI Group (UK) Ltd, Croydon, CR0 4YY

Links to third party websites are provided by Oxford in good faith and
for information only. Oxford disclaims any responsibility for the materials
contained in any third party website referenced in this work.

Contents

Preface — ix
List of Illustrations — xi
List of Abbreviations — xvii
Notes on Contributors — xxv

1. Introduction — 1
   Patrick Emmenegger, Flavia Fossati, Silja Häusermann, Yannis Papadopoulos, Pascal Sciarini, and Adrian Vatter

PART I. FOUNDATIONS

2. Switzerland: A Paradigmatic Case of Political Integration — 15
   Wolf Linder and Sean Mueller

3. The Historical and Institutional Formation of Swiss Political Culture — 33
   Irène Herrmann

4. The Political Culture of Switzerland in Comparative Perspective — 50
   Markus Freitag and Alina Zumbrunn

5. The Structural Shifts in Switzerland's Economy and Society, 2000–2020 — 73
   Daniel Oesch

6. Switzerland's Position in Europe and the World — 94
   Thomas Bernauer and Stefanie Walter

7. The Ideological Space in Swiss Politics: Voters, Parties, and Realignment — 116
   Delia Zollinger and Denise Traber

PART II. INSTITUTIONS

8. Federalism — 139
   ADRIAN VATTER

9. Direct Democracy — 156
   ISABELLE STADELMANN-STEFFEN AND LUCAS LEEMANN

10. Parliament — 174
    STEFANIE BAILER AND SARAH BÜTIKOFER

11. Federal Government — 195
    YANNIS PAPADOPOULOS AND FRITZ SAGER

12. Judicial System — 214
    MARTINA FLICK WITZIG, CHRISTINE ROTHMAYR ALLISON, AND FRÉDÉRIC VARONE

PART III. CANTONS AND MUNICIPALITIES

13. Cantons — 235
    ADRIAN VATTER

14. Municipalities — 254
    ANDREAS LADNER AND NICOLAS KEUFFER

15. Metropolitan Areas — 276
    DANIEL KÜBLER

PART IV. ACTORS

16. Federal Administration — 299
    FRÉDÉRIC VARONE AND DAVID GIAUQUE

17. Parties and Party Systems — 317
    ANDREAS LADNER, DANIEL SCHWARZ, AND JAN FIVAZ

18. Interest Groups — 337
    ANDRÉ MACH AND STEVEN EICHENBERGER

19. Social Movements — 355
    MARCO GIUGNI

20. Media and Political Communication 372
REGULA HÄNGGLI FRICKER AND ALEXANDRA FEDDERSEN

PART V. ELECTIONS AND VOTES

21. National Elections 391
GEORG LUTZ AND ANKE TRESCH

22. Direct-Democratic Votes 410
PASCAL SCIARINI AND ANKE TRESCH

23. Digital Democracy 430
FABRIZIO GILARDI AND ALEXANDER H. TRECHSEL

PART VI. DECISION-MAKING PROCESSES

24. Decision-Making Process 451
PASCAL SCIARINI

25. Implementation and Evaluation of Public Policies 471
ANDREAS BALTHASAR

PART VII. PUBLIC POLICIES

26. Foreign Policy 491
LAURENT GOETSCHEL

27. Switzerland and the European Union 506
FABIO WASSERFALLEN

28. Security Policy and Politics 523
ANDREAS WENGER

29. Economic Policy 543
PATRICK EMMENEGGER

30. Banking and the Swiss Financial Centre 563
ROY GAVA

31. Infrastructure Policy: Transport and Energy 585
FRITZ SAGER AND DAVID KAUFMANN

32. Education Policy ANJA GIUDICI AND PATRICK EMMENEGGER	604
33. Research, Technology, and Innovation Policies LUKAS BASCHUNG AND JEAN-PHILIPPE LERESCHE	623
34. Environmental and Spatial Planning Policies KARIN INGOLD AND STÉPHANE NAHRATH	642
35. Migration Policy SANDRA LAVENEX	658
36. Integration Policy ANITA MANATSCHAL	677
37. Social Policy GIULIANO BONOLI AND FLAVIA FOSSATI	695
38. Health Policy PHILIPP TREIN, CHRISTIAN RÜEFLI, AND ADRIAN VATTER	714
39. Family Policy SILJA HÄUSERMANN AND RETO BÜRGISSER	733
40. Gender and Equality+ Policy ISABELLE ENGELI	753

PART VIII. EPILOGUE

41. Switzerland, *quo vadis*? Current Challenges and Potential Solutions for Swiss Politics RAHEL FREIBURGHAUS AND SEAN MUELLER	773
42. An Outside Perspective on Swiss Politics. How Successful Is Switzerland's Political System? HERBERT OBINGER	795
43. Chocolate Democracy DANIEL BOCHSLER	811
Index	831

Preface

The *Oxford Handbook of Swiss Politics* is the most comprehensive and up-to-date English language collection on Swiss politics. However, it did not emerge *ex nihilo*. Launched as early as in the 1980s as a four-volume bilingual (German/French) compendium, it was published under the title *Handbuch politisches System der Schweiz/ Manuel système politique de la Suisse*. Closer in its format to this *Handbook*, a *Handbuch der Schweizer Politik/Manuel de la politique suisse* appeared for the first time in a single volume in 1999, followed by several updated editions, with the last one published in 2022. The editors of that bilingual volume then approached Oxford University Press (OUP) and submitted a proposal for an *Oxford Handbook of Swiss Politics* mainly for two reasons. First, many features or even peculiarities of the Swiss political system (such as its direct-democratic and power-sharing institutions, its liberal-democratic corporatism, and its non-membership in the European Union) have received strong international attention. Second, several developments in Switzerland have foreshadowed similar trends across Western Europe, such as the early rise of right-wing populism, the transformation of the political left, and the ensuing strong party polarization. For both reasons, we are convinced that the Swiss case is of interest to a wider audience and has a strong added value for comparative research.

Our proposal received enthusiastic feedback from the reviewers and full support from Dominic Byatt of OUP, whom we would like to thank for efficiently handling our project. The chapter structure of the present *Handbook* largely follows the structure of the 2022 bilingual edition, but the chapters are by far not mere translations from German or French. Every chapter has been fundamentally rethought and enriched under the editors' guidance to study Switzerland from a comparative angle, speak to broader scholarly debates, and target an international audience. Moreover, the *Handbook* includes several new chapters to address major current developments that characterize the Swiss case in international comparison and a new epilogue with three reflective chapters on the relevance of the Swiss case in the landscape of developed Western economies.

We are obliged to NZZ Libro, who holds the rights for the edition of the *Handbuch/ Manuel* and granted permission to proceed with our project. We are also grateful for the funding that the Swiss Academy of Humanities and Social Sciences generously provided. Topped with funding from the research accounts of Silja Häusermann (University of Zurich) and Pascal Sciarini (University of Geneva), the Academy's very substantial contribution allowed us to entrust Martina Flick Witzig with the final scrutiny of chapter manuscripts. We are grateful for as well as impressed by her professionalism. We would also like to thank Saskia Buchmüller for layout support and Vicki Sunter for the flawless communication with OUP. The project of periodically publishing handbooks on the Swiss political system has been running since the beginning under the auspices of the Swiss Political Science Association. We are thankful for the association's continuous support.

It is with great sadness that we learned, while this *Handbook* was being prepared, of the death of our dear colleague Andreas Ladner, who was among the contributors. Andreas inspired and motivated several generations of political scientists with his enthusiasm, curiosity, and personal support. With his numerous works on political parties, municipalities, federalism, and public administration, Andreas always showed breadth of vision and intellectual creativity. He was a strongly appreciated colleague and instructor, and for many of us a close friend. We will miss him and wish to dedicate this *Handbook* to his memory.

We hope the *Oxford Handbook of Swiss Politics* has become what we wanted it to be—namely, a reference work that is easily accessible outside Switzerland and helpful for the general public to understand better some of the (seeming) peculiarities of this country and its value to comparative research.

Patrick Emmenegger, Flavia Fossati, Silja Häusermann,
Yannis Papadopoulos, Pascal Sciarini, and Adrian Vatter

Illustrations

Figures

4.1	Support for direct democracy, federalism, and consociationalism, 1981–2016	56
4.2	Satisfaction with democracy in comparative perspective, 2018	58
4.3	Technocracy in comparative perspective, 2017–2020	59
4.4	National pride in comparative perspective, 2017–2020	60
4.5	Trust in the government in comparative perspective, 2017–2020	62
4.6	Trust in the legal system in comparative perspective, 2018	63
4.7	Trust in political parties in comparative perspective, 2018	64
4.8	Party identification in comparative perspective, 2018	65
4.9	State interventionism in comparative perspective, 2019	66
4.10	Attitudes towards openness in foreign policy, the EU, and the environment, 1993–2019	67
5.1	Annual changes in GDP, GDP per capita, and population in Switzerland (in per cent)	75
5.2	Contribution of demand components to real GDP growth in Switzerland	76
5.3	Net migration (immigration minus emigration) in Switzerland, number of persons 1945–2020	78
5.4	Foreign resident population in Switzerland by nationality	78
5.5	Number of new immigrants (aged 20–64) to Switzerland per year, by education	79
5.6	Highest completed education of the population aged 25–64 (in per cent), 1996–2020	81
5.7	Highest level of education completed by the resident population aged 25–34	81
5.8	Employment in different sectors as proportion of total employment, 1991–2019	83

5.9	Change in the number of employed persons with Swiss nationality by social class	86
5.10	Annual change in wages and consumer prices in Switzerland (in per cent)	88
5.11	Share of pre-tax national income going to the bottom 50 per cent and top 10 per cent of Switzerland's adult population	89
6.1	Average degree of democracy (Polity IV-Score) in 1900–2018	95
6.2	Per capita income, 1980–2018 (in US$, 2010 exchange rate)	97
6.3	Ambitious environmental policy, competitiveness, and ecological innovation	98
6.4	Military spending as a percentage of GDP, 1988–2018	99
6.5	Expenditure for development assistance as a percentage of GDP (2017)	100
6.6	Switzerland's most important trading partners (2018)	102
6.7	Population by migration status (2018), permanent resident population ≥ age 15	103
6.8	Degree of globalization according to de jure KOF Globalization Index, 1970–2019	104
6.9	Support for foreign policy openness, percentage of respondents	108
7.1	Expansion of tertiary education	119
7.2	Occupational change	120
7.3	Educational composition of major Swiss parties	121
7.4	Evolution of voter preferences	123
7.5	Evolution of issue salience: most important issue	126
7.6	The Swiss two-dimensional political space over time (distance from the party-system mean, standardized)	127
7.7	The main Swiss parties in the two-dimensional political space of Western Europe	129
9.1	Lines show the moving averages (± four years) of votes per year	161
9.2	Direct democracy in the representative cantons, 1848–2015	165
9.3	Subnational Index of Direct Democracy (snDDI) according to Leemann and Stadelmann-Steffen (2022)	167
10.1	Party-political composition Federal Assembly/Federal Council compared to party preferences	180
10.2	Institutional Power of Parliament Index	184
10.3	Average length of stay in parliament in years	186
10.4	Interest group organizations of National Councillors and Councillors of States over time	187

12.1	Administrative law claims	216
14.1	Performance limits by municipality size (1994 and 2017)	256
14.2	Profiles of municipal autonomy in the cantons of AR, ZH, NE, and GE	258
14.3	Average size of the executive branch by size of municipality	266
14.4	Average voter turnout for communal, cantonal, and national elections by municipality size (2017)	268
15.1	Large urban regions (dark) and metropolitan areas (light)	279
17.1	Voter shares of the five largest parties, 1919–2019 (in per cent)	322
17.2	Effective number of parties at national level and mean value of the effective number of parties in the cantons	324
17.3	Volatility of the Swiss party system, National Council elections and mean value of cantonal parliamentary elections (in per cent)	325
17.4	Political profiles of CVP, FDP, SVP, SP, GPS, and GLP	331
20.1	Actors and interactions in political communication	373
20.2	Main source of political information	381
21.1	Turnout in national elections and popular votes, 1919–2019	396
21.2	Share of votes in the National Council, 1919–2019	397
21.3	Share of seats in the Council of States, 1919–2019	399
22.1	Success rate of federal authorities and number of direct-democratic votes, 1850–2020	413
22.2	Success rate of federal authorities by direct-democratic institutions, 1947–2019	414
23.1	Number of ongoing WeCollect projects over time	436
23.2	Number of signatures for national WeCollect projects, over time	436
29.1	Swiss unemployment rate (in per cent), 1920–2018	547
29.2	Real GDP growth (in per cent), 1965–2019	547
29.3	Swiss public debt (in per cent of GDP), 1973–2019	548
29.4	Currency exchange rates, yearly average, in Swiss francs, 1999–2021	551
29.5	Swiss National Bank balance sheet (in million CHF), December 1996 to January 2022	551
29.6	Employment rate by gender (in per cent of population aged 15-64), 1991–2020	557
30.1	Size of the financial industry	565
30.2	National banking sectors: size and concentration	566
30.3	Diversity in the Swiss banking sector	568

30.4	Stock of financial regulation	575
30.5	Media coverage to actors of Swiss financial regulation	577
30.6	Congruence between SBA and parliamentary groups, 2017–2021	579
31.1	Density of rail network in OECD countries	587
31.2	Density of road network in OECD countries	587
31.3	Movements in Swiss passenger transport, 1970–2018	589
31.4	Share of rail passengers and road passengers in OECD countries	589
31.5	Gross energy consumption 1910–2019 (SFOE 2019a)	594
33.1	Position of the Swiss R&I system actors	629
33.2	R&D Intensity (per cent of Gross Domestic Product) in international comparison	635
35.1	Share of foreigners in the total permanent resident population since the end of December 1900 (in per cent)	659
35.2	Immigration, family reunification, emigration, and naturalizations, 1988–2020	660
35.3	Asylum applications at the end of the year, 1996–2019	668
36.1	Two-dimensional typology of immigrant integration policy regimes	679
36.2	Integration policies in Western Europe	680
37.1	Compulsory private and public social expenditure in Switzerland and OECD average as a percentage of GDP, 2017	696
38.1	Swiss health expenditure in a comparative perspective	715
38.2	Stringency of public health regulation during the Covid-19 crisis	716
39.1	Public expenditure by type of family policy (in per cent of GDP 2017)	736
39.2	Total family benefits for two children (aged 6 and 9) as a per cent of average full-time earnings, 2018	737
39.3	Length of statutory paid maternity and parental leave for women after birth (in weeks)	738
39.4	Public expenditure on childcare (as a per cent of GDP)	739
39.5	Out-of-pocket childcare costs for a two-earner two-child family, 2021	740
39.6	Cantonal childcare coverage rate for children of pre-school age, 2015–2017	744
41.1	Turnout in cantonal parliamentary elections and referendums, 1976 and 1978—March 2022 (in per cent)	775
41.2	Development of (de-)centralization in Switzerland, 1850–2010	776
41.3	Readiness for 'Frontier Technologies' Index, 2021	778
41.4	KOF Globalisation Index—Switzerland vs. EU-27, 1970–2021	779
41.5	Combined seat share of pole parties across key federal institutions, 1919–2021 (in per cent)	781

41.6	The most pressing challenges (for experts)	783
41.7	Predefined challenges, as assessed by experts	783
41.8	Swiss institutions that experts regard as most in need of reform (weighted)	786
41.9	Swiss actors and processes that experts regard as most in need of reform (weighted)	787
41.10	Swiss policy areas that experts regard as most in need of reform (weighted)	788
42.1	Having a say in what the government does, ca. 2018	797
42.2	Gini coefficient (after taxes and transfers) and tax ratio 2017 in twenty OECD countries	806
42.3	Trust in Government in OECD Countries, ca. 2018	806
43.1	What citizens expect from democracy	813
43.2	The size of federal countries and their (median) autonomous units, global comparison	822

Tables

2.1	Proportional representation of linguistic groups (in per cent)	20
2.2	Use of the proportional rule: institutions and criteria	26
5.1	Share of occupational classes in total employment, 1991/2 and 2018/9	85
6.1	Economic freedom according to the Index of Economic Freedom (2020)	96
8.1	Popular votes with conflicting popular and cantonal majorities	144
9.1	Referendums and popular initiatives, 1848–2021	160
12.1	Constitutional review in comparison	218
13.1	Overview of the most important popular rights in the cantons (status: 2019)	243
14.1	Resident population in municipalities by canton, 2018	260
14.2	Execution of municipal tasks internally (grouped by percentage of municipalities performing tasks themselves in the specified areas of responsibility)	263
14.3	Number of municipalities per canton in 2020 and difference with 1990	271
15.1	The ten largest Swiss metropolitan areas	278
15.2	Institutional fragmentation of major metropolitan areas, international comparison (data for metropolitan areas over 200,000 inhabitants for the year 2000 or near)	281
15.3	Centrality charges of core cities and surrounding municipalities in Swiss metropolitan areas in 2013, indexed (mean of all municipalities in the same canton [excluding core cities] = 100)	282

15.4	City-suburb amalgamations in Swiss metropolitan areas since 1893	285
16.1	Evolution of the workforce (full-time, permanent employees)	302
16.2	Distribution of employees and expenditure (in billions of Swiss francs) by department, 2018	303
16.3	Services that have answered directly to department heads, 1928–2018	304
20.1	Most important print and online media by language region, 2022	377
22.1	Frequency of direct-democratic votes, 1848–2020	412
22.2	Voters' sources of information (in per cent)	416
23.1	Percentage of candidates with social media accounts (2019 national elections)	432
23.2	Top ten WeCollect projects by number of signatures	437
24.1	Importance of decision-making phases (percentage of interview partners who mention a specific sub-phase as 'one of the three most important')	454
24.2	Initiation of decision-making processes (in per cent)	456
24.3	Percentage of legislative acts that gave rise to a pre-parliamentary procedure	458
24.4	Duration of decision-making processes, in total and by phase (in months)	459
24.5	Percentage of voting recommendations running counter to the Federal Council (number of votes in parenthesis)	463
27.1	Votes on EU proposals with the 'yes' percentages for voters	516
30.1	Main BIAs of the Swiss financial sector	573
33.1	*Intramuros* research and development expenditures (in billion CHF) in Switzerland according to the activity sector, 2000–2019	636
33.2	Swiss universities' places in international rankings	637
34.1	The different categories of substantive environmental policy instruments	649
34.2	Current status (2018) of implementation of key environmental policies	652
35.1	Development of the right of residence and right of establishment	664
35.2	Federal popular initiatives around migration policy since 1968	666
36.1	Federal popular initiatives in the field of integration and citizenship policy since 1968	685
37.1	Political institutions and delay in the adoption of the main social laws	700
37.2	Statistics on relative poverty (per cent) in Switzerland compared to the EU average	708
38.1	Main reforms regarding health insurance and public health in Switzerland	720
39.1	Participation rates in formal childcare rates (0 to 2 year olds) by income (2019)	741
42.1	An international comparative look at Switzerland	800

Abbreviations

ABRS	Association of Regional Swiss Banks
ACS	Automobile Club of Switzerland
AFMP	Agreement on the Free Movement of Persons
AG	Argovia
AI	Appenzell Inner-Rhodes
AIG	Foreign Nationals and Integration Act
AMAS	Asset Management Association
AMLCA	Anti-Money Laundering Control Authority
ANAG	Federal Act on the Residence and Settlement of Foreigners
AR	Appenzell Outer-Rhodes
ARE	Federal Office for Spatial Development
armasuisse	Federal Office for Defence Procurement
ART	Assisted Reproductive Technology
Art./art.	Article
ASTAG	Swiss Road Transport Association
AuG	Federal Act on Foreign Nationals—Foreign Nationals Act
AUS	Australia
AUT	Austria
AVES	Campaign for Sensible Energy Policy Switzerland
BAKOM	Federal Office of Communications
BDP	Conservative Democratic Party (Bürgerlich-Demokratische Partei)
BE	Bern
BEL	Belgium
BFF	Federal Office for Refugees
BFM	Federal Office for Migration
BFS	Federal Statistical Office
BG	Border Guard Corps
BGB	Party of Farmers, Traders and Independents
BGE	Collection of the Federal Supreme Court's Decisions

BIA	Business interest association
BIGA	Federal Office for Industry, Trade, and Labour
BL	Basle-Country
BS	Basel-City
BüG	Swiss Citizenship Act
c.f.	compare
CAN	Canada
CEDAW	Convention on the Elimination of All Forms of Discrimination Against Women
CERN	European Organization for Nuclear Research
CH	Switzerland
CHF	Swiss Francs
CHL	Chile
CLUP	Communal Land Use Plan
CMP	Cantonal Master Plan
COFF	Federal Commission for the Coordination of Family Affairs
COL	Colombia
CP	Convention-Programs
CSCE	Conference on Security and Cooperation in Europe
CSDE	Swiss Conference of Gender Equality Delegates
CSP	Christian Social Party (Christlich-soziale Partei der Schweiz)
CTP	Coordinated Transport Policy
CVP	Christian Democratic People's Party (Christlichdemokratische Volkspartei)
CZE	Czech Republic
DDPS	Federal Department of Defence, Civil Protection, and Sport
DETEC	Federal Department of the Environment, Transport, Energy, and Communications
DIL	Directorate for International Law
DNK	Denmark
DP	Democratic Party
e.g.	for example
EAER	Department of Economic Affairs, Education, and Research
EC	European Community
ECHR	European Convention on Human Rights

EDK	Conference of Cantonal Ministers of Education (Konferenz der kantonalen Erziehungsdirektoren)
EDU	Federal Democratic Union of Switzerland
EEA	European Environment Agency
EEA	European Economic Area
EFTA	European Free Trade Association
EKM	Federal Commission on Migration
EKR	Federal Commission against Racism
EMBO	European Molecular Biology Organization
EPA	Federal Act on the Protection of the Environment
EPFL	Federal Institute of Technology Lausanne
ESA	Electricity Supply Act
ESP	Spain
EST	Estonia
etc.	et cetera
ETHZ	Federal Institute of Technology Zürich
EU	European Union
Euratom	European Atomic Energy Community
FABI	Financing and Expansion of the Railway Infrastructure
FC	Federal Constitution
FCWI	Federal Commission for Women's Issues
FDF	Federal Department of Finance
FDFA	Federal Department of Foreign Affairs
FDHA	Federal Department of Home Affairs
FDI	Foreign Direct Investment
FDJP	Federal Department of Justice and Police
FDK	Swiss Conference of Cantonal Directors of Finance (Konferenz der kantonalen Finanzdirektorinnen und Finanzdirektoren)
FDP	Free Democratic Party—Liberal Party (Freisinnig-Demokratische Partei)
fedpol	Federal Office of Police
FEDRO	Federal Roads Office
FFA	Federal Finance Administration
FIN	Finland
FINMA	Swiss Financial Markets Supervisory Authority
FIT	Federal Institute of Technology
FITSU	Federal IT Steering Unit

FMD	Federal Military Department
FOCBS	Federal Office for Customs and Border Security
FOCJ	Functional Overlapping Competing Jurisdictions
FOCP	Federal Office for Civil Protection
FOEN	Federal Office for the Environment
FOGE	Federal Office for Gender Equality
FOPI	Federal Office of Private Insurance
FOT	Federal Office of Transport
FR	Freiburg
FRA	France
FSC	Federal Supreme Court
FSO	Federal Statistical Office
G7	Group of Seven
GAL-TAN	'Green Alternative Libertarians' and 'Traditionalist Authoritarian Nationalists'
GATT	General Agreement on Tariffs and Trade
GDK	Conference of the Cantonal Ministers of Public Health (Konferenz der kantonalen Gesundheitsdirektorinnen und Gesundheitsdirektoren)
GDP	Gross Domestic Product
GE	Geneva
GEA	Federal Gender Equality Act
GER	Germany
GFC	Global Financial Crisis
GL	Glarus
GLP	Green Liberal Party (Grünliberale Partei)
GMEB	Management by Performance Mandate and Budget Envelope
GPS	Green Party of Switzerland (Grüne Partei der Schweiz)
GR	Grisons
GRC	Greece
HarmoS	Intercantonal Agreement on the Harmonization of Compulsory Schooling
HDI	Human Development Index
HGVC	Heavy Goods Vehicle Charge
HUN	Hungary
i.e.	id est, that is
ibid.	ibidem, in the same place
ICT	Information and Communications Technology

IHL	International Humanitarian Law
Innosuisse	Swiss Innovation Agency
IRL	Ireland
ISCED	International Standard Classification of Education
ISCO	International Standard Classification of Occupations
ISL	Iceland
ISR	Israel
IT	Information Technology
ITA	Italy
JPN	Japan
JU	Jura
KdK	Conference of Cantonal Governments (Konferenz der Kantonsregierungen)
KOR	Republic of Korea
LdU	Alliance of Independents (Landesring der Unabhängigen)
LGTBQ	lesbian, gay, bisexual, transgender, queer
LOA	Federal Act on the Organisation and Management of the Federal Council and Federal Administration
LOGA	Law on the Organisation of Government and Administration
LOS	Lesbian Organization Switzerland
LP	Liberal Party
LPers	Federal Personnel Law
LTU	Lithuania
LU	Lucerne
LUX	Luxembourg
LVA	Latvia
MCG	Geneva Citizens' Movement (Mouvement Citoyens Genevois)
MCP	Multiculturalism Policy Index
MEX	Mexico
MP	Member of Parliament
NA	National Action (Nationale Aktion für Volk und Heimat)
NAF	National Road and Agglomeration Transport Fund
NATO	North-Atlantic Treaty Organization
NCS	National strategy for the protection of Switzerland against cyber risks
NCSC	National Cyber Security Center
NE	Neuenburg

NEA	Nuclear Energy Act
NFA	National Fiscal Equalization and Task-Sharing between the Federation and the cantons
NGO	Non-Governmental Organization
NLD	The Netherlands
NMG	New Management Model
NOR	Norway
NPM	New Public Management
NRLA	Federal Decree on the Construction of the New Transalpine Rail Link
NRP	National Research Programmes
NW	Nidwalden
NZ	New Zealand
OASI	Old-Age and Survivors' Insurance
OECD	Organisation for Economic Co-operation and Development
OSCE	Organization for Security and Co-operation in Europe
OUP	Oxford University Press
OW	Obwalden
p., pp.	page, pages
para.	Paragraph
PET	Professional Vocational Education and Training
PISA	Programme for International Student Assessment
PITF	Integrated Task and Financial Plan
PMSC	Private Military Security Companies
POCH	Progressive Organizations of Switzerland (Progressive Organisationen der Schweiz)
POL	Poland
PPDB	Political Party Database
PR	Proportional Representation
PRT	Portugal
PTT	Swiss Postal Telegraph and Telephone Agency
PYLL	Potential years of life lost
R&D	Research and Development
R&I	Research and Innovation
RGA	Reform of Government and Administration
RIF	Rail Infrastructure Fund

RIPA	Federal Act on the Promotion of Research and Innovation
SBA	Swiss Bankers' Association
SBB	Swiss Federal Railways (Schweizerische Bundesbahnen)
SDC	Swiss Agency for Development and Cooperation
SDES	Society for the Development of the Swiss Economy
SECO	State Secretariat for Economic Affairs
Selects	Swiss Election Study
seq.	the following
SERI	State Secretariat for Education, Research, and Innovation
SFBC	Swiss Federal Banking Commission
SFOE	Swiss Federal Office of Energy
SG	St Gallen
SGB	Swiss Federation of Trade Unions (Schweizerischer Gewerkschaftsbund)
SGI	Sustainable Governance Indicators
SH	Schaffhausen
SIF	State Secretariat for International Financial Matters
SME	Small and medium-sized enterprise
SNB	Swiss National Bank
snDDI	Subnational Index of Direct Democracy
SNSF	Swiss National Science Foundation
SO	Solothurn
SP	Social Democratic Party (Sozialdemokratische Partei)
SPA	Federal Act on Spatial Planning
SR	Systematic Compilation of Federal Legislation
SVK	Slovakia
SVN	Slovenia
SVP	Swiss People's Party (Schweizerische Volkspartei)
SWE	Sweden
SZ	Schwyz
TAK	Tripartite Agglomeration Conference
TCS	Touring Club of Switzerland
TG	Thurgovia
TI	Ticino
TRTA	Federal Act on Road Transit Traffic in the Alpine Region
TUR	Turkey

UAS	Universities of Applied Sciences
UBCS	Association of Swiss Cantonal Banks (Union des Banques Cantonales Suisses)
UK	United Kingdom
UN	United Nations
UNI	Universities
UPS	Swiss Employers' Association
UR	Uri
US—USA	United States (of America)
USAM	Swiss Industry and Trade Association
USCI	Swiss Federation of Commerce and Industry (economiesuisse since 2000)
USP	Swiss Farmers' Unions
USS	Swiss Federation of Trade Unions
UTE	Universities of Teacher Education
VAA	Voting Advice Application
VD	Vaud
VET	Vocational Education and Training
VIntA	Ordinance on the Integration of Foreign Nationals
VOC	Volatile Organic Compounds
VS	Valais
vs.	versus
WEA	Armed Forces Development Programme
WWF	World Wildlife Fund For Nature
WWI—WWII	First/Second World War
ZG	Zug
ZH	Zurich

Notes on Contributors

Stefanie Bailer is a professor of political science at the University of Basel. Her research interests are parliamentarism and in particular decision-making by parliamentarians, party group discipline, and careers, as well as international decision-making and negotiations, in particular in the EU and other negotiations. She is currently analysing social media use by politicians and voters' perceptions of it, as well as voters' trust in politicians. Her work has appeared in journals such as *British Journal of Political Science*, *European Journal of Political Research*, *European Union Politics*, *Electoral Studies*, and *Legislative Studies Quarterly*.

Andreas Balthasar is a titular professor at the University of Lucerne. Balthasar is also a senior consultant in Interface Policy Studies Research Consulting, a company he founded in Lucerne. From 2000 to 2008 he was president of the Swiss Evaluation Society SEVAL. His work focuses on evaluation research, evidence-informed policy-making, and policy analysis. Among his publications are 'Critical Friend Approach: Policy Evaluation Between Methodological Soundness, Practical Relevance, and Transparency of the Evaluation Process' (*German Policy Studies* 7(3), 2011), 'Energy Transition in Europe and the United States: Policy Entrepreneurs and Veto Players in Federalist Systems' (with Miranda A. Schreurs and Frédéric Varone, *Journal of Environment & Development*, 2019).

Lukas Baschung is an associate professor at Haute école de gestion Arc (HEG Arc) in Neuchâtel, which is part of the University of Applied Sciences and Arts Western Switzerland/HES-SO. He teaches public management and works on research topics in the field of public quality management, strategy and collaborative management, and local economic development as well as higher education and research policies. In addition, he is head of a Masters major programme, 'Business in Eurasia'. Recently, he published a contribution on the strategic collaboration of large Swiss municipalities in *Local Government Studies* (together with Jérôme Heim).

Thomas Bernauer is a professor of political science at ETH Zurich in Switzerland. He was the founding director of ETH Zurich's Institute of Science, Technology and Policy (ISTP) and is a lead author in IPCC working group II. His research focuses on environmental policy and international trade issues, based on macro-level quantitative research, micro-level survey embedded experiments, case study research, and interaction with policymakers and stakeholders. He has published around 150 articles, mainly in political science and environmental sciences journals, received an ERC Advanced

Grant, and received the American Political Science Associations' Elinor Ostrom career achievement award.

Daniel Bochsler is an associate professor of nationalism studies and political science at Central European University (CEU) in Vienna, a professor of political science at the University of Belgrade, and Privatdozent at the University of Zurich. His research deals primarily with political institutions in heterogeneous societies, with a regional focus on Central and Eastern Europe. He has worked on Swiss politics, in particular on federalism and on elections. His recent work has been published in, among others, *Comparative Political Studies* and the *European Journal of Political Research*.

Giuliano Bonoli is a professor of social policy at the Swiss graduate school for public administration at the University of Lausanne. He has been involved in several national and international research projects on social policies. His work has focused on pension reform, the labour market, and family polices. He has published some fifty articles in journals such as *Politics & Society, Journal of European Public Policy, European Sociological Review*, and *Journal of European Social Policy*.

Reto Bürgisser is a postdoctoral researcher at the Department of Political Science at the University of Zurich. He holds a PhD from the European University Institute (EUI). His research focuses on the politics of welfare state recalibration in Continental and southern Europe, fiscal and environmental policy preferences, technological change, and growth models. More information can be found here: www.retobuergisser.com.

Sarah Bütikofer is a political scientist with a focus on Swiss politics and parliamentary research. Since 2015, she has been the editor-in-chief of DeFacto, the online knowledge platform of Swiss political sciences, which is part of the Swiss Political Science Association. She teaches courses on Swiss politics and science communication for social scientists at various institutions, including the universities of Basel, Zurich, and ETH Zurich. She also conducts research projects on Swiss politics, legislative behaviour, professionalization, and the political careers of parliamentarians, and acts in various roles for the communication of research results from political science.

Steven Eichenberger is a lecturer at the Department of Political Science and International Relations of the University of Geneva. His research focuses on Swiss politics, interest groups, and legislative organization. His research has been published in, among others, *Party Politics, Governance* and the *Swiss Political Science Review*.

Patrick Emmenegger is a professor of comparative political economy and public policy at the University of St Gallen in Switzerland. His research focuses on the political economy of welfare and skills, labour market regulation, industrial relations, democratization, state-building, the politics of taxation, and institutional theory. He has published *The Age of Dualization: The Changing Face of Inequality in Deindustrializing Societies* (2012, Oxford University Press) and *The Power to Dismiss: Trade Unions and the Regulation of Job Security in Western Europe* (2014, Oxford University Press).

Isabelle Engeli is a professor of public policy at the Department of Social and Political Sciences, Philosophy, and Anthropology at the University of Exeter. She leads, with Amy Mazur, the Research Network on Gender Equality Policy in Practice, which investigates the politics of implementing gender equality in the corporate world in Europe and North America. Her research appears in journals such as *European Journal of Political Research*, *European Journal of Politics and Gender*, *Journal of European Public Policy*, *Regulation & Governance*, *Revue Française de Science Politics*, and *West European Politics*. She is editor-in-chief of the *European Journal of Political Research*, and founding editor of the *European Journal of Politics and Gender*.

Alexandra Feddersen studied political science at the University of Geneva and has been an assistant professor in political communication and media at the University of Fribourg since 2019. In her research, she is mainly interested in the communication strategies of political parties, as well as in the interactions between the elites and public opinion. She has published her (co-authored) work on the (in)stability of voters' issue-ownership perceptions, political parties' strategies when communicating position changes, public opinion cueing, and backlash effects in response to party messages in several leading scientific journals in the field (e.g. *Political Communication*, *Party Politics*, and *Electoral Studies*).

Jan Fivaz is a research associate at the KPM Centre for Public Management at the University of Bern and at the Bern University of Applied Sciences (BFH Wirtschaft). He is a co-founder of the online voting advice application 'smartvote'. He worked for several research projects funded by the Swiss National Science Foundation on digital democracy, digital decision-making, and political parties. Beyond that, his research interests include electoral research and democratic representation. He is co-author of several publications about voting advice applications and digital democracy as well as co-editor of the book *Political Representation. Roles, Representatives and the Represented* (2016, Routledge).

Martina Flick Witzig is a postdoc at the Institute of Political Science, University of Bern. She teaches and conducts research on party systems, direct democracy, the Swiss militia system, and the interplay of democracy and the rule of law. Her research has been published in *Politics* and the *Swiss Political Science Review*, as well as in various edited volumes and monographs.

Flavia Fossati is an assistant professor of inequality and integration studies at the University of Lausanne (Switzerland) and at the Swiss Centre of Expertise in Life Course Research (CIR-LIVES). Previously, she has been appointed as an assistant professor of social policy at the University of Vienna. She has been a visiting fellow at EUI and Malmö University. Her research interests include social and immigration policies, deservingness and welfare state chauvinism, and survey experiments. Her research is published in, among others, *Cambridge University Press*, *European Sociological Review*, *Socio-Economic Review*, and *International Migration Review*. More information can be found here: https://orcid.org/0000-0002-9218-5422.

Rahel Freiburghaus is a postdoctoral researcher at the Institute of Political Science, University of Bern. She specializes in Swiss politics, federalism, and subnational lobbying, as well as in the comparative study of political institutions and democracy, respectively. Her research has appeared in *West European Politics*, *Democratization*, and *Regional & Federal Studies*, among other journals. She is currently co-editing a *Handbook of Comparative Political Institutions* that brings together both leading authorities in the field and up-and-coming academics. She teaches courses on the challenges facing Swiss politics, as well as potential solutions that operate at the science-policy interface, addressing students, established scholars, and practitioners alike.

Markus Freitag is a full professor of political sociology and political psychology at the Institute of Political Science, University of Bern. He has published on trust, social capital, volunteering, direct democracy, war time experiences, political behaviour and attitudes, emotions, and personality in, among others, the *British Journal of Political Science*, *Comparative Politics*, *Comparative Political Studies*, *European Journal of Political Research*, *European Union Politics*, *Journal of Conflict Resolution*, *Journal of Politics*, *Journal of Ethnic and Migration Studies*, *Political Behavior*, *Public Opinion Quarterly*, and *West European Politics*.

Roy Gava is an assistant professor in business and politics at the School of Economics and Political Science of the University of St Gallen. His research interests include comparative public policy, financial regulation, and interest groups. His work has appeared in, among others, *European Journal of Political Research*, *West European Politics*, *Political Science Research and Methods*, and *Regulation & Governance*.

David Giauque is a full professor of public management and human resources management at the Swiss Graduate School of Public Administration (University of Lausanne). A political scientist and sociologist by training, he teaches and conducts research mainly on the following topics: human resources management in the public sector; well-being and performance; high performance HR practices; new ways of working; and organizational regulation. He is the author of numerous books and scientific articles on these different themes.

Fabrizio Gilardi is a professor of policy analysis in the Department of Political Science at the University of Zurich. His research agenda focuses on the implications of digital technology for politics and democracy, which he studies particularly in the context of the ERC Advanced Grant 'Problem Definition in the Digital Democracy' (PRODIGI, 2021-2025). His work has been published in journals such as the *American Journal of Political Science*, *British Journal Political Science*, *Political Communication*, and *Proceedings of the National Academy of Sciences*. His latest book is *Digital Technology, Politics, and Policy-Making* (Elements in Public Policy Series, Cambridge University Press, 2022).

Anja Giudici is a lecturer (assistant professor) in education at the School for Education, Communication and Language Sciences at Newcastle University. She previously worked as a postdoctoral research fellow at the Department of Politics and International

Relations at the University of Oxford. Her research focuses broadly on the politics and history of education systems. Her work on the politics of education and its interactions with educational stakeholders such as teachers and parents has been published in journals including the *Journal of Education Policy*, *Comparative Politics*, and the *European Educational Research Journal*.

Marco Giugni is a professor in the Department of Political Science and International Relations and director of the Institute of Citizenship Studies (InCite) at the University of Geneva. His research focuses on social movements and political participation. He recently co-edited, together with Maria Grasso, *The Oxford Handbook of Political Participation* (Oxford University Press 2022).

Laurent Goetschel is Director of Swisspeace and Professor of Political Science at the University of Basel. He directed a Swiss National Science Foundation's research program on Swiss foreign policy from 1997 to 2000 and served as the political advisor of Swiss Minister for Foreign Affairs Micheline Calmy-Rey from 2003 to 2004. He is a member of the Swiss Commission for Research Partnerships with Developing Countries of the Swiss Academy of Sciences.

Regula Hänggli Fricker is a Professor in Political Communication at the University of Fribourg. She was previously a professor at Amsterdam School of Communication Research (ASCoR). Her research interests include political communication in a comparative perspective, (digital) democracy, the role of media and communication, and societal aspects of digital transformation. Her published work deals with the shaping of public debates on unemployment (Cambridge University Press), the origin of dialogue in the news media (Palgrave), the framing of debates on Islam, or ethics of smart cities.

Silja Häusermann is a professor of political science at the University of Zurich. She studies welfare state politics and party system change in advanced capitalist democracies. She directs the ERC project, 'welfarepriorities' and is the co-director of the UZH University Research Priority Programme 'Equality of Opportunity'. She is the co-editor of *The Politics of Advanced Capitalism* (Cambridge University Press 2015) and *The World Politics of Social Investment* Vols I and II (Oxford University Press 2022). More information can be found here: www.siljahaeusermann.org.

Irène Herrmann is a full professor of Swiss transnational history at the University of Geneva, having graduated there in both Russian and history. She was visiting professor at the University Laval (Canada), lecturer at the Graduate Institute of International Studies (Geneva), fellow from the SNF at the Russian State University for Humanities (Moscow), and SNF professor at the University of Fribourg. She has published more than 150 scientific articles, ten edited books, and five monographs. Her work focuses mainly on solidarity, humanitarianism, conceptual history, conflict management, and the political uses of the past in Switzerland and in post-Soviet Russia.

Karin Ingold is a professor of policy analysis with a focus on the environment at the Institute of Political Science at the University of Bern. She is vice-president of the

Oeschger Center for Climate Research at the University of Bern and heads a research group at Eawag, the ETH Domain's water research institute in Dübendorf. In her research, she is interested in decision-making processes around climate change, energy, sustainability, and other areas and has published in journals like *Science*, *Nature Climate Change*, *Policy Studies Journal*, and the *Journal of Public Administration Research and Theory*.

David Kaufmann is an assistant professor of spatial development and urban policy at ETH Zürich. His research examines the intersections of public policy, urban politics, spatial planning, and migration studies. David Kaufmann studied political science at the University of Zürich and the University of Lund. He obtained his PhD from the University of Bern. He was guest researcher at Leiden University, Virginia Tech, University of Ottawa, and University of Toronto. His work has been published in journals such as *PNAS*, *Public Administration Review*, *British Journal of Political Science*, *Governance*, and *Urban Studies*.

Nicolas Keuffer works as a senior research fellow at IDHEAP, University of Lausanne. His research areas include local autonomy in Europe and Switzerland, local politics, intergovernmental relations, decentralization, and institutional and administrative reforms. He is the co-author of *Zustand und Entwicklung der Schweizer Gemeinden. Ergebnisse des nationalen Gemeindemonitorings 2017* (Somedia 2020) or *Patterns of Local Autonomy in Europe* (Palgrave Macmillan 2019). His research has been published in, among others, *Local Government Studies*, *Regional & Federal Studies*, and *International Review of Administrative Sciences*.

Daniel Kübler has been a professor at the Department of Political Science at the University of Zurich since 2009 and co-directs the Centre for Democracy Studies in Aarau. He has held visiting positions at the University of Constance, the University of New South Wales, and Science Po Paris. His research interests are urban and metropolitan politics and governance, democracy and democratic innovations, and public policy analysis and evaluation, as well as representative bureaucracy. On the subject of his chapter in this *Handbook*, he co-authored 'Inequality and governance in the metropolis' (2017, Palgrave Macmillan, co-edited with Jefferey M. Sellers, Marta Arretche, and Eran Razin), 'The political ecology of the metropolis' (2013, ECPR Press, co-edited with Jefferey M. Sellers, Melanie Walter-Rogg, and R. Alan Walks), and 'Metropolitan governance' (2005, Routledge, co-edited with Hubert Heinelt) as well as articles recently published in *Comparative European Politics*, *Territory Politics Governance*, *Urban Affairs Review*, *Journal of Urban Affairs*, and *Urban Research and Practice*.

Andreas Ladner was a full professor for Swiss political institutions and public administration at the Swiss Graduate School of Public Administration (IDHEAP) at the University of Lausanne. His areas of research included the quality of democracy, local government, institutional change, political parties, and voting advice applications. He conducted several major research projects of the Swiss National Science Foundation and authored books and articles on these topics. He was co-author of the books *Size* *and Local Democracy* (Edward Elgar 2014) and *Patterns of Local Autonomy in Europe* (Palgrave Macmillan 2019).

Sandra Lavenex is a professor of European and international politics at the University of Geneva and a visiting professor at the Collège d'Europe. Her current research focuses on European and international migration policy, EU external relations, and differentiated regional integration. More information can be found here: https://www.unige.ch/sciences-societe/speri/membres/professeures-et-professeurs/sandra-lavenex/.

Lucas Leemann is an associate professor of comparative politics with a special focus on the empirical study of democracy in the Department of Political Science at the University of Zurich. His research interests focus on how citizens form opinions and how these opinions translate into policies. His research ranges from questions of how to measure preferences, to direct democracy, to questions about how certain political institutions emerged in the nineteenth century in the first place. His research has been published in leading journals (e.g. *American Political Science Research*, *American Journal of Political Science*, and *Journal of Politics*). He is also an editor of the *British Journal of Political Science*.

Jean-Philippe Leresche is a full professor at the Institute of Political Studies (IEP) and at the Observatoire science, politique et société (OSPS) of the University of Lausanne. Currently, his work focuses on higher education and research policies in Switzerland. He has co-published twenty-five books on topics as diverse as metropolitan and cross-border governance, sustainable urban development, food policies, the use value of science, the evolution of academic disciplines, the internationalization of research and higher education, and university/faculty governance. Recently, he published an article on the evolution of national higher education models in the *Revue internationale de politique comparée* (with Cécile Crespy).

Wolf Linder, Professor Emeritus, studied Law and Political Science. After research activities at the University of Constance and the ETH Zurich, he was professor at the Institut de hautes études en administration publique (Lausanne). From 1987 to 2009, he was director at the Institute of Political Science at the University of Bern. Besides his academic research, he worked as an expert for Swiss institutions and international organizations in developing countries. His main fields are Swiss politics as well as institutions of federalism and decentralization. His book *Swiss Democracy—Possible Solutions to Conflict in Multicultural Societies* (4th ed., Palgrave, 2021, with Sean Mueller) has been translated into several languages, including Arabic and Azerbaijani.

Georg Lutz is Director of 'FORS' and Professor of Political Science at the University of Lausanne. He was previously principal investigator of the Swiss election study 'Selects' for many years. His work focuses on political institutions and political behaviour in a comparative perspective as well as Swiss politics and survey research methods. His research is published in, among others, the *Swiss Political Science Review* and *Representation*, as well as in contributions to different edited volumes.

André Mach is an associate professor at the Institute of Political Studies of the University of Lausanne. His areas of research include interest group politics, the study of elites, comparative political economy, and Swiss politics. His research has been published in, among others, *Politics and Society, Regional and Federal Studies, Interest Groups & Advocacy, Governance, Actes de la recherche en sciences sociales, Higher Education, Economy and Society*, and *Swiss Political Science Review*.

Anita Manatschal is a full professor in migration policy analysis at the Swiss Forum for Migration and Population Studies at the University of Neuchâtel, where she also serves as deputy director. Located at the intersection of political sociology and comparative politics, her research interests include migration policy analysis, immigrant civic and political engagement, discrimination, and xenophobia. Recent publications appeared in the *Journal of European Public Policy, Political Psychology, European Union Politics, The Journal of Personality and Social Psychology, Regional Studies*, and *Comparative Migration Studies*, as well as in various edited volumes and monographs.

Sean Mueller is an assistant professor at the Institute of Political Studies of the University of Lausanne. He obtained his PhD from the University of Kent, UK (2013), and his habilitation from the University of Bern (2022). His main research areas are Swiss politics, federalism, and direct democracy. Together with Wolf Linder, he co-authored *Swiss Democracy* (Palgrave 2021). Articles of his have appeared in, amongst others, the *Journal of Democracy, Government & Opposition, Comparative Political Studies, West European Politics, Publius*, and *Regional & Federal Studies*.

Stéphane Nahrath is a professor of public policy and sustainability at the Swiss Graduate School of Public Administration (IDHEAP) at the University of Lausanne. His teaching, research, and publications relate to environmental and spatial planning policies, urban governance, and circular economy, as well as to the analysis of various kinds of institutional resource regimes (soil, water, air, forest, landscape, biodiversity, climate, and networks infrastructures). His work has been published in journals such as *Policy Sciences, Ecological Economics, Environmental Science & Policy, Environment and Planning A, Resources, Conservation & Recycling, Journal of Cleaner Production*, and *International Journal of the Commons*.

Herbert Obinger is a professor of comparative public and social policy at the Research Center on Inequality and Social Policy (SOCIUM), University of Bremen. He is co-editor of the *Oxford Handbook of the Welfare State* (2021).

Daniel Oesch is a professor of economic sociology at the University of Lausanne. He is the author of *Occupational Change in Europe* (Oxford University Press 2013) and *Redrawing the Class Map* (Palgrave Macmillan 2006) and has widely published on social stratification, class voting, and the consequences of unemployment. He currently serves as director of the Swiss Centre of Expertise in Life Course Research (https://centre-lives.ch).

Yannis Papadopoulos is a professor of Swiss politics and public policy at the Institute of Political Studies of the University of Lausanne and a member of the Laboratory for Analysis and Public Policy (LAGAPE). His research concentrates on recent developments in Swiss policy-making and on the broader implications of governance transformations for accountability and democracy. He has recently published *Understanding Accountability in Democratic Governance* (Elements series in Public policy, Cambridge University Press 2023) and co-edited the *Handbuch der Schweizer Politik-Manuel de la politique suisse* (NZZ Libro 2022).

Christine Rothmayr Allison is a professor of political science at the Université de Montréal. Her main fields of interest are comparative public policy, law and politics, and policy evaluation in Europe and North America. Her current research looks at the politicization of courts in Europe and the impact of court decisions on policy change. She holds a PhD from the University of Zurich and worked for several years at the University of Geneva.

Christian Rüefli is an independent public policy analyst and evaluator. After completing his studies in political science and economics at the University of Berne in 2000, he joined Büro Vatter, Politikforschung & -beratung, a private agency for public policy research and consulting, becoming the managing director in 2008. His main fields of interest and expertise are health (care) policy and institutional aspects of governance, regulation/legislation, and evaluation. He has produced numerous studies and evaluation reports on behalf of public agencies, parliamentary bodies, and NGOs and co-authored several journal articles and handbook chapters on Swiss health policy.

Fritz Sager is a professor of political science at the KPM Center for Public Management at the University of Bern, and vice-rector of the same University. His research focuses broadly on public policy and public administration. Specific fields of interest are the politics of expertise, policy implementation, evaluation, and the history of administrative ideas. He has published in numerous international political science, public administration, and public policy journals. Recent research regards executive politics, blame avoidance, and evidence-based policy-making during the COVID-19 pandemic in Switzerland and abroad. More information can be found here: https://orcid.org/0000-0001-5099-6676

Daniel Schwarz is a research associate at the KPM Centre for Public Management at the University of Bern and at the Bern University of Applied Sciences (BFH). He is a co-founder of the online voting advice application 'smartvote' and focuses his research on parliaments, political parties, political institutions, and e-democracy. He is co-author of several publications on voting advice applications, digital democracy, and legislative behaviour.

Pascal Sciarini is a professor of Swiss and comparative politics and dean of the School of Social Sciences at the University of Geneva. His main research topics are decision-making processes, direct democracy, Europeanization, and electoral behaviour. His work has appeared in several journals, such as *Comparative Political Studies, The Journal of Politics, British Journal of Political Science, European Journal of Political Research, West European Politics, Electoral Studies,* and *Social Networks*. He is co-author of Political *Decision-Making in Switzerland: The Consensus Model under Pressure* (Palgrave Macmillan 2015).

Isabelle Stadelmann-Steffen is a professor of comparative politics at the Institute of Political Science at the University of Bern. Her research interests lie in the areas of public policy (especially welfare state policy and energy policy), direct democracy, political behaviour, and research on attitudes. In her ongoing research projects, she works at the intersections of these focus areas. For example, she investigates how the content of family policy and energy policy influences citizens' political preferences and behaviour. Her research has been published in leading journals like *Comparative Political Studies, Socio-Economic Review, Nature Climate Change,* and *Energy Research & Social Science*.

Denise Traber is an assistant professor of political science at the University of Basel. Her research focuses on political behaviour and party competition in the context of societal and economic changes. She currently directs the SNF project 'Class identity politics: the (new) political role of social class in Western Europe'. Her work has been published in, among others, the European Journal of Political Research, Comparative Political Studies, West European Politics, and Political Science Research and Methods. She is the co-author of Political Decision-Making in Switzerland. The Consensus Model under Pressure (Palgrave MacMillan 2015). More information can be found here: www.denisetraber.net.

Alexander H. Trechsel is professor and chair of political science and vice-rector of research at the University of Lucerne. His research focuses on democracy and comparative politics, with an emphasis on new technologies and voting behaviour, political communication, political parties, and direct forms of citizen participation. He has published widely on Swiss politics, the European Union, and digitalization and politics, as well as direct democracy. He is the author of several monographs, edited volumes, and research articles published by university presses and journals in the United States and Europe.

Philipp Trein is an assistant professor in public administration and policy at the IEP (Institute of Political Studies) of the University of Lausanne and a senior fellow at the IES (Institute of European Studies) at UC Berkeley. His research interests cover comparative public policy and administration, digitalization, health policy, and social policy, as well as multilevel governance and federalism. His latest research project deals with the integration of artificial intelligence into public policy. More information can be found here: https://www.philipptrein.com/publications/.

Anke Tresch is an associate professor of political sociology at the Institute of Political Studies at the University of Lausanne and head of the 'Political Surveys' group at the Swiss Centre of Expertise in the Social Sciences (FORS). She directs the Swiss national election study Selects and co-leads a research project on Swiss Direct Democracy in the 21st Century. Her research focuses on political communication, opinion formation, and voting behaviour in elections and referendums. Her research is published in, among others, *Political Communication*, *Electoral Studies*, and *Party Politics*.

Frédéric Varone is a full professor of political science at the University of Geneva, where he leads the interdisciplinary Master in public management. He also holds an elective mandate as deputy magistrate at the Geneva Court of Auditors for the period 2019–2024. An economist and political scientist by training, his teaching and research interests focus on comparative public policy analysis, public sector reform, programme evaluation, interest group strategies, and the behaviour of elected parliamentarians. He co-published with Michael Hill the eighth edition of *The Public Policy Process* (Routledge 2021).

Adrian Vatter is a full professor of political science (Swiss politics) at the Institute of Political Science, University of Bern. He studied political science and economics at the University of Bern and was professor at the University of Konstanz, Germany (2003–2007) and at the University of Zurich (2008–2009). He has published on Swiss politics, federalism, direct democracy, consensus democracy, subnational politics, and comparative public policy in leading journals. He is the author of *Swiss Federalism* (Routledge 2018) and *Power Diffusion and Democracy* (Cambridge University Press 2019; co-authored with Julian Bernauer).

Stefanie Walter is a full professor of international relations and political economy at the Department of Political Science at the University of Zurich. Her research examines distributional conflicts, political preferences, and policy and negotiation outcomes related to globalization, financial crises, European integration, and international cooperation. Her work has been published in journals such as the *Annual Review of Political Science*, *American Journal of Political Science*, *Comparative Political Studies*, and *International Organization*. She is the author of *Financial Crises and the Politics of Macroeconomic Adjustments* (Cambridge University Press 2013) and co-author of *The Politics of Bad Options* (Oxford University Press 2020).

Fabio Wasserfallen is an associate professor of European politics and director of the Institute of Political Science at the University of Bern. Previously, he was associate professor of political economy at the Salzburg Centre of European Union Studies, professor of comparative politics at Zeppelin University, and Fung global fellow at Princeton. The findings of his research have been published in journals such as the *American Political Science Review*, *American Journal of Political Science*, *British Journal of Political Science*, *European Journal of Political Research*, *European Union Politics*, and *Journal of European Public Policy*.

Andreas Wenger is a professor of international and Swiss security policy at ETH Zurich and has been the director of the Center for Security Studies (CSS) at ETH Zurich since 2002. He studied history, political science, and German literature at the University of

Zurich. The focus of his main research interests lies on security and strategic studies and the history of international relations. He teaches seminars on political violence and security policy and is a delegate of the MAS ETH Mediation in Peace Processes course.

Delia Zollinger is a postdoctoral researcher at the Department of Political Science, University of Zurich. Her research focuses on political behaviour and party system change in advanced democracies. She has published work on the political landscape of Switzerland in *Comparative Political Studies* and the *American Journal of Political Science*, and she is the co-author of a book on social democracy in Switzerland.

Alina Zumbrunn is a PhD candidate at the Institute of Political Science, University of Bern. Her research interests lie in the fields of the rural–urban divide, political culture, political psychology, political support, and support for democracy. She has published on personality and political interest in the journal *Politics*.

CHAPTER 1

INTRODUCTION

PATRICK EMMENEGGER, FLAVIA FOSSATI,
SILJA HÄUSERMANN, YANNIS PAPADOPOULOS,
PASCAL SCIARINI, AND ADRIAN VATTER

THIS volume aims to provide an unprecedented breadth of analysis on the development of modern Swiss politics. Throughout the forty-three chapters, contributors provide authoritative accounts of Switzerland's political system, and they explore its distinctive politics at all levels and across many themes, thereby offering the most wide-ranging treatment available of an intriguing country. The volume examines the factors that make Swiss politics unique and complex while firmly placing these in an international context. Without a doubt, Switzerland is one of the most unusual political systems in the world because of its federal structure, direct democracy, assembly-independent federal council as government, multicultural population, non-membership in the European Union (EU), and formal neutrality in the international system, to name but a few. Couched within comparative and conceptual frames in conversation with the broader scholarly literature, this volume's contributions explore these and many additional features. Moreover, this volume presents the case of Switzerland to a wider audience.

Although the Swiss political system has long been widely commended for its exceptional stability, fairness, and inclusiveness, today it is surprisingly polarized, and developments in Swiss politics have foreshadowed major trends that mark current European politics. Examples include the rise of right-wing populism and of the 'new left', or the increasing use of popular referenda on matters related to supranational integration. Moreover, this volume's contributions show that politics and political behaviour in Switzerland are less exceptional today in international comparison than they may have been a few decades ago. This goodbye to the Swiss *Sonderfall* (special case) has been more evolutionary than abrupt, but Swiss politics is no longer as unique as it used to be. Instead, Switzerland has become a test case of democracy in divided societies and fragmented politics. In this way, the *Oxford Handbook of Swiss Politics* provides a necessary corrective to the often rather idealized and sometimes outdated perception of Swiss politics—among both international and Swiss readers.

Switzerland is home not only to an intriguing political system but also to a highly successful economy, leading international rankings in aspects such as innovation capacity, competitiveness, and wealth. At first sight, the Swiss economy seems far more liberal than its continental European neighbouring countries; however, rather than being a typical liberal market economy, Switzerland features a fascinating mixture of public and private forms of cooperation and a possibly surprising amount of state regulation. The close interlinkages of this political economy regime and the political system are key to understanding Swiss politics and have too long been overlooked by studies focusing on political institutions only. Moreover, although deeply integrated into international markets, Switzerland is a surprisingly reluctant member of the international political community due to its focus on preserving sovereignty and direct democracy. Switzerland's relationship with the EU is a case in point. Deeply integrated in the single market and geographically at the heart of Europe, Switzerland refuses to join the union and is currently struggling more than ever to find a sustainable political relationship with it.

The *Oxford Handbook of Swiss Politics* is thus ideal for an international readership to gain an overview of all aspects related to Swiss politics; to learn about the most important developments, ongoing debates, and recent trends; and to acquire pointers for relevant further reading. Its breadth offers analyses relevant not only to political science but also to international relations, European studies, history, sociology, law, public policies, and economics. To cover all aspects of Swiss politics, this volume brings together a diverse set of more than fifty leading experts in their respective areas, each of whom has significantly contributed to the field about which they write. Overall, the *Oxford Handbook of Swiss Politics* offers the most comprehensive and thorough English language collection on Swiss politics to date and may serve as a reference point for some time to come.

1 WHY SWITZERLAND?

Beyond the political system, Switzerland offers several core features that are worthwhile to examine. In particular, four such features convincingly speak for an in-depth analysis of Switzerland (cf. Vatter 2020, 27–30).

1.1 Switzerland as a political 'nation of will' on a multicultural basis

Unlike most nation-states, a common language, denomination, ethnicity, or culture do not unite Switzerland. Rather, its national identity and its political self-image are based on the definition of a genuinely political 'nation of will'. This contrasts with the cultural national models still common in Europe today. Switzerland's national identity is thus only partly based on a common historical past and national myths and symbols, which, moreover, were mostly created after the nation-state was founded in the nineteenth century (Zimmer 2003; Wimmer 2011). Rather, its political institutions of power-sharing such as the extended popular rights, federalism with the autonomous position of the cantons, and the principle of proportionality in allocating political resources have contributed significantly to the formation of a functioning nation-state over the course of the last 170 years, and to the emergence of this shared national political identity. Three specific features appear as particularly important: the Swiss population's political rights to vote on the same issues throughout the country and to elect their representatives to the federal parliament, the simultaneously large degree of autonomy and territorial protection of national minorities that the federal institutions guarantee to the culturally and structurally different cantons, and the consociational principle of amicable agreement and proportional power-sharing for the peaceful settlement of political conflicts (Linder and Mueller 2021, 263).

Primarily due to its political institutions, Switzerland is often considered a paradigmatic case of political integration (Deutsch 1976). From a political science perspective, Switzerland is of particular interest because it represents one of the rare examples of a political nation's successful formation on a multicultural basis. Its state-building did not take place through ethnic, linguistic, or confessional unification processes (e.g. Weber 1976; Hobsbawm 1990) but mainly through the successful development and interaction of political institutions, which aimed to facilitate integration in a plural society that was strongly divided along linguistic, religious, geographic, and economic lines. Power-sharing—vertically between jurisdictional levels and, over time, also horizontally between the major political parties—and the political authorities' tradition of formalized and extensive consultation with civil society when formulating policies, have allowed Switzerland to overcome these divisions. These political institutions and the resulting culture of amicable agreement allow the Swiss, in the words of Ernest Gellner (1964, 174), to 'speak "the same language" even if they do not do so in a literal sense'.

However, it is often overlooked that it took Switzerland more than a century to transform into this consensus democracy (Vatter et al. 2020). Modern Switzerland's creation in 1848 followed a domestic military conflict. Although Joachim Remak (1993, 1) famously called the *Sonderbund* war a 'very civil war', it was a war nonetheless, which was followed by decades of discrimination of the losing side. Admittedly, the liberal victors installed the institutions of modern democracy, but they clearly had a majoritarian system in mind. Moreover, they did not hesitate to engage in electoral manipulation to exclude the conservative 'forces of darkness' (Gruner 1978, 315). The cantons' strong role in the Swiss polity was a concession needed to gain support for the nation-building project, and the expansion of direct democratic institutions as well as the adoption of proportional representation were the outcome of the minority groups' successful mobilization (Gruner 1978; Bolliger and Zürcher 2004; Holenstein 2018; Emmenegger and Walter 2021). Hence, not only is Switzerland a rare example of the successful formation of a political nation on a multicultural basis, but it also offers rich lessons about the conflicts and struggles leading to the creation of political institutions and to the development of a culture of amicable agreement. Moreover, Switzerland's conflict-laden path to today's consensus democracy clearly shows that this model of political integration's survival cannot be taken for granted.

1.2 Switzerland in Europe, Switzerland in the world

Given its considerable political, cultural, and social heterogeneity contained in a small-scale federal system, Switzerland presents an ideal research laboratory for political science. Bearing in mind the complexities of the EU integration process, calls from prominent representatives of the social sciences and humanities in the 1970s to study the dynamics of the European integration process regarding the Swiss experience take on new significance. The Norwegian political scientist Stein Rokkan (1970) and the Swiss philosopher Denis de Rougemont (1970), for instance, argued that Switzerland could be regarded as a microcosm of Europe with its cultural, linguistic, and regional diversity. After all, the Swiss Confederation had already successfully gone through the difficult process of unifying several sovereign states into a federal state in the nineteenth century. Rokkan (1970) recommended that anyone who wanted to understand the dynamics and problems of the European integration of heterogeneous or multicultural states should first study Swiss politics. De Rougemont (1970) went one step further, advocating the use of Switzerland's political system as a model for European unification. The German sociologist Jürgen Habermas (1992) made a similar claim when portraying Switzerland as a case of 'constitutional patriotism' (similar to the notion of the genuinely political Swiss national identity developed in the section above), one that might serve as an example for constructing a European identity (Sciarini et al. 2001). In view of the current simultaneous and contrasting trends of further integration and selective disintegration, these statements do not seem to have lost their validity. European political theorists (e.g. Lacey 2017) and political practitioners (e.g. Fischer 2014) make this clear as they praise Swiss democracy as a model for the EU.

Beyond the interest in Switzerland as a historical case of political integration, the country also holds ample insights regarding the tensions an increasing number of countries are experiencing between an ever-stronger economic integration in international markets and their political sovereignty. Switzerland hosts several international organizations and is among the most globalized countries in the world (Gygli et al. 2019). However, at the same time, Switzerland continues to be deeply concerned about preserving its neutrality and political sovereignty in the face of global developments and it is historically suspicious of institutionalized forms of international cooperation. Switzerland's complicated relationship with the EU offers a powerful example of this tension. Although among the economically most-integrated countries in the European Single Market, Switzerland stoutly refuses to join the EU, constantly trying to find ever-new ways to achieve increasing economic integration while (seemingly) retaining as much political sovereignty as possible. This includes the formally autonomous transposition ('autonomer Nachvollzug') of EU laws, which often leads, however, to de facto generalized alignment with EU legislation.[1]

Switzerland has traditionally handled this tension between economic integration and political sovereignty via a hybrid strategy of liberal regulations for export markets and protectionism for domestic markets (Bonoli and Mach 2000; Armingeon and Emmenegger 2007). However, the increasing economic integration of world markets challenges this model. The pressure to expose domestic markets, wages, and systems of social security to the vagaries of international markets or subject them to the international organizations' control has given rise to political movements that want to 'take back control' even if such political control comes at the cost of economic welfare. Individuals who perceive themselves as 'losers of globalization' (Kriesi et al. 2008) nowadays compose a significant part of the electorate in advanced democracies, and they regularly express their discontent in elections or referenda. These dynamics of contested political integration and disintegration play out in Switzerland and in countries as diverse as Great Britain, Hungary, and Italy in a way that is likely to intensify in many other advanced democratic economies as well.

1.3 Switzerland as a laboratory of democratic innovations

Switzerland's political system is of particular interest not only from a historical-political and European-international perspective but also regarding the current diagnosis of a democratic deficit of established representative democracies. The political, social, and economic problems in numerous states resulted in the Swiss institutions, such as direct democracy, federalism, and consociationalism, becoming much more appealing in recent times. With the transfer of competencies to inter- and supranational organizations, the importance of the nation-state has diminished. This has also led to fewer opportunities for lower levels of government and especially citizens to exert influence. At the same time, criticism of established parties is on the rise, the legitimacy of representative democratic institutions is declining, and the proportion of non-voters disenchanted with politics and the number of protest voters are increasing. In many places, these factors have aroused interest in democratic innovation more generally and the model of democracy 'à la Suisse' more specifically.

Today, in particular, the Swiss institution of direct democracy is drawing attention to this country, and there is no doubt that the great appeal of direct citizens' participation in political matters has given rise to the desire for popular votes in many countries. The possibility of voting on issues as important and diverse as the level of taxes and wages, the duration of holidays, the relationship with the EU, and the abolition of the country's army has led Switzerland to be regarded as a political laboratory, particularly in view of the effects of popular rights. This is expressed, for example, in the introduced European Citizens' Initiative, even though it is a pale imitation of Swiss popular initiatives as European authorities retain—at least formally—the option to ignore Citizens' initiatives (Tosun et al. 2022).

In his influential work on democracy research, Manfred G. Schmidt (2019, 353, own translation) argues that 'anyone who wants to test judgements about direct democracy against practice in the context of a prosperous country with a long democratic tradition can regard Switzerland as a quasi-experiment'. This *Handbook* provides a differentiated view of Swiss democracy. To be sure, Switzerland has been a forerunner in introducing universal male suffrage in 1848 (but a laggard with regard to female suffrage, introduced only in 1971), direct democracy, formalized procedures for the consultation of civil society, and other institutions of power-sharing. This democratization of decision-making has certainly contributed to citizens' satisfaction with the quality of democracy and governmental performance. Direct democracy, in particular, allows for citizens' ownership over policy and is more generally seen as a cement of political identity. Nevertheless, it should not be mythicized because it reproduces or even creates inequalities. Most notably, direct democracy entails social selectivity, considering survey evidence suggests that citizens with a low educational level and limited political skills turn out to vote less frequently. It does not completely escape the risk of 'majority tyranny' either, with direct democratic decisions being more harmful than the—often criticized as elitist—procedures of representative democracy to minorities ('out-groups') with which the median citizen does not identify (Vatter and Danaci 2011; Hainmueller and Hangartner 2019).

Finally, one would expect Switzerland to continue being at the forefront of innovations concerning political participation. However, this does not seem to be the case. Although participatory forums aimed at increasing the deliberative quality of debates and decision-making flourish around the world (including in political systems with similar mechanisms of direct democracy, such as some states in the US), it is only recently that 'mini-publics' involving a randomly selected sample of people have been established in this country (Stojanovic 2023). Probably the existence of direct democratic tools, coupled with the usually inclusive consultation of civil society organizations, has alleviated the functional pressure for such devices but has also, to some extent, caused prejudice to the reflection on the coupling between public deliberation and democratic participation. This is an area in which learning potential from experiences abroad subsists for Switzerland.

1.4 Switzerland and the new party politics

Although the Swiss political system has long been appreciated for including political minorities and for finding widely shared compromises, stronger tensions have emerged in recent years. In many ways, Swiss politics are less exceptional today than they were a few decades ago. Switzerland has been undergoing changes also observed in other countries and, more specifically, this country has been at the forefront of developments regarding the reconfiguration of the political space that is of transnational relevance (Hooghe and Marks 2018). The country's rapid and sweeping economic and socio-structural transformation towards a service-based knowledge economy has fuelled political conflict over the reallocation of opportunities and constraints in society between low- and high-skilled industries and services, natives and immigrants, et cetera. Hence, conflicts over socio-cultural matters have come to play an increasingly important role in Swiss politics, overshadowing concerns over economic-distributive matters. Nowhere do these cultural conflicts become more visible than in Switzerland's difficult relationship with the EU, which has been a 'work in progress' for half a century now.

Cultural conflicts have given rise to populism and sustained political polarization. National-populist parties emerged in Switzerland as early as the 1970s, before the rise of the French *Front National* in the 1980s. Those were admittedly fringe parties, but they mobilized around their claims far beyond their own electorate in referendum votes (Joye and Papadopoulos 1991). Today, Switzerland features the electorally most successful far-right party in Europe, openly challenging the country's famed consensus model of democracy. The Swiss People's Party is the largest party in terms of votes and, remarkably, it continues to be part of the federal and of many cantonal governments despite its antiestablishment turn that manifests itself most prominently in electoral and referendum campaigns.

The comparatively forceful politicization in Switzerland of the 'GAL-TAN' divide between 'Green Alternative Libertarians' and 'Traditionalist Authoritarian Nationalists' (Hooghe and Marks 2018) has been at the forefront of partisan realignment on the other end of the partisan spectrum as well. Switzerland is the first country in which a Green deputy was elected to a national parliament (in 1979). As in many countries, not only has the early emergence of post-materialist and 'new left' values given birth to green parties and environmental movements, but the Swiss Social Democratic Party has strategically aligned its programmatic orientation with the left-libertarian progressive agenda as well. The latter's ideological profile is today almost identical to the Green Party's profile, and both parties compete in the same ideological space and for the same segment of the electorate (Bochsler and Sciarini 2010; Petitpas and Sciarini 2022; Sciarini 2010; Häusermann et al. 2022).

For the last thirty years, the opposition between a nativist far right and a culturally progressive new left has dominated Swiss politics and these developments have put a strain on the integrative function of Swiss political institutions (Bochsler et al. 2015). At the same time, these enduring institutions continued to imprint their mark on how policy-making unfolds in Switzerland. Despite the huge gap in their political positions and policy preferences, the left-wing Social Democrats and the right-wing populist Swiss People's Party continue to be governmental coalition partners at the federal and cantonal levels. Under such conditions of high polarization, one would expect deadlock to threaten the Swiss decision-making system with many veto points. However, the combination of the social-economic and the social-cultural cleavage resulted in a tripolar configuration of party competition that potentially allows for changing majorities (Bühlmann et al. 2019), generally sufficiently large in parliament to avoid or overcome the veto point of direct democracy. Despite polarization, only a very small amount of federal legislation is challenged by a referendum, and even when a referendum vote takes place, the voters often follow the government and the parliamentary majority. Therefore, we observe a decoupling between the increasingly polarized sphere of politics and the still predominantly accommodative logic of policy-making in several policy fields (Maggetti and Papadopoulos 2018; Sciarini et al. 2015). However, in several key areas of policy-making (such as old-age pensions, environmental policy, or relations with the EU), the country has indeed increasingly suffered from a declining reform capacity.

2 La Suisse existe— La Suisse n'existe pas

'*La Suisse n'existe pas*' was the motto of the Swiss Pavilion at the Seville Expo in 1992. The motto problematized questions of national identity in a country featuring four linguistic regions. Today, questions of identity and co-existence remain as topical as ever. Switzerland, as a microcosm of Europe, successfully underwent the process of political integration from a loose confederation of states to a federal state as early as the nineteenth century. It is also regarded as a successful case of political integration through the forming of power-sharing institutions throughout the course of the twentieth century, as well as a pioneer for contemporary forms of direct citizen participation and the peaceful resolution of conflicts in multicultural societies. In many ways, Switzerland is a success story. There are very few countries in the world that have achieved a comparable performance in diverse fields such as wealth, quality of life, and satisfaction with democracy.

However, Swiss politics are not short of conflicts. Most of its political institutions, cherished and celebrated today, were the result of intense and protracted struggles. Its economy, among the most globalized and successful in the world, rests on a delicate compromise between outward-looking and inward-looking segments of society. Switzerland features one of the most diverse and multicultural populations in the world, but the country has never ceased to be a 'reluctant country of immigration' (Cornelius et al. 2004) and it hesitates to embrace its new multicultural identity, especially by retaining big hurdles for immigrants who wish to naturalize. Moreover, in recent years, Switzerland has also been undergoing significant changes, leading to increased levels of political polarization and the rise of populism and the far right. In short, Switzerland might be a bit less unusual today than it was in the past, and maybe Switzerland's past is not as unusual as people sometimes tend to think. Today, Switzerland faces similar struggles to most other advanced democracies, although occasionally, Switzerland has created new and surprising solutions to these challenges. As a country located in the heart of Europe but outside the EU, we believe that Switzerland offers considerable potential for fruitful analysis from a political science perspective.

3 STRUCTURE OF THE BOOK

The *Handbook* aims to provide the reader with detailed knowledge and understanding of the many different facets of the Swiss political system. It presents an account of Swiss politics that recognizes its inherent diversity by taking a thematic approach in seven parts and an epilogue. However, by presenting new arguments, insights, and data, the forty-three chapters also make contributions in their own right. The seven parts are: foundations (chapters 2 to 7), institutions (chapters 8 to 12), cantons and municipalities (chapters 13 to 15), actors (chapters 16 to 20), elections and votes (chapters 21 to 23), decision-making processes (chapters 24 and 25), and public policies (chapters 26 to 40); and three concluding chapters compose the epilogue (chapters 41 to 43).

Following this introductory chapter, the part on foundations starts with three chapters on political history and culture. Chapter 2 discusses the role of Swiss institutions in pacifying conflicts in the past and today. Chapter 3 explains how the political history of citizen empowerment and integration in Switzerland forged its political culture. Chapter 4 explores the key features of this political culture in a comparative perspective. Chapters 5 to 7 then present the key developments in structural and political foundations over the past three decades, with chapter 5 focusing on the economic and socio-structural challenges, chapter 6 discussing Switzerland's position in Europe and the world, and chapter 7 presenting the profoundly realigned and polarized ideological and partisan space of Swiss politics. With these six chapters, the first part of this *Handbook* characterizes the background against which the subsequent chapters focus on specific aspects of the political system.

Part II first concentrates on studying the core institutions of Swiss federalism (chapter 8) and direct democracy (chapter 9). It then examines the federal parliament (chapter 10), the collegial government (chapter 11), and the judiciary (chapter 12). Part III includes chapters on the subnational units: cantons (chapter 13) and municipalities (chapter 14), but also agglomerations (chapter 15) that are increasingly important functionally for problem-solving and strive to gain recognition as legitimate decisional levels. Part IV presents chapters addressing the central actors in federal decision-making: the public bureaucracy (chapter 16), political parties (chapter 17), interest groups (chapter 18), and social movements (chapter 19). Given the mediatization of politics that also affects the Swiss system, chapter 20 is dedicated to studying the media and political communication.

The chapters in Part V study political behaviour both in national elections (chapter 21) and in direct democratic votes that are crucial for the Swiss political system (chapter 22). To keep up with recent developments, the part also includes a chapter on E-democracy (chapter 23). Part VI surveys the decision-making processes: how policies are formulated at the federal level (chapter 24), but also how they are implemented—mostly at the cantonal level—and sometimes also evaluated (chapter 25). Part VII, on public policies, presents a series of chapters on important policy areas. The first three chapters are devoted to Switzerland's international relations: foreign policy (chapter 26), its complicated relationship with the EU (chapter 27), and security policy (chapter 28). Subsequently, the focus turns to more domestic policies. Switzerland relies on surprisingly unorthodox economic policies (chapter 29) and is home to one of the largest financial centres (chapter 30). The subsequent chapters examine infrastructure policies (chapter 31), education policy (chapter 32), research, technology, and innovation policies (chapter 33), and environmental and spatial planning policies (chapter 34). Immigration policies (chapter 35) and integration policies (chapter 36) are of particular importance in a multicultural country such as Switzerland. The last chapters in this section address different aspects related to the Swiss welfare state and to equality policy: social policy (chapter 37), health policy (chapter 38), family policy (chapter 39), and gender equality (chapter 40).

The volume concludes with three chapters. The first concluding chapter identifies current challenges to Swiss democracy and suggests likely future developments (chapter 41). The second examines the performance of the Swiss polity against numerous benchmarks and by comparing it to other countries (chapter 42). Finally, the third concluding chapter critically reflects on some of the 'myths' about Switzerland and whether and how these myths measure up with reality (chapter 43).

Note

1. It has not been established thus far that Switzerland's 'autonomer Nachvollzug' leaves more room for discretion to national authorities than the 'customized' implementation of European legislation by EU member states does (Zhelyazkova and Thomann 2022).

References

Armingeon, Klaus, and Patrick Emmenegger. 2007. 'Wirtschaftspolitik: Die Erosion des schweizerischen Modells'. In *Schweizer Wirtschaft—Ein Sonderfall?*, edited by Hanno Scholtz, and Michael Nollert, pp. 175–207. Zurich: Seismo.

Bochsler, Daniel, and Pascal Sciarini. 2010. 'So Close but so Far: Voting Propensity and Party Choice for Left-Wing Parties in the Swiss National Elections 2003–2007'. *Swiss Political Science Review* 16 (3): pp. 373–402.

Bochsler, Daniel, Regula Hänggli, and Silja Häusermann. 2015. 'Introduction: Consensus Lost? Disenchanted Democracy in Switzerland'. *Swiss Political Science Review* 21 (4): pp. 475–490, doi: 10.1111/spsr.12191.

Bolliger, Christian, and Regula Zürcher. 2004. 'Deblockierung durch Kooptation? Eine Fallstudie zur Aufnahme der Katholisch-Konservativen in die schweizerische Landesregierung 1891'. *Swiss Political Science Review* 10 (4): pp. 59–92.

Bonoli, Giuliano, and André Mach. 2000. 'Switzerland: Adjustment Policies within Institutional Constraints'. In *Welfare and Work in the Open Economy: Diverse Responses to Common Challenges*, edited by Fritz W. Scharpf, and Vivien A. Schmidt, pp. 131–174. Oxford: Oxford University Press.

Bühlmann, Marc, Anja Heidelberger, and Hans-Peter Schaub. 2019. 'Konkordanz im Parlament – Entscheidungsfindung zwischen Kooperation und Konkurrenz'. In *Konkordanz im Parlament – Entscheidungsfindung zwischen Kooperation und Konkurrenz*, edited by Marc Bühlmann, Anja Heidelberger, and Hans-Peter Schaub, pp. 13–56. Zurich: NZZ Libro.

Cornelius, Wayne A., Philip L. Martin, and James F. Hollifield. 2004. *Controlling Immigration: A Global Perspective*. Stanford: Stanford University Press.

De Rougemont, Denis. 1970. *La Suisse, ou l'histoire d'un peuple heureux*, 2nd ed. Paris: Hachette.

Deutsch, Karl W. 1976. *Die Schweiz als paradigmatischer Fall politischer Integration*. Bern: Haupt.

Emmenegger, Patrick, and André Walter. 2021. 'Disproportional Threat: Redistricting as an Alternative to Proportional Representation'. *Journal of Politics* 83 (3): pp. 917–933.

Fischer, Joschka. 2014. *Scheitert Europa? Europa am Scheideweg*. Köln: Kiepenheuer & Witsch.

Gellner, Ernest. 1964. *Thought and Change*. London: Weidenfeld and Nicolson.

Gruner, Erich. 1978. *Die Wahlen in den schweizerischen Nationalrat, 1848–1919*. Vol. 1. Bern: Francke.

Gygli, Savina, Florian Haelg, Niklas Potrafke, and Jan-Egbert Sturm. 2019. 'The KOF Globalisation Index—Revisited'. *Review of International Organizations* 14 (3): pp. 543–574.

Habermas, Jürgen.1992. 'Citizenship and National Identity'. *Praxis International* 12 (1): pp. 7–19.

Hainmueller, Jens, and Dominik Hangartner. 2019. 'Does Direct Democracy Hurt Immigrant Minorities? Evidence from Naturalization Decisions in Switzerland'. *American Journal of Political Science* 63 (3): pp. 530–547. doi: 10.1111/ajps.12433.

Häusermann, Silja, Tarik Abou-Chadi, Reto Bürgisser, Matthias Enggist, Reto Mitteregger, Nadja Mosimann, and Delia Zollinger. 2022. *Wählerschaft und Perspektiven der Sozialdemokratie in der Schweiz*. Zurich: NZZ Libro.

Hobsbawm, Eric. 1990. *Nations and Nationalities since 1780: Programme, Myth, Reality*. Cambridge: Cambridge University Press.

Holenstein, Rolf. 2018. *Die Stunde Null: Die Neuerfindung der Schweiz 1848*. Basel: Echtzeit.

Hooghe, Liesbet, and Gary Marks. 2018. 'Cleavage Theory Meets Europe's Crises: Lipset, Rokkan, and the Transnational Cleavage'. *Journal of European Public Policy* 25 (1): pp. 109–135, doi: 10.1080/13501763.2017.1310279.

Joye, Dominique, and Yannis Papadopoulos. 1991. 'Quel rôle pour les petits partis dans la démocratie directe?' *Annuaire suisse de science politique* 31: pp. 131–150.

Kriesi, Hanspeter, Edgar Grande, Romain Lachat, Martin Dolezal, Simon Bornschier, and Timotheos Frey. 2008. *West European Politics in the Age of Globalization*. Cambridge: Cambridge University Press.

Lacey, Joseph. 2017. *Centripetal Democracy. Democratic Legitimacy and Political Identity in Belgium, Switzerland, and the European Union*. Oxford: Oxford University Press.

Linder, Wolf, and Sean Mueller. 2021. *Swiss Democracy. Possible Solutions to Conflict in Multicultural Societies*, 4th rev. ed. Basingstoke: Palgrave Macmillan.

Maggetti, Martino, and Yannis Papadopoulos. 2018. 'Policy Style(s) in Switzerland: Under Stress'. In *Policy Styles and Policy-Making: Exploring the Linkages*, edited by Michael Howlett, and Jale Tosun, pp. 157–179. Abingdon: Routledge.

Petitpas, Adrien, and Pascal Sciarini. 2022. 'Competence Issue Ownership, Issue Positions and the Vote for the Greens and the Social Democrats'. *Swiss Political Science Review* (early view). doi: 10.1111/spsr.12509.

Remak, Joachim. 1993. *The Swiss Sonderbund War of 1847: A Very Civil War*. London and New York: Routledge.

Rokkan, Stein. 1970. *Citizens, Elections, Parties: Approaches to the Comparative Study of the Processes of Development*. New York: McKay.
Schmidt, Manfred G. 2019. *Demokratietheorien. Eine Einführung*, 6th ed. Wiesbaden: Springer VS Verlag.
Sciarini, Pascal. 2010. 'La concurrence au sein de la gauche'. In *Le destin électoral de la gauche. Le vote socialiste et vert en Suisse*, edited by Sarah Nicolet, and Pascal Sciarini, pp. 131–177. Genève: Georg.
Sciarini, Pascal, Manuel Fischer, and Denise Traber (eds). 2015. *Political Decision-Making in Switzerland: The Consensus Model Under Pressure*. Basingstoke/New York: Palgrave Macmillan.
Sciarini, Pascal, Simon Hug, and Cédric Dupont. 2001. 'Example, Exception or Both? Swiss National Identity in Perspective'. In *Constructing Europe's Identity: The External Dimension*, edited by Lars-Erik Cedermann, pp. 57–88. Boulder, Colorado: Lynne Rienner.
Stojanovic, Nenad. 2023. 'Citizens Assemblies and Direct Democracy'. In *Handbook of Citizens' Assemblies*, edited by Min Reuchamps, Julien Vrydagh, and Yanina Welp, pp. 183–195. Berlin: De Gruyter.
Tosun, Jale, Daniel Béland, and Yannis Papadopoulos. 2022. 'The Impact of Direct Democracy on Policy Change: Insights from European Citizens' Initiatives'. *Policy & Politics* 50 (3): pp. 323–340. doi: 10.1332/030557321X16476244758073.
Vatter, Adrian. 2020. *Das politische System der Schweiz*, 4th ed. Baden-Baden: Nomos.
Vatter, Adrian, and Deniz Danaci. 2011. 'Mehrheitsdemokratisches Schwert oder Schutzschild für Minoritäten? Minderheitenrelevante Volksentscheide in der Schweiz'. In *Vom Schächt- zum Minarettverbot. Religiöse Minderheiten in der direkten Demokratie*, edited by Adrian Vatter, pp. 215–237. Zurich: Verlag Neue Zürcher Zeitung.
Vatter, Adrian, Rahel Freiburghaus, and Alexander Arens. 2020. 'Coming a Long Way: Switzerland's Transformation from a Majoritarian to a Consensus Democracy (1848–2018)'. *Democratization* 27 (6): pp. 970–989.
Weber, Eugen. 1976. *Peasants into Frenchmen: The Modernization of Rural France, 1870–1914*. Stanford: Stanford University Press.
Wimmer, Andreas. 2011. 'A Swiss Anomaly? A Relational Account of National Boundary-Making'. *Nations and Nationalism* 17 (4): pp. 718–737.
Zhelyazkova, Asya, and Eva Thomann. 2022. '"I Did It My Way": Customisation and Practical Compliance with EU Policies'. *Journal of European Public Policy* 29 (3): pp. 427–447.
Zimmer, Oliver. 2003. *A Contested Nation: History, Memory and Nationalism in Switzerland, 1761–1891*. Cambridge: Cambridge University Press.

PART I
FOUNDATIONS

CHAPTER 2

SWITZERLAND

A paradigmatic case of political integration

WOLF LINDER AND SEAN MUELLER

1 INTRODUCTION

THE central thesis of this chapter is that, despite its many cleavages, Switzerland is stable, peaceful, democratic, and prosperous. More specifically, we suggest that this can be attributed to the political institutions that were created—some copied, others invented—and adjusted to accommodate the country's linguistic, religious, territorial, economic, and political diversity. But rather than presenting the Swiss case as a model to be imitated by others, the purpose of this chapter is to provide an analytic description of how this cultural diversity might be reconciled with political, social, and national unity. The Swiss case illustrates how the political integration of various social groups can happen without eliminating or marginalizing sub-national identities. At the same time, it also underscores the many conflicts and struggles that needed to be settled so that integration could advance. However, even today, we can see that there are clear limits to what the principle of proportionality can achieve for certain groups.

First, let us say a word about stability. With only a short interruption, the seven-member Swiss government has been composed of the same four parties for over sixty years, since 1959 (e.g. Giudici and Stojanović 2016 and own updates). Together, these four parties have represented between 70 and 90 per cent of the Swiss electorate (FSO 2022). The longest-serving party, the Liberals, has been in government without interruption since 1848. Moreover, although every year the people directly vote on some six proposals to change the federal constitution (average for 2000–2021; Swissvotes 2022), Switzerland is not a country of political revolutions—most policy areas are characterized by piecemeal adjustment.[1]

That said, as well as conflict between urban and rural cantons, there is no single *lingua franca*, but rather four distinct linguistic regions (German, French, Italian, Romansh). Also, the religious divide between Protestants and Catholics, which played an important role during the civil war of 1847 and preceding centuries (e.g. Church and Head 2013), continues to impact the party system today. Yet outsiders wonder about not only Swiss conservatism but also the seeming absence of serious social, economic, or cultural conflicts. In the context of Swiss history, this outcome is all the more puzzling, since the initial conditions for state- and nation-building were anything but favourable. It would thus be fundamentally wrong to think of Switzerland as a country without historical conflicts. Modern Switzerland was *not* created by one homogeneous ethnic people, but by different groups speaking different languages and adhering to different religions. Nation-building was a slowly evolving, bottom-up process. Moreover, just as in other countries, nation-building and the processes of urbanization, industrialization, and modernization were accompanied by sundry societal conflicts.

Karl Deutsch (1976), a scholar looking at Switzerland from the outside, noted that Switzerland represented a 'paradigmatic case of political integration'. Yet the Swiss became a nation with its own, distinct identity *only through and because of its political institutions*. The role of institutions was fundamental in uniting territorial communities of four different languages, two different religions, and many disparate regional—cantonal and local—histories. Perhaps most spectacularly, these political institutions managed to turn the disadvantages of cultural diversity, such as fragmentation and conflict, into advantages, such as experimentation and tolerance.

The remainder of this chapter is structured around the three main cleavages in Switzerland—religion, language, and class (sections 2–4)—that have given rise to political contestation and to their institutional solutions. We then discuss one crucial institutional component that enabled political integration: proportionality (section 5). The final section concludes with general insights regarding political integration, where its limits lie today, and what broader lessons we may be able to draw from the Swiss case.

2 Political Catholicism: from segmentation to integration

In the middle of the nineteenth century, the Catholic minority comprised about 40 per cent of the Swiss population. The existing twenty-five cantons more or less represented religiously uniform entities. In 1860, ten cantons had over 75 per cent Protestants, eleven rather smaller cantons had over 75 per cent Catholics. Only four (Geneva, Grisons, Aargau, St. Gall) had a more even distribution. Eight of the most Catholic cantons had previously formed a special alliance (*Sonderbund*) to preserve the confederal status quo but were defeated in the 1847 civil war by urban-protestant centralizers. Although Catholic Conservatives achieved a satisfying constitutional compromise in the form of the 1848 federal constitution, their integration was at first hampered by self-segregation. Politically, they retired to the strongholds of 'their' cantons and let the Radical majority (from which the Liberal Party later emerged) take the initiative in forging national unity for the new federal state.

Catholic regions were mostly rural and cut off from the process of industrialization with which the more progressive, Protestant, and increasingly urban counterparts were mainly concerned. The First Vatican Council of the Catholic Church, held in Rome in 1871, was hostile to the modernization of society and to scientific progress, opposed the separation of religion and state, and tried to enforce the Pope as the sole and binding authority on all aspects of life. This led to isolation and segregation. Many Catholic cantons continued to let the Catholic Church run public education, or they maintained segregated primary and secondary schools. Even in the few mixed cantons, religious segregation in public schools continued well into the second half of the twentieth century (see also 'Education Policy' in this volume). The first Catholic university was founded in Fribourg in 1889, and a tight web of social organizations kept Catholics together and close to the Church—both in their home cantons and in the diaspora regions where Catholics constituted a minority.[2]

Catholics not only had their own political party, the Catholic Conservatives (from which the Christian-Democrats later emerged). They also had their own trade unions, newspapers, and bookshops. In mixed regions, they remained loyal to the Catholic butcher, restaurant, plumber, and carpenter—even when the quality of a Protestant competitor was said to be better (Altermatt 1991, 147). This kind of segmentation also existed among Protestants, but to a much lesser extent: Protestant Switzerland lacked both the political leadership of a single confessional party and the moral pressure of a universalist Church to integrate all social classes on a continuing basis.

No wonder, then, that conflicts over religious issues, especially in the mixed cantons, became acute. Swiss history books speak of the 'cultural struggle' (*Kulturkampf*), for the divide went far beyond religion and extended to different views of the role of the state in and for society. This struggle heavily influenced the first total revision of the federal constitution in the 1870s, which reached its peak just then. The constitution of 1874 aimed at a fully secularized state and eliminated most public functions of the Church. Several articles of the constitution confirmed the anti-clerical character of the federation and the isolation of Catholics.

Insofar as these provisions discriminated against Catholics, they were eliminated from the constitution in the second half of the twentieth century. Today, the regulation of the relationship between the Church and the state is the sole responsibility of the cantons. These relations, therefore, vary from canton to canton. Usually, there is an incomplete separation of state and Church: Protestant, Roman-Catholic, and small Christ-Catholic Churches are all recognized as public institutions, called *Landeskirchen*. Some cantons, for instance Zurich, have given a similar status to the Jewish community, but not to the Muslim community, which has grown rapidly in the last few decades.

The historical conflict between Catholics and Protestants, at least in its early form, has since faded away. The establishment of a modern, liberal democracy has settled many of the issues, which reduced the direct influence of religious organizations on the state. However, the more than four generations during which federalism permitted 'in-between' solutions to these conflicts need to be noted. Thus, it is less accurate to claim that cultural issues were 'settled' than to say that they were simply given time to cool down.

Several factors aided the decline of the confessional schism. First, modernization helped to overcome the separation of society into Catholic and Protestant 'pillars'. A strong and steady migration between Catholic and Protestant regions also increased religious tolerance and cooperation. Internal migration led to desegregation, which further helped integration. The declining influence of religion on people's lives opened up the path to pragmatic solutions: smaller communities, instead of building two churches, constructed one for both Catholics and Protestants. Marriage between Protestants and Catholics became more common. Industrialization and the modern economy did not distinguish between Catholic and Protestant money. Divisions also disappeared as more and more Catholics gained equal access to those economic and social activities which had once been seen as typically Protestant. Cultural and political Catholicism itself developed pluralist attitudes towards the state. At the beginning of the 1970s, the Catholic Conservative Party renamed itself the Christian-Democratic Party. The new label suggested more universal values of Christian belief and culture, signalling the acceptance of a clear separation between state and religion. This resembled the programmes of Christian-Democrats in Germany and Italy after WWII. In 2020, Swiss Christian-Democrats went even further and merged with the Citizen-Democrats (BDP) into a new party called 'The Centre' (*Die Mitte/Le Centre*, cf. e.g. Swissinfo 2020), demonstrating just how much religion had become less relevant for political mobilization.

The second factor was more political. Federalism, and more precisely extensive levels of self-rule or regional autonomy in areas such as education, culture, and language (Dardanelli and Mueller 2019), permitted Catholics to maintain the particularities of their culture in their 'own' cantons during the first decades of the nation-state. Later, the devices of direct democracy permitted the Catholic minority to participate, with considerable success, in federal decision-making. Notably, the introduction of the facultative referendum in 1874 enabled Catholic Conservatives to successfully challenge proposals by the Radical-dominated parliament. Simple majoritarian politics, therefore, became increasingly unmanageable—Catholics had to be integrated through participation in the government. Moreover, in 1918 a coalition of Catholic Conservatives and Social-Democrats succeeded in imposing proportionality rules for elections to the National Council—this time using the popular initiative. That spelled the end of an absolute majority for the Radicals in the Swiss parliament, while for Catholics it marked the commencement of real power-sharing (Altermatt 2021). Finally, with class struggles growing in importance (see below, section 4), the Catholic opponent of the nineteenth century became the closest ally of the Radicals in the twentieth century. The political integration of Catholic Conservatives into the federal executive thus occurred, above all, via struggles in the direct-democratic arena.

Beyond participation in the Federal Council—one seat out of seven in 1891, a second one in 1919 (Vatter 2020, 203)—and other key positions in the federal administration, power-sharing meant compromises on legislative issues between Radicals and Catholic Conservatives. Power-sharing thus brought significant political influence, recognition, and success to the Catholic part of society, which have endured to the present.

Although religious cleavages have largely disappeared, the former Christian-Democratic Party (now The Centre) still constitutes one of the four governing parties and is the largest party in the Council of States (FSO 2022). Economically, they have become advocates of business interests almost as much as their Radical partners in government; at the same time, they often defend social policies together with the Left. Even before the merger with the BDP and the name change to The Centre in 2020, the Christian-Democratic Party was a pragmatic centrist party. Nevertheless, it should be noted that some crucial questions of the cultural schism—such as the prohibition of Jesuits, who in the nineteenth century were regarded by Protestants as conspiratorial promoters of counter-reformation—were only resolved long after the practical relevance of the issue had disappeared. In short, in Switzerland disputes regarding fundamental values and religious beliefs were not resolved overnight, but it took considerable time and effort before they could be considered more or less settled.

3 Multilingualism: understandings and misunderstandings

Multilingualism constitutes a second component of the integration of cultural minorities into Swiss society (McRae 1964; Windisch 1992; Du Bois 1999). Today, approximately 73 per cent of Swiss citizens speak German, 21 per cent French, 4 per cent Italian,[3] and 0.6 per cent Romansh.[4] The issue of multilingualism differs in two ways from the question of religion: With the important exception of the Jura problem (see Linder and Mueller 2021, 38–40), language never became as divisive as religion. However, the issue never really cooled down and it remains an important aspect of Swiss politics to this day (e.g. Mueller and Heidelberger 2022).

Switzerland affords numerous institutional protections for linguistic minorities. First, federalism and local autonomy again permit the Romansh-, Italian-, and French-speaking minorities to live according to their own culture within the boundaries of 'their' cantons and municipalities. Moreover, as a majority in several cantons, they also have a political voice in the decision-making of the central government. The historical importance of this kind of voice is well illustrated by the fact that, until 1974, the members of the National Council were seated in linguistic blocs (Swiss Federal Archives 2011, 2).

Second, there are statutory rights for linguistic minorities. The principle of 'territoriality' guarantees linguistic autonomy, and the cantons are obliged to guarantee the traditional language(s) of their region. Hence, newcomers need to adjust to whatever language is spoken in a given territory, and no municipality can be forced to change its official language. German, French, Italian, and Romansh are all defined as national languages.[5] Banknotes and the most important federal government documents are worded in all four languages, whereas less important legal texts are translated 'only' into German, French, and Italian.

Third, proportionality leads to political quotas. An unwritten rule says that two of the seven members of the Federal Council should be French- or Italian-speakers, and over time this has been largely observed (Giudici and Stojanović 2016; Altermatt 2019). In governmental expert and parliamentary committees, too, linguistic proportions are observed. Complaints about 'German predominance'—more common among French- than Italian-speakers—are not well founded when looking at federal personnel statistics: at all levels of government, proportionality is observed to a high degree (Table 2.1). Nonetheless, in daily interactions and informally, German and especially Swiss-German can become dominant (Kübler et al. 2020, 45ff.).

In contrast to many other countries, the Swiss quota system is not based on hard legal rules. While some quotas are written as general regulations in law, most are informal, that is, they are obeyed as a matter of political custom. As Table 2.1 illustrates, these general regulations and informal quotas produce astonishing results in terms of the fair representation of different cultural groups. Yet proportional representation does not necessarily translate into proportional *influence*. Take, for example, the Federal Council with seven members, of which in 2022 two were French- and one is Italian-speaking. Here, the proportionality rule favours linguistic minorities. However, the four German-speakers could easily overrule them, without even talking to or listening to

Table 2.1: Proportional representation of linguistic groups (in per cent)

	German	French	Italian	Romansh
Swiss population (5.4 million)	71.5	23.7	6.1	0.6
Federal Council (7 members)	57.1	28.6	14.3	0
National Council (200 members)	73.0	23.0	4.0	0.5
Council of States (46 members)	73.9	21.7	4.3	0
Federal Supreme Court (38 members)	60.5	31.6	7.9	0
Expert committees (ca. 1900 people)	65.1	25.5	8.6	0.8
Federal administration (ca. 40 000 employees/36 000 Full-Time Equivalents):				
- All personnel (2021)	70.1	22.7	6.7	0.5
- Top management (2018)	70.3	24.0	5.7	0

Note: Population data only for Swiss citizens who are 15 years and older (2020); data for the Federal Council and parliament from February 2019; data for expert committees from 2016. Population totals greater than 100% since more than one main language could be indicated.
Data source: Own calculations based on OFS (2022), Federal Council (2016), Delegate for Plurilinguism (2019), Federal Personnel Office (2022).

the French- and Italian-speakers. Moreover, the latter might be forced to learn German just to understand the discussions. Of course, minority representatives have the *formal* right to speak their language, but being able to present a key argument in German is advantageous. Even learning 'high' German may not suffice, since French- and Italian-speakers may also face a situation when the German-speaking majority begins to converse in their regional dialect(s), which even French- and Italian-speakers fluent in 'high' German would find barely intelligible. By contrast, some German-speakers may willingly speak French with their counterparts, and even make it the official language of discussions (Linder and Mueller 2021, 37).[6]

At the federal level, discussions in the National Council are simultaneously translated into all three official languages. Although the official record of Swiss laws and regulations is published in Italian, French, and German, the documentation for parliamentarians is frequently available in only one or two languages. The same is true of many government reports. Canada, for instance, goes much further, requiring every official document to be published in both English and French.

The Swiss are very conscious of the need for multilingualism: in schools, children are instructed in at least two languages. It is a myth, however, that these efforts have produced widespread bi- or trilingualism (Werlen 2008, 211f.). Most people rarely read newspapers or listen to the news in a language other than their own, which means that they perceive politics according to different media systems in the three linguistic regions. When face to face with a person speaking another language, one often observes a greater effort to be multilingual. Traditionally, German-speakers try to speak French to a *Romand*, even if their French is poor (the term *français federal* captures such efforts). Today, young people, all of whom are taught English at school, tend to use English as the informal *lingua franca* among themselves. Incidentally, the same appears true in the federal administration (Kübler et al. 2020, 84ff.).

The Swiss are rather proud of the multilingual aspect of their society and would find the question of whether German-, Italian-, French-, or Romansh-speakers are 'better' Swiss people rather silly (cf. also Schmid 2001). Multilingualism requires public expenditure and fiscal redistribution in favour of minorities, both of which the Swiss have been willing to bear. There are four complete public radio and television networks, one for each linguistic group. The networks of the linguistic minorities get a more-than-proportional share of the national budget. For instance, in 2018, *Radio Télévision Suisse* generated only 23 per cent of all revenue but received 33 per cent (SRG 2019, 41).

Cultural differences also extend to lifestyle (Windisch 1992). There is a popular saying that German-speakers live to work, whereas French- and Italian-speakers work to live. While these and other distinctions may sometimes create difficulties in communicating, they are accepted as part of normal life and enrich Swiss society. Whereas religious cleavages have become less salient, linguistic diversity and segmentation have not disappeared but instead are maintained and protected within the boundaries of cantons and municipalities (e.g. Mueller 2022). Finally, differences also appear in political behaviour. For instance, French-speakers favour a more open foreign policy, while on the armed forces they are more sceptical than German-speakers. Also, green and left-wing parties have consistently fared better in the West than in the rest.[7]

With one important exception (the Jura case, see Linder and Mueller 2021, 38–40), language has not been a major political problem for Swiss society. The virtues of pluralism may lie partly in the fact that the different cultures are separated from each other by the political autonomy of their cantons and, in multilingual cantons, of their municipalities. It may also be true that globalization makes many societal differences between the cantons diminish or even disappear. Still, federalism provides a kind of horizontal segmentation that enables the three main regions of German-, French-, and Italian-speakers to live simultaneously apart and together (Watts 1991; Schmid 2001; Windisch 1992).

4 The challenges of socio-economic inequality

4.1 A working class without a homeland

Compared to other European countries, the industrialization of Switzerland took place earlier and was in some ways distinct. Instead of concentrating in urban areas, important industries—watchmaking, textiles, embroidery—tended to thrive in rural areas. This decentralized industrialization prevented the sudden concentration of a mass proletariat in cities. But, as in every capitalist country, industrialization led to growing inequalities and the impoverishment of a new social class of workers, whose jobs were insecure and whose earnings were low. As in other countries, democracy did not protect workers from economic exploitation and inhumane working conditions.

In mid-nineteenth century Switzerland, neither a socialist party nor a strong trade union for workers existed. However, a faction of the Radical Party sought to defend the interests of the working class through a policy of 'entrepreneur-socialism'. That faction was the driving force behind the first regulations to protect workers and ban the use of child labour. The liberal wing strongly opposed these policies and, in the fashion of 'Manchester liberalism', wanted to avoid any government intervention in the free market. This period marks the emergence of two new economic questions, which slowly superseded the older cultural schisms in Swiss politics: First, to what extent should the government protect Swiss industries against international competition and intervene in the free market? Second, what role should the government play in compensating for growing social inequalities created by competition?

Business itself was divided on the question of the free market. Whereas some export industries pushed for unconditional liberalization, farmers wanted to be protected from international competitors through import tariffs. Small trades and crafts were organized into corporations and also sought protectionist regulations. The first vocational schools, for instance, were run by trade and craft corporations, but the state provided subsidies and declared professional schools mandatory for apprentices. This eliminated the problem of free riders—enterprises that abstained from investing in professional training, but which would hire employees from other enterprises that had invested in them (Linder and Mueller 2021).

Thus, from the very beginning, Switzerland's economy tended to develop organized relations with the state. In a kind of highly fragmented corporatism, many professional and business organizations cooperated with the state. They sought specific advantages through state regulations or subsidies, attempting to eliminate some of the risks arising from competition. In return, they helped implement government activities. The farmers' association, for instance, furnished the statistical data used for drafting agricultural policies, which helped to keep the number of public administration staff at bay. The strong and influential relations of organized professions and businesses with the national government have persisted until today, despite their rhetoric of economic liberalism and anti-statism (Farago 1987; Church 2004, 71–81; see also 'Interest Groups' in this volume).

In the race for the organizational protection of economic interests, workers came late and did not organize until the end of the nineteenth century. Although they had a common interest to defend—the betterment of their economic conditions—, it proved more difficult for them to organize. Workers were spread out all over the country and were to a large degree isolated in smaller towns and villages. While traditional social ties and paternalist patterns dampened the effects of economic inequality, they also hampered the collective identity formation among and political organization of the new working class. When the Social-Democratic Party was eventually founded in 1888 (Vatter 2020, 107), however, it achieved rapid electoral success. Social-Democrats and trade unions were also among the first to use the new instrument of the popular initiative at the federal level. In 1894, they demanded the right to work and a proper industrial policy—forty years before Keynes. But the hope that direct democracy would be the lever of social reform was soon dashed: over 80 per cent of voters and all cantons rejected the Social-Democratic proposal (Federal Chancellery 2019).

Another reason for the relatively late organization of the working class was that cultural ties often proved stronger than shared economic interests. The Catholic Conservative Party and its trade unions successfully united Catholic workers, but not other workers. Thus, the working class movement was divided. While this did not prevent the Social-Democrats from becoming one of the largest parties, they never managed to form a coalition of equal strength to the centre-right, bourgeois forces. Neither did trade unions succeed in influencing industrial policy as much as businesses did. This minority position of labour in politics and industrial relations has remained a core characteristic of Swiss politics (Farago 1987; Kriesi 1980). By contrast, other small European countries, such as The Netherlands, Austria, Norway, or

Sweden, have established more of an equilibrium between labour and capital, and between the political left and right. Territorial decentralization and cultural segmentation were thus two obstacles to the organization of the Left in Switzerland, and labour has never been able to catch up with the organizational strength of either businesses or farmers.

4.2 From class struggle to economic partnership

During the first decades of the twentieth century, conditions for the Swiss working class worsened. Regarding the period before WWI, historians have noted the development of a conservative, nationalist, and sometimes reactionary and anti-democratic political right, which engaged in a 'class struggle from above' (Gruner 1977; Jost 1992). Politically marginalized by bourgeois forces, the Social-Democrats and trade unions could not prevent the working class from bearing most of the burden of the economic setbacks during and after WWI.

The worldwide economic crisis of the 1930s also brought mass unemployment to Switzerland. Federal troops suppressed several strikes, more than once ending in bloodshed. The Left was denied what Catholics (in 1891) and farmers (in 1929) had achieved: recognition, participation, and political influence in the Federal Council. Proportional principles were used to integrate cultural minorities, but not yet to address the growing socio-economic cleavage.

On top of all that, the Socialist movement was itself divided. A communist faction criticized bourgeois democracy as fake and an instrument of the capitalist class, arguing that the betterment of the working class could arrive only through political and economic revolution. Mainstream Social-Democrats, on the other hand, insisted on proportional participation in all democratic institutions and trusted in limited reforms, even if the state remained dominated by a bourgeois majority. Social-Democrats also aspired to have a mixed economy, with a strong public sector and state intervention to minimize social equality (Nobs 1943). This would not only improve the situation of workers but also protect the Swiss economy from the worldwide market crisis that at the time seemed inevitable.

For almost four decades, that is until WWII, the workers' movement, politically discriminated against and internally divided, wavered between radicalizing the class struggle and cooperating in the hope of achieving integration. In the end, outside events gave the latter strategy the upper hand. Faced with the threat from Hitler's Germany, the Social-Democrats modified their pacifist stand and supported the modernization of the army. An important treaty between the employers' organizations and trade unions in the mechanical-engineering industry was signed in 1937: The so-called 'Labour Peace Convention' (*Friedensabkommen*) accepted unions as representative organizations for workers, proposed to resolve all conflicts by negotiation, and vowed to end all strikes. Economic and social inequalities—the predominant political issues of the twentieth century—thus finally began to be addressed through cooperation and integration, the tried and tested means of accommodation. The Social-Democrats accordingly obtained their first seat in the Federal Council during WWII and adequate, i.e. proportional, representation as of 1959. They have held onto these two seats until this day.

In hindsight, the unifying experience of the generation that defended Swiss independence and neutrality between 1939 and 1945 may also have had a benevolent effect on the integration of the Left. By the 1950s, ideological differences between the political left and right had shrunk. A broad consensus amongst all political forces allowed for the creation of social security, health care, and higher education systems, which collectively addressed many areas of social and economic inequality. Coupled with the continued use of direct democracy to press for government inclusion—this time by trade unions—, economic growth gradually led employers' and workers' organizations away from confrontation towards more cooperation. Collective contracts, similar to the 1937 Labour Peace Convention, became the norm. Even though the labour force was less unionized than in other European countries, Swiss workers and employees obtained a fair share in the growth of prosperity (Linder 1983). By the late 1950s, the number of working days lost due to strikes across Switzerland had basically reached zero—from a high of eighty per 1,000 workers just after World War II (Vatter 2020, 162).

By the early 1970s, the highest-ever degree of integration across different social classes in Switzerland had been achieved. Employers and workers had become accustomed to partnership, and the Left had been integrated into the once purely bourgeois state. Political parties and economic organizations were able to achieve consensus by compromise, and power-sharing seemed to prove effective. However, since that time, the level of social integration in Swiss society has noticeably declined. When economic growth turned into a recession in 1974, the Left learned that proportional participation did not mean proportional influence. In 1984, a minority of the Social-Democrats even considered quitting the Federal Council because political power-sharing had not shifted influence from the 'haves' to the 'have-nots'. Unions, willing to share the burden of recession by accepting pay cuts, were losing members and political influence. In recent decades, while achieving less from employers by way of contracts, unions have instead tried to promote social policy by way of legislation. This has led to a shift from a liberal to a post-liberal welfare regime in which social partnership plays a slightly less important role (Trampusch 2010; see also 'Interest Groups' in this volume).

In the last three decades, finally, globalization and liberalization have led to new conflicts between capital and labour and between urban and rural areas.[8] Despite polarization between the Right and the Left, political power-sharing has persisted thus far, but the partnership between employers and unions has become more difficult to sustain, and the Swiss model of political integration has increasingly confronted limits to what it can achieve.

5 Proportional representation: the key to the doors to power

In the preceding sections, we observed how linguistic and religious minorities were politically and socially integrated, and then how conflicts arising from industrialization were resolved. Conflict resolution in Switzerland relies very much on power-sharing rather than on a winner-take-all approach. This section takes a closer look at the proportionality rule that underpins Swiss power-sharing.

The proportional rule is the key that unlocks the door to almost all political institutions. As Table 2.2 shows, proportionality applies to different criteria—or groups—in the same body. Party membership is, of course, the main affiliation that aspiring political representatives must possess—whatever a person's specific party stands for at any given moment (e.g. a specific religion or class, historically, or a given area, today). Yet, even in the 'magic formula' of the seven-member Federal Council, party affiliation is not the only criterion. The Federal Assembly also follows the rule of linguistic proportionality, normally granting French- and Italian-speakers two or three seats. Until 1999, a provision in the constitution stated that there could not be more than one representative from the same canton. This criterion has been abandoned in favour of a new rule stipulating appropriate representation for the various language regions. Gender balance has not (yet) become a formal rule but is increasingly important; in 2010, there briefly was a female majority in the Federal Council. Not only candidates for the Federal Council, but also high officials of the federal government must fulfil one or more criteria of proportionality to be eligible for a position. Proportionality is also practised in many cultural organizations and sports. It would be unimaginable, for instance, that the executive committee of the Swiss Football Association consisted of German-speakers only.

Table 2.2: Use of the proportional rule: institutions and criteria

Institution	Language	Party	Gender
Federal Council	x	x	x
National Council	(x)	x	(x)
Council of States	x	x	(x)
Federal Supreme Court	x	x	x
Parliamentary committees	x	x	(x)
Expert committees	x	(x)	x
Nomination of high government officials	x	(x)	x

Note: x = criteria normally used, (x) = criteria sometimes important.

There is some criticism that this system means that the 'real' job requirements are all too often neglected. Yet there is flexibility in this approach, which permits over- or under-representation temporarily insofar as it is compensated over time. Nor is there necessarily a tendency towards reification of objective identity markers, which is commonly found with more rigid or 'corporate' quotas (Stojanović 2021, ch. 8). Indeed, we cannot even speak of formal 'group rights' because, in most cases, these are mere political claims that cannot be enforced by law (but are respected nonetheless). Also, the great majority of Swiss are opposed to rigid legal quotas and prefer the idea that all groups of society should be fairly represented in public bodies. Proportionality, therefore, is an element of political culture rather than legal practice.

There are two more fundamental criticisms of proportionality as practised in Switzerland. First, with six rather than four main political parties (i.e. including the Greens and Green-Liberals), practising proportional representation in government and elsewhere has become more difficult. Second, needing to rely on inter-elite bargaining always carries the risk of a populist backlash. Indeed, populism had an early rise in Switzerland but is usually tamed by direct-democratic voting (e.g. Stojanović 2021, 67–70).

6 Conclusion

Until the middle of the nineteenth century, Switzerland was neither a unified society nor an integrated state. It was composed of several small societies with differing traditions, languages, and religions that had become too limited to survive independently. The state created in 1848 was based on a common constitution, but *not* on a common language or religion. It was artificial, a product of historical circumstances, and could easily have failed. It lacked a coherent social basis. Finally, surrounded by much more powerful cultural nations, the Swiss political project could simply have been divided up among larger kin nations (Altermatt 1996).

Yet, thanks to its political institutions and several fortunate circumstances, including cross-cutting cleavages, Switzerland found its own identity as a modern society, and became an example of how different cultures can be successful integrated and how socio-economic inequalities can be redressed.

The key to this process, we have suggested, was *proportional representation*. It was introduced, fought for, and won, mainly through referendums—step by step—for all institutions of the central state. By now, it encompasses parliament and its committees, the government, the courts, and expert committees as well as the federal administration. Proportional representation is applied not only to party affiliation but also to linguistic groups, and belatedly also to gender, thus giving different societal groups adequate recognition, voice, and influence.

With these developments also came a more general shift to *political power-sharing* broadly understood. Swiss democracy developed differently from the majoritarian or 'Westminster' model of parliamentary government. Instead of competition between government and opposition, where 'the winner takes all' for at least four years, Switzerland possesses an oversized government coalition which, ironically, needs to bargain its way through parliament for each individual proposal (see also 'The Federal Government' in this volume). Rather than majoritarian or even plurality politics, decision-making in Swiss politics is fundamentally characterized by negotiation, consensus-seeking, and compromise. Unlike competitive democracy, power-sharing has thus far largely managed to avoid the alienation of minorities that can easily arise from a perpetually winning majority.

Two further political institutions enabled this development. The first is *a non-ethnic concept of the nation-state*. Switzerland never had the choice of building a state based on one religion, one culture, or one language. Forming a nation-state on that basis, even if it were possible, would have entailed excessive social cost. Instead, the different peoples of the cantons recognized each other as having equal rights regardless of differences in religion, language, or cultural heritage. Switzerland is thus above all a political nation, held together by the political will to live under the same constitution.

The second facilitating institution is *federalism*. Regional self- and shared rule were essential for the bottom-up process of nation-building and for anchoring proportionality and power-sharing. Federalism allowed for a compromise between the opponents and advocates of a strong central state and it still provides the cantons and their different cultures with the utmost autonomy, while also ensuring national unity. In cutting across linguistic regions, federalism also contributes to weakening the potential for cultural conflict (e.g. Mueller 2022).

What general lessons can we distil from the Swiss case? First, it took time to overcome the deep conflicts between Catholics and Protestants and between capital and labour. While the religious and linguistic cleavages have cooled down, the class cleavage has become more salient—and might ignite again if material inequalities continue to widen and overlap with new value divisions and urban–rural polarization. Second, while integration was successful for the main linguistic and religious groups of civil society, other minorities remained discriminated against. Women, for instance, received their political rights much later than in other countries. Immigration equally represents a new challenge for Swiss integration precisely because it cannot easily be solved by the political mechanisms deployed for the integration of indigenous groups.

Finally, external factors which once helped create and maintain national unity today threaten it. Pressure from the outside was one of the main motivations for the creation of the federation in 1848: The Swiss cantons, surrounded by much bigger nation-states, wanted to keep their autonomy and independence. Armed neutrality also allowed Switzerland to stay out of the wars between Germany and France. With the end of the Cold War and NATO enlargement, armed neutrality lost much of its practical importance in foreign policy, yet it is still a commonly shared value of all Swiss citizens (see also 'Switzerland's Position in Europe and the World' in this volume).

Yet today, pressure from the outside has a fundamentally different effect. Instead of unifying, it is dividing the country. For the last thirty years, Switzerland has been undecided on the question of European integration, split between (a dwindling number of) protagonists of full EU membership and those who prefer bilateral treaties with the EU. Globalization has changed Swiss politics more than anything else. It has led to new social tensions between 'winners' (especially the highly qualified in cities) and 'losers' (the less skilled in the countryside, mainly). Even political neutrality, the long-standing constant in Swiss foreign affairs, is now being questioned.

These dividing pressures from the outside have accompanied the rising political polarization and populist challenges from the inside. If elite political behaviour no longer finds or even seeks consensus, blockages ensue. While many deplore the dwindling persuasiveness of political compromise, Clive Church (2016) went further and declared the Swiss model of societal integration dead (see also Bochsler et al. 2015).

We are less pessimistic. The main problem lies in the fact that politics has fundamentally changed in Switzerland, while the basic political institutions and standard solutions have not: Proportional representation, direct democracy, and federalism have remained in place. As seductive as majoritarian politics may appear to some Swiss, it is an institutional non-starter. As a result, the Swiss have no other choice than to revive their lost political culture of consensus politics and compromise. To this day, the Swiss are constitutional patriots and feel as a 'nation of political will', as 'being different from others'. While lacking a common language or religion and despite inevitable conflicts, the Swiss are proud of what they all share as citizens: their political architecture and its attendant civic rights.

However, this traditional narrative of national *political* integration must be revitalized with convincing arguments for the future. Ironically, the very same issues that today often cause heated debates could provide the framework; for instance: What does it mean to be neutral in today's increasingly interdependent world? What place to accord to federalism and cantonal autonomy in an internationalized society where local particularisms have lost much of their meaning and where the integration of immigrants remains a challenge? And how can the absolutist notions of sovereignty and independence be transformed into more pragmatic and flexible definitions of national autonomy and international cooperation?

Adhering to the traditional narratives and instruments that have permitted Switzerland to become integrated also means constantly re-evaluating, re-thinking, and re-affirming those very elements of Swiss political nationalism. This task is all too often forgotten or decried as heresy.

Notes

1. See 'Social Policy', 'Family Policy', and 'Gender and Equality+ Policy' in this volume. More generally, see 'The Historical and Institutional Formation of Swiss Political Culture' in this volume.
2. For further details, see Linder and Mueller (2021, 31ff.).
3. If the total population, including the 25 per cent foreign nationals, is taken into consideration, the share of Italian-speakers doubles, whereas the proportion of German-speakers decreases.

4. Romansh is a language largely descending from Latin and rooted in some Alpine regions of south-eastern Switzerland.
5. In 1938, Romansh was added as the fourth national language of Switzerland. This was the result of a 1935 request by the executive of Canton Grisons, at the height of Italian fascism under Mussolini. The initiators understood the request 'primarily as an aid to Romansh in its uphill struggle for survival against the inroads of modern communications and tourism' (see McRae 1964, 9). With an amendment to the constitution in 1996, Romansh also became the official language for state authorities 'when communicating with persons who speak Romansh' (Art. 70 para. 1 Cst.).
6. This is much less likely to occur with Italian.
7. Between 1971 and 2019, left-wing parties (Social-Democrats, Greens, and radical left) scored an average of 28 per cent of the National Council vote in German-speaking versus 35 per cent in French-speaking Switzerland. Their combined score in 2019 was 29 per cent in the former but a record 42 per cent in the latter (FSO 2022).
8. See Linder et al. 2008, who observed steep rises for both of these conflict dimensions. See also 'The Ideological Space in Swiss Politics: Voters, Parties, and Realignment' in this volume.

References

Altermatt, Urs. 1991. *Katholizismus und Moderne*. Zurich: Benziger.
Altermatt, Urs. 1996. *Das Fanal von Sarajevo: Ethnonationalismus in Europa*. Zurich: NZZ Verlag.
Altermatt, Urs. 2019. *Das Bundesratslexikon*. Zurich: NZZ Verlag.
Altermatt, Urs. 2021. *Der lange Weg zum historischen Kompromiss: Der schweizerische Bundesrat 1874–1900*. Zurich: NZZ Libro.
Bochsler, Daniel, Regula Hänggli, and Silja Häusermann. 2015. 'Introduction: Consensus Lost? Disenchanted Democracy in Switzerland'. *Swiss Political Science Review* 21 (4): pp. 475–490. doi: https://doi.org/10.1111/spsr.12191
Church, Clive H. 2004. *The Politics and Government of Switzerland*. Basingstoke/New York: Palgrave-Macmillan.
Church, Clive H. 2016. *Political Change in Switzerland*. London: Routledge.
Church, Clive H., and Randolph C. Head. 2013. *A Concise History of Switzerland*. Cambridge: Cambridge University Press.
Dardanelli, Paolo, and Sean Mueller. 2019. 'Dynamic De/Centralisation in Switzerland, 1848–2010'. *Publius: The Journal of Federalism* 49 (1): pp. 138–165. doi: https://doi.org/10.1093/publius/pjx056
Delegate for Plurilinguism. 2019. *Förderung der Mehrsprachigkeit innerhalb der Bundesverwaltung*. Bern, at https://www.plurilingua.admin.ch/plurilingua/de/home/debatten-aktualitaet/nsb-news_list.msg-id-77659.html (accessed 20 December 2019).
Deutsch, Karl. 1976. *Die Schweiz als paradigmatischer Fall politischer Integration*. Bern: Haupt.
Du Bois, Pierre. 1999. *Alémaniques et Romands entre unité et discorde: histoire et actualité*. Lausanne: Favre.
Farago, Peter. 1987. *Verbände als Träger öffentlicher Politik*. Grüsch: Rüegger.
Federal Chancellery. 2019. Various data, at https://www.bk.admin.ch (accessed 1 October 2019).
Federal Council. 2016. *Bericht über die vom Bundesrat im Rahmen der Gesamterneuerungswahlen für die Amtsperiode 2016–2019 gewählten ausserparlamentarischen Gremien*. Bern, at https://www.admin.ch/opc/de/federal-gazette/2016/4183.pdf (accessed 1 October 2019).

Federal Personnel Office. 2022. Reporting Personalmanagement 2021. At https://www.epa.admin.ch/epa/de/home/themen/das-bundespersonal-in-zahlen.html (accessed 15 March 2022).
FSO [Federal Statistical Office]. 2022. Various data, at https://www.bfs.admin.ch (accessed 10 March 2022).
Giudici, Anja, and Nenad Stojanović. 2016. 'Die Zusammensetzung des Schweizerischen Bundesrates nach Partei, Region, Sprache und Religion, 1848–2015'. *Swiss Political Science Review* 22 (2): pp. 288–307. doi: https://doi.org/10.1111/spsr.12214
Gruner, Erich. 1977. *Die Parteien in der Schweiz*. Bern: Francke.
Jost, Hans Ulrich. 1992. *Die reaktionäre Avantgarde: Die Geburt der neuen Rechten in der Schweiz um 1900*. Zurich: Chronos.
Kriesi, Hanspeter. 1980. *Entscheidungsstrukturen und Entscheidungsprozesse in der Schweizer Politik*. Frankfurt/New York: Campus Verlag.
Kübler, Daniel, Emilienne Kobelt, and Roman Zwicky. 2020. *Les langues du pouvoir: Le plurilinguisme dans l'administration fédérale*. Lausanne: PPUR.
Linder, Wolf. 1983. 'Entwicklung, Strukturen und Funktionen des Wirtschafts- und Sozialstaats in der Schweiz'. In *Handbuch Politisches System der Schweiz: Vol. I*, edited by Alois Riklin, pp. 255–382. Bern/Stuttgart: Haupt.
Linder, Wolf, Christian Bolliger, and Regula Zürcher. 2008. *Gespaltene Schweiz—geeinte Schweiz*. Zurich: Hier + Jetzt.
Linder, Wolf, and Sean Mueller. 2021. *Swiss Democracy: Possible Solutions to Conflict in Multicultural Societies*, 4th rev. ed. London: Palgrave.
McRae, Kenneth D. 1964. *Switzerland: Example of Cultural Coexistence*. Toronto: The Canadian Institute of International Affairs.
Mueller, Sean. 2022. 'The Paradox of Cooperation: Intergovernmental Relations and Identity Conflicts in Switzerland'. In *Intergovernmental Relations in Divided Societies*, edited by Yonatan T. Fessha, Karl Kössler, and Francesco Palermo, pp. 1–29. London: Palgrave.
Mueller, Sean, and Anja Heidelberger. 2022. 'Den Röschtigraben vermessen: Breite, Tiefe, Dauerhaftigkeit'. In *Direkte Demokratie in der Schweiz: Neue Erkenntnisse aus der Abstimmungsforschung*, edited by Hans-Peter Schaub, and Marc Bühlmann, pp. 137–157. Zurich/Geneva: Seismo.
Nobs, Ernst. 1943. *Helvetische Erneuerung*. Zurich: Oprecht.
Schmid, Carol L. 2001. *The Politics of Language: Conflict, Identity, and Cultural Pluralism in Comparative Perspective*. New York: Oxford University Press.
SRG. 2019. *Geschäftsbericht 2018*. At https://www.srgssr.ch (accessed 1 October 2019).
Stojanović, Nenad. 2021. *Multilingual Democracy: Switzerland and Beyond*. London and New York: ECPR Press/Roman and Littlefield.
Swiss Federal Archives. 2011. 'Der Bund, das Parlament und seine Stühle'. *Geschichte aktuell*, at https://www.bar.admin.ch (accessed 1 October 2019).
Swissinfo. 2020. 'CVP schliesst sich mit BDP zur "Die Mitte" zusammen'. At https://www.swissinfo.ch/ger/cvp-schliesst-sich-mit-bdp-zur--die-mitte--zusammen/46190824 (accessed 10 March 2022).
Swissvotes. 2022. *Database on Swiss Popular Votes*. Année Politique Suisse, University of Bern. Online at https://www.swissvotes.ch (accessed 10 March 2022).
Trampusch, Christine. 2010. 'The Welfare State and Trade Unions in Switzerland. A Historical Reconstruction of the Shift from a Liberal to a Post-Liberal Welfare Regime'. *Journal of European Social Policy* 20 (1): pp. 58–73. doi: https://doi.org/10.1177/0958928709352539
Vatter, Adrian. 2020. *Das politische System der Schweiz*, 4th ed. Baden-Baden: Nomos.

Watts, Richard J. 1991. 'Linguistic Minorities and Language Conflict in Europe: Learning from the Swiss Experience'. In *Language Policy for the EC*, edited by Florian Coulmas, pp. 75–102. Berlin: Mouton de Gruyter.

Werlen, Iwar. 2008. 'Englisch als Fremdsprache bei Erwachsenen in der Schweiz'. In *Sprachkontakt und Mehrsprachigkeit*, edited by Sandro Moraldo, pp. 193–214. Heidelberg: Winter.

Windisch, Uli. 1992. *Les relations quotidiennes entre Romands et Alémaniques*. Lausanne: Editions Payot.

CHAPTER 3

THE HISTORICAL AND INSTITUTIONAL FORMATION OF SWISS POLITICAL CULTURE

IRÈNE HERRMANN

1 INTRODUCTION

SWISS citizens are widely known to enjoy particularly extensive democratic rights. Not only can they vote and be elected to government, but they can also reject laws and even propose changes to their constitution. Ever since these national prerogatives were introduced in the second half of the nineteenth century, foreign observers have looked at them with interest as well as suspicion, wondering whether the Swiss had opened the door to a political paradise or, more likely, to chaos by allowing citizens such a broad spectrum of liberties (Kurunmäki and Herrmann 2018).

To the surprise of many, these exceptional rights did not lead to complete disarray. Progressive minds idealized direct democracy, though in practice it led to the expression of conservative, if not reactionary, tendencies which were apparently contrary to the citizens' immediate interests. Notably, these instruments of direct democracy were used to impose mandatory sobriety, accept tax increases, and refuse to reduce working hours.

Of course, this attitude did not go unnoticed among scholars. Broadly speaking, there are two theories to explain it. The classic thesis sees this counterintuitive political behaviour as the culmination of many centuries of history. According to this viewpoint, the Swiss people, heirs to a republican system reaching back centuries, have developed an exceptional capacity for 'political reasonableness', namely, sacrificing short-term interests in exchange for long-term benefits. They have learned to handle institutional instruments for so long that this 'political maturity' has become somewhat natural to them (Kirchgässner et al. 1999, 192–200). This ontological viewpoint is doubtful and, from a historical perspective, all the less credible, as the Swiss have long been known to be quarrelsome.

In the 1960s and 1970s, another, more politically left-leaning theory took hold. Its proponents understood political behaviour against the immediate interests of voters as being the result of manipulative propaganda subtly engineered by the elites and for their benefit (Masnata and Masnata-Rubattel 1978, 17). However, this interpretation is inadequate, as the Swiss have a porous political system that allows them to avoid excessive elite pressure. Moreover, several measures intended to benefit the population were proposed by the governments themselves and subsequently rejected by the very voters whose plight they were intended to alleviate.

For these reasons, the 'left-wing' analysis of this popular self-restraint is as unsatisfactory as the 'classical' interpretation. However, both theories encompass a promising historical dimension, as each in its own way emphasises that the strange political attitudes of Swiss citizens have been built over time.

The aim of this chapter is therefore to place the development of Swiss political institutions in the context of their time. This will help to understand what led the Swiss to democratize earlier and more completely than others. This chapter will also explore the concurrent socio-politically 'ultra-moderate' use of institutional tools. The analysis is split into two parts, the first devoted to the nineteenth century, when this political edifice developed, and the second covering most of the twentieth century, when the political ethos in question found more obvious expression, namely the distinctive traits which are still present to day.

2 Empowering citizens (1798–1891)

Proponents of the 'historical school' rightly emphasize the long history of building democratic structures in Switzerland. As in other European territories, some communities in what is now Switzerland already had democratic decision-making institutions in the Middle Ages. The most long-lasting of these was the Landsgemeinde, an assembly where men who could bear arms voted by a show of hands on measures concerning management of community life (Roca 2011, 3ff.). The right to participate in this decision-making process was granted by inheritance. In this system, numerous mechanisms were established to guarantee the outcome of votes. The ultimate aim was not to express an individual opinion but to reinforce an established order in which everyone acknowledged the place they were meant to occupy (Christin 2014).

The principles of equality and individual independence were introduced as late as 1798 when the troops of the French Directory invaded Switzerland. These values, imported from abroad and by force, would form the basis of democracy in Switzerland today.

The progressive elites leaned on the conceptual ideal of 'freedom', which was supposed to form the central element of the nation's identity, to forge political institutions by and through which this 'age-old' aspiration for liberty was expressed. However, its fullest manifestation—direct democracy—was also the consequence of pressures from the opposing conservative camp. As for the people, influenced by a historical narrative of being worthy of the rights they had been granted, they seemed to view this incredibly expansive gamut of legislative freedoms as the natural result of their own sense of duty and overall exceptionality. Consequently, they had come to feel responsible for the well-being of Switzerland, and that the quality of their lives depended on that responsibility (Herrmann 2006). They accepted the key principle of the system, which delegates part of the state's prerogatives to the citizens while requiring in return that they assume their responsibilities towards the community.

2.1 The Helvetic Republic or the empowerment of the nation (1798–1802)

In 1798, the French Directory continued its policy of conquering neighbouring territories and, after Savoy, the Netherlands, and Italy, decided to invade Switzerland. On 5 March 1798, Berne, the most important canton of the Helvetic Corps, fell and the entire Old Regime Confederation fell along with it. This military incursion had a strategic purpose. However, the official pretext was to help local patriots free themselves from the oppression of the patriciate.

In fact, Paris relied on its Swiss supporters to seize control of Switzerland. This domination involved a fundamental overhaul of institutions, which was ratified by the country's first constitution on 16 April 1798. This document, inspired and supervised by France, completely revolutionized the way Switzerland was organized. The most obvious change was the transformation of the former conglomerate of cantons, linked by loose alliances, into a centralized state, the Helvetic Republic (*Helvetik*). The cantons became mere administrative divisions governed by a national executive body, supported by a bicameral parliament, itself elected in several selective rounds by the people, to whom sovereignty belonged. In addition, the constitution declared legal, linguistic, and religious equality for citizens.

However, this political edifice broke before it could be implemented, as these reforms took place in a context of not only military occupation but also European wars and domestic political instability. In 1799, the Coalition War was waged in the eastern cantons, and between 1800 and 1802, the country was shaken by four coups d'état. Therefore, any major political or economic changes were often implemented by simply eradicating the previous system. This led to half measures if they were not completely killed off in all the chaos (Simon 1995–1998).

Under these circumstances, various tensions resulted in underlying violence that quickly degenerated into civil war. In July 1802, after the fourth coup d'état, the new authorities sought to consolidate their position by passing a new constitution. As soon as it was accepted, Bonaparte withdrew his men and the country sank into a civil conflict between the official supporters of the revolutionary reforms and their many detractors. Unable to quell this rebellion, the legitimate representatives of power requested the armed intervention of the First Consul, who obliged ... and put an end to the regime of the Helvetic Republic.

In retrospect, this five-year period stands out as both an incredibly innovative interlude and one of the most violent episodes in Swiss history. This dichotomy explains the quandary which vexed subsequent leaders who based their principles on this chaotic period. Even after updating these ideas, they were reluctant to admit where they came from.

2.2 Restoration and regeneration or the empowerment of the cantons (1803–1847)

Most observers interpreted the failure of the Helvetic Republic as a clear indication of the incompatibility between Switzerland and centralization. Federalism was the basis of the new constitution Bonaparte imposed on Switzerland on 19 February 1803, the Act of Mediation. The main purpose of this law was to guarantee Swiss soldiers to the French armies, but it also promoted St Gallen, Aargau, Thurgau, Ticino, Vaud, and Graubünden to the rank of cantons. In addition, all cantons were now considered equal. They had once again become masters of their internal organization. These provisions also prevented political freedoms from becoming a threat to those in power by introducing certain safeguards, thus guaranteeing the proper use of prerogatives granted to the population.

In this conservative turn, which was also taking place in France, the cantons returned to their original structures. The old patrician states, such as Berne, reinstated a strict oligarchy. In the lands of 'pure democracy', such as Uri and Schwyz, Landgemeindes were reunited. As for most of the newly created cantons, they favoured a representative system inherited from France but with safeguards in place, such as a suffrage based on a tax threshold. From a political perspective, this Mediation regime represented a retreat into the cantonal space and to mechanisms of citizen participation reminiscent of the Ancien Régime (Tornare 2005).

This conservative regression became even more pronounced in 1814, when a defeated Napoleon had to abandon his control over the Confederation. Left to their own devices, the cantons began to repeal the Act of Mediation and threatened to descend into civil war once again. Thanks to the comminatory intervention of the Great Powers, they ended up, after a year of negotiations, with a new fundamental law: the Federal Pact. Officially signed into law on 7 August 1815, the text reflected the geo-political pressures prevalent as it was being drafted.

Firstly, it echoed the state of mind of the victorious monarchs: they advocated the consolidation of international order on the Continent. For this reason, they officially guaranteed Swiss neutrality and decided to reinforce the country's western border by adding to it the cantons of Valais, Neuchâtel, and Geneva. For the same reason, they also committed the Swiss to building a more efficient army and to founding an officers' school. Above all, they wanted to restore pre-revolutionary legitimacy. Thus, Switzerland remained the only republic on the Continent, while the cantons were encouraged to reserve political and economic rights for the ruling elites (Humair 2018, 13ff.).

Most Swiss leaders gladly agreed with the Great Powers' wishes. The Federal Pact they drafted was very conservative-oriented, devoid of a revision clause, and provided for only one common political institution in the form of an intermittent and weak diet. Moreover, the cantons strengthened the conservative tendencies of their internal political systems. They nevertheless remained mutually equal and their elites, aware of the risks inherent in popular discontent, denied the common people access to institutions, while striving to improve agricultural techniques and reinforcing the influence of the Church (Herrmann 2016).

This management of public dissatisfaction by means of Christian edification frustrated those who had taken advantage of the Helvetic Republic to explore new horizons. Members of the bourgeoisie and entrepreneurs aspired to having greater political rights. Some governments, such as that in Geneva, understood the underlying danger this desire represented to public order. They relaxed the conditions for participation in the res publica, introducing measures such as publicity of parliamentary debates. And when revolution broke out in Paris in July 1830, it was replicated in most of the (proto-)industrialized regions of the Confederation in the north-east and the Central Plateau (Kölz 2006, 227ff.).

In these areas, the discontented populace gathered to protest. Supported by the crowd, leaders imbued with liberal ideas demanded an increase in the rights of the population. In some cantons (TI, TG, AG, LU, ZH, SG, FR, VD, SO, BE, SH) the authorities abdicated. Liberal constituents immediately drew up constitutions that gave them a considerable number of freedoms and the means to preserve them, thus abolishing the Restoration (of the Ancien Régime) in favour of a so-called 'regenerated' regime. In most cases, as in Zurich, a representative system based on universal (male) suffrage was established. Similarly, the cities were no longer favoured at the expense of the countryside. Finally, the new constitutions ensured that the industrialization of the cantonal economy could proceed unhindered. However, this increase in power was limited by restrictions on access to the ballot and by the weakness of the powers placed in the hands of the voters. In reality, the liberals used mob pressure to gain political and economic rights which would benefit them at the expense of those who had brought them to power (Herrmann 2014).

These constitutional changes provoked fierce opposition. In the cantons of Neuchâtel, Schwyz, and Basel, the turmoil led to federal military intervention to restore order. However, this measure did not prevent a civil war from breaking out in Basel, resulting in the division of the canton (1833). At the federal level, the 'regenerated' cantons wanted to amend the 1815 Pact to make it more progressive but the conservatives adamantly refused to do so. The absence of a revision clause allowed the latter to block political change. Moreover, the Landsgemeinde cantons believed that they were the only true bearers of democracy and distrusted the 'French' representative system. Conservatives also entrenched their position even further due to an additional religious dimension, which exacerbated ideological disagreements from the mid-1830s onwards.

In January 1834, representatives from Bern, Lucerne, Solothurn, Basel-Land, St. Gallen, Aargau, and Thurgau met in Baden and signed fourteen articles aimed at 'nationalizing religion'. This act irritated even the Pope, who expressed his strong displeasure in the encyclical Commissum divinitus of 17 May 1835. The Pope's intervention in Swiss debates made an impression on both the clergy and the faithful, thus polarizing the country into two camps: the conservatives, followers of an order 'willed by God', and their opponents, who advocated the primacy of individual reason. The basic conflict was not strictly split along religious lines, although the former tended to be more Catholic and the latter more Protestant (Panzera 2000, 272–276).

At the beginning of the 1840s, an economic crisis aggravated the situation. Seven conservative cantons—Uri, Schwyz, Unterwald, Lucerne, Zug, Fribourg, and Valais—decided to form a separate alliance, known as the Sonderbund. The other cantons became aware of the existence of this alliance in the spring of 1846, which provoked an outcry among the 'regenerate' camp who demanded its dissolution. After several months of fruitless negotiations, it became clear that both sides were considering settling the problem by force of arms. For some, a civil conflict was the only way to preserve 'true religion' and cantonal sovereignty; for others, it was a means of transforming the Confederation into a nation state.

It was against this background that the Sonderbund War broke out on 3 November 1847. The hostilities lasted less than three weeks because the conservatives were ill-prepared, while their opponents, wanting to build a united country, tried actively to prevent a vicious cycle of revenge. This rapidity precluded armed intervention by the great European powers, who were also occupied by the emergence of the 'People's Spring' of 1848. To be certain of this, the defeated parties had to pay compensation and appoint local governments favourable to the victors. Nevertheless, the new nation would be built with some fears of the defeated in mind. Overall, the Confederation would remain resolutely federalist, as ratified by the 1848 constitution (Remak 1997).

2.3 The federal state or the empowerment of citizens (1847–1891)

This constitution was the tripartite result of the 1847 conflict. Firstly, the origin of these hostilities lay in the immutability of the Federal Pact and, consequently, in the intense desire to be able to change fundamental law. Secondly, the victors were aware that they had just taken over the country through a civil and highly illegal conflict. Finally, they knew that their country was extremely poor and vulnerable. It was therefore regarded as important to enact new laws that would quickly anchor the victors' aspirations in legislation and for the future (Humair 2009).

No sooner had hostilities ceased and the threat of foreign intervention subsided than the constituents set to work in February 1848. All the cantons were called upon to send their representatives, except Neuchâtel and Appenzell Innerrhoden, which were guilty of remaining neutral during the conflict. However, the defeated cantons participated in the discussions, as the victorious camp wanted the constitution, which was supposed to underpin the (re)construction of a true nation, to forge unity; moreover, the liberals feared the extremism of the 'Radicals' on their left wing and counted on the conservatives to maintain the balance in the centre, i.e. closer to their own aspirations. As a result, the constitution was a solution built on compromise (Kreis 1986, 88–89).

The influence of the defeated parties is evident in several measures, such as the refusal to entrust the control of education or the police to the Confederation. Others were clearly inspired by radicalism, such as the abolition of the death penalty on ideological grounds. As for economic considerations, most echoed liberal concerns. The bicameralism now emblematic of the Swiss political system, which seemed expensive and exotic at the time, was first put in place as a temporary solution (Kölz 2006, 614ff.). In any case, all male Swiss citizens who had reached their majority and were solvent and established were now entitled to elect the federal parliament and to vote on a new constitution. The exclusion of bankrupts, servants, itinerant populations, and Jews is an indication of the values of the new masters of the country. They feared the influence of dependency on the ballot and aspired to a political life shaped by free individuals, guided by a 'reasonable' Christian faith (Herrmann 2013).

The circumstances in which the text was ratified, its moderation, and the institutional safeguards it established explain why its proponents had the time to establish the regime it introduced and its new leaders. Yet the need for change became an urgent matter in the early 1860s, primarily because the elites of the defeated cantons wanted to break out of the 'cantonal straitjacket' and influence the federal sphere. This desire coincided with the emergence of the democratic movement, a composite group of people who were determined to combat the power of the now dominant Radicals by introducing instruments of direct democracy.

The signal for change came in 1864, when Switzerland ratified a trade treaty with France. This agreement included a 'most-favoured-nation' clause, which gave French Jews the freedom to settle on Swiss soil, a right that Swiss Jews themselves did not enjoy. In 1866, in order to rectify this incongruity, the federal authorities submitted a partial revision of the constitution to their citizens. They agreed to grant settlement rights to Swiss Jews, but refused to introduce other liberties, such as freedom of worship. This decision was therefore less a reflection of philosemitism than an expression of their concern to maintain the socio-political prerogatives of nationals.

Work to improve the constitution was boosted by the Franco-Prussian war of 1870–1871. This conflict demonstrated the weakness of the Confederation by showing the degree to which respect for neutrality depended on the goodwill of external players and by exposing inadequacies in the Swiss army. These considerations prompted the government to propose a new constitution, one that would reduce the primacy of federalism. On 12 May 1872, the project was rejected both by Catholics who feared for their religion and by the Romands, who saw it as an attempt to 'Prussianise' Switzerland. The drafters of this document quickly set to work once again and succeeded in passing a totally revised constitution by 29 May 1874 (Rielle 2010).

In the second draft, the framers of the constitution moderated their positions considerably. They took care to tone down their aspirations for centralization as well as their desire to increase popular prerogatives—which nevertheless remained considerable. Citizens were granted freedom of belief, conscience, trade, industry, and, above all, the right to a legislative referendum granting the right for a rejection of federal laws to be proposed if put forward by a minimum of 30,000 Swiss voters (5 per cent of the electorate). This could be seen as a progressive measure. However, the opponents of radicalism soon made use of this tool to block the Federal Council's policies. In the early 1880s, the referendum was used so efficiently that it made a laughing stock of the administration (Graber 2017, 135ff.).

In order to overcome this major obstacle, the authorities decided in 1891 to introduce the 'right of constitutional initiative', allowing amendments to the constitution to be made if proposed by a minimum of 50,000 voters. This particular right also served the wishes of the conservatives, who saw this right as the heir to Swiss mediaeval 'democracy', not to mention that it was already in place in many cantons. This achievement was unprecedented in Europe and had significant implications. On the one hand, it granted a greater importance to a new political structure: the party. Only the party had enough reach to collect the required number of signatures and enough knowledge to take a stand in public debate. On the other hand, the threat of referendums and initiatives required parliamentarians to reach a certain level of agreement among themselves. Some scholars see this need as the origin of the fundamental role played by consensus (Moeckli 2016).

In the mind of the elite, the best way to ensure a 'reasonable' use of these extensive rights was to sell them as inherently 'Swiss'. The thinking was that this process would subliminally reinforce the pride the voters felt in exercising these exceptional rights and discourage them from squandering their fine political legacy (Marchal 2006). However, it simultaneously generated a reticence to share these exceptional rights. Therefore, if Swiss political reasonableness came with a broad spectrum of rights, it would not facilitate the second phase of Swiss democratization, when the goal shifted from increasing political freedoms to expanding the number of those who would benefit from them.

3 Integration (1891–1991)

Events in the first few decades of direct democracy seem to lend themselves to the left-wing-based view of Swiss politics, which presents them as the result of calculations by the elite to maintain power. By astutely integrating minority leaders, the authorities managed to maintain their stability and their opportunities to influence their fellow citizens for an extended period. The first initiatives seem to confirm this view, as they were used surprisingly sparingly in a society that was the first in Europe to exercise such extensive rights. Of the eleven initiatives launched between 1891 and 1914, only two were signed into law. Moreover, the very nature of these laws is surprisingly conservative: the first prohibits the ritual slaughter of cattle (1893) and the second the sale of absinthe (1908). The latter corresponded to the wishes of the government. However, the former testified to a latent anti-Semitism and to issues concerning integration into the national body.

This vote signalled a great reluctance to broaden the electoral base as though, having secured the loyalty of the initial core of (male) citizens, it was difficult to rely on the loyalty of others. Indeed, the question of inclusion marks much of twentieth century Swiss political development. It is so central, in fact, that it serves as the measure of democratization that underlies Swiss socio-political life, just as the growth of popular rights did in the previous century.

3.1 The majority system or the integration of Catholics (1891–1918)

The prohibition of certain groups from participating in the electoral system is a phenomenon that appeared long before the introduction of the legislative initiative, as limiting the number of voting citizens is a means of controlling the ballot. After the revolutionary period, a system restricting access to full rights by means of heredity or financial independence was still in vogue. When, in the wake of the 'regenerative' regime change, most liberal cantons proclaimed universal suffrage, they managed the risks inherent in this legislative generosity by deploying an arsenal of measures that silenced whole demographics considered to be 'insecure' because they were unstable and/or financially dependent (Herrmann 2014). The winners of the Sonderbund conflict relied on a majority system to stay in power and therefore skilfully manipulated the mapping of electoral boundaries, a move which secured them a notable longevity in the Federal Assembly (Tanner 1998, 63ff.).

Despite this, the results at the ballot box did not always correspond to Berne's expectations. The rejection of the 1872 draft of the constitution provoked intense reflection on how to win a vote, as exclusion of 'undesirable' citizens no longer appeared to be sufficient to maintain the status quo. As the rejection of the draft was the result of the alliance between the French-speaking cantons and the small Catholic cantons, it provoked the authorities into make concessions to the former by feeding the hatred that Ultramontanism—the supranational power of the Pope—inspired in the latter (Stadler 1996). Following this tactic's success in 1874, it was turned into a strategy: if the government wanted to be sure that measures would be accepted, it had to secure a majority and, if necessary, set one part of the country against the other.

This specific strategy was used again some fifteen years later to include the Catholics. The intransigent Radicals of 1848 were gradually replaced by wealthier leaders who were uncomfortable with the development of internationalist, anarchist, and left-wing ideas.

As the defence of the working class became more organized, the authorities looked to the Catholic cantons for support in defending the country against the 'red peril'. Moreover, the former Sonderbund cantons were reintegrated into the grand narrative of the Swiss past. In 1891, as the authorities introduced the right of constitutional initiative, they also celebrated the 600th anniversary of the founding of the Confederation, an event which supposedly took place in the middle of Sonderbund territory in early August 1291. In addition to all of this, they promoted the appointment of the first conservative Catholic (Josef Zemp) in the Federal Council.

This appointment can be interpreted as the effect of an inclusion mechanism. However, the Federal Council remained otherwise exclusively composed of Radicals. In a strictly majority system, the presence of a Catholic was a way of giving him the opportunity to express himself without having to give his opinions any serious consideration. Better still, it was a way of keeping the minority he represented in check: they had a spokesperson at the highest level of state and therefore, in theory, had no reason to complain (Herrmann 2006, 155). In reality, the wholesale integration of Catholics would take a few more years.

Authorities intensified the integrating potential of history. While the turn of the nineteenth and twentieth centuries saw the emergence of an increasingly scientific and professional historiography, it was also a time of active invention of tradition, namely a poorly defined and idealized past. The intention of this Swiss tradition was to anchor the average citizen, the bearer of progress, and the future of Switzerland to a mythical and harmonious 'old time'. Tradition was highlighted in theatrical performances and museum exhibitions, glorifying the united ancestors of a democratic and prosperous Switzerland, as exemplified by the second national exhibition in 1896 (el-Wakil and Vaisse 2001).

That notwithstanding, the idealization of Swiss tradition correlated directly to the ever-increasing dissension generated by rapid industrialization in the country. The period leading up to the First World War was marked by a large number of strikes. As in the rest of Europe, Switzerland experienced a momentary social calm in 1914, thanks to the Swiss Sacred Union, a political truce caused by the outbreak of war. However, this short-lived respite came to an end when conflict flared up between pro-French French-speakers and pro-German German-speakers who now found themselves on their own respective sides of an antagonistic divide. This schism worried the authorities who tried to reunite their citizens by brandishing the threat of an enemy attack, workers' discontent, and revolution. In fact, due to supply shortages during the war, Switzerland was wracked with economic difficulties and most workers found themselves utterly impoverished. The Soviets' accession to power, driven by internationalist (and hence anti-national) aspirations, ideologized their struggle, which worried the Swiss authorities deeply. On 10 November 1918, discontented workers and employees decided to go on general strike, so the government called in the troops (Gautschi 1988).

This strike did not frighten only the leaders. Part of the general population was also concerned about the idea of a Bolshevik invasion. This fear reinforced a tendency towards conservatism, which could already be read in the rejection of most of the social improvements proposed by the government at the turn of the century. Hence, in 1918, the official discourse succeeded in portraying the strikers as agitators, aiming to destroy Swiss democracy and the protection and rights it guaranteed to its citizens. In the face of this existential danger, other divisions seemed insignificant, thus greatly helping to unite the two linguistic communities of Switzerland, and giving Catholics a definitive place in Swiss political life (Rossfeld et al. 2018).

3.2 The proportional system or the integration of the socialist left (1918–1959)

However understandable, the fear of the 'red menace' had no foundation. The demands expressed by the strikers remained mostly moderate, notably wishing for the introduction of rights already present in other non-communist countries, such as women's suffrage, and the application of rights that the Swiss had already voted for. The strikers' first demand called for the immediate renewal of the National Council by proportional representation, an electoral system which the Swiss population had already accepted on 13 October 1918. This system was the result of a process dating back to the second half of the nineteenth century when opponents of the Radicals sought to dismantle the majority system that gave them a hegemonic position. Because of this pressure and because the proliferation of parties made the outcome of elections less predictable, the Radicals resigned themselves to this solution which, in the long run, presented fewer risks. Before 1914 two initiatives were launched to apply the proportional electoral system at the federal level, but without success. Following a political mechanism that would become customary, the measure was re-proposed and adopted in the third attempt. Thus, the strikers' demands were more legalistic than revolutionary; however, the consequences of meeting them would profoundly change the Swiss political reality (Dubosson 1993/1994).

In 1919, elections to the National Council were held using the proportional system and resulted in a clear diversification of political power. The Radicals lost their absolute majority and the Left quickly assumed a crucial role. Therefore, the classic representatives of the prior government now had to deal with other parties. Furthermore, they had to position themselves in relation to the Socialists. Drawing on their strategy of 'inclusion through exclusion' (of the Left), which had begun more than forty years previously, authorities were looking for alliances in the centre and in the conservative camp. In spite of that, during the interwar period, the Socialist Party regularly won between 21 and 29 per cent of the votes and was even considered to be the most influential political party in the country at the beginning of the 1930s. However, it would take another three decades of negotiation before the Socialists were considered an essential part of the country's institutional life.

In the aftermath of the general strike, there was no time for conciliation. The Socialist Party, (re)founded in 1888, fought to establish a genuine dictatorship of the proletariat. However, it refused to be 'subservient' to Moscow and this position alienated its leftmost wing, which formed the Swiss Communist Party on 6 March 1921. Despite this split, the Left refused to compromise with the government: strikes and demonstrations proliferated without improving workers' living conditions at all. Around 1935, at a time when Hitler was dominating Germany and authoritarian models were being emulated by frontist (fascist) movements in Switzerland, the Left decided to support democracy and national defence. This stance was also characteristic of the trade unions, so that in 1937 the metal industry concluded a 'labour peace'—an agreement providing for the resolution of conflicts through negotiation—a model which spread to other industrial sectors. This rapprochement reached its zenith with the appointment of the Socialist Ernst Nobs to the Federal Council on 15 December 1943 (Halle 2011).

However, just as the accession of a conservative Catholic to the national executive had been only the first step in a longer integration process, the election of Nobs did not immediately result in the wholesale integration of the left. In neutral and unoccupied Switzerland, war had not dulled the hatred of the communists. The Swiss Communist Party had been banned in November 1940 and despite its reinvention four years later under the name of the Labour Party, its members were still under suspicion. Actually, at the end of WWII, Switzerland plunged into a sort of 'self-satisfied conservatism' based on the prosperity that its status as a privileged creditor of devastated states granted. In 1953, the Socialist Party withdrew its representative from the Federal Council because of its powerlessness. However, the party still won more than a quarter of the votes, and its ideological stance tended to be in line with that of the government, merely advocating better living conditions while professing a strong anti-Soviet stance. And when, in December 1959, four federal councillor seats became available, two of them went to the Socialists, who shared power with two Radicals, two Christian Democrats and an Agrarian (traditional right). This time, the Socialists' inclusion was destined to last, as this composition, known as the 'magic formula', remained in force until 2003.

The magic formula can be seen as the transposition of the proportional system to the highest level of the state and somehow compensated for the fact that Swiss voters do not elect their executive, let alone their president. The influence it gave to the Left was reflected in a shift of leftist policy towards the centre. Moreover, the citizens massively supported the governmental parties while continuing to shun the social improvements the government proposed. In 1948, Swiss voters signed the AHV (social security for pensioners) into law, a vote initially rejected in 1931. In contrast to this, they voted against the adoption of the 44-hour working week, a vote entirely according to the wishes of the government in charge at the time. In addition, Swiss women still did not have the right to vote, and the country's prosperity was based heavily on the labour of immigrants who were not allowed to integrate. At the dawn of the 1960s, the 'oldest democracy in Europe' still did not guarantee equality and basic political rights for all.

3.3 Universal integration? (1959–1992)

As the Socialists were entering the Federal Council, they suffered a bitter defeat. In February 1959, the people had rejected the introduction of women's suffrage by two-thirds of the votes. Admittedly, the Federal Council's support for this cause was rather weak (Boucherin 2012), while the Left had been fighting for it since 1912. At the end of WWI, after which several countries gave women the right to vote and to be elected to political office, several cantons put the question to the electorate but in vain. The Second World War accentuated this trend in a paradoxical way. Firstly, neutrality avoided full mobilization so it did not seem necessary to reward women for their efforts during the hostilities. Moreover, the Swiss army was idealized and this mythological narrative reinforced the ancient bond between citizen and soldier. In addition to this, in contrast to other Western countries, the Confederation remained wary of communism and therefore of its ideas on gender equality (Studer 2020, 89ff.).

However, in the midst of the Cold War, the authorities thought they could better protect the country by strengthening its civil service, which involved women. The discussion highlighted the potential role of Swiss women in the defence of their country as almost equal to their male (military) counterparts. Caught in its own web, the government submitted the question to the citizens. The Swiss were the only men on the Continent whose vote controlled the political rights of their female compatriots. And they refused, making Switzerland one of the only Western states to retain an exclusively male electorate at the national level (Studer 2020).

Vaud, however, took advantage of the 1959 referendum to give women the right to vote at the cantonal level and was quickly followed by Neuchâtel and Geneva. These cantons thus proved through practice that female participation did not change the distribution of political power. Consequently, more and more cantons followed this example, so that the absence of women in federal elections became a domestic oddity, while at the same time being a major international embarrassment. Throughout the world, women's suffrage was a sign of true democracy. It was a requirement for signing the European Convention on Human Rights, to which the Swiss government wished to accede. This is why it put the question to the voters again, this time with conviction. Its endeavour was facilitated by fervent public protests by feminists and by a generational shift in parliament, as well as among citizens. The ideas and fears of the WWII era were fading, more and more women were working, and almost all democracies had already given women the vote. On 7 February 1971, two-thirds of voters secured women the right to vote.

The importance of the country's reputation was highlighted further as the Swiss had just been internationally disgraced for their reluctance to accept immigrants. Until the end of the nineteenth century, the only immigrants were religious or political refugees to whom the porous nature of federalism and the republican system guaranteed a degree of security, endorsed by a tradition of asylum. But from the turn of the twentieth century onwards, more and more immigrants had economic motivations. They indicated and increased the recent prosperity of Switzerland. They also exacerbated xenophobic reflexes, which were first counterbalanced by the authorities' conviction of the power of assimilation through adherence to Swiss ideals. However, after WWI, the integration of foreigners was perceived as difficult and undesirable. When, in the aftermath of WWII, the country made active use of immigrant labour, these views became even more pronounced. In the 1950s and 1960s, when the proportion of foreigners rose from 6 to 11 per cent of the Swiss population, this flux was accompanied by a distrust that was perceptible both in the harshness of the living conditions put in place by the authorities and in the liveliness of xenophobic prejudices within Swiss society (Arlettaz and Arlettaz 2010).

In 1964, several partially contradictory developments occurred. On the one hand, the European Community signed an agreement on the free movement of people, which reduced Switzerland's attractiveness. As the country needed more workers to support the development of its industry, Berne negotiated a treaty with Rome, improving the overall condition for Italians, who then made up almost 60 per cent of the immigration. On the other hand, this text reinforced the intransigence of many nationals with regard to foreigners who, they believed, could 'denature' their homeland (Überfremdung). This fear found its political expression in an initiative drafted by the far-right MP James Schwarzenbach, who called for a limit on the number of immigrants to 10 per cent of the population. Even though Swiss government and business circles were vehemently opposed to a measure they considered counterproductive for the Swiss market and international reputation, the public gave the measure more support than expected. On 7 June 1970, to the great surprise of the country's elites, this xenophobic initiative was defeated by a mere 54 per cent of the votes (Buomberger 2004).

Immediately, Schwarzenbach set out to re-launch a similar initiative. But his second attempt was clearly rejected by the people. This reversal was due to the oil crisis of 1973, which significantly slowed down the flow of migration and reduced the relevance of a strict quota for foreigners. This attitude marked the beginning of a growing openness in Switzerland towards the world, an attitude notable in the 1976 law on development cooperation and the 1979 law on asylum. This socio-political trend was also perceptible in the efforts made by the leaders, from the mid-1970s to the mid-1980s, to associate the country with various international alliances.

At the end of the Cold War, signs of popular tension reappeared. In 1986, the citizens declined to join the UN, and on 6 December 1992, they opposed the wishes of the governmental and economic elites by refusing to join the EEA and, by extension, the European Community. This decision, taken by the people, dismayed the establishment: not only did Switzerland no longer occupy a privileged place between the two blocs, but the Swiss themselves were increasingly distancing themselves from their authorities and digging themselves deeper into a position they believed to be traditional.

In so doing, the citizens were placing their trust in a specific party, the People's Party (SVP). On the pretext of returning to the true and essential values of Swiss history (Marchal 2005, 131–148), this party had decisively changed the decade-long functioning of Swiss politics, the omnipresent consensus, and the alliances between the Socialists and the right-wing parties. Thus, the 'responsibility' that had so long characterized the Swiss socio-political reality seemed to vanish as from 1991 onwards the Swiss population was increasingly attracted to this party and its populist anti-establishment programme that supposedly emulated the national past. Making this party a determining leading political force in Switzerland was a way of allegedly 'historicizing' and hence 'legitimizing' the reluctance of the twentieth century Swiss citizens to integrate populations or habits that were seen as likely to squander the political and material wealth of democracy. Their reluctance was rooted not in history but in its misinterpretation, and it was contrary to the wishes of the rest of the political authorities, as evidenced by the elite integration policy they had, mutatis mutandis, been pursuing.

4 Conclusion

Swiss political behaviour at the end of the twentieth century suggests that the Swiss people did not possess some kind of permanent self-restraint. Neither were they manipulated by their governments. Rather, it is as if they had over-internalized the injunctions of individual responsibility based on the duty of being worthy of their glorious ancestors.

This sense of responsibility was the necessary complement to political developments that gave them more and more rights: male citizens were granted the right to elect their representatives, then refuse laws, and ultimately propose changes to their constitutions. These exceptionally generous rights, as well as their moral-historical safeguard, were mostly characteristic of a country that had long been very poor and whose state had had to delegate to its citizens the share of responsibility that it could not assume for them.

The system, born out of poverty, which led to a simultaneous increase in the rights and responsibilities of male citizens, reached its peak and demanded to be extended to other categories of the population at the same time as the country was becoming rich. The authorities, sometimes painfully, understood that it was in their interest to share their power with minority elites emboldened by this new wealth, especially since the ethic of responsibility would incite them to exercise it with great restraint.

At the same time, Swiss people began to understand their unexpected prosperity as undeniable proof of their superior political (and economic) reasonableness. This interpretation of reality led them to maintain or even accentuate their self-restraint and to distrust others' sense of responsibility. This is why women were refused the right to vote until very late, and why foreigners, who did not share the same history, were regarded with suspicion, even though they decisively contributed to the wealth of Switzerland, which seemed to prove the benefits of the Swiss' sense of responsibility.

These possibly counterproductive and harmful results were only very indirectly brought about by elite pressures and medieval 'democratic experiments'. In fact, they emerged from a distorted understanding of a historical narrative that was itself biased, both of which were perfectly in tune with a history more than two centuries old.

REFERENCES

Arlettaz, Gérald, and Silvia Arlettaz. 2010. *La Suisse et les étrangers: immigration et formation nationale (1848-1933)*. Lausanne: Ed. Antipodes & Société d'histoire de la Suisse romande.

Boucherin, Nadine. 2012. *Les stratégies argumentatives dans les débats parlementaires suisses sur le suffrage féminin (1945-1971)*. Doctoral thesis, Université de Fribourg. https://folia.unifr.ch/unifr/documents/302695.

Buomberger, Thomas. 2004. *Kampf gegen unerwünschte Fremde: Von James Schwarzenbach bis Christoph Blocher*. Zurich: Orell Füssli Verlag.

Christin, Olivier. 2014. *Vox populi. Une histoire du vote avant le suffrage universel*. Paris: Seuil.

Dubosson, Françoise. 1993/1994. 'L'introduction de la représentation proportionnelle à Genève (1865-1892)'. *Bulletin de la Société d'histoire et d'archéologie de Genève* 23/24: pp. 69-89.

el-Wakil, Leila, and Pierre Vaisse. 2001. *Genève 1896: regards sur une exposition nationale*. Genève. Paris: Georg.

Gautschi, Willi. 1988. *Der Landesstreik, 1918*. Zurich: Chronos Verlag.

Graber, Rolf. 2017. *Demokratie und Revolten. Die Entstehung der direkten Demokratie in der Schweiz*. Zurich: Chronos Verlag.

Halle, Marianne. 2011. 'Les incitations politiques en Suisse pendant l'Entre-deux-guerres: études de cas et analyse comparative'. *Revue suisse d'histoire* 61 (1): pp. 90-107.

Herrmann, Irène. 2006. *Les cicatrices du passé. Essai sur la gestion des conflits en Suisse (1798-1918)*. Berne: Peter Lang.

Herrmann, Irène. 2013. 'Les fluctuations de la tolérance politique en Suisse (1848-1945)'. In *Les frontières de la tolérance*, edited by Simone de Reyff, Michel Viègnes, and Jean Rimez, pp. 149-160. Neuchâtel: Alphil – Presses universitaires suisses.

Herrmann, Irène. 2014. 'Zwischen Angst und Hoffnung: Eine Nation entsteht (1798-1848)'. In *Geschichte der Schweiz*, edited by Georg Kreis, pp. 371-421. Bâle: Schwabe Verlag.

Herrmann, Irène. 2016. *12 septembre 1814: la Restauration: la Confédération réinventée*. Lausanne: Presses Polytechniques et Universitaires Romandes.

Humair, Cédric. 2009. *1848. Naissance de la Suisse moderne*. Lausanne: Antipodes.

Humair, Cédric. 2018. *La Suisse et les puissances européennes: aux sources de l'indépendance (1813-1857)*. Neuchâtel: Éditions Livreo-Alphil.

Kirchgässner, Gebhard, Lars P. Feld, and Marcel R. Savioz (eds). 1999. *Die direkte Demokratie. Modern, erfolgreich, entwicklungs- und exportfähig*. Bâle, Genève, Munich: Helbing & Lichtenhahn.

Kölz, Alfred. 2006. *Histoire constitutionnelle de la Suisse moderne. Ses fondements idéologiques et son évolution institutionnelle dans le contexte européen, de la fin de l'Ancien Régime à 1848*. Berne: Stämpfli et Bruxelles: Bruylant.

Kreis, Georg. 1986. *Le siècle où la Suisse bougea: Un nouveau regard sur le XIXe siècle*. Lausanne: Editions 24 heures.

Kurunmäki Jussi, and Herrmann Irène. 2018. 'Birthplaces of Democracy. The Rhetoric of Democratic Tradition in Switzerland and Sweden'. In *Democracy in Modern Europe, a Conceptual History*, edited by Jussi Kurunmäki, Jeppe Nevers, and Henk te Velde, pp. 88-112. New York, Oxford: Berghahn.

Marchal, Guy. 2005. 'Die Schweizer und ihr Mittelalter: Missbrauch der Geschichte?' *Revue suisse d'histoire* 55 (2): pp. 131-148.

Marchal, Guy. 2006. *Schweizer Gebrauchsgeschichte: Geschichtsbilder, Mythenbildung und nationale Identität*. Basel: Schwabe Verlag.

Masnata, François, and Claire Masnata-Rubattel. 1978. *Le pouvoir suisse. Séduction démocratique et répression suave*. Paris: C. Bourgeois.

Moeckli, Silvano. 2009. Formation de la volonté politique. In *Dictionnaire historique de la Suisse (DHS)*. SAGW. https://hls-dhs-dss.ch/fr/articles/017367.php [23.06.2023].

Panzera, Fabrizio. 2000. 'L'Eglise en Suisse, de la fin de l'Ancien Régime à la Restauration (1798-1835)'. In *Histoire religieuse de la Suisse. La présence des catholiques*, edited by Guy Bedouelle, and François Walter, pp. 259-276. Paris: Editions du Cerf, Fribourg: Editions universitaires.

Remak, Joachim. 1997. *Bruderzwist nicht Brudermord. Der Schweizer Sonderbundskrieg von 1847*. Zurich: Orell Füssli Verlag.

Rielle, Yvan. 2010. '"Il nous faut les Welsches" – Kompromisse ebnen der neuen Bundesverfassung den Weg'. In *Handbuch der eidgenössischen Volksabstimmungen 1848-2007*, edited by Wolf Linder, Christian Bolliger, and Yvan Rielle, pp. 34-37. Bern: Haupt.

Roca, René (ed.). 2011. *Wege zur direkten Demokratie in den schweizerischen Kantonen*. Zurich: Schulthess.

Rossfeld, Roman, Christian Koller, and Brigitte Studer (eds). 2018. *Der Landesstreik. Die Schweiz im November 1918*. Baden: Hier und Jetzt.

Simon, Christian (ed.). 1995-1998. *Dossier helvétique*. Bâle: Helbing & Lichtenhahn puis Schwabe Verlag.

Stadler, Peter. 1996. *Der Kulturkampf in der Schweiz: Eidgenossenschaft und katholische Kirche im europäischen Umkreis, 1848-1888*. Zurich: Chronos Verlag.

Studer, Brigitte. 2020. *La conquête d'un droit: le suffrage féminin en Suisse*. Neuchâtel: Éditions Livreo-Alphil.

Tanner, Albert. 1998. 'Ein Staat nur für die Hablichen? Demokratie und politische Elite im frühen Bundesstaat'. In *Etappen des Bundesstaates. Staats- und Nationsbildung der Schweiz, 1848-1998*, edited by Brigitte Studer, pp. 63-88. Zurich: Chronos Verlag.

Tornare, Alain Jacques (ed.). 2005. *Quand Napoléon Bonaparte recréa la Suisse: la genèse et la mise en œuvre de l'Acte de médiation: aspects des relations franco-suisses autour de 1803*. Paris: Société des études robespierristes.

CHAPTER 4

THE POLITICAL CULTURE OF SWITZERLAND IN COMPARATIVE PERSPECTIVE

MARKUS FREITAG AND ALINA ZUMBRUNN

1 INTRODUCTION

THE study of political culture is not part of the standard repertoire of Swiss political science literature. Three reasons are likely for this: The vagueness of the concept and its ramifications, insufficient data sources, and the often-invoked diversity of the Swiss culture.

With regard to conceptual clarity, the bon mot of 'the jelly that is difficult to nail to the wall' is often used to refer to political culture (Kaase 1983). First of all, the concept of political culture exists and is used in both a normatively moralizing and a neutrally descriptive and more empirically oriented form (Pickel and Pickel 2006; Seitz 1997). On the one hand, the label of political culture applies to the quality of political debates or the particularly stylish or moral handling of political power. On the other hand, the focus is solely on individual attitudes towards the political system that is on the 'subjective orientations to politics' (Verba 1965, 513). In academic as well as more essayistic writings, we find both basic convictions in Switzerland, which has not been conducive to the systematic development of the concept (Seitz 2006). From a genuinely empirical political science perspective, however, only the second form ought to be used. To put it bluntly: When it comes to the tonality and semantic level of political conflicts, one may speak of political style or political togetherness, but not of political culture in the sense of a modern political science understanding (Dachs 2009, 5).

Until the beginning of the 1980s, population surveys in Switzerland were not available in such abundance as today, not least due to Switzerland's systematic involvement in international survey projects. Moreover, surveys conducted in the wake of referendums and national elections focused mainly on the motivations behind the respective electoral or voting decision and less on attitudes towards the political system. This may also explain why there are only a few data-saturated empirical contributions on components of Switzerland's political culture and why there have been few broad research programmes of empirical political science cultural research thus far. Moreover, the contributions to date focus only fragmentarily on subjective orientations to Swiss politics (Bauer et al. 2018; Brunner and Sgier 1997; Coromina and Kustec 2020; Freitag 2001; Longchamp and Rousselot 2010; Scheidegger and Staerklé 2011; Staubli 2016; Widmer and de Carlo 2010).

Furthermore, the statements of political culture research refer primarily to the political community of a whole nation (Almond and Verba 1963, 13). This contrasts with the apparent segmentation of political culture in Switzerland (Linder and Steffen 2006, 20). The three language areas (German, French, and Italian) are culturally largely autonomous and comparatively self-contained systems 'with their backs to one another' (Steiner 2001, 145). Various studies show that the three language regions are sometimes more similar to their neighbouring countries Germany, France, and Italy than to their Swiss neighbours in terms of civic and cultural aspects, thus at least calling into question the internal homogeneity of Swiss political culture (Freitag and Stadelmann-Steffen 2008; Stadelmann-Steffen and Gundelach 2015).

These observations are the starting point for this contribution to political culture in Switzerland in comparative perspective. As we understand it, political culture research is associated with the subjective side of politics and thus deals with the attitudes of individuals towards the political system (Pickel and Pickel 2006). Political culture is not defined as a highly developed cultivation of political will-formation and decision-making. Rather, following the research tradition founded by Almond and Verba (1963), we conceptualize political culture as the *totality of citizens' values, beliefs, and attitudes towards the political system, political actors, processes, and political objects*.[1] In this sense, attitudes form the basic category in the present analysis of political culture (Faas et al. 2020; Gabriel 2008, 182; Welch 2013). Moreover, while political attitudes can be interpreted as characteristics of individuals, political culture as a collective characteristic denotes a distribution pattern of individual attitudes within a political community. Against this background, it is the collective relationships that are of particular interest and less so insights into the orientations of individual persons.

While our understanding of political culture frees the concept from normative charges, it also has limitations. For example, a survey of political opinions, attitudes, and values does not reach the historical depth of structures that shape a political culture and can explain the individual convictions measured (Rohe 1990) (see also 'The Historical and Institutional Formation of Swiss Political Culture' in this volume). Knowing that there is an alternative understanding of political culture that is both inherent in science and commonplace, the *jelly* conceived here sometimes appears to be difficult to digest. Moreover, such an analytical understanding of concepts precludes research into political action. Political behaviour may indeed derive from these attitudes, but by definition, it does not belong to political culture (Pickel and Pickel 2006, 58; Seitz 1997, 270; Westle 2010, 307). In this way, the present contribution follows the conventions of international political culture research and departs from the specifically Swiss tradition of analysing social cleavages as a foundation of electoral and voting behaviour under the label of political (voting) culture (see e.g. Linder et al. 1991; Linder and Steffen 2006; Seitz 1997).[2] Finally, attitudes towards other social subsystems such as the economy and religion, educational principles, and basic moral convictions are not included in the analysis.

In summary, the present contribution deals with the presentation of the distribution of orientations of the Swiss population towards the political system. The next section first presents the core ideas of the concept of political culture, then we discuss measurements and data stocks of political culture, and illustrate the situation in Switzerland from a comparative perspective. A conclusion completes the observations.

2 On the Concept of Political Culture

The concept of political culture was first introduced into political science by Almond (1956, 396) in the 1950s. Nevertheless, the main features of empirical research on political culture are based on the work of Almond and Verba (1963) and their study *The Civic Culture* (Reisinger 1995; Seitz 1997). Scientific reasons and political developments were both relevant for this first systematic consideration of the population as a political corpus. In addition to the emergence of the system theory, the spread of behaviourism, and the development of survey research, a major driving force lay in the history of the twentieth century with its totalitarian regimes in Germany, Russia, and Italy (Westle 2010). Institutional and modernization theory perspectives could not explain why some democracies with similar structures had survived and others had not. New considerations and approaches were needed to discuss the conditions of system stability. Almond and Verba (1963) looked for these factors in the orientations of the population towards politics. Of particular importance was how members of a political community assessed the institutional architecture, how they judged its performance, and whether they exhibited certain civic virtues.

The research agenda on political culture developed by Almond and Verba (1963; 1980) against this background is based on the following core ideas (Fuchs 2007, 163; Linder and Steffen 2006, 32; Pickel and Pickel 2006, 58): (1) The stability of a (democratic) political system depends on the congruent relationship between political structure and political culture, i.e. between the orientations of the population towards politics and the institutional structure. (2) The political culture of a political community stems from the political attitudes of its members. (3) These political attitudes, opinions, and beliefs are the result of early childhood socialization, education, media influence, and adult life experiences with the performance of the political system. As a direct consequence, these core elements of political culture cannot change in the short term but only through long-term learning processes and generational exchange. (4) Political culture is a macro-level phenomenon. Only as a contextual phenomenon is political culture able to control system stability. (5) Subjective orientations to the political system aggregated to the macro level form the basis of knowledge on political culture.

Almond and Verba (1963, 13) define political culture as 'the particular distribution of patterns of orientation toward political objects among the members of the nation', distinguishing between four political objects of attitudes and three orientations. The latter include *cognitive* (knowledge and perceptions), *affective* (positive and negative emotions), and *evaluative* (morally based judgements) types of attitudes. With regard to the objects of attitudes, the *system as a whole* comprises the (national) political community and the mode of governance. *Input* includes the institutions through which the population can submit demands and wishes to politics (parties and interest groups). *Output* concerns the concrete achievements of politics and the institutions and actors involved in its implementation (government, administration, parliament, and legal system). The *self as a political actor* focuses on the individuals' assessments of their political competence and political involvement. The combination of types of attitudes and objects of attitudes results in a matrix that can be used to identify the respective political culture.

Critical comments and further development of the research programme through the work on political support by Easton (1965; 1975) led to conceptual improvements of earlier considerations (Almond 2000; Fuchs 2007; Dalton 2004; Gabriel 2008, 182–183; Norris 2017). As far as the objects of orientation are concerned, political culture research has recently returned to the tripartite division of a *polity, policy, and politics culture*. Attitudes towards the political system are considered to be of particular importance with regard to system maintenance, although we lack assertions about the exact level of support. The *polity culture* comprises two elements: attitudes towards the political regime and towards the political community. While the political regime refers to fundamental characteristics of politico-institutional orders (fundamental rights, order of rule), the political community represents the community to which individuals relate and to which they express their loyalty (nation, region, ethnicity, etc.). A second set of orientations is directed towards the *policy culture*, i.e. the content of political decisions. Examples would be attitudes towards decisions on nuclear energy, political openness, or environmental protection. Finally, all attitudes towards the process of policy-making, articulation of interests, and demanding and enforcing binding decisions make up the *politics culture*. Various actors are involved in the policy-making process who can influence the individual's opinion: the range extends from the voter to political organizations such as parties and associations, mass media, and courts, to government, parliament, and administration.

At the attitudinal level, the concept of political support has been systematized since the studies of Easton (1965; 1975) and divided into a specific and a diffuse assessment (Dalton 2004; Norris 2017). While specific political support refers solely to the rulers and is sometimes subject to considerable fluctuations, diffuse political support remains largely stable without the occurrence of massive events (such as wars or political and economic crises, for example) and targets all objects. Diffuse support also plays a key role with regard to the legitimacy and stability of the political system: this type of support enables the stability of political systems despite dissatisfaction with temporary performance deficits of political actors (and the associated limited specific political support).

The approaches of Almond, Verba, and Easton very quickly found their way into the comparative analysis of political systems and have been established in empirically oriented political science research for decades. With the increasing popularity of the concept, however, its contours began to blur to such an extent that political culture increasingly became a catch-all term (Kaase 1983; Reisinger 1995). Not least for this reason, critics have always accompanied the research programme of political culture research, which attempts to determine political culture solely through individual attitudes and thereby proceeds value-free. Here, above all, historically and socio-culturally oriented perspectives express their viewpoints and point to the methodological and content-related fuzziness (Pickel and Pickel 2006; Westle 2010). Concentrating solely on attitudes towards politics remains too superficial and neglects deep structures, such as the development of world views, concepts of order, and linguistically constructed political realities, in the sense of a more comprehensive concept of culture (e.g. Rohe 1990). In this view, political culture research should devote itself more to the identification of complex ideas instead of concentrating solely on the mere querying and summing up of short-lived individual opinions and attitudes. In addition, concept-immanent inadequacies of the research programme are also repeatedly evaluated. They primarily question the conceptual architecture of political culture based on poorly developed indicators regarding the distinct objects (Faas et al. 2020; Tong 2019; Westle 2010).

3 Measurement and Data

The measurement of political culture and the accompanying methods of data collection depend to a decisive degree on the analytical approach and can vary between idiographic procedures of document analysis (using textbooks, sagas, proverbs, songs, etc.), observation, and standardized population surveys. While more idiographic methods are associated with a deeper understanding of single aspects, quantitative approaches allow the collection of opinions of numerous individuals over time and in this way also enable systematically comparative studies.

The empirical exploration of the concept of political culture by means of survey data focuses overall less on the distribution of political orientations to capture different types of political culture than on the legitimacy of political regimes, political institutions, and actors or on the individual in his or her political role (Westle 2010, 314). The focus of analysis thus lies mainly on forms of political support in the tradition of Easton (1965; 1975). The concrete indicators used to measure the diverse cognitive, evaluative, and affective orientations are still the subject of intense debate within survey research (Dalton 2004; Westle 2010). If the choice of objects follows a systematic approach at all, it is usually along the lines of the classic objects 'system as a whole', 'output', 'input', and the 'self as a political actor'. In addition, the threefold division of polity, policy, and politics guides newer approaches in their selection of indicators (Almond and Verba 1980; Gabriel 2008).

With regard to the database, it should first be noted that data availability has improved considerably in recent decades. This applies both to national data and to international comparative surveys, which form a basis for fruitful comparative research on political culture. In Switzerland, the most important national data sets include the Vox and Voto surveys conducted after each referendum (since 1977), the Swiss Electoral Studies conducted after each national election (since 1995), and the annual Swiss Household Panel (since 1999). The particular benefit of these Swiss survey programmes lies in the recurrence of the surveys according to a predefined time grid in the sense of a trend or panel design. The most important international comparative surveys with (ir)regular Swiss participation include the World Values Survey (WVS, since 1981), the European Values Study (EVS, since 1981), the European Social Survey (ESS, since 2002), the International Social Survey Programme (ISSP, since 1984), and the Eurobarometer (since 1973).

The present chapter will focus its evaluations on some core elements of political culture in Switzerland. Whenever possible, we will take both a diachronic and a synchronic approach. The longitudinal observations examine the development of political culture in Switzerland over time, while the cross-sectional observations compare Switzerland with European or OECD countries. The analytical interest focuses on elements of polity and politics culture as well as selected policy aspects between 1981 and 2020.[3] In addition to attitudes towards the form of government and political community (nation, language region, canton, and municipality), orientations towards various political institutions (government, parliament, the legal system, police, administration, cantonal and local authorities, parties, interest groups, politicians), and the political role of the electorate (party identification, political interest, political competence, political influence), the empirical presentation of Switzerland's political culture also includes attitudes towards political openness and environmental policy.

4 Political Culture in Switzerland in Comparative Perspective

With regard to the polity culture, for the period between 1999 and 2019, it can first be stated that the Swiss have, on average, been fairly satisfied with the way democracy works (see online appendix).[4] Satisfaction even tends to increase over the years. With regard to identification with the political community, Swiss citizens have recently also tended to show more pride in their country. When differentiating according to the level of identification in federalist Switzerland, the attachment to the country, language region, canton, and municipality have reached consistently high levels over the last few years, although ties to the nation seem to be the strongest (see online appendix).[5]

However, the unique feature of the Swiss political system lies indisputably in the triad of power-sharing elements consociationalism, federalism, and direct democracy (Linder and Müller 2017; Vatter 2020) (see also 'Switzerland: A Paradigmatic Case of Political Integration' in this volume). The procedures for political decision-making laid down therein find convincing support amongst the population (see

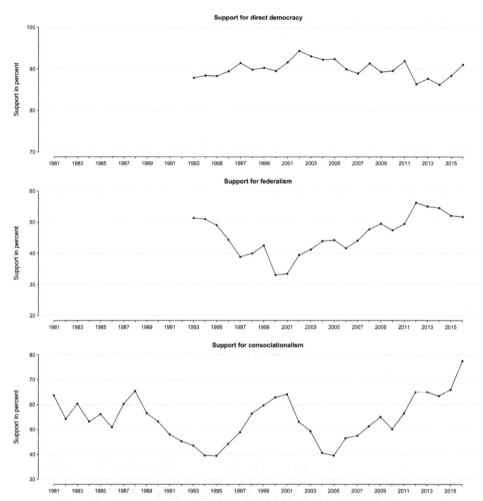

FIGURE 4.1: Support for direct democracy, federalism, and consociationalism, 1981–2016
Questions: *(1) I would now like to ask you some questions about different aspects of Swiss society. For each aspect, I would like you to answer what you would like to see in Switzerland. Please answer by giving us the number that most closely corresponds to your opinion. If you agree with the first part of the prompt, choose number 1 or a number close to 1. If you agree with the second part of the prompt, choose number 7 or a number close to 7. What do you want for Switzerland? A Switzerland with citizen participation in important governmental decisions (1), or a Switzerland without citizen participation in important governmental decisions (7)?* Depicted is the percentage of respondents in categories 1, 2, and 3; *(2) What kind of Switzerland would you like to see? A Switzerland where the federal state has more power (1) or a Switzerland where the cantons have more power (7)?* Depicted is the percentage of respondents in categories 5, 6, and 7; *(3) I am now going to read you two views that one hears quite often about our government. Which one do you agree with most? The first view is: I can mostly rely on the Federal Council. It acts to the best of its knowledge and conscience, for the good of all. And the second view is: Within the Federal Council, more and more decisions are made against the people and less and less in their favour. The Federal Council no longer knows our concerns and wishes.* Depicted is the percentage of respondents agreeing with the first view.

Data source: Kriesi, Brunner and Lorétan (1981–2016).

Figure 4.1). There is particularly high support for direct democratic rights. Almost 90 per cent of the Swiss population would like to see strong citizen participation in the political decision-making process. Longchamp and Rousselot (2010, 249) also report that 79 per cent consider direct democratic rights to be an important check on elected representatives. Furthermore, an average of 45 and 55 per cent respectively support federalism as the preferred form of governance and see the Federal Council as an organ of consociationalism that pursues general rather than special interests in its policies. The rather unsteady support for federalism and consociationalism compared to direct democracy can partly be attributed to political developments. Up to the turn of the millennium, increasing Europeanization and globalization found expression in the desire for a stronger central government capable of acting in the face of growing international challenges. Launched by the new Federal Constitution in the mid-1990s, negotiations on the reform of the National Fiscal Equalization (NFA) system revitalized the subnational-cantonal relevance in federal policy-making. Nevertheless, figures over the last ten years show a slight decline in support for federalism as an organizational principle amongst the Swiss population. In turn, declining support for the Federal Council as an instance of consociationalism in the 1990s can sometimes be linked to the rejection of EEA accession (1992) and the failure of the envisaged governmental reform (1996). The successful process and completion of bilateral treaties with the European Union (EU) at the end of the 1990s brought the Federal Council, as guardian of the common good, high approval ratings once again. However, the confusion surrounding the legitimacy and interpretation of the magic formula (*Zauberformel*) in the form of the non-re-election of Christian Democrat Ruth Metzler and the inauguration of Christoph Blocher (Swiss People's Party) probably led to temporary losses in political support. In the era after Christoph Blocher, however, the Federal Council again experienced growing support, reaching a new peak in 2016 with the loss of the Conservative Democratic Party seat to the Swiss People's Party and the re-establishment of the magic formula.

As far as the judgement of the form of the regime is concerned, at least two other aspects are relevant in addition to the question of democratic satisfaction. On the one hand, the evaluation of the democratic model vis-à-vis other alternative regimes (autocracy, technocratic regime) is of interest. On the other hand, the perception of the decision-making process and the performance of the democratic model are also important.

In Switzerland as well as in other nations, democracy enjoys very broad support (see online appendix). Nevertheless, there is some variance between the respective nations. While democracy enjoys a very high level of acceptance in Albania, Sweden, Norway, Iceland, Denmark, and Germany in the European Values Study survey from 2017 to 2020, it receives considerably less support in Georgia, Slovakia, and Russia. Referring to satisfaction with democracy, Switzerland leads the field among European countries (Figure 4.2). Only in Norway do people express a similarly pronounced level of comfort with the way democracy works. According to the data of the European Social Survey 2018, Serbs, Croatians, and Bulgarians

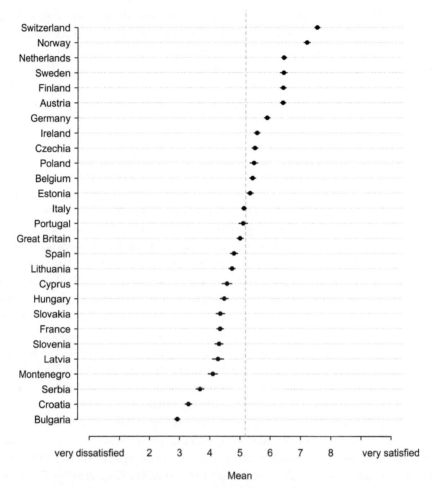

FIGURE 4.2: Satisfaction with democracy in comparative perspective, 2018
Question: *On the whole, how satisfied are you with the way democracy works in [country]? Still use this card.*

Data source: ESS (2018).

in particular express dissatisfaction with their democracy. But respondents in Slovakia, France, Slovenia, Latvia, and Montenegro are also critical when it comes to the functioning of their democracy. Finally, in Switzerland, the style of governance is also seen as very democratic. However, people in Denmark, Norway, and Sweden are even more favourable about their countries' decision-making process in the European Values Study 2017–2020. According to the respective respondents, governance is less democratic in Croatia, Northern Macedonia, Albania, Armenia, and Bosnia and Herzegovina. Regarding technocracy as an alternative form of government, Figure 4.3 reveals that the Swiss respondents are very reluctant about the

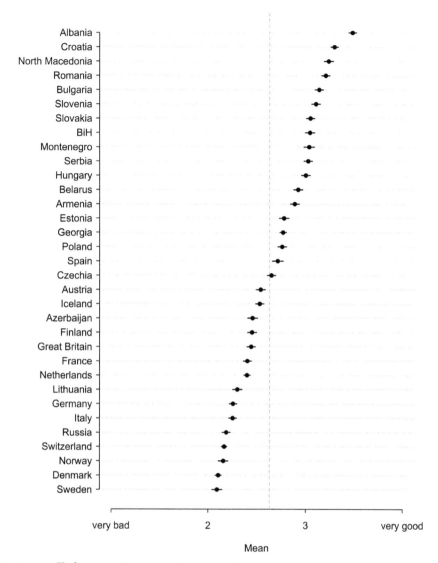

FIGURE 4.3: Technocracy in comparative perspective, 2017–2020
Question: *I'm going to describe various types of political systems and ask what you think about each as a way of governing this country. For each one, would you say it is a very good, fairly good, fairly bad or very bad way of governing this country? Having experts, not government, make decisions according to what they think is best for the country.* The country abbreviation BiH stands for Bosnia and Herzegovina.

Data source: EVS (2022).

idea of governance by unelected experts. According to data from the European Values Study 2017–2020, only Norway, Denmark, and Sweden are less supportive of such a political regime. To the contrary, in particular eastern European countries show technocratic preferences.

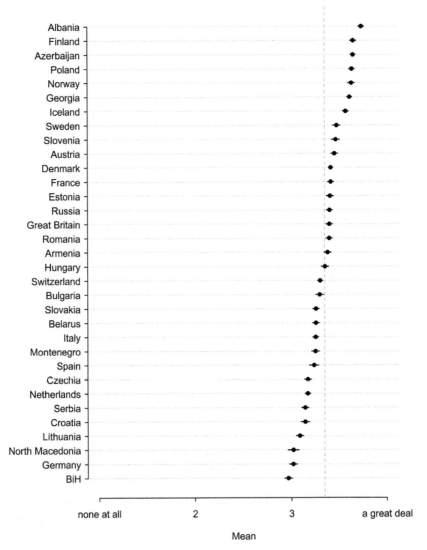

FIGURE 4.4: National pride in comparative perspective, 2017–2020
Question: *How proud are you to be a [COUNTRY] citizen?* The country abbreviation BiH stands for Bosnia and Herzegovina.

Data source: EVS (2022).

Moreover, national pride is not particularly pronounced in Switzerland from a comparative perspective (Figure 4.4). Although the Swiss are proud of their country (and more so than their German and Italian neighbours, for example), the Swiss tend to place in the middle of the international ranking according to the data of the European Values Study 2017–2020. Albanians, Finns, Azerbaijanis, Poles, Norwegians, Georgians, and Icelanders are all more proud of their national affiliation.

Even more than through the comparatively abstract concepts of democracy and nation, actors within political institutions affect the everyday experiences of citizens. In the context of the *politics culture*, the distinction between legal and partisan, or representational, institutions is crucial (Gabriel 2008, 194; Longchamp and Rousselot 2010; Rothstein and Stolle 2008). Partisan or representational institutions are home to different interests and values as well as the resulting political conflicts that accompany the political decision-making process. Legal institutions, on the other hand, have the function of regulating social conflicts in a binding manner and guaranteeing compliance with the law. Their activity is usually exempt from partisan political controversies. While individual and group-specific preferences strongly influence attitudes towards partisan institutions, orientations towards legal institutions tend to reflect generally binding values and norms. Accordingly, the police and the legal system regularly occupy top positions in the trust hierarchy, followed by governments and parliaments (Freitag 2001; Listhaug and Wiberg 1995).

A look at the respective institutions referring to the politics culture confirms these considerations in the Swiss context. Levels of trust are highest for the legal system and police, followed by the Federal Council, local and cantonal authorities, and the Federal Parliament (see online appendix). In contrast, the parties face a comparatively high level of distrust. The relatively contested role of parties in Switzerland is also reflected in the evaluations on party identification: the majority of respondents state that they have not been particularly close to any party in the last twenty-five years (see online appendix). In 2019, the proportion of those attached to a party stabilized at just under 40 per cent. A citizen's relationship to politics is further revealed by their self-attested political interest and ascribed political competence. Political interest creates the basis for individuals to engage with political issues and become politically active when necessary (Gabriel 2008, 201; Prior 2019; Westle 2020, 276–277). However, political interest leads to political participation in particular when a citizen is convinced that he or she understands political issues and is able to influence them through his or her actions. Between 1995 and 2019, Swiss people were on average definitely interested in politics. They were also inclined to believe that it is possible to influence politics through elections, as it makes a difference in who is elected (see online appendix).[6]

The Europe-wide classification of the developments regarding facets of the politics culture reported so far shows that Switzerland consistently occupies one of the top positions in the area of trust in political institutions and actors, regardless of the data source. In international comparisons, the Swiss trust their government, parliament, and politicians the most (Figure 4.5, see also online appendix). When it comes to trust in the legal system and political parties, Switzerland is one of the nations with above-average values and regularly ranks among those nations with the highest levels of trust (Figure 4.6 and Figure 4.7). However, in a comparison between legal and partisan institutions, the former enjoy higher esteem among industrialized countries (see also online appendix). Among partisan institutions, parties and politicians score the

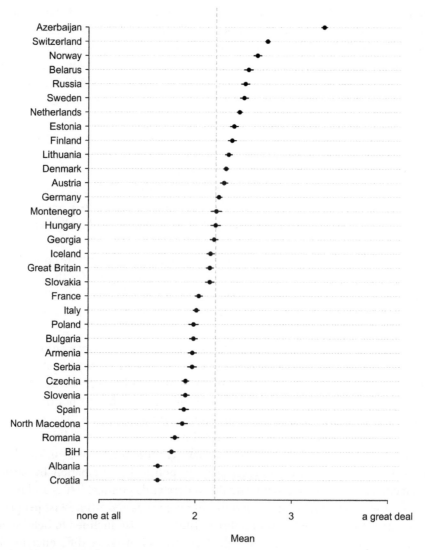

FIGURE 4.5: Trust in the government in comparative perspective, 2017–2020
Question: *Please look at this card and tell me, for each item listed, how much confidence you have in them, is it a great deal, quite a lot, not very much or none at all?...government.* The country abbreviation BiH stands for Bosnia and Herzegovina.

Data source: EVS (2022).

lowest. In addition, European citizens show varying degrees of party identification, with Scandinavian countries Sweden and Norway and southern European countries Portugal and Spain being the most likely to feel party attachment. According to the analyses of the 2018 European Social Survey, Switzerland ranks in the middle in this form of political identity (Figure 4.8).[7] Party identification is rather low in Poland, Montenegro, Latvia, and Lithuania, among others, according to the available data.

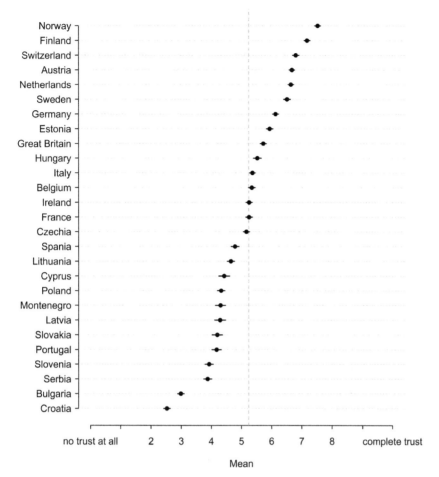

FIGURE 4.6: Trust in the legal system in comparative perspective, 2018
Question: *Using this card, please tell me on a score of 0–10 how much you personally trust each of the institutions I read out. 0 means you do not trust an institution at all, and 10 means you have complete trust. ...the legal system?*

Data source: ESS (2018).

In terms of political interest, European citizens as a whole are rather moderately interested in political events and only a minority shows above-average political interest (see online appendix). This includes the populations of Sweden, Finland, Norway, Germany, the Netherlands, and the United Kingdom, as well as Switzerland. In contrast, the political interest of Hungarians, Serbs, Czechs, and Montenegrins is rather low (European Social Survey 2018). The feeling of subjective political competence and political influence is above average among Swiss citizens compared to other countries (see online appendix). Germany, Norway, Sweden, and Austria have similarly high levels of political competence (European Social Survey 2018).

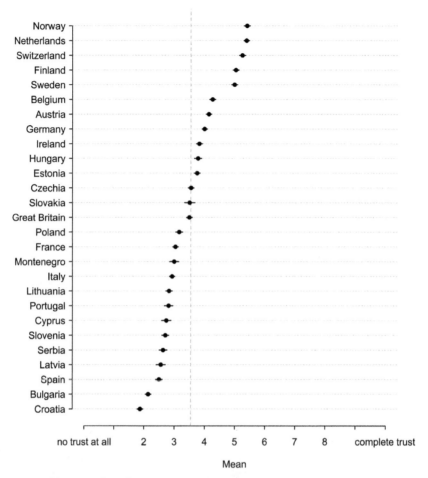

FIGURE 4.7: Trust in political parties in comparative perspective, 2018
Question: *Using this card, please tell me on a score of 0–10 how much you personally trust each of the institutions I read out. 0 means you do not trust an institution at all, and 10 means you have complete trust. ... political parties?*

Data source: ESS (2018).

The populations of Norway, Sweden, and Finland, as well as the Netherlands and Germany, also report a high level of self-ascribed political influence (European Social Survey 2018; see online appendix).

Finally, we focus on selected aspects of Swiss policy culture. With regard to the question of how much the state should intervene in the economy, Switzerland, together with Taiwan, Japan, New Zealand, and Denmark, is among the countries most in favour of liberalism (Figure 4.9). Russia, Bulgaria, Croatia, and Slovenia display the strongest preference for state intervention in the economy. When it comes to political decisions that have been at the centre of public debate in recent years such as

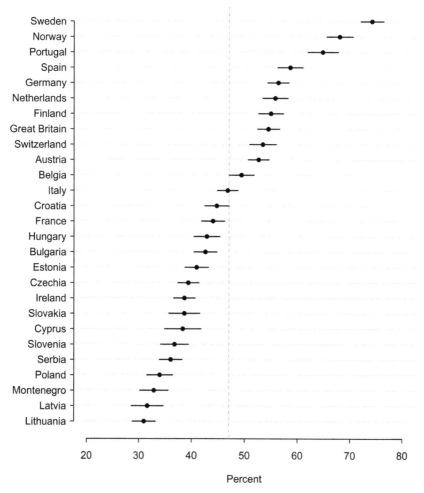

FIGURE 4.8: Party identification in comparative perspective, 2018
Question: *Is there a particular political party you feel closer to than all the other parties?* Depicted is the percentage of respondents who answered yes.

Data source: ESS (2018).

the question of joining the EU, the Swiss population has been very hesitant for some time. In 2019, just under 20 per cent still supported joining the EU. Nevertheless, since 1995, a roughly constant proportion of up to 80 per cent has been in favour of opening up the country. With regard to the decision to protect the environment at the expense of economic development, the data also reveals a clear picture: Over the past twenty-five years, between 70 and 80 per cent of the Swiss population have regularly prioritized the protection of the environment over the well-being of the economy (Figure 4.10).

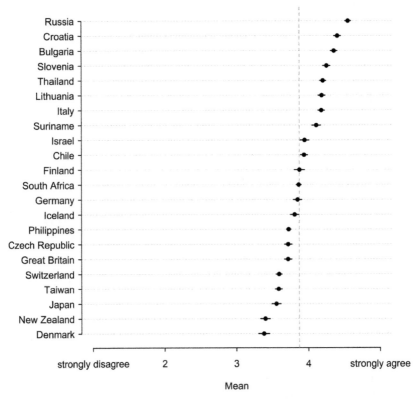

FIGURE 4.9: State interventionism in comparative perspective, 2019
Question: *To what extent do you agree or disagree with the following statements? It is the responsibility of the government to reduce the differences in income between people with high incomes and those with low incomes. Scale from strongly disagree (1) to strongly agree (5).*

Data source: ISSP Research Group (2021).

In terms of attitudes towards further integrating the EU, Switzerland tends to position itself in the lower third of the European countries surveyed (see online appendix). Eastern countries such as Albania, Bosnia and Herzegovina, Bulgaria, Northern Macedonia, and Romania are particularly in favour of further integration. Long-standing members of the EU such as the Netherlands, France, or Finland, but also the Czech Republic and Russia, are, on the other hand, rather critical of EU integration. Regarding environmental protection, together with Sweden and Iceland, Switzerland prioritizes ecological over economic well-being the most from a comparative perspective (see online appendix). Serbia, Armenia, Bosnia and Herzegovina, and Lithuania, on the other hand, tend to prefer a flourishing economy to a clean environment.

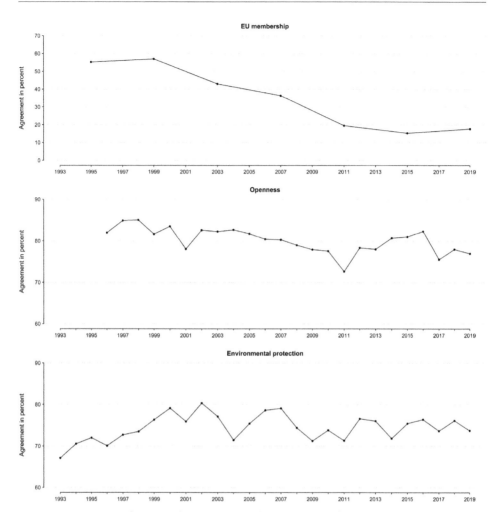

FIGURE 4.10: Attitudes towards openness in foreign policy, the EU, and the environment, 1993–2019

Question: (a) *Are you in favour of Switzerland joining the EU or going it alone?* 'Very much in favour of joining the EU' (1), 'Rather in favour of joining the EU' (2), 'Neither nor' (3), 'Rather in favour of going it alone' (4), 'Very much in favour of going it alone' (5). Depicted is the percentage of respondents in categories 1 and 2; (b) *I would now like to ask you some questions about various aspects of Swiss society. Please tell me what you would like to see in Switzerland. If you agree with the first part of the question, choose the number 1 or close to 1. If you agree with the second part of the question, choose the number 7 or close to 7. Do you want Switzerland to open up more to the outside world (1) or to close itself off more (7)?* Depicted is the percentage of respondents in categories 1, 2, and 3; from 2017: *Do you want Switzerland to open up more to the outside world (1) or to close itself off more (6)?* Depicted is the percentage of respondents in categories 1, 2, and 3; *A Switzerland where environmental protection is more important than economic prosperity (1) or a Switzerland where economic prosperity is more important than environmental protection (7)?* Depicted is the percentage of respondents in categories 1, 2, and 3; from 2017: *A Switzerland where environmental protection is more important than economic prosperity (1) or a Switzerland where economic prosperity is more important than environmental protection (6)?* Depicted is the percentage of respondents in categories 1, 2, and 3.

Data sources: Question on joining the EU: Selects (2021); others: until 2016 Kriesi, Brunner and Lorétan (1981–2016), from 2017 FORS and ZDA (2017–2020).

5 Conclusion

This chapter deals with aspects of Swiss political culture in the research tradition of Almond and Verba (1963; 1980) as well as Easton (1965; 1975), meaning that the empirical analysis of individual attitudes towards the political regime was the focus of analytical interest. Using data from different national and international surveys, we can report two central findings: First, it should be noted that orientations towards the democratic form of government and political community, and towards institutions and actors involved in the process of influencing politics, have been characterized by a high degree of stability over the past decades. Secondly, the diverse analyses have also made it clear that Switzerland reveals a high degree of political culture in a comparative perspective. This is true with regard to the degree of approval of democratic governance, trust in institutions, and in questions of political involvement. Switzerland can thus be labelled as a stronghold of a political culture with an extraordinary level of support and trust.

This position of the Swiss political culture in comparative perspective calls for an explanation. In addition to advantageous socio-economic constellations, attention should be focused on the institutional configurations of the political system (Dachs 2009; Linder and Steffen 2006; Vatter 2020). Here, the focus is on the so-called militia-system (*Milizsystem*) and the unique combination of consociationalism, direct democracy, and federalist state architecture as catalysts of political trust and high approval ratings (Freitag et al. 2019; Linder and Müller 2017; Vatter 2008; Vatter 2018; Vatter 2020; Vatter et al. 2019). The militia-system ensures that economic, social, and political interests are closely intertwined and forms an effective barrier against the political class becoming disengaged. These enmeshed connections between the respective subsystems provide broad acceptance of negotiated political decisions across the population's interests and lead to a high level of approval for democratic procedures and political institutions.

Opportunities for building political support and consent also arise through different ways and means of access to political participation. If the political framework promises incentives to participate in the political process, individuals take advantage of institutionalized opportunities to overcome any reservations they may have about the political system. Strongly decentralized communities ensure the continuity of political, cultural, and social interests by providing access to the political decision-making process at different levels. Direct democratic participation procedures create, for example, opportunities for constant scrutiny of policies and prevent the interests of those exercising power and those subjected to it from diverging. As a side effect, this control mechanism induces the generation of support and advances of trust in the political system and in the actors. Finally, power-sharing institutions and minority-protecting mechanisms contribute to the formation of political trust. As soon as person A realizes that person B is always better off as a result of political decisions and that decision-making is biased, person A will lose trust in the responsible political institutions. In other words: If the political framework creates the impression of favouritism as well as the systematic exclusion of interests and encourages a 'winner takes it all' mentality, it generates distrust among the disadvantaged actors. However, as long as the people perceive the decision-making process as impartial and fair, even a disadvantageous outcome is accepted and does not lead to a loss of trust.

Given the comprehensive inclusion of political, social, and economic interests under the maxim of amicable agreement, consensual organizational structures are assumed to promote political trust. More Westminster-oriented models of democracy emphasize the competitive and conflictual character and the low capability to include various interests instead. However, these features stand as obstacles to comprehensive political support. This is all the more the case when the given organizational structure of the political regime denies minorities the chance to participate and does not provide an institutional bar to the systematic exploitation of minorities by the majority. Consociational democracies take greater account of the concerns of minorities, represent heterogeneous interests, and lead overall to societies that appreciate the values, norms, and rules of the game of democratic regimes in a special way (Bernauer and Vatter 2019).

Finally, institutions such as direct democracy, federalism, and consociationalism shape the way in which political debate takes place. Each of the three aspects mentioned stands for the openness of the political system and promotes deliberation and communication between political actors. These institutional peculiarities of Switzerland structure political debate and the respectful and sensitive handling of political power at every level of the political system. The way in which conflicts are dealt with in this institutionally prescribed way ensures a high level of acceptance of the basic democratic order and strong approval of the country's political institutions. Hence, the *manner of political coexistence* lays a significant foundation for such a high level of *political culture*.

Notes

1. We refer here to the narrow definition of culture in general by the founding fathers of political culture research: 'We employ the concept of culture in only one of its meanings: that of psychological orientations towards social objects' (Almond and Verba 1963, 13). Political culture 'thus refers to the specifically political orientations' (Almond and Verba 1963, 12). In the following, the terms 'attitudes' and 'orientations' are used synonymously, although the latter rather captures the deeper and more stable dispositions.
2. Characteristic of this focus in Swiss political science is the study by Seitz (1997), which, in addition to a history of concepts in political culture research, places Swiss voting behaviour in this context in order to obtain information on 'regional political cultures' (Seitz 1997, 275).
3. The periods analysed vary according to the available data. We strive to evaluate the most current data in each case.
4. The figures provided display unweighted values. The use of weights leads to almost identical findings.
5. For reasons of space, we only present a selection of the evaluations referred to in this article. The illustrations of the other data and findings on political culture discussed in the text

are available at the first author's website at www.ipw.unibe.ch/freitag in a separate online attachment. Their order follows the order in the article.

6. In Swiss direct democracy, popular votes are usually considered to have an even greater influence on the political process than elections (Freitag and Stadelmann-Steffen 2010; Vatter et al. 2019). Unfortunately, such data on the importance of direct democratic measures are not available in the longitudinal section.

7. The differences to the findings from the evaluations of the SELECTS electoral study should be noted.

References

Almond, Gabriel. 1956. 'Comparative Political Systems'. *Journal of Politics* 18 (3): pp. 391–409.

Almond, Gabriel. 2000. 'The Study of Political Culture'. In *Culture and Politics*, edited by Lane Crothers, and Charles Lockhart, pp. 5–20. New York: Palgrave Macmillan.

Almond, Gabriel, and Sidney Verba. 1963. *The Civic Culture, Political Attitudes and Democracy in Five Nations*. Newbury Park: Sage Publications.

Almond, Gabriel, and Sidney Verba. 1980. *The Civic Culture Revisited*. Boston/Toronto: Little, Brown.

Bauer, Paul C., Markus Freitag, and Pascal Sciarini. 2018. 'Political Trust in Switzerland: Again a Special Case?' In *Identities, Trust, and Cohesion in Federal Systems: Public Perspectives*, edited by Jack Jedwab, and John Kincaid, pp. 115–145. Kingston: Queen's University.

Bernauer, Julian, and Adrian Vatter. 2019. *Power Diffusion and Democracy. Institutions, Deliberation and Outcomes*. Cambridge: Cambridge University Press.

Brunner, Matthias, and Lea Sgier. 1997. 'Crise de confiance dans les institutions politiques suisses? Quelques résultats d'une enquête d'opinion'. *Schweizerische Zeitschrift für Politische Wissenschaft* 3 (1): pp. 105–113.

Coromina, Lluís, and Simona Kustec. 2020. 'Analytical Images of Political Trust in Times of Global Challenges. The Case of Slovenia, Spain and Switzerland'. *Journal of Comparative Politics* 13 (1): pp. 102–118.

Dachs, Herbert. 2009. 'Politische Kultur. Begriff – Dimensionen – Entstehen'. *Informationen zur Politischen Bildung* 30: pp. 5–7.

Dalton, Russell J. 2004. *Democratic Challenges, Democratic Choices: The Erosion of Political Support in Advanced Industrial Democracies*. Oxford: Oxford University Press.

Easton, David. 1965. *A Systems Analysis of Political Life*. New York: John Wiley and Sons.

Easton, David. 1975. 'A Re-Assessment of the Concept of Political Support'. *British Journal of Political Science* 5 (4): pp. 435–457.

ESS. 2018. *ESS Round 9: European Social Survey Round 9 Data (2018)* [Dataset]. Sikt – Norwegian Agency for Shared Services in Education and Research, Norway – Data Archive and distributor of ESS data for ESS ERIC. Data file edition 3.1. doi:10.21338/NSD-ESS9-2018.

EVS. 2022. *European Values Study 2017: Integrated Dataset (EVS2017)* [Dataset]. GESIS Data Archive, Cologne. ZA7500 Data file Version 5.0.0. doi:10.4232/1.13897.

Faas, Thorsten, Oscar W. Gabriel, and Jürgen Maier (eds). 2020. *Politikwissenschaftliche Einstellungs- und Verhaltensforschung: Handbuch für Wissenschaft und Studium*. Baden-Baden: Nomos.

FORS and ZDA. 2017–2020. *Surveys on the Swiss Popular Votes, 12 February 2017, 21 May 2017, 24 September 2017, 4 March 2018, 10 June 2018, 23 September 2018, 25 November 2018, 10 February 2019, 19 May 2019, 9 February 2020* [Datasets]. FORS – Centre of expertise in the social sciences, Centre for democracy Studies Aarau (ZDA), University of Zurich. Distributed by FORS, Lausanne. https://www.swissubase.ch/en/catalogue/studies/12471/13712/datasets.

Freitag, Markus. 2001. 'Das soziale Kapital der Schweiz. Vergleichende Einschätzungen zu Aspekten des Vertrauens und der sozialen Einbindung'. *Schweizerische Zeitschrift für Politikwissenschaft* 7 (4): pp. 87–117.

Freitag, Markus, Pirmin Bundi, and Martina Flick Witzig. 2019. *Milizarbeit in der Schweiz—Zahlen und Fakten zum politischen Leben in der Gemeinde*. Zürich: NZZ Libro.

Freitag, Markus, and Isabelle Stadelmann-Steffen. 2008. 'Schweizer Welten der Freiwilligkeit: das freiwillige Engagement der Schweiz im sprachregionalen Kontext'. In *Sozialbericht 2008*, edited by Christian Suter, Silvia Perrenoud, René Levy, Ursina Kuhn, Dominique Joye, and Pascal Gazareth, pp. 170-190. Zürich: Seismo.

Freitag, Markus, and Isabelle Stadelmann-Steffen. 2010. 'Stumbling Block or Stepping Stone? The Influence of Direct Democracy on Individual Participation in Parliamentary Elections'. *Electoral Studies* 29 (3): pp. 472–483.

Fuchs, Dieter. 2007. 'The Political Culture Paradigm'. In *The Oxford Handbook of Political Behavior*, edited by Russel J. Dalton, and Hans-Dieter Klingemann, pp. 161-184. Oxford: Oxford University Press.

Gabriel, Oscar W. 2008. 'Politische Einstellungen und politische Kultur'. In *Die EU-Staaten im Vergleich: Strukturen, Prozesse, Politikinhalte*, edited by Oscar W. Gabriel, and Sabine Kropp, pp. 181–214. Wiesbaden: VS Verlag für Sozialwissenschaften.

ISSP Research Group. 2021. *International Social Survey Programme: Social Inequality V - ISSP 2019* [Dataset]. GESIS Data Archive, Cologne. ZA6980 Data file Version 2.0.0, https://doi.org/10.4232/1.13322.

Kaase, Max. 1983. 'Sinn oder Unsinn des Konzepts "Politische Kultur" für die vergleichende Politikforschung, oder auch: Der Versuch einen Pudding an die Wand zu nageln'. In *Wahlen und politisches System - Analysen aus Anlass der Bundestagswahl 1980*, edited by Max Kaase, and Hans-Dieter Klingemann, pp. 144–171. Opladen: Westdeutscher Verlag.

Kriesi, Hanspeter, Matthias Brunner, and François Lorétan. 1981–2016. *VoxIt 1981–2016* [Dataset]. Université de Genève – Faculté des Sciences de la Société – SdS – Département de science politique et relations internationales, Universität Zürich – Philosophische Fakultät – Institut für Politikwissenschaft – IPZ – Lehrstuhl für Vergleichende Politikwissenschaft, FORS – Centre de compétences suisse en sciences sociales. Distributed by FORS, Lausanne. https://doi.org/10.23662/FORS-DS-689-2.

Linder, Wolf, Claude Longchamp, and Regula Stämpfli. 1991. *Politische Kultur im Wandel am Beispiel des selektiven Urnengangs*. Basel: Schweizerischer Nationalfonds (Reihe Kurzfassungen NFP 21).

Linder, Wolf, and Sean Müller. 2017. *Schweizer Demokratie: Institutionen – Prozesse – Perspektiven*, 4th ed. Bern: Paul Haupt Verlag.

Linder, Wolf, and Isabelle Steffen. 2006. 'Politische Kultur'. In *Handbuch der Schweizer Politik*, edited by Ulrich Klöti, Peter Knoepfel, Hanspeter Kriesi, Wolf Linder, Yannis Papadopoulos, and Pascal Sciarini, pp. 15–34. 4th ed. Zürich: Verlag Neue Zürcher Zeitung.

Listhaug, Ola, and Matti Wiberg. 1995. 'Confidence in Political and Private Institutions'. In *Beliefs in Government. Vol. 1: Citizen and the State*, edited by Hans-Dieter Klingemann, and Dieter Fuchs, pp. 298–322. Oxford: Oxford University Press.

Longchamp, Claude, and Bianca Rousselot. 2010. 'Bürger und Politik in der Schweiz'. In *Deutschland, Österreich und die Schweiz im neuen Europa: Bürger und Politik*, edited by Oscar W. Gabriel, and Fritz Plasser, pp. 217–264. Baden-Baden: Nomos.

Norris, Pippa. 2017. 'The Conceptual Framework of Political Support'. In *Handbook on Political Trust*, edited by Sonja Zmerli, and Tom van der Meer, pp. 19–32. Cheltenham: Edward Elgar Publishing.

Pickel, Susanne, and Gert Pickel. 2006. *Politische Kultur- und Demokratieforschung: Grundbegriffe, Theorien, Methoden. Eine Einführung*. Wiesbaden: VS Verlag für Sozialwissenschaften.

Prior, Markus. 2019. *Hooked. How Politics Captures People's Interest*. Cambridge: Cambridge University Press.

Reisinger, William M. 1995. 'The Renaissance of a Rubric: Political Culture as Concept and Theory'. *International Journal of Public Opinion Research* 7 (4): pp. 328–352.

Rohe, Karl. 1990. 'Politische Kultur und ihre Analyse. Probleme und Perspektiven der politischen Kulturforschung'. *Historische Zeitschrift* 250 (2): pp. 321–346.

Rothstein, Bo, and Dietlin Stolle. 2008. 'The State and Social Capital: An Institutional Theory of Generalized Trust'. *Comparative Politics* 40 (4): pp. 441–459.

Scheidegger, Régis, and Christian Staerklé. 2011. 'Political Trust and Distrust in Switzerland: A Normative Analysis'. *Swiss Political Science Review* 17 (2): pp. 164–187.

Seitz, Werner. 1997. *Die politische Kultur und ihre Beziehung zum Abstimmungsverhalten: Eine Begriffsgeschichte und Methodenkritik*. Zürich: Realtopia Verlagsgenossenschaft.

Seitz, Werner. 2006. 'Elemente der politischen Kultur der Schweiz. Eine Annäherung'. In *Wes Land ich bin, des Lied ich sing? Medien und politische Kultur, Berner Texte zur Kommunikations- und Medienwissenschaft, Band 10*, edited by Roger Blum, Peter Meier, and Nicole Gysin, pp. 51–64. Bern: Haupt Verlag.

Selects. 2021. *Swiss Election Study, cumulative dataset 1971–2019* [Dataset]. Distributed by FORS, Lausanne. https://doi.org/10.48573/pcbm-2280.

Stadelmann-Steffen, Isabelle, and Birte Gundelach. 2015. 'Individual Socialization or Politico-Cultural Context? The Cultural Roots of Volunteering in Switzerland'. *Acta Politica* 50 (1): pp. 20–44.

Staubli, Silvia. 2016. 'Vertrauen in die Schweizer Polizei: Zur Rolle institutioneller Anerkennung, prozeduraler Gerechtigkeit und sozialem Vertrauen'. *Soziale Probleme* 27 (1): pp. 49–74.

Steiner, Jürg. 2001. 'Switzerland and the European Union: A Puzzle'. In *Minority Nationalism and the Changing International Order*, edited by Michael Keating, and John McGarry, pp. 137–154. Oxford: Oxford University Press.

Tong, Dezhi. 2019. *Introduction to Comparative Political Culture: The Theoretical Reflection on the Plurality of Democracy*. Singapore: Higher Education Press and Springer Nature.

Vatter, Adrian. 2008. 'Vom Extremtyp zum Normalfall? Die schweizerische Konsensusdemokratie im Wandel: Eine Re-Analyse von Lijpharts Studie für die Schweiz von 1997 bis 2007'. *Schweizerische Zeitschrift für Politikwissenschaft* 14 (1): pp. 1–47.

Vatter, Adrian. 2018. *Swiss Federalism. The Transformation of a Federal Model*. London and New York: Routledge.

Vatter, Adrian. 2020. *Das politische System der Schweiz*, 4th ed. Baden-Baden: Nomos.

Vatter, Adrian, Bianca Rousselot, and Thomas Milic. 2019. 'The Input and Output Effects of Direct Democracy: A New Research Agenda'. *Policy & Politics* 47 (1): pp. 169–186.

Verba, Sidney. 1965. 'Comparative Political Culture'. In *Political Culture and Political Development*, edited by Lucian W. Pye, and Sidney Verba, pp. 512–560. Princeton: Princeton University Press.

Welch, Stephen. 2013. *The Theory of Political Culture*. Oxford: Oxford University Press.

Westle, Bettina. 2010. 'Politische Kultur'. In *Vergleichende Regierungslehre: Eine Einführung*, edited by Hans-Joachim Lauth, pp. 306–325. 3rd ed. Wiesbaden: VS Verlag für Sozialwissenschaften.

Westle, Bettina. 2020. 'Kognitives politisches Engagement'. In *Politikwissenschaftliche Einstellungs- und Verhaltensforschung: Handbuch für Wissenschaft und Studium*, edited by Thorsten Faas, Oscar W. Gabriel, and Jürgen Maier, pp. 273–295. Baden-Baden: Nomos.

Widmer, Eric D., and Ivan de Carlo. 2010. 'Why Do the Swiss Trust their Government Less and Other People More than They Used To?'. In *Value Change in Switzerland*, edited by Simon Hug, and Hanspeter Kriesi, pp. 171–190. Plymouth: Lexington Books.

CHAPTER 5

THE STRUCTURAL SHIFTS IN SWITZERLAND'S ECONOMY AND SOCIETY, 2000–2020

DANIEL OESCH

1 INTRODUCTION

OVER the last decades, Switzerland experienced strong growth in several areas. The economy expanded almost without interruption between 2000 and 2019, employment increased at a rate that has been called the 'jobs miracle' (Siegenthaler 2017), educational attainment rose, and the population grew by over a fifth.[1]

A driving force behind this growth were women. In the last twenty years, young women not only caught up with young men in terms of education, but overtook them. In 2020, significantly more young women than men had a university degree in Switzerland, and women converted their higher education into higher rates of labour market participation. Women thus contributed to a larger extent to the jobs boom of the last two decades than men. However, the gender revolution is still incomplete (Esping-Andersen 2009). Similar to the Netherlands, Switzerland remains a part-time economy, with most men with children working full-time and most women with children working part-time (Visser 2002).

The second driving force behind Switzerland's growth has been immigration. In the decade of the 2010s, migration reached levels last seen during the post-war boom of the early 1960s. Between 2010 and 2018, 180,000 people immigrated and 110,000 people emigrated each year. The special feature of the latest wave of immigration, however, is not its extent but its skill structure. Since the beginning of the twenty-first century, Switzerland has mainly attracted highly qualified migrants: more than half of the adults immigrating each year had a university degree. The concentration of immigrants in the lower hierarchical rungs of Swiss society is becoming a thing of the past.

Over the last two decades, Switzerland's GDP grew thanks to a large population increase which, in turn, was made possible by sustained immigration that responded to the Swiss economy's strong demand for foreign labour. As a result, per capita income rose only moderately, and the evolution of wages was even weaker—despite rising employment and low unemployment. As the costs for health care and housing increased at the same time, it is uncertain whether the majority of Switzerland's population experienced the last two decades as a boom period. This is especially true for the losers of structural change in the economy, the traditional working class on the one hand and the lower middle class of office clerks on the other. Their employment prospects have deteriorated in Switzerland as elsewhere in Western Europe, notably in Germany, Sweden, and the UK (Oesch and Piccitto 2019). In parallel, the upper middle class continued to grow, benefiting from strong job growth in health, education, and business-related services such as consulting and information technology.

This chapter reveals how Switzerland's economic and social structure has transformed over the last two decades. The changes are documented with data series taken from the freely accessible Internet databases of the Swiss Federal Statistical Office (FSO) and the Organisation for Economic Co-operation and Development (OECD). For the sake of simplicity, these sources are cited as FSO and OECD. All data sets are available from the author.

2 Economic growth across the board

Unlike in most European countries, the boom of the post-war decades did not end in Switzerland until the early 1990s. The two oil price crises in 1973/74 and 1979/80 had led to short and deep recessions in Switzerland (Flückiger 1998). In the 1980s, however, full employment prevailed again and by the end of the decade, the economy was booming with growth rates of 3 to 4 per cent and an official unemployment rate of less than half a per cent. The long recession of the 1990s was all the more drastic. Between 1991 and 1996, the economy stagnated for six consecutive years. This led to an unemployment rate of over 5 per cent in 1997—the highest level since the 1930s—and to rising numbers of people depending on social assistance and disability insurance, as well as to deficit-ridden public finances (Lampart 2006).

Just as the discussion of Switzerland's lack of economic dynamism was in full swing, a period of steady GDP growth set in at the end of the 1990s, interrupted only briefly by the bursting of the IT bubble in 2002/03 and the financial crisis of 2008/09. Figure 5.1 shows that Switzerland's GDP grew by an average of 1.8 per cent annually between 2000 and 2018. This means that, in price-adjusted terms, Switzerland's GDP in 2018 was 50 per cent larger than in 2000. The growth rate of 1.8 per cent was not only higher than the average in the 1970s and 1990s, but also exceeded the annual GDP growth in 2000–2018

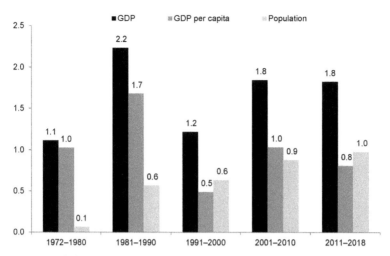

FIGURE 5.1: Annual changes in GDP, GDP per capita, and population in Switzerland (in per cent)
GDP figures are adjusted for inflation.
Data source: FSO.

achieved by Switzerland's neighbours Austria (1.6 per cent), Germany (1.4 per cent), France (1.4 per cent), and Italy (0.4 per cent).

Switzerland's economic growth was made possible because consumers abroad increased their demand for Swiss goods and services, and recent immigrants contributed to increasing the supply of Swiss goods and services. A breakdown of GDP growth into the individual demand components of private consumption, investment, government spending, and foreign trade shows the increasing importance of export surpluses, that is the amount by which the value of exports exceeds that of imports (see Figure 5.2). Export surpluses made no contribution to economic growth in Switzerland in the 1970s and 1980s when just as many goods and services were imported as exported. Since then, export surpluses have become more important for Switzerland every decade and foreign trade contributed annually an average of 0.5 percentage points to GDP growth between 2001 and 2018. This was possible because Switzerland achieved massive export surpluses (that is, surpluses in its current account) of 10 per cent annually during the same period.

Foreign trade thus contributed almost as much to GDP growth as private consumption. Between 2001 and 2018, demand from private households contributed 0.6 to 0.8 percentage points annually to growth—only half as much as in the 1970s and 1980s—whereas government spending played a subordinate role. Similar to Germany, Switzerland has thus adopted a neo-mercantilist growth model that combines wage restraint, consumption moderation, and high export surpluses. Unlike the consumption-based growth models in the United Kingdom, Sweden, or the USA, Swiss economic policy in the last two decades has primarily relied on growth impulses from abroad (Baccaro and Pontusson 2016).

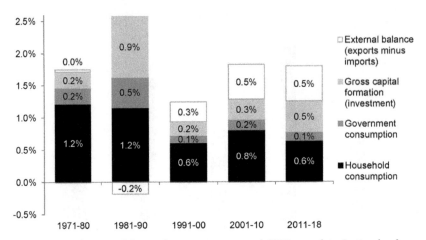

FIGURE 5.2: Contribution of demand components to real GDP growth in Switzerland

Data source: OECD.

The Swiss economy expanded strongly over the last two decades, but this expansion was mainly due to strong growth in the volume of labour. Hence, the GDP per capita in Switzerland has not grown substantially more than in Germany, France, or Austria, rising by about 1 per cent annually since 2000 (OECD).

If working hours per capita remain constant over time, the evolution of GDP per capita corresponds to the evolution of labour productivity. With an annual increase of 1 per cent, these productivity advances between 2000 and 2018 were slower than media reports about 'rapid digitalization' suggested. An annual increase in GDP per capita and labour productivity of 1 per cent seems modest at first glance. However, the comparison with the spectacular catch-up growth of the economic miracle years between 1948 and 1973 is misleading. Productivity advances of 3 to 4 per cent annually were not achieved in Western Europe for any length of time, either before or since these post-war decades (Inklaar et al. 2018). Moreover, even per capita growth of 1 per cent per year means that over the course of thirty years, the available economic output per inhabitant increases by one-third. A succeeding generation thus has over a third more goods and services at its disposal than the previous generation (Piketty 2013).

3 STRONG POPULATION GROWTH

The robust economic growth since the turn of the millennium is closely linked to the strong population growth. Between 2000 and 2020, the resident population in Switzerland increased by a full 20 per cent, from 7.2 to 8.7 million. Two geographical poles in particular were responsible for this growth: the Zurich agglomeration (with the cantons of Zurich, Aargau, Zug, and Schwyz) and the Lake Geneva region (with the cantons of Vaud, Geneva, Fribourg, and Valais). Population growth was below average in the Jura Arc (Jura, Neuchâtel), most of the Alpine mountain cantons (Grisons, Uri, Appenzell, Glarus), and the canton of Bern.

The uneven demographic development reflects the geographical differences in economic dynamics. In the last two decades, the two growth poles around Zurich and Geneva-Lausanne attracted many domestic and foreign workers. Consequently, the economy's strong demand for labour acted as an engine of population growth—a demand that led companies to increasingly recruit foreign workers because the Swiss labour market had dried up.

Until the end of the 1970s, population growth in Switzerland was more strongly influenced by the birth surplus (births minus deaths) than the migration balance (immigration minus emigration). However, starting from the 1980s, immigration contributed more to population growth than did birth surplus (Fux 2007; Babel 2019). Contrary to a common expectation, the birth rate in Switzerland has remained almost unchanged over the last four decades. Since the abrupt decline in the mid-1970s, the number of children per woman has remained stable at 1.5. Only the average age of mothers at the birth of children has risen: from twenty-eight years in 1980 to thirty-two years in 2018.

4 THE INCREASE IN HIGHLY SKILLED IMMIGRATION

Switzerland has been a country of immigration since the end of the nineteenth century. Since 1890, the number of immigrants has tended to exceed that of emigrants, with the exception of the war decades 1914–1945 and the first oil price crisis in 1974–78. Figure 5.3 shows for the period after 1945 that immigration dwarfed emigration, particularly during the post-war boom in the 1960s with positive net migration of 100,000 persons in 1961 and 80,000 persons in 1962.

After the two slumps in the crisis decades of the 1970s and 1990s, immigration picked up again at the beginning of the twenty-first century. In the peak years from 2007 to 2009 and 2012 to 2016, net migration reached levels similar to those of the 1960s, with a net balance of 70,000 to 80,000 migrants per year. However, net migration conceals large movements: on average, 180,000 people immigrated and 110,000 people emigrated annually between 2010 and 2018.

This strong immigration is primarily explained by Switzerland's booming labour market after 2000. It is also related to institutional changes and notably the agreement on the free movement of persons between Switzerland and the EU, which came into force in 2002 and allowed EU citizens non-discriminatory access to the Swiss labour market and vice versa. The majority of immigrants were thus EU citizens: during the 2010s, they were responsible for three-quarters of net migration (Babel 2019, 20).

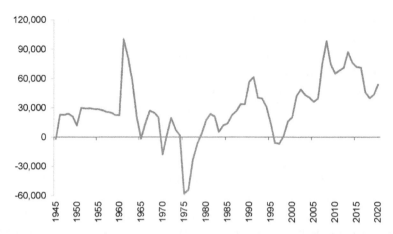

FIGURE 5.3: Net migration (immigration minus emigration) in Switzerland, number of persons 1945–2020

Data source: FSO.

As a result of the various waves of immigration, the proportion of foreigners in the Swiss population has risen steadily, exceeding 20 per cent for the first time in 1994 and reaching 25.5 per cent in 2020. The foreign resident population has also increased in absolute numbers, from 1.4 million in 2000 to 2.2 million in 2020. A growing proportion of foreigners can be observed not only in Switzerland but also in most other Western European countries. In 2020, according to Eurostat, the proportion of foreigners was 16.6 per cent in Austria, 12.5 in Germany, 8.4 in Italy, and 7.6 per cent in France.

Immigration to Switzerland has diversified considerably in recent decades. In 1980, almost half of all foreigners living in Switzerland came from Italy and, at 11 per cent, Spaniards were the second largest group of foreigners (see Figure 5.4). Four decades later, Italians were still the largest immigrant group, but at 15 per cent of all foreigners,

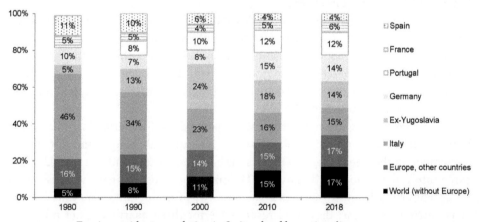

FIGURE 5.4: Foreign resident population in Switzerland by nationality

Data source: FSO.

their share is much smaller and hardly stands out against the almost equally numerous nationals from Germany (14 per cent) and Portugal (12 per cent). The latter two groups, as well as French nationals, increased their immigration after the European Union and Switzerland signed the agreement on the free movement of persons in 2002. European citizens continue to make up the large majority of all foreigners in Switzerland, but the weight of non-European immigration has increased since 1980—in relative and absolute terms. Switzerland has become globalized not only in its economic relations but also in the origin of its population.

Immigration to Switzerland is strongly driven by the needs of the economy. Thus, the vast majority of immigrants come to Switzerland for employment reasons. Among people with a university education who immigrated in recent years, more than half already had an employment contract or a job offer from Switzerland before entering the country (Wanner and Steiner 2018, 9). The second most important reason for immigrating to Switzerland is family reunification. Other reasons such as education or asylum application come third and fourth, but play a quantitatively subordinate role.

In the boom of the post-war decades, Swiss employers recruited mainly low-skilled immigrants for industry and construction, the hospitality industry, and agriculture. The result was the creation of a foreign underclass that clustered at the low-end jobs of Switzerland's occupational structure (Flückiger 1998; Hoffmann-Nowotny 1973; Wanner and Steiner 2018). This model was all the more effective because the residence permits of many foreign workers—both annual residents and seasonal workers—were tied to a job. Only foreigners with a settlement permit were free to change jobs. Foreigners with a settlement permit were a small minority up to the oil crisis (22 per cent in 1970), but since the mid-1990s their share has stabilized at around two-thirds of the resident foreign population (FSO).

In a drastic turn of tendencies, highly skilled migrants have come to dominate immigration to Switzerland over the last few decades. Figure 5.5 shows that people with tertiary

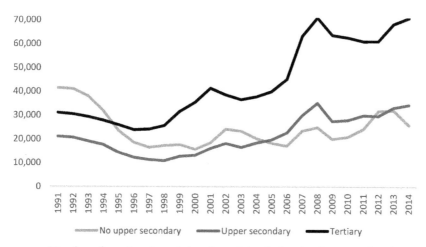

FIGURE 5.5: Number of new immigrants (aged 20–64) to Switzerland per year, by education

Data source: Wanner and Steiner (2018, 6).

education—usually a university degree—have been the majority of new immigrants each year since the end of the 1990s. However, they also emigrate more frequently than lower educated immigrants do. The number of immigrants with low and medium qualifications newly arriving in Switzerland has changed little over the past twenty-five years. Therefore, the strong increase in immigration is almost exclusively due to the high-skilled group. In the 2010s, around half of the net migration for 25–64 year olds consisted of people with tertiary qualifications (Babel 2019, 22). In some fields of education, more people with tertiary degrees immigrated each year than were trained domestically in the same year, especially in computer science, medicine, engineering, and natural sciences (Babel 2019, 23–24).

5 Ongoing educational expansion

Educational attainment has not only increased in recent waves of immigration. The domestic population also continued to benefit from educational expansion. Figure 5.6 shows that between 1996 and 2020, the proportion of 25–64 year olds with a tertiary degree in Switzerland tripled, growing from 10 to 30 per cent. If professional vocational education and training (PET) is also defined as tertiary education—as is common in Switzerland, but not in Germany—45 per cent had a tertiary degree in 2019 (see 'Education Policy' in this volume for an overview of Switzerland's education system). And the educational expansion is still in full swing: by the end of the 2020s, more than half of adults in Switzerland are expected to have a degree from a university, university of applied sciences, or in PET (Babel 2019, 43).

Surprisingly, the growing share of people with tertiary education has only led to a weak decrease in the share of people without post-compulsory education. Despite efforts by the cantonal governments to keep more young people in education beyond the end of compulsory schooling, this proportion of early education-leavers has stagnated at over 10 per cent. Instead, the growth in tertiary education has been at the expense of initial vocational training at the upper-secondary level of education—at least at first glance. Whereas in 1996 54 per cent of 25- to 64-year-olds had an apprenticeship as their highest qualification, in 2020 this was only the case for 36 per cent. However, a second glance shows that over the same period of time, about two-thirds of every cohort of young people continued to choose a VET programme after compulsory schooling—a proportion that remained almost unchanged over time (Babel 2019, 13). As a result, the importance of vocational training (apprenticeships) as *initial* post-compulsory education has declined only slightly. What has changed is that for a growing proportion of young people it is merely a stepping stone towards tertiary education—thanks, among other things, to the strong expansion of vocational baccalaureates and universities of applied sciences.

Switzerland, therefore, remains a showcase for a collective system of skills education (Busemeyer and Trampusch 2012). In no other country in the OECD does such a high proportion of young people complete basic vocational education and training. And even more so than in other apprenticeship-countries (such as Denmark, Germany,

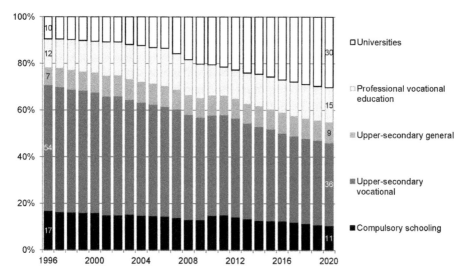

FIGURE 5.6: Highest completed education of the population aged 25–64 (in per cent), 1996–2020

Data source: FSO.

the Netherlands, or Austria), VET takes place in a dual system (i.e. in companies and schools), continues to be developed with the close involvement of employers' associations, and leads to nationally recognized diplomas (Korber and Oesch 2019).

The expansion of education in recent decades has been driven primarily by women. This is shown by comparing two different birth cohorts that were aged 25–34 years in 1999 and in 2019 respectively (see Figure 5.7). In 1999, young women were more likely than young men to have stopped after compulsory schooling or initial vocational education and training, while young men were more likely to have completed higher education. Twenty years later, young women had not only made up for the educational gap, but overtaken men. In 2019, more young women than young men had a university degree.

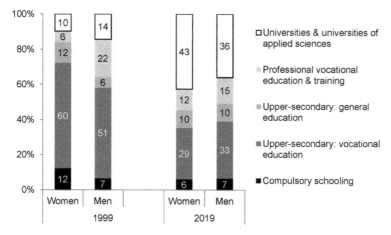

FIGURE 5.7: Highest level of education completed by the resident population aged 25–34

Data source: FSO.

Despite the ongoing educational expansion in Switzerland, the providers of tertiary degrees did not succeed in satisfying the economy's strong demand for workers with higher education (Kriesi and Leemann 2020; Meyer 2018). The skills structure of the latest wave of immigration suggests that the Swiss economy demands far more workers with tertiary degrees than are being trained domestically. Thus, there is a shortage of skilled workers in most occupations that require tertiary education. At the same time, labour demand stagnates in many occupational fields that require an apprenticeship, notably in the two most frequently chosen vocational apprenticeships in Switzerland: for commercial employees and retail trade employees (SECO 2016; SBFI 2017; Babel 2019).

In recent decades, a degree from a university opened up bright salary and employment prospects in Switzerland (Korber and Oesch 2019). Young people and their families clearly perceived these labour market signals. As a consequence, the educational system has become a crucial front in the class struggle, which played out in access to gymnasiums that deliver entry tickets to higher education. With gymnasium-based baccalaureate rates of only 15 to 20 per cent of a given birth cohort, the German-speaking cantons of Switzerland (with the exception of Basel) set a narrow numerus clausus for the direct route to universities. This has the consequence that many young people are frustrated in their aspiration of obtaining a university education, while many employers are frustrated in their search for domestic staff with a university education.

A second consequence is that social origin has a particularly strong influence on who obtains a university degree in Switzerland (Becker and Schoch 2018). Young people who achieve the same school grades and PISA test scores at age sixteen are twice as likely to have a university degree by age thirty if their parents belong to the upper middle class rather than the working class (Combet and Oesch 2021). Switzerland is thus one of the European countries where the influence of parental resources on educational pathways and attainment is particularly strong (Pfeffer 2008). Difficult access to Swiss higher education is socially and economically suboptimal. It discourages many children from modest class backgrounds from studying and, at the same time, forces many companies to recruit tertiary-educated workers abroad (Kriesi and Leemann 2020).

6 Sectoral change in the labour market

During the last twenty years, not only were GDP, population, and educational attainment growing, but the labour market also experienced a boom. After the crisis-ridden decade of the 1990s in which employment stagnated, the number of jobs began to expand again at the turn of the millennium. Between 2000 and 2021, employment in Switzerland increased by a quarter, from 4.1 to 5.2 million workers (from 3.3 to 4.0 million in full-time equivalents).

A distinction by sector shows the extent of structural change in the labour market. Two sectors, in particular, were responsible for the employment boom. First, the number of jobs in health care, education, social services, and public administration increased by more than 50 per cent between 2000 and 2019 (in full-time equivalents). Second, employment grew by more than 40 per cent in business-related services that include the financial sector, communications, IT, consulting, and research.

In contrast, employment in manufacturing, construction, transport, retail trade, and personal services remained constant. Contrary to popular belief, there has been neither strong growth in low-skilled personal service jobs nor a slump in industrial employment in Switzerland over the past twenty years. On the contrary, after a massive wave of de-industrialization in the early 1990s, Switzerland experienced a small re-industrialization at the beginning of the 2000s, which was slowed down a first time by the financial crisis in 2009 and a second time by the appreciation of the Swiss franc in 2015 (which made Swiss exports less cost-competitive). At the same time, a radical change took place within industry. While the pharmaceutical and watch industries created many jobs, employment fell in the printing, metal, and machine industries.

In a growing labour market, stable employment figures for a sector still mean a decreasing share of total employment. Figure 5.8 shows that the share of industry shrank from 25 per cent of total employment in 1991 to 17 per cent in 2019. Similarly, the share of retail trade and transport (from 22 to 18 per cent) and that of personal services (from 11 to 9 per cent) declined. In contrast, the employment share of construction remained almost constant after the mid-1990s. Since the end of the housing crisis in the early 1990s, this sector has employed 8 to 9 per cent of all workers.

Women have not only caught up in terms of educational attainment but have also played a decisive role in the recent employment boom. Between 2000 and 2021, the number of women in paid employment rose by 630,000 in Switzerland, compared to a rise of 470,000 among men. While the male employment rate fell in the 1990s and remained constant at 85 per cent after the early 2000s, the proportion of women in

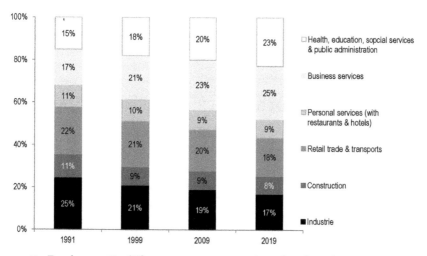

FIGURE 5.8: Employment in different sectors as proportion of total employment, 1991–2019

Data source: FSO, in full-time equivalents.

employment increased by ten percentage points between 1991 and 2021, from 66 to 76 per cent (age group 15–64, FSO).

Among childless women, more than 70 per cent were already in employment in the 1990s. Consequently, the increase in employment was almost exclusively due to mothers who have become less likely to withdraw from the labour market after the birth of children. The proportion of employed mothers of pre-school age children thus increased from 50 to 75 per cent between 1990 and 2021 (FSO; Giudici and Schumacher 2017).

However, gender differences in the labour market have not disappeared, as the growth in female employment has mainly taken place in part-time jobs. While 49 per cent of women worked part-time in 1991, 59 per cent did so in 2021. In contrast, the vast majority of men continue to work full-time (despite a small increase in male part-time work from 8 to 18 per cent between 1991 and 2021). In Switzerland, this evolution has solidified the model of one and a half jobs per household: fathers work full-time in a paid job; mothers work half-time and do most of the housework. Switzerland is thus the second part-time economy in the world, after the Netherlands (where 74 per cent of women work part-time), but ahead of Germany and Austria (both with 47 per cent female part-time work) (OECD).

Despite the increase in part-time work, Switzerland's employment boom remains impressive if measured in terms of total working hours instead of the number of people in employment. Between 1960 and 2005, the total volume of paid work in Switzerland hardly changed (except for a dip in the mid-1970s to mid-1980s). A larger number of employees worked fewer hours per year on average. Between 2005 and 2015, however, the volume of work increased sharply—by around 20 per cent and thus as much as during the post-war boom of the 1950s and early 1960s (Siegenthaler 2017). Thus, after the turn of the millennium, Switzerland experienced a 'job miracle that even dwarfs that in Germany' (Siegenthaler 2017, 8).

These findings run diametrically counter to the discussion on the end of work. While colourful scenarios of technological unemployment are outlined in the media, more people are working in Switzerland than ever before—in front of computers, next to assembly lines, and in tandem with robots. As in earlier phases of technological upheaval, the volume of work has also increased in the current wave of innovation, in Switzerland as well as in other Western countries.

7 Upgrading the occupational structure

Of particular interest is how the change in employment and education has affected social stratification. A popular thesis in economics claims that technological change is leading to an increasing polarization of the occupational structure. New jobs would be created at the margins of the labour market, while employment in intermediate occupations would decline. Research for the US and the UK indeed suggests that employment growth has been strongest in high-wage occupations and weakest in middle-wage occupations (Goos and Manning 2007; Autor and Dorn 2013).

However, the developments in the two Anglo-Saxon labour markets do not translate well to Western Europe. The polarization in the US and the UK is closely related to the education system (weak supply at intermediate skill levels), wage-setting institutions (low statutory minimum wages and few collective agreements), and migration policies (polarized immigration of low- and high-skilled workers) (Oesch 2013). Empirical studies thus refute the polarization thesis for Switzerland. With the exception of the 1980s, Switzerland's occupational structure has steadily upgraded since 1970. Only during the construction and consumption boom of the 1980s did employment increase strongly, not only in high-paid but also in low-paid occupations. In the two decades that followed, by contrast, nowhere were so few jobs created as in low-paid occupations (Murphy and Oesch 2018).

In Table 5.1, we trace the change in the employment structure between 1991 and 2019. It shows that occupational upgrading was driven by the strong growth of the salaried middle class, consisting of three occupational categories: (i) (associate) managers and administrators,

Table 5.1: Share of occupational classes in total employment, 1991/2 and 2018/9

	Interpersonal service logic	Technical work logic	Administrative work logic	Independent work logic		
	Socio-cultural (semi-)professionals	Technical (semi-)professionals	(Associate) managers	Liberal professionals and large employers	Tertiary	*Educational requirement of occupations*
	Medical doctors Teachers Social workers	*Engineers Architects IT-specialists*	*Administrators Consultants Accountants*	*Entrepreneurs Lawyers Dentists*		
1991/92	10.3%	10.9%	13.0%	3.4%		
2018/19	13.5%	13.7%	16.8%	4.0%		
Change	+3.2	+2.8	+3.8	+0.6		
	Service workers	Production workers	Office clerks	Small business owners and farmers	Secondary	
	Waiters Nursing aides Shop assistants	*Mechanics Carpenters Assemblers*	*Secretaries Receptionists Mail clerks*	*Shop owners Independent artisans Farmers*		
1991/92	12.8%	22.8%	16.5%	10.4%		
2018/19	14.1%	15.5%	13.0%	9.4%		
Change	+1.3	-7.3	-3.5	-1.0		

Note: The table shows the share of each occupational class in total employment (18- to 65-year-olds working at least twenty hours per week). We calculate the average for 1991 and 1992 on the one hand, and 2018 and 2019 on the other, in order to reduce the influence of annual fluctuations. The calculations are based on detailed occupation codes (at the ISCO 4-digit level).

Data source: Swiss Labour Force Survey 1991, 1992, 2018, 2019.

whose share in total employment grew by 4 percentage points; (ii) socio-cultural (semi-) professionals such as medical doctors, teachers, social workers, or nurses, whose share increased by 3 percentage points; (iii) technical (semi-)professionals such as engineers, computer scientists, architects, or technicians, whose share increased by 3 percentage points.

In contrast, the employment share of two classes decreased: that of production and construction workers by 7 percentage points and that of office clerks by 3.5 percentage points. These two shrinking occupational groups do not constitute the core of the middle class, but the traditional working class on the one hand and the lower middle class on the other.

The employment share of the self-employed remained stable and growth in personal service jobs was modest at one percentage point. This growth in lower skilled service jobs was too weak to compensate for the reduction in routine agricultural, industrial, and back-office jobs. Like other Western European countries, Switzerland was thus most successful in automating and outsourcing low-skilled occupations, and thus in replacing the jobs of farm workers and plant operators, data entry clerks, and shop assistants. New jobs were created mainly in highly skilled service occupations, programmers and engineers, consultants and analysts, medical doctors and teachers. As a result, the employment structure in Switzerland was upgraded—very similarly to Germany, Spain, or Sweden (Oesch and Piccitto 2019).

In Figure 5.9, the occupational categories are grouped into larger classes and only include employed persons entitled to vote, i.e. the workforce with a Swiss passport. This shows how the gainfully employed electorate in Switzerland has changed in terms of social class. In the early 1990s, the working class slightly outnumbered the salaried middle class. But while the share of the working class shrank by 6 percentage points in the following three decades, the proportion of the salaried middle class increased by 10 points. As a result, the salaried middle class today comprises about 44 per cent of the Swiss workforce compared to 30 per cent of the working class. The rest is made up of 13 per cent of office clerks and 13 per cent of employers and self-employed.

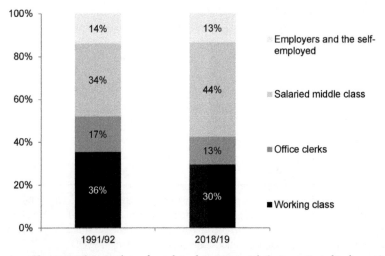

FIGURE 5.9: Change in the number of employed persons with Swiss nationality by social class

For source and data, see notes to Table 5.1. Managers, socio-cultural, and technical professionals are grouped into the salaried middle class; production workers and personal service workers into the working class; and large employers, the liberal professions, and small business owners into employers and the self-employed.

8 Moderate wage inequality, high wealth inequality

Switzerland's strong expansion of GDP and employment growth over the last twenty years is beyond doubt. Nevertheless, it is questionable whether a large part of the population experienced these two decades as a boom period. The reason lies in the weak growth of earnings. This becomes clear from Figure 5.10, which shows the development of nominal wages, inflation, and the resulting real wages since 1950. During the decades of the post-war boom, real wages grew, on average, by 1.7 per cent annually in the 1950s, 3.3 per cent in the 1960s, and 2.3 per cent in the 1970s. The two oil price crises of the 1970s put an end to the post-war boom and wage growth flattened out. Real wage increases fell to 0.9 per cent annually in the 1980s and 0.2 per cent in the crisis decade of the 1990s. Surprisingly, even in the two decades of the jobs miracle—the 2000s and 2010s—real wage growth did not exceed 0.6 per cent annually.

While real wage growth was held back by inflation in earlier decades, this factor fell away between 2000 and 2020. In Switzerland, the annual increase in consumer prices between 1960 and 1990 averaged over 3 per cent. After 1993, however, inflation fell steadily, averaging 1 per cent in the 2000s and 0 (!) per cent in the 2010s—with negative inflation in four years between 2012 and 2016. This means that real wages stopped growing since the mid-1990s because negotiated wages—nominal wages—stagnated. This stagnation is puzzling to economists, who expect wages and prices to rise as labour markets dry up and workers become increasingly scarce. Yet despite an official unemployment rate that fell from a low 3.5 to an even lower 2.3 per cent between 2010 and 2019, wage growth in Switzerland remained weak and there was no inflationary pressure.

One possible reason for the absence of a wage-price spiral is immigration policy and the free movement of persons between Switzerland and the European Union. Thanks to the possibility of recruiting workers in Lyon, Milan, or Stuttgart at any time, there was never any real shortage on the Swiss labour market even when unemployment was low. A second reason is the weaker bargaining power of trade unions and the lesser importance of collective wage bargaining. Notably over the 1990s, wage setting in Switzerland was increasingly shifted to the company level, and individual wage agreements replaced collective wage bargaining between trade unions and employer associations in many sectors and firms (Oesch 2011).

FIGURE 5.10: Annual change in wages and consumer prices in Switzerland (in per cent)
The consumer price index measures inflation and real wages show the rise in wages corrected for inflation.
Data source: FSO (Swiss wage index).

Figure 5.10 is based on the Swiss wage index, which measures the wage evolution for a given occupational activity and consequently ignores structural change—that is, shifts between occupations and sectors as well as and shifts in occupational activity such as promotions. These two aspects are taken into account in Switzerland's wage structure survey and this leads to somewhat higher wage increases. In the twenty years between 1996 and 2016, median wages (p50) grew by 0.8 per cent annually in price-adjusted terms. For low-wage (p10) and high-wage (p90) employees, real wages grew slightly more, by 1 and 1.2 per cent respectively. Wage growth was strongest among employees in the top 1 per cent (p99), whose incomes increased by 2.3 per cent annually in price-adjusted terms (SGB 2018, 5). These averages come closer to measures of annual GDP growth per capita of around 1 per cent over the same period (see Figure 5.1).

Labour income developed somewhat more positively over time at the household level than the individual level because of women's increased labour force participation. At the same time, the tax burden also increased at the household level, especially because of the rising cost of health insurance. Since compulsory health insurance came into force, annual costs have risen by an average of 3.8 per cent annually between 1996 and 2020 (Federal Office of Public Health). Higher health expenditure, together with increased housing costs, have eaten away most of the income gains between 2000 and 2016 (SGB 2018, 33).

Finally, there is the question of the distribution of income in Switzerland. Figure 5.11 compares the share of national income accruing to the lower half of the population and that obtained by the richest 10 per cent. Over the last four decades, the lower half received a constant share of about 24 per cent. In 2017, Switzerland had thus a

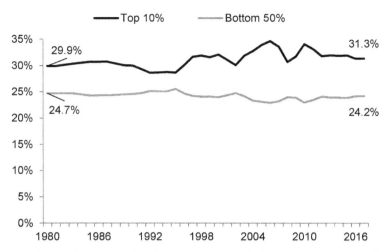

FIGURE 5.11: Share of pre-tax national income going to the bottom 50 per cent and top 10 per cent of Switzerland's adult population

Data source: World Inequality Database (https://wid.world).

comparable distribution of incomes as Austria, France, or Sweden. In contrast, the lower half of the population received significantly smaller shares of national income in Germany (18.5 per cent), Italy (20.6 per cent), and above all the USA (12.7 per cent) than in Switzerland. Over the same period, Switzerland's richest 10 per cent secured a slightly increasing share of national income of 30 to 31 per cent. This growth was entirely due to the richest 1 per cent, which increased its share of national income from 10 to 11 per cent (Foellmi and Martinez 2017; Martinez 2017; World Inequality Database).

An analysis of seven national surveys and tax data concludes that income inequality at the household level changed little in Switzerland between 1990 and 2012. The disproportionate growth in very high wages led to an increase in income inequality, whereas the increased workforce participation of women led to a decrease (Kuhn and Suter 2015). While income inequality remained stable in Switzerland, it rose sharply in Germany, Italy, Sweden, and the USA.

In terms of income inequality, Switzerland is close to the OECD average (OECD). Yet the situation is very different with regard to the distribution of *wealth*. Since the 1980s, overall wealth has grown strongly in Switzerland and the inequality in the distribution of wealth increased significantly. The richest 1 per cent of taxpayers in Switzerland owned 42 per cent of total private assets in the mid-2010s, compared to 34 per cent at the beginning of the 1990s. Such a concentration of wealth in the hands of a small group is also unusual internationally. Wealth concentration in the hands of the top 1 per cent is not only much stronger in Switzerland than in the UK (23 per cent) or France (20 per cent), but it also exceeds the level of the US (39 per cent) (figures for the mid-2010s, Brülhart 2019, 9).

9 Conclusion

How can we interpret the changes in Switzerland's economic and social structure since 2000? The first two decades of the twenty-first century in Switzerland were indisputably characterized by growth: the economy expanded, employment rose, immigration accelerated, and the population increased. Unlike in parts of Southern Europe, the last twenty years in Switzerland will not go down in history as a time of crisis. The financial crisis of 2008–2009 and the appreciation of the Swiss franc in 2015 led only to brief dips in the economy's growth trajectory.

A positive conclusion suggests itself with regard to the labour market. Many new jobs were created and unemployment remained at low levels, the official unemployment rate never exceeding 4 per cent in the last twenty years (SECO 2019, 15). Over the same period, the occupational structure upgraded as employment disproportionately grew in higher-skilled fields of the labour market.

The growth of the economy and employment also had a positive impact on public finances. Between 1990 and 1999, the state sector (including government at the federal, cantonal, and municipal level as well as public social security funds) incurred, on average, an annual deficit of 2 per cent. This changed after the turn of the millennium as public budgets were balanced, on average, between 2000 and 2009. Between 2010 and 2018, they achieved an average annual surplus of half a per cent. Consequently, prior to the COVID-19 crisis, Switzerland's debt-to-GDP ratio continuously shrank, from 45 per cent in 2000 to 27.5 per cent in 2018 (FSO), putting it far below the EU's debt ratio of 80 per cent (Eurostat).

However, the boom of the 2000s left smaller traces in people's private purses than earlier growth periods, notably real wages increased much more slowly in the last twenty years than in the post-war decades. Because health and housing costs rose at the same time, the evolution in disposable incomes was less spectacular than what could be expected from an extended economic boom period. For parts of the population, the negative side effects of the boom may thus have predominated. The term 'density stress' was used in the 2010s to describe dissatisfaction with overcrowded trains and long traffic jams, overbuilt green spaces, and expensive housing. This dissatisfaction was expressed most strongly in a national popular referendum held in 2014 that aimed at limiting 'mass immigration' and that was accepted by a short margin.

Regardless of how the growth boom is assessed, Switzerland's population structure has changed fundamentally over the past two decades. Three structural changes in particular are noteworthy. First, the distribution of educational attainment in Switzerland has risen sharply. Educational expansion has further accelerated at the level of universities and universities of applied sciences, and their graduates were joined by immigrants amongst whom a majority also held university degrees. As a result, tertiary education is becoming the new norm in Switzerland, replacing apprenticeships as the highest level of educational attainment for a majority of the population.

Secondly, the population in Switzerland has become more diverse under the influence of strong immigration, where no longer does any single country of origin dominate. Increasingly high-skilled immigration from a growing number of countries is putting an end to the historical clustering of migrants in low-paid and low-skilled jobs. This means that the term 'migration background' is no longer synonymous with low socio-economic status as it used to be in Switzerland in the post-war decades.

Finally, structural change in the labour market has also altered Switzerland's class structure. Strong job growth in health, education, and business-related services has mainly benefited higher-skilled workers. While the ranks of the salaried middle class expanded, the traditional working class and lower middle class of clerical workers lost ground. Consequently, the big loser of technological change in recent decades has been not the middle class but the working class. In Switzerland, as in the rest of Western Europe, it has lost its majority class status and is increasingly being put on the defensive (Castel 1999).

Note

1. Earlier versions of this chapter benefited from helpful comments by Jacques Babel, Silja Häusermann, Daniel Lampart, and Andreas Rieger. We are grateful for their help.

References

Autor, David, and David Dorn. 2013. 'The Growth of Low-Skill Service Jobs and the Polarization of the US Labor Market'. *American Economic Review* 103 (5): pp. 1553–1597.

Babel, Jacques. 2019. *Demografische Entwicklung und Auswirkungen auf den gesamten Bildungsbereich Bericht des Bundesrats in Erfüllung des Postulats 12.3657 vom 17. August 2012.* Bern: Bundesamt für Statistik.

Baccaro, Lucio, and Jonas Pontusson. 2016. 'Rethinking Comparative Political Economy: The Growth Model Perspective'. *Politics & Society* 44 (2): pp. 175–207.

Becker, Rolf, and Jürg Schoch. 2018. *Soziale Selektivität. Empfehlungen des Schweizerischen Wissenschaftsrates.* Bern: Schweizer Wissenschaftsrat. https://wissenschaftsrat.ch/images/stories/pdf/de/Politische_Analyse_SWR_3_2018_SozialeSelektivitaet_WEB.pdf, accessed 15 May 2022.

Brülhart, Marius. 2019. 'Erbschaften in der Schweiz: Entwicklung seit 1911 und Bedeutung für die Steuern'. *Social Change in Switzerland* 20. doi: 10.22019/SC-2019-00008.

Busemeyer, Marius, and Christine Trampusch. 2012. *The Political Economy of Collective Skill Formation.* Oxford: Oxford University Press.

Castel, Robert. 1999. 'Pourquoi la classe ouvrière a-t-elle perdu la partie?'. *Actuel Marx* 26: pp. 15–24.

Combet, Benita, and Daniel Oesch. 2021. 'The Social-Origin Gap in University Graduation by Gender and Immigrant Status: A Cohort Analysis for Switzerland'. *Longitudinal and Life Course Studies* 12 (2): pp. 119–146.

Esping-Andersen, Gøsta. 2009. *The Incomplete Revolution: Adapting Welfare States to Women's New Roles.* Princeton: Polity Press.

Flückiger, Yves. 1998. 'The Labour Market in Switzerland: The End of a Special Case?'. *International Journal of Manpower* 19 (6): pp. 369–395.

Foellmi, Reto, and Isabel Martínez. 2017. 'Volatile Top Income Shares in Switzerland? Reassessing the Evolution Between 1981 and 2010'. *Review of Economics and Statistics* 99 (5): pp. 793–809.

Fux, Beat. 2007. 'Population Projections Revisited: Eine wissenssoziologische Analyse schweizerischer Bevölkerungsprognosen oder weshalb die Demographie der Bevölkerungswissenschaft bedarf'. *Zeitschrift für Bevölkerungswissenschaft* 32 (3–4): pp. 597–620.

Giudici, Francesco, and Reto Schumacher. 2017. 'Erwerbstätigkeit von Müttern in der Schweiz: Entwicklung und individuelle Faktoren'. *Social Change in Switzerland* 10. doi:10.22019/SC-2017-00006.

Goos, Maarten, and Alan Manning. 2007. 'Lousy and Lovely Jobs: The Rising Polarization of Work in Britain'. *Review of Economics and Statistics* 89 (1): pp. 118–133.

Hoffmann-Nowotny, Hans-Joachim. 1973. *Soziologie des Fremdarbeiterproblems: eine theoretische und empirische Analyse am Beispiel der Schweiz*. Stuttgart: Enke.

Inklaar, Robert, Herman de Jong, Jutta Bolt, and Jan van Zanden. 2018. 'Rebasing "Maddison": New Income Comparisons and the Shape of Long-Run Economic Development', *Maddison Project Working paper* 10, University of Groningen.

Korber, Maïlys, and Daniel Oesch. 2019. 'Vocational versus General Education: Employment and Earnings Over the Life Course in Switzerland'. *Advances in Life Course Research* 40: pp. 1–13.

Kriesi, Irene, and Regula Leemann. 2020. 'Tertiarisierungsdruck. Herausforderungen für das Bildungssystem, den Arbeitsmarkt und das Individuum'. *Swiss Academies Communications* 15 (6): pp. 1–53.

Kuhn, Ursina, and Christian Suter. 2015. 'Die Entwicklung der Einkommensungleichheit in der Schweiz'. *Social Change in Switzerland* 2. doi:10.22019/SC-2015-00004.

Lampart, Daniel. 2006. *Handlungsspielräume und-restriktionen der Schweizer Konjunkturpolitik in der langen Stagnation der 1990er Jahre: eine modellbasierte Evaluation*. Doctoral thesis, University of Zürich.

Martínez, Isabel. 2017. 'Die Topeinkommen in der Schweiz seit 1980: Verteilung und Mobilität'. *Social Change in Switzerland* 11. doi:10.22019/SC-2017-00008.

Meyer, Thomas. 2018. 'Von der Schule ins Erwachsenenleben: Ausbildungs- und Erwerbsverläufe in der Schweiz'. *Social Change in Switzerland* 13. doi:10.22019/SC-2018-00002.

Murphy, Emily, and Daniel Oesch. 2018. 'Is Employment Polarisation Inevitable? Occupational Change in Ireland and Switzerland, 1970-2010'. *Work Employment and Society* 32 (6): pp. 1099–1117.

Oesch, Daniel. 2011. 'Swiss Trade Unions and Industrial Relations After 1990: A History of Decline and Renewal'. In *Switzerland in Europe. Continuity and Change in the Swiss Political Economy*, edited by Christine Trampusch, and André Mach, pp. 82–102. London: Routledge.

Oesch, Daniel. 2013. *Occupational Change in Europe. How Technology and Education transform the Job Structure*. Oxford: Oxford University Press.

Oesch, Daniel, and Giorgio Piccitto. 2019. 'The Polarization Myth: Occupational Upgrading in Germany, Spain, Sweden and the UK, 1992–2015'. *Work and Occupations*, 46 (4): pp. 441–469.

Pfeffer, Fabian. 2008. 'Persistent Inequality in Educational Attainment and Its Institutional Context'. *European Sociological Review* 24 (5): pp. 543–565.

Piketty, Thomas. 2013. *Le capital au XXIe siècle*. Paris: Seuil.

SBFI. 2017. 'Berufsbildung in der Schweiz. Fakten und Zahlen 2017'. https://www.sbfi.admin.ch/dam/sbfi/de/dokumente/2017/04/Fakten_Zahlen_BB2017.pdf.download.pdf/Fakten_Zahlen_BB2017_dt.pdf, accessed 15 May 2022.

SECO. 2016. 'Fachkräftemangel in der Schweiz, Indikatorensystem zur Beurteilung der Fachkräftenachfrage'. https://www.seco.admin.ch/seco/de/home/Publikationen_Dienstleistungen/Publikationen_und_Formulare/Arbeit/Arbeitsmarkt/Fachkraeftebedarf/indikatorensystem-zur-beurteilung-der-fachkraeftenachfrage.html, accessed 15 May 2022.

SECO. 2019. 'Bericht des Observatoriums zum Freizügigkeitsabkommen Schweiz – EU. Auswirkungen der Personenfreizügigkeit auf den Schweizer Arbeitsmarkt'. https://www.seco.admin.ch/seco/de/home/Publikationen_Dienstleistungen/Publikationen_und_Formulare/Arbeit/Personenfreizuegigkeit_und_Arbeitsbeziehungen/observatoriumsberichte/15_Bericht_Observatorium.html, accessed 15 May 2022.

SGB. 2018. 'Verteilungsbericht 2018. Die Verteilung der Löhne, Einkommen und Vermögen sowie die Belastung durch Steuern und Abgaben in der Schweiz. SGB-Dossier 130'. https://www.sgb.ch/themen/arbeit/detail/dossier-130-verteilungsbericht-2018, accessed 15 May 2022.

Siegenthaler, Michael. 2017. 'Vom Nachkriegsboom zum Jobwunder – der starke Rückgang der Arbeitszeit in der Schweiz seit 1950'. *Social Change in Switzerland* 9. doi:10.22019/SC-2017-00004.

Visser, Jelle. 2002. 'The First Part-Time Economy in the World: A Model to be Followed?'. *Journal of European Social Policy* 12 (1): pp. 23–42.

Wanner, Philippe, and Ilka Steiner. 2018. 'Ein spektakulärer Anstieg der hochqualifizierten Zuwanderung in die Schweiz'. *Social Change in Switzerland* 16. doi: 10.22019/SC-2018-00008.

CHAPTER 6

SWITZERLAND'S POSITION IN EUROPE AND THE WORLD

THOMAS BERNAUER AND STEFANIE WALTER

1 INTRODUCTION

GLOBAL economic integration and global political restraint—this fine balance has characterized Switzerland's relationship with the international community since the Swiss federal state was founded in 1848.[1] Geopolitical change and crises, globalization, and the European integration process, however, have increasingly challenged this traditional model of Swiss foreign relations. With its entry into the United Nations (UN) (2002) and two sets of bilateral treaties with the European Union (EU) (2000, 2005), Switzerland has taken significant steps towards a stronger political involvement in the international arena, even if a clear majority of Swiss voters, parliament, and the government remain opposed to EU membership.

This chapter situates Switzerland in the global economy and in international politics. It begins by contextualizing Switzerland in its international environment and comparing it with its neighbours as well as some additional countries. The chapter then shows that Switzerland is one of the most 'globalized', i.e. most open countries in the world. Finally, it shows that the political system of Switzerland has slowly but noticeably reacted to European as well as the global political and economic changes of the recent past. Nevertheless, with respect to foreign policy, voters remain divided into two camps; these camps view the implications of increasing integration into the European and global arena very differently, in particular with regard to the consequences for sovereignty, neutrality, federalism, and direct democracy. This division generates considerable political controversies about the challenges Switzerland faces.

2 Switzerland in international perspective

Switzerland is located in the heart of Europe, bordering on Austria, France, Italy, Germany, and Liechtenstein. With an area of 41,000 km² and a population of about 8.7 million it is one of the smaller European states. Yet, both its economic output (in 2019, the World Bank (2020) ranked Switzerland's economy as thirty-seventh worldwide in terms of real GDP) and its role as an important transit route across the Alps contribute to the country's relevance in Europe. To situate Switzerland in this context, the next section compares Switzerland with its neighbouring countries, as well as the United Kingdom (UK) and the United States (US), in five areas: political and economic freedom, economic output, environmental protection, defence, and developmental assistance.

2.1 Political and economic freedom

Until the end of World War II, Switzerland was one of the very few European countries to have experienced a continuous tradition of liberalism, democracy, and constitutionalism for over 100 years. In the past seventy-five years, Switzerland's political freedom has become the European norm rather than the exception, however. Well-established measures for the degree of democracy (e.g. Freedom House Index, Polity IV Index, Democracy Barometer) show that most other advanced industrialized countries now also achieve very high scores. However, Figure 6.1 shows that Switzerland has a

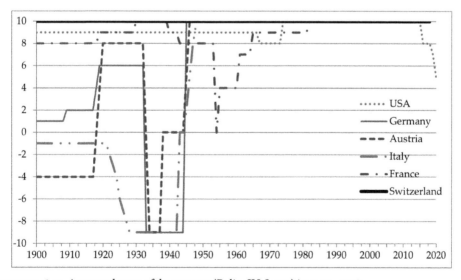

FIGURE 6.1: Average degree of democracy (Polity IV-Score) in 1900–2018
This index varies from -10 (full autocracy) to +10 (full democracy).
Data source: Center for Systemic Peace (2020).

Table 6.1: Economic freedom according to the Index of Economic Freedom (2020)

	Switzerland	Austria	France	Germany	Italy	UK	USA
Global Rank	5	4	64	27	74	7	17
Overall Score	82	82.6	66	73.5	63.8	79.3	76.6
Property Rights	87.4	82.8	85.9	80.5	75.4	92.2	81.8
Judicial Effectiveness	81.5	86.1	71.2	74.3	51.3	82.7	83.7
Government Integrity	90.1	89.3	83.3	82.8	62.2	89.9	77.2
Tax Burden	70.1	63	48.8	60.9	56	64.7	74.6
Government Spending	65.3	61.6	4.5	42.2	28.5	49.5	56.5
Fiscal Stability	96.7	91.8	67.1	92.9	71.1	78.1	54.3
Business Freedom	74.2	87.8	82.5	82.8	70.4	94.7	83.3
Labour Freedom	72.4	84	46.1	53	50.9	73.1	87.9
Price Stability	84.4	86.2	76.7	76.7	83.2	80.3	75.5
Trade Freedom	86.6	88.2	81.4	86.4	86.4	86.4	79.8
Investment Freedom	85	80	75	80	80	80	85
Financial Freedom	90	90	70	70	50	80	80

Data source: Miller et al. (2020). This index ranks 179 countries and varies from 0 to 100, whereby 100 denotes maximum economic freedom.

particularly long democratic tradition: In an international comparison of the average degree of democracy for the period 1900–2018, Switzerland ranks among the top-most countries.

Switzerland also ranks highly regarding economic freedom. According to the Index of Economic Freedom, which measures the extent of public intervention in the economy, Switzerland ranks fifth of 179 countries in 2020 (Miller et al. 2020). Table 6.1 shows that Switzerland ranks highly in most of the dimensions of this index. In other words, by international standards, Switzerland offers its citizens both comprehensive political and economic freedoms.

2.2 Economic output

With a per capita income of over 80,000 CHF per year (FSO 2020a), Switzerland is one of the richest countries in the world. Even though Switzerland lost some of its lead in the 1990s and during the first years of the new millennium due to slow economic growth, most notably in inward-oriented sectors, Switzerland's per capita income in 2018 was still about one-third higher than the average per capita income among EU member states (World Bank 2020; Figure 6.2). In the 2010s, the average rate of economic growth of 1.9 per cent ranked above the EU average of 6.6 per cent but below the Organisation

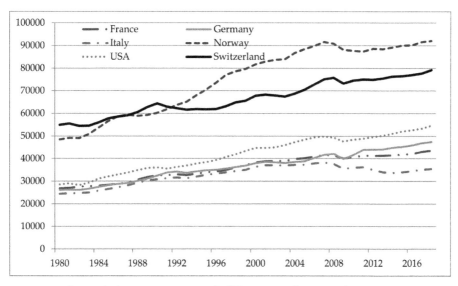

FIGURE 6.2: Per capita income, 1980–2018 (in US$, 2010 exchange rate)

Data source: World Bank (2020).

for Economic Co-operation and Development (OECD) average of 2.0 per cent (World Bank 2020). Compared to other countries, the unemployment rate in Switzerland is low (for details see 'The Structural Shifts in Switzerland's Economy and Society, 2000–2020' in this volume). Considering again the 2010s, Switzerland's unemployment rate was on average 4.7 percentage points lower than the EU average and 2.3 percentage points lower than the OECD average (World Bank 2020). In 2020, Switzerland's unemployment rate was significantly lower than the French and Italian rates and similar to the Austrian and German unemployment rates.

Switzerland also exhibits a high degree of both economic and political stability, which—in addition to its economic competitiveness and flourishing foreign trade— forms the basis for the country's prosperity. With an average of 0.03 per cent, the rate of inflation during the 2010s was very low (World Bank 2020), and while inflation rates increased in 2022 like in other countries, it has remained well below the levels seen in the US or the Eurozone. At the same time, the Swiss franc as a 'safe haven currency' has been appreciating significantly relative to both the euro and the US dollar in the last decade. Even though this has caused problems for the export industry and negatively affected Switzerland's overall economic development,[2] Switzerland is still considered an attractive investment destination: in 2020, the country ranked third in the International Institute for Management Development's World Competitiveness Ranking, which considers 337 different criteria pertaining to the macroeconomic environment, political efficiency, efficiency of the economic system, and quality of infrastructure (IMD 2020).

Switzerland also scores well with regard to socio-economic developments. The 2019 Human Development Index, which considers life expectancy and education in addition to economic output, ranks Switzerland as second of 187 states (UNDP 2020).

A similar picture emerges with regard to Switzerland's international competitiveness in research and development. Switzerland ranks eighth among OECD countries in terms of expenses for research and development (R&D) as a share of GDP (FDFA 2020a). Globally, Switzerland holds by far the most patents per capita and is the world leader with regard to the number of publications in high-quality scientific journals per year relative to the number of inhabitants (FDFA 2020b). In addition, several of the top-ranked universities in continental Europe are located in Switzerland.

2.3 Environmental protection

Environmental protection and sustainable development tend to play an important role in Switzerland, as data on environmental legislation and environmental quality, as well as public opinion data, show (Bernauer et al. 2020; EEA 2020). According to data from the European Environment Agency and the OECD (Figure 6.3), for instance, Switzerland ranks among those European countries most capable of combining a high degree of environmental protection with strong economic competitiveness.

Switzerland's high level of environmental protection is also reflected in the Environmental Performance Index rankings (Wendling et al. 2018), where the country regularly occupies a top position and was ranked number one worldwide in 2018. That said, it should be noted that environmental protection in Switzerland comes partly at the expense of foreign countries. Around 75 per cent of the environmental impact of Swiss consumption is currently offloaded abroad. For instance, while Switzerland's greenhouse gas emissions have decreased somewhat compared to 1990, the total global emissions caused by Swiss consumption have increased (FOEN 2018).

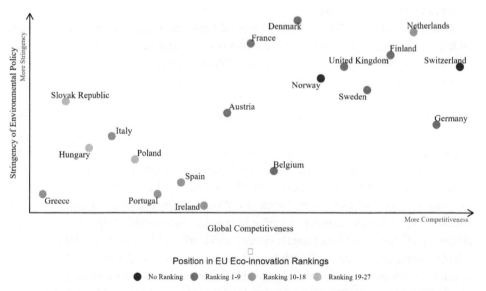

FIGURE 6.3: Ambitious environmental policy, competitiveness, and ecological innovation

Data source: European Commission (2020); OECD (2020a); WEF (2020).

2.4 Defence

Political science research on the determinants of military spending has argued that small countries, particularly members of military alliances, tend to free ride, letting their larger alliance partners bear a larger part of the security burden (e.g. Hartley and Sandler 1995). The extent to which this proposition explains Swiss military spending has not yet been sufficiently explored. On the one hand, given its neutrality, Switzerland cannot rely on large alliance partners. On the other hand, most observers of Swiss security policy believe that Switzerland to some extent profits from NATO's 'security shield' (Spillmann et al. 2001). In comparison to other countries, Swiss military spending is rather low (Figure 6.4). At less than 1 per cent of GDP, it amounted to less than one-quarter of the US military spending ratio in 2018 and has been even slightly below Austria's military expenditures since 2007 (a similarly neutral, centrally located, small state in Europe). A study by Bernauer et al. (2009) concludes, however, that other countries' military expenses have no statistically significant effect on Swiss military spending. What makes Switzerland unique internationally is the fact that the existence of the Swiss army as such became the subject of a referendum in 1989, in which a sizeable minority of 36 per cent voted for the abolition of the army. This result triggered a reform process that ultimately led to a significant downsizing of the armed forces and a reduction in defence spending. Because the Ukraine war has highlighted security risks to Switzerland, however, there have recently been significant debates on whether and how to increase military spending and seek closer ties with NATO.

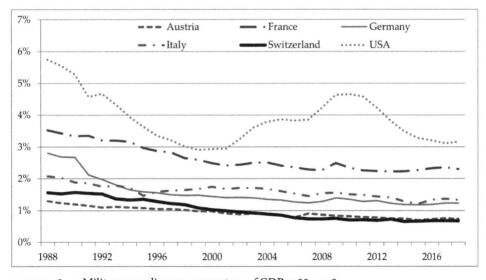

FIGURE 6.4: Military spending as a percentage of GDP, 1988–2018

Data source: SIPRI (2020).

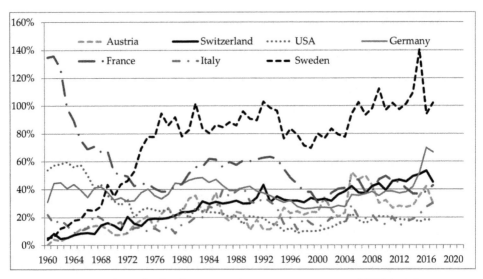

FIGURE 6.5: Expenditure for development assistance as a percentage of GDP (2017)

Data source: OECD (2020b).

2.5 Development assistance

In response to criticism of being a rich, neutral 'cherry-picker', Switzerland's foreign policy has emphasized solidarity with poorer countries since World War II and particularly since the 1970s. Nevertheless, Switzerland only holds an average position when comparing its level of development assistance to poorer states with other OECD countries (Figure 6.5). In 2017, it spent around 3.1 billion US dollars (approximately 2.8 billion CHF) on development assistance. This represents around 0.47 per cent of GDP (OECD 2020b, compared to 0.32 per cent in 1990), and is significantly less than the UN's recommendation of 0.7 per cent. In 2019, nearly 60 per cent of development assistance funds flowed into bilateral assistance, whereas the remaining 40 per cent were contributions to multilateral organizations. Of course, development assistance only measures the quantity, not the quality of this assistance.

3 Swiss foreign policy between continuity and change

The literature on Swiss foreign policy has long painted the picture of a country that is highly integrated into the world market economically, but only feebly involved with the world in political terms (e.g. Gabriel 1997; Goetschel et al. 2005; Schwok 2014). Switzerland's non-membership in the EU and NATO as well as Switzerland's decision not to join the European Economic Area (EEA) in December 1992 lie at the heart of this line of argument. Another case in point is the fact that Switzerland's largest political party, the national-conservative Swiss People's Party (SVP) with a decidedly nationalist agenda, has managed to increase its voter share up to around 30 per cent.

Yet, since the end of the Cold War this approach has begun to change to some extent: Switzerland has joined important international organizations such as the UN, the World Bank, and the International Monetary Fund and concluded two far-reaching sets of bilateral agreements with the EU.

A majority of citizens supports this change towards a somewhat more involved foreign policy. With 54.6 per cent Yes-votes overall and a narrow cantonal majority (twelve cantons voted yes, eleven voted no), UN membership was narrowly approved on 3 March 2002. The first set of bilateral treaties with the EU was accepted in a May 2000 referendum (67.2 per cent Yes-votes), and the second set of treaties (or, more precisely, those provisions concerning the Schengen/Dublin agreement) in June 2005 with 54.6 per cent Yes-votes. And while several policy decisions and direct-democratic votes have sought to limit Switzerland's international commitments in recent years, many proposals whose implementation would have questioned Switzerland's existing international obligations were either implemented in accordance with international treaties (such as the 2014 initiative 'against mass immigration' (*Masseneinwanderungsinitiative*)), or rejected at the ballot box (such as the 2018 'self-determination' initiative (*Selbstbestimmungsinitiative*), or the 2020 initiative for limiting immigration ('limitation initiative', *Begrenzungsinitiative*)). Most recently, Switzerland also joined the EU and other Western countries in sanctioning Russia over its invasion of Ukraine.

What has caused this (moderate) change in Swiss foreign policy? How far is Switzerland willing to go in terms of political integration into the international community? The next section argues that Switzerland has very close socio-economic ties with the outside world, and that this has eventually also led to stronger political ties to the international arena. Since this change has frequently been the subject of domestic political controversies and resistance, we also look at political opposition to foreign policy openness.

3.1 Switzerland between globalization and demarcation

Small countries tend to be more open economically than large countries with a similar economic structure (e.g. Bernauer 2000), and Switzerland is no exception. Important sectors of the Swiss economy have traditionally had a very strong outward orientation, notably, the banking, chemical, pharmaceutical, and machine building industries (see 'Economic Policy' in this volume). In 2019, Switzerland's exports in goods and services amounted to over 300 billion CHF (FSO 2020b), and international transactions contributed between 40 and 50 per cent to Switzerland's GDP. Economic exchange with the EU is particularly strong. In 2018, 52 per cent of Swiss exports were destined for EU countries, while 70 per cent of imports originated in EU member states (FDFA 2020c). About half (51 per cent) of total Swiss foreign direct investment (FDI) in 2017 flowed into the EU, while three-quarters of FDI in Switzerland came from the EU (FDFA 2019). In terms of countries, Switzerland's most important trading partners are Germany, the US, China, France, Italy, and the UK (Figure 6.6). Comparing foreign trade to GDP ratios, a common measure of trade openness, Switzerland ranks ahead of all its neighbours (World Bank 2020). International capital flows are equally important for Switzerland. The country is popular with foreign investors. In 2019, Swiss banks reported a net capital import of 49 billion CHF (SNB 2020). Switzerland also holds important investments abroad, for example in the form of foreign subsidiaries of Swiss companies. The capital yield from those investments abroad amounted to 104 billion CHF in 2018, almost one-seventh of Swiss GDP (SNB 2019). All these indicators attest to the importance of international trade and finance for the Swiss economy.

Similarly, Switzerland's labour market is closely intertwined with that of other countries. As Figure 6.7 shows, around one-third of the Swiss population aged 15 and older has a migration-related background. In 2018, approximately one-quarter (25.1 per cent) of Switzerland's 8.54 million inhabitants were foreign nationals, of which about two-thirds carry an EU or European Free Trade Association (EFTA) passport. The share of non-European foreigners has increased sixfold since 1980 and currently accounts for about 20 per cent of the foreign population residing in Switzerland (FSO 2020c). Compared to the EU-27 average of 4.9 per cent and other European countries, this proportion of foreigners is indeed very high. Within Europe, only Luxembourg with 47 per cent and Liechtenstein with around 35 per cent exceed Switzerland's share of foreigners residing in the country. That said, the large share of foreign nationals is also related to Switzerland's very restrictive naturalization policy, which means that it takes very long and is very difficult for foreigners to obtain a Swiss passport.

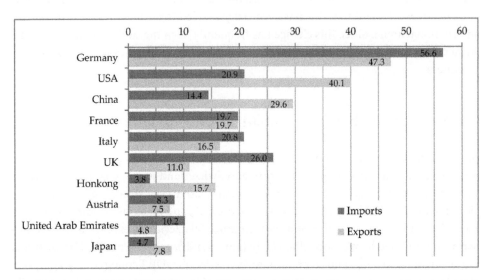

FIGURE 6.6: Switzerland's most important trading partners (2018)

Figures in billions of Swiss francs.

Data source: FSO (2020b).

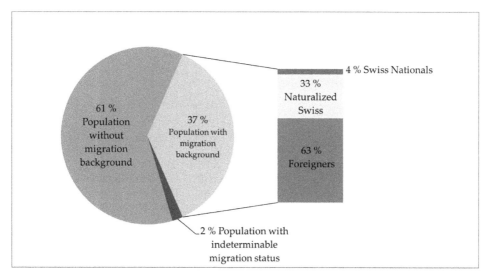

FIGURE 6.7: Population by migration status (2018), permanent resident population ≥ age 15

Data source: FSO (2020c).

Switzerland's deep integration with the outside world is not limited to the economy, however. Rather, it exhibits an exceptionally strong international orientation in other areas as well. The KOF Globalization Index recognizes that global integration consists of various non-economic aspects and therefore measures the interdependence of states comprehensively, taking economic, social, and political dimensions of globalization into account (Gygli et al. 2019). In the 2017 ranking, Switzerland was placed first among 197 countries and is hence the most 'globalized' country in the world. Figure 6.8 compares the *de jure* economic, political, and social globalization levels in Switzerland, the OECD, and the EU countries on average. In each case, the index focuses on *de jure* policies that may differ from *de facto* globalization measures (e.g. in terms of actual flows in trade, financial activities, or persons). The sub-index for *de jure* economic globalization considers policies that facilitate and promote trade flows between countries as well as the country's openness to international financial flows and investment. Political globalization measures the country's ability to engage in international political cooperation, as reflected, for example, in the number of multilateral treaties or memberships in international organizations. Finally, social globalization encompasses policies and resources that promote direct interactions between people from different countries, cross-national information sharing and cultural influences (Gygli et al. 2019, 556–558). As Figure 6.8 shows, Switzerland exhibits a very high level in all three dimensions of globalization over time, even if *de jure* globalization in the economic sphere has declined somewhat in recent years and has been subject to strong fluctuations—similar to the comparison values. This is not reflected in *de facto* developments, however, where economic interdependence has risen sharply in all four states since 2000.

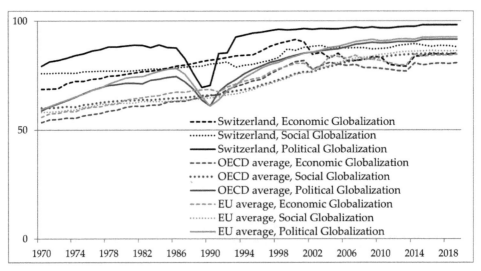

FIGURE 6.8: Degree of globalization according to de jure KOF Globalization Index, 1970–2019

Data source: Gygli et al. (2019).

3.2 Switzerland's foreign policy strategy: continuity and change

Both continuity and change have characterized Swiss foreign policy. In terms of continuity, the most important concept guiding Swiss foreign policy for more than two hundred years has been neutrality. This concept originally had a purely instrumental (means to an end) character. Napoleon's forces had occupied Switzerland in the late eighteenth century, after they had met rather little resistance, in part because of Switzerland's internal political fragmentation. At the Vienna congress in 1815, it was decided that Switzerland should be neutral, not least to provide a buffer zone between Europe's great powers. In 1847 there was a (rather small-scale and short) civil war between conservative rural and liberal urban cantons. When the modern Swiss state was established in 1848, foreign policy abstinence as embodied by neutrality was therefore seen as an important means for avoiding conflict both domestically and in relation to other states. In the First and Second World War, and similarly in the Cold War, neutrality, combined with a strong army, became the central pillar of Swiss foreign policy (Spillmann et al. 2001; Widmer 2003). Indeed, the fact that Switzerland has managed to stay out of any war since the early nineteenth century on an otherwise war-stricken continent has been widely interpreted as a direct result of neutrality and a strong army.

After World War II, the principle of neutrality became such a central component of Swiss foreign policy that Switzerland strongly hesitated to join even those international organizations that were fully in line with its social, political, and economic value system and important to its foreign economic relations. It joined the European Council only fourteen years, the GATT (today's World Trade Organization) nineteen years, and the Bretton Woods institutions forty-seven years after they were founded. Its reluctance to become involved in foreign security policy is also obvious from the fact that, even thirty years after the end of the Cold War, only about 250 out of approximately 140,000 Swiss soldiers were involved in international peacekeeping or observer missions in 2019 (DDPS 2020). This is significantly less than Austria's contribution, which is also a small neutral state but deployed 889 soldiers abroad in 2020 (Bundesministerium für Landesverteidigung 2020). Nevertheless, peacebuilding constitutes an important Swiss foreign policy objective. Switzerland has acted as an international mediator in several conflicts: between 2016 and 2019, it was involved, on average, in seventeen peace processes per year (Graf and Lanz 2013; Swiss Confederation 2020).

Since the mid-1980s, major global transformations have increasingly laid bare the tension between the benefits of intensified international cooperation and the constraints this could impose on national sovereignty, however, and have led to changes in Swiss foreign policy strategy. These changes are visible both in government documents on the conceptual foundations of Swiss foreign policy as well as actual foreign policy decisions. In a foreign policy report issued in 1993, the Federal Council (Switzerland's collective presidency) stated for the first time that Switzerland's important position in the global economy may not be fully compatible with its absence in important international decision-making fora such as the EU and the UN. It also noted that, at least in the long run, Swiss interests may be better served by participating in those decision-making processes than by merely implementing (albeit by autonomous decision) what other states and international organizations had decided (*autonomer Nachvollzug*, henceforth 'autonomous implementation'). The increasing interdependence in the world economy (globalization) and geopolitical changes thus have engendered substantial adjustment processes in Swiss foreign policy in the past decades.

The first two major attempts at greater political integration into the international community ended in a veritable debacle for the Swiss government, however. In 1986, the government's proposal to join the United Nations was rejected in a national referendum, even though Switzerland had been a member of most special UN agencies for many years. In 1992, a proposal to join the EEA suffered the same fate. This stood in stark contrast to other neutral European countries—Austria, Ireland, Finland, and Sweden—which had joined the UN a long time before and had already become members of the EU in 1973 (Ireland) or were joining the Union in 1995 (Austria, Finland, and Sweden).

A lot has changed since. Since the turn of the millennium, Switzerland has therefore pushed forward its international political integration, at least to some extent. Its foreign policy is driven more strongly by both values and interests and reaches beyond mere economic and security policies to also include multilateral cooperation. This is exemplified both by Switzerland's explicit goal to obtain a (temporary) seat on the UN Security Council (FDFA 2020d) and by Switzerland's decision to participate in international sanctions against countries such as Syria, Libya, Myanmar, Belarus, and most recently Russia. Switzerland also joined the International Monetary Fund and the World Bank in 1992 and, on the second attempt, the UN in 2002. Between 2000 and 2005, it negotiated two sets of bilateral treaties with the EU. These agreements go far beyond the trade liberalization measures agreed in the context of EFTA.

More generally, Swiss foreign policy has been updated repeatedly in view of changes in the international environment, such as the growing relevance of the fight against international terrorism, Switzerland's UN membership, the Sustainable Development Goals of the UN, the emergence of new geopolitical powers, most notably China and India, and the resulting great power competition, EU enlargement and intensified EU integration, and Russia's invasion of Ukraine. The Federal Council's foreign policy strategy 2020–2025 sets priorities in areas such as peace and security, prosperity and the maintenance of rules-based international economic structures, sustainability, environmental protection, and digitization. The supreme objective remains preserving Switzerland's independence and welfare, as stated in the current federal constitution of 1999. More strongly and clearly than in the past, Switzerland is now trying to define its strategic priorities with respect to specific regions and countries beyond Europe. It also seeks to actively shape the design of global framework conditions.

This often implies a balancing act between preserving neutrality and further integrating into the international community (Schwok 2014), a feat that is further complicated by increasing geopolitical tensions. For example, in the most recent Swiss foreign policy strategy, neutrality as a means of Swiss foreign policy continues to be a relevant principle, but in contrast to previous reports is clearly no longer identified as the central element of Swiss foreign policy. Russia's war of aggression against Ukraine, which started in February 2022, and the response by the EU, NATO, and G7 countries have led to a resurgent focus on neutrality, however, leading to a heated debate in Switzerland about what neutrality means when facing fundamental challenges to principles of the liberal world order and massive violations of international law. It has also led to debates on whether and how to seek closer ties with the EU and NATO, whose importance for Swiss prosperity and security have become acutely apparent (Bernauer et al. 2022; Bernauer 2023).

3.3 Swiss foreign policy in practice

In addition to developments at the 'declaratory' and strategic level, such as discussed above, it is insightful to also look at adjustments in the political decision-making system, which take the heightened need for coordination into account. Indeed, foreign policy decision-making today appears more complex than during the Cold War. For one, the direct-democratic component of Swiss foreign policy has been enhanced by an expansion of opportunities for referenda in 2003 (*Staatsvertragsreferendum*, as set forth in articles 141 and 141a of the Swiss constitution).

Moreover, several more subtle developments are noteworthy. Hirschi et al. (1999) and Klöti et al. (2005) examined 802 international agreements between Switzerland and other countries or international organizations in the 1980s and 1990s. They found that the number of agreements has almost doubled since the 1980s. Yet, they observed neither a thematic expansion nor a trend away from neighbouring states and Western Europe as a whole as its most important partners. Thus, in practice a trend towards more multilateral cooperation cannot be observed. At the same time, Sciarini (2014) concluded that the share of directly or indirectly internationalized decision-making processes in Switzerland had increased massively over the previous thirty years. In comparison to domestic policy decisions, however, decision-making in foreign policy remains more isolated from participation across different levels of policy-making, though more administrative units of the federal government are involved.

The Federal Council and the federal administration remain the central actors in foreign policy, while the parliament, the cantons, interest groups, and the wider public are involved to a lesser extent. Previous studies investigating Swiss laws passed by parliament and subject to direct-democratic decision-making come to similar conclusions. They find that, except for laws implementing EU standards (measures of 'autonomous implementation', see above), laws with a stronger international component were associated with less consultations at the pre-parliament stage and less conflict in parliament (Sciarini et al. 2002; Vögeli 2007; Widmer 2008). Swiss foreign policy thus remains more centralistic and executive-dominated than domestic policy areas. The big exception is legislation with a European link. Here, domestic policy is becoming increasingly Europeanized, which has resulted in a strong integration of Switzerland with EU law (Oesch 2020). Out of 1124 domestic policy reforms adopted between 1990 and 2010, about one-third were directly or indirectly Europeanized (Jenni 2014).

3.4 Public opinion on Switzerland's international role

The central elements of the Swiss political system, in particular direct democracy, federalism, and consociational democracy, turn public opinion into a key factor for Swiss foreign policy adjustments. Even though many foreign policy issues and decisions are not substantially noticed by the wider public, fundamental decisions in Swiss foreign policy are directly dependent, via initiatives and referenda, on the public's political consent. In addition, certain decisions, especially joining collective security organizations and supranational organizations, require the consent of the majority of cantons (the so-called *Ständemehr*, expressed by the majority of votes in each of these cantons) in addition to the majority of votes in Switzerland as a whole. This grants small, rural (and usually more conservative) cantons disproportionate influence. This strong direct-democratic component requires that important foreign policy decisions are supported by a large part of the population. It also implies, however, that far-reaching changes to the status quo in foreign policy are often very hard to achieve.

From this perspective, the very slow adjustment of Swiss foreign policy to global changes is primarily due to the fact that a considerable part of the Swiss population (e.g. Tresch et al. 2021) and the political elite (e.g. Bornschier 2015) remain sceptical with respect to further foreign policy openness. Surveys show that the share of

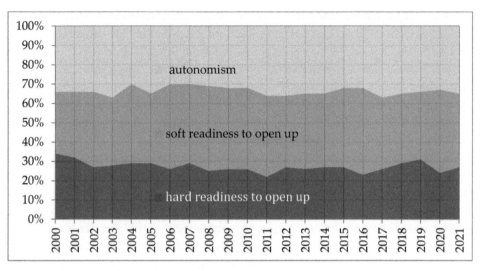

FIGURE 6.9: Support for foreign policy openness, percentage of respondents

Data source: Tresch et al. (2021).

strong opponents to further political integration into the international system has remained quite stable at around one-third over the past twenty years (Figure 6.9). Almost 40 per cent are willing to support a cautious integration, while the remaining 30 per cent can be classified as supporters of a more fast-paced opening process in Swiss foreign policy.

Surveys on neutrality demonstrate that neutrality has become much more than a means to an end (as originally envisaged), but part of the country's political identity. More than 85 per cent of respondents in various surveys claim that neutrality is inextricably linked to the Swiss state (Tresch et al. 2022). In addition, the share of respondents who think that Switzerland should remain as economically and politically independent as possible from other states has risen steadily over the past twenty years and reached 77 per cent in 2020 (Tresch et al. 2020). These survey findings do not imply, however, that Swiss voters are generally opposed to international engagement. In a 2022 survey, for example, around 66 per cent of the respondents were in favour of Switzerland providing more development assistance. More than 70 per cent of the respondents called for a more active role in international conferences and mediation in conflicts. In contrast, the willingness to cooperate in defence policy was much lower, with only about one-third in favour of moving closer to NATO (Tresch et al. 2022). In light of Russia's war against Ukraine, the willingness to cooperate with other European states in security issues has increased, however. In June 2022, for example, 56 per cent of voters supported a closer cooperation with NATO, even though 50 per cent of respondents continued to oppose NATO membership (Frenzel and Walter 2022). Likewise, the Swiss government's decision to implement EU sanctions against Russia are widely supported among the Swiss population, with almost two-thirds voicing support in June 2022 (Frenzel and Walter 2022).

4 Switzerland's relationship with the EU

Switzerland's relationship with the EU is ambivalent. In contrast to most European states, which have opted for close cooperation and a 'pooling of sovereignty' within the framework of the EU, Switzerland has chosen a more sovereignty-protecting approach. In lieu of EU membership, Switzerland maintains close relations with the EU at the political, economic, and cultural level through a set of bilateral agreements and arrangements. By means of the bilateral agreements I and II, Switzerland is not only part of the Schengen area but also profits from extensive access to the EU internal market. Hence, the bilateral agreements allow Switzerland to cooperate closely with the EU without formal membership, thus maintaining a custom-made relationship that is much less integrated with the EU than most other European states. Switzerland's bilateral approach enjoys strong support among the Swiss population (Tresch et al. 2022). At the same time, a clear majority rejects EU membership for Switzerland. Whereas in the 1990s just about half of the population wanted to join the EU, the support dwindled to only around 16 per cent in 2022 (Tresch et al. 2022). Although the Swiss population is very aware of the trade-offs with regard to the bilateral agreements (Lauener et al. 2022), it is clearly less willing to give up some sovereignty than many of its neighbours.

Over the past ten years, however, Switzerland–EU relations have become more tenuous and conflictual. The trade-off between Switzerland's independent immigration control and the free movement of persons stipulated in the bilateral agreements became highly contentious in the 2010s (Emmenegger et al. 2018; Milic 2015; Sciarini et al. 2015) and repeatedly gave rise to fierce political disputes. The scepticism towards Europe (and international treaty obligations in general) has been politically reflected in a significant number of popular initiatives aimed at limiting or even terminating such obligations (Walter 2021). Examples include the initiative 'against mass immigration' (*Masseneinwanderungsinitiative*) and the 'ECOPOP' initiative ('*Stopp der Überbevölkerung*') in 2014, the 'enforcement' initiative (*Durchsetzungsinitiative*) in 2016, the 'self-determination' initiative (*Selbstbestimmungsinitiative*) in 2018, or the 'limitation' initiative (*Begrenzungsinitiative*) in 2020. With the vote in favour of the 2014 mass immigration initiative, a particularly conflictual period in Switzerland-EU relations started, even if this initiative was ultimately implemented in such a way that obligations towards the EU concerning the free movement of persons were not called into question (Armingeon and Lutz 2019). And although most other attempts to limit or undermine existing international obligations have been rejected by voters, their overall scepticism towards the EU has made it difficult to evolve and intensify relations. Bilateral negotiations between Switzerland and the EU have come to a virtual standstill since the adoption of the second package of bilateral treaties in 2004.

These difficulties are most apparent in the failed efforts to intensify bilateral relations and modernize the bilateral agreements within a larger, more robust institutional framework. The increased number of EU member states and, consequently, the growing heterogeneity of interests, have rendered the resolution of cross-border problems between Switzerland and EU member states through the bilateral approach more time-consuming, complicated, and sometimes practically impossible, challenges that have been further exacerbated by the eurozone crisis in 2008, the Covid-19 pandemic, and the recent energy crisis.

Recognizing the resulting need for deeper and more institutionalized relations, Switzerland and the EU engaged in negotiations about an encompassing framework agreement in 2014. The EU members and the Commission sought to bundle existing and further bilateral agreements into an institutional framework agreement that should have linked previous treaties to future legal developments in the EU and also envisaged the creation of a dispute settlement mechanism between Berne and Brussels. In contrast, the Swiss government as well as the majority in the Swiss parliament and population preferred the status quo of individual treaties or treaty packages without automatic implementation of future EU law.

Reflecting a widespread perception among the public that Switzerland can benefit from the advantages of European integration without having to accept some disadvantages, and confidence that the EU will accommodate Swiss demands (Malet and Walter 2021), the Swiss government unilaterally terminated negotiations with the EU over the institutional framework agreement in spring 2021, after seven years of bargaining. This has given rise to resentments in Swiss–EU relations and resulted in the EU taking a tougher stance towards Switzerland. Since 2019, for example, the EU has refused to grant Switzerland stock market equivalence. In 2021, the Swiss medical technology sector also lost its previously barrier-free access to the EU's single market, and Swiss researchers lost full access to the Horizon Europe programme as the EU is no longer willing to update any bilateral agreements with Switzerland or conclude new ones until the 'institutional questions' about Swiss–EU relations are resolved. By 2022 alone, this stance by the EU has already led to a noticeable erosion of bilateral relations (Avenir Suisse 2022). Should the EU further object to continuing the current bilateral path, Switzerland will have to engage in a fundamental debate on how to maintain a mutually beneficial relationship with the EU in the coming years.

5 Outlook

Switzerland's position in the world is characterized by contradictions. While it is one of the most 'globalized' countries from a socio-economic viewpoint, the political adjustment process to global geopolitical and economic changes over the past decades has been slow and protracted. Notwithstanding its decision to become a member of the Bretton Woods institutions and the UN, as well as to ratify two comprehensive sets of bilateral treaties with the EU, Swiss voters and their policymakers shy away from seeking membership in the European Union for fear of losing sovereignty and autonomy. This reluctance persists despite the fact that the EU is the most important political institution in Europe beyond the traditional nation state, that the EU's socio-economic and political value system is fully in line with Switzerland's, and that the EU is by far Switzerland's biggest trading partner.

Most European states believe that socially and ecologically benign market integration, economic growth, prosperity, and sustainable development in general can best be achieved by giving up some national sovereignty in return for the ability to gain some influence on the behaviour of other states. These states believe, furthermore, that this process, the so-called 'pooling of sovereignty', can be organized more efficiently and effectively in a supranational organization like the EU than through a bilateral network of (to date) twenty-seven EU member states and hence 351 country dyads. Similarly, they assume that within the framework of the EU they will be better able to deal with international conflicts caused by existing (e.g. the US), rising (e.g. China), or declining (e.g. Russia) great powers, or unstable regional powers (e.g. Turkey, Iran). While this approach is not without controversy, as Brexit or the debates over the judiciary and the rule of law in Hungary and Poland show, it seems to dominate the actions of most European governments. Switzerland, on the other hand, highly values its sovereignty and is therefore more willing to forego gains from international cooperation.

While deepening cooperation between Switzerland and the EU, the aborted institutional framework agreement would have also resulted in an even stronger Europeanization of Swiss legislation. At the same time, however, Switzerland's influence on other countries and their joint decisions in the EU would have remained very limited under the framework agreement rather than full EU membership, since the development of EU law is the exclusive realm of EU member states. Ultimately, third countries such as Switzerland cannot shape EU law, even within the framework of association agreements such as the EEA (from which Switzerland has abstained) or bilateral treaties. Rather, they can simply adopt it (more or less) voluntarily. The idea that Switzerland may influence EU legal developments in crucial policy areas before adopting the respective laws has largely proved to be a pipe dream.

On a more fundamental level, it appears dubious whether focusing present debates over issues of sovereignty, neutrality, federalism, and direct democracy (and hence, presumably, Swiss identity) mainly on the EU-membership issue lives up to Switzerland's position in the global political and economic system (cf. Linder 2012). Doing so ignores the end of the Cold War, the increasing importance of dynamically evolving regional and global security challenges and collective security systems, and increased geopolitical rivalry between liberal democracies (above all the US and EU countries) and China. In addition, the war of aggression by Russia against Ukraine has rendered the usefulness of Switzerland's neutrality as a means to an end (prosperity, security) very questionable—no matter whether Switzerland decides to join the EU or not (Bernauer et al. 2022).

While the 'autonomous implementation' of EU law allows for the preservation of formal sovereignty, this is not the case for material sovereignty as has been exemplified by the high degree of Europeanization in Swiss legislation (Jenni 2014). Global markets are becoming increasingly integrated and the resulting competitive pressure acts on a global scale and is not limited to the EU, despite Covid-19-induced and war-related setbacks. Yet, whereas the EU member states, which taken together form the world's largest market, possess substantial leverage in regional and global institutions regulating this process, Switzerland is forced to follow behind the superpowers and particularly the EU in order to protect its interests. Whether standing apart from the EU really protects Swiss sovereignty is therefore an open question.

It can thus be argued that globalization and geopolitical changes, and not EU membership, has been shifting decision-making authority away from European nation states to international and supranational institutions. The same trend can be observed domestically, where the Swiss national executive is gaining competencies that were previously the domain of parliament, interest groups, and cantonal and municipal institutions. This shift undoubtedly causes tensions between federal and direct-democratic decision-making structures and international or supranational institutions. Considering ongoing global and geopolitical challenges, it thus seems important to guide the public debate towards the question of how Switzerland can best ascertain a high level of social welfare, prosperity, environmental quality, and sovereignty in the face of these global rather than EU-induced political and economic changes. EU membership might then well appear more beneficial than in the current debate that is dominated by analysis of the short-term economic advantages and disadvantages of such a policy decision.

Notes

1. We would like to thank Jana R. Kissling and Maja Schoch for excellent research assistance.
2. For this reason, the Swiss National Bank set a floor for the exchange rate of the Swiss franc relative to the euro in the fall of 2011, which was partly enforced through massive interventions on the foreign exchange market. In January 2015, the floor in exchange rate was lifted again, which led to a strong appreciation of the Swiss franc.

References

Armingeon, Klaus, and Philipp Lutz. 2019. 'Muddling Between Responsiveness and Responsibility: The Swiss Case of a Non-Implementation of a Constitutional Rule'. *Comparative European Politics* 18 (2): pp. 256–280.

Avenir Suisse. 2022. *Erosionsmonitor #3*. https://www.avenir-suisse.ch/publication/erosions monitor-juni-22-verhaeltnis-schweiz-eu-schwerpunkt-nordwestschweiz/

Bernauer, Thomas. 2000. *Staaten im Weltmarkt*. Opladen: Leske und Budrich.

Bernauer, Thomas, Vally Koubi, and Fabio Ernst. 2009. 'Does Neutrality Make a Difference? Explaining Patterns of Swiss Defense Spending in 1975–2001'. *Defence and Peace Economics* 20 (5): pp. 413–422.

Bernauer, Thomas, Lukas Rudolph, Lukas Fesenfeld, and Franziska Quoß. 2020. *ETH-Studie Schweizer Umweltpanel*. Zürich: ETH Zürich.

Bernauer, Thomas, Katja Gentinetta, and Joëlle Kuntz. 2022. *Swiss Foreign Policy for the 21st Century*. Basel: NZZ Libro.

Bernauer, Thomas. 2023. 'Austrian and Swiss Foreign Policy: A Comparison and Research Agenda'. *Austrian Journal of Political Science*. 51 (4): pp. 33–38.

Bornschier, Simon. 2015. 'The New Cultural Conflict, Polarization, and Representation in the Swiss Party System, 1975–2011'. *Swiss Political Science Review* 21 (4): pp. 680–701.

Bundesministerium für Landesverteidigung. 2020. *Auslandeinsätze des Bundesheeres. Zahlen, Daten, Fakten*. Vienna: Bundesministerium für Landesverteidigung.

Center for Systemic Peace. 2020. *Polity5: Regime Authority Characteristics and Transitions Datasets*. http://www.systemicpeace.org/inscrdata.html [17.11.2020].

DDPS – Federal Department of Defence, Civil Protection and Sport. 2020. *Militärische Friedensförderung*. Bern: DDPS.

EEA – European Environmental Agency. 2020. *The European Environment—State and Outlook 2020: Knowledge for Transition to a Sustainable Europe*. Copenhagen: EEA.

Emmenegger, Patrick, Silja Häusermann, and Stefanie Walter. 2018. 'National Sovereignty vs. International Cooperation: Policy Choices in Trade-Off Situations'. *Swiss Political Science Review* 24 (4): pp. 400–422.

European Commission. 2020. *Environment Eco-innocation Action Plan: Eco-Innocation Index 2019*. https://ec.europa.eu/environment/ecoap/indicators/index_en [16.11.2020].

FDFA – Federal Department of Foreign Affairs. 2019. *Schweiz–EU in Zahlen. Statistiken zu Handel, Bevölkerung und Verkehr*. Bern: FDFA.

FDFA – Federal Department of Foreign Affairs. 2020a. *Wissenschaft und Forschung der Schweiz – Fakten und Zahlen*. Bern: FDFA.

FDFA – Federal Department of Foreign Affairs. 2020b. *Publikationen und Patente*. Bern: FDFA.

FDFA – Federal Department of Foreign Affairs. 2020c. *Wirtschaft und Handel – eine wichtige Partnerschaft*. Bern: FDFA.

FDFA – Federal Department of Foreign Affairs. 2020d. *Schweizer Aussenpolitik: Strategien und Grundlagendokumente*. Bern: FDFA.

FOEN – Federal Office for the Environment. 2018. *Umwelt-Fussabdrücke der Schweiz. Zeitlicher Verlauf 1996–2015*. Bern: FOEN.

Frenzel, Sabine, and Stefanie Walter. 2022. 'Neutral auf der Seite der Völkerrechts: Ungebrochene Unterstützung für die Ukraine in der Schweizer Bevölkerung'. *De facto blog*, 24 June 2022. https://www.defacto.expert/2022/06/24/neutral-auf-der-seite-der-voelkerrechts-ungebrochene-unterstuetzung-fuer-die-ukraine-in-der-schweizer-bevoelkerung/ [05.11.2022].

FSO – Federal Statistical Office. 2020a. *Volkswirtschaft*. https://www.bfs.admin.ch/bfs/de/home/statistiken/volkswirtschaft.html [16.11.2020].

FSO – Federal Statistical Office. 2020b. *Aussenhandel*. https://www.bfs.admin.ch/bfs/de/home/statistiken/industrie-dienstleistungen/aussenhandel.html [16.11.2020].

FSO – Federal Statistical Office. 2020c. *Migration und Integration*. https://www.bfs.admin.ch/bfs/de/home/statistiken/bevoelkerung/migration-integration.html [17.11.2020].

Gabriel, Jürg. 1997. *Sackgasse Neutralität*. Zürich: VDF.

Goetschel, Laurent, Magdalena Bernath, and Daniel Schwarz. 2005. *Swiss Foreign Policy: Foundations and Possibilities*. London/New York: Routledge.

Graf, Andreas, and David Lanz. 2013. 'Conclusions: Switzerland as a Paradigmatic Case of Small-State Peace Policy?' *Swiss Political Science Review* 19 (3): pp. 410–423.

Gygli, Savina, Florian Haelg, Niklas Potrafke, and Jan-Egbert Sturm. 2019. 'The KOF Globalisation Index—Revisited'. *Review of International Organizations* 14 (3): pp. 543–574.

Hartley, Keith, and Todd Sandler. 1995. *The Economics of Defense*. Cambridge: Cambridge University Press.

Hirschi, Christian, Uwe Serdült, and Thomas Widmer. 1999. 'Schweizerische Aussenpolitik im Wandel: Internationalisierung, Globalisierung und Multilateralisierung'. *Swiss Political Science Review* 5 (1): pp. 31–56.

IMD. 2020. World Competitiveness Rankings 2020. Lausanne: IMD.

Jenni, Sabine. 2014. 'Europeanization of Swiss Law-Making: Empirics and Rhetoric Are Drifting Apart'. *Swiss Political Science Review* 20 (2): pp. 208–215.

Klöti, Ulrich, Christian Hirschi, Uwe Serdült, and Thomas Widmer. 2005. *Verkannte Aussenpolitik: Entscheidungsprozesse in der Schweiz*. Zürich/Chur: Rüegger.

Lauener, Lukas, Patrick Emmenegger, Silja Häusermann, and Stefanie Walter. 2022. 'Torn Between International Cooperation and National Sovereignty: Voter Attitudes in Trade-off Situations in Switzerland'. *Swiss Political Science Review* 28 (2): pp. 277–295.

Linder, Wolf. 2012. Schweizerische Demokratie: Institutionen, Prozesse, Perspektiven. Bern: Haupt.

Malet, Giorgio, and Stefanie Walter. 2023. Have your Cake and Eat It, Too? Switzerland and the feasibility of differentiated integration after Brexit *West European Politics*. DOI: 10.1080/01402382.2023.2192083.

Milic, Thomas. 2015. '"For They Knew What They Did"—What Swiss Voters Did (Not) Know About The Mass Immigration Initiative'. *Swiss Political Science Review* 21 (1): pp. 48–62.

Miller, Terry, Anthony B. Kim, and James M. Roberts. 2020. *2020 Index of Economic Freedom*. Washington DC: The Heritage Foundation. https://www.heritage.org/index/explore [17.11.2020].

OECD – Organisation for Economic Co-operation and Development. 2020a. *Environmental Policy Stringency Index*. https://stats.oecd.org/Index.aspx?DataSetCode=EPS [16.11.2020].

OECD – Organisation for Economic Co-operation and Development. 2020b. *Development Finance Data*. https://www.oecd.org/dac/financing-sustainable-development/development-finance-data/ [16.11.2020].

Oesch, Matthias. 2020. *Schweiz–Europäische Union: Grundlagen, Bilaterale Abkommen, Autonomer Nachvollzug*. Zürich: EIZ.

Sciarini, Pascal. 2014. 'Eppure Si Muove: the Changing Nature of the Swiss Consensus Democracy'. *Journal of European Public Policy* 21 (1): pp. 116–132.

Sciarini, Pascal, Simon Lanz, and Alessandro Nai. 2015. 'Till Immigration do us Part? Public Opinion and the Dilemma between Immigration Control and Bilateral Agreements'. *Swiss Political Science Review* 21 (2): pp. 271–286.

Sciarini, Pascal, Sarah Nicolet, and Alex Fischer. 2002. 'The Impact of Internationalization on the Swiss Decision-Making Process: A Quantitative Analysis of Legislative Acts, 1995–1999'. *Swiss Political Science Review* 8 (3/4): pp. 1–34.

Schwok, René. 2014. *Die Schweizer Aussenpolitik nach Ende des Kalten Kriegs*. Zürich: NZZ Libro.

SIPRI. 2020. *SIPRI Military Expenditure Database*. https://www.sipri.org/databases/milex [16.11.2020].

SNB – Swiss National Bank. 2019. *Direktinvestitionen 2018*. Zürich: SNB.

SNB – Swiss National Bank. 2020. *Zahlungsbilanz und Auslandvermögen der Schweiz 2019*. Zürich: SNB.

Spillmann, Kurt, Andreas Wenger, and Christoph Breitenmoser. 2001. *Schweizer Sicherheitspolitik seit 1945*. Zürich: Verlag Neue Zürcher Zeitung.

Swiss Confederation. 2020. *Aussenpolitischer Bericht 2019*. https://www.eda.admin.ch/dam/eda/de/documents/publications/SchweizerischeAussenpolitik/20200424-aussenpolitischer-bericht-2019-EDA_DE.pdf [05.11.2022].

Tresch, Tibor Szvircsev, Andreas Wenger, Stefano De Rosa, Thomas Ferst, and Jacques Robert. 2020. *Sicherheit 2020. Aussen-, Sicherheits- und Verteidigungspolitische Meinungsbildung im Trend*. Zürich: ETH Zürich.

Tresch, Tibor Szvircsev, Andreas Wenger, Stefano De Rosa, Thomas Ferst, Céline Gloor, and Jacques Robert. 2021. *Sicherheit 2021. Aussen-, Sicherheits- und Verteidigungspolitische Meinungsbildung im Trend*. Zürich: ETH Zürich.

Tresch, Tibor Szvircsev, Andreas Wenger, Stefano De Rosa, Thomas Ferst Jacques Robert, and Patric Rohr. 2022. *Sicherheit 2022. Aussen-, Sicherheits- und Verteidigungspolitische Meinungsbildung im Trend*. Zürich: ETH Zürich.

UNDP – United Nations Development Programme. 2020. *Human Development Report 2019: Beyond Income, Beyond Averages, Beyond Today. Inequalities in Human Development in the 21st Century*. New York: UNDP.

Vögeli, Chantal. 2007. *Vom Inhalt zur Struktur? Eine komparative Analyse schweizerischer innen- und aussenpolitischer Entscheidungsprozesse*. Dissertation, Universität Zürich.

Walter, Stefanie. 2021. 'Brexit Domino? The Political Contagion Effects of Voter-Endorsed Withdrawals from International Institutions'. *Comparative Political Studies* 54 (13): pp. 2382–2415.

World Bank. 2020. *World Development Indicators*. Washington DC: World Bank. https://data.worldbank.org/indicator [16.11.2020].

Wendling, Zachary A., Daniel C. Esty, John W. Emerson, Marc A. Levy, Alex de Sherbinin, et al. 2018. *2018 Environmental Performance Index*. New Haven, CT: Yale Center for Environmental Law and Policy.

Widmer, Paul. 2003. *Schweizer Aussenpolitik und Diplomatie von Pictet de Rochemont bis Edouard Brunner*. Zürich: Ammann.

Widmer, Thomas. 2008. 'Evaluation in der Außenpolitik: Gründe für eine Evaluationslücke'. *Zeitschrift für Internationale Beziehungen* 15 (1): pp. 125–138.

WEF – World Economic Forum. 2020. *GCI Global Competitiveness Index*. http://reports.weforum.org/global-competitiveness-report-2015-2016/competitiveness-rankings/ [16.11.2020].

CHAPTER 7

THE IDEOLOGICAL SPACE IN SWISS POLITICS

Voters, parties, and realignment

DELIA ZOLLINGER AND DENISE TRABER

1 INTRODUCTION

DESPITE its particular government institutions, political conflicts in Switzerland bear many similarities to other West European democracies. As we will show in this chapter, Switzerland is interesting from a comparative perspective because it exemplifies structural and political transformations that have reached most advanced democracies by now. Long-term changes in the economy and society became apparent early on in Switzerland. These structural changes have—together with the effects of globalization that became salient in the early 1990s—transformed the electoral landscape and underpinned a fundamental restructuring of ideological conflicts.

Switzerland's transition from an industrial to an increasingly globally connected, knowledge-based society has been among the earliest and most far-reaching in Western Europe. Deindustrialization and growing reliance on human capital for growth and productivity (besides new technologies) laid the foundation for the far-reaching social change that came with an increasingly high-skilled, service-based, and feminized workforce. Switzerland has experienced exemplary growth of such a 'new' middle class of highly educated professionals who are socially progressive, supportive of open borders, and whose lives do not typically follow the traditional male-breadwinner model of the industrial era. Early on, this development created incentives for leftwing parties (including established ones like the Swiss Social Democrats) to cater to this growing electoral potential by not only championing socioeconomic egalitarianism but adopting a broader universalist platform that advances minority rights, supports diversity, and promotes sociocultural openness. At the same time, the backlash against this broad trend of social liberalization has been powerful and sustained, with nativist-traditionalist far-right mobilization falling on fertile ground, particularly among groups of lower-educated production workers and small business owners.

Since as early as the 1990s, Swiss voters have become polarized along what is by now frequently seen as a 'second dimension' of politics emerging across Western Europe—a dimension centred on issues such as immigration, European integration, environmental protection, or gender equality. Indeed, the electorates of the parties situated at the left and right poles of the Swiss political system have consistently been more divided over such issues for the last three decades than over issues associated with the traditional 'first' state–market dimension (e.g. classic conflicts over redistribution and state intervention in the economy). In addition, Swiss voters have long perceived issues such as immigration or supranational integration as particularly important.

Political actors in Switzerland have responded and contributed to shaping this changing ideological landscape in ways that are paradigmatic of developments across much of Western Europe. A forceful 'new left' impetus advancing socially progressive positions initially gave rise to a number of new parties, including the Greens throughout the 1970s and 1980s. However, alongside the meanwhile established Greens, the main party of the left—the Social Democrats—also adopted a socially progressive position early on, beginning to tap into a growing new middle-class electorate well before the turn of the century. Electoral realignment is hence particularly pronounced and advanced in the Swiss case. A socially liberal new middle class has gained relative importance within the left's electoral base. As a consequence of this electoral realignment, counter-mobilization against the new left's embrace of diversity and cosmopolitanism gained momentum in the 1990s, when the Swiss People's Party (historically an agrarian party) began to transform its platform by campaigning against European integration and for restrictive immigration policy. With dramatic increases in the party's vote shares over subsequent decades it has become the largest party in the Swiss federal assembly and one of the strongest far-right parties in Western Europe.

In Switzerland, parties at the universalist new left and particularist far right poles respectively have consolidated their success over the last decades, becoming strong, stable, and decidedly polarized party blocs. The much-discussed fragmentation and decline of mainstream parties can today be observed primarily among centre-right parties. The Liberals and the Christian Democrats—while struggling to define their positions on second-dimension issues—have lost their positions as the historically dominant parties in Switzerland. With the emergence of the Green Liberals in the 2010s, divisions on the right over social progressivism versus conservative nationalism have become even more fraught.

In sum, the Swiss trajectory of the last few decades shows a clear pattern of polarized political competition primarily over second-dimension issues. The new left caters to highly educated, socially progressive (and economically left-wing) professionals, and the far right mobilizes disproportionately among conservative lower-educated groups who feel threatened by social change. A fragmented centre-right third pole is caught between these two extremes. From a comparative perspective, the Swiss case hence traces a path of profound restructuration of politics, in which even certain redistributive conflicts become embedded in the universalist versus particularist competition. The most recent developments in Swiss party politics, notably the emergence of the centre-right Green Liberals, might further be indicative of developments in Western Europe. In other words, it remains to be seen how newly salient issues such as environmental/climate protection or European integration are absorbed by—or else further transform—a political space that has already been fundamentally reconfigured in the post-industrial era.

This chapter proceeds to trace various elements of a transforming Swiss political space: structural changes in the economy and society, changes in the composition of party electorates and voter preferences, developments in issue salience, and the evolving positions of major parties. Our empirical evidence spans the period from 1990 to 2020 and is based on data from voter and expert surveys, as well as coded party programmes. We complement a temporal perspective with a comparative one that situates the Swiss case in Western Europe. We end with a more speculative discussion of whether and how studying the Swiss case can be useful for assessing developments in other countries that share key aspects of the country's trajectory of change in an ongoing era of knowledge-based growth.

2 A STRUCTURALLY TRANSFORMED ELECTORAL LANDSCAPE

Switzerland exemplifies the advanced democracies' transformation from industrial to post-industrial, globally connected, and increasingly knowledge-based economies (Kriesi et al. 2008; Iversen and Soskice 2019; Garritzmann et al. 2021). It belongs to those countries where structural shifts started early and have progressed furthest. Changes in social structure paved the way for new issues, grievances, and demands to be mobilized by political parties. In other words, they changed parties' incentives and opportunities to cater to specific segments of the electorate (cf. Beramendi et al. 2015). Specifically, key structural changes have provided the basis for a fundamental transformation of the left, as well as for the rise of the far right in Switzerland. On the one hand, the expansion of a socially progressive educated middle class has created a new voter base for left-wing parties that embrace green/left-libertarian positions; on the other hand, the far right's success is based on its nativist-traditionalist appeals to groups relatively disadvantaged by structural change.

As is the case across many advanced democracies, three important and interrelated changes have taken place since the mid-twentieth century: educational expansion, a sectoral shift from the industrial to the service sector, and a feminization of the workforce. Figure 7.1 depicts the expansion of tertiary education in Switzerland, situating the trend in comparison to a selection of countries in Northern, Western, and Southern Europe. It shows how the share of the Swiss population with higher education more

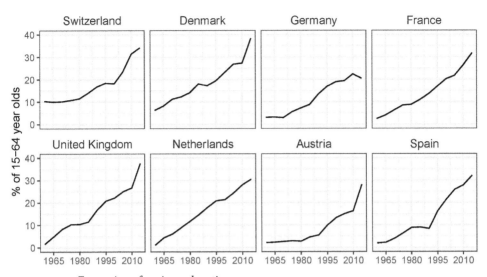

FIGURE 7.1: Expansion of tertiary education

Data source: Barro and Lee (2021).

than tripled between 1960 and 2015, with over a third of over-fifteen year olds holding a higher-level degree by the end of the period. The trajectory of educational expansion at the tertiary level roughly tracks that in other countries, surpassing several of them.[1] By 2030, at least 50 per cent of adults in Switzerland aged between twenty-five and sixty-four are projected to hold a tertiary degree (higher vocational education or university) (FSO 2020b).

Second, technological change has dramatically diminished employment in industry, while boosting job creation in other parts of the Swiss economy (Oesch 2006a). Since the early 1990s, the share of jobs with routine (easy to automate) task profiles has diminished considerably; routine occupations now make up less than a third of employment (see Figure 7.2). The industrial working class in Switzerland has dwindled in numerical and organizational strength (Oesch 2007, 2006b; Rennwald 2014). By now, more than 50 per cent of jobs in Switzerland belong to a non-routine cognitive category associated with knowledge-based work. Finally, this shift from semi-skilled manual work to highly skilled service sector jobs has also facilitated women's labour force participation: over 80 per cent of women participate in the workforce today, up from just under 70 per cent in the early 1990s (FSO 2019).[2]

From a comparative perspective, the Swiss trajectory exemplifies the growth of a highly educated middle class occupied primarily in high-skilled services at the expense of working- and lower-middle classes in semi-skilled production and clerical work. As shown in Figure 7.2, Switzerland is comparable to Denmark or the UK, and structural shifts happened earlier and/or more strongly than in Austria, Germany, or France. In Southern Europe, trajectories have been somewhat different (see e.g. Spain in Figure 7.2): strong educational expansion was not met by equally clear-cut job growth

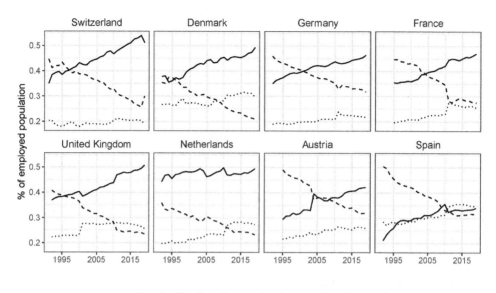

FIGURE 7.2: Occupational change
Data source: adapted from Garritzmann et al. (2021); data: International Labour Organization (2021).

in high-skilled services (Garritzmann et al. 2021; Ansell and Gingrich 2018), creating a different set of political pressures.

In Switzerland, educational expansion and the related growth of a high-skilled service sector have produced entirely new electoral potentials within an expanding and diversifying middle class (Oesch 2006a, b, Kitschelt 1994; Gingrich and Häusermann 2015; Abou-Chadi and Hix 2021). It is important to highlight, meanwhile, the comparatively low and stable share of non-routine manual work (see Oesch 2015). In contrast to some other countries (see e.g. the UK, France, or the Netherlands), technological change has not led to the emergence of a new service sector precariat in Switzerland (Oesch 2015; Garritzmann et al. 2021). In other words, the emergence of a 'new (educated) middle class' has not been accompanied by the rise of a 'new proletariat', which, notably, has implications for left-wing parties.

3 Realigned electorates and their preferences

3.1 Composition of party electorates in a transforming society

How have parties' electorates evolved in the face of such social transformations? This section examines how the composition of Swiss parties' electorates has changed over the last few decades, notably revealing how the left has started to cater successfully to an expanding highly educated new middle class, while the far right has become the party of the old middle class and—increasingly—the working classes. For this examination of electoral 'realignment' (long-term transformation of voter–party linkages), we focus on the four major Swiss parties that have held at least one seat in the Swiss government since 1944:[3] the Social Democrats (SP), the Christian Democrats (CVP), the Liberals (FDP), and the Swiss People's Party (SVP). The social democratic SP and the far-right SVP are of particular interest. Their changing mobilization efforts have fuelled the reconfiguration of the Swiss political space (along with comparatively newer parties, such as the Greens, that we discuss later on).

To illustrate the changing voter composition, we focus on educational attainment, the most widely recognized predictor of deepening sociocultural divides across advanced democracies (Häusermann and Kriesi 2015; Marks et al. 2022; Stubager 2009). Figure 7.3 shows how the SP has become a party of the highly educated over the last three decades, today looking not unlike the liberal FDP in this regard.[4] The similarity is striking, considering how these parties have historically been the main antagonists in the Swiss class conflict (Rennwald 2014). Educational upgrading is also reflected (more moderately) among the CVP. In stark contrast, the SVP has remained firmly anchored among voters with medium education. Overall, the major shifts have occurred between the tertiary and secondary levels, while the share of low-educated voters is small over the whole period under study.

From a comparative perspective, changes in voter composition are especially noteworthy for the SP. For an established social democratic party historically associated with the working class, this shift in voter base is remarkably clear-cut (Nicolet and Sciarini 2010; Rennwald and Evans 2014; Rennwald 2020; Häusermann et al. 2022), resulting not just from structural trends but also from targeted appeals to a growing middle class with increasingly green/socially progressive as well as economically left-wing positions. On the other side of the political spectrum, those with medium education—which notably includes apprenticeship training in the Swiss case—consistently made up a solid two-thirds of the SVP electorate as the party grew its vote share in national elections from 15 (1995) to 30 per cent (2015) with an increasingly nationalist and nativist platform.

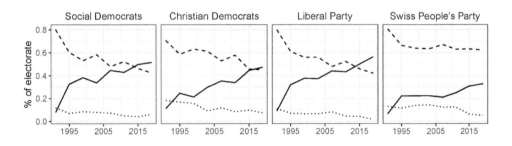

FIGURE 7.3: Educational composition of major Swiss parties

Data source: Tresch et al. (2020).

This already speaks to how Switzerland exemplifies electoral realignment: a rich body of research has mapped different partisan and socio-structural groups in a two-dimensional preference space (Kriesi et al. 2006; Van Der Brug and Van Spanje 2009; Oesch and Rennwald 2010; Kriesi et al. 2008; Häusermann et al. 2022; Bornschier 2015; Oesch and Rennwald 2018) and shown how structural change has transformed party–voter linkages. These studies consistently provide evidence of increasingly tripolar political competition at the level of voters. Parties occupying three poles—the left, centre right, and the radical right—are supported by specific educational/occupational segments of the electorate, who hold distinct ideological preferences (Oesch and Rennwald 2018). Sociocultural professionals (in the new educated middle class) and urban people have become the main supporters of social democratic and green parties. These voters are more economically left-wing and socially progressive than (also highly educated) managers and self-employed professionals—the core voter base of centre-right Christian Democratic and Liberal parties. Further to the right, the main clientele of the SVP consists of production and service workers, small business owners/artisans, and rural voters with lower levels of education. These voters are the most conservative, particularly regarding social and cultural questions.

3.2 Voter polarization over sociocultural issues

Electoral realignment occurred in Switzerland as voters became increasingly polarized over social and cultural issues comprising a 'second' dimension of electoral competition alongside the traditional 'first' state–market dimension. Again focusing on long-standing government parties, this section shows how, as early as the 1990s, polarization between the left and the far right over social issues (e.g. immigration, Europe) was already greater than that between the left and the centre right over economic ones (e.g. state intervention in the economy).

Using combined data from the Voxit (1994–2016) and Voto (2016–2020) studies,[5] we examine the political preferences of Swiss voters regarding four issues: immigration, openness to international influences, economic liberalism, and the environment (see Figure 7.4). The first three issues are generally associated with the second and first dimensions of political conflict (Kriesi et al. 2008; Häusermann and Kriesi 2015; Hooghe and Marks 2018), while questions regarding the environment have recently become more important and polarizing (see Giger et al. 2022).

The top left graph in Figure 7.4 shows average positions regarding the question of whether one would rather want equal opportunities for immigrants and Swiss people (1) or better opportunities for Swiss people compared to immigrants (6).[6] Swiss social democratic voters have been consistently most in favour of equal opportunities for immigrants. This is striking, looking as far back as the 1990s, and reflects the party's early adoption of socially liberal positions. On the other side of the political spectrum, the SVP, having put immigration on the agenda, has been able to mobilize voters who prioritize Swiss citizens over immigrants. Considering the SVP's rapidly expanding

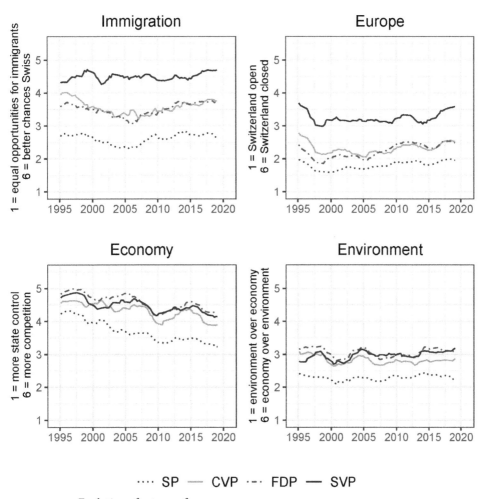

FIGURE 7.4: Evolution of voter preferences

Data source: Kriesi et al. (2017), FORS (2020).

electorate over this time period, the lack of moderation in attitudes is remarkable; the SVP appears to have articulated and strengthened an existing electoral potential with its nativist stance (Bornschier 2010).

Further, the top right graph in Figure 7.4 presents average positions regarding the question of whether Switzerland should be open or closed to international influences.[7] Opposition towards international integration was at its highest level in the years after 1992, the time of the historic direct-democratic vote about Switzerland's membership in the European Economic Area. The rejection of the treaty by 50.3 per cent of Swiss voters was largely a consequence of the SVP's successful campaign and proved to be the beginning of the SVP's steep rise in consecutive elections. The graph further illustrates a general trend towards more openness in the late 1990s and early 2000s, after negotiations of the bilateral treaties with the EU were settled and accepted as an alternative to full integration. However, as with immigration, polarization regarding EU positions is consistently strong (especially comparing SP and SVP electorates) and it increased after 2015, especially due to a right-wing shift among SVP voters.

Turning to traditional economic conflict, the bottom left graph in Figure 7.4 shows the average position of the four party electorates on a continuum between more state control of the economy (1) and more economic competition (6).[8] On this question, liberal FDP voters are most distant from Social Democrats, but compared to preferred levels of immigration and international integration, (centre)-right and social democratic electorates have generally been far less divided over the role of the state in the economy. This is consistent with insights that political competition in Switzerland (notably between the pole parties SVP and SP) has played out primarily on the second dimension. That being said, we do observe a continuous shift to the left among SP voters over the last twenty-five years. This indicates that the SP's increasingly pronounced positions on the first dimension have contributed to the polarization of the Swiss party system (Traber 2015; Traber et al. 2022). Importantly, the SP electorate has become more economically left-wing even as it has become more highly educated. This is noteworthy because it supports empirical evidence from comparative studies showing that the increasing importance of middle-class voters for the left does not undermine a generous welfare state or social embeddedness of markets, but rather provides a new basis for it (Gingrich and Häusermann 2015). In sum, the two top graphs and the bottom left graph in Figure 7.4 illustrate how, already in the mid-1990s, socio-cultural divisions separated Swiss voters more than traditional state–market conflict, and how attitudes—and therefore attitude polarization—remained relatively stable until around 2015, when they started to diverge again.

The last issue we consider here is the environment. The bottom right graph in Figure 7.4 considers an item asking respondents whether they would privilege the environment over the economy, or vice versa.[9] This trade-off question appears sub-optimal and outdated from today's perspective, but it offers an opportunity to track preferences over a longer time period. Environmental concerns have long been associated with second-dimension politics, in part because of the new social movements that put social as well as environmental issues on the political agenda from the 1970s onwards. Figure 7.4 indicates that, among the established major parties, voters of the Social Democrats favoured environmental protection most clearly and consistently over the observed time period. This is in line with the notion that the SP took on board the concerns of these social movements well before the start of the time series presented. What might seem surprising are the otherwise moderate partisan differences. In fact, in the Swiss case, preferences on environmental policy were long more aligned with traditional state–market divisions (Kriesi et al. 2008). This may be partly due to dynamics on the political supply side: before the emergence of the Green Liberals in the 2000s/2010s, the lack of a pro-environment/pro-market electoral option meant that opposition over environmental politics coincided with traditional economic left–right politics.

Despite the relative stability evident from Figure 7.4, the politics surrounding the environment and climate action are interesting because they are key to further change in the ideological space in Switzerland. The national election of 2019 was marked by mobilization around climate change and increased salience of environmental concerns (Tresch et al. 2020; Giger et al. 2022). The election saw the Greens and also the Green Liberal Party make significant electoral gains. This includes gains at the expense of the Social Democrats, who are just as pro-environment as the Greens but rate as less competent on environmental and climate issues (Häusermann et al. 2022; Lachat 2014). The Swiss People's Party has since also (successfully) opposed other major parties over a milestone proposal for climate policy legislation that was put to a direct-democratic vote in 2021, criticizing the proposed measures as too costly for normal citizens. The more outspoken policy stance is likely reflected in Figure 7.4, which shows polarization of preferences between SP and SVP voters in the most recent years.

3.3 Relative salience of sociocultural issues

Besides ideological positions, the salience and politicization of issues have been important drivers of the remarkable changes in the Swiss political space. Political conflicts or electoral realignment do not simply emerge from positional shifts; what matters in addition is how parties emphasize or ignore certain issues and how this translates into voters' perceived importance of issues (Schattschneider 1960; Ansolabehere and Iyengar 1994; Wagner and Meyer 2014). Figure 7.5 depicts for four policy areas the share of voters who considered these issues the most important at the time of eight elections between 1991 and 2019. Immigration and asylum issues were considered most important in the majority of elections (not surprisingly, especially by far-right voters), with the exception of 2019, when environment and energy took over. The combined results illustrate nicely how second-dimension issues have dominated Swiss politics since the late twentieth century, and how issue salience has been an important factor in the realignment process. Compared to immigration, European integration became less important in the early 2000s, though its salience has increased in recent years. The economy and finances were crucial in the early 1990s when Switzerland experienced a severe recession—and again in 2011 during the most recent economic crisis. However, from a comparative perspective, it is important to note that the salience of economic issues (and hence first-dimension politics) is relatively low, whereas the economy is usually considered the most important issue in many European countries (Traber et al. 2018). Regarding environmental and energy issues, two important aspects stand out from Figure 7.5. First, it is striking how social democratic voters already had a strong focus on these issues in the early 1990s. Second, we see a clear increase in perceived importance in the most recent election, which took place before the Covid pandemic, in a year when the climate strike movement was at its height. There are, however, important differences between the two parties at the ideological poles: while environmental issues were most important for left voters, among the far right, immigration and European integration were still the dominating concerns in 2019.

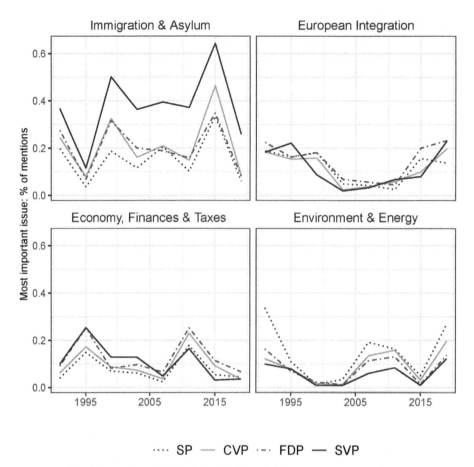

FIGURE 7.5: Evolution of issue salience: most important issue

Data source: Tresch et al. (2020).

4 A RECONFIGURED SPACE OF PARTY COMPETITION

Switzerland has not only experienced the structural transformations and new issue conflicts typical for advanced democracies but it also represents an emblematic case of changes in party politics that have emerged to a varying degree across Western and Northern Europe. This has to do with established political actors' changing mobilization efforts, as well as with the successes of new parties.

As already shown, a 'second', sociocultural dimension of politics (centred around issues such as immigration, supranational integration, gender equality, or LGTBQ rights) has increasingly come to characterize party politics in Switzerland, complementing the traditional economic dimension over redistribution and state intervention in the economy

(Kriesi et al. 2008; Bornschier 2010; Bornschier et al. 2021; Oesch and Rennwald 2018). While this is by now a common trend across advanced democracies (see also Kitschelt 1994; Hooghe and Marks 2018), the Swiss case stands out, due to the highly distinctive positions of parties at the opposing left versus far-right poles. Politicization of the second ideological dimension started earlier and is more pronounced compared to other European countries.

Figure 7.6 shows a two-dimensional placement of parties based on the Manifesto Project Dataset (Volkens et al. 2021).[10] While expert data provides broadly consistent mappings of the Swiss political space today, manifestos offer a basis for contrasting party positions over three decades. In Switzerland, the main shifts in party positions, profiles, and electorates occurred in two waves: one starting in the late 1970s as a consequence of structural changes in the post-war period, the cultural revolution, and value change that ensued; and a second one starting in the 1990s, mainly driven by globalization and increasing international integration (Häusermann and Kriesi 2015; Lauener et al. 2022).

In a first wave of mobilization, the new social movements of the 1970s and 1980s put issues of social liberalization, gender equality, or environmental protection on the agenda (Kitschelt 1994; Kriesi 1998). Along with the then emerging Greens, the Swiss Social Democrats came to absorb much of the electoral potential in a growing educated middle class by adopting socially progressive positions early on (Nicolet and Sciarini 2010; Rennwald and Evans 2014; Häusermann et al. 2022; see 'Political Parties and Party Systems in Switzerland' in this volume). As can be seen in Figure 7.6, since the 1990s, the Social Democrats and Greens have increasingly taken overlapping positions that are on the top left of the other major parties. A second wave of mobilization along the second dimension also played out in exemplary fashion in the Swiss case, largely due to the Swiss People's Party's electoral rise after its conversion from an agrarian, conservative

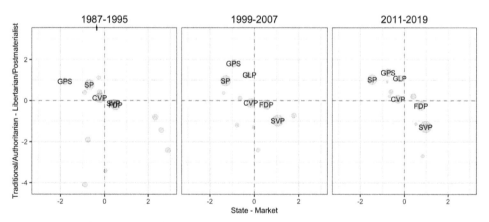

FIGURE 7.6: The Swiss two-dimensional political space over time (distance from the party-system mean, standardized)

GPS = Green Party; SP = Social Democrats; GLP = Green Liberal Party;
CVP = Christian Democrats; FDP = Liberal Party; SVP = Swiss People's Party.

Data source: Volkens et al. (2021).

centre-right to a nativist-nationalist far-right party (Kriesi et al. 2008; Skenderovic 2009; Bornschier 2010; 'Political Parties and Party Systems in Switzerland' in this volume). The party's early and strong shift regarding socio-cultural positions from centrist to far right over the last three decades represents the most impressive party trajectory in Figure 7.6. As we have discussed in the last section, this transformation into a typical far-right party allowed the SVP to establish a firm voter base among groups with medium levels of education, as well as among production workers, small business owners, and voters living outside core cities (Oesch 2008; McGann and Kitschelt 2005).

Regarding party strength, Figure 7.6 shows that there has been consolidation at the left-libertarian and right-authoritarian poles of the Swiss party system. The Greens and Social Democrats combined and the Swiss People's Party have each garnered between 25 and 30 per cent of the vote share in recent national elections (Kriesi 2015; Tresch et al. 2020; Giger et al. 2022). By contrast, the historically dominant Liberal and Christian Democratic parties have seen their electoral fortunes decline over the last few decades. This is not least due to these parties' difficulty in defining their position with regard to newly emerging socio-cultural issues (Oesch and Rennwald 2018; Gidron et al. 2020; Rennwald 2014; 'Political Parties and Party Systems in Switzerland' in this volume).

As a consequence, two electorally strong and clearly polarized left and far-right blocs have emerged over time, after an initial, transitory phase of party system fragmentation in Switzerland. This is notable, especially given current tendencies toward party system fragmentation in many advanced democracies (e.g. de Vries and Hobolt 2020). The electoral strength of party blocs at the two opposite poles has resulted in fiercer election campaigns and increasing conflict in parliamentary decision-making (Häusermann et al. 2004; Linder and Schwarz 2008; Traber et al. 2014; Afonso and Papadopoulos 2015; Bornschier 2015; Traber 2015; Sciarini et al. 2015; Vatter 2016). Today, centre-right parties are weaker and more fragmented. As the Swiss People's Party has moved markedly to the right on socio-cultural issues (see Figure 7.6), the Christian Democrats and especially the Liberals have ceded their positions as the major right-wing parties opposing the left. Competition has become even fiercer since the emergence of the Green Liberal Party in the 2000s/2010s, which is socially progressive but more pro-market than the Social Democrats and Greens (Figures 7.6 and 7.7). Studies of voter flows in Switzerland show that far-right electoral gains have come primarily from centre-right parties, more so than from left ones (Bischof and Kurer 2022). The presence of the Green Liberals exacerbates the difficulty of centre-right parties to appeal to socially conservative voters without at the same time alienating pro-market cosmopolitans (let alone without further normalizing far-right positions; see Krause et al. 2022).

Figure 7.7 illustrates that, from a comparative perspective, Switzerland has become a prime example of 'tripolar' competition in a two-dimensional political space (left—centre right—far right; Oesch and Rennwald 2018; Bornschier et al. 2021; Zollinger 2022). Based on the most recent Chapel Hill Expert Survey from 2019, it shows the major Swiss parties' distinctive positions (grey circles) in a two-dimensional political space compared to other West European countries (white circles).[11] On the left, the Social Democrats' as well as the Greens' positions are distinctively universalist and

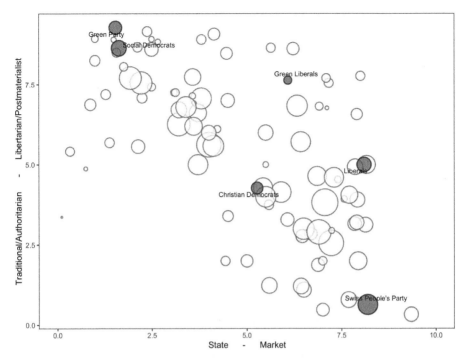

FIGURE 7.7: The main Swiss parties in the two-dimensional political space of Western Europe
Data source: adapted from Zollinger (2022); data: CHES, Bakker et al. (2020).

pro-state, whereas, on the right, the Swiss People's Party is among the most right-wing parties in terms of particularistic as well as economically liberal positions. Among the five largest parties in Switzerland, the remaining three—the Green Liberals, Christian Democrats, and the Liberals—are placed roughly on or slightly to the right of the diagonal between the universalist left and the particularistic right. Figure 7.7 thus illustrates, first, the tripolar character of the Swiss political space (Oesch and Rennwald 2018), and second, points to the emergence of a starkly pronounced new ideological dimension that summarizes the economic and cultural conflicts and stretches between two poles: culturally conservative/economically right-wing positions on one side and culturally liberal/economically left-wing on the other.

5 THE NEW IDEOLOGICAL SPACE IN SWISS POLITICS

This chapter has situated the Swiss case from a comparative perspective with regard to structural and political developments and it has traced the changing composition and attitudes of party electorates as well as party positions over the last few decades. We have suggested that Switzerland is in many ways emblematic of transformations observable across other advanced democracies in Western Europe.

In this concluding section, we discuss some of the most recent developments in Swiss politics, as well as what they might signal for ongoing and potential future developments of the political space. One question that (re-)emerges from this chapter is whether the Swiss political space is indeed still best described as two-dimensional, or whether the salient conflict in which the left (Social Democrats and Greens) and far right (Swiss People's Party) are situated at the poles has, in fact, become so all-encompassing that it dominates the political space in the form of one single 'diagonal' main dimension running from left/progressive to right/authoritarian (cf. Kitschelt 1994).

Evidence that polarization along a sociocultural dimension has come to affect many other policy domains stems in part from the fact that this dimension by now incorporates or shapes many distributive conflicts, including questions of who should have primary access to the welfare state (e.g. welfare chauvinism) or whether 'social investments' in education, childcare, etc. should be prioritized over traditional compensatory policies such as unemployment insurance (Häusermann and Kriesi 2015; Häusermann et al. 2020). This is clearly evident in the Swiss case:[12] left-wing parties in Switzerland continue to advocate an important role for the state in fostering equality and social justice, but they increasingly do so in a way that is compatible with a culturally liberal vision of society (Häusermann et al. 2022; Rennwald and Evans 2014; Nicolet and Sciarini 2010). The Swiss People's Party, meanwhile, has adopted welfare chauvinist positions like many other far-right parties, and it typically advocates a more traditional, status-preserving, and protection-oriented form of the welfare state that serves its core constituency in the manual working and small business classes (cf. Enggist and Pinggera 2022).

Furthermore, research indicating that the second dimension of ideological competition not only bundles a new set of (social as well as distributive) issues but has also come to shape how Swiss voters think about their own group belonging suggests that the universalism–particularism divide in Switzerland today resembles a full-blown 'cleavage' (Bornschier et al. 2021; Zollinger 2022). In other words, collective identities translate structural divides into politics (Bartolini 2005; Bartolini and Mair 1990). Socio-cultural group categories—relating, for instance, to national or rural identity and 'down-to-earthness' as opposed to cosmopolitan identity—by now appear to be more divisive in the Swiss electorate than traditional identities related to the old class and religious cleavages (cf. Lipset and Rokkan 1967). All of this indicates that universalist-particularist divisions will likely structure Swiss politics for a long time to come, providing a prism through which voters view their social position and evaluate their interests, and hence constraining parties' opportunities to mobilize electoral groups who have already found their political home.

Despite evidence for the emergence of a new dimension of political contestation—the 'diagonal'—however, there are still clear indications of tripolar political competition, and new actors' positions or the renewed salience of specific issues is at times perpendicular to the oppositions comprised in a new cleavage. The Green Liberals' appearance on the political scene strengthens a largely socially progressive but more right-wing political offering that might lead to greater articulation of divisions over the size and role of the state among the highly educated. The Green Liberals' stance in favour of climate protection as well as their endorsement of close cooperation and integration with the European Union also makes for interesting actor constellations with regard to issue areas whose recently increased salience is likely to persist or grow further in the foreseeable future. It seems somewhat open how exactly specific divisions related to climate change or European integration (including distributive ones) become aligned with other dimensions of Swiss politics; whether these broader issue complexes come to align with a left-progressive/right-authoritarian diagonal and/or whether specific divides over policies, costs, and distributive consequences activate more cross-cutting divides.

Hence, from a comparative perspective, Switzerland's trajectory over the past few decades might represent a path of increasingly dominant, all-encompassing left-versus-far-right polarization. However, signs of a re-emerging liberal pole around climate and Europe also indicate reinvigorated tripolarity as a possible scenario for the near future. Successes of far-right and left-libertarian/green parties across advanced democracies over the past few decades seem to trace the Swiss experience of the late twentieth century, but, for instance, Macron's En Marche/Renaissance in France or recent successes of the German Liberals also indicate that the Swiss Green Liberals increasingly establishing themselves in demarcation from both the far right and the left might form part of a more general trend. This would signal heightened electoral competition over an expanding electoral middle class (between the left and centre right), but potentially also (as the recent German government coalition signals), room for alliances between (broadly) socially progressive forces on the left and right. In Switzerland, such strengthened tripolarity could also attenuate and disperse the entrenched polarization that today characterizes electoral politics and policy-making.

Notes

1. Based on own calculations using the 2021 update of the Barro and Lee 2013 Educational Attainment Data.
2. That said, a comparatively high share of working women in Switzerland (63 per cent in 2019) work part-time (FSO 2020a).
3. With the exception of the years between 1954 and 1958, when the SP was not represented, and the year 2008, when the SVP had no seat in government.
4. The coding is as follows: Below secondary: 'primary school', 'compulsory education'; Secondary: 'basic vocational training', 'vocational education', 'diploma school', 'high school'; Tertiary: 'higher vocational training', 'vocational college', 'university'.
5. Surveys are conducted two to four times a year; we present moving averages of quarterly data.
6. The literal question is: 'Möchten Sie eine Schweiz mit gleichen Chancen für Ausländer und Ausländerinnen ODER eine Schweiz mit besseren Chancen für die Schweizer und Schweizerinnen?'

7. The literal question is: 'Möchten Sie eine Schweiz, wo sich vermehrt nach aussen öffnet, ODER eine Schweiz, wo sich vermehrt verschliesst?'
8. Literal question: 'Möchten Sie eine Schweiz mit mehr Staatseingriffen in die Wirtschaft ODER eine Schweiz mit mehr Wettbewerb auf dem Markt?'
9. Literal question: 'Möchten Sie eine Schweiz, wo der Umweltschutz wichtiger ist als der wirtschaftliche Wohlstand ODER eine Schweiz, wo der wirtschaftliche Wohlstand wichtiger ist als der Umweltschutz?'
10. Positions are calculated as follows (see Codebook: https://manifesto-project.wzb.eu/down/data/2021a/codebooks/codebook_MPDataset_MPDS2021a.pdf): First, positions on the cultural dimension are: (per107 + per108 + per501 + per502 + per503 + per602 + per604 + per607)−(per109 + per110 + per601 + per603 + per605 + per608); positions on the economic dimension are: (per401 + per402 + per410 + per414 + per505)−(per403 + per404 + per409 + per412 + per413 + per416 + per504). Second, we calculate the weighted (by vote share) party system mean on each dimension and election. Figure 7.6 finally shows for each party the normalized distance from the party system mean (averaged over three elections in each panel). All parties in the dataset of the Comparative Manifesto Project are included in the graphs; labelled are the six largest parties in the latest period.
11. The EU-15, Switzerland, and Norway are included. The size of circles illustrates party strength. Traditional/authoritarian versus libertarian/postmaterialist positions are based on the CHES variable GALTAN. State-market positions are based on the variable LRECON (see codebook).
12. This is noteworthy because the background of austerity and (perceived) fiscal constraints— exacerbated in the 2010s—that supposedly fuelled this blurring of socioeconomic and sociocultural conflicts was less pronounced in the Swiss case than elsewhere.

References

Abou-Chadi, Tarik, and Simon Hix. 2021. 'Brahmin Left versus Merchant Right? Education, Class, Multiparty Competition, and Redistribution in Western Europe'. *British Journal of Sociology* 72 (1): pp. 79–92.

Afonso, Alexandre, and Yannis Papadopoulos. 2015. 'How the Populist Radical Right Transformed Swiss Welfare Politics: From Compromises to Polarization'. *Swiss Political Science Review* 21 (4): pp. 617–635.

Ansell, Ben, and Jane Gingrich. 2018. 'Skills in Demand? Higher Education and Social Investment in Europe'. In *Welfare Democracies and Party Politics: Explaining Electoral Dynamics in Times of Changing Welfare Capitalism*, edited by Philip Manow, Bruno Palier, and Hanna Schwander, pp. 225–256. Oxford: Oxford University Press.

Ansolabehere, Stephen, and Shanto Iyengar. 1994. 'Riding the Wave and Claiming Ownership Over Issues: The Joint Effects of Advertising and News Coverage in Campaigns'. *The Public Opinion Quarterly* 58 (3): pp. 335–357.

Bakker, Ryan, Liesbet Hooghe, Seth Jolly, Gary Marks, Jonathan Polk, Jan Rovny, Marco Steenbergen, and Milada A. Vachudova. 2020. *2019 Chapel Hill Expert Survey, Version 2019.3* [Dataset]. Chapel Hill, NC: University of North Carolina.

Barro, Robert J., and Jong W. Lee. 2013. 'A New Data Set of Educational Attainment in the World, 1950–2010'. *Journal of Development Economics* 104: pp. 184–198.

Barro, Robert J., and Jong W. Lee. 2021. *September Update: Barro-Lee Estimates of Educational Attainment for the Population Aged 15–64 from 1950 to 2015*. www.barrolee.com (accessed 31 October 2022).

Bartolini, Stefano. 2005. 'La formations des clivages'. *Revue internationale de politique comparée* 12 (1): pp. 9–34.

Bartolini, Stefano, and Peter Mair. 1990. *Identity, Competition and Electoral Availability: The Stabilisation of European Electorates 1885–1985*. Cambridge: Cambridge University Press.

Beramendi, Pablo, Silja Häusermann, Herbert Kitschelt, and Hanspeter Kriesi. 2015. *The Politics of Advanced Capitalism*. New York: Cambridge University Press.

Bischof, Daniel, and Thomas Kurer. 2022. 'Lost in Transition – Where Are All the Social Democrats Today?' In *Beyond Social Democracy: Transformation of the Left in Emerging Knowledge Societies*, edited by Silja Häusermann, and Herbert Kitschelt. Manuscript.

Bornschier, Simon. 2010. *Cleavage Politics and the Populist Right: The New Cultural Conflict in Western Europe*. Philadelphia: Temple University Press.

Bornschier, Simon. 2015. 'The New Cultural Conflict, Polarization, and Representation in the Swiss Party System, 1975–2011'. *Swiss Political Science Review* 21 (4): pp. 680–701.

Bornschier, Simon, Céline Colombo, Silja Häusermann, and Delia Zollinger. 2021. 'How "Us" and "Them" Relates to Voting Behavior—Social Structure, Social Identities, and Electoral Choice'. *Comparative Political Studies* 54 (12): pp. 2087–2122.

De Vries, Catherine E., and Sara B. Hobolt. 2020. *Political Entrepreneurs: The Rise of Challenger Parties in Europe*. Princeton: Princeton University Press.

Enggist, Matthias, and Michael Pinggera. 2022. 'Radical Right Parties and Their Welfare State Stances–Not So Blurry After All?' *West European Politics* 45 (1): pp. 102–128.

FORS. 2020. *VOTO Studies: Standardized Post-Vote Surveys, 2016–2020 [Dataset]*. Lausanne: FORS.

FSO. 2019. 'Auf dem Weg zur Gleichstellung von Frau und Mann. Stand und Entwicklung'. Technical Report May. Neuchâtel: Swiss Federal Statistical Office. https://www.bfs.admin.ch/asset/de/8288359 (accessed 26 September 2022).

FSO. 2020a. 'Erwerbsbeteiligung der Frauen 2010–2019. Technical Report November'. Neuchâtel: Swiss Federal Statistical Office. https://www.bfs.admin.ch/asset/de/14941826 (accessed 26 September 2022).

FSO. 2020b. 'Szenarien für das Bildungsniveau der Bevölkerung'. Neuchâtel: Swiss Federal Statistical Office. https://www.bfs.admin.ch/bfs/de/home/statistiken/bildung-wissenschaft/szenarien-bildungssystem/szenarien-bildungsstand.html (accessed 26 September 2022).

Garritzmann, Julian L., Silja Häusermann, Thomas Kurer, Bruno Palier, and Michael Pinggera. 2021. 'The Emergence of Knowledge Economies: Educational Expansion, Labor Market Changes, and the Politics of Social Investment'. In *The World Politics of Social Investment*, edited by Julian L. Garritzmann, Silja Häusermann, and Bruno Palier, pp. 251–284. Oxford: Oxford University Press.

Gidron, Noam, James Adams, and Will Horne. 2020. *American Affective Polarization in Comparative Perspective*. Cambridge: Cambridge University Press.

Giger, Nathalie, Denise Traber, and Anke Tresch. 2022. 'Introduction to the Special Issue "The 2019 Swiss National Elections"'. *Swiss Political Science Review* 28(2): pp. 157–168.

Gingrich, Jane, and Silja Häusermann. 2015. 'The Decline of the Working-Class Vote, the Reconfiguration of the Welfare Support Coalition and Consequences for the Welfare State'. *Journal of European Social Policy* 25 (1): pp. 50–75.

Häusermann, Silja, Tarik Abou-Chadi, Reto Bürgisser, Matthias Enggist, Reto Mitteregger, Nadja Mosimann, and Delia Zollinger. 2022. *Wählerschaft und Perspektiven der Schweizer Sozialdemokratie*. Zürich: NZZ Libro.

Häusermann, Silja, and Hanspeter Kriesi. 2015. 'What Do Voters Want? Dimensions and Configurations in Individual-Level Preferences and Party Choice'. In *The Politics of Advanced Capitalism*, edited by Pablo Beramendi, Silja Häusermann, Herbert Kitschelt, and Hanspeter Kriesi, pp. 202-230. New York: Cambridge University Press.

Häusermann, Silja, André Mach, and Yannis Papadopoulos. 2004. 'From Corporatism to Partisan Politics: Social Policy Making under Strain in Switzerland'. *Swiss Political Science Review* 10 (2): pp. 33-59.

Häusermann, Silja, Michael Pinggera, Macarena Ares, and Matthias Enggist. 2020. 'The Limits of Solidarity: Changing welfare coalitions in a transforming European party system'. *Swiss Political Science Association. Annual Meeting, Luzern, 3 February 2020 - 4 February 2020*, https://www.zora.uzh.ch/id/eprint/194708/ (accessed 26 September 2022).

Hooghe, Liesbet, and Gary Marks. 2018. 'Cleavage Theory Meets Europe's Crises: Lipset, Rokkan, and the Transnational Cleavage'. *Journal of European Public Policy* 25 (1): pp. 109-135.

International Labour Organization. 2021. *Data: Employment by Sex and Education*. https://www.ilo.org/ilostat-files/Documents/Bulk_ilostat_en.html (accessed 31 October 2022).

Iversen, Torben, and David Soskice. 2019. *Democracy and Prosperity: Reinventing Capitalism Through a Turbulent Century*. Princeton: Princeton University Press.

Kitschelt, Herbert. 1994. *The Transformation of European Social Democracy*. New York: Cambridge University Press.

Krause, Werner, Denis Cohen, and Tarik Abou-Chadi. 2022. 'Does Accommodation Work? Mainstream Party Strategies and the Success of Radical Right Parties'. *Political Science Research and Methods* 11 (1): pp. 1-8. doi: 10.1017/psrm.2022.8.

Kriesi, Hanspeter. 1998. 'The Transformation of Cleavage Politics: The 1997 Stein Rokkan Lecture'. *European Journal of Political Research* 33 (2): pp. 165-185.

Kriesi, Hanspeter. 2015. 'Conclusion: The Political Consequences of the Polarization of Swiss Politics'. *Swiss Political Science Review* 21 (4): pp. 724-739.

Kriesi, Hanspeter, Edgar Grande, Romain Lachat, Martin Dolezal, Simon Bornschier, and Timotheus Frey. 2006. 'Globalization and the Transformation of the National Political Space: Six European Countries Compared'. *European Journal of Political Research* 45 (6): pp. 921-956.

Kriesi, Hanspeter, Edgar Grande, Romain Lachat, Martin Dolezal, Simon Bornschier, and Timotheus Frey. 2008. *West European Politics in the Age of Globalization*. Cambridge: Cambridge University Press.

Kriesi, Hanspeter, Matthias Brunner, and François Lorétan. 2017. *Standardisierte Umfragen VoxIt 1981-2016 [Dataset]*. Lausanne: FORS.

Lachat, Romain. 2014. 'Issue Ownership and the Vote: The Effects of Associative and Competence Ownership on Issue Voting'. *Swiss Political Science Review* 20 (4): pp. 727-740.

Lauener, Lukas, Patrick Emmenegger, Silja Häusermann, and Stefanie Walter. 2022. 'Torn Between International Cooperation and National Sovereignty: Voter Attitudes in Tradeoff Situations in Switzerland'. *Swiss Political Science Review* 28 (2): pp. 277-295.

Linder, Wolf, and Daniel Schwarz. 2008. 'Möglichkeiten parlamentarischer Opposition im schweizerischen System'. *Parlament—Mitteilungsblatt der Schweizerischen Gesellschaft für Parlamentsfragen* 11 (2): pp. 4-10.

Lipset, Seymour M., and Stein Rokkan. 1967. *Party Systems and Voter Alignments: Cross-National Perspectives*. New York: Free Press.

Marks, Gary, David Attewell, Liesbet Hooghe, Jan Rovny, and Marco Steenbergen. 2022. 'The Social Bases of Political Parties: A New Measure and Survey'. *British Journal of Political Science* 53 (1): pp. 1-12. doi:10.1017/S0007123421000740.

McGann, Anthony J., and Herbert Kitschelt. 2005. 'The Radical Right in the ALPS: Evolution of Support for the Swiss SVP and Austrian FPÖ'. *Party Politics* 11 (2): pp. 147–171.

Nicolet, Sarah, and Pascal Sciarini. 2010. *Le destin électoral de la gauche. Le vote Socialiste et Vert en Suisse*. Chêne-Bourg: Georg Editeur.

Oesch, Daniel. 2006a. 'Coming to Grips with a Changing Class Structure: An Analysis of Employment Stratification in Britain, Germany, Sweden and Switzerland'. *International Sociology* 21 (2): pp. 263–288.

Oesch, Daniel. 2006b. *Redrawing the Class Map. Stratification and Institutions in Britain, Germany, Sweden and Switzerland*. London: Palgrave Macmillan.

Oesch, Daniel. 2007. 'Weniger Koordination, mehr Markt? Kollektive Arbeitsbeziehungen und Neokorporatismus in der Schweiz seit 1990'. *Swiss Political Science Review* 13 (3): pp. 337–368.

Oesch, Daniel. 2008. 'Explaining Workers' Support for Right-Wing Populist Parties in Western Europe: Evidence from Austria, Belgium, France, Norway, and Switzerland'. *International Political Science Review* 29 (3): pp. 349–373.

Oesch, Daniel. 2015. 'Welfare regimes and Change in the Employment Structure: Britain, Denmark and Germany since 1990'. *Journal of European Social Policy* 25 (1): pp. 94–110.

Oesch, Daniel, and Line Rennwald. 2010. 'The Class Basis of Switzerland's Cleavage between the New Left and the Populist Right'. *Swiss Political Science Review* 16 (3): pp. 343–371.

Oesch, Daniel, and Line Rennwald. 2018. 'Electoral Competition in Europe's New Tripolar Political Space: Class Voting for the Left, Centre-Right and Radical Right'. *European Journal of Political Research* 57 (4): pp. 783–807.

Rennwald, Line. 2014. 'Class (Non)Voting in Switzerland 1971–2011: Ruptures and Continuities in a Changing Political Landscape'. *Swiss Political Science Review* 20 (4): pp. 550–572.

Rennwald, Line. 2020. *Social Democratic Parties and the Working Class: New Voting Patterns*. Cham: Springer Nature.

Rennwald, Line, and Geoffrey Evans. 2014. 'When Supply Creates Demand: Social Democratic Party Strategies and the Evolution of Class Voting'. *West European Politics* 37 (5): pp. 1108–1135.

Schattschneider, Elmer E. 1960. *The Semisovereign People*. New York: Holt, Rinehart and Winston.

Sciarini, Pascal, Manuel Fischer, and Denise Traber. 2015. *Political Decision-Making in Switzerland: The Consensus Model under Pressure*. Houndsmill, Basingstoke: Palgrave Macmillan.

Skenderovic, Damir. 2009. *The Radical Right in Switzerland: Continuity and Change, 1945–2000*. New York, Oxford: Berghahn Books.

Stubager, Rune. 2009. 'Education-based Group Identity and Consciousness in the Authoritarian-Libertarian Value Conflict'. *European Journal of Political Research* 48 (2): pp. 204–233.

Traber, Denise. 2015. 'Disenchanted Swiss Parliament? Electoral Strategies and Coalition Formation'. *Swiss Political Science Review* 21 (4): pp. 702–723.

Traber, Denise, Nathalie Giger, and Silja Häusermann. 2018. 'How Economic Crises Affect Political Representation: Declining Party-Voter Congruence in Times of Constrained Government'. *West European Politics* 41 (5): pp. 1100–1124.

Traber, Denise, Simon Hug, and Pascal Sciarini 2014. 'Party Unity in the Swiss Parliament: The Electoral Connection'. *The Journal of Legislative Studies* 20 (2): pp. 193–215.

Traber, Denise, Lukas F. Stoetzer, and Tanja Burri. 2022. 'Group-Based Public Opinion Polarisation in Multi-Party Systems'. *West European Politics* 46 (4): pp. 652–677. doi: 10.1080/01402382.2022.2110376

Tresch, Anke, Georg Lutz, Lukas Lauener, Nicolas Pecari, Robert Baur, Thomas De Rocchi, and Andreas Goldberg. 2020. *Swiss Election Study (Selects), Cumulative Dataset 1971–2019* [Dataset]. Lausanne: FORS.

Tresch, Anke, Lukas Lauener, Laurent Bernhard, Georg Lutz, and Laura Scaperrotta. 2020. *Eidgenössische Wahlen 2019. Wahlteilnahme und Wahlentscheid [Dataset]*. Lausanne: Selects – FORS.

Van Der Brug, Wouter, and Joost Van Spanje. 2009. 'Immigration, Europe and the "New" Cultural Dimension'. *European Journal of Political Research* 48 (3): pp. 309–334.

Vatter, Adrian. 2016. *Das politische System der Schweiz*. Baden-Baden: Nomos.

Volkens, Andrea, Tobias Burst, Pola Lehmann, Bernhard Weßels, and Lisa Zehnter. 2021. *The Manifesto Data Collection. Manifesto Project (MRG/CMP/MARPOR). Version 2021a [Dataset]*. Berlin: Wissenschaftszentrum Berlin Für Sozialforschung (WZB).

Wagner, Markus, and Thomas Meyer. 2014. 'Which Issues do Parties Emphasise? Salience Strategies and Party Organisation in Multiparty Systems'. *West European Politics* 37 (5): pp. 1019–1045.

Zollinger, Delia. 2022. 'Cleavage Identities in Voters' Own Words. Harnessing Open-Ended Survey Responses'. *American Journal of Political Science*. doi: 10.1111/ ajps.12743.

PART II
INSTITUTIONS

CHAPTER 8

FEDERALISM

ADRIAN VATTER

1 The foundations of Swiss federalism

1.1 Historical roots

During the eventful first half of the nineteenth century, the territory of present-day Switzerland passed through various forms of governance, from a loose-knit federation to a centralized, unitary state modelled after the French state ('Helvetic Republic'; 1798–1803). The 1847 military defeat of the Catholic-conservative cantons of the *Sonderbund* paved the way for creating a modern federation. In contrast to post-Westphalian nation-states that were created in the surrounding countries, the newly created federation did not adopt the vision of a Swiss nation, unified by language, ethnicity, or culture, but pursued the idea of a 'multicultural state' from the very beginning (Linder and Mueller 2021, 16). At the same time, the 1848 federal constitution was based on a constitutional compromise between a majority of liberal-Protestant federalists and a minority of conservative-Catholics favouring cantonal autonomy. Thus, the tasks of the central government remained largely in the hands of the cantons. However, through the abolition of internal customs duties and the harmonization of external ones, the new constitution created the conditions for a single economic area. It also assigned several new responsibilities to the federal level in the fields of foreign policy, customs policy, postal and coinage prerogatives, and parts of the military (see Dardanelli and Mueller 2019).

The constitution of 1848 was characterized above all by a combination of two core elements, which had different origins (Häfelin et al. 2016):

- The basic principles of democracy and the rule of law (constitutionalism) were already embodied in the constitutions of the liberal cantons (revised during the 'Regeneration' years of the 1830s). These principles included a compulsory

referendum on constitutional matters, representative democracy, division of powers, legal equality, and basic constitutional rights.
- The federal structure followed the lines of the 1787 US constitution, with a bicameral system.

The 1848 federal constitution also determined the relationship between the different political institutions according to the principle of the division of powers, a relationship that is basically still valid today (Vatter et al. 2020). Following the US example, the Federal Assembly (parliament) was created as a bicameral system in which the two chambers, the National Council and the Council of States, have equal rights. Beyond bicameralism, the close combination of federalism and democracy finds its expression in the double majority: any proposal to amend the federal constitution must be submitted and approved by both 'a majority of those who vote and a majority of the cantons' (Art. 142.2). This constitutional compromise, embodying non-centralization and the granting of extensive autonomy at the cantonal and subnational levels, gradually alleviated the tensions between Protestants and Catholic-conservatives and between federalists and 'cantonalists'. It also allowed for distinct social and cultural developments within the different cantons, which were the relevant modernizing agencies in the nineteenth century (Church and Head 2013). At the same time, the federation favoured the creation of a Swiss multicultural society (Linder and Mueller 2021). The 1874 full revision of the federal constitution spurred legal harmonization. Ever since, the federation has been responsible not only for the military and legal systems but also for legislation in fields such as social security or transport. With the 1874 introduction of the optional referendum—and the popular initiative for constitutional amendments in 1891—direct democracy was also significantly strengthened. The extension of basic constitutional rights (e.g. freedom of religion, conscience, and trade) and the expansion of the federal Supreme Court's power were additional core features of the 1874 federal constitution. By the time it was replaced in 1999, the 1874 federal constitution had been amended 155 times (Dardanelli and Mueller 2019, 151)—usually fostering legislative centralization at the expense of the cantons. Yet the 1999 federal constitution enshrined the involvement of the cantons in foreign policy.

In sum, the 1848 Swiss federation was characterized by multi-ethnic federalism, which stood in sharp contrast to the predominant nationalist integration strategy elsewhere in Europe at the time; the simultaneously strong autonomy and the cantons' involvement in federal policy-making by, e.g. US-style bicameralism; as well as the principle of popular sovereignty unique in the European context (Vatter et al. 2020)—thus the foundations of Swiss federalism that are still valid today.

1.2 The basic principles of Swiss federalism

Federalism means the division of power through the vertical separation of powers by granting extensive territorial autonomy while also allowing for co-decision-making.

In short, federalism realizes a distinct combination of self-rule *and* shared rule (Watts 2008, 8; cf. Elazar 1987). In hardly any other federal state do the constituent units have such extensive competencies as in the twenty-six Swiss cantons (Dardanelli and Mueller 2019; Hooghe et al. 2016). The far-reaching autonomy of and equality among the cantons, their rights to participate in federal policy-making, and their duty to cooperate form the core of the Swiss federation (Häfelin et al. 2016). The guiding principle of cantonal autonomy is based on article 3 of the federal constitution, enshrining that the cantons are sovereign except to the extent that their sovereignty is limited by the federal constitution. The cantons exercise all rights that are not vested in the federation—and the cantons may pass some of their original powers on to the local level (i.e. municipalities). Whenever the federation seeks to take on a new task, it must be explicitly transferred to the federal level by means of a constitutional amendment approved by a double majority (see above). Joint responsibilities became widespread as well. However, the 2004/08 landmark federal reform—a reform that tackled both fiscal equalization and the division of powers between the federation and the cantons (Wasserfallen 2015; Mueller et al. 2017)[1]—sought to disentangle them. While the federal reform was the most far-reaching one, it has not fundamentally changed power relations among the cantons and among the cantons and the federation, respectively (Arens 2020; Arnold et al. 2019; Arnold 2020). From a constitutional perspective, the basic constitutional principles of cantonal autonomy can still be specified as follows:

- *The existence and the equality of the cantons are guaranteed (art. 1).* Federal legislation cannot abolish or amalgamate the cantonal level. Changes to cantonal territories have to be approved by the majority of the people and of the cantons (e.g. the 1978/79 creation of the canton of Jura; art. 53.2). Moreover, the cantons enjoy equal rights irrespective of, e.g. their size.[2]
- *The cantons are free to choose their internal organization.* The cantons decide upon their own constitution within the loosely defined borders of a 'democratic constitution' (art. 51.1), their political system, the political rights of their citizens, and the extent of local autonomy. Moreover, they are free to choose their staff independently. The federation, e.g. cannot dismiss a cantonal government. However, cantonal freedom of internal organization is not unlimited, as the cantons need to guarantee the rule of law and basic rights.
- *The cantons have far-reaching responsibilities.* The aforementioned article 3 functions as an actual rule for the division of powers according to the subsidiarity principle. Political issues should be dealt with at the most immediate level that is consistent with their resolution. The federation, in turn, should only step in if there is abundant proof that the cantons are not competent. In that case, the cantons still enjoy considerable leeway in implementing federal laws.
- *The cantons have their own financial resource.* The cantons and even the municipalities have the power to levy taxes.
- *The cantons are not subject to political control.* Without legal authority, the federation cannot interfere in the political process of the cantons or 'correct' unwelcome

political decisions. It may, however, use more subtle 'disciplinary' measures through, e.g. cooperative arrangements, federal grants, or, more generally, the power of the purse.
- *The cantons participate in federal decision-making.* The cantons participate in federal decision-making, in particular in the legislative process (art. 45). To this end, the cantons have several vertical institutions at their disposal that are constitutionally guaranteed (see below). Yet, in practice, they increasingly revert to a broad, multifaceted, and ever-changing toolkit of both more recent instruments of 'formalized vertical cooperation' (Mathys 2016; Ladner 2018) and 'subnational lobbying' in its purest form (Freiburghaus et al. 2021a, b; Freiburghaus 2024).

Besides these structural principles, two other basic characteristics of Swiss federalism must be mentioned. First, on the *process level,* there is a complex, highly dynamic web of intergovernmental relations that has, over time, developed towards 'cooperative federalism' in the realms of both policy-making and implementation (e.g. Arens 2020; Vatter 2018). Second, on the *political-cultural level,* there is a strong 'anti-statist ideology' leaning towards the non-centralization of political power as well as distinct parallelism of both 'competition' (e.g. in tax competition) and 'solidarity' (e.g. through fiscal equalization).

2 THE INSTITUTIONS OF SWISS FEDERALISM

In order to materialize practically, the foundations and the basic principles of Swiss federalism require certain institutional arrangements. More concisely, there must be vertical institutions that ensure the cantons' participation in federal decision-making—and there are horizontal institutions facilitating intergovernmental cooperation between the cantons (Linder and Vatter 2001; Vatter 2005, 2006, 2018). This section illustrates the vertical and horizontal institutions of Swiss federalism and considers a number of problems and projects for reform.

2.1 The vertical institutions of Swiss federalism

2.1.1 *The Council of States (bicameralism)*
The Federal Assembly consists of two equally powerful chambers: the National Council representing the people and the Council of States representing the cantons. As in other federations, bicameralism is seen a core feature of shared rule, enabling the cantons to influence federal policy (see Mueller and Vatter 2020). The Council of States comprises forty-six members, meaning that each canton delegates two members of parliament (MP) except for six cantons delegating but one MP[2]. Cantonal laws regulate their voting procedures and salaries. Until the 1970s, the Councillors of State of

some cantons were elected by the cantonal parliaments, but now all elections are based on direct popular vote. With the exception of the canton of Jura and, since 2010, of Neuchâtel, all cantons follow the majority rule. The term of office is four years in all cantons, and, with few exceptions, elections are held at the same time as the elections for the National Council.

The Swiss bicameral system is the result of the constitutional compromise (see section 1). Historically, the upper house was supposed to form an effective barrier to safeguard cantonal autonomy through cantonal representation at the federal level. At the same time, however, the federal constitution stipulated that federal MPs vote without instructions (including instructions provided by the cantonal governments). The successive introduction of direct popular elections, too, pushed back the cantonal authorities' influence in federal policy-making. This 'Senate principle' is a key difference to Germany, where the *Bundesrat* is composed of delegates from the *Länder* governments with a bound mandate. Accordingly, empirical studies emphasize that the interests of the cantons are hardly articulated any differently in the Council of States than they are in the National Council and that the Council of States, therefore, fulfils its purpose as a representative of cantonal interests only to a limited extent (e.g. Vatter et al. 2017; Mueller and Vatter 2020). At least, the Council of States can be, in practice, considered to be more influential than the lower house (Mueller et al. 2020), leaving some yet limited leeway to shape federal policy in a mainly symbolic way (Freiburghaus et al. 2021b). In terms of an overall assessment, the following can be maintained: due to its institutional architecture (e.g. popular elections of MPs), the Council of States manages to fulfil certain functions of second chambers (e.g. fostering political consensus, enhancing the quality of legislation). Yet the Council of States fails to deliver on its *raison d'être*, as it neither effectively advocates nor safeguards cantonal interests in federal policy-making. While the Council of States does not live up to its premise (anymore), the cantonal governments increasingly try to compensate for this lack of cantonal interest representation by lobbying 'their' MPs in the Council of States more fiercely (Freiburghaus 2024).

2.1.2 *The cantonal vote on constitutional amendments (double majority)*

As detailed in section 1, any constitutional amendment must be approved by both a majority of the voters and a majority of the cantons. While the double-majority rule remained uncontested for about 100 years and had almost no practical consequences, it has come under strong attack from various sides in the last thirty years. The most important arguments that have been advanced in favour of revising (or even abolishing) can be summarized as follows (see Vatter and Sager 1996; Vatter 2020).

The first argument points to the unequal demographic development as a result of industrialization and subsequent migration to urban areas. This can be illustrated with the frequently quoted example that a vote cast in Appenzell Innerrhoden counts about forty times more than one cast in Zurich if a double majority is required. A direct consequence of this growing population imbalance between small and large cantons is that an ever-declining number of voters can block a double-majority bill. Today, the 'smallest theoretically possible blocking minority' lies at about 9 per cent of the voting population if the 'no'-votes are distributed optimally among the small cantons. According to Linder and Mueller (2017, 225), in the last thirty years, the effective blocking minority lies between 18 and 25 per cent. A second argument lies in the steady increase of double-majority votes. While there were only forty-six double-majority votes between 1951 and 1969, that number rose to 124 for the period between 2001 and 2022 (Swissvotes 2022). Not only has the number of actual bills submitted to vote, to both eligible voters and the canton, risen steadily, but the scope of the respective bills has also risen (Wili 1988, 157; see Vatter 2018). For example, since 1977, the double-majority clause also applies when Switzerland's accession to organizations for collective security or to supranational communities is at stake (art. 140.1); a co-decision right guaranteed to the cantons (or, more precisely, their eligible citizens) that poses high hurdles for the country's integration into multilateral (or EU-related) frameworks. A total of ten bills have been rejected as a result of the cantonal majority requirement since 1848. In the late 1980s, Wili (1988, 240) was still able to maintain that, as a rule, an exclusively cantonal veto could have only a delaying effect since, in most cases, a rejected bill would be re-submitted to the people and the cantons relatively quickly and often successfully. However, in the light of voting results in recent years, this assessment seems too optimistic (e.g. European policy).

An analysis by the cantons of the voting results for the ten bills that failed due to the cantonal majority requirement identifies the 'winners' and 'losers' of the double-majority clause (see Table 8.1; Vatter 2020; Vatter and Sager 1996). Among the 'winners'

Table 8.1: Popular votes with conflicting popular and cantonal majorities

Bill	Year	Per cent 'yes'-population	Cantons
Weights and measures	1866	50.5	9.5:12.5
Proportionality rule for National Council	1910	47.5	12:10
Protection of tenants and consumers	1955	50.2	7:15
Civil protection	1957	48.1	14:8
Fiscal policy of the federation	1970	55.4	9:13
Federal responsibilities for education	1973	52.8	10.5:11.5
Articles on economic policy	1975	52.8	11:11
Article on energy policy	1983	50.9	11:12*
Cultural policy	1994	51.0	11:12
Facilitation of naturalization	1994	52.8	10:13
Family article	2013	54.3	10:13
Responsible business initiative	2020	50.7	8.5:14.5

* From 1978/79 onwards, the canton of Jura is counted as the twenty-third canton.
Data sources: Vatter (2020); Swissvotes (2022).

were, first of all, the cantons of the former *Sonderbund*—in particular, the rather small, rural, and rather conservative cantons such as Uri, Schwyz, Obwalden, Nidwalden, Glarus, Zug, and the two Appenzell. In this sense, the cantonal majority requirement remains a very efficient protection of the former *Sonderbund* and mainly Catholic cantons of central and eastern Switzerland. On the other hand, the exclusively French-speaking cantons of western Switzerland, as well as Ticino, are definitely among the losers under the double-majority rule. For instance, regarding the bills on energy policy, cultural policy, and naturalization policy, the four French-speaking cantons, which have almost ten times as many voters as the mountainous cantons of central Switzerland, were on the losing side. This same pattern is also valid for the various 'quasi-conflicts' in recent years. Apart from the French-speaking and Italian-speaking minorities, densely populated urban areas with progressive, cosmopolitan attitudes (i.e. Zurich, Bern, Basel, and Geneva) stand out as another group of losers. In double-majority votes, they are often outvoted not only by the smaller cantons but, in many cases, also by the rural populations of their own cantons.

2.1.3 *The cantonal initiative*

The cantonal initiative was introduced in 1848 to compensate for the fact that the cantons did not have the right to impose mandates on their delegates in the Council of States. It gives every canton the right to submit an initiative to the Federal Assembly. In the overwhelming majority of the cantons, it is the cantonal parliament that exerts this right; sometimes, it is simultaneously vested in the eligible voters or, in two cantons, in the cantonal government. In contrast to the popular initiative, the cantonal initiative is not an actual initiative but only an instrument to 'lobby the Swiss parliament' (Mueller and Mazzoleni 2016, 50) by proposing a bill on a given matter. If one of the two chambers dismisses the proposal, or if no common decision is reached by the two chambers, the cantonal initiative is rejected, and no federal bill is prepared.

Until the 1970s, an average of just under a dozen cantonal initiatives were submitted per decade. In the 1980s, the number rose to forty-seven and doubled in the 1990s to 103, and again in the 2000s to 182 cantonal initiatives. Recently, a total of 309 cantonal initiatives were submitted between 2010 and 2021 (Vatter 2020). However, cantonal initiatives hardly ever succeed and are often dismissed by the national MPs as mere 'peripheral protests' (Mueller and Mazzoleni 2016). For the period from 1970 to 2001, only one-third of all cantonal initiatives achieved a certain effect, for instance, by triggering a postulate or a motion in the Federal Assembly (Neuenschwander 2006). A follow-up study confirms the overall small direct effect for the years 1990 to 2010: parliament only complied with just under 20 per cent of all cantonal initiatives submitted during this period. This downward trend has become even more pronounced in recent times: in less than 7 per cent of the cantonal initiatives settled between 2008 and 2019 did both chambers decide to 'follow up' on the cantons' proposal. Overall, the cantonal initiative has three functions: a protest against unwelcome federal laws (e.g. health insurance law); political marketing attempts to raise federal MP's awareness of regional needs; and the possibility for cantonal parliaments to participate in and to influence ongoing federal legislative processes (Mueller and Mazzoleni 2016).

2.1.4 The cantonal referendum

According to the federal constitution, 50,000 voters or, alternatively, a minimum of eight cantons can trigger a popular vote on, e.g. an (emergency) federal act, certain federal decrees, and/or certain international treaties (e.g. if the latter provides accession to an international organization). The cantons themselves can decide which authority is responsible for triggering such an optional referendum; accordingly, various regulations apply. Given the required quorum of eight cantons, the cantons repeatedly tried but never succeeded in triggering a cantonal referendum until 2004. Then, in fear of substantial tax losses caused by a new federal tax law (*Steuerpaket 03*), a total of eleven cantons launched a successful cantonal referendum for the first time. Together with the left-leaning parties disfavouring tax cuts the cantons won a majority of votes in the popular vote of 16 May 2004, rejecting the tax laws proposed by the federation. Besides the essential leadership and considerable coordination efforts of the Conference of Cantonal Government (KdK), the first (and since 2004 also the last) successful cantonal referendum was also enabled and fostered by the cantons' institutional reforms, which made it easier to launch referendums, as well as by the dominance of party political interests over cantonal interests in the Council of States (Fischer 2006).

2.1.5 The cantons in the pre-parliamentary decision-making process

During the twentieth century, as a consequence of welfare state development, the pre-parliamentary consultation procedure (*Vernehmlassungsverfahren*) has become an important channel through which organized interests influence federal decision-making. The 1947 revisions of the constitutional provisions on economic policy made consultations with the cantons and with economic interest groups compulsory, a participatory right that was, over time, further strengthened (e.g. in the 1999 full revision of the federal constitution). In any case, the consultation procedure shall reduce the likelihood of an optional referendum—just as it shall ensure that federal bills are sensibly drafted and easy to implement.

The official position of the cantons—i.e. of the agencies that implement a significant part of federal legislation—is of great importance in the Swiss federal system. The main reason is that, in the consultation process, the cantonal governments can express their will in a direct and undistorted manner. While today, the cantonal governments still participate very frequently (Freiburghaus 2024), the consultation procedure does not always live up to its inclusive function. The basic problem from the point of view of the cantons is twofold (see Sager and Steffen 2006). On the one hand, the federation overwhelms the cantons with a huge and steadily increasing number of consultations. Although the main aim of the 2004 Consultation Act was to streamline the pre-parliamentary consultation phase in the sense of reducing the number of consultations, this goal has not been achieved to date. On the other hand, the cantons' objections and preferences are often only insufficiently taken into account, especially if compared to (business) interest groups. Generally speaking, federal decision-making is dominated by a limited number of actors, with the pre-parliamentary stages being particularly selective and open to just a few of the most influential political actors (Sciarini et al. 2015). There are no commonly agreed and/or formalized criteria according to which the federation evaluates the many statements it receives—and has an incentive to give disproportionate weight to the statements made by those political actors who are capable of triggering a referendum. While the responsible federal authorities, consulted experts, and interest groups are all usually accorded a strong position, other actors, such as the cantons or the parties, find themselves in a comparatively weak situation. The limited cantonal influence in comparison with interest groups is also a consequence of the latter's greater organizational capacity and ability to put forward powerful arguments. In contrast to interest groups, the cantons cannot specialize in, e.g. one core issue, but they have to represent heterogeneous interests and are thus obliged to adopt contradictory positions reflecting broad compromises worked out in the collegial multi-party governments of the cantons (Sager and Steffen 2006). In order to have an actual say, the cantons must thus 'accommodate [their] collective and individual voice[s]' (Freiburghaus et al. 2021a, 223): If they form some kind of 'consultation cartel' and submit a joint statement (e.g. formulated in the name of a given intercantonal conference), the cantons are likelier to be heard *collectively* (see also Schnabel et al. 2022). But in order to arrive at such jointly formulated statements, the individual canton unavoidably has to give up some of its particular, regionally distinct interests such as, e.g. technical questions on the actual feasibility and implementation of a federal bill (see Freiburghaus 2024). Moreover, especially during crises, the Federal Council often sets very tight deadlines. Hence, the cantons have too little time to submit well-founded comments, which, again, reduces the odds of their statement(s) being taken into account by the federal authorities.

2.1.6 *The implementation of federal bills by the cantons*

While the federation holds the legislative power in many areas, responsibility for implementing federal policies resides to a large extent with the cantons. For the federation, 'administrative decentralization' (Dardanelli and Mueller 2019) has the advantage of reducing its workload; for the cantons, the advantage lies in controlling their own programme priorities and in adapting policy implementation to the local context (Linder and Mueller 2017). The federation supervises the cantonal implementation of policies. However, given the necessity of maintaining vertically smooth cooperation over the long term, implementation control is limited in scope and politically difficult to execute. The federation, therefore, prefers cooperative to conflictual strategies and hardly ever sanctions the cantons for non-compliance.

In any case, the implementation of federal bills is based on cooperation between programming and implementing agencies and resembles implementation processes in general, which are characterized by divergent interests, low predictability, and the need to mobilize sufficient political will. The cantons enjoy considerable leeway—and they are able to adapt the political programmes of the federation according to their distinct regional needs within the scope of usually quite loose federal framework regulation.

Thus, in carrying out federal policies, the cantons act not only as implementing but also as *programming* agencies (Sager and Rüefli 2005).

The drawbacks of the cantonal implementation of federal bills are quite obvious. Yet the factors that lead to implementation deficits and/or non-compliance of the cantons are very complex (e.g. Vatter and Wälti 2003; Sager et al. 2019). To begin with, the inadequate cooperation between the federation and the cantons in implementing federal policies can be explained by the unclear delineation of tasks between the two levels of the federal system. As a consequence, new tasks are passed back and forth between the cantons and the federation (referred to as the *'föderalistisches Schwarz-Peter-Spiel'*; see Bussmann 1986). New tasks are first assigned to the cantons, but when the strain on the cantons increases, they turn to the federation, which has to (financially) assist even though the responsibility lies with the cantons. The federation then enacts a federal law but continues to delegate the responsibility for its implementation to the cantons while providing financial assistance in return. Whereas active cantons benefit from these federal subsidies, others fall behind and call for more help from the federation. This, in turn, makes it necessary for the federation to provide further support and sanctions. While the 2004/08 NFA[1] sought to disentangle the tasks between the federation and the cantons (see above), it remains questionable to what extent a clearer, less overlapping division of powers is realistic given the manifold interdependencies in the ages of high mobility, digitalization, and internationalization (Arnold et al. 2019). Other factors that lie at the root of implementation problems include inadequate horizontal coordination, overly complex procedures, large disparities among the cantonal administrations in terms of financial, legal, and human resources, the politically limited (sanction) capacity of the federation, obvious flaws and faults in the federal framework regulation, and insufficient regard for the specific regional contexts (see Sager et al. 2019).

Overall, the cantonal implementation of federal bills certainly has highly integrative effects. However, this arrangement usually allows for only incremental adaptation to new circumstances and thus limits the innovation and decision-making capacity of Swiss politics (Vatter and Wälti 2003). However, limited innovation is not a feature of the federalist system of implementation as such. Rather, it depends to a great extent on the various constellations of political conflict and consensus at the different territorial levels (Linder and Mueller 2017). The effectiveness of federal implementation is most likely to be enhanced by incorporating the results of evaluation results and/or scientific evidence into revisions of federal policy; by identifying potential implementation problems at an early stage of policy formulation; and by including the cantons from the very beginning as future implementation agencies in the debate about federal policies. Moreover, new studies indicate that secondary harmonization processes can minimize differences in cantonal policy implementation (see Balthasar 2003; Sager 2003; Sager et al. 2019).

However, the toolkit that enables cantonal participation in federal decision-making is not limited to the vertical institutions laid down in the federal constitution. The Council of States, the double majority, the cantonal initiative, the cantonal referendum, the consultation procedure, and the implementation of federal bills by the cantons are all, in one way or another, enshrined in, and prescribed by, the federal constitution. Yet besides these institutionalized channels, there is a broad, multifaceted, and ever-changing range of both more recent forms of 'formalized' vertical cooperation and informal genuine advocacy (or lobbying) tactics in how the cantons seek to make themselves heard. One of the most striking examples of such recent 'formalized' vertical cooperation is that of the so-called 'convention-programs' (CPs); an instrument introduced by the 2004/08 NFA reform (art. 46.2). CPs are public law contracts signed by the federation with each canton, based on the provision of earmarked federal grants. CPs are valid for a limited period of usually three to four years (Mathys 2016; Ladner 2018). They should, first and foremost, foster multi-level coordination in the nineteen shared tasks that remained in place post-NFA (e.g. regional traffic, nature, and wildlife protection, flood protection; see Mueller and Vatter 2020 for a detailed overview). Regarding 'new, informal channels' (Vatter 2018, 247) and 'subnational lobbying' (Freiburghaus et al. 2021a, b), the cantons increasingly fall back on and revert to basically everything possible to exert influence at the federal level (Freiburghaus 2024). According to Freiburghaus (2024), the most important advocacy tactics include face-to-face lobbying, intergovernmental councils, regional offices in downtown Bern (i.e. the de facto capital), and public-funded lobbyists, as well as the media (e.g. by 'going public' and/or by mobilizing voters ahead of federal ballots).

2.2 The horizontal institutions of Swiss federalism

At the latest, since the second half of the twentieth century, intercantonal (or horizontal) cooperation has become increasingly important (see Arens 2020; Arnold et al. 2019; Pfisterer 2015; Schnabel 2020a, b; Schnabel et al. 2022; Wasserfallen 2015). The horizontal institutions of Swiss federalism fulfil three functions in particular: exchange of information and experience among the cantons; coordination among the cantons in their own policy areas; and joint representation of interests vis-à-vis the federal government (Vatter 2018). Recently, they have also increasingly served to organize the joint execution of tasks (e.g. by means of joint police academies or joint teacher training colleges).

2.2.1 *Intercantonal agreements ('Konkordate')*

Intercantonal agreements (*Konkordate*) represent the most important aspect of horizontal cooperative federalism. Today, there are more than 800 intercantonal agreements in force, the vast majority of which are less than forty years old (Arens 2020). They are primarily an instrument of regional cooperation. Three-quarters of post-1848 intercantonal agreements are bilateral while a mere dozen treaties include all cantons. A spatial analysis identifies four groups of particularly strongly interlinked cantons: the cantons of eastern Switzerland, the French-speaking and Italian-speaking cantons (as one group), and the cantons of northwestern and central Switzerland, respectively. According to Arens (2020), intercantonal cooperation by means of concordats mainly takes place within functional, linguistically closed, and geographically delimited areas where there is a high degree of proximity and mobility. Political factors, in turn, hardly play a role (see Bochsler 2009). Thus, intercantonal agreements can best be described as measures for regional policy-making within functional areas, which usually deal with technical but less so with politically sensitive issues. Most of the treaties deal with finance and tax issues, but many also concern education and cultural issues (Arens 2020).

The cantons have the right to make agreements on all matters within their competence. However, the federal constitution imposes certain limits. The cantons do not have the right to make political agreements that would alter the political balance of power between the cantons. Moreover, such treaties must be compatible with federal law, federal interests, or the rights of other cantons (Häfelin et al. 2016).

Besides geographic and functional motivations, intercantonal treaties are often used to prepare regulations at the federal level. In recent years, such treaties increasingly serve to defend cantonal powers and thus to prevent federal encroachment in a given policy (e.g. the intercantonal agreement on the exclusion of tax conventions; Häfelin et al. 2016).

2.2.2 Intercantonal conferences

Historically, the Swiss cantons have a long tradition of coming together for the joint discussion and/or coordination of politically salient matters. As in other federations, such intergovernmental councils—called intercantonal conferences in Switzerland—can be differentiated according to, e.g. their purpose and the direction of action (Behnke and Mueller 2017). In terms of purpose, there is the generalist, vertically and horizontally oriented Conference of Cantonal Government (KdK). The KdK is not a real 'peak council' that directs other councils (Schnabel et al. 2022). Rather, in the dense and highly institutionalized web of Swiss intercantonal conferences, there are also sectoral, policy-specific conferences formed by the respective ministers from each canton (called 'directors' in Switzerland), e.g. in the domains of education, economy, or transports. Such sectoral, policy-specific conferences are both vertically and horizontally oriented (Schnabel and Mueller 2017; see Schnabel 2020a, b).

The KdK was founded in 1993, mostly because the cantons felt excluded from the talks and negotiations between the EU (then EC) and Switzerland. Each canton is entitled to one seat, irrespective of its population size. Resolutions of the plenary conference, adopted by a qualified majority of eighteen cantonal governments, are considered opinions of the KdK, whereby the right of the cantons to express their own, sometimes exclusive, opinions is preserved (Schnabel 2020a, b). The KdK's purpose is, e.g. to promote cooperation between the cantons and to ensure the necessary coordination and flow of information; the further development of federalism; and the formation of wills and the preparation of decisions in the Confederation. The KdK also submits statements in the aforementioned consultation procedure and often coordinates the cantonal implementation of federal policy. The KdK also plays a particularly important role in foreign and integration policy, which was reflected, for example, in its intensive involvement in the drafting of the Bilateral Agreements II with the European Union or in the negotiating mandate for the (failed) Institutional Agreement. Overall, the activities of the KdK have recently led to increased consideration of the cantons at the federal policy level. However, the individual canton(s) must put their particular interests behind them order to forge a common front as a collective of all twenty-six cantons (Schnabel 2020b, Schnabel et al. 2022). This high degree of institutionalization, which is also striking in an international comparison (Bolleyer 2009), and the direct involvement of cantonal government members are seen as success factors. This is why the KdK today is 'by all means the better Council of States' (Schnabel 2020b, own translation)—better because the KdK is more effective in safeguarding and representing territorial interests in federal policy-making than the second chamber.

The sectoral, policy-specific conferences bring together the members of the cantonal governments in charge of a given portfolio (or ministry), often also joined by the respective Federal Councillor (Vatter 2018). Sectoral, policy-specific conferences mainly serve to facilitate the exchange of information, coordination, and, eventually, joint action (e.g. by means of resolutions or an intercantonal agreement). Well-known examples include the Conference of the Cantonal Ministers of Education (EDK; 1897–), the Conference of the Cantonal Ministers of Public Health (GDK; 2019–), or the Conference of Cantonal Finance Directors (FDK; 1910–). They all operate according to formally established rules, have a permanent office (sometimes even scientific staff), and use working groups to prepare plenary sessions, while decisions are taken by a simple majority (Schnabel and Mueller 2017, 553).

Importantly, the parallelism of generalist and sectoral, policy-specific intercantonal conferences does not only exist at the national level. In contrast to most other federations, Switzerland has many regional councils that 'mirror' countrywide councils. For example, besides the national GDK, there are four regional sectoral GDKs: one in western Switzerland, one in northwestern Switzerland, one in eastern Switzerland (including the Principality of Liechtenstein), and one in central Switzerland. The four generalist regional conferences have even existed longer than the KdK.

Finally, there are also the intercantonal conferences of experts, which are organized at the various administrative levels and which are highly technocratic in nature. Overall, there are well over 500 such bodies in very diverse fields of administration, which thus form a dense network of liaison bodies between the cantonal offices.

Besides the intercantonal agreements and intercantonal conferences—i.e. the most important horizontal institutions of Swiss federalism—the cantons also run joint institutions, such as specialized colleges and prisons. These forms of intercantonal collaboration are many and diverse and allow for flexible cooperation adapted to the local context. They can also be seen as decentralized alternatives to harmonization at the federal level. However, these collaborative mechanisms have proved to be cumbersome, especially in cases of politically controversial issues. Moreover, intercantonal agreements have not been very effective in preventing federal encroachment, as the experience of recent years has shown.

3 Challenges to Swiss federalism

Federalism is still one of the core elements of Switzerland's political culture and its political system. However, more than 170 years after the creation of the Swiss federation, Swiss federalism is confronted with many challenges and appears to be in need of reform (Ladner 2018; Vatter 2018; see also 'Switzerland, *quo vadis*? Current Challenges and Potential Solutions for Swiss Politics' in this volume). For the years to come, issues such as ongoing (legislative) centralization, a potential renewal of fiscal equalization, further unravelling of the division of tasks between the federation and the cantons, closer horizontal cooperation, more effective participation of the cantons in federal decision-making, and/or waning public acceptance of federalism as a distinct form of governance will increasingly come to the fore in the debate. In fact, there are some quite basic challenges that call for a debate of principle on the meaning and purpose of federalism today. The self-evident demographic shifts between the cantons, growing interdependencies between the supranational, federal, and subnational level(s), and the increasingly frequent conflicts between the popular and cantonal majorities in constitutional votes, as well as fundamental transformations in the understanding of the notion of democracy, have aggravated the tension between the two basic political principles of democracy and federalism, and have underscored the urgent need for reform. Further problems for the future of Swiss federalism are the increasing loss of solidarity among the cantons, the replacement of this solidarity by competition (e.g. on taxes), and the role of cantonal legislatures being severely pushed back in light of 'cooperative federalism', which is, despite the reforms of enhanced parliamentary scrutiny in intergovernmental affairs (Arens 2020), still the domain of executives. More generally, and given the extent of legislative centralization (Dardanelli and Mueller 2019), the cantons are becoming increasingly limited to mere political implementation, which clearly contradicts the cantons' claims to sovereignty. Finally, the increasing importance of non-territorial minorities and the complexity of socio-economic and cultural conflicts that escape the traditional territorial logic of federal (which is: territorial) conflict resolution are putting the existing federal institutions under still greater pressure. There is also increasing tension between the growing importance of urban areas and their dismissed, marginalized role in the institutional architecture of Swiss federalism. The invigoration of federalism by adapting federalist structures to the new realities of large urban settlements and regions, as well as to ever-increasing interdependencies, and by strengthening pluralist, democratic decision-making that is more sensitive to the needs of increasingly significant non-territorial minorities will therefore constitute the fundamental, long-term challenge to Swiss federalism.

Notes

1. The federal reform was entitled '*Neugestaltung des Finanzausgleichs und der Aufgabenteilung*' (NFA) and approved by 64.4 per cent of the voters and 20.5 cantons in a mandatory referendum held in November 2004. The NFA took effect in 2008.

2. The cantons of Obwalden, Nidwalden, Basel-Stadt, Basel-Landschaft, Appenzell Ausserrhoden, and Appenzell Innerrhoden (formerly called 'half-cantons') are historical peculiarities. They each have half a cantonal vote when it comes to the double majority and they have only one instead of two MPs in the Council of States.

References

Arens, Alexander. 2020. *Federalism and Intergovernmental Relations: An Analysis of Intercantonal Cooperation and Parliamentary Participation in Subnational Switzerland*. Dissertation, Institut für Politikwissenschaft, Universität Bern.

Arnold, Tobias. 2020. 'Reforming Autonomy? The Fiscal Impact of the Swiss Federal Reform'. *Regional & Federal Studies* 30 (5): pp. 651–674. doi: https://doi.org/10.1080/13597566.2019.1630612.

Arnold, Tobias, Alexander Arens, Sean Mueller, and Adrian Vatter. 2019. 'Schweizer Föderalismus im Wandel: Die versteckten politischen Effekte der NFA'. In *Jahrbuch des Föderalismus 2019, Föderalismus, Subsidiarität und Regionen in Europa*, edited by Europäisches Zentrum für Föderalismus-Forschung Tübingen EZFF, pp. 165–174. Baden-Baden: Nomos.

Balthasar, Andreas. 2003. 'Die Prämienverbilligung im Krankenversicherungsgesetz: Vollzugsföderalismus und sekundäre Harmonisierung'. *Swiss Political Science Review* 9 (1): pp. 335–353. doi: https://doi.org/10.1002/j.1662-6370.2003.tb00410.x.

Behnke, Nathalie, and Sean Mueller. 2017. 'The Purpose of Intergovernmental Councils: A Framework for Analysis and Comparison'. *Regional & Federal Studies* 27 (5): pp. 507–527. doi: https://doi.org/10.1080/13597566.2017.1367668.

Bochsler, Daniel. 2009. 'Neighbours or Friends? When Swiss Cantonal Governments Cooperate with Each Other'. *Regional & Federal Studies* 19 (2): pp. 349–370. doi: https://doi.org/10.1080/13597560902957476.

Bolleyer, Nicole. 2009. *Intergovernmental Cooperation: Rational Choices in Federal Systems and Beyond*. Oxford: Oxford University Press.

Bussmann, Werner. 1986. *Mythos und Wirklichkeit der Zusammenarbeit im Bundesstaat. Patent oder Sackgasse?* Bern/Stuttgart: Haupt.

Church, Clive H., and Randolph Head C. 2013. *A Concise History of Switzerland*. Cambridge: Cambridge University Press.

Dardanelli, Paolo, and Sean Mueller. 2019. 'Dynamic De/Centralisation in Switzerland, 1848–2010'. *Publius: The Journal of Federalism* 49 (1): pp. 138–65. doi: https://doi.org/10.1093/publius/pjx056.

Elazar, Daniel J. 1987. *Exploring Federalism*. Tuscaloosa, AL: The University of Alabama Press.

Fischer, Alex. 2006. 'Das Kantonsreferendum: Wirkungsweise und Reformansätze'. In *Föderalismusreform. Wirkungsweise und Reformansätze föderativer Institutionen in der Schweiz*, edited by Adrian Vatter, pp. 132–151. Zürich: NZZ Verlag.

Freiburghaus, Rahel. 2024. *Lobbyierende Kantone? Subnationale Interessenvertretung in der Schweiz*. Baden-Baden: Nomos.

Freiburghaus, Rahel, Sean Mueller, and Adrian Vatter. 2021a. 'Overnight Centralisation in One of the World's Most Federal Countries'. In *Federalism and the Response to COVID-19. A Comparative Analysis*, edited by Rupak Chattopadhyay, Felix Knüpling, Diana Chebenova, Liam Whittington, and Phillip Gonzalez, pp. 217–228. London/New York: Routledge.

Freiburghaus, Rahel, Alexander Arens, and Sean Mueller. 2021b. 'With or Without their Region? Multiple-Mandate Holders in the Swiss Parliament, 1985–2018'. *Local Government Studies* 47 (6): pp. 971–992. doi: https://doi.org/10.1080/03003930.2020.1832891.

Häfelin, Ulrich, Walter Haller, Helen Keller, and Daniela Thurnherr. 2016. *Schweizerisches Bundesstaatsrecht. Ein Grundriss*, 8th ed. Zürich /Basel/Geneva: Schulthess.

Hooghe, Liesbet, Gary Marks, Arjan H. Schakel, Sandra Chapman-Osterkatz, Sara Niedzwiecki, and Sarah Shair-Rosenfield. 2016. *Measuring Regional Authority*. Oxford: Oxford University Press.

Ladner, Andreas. 2018. *Der Schweizer Föderalismus im Wandel. Überlegungen und empirische Befunde zur territorialen Gliederung und der Organisation der staatlichen Aufgabenerbringung in der Schweiz*. Lausanne: IDHEAP.

Linder, Wolf, and Adrian Vatter. 2001. 'Institutions and Outcomes of Swiss Federalism: The Role of the Cantons in Swiss Politics'. *West European Politics* 24 (2): pp. 95–122. doi: https://doi.org/10.1080/01402380108425435.

Linder, Wolf, and Sean Mueller. 2017. *Schweizerische Demokratie. Institutionen, Prozesse und Perspektiven*. 4th ed. Bern/Stuttgart: Haupt.

Linder, Wolf, and Sean Mueller. 2021. *Swiss Democracy. Possible Solutions to Conflict in Multicultural Societies*. Houndsmills: Palgrave.

Mathys, Laetitia. 2016. *Les conventions-programmes: Un nouvel outil pour la collaboration verticale en Suisse*. Lausanne: IDHEAP.

Mueller, Sean, and Oscar Mazzoleni. 2016. 'Regionalist Protest through Shared Rule? Peripherality and the Use of Cantonal Initiatives in Switzerland'. *Regional and Federal Studies* 26 (1): pp. 45–71. doi: https://doi.org/10.1080/13597566.2015.1135134.

Mueller, Sean, and Adrian Vatter (eds). 2020. *Der Ständerat: Die Zweite Kammer der Schweiz*. Basel: NZZ Libro.

Mueller, Sean, Adrian Vatter, and Charlie Schmid. 2017. 'Self-Interest vs. Solidarity? The Referendum on Fiscal Equalisation in Switzerland'. *Statistics, Politics, and Policy* 7 (1/2): pp. 3–28. doi: https://doi.org/10.1515/spp-2016-0003.

Mueller, Sean, Sereina Dick, and Rahel Freiburghaus. 2020. 'Ständerat, stärkerer Rat? Die Gesetzgebungsmacht der Zweiten Kammer im Vergleich zu National- und Ständerat'. In *Der Ständerat. Die Zweite Kammer der Schweiz*, edited by Sean Mueller, and Adrian Vatter, pp. 119–145. Basel: NZZ Libro.

Neuenschwander, Peter. 2006. 'Die Standesinitiative: Wirkungsweise und Reformansätze'. In *Föderalismusreform. Wirkungsweise und Reformansätze föderativer Institutionen in der Schweiz*, edited by Adrian Vatter, pp. 99–131. Zürich: NZZ Verlag.

Pfisterer, Thomas. 2015. 'Intergovernmental Relations in Switzerland: An Unfamiliar Term for a Necessary Concept'. In *Intergovernmental Relations in Federal Systems. Comparative Structure and Dynamics*, edited by Johanne Poirier, Cheryl Saunders, and John Kincaid, pp. 379–419. Don Mills: Oxford University Press.

Sager, Fritz. 2003. 'Kompensationsmöglichkeiten föderaler Vollzugsdefizite. Das Beispiel der kantonalen Alkoholpräventionspolitiken'. *Swiss Political Science Review* 9 (1): pp. 309–332. doi: https://doi.org/10.1002/j.1662-6370.2003.tb00409.x.

Sager, Fritz, and Rüefli, Christian. 2005. 'Die Evaluation öffentlicher Politiken mit föderalistischen Vollzugsarrangements'. *Swiss Political Science Review* 11 (2): pp. 101–129. doi: https://doi.org/10.1002/j.1662-6370.2005.tb00357.x.

Sager, Fritz, and Isabelle Steffen. 2006. 'Die Kantone im Vernehmlassungsverfahren des Bundes: Wirkungsweise und Reformansätze'. In *Föderalismusreform. Wirkungsweise und Reformansätze föderativer Institutionen in der Schweiz*, edited by Adrian Vatter, pp. 132–152. Zürich: NZZ Verlag.

Sager, Fritz, Christian Rüefli, and Eva Thomann. 2019. 'Fixing Federal Faults. Complementary Member State Policies in Swiss Health Care Policy'. *International Review of Public Policy* 1 (2): pp. 147–172. doi: https://doi.org/10.4000/irpp.426.

Schnabel, Johanna. 2020a. *Managing Interdependencies in Federal Systems. Intergovernmental Councils and the Making of Public Policy*. Houndsmills: Palgrave Macmillan.

Schnabel, Johanna. 2020b. 'Die Konferenz der Kantonsregierungen als der bessere Ständerat? Territoriale Mitbestimmung im schweizerischen Föderalismus'. In *Der Ständerat. Zweite Kammer der Schweiz*, edited by Sean Mueller and Adrian Vatter, pp. 181–202. Basel: NZZ Libro.

Schnabel, Johanna, and Sean Mueller. 2017. 'Vertical Influence or Horizontal Coordination? The Purpose of Intergovernmental Councils in Switzerland'. *Regional & Federal Studies* 27 (5): pp. 549–572. doi: https://doi.org/10.1080/13597566.2017.1368017.

Schnabel, Johanna, Rahel Freiburghaus, and Yvonne Hegele. 2022. 'Crisis Management in Federal States: The Role of Peak Intergovernmental Councils in Germany and Switzerland During the COVID-19 Pandemic'. *DMS – Der Moderne Staat* 15 (1): pp. 42–61. doi: https://doi.org/10.3224/dms.v15i1.10.

Sciarini, Pascal, Manuel Fischer, and Denise Traber. 2015. *Political Decision-Making in Switzerland. The Consensus Model under Pressure*. Houndsmills: Palgrave.

Swissvotes. 2022. *Dataset*. https://www.swissvotes.ch/page/dataset (accessed 2 September 2022).

Vatter, Adrian. 2005. 'The Transformation of Access and Veto Points in Swiss Federalism'. *Regional and Federal Studies* 15 (1): pp. 1–18. doi: https://doi.org/10.1080/13597560500083758.

Vatter, Adrian (ed.). 2006. *Föderalismusreform. Wirkungsweise und Reformansätze föderativer Institutionen in der Schweiz*. Zürich: NZZ Verlag.

Vatter, Adrian. 2018. *Swiss Federalism. The Transformation of a Federal Model*. London/ New York: Routledge.

Vatter, Adrian. 2020. *Das politische System der Schweiz*, 4th ed. Baden-Baden: Nomos.

Vatter, Adrian, and Fritz Sager. 1996. 'Föderalismusreform am Beispiel des Ständemehrs'. *Schweizerische Zeitschrift für politische Wissenschaft* 2 (2): pp. 165–200. doi: https://doi.org/10.1002/j.1662-6370.1996.tb00179.x.

Vatter, Adrian, and Sonja Wälti (eds). 2003. 'Schweizer Föderalismus in vergleichender Perspektive', *Swiss Political Science Review* Sonderheft, 1 (9): pp. 1–25.

Vatter, Adrian, Rahel Freiburghaus, and Alexander Arens. 2020. 'Coming a Long Way: Switzerland's Transformation from a Majoritarian to a Consensus Democracy (1848–2018)'. *Democratisation* 27 (6): pp. 970–989. doi: https://doi.org/10.1080/13510 347.2020.1755264.

Vatter, Adrian, Rahel Freiburghaus, and Ladina Triaca. 2017. 'Deutsches Bundesrats- vs. Schweizer Senatsmodell im Lichte sich wandelnder Parteiensysteme: Repräsentation und Legitimität Zweiter Kammern im Vergleich'. *Zeitschrift für Parlamentsfragen* 48 (4): pp. 741–763. doi: https://doi.org/10.5771/0340-1758-2017-4-741.

Wasserfallen, Fabio. 2015. 'The Cooperative Capacity of Swiss Federalism'. *Swiss Political Science Review* 21 (4): pp. 538–555. doi: https://doi.org/10.1111/spsr.12187.

Watts, Ronald L. 2008. *Comparing Federal Systems*, 2nd ed. Montréal: McGill-Queen's University Press.

Wili, Hans-Urs. 1988. *Kollektive Mitwirkungsrechte von Gliedstaaten in der Schweiz und im Ausland: Geschichtlicher Werdegang, Rechtsvergleichung, Zukunftsperspektiven. Eine institutsbezogene Studie*. Bern: Stämpfli.

CHAPTER 9

DIRECT DEMOCRACY

ISABELLE STADELMANN-STEFFEN AND
LUCAS LEEMANN

1 A REPRESENTATIVE SYSTEM WITH DIRECT-DEMOCRATIC INSTITUTIONS

THE idea of enriching representative systems with direct-democratic elements is part of the 1793 Girondiste constitutional proposal during the French Revolution.[1] Thomas Paine (1736/37–1809) and the Marquis of Condorcet (1743–1794) were two prominent members of the committee that drafted the proposal. The latter sought to break pure representation by granting citizens the opportunity to decide directly on (some) policy questions (Kölz 1992, 79). France eventually adopted a different constitution but it did not take long before this idea was included in the constitution of a larger representative system. In 1831, the constitutional convention of the canton of St Gallen adopted the veto right, which was a very weak form of the optional referendum. Subsequently, during the nineteenth century, all purely representative Swiss cantons adopted direct-democratic institutions (Leemann 2022). Nowadays, the extensive direct-democratic rights are one of the defining features of Swiss politics at both the national and the subnational level.

Switzerland is an outlier in international comparisons and allows citizens to vote by far the most on substantive issues (Altman 2019). Nevertheless, we cannot speak of a pure popular rule, as Rousseau conceived of direct democracy. Rather, direct-democratic institutions complement the inherently representative political system: while the people, thus, play an important (direct or indirect) role in most political decisions, parliament and government also play a central role. Over time, the system has evolved in a way that allows the three main decision-making bodies to work together in a differentiated manner (Linder and Wirz 2014): The electorate has the right to participate in all major decisions, especially those concerning the federal constitution. Parliament essentially decides on laws, the second most important decisions. In many cases, these representatives make final decisions, unless the people demand co-determination through a referendum. Finally, the government is responsible for other decisions, such as decrees, which are, at least formally, of the least material importance and are not subject to direct democracy. In principle, therefore, the electorate decides on the most important issues, parliament on the important ones, and the executive on the less important ones (Linder and Mueller 2017; Linder and Wirz 2014).[2]

2 Direct-democratic institutions

A large variety of different direct-democratic institutions exists around the world, and their exact design differs across contexts. From a comparative perspective, however, these different direct-democratic instruments can be classified into four categories (e.g. Hug 2004; Altman 2017; Morel 2018): (i) parliamentary decisions on which citizens can vote by constitution (mandatory referendums), (ii) parliamentary decisions that people can vote on only if enough signatures are collected (facultative referendums),[3] (iii) proposals that are submitted directly by the electorate (popular initiatives),[4] and (iv) proposals that the government submits directly to the electorate (plebiscites).[5] According to Hug (2004), the classification of the different instruments is based on two criteria. The first criterion concerns whether the vote is actively initiated, for example by collecting enough signatures, or automatically prescribed by the constitution. This criterion differentiates the facultative referendum and the popular initiative from the mandatory referendum. The second criterion refers to whether the vote concerns a law that has already been passed in parliament or a new proposal. This criterion distinguishes the mandatory and facultative referendums from the popular initiative, which enables citizens and organizations to propose a constitutional change.

The right of recall is a special case. If enough signatures are collected, this instrument can be used to force a vote on the continuation of an elected office holder. If a majority votes against the office holder remaining in office, their term ends early and a replacement election must take place. The right of recall often is not considered a direct-democratic institution in the strict sense, since the vote is not about substantive policy, but elected representatives. For Kölz (1996), however, the right of recall also demonstrates that representative and direct democracy cannot be separated easily.

In Switzerland, direct-democratic institutions exist at the national, the cantonal, and the local levels. In the following section, we mostly focus on the national level but we also delve into existing cantonal differences when we discuss the historic adoption of these institutions in section 3.

2.1 Direct-democratic institutions at the national level

In Switzerland, the mandatory referendum, the facultative referendum, and the popular initiative to request an amendment to the federal constitution all take place at the national level. Conversely, there is no plebiscite and no right of recall for national office holders.[6] In the following, we describe these three most common instruments of direct democracy, but do not elaborate on special cases, such as the resolutive referendum for urgent federal decisions or urgent decisions without sufficient constitutional basis (Linder and Wirz 2014). For a discussion of direct-democratic rights at the cantonal level, see 'The Cantons' in this volume.

2.1.1 *Mandatory referendums*

Whenever the Swiss parliament decides to amend the federal constitution, a ballot vote is held to confirm or reject this decision. The same procedure applies to decisions regarding Switzerland's accession to organizations for collective security or to supranational communities. Thus, such deviations from the status quo only come into force after they have also been approved by a 'majority of those who vote and a majority of the cantons' (art. 142 para. 2). This so-called double majority, i.e. where both the population and a majority of the constituent units need to agree, is required because these changes are considered particularly important—and territorial minorities should have a say thereon.

As far as the required majority of the cantons is concerned, each canton has one vote, while those formerly called 'half-cantons'—Ob- and Nidwalden, Appenzell Innerrhoden and Ausserrhoden, Basel Stadt, and Land—only have half a vote each. Since the votes of the cantons are independent of the cantons' size, less populous cantons receive a greater weight. This rule is a relic of the history of the Swiss federation, which was constituted in 1848 in the aftermath of a short civil war (cf. Vatter 2020). Originally, this double majority served to protect the Catholic-conservative opposition from the liberal majority. However, Bochsler (2013) relies on cantonal elections to show that this decision rule has increasingly been used a veto instrument of the nationalist conservatives. This pattern is best observed on issues that run along the cleavage between 'social liberals' and conservatives who advocate for traditional values.

The mandatory referendum is the oldest direct-democratic instrument in post-1848 Switzerland. The first mandatory referendums took place as early as 1866, and up until World War II, there was on average less than one such ballot decision per year (see Figure 9.1).[7] In the post-war period, the number of mandatory referendums has increased significantly. However, this upward trend goes hand in hand with a similarly increasing number of federal decisions subject to referendum, which can be understood as a quantitative measure of legislative activity.

2.1.2 *Optional referendums*

When the parliament passes federal acts, issues federal decrees (provided that the federal constitution or an act so requires), or ratifies international treaties of unlimited duration, these decisions are subject to an optional referendum. A referendum is held if 50,000 signatures are collected within 100 days of the enactment's official publication.[8]

If a referendum vote is held, the proposal requires the approval of a simple majority of those voting in order to eventually get introduced. Neidhart (1970) describes the optional legislative referendum as a 'sword of Damocles' hanging over Swiss policy-making (cf. section 2.2, where we discuss the referendum's direct and indirect effects in more detail).

In Figure 9.1, we see that the optional referendum experienced a first boom towards the end of the nineteenth century, just before the Catholic Conservatives were conceded one seat in the national government (see Swissvotes 2022 and Bolliger and Zürcher 2004, for the articulation of this claim). Its use surged again after World War II, peaking in the 1990s during a period of intense partisan conflict and competition (Leemann 2015).

2.1.3 *Popular initiative*

The popular initiative allows 100,000 citizens to demand a partial or a complete revision of the federal constitution. If the necessary signatures are collected within eighteen months, the popular initiative is put to a popular vote. Like in the case of the mandatory referendum, constitutional amendments in tune with the initiators' demands require a double majority, i.e. a majority of voters as well as a majority of the cantons. Both the federal parliament and the Federal Council discuss the proposal and usually issue a negative voting recommendation.[9] The parliament also has the option to issue a counter-proposal in response to the concerns raised by the popular initiative. This allows the parliamentary majority to offer a more moderate version if it considers the topic relevant and/or if it fears that the initiative will be adopted.

The popular initiative differs from the other direct-democratic instruments in that it enables social actors to directly make a 'bottom-up' proposal and not merely react to parliamentary proposals, like in the case of optional referendums. Hence, the popular initiative embodies Altman's (2019) 'citizen-initiated mechanism of direct democracy'. In this vein, the initiative can serve to introduce a new or neglected issue into the political discourse. It is evident that the use of the initiative often increases during periods of larger changes in parties' vote shares and when party competition intensifies (Leemann 2015). Figure 9.1 depicts the use of the popular initiative since 1893.

2.1.4 *Development of the use of direct-democratic instruments*

Each year, Swiss voters decide on a wide variety of substantive issues at the federal level on three to four dates.[10] Table 9.1 provides an overview of the number of referendums and popular initiatives between 1848 and 2021.

Over the past twenty years, the Swiss electorate has decided on an average of about one mandatory referendum, three optional referendums, and almost five popular initiatives per year. The use of direct democracy has increased significantly over time (Figure 9.1). The grey area in Figure 9.1 depicts the number of federal decisions that could potentially be subject to a referendum. It enables us to put the use of popular rights in relation to the general legislative activity of the parliament. We can thus see that

Table 9.1: Referendums and popular initiatives, 1848–2021

Mandatory referendums	
Put to the vote	224[a]
Accepted by the people and cantons	168[a]
Rejected	56[a]

Popular initiatives	
Launched	491
At the signature stage	10[b]
Signature collection not successful	133[b]
Signature collection successful	347[b]
Withdrawn	104[b]
Invalidated, depreciated	6[b]
Pending before parliament	4[b]
Put to the vote	226[a]
Accepted by the people and cantons	24[a]
Rejected	202[a]
Parliament's counterproposals	16[a]
Accepted by the people and cantons	6[a]
Declined	10[a]

Optional referendums	
Parliamentary resolutions subject to an optional referendum	3,174[b]
Number of referendums taken	238[b]
Signature collection successful	203[b]
Rejected	84[a/c]
Accepted	116[a/c]

Note: As of 31.12.2021.
Data source: Federal Statistical Office (2022) ([a]), Federal Chancellery (2022) ([b]), Swissvotes (2022) ([c])

the popular initiative was used with increasing frequency in the 1970s and 1980s, as well as after 2000. Both periods are characterized by substantial social and political conflicts, and a high number of initiatives pertain to the cultural dimension (e.g. issues related to immigration and the environment). Likewise, the chart shows that the greater use of optional referendums, especially from the 1980s onwards, was accompanied by equally intensive overall legislative output.

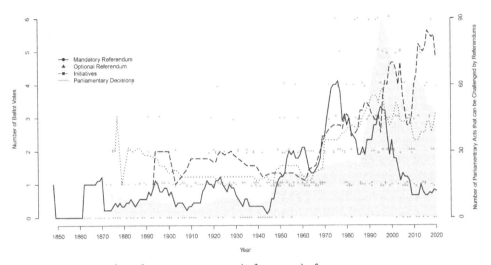

FIGURE 9.1: Lines show the moving averages (± four years) of votes per year

Data source: Swissvotes (2022).

2.2 Direct and indirect effects of direct-democratic instruments

Originally conceived as an instrument of control and opposition (see section 2), today direct democracy makes up a central element of Switzerland's consociational democracy. It constitutes the basis of a power-sharing system that shapes both the pre-parliamentary and parliamentary phases of policy-making and the federal implementation of national policies in important ways (Vatter et al. 2019). As a result, and as the following paragraphs explain in greater detail, not only does direct democracy directly impact Switzerland's policy-making (i.e. through specific decisions), but it also generates indirect effects.

2.2.1 Direct effects of direct democracy

Various studies suggest that direct-democratic decision-making makes a difference in terms of content: i.e. that the strong involvement of the voting population leads to different policy outcomes than we would expect to see in a purely representative system. In particular, direct democracy's influence on public policy has been studied quite extensively. The findings, which are often based on cantonal comparisons, suggest that the impact of direct democracy is context-specific and varies depending on which direct-democratic instrument is used. For example, various studies show that (financial) referendums have an inhibiting effect on government spending (Emmenegger et al. 2022; Freitag et al. 2003) as well as on public debt (Feld and Kirchgässner 2001). Conversely, popular initiatives have the potential to stimulate government spending because minority groups can also put their spending preferences on the political agenda.

This mechanism is activated mainly when the governing coalition is small (Emmenegger et al. 2022). In the same vein, Emmenegger et al. (2021) document that direct democracy was decisive for the introduction of direct taxes in the cantons, which, in turn, formed the basis for state investments in infrastructure and education.

Theoretically, these direct effects on policy outcomes are explained by the fact that direct democracy brings policy outcomes closer to citizens' preferences, i.e. it increases the congruence between policy design and popular ideas (Frey and Stutzer 2000; Leemann and Wasserfallen 2016). Indeed, Leemann and Wasserfallen (2016) show that the effect of direct democracy on congruence is particularly strong when the political elite and the voting population disagree. Such situations are most common on issues that do not play a major role in elections. This once again emphasizes the controlling and corrective potential of direct-democratic instruments.

Finally, it is worth mentioning that the consensual orientation of Swiss democracy, which is mainly embodied in the referendum (Neidhart 1970), is in tension with the fact that referendums basically follow a majoritarian logic. In other words, while Switzerland's direct democracy requires and encourages compromise and cooperation at the elite level, referendums make conflicts particularly visible and tangible at the citizen level. In principle, a narrow majority can make decisions that affect the defeated minority in an immediate and negative way.[11] In this respect, the cross-cutting nature of the classic political cleavages in Switzerland is seen as a favourable condition (Linder and Mueller 2017). This means that, for example, language regions and religious affiliations do not coincide and, accordingly, linguistic and religious minorities do not overlap. More generally, Switzerland's multidimensional cleavage space and frequent direct-democratic decisions mean that rather than constantly winning or losing out, most political groups will win some ballot votes and lose others (see Kern et al. 2021).

Nevertheless, this pattern does not necessarily hold for all social groups. Indeed, the potential for a 'tyranny of the majority' (Vatter and Danaci 2010) seems to be especially relevant to the particularly sensitive field of minority rights and more specifically the rights of out-groups. In this vein, Hainmueller and Hangartner (2019) demonstrate that naturalization decisions differ systematically, contingent on whether a commission decides on naturalization applications or municipal citizens can make these decisions at the ballot box—a practice that some municipalities used until 2003.

2.2.2 *Indirect effects of direct democracy*

It is often argued that direct democracy shapes the Swiss-style system of government and influences political processes through indirect effects that are just as important as its direct effects. The existence of the (optional) referendum makes it possible for a parliamentary minority to have an undesirable decision examined by the population. This 'threat of referendum' generates the incentives for, and even forces, parliamentary majorities to search for compromises in order to avoid a referendum and, thus, political inertia. The aforementioned consensus effect also explains why the optional referendum has been a very effective opposition tool even when it is not actually used (Neidhart 1970).

While in the first years after its introduction, in 1874, the referendum helped the Catholic Conservatives to block the liberal parliamentary majority (and thus to press for their political inclusion), the instrument's blocking effect was later reduced by the systemic inclusion of all stakeholders who are, in principle, able to call for a referendum (Linder and Wirz 2014). To this day, the referendum still forces political actors in Switzerland to foster consensus and, thus, solutions with majority support. Recent examples are the failed 2017 pension provision reform and the rejected revision of the CO_2 Act in 2021, which convincingly illustrate that major reform projects in particular may not pass the direct-democratic hurdle if they are only supported by narrow parliamentary majorities. In this sense, referendums' general tendency to complicate—or at least delay—state reforms and, hence, to overprotect the status quo (Kirchgässner 2008; Obinger 1998) are two main criticisms levelled against direct-democratic instruments. At the same time, however, Table 9.1 shows that in the vast majority of cases, the parliament succeeds in passing proposals that are widely accepted by all parliamentary actors and are not challenged by referendums.

In principle, direct democracy weakens the relevance of representative institutions, processes, and actors (Freitag and Stadelmann-Steffen 2010; Linder and Mueller 2017). The more often the people decide directly at the ballot box, the less relevant elections and elected representatives are. This trade-off between electoral and direct democracy is highlighted as one of the reasons why Switzerland has an exceptionally low voter turnout in comparison to other countries (Blais 2014; Freitag and Stadelmann-Steffen 2010).

However, direct-democratic instruments also offer some actors, especially political parties, additional (campaigning) opportunities to put their own issues on the political agenda or to use referendums and initiatives to mobilize their electorates. Leemann (2015) demonstrates that political parties' use of the initiative has increased since the twentieth century. Research on more recent years comes to a very similar conclusion (Braun Binder et al. 2020). Ladner and Brändle (1999) also use a comparison of cantonal parties to show that expanded direct democracy is accompanied by more professional and formalized party organizations. Fatke's (2014) findings thereby imply that direct democracy may not only offer parties campaigning opportunities but may also increase their need to make use of such opportunities, as direct democracy reduces the relevance of parties' representative function and therewith individual party identification.

3 THE HISTORICAL DEVELOPMENT OF DIRECT DEMOCRACY

Historically, the constitutional referendum is the oldest form of popular participation. Such a vote took place in the Helvetic Republic (1798–1803) as early as 1802 and the federal constitution of 1848 was adopted in a mandatory referendum (although the latter can hardly be compared to today's votes). The first compulsory referendums took place in 1866 and, in principle, all Swiss males could participate in them. The complete revision of the federal constitution in 1874 decreed the optional right of referendum, and the right of popular initiative to request a partial revision of the federal constitution was added in 1891.

Today, it is hard to imagine Switzerland without direct democracy, but direct democracy only developed to the important institutional element it is today during the nineteenth century. Thus, a closer look at what happened in the nineteenth century, especially at the cantonal level, allows us to understand how and why these institutions were originally introduced and developed. The Helvetic Republic collapsed in 1803 and Napoleon Bonaparte (1769–1821) wrote a constitution for all twenty-one cantons that existed at that time as part of the Act of Mediation (de Capitani 2006).[12] The six Landsgemeinde cantons got the Landsgemeinde back, while all other cantons were given purely representative constitutions (Kölz 1992). Consequently, over 90 per cent of the Swiss population lived in cantons with purely representative constitutions (de Capitani 2006, 519) and this only changed slowly. Older historiography tends to describe this process as quasi-natural and continuous (e.g. Blickle 2000). More recent historical and political science research instead emphasizes the disruptive nature of, and the role of conflict in, this development, as these political institutions distributed power differently for the foreseeable future (Suter 2012; Graber 2017).

The individual cantonal constitutions differ in how easy they made the use of these instruments (i.e. the number of required signatures and the period during which they were to be collected). Figure 9.2 shows the 'historical direct democracy index', meant to visualize these differences in the extent of direct democracy across cantons and over time. Two insights can be gained. First, direct democracy changed most dramatically in the nineteenth century and changes only resumed at the end of the twentieth century. Second, referendum and initiative rights were either introduced at the same time or referendum rights were incorporated into constitutions first (Schwyz and Vaud are two exceptions).

Why did this development occur and why were direct-democratic instruments increasingly expanded in the nineteenth century? Here, Leemann (2022) argues that the impetus came from smaller parties that were disadvantaged in a system of majority voting. Since proportional representation had not been introduced at that time, the only option left for these disadvantaged groups was to demand more direct participation. They did so in the hopes that political decisions would be taken in favour of the voters rather than in favour of the elected representatives. Therefore, this explanation identifies these parties (which, at the time, looked like very loose alliances) as the driving force behind the development of direct democracy. Contrary to this account, Gruner (1964, 208) argued that the presence of direct-democratic institutions stimulated the creation of political parties and coined the phrase 'Swiss parties are the children of Swiss direct democratic rights'.

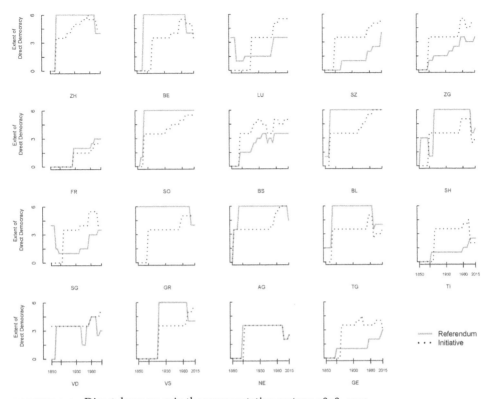

FIGURE 9.2: Direct democracy in the representative cantons, 1848–2015

Data source: Leemann (2022).

4 SWITZERLAND FROM AN INTERNATIONAL PERSPECTIVE

This section eventually examines Switzerland and its direct-democratic institutions from an international perspective. It is worth mentioning that comparing Switzerland to other countries comes with several challenges. First, the variation in direct-democratic rights across countries makes the Swiss case an outlier in terms of both the availability and the use of direct-democratic rights (Altmann 2011, 2019). Second, the Swiss case is also rather peculiar with respect to how direct-democratic instruments are institutionally embedded into the political process. Initiatives and referendums form an integral part of the standard policy-making process and of its strong consensual orientation. This set-up differs fundamentally from, for example, the US context, where direct-democratic rights have not led to power-sharing, but actually offer a way to 'get around' the legislature, or—as discussed in more detail below—from referendums in the context of European integration (Heidbreder et al. 2019; Leemann and Stadelmann-Steffen 2022). Third, partly due to data issues, research on direct democracy often becomes subnational research for countries in which direct democracy is extensively developed (i.e. Switzerland and the US), and/or is based on single country studies (at the national or subnational level; see Leemann and Stadelmann-Steffen 2022). This tendency has hampered comparative research and, thus, limits our understanding of how direct-democratic institutions interact with other elements of representative democracy (Hug 2009).

Against this background, we assume two different comparative perspectives in this section. We first look at direct-democratic institutions at the national level and concentrate on their institutional embeddedness in Switzerland compared to other countries. We then compare direct-democratic institutions at the national and the subnational levels in Switzerland and three other countries with relatively extended direct-democratic rights (Austria, Germany, and the US).

4.1 Switzerland in international perspective

From an international perspective, Switzerland is often considered 'the world champion of direct democracy' (Altman 2008b). While the discussion above showed that despite its strong reliance on direct democracy, the Swiss political system still has representative democracy at its core, this section specifically compares the Swiss system with what direct democracy looks like and how it functions in other countries. In fact, national government decisions in a number of countries are more or less regularly confirmed or rejected at the ballot box. It is striking that, in addition to Switzerland, Lichtenstein, and Italy, direct-democratic rights are quite widespread, especially in Central and Eastern Europe. Moreover, direct-democratic institutions can also be found in some countries in South America. However, their origins and the way direct democracy influences each country's representative system are different (Ruth-Lovell et al. 2017). We discuss such context-specific aspects of direct democracy in more detail below.

The use of direct-democratic instruments has increased sharply in recent decades, both in Switzerland and worldwide alike (Altman 2011). This is not least due to the fact that direct democracy is repeatedly seen as an instrument meant to counteract legitimacy deficits or even democratic deficits (Leininger 2015). In this context, Switzerland is often viewed as a 'living proof' of the fact that direct democracy 'works'. Nevertheless, recent practical examples, above all the Brexit referendum, have raised doubts about its efficacy and given new impetus to old criticism of direct democracy (Vatter et al. 2019, 170). This apparent inconsistency can be explained with the aforementioned highly context-dependent impact of direct democracy (Heidbreder et al. 2019). Most EU referendums are not embedded in the institutionalized processes of national representative systems, but constitute exceptional moments in which citizens assume the decision-making role. In this context, referendums do not exert consensual pressures, but rather tend to further deepen ideological divides. However, by comparing Uruguay and Switzerland, Altman (2008a) shows that different consequences are possible even in the presence of similar institutional structures. This finding emphasizes the relevance of non-institutional contextual aspects and highlights the need to investigate how direct-democratic instruments interact with representative institutions (Hug 2009).

4.2 Subnational direct democracy in international comparison

Subnational units with direct democracy can also be found in other federal systems. In a recent project, Stadelmann-Steffen and Leemann (2022) measured and compared the extent of direct democracy in subnational units in Austria, Germany, Switzerland, and the United States based on a comprehensive 'Subnational Index of Direct Democracy' (snDDI).

Figure 9.3 shows the extent of direct democracy in the subnational units of these four countries. Three descriptive findings stand out. First, the average extent of direct democracy is greatest in the Swiss cantons. Second, in comparison with the rest of the studied countries, Germany and Austria only have very limited forms of subnational direct democracy. And third, subnational entities with direct democracy that is equally or even more pronounced than that of the Swiss cantons do exist. The US states of Arizona, Colorado, Michigan, and California score higher on the subnational direct democracy index than all Swiss cantons—except for the canton of Glarus, one of the two remaining Landsgemeinde cantons.

FIGURE 9.3: Subnational Index of Direct Democracy (snDDI) according to Leemann and Stadelmann-Steffen (2022)

5 Concluding remarks

The distinctive direct-democratic instruments significantly, and also famously, characterize Swiss democracy and make it look like a 'different' democracy compared to purely representative democracies. This is not only because eligible voters decide directly on substantive proposals or even shape such proposals, but also because the direct-democratic institutions in Switzerland exhibit indirect effects on the representative system and the policy-making process. However, what these effects specifically look like largely depends on the actual instrument at hand. Thus, for example, it would be too simplistic to attribute an exclusively inhibiting effect on change and the status quo to direct democracy. On the one hand, the national popular initiative and the legislative initiative, which takes place at the cantonal level, are instruments that put new or neglected issues on the political agenda. On the other hand, history largely shows that direct democracy does have the potential to produce major changes in certain political situations and under certain circumstances. The last point once again illustrates the context dependence of direct-democratic effects and processes. This is especially important when we compare the Swiss semi-direct democracy to direct-democratic instruments and decisions elsewhere.

A look at the last 150 years makes it clear that direct democracy in Switzerland only became what it is today over time. More recently, it has proven to be much more stable than one might expect it to be against the backdrop of societal megatrends such as globalization, demographic and societal evolutions, or digitalization. Just like scientific and political debates, current developments reflect tensions that have arisen as a result of these trends. One example is the handling of popular initiatives that are problematic in terms of fundamental rights and, related to this, the (in-)compatibility between popular initiatives and supranational law, especially the bilateral agreements between Switzerland and the EU (Leupold and Besson 2011). Such incompatible popular initiatives have grown in number in recent years, as the well-known examples of the so-called minaret initiative (2009), the 'deportation initiative' (2010), the popular initiative against 'mass immigration' adopted in 2014, and the 'burka ban' (2021) illustrate. The reasons for this growth are at least twofold: first, there are hardly any legal limits on a popular initiative's domain; second, the signature hurdle has in fact constantly decreased given Switzerland's steady population growth (Leemann 2015), while polarization has increased (Dostal and Champod 2015). Experts on constitutional law have proposed reforming the legal principles of popular initiatives by changing the formal preliminary examination, the procedure of the admissibility check, or the substantive limit of initiatives (Möckli 2018), but the high majority requirement through the double majority makes such reforms politically difficult. In the past, these tensions were resolved through a 'harmonizing interpretation' (Epiney 2016), i.e. by failing to implement the respective popular decisions or by only implementing a toned-down version.

Digitalization represents a second example of a changing context that foments the political and scientific debate on the future development of direct democracy (see also 'Switzerland, *quo vadis*? Current Challenges and Potential Solutions for Swiss Politics' in this volume). Current developments in the field of digitalization may not change the basic features of direct-democratic institutions, but may further alter the processes associated with them. On the one hand, this affects the process of opinion formation: the role of social media, the danger of selective information, and the so-called echo chambers are intensively discussed and studied in this realm (Taber and Lodge 2006; but see also Guess et al. 2018 on echo chambers in general). On the other hand, these changes increasingly affect the way direct-democratic instruments are launched. For example, Milic et al. (2019) defined the 2018 referendum on the legal basis for monitoring insured persons as the first 'internet referendum' because four people managed to practically single-handedly gather enough people and signatures by using online tools. The next step—actual digital signature collection (e-collecting)—is not currently possible at the national or the cantonal level,[13] but could greatly simplify the launch of direct-democratic decisions and provide new actors with an important role in signature collection (Bisaz and Serdült 2017). Civil society initiatives such as www.wecollect.ch and the Foundation for Direct Democracy provide important software infrastructure and keep launching the digitalization debate anew. Conveniently for the foundation, these impulses come from civil society and not from political parties or the executive. It seems likely that such a digitalization of direct democracy would trigger further changes in today's finely tuned structure.

Notes

1. We thank Oliver Strijbis for helpful comments and Angela Odermatt and Moira Ettlin for their help in creating this chapter.
2. See also 'The Federal Government' in this volume, or the 'executive dominance' thesis.
3. Sometimes also referred to as optional referendums, popular referendums, veto referendums, petition referendums, or *abrogativos*.
4. Sometimes also referred to as citizens' or voters' initiatives.
5. A possible fifth category is the recall where citizens can vote on whether an elected office holder must step down. It is unique in that it uses the methods of direct-democratic institutions (i.e. the ballot vote) but is directed towards the representative system as its object is not a law but rather a representative (Kölz 1996, 105).
6. The recall still exists in six cantons but was never as widespread as it is at the state level in the US, and is also hardly ever used in Switzerland.
7. Formally, it can be argued that the first mandatory referendum took place in 1848, i.e. when the cantons decided on the 1848 federal constitution. However, only fourteen cantons and two 'half-cantons' voted at the ballot box. In Lucerne, the liberal government counted the citizens who did not go to the polls as yes-voters. In the Landsgemeinde cantons (at that time Uri, Obwalden, Nidwalden, Glarus, and both Appenzells), voting took place at the Landsgemeinde, and in Fribourg and the Grisons, the parliament voted on the new national constitution (Rielle 2010).

8. Another possibility is that eight cantons can demand a referendum. This has only happened once since 1874 – in 2003, concerning a tax package that would have caused the cantons to bear high tax losses (Dubach 2010).
9. The Popular Initiative for UN Accession (2002) and the 1 August Initiative (1993) were two exceptions, as the Federal Assembly recommended the adoption of the proposals.
10. For brief descriptions of all votes between 1848 and 2007, see Linder et al. (2010). Information about all votes, especially newer ones, is available from Swissvotes (2022) and the Center for Research on Direct Democracy (2022).
11. Naturally, there are significant differences between votes for which a popular majority is sufficient and votes that are subject to the double majority. In particular, initiatives that require both a popular majority and a majority of the cantons deviate from the aforementioned simple majority logic (Vatter 2000; Vatter 2009).
12. The Cantons of Unterwalden (NW, OW) and the Appenzell (AI, AR) were each given a joint constitution, stipulating that their territories split into two different parts. Geneva joined France, Valais was an independent republic, Neuchâtel was part of Prussia, Basel was still a full canton, and the canton of Jura was yet to be formed.
13. The Canton of Schaffhausen was the first canton to introduce a digital identity in 2018. In 2020, a popular motion was used to introduce a legal basis for electronic voting, whereby the initiators also provided a prototype.

References

Altman, David. 2008a. 'Collegiate Executives and Direct Democracy in Switzerland and Uruguay: Similar Institutions, Opposite Political Goals, Distinct Results'. *Swiss Political Science Review* 14 (3): pp. 483–520.

Altman, David. 2008b. *Uruguay: A Prodigious User of Direct Democracy Mechanisms*. c2d Working Papers Series 24, Centre for Democracy Studies Aarau (ZDA) at the University of Zurich.

Altman, David. 2011. *Direct Democracy Worldwide*. Cambridge: Cambridge University Press.

Altman, David. 2017. 'The Potential of Direct Democracy: A Global Measure (1900-2014)'. *Social Indicators Research* 133 (3): pp. 1207–1227.

Altman, David. 2019. *Citizenship and Contemporary Direct Democracy*. Cambridge/New York: Cambridge University Press.

Bisaz, Corsin, and Uwe Serdült. 2017. 'E-Collecting als Herausforderung für die direkte Demokratie der Schweiz'. *LeGes* 28 (3): pp. 531–545.

Blais, André. 2014. 'Why is Turnout So Low in Switzerland? Comparing the Attitudes of Swiss and German Citizens Towards Electoral Democracy'. *Swiss Political Science Review* 20 (4): pp. 520–528.

Blickle, Peter. 2000. *Kommunalismus. Skizzen einer gesellschaftlichen Organisationsform*. München: Oldenbourg.

Bochsler, Daniel. 2013. 'Die CVP verliert das Wallis und das Ständemehr'. *Neue Zürcher Zeitung* 5 March 2013: p. 9.

Bolliger, Christian, and Regula Zürcher. 2004. 'Deblockierung durch Kooptation? Eine Fallstudie zur Aufnahme der Katholisch-Konservativen in die schweizerische Landesregierung 1891'. *Swiss Political Science Review* 10 (4): pp. 59–92.

Braun Binder, Nadja, Thomas Milic, and Philippe E. Rochat. 2020. *Die Volksinitiative als (ausser)parlamentarisches Instrument?* Zürich: Schulthess.

Center for Research on Direct Democracy. 2022. *Database.* https://c2d.ch/.

De Capitani, François. 2006. 'Beharren und Umsturz (1648-1815)'. In *Geschichte der Schweiz und der Schweizer*, edited by Beatrix Mesmer, and Ulrich Im Hof, pp. 447–526. Basel: Schwabe Verlag.

Dostal, Jörg Michael, and Marc Champod. 2015. 'The Conflict between Direct Democracy and International Law: Analysing the Swiss Case'. *Journal of the Korean-German Association for Social Sciences* 25 (3): pp. 3–38.

Dubach, Roswitha. 2010. 'Allianz von Kantonen und der Linken versenkt das "Steuerpaket 2001"'. In *Handbuch der eidgenössischen Volksabstimmungen 1848-2007*, edited by Wolf Linder, Christian Bolliger, and Yvan Rielle, pp. 646–647. Bern: Haupt.

Emmenegger, Patrick, Lucas Leemann, and André Walter. 2021. 'No Direct Taxation without New Elite Representation: Industrialization and the Domestic Politics of Taxation'. *European Journal of Political Research* 60 (3): pp. 648–669.

Emmenegger, Patrick, Lucas Leemann, and André Walter. 2022. 'Coalition Size, Direct Democracy, and Public Spending'. *Journal of Public Policy* 42 (2): pp. 224–246.

Epiney, Astrid. 2016. 'Initiativrecht unter Wahrung der Rechtsstaatlichkeit. Überlegungen zu den Anforderungen an die Gültigkeit von Volksinitiativen'. In *Reformbedürftige Volksinitiative. Verbesserungsvorschläge und Gegenargumente*, edited by Georg Kreis, pp. 93–112. Zürich: NZZ Libro.

Fatke Matthias. 2014. 'Allure or Alternative? Direct Democracy and Party Identification'. *Party Politics* 20 (2): pp. 248–260.

Federal Chancellery. 2022. *Volksabstimmungen*, https://www.bk.admin.ch/bk/de/home/politische-rechte/volksabstimmungen.html (accessed 24 August 2022).

Federal Statistical Office. 2022. *Abstimmungen*, https://www.bfs.admin.ch/bfs/de/home/statistiken/politik/abstimmungen.html (accessed 24 August 2022).

Feld, Lars P., and Gebhard Kirchgässner. 2001. 'Does Direct Democracy Reduce Public Debt? Evidence from Swiss Municipalities'. *Public Choice* 109 (3): pp. 347–370.

Freitag, Markus, Adrian Vatter, and Christoph Müller. 2003. 'Bremse oder Gaspedal? Eine empirische Untersuchung zur Wirkung der direkten Demokratie auf den Steuerstaat'. *Politische Vierteljahresschrift* 44 (3): pp. 348–369.

Freitag, Markus, and Isabelle Stadelmann-Steffen. 2010. 'Stumbling Block or Stepping Stone? The Influence of Direct Democracy on Individual Participation in Parliamentary Elections'. *Electoral Studies* 29 (3): pp. 472–483.

Frey, Bruno S., and Alois Stutzer. 2000. 'Happiness, Economy and Institutions'. *The Economic Journal* 110 (10): pp. 918–938.

Graber, Rolf. 2017. *Demokratie und Revolten. Die Entstehung der direkten Demokratie in der Schweiz*. Zürich: Chronos Verlag.

Guess, Andy, Brendan Nyhan, Benjamin Lyons, and Jason Reifler. 2018. *Avoiding the Echo Chamber about Echo Chambers*. Miami: Knight Foundation.

Gruner, Erich. 1964. 'Eigentümlichkeiten der schweizerischen Parteienstruktur: zur Typologie frühliberaler Massenparteien'. *Politische Vierteljahresschrift* 5 (2): pp. 203–217.

Hainmueller, Jens, and Dominik Hangartner. 2019. 'Does Direct Democracy Hurt Immigrant Minorities? Evidence from Naturalization Decisions in Switzerland'. *American Journal of Political Science* 63 (3): pp. 530–547.

Heidbreder, Eva G., Isabelle Stadelmann-Steffen, Eva Thomann, and Fritz Sager. 2019. 'EU Referendums in Context: What Can We Learn from the Swiss Case?' *Public Administration* 97 (2): pp. 370–383.

Hug, Simon. 2004. 'Occurrence and Policy Consequences of Referendums. A Theoretical Model and Empirical Evidence'. *Journal of Theoretical Politics* 16 (3): pp. 321–356.

Hug, Simon. 2009. 'Some Thoughts about Referendums, Representative Democracy, and Separation of Powers'. *Constitutional Political Economy* 20 (9): pp. 251–266.

Kirchgässner, Gerhard. 2008. 'Direct Democracy: Obstacle to Reform?' *Constitutional Political Economy* 19 (2): pp. 81–93.

Kern, Anna, Lala Muradova, and Sofie Marien. 2021. 'The Effect of Accumulated Losses on Perceptions of Legitimacy'. *SSRN Electronic Journal*: pp. 1–57. http://dx.doi.org/10.2139/ssrn.3762746.

Kölz, Alfred. 1992. *Neuere schweizerische Verfassungsgeschichte. Ihre Grundlinien vom Ende der alten Eidgenossenschaft bis 1848*. Bern: Stämpfli.

Kölz, Alfred. 1996. 'Die Bedeutung der Französischen Revolution'. In *Die Ursprünge der schweizerischen direkten Demokratie*, edited by Andreas Auer, pp. 105–117. Basel: Helbing & Lichtenhahn.

Ladner, Andreas, and Michael Brändle. 1999. 'Does Direct Democracy Matter for Political Parties? An Empirical Test in the Swiss Cantons'. *Party Politics* 5 (3): pp. 283–302.

Leemann, Lucas. 2015. 'Political Conflict and Direct Democracy: Explaining Initiative Use 1920-2011'. *Swiss Political Science Review* 21 (12): pp. 596–616.

Leemann, Lucas. 2022. *Direct Democracy and Political Conflict – Institutional Evolution in the 19th Century*. Unpublished manuscript, University of Zurich.

Leemann, Lucas, and Isabelle Stadelmann-Steffen. 2022. 'Satisfaction With Democracy: When Government by the People Brings Electoral Losers and Winners Together'. *Comparative Political Studies* 55 (1): pp. 93–121.

Leemann, Lucas, and Fabio Wasserfallen. 2016. 'The Democratic Effect of Direct Democracy'. *American Political Science Review* 110 (4): 750–762.

Leininger, Arndt. 2015. 'Direct Democracy in Europe: Potentials and Pitfalls'. *Global Policy* 6 (1): pp. 17–27.

Leupold, Michael, and Michel Besson. 2011. 'Gefährden Volksinitiativen die "gute Ordnung" der Verfassung?' *LeGes* 22 (3): pp. 389–407.

Linder, Wolf, and Sean Mueller. 2017. *Schweizerische Demokratie. Institutionen, Prozesse, Perspektiven*, 4th ed. Bern: Haupt.

Linder, Wolf, and Rolf Wirz. 2014. 'Direkte Demokratie'. In *Handbuch der Schweizer Politik. Manuel de la politique Suisse*, edited by Peter Knoepfel, Yannis Papadopoulos, Pascal Sciarini, Adrian Vatter, and Silja Häusermann, pp. 145–167. Zürich: NZZ Libro.

Linder, Wolf, Christian Bolliger, and Yvan Rielle. 2010. *Handbuch der eidgenössischen Volksabstimmungen 1848–2007*. Bern: Haupt.

Milic, Thomas, Alessandro Feller, and Daniel Kübler. 2019. *VOTO-Studie zur eidgenössischen Volksabstimmung vom 25. November 2018*. Aarau/Lausanne/Luzern: FORS, ZDA, LINK Institut.

Möckli, Daniel. 2018. 'Völkerrechtliche Verpflichtungen als Grenzen für Volksabstimmungen in der Schweiz'. In *Demokratische Kontrolle völkerrechtlicher Verträge: Perspektiven aus Österreich und der Schweiz*, edited by Andreas T. Müller, and Werner Schröder, pp. 80–98. Zürich/Wien/Baden-Baden: Nomos.

Morel, Laurence. 2018. 'Types of Referendums, Provisions, and Practices at the National Level Worldwide'. In *The Routledge Handbook to Referendums and Direct Democracy*, edited by Laurence Morel, and Matt Qvortrup, pp. 27–59. London/New York: Routledge.

Neidhart, Leonhard. 1970. *Plebiszit und pluralitäre Demokratie. Eine Analyse der Funktion des schweizerischen Gesetzesreferendums*. Bern: Francke Verlag.

Obinger, Herbert. 1998. 'Federalism, Direct Democracy, and Welfare State Development in Switzerland'. *Journal of Public Policy* 19 (3): pp. 241–263.

Rielle, Yvan. 2010. 'Die Gründung des schweizerischen Bundesstaates 1848'. In *Handbuch der eidgenössischen Volksabstimmungen 1848–2007*, edited by Wolf Linder, Christian Bolliger, and Yvan Rielle, pp. 19–20. Bern: Haupt Verlag.

Ruth-Lovell, Saskia P, Yanina Welp, and Laurence Whitehead (eds). 2017. *Let the People Rule? Direct Democracy in the Twenty-first Century*. Lanham: Rowman & Littlefield.

Suter, Andreas. 2012. 'Die Genese der direkten Demokratie – Aktuelle Debatten und wissenschaftliche Ergebnisse'. *Schweizerische Zeitschrift für Geschichte* 62 (3): pp. 456–73.

Swissvotes. 2022. *Data set*. https://swissvotes.ch/page/home (accessed 12 April 2022).

Taber, Charles S., and Milton Lodge. 2006. 'Motivated Skepticism in the Evaluation of Political Beliefs'. *American Journal of Political Science* 50 (7): pp. 755–769.

Vatter, Adrian. 2000. 'Consensus and Direct Democracy: Conceptual and Empirical Linkages'. *European Journal of Political Research* 38 (1): pp. 171–192.

Vatter, Adrian. 2009. 'Lijphart Expanded: Three Dimensions of Democracy in Advanced OECD Countries?' *European Political Science Review* 1 (1): pp. 12–5154.

Vatter, Adrian. 2020. *Das politische System der Schweiz*, 4th ed. Baden-Baden: Nomos.

Vatter, Adrian, and Deniz Danaci. 2010. 'Mehrheitstyrannei durch Volksentscheide? Zum Spannungsverhältnis zwischen direkter Demokratie und Minderheitenschutz'. *Politische Vierteljahresschrift* 51 (2): pp. 205–222.

Vatter, Adrian, Bianca Rousselot, and Thomas Milic. 2019. 'The Input and Output Effects of Direct Democracy: A New Research Agenda'. *Policy & Politics* 47 (1): pp. 169–186.

CHAPTER 10

PARLIAMENT

STEFANIE BAILER AND SARAH BÜTIKOFER

1 INTRODUCTION

WHEN the Covid-19 pandemic reached Europe in the spring of 2020 the hour of the executive had come.[1] Little was heard from parliaments and their members. In Switzerland, the Federal Assembly broke off its ongoing spring session and invoked the emergency decrees issued by the Federal Council. At first, it seemed as if there were no need for the parliament at all—the sceptre laid solely with the Federal Council. Yet, from the summer session of 2020 onwards, the parliament re-assumed its constitutionally strong role, which permits parliament to declare the state of emergency and to adopt its own emergency measures. It passed the Covid-19 Act in an emergency procedure;[2] an act which anchors in ordinary law those Covid-19-related measures that cannot be taken based on the Epidemics Act (Bolleyer and Salát 2021). While this was a rather surprising and hopefully rare event of a global crisis, we are curious to investigate whether this interruption of an ordinary parliamentary session was symptomatic of a weakness of parliament at a time of crisis or whether it was primarily due to the extraordinary circumstances of the Covid-19 pandemic.

This chapter examines the role of the parliament not only in times of crisis, but also as a political actor alongside the citizens in the country with the most extensive form of direct democracy in the world. First, we introduce the institutional characteristics and functioning of the National Council and the Council of States, the two parliamentary chambers at the national level. Second, we measure the institutional power of the Swiss parliament and compare the result with qualitative estimates by political experts to provide an encompassing estimate of the power of parliament. Third, we present two central developments for the Swiss parliament: increasing professionalization, as well as the growing influence of interest groups.

2 THE SWISS FEDERAL ASSEMBLY: THE SUPREME POWER IN THE CONFEDERATION

The federal constitution of the Swiss Confederation enshrines the supremacy of parliament by stipulating that the Federal Assembly 'is the supreme authority of the Confederation' (art. 148,1), subject only to the rights of the eligible people and the cantons. Consequently, the Federal Assembly has a dominant position (Lüthi 2017), which is also evident from the fact that the legislature is the electoral body of the executive and judiciary (Vatter 2020). The Swiss political system has been called a hybrid between a parliamentary and presidential system (Lijphart 1999, 119) or an 'assembly-independent regime' (Shugart and Carey 1992, 160). On the one hand, it shares the characteristics of a parliamentary system, where the parliament elects government. Yet, parliament cannot bring the government to fall with a vote of no confidence as in parliamentary democracies; a feature that is similar to presidential systems, where parliament cannot dismiss the government. On the other hand, the Swiss government does not have the same independence as a president in a presidential system because it is not elected by the citizens directly, but by parliament. Moreover, and unlike the situation in a presidential system such as the US, the government has no right to veto the decisions of the Federal Assembly.

In contrast to many other parliamentary democracies, in which cabinet members may serve in parliament while being cabinet members, a personal division of power between the legislative and the executive is realized in Switzerland (art. 144, 1 of the federal constitution: incompatibility). Government members are not allowed to serve in parliament (Andeweg and Nijzink 1995). The legislative cycle is generally fixed for four years and early parliamentary elections can only be called when citizens ask for a complete revision of the constitution (art. 193, 3 of the constitution). The Federal Assembly is also largely independent vis-à-vis the judiciary. Constitutional jurisdiction in Switzerland is limited in terms of subject matter (art. 190 of the federal constitution[3]), since federal laws must be applied even if they may be unconstitutional (Reich 2020).

2.1 The united Federal Assembly: the two chambers of the Swiss parliament

The Swiss legislature consists of two equal parliamentary chambers. The National Council, the lower house, is made up of 200 mostly proportionally[4] elected representatives of the people, while the upper house, the Council of States, is made up of forty-six representatives from the twenty-six cantons. The cantons are free to determine their own electoral system but, as a matter of fact, almost everywhere a majoritarian system is applied. Hence, the two chambers are quite comparable to the set-up of the

US House of Representatives and the US Senate. The two councils only hold joint proceedings as the Federal Assembly in particular circumstances: to conduct elections (see below), to decide on conflicts of jurisdiction between the highest federal authorities, and to decide on applications for pardons. Usually, the two chambers of parliament deal with all bills separately but have to come to an agreement to pass a bill. The two presidents of the council determine which council is to be given first consideration, usually based on the criteria of business load and urgency. In case of disagreement, the first chamber to process a bill is decided by lot. First consideration may bring on important agenda-setting power, giving either chamber particular influence over specific bills. The Council of States is currently considered to have more influence, as it is more often the first chamber to deliberate on bills (Mueller et al. 2020).

2.2 The tasks of the Federal Assembly

The activities of the Federal Assembly, as laid down in the federal constitution and the Parliament Act, are split into four central core areas including legislative, electoral, control, and representative functions. In addition, there are newer tasks, such as participation in foreign policy and the planning of state activities (Vatter 2020).

2.3 Legislation

As Switzerland is a semi-direct democracy, both parliament and the people are responsible for legislation: federal laws are enacted by the Federal Assembly, but are subject to an optional referendum. Parliament can also propose amendments to the federal constitution and submit them to a vote of the people and the cantons, issue federal decrees, and approve international agreements.

The legislative process comprises four phases. In the first phase, the legislative process is initiated either by the Federal Council or by parliament. In comparison to other parliaments, Swiss parliamentarians have a substantial number of individual legislative instruments to initiate laws, namely parliamentary initiatives and parliamentary requests (i.e. motions, postulates, interpellations, questions). In recent decades, significantly more proposals have been submitted by members of parliament (MP) than in the past (Vatter 2020; Lüthi 2017) because MPs use these parliamentary instruments to distinguish themselves (Zumbach et al. 2019; Vatter 2020). In the second phase, either the Federal Council or a parliamentary committee takes the lead in steering the bill through the legislative debates; followed by the consultation procedure (*Vernehmlassung*), in which all political actors have the opportunity to comment on the first draft of a proposed law. This consultation procedure serves as an instrument to make the law 'referendum-proof', so that as few political stakeholders as possible will initiate a referendum after the law has been passed. Due to the existence of this consultation procedure, the pre-parliamentary phase takes considerably more time than the subsequent parliamentary deliberation (Sciarini 2014). In the third phase, the Federal Council submits the new draft acts to the Federal Assembly, together with a Federal Council dispatch, i.e. an explanatory memorandum that provides an explanation of the bill. If a parliamentary committee has drafted the bill, it submits it to its council with an explanatory report, which must meet the same requirements as a memorandum from the Federal Council.

During the fourth phase, the two chambers of parliament discuss the draft bill in separate proceedings. Both chambers must agree on the same wording, and they do so in the majority of cases. If there are still differences between the chambers after a maximum of three discussions, a conciliation conference must reach a final compromise. The proportion of drafts dealt with in conciliation conferences has increased recently compared to previous legislative periods. This indicates a slightly higher potential for conflict between the two councils (Dick 2018). In recent years, the position of the Council of States has more often prevailed over that of the National Council in the conciliation conferences (Freiburghaus 2018). As soon as the National Council and the Council of States have reached unanimous decisions (full agreement) and have approved the wording revised by the drafting committee, both councils hold the final vote on the same day. Subsequently, the adopted legislative text is published. After this, the law can be stopped from coming into force by an optional referendum, which can be requested by 50,000 voters or any eight cantons within 100 days of the official publication. This happens for approximately 7 per cent of bills, of which approximately two out of five are successful (Linder and Mueller 2017; Vatter 2020).[5] In this case, the law previously drafted by parliament does not enter into force and the process begins anew.

2.4 Elections

The members of the Federal Assembly elect a substantial number of positions. While these include the position of the President of the Confederation, the Federal Chancellor, members of the Federal Supreme Court, and in the event of war, the General of the Swiss Armed Forces, the most important body they elect is the government, the Federal Council.

2.5 Control function

Parliament exercises oversight of the Federal Council and the Federal Administration, the federal courts, and other bodies entrusted with the tasks of the Confederation (art. 169 of the federal constitution). Typically, in parliamentary democracies, the opposition parties have the task of critically assessing the government's activities and discussing them in public with the next elections in mind. As a last resort, the opposition can even overthrow the government. Swiss-style consociationalism built on the inclusion of all important political forces in the government, in turn, has transferred the responsibility for government control to the whole Federal Assembly (Vatter 2020; Storz and Mueller 2018). The Federal Assembly has various bodies at its disposal to fulfil this responsibility.

As in other parliaments, both chambers may appoint a special parliamentary investigation committee in events of importance (Lüthi 2017). The most famous example of such a parliamentary investigation committee dealt with the 'secret files scandal' (*'Fichenaffäre'*) in which federal authorities had excessively documented (or: surveilled) citizens they considered to be more or less suspicious (Mangold 2015). As a result of this scandal, a control (or: audit) committee was created in 1991 to scrutinize the conduct of business by e.g., the Federal Council and the Federal Administration (Vatter 2020). Besides these committees, parliamentarians can scrutinize the government by means of oral and written questions. Quite frequently, parliamentarians use this tool to obtain information from the Federal Administration or as a platform to present themselves (Bailer 2011, 303).

3 The composition and organization of the council chambers

The members of the two chambers of parliament represent both their electorate and their canton of origin and are elected by the voters in the respective cantons. The 200 seats of the National Council are distributed proportionally to the number of inhabitants per canton being the constituency, with each canton being entitled to at least one seat. The number of seats varies from one seat to twenty-four (Berne), and thirty-five seats (Zurich) in the largest cantons (as of 2022). The voters may cast as many votes as the canton has seats, and they are free to modify the party lists in two aspects: the voters can either cumulate votes by listing individual candidates twice or they can allocate their voters to candidates across different party lists on their open list ballots (panachage). These possibilities increase the incentive to cultivate a personal vote (Carey and Shugart 1995), meaning that candidates from the same party campaign harder for voters from the same party, e.g. by spending time in the constituency leading to more intraparty competition (André and Depauw 2013).

The proportional representation system in the National Council promotes the chances of new political forces entering parliament and hence party fragmentation. In small cantons with few seats, candidates from only one to three parties are usually sent to the National Council, while National Council delegations in the more populous cantons are composed of members from up to eight parties. Until the early 1990s, the distribution of seats in the National Council was very stable, with the traditional centre parties accounting for about two-thirds of the seats and the left for one-third (Vatter 2020). Afterwards, an increasing polarization and party fragmentation took place (see 'Political Parties and Party Systems in Switzerland' in this volume).

The forty-six Councillors of States are mainly elected by a majority vote (except for the cantons of Jura and Neuchâtel), determined by cantonal law. All cantons are represented by two seats, with former 'half-cantons' having only one seat each. The majoritarian system favours candidates who, due to their personality and/or seniority, can win votes beyond their own parties. Hence, each canton has representatives elected by proportional representation (PR) in the National Council, and representatives elected mostly by majority vote in the Council of States. The party-political composition of the Council of States differs from that of the National Council and has traditionally been dominated by centre parties. Yet, in the elections of 2019, the Christian Democratic People's Party (CVP) and the Free Democratic Party (FDP), with twenty-five of the forty-six seats, obtained fewer seats than ever before, while the Green Party gained substantial five seats (Vatter and Ladner 2020).

3.1 Upheavals in the party system

Recent decades were marked by major upheavals in the party system. The Swiss People's Party (SVP) has strongly increased its vote share since the mid-1990s. Even though it suffered losses in the most recent elections in 2019, it has been the strongest force in the National Council since 2003, while both the FDP and the CVP have obtained fewer seats over time. Similar to other political systems in Western Europe, the Swiss party landscape has become highly polarized in recent decades, resulting in the coalition of the major parties seeing a 30-percentage point reduction in their majority since the 1990s. This party polarization has led to a significantly higher level of conflict in parliament (Traber 2015). The Green Party entered the National Council for the first time in 1979, steadily increasing its delegation. Ever since, the losses of the Social Democratic Party (SP) have often gone to the Greens as gains, but because temporary Green losses offset SP gains, the left camp has remained relatively unchanged. The last elections in 2019 brought unusually large seat shifts and were dominated by the 'climate and women's vote' (Vatter 2020). The Green Liberals (GLP), founded in 2004, managed to double their vote share in just under two decades. At the same time, the pole parties (SVP, SP) lost a substantial number of seats. Figure 10.1 shows the current party-political composition of the Federal Assembly and the Federal Council in relation to party strength in the overall population.

3.2 Parliamentary party groups

The organs of the Federal Assembly include the parliamentary groups. Members of the same party, or of parties that are ideologically close to each other, may form a parliamentary party group if at least five parliamentarians join it. Membership in a parliamentary party group is a prerequisite for National Councillors to be able to sit on committees. Parliamentary party groups enjoy various institutional rights in the national parliament

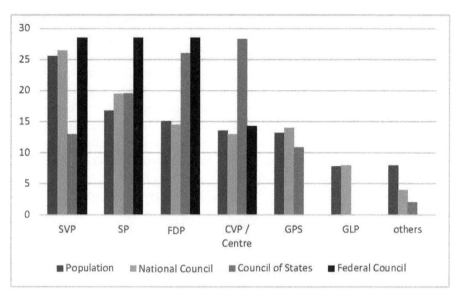

FIGURE 10.1: Party-political composition Federal Assembly/Federal Council compared to party preferences

regarding the submission of parliamentary procedural requests or participation in parliamentary coordination functions, which is why it is attractive for members of parliament to belong to such a group.

3.3 Votes

The National Council belongs to the minority of parliaments in the world where the standard operating procedure for votes is electronic roll call votes, which are all published (Hug and Wüest 2014; Ainsley et al. 2020). Over the last few decades, the parliamentary groups in the National Council have developed higher voting unity than in the past (Traber et al. 2014). This has also become evident when we consider their speeches, where they present themselves usually less homogeneously (Schwarz et al. 2017).[6] This is explained by the increasing polarization of the conflict between the parliamentary groups so that internal unity matters more (Traber 2015). Stricter disciplinary measures within the parliamentary groups also play a role (Bailer 2018; Bailer and Bütikofer 2015).

In the Council of States, parliamentarians introduced electronic roll call voting in 2014 (later than in the National Council) but they felt compelled to do so after a couple of embarrassing vote-counting mistakes. Only isolated studies are available on the voting behaviour of the Council of States from before the introduction of electronic voting, which are based on the observation of video tapes (Bütikofer and Hug 2010; Bütikofer 2014). Since 2022, all votes of the Council of States are not only recorded but also published; until then, individual voting decisions were only published in the case of overall or final votes. The introduction of the publication of individual voting decisions has been shown to lead to more uniform voting by members of the same party, not only in the National Council (Hug and Wüest 2014) but also in the Council of States (Benesch et al. 2020).

3.4 Representation

While the linguistic regional minorities in the Federal Assembly are represented in line with the population, a representation deficit can be observed for other characteristics. The fact that the prevailing ideal of the national parliamentarian position is still a part-time occupation has a reinforcing effect on unequal opportunities. A large proportion of the population has neither the financial and time resources, as well as the flexibility necessary for a political mandate in addition to their main employment nor the ability to give up completely the security or income offered by their main occupation.

As in other national parliaments, male academics aged between forty and sixty-five are clearly overrepresented, as well as farmers and the self-employed. Full-time politicians outnumber salaried employees in the Federal Assembly (Pilotti 2017). Many population groups, such as citizens with migration backgrounds as well as members of less privileged social classes, are underrepresented. Over time, it is not only the party-political but also the sociological composition of the two chambers that has changed. There are now significantly more people in parliament who, at a relatively young age, have already set their sights on a political career in the national legislature and are pursuing politics full-time.

Measured against their share in the population, women in Switzerland are particularly underrepresented (Seitz 2020). Since the introduction of active and passive women's suffrage in 1971, their share in the Federal Assembly has steadily increased to 42 per cent in the National Council (2019–2023), but only to 26 per cent in the Council of States. The strong rise of female parliamentarians in the 'women's election' in 2019 resulted from a larger share of women being nominated on electoral lists (40 per cent; see Giger et al. 2022). In the year preceding the 2019 elections, a campaign to increase female representation ('*Helvetia ruft*') and the large demonstrations of the 2019 'women's strike' signalled to parties that they needed to take action on the issue of female candidatures. Hence, in this election, the parties specifically promoted female candidates by placing them on promising list positions. This illustrates that female candidates need good list positions even more than male candidates in order to be elected (Gilardi et al. 2019). The women-friendly effect of PR, therefore, occurs mainly in large cantons, since there is great competition for lists, and parties can specifically promote women by means of attractive list positions in contrast to small constituencies (Bütikofer et al. 2008, 656). Moreover, voters (especially female ones) considered women in the 2019 election as more fit for political office, with women about one percentage point more likely to be elected than men (Tresch et al. 2020; Giger et al. 2022). Yet, the success of female candidates was not a consequence of increased female voter participation: in 2019, the voter participation of women was actually lower than that of men.

3.5 Parliamentary services

The parliamentary services support both chambers in the fulfilment of their tasks. With a staff of 238 positions (as of 2022), the parliamentary services are extremely small compared to those of countries and legislatures of a similar size, e.g. Austria (485 positions), Belgium (603 positions), or the Czech Republic (361 positions)[7] (see also Z'graggen 2009; Flick Witzig and Bernauer 2018). This is surprising considering that Swiss part-time parliamentarians should need more administrative and scientific support to conduct their work. Yet, attempts to increase parliamentary staff numbers or the introduction of personal assistants for parliamentarians have so far often been rejected.

3.6 Sessions

The National Council and the Council of States are the only national chambers of parliament still based on the semi-professional principle. They meet four times a year for ordinary three-week sessions, in cases of emergency, and for extraordinary sessions. In between, parliament does not sit, but parliamentarians meet for office, caucus, and committee meetings depending on their function and membership. The meetings of the two chambers of the parliament are public and are run according to their own standing rules, e.g. there is no speaking time limit in the Council of States and members speak from their seats. These rather unusual rules contribute to a different debate culture in the Council of States (similar to a 'chambre de réflexion) in contrast to the National Council (Bütikofer and Hug 2010).

3.7 Committees

Committees, denoted 'commissions', are committees of parliament which provide preliminary advice on the business assigned to their area of expertise. In recent years, the political process has tended to shift from the pre-parliamentary phase to deliberations in the Federal Assembly, which has also strengthened the parliamentary committees (Mach et al. 2020). Unlike in other parliaments, where the size of the committees varies according to their importance, each committee has the same number of members: thirteen in the Council of States and twenty-five in the National Council. The term of office for members is four years, and re-election is possible. The committee presidents may only remain in office for two years. Within the parliamentary groups, the proportional allocation of MPs to the individual committee is not always free of conflict, as the attractiveness of the committee varies, and various criteria such as seniority, expertise, and behaviour within the parliamentary group play a role (Bailer 2018). The meetings of the committees are strictly confidential to facilitate the elaboration of factual and politically feasible solutions.

4 The power of the Federal Assembly

A key question regarding the Federal Assembly concerns its power. As a part-time national parliament with meagre administrative resources and limited by strong direct-democratic tools, it has long been considered a weak parliament (Kriesi and Trechsel 2008, 72). In contrast, recent studies attest it has more power, e.g. in legislation (Gava et al. 2020; Vatter 2018). In the following section, we discuss this controversy and analyse the institutionally defined formal power of parliament, and how this corresponds to its actual, de facto power according to expert opinions.

There are various approaches to measuring the power of the Federal Assembly in relation to other political actors and in international comparison to other parliaments. With the *Reputational Power Index* (Sciarini et al. 2015) based on expert assessments, it can be shown that the power of parliament has increased since the 1980s in comparison to other political actors. However, this *Reputational Power Index* does not allow for an international comparison, as this expert survey has not yet been conducted on a comparative basis. Other analyses examining Switzerland in international comparison only partly confirm the finding. Flick Witzig and Bernauer (2018) distinguish between formal power, i.e. power defined in rules and regulations, and de facto power, i.e. power actually exercised, and show that although the Federal Assembly is formally strong, its de facto power is rather average in international comparison. However, the assessment of the de facto power actually exercised is partly based on the assessment of a single expert (Sebaldt 2009). The finding that the de facto influence of parliament is mediocre contrasts with the analysis of Gava et al. (2020), who measure the influence of parliament on draft laws with the help of a text analysis and attest to its extraordinarily high influence and, thus, power in the law-making process—especially in the amendment of laws. As a further contribution to this ongoing debate on the assessment of the power of the Federal Assembly, we present here in a first step the newly calculated *Institutional Power of Parliament Index* for Switzerland (derived from parliamentary rules) according to Sieberer (2011), which facilitates international comparison. In this way, we measure the formal power of a parliament in a comprehensible way; based on analyses of institutional rules and powers. In a second step, we conducted an expert survey to show whether political experts from Switzerland consider our calculation of the formal power value to be an accurate depiction of the de facto power.

With the *Institutional Power of Parliament Index* (Sieberer 2011), we measure various aspects of power with fourteen different items. These include the areas of policy influence, electoral power, control, and committee power.[8] Using a factor analysis, we reduce

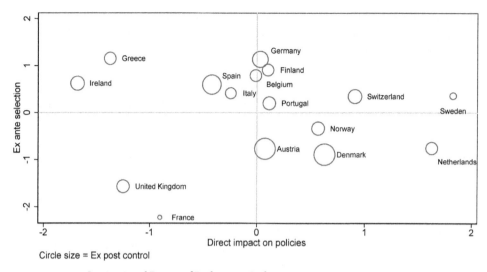

FIGURE 10.2: Institutional Power of Parliament Index

the fourteen questions to the power dimensions of *direct impact on policies, electoral powers (ex ante selection)*, and *control*, as shown in Figure 10.2:

The index shows an above-average value for Switzerland in an European comparison in the areas of legislation and electoral powers. The area of government control is somewhat weaker.

In order to compare this assessment of formal power derived from rules of procedure and authority with the actual, factual power exercised, we conducted an expert survey.[9] When experts from the fields of journalism, political consulting, and lobbying were confronted with the results of our index calculation and asked about their own assessment of how the Swiss parliament had exercised its power in the last ten years, they largely agreed with our calculations.[10]

We asked the experts whether the influence of the Federal Assembly had increased or decreased over the last ten years. Two-thirds of the respondents believe that the Federal Assembly exerts a stronger influence on legislation today than it did ten years ago, while the remaining third believes its influence is less strong nowadays. Respondents explained the rising influence on legislation[11] by more intense party competition (three out of eighteen respondents), as well as by the increased ambition (four out of eighteen respondents) and self-confidence of MPs (three out of eighteen respondents). The few respondents who assume a decrease in influence attribute this predominantly to the polarization in the Federal Assembly.

In order to additionally examine the relationship between formal and de facto power, we asked the experts whether they agreed with the statement that the Federal Assembly has only a mediocre influence on legislation despite its strong formal power (see Flick Witzig and Bernauer 2018). One-third of the respondents agreed with this statement. But half of the respondents rejected the statement and instead confirmed the strong formal power. We were also particularly interested in the question of who influences the political agenda of the National Council and the Council of States. Here, over 80 per cent of respondents agreed with the statement that the Federal Assembly is successful in putting its own issues on the political agenda. In addition, 70 per cent of respondents agreed with the statement that the Federal Assembly is more successful in setting its own issues today than it was ten years ago. The most frequent explanations given for this stronger role in agenda-setting were the parties, which provide stronger impetus through a stronger will to shape the agenda and greater polarization.

Our experts share the significantly weaker formal assessment of the control function of the Federal Assembly in the *Institutional Power of Parliament Index*. Their opinions on the Federal Assembly's control capacities are divided. Just under half of the respondents agreed with the statement that the Federal Assembly is successful in controlling the Federal Council. Thirty per cent neither agreed nor disagreed with the statement, and 20 per cent disagreed. Only a minority of about 40 per cent thinks that the Federal Assembly is doing a better job of controlling the government today compared to ten years ago. Just under half of the respondents think there is no change, and 15 per cent think it is less successful. In conclusion, we note that the Federal Assembly is a powerful legislature, both formally measured and as confirmed by expert assessments. In particular, its great influence over the legislative process stands out. This is in contrast to a rather low level of power in the area of government control. Furthermore, we show that the power of the Federal Assembly has increased over the years, especially in the area of law-making (including agenda-setting), but to a lesser degree in the area of control.

After the description of the central characteristics of the Swiss parliament and an analysis of its power, we outline in the last section two central tendencies shaping the Federal Assembly today: increasing professionalization and the influence of interest groups.

5 Professionalization

Despite the semi-professional status of the Swiss parliament similar to US subnational parliaments according to Squire's corrected professionalization index (Huwyler et al. 2022), an increasing professionalization at the individual level can be observed in the Federal Assembly. The average parliamentary workload has risen in both chambers: estimates vary between 70 and 80 per cent of normal working hours (Sciarini et al. 2017) while most observers assume that the workload is higher in the Council of States, e.g. due to the higher number of committee memberships (Vatter 2020, 270; Pilotti and Di Capua 2019). The increasing level of professionalization is also noticeable by the decreasing average age of MPs. In the 1960s, the average age was between sixty-three to sixty-five years. Today, the average age of National Councillors has fallen to fifty-one and for the Councillors of States to fifty-six (Turner-Zwinkels et al. 2022). We interpret this downward trend as a sign both of increasing professionalization (Saalfeld 1997) and of the growing attractiveness of the parliamentary mandate. Ever-younger politically engaged people aspire to hold office and to pursue a professional political career with a focus on fewer but more important offices (Di Capua et al. 2022). The declining average age is typical of professionalized parliaments as in Germany or the Netherlands (Ohmura et al. 2018; Turner-Zwinkels et al. 2022).

A higher average age may also indicate that parliamentarians need to be more professional and experienced to climb up on the political career ladder. This reasoning is reflected in the elevated average age of members of the Council of States compared to the National Council, which, in turn, reflects the higher prestige of the Council of States. The latter is considered more attractive because it exerts more influence, a result confirmed by our expert survey.

If we look at the average term of office in the two chambers, the usual measure for professionalization (Figure 10.3) (Saalfeld 1997; Allen et al. 2020), we see a decreasing average age in the National Council and a rising one in the Council of States.

The longer term of office is interpreted as a sign of increasing professionalization of MPs as well as of efforts of parliamentarians to spend a longer time in an attractive institution (Allen et al. 2020). This seems particularly to be the case for the more attractive Council of States. In contrast, tenure in the National Council has fallen significantly over the last seventy years. Equivalent chambers in other countries, such as the Netherlands, show similar patterns.

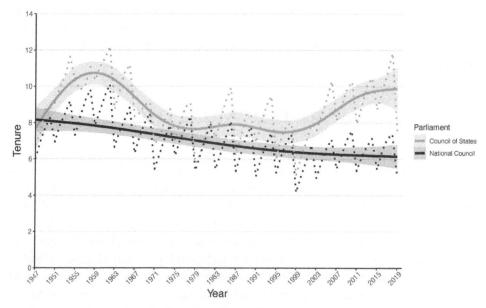

FIGURE 10.3: Average length of stay in parliament in years

Data source: Turner-Zwinkels et al. (2022).

6 THE INFLUENCE OF INTEREST GROUPS

Switzerland has always stood out for its marked lack of transparency when it comes to links between vested interests and MPs. This regularly provokes criticism from international organizations such as the Council of Europe as well as from NGOs such as *Transparency International Switzerland* or *Lobbywatch*.[12] In other countries, all contacts between lobby groups and MPs must be publicly documented in type and length (e.g. Ireland) or the financial supplementary incomes of MPs are published (e.g. Germany) (Chari et al. 2020); in contrast, Swiss MPs have only been obliged to disclose seats on boards of directors and foundations since 1985.[13] The insufficient transparency in party and campaign financing is becoming an increasingly important topic of discussion; party financing laws have been initiated in six cantons,[14] and a new national—rather weak—regulation was finally adopted in 2021.[15]

Over the last twenty-five years, the links between MPs and interest groups have intensified significantly (Gava et al. 2017; Eichenberger and Mach 2017; Huwyler and Turner-Zwinkels 2020). What is remarkable are not only the extensive links with business associations and companies but also those with interest groups representing

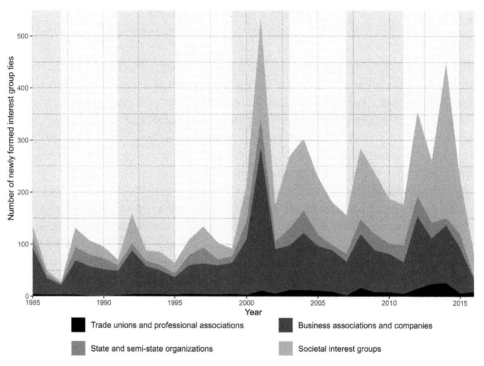

FIGURE 10.4: Interest group organizations of National Councillors and Councillors of States over time

Data source: Huwyler (2021).

so-called public goods such as environmental protection ('societal interest groups') (Figure 10.4). Such direct links between interest groups and MPs increase over the course of an individual parliamentary career, with MPs standing in the political centre as well as on the right having significantly more contacts with interest groups; especially with companies. MPs who are politically more to the left have fewer connections on average and are also significantly less connected to companies (Huwyler and Turner-Zwinkels 2020).

MPs' connections with interest groups do not remain without effect on political action in the committees and in the plenum (Eichenberger and Mach 2017). Recent studies show that as soon as they enter into an association with an interest group, MPs on average submit more parliamentary proposals (Huwyler et al. 2022) in precisely the policy area in which they are associated with the interest group and request more policy evaluations (Varone et al. 2020). Similarly, they are more likely to co-sponsor legislative initiatives with colleagues with whom they have already collaborated and networked in interest groups (Fischer et al. 2019).

7 Conclusion: An influential pseudo-militia parliament with modest resources

The Federal Assembly is a powerful parliament by international standards, with a strong influence especially in the area of legislation, which seems to have increased in the last ten years. Experts explain this increase in power with the emergence of more intense and polarized party competition on the one hand, and with the presence of more ambitious and self-confident MPs on the other. It is therefore all the more urgent to ask how the National Council and the Council of States can legitimately exercise this role and, for example, live up to their task even in a crisis. In our opinion, greater representativeness and a move towards a more professionalized and transparent parliament are part of the answer to this question: in terms of socio-demographic characteristics, the Federal Assembly does not meet the representation ideal of a parliament composed of all social classes. Although the representation of women, younger people, and citizens with migration backgrounds has improved recently, the Federal Assembly is a highly socially selective body; composed mainly of academics, the self-employed, and increasingly (quasi-)full-time politicians. Structural changes would be necessary to remedy the situation. These include an adequate compensation system for politicians and their staff, attractive pension schemes, stronger parliamentary services, and a rethinking of the session rhythm. Equally crucial is the political will of the parties to promote more diversity in the nomination of candidates. Given the increased representation of women after the 2019 elections, it is evident that this path can be successful.

Switzerland may have the only remaining part-time parliament (also called 'militia parliament') but even it cannot avoid the change towards a professional parliament. The number of full-time parliamentarians has steadily gone up for some time, and the people's representation is developing into a 'pseudo-militia' parliament. It is staffed by people who can afford to engage in a temporary and time-consuming office. Others have to cut back on their professional activities and are partly dependent on additional income, i.e. in the form of mandates in interest groups, trade unions, or companies. The comparatively modestly equipped parliamentary services and parliamentary groups as well as the lack of parliamentary assistants means that MPs are dependent on the expertise of interest groups or intransparent arrangements to obtain relevant information. Both developments—the additional income thanks to connections to interest groups and the information dependence on external sources—leads to stronger influence from organized interests. In addition, the better-educated and self-employed benefit from this system, as they can often also draw on an already existing infrastructure for research and administrative work (i.e. in the case of lawyers, who are strongly represented in the National Council). Better equipping MPs and the parliamentary services would additionally arm the legislature with more expertise and information vis-à-vis the Federal Administration when drafting laws, and vis-à-vis the Federal Council when monitoring and overseeing it.

Expertise not directly offered by organized interests and better structural framework conditions could contribute to a better representation of the non- or less-well-organized and financially weaker parts of the population and sectors (e.g. single parents, people with a migration background, employees). Another measure would be more far-reaching: stricter disclosure rules for interest group contacts and more comprehensive recording of party and campaign financing. After all, it is legitimate to give voters insight into contacts and money flows between interest groups of any colour and 'their' MPs, so that they can assess which voices the people's representation actually listens to.

Notes

1. We would like to thank Reja Wyss for her excellent research assistance for this chapter. Many thanks to Clint Claessen and Daniel Höhmann for their support with the graphics. We would also like to thank Dr Ruth Lüthi of the parliamentary services and Peter Schwendener of the Federal Finance Administration for their assessment, and Prof Ulrich Sieberer (University of Bamberg) for the data of the power index for the EU countries. In addition, Prof. Adrian Vatter, Dr Ruth Lüthi, Dr Daniela Eberli and Prof. Denise Traber also critically reviewed the chapter, for which we are very grateful. A big thank you also goes to all the experts who took part in our survey for their valuable assessments of Swiss parliamentary life.
2. Federal Act of 25 September 2020 on the legal basis for ordinances of the Federal Council to deal with the Covid-19 epidemic (COVID-19 Act). The Federal Assembly set accents, for example by introducing a hardship clause for companies or support for professional sports clubs. In addition, it stipulated that the Federal Council would inform parliament

early, regularly, and comprehensively about the implementation of the law and would consult the competent committees before issuing ordinances.
3. Article 190 of the federal constitution: 'Federal laws and international law are authoritative for the Federal Supreme Court and the other authorities applying the law.'
4. Since six cantons are only allowed to be represented by one parliamentarian due to their small size, these representatives are in fact elected by majority vote.
5. For an overview: https://www.parlament.ch/de/%C3%BCber-das-parlament/fakten-und-zahlen/zahlen-volksabstimmungen
6. For current measurements of party unity, see https://smartmonitor.ch/de.
7. Direct information from the respective parliamentary services.
8. The individual questions cover the areas of policy influence (control plenary agenda, control committee agenda, termination of plenary debates, influence on the budget process), electoral powers (parliamentary freedom of choice, government restriction), control (control structures, control resources, control rights, subpoenaing of witnesses), and committee power (committee rights to amend bills, right of committees to initiate legislation, calling for documents). The corresponding response values for the question items were calculated as values for the different areas using factor analyses.
9. In September 2020, we surveyed forty political experts who have many years of professional experience in the fields of journalism, especially federal house reporting, political consulting and communication, and parliament-related, public administration. We asked them to answer four key questions about the power of parliament using an online survey. Twenty-three people took part in our survey (57 per cent response rate).
10. We focused on the aspects of policy influence and control in the expert survey, as the electoral powers (of the Federal Council) are uncontroversial.
11. We offered the following explanations (as well as an open answer option) as answer options: 'stronger self-confidence of parliamentarians', 'ambitious parliamentarians', 'raising the profile of party competition'.
12. https://www.coe.int/en/web/greco/evaluations/switzerland.
13. Accessible in the register of vested interests: https://www.parlament.ch/centers/documents/de/interessen-sr.pdf.
14. https://www.swissinfo.ch/ger/direktedemokratie/parteienfinanzierung_kantone-preschen-bei-finanztransparenz-vor/43931472.
15. https://www.fedlex.admin.ch/eli/fga/2021/1492/de.

References

Ainsley, Caitlin, Clifford J. Carrubba, Brian F. Crisp, Betul Demirkaya, Matthew J. Gabel, and Dino Hadzic. 2020. 'Roll-Call Vote Selection: Implications for the Study of Legislative Politics'. *American Political Science Review* 114 (3): pp. 691–706. doi: 10.1017/S0003055420000192.

Allen, Nicholas, Gabriele Magni, Donald Searing, and Philip Warncke. 2020. 'What is a Career Politician? Theories, Concepts, and Measures'. *European Political Science Review* 12 (2): pp. 199–217. doi: 10.1017/S1755773920000077.

Andeweg, Rudy B, and Lia Nijzink. 1995. 'Beyond the Two-Body Image: Relations between Ministers and MPs'. In *Parliaments and Majority Rule in Western Europe*, edited by Herbert Döring, pp. 152–178. Frankfurt: Campus.

André, Audrey, and Sam Depauw. 2013. 'District Magnitude and Home Styles of Representation in European Democracies'. *West European Politics* 36 (5): pp. 986–1006. doi: 10.1080/01402382.2013.796183.

Bailer, Stefanie. 2011. 'People's Voice or Information Pool? The Role of, and Reasons for, Parliamentary Questions in the Swiss Parliament'. *The Journal of Legislative Studies* 17 (3): pp. 302–314. doi: 10.1080/13572334.2011.595123.

Bailer, Stefanie. 2018. 'To Use the Whip or not: Whether and When Party Group Leaders Use Disciplinary Measures to Achieve Voting Unity'. *International Political Science Review* 39 (2): pp. 163–177.

Bailer, Stefanie, and Sarah Bütikofer. 2015. 'From Loose Alliances to Professional Political Players: How Swiss Party Groups Changed'. *Swiss Political Science Review* 21 (4): pp. 556–577.

Benesch, Christine, Monika Bütler, and Katharina E. Hofer. 2020. 'Licht ins Dunkel: Transparenteres Abstimmungsverhalten im Ständerat'. In *Der Ständerat. Zweite Kammer der Schweiz*, edited by Sean Mueller, and Adrian Vatter, pp. 71–92. Basel: NZZ Libro.

Bolleyer, Nicole, and Orsolya Salát. 2021. 'Parliaments in Times of Crisis: COVID-19, Populism and Executive Dominance'. *West European Politics* 44 (5-6): pp. 1103–1128. doi: 10.1080/01402382.2021.1930733.

Bütikofer, Sarah. 2014. *Das Schweizer Parlament. Eine Institution auf dem Pfad der Moderne*. Baden-Baden: Nomos.

Bütikofer, Sarah, Isabelle Engeli, and Thanh-Huyen Ballmer-Cao. 2008. 'L'impact du mode de scrutin sur l'élection des femmes à l'Assemblée fédérale Suisse (1995–2003)'. *Swiss Political Science Review* 14 (4): pp. 631–661. doi: 10.1002/j.1662-6370.2008.tb00115.x.

Bütikofer, Sarah, and Simon Hug. 2010. 'The Swiss Upper House. "Chambre de Réflexion" or Conservative Renegades?' *Journal of Legislative Studies* 16 (2): pp. 176–194.

Carey, John M., and Matthew S Shugart. 1995. 'Incentives to Cultivate a Personal Vote: A Rank Ordering of Electoral Formulas'. *Electoral Studies* 14 (4): pp. 417–439.

Chari, Raj, John Hogan, Gary Murphy, and Michele Crepaz. 2020. *Regulating Lobbying: A Global Comparison*. Manchester: Manchester University Press.

Di Capua, Roberto, Andrea Pilotti, André Mach, and Karim Lasseb. 2022. 'Political Professionalization and Transformations of Political Career Patterns in Multi-Level States: The Case of Switzerland'. *Regional & Federal Studies* 32 (1): pp. 95–114. doi: 10.1080/13597566.2020.1771312.

Dick, Seraina. 2018. 'Der Ständerat im Schatten der Volkskammer? Die Gesetzgebungsmacht der Zweiten Kammer'. In *Das Parlament in der Schweiz. Macht und Ohnmacht der Volksvertretung*, edited by Adrian Vatter, pp. 233–261. Zürich: NZZ Libro.

Eichenberger, Steven, and André Mach. 2017. 'Formal Ties Between Interest Groups and Members of Parliament: Gaining Allies in Legislative Committees'. *Interest Groups & Advocacy* 6 (1): pp. 1–21. doi: 10.1057/s41309-017-0012-2.

Fischer, Manuel, Frédéric Varone, Roy Gava, and Pascal Sciarini. 2019. 'How MPs' Ties to Interest Groups Matter for Legislative Co-Sponsorship'. *Social Networks* 57: pp. 34–42. doi: https://doi.org/10.1016/j.socnet.2018.12.001.

Flick Witzig, Martina, and Julian Bernauer. 2018. 'Aus der Balance? Das Verhältnis von Parlament und Regierung im internationalen Vergleich'. In *Das Parlament in der Schweiz*, edited by Adrian Vatter, pp. 425–454. Zürich: NZZ Libro.

Freiburghaus, Rahel. 2018. 'Ein grosser Scherbenhaufen? Einigungskonferenzen im schweizerischen Zweikammersystem'. In *Das Parlament in der Schweiz*, edited by Adrian Vatter, pp. 197–232. Zürich: NZZ Libro.

Gava, Roy, Julien M Jacquet, and Pascal Sciarini. 2020. 'Legislating or Rubber-Stamping? Assessing Parliament's Influence on Law-Making with Text Reuse'. *European Journal of Political Research* early view. doi: 10.1111/1475-6765.12395.

Gava, Roy, Frédéric Varone, André Mach, Steven Eichenberger, Julien Christe, and Corinne Chao-Blanco. 2017. 'Interests Groups in Parliament: Exploring MPs' Interest Affiliations (2000-2011)'. *Swiss Political Science Review* 23 (1): pp. 77–94. doi: doi:10.1111/spsr.12224.

Giger, Nathalie, Denise Traber, Fabrizio Gilardi, and Sarah Bütikofer. 2022. 'The Surge in Women's Representation in the 2019 Swiss Federal Elections'. *Swiss Political Science Review* 28 (2): pp: 361–376.

Gilardi, Fabrizio, Sarah Bütikofer, and Alessandro Feller. 2019. *Die Frauenwahl 2019*. https://www.defacto.expert/2019/10/23/die-frauenwahl-2019/ (accessed 21 October 2022).

Hug, Simon, and Reto Wüest. 2014. 'Party Pressure in Roll Call Votes'. Annual Meeting of the Midwest Political Science Association, Chicago, 3–6 April 2014.

Huwyler, Oliver. 2022. 'Interest Groups' Recruitment of Incumbent Parliamentarians to Their Boards'. *Parliamentary Affairs* 75 (3): pp. 634–654. doi: 10.1093/pa/gsab031.

Huwyler, Oliver, and Tomas Turner-Zwinkels. 2020. 'Political or Financial Benefits? Ideology, Tenure, and Parliamentarians' Choice of Interest Group Ties'. *Swiss Political Science Review* 26 (1): pp. 73–95. doi: 10.1111/spsr.12391.

Huwyler, Oliver, Tomas Turner-Zwinkels, and Stefanie Bailer. 2022. 'No Representation without Compensation: The Effect of Interest Groups on Legislators' Policy Area Focus'. *Political Research Quarterly*. doi: https://doi.org/10.1177/10659129221137035.

Kriesi, Hanspeter, and Alexander H. Trechsel. 2008. *The Politics of Switzerland*. Cambridge: Cambridge University Press

Lijphart, Arend. 1999. *Patterns of Democracy. Government Forms and Performance in Thirty-Six Countries*. Yale: Yale University Press.

Linder, Wolf, and Sean Mueller. 2017. *Schweizerische Demokratie. Institutionen, Prozesse, Perspektiven*. Bern: Haupt.

Lüthi, Ruth. 2017. 'Parlament'. In *Handbuch der Schweizer Politik*, edited by Peter Knoepfel, Yannis Papadopoulos, Pascal Sciarini, Adrian Vatter, and Silja Häusermann, pp. 169–192. Zürich. Verlag Neue Zürcher Zeitung.

Mach, André, Frédéric Varone, and Steven Eichenberger. 2020. 'Transformations of Swiss Neo-corporatism: From Pre-parliamentary Negotiations towards Privileged Pluralism in the Parliamentary Venue'. In *The European Social Model under Pressure: Liber Amicorum in Honour of Klaus Armingeon*, edited by Romana Careja, Patrick Emmenegger, and Nathalie Giger, pp. 51–68. Wiesbaden: Springer Fachmedien Wiesbaden.

Mangold, Hannes. 2015. 'Monster in the Box: The Card Index Affair and the Transformation of Switzerland's Intelligence Information System, 1989–1994'. *Journal of Intelligence History* 14 (2): pp. 129–138. doi: 10.1080/16161262.2015.1035517.

Mueller, Sean, Seraina Dick, and Rahel Freiburghaus. 2020. 'Ständerat, stärkerer Rat? Die Gesetzgebungsmacht der Zweiten Kammer im Vergleich zu National- und Bundesrat'. In *Der Ständerat. Die Zweite Kammer der Schweiz*, edited by Sean Müller, and Adrian Vatter, pp. 119–145. Zürich: NZZ Libro.

Ohmura, Tamaki, Stefanie Bailer, Peter Meissner, and Peter Selb. 2018. 'Party Animals, Career Changers, and other Political Career Patterns'. *West European Politics* 41 (1): pp. 169–195. doi: 10.1080/01402382.2017.1323485.

Pilotti, Andrea. 2017. *Entre démocratisation et professionnalisation: le Parlement suisse et ses membres de 1910 à 2016*. Zürich/Genf: Seismo.

Pilotti, Andrea, and Roberto Di Capua. 2019. 'Die sozio-professionelle Zusammensetzung des Nationalrats 2019–2023'. https://www.defacto.expert/2019/11/08/die-sozio-professionelle-zusammensetzung-nationalrat/ (accessed 21 October 2022).

Reich, Johannes. 2020. 'Verhältnis von Demokratie und Rechtsstaatlichkeit'. In *Verfassungsrecht der Schweiz/Droit constitutionnel suisse*, edited by Oliver Diggelmann, Maya Hertig Randall, and Benjamin Schindler, pp. 333–355. Zürich/Basel/Genf: Schulthess.

Saalfeld, Thomas. 1997. 'Professionalisation of Parliamentary Roles in Germany: An Aggregate-Level Analysis, 1949–94'. In *Members of Parliament in Western Europe*, edited by Wolfgang C. Müller, and Thomas Saalfeld, pp. 32–54. London: Frank Cass.

Schwarz, Daniel, Denise Traber, and Kenneth Benoit. 2017. 'Estimating Intra-Party Preferences: Comparing Speeches to Votes'. *Political Science Research and Methods* 5 (2): pp. 379–396. doi: 10.1017/psrm.2015.77.

Sciarini, Pascal. 2014. 'Processus législatif'. In *Manuel de la politique suisse*, edited by Pascal Sciarini, Peter Knoepfel, Yannis Papadopoulos, Adrian Vatter, and Silja Häusermann, pp. 525–561. Zürich: NZZ Libro.

Sciarini, Pascal, Manuel Fischer, and Denise Traber. 2015. *Political Decision-Making in Switzerland: The Consensus Model under Pressure*. Houndmills, Basingstoke: Palgrave Macmillan.

Sciarini, Pascal, Frédéric Varone, Luzzi Ferro, Fabio Cappelletti, Vahan Garibian, and Ismail Muller. 2017. *Studie über das Einkommen und den Arbeitsaufwand der Bundesparlamentarierinnen und Bundesparlamentarier, Schlussbericht zu Handen der Parlamentsbibliothek der Parlamentsdienste der Bundesversammlung*. Genf: Universität Genf.

Sebaldt, Martin. 2009. *Die Macht der Parlamente*. Wiesbaden: VS Verlag.

Seitz, Werner. 2020. *Die Frauen bei den eidgenössischen Wahlen 2019: Ein grosser Schritt nach vorne - im Bundeshaus. Mit einem Exkurs zu den Frauen bei den Wahlen in die kantonalen Parlamente und Regierungen 2015/2019*. Bern: Schweizerische Eidgenossenschaft.

Shugart, Matthew Soberg, and John M Carey. 1992. *Presidents and Assemblies: Constitutional Design and Electoral Dynamics*. Cambridge: Cambridge University Press.

Sieberer, Ulrich 2011. 'The Institutional Power of Western European Parliaments: A Multidimensional Analysis'. *West European Politics* 34 (4): pp. 731–754.

Storz, Anna, and Sean Mueller. 2018. 'Parlamentarische Untersuchungskommissionen in der Schweiz'. In *Das Parlament in der Schweiz*, edited by Adrian Vatter, pp. 165–196. Zürich: NZZ Libro.

Traber, Denise. 2015. 'Disenchanted Swiss Parliament? Electoral Strategies and Coalition Formation'. *Swiss Political Science Review* 21 (4): pp. 702–723. doi: https://doi.org/10.1111/spsr.12185.

Traber, Denise, Simon Hug, and Pascal Sciarini. 2014. 'Party Unity in the Swiss Parliament: The Electoral Connection'. *The Journal of Legislative Studies* 20 (2): pp. 193–215. doi: 10.1080/13572334.2013.837259.

Tresch, Anke, Lukas Lauener, Laurent Bernhard, Georg Lutz, and Laura Scaperotta. 2020. *Eidgenössische Wahlen 2019. Wahlteilnahme und Wahlentscheid*. Lausanne: FORS.

Turner-Zwinkels, Tomas, Oliver Huwyler, Elena Frech, Philip Manow, Stefanie Bailer, Niels D. Goet, and Simon Hug. 2022. 'Parliaments Day-by-Day: A New Open Source Database to Answer the Question of Who Was in What Parliament, Party, and Party-group, and When'. *Legislative Studies Quarterly* 47 (3): pp. 761–784 doi: https://doi.org/10.1111/lsq.12359.

Varone, Frédéric, Pirmin Bundi, and Roy Gava. 2020. 'Policy Evaluation in Parliament: Interest Groups as Catalysts'. *International Review of Administrative Science* 86 (1): pp. 98–114. doi: 10.1177/0020852317750461.

Vatter, Adrian. 2018. *Das Parlament in der Schweiz. Macht und Ohnmacht der Volksvertretung.* Zürich: NZZ Libro.

Vatter, Adrian. 2020. *Das politische System der Schweiz*, 2nd ed. Baden-Baden: Nomos.

Vatter, Adrian, and Andreas Ladner. 2020. 'Vom Gesandtenkongress zur gewählten Volkskammer: Der Ständerat im Wandel der Zeit'. In *Der Ständerat. Zweite Kammer der Schweiz*, edited by Sean Mueller and Adrian Vatter, pp. 35–69. Zürich: NZZ Libro.

Z'graggen, Heidi. 2009. *Die Professionalisierung von Parlamenten im historischen und internationalen Vergleich.* Bern: Haupt Verlag.

Zumbach, David, Anja Heidelberg, and Marc Bühlmann. 2019. 'Da setze ich meinen Namen drunter! Mitunterzeichnen als Indikator der Kompromissbereitschaft'. In *Konkordanz im Parlament*, edited by Marc Bühlmann, Anja Heidelberger, and Hans-Peter Schaub, pp. 171–196. Zürich: NZZ Libro.

CHAPTER 11

FEDERAL GOVERNMENT

YANNIS PAPADOPOULOS AND FRITZ SAGER

1 INTRODUCTION

THIS chapter deals with the Swiss federal executive.[1] Since the creation of the Swiss federation in 1848, the seven-member Federal Council has assumed the role of government at the national level: it is *de jure* the 'supreme governing and executive authority of the Confederation' (art. 174 of the federal constitution). Its peculiar collegial nature, the stability of its format since 1848, and the longevity of the grand coalition that has been ruling since 1959 (with only relatively minor changes in the last two decades), all make the Swiss federal government an intriguing object for political science research.

The chapter first presents the—to a large extent unique—Swiss governmental system. Focusing on the election of the members of the Federal Council and on the evolving composition of the executive, it highlights the gradual implementation of the 'consociational' norm of power-sharing among the major political parties. The second section focuses on the position of the executive within the broader political system; an increasingly polarized system that includes many veto points. The contribution then zooms into the government's internal organization: in section 3, we assess the operation of the collegial principle—which is distinctive to that form of government—and identify the challenges affecting the decision-making and organizational processes inside the political-administrative apparatus. Section 4 concentrates on the repeated and mostly unsuccessful efforts at governmental reform, mainly in view of enhancing governmental performance. The chapter concludes with the latest developments impacting governmental activities and with the main prospects.

2 THE GOVERNMENTAL SYSTEM

One encounters the Swiss collegial system of government not only at the federal but also at subnational levels. However, unlike the federal government, cantonal and municipal executives are directly elected by voters and therefore enjoy direct popular legitimacy (as popularly elected presidents do). Another difference is that, in some cases, the officials that preside over them have stronger prerogatives and are more visible in their role as city mayor, for example. The collegial form of government was originally inspired by the *Directoire* ('Directory') in revolutionary France. It was first imported into Switzerland at the end of the eighteenth century under the short-lived centralized regime of the *République helvétique*, before being adopted at the cantonal level and becoming the form of government of the 1848 federation. Since then, it has remained unchanged in its core institutional features and is 'the most significant collegial executive in modern times' (Altman 2020, 317), with only a handful of countries sharing a relatively similar system of government.[2] One of the main peculiarities is the individual and sequential majority-rule election of the college members who also hold ministerial portfolios.

2.1 Mode of election

The differences between the Swiss system of government and both parliamentary and presidential systems are already visible in the mode of election of the government. The Federal Assembly elects each of the seven members of the Federal Council in individual elections. Complete re-elections take place in a joint session of the two parliamentary chambers (the National Council and the Council of States) that convenes shortly after the election of the National Council every four years. The elections, which are unavoidably personalized, are also frequently competitive in many respects. Competition can already be tough within parties for the designation of candidates. As an absolute majority of the members of the Federal Assembly is required to be elected, several rounds of voting may be necessary. In around 15 per cent of cases, the assembly has not put the party seat into question but has opted for candidates other than those officially proposed by this party's parliamentary group (Vatter 2020b, 88). To reduce such a risk, many parliamentary groups have switched to nominating more than one candidate for the Federal Council seat that is allocated to them. The Federal Assembly also gets to elect the federal chancellor—often denominated as 'shadow federal councillor'—and two vice-chancellors, each with a four-year term. The chancellor acts as the Federal Council's chief of staff. He or she, too, attends the weekly meetings of the Federal Council in an advisory capacity, but also has the right to table motions.

The Federal Council is elected for a fixed four-year term. Parliament cannot dismiss it with a vote of no confidence. In return, the government does not have the power to dissolve parliament. Thus, government and parliament in Switzerland are—at least formally—independent of each other. This distinguishes the Swiss system from parliamentary systems such as the United Kingdom or Germany (Sager and Vatter 2019, 196–197). Switzerland also differs from presidential systems such as the United States in that its federal government is not elected directly by the people. The reason given for the parliamentary election of the Federal Council is that the various language communities, regions, and party groups can be better represented than in a popular election. Claims for a popular election of the Federal Council have been recurring but have remained unsuccessful; the drafters of the 1848 federal constitution rejected the popular election, although by a very narrow margin. Ever since, three popular initiatives and several parliamentary bills with similar claims have failed as well.

2.2 'Consociationalism' and 'magic formula'

Consociationalism is the international label for what the Swiss call 'concordance', namely a defining feature of this country's political culture that is also reflected in the structure and operation of the executive. It can be seen as a specific manifestation of consensus democracy, which Lijphart (1968, 2012) contrasts with majoritarian democracy. In policy-making, this term denotes a deliberate search for compromises likely to be supported by as large a majority as possible; including interest groups and relevant stakeholders (Papadopoulos 1997; Sager and Vatter 2019, 197). The durability of consociationalism—synonymous with negotiation, compromises, and inclusion—is usually explained by institutional constraints, and more specifically by three elements shaping Swiss politics:

- First and foremost is direct democracy and in particular the instrument of the optional referendum, which gives Swiss voters the opportunity to vote on parliamentary decisions if requested. As the outcome of referendums is often uncertain, decision-makers seek to avoid them by involving all oppositional forces that have the reputational power to win referendums. The 'referendum constraint' (Neidhart 1970) is also reflected in the composition of the Federal Council: The largest political parties are all represented in the federal government in order to prevent deadlock.
- The second institutional element is proportional representation. Ever since the 1919 shift from a first-past-the-post system to proportional representation for the election of the first chamber (National Council), no party has succeeded in winning an absolute majority.
- Last but not least, federalism is also an important institutional determinant. Because Switzerland is a pluralistic society, efforts were made very early on to establish mechanisms that strike a balance between the different linguistic and/or confessional communities.

According to Keman (1996), Swiss 'Konkordanzdemokratie' has three main pillars: the cooperative behaviour of the members of the governing coalition despite the lack of a coalition agreement, the consideration of minorities, and a mirror-image representation of society in the political system. Consociationalism manifests itself prominently in the composition of the Federal Council. Not only are the various regions represented, but the largest political parties have also been uninterruptedly represented for several decades in the government according to their share of the electorate. In recent decades, however, it has become increasingly apparent that Switzerland has evolved from a prototypical case to a more moderate form of consensus democracy (Vatter 2008; Vatter et al. 2020).

2.3 A short electoral history

Switzerland's oldest party—the FDP as the major representative of the liberal family—has been part of the national government without interruption for more than 170 years (Vatter and Milic 2019, 235). For over four decades, the so-called 'magic formula' (Burgos 2018; Burgos et al. 2011) ensured that the FDP, the Social Democrats (SP), and the Christian Democrats (CVP; now 'Die Mitte-Le Centre') each had two seats in the Federal Council, while the Swiss People's Party (SVP) was entitled to one seat. Although it was repeatedly criticized, for a long time no party succeeded in overturning the 'magic formula' that had been in force since 1959. However, since the turn of the millennium, major challenges have put this long-term stability under pressure. They originate in the concomitant electoral rise and radicalization of the SVP, which became the strongest party in 2003 (27.7 per cent of votes in the election to the National Council). Even if in earlier times, electoral success never translated directly into seat gains (Caluori and Hug 2003), the SVP was conceded a second representative in the Federal Council in 2003 with its charismatic leader Christoph Blocher. The Christian Democrats, in turn, lost one of their two seats. The new composition of the government did justice to the principle of proportional representation by mirroring changes in the relative strength of parties (Vatter and Milic 2019, 250). However, the SVP persisted in its confrontational course despite its stronger representation in government (Church und Vatter 2009).

Therefore, in the next 2007 complete re-election, the partisan composition of the government changed again. Even though non-re-elections of incumbent government members had been very exceptional events, Christoph Blocher was replaced by a more moderate SVP member, Eveline Widmer-Schlumpf. Yet shortly thereafter, she was excluded from the SVP, and contributed to the foundation of a new albeit minor party: the Bürgerlich-Demokratische Partei (BDP; now merged with Die Mitte). Hence, in 2007, the SVP lost its second seat and even ceased to be represented in government for a short period after its remaining member also joined the BDP, and it was only in 2015 that it recovered its second seat. The governmental formula incarnated anew the principle of proportionality, but in 2019 the Greens gathered more votes than the Christian

Democrats in the National Council election, and since then have been lining themselves up for seats in the seven-member cabinet.

Developments around the composition of the government over the last two decades—including shifts in representation plus more frequent pre-full-term resignations—indicate that Swiss politics in general has become undeniably more confrontational and less predictable. At the beginning of the magic formula, the four parties represented in the Federal Council gathered around 85 per cent of the seats in the National Council. Since the 2019 elections, this representation has fallen to a historic low point of less than 70 per cent. From an international perspective, Switzerland clearly continues to be a case of an oversized coalition, but within the country, political parties are fussing over cabinet seats on a scale seldom seen before.

2.4 Descriptive representation matters (too much?)

The principle of proportionality not only applies to partisan representation in the Federal Council. The cantonal origin of its members has also been an important criterion. Until 1999, the federal constitution even enshrined that a canton could not have more than one representative in government. Since the total revision of 1999, however, the rule became more flexible as the Constitution now stipulates that 'care must be taken to ensure that the various geographical and language regions of the country are appropriately represented' (art. 175 para. 4). At the level of larger regions this works: the three largest cantons (i.e. Bern, Vaud, Zurich) have always been part of the federal government, with few interruptions, and only a minority of small cantons have never been represented. Although they have almost always had a seat, the cantons of Zurich and Geneva are among the most clearly underrepresented cantons given their population size, while the cantons of Vaud and Neuchâtel count among the most overrepresented (Altermatt 2019a; Vatter 2020b). Closely linked to cantonal and regional origin is the criterion of language (Giudici and Stojanović 2016). There is an unwritten rule that at least two members should come from Latin-speaking Switzerland. The mother tongue of the Federal Councillors also matters because it influences the working language in their departments (ministries).

Another criterion that played a decisive role in the composition of the Federal Council until well into the twentieth century was denomination. In terms of confessional representation, a '5:2 formula' with a Protestant majority and a Catholic minority quickly settled (Vatter 2020b, 131). Today, confessional affiliation plays only a subordinate role. By contrast, gender became an important electoral criterion following the 1971 introduction of women's suffrage at the federal level. The first woman was elected to the Federal Council in 1984 but had to resign five years later. Until 1998, with few interruptions, women were only represented with one Federal Council seat out of seven. The claim for greater representation of women was asserted at each new election and, for a short time between 2010 and 2011, there were even more women than men in the

Federal Council. Since then, not more than three members of the Federal Council have been women.

Finally, given the high levels of personalization built into the Federal Council's mode of election, the reputation of the candidates certainly plays a role; albeit difficult to identify. In his typology of personality profiles of Federal Councillors, Vatter (2020b, 211–213) suggests that in the heyday of consociationalism between 1960 and the end of the 1980s, an above-average number of persons were elected who corresponded to the type of pragmatic public manager and policy broker. More recently, the prevailing profile has tended to change, as charismatic, extroverted, and dominant personalities have more often been elected; reflecting overall trends towards polarization and mediatization (Vatter 2020b, 338).

There is no doubt that the circle of eligible candidates is severely limited by the combination of the various criteria related to descriptive representation listed above, so that it is not necessarily the most competent who manage to get elected. To be sure, this is probably not what is primarily expected from party government, but the need for management and leadership qualities cannot be ignored either, especially if we keep in mind the wide area of competences of the individual Swiss ministries (see below). It may be that this leads to a more influential role for the bureaucracy—a more general trend nowadays, that is, however, difficult to evaluate. The reputational power of 'state executive actors'—as measured through surveys of insiders who are familiar with the business of politics (Sciarini et al. 2015, chapter 9)—remained steadily quite high compared with other actors involved in the policy process. Still, these findings do not allow one to distinguish between ministerial leadership and bureaucratic influence.

3 Position of the Government in the Federal Political System

As a body with strategic ambitions to plan and coordinate state policy, the Federal Council is a core decision-maker in the Swiss political system. Due to its formal independence from parliament, it has a comparatively strong institutional position. To be sure, the Federal Assembly has been able to strengthen its position vis-à-vis the government through a number of internal reforms since the end of the twentieth century, whose purpose was mainly to rehabilitate its legislative and control functions. In that sense, the Federal Assembly followed a path quite similar to that of many of its counterparts in democratic systems; it underwent a learning process and sought to 'strike back' against trends toward 'deparliamentarization'.[3] However, the re-empowerment of parliament vis-à-vis the government has been uneven. For example, there has been an increasing 'reparliamentarization' of decision-making processes in the area of social policy, attributed to the declining capacity of the neo-corporatist circuit to forge compromises between business and labour (Papadopoulos 2008; Afonso et al. 2010). By contrast, in policy areas that are strongly impacted by European integration, the influence of the government has increased significantly as the Federal Council is the only domestic actor involved in the intergovernmental arena of negotiations, and parliamentary influence on international agreements is constrained by their 'take it or leave it' character (Fischer and Sciarini 2019).

For parliament, empowerment vis-à-vis the government may thus be necessary yet not sufficient. If we consider the different sequences of the policy process in greater detail, it becomes apparent that the Federal Council is involved as an important actor in all of them (see 'Decision-Making Process' in this volume). The government first plays a central role in agenda-setting (Jaquet et al. 2019): on the one hand, it is frequently at the origin of new legislation, and, on the other hand, it exercises a filter function by only addressing a limited number of societal problems. However, it must be noted that the role of governments in initiating legislation tends to be even more prominent in pure parliamentary systems. We must also take into account that with the internationalization of policy processes, the share of Swiss legislation that is externally initiated has increased. Still, the government remains the key mediator between the external and the internal arena.

The Federal Council also plays a decisive role in the phase of policy formulation. In the so-called 'pre-parliamentary' procedure, it leads and manages the increasingly frequent consultation processes, in which cantons, parties, and interest as well as stakeholder groups express their views on proposed legislation. The administration, politically overseen by the government, then weights these views—having significant latitude to play a gatekeeping role at this phase (Bieri 2020). With the exception of parliamentary initiatives, the government subsequently formulates the draft piece of legislation addressed to parliament and justifies the proposed policy measures in an accompanying message.

Of course, Parliament is formally free to reject or amend the proposals of the Federal Council. Indeed, it acts as a veto point, especially with regard to important reforms (Gava et al. 2021), and the greater polarization of parliament made Swiss-style governing more challenging. A striking peculiarity of the Swiss system that would be inconceivable in parliamentary systems is that the two largest governmental parties SP and SVP, which are also at distant ideological poles, often behave as opposition parties, both in parliament and in direct-democratic votes. Whereas in the 1970s the government was usually backed by a dominant coalition of centre and right-wing parties, today the coalitions that support governmental bills are fluctuating.[4]

In Switzerland, legislation initiated by the government proves to be more robust than in the US presidential system in which executive and parliament are also largely independent from each other. Governmental bills that are rejected by parliament remain the exception (Schwartz et al. 2011). Representatives of the executive and the administration attend parliamentary committee meetings, which are considered to be the most important phase of the policy process (Sciarini et al. 2015) and are also influential therein because parliamentarians suffer from information gaps vis-à-vis the executive. As the

Federal Council can actively push through its goals in the plenary sessions of the Federal Assembly, its influence on the legislative process cannot be denied.

The indirect effect of direct democracy on the government's freedom to shape the content of policy should not be underestimated, either. In order to prevent a referendum from being triggered, the government must take into account at an early stage the claims of various organized actors, especially those who are notorious for successfully campaigning against and eventually voting down government-sponsored bills. At the same time, the government is not powerless in the face of popular opposition. It may, for example, strategically time the vote and skilfully put together voting packages in order to reduce the risk of failure at the ballot box. Moreover, it prominently develops its arguments in the official voting brochure, which most voters consider to be a reliable source and widely use as an information cue. In addition, individual members of the government are active in referendum campaigns (e.g. by delivering speeches or going on TV). Furthermore, the government retains relatively large leeway after a law goes into force as it has the formal authority to draft ordinances. Laws often leave open questions beyond mere 'technical' issues, and therefore the ability to shape the content of ordinances may translate into non-negligible policy influence.[5] Attempts by parliament to keep a closer eye on the Federal Council in the case of ordinances with the establishment of veto rights have so far failed.

In sum, the Federal Council can exert considerable influence in different forms at all stages of the policy process. Still, its power is constrained. Its effect on legislation varies across policy sectors and is context-dependent. Either way, the image of an unchallenged hierarchical body that exercises its power in a top-down mode would not be an adequate description. Rather, the Federal Council should be seen as a core node that is part of a complex web of actors and negotiations, using its position to seek consensus whenever possible or at least sufficient support for its goals and policies. The Swiss government's leadership function means establishing and consolidating influence through intermediation procedures rather than imposing ideological agendas.

4 Internal organization

The Constitution sets out the government's most important organizational principles: the collegial, the departmental, and the delegation principles. We discuss the three principles and their implications for the structural and procedural organization of the executive.

4.1 Principle of collegiality

The principle of collegiality is a core specificity of the Swiss government system. It can be disaggregated into two relatively simple legal principles (Vatter 2020b), although the translation of these principles into concrete political practice may not always be straightforward.

Firstly, the constitution prescribes that the government reaches its decisions as a collegial body (art. 177). Although majority decisions are formally possible, there is a strong imperative for consensus whenever possible, and majority rule should apply only exceptionally whenever internal conflicts cannot be surmounted otherwise. Actually, we do not know how often a vote is necessary because discussions within the college are confidential to favour a deliberative atmosphere, and in all likelihood they involve some give and take.

Secondly, the college members are required to support governmental decisions, even if these may be contrary to a member's personal or party-political views, as the Government and Administration Organization Act stipulates. This means that, once taken, a minister is bound by a collegial decision and he or she must defend it in public even if he or she was outvoted within the governmental college. There have been some breaches of that principle, although this is quite unusual.

Within the college, each of the seven ministers has one vote, while in other countries, heads of the executive branch have the power to impose their decisions on the cabinet (Altermatt 2019b, 31). The Federal Assembly elects the president of the Swiss Confederation among the seven members of the government every year according to the seniority principle that was established at the end of the nineteenth century (Altermatt 2021). Although the degree of support from parliament may vary, the principle of a yearly rotation—designed to avoid power concentration—is not contested in practice, thus the election is not competitive.[6] Initially, the president was a stronger figure compared to today's standards, leading a dedicated department in charge of foreign affairs and security matters. However, about a century ago, it was established that the function is just that of a 'primus inter pares': he or she mainly has a representative role and chairs the Federal Council's meetings. The president does not benefit politically from that position. Even if it allows him or her to shape to some extent the debates in the college or strengthen its international reputation, it is difficult to assess whether that prerogative truly gives an advantage, which should not be in any way substantial and surely is not systematic. Politicians and commentators often claim that the presidential position should be strengthened, mainly with an extension of the mandate's term, but as with other proposals to reform the government, no concrete steps have been undertaken thus far.

There are advantages to this peculiar 'collegial' governmental style (and form) that are more generally apparent in collaborative modes of governance (Papadopoulos 2012). Power is not concentrated and unlike in other countries, it remains unaffected by the 'presidentialisation' of politics (Poguntke and Webb 2005), which is reflected in the advent of the 'court' government (Savoie 2008) in which the prime minister and a small group of persons around him or her dominate (e.g. a few ministers, policy professionals, public relations specialists). There is better representativeness and greater pluralism through the broad inclusion of various regional, cultural, and partisan interests. Continuity also profits from the collegial system. Furthermore, the decisions' overall epistemic quality is higher because the skills and experience of several people can be pooled within the college; although, we have seen that conciliating multiple representation criteria may come to the detriment of selecting the most competent individuals.

However, there are downsides to the collegial mode of government, too. Power fragmentation within the governmental college may lead to mutual obstruction, and ultimately to policy blockade because the internal procedures of office consultation and co-report can be instrumentalized for promoting or preserving narrow partisan or bureaucratic interests (see below). To avoid this, haggling becomes inevitable. In the absence of hierarchical coordination, ministers primarily seek to avoid damage caused to matters under their responsibility, and ultimately it is just 'negative' coordination that tends to prevail. Given that the college's internal veto points add up to the parliamentary and direct-democratic veto points to inhibit far-reaching reforms, there is a risk of suboptimal outputs to the detriment of comprehensive and forward-looking policies.

Finally, the more recent phenomenon of the mediatization has not left the Swiss government system unaffected and has put the collegial principle under pressure (Landerer 2015). Disagreements within the college are obviously newsworthy for the media, and are therefore increasingly disclosed and commented. They aliment the public debate, while confidentiality is a prerequisite for the collegial government's smooth operation. As the phenomenon of mediatization coincides with that of polarization, the members of the Federal Council are caught between the government's collective opinion and their own party preferences (Sager and Vatter 2019, 208). This is even more true because the Swiss multiparty government—unlike in parliamentary systems—does not have a coalition agreement to which all coalition partners have agreed to commit.

4.2 Departmental and delegation principle

Similar to the collegial principle, the departmental principle is anchored in the federal constitution (art. 177), but their coexistence is not without ambiguities and frictions. To a certain extent, the departmental principle forms a counterweight to the collegial principle (Sager and Vatter 2019, 204; Vatter 2020b, 239ff) because it gives the seven ministers the opportunity to incorporate their ideological beliefs and personal preferences in their policy choices, even though they may fade into the background in the governmental college. In concrete terms, the principle entails that the governmental business is divided among the ministries (called 'departments' in Switzerland). In addition, the principle of delegation, closely linked to the departmental principle, states that the treatment of individual policy issues can formally be delegated to the departments. The departmental heads may in turn delegate the formulation of policy proposals to the departmental administration, mostly to the numerous federal offices that are part of the department's hierarchical structure. This of course raises the issue of administrative power, especially because—also due to the ever-increasing number of federal tasks—the administration has expanded and become more differentiated, above all vertically (Ladner et al. 2013; for the vertical dimension see 'Federal Administration' in this volume).

The strong vertical differentiation contrasts with the limited horizontal differentiation, as the number of government members and departments has been limited to seven since 1848, and cannot increase without amending the federal constitution. Hence, all areas of responsibility of the modern federal state must be distributed among only seven departments, and this peculiarity leads to tasks accumulating in the individual departments. The most emblematic cases of 'mammoth' ministries are those of the Federal Department of the Environment, Transport, Energy, and Communications and of the Federal Department of Home Affairs, which includes many diverse and unrelated areas. Moreover, economy, education, and research are concentrated in the Department of Economic Affairs, and Defence, Civil Protection, and Sport is a single ministry as well.

The heterogeneity of ministries has advantages and disadvantages regarding efficacy. First, coordination problems can possibly be solved within a single department, which to a certain extent relieves the governmental college of such tasks. Important reforms in recent years in several established democracies have strengthened the cohesion of governmental action (the 'joined-up government' or 'whole of government' approaches). They have strengthened the centre ('core executive') and have developed organizations and mechanisms aimed at integrating governmental policies and mediating and arbitrating between 'baronies' (see Elgie 2011). This movement did not really affect Switzerland, simply because the weak horizontal differentiation reduced the functional pressure. Conversely, the internal heterogeneity obviously increases the workload of government members. Repeatedly, departmental responsibilities were reorganized, but as long as the governmental college is not extended to include more members, there is no foreseeable improvement regarding the problem of overload.

4.3 Organizational processes

The diverse internal processes make the Swiss executive a highly complex system. As a rule, lengthy and elaborate rounds of consultation precede Federal Council decisions, which in principle are open to all interested parties. One should mainly distinguish two successive and strongly codified coordination and negotiation procedures within the administrative apparatus (Bundesamt für Justiz 2019): office consultation and co-report procedure.

In the preliminary so-called office consultation (*Ämterkonsultation*), the federal office (subdivision) that has the lead on a bill submits its proposal to the interested offices within the federal administration for their comments. Considering the clarification of substantial matters and the elimination of any differences is relatively time-consuming, this initial procedure usually takes about two months. Once office consultation is concluded, the so-called co-report procedure (*Mitberichtsverfahren*) begins with an official proposal that incorporates feedback from the previous procedure, sent to the Federal Chancellery and to all seven departments. The Federal Chancellery explicitly invites departments that have a particular interest in a matter to submit a 'co-report', but all departments can formulate comments. Co-reports are then sent to all departments, the lead department can draft a statement on the opinions expressed in the co-reports, and the various departments can in turn react to the lead department's views.

This iterative process is necessary for internal consensus-building (or at least for identifying controversial points) before the heads of the departments meet in the collegial executive to take decisions. It reduces the Federal Council's workload, which can thus address uncontroversial business swiftly. However, the rising polarization that is also reflected in the debates within the Federal Council has weakened the internal coordination mechanisms by making it more difficult to reach agreement in advance. Although hard data are not available, it seems that the frequency of majority decisions within the governmental college has increased, albeit not steadily so and heavily depending on incumbents' personality traits (Vatter 2020b).

It can be objected that, in most cases, the inter-ministerial policy coordination procedures remain effective and lead to decisions upon which all government members can agree. However, these procedures have some disadvantages. Unsurprisingly, the departments tend to be interested only in those matters that directly affect them, and inter-ministerial coordination procedures do not seem to offset the increasing departmentalization (Brühl-Moser 2019). Consequently, the Federal Council has begun to address strategic issues in internal discussions that take place in advance of formal decision-making processes. However, this occurs with no guarantee that such discussions lead to broadly supported decisions likely to survive the successive veto points.

5 Governmental reform

5.1 Limits to effectiveness

The unique Swiss collegial government system combined with a permanent grand coalition has clearly deployed integrative effects. It has not only ensured a high degree of political stability but has also contributed to taming political conflict. Nevertheless, this system is criticized for its lack of transparency, adaptability, and innovation capacity. Not only is the departmentalization seen as undermining the coherence of government actions, but critics also point out the chronic overburdening of the Federal Council. Therefore, the government's activities have been the subject of various reports by parliamentary control committees and by the office in charge of parliamentary control of the administration since the 1990s. Among other criticisms, they have blamed the government for not performing its functions adequately, especially in crises, and for only providing limited strategic guidance and adequate information (e.g. GPK 2010; PVK 2009).[7] The observed weaknesses relate to different challenges.

First, there is the volume of work related to the increasing complexity of policy problems. From the 1990s onwards, there has been a significant increase in legislative activities (Linder 2014). This leads to considerable interdependencies between policy areas, which makes planning and implementing policy measures much more difficult, resulting in greater efforts for government and administration to coordinate. This is no Swiss specificity of course, but departmentalization inhibits such efforts. Although ministerial 'baronies' are common in most democratic government systems, the absence of strong leadership in the collegial form of government causes an additional problem. Increasing Europeanization and internationalization pose a further problem for the government. Whereas in the past it was primarily the Department of Foreign Affairs, often joined by the Department of Defence, that was responsible for foreign policy, today almost all departments are involved in some form or another. Furthermore, domestic polarization challenges the Swiss policy style, which relies on bargaining and side-payments. For example, reforms to ensure the sustainability of the pension system have been on the agenda for several decades now, but the status quo still prevails in many areas due to opposition from different sides. In summary, the demands have grown on government for many reasons; however, the government is not well equipped to cope with that increase.

5.2 Reform proposals

In view of the above-mentioned challenges, repeated efforts to reform the government and the administration are not surprising.[8] The Federal Chancellery was significantly upgraded as a coordination body, and there were some reforms of the administrative structure. However, the structure of the Federal Council remained unchanged despite the recurrence of reform proposals.

Starting as early as the 1880/90s, numerous reform initiatives failed. Unsurprisingly, relatively radical proposals such as that of a shift to a parliamentary or a presidential system were rejected quite early (APS 1992, 33; 1993, 36), but in 1996, the electorate rejected an even more modest proposal to strengthen governmental capacity with the nomination of more state secretaries. The Government and Administration Organization Act was finally reformed in 1997, mostly paving the way for managerialist reforms of the federal administration.

In the process of the total revision of the Constitution, the government saw an opportunity to present its own reform proposal. In 1998, it thus envisaged the separation of strategic from operational tasks that would be delegated to 'ministers' assisting the seven government members. However, the parliament rejected the governmental proposal at the beginning of 2004, and claimed new reform options from the government. The Federal Council presented five reform proposals in 2010, one of which was to extend the term of office of the Federal Presidency from one year to two.[9] These—relatively unambitious—efforts shared the fate of other reform proposals: they were reduced to a mere administrative reform (Thom and Ritz 2017, 26). Parliament rejected the extension of the president's and vice-president's term of office, and it limited itself to strengthening the Federal Chancellery (e.g. adding a Presidential Service Unit) and to creating more state secretary positions.

Overall, the Federal Council has proved extremely resistant to reform (Brühl-Moser 2019, 126), and whenever the government took some initiatives, they were countered by veto points; be it in parliament or in a referendum. Therefore, it is hardly surprising that more recent reform endeavours, which aim to increase the size of the Federal Council (from seven to nine members, for example), have negligible chances as well, although they also appear on the political agenda at regular intervals. Parliamentary motions and cantonal initiatives have called for an increase in the comparatively small size of the federal executive, too. This is a simple reform that pursues different objectives: reduce the workload of the government's individual members, optimize the division of departments according to policy areas, and increase the representativeness of the governing body. Less noble partisan considerations also militate for such an increase because a nine-member body would more easily satisfy smaller parties such as the Greens, whose claim to be represented in the government following their electoral successes could then be accommodated without any prejudice for the representation of the other parties.

6 Conclusion

Switzerland owes its political stability not least to its unique system of government—combining the formal collegial principle with a grand coalition—in addition to direct democracy and federalism. This country has demonstrated its ability to integrate successfully various minorities and to involve them in politics, to build a performant state, and to maintain economic prosperity. This is reflected in the confidence in political actors and institutions, which (according to European Social Survey data) is high by international standards and has even increased regarding trust in government operations.[10]

However, one should not underestimate the negative effect of partisan polarization on a system of government that, although designed to mitigate conflict, cannot operate smoothly when the governing parties are drifting apart. For example, conflict among governmental parties, combined with the absence of strong governmental leadership, led to an unresolved relationship with the European Union and consequently to the country's relative political isolation. More generally, governing has become more difficult in recent years. The governing parties support the Federal Council's position less and less in parliamentary debates and referendum campaigns (Vatter 2020a, 540–41). This is particularly true for the SVP and the Social Democrats—the two parties with the highest share of the vote in elections and most seats in the National Council. Thus, in the last decade, less than 20 per cent of all bills were supported by all governing parties in the National Council, which is striking for observers familiar with how parliamentary systems function (Papadopoulos and Maggetti 2018). Together with the increasing mediatization and personalization in Swiss politics, such tendencies may further reinforce the centrifugal forces that departmentalization entails (Hinterleitner and Sager 2019). Therefore, the Federal Council can only fulfil its strategic leadership role with difficulty, especially in view of existing structural constraints: an excessive workload due to the limited number of members of the executive and the very broad area of competence of most governmental departments.

A reform of the federal government, which has remained almost unchanged for more than 170 years, seems increasingly necessary. Realistically, such innovations can only be brought about gradually (Bär 2011). However, the perception that the government's capabilities must be enhanced—which appears especially in times of crisis such as the COVID-19 pandemic (KSBC 2020; Sager and Mavrot 2020)—stands in contrast to the so-far half-hearted and very modest concrete reform proposals. The Federal Council does not seem to have an urgent appetite for reform because reforms potentially involve a certain loss of power (e.g. burden-sharing with yet another colleague that would get 'a piece of the pie'). However, governmental ownership of reforms is a necessary condition for their success, even though by no means a sufficient one in a system with as many veto points as the Swiss one. It is therefore reasonable to assume that the governmental and administrative structures described in this chapter and the related processes will continue to exist in their current form for quite some time. This is also plausible because the Federal Council still enjoys a particularly high level of trust among Swiss citizens (see 'The Political Culture of Switzerland in Comparative Perspective' in this volume), which is an important resource for addressing the numerous challenges confronting it.

Notes

1. We are grateful to Adrian Vatter for his insightful comments, and to Lysiane Adamini and Deborah Fritzsche for research assistance. For more extensive developments on the Swiss federal government see the contributions in Ritz, Haldemann, and Sager (2019) and the book by Vatter (2020b).
2. Collegial executives existed intermittently in Uruguay (inspired by the Swiss model), and one finds collegial features today in the executives of multi-ethnic Bosnia-Herzegovina and of the micro-states Andorra and San Marino.
3. In European parliamentary systems the decline of parliamentary influence is mainly attributed to the prominent role of executives in European integration: on parliamentary reaction see Auel and Benz (2005). One observes, though, a more assertive role of Congress in the US separation of power system of government too: see for instance Kriner and Schickler (2017) regarding the control function.
4. It is now quite exceptional that all governmental parties support a bill in a referendum vote, but in votes in which three of the four governing parties supported the bill, citizens

voted in favour of the governmental option in around 80 per cent of cases (Papadopoulos and Maggetti 2018).
5. See the comparative study of Huber and Shipan (2002).
6. The elected vice-president is elected as president the year after.
7. For example, the Swiss federal audit office evaluated the administration's prospective impact assessments conducted for legislative projects and found that the available assessment tools were under-used. Moreover, where they were used, the reliability of their results was questionable (Contrôle fédéral des finances 2016).
8. See Vatter (2020b, 283–330), who presents a systematic evaluation of the existing proposals for governmental reform. Their assessment is based on predefined criteria and the author formulates his own proposals on the same basis.
9. This option has been recurrently on the agenda, particularly in view of the internationalization of policy-making and the ensuing necessity of continuity in the interactions between the Swiss Presidency and the foreign Heads of state and government (Vatter 2020b, 283–285).
10. See https://www.defacto.expert/2018/05/28/vertrauen-regierung-parlament/ (accessed 17 August 2023).

References

Afonso, Alexandre, Marie-Christine Fontana, and Yannis Papadopoulos. 2010. 'Does Europeanisation Weaken the Left? Changing Coalitions and Veto Power in Swiss Decision-Making Processes'. *Policy & Politics* 38 (4): pp. 565–582. doi: 10.1332/030557310X501794.

Altermatt, Urs (ed.). 2019a. *Das Bundesratslexikon*. Zurich: NZZ Libro.

Altermatt, Urs. 2019b. 'Von der Koalitionsregierung von 1848 zur Konkordanzregierung von 1959'. In *Blackbox Exekutive*, edited by Adrian Ritz, Theo Haldemann, and Fritz Sager, pp. 29–48. Zurich: NZZ Libro.

Altermatt, Urs. 2021. 'Zwei Klassen von Bundesräten'. *Neue Zürcher Zeitung*, 9 December 2021, p. 7.

Altman, David. 2020. 'Checking Executive Personalism: Collegial Governments and the Level of Democracy'. *Swiss Political Science Review* 26 (3): pp. 316–338. doi: 10.1111/spsr.12406.

APS – Année politique suisse. various years. https://anneepolitique.swiss/. Bern: Institut für Politikwissenschaft.

Bär, Theo. 2011. *Die Regierungsreform im Bund in kleinen Schritten und auf einem engen Pfad, Inkrementalismus und Pfadabhängigkeit*. Lausanne: Cahier de l'IDHEAP.

Auel, Katrin, and Arthur Benz. 2005. 'The Politics of Adaptation: The Europeanisation of National Parliamentary Systems'. *The Journal of Legislative Studies* 11 (3/4): pp. 372–393. doi: 10.1080/13572330500273570.

Bieri, Niklaus. 2020. 'Die Verwaltung als Gatekeeper im Vernehmlassungsverfahren'. *Swiss Yearbook of Administrative Sciences* 11 (1): pp. 1–11. doi: 10.5334/ssas.134.

Brühl-Moser, Denise. 2019. 'Staatsleitungen im internationalen Vergleich'. In *Blackbox Exekutive*, edited by Adrian Ritz, Theo Haldemann, and Fritz Sager, pp. 97–139. Zurich: NZZ Libro.

Bundesamt für Justiz. 2019. *Gesetzgebungsleitfaden. Leitfaden für die Ausarbeitung von Erlassen des Bundes*. Bern: EDMZ.

Burgos, Elie. 2018. *La composition partisane du Conseil fédéral et la 'formule magique'. Le consensus helvétique en question*. PhD thesis, University of Lausanne.

Burgos, Elie, Oscar Mazzoleni, and Hervé Rayner. 2011. *La formule magique. Conflits et consensus dans l'élection du Conseil fédéral*. Lausanne: Presses polytechniques et universitaires romandes.

Caluori, Ladina, and Simon Hug. 2003. 'Changes in the Partisan Composition of the Swiss Government: 1891, 1919, 1929, 1943, 1959, 2003 ... ?'. *Swiss Political Science Review* 11 (3): pp. 101–121. doi: 10.1002/j.1662-6370.2005.tb00364.x.

Church, Clive, and Adrian Vatter. 2009. 'Opposition in Consensual Switzerland: A Short but Significant Experiment'. *Government and Opposition* 44 (4): pp. 412–437. doi: 10.1111/j.1477-7053.2009.01295.x.

Contrôle fédéral des finances. 2016. *Prévisions dans les messages du Conseil fédéral. Evaluation des analyses prospectives de l'impact des projets législatifs*. https://www.efk.admin.ch/images/stories/efk_dokumente/publikationen/evaluationen/Evaluationen%20(50)/14486BE_f.pdf (accessed 17 August 2023).

Elgie, Robert. 2011. 'Core Executive Studies Two Decades On'. *Public Administration* 89 (1): pp. 64–77. doi: 10.1111/j.1467-9299.2011.01899.x.

Fischer, Manuel, and Pascal Sciarini. 2019. 'Die Position der Regierung in Entscheidungsstrukturen'. In *Blackbox Exekutive*, edited by Adrian Ritz, Theo Haldemann, and Fritz Sager, pp. 49–64. Zurich: NZZ Libro.

Gava, Roy, Jaquet, Julien, and Pascal Sciarini. 2021. 'Legislating or Rubber-Stamping? Assessing parliament's Influence on Law-Making with Text Reuse'. *European Journal of Political Research* 60 (1): pp. 175–198. doi: 10.1111/1475-6765.12395.

Giudici, Anja, and Nenad Stojanović. 2016. 'Die Zusammensetzung des Schweizerischen Bundesrates nach Partei, Region, Sprache und Religion, 1848–2015'. *Swiss Political Science Review* 22 (2): pp. 288–307. doi: 10.1111/spsr.12214.

GPK – Geschäftsprüfungskommissionen des Nationalrates und des Ständerates. 2010. *Die Behörden unter dem Druck der Finanzkrise und der Herausgabe von UBS-Kundendaten an die USA. Bericht der Geschäftsprüfungskommission des Nationalrates und des Ständerates vom 30. Mai 2010*. https://www.parlament.ch/centers/documents/de/bericht-gpk-ns-ubs-kundendaten-usa-2010-05-30-d.pdf (accessed 17 August 2023)..

Hinterleitner, Markus, and Fritz Sager. 2019. 'Krisenmanagement und Risikovermeidung'. In *Blackbox Exekutive*, edited by Adrian Ritz, Theo Haldemann, and Fritz Sager, pp. 409–427. Zurich: NZZ Libro.

Huber, John D., and Charles R. Shipan. 2002: *Deliberate Discretion? The Institutional Foundations of Bureaucratic Autonomy*. Cambridge: Cambridge University Press.

Jaquet, Julien M., Pascal Sciarini, and Frédéric Varone. 2019. 'Policy-Agenda-Setting: Regierung als Hauptinitiator von Entscheidungsprozessen?'. In *Blackbox Exekutive*, edited by Adrian Ritz, Theo Haldemann, and Fritz Sager, pp. 213–233. Zurich: NZZ Libro.

Keman, Hans. 1996. 'Konkordanzdemokratie und Korporatismus aus der Perspektive eines rationalen Institutionalismus'. *Politische Vierteljahresschrift* 37 (3): pp. 494–516.

Kriner, Douglas L. and Eric Schickler. 2017 *Investigating the President: Congressional Checks on Presidential Power*. Princeton: Princeton University Press.

KSBC – Krisenstab des Bundesrats Corona. 2020. *Schlussbericht*. https://www.newsd.admin.ch/newsd/message/attachments/61814.pdf (accessed 17 August 2023).

Ladner, Andreas, Jean-Loup Chappelet, Yves Emery, Peter Knoepfel, Luzius Mader, Nils Soguel, and Frédéric Varone (eds). 2013. *Handbuch der öffentlichen Verwaltung in der Schweiz*. Zurich: NZZ Libro.

Landerer, Nino. 2015. *Mass Media and Political Decision-Making: Analyzing Mediatization in Switzerland*. Baden-Baden: Nomos.

Lijphart, Arend. 1968. *The Politics of Accommodation: Pluralism and Democracy in the Netherlands*. Berkeley, CA: University of California Press.

Lijphart, Arend. 2012. *Patterns of Democracy: Government Forms and Performance in Thirty-Six Countries*. New Haven/London: Yale University Press.

Linder, Wolf. 2014. 'Swiss Legislation in the Era of Globalisation: A Quantitative Assessment of Federal Legislation'. *Swiss Political Science Review* 20 (2): pp. 223–231. doi: 10.1111/spsr.12100.

Neidhart, Leonard. 1970. *Plebiszit und pluralitäre Demokratie. Eine Analyse der Funktion des Schweizerischen Gesetzesreferendums*. Bern: Francke.

Papadopoulos, Yannis. 1997. *Les processus de décision fédéraux en Suisse*. Paris: L'Harmattan.

Papadopoulos, Yannis. 2008. 'Europeanisation? Two Logics of Change of Policy-Making Patterns in Switzerland'. *Journal of Comparative Policy Analysis* 10 (3): pp. 253–276. doi: 10.1080/13876980802231107.

Papadopoulos, Yannis. 2012. 'The Democratic Quality of Cooperative Governance'. In *The Oxford Handbook of Governance*, edited by David Levi-Faur, pp. 512–526. Oxford: Oxford University Press.

Papadopoulos, Yannis, and Martino Maggetti. 2018. 'Policy Style(s) in Switzerland: Under Stress'. In *Policy Styles and Policy-Making: Exploring the Linkages*, edited by Michael Howlett, and Jale Tosun, pp. 157–179. Abingdon: Routledge.

Poguntke, Thomas and Paul Webb (eds). 2005 *The Presidentialization of Politics. A Comparative Study of Modern Democracies*. Oxford: Oxford University Press.

PVK – Parlamentarische Verwaltungskontrolle. 2009. *Die strategische politische Steuerung des Bundesrates. Bericht der Parlamentarischen Verwaltungskontrolle zuhanden der Geschäftsprüfungskommission des Nationalrates vom 15. Oktober 2009*. https://www.parlament.ch/centers/documents/de/pvk-strateg-polit-steuerung-bundesrat-2009-10-15-d.pdf (accessed 17 August 2023).

Ritz, Adrian, Theo Haldemann, and Fritz Sager (eds). 2019. *Blackbox Exekutive*. Zurich: NZZ Libro.

Sager Fritz, and Céline Mavrot. 2020. 'Switzerland's COVID-19 Policy Response: Consociational Crisis Management and Neo-corporatist Reopening'. *European Policy Analysis* 6 (2): pp. 293–304. doi: 10.1002/epa2.1094.

Sager, Fritz, and Adrian Vatter. 2019. 'Regierungshandeln im Spannungsfeld von Partei- und Exekutivpolitik am Beispiel des Bundesrats'. In *Blackbox Exekutive*, edited by Adrian Ritz, Theo Haldemann, and Fritz Sager, pp. 195–211. Zurich: NZZ Libro.

Savoie, Donald. 2008. *Court Government and the Collapse of Accountability in Canada and the United Kingdom*. Toronto: University of Toronto Press.

Schwartz, Daniel, André Bächtiger, and Georg Lutz. 2011. 'Agenda-Setting Power of the Government in a Separation-of-Powers Framework'. In *The Role of Governments in Legislative Agenda-Setting*, edited by Bjorn Erik Rasch, and George Tsebelis, pp. 127–143. Abingdon: Routledge.

Sciarini, Pascal, Manuel Fischer, and Denise Traber. 2015. *Political Decision-Making in Switzerland. The Consensus Model under Pressure*. Basingstoke: Palgrave.

Thom, Norbert, and Adrian Ritz. 2017. *Public Management. Innovative Konzepte zur Führung im öffentlichen Sektor*. Wiesbaden: Gabler.

Vatter, Adrian. 2008. 'Vom Extremtyp zum Normalfall? Die schweizerische Konsensusdemokratie im Wandel: Eine Re-Analyse von Lijpharts Studie für die Schweiz von 1997 bis 2007'. *Swiss Political Science Review* 14 (1): pp. 1–47. doi: 10.1002/j.1662-6370.2008.tb00095.x.

Vatter, Adrian. 2020a. *Das politische System der Schweiz*. Baden-Baden: Nomos.

Vatter, Adrian. 2020b. *Der Bundesrat. Die Schweizer Regierung*. Zurich: NZZ Libro.

Vatter, Adrian, Rahel Freiburghaus, and Alexander Arens. 2020. 'Coming a Long Way: Switzerland's Transformation from a Majoritarian to a Consensus Democracy (1848–2018)'. *Democratization* 27 (6): pp. 970–989. doi: 10.1080/13510347.2020.1755264.

Vatter, Adrian, and Thomas Milic. 2019. 'Regierungskoalitionen in der Schweiz'. In *Blackbox Exekutive*, edited by Adrian Ritz, Theo Haldemann, and Fritz Sager, pp. 235–254. Zurich: NZZ Libro.

CHAPTER 12

JUDICIAL SYSTEM

MARTINA FLICK WITZIG,
CHRISTINE ROTHMAYR ALLISON, AND
FRÉDÉRIC VARONE

1 INTRODUCTION

SINCE the mid-1990s, political scientists have become increasingly interested in analysing legal institutions from a comparative perspective—and this is particularly true outside of the US context (e.g. Tate and Vallinder 1995; Shapiro and Stone 1994). The rising worldwide influence of constitutional courts and supranational courts has led to many empirical case studies and much comparative research (e.g. Kagan and Axelrad 2001; Tate 2002; Ginsburg 2003; Hirschl 2004; Kelemen 2011; Burke and Barnes 2017; Brouard and Hönnige 2017). These studies all confirm that courts and judges are influential actors in the political process and demonstrate that the methodological tools commonly applied in political science can be successfully used to research the role and impact of courts (Shapiro and Stone 1994, 398), including experiments (Engst et al. 2020).

In Switzerland, we also observe a growing political science interest in research on the judiciary. Various qualitative studies are available on the influence of the judiciary (Rothmayr 1999 and 2001; Tornay 2008; Flückiger et al. 2000; Tanquerel et al. 2008; Rothmayr and L'Espérance 2017). Other studies address legal mobilization (Fuchs 2013, 2019) or the election of judges (Vatter and Ackermann 2014). Researchers may be interested in judges as part of the political elite (Tippenhauer 2010) or in analysing the constitutional jurisdiction at the cantonal level (Flick Witzig and Vatter 2020). Concerning administrative justice, we have data on the development of case numbers and success rates, which allow us to discuss hypotheses on judicialization and legal mobilization (Tanquerel et al. 2011; Byland and Varone 2012; Varone and Byland 2019). Moreover, various evaluation studies have contributed to a better understanding of judicial reforms and their effects (Lienhard et al. 2012). Much of this research is interested in the area of constitutional and administrative law, to which we limit our elaborations below as well.

Our contribution aims to outline the basic features of the organization of the judiciary in Switzerland. In addition, we address aspects of judicialization, a phenomenon that has strongly shaped political science research on courts in recent decades. In doing so, we address the competencies of the Federal Supreme Court in its role as a constitutional court, the modalities of appointing judges, and the influence of internationalization. We conclude with a brief comparative assessment of the central features of the Swiss judicial system.

2 STRUCTURE AND ORGANIZATION OF THE JUDICIARY

In March 2000, a majority of 84 per cent of the voters approved amendments to the Swiss federal constitution (FC), with some articles reforming the judiciary and its structure at the federal level and, to a limited extent, also in the cantons. This reform, which entered into force on 1 January 2007,[1] significantly strengthened the independence of the judiciary, harmonized important elements that were somewhat disconnected in the past, and contributed to further differentiation of the Swiss judicial system. Following the reform, Switzerland now has four federal courts: the Federal Supreme Court (into which the formerly independent Federal Insurance Court is now incorporated), the Federal Administrative Court, the Federal Criminal Court, and the Federal Patent Court.

The Federal Supreme Court (FSC), based in Lausanne, is, according to article 188 FC, the 'highest federal judicial authority'. The FSC, consisting of thirty-eight ordinary judges and nineteen deputy judges (FSC 2022), is the court of final appeal, and it thus watches over the correct and uniform application of federal civil, criminal, and administrative law. In addition but to a limited extent, it exercises the powers of constitutional review (see below).

The second federal court, the Federal Administrative Court based in St. Gallen, took up its work in 2007. With its seventy-six judges, it is the largest court of the Swiss Federation. It reviews the decisions of the federal administration. In specific fields, it may also hear complaints against decisions made by cantonal governments (e.g. matters of health insurance; Federal Administrative Court 2022; see Figure 12.1). The judgements of the Federal Administrative Court can in most cases be appealed to the FSC. However, in some realms like asylum law, the decisions of the Federal Administrative Court are final. The creation of the Federal Administrative Court is the culmination of a long and complex process of allowing independent courts to control administrative decisions by shifting this power away from the executive (i.e. the Federal Council, extra-parliamentary commissions (see Rebmann and Mach 2013) or cantonal governments). Now, there is access to independent courts in all cases, except for cases of a genuine political character. Indeed, a new constitutional provision (art. 29a FC) guarantees such access as an enforceable individual right.

The third federal court, the Federal Criminal Court, is based in Bellinzona and has been operational since 2004. With its eighteen judges, it is a court of the first instance competent to decide criminal cases assigned to it by law (art. 191a FC), including crimes of an especially serious nature. The Federal Criminal Court performs several additional tasks, such as hearing complaints against the Federal Prosecutor, ordering compulsory measures in federal penal procedures, and resolving jurisdictional conflicts between federal and cantonal criminal authorities. Its decisions may be appealed to the FSC (Federal Criminal Court 2022).

Finally, the Federal Patent Court has exclusive jurisdiction in civil matters relating to the validity and the infringement of patents. Based in St Gallen, the Court took up its work in 2012 with two permanent and forty-one non-permanent judges. Its decisions can be appealed to the FSC (Federal Chancellery 2021).

Due to the establishment of the new courts at the federal level, two major goals of the judicial system reform have been achieved. First, the overburdened FSC is relieved from certain tasks, such as having to act in some cases as a court of first instance. This allows the FSC to maintain its efficiency as the highest court. Second, legal protections are enhanced by granting private parties access to courts in all areas of law, which had not been the case prior to the reform.

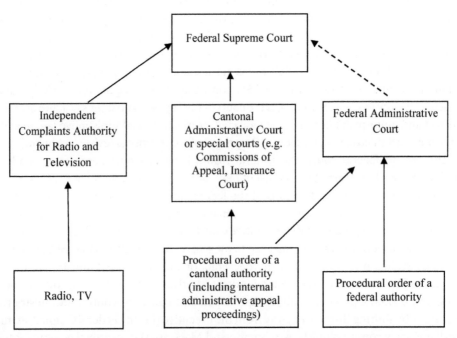

FIGURE 12.1: Administrative law claims

In certain cases, explicitly mentioned in art. 83 of the Federal Supreme Court Act, the Federal Administrative Court decides as the final complaints body (e.g. rulings on ordinary naturalization, in the fields of immigration and asylum law, etc.).

Data source: Adapted from Tanquerel et al. (2011, 26) and FSC (2019, 26).

Except for the federal courts just presented, the cantonal law establishes all Swiss judicial authorities. The cantons enjoy extensive autonomy in the organization of the judiciary, but they usually have two levels of courts in their judicial organization, for both civil and criminal cases. The judicial system is often divided between lower courts, which are organized by districts or regions, and the Cantonal Court, a single higher authority. For administrative matters, cantonal administrative authorities may act as courts of first instance. Typically, the cantonal administrative court as the last cantonal instance before an appeal to the FSC (Mahon 2019, 145f.) supervises their activities and decisions.

3 Aspects of Judicialization and Politicization

3.1 Restricted constitutional review

Due to its jurisdictional limitations, the FSC differs from the highest courts in other countries. Because federal laws are excluded from the constitutional review of all courts, the FSC is limited to examining the constitutionality of cantonal laws and federal ordinances:[2] the FSC cannot and must not apply unconstitutional ordinances of the Federal Council or Federal Assembly (Tanquerel 2020, 226). However, as far as laws adopted by the Federal Assembly are concerned, the FSC has no power to annul them if they are unconstitutional, and it can't even refuse to apply them (art. 190 FC). The constitution, therefore, obliges judges to apply federal laws, but it does not prohibit them from ruling on their compliance. In other words, if the FSC finds a federal law to be in conflict with the constitution, it can state this in a decision and thus call on the legislature to remedy the situation. In this sense, the Swiss concept differs fundamentally from the 'European' and the 'American' models of constitutional jurisdiction (Epstein et al. 2001). In other respects, the Swiss system combines elements characteristic of both models, as Table 12.1 below reveals. Regarding cantonal legislation, Switzerland is in line with the European model as far as the timing and type of constitutional review are concerned. The Swiss institutional structure is, however, closer to the American model.

The instruments of direct democracy, i.e. the initiative and referendum, are traditionally seen as the main reasons for the limitation of constitutional jurisdiction (Ehrenzeller 2020, 74). When the federal constitution of 1874 was drafted, the reformers wanted to ensure that the FSC would not be able to review federal laws legitimized by popular referendum (for an overview of direct democratic institutions today, see 'Direct Democracy' in this volume). Majority-democratic principles were prioritized over liberal-democratic values. In addition, the Liberal Party, a right-wing party promoting liberal democracy and free markets together with social responsibility, held a solid political majority at the time of the reform debate, therefore rendering the political landscape

Table 12.1: Constitutional review in comparison

	American System	European System	Switzerland
Institutional Structure	Diffuse: Ordinary courts can review constitutionality.	Concentrated: Only the Constitutional Court reviews constitutionality.	Elements of both diffuse and concentrated review.
Timing	*A posteriori:* Constitutional review can only take place after the enactment of the law concerned.	Mainly *a posteriori:* A law can be reviewed after its enactment. Some countries allow for a priori control (before the law's enactment).	*A posteriori* (mainly for cantonal provisions). Federal laws are excluded from the constitutional review of all courts.
Type	Concrete judicial review, i.e. the constitutionality of a provision can be reviewed only in conjunction with its application.	Judicial review can be concrete or abstract (independently of the law's application).	Abstract and concrete judicial review of cantonal laws. Provisions of federal ordinances can only be reviewed in cases of application.
Standing (*locus standi*)	Affected persons.	Authorities, parliament, citizens, courts, and affected persons.	Affected and unaffected citizens*, and in some cases authorities.

* In the case of an abstract review, it is sufficient for the applicant to be affected virtually, i.e. the requirements are met if there is at least a minimal probability that the applicant's interests could be affected by the contested regulation at some time in the future. (BGE 135 II 243 E. 1.2; 133 I 206 E. 2.1).

Data source: Adapted from Epstein et al. (2001).

very homogenous (Auer 1983, 60–61; Reich 2020, 353). Only the introduction of the proportional election system at the federal level in 1918 with its ensuing losses for the political party in power and stronger competition between the different parties triggered a debate on the issue of constitutional review. This debate culminated in a popular initiative demanding the introduction of full constitutional review; however, the initiative failed at the ballot box in 1939. Afterwards, the discussion subsided for several decades. This may be attributed to the heightened integration of different social interests into the political process, itself a consequence of the 'magic formula' to form a government coalition with the same four parties: Liberal Democratic Party, Christian Democratic Party, Social Democratic Party, and Swiss People's Party (Auer 1983, 65–66).

Discussions about a new constitution in the 1970s included a debate on the expansion of judicial review, but the reform efforts failed. It was only in preparation for the judicial reform of 2000 that the Federal Council (Government) proposed the introduction of constitutional review of federal laws at the time of their application (i.e. concrete review). Although the concrete review proposal was at first supported by a majority in both chambers of the parliament, the Federal Assembly finally rejected it because it feared that the voters would reject such an amendment to the constitution as being incompatible with their direct democratic rights. In particular, the Social Democratic Party and the Swiss People's Party opposed any expansion of constitutional review and stressed the incompatibility between direct democracy and the 'rule of judges'. The opposition of these two parties may also be related to them being the most frequently excluded from the winning coalition in the Federal Council (Linder and Mueller 2017, 265). Considering the conservative trend of many of the FSC's judgements and its political composition, and in the light of powerful direct democratic institutions, expanding the possibilities for constitutional review might not be seen as an auspicious instrument for obtaining political gains.

Do the restricted competencies of the FSC regarding judicial review imply that it is a weak court? Various arguments speak against this assessment. First, the FSC plays a key role as a constitutional court for cantonal laws. The FSC indeed fosters the uniform application of federal laws in all cantons with its interpretation of federal criminal, private, and administrative law. In an empirical study, Byland et al. (2015) focus on the disability insurance benefits granted by cantonal administrations and the related judicial rulings by both cantonal courts and the FSC. The findings suggest that the FSC judgements have a limited but positive impact on the harmonization of cantonal policy outputs when a significant policy change is implemented (i.e. granting or not granting a disability benefit; Byland et al. 2015). Furthermore, cantons have to observe minimum fundamental rights standards established by the FSC in most areas, i.e. for cantonal elections and direct democratic institutions. Although the federal constitution essentially leaves the shaping of political rights to the cantons, the FSC has developed a whole set of principles and rules to protect the free formation and expression of the electorate's will. Based on these specifications, various cantons have had to undertake comprehensive reforms of their electoral systems over the past twenty years (Leuzinger 2018). They mainly aimed at eliminating impairments of electoral equality due to very different sizes of electoral districts within the individual cantons. In the area of direct democracy, Tornay (2008) systematically examined the jurisprudence of various courts (FSC, upper cantonal courts, and administrative courts) as well as the decisions of executive authorities. Her dataset includes 510 decisions between 1990 and 2007, concerning, among other things, initiative and referendum rights, freedom to vote, or naturalization by referendum at the cantonal and local levels. The author concludes that the FSC performs an important function in safeguarding direct democratic rights.

In addition, the FSC found ways to broaden the scope of constitutional review in Switzerland. In a decision from 1886, the FSC had already established that all courts were obliged to review the compatibility of cantonal laws with the federal constitution in the context of concrete review (Auer 2016, 596; Flick Witzig and Vatter 2020, 405). Today, a corresponding provision in the constitution itself stipulates its supremacy (art. 5 para. 2 and art. 49 para. 1 FC). Another FSC method that has contributed to expanding its influence is the constitutional interpretation of laws, which the court has been practising since the late 1960s. When faced with several interpretations of a legal text, this technique allows the judges to choose the one that best reconciles the meaning of the norm with the federal constitution. The presumption of conformity of federal laws with the constitution thus goes hand in hand with a control of the interpretation of laws, which aims as far as possible to coordinate the meaning of the law with the constitution. Moreover, the Court imposed a new understanding of the rule of immunity from federal law in the early 1990s. As mentioned above, the constitution obliges judges to apply federal laws. However, if the FSC finds a federal law to be in conflict with the constitution, it can state this in a decision and thus call on the legislature to remedy the situation. Thus, article 190 FC only prevents a sanction at the judicial level (Hottelier 2020, 204).

Last but not least, the Court played an active part in the development of fundamental rights, sparsely and incompletely enunciated in the constitution of 1874, which contributed to the expansion of fundamental rights and to the recognition of fundamental rights not yet codified (Müller 2020). The FSC's jurisprudence thus did not follow a strictly interpretative model. On the contrary, the Court displayed considerable judicial activism. We can even refer to a 'rights revolution' in Switzerland (Epp 1998), though the now much more detailed list of fundamental and social rights in the federal constitution in force since 2000 leaves less room for judicial activism. As Shapiro argues, one explanation for the increasing importance of constitutional courts is linked to what he calls 'rights-generated review'. The expansion of fundamental rights increases the opportunities for constitutional review, which in turn augments the influence and power of the highest courts (Shapiro 1999, 200).

3.2 The political nature of judicial appointments

While the FSC's restricted competencies for judicial review are likely to cause a low degree of judicialization, the opposite is true for the way its judges are selected. The political nature of judicial appointments is a preeminent characteristic of the Swiss judicial system:

- Usually, judges are elected by the legislature (or, on the cantonal level, by the people). There is no self-recruiting system for judges, with a few exceptions on the cantonal level.[3] In other words, the selection of judges is not made by higher judicial instances or magisterial commissions, as is the case in Spain, France, and Italy (Guarnieri and Pederzoli 1996).
- Commonly, the political parties endorse the candidates. Party membership or ideological closeness to the party endorsing the candidate is the rule. The distribution of seats on the federal courts among the parties mirrors the one held by the parties in the Swiss parliament. If parties are under-represented in courts as a result of parliamentary elections, subsequent judicial elections seek to compensate for this (Vatter and Ackermann 2014). Because of the electoral successes of the right-wing populist Swiss People's Party, its representation in the FSC tripled within

two decades (1999–2019). Since 2011, it has provided the largest contingent of FSC judges (Vatter 2020, 495).
- The close connection between judges and their supporting parties is further accentuated by the fact that judges pay a contribution to their parties during their term of office ('mandate tax'). This constitutes an important source of income for the parties since Switzerland only provides rudimentary state funding for political parties. The exact amount of the mandate taxes is not disclosed; it varies depending on the party (Racioppi 2017).
- Candidates regularly come from the judicial system, i.e. judges of lower courts. Still, they may also come from a larger judicial community (lawyers, administrators, university professors). In contrast to other European countries, there is no fixed career path in Switzerland for judges with initial specialized training (as is the case, once again, in France, Italy, and Spain). Experience as a judge matters, but it is not a precondition.
- Judges serve for a fixed term with the possibility of re-election. Switzerland neither has life appointments (as in the US for the Supreme Court and federal judges) nor limits the number of terms one can serve as a judge (as with the German Federal Constitutional Court).

The political nature of judicial appointments and the relative openness of access to the judicial bench are typical for countries with a common-law tradition (especially the US). However, in most common-law countries, extensive prior experience as an advocate is of comparably greater importance, if not a precondition. In contrast to countries with a common-law tradition, the involvement of laypeople remains limited (lay judges, but also juries—see Hauser and Schweri 1999, 78 et seq.).

The Federal Assembly elects the judges of the FSC for a term of six years (art. 168 FC). The eligibility criteria that candidates must meet are modest: it is sufficient to fulfil the same standards that apply to candidates seeking to serve on the National Council (i.e. the lower chamber of parliament). However only persons with judicial training and experience are really considered (judges, lawyers, professors, and administrators—see Schmid 1984, 130). Re-election is possible and common (Luminati and Contarini 2021). Between 1848 and 2013, judges of the FSC served an average of twenty years (Vatter and Ackermann 2014), which implies several terms. Next to proportional party representation, the appropriate coverage of the three language regions (German-, French-, and Italian-speaking cantons) is another goal. The proportion of women on the court was very low for a long time. Its first female judge took office in 1975 and remained the only woman at the FSC for ten years (FSC 2021). The proportion of women gradually increased afterwards and currently stands at 42 per cent (as of January 2022; FSC 2022).

The party-political affiliation of federal judges in combination with the re-election requirement repeatedly prompts debates:

- One goal of the reform of the legal system adopted in 2000 was to reduce the political character of the election. The Federal Council proposed itself as the electoral body for the newly created federal courts' judges. During the debate regarding this reform, this proposal was replaced by the proposition to create an independent judicial committee within the Federal Assembly, and this proposition prevailed. The Judicial Committee, created in 2003, is part of the Federal Assembly and is composed of elected members of both chambers of parliament. It prepares the election of the judges to the federal courts, especially by examining the qualifications of the candidates. However, the election still takes place based on the proposal of a political party by the Federal Assembly. In short, the political character of the election remains unchanged.

- From an international perspective, the GRECO (Groupe d'États contre la corruption) criticizes the Swiss system, recommending, in particular, the abolition of mandate taxes as well as the re-election requirement (GRECO 2016). In addition, international comparative research places Switzerland in a critical position regarding the *de jure* independence of the judiciary. According to Voigt et al. (2015), Switzerland ranks only 106th among 124 countries surveyed.
- The election modalities also remain under pressure in domestic politics. The Swiss Association of Judges (2019) recently called for the abolition of the mandate tax to avoid the appearance of a lack of political independence. A parliamentary initiative submitted in 2020 pursues the same goal, yet its consideration in parliament is currently pending (as of January 2022). The issue also received considerable attention through a popular initiative (the Justice-Initiative). It sought to replace the requirement of periodical re-election with a one-time appointment. Judges of the FSC could have remained in office until five years after reaching the ordinary retirement age. This provision was supplemented by an impeachment clause, i.e. the possibility of the Federal Assembly to remove judges from office in the event of a serious breach of official duty or if the person had permanently lost the ability to exercise the office. In addition, the popular initiative aimed to limit party politics' influence on the appointment of judges by replacing the election with a lottery. An expert commission would have decided about the candidates' admission to the lottery pot based on the objective criteria of professional and personal suitability (Federal Chancellery 2022). However, the initiative clearly failed at the ballot box in November 2021, receiving an approval rate of only 32 per cent (Swissvotes 2022).
- One incident regularly mentioned during the campaign for the Justice-Initiative, was the case of the FSC judge Yves Donzallaz. As mentioned above, re-election is standard for judges seeking to renew their mandate after a first and second term. In September 2020, for the first time ever, the Swiss People's Party did not recommend one of its judges for re-election because the party disagreed with the judge's decisions, particularly on immigration issues. The judge, however, easily managed his re-election with the votes of the other parties. Furthermore, he was elected vice-president of the FSC in 2021, the president and vice-president of the FSC being elected by the Federal Assembly on a proposition by the FSC. These circumstances illustrate the potential for politicization inherent in the current

model of appointing judges. If the parties start to challenge re-elections systematically based on ideological grounds, this weakens the independence of federal judges.

The recent discussions reflect various developments. Changes in the party-political composition of the Federal Assembly and the Federal Council have intensified conflicts over the composition of the Federal Supreme Court. As the strengths of some parties increase, while others are losing support, the winning parties seek better representation on the highest courts in subsequent judicial elections (Vatter and Ackermann 2014). The recommendations and analyses of international bodies are also heating the discussions. International comparative studies, however, suggest that the actual independence of courts is not simply the result of selection and nomination procedures. Undesirable political influence takes various forms, for example through media campaigns, and it is not limited to formal institutions. The politicization of the judiciary, as seen in various European countries and partly driven by populist parties (i.e. the Swiss People's Party in Switzerland; e.g. Popova and Rothmayr Allison forthcoming), sharpens the focus on the issue of judicial independence and the institutional conditions that best guarantee it.

For Switzerland, it can be noted that judges are generally re-elected, which takes away some of the political character of their appointment. This also contributes to the fact that the *de facto* independence of the Swiss judiciary is considered to be high in international comparison (Voigt et al. 2015). In addition, the biographies of federal judges suggest that recruitment from outside the judiciary is the exception. Experience and professional competencies are thus important in the selection process. This also applies to the Federal Administrative Court. As Tippenhauer (2010, 57–59) found, only seven out of its seventy-three judges did not have judicial experience at the time of their election. Thus, judicial experience is of great importance for recruitment to the Federal Administrative Court, too.

So far, we do not know much about the influence of the party-political composition of the judges' panel on the case law. New research for the Federal Administrative Court detected notable differences in decision-making behaviour by party affiliation, at least in some legal areas. Especially in asylum law cases, left-wing judges decide more often in favour of asylum seekers than right-wing judges do (Fankhauser 2021; Hangartner et al. 2019; Spirig 2018; Fankhauser et al. 2022). In social security cases, a similar but less strong correlation is visible (Gertsch 2021). For the FSC, corresponding studies are missing so far.

3.3 Internationalization

Lately, the implications of internationalization and European integration on the political processes in Switzerland have been increasingly examined (Fischer 2007; Linder 2011; Gava et al. 2014). Its lasting effect on domestic policies is also eminent in the area of the judiciary. Internationalization contributed to the expansion of constitutional review in the case law of the FSC, which in turn was conducive to the harmonization of cantonal policies.

The Swiss legal system has a monist character. Thus, international law does not need to be transposed into national law by means of a legislative act but applies directly and is binding on all authorities (art. 190 FC). Since the entry into force of the current federal constitution on 1 January 2000, article 5 paragraph 4 also expressly stipulates that the Confederation and the cantons must observe international law. In principle, the FSC had already recognized the direct applicability of international law in earlier decisions (BGE 3 270, pp. 285–286; BGE 7 774, pp. 781–782; BGE 27 I 192, p. 194; BGE 35 I 411, p. 415 E. 3; Federal Council 2010, 2302). On the other hand, the question of the rank of international law within the Swiss hierarchy of norms is less clear, as the federal constitution does not explicitly state the primacy of international law over national law (Federal Council 2010, 2305). The FSC contributed to the clarification of this question on various occasions and generally assumed the primacy of international law (Federal Council 2010, 2310). However, this principle does not apply without exceptions:

- In the Schubert case (1973), the Court decided that a federal law must be applied—even where it violates international law—if the Federal Assembly deliberately sought to legislate in contravention of Switzerland's international obligations (BGE 99 Ib 39; see Epiney 1994, 537ff.; Seiler 1995, 451; Achermann 2001, 44 ff.).
- In a 1999 decision, the FSC partially departed from the so-called Schubert practice. Confronted with a case where a Swiss law conflicted with a provision of the European Convention on Human Rights (ECHR), it ruled that the latter takes precedence regardless of whether the provision of national law was enacted before or after the international treaty (BGE 125 II 417).

The fundamental supremacy of international law over national law plays an important role when the people have adopted initiatives by direct democratic means that are in tension with international law provisions. This has been the case several times in recent decades. In 2004, for example, an initiative was adopted that provided for the lifelong detention of offenders in the case of severe crimes. Cancellation of custody should only be possible in highly exceptional cases. In 2010, the majority of the people and the cantons adopted the popular initiative 'For the deportation of criminal foreigners'. In 2014, the 'Mass immigration initiative' followed, which wanted to regulate or limit immigration by introducing quotas. All three initiatives contradicted Switzerland's obligations under international law, which made it difficult for the parliament to implement them. Dissatisfied with this situation, the Swiss People's Party, which had initiated or supported the aforementioned initiatives, launched another one. This initiative's aim was to establish the primacy of the Swiss constitution over international law (except for mandatory international law). However, it failed in the referendum in 2018 (Burger 2019). These popular initiatives are related to the Swiss People's Party's electoral success, which has shifted power in the Federal Council and the National Council. The party won a second seat in the Federal Council in 2003 at the expense of the Christian Democrats and became the strongest party in the National Council (see 'Political Parties and Party Systems in Switzerland' in this volume). The Swiss People's Party sees EU institutions and international judges as potential threats to vital Swiss institutions, such as direct democracy, and to Swiss sovereignty more broadly.

The recognition of the primacy of international law by the FSC prior to its incorporation into the text of the 1999 constitution has contributed considerably to Switzerland's opening to new regions of the World, and to its integration into new internationally regulated areas. The consistent application of the ECHR has played an important role, for example, in the modernization of the Swiss jurisprudence regarding fundamental rights and the harmonization of cantonal codes of procedure. Moreover, and as described above, this practice has widened the FSC's constitutional jurisdiction: the Court now examines the compliance of federal laws with the ECHR, within its limits of constitutional review (Hertig Randall 2010). This confirms the general assumption that the adoption of international norms (such as the ECHR) and the introduction of international court instances (such as the European Court of Human Rights) are important factors to explain the increasing influence of courts on the national level (Volcansek 1997).

However, these integration and modernization effects did not materialize in all areas. The FSC declared certain norms of international law to be not directly applicable as is the case of the free trade agreement with the European Economic Community (BGE 112 Ib 183; 105 II 49; for criticism of these judgements, see Jacot-Guillarmod 1993, 352ff.; see also Schweizer 1993, 577ff.).[4] With this restrictive stance, the FSC missed an opportunity to bring Switzerland closer to Europe, at least in the area of the free movement of goods, in the 1970s and 1980s.

To sum up, internationalization has changed the opportunity structures for the FSC concerning domestic policies. It has utilized its new opportunities differently from case to case. On the one hand, it has expanded its capacity to review the constitutionality of federal laws and to modernize its jurisprudence. On the other hand, it has associated itself with the politically dominant opinion of a slow and prudent rapprochement of Switzerland towards Europe. The FSC is indeed characterized by a combination of an aggressive and creative case law, together with judicial deference to political decisions. It reinforces the admonition discussed earlier in this chapter that the limited constitutional review of federal legislation should not be equated with minor political influence.

4 CONCLUSION

In several respects, the Swiss judiciary appears to be a Janus-faced phenomenon. At first glance, the seeming lack of constitutional jurisdiction due to article 190 FC makes the FSC look like a pale player compared to other highest courts, such as the German Federal Constitutional Court, the American Supreme Court, or the French Conseil Constitutionnel. However, this contrasts with the great influence that the FSC exercises in various policy fields. Moreover, through its case law, the FSC has largely succeeded in extending the limits imposed by article 190 FC. It must also be taken into account that the cantons enjoy considerable legislative competencies and that the constitutional jurisdiction vis-à-vis cantonal legislation is comprehensive. These opposing points of view are also reflected in divergent assessments on the extent of constitutional jurisdiction in Switzerland: some authors assume that constitutional review is non-existent (Kneip 2016, 368; Lijphart 2012, 215) or weak (Vatter 2020, 512). Alivizatos (1995, 575) describes Swiss constitutional jurisdiction as limited, while Lhotta (2001) attributes a medium reach. Mahon (2019, 146) even speaks of 'an extensive review with a notable exception'. If we include the points outlined above, the Swiss constitutional review appears to be *de facto* at least of medium strength.

The Swiss judicial system is also Janus-faced with regard to its degree of politicization. On the one hand, there are close links between political parties and judges. They are particularly evident in the election of judges by political authorities, and the *de facto* obligation for judges to represent a political party. Moreover, mandate taxes and periodic re-elections underline the significance of political parties for judicial appointments and retention. On the other hand, the recall of judges is a very rare exception, which weakens the political character of the judiciary as much as the fact that legal experience and education are *de facto* key requirements for a judicial office. The Swiss judiciary also presents a contradictory picture when it comes to assessing its independence. While on the *de jure* dimension it only achieves 106th place among 124 countries surveyed, on *de facto* independence, Switzerland remarkably occupies 17th place out of the 108 countries assessed (Voigt et al. 2015). Indeed, the Swiss judicial system is a prime example of how important it is to differentiate between 'rules in form' and 'rules in use'. Finally, while Swiss political institutions, including the judicial system, have their peculiarities, the political debates about the Swiss judicial system are not fundamentally different from those observed elsewhere in Europe. Judicialization has given place to more political attention on the courts and closer scrutiny of *de facto* and *de jure* independence. This increased political salience is met by greater scholarly efforts to study judicial behaviour and judicial institutions in Switzerland empirically.

Notes

1. The adoption of new laws and the actual establishment of new federal courts required several years of preparation.
2. Federal ordinances can be adopted by the Federal Council or the Federal Assembly. Parliamentary ordinances, which are rare in practice, are acts of parliament, mostly on issues of minor importance that are not subject to the referendum (arts 163 and 164 FC).
3. In a few cantons, candidates for certain positions on the bench are appointed or elected by a court or a special electoral committee. For example, in the cantons of Vaud and Valais, judges of first instance are appointed by the Cantonal Court. In the canton of Fribourg, a special electoral committee is in charge of the election of district judges and justices of the peace (Bezirks- und Friedensrichter).

4. In accordance with consistent jurisprudence, appellants before the Federal Court are only permitted to base their claims on international treaties that are 'self-executing' (see, e.g. BGE 111 V 201; 106 Ib 182).

References

Achermann, Alberto. 2001. 'Der Vorrang des Völkerrechts im schweizerischen Recht'. In *Der Staatsvertrag im schweizerischen Verfassungsrecht*, edited by Thomas Cottier, Alberto Achermann, Daniel Wüger, and Valentin Zellweger, pp. 33–92. Bern: Stämpfli.
Alivizatos, Nicos C. 1995. 'Judges as Veto Players'. In *Parliaments and Majority Rule in Western Europe*, edited by Herbert Döring, pp. 566–589. Frankfurt am Main: Campus.
Auer, Andreas. 1983: *La juridiction constitutionnelle en Suisse*. Basel: Helbing & Lichtenhahn.
Auer, Andreas. 2016. *Staatsrecht der schweizerischen Kantone*. Bern: Stämpfli.
Brouard, Sylvain, and Christoph Hönnige. 2017. 'Constitutional Courts as Veto Players: Lessons from the United States, France and Germany'. *European Journal of Political Research* 56 (3): pp. 529–552.
Burger, Rudolf, 2019. 'Das Völkerrecht wird dem Landesrecht nicht untergeordnet'. *Swissvotes – die Datenbank der eidgenössischen Volksabstimmungen*. https://swissvotes.ch/attachments/0c532b1bc76fccf34010c4771876062485b4a0e97674dee65f6b0fc41a3ea0c3 (accessed 1 February 2022).
Burke, Thomas F., and Jeb Barnes. 2017. *Varieties of Legal Order: The Politics of Adversarial and Bureaucratic Legalism*. New York: Routledge.
Byland, Karin, Roy Gava, and Frédéric Varone. 2015. 'Impacts of Courts on Policy Implementation in a Federal State: Evidence from Disability Insurance in Switzerland'. *Yearbook of Swiss Administrative Sciences 2015*: pp. 167–180.
Byland, Karin, and Frédéric Varone. 2012. 'Research note: Judiciarisation de l'action publique en Suisse: une analyse du contentieux adminisitratif au Tribunal Fédéral'. *Revue suisse de science politique* 18 (1): pp. 78–100.
Ehrenzeller, Bernhard. 2020. 'Bundesversammlung'. In *Verfassungsrecht der Schweiz*. Vol. 3, edited by Oliver Diggelmann, Maya Hertig Randall, and Benjamin Schindler, pp. 69–91. Zürich: Schulthess.
Engst, Benjamin G., Thomas Gschwend, and Sebastian Sternberg. 2020. 'Die Besetzung des Bundesverfassungsgerichts'. *Politische Vierteljahresschrift* 61 (1): pp. 39–60.
Epiney, Astrid, 1994. 'Das Primat des Völkerrechts als Bestandteil des Rechtsstaatsprinzips'. *Schweizerisches Zentralblatt für Staats- und Verwaltungsrecht* 95: pp. 537–561.
Epp, Charles R. 1998. *The Rights Revolution. Lawyers, Activists, and Supreme Courts in Comparative Perspective*. Chicago: University of Chicago Press.
Epstein, Lee, Jack Knight, Olga Shvetsova. 2001. 'The Role of Constitutional Courts in the Establishment and Maintenance of Democratic Systems of Government'. *Law & Society Review* 35 (1): pp. 117–164.
Fankhauser, Myriam. 2021. *Der Einfluss der Parteizugehörigkeit von RichterInnen auf die Rechtsprechung am Bundesverwaltungsgericht*. Masterarbeit. Universität Bern.
Fankhauser, Myriam, Martina Flick Witzig, and Adrian Vatter. 2022. 'Richterliche Parteizugehörigkeit und Rechtsprechung in Asylverfahren'. *Justice - Justiz - Giustizia* 2022 (2), https://richterzeitung.weblaw.ch/rzissues/2022/2/richterliche-parteiz_300ca64c8c.html__ONCE (accessed 05 July 2022).

Federal Administrative Court. 2022: 'Tasks of the Federal Administrative Court'. https://www.bvger.ch/bvger/en/home/about-fac/tasks-jurisdiction.html (accessed 17 February 2022).

Federal Chancellery. 2021: 'Das Bundespatentgericht'. https://www.ch-info.swiss/edition-2021/die-gerichte-des-bundes/bundespatentgericht (accessed 30 March 2022).

Federal Chancellery. 2022. 'Eidgenössische Volksinitiative "Bestimmung der Bundesrichterinnen und Bundesrichter im Losverfahren (Justiz-Initiative)"'. https://www.bk.admin.ch/ch/d/pore/vi/vis486t.html (accessed 21 January 2022).

Federal Council. 2010. 'Das Verhältnis von Völkerrecht und Landesrecht. Bericht des Bundesrates'. BBl. 2010: pp. 2263–2342. https://www.eda.admin.ch/dam/eda/de/documents/aussenpolitik/voelkerrecht/La-relation-entre-droit-international-et-droit-interne_de.pdf (accessed 01 February 2022).

Federal Criminal Court. 2022. 'Overview'. https://www.bstger.ch/en/il-tribunale/il-tribunale-penale-federale-in-breve.html (accessed 27 January 2022).

Federal Supreme Court. 2019. 'Die Wege zum Bundesgericht. Kurzer Überblick über die Organisation der Rechtspflege in der Schweiz'. https://www.bger.ch/files/live/sites/bger/files/pdf/de/BG_Brosch%c3%bcreA5_D_Onl.pdf (accessed 16 January 2022).

Federal Supreme Court. 2021. 'Liste der ehemaligen Bundesrichter'. https://www.bger.ch/index/federal/federal-inherit-template/federal-status/federal-richter-altebundesrichter/federal-richter-altebundesrichter-liste.htm (accessed 03 May 2021).

Federal Supreme Court. 2022. 'Gerichtsmitglieder und Personal'. https://www.bger.ch/index/federal/federal-inherit-template/federal-richter.htm (accessed 16 February 2022).

Fischer, Alex. 2007. 'Internationalization of Swiss Decision-Making Processes'. In *Handbook of Swiss Politics*, edited by Ulrich Klöti, Peter Knoepfel, Hanspeter Kriesi, Wolf Linder, and Yannis Papadopoulos, pp. 547–567. Zurich: NZZ Libro.

Flick Witzig, Martina, and Adrian Vatter. 2020. 'Verfassungsgerichtsbarkeit in den Schweizer Kantonen'. In *Verfassungsgerichtsbarkeit in Bundesländern. Theoretische Perspektiven, methodische Überlegungen und empirische Befunde*, edited by Werner Reutter, pp. 401–426. Wiesbaden: Springer.

Flückiger, Alexandre, Charles-Albert Morand, and Thierry Tanquerel. 2000. *Évaluation du droit de recours des organisations de protection de l'environnement*. Bern: OFEFP.

Fuchs, Gesine. 2013. 'Strategic Litigation for Gender Equality in the Workplace and Legal Opportunity Structures in Four European Countries'. *Canadian Journal of Law and Society* 28: pp. 189–208.

Fuchs, Gesine. 2019. *Gleichstellungspolitik in der Schweiz*. Opladen: Barbara Budrich.

Gava, Roy, Pascal Sciarini, and Frédéric Varone. 2014. 'Twenty Years After the EEA Vote: The Europeanization of Swiss Policy-Making'. *Swiss Political Science Review* 20 (2): pp. 197–207.

Gertsch, Gabriel. 2021. 'Richterliche Unabhängigkeit und Konsistenz am Bundesverwaltungsgericht: eine quantitative Studie'. *Schweizerisches Zentralblatt für Staats- und Verwaltungsrecht* 122: pp. 34–56.

Ginsburg, Tom. 2003. *Judicial Review in New Democracies: Constitutional Courts in Asian Cases*. Cambridge: Cambridge University Press.

GRECO. 2016. *Vierte Evaluationsrunde. Prävention von Korruption bei Mitgliedern von Parlamenten, Gerichten und Staatsanwaltschaften. Evaluationsbericht Schweiz*. Strassburg: GRECO.

Guarnieri, Carlo, and Patrizia Pederzoli. 1996. *La Puissance de juger: Pouvoir judiciaire et démocratie*. Paris: Editions Michalon.

Hangartner, Dominik, Benjamin E. Lauderdale, and Judith Spirig. 2019. 'Inferring Individual Preferences from Group Decisions: Judicial Preference Variation and Aggregation in Asylum

Appeals'. http://benjaminlauderdale.net/files/papers/SwissAsylumPanels.pdf (accessed 21 January 2021).

Hauser, Robert, and Erhard Schweri. 1999. *Schweizerisches Strafprozessrecht*. Basel: Helbing und Lichtenhahn.

Hertig Randall, Maya. 2010. 'L'internationalisation de la juridiction constitutionnelle: défis et perspectives'. *Revue de droit suisse, Halbbd* 2: pp. 221–380.

Hirschl, Ran. 2004. *Towards Juristocracy: The Origin and Consequences of the New Constitutionalism*. Massachusetts: Harvard University Press.

Hottelier, Michel. 2020. 'La juridiction constitutionnelle fédérale'. In *Verfassungsrecht der Schweiz. Vol. 2*, edited by Oliver Diggelmann, Maya Hertig Randall, and Benjamin Schindler, pp. 191–221. Zürich: Schulthess.

Jacot-Guillarmod, Olivier. 1993. 'Le juge suisse face au droit européen'. *Zeitschrift für Schweizerisches Recht* 134 (II): pp. 227–576.

Kagan, Robert A., and Lee Axelrad (eds). 2001. *Regulatory Encounters. Multinational Corporations and American Adversarial Legalism*. Berkeley: University of California Press.

Kelemen, R. Daniel. 2011. *Eurolegalism: The Transformation of Law and Regulation in the European Union*. Cambridge: Harvard University Press.

Kneip, Sascha. 2016: 'Verfassungsgerichte in der Vergleichenden Politikwissenschaft'. In *Handbuch Vergleichende Politikwissenschaft*, edited by Hans-Joachim Lauth, Marianne Kneuer, and Gert Pickel, pp. 361–372. Wiesbaden: Springer VS.

Leuzinger, Lukas. 2018. 'Die Auswirkungen des Doppelproporzes bei kantonalen Parlamentswahlen'. *Parlament, Parlement, Parlamento* 21 (3): pp. 38–47.

Lhotta, Roland. 2001. 'Verfassungsgerichte im Wandel föderativer Strukturen — eine institutionentheoretische Analyse am Beispiel der BRD, der Schweiz und Österreichs. Konferenzpapier zur gemeinsamen Tagung von DVPW, ÖGPW und SVPW am 8./9. Juni 2001'. Berlin. www.hsu-hh.de/lhotta/index_INdteTjIda6pwHJE.html (accessed 16 July 2013).

Lienhard, Andreas, Stefan Rieder, Martin Killias, Christof Schwenkel, Sophie Nunweiler, and Andreas Müller. 2012. *Evaluation der Wirksamkeit der neuen Bundesrechtspflege. Zwischenbericht II zuhanden des Bundesamtes für Justiz*. Bern, Luzern und Zürich: KPM, Interface und Universität Zürich.

Lijphart, Arend. 2012. *Patterns of Democracy. Government Forms and Performance in Thirty-Six Countries*. New Haven/London: Yale University Press.

Linder, Wolf. 2011. 'Europe and Switzerland. Europeanization without EU Membership'. In *Switzerland in Europe. Continuity and Change in the Swiss Political Economy*, edited by Christine Trampusch, and André Mach, pp. 43–59. New York: Routledge.

Linder, Wolf, and Sean Mueller. 2017. *Schweizerische Demokratie. Institutionen - Prozesse - Perspektiven*. Bern: Haupt.

Luminati, Michel, and Filippo Contarini. 2021. 'Die Bundesrichterwahlen im Wandel: "Kampfwahlen", "Denkzettel" und andere Eigentümlichkeiten'. *Schweizerisches Zentralblatt für Staats- und Verwaltungsrecht* 122 (1): pp. 3–33.

Mahon, Pascal. 2019. 'Judicial Federalism and Constitutional Review in the Swiss Judiciary'. In *Swiss Public Administration*. edited by Andreas Ladner, Nils Soguel, Yves Emery, Sophie Weerts, and Stéphane Nahrath, pp. 137–155. Cham: Palgrave Macmillan.

Müller, Jörg Paul. 2020. 'Entstehung und Entwicklung der Grundrechte in der Schweiz'. In *Verfassungsrecht der Schweiz. Vol. 2*, edited by Oliver Diggelmann, Maya Hertig Randall, and Benjamin Schindler, pp. 263–287. Zürich: Schulthess.

Popova, Maria, and Christine Rothmayr Allison (forthcoming). 'Politicisation of Courts in European Democracies'. In *Handbook of Law and Political Systems*, edited by Rebecca Reid, Kirk Randazzo, and Robert Howard. Cheltenham: Edgar Elgar.

Racioppi Giuliano. 2017. 'Die moderne "Paulette": Mandatssteuern von Richterinnen und Richtern'. *Justice - Justiz - Giustizia* 2017 (3); https://richterzeitung.weblaw.ch/rzissues/2017/3/die-moderne--paulett_of1d31e065.html__ONCE (accessed 30 March 2022).

Rebmann, Frédéric, and André Mach. 2013. 'Commissions extra-parlementaires fédérales'. In *Manuel d'administration publique suisse*, edited by Andreas Ladner, Jean-Loup Chappelet, Yves Emery, Peter Knoepfel, Luzius Mader, Nils Soguel, and Frédéric Varone, pp. 161–176. Lausanne: Presses Polytechniques Universitaires Romandes.

Reich, Johannes. 2020. 'Verhältnis von Demokratie und Rechtsstaatlichkeit'. In *Verfassungsrecht der Schweiz. Vol. 1*, edited by Oliver Diggelmann, Maya Hertig Randall, and Benjamin Schindler, pp. 333–355. Zürich: Schulthess.

Rothmayr, Christine. 1999. *Politik vor Gericht. Implementation und Wirkung von Entscheiden des Schweizerischen Bundesgerichts in den Bereichen Fortpflanzungsmedizin, Lohngleichheit von Frau und Mann und Sonntagsarbeit*. Bern: Haupt.

Rothmayr, Christine. 2001. 'Towards the Judicialisation of Swiss Politics?' In *The Swiss Labyrinth. Institutions, Outcomes and Redesign*, edited by Jan-Erik Lane, pp. 77–94. London: Frank Cass.

Rothmayr Allison, Christine, and Audrey L'Espérance. 2017: 'Regulating Assisted Reproduction in Canada, Switzerland, and the USA: Comparing the Judicialization of Policy-Making'. *Journal of Comparative Policy Analysis: Research and Practice* 19 (3): pp. 262–276.

Schmid, Gerhard. 1984. 'Justiz'. In *Handbuch Politisches System der Schweiz. Band 2*, edited by Ulrich Klöti, pp. 117–134. Bern/Stuttgart: Haupt.

Schweizer, Rainer J. 1993. 'Die schweizerischen Gerichte und das europäische Recht'. *Zeitschrift für schweizerisches Recht* 112: pp. 577–766.

Seiler, Hansjörg, 1995. 'Noch einmal: Staatsvertrag und Bundesgesetz'. *Schweizerisches Zentralblatt für Staats- und Verwaltungsrecht* 96: pp. 451–456.

Shapiro, Martin. 1999. 'The Success of Judicial Review'. In *Constitutional Dialogues in Comparative Perspective*, edited by Sally J. Kenney, William M. Reisinger, and John C. Reitz, pp. 193–219. Houndsmills: Macmillan Press.

Shapiro, Martin, and Alec Stone. 1994. 'The New Constitutional Politics of Europe'. *Comparative Political Studies, Special Issue: The New Constitutional Politics of Europe* 26 (4): pp. 397–420.

Spirig, Judith. 2018. *Like Cases Alike or Asylum Lottery? Inconsistency in Judicial Decision Making at the Swiss Federal Administrative Court*. Dissertation, Universität Zurich.

Swiss Association of Judges. 2019. 'Stellungnahme: Mandatssteuern'. http://www.svr-asm.ch/de/index_htm_files/Mandatssteuern.pdf (accessed 27 March 2019).

Swissvotes. 2022. 'Justizinitiative'. https://swissvotes.ch/vote/649.00 (accessed 21 January 2022).

Tanquerel, Thierry, 2020. 'La juridiction constitutionnelle dans les cantons'. In *Verfassungsrecht der Schweiz. Vol 2*, edited by Oliver Diggelmann, Maya Hertig Randall, and Benjamin Schindler, pp. 223–242. Zürich: Schulthess.

Tanquerel, Thierry, Alexandre Flückiger, Karin Byland, and Arun Bolkensteyn. 2008. 'Droit de recours des organisations écologistes'. http://www.news.admin.ch/NSBSubscriber/message/attachments/13444.pdf (accessed 17 July 2013).

Tanquerel, Thierry, Frédéric Varone, Arun Bolkensteyn, and Karin Byland. 2011. *Le contentieux administratif judiciaire en Suisse: une analyse empirique*. Genève: Schulthess.

Tate, Neal C. 2002. 'Past, Present and Future with the "Comparative Advantage"'. *Law and Courts, Newsletter of the Law and Courts Section of the APSA* 12 (3): pp. 1–13.
Tate, Neal C., and Torbjörn Vallinder. 1995. 'The Global Expansion of Judicial Power: The Judicialization of Politics'. In *The Global Expansion of Judicial Power*, edited by Neal C. Tate, and Torbjörn Vallinder, pp. 1–10. New York, New York University Press.
Tippenhauer, Laurent. 2010. *Les Élites Judiciaires Suisses: Des Commissions de Recours Fédérales au Tribunal Administratif Fédéral, entre changement et continuité*. Mémoire de Master en management public, Université de Genève.
Tornay, Bénédicte. 2008. *La démocratie directe saisie par le juge*. Zurich: Schulthess.
Varone, Frédéric, and Karin Byland. 2019. 'Evolution du contentieux administratif judiciaire au Tribunal fédéral (1990–2017)'. In *Etudes en l'honneur du Professeur Thierry Tanquerel*, edited by Michel Hottelier, Maya Hertig Randall, and Alexandre Flückiger, pp. 407–415. Genève: Schulthess.
Vatter, Adrian. 2020. *Das politische System der Schweiz*. Baden-Baden: Nomos.
Vatter, Adrian, and Maya Ackermann. 2014. 'Richterwahlen in der Schweiz: Eine empirische Analyse der Wahlen an das Bundesgericht von 1848–2013'. *Zeitschrift für schweizerisches Recht* 133 (1): pp. 517–537.
Voigt, Stefan, Jerg Gutmann, and Lars. P. Feld. 2015. 'Economic Growth and Judicial Independence, A Dozen Years on: Cross-Country Evidence Using an Updated Set of Indicators'. *European Journal of Political Economy* 38 (June): pp. 197–211.
Volcansek, Mary L., 1997. 'Supranational Courts in a Political Context'. In *Law above Nations. Supranational Courts and the Legalization of Politics*, edited by Mary L. Volcasek, pp. 1–19. Gainesville: University Press of Florida.

PART III
CANTONS AND MUNICIPALITIES

CHAPTER 13

CANTONS

ADRIAN VATTER

1 The federation and its member states

1.1 The cantons' status in the federation

In hardly any federal state do member states dispose of such far-reaching competencies and self-rule as the twenty-six cantons in the Swiss Confederation.[1] Cantonal autonomy in the framework of the federal constitution and the cantons' equality, their participation in federal decision-making (shared rule), and the duty to cooperate with the federation and each other continue to be deemed the most important centrepieces of the Swiss Confederation. Switzerland is thus both a prime and an extreme example of a federal state (Lijphart 2012; Vatter 2018, 2020; Watts 2008). Historically, the Swiss federation grew from the '*Orte*' of the old Confederation. Despite the 1848 formation of the modern federal state, the cantons have retained their state sovereignty (albeit not unlimited), which is moreover expressly protected in the 1999 federal constitution (Häfelin et al. 2016). The Swiss cantons have their own territories; they adopt their own constitutions and legal systems. They enjoy organizational leeway just as sovereignty to employ and dismiss staff as they please. Moreover, they are free to choose their proper political institutions in the executive, legislative, and judicial branches of government (within the borders of a 'democratic constitution', as prescribed by the federal constitution). In short, the cantons dispose of numerous properties of a state. 'Each canton constitutes a State equipped with a constitution (...) and is equivalent to a small nation; and although this is not the case, each canton is nevertheless endowed with a strong identity' (Seiler 1991, 348, own translation). In this respect, the sovereignty of the cantons is also expressed through the historically accrued basic self-understanding of Swiss citizens as well as in the strong ceremonial symbolism of the cantonal statehoods.

Although the significance of the central state has increased due to the rapid technical, economic, and social developments of the twentieth century, 'one must be cautious in imagining the existence of a continuous centralization process which assigns ever more room for manoeuvre to the federation and ever less to the cantons' (Germann 1999, 392, own translation). In fact, in an international comparison, Switzerland remains highly decentralized in terms of revenue and expenditure structures, and there are various indications that the cantons have regained importance vis-à-vis the federation (Arnold 2020; Koller et al. 2012; Linder and Mueller 2017; Vatter 2020). The reform of the system to distribute finances and tasks more equally (*Neuer Finanz- und Lastenausgleich, NFA*), in force since 2008, has continued to strengthen the position of the cantons by slightly increasing subnational expenditure and non-earmarked federal government grants. At the same time, however, revenue has not increased correspondingly (Arnold 2020). Moreover, the cantons have not yet managed to stop the process of centralization, especially visible in the realm of legislative competencies (Dardanelli and Mueller 2019). Still, the cantons have retained considerable room for manoeuvre in significant political areas (e.g. education, culture, health, justice, and police), and they keep being in charge of the implementation of federal orders. All this points to a continued high significance of the cantons (Arnold 2020; Arens et al. 2021).

1.2 Differences between confederate and cantonal political structures

Although there are great similarities between the basic features of the federation's and the cantons' decision-making processes, and although the typical characteristics of Swiss politics such as direct democracy and consociationalism are particularly developed at the subnational level, there are nevertheless significant institutional differences between the two federal levels (Linder and Mueller 2017; Vatter 2002, 2018, 2020). The most palpable differences can be summarized as follows.

1.2.1 *Direct popular election of the executive and strong status of the government*

The most important institutional difference between the federation and the cantons is the procedure by which the government is elected. While the Federal Assembly (*Bundesversammlung*) elects the Federal Council (*Bundesrat*) for a fixed period of four years, the cantonal executives are determined directly by the eligible voters (Vatter 2020). In this way, the cantonal governments dispose of greater independence vis-à-vis the legislature (as compared to the Federal Council) but are at the same time directly responsible to the voters. 'Popular election of the governments constitutes one of the characteristics of the cantons' political systems and accords the governments a legitimacy of their own vis-à-vis the parliaments, which in turn reinforces their strong position within the canton' (Delley and Auer 1986, 95, own translation). Popular election thus causes the cantons' political systems generally to react more sensitively to political changes than the federation, as the incumbents are always 'afraid of electoral sanctions' (Freiburghaus et al. 2021, 217).

1.2.2 No second parliamentary chamber and the weak status of the parliament

Unlike the bicameral Federal Assembly, unicameralism prevails at the cantonal level. There is no second chamber to cater for the interests of the lower state level (e.g. municipalities). Yet, as a rule, there are 'second readings' in the course of parliamentary deliberations. Moreover, local interests are protected by multiple-mandate holders, i.e. members of a cantonal parliament (MP) who preside, at the same time, over a given municipality (Arnold 2018) and through local autonomy, which is, as a rule, highly developed (Mueller 2015). Altogether, due to the direct popular election of the government and the highly developed direct democracy, the parliament occupies a comparatively weak position in the cantonal political system.

1.2.3 More homogenous party-political relationships

In general, party politics and party-political competition on the cantonal level are less pronounced than they are on the federal level (Ladner 2003, 2004; Vatter 2002, 2020). The simpler and, in particular, more homogenous party-political majorities, the more strongly developed popular rights, and the less formalized access of interest groups provide more favourable conditions for the parties to exert influence than at the federal level. However, Neidhart (1986, 40, own translation) considers the role of cantonal parties to be limited by the same three factors which also limit the power of the cantonal legislatures: 'Firstly through the self-confidence and the competitiveness between the canton, its large cities and its municipalities, secondly through—very widespread—direct democracy (popular election of the executives, legislative referendums), and thirdly through the marked gap between, on the one hand, the strong governments and their sizeable administrations which also co-execute federal law, and on the other hand the cantonal parliaments, which with the exception of a few large cantons are militia-type parliaments and as such rather weak.'

1.2.4 More strongly developed and more successful direct democracy

Popular initiatives and optional referendums originated in the cantons and have prevailed, especially in German-speaking Switzerland, over the 'Latin' model of liberal-representative democracy (Bühlmann et al. 2014). Thus, even today, the barriers to the use of referendums and initiatives are lower in German-speaking Switzerland than in Western Switzerland (cf. appendix). Moreover, direct democracy is more strongly developed in the cantons than on the federal level and displays numerous variations (Vatter 2018, 2020; Stadelmann-Steffen and Leemann 2022). What is more, the success rate of citizen-initiated bills is considerably higher at the cantonal than at the federal level, reflecting the less polarized and less competitive nature of cantonal politics anew.

1.3 The differences between the cantons

Switzerland's federal state structure has led to a diversity of different political systems in the cantons. Thus, Linder and Mueller (2017, 172, own translation) conclude that the 'continuing cantonal liberties of having own organizations, electing authorities and fulfilling tasks (. . .)' have caused 'an extraordinary diversity of cantonal-political institutions to arise'. Until now, the most striking institutional difference lies in the way the legislature is organized: parliamentary ballot-box democracy versus a long-standing 'assembly tradition' (Bühlmann et al. 2014, 410) that is reflected in the two remaining popular assembly cantons of Appenzell Inner-Rhodes and Glarus (Schaub 2016; Vatter et al. 2020).

Besides such institutional differences (addressed in the following sections), there are strong socio-structural, socio-cultural, economic, and administrative disparities between the cantons, which give rise to regular discussions and have also led to calls for cantonal mergers (Blöchliger 2005). The huge differences between the cantons can be illustrated, for instance, using the example of population size: while Appenzell Inner-Rhodes has just over 16,000 inhabitants, the canton Zurich has over 1.5 million. The mere number of administrative employees in Zurich thus exceeds the number of inhabitants in the smallest canton. Accordingly, the sparsely populated cantons have far fewer possibilities to differentiate their administrative structures and possess only modest resources for the fulfilment of their many duties (Koller 2013).

2 THE POLITICAL INSTITUTIONS IN THE CANTONAL DEMOCRACIES

2.1 The cantonal governments

Delley and Auer (1986, 95, own translation) describe the main duties of the cantonal government as follows: 'The State Council (*Conseil d'État*) is the highest executive and administrative authority of the canton. It directs and supervises the canton's administration and appoints the canton's officials. It represents the canton externally.' The cantonal executives are directly elected by the eligible voters. Geneva introduced a direct election, to be carried out in secret as early as 1847. Nonetheless, the transition to popular election took more than seventy years in the other cantons. The wave of democratization of governmental elections reached its conclusion in the 1920s when the people of Fribourg and Valais were granted the right to directly elect their executives (Garrone 1991; Vatter 2020).

The principle of majority voting is the predominant electoral system in the appointment of the cantonal executive (Felder 1993; Garrone 1991; Vatter 2002, 2020). Ticino is the only canton in which, since the end of the nineteenth century, the government has been elected based on proportional representation (PR; cf. appendix). In the popular assembly canton Appenzell Inner-Rhodes, the government is elected by an open show of hands, while elsewhere, it is elected in secret according to the majority vote principle. As a rule, in the case of majority voting, there are two ballots. The first ballot requires an absolute majority, while in the run-off, a relative majority of the submitted candidate votes or ballot papers is sufficient. Whereas in the nineteenth century, cantonal governments had up to twenty-five members, today they consist without exception of seven or five people. The development of smaller cabinets is mainly due to the professionalization of government activity, i.e. the change from the exercise of governmental duties as a secondary to a primary office (Bochsler et al. 2004).

The cantons' governmental systems are, without exception, integrated combinations of collegial and departmental systems in which each member of government leads one department. In around half of the cantons, the principle of collegiality without any hierarchical setting is enshrined in the cantonal constitutions. The president of the government changes annually and, as a rule, does not hold any significant prerogative apart from the leadership of governmental meetings.

In most of the cantons, the transition from the hegemonial one-party system to the two-party and later broadly supported broad, oversized multi-party cabinets represents the typical pattern of progress in the twentieth century. However, in individual cantons, this voluntary transfer of governmental power to the large parties took place only partially or for certain periods (Vatter 2002, 2020). A particularly salient model for a canton dominated by one majority party is Valais, where the Catholic Conservatives (later the Christian Democratic People's Party (*Christlichdemokratische Volkspartei der Schweiz, The Centre*)) asserted the right to exercise sole governmental power for almost the entire second half of the twentieth century with a share of the electorate of less than 60 per cent. Nevertheless, the typical pattern of development in the cantons was the voluntary assignment of governmental power by the majority parties to the smaller party-political and regional minorities for the formation of broadly supported, yet usually right-leaning, multi-party collegial governments. The fact that the majority parties, as a rule, integrated important political, confessional, linguistic, and regional minorities into the cantonal governments (Felder 1993; Vatter 2002, 2020) can be attributed above all to the highly developed direct democracy. The strong segmentation of Swiss society into numerous subcultures and regional disparities, as well as the proportional representation (PR) formula applied in cantonal parliamentary elections, contributed to this development. While the party-political composition of the cantonal governments was very stable for a long time, from the mid-1980s, there was an increasing trend away from pure confirmation elections (*reine Bestätigungswahl*). As a direct consequence of the increased competitiveness of cantonal government elections, the formerly stable composition of cantonal governments eroded. Thus, at the beginning of the 1990s, governmental instability in the cantons was higher than in the entire preceding fifty years, with fourteen party-political changes in one legislative term (Vatter 1998a). However, the degree of these transformations needs to be qualified. In fact, the overall balance of power between right-leaning and left-wing parties hardly changed. While the ratio of governmental seats occupied by right- and left-wing parties was 80 per cent to 20 per cent over thirty years until the turn of the millennium, it has shifted to a 70 to 30 per cent ratio since then. Generally, a trend away from the absolute majority parties can be observed in the course of the last few decades (Vatter 2020). Whereas in the 1960s, the electoral strength of the executive parties as a mean value for all the cantons was still higher than 90 per cent, it sank to 86 per cent in the mid-1990s and eroded further to around 75 per cent in 2020 (cf. appendix). The continuous losses suffered by the traditional governing parties, the inroads made by new parties, and the strong increase in the competitiveness of cantonal government elections have led to an increasing polarization between the large blocks and to a certain weakening of the predominant 'consociational model' with a right-leaning majority and a left-wing minority. In some cantons, they also have made it possible to try out new cabinet formulas previously unknown in Switzerland.

2.2 Cantonal parliaments

The present-day structures of the cantonal legislatures are, above all, the consequence of the historical upheavals of the nineteenth century, in that the liberal 'Regeneration period' helped to bring about the breakthrough of parliamentary supremacy. Originally, the primary function of the 'Grand Councils' (*Grosse Räte*) was to support and execute the decisions of the governments (i.e. the 'Small Councils' or *Kleine Räte*). Only later did the cantonal legislatures secure proper legislative and controlling functions. It is striking how different the status of the parliaments was in the individual cantons. While 'the new cantons', founded after the Napoleonic invasion, as well as the city cantons, approached an equilibrium between the executive, the legislature, and the population after the period of the 1860s' 'Democratic Movement', parliament was never able to establish itself properly in the popular assembly cantons (Linder and Hättenschwiler 1990; Vatter 2002, 2020).

Compared to the federal parliament, the cantonal parliaments have a relatively weak position vis-à-vis the other political actors, mainly due to two institutional factors (Wirz 2018). Their law-making capabilities are limited not only by the strongly developed popular rights but also by the cantonal government, elected directly by the eligible voting population. The executive is thus independent of parliament. At the same time, parliament cannot decide on its own dissolution, nor can it call new elections. According to Linder and Hättenschwiler (1990, 197, own translation), the 'popular election of the government, the obligatory legislative referenda of many cantons, the openness of the popular initiative for laws and administrative acts (...) are factors which qualify the status of the cantonal parliaments and which have always limited their leadership responsibilities in the State'. Moreover, the cantonal parliaments still suffer from the 'executive-driven' logic of intercantonal cooperation, even though they managed to implement certain steps towards enhanced parliamentary scrutiny rights (Arens 2020). Usually, the cantonal parliaments only get to appoint the highest cantonal court and, in a few German Swiss cantons and Jura, the election of the president of the government (Leuzinger and Kuster 2020). What is more, the cantonal parliaments continue to be only weakly professionalized, with the average cantonal MP spending some 15 per cent of a full-time job on legislative work, albeit there is a great variance from about 7 to even 70 per cent in Appenzell Inner-Rhodes and Geneva, respectively (Bundi et al. 2017).

In the election of the cantonal legislatures, PR is dominant; recently further refined by the even more proportional biproportional apportionment ('*doppelter Pukelsheim*'; Glaser 2018; Vatter 2002, 2020; Vatter et al. 2020; Walter and Emmenegger 2019). In principle, PR should guarantee distribution of seats corresponding to the parties' electoral strength based on the number of listed votes. Today, Appenzell Inner-Rhodes is the only canton which continues to elect MPs exclusively by majority election. Appenzell Outer-Rhodes, in turn, has a mixed electoral system.

Only the cantons Ticino and Geneva consist of a single cantonal constituency, whereas the territories of the other cantons are divided into several multi-member constituencies. However, in practice, small constituencies in the eastern and central Swiss cantons strongly limit proportionality, increasing the hurdles for small parties.

The size of the cantonal legislatures varies between fifty (Appenzell Inner-Rhodes) and 180 seats (Zurich; cf. appendix). In the last few decades, numerous cantons have decided to reduce the size of their parliaments. In view of the weak professionalization, however, it remains to be seen whether this measure will increase the efficiency and effectiveness of legislative work, a burden which is, in fact, quite unevenly distributed across the cantonal parliaments. While the legislature in Geneva processed over 200 bills in 2008, the cantons Argovia, Schwyz, and Thurgovia passed only a few laws (CHStat 2020).

2.3 Cantonal party systems

Generally, the cantonal party systems in the twentieth century showed a high degree of diversity (Gruner 1977; Ladner 2003, 2004; Vatter 2002, 2020; Vatter et al. 2020). Thus, bipolar two-party systems, moderate three-party, and fragmented multi-party systems existed side by side in the cantons. At the turn of the twentieth century, and mainly so in the cantons particularly affected by industrialization and modernization, the conflict between the working and the middle classes became the most important cleavage, while in the Catholic cantons, cultural tensions between the liberals and conservatives continued to dominate. Until well into the twentieth century, the rural Catholic cantons displayed a more or less hegemonial two-party system, mostly dominated by conservative parties and clearly influenced by the prevalent uniform confessional, linguistic, and socio-economic structures. The second half of the twentieth century was then marked by an increasing fragmentation and volatility of cantonal party systems and the temporary appearance of small parties (*Progressive Organisationen der Schweiz [POCH]*, *Landesring der Unabhängigen [LdU]*, Republicans, *Nationale Aktion [NA]*). However, the fragmentation of the party systems in the small agricultural cantons generally took place more slowly than in the densely populated ones. In general, the less fragmented cantonal party systems did not only display smaller proportions of left-wing parties but they were also until recently dominated by ongoing tensions between liberal and conservative parties. Finally, various crosscutting cleavages characterized the cantons with a medium degree of fractionalization. During the first third of the twentieth century, either these cantons were marked by 'middle class versus farmers' disputes between the Progressive Democratic Party and the later Swiss People's Party (*Schweizerische Volkspartei [SVP]*) or—in the case of the larger, both urban and rural cantons—they witnessed left-wing/right-wing conflicts in the urban areas at the same time as Catholic-liberal tensions in the rural areas.

The rise of the SVP in many cantons since the 1990s is a symptom both of social change and of a nascent 'cultural divide', opening up between advocates and opponents of globalization, Europeanization, and cosmopolitism (Kriesi et al. 2005; Sciarini et al. 2003). In the course of just a few years, the formerly protestant Swiss-German party ('*Deutschschweizerpartei*') has succeeded, by means of a consistent fuelling of this new divide, in gathering the opponents of pro-European foreign policy even in the French-speaking and Catholic cantons and thus becoming one of the strongest right-wing populist parties in Europe (Kriesi et al. 2005; Giger et al. 2011, 268). In light of the climate change crisis, in the 2020s, green parties started to make considerable inroads at the expense of the social democratic party.

Empirical investigations of the reasons for the different degrees of fragmentation of cantonal party systems conclude that the number of parties in the cantons can best be explained by differences in terms of confessional heterogeneity and the average size of constituencies (Vatter 1998b, 2003). For the more recent period, the study by Flick Witzig and Vatter (2018) shows that, in addition to the size of the constituencies, electoral quotas, as well as the population density, have a particularly strong influence on cantonal party diversity, while the existence of different language groups hardly plays a role. In addition to institutional differences, the fragmentation reflects, above all, the varying degrees of socio-economic modernization and urbanization of the cantonal democracies, while the historical confessional differences have clearly lost significance with the nationwide rise of the SVP.

2.4 Direct democracy in the cantons

The direct-democratic rights of citizens are more strongly developed on the cantonal than on the federal level. Thus, the cantons allow not only for constitutional initiatives and (optional or compulsory) legislative referendums but also for legislative initiatives and/or financial referendums (Fuhrer 2019; Linder and Mueller 2017; Stutzer 1999; Trechsel 2000; Vatter 2002, 2020; Vatter et al. 2020). Besides the financial referendum, numerous cantons also have further forms of a referendum, such as the referendum for administrative acts, the referendum for international treaties ('*Staatsvertragsreferendum*'), and referendums against intercantonal treaties ('*Konkordate*') and for the triggering of cantonal referendums (and/or cantonal initiatives). Finally, various cantons also use further forms of an initiative such as recall. Table 13.1 provides a general overview of the most important popular rights in the cantons.

Table 13.1: Overview of the most important popular rights in the cantons (status: 2019)

Canton	Constitutional Referendum	Legislative Referendum	Finance Referendum	Constitutional Initiative	Legislative Initiative	Initiative for the Triggering of a Cantonal Referendum
ZH	C	C/O	O	Yes	Yes	P
BE	C	O	O	Yes	Yes	–
LU	C	O	C/O	Yes	Yes	–
UR	C	C/O	C/O	Yes	Yes	P
SZ	C	C/O	C/O	Yes	Yes	P
OW	C	O	O	Yes	Yes	P
NW	C	O	C/O	Yes	Yes	–
GL	C	C	C	Yes	Yes	–
ZG	C	O	O	Yes	Yes	P
FR	C	O	C/O	Yes	Yes	–
SO	C	C/O	C/O	Yes	Yes	–
BS	C	C/O	O	Yes	Yes	–
BL	C	O	O	Yes	Yes	–
SH	C	C/O	C/O	Yes	Yes	P
AR	C	C/O	C/O	Yes	Yes	–
AI	C	O	C	Yes	Yes	–
SG	C	O	C/O	Yes	Yes	–
GR	C	O	C/O	Yes	Yes	P
AG	C	C/O	C/O	Yes	Yes	–
TG	C	O	C/O	Yes	Yes	P
TI	C	O	O	Yes	Yes	–
VD	C	O	O	Yes	Yes	–
VS	C	O	O	Yes	Yes	–
NE	C	O	O	Yes	Yes	–
GE	C	O	O	Yes	Yes	–
JU	C	O	C/O	Yes	Yes	P

Note: O = optional; C = compulsory; P = popular.
Data source: Vatter (2020, 363); Vatter et al. (2020).

In general terms, there has been a continuous increase in direct-democratic votes in the cantons during the twentieth century, lasting until the beginning of the 1980s (Eder 2010; Vatter 2002, 2020). The number of cantonal referendums doubled in certain cantons between 1960 and 1980. Since then, it has stagnated at a high level. Between 1990 and 2010, mandatory referendums accounted for two-thirds, popular initiatives for one-fifth, and optional referendums for about one-seventh of the total. More than half of all cantonal referendum votes relate to bills at the legislative level, while the optional financial referendum only accounts for a good third and the optional administrative referendum for less than 10 per cent of the cases. In terms of initiatives, the picture is even clearer: two-thirds of all cases are legislative initiatives, while only a scant quarter are initiatives at the constitutional level. Status and administrative initiatives account for less than 10 per cent of all cantonal popular initiatives.

The issues brought forward by means of citizen-initiated instruments of direct democracy focused on three political areas: state order and democracy, financial and especially tax policy, and the social and health system. The most frequent subject concerns the reform and, above all, the expansion of democratic inclusion. At the beginning of the nineteenth century, the focus was still on consolidating and establishing easier access to the institutions of direct democracy. From the beginning of the twentieth century, the initiatives aiming at the introduction of PR-electoral systems became the focus of attention (Vatter 2002). Subsequently, there were several—often initially unsuccessful—attempts to introduce women's suffrage, grant voting rights to non-Swiss citizens and/or persons with disabilities, lower the voting age to sixteen—and/or even to securing basic civil rights for non-human primates (i.e. monkeys). Finally, the material expansion of popular rights keeps playing an important role, involving the development of financial referendums and referendums for administrative acts as well as the required participation of the population in the construction of large infrastructural facilities (e.g. deep geological repositories for hazardous or radioactive waste). All in all, direct democracy at the cantonal level is specifically used to reform and expand *political inclusion and democracy itself*. In this way, it exerts a significant influence on the changing balance of power between the various authorities.

The change in the subjects of cantonal referendums in the course of the twentieth century is also an expression of a superordinate shift from the 'distribution paradigm' to the 'governance paradigm' (Epple 1997; Vatter 2002): the more urban and economically developed a given canton, the more quickly questions of inequality and income distribution displaced issues of power allocation. During the last third of the twentieth century, these two paradigms were, in turn, overshadowed by disputes regarding growth management, fought at the ballot box. While socio-political bills leading to the further development of the welfare state were still strongly controversial in the first half of the twentieth century, they met with broad acceptance after World War

II. Only with the economic crisis of the 1970s did the socio-political consensus end. From this time on, and especially in the urban German Swiss cantons, environmental bills increasingly became the focus of attention. However, this applies less to the Latin cantons, in which initiatives and referendums were used mainly for reforms of social and financial policy. A different scenario again applied in the rural cantons; first, the development of democratic rights continued to play an important role until well into the second half of the twentieth century; second, bills related to distribution policy were generally less important due to the relative weakness of the left-wing parties in these cantons; and third, environmental issues were all but completely absent until the beginning of the 1980s.

A glance at the focal issues of recent times shows that ecological concerns temporarily lost importance in the course of the 1990s and at the beginning of the twenty-first century, even in urban cantons. By contrast, economic and migration policy issues became more relevant at that time. The extent of the economic liberalization and the relationship between Swiss and non-Swiss population segments became new focal points of cantonal referendums. Since the 1990s, the topics of direct-democratic bills shifted from the ecology debate to the new 'cultural divide'. In the first two decades of the twenty-first century, the focus was again strongly on reforms of the state order and infrastructure projects, as well as financial and tax proposals, which means that a certain return to the original issues of initiative and referendums can be observed.

Generally speaking, success rates vary according to the policy in question (Vatter 2002). Referendums on core state-political and economic issues, particularly on reforms of civic rights with direct, short-term consequences for individual citizens (such as political participation in elections, referendums, and tax questions), have differing, but altogether the highest success rates, while reform issues gear towards the medium. In contrast, direct-democratic bills with long-term implications on cultural matters and/or favouring minorities (e.g. non-Swiss citizens) often clearly fail at the ballot box (Vatter 2011).

It is mainly left-wing parties, most of all the Social Democrats, that exert extra-parliamentary pressure on the political decision-making process in the cantons by means of initiatives and referendums (Vatter 2020). Around 60 per cent of all referendums originate in the red-green camp. However, the use of popular rights by left-wing and green parties is disproportionate to the latter's ballot success. While they are among the losers in just under two-thirds of all ballots, right-leaning government parties are on the winning side in two out of three cases. Thus, the use of popular rights, particularly by marginalized left-wing and green parties, stands in constant tension with their success rates. While the left-wing and green parties, often joined by interest groups, unions, and/or the organized civic society, are mainly responsible for the active use of popular rights in the cantons, it is ultimately the right-leaning party-political majority which wins the direct-democratic decisions. This, in turn, further motivates the defeated to come up with new citizen-initiated bills (Vatter 2002).

Empirical analyses clearly show that cantonal referendums, particularly popular initiatives, have quite high success chances, higher than at the federal level. On average, each fourth initiative and each second optional referendum achieves a majority among the voting population. The cantonal population agrees to compulsory referendum bills in nine out of ten cases. If we take into account all cantonal bills, the opinions of the government and the majority of the population coincide in around four out of five ballots (Vatter et al. 2020).

Regarding the frequency of the ballots, there are considerable differences between the cantons. Thus, between 1990 and 2018, an average of more than five ballots per year took place in eleven cantons,[2] between two and five in thirteen cantons,[3] and less than two in Fribourg and Jura. Empirical analyses illustrate that institutional barriers (e.g. the number of signatures required, collection deadlines) hardly influence the number of referendums in the cantons (Eder 2010; Barankay et al. 2003; Trechsel 2000; Vatter 2000). Socio-structural features (e.g. population size, degree of urbanization), as well as political characteristics such as the strength of the governing coalition or municipal autonomy, display more explanatory power.

3 Challenges for the Swiss cantons

Profound social, economic, and political changes pose major challenges for the cantons. The conclusion briefly outlines three of these structural problems, which bring the Swiss federation with its constituent states to its limits (see Vatter 2018).

3.1 Small is not always beautiful

The average population of a Swiss canton is less than 300,000 inhabitants, which is a very small size for a constituent state by international standards. While about half of all Austrian states have more than one million inhabitants, this is true for only two of twenty-six cantons (namely Zurich and Bern). At the same time, due to rapid social and economic changes, the small cantons have lost their original significance as a comprehensive living and political decision-making area. People are less rooted in their own home cantons due to higher mobility, and a large part of the population lives and works in different regions. As a result, political and functional spheres of action diverge increasingly. Due to the coordination pressure, this development has led to an increase in multiple forms of horizontal, executive-driven intercantonal cooperation, bringing about significant changes in the power configurations in the political systems of the cantons, oftentimes at the (further) expense of the cantonal parliaments.

3.2 The ratio 1:100

Huge intercantonal differences pose another major challenge. In 1850, the ratio between the smallest (Appenzell Inner-Rhodes) and the largest canton (Bern) in terms of population was about 1:40; soon, this factor will reach 1:100 (Appenzell Inner-Rhodes versus Zurich). It is therefore not surprising that the divergent capacities of the cantons' administrations have led to considerable problems in the implementation of federal decrees. In addition, there are also increasing differences in economic and financial strength that keep challenging the federal balance.

3.3 Retaining self-rule in the (quasi-)absence of shared rule

Finally, the Swiss cantons are also facing major challenges in terms of how they participate in federal decision-making (or, more generally, collaborate with the federation). There are hardly any remaining *institutionalized* 'access points' (Vatter 2005) anymore, i.e. strong, effective vertical institutions that would safeguard the cantons' say at the national level (see 'Federalism' in this volume). Unlike elsewhere (e.g. Germany), the cantonal governments are not directly represented in the Federal Assembly. Hence, they cannot block (or: veto) legislation that further spurs the strong (legislative) centralization tendencies, a trend that has been clearly visible since the 1848 outset of the Swiss Federation (Dardanelli and Mueller 2019). Put differently, in the (quasi-)absence of constitutionally enshrined shared rule, cantonal self-rule will continue to diminish. If the cantons do not have a real say in federal policy-making, the obvious structural challenges, such as the huge size differences, will most likely intensify. The reason is this: without institutionalized 'access points', some cantons fail to make themselves heard so that the Federal Assembly will keep passing federal laws the cantons simply cannot implement, e.g. because they lack the resources and/or knowledge to do so.

Appendix: Overview of political institutions of the Swiss cantons

Canton	Electoral system (government)	Number of cabinet ministers	Number of departments	Number of governing parties, 2009–2018	Voter shares of the governing parties in per cent, 2009–2018	Electoral system (parliament)	Number of parliamentary seats	Effective number of legislative parties, 2009–2018	Number of signatures required to launch a popular initiative in %	Number of popular initiatives, 2009–2018	Quorum in per cent
Zurich	M	7	7	4.0	72.4	PR	180	9.8	0.7	44	5**
Bern	M	7	7	5.0	71.5	M+PR	100	9.3	2.6	27	–
Lucerne	M	5	5	4.0	69.1	PR	120	5.8	1.6	21	–
Uri	M	7	7	3.7	84.3	M+PR	64	5.7	2.3	5	1
Schwyz	M	5	5	3.0	75.2	M+P	60	8.3	2.0	14	–
Obwalden	M	5	5	3.3	67.7	PR	55	5.0	2.0	2	–
Nidwalden	M	7	7	3.1	84.5	PR	60	5.2	0.8	8	–
Glarus	M	5	5	4.0	67.3	PR	60	6.7	–	93	–
Zug	M	7	7	3.9	81.9	PR	80	6.9	2.8	7	3/5**
Fribourg	M	7	7	3.9	69.6	PR	110	8.5	3.3	2	–
Solothurn	M	5	5	3.2	66.7	PR	100	7.6	1.7	8	–
Basel-City	M	5	5	4.2	70.5	PR	90	7.8	0.8	27	4*
Basel-Country	M	7	7	5.0	80.9	PR	160	9.8	2.1	10	–

Schaffhausen	M	7	7	4.0	85.9	PR	120	7.4	1.9	8	–
Appenzell AR	M	5	7	3.4	76.9	M+PR	65	6.0	0.8	5	–
Appenzell IR	M	7	7	1.8	–	M	50	–	–	7	–
St. Gallen	M	7	7	3.3	88.3	M+PR	100	5.7	2.1	14	–
Grisons	M	5	5	4.0	–	PR	120	7.1	2.2	8	–
Argovia	M	5	5	4.7	82.7	PR	140	8.4	0.8	18	3/5**
Thurgovia	M	5	5	4.0	75.2	PR	130	8.7	2.5	6	–
Ticino	PR	5	5	4.0	85.0	PR	90	6.8	3.3	8	–
Vaud	M	5	5	3.0	77.2	PR	130	6.6	2.0	3	5*
Valais	M	7	7	4.0	73.9	PR	150	10.0	3.0	6	8*
Neuchâtel	M	5	5	2.2	59.7	PR	115	7.2	4.1	6	3
Geneva	M	7	7	4.9	69.3	PR	100	8.2	4.2	12	7
Jura	M	5	5	3.5	70.4	PR	60	7.5	4.0	3	–

Note: M = majority representation, PR = proportional representation; * in the respective constituency; ** in at least one constituency

Data source: Vatter (2020, 70); Vatter et al. (2020).

Notes

1. The designation 'cantons' for the individual federal states of the Swiss Confederation is documented from the sixteenth century onwards as are, until the eighteenth century, the designations 'place' (*Ort*), 'region' (*Gebiet*), and 'area' (*Stand*). The word stems from the French *canton* ('corner, nook; district, area'), which is in turn borrowed from the synonymous Italian *cantone*, an enlargement of *canto* (nook, corner).
2. Zurich, Uri, Glarus, Solothurn, Basel-City, Basel-Country, Schaffhausen, Appenzell Inner-Rhodes, Grisons, Argovia, Geneva.
3. Bern, Lucerne, Schwyz, Obwalden, Nidwalden, Zug, Appenzell Outer-Rhodes, St Gallen, Thurgovia, Ticino, Vaud, Valais, Neuchâtel.

References

Arens, Alexander. 2020. *Federalism and Intergovernmental Relations: An Analysis of Intercantonal Cooperation and Parliamentary Participation in Subnational Switzerland*. Dissertation, Institut für Politikwissenschaft, Universität Bern.

Arens, Alexander, Sean Mueller, and Adrian Vatter. 2021. 'Finanzausgleich mal anders: Interkantonale Zusammenarbeit mit Lastenausgleich'. In *Jahrbuch des Föderalismus 2021*, edited by Europäisches Zentrum für Föderalismus-Forschung Tübingen EZFF, pp. 303–315. Baden-Baden: Nomos.

Arnold, Tobias. 2018. 'Föderales Schwarz-Peter-Spiel? Der Einfluss der lokalen Politikerinnen und Politiker auf die kantonalen Parlamente'. In *Das Parlament in der Schweiz. Macht und Ohnmacht der Volksvertretung*, edited by Adrian Vatter, pp. 367–390. Zürich: NZZ Libro.

Arnold, Tobias. 2020. 'Reforming Autonomy? The Fiscal Impact of the Swiss Federal Reform 2008'. *Regional & Federal Studies* 30 (4): pp. 651–674. doi: https://doi.org/10.1080/13597566.2019.1630612.

Barankay, Iwan, Pascal Sciarini, and Alexander Trechsel. 2003. 'Institutional Openness and the Use of Referendums and Popular Initiatives: Evidence from Swiss Cantons'. *Schweizerische Zeitschrift für Politische Wissenschaft* 9 (1): pp. 169–199. doi: https://doi.org/10.1002/j.1662-6370.2003.tb00404.x.

Blöchliger, Hansjörg. 2005. *Baustelle Föderalismus*. Zürich: Verlag Neue Zürcher Zeitung.

Bochsler, Daniel, Christophe Koller, Pascal Sciarini, Sylvie Traimond, and Ivar Trippolini. 2004. *Die Schweizer Kantone unter der Lupe. Behörden, Personal, Finanzen*. Bern/Stuttgart: Haupt.

Bühlmann, Marc, Adrian Vatter, Oliver Dlabac, and Hans-Peter Schaub. 2014. 'Liberal and Radical Democracies: The Swiss Cantons Compared'. *World Political Science Review* 10 (2): pp. 385–423. doi: https://doi.org/10.1515/wpsr-2014-0017.

Bundi, Pirmin, Daniela Eberli, and Sarah Bütikofer. 2017. 'Between Occupation and Politics: Legislative Professionalisation in the Swiss Cantons'. *Swiss Political Science Review* 23 (1): pp. 1–20.

CHStat. 2020. *Datenbank über die Schweizer Kantone und Städte*. Lausanne: Cahier de l'IDHEAP.

Dardanelli, Paolo, and Sean Mueller. 2019. 'Dynamic De/Centralisation in Switzerland, 1848–2010'. *Publius: The Journal of Federalism* 49 (1): pp. 138–165. doi: https://doi.org/10.1093/publius/pjx056.

Delley, Jean-Daniel, and Andreas Auer. 1986. 'Structures politiques des cantons'. In *Handbuch Politisches System der Schweiz, Bd. 3, Föderalismus*, edited by Raimund E. Germann, and Ernst Weibel, pp. 85–105. Bern/Stuttgart: Haupt.

Eder, Christina. 2010. *Direkte Demokratie auf subnationaler Ebene. Eine vergleichende Analyse der unmittelbaren Volksrechte in den deutschen Bundesländern, den Schweizer Kantonen und den US-Bundesstaaten*. Baden-Baden: Nomos.

Epple, Ruedi. 1997. 'Der Paradigmenwechsel im Abstimmungsverhalten - Aspekte der politischen Kultur des Kantons Basel-Landschaft'. *Schweizerische Zeitschrift für Politische Wissenschaft* 3 (2): pp. 31–56. doi: https://doi.org/10.1002/j.1662-6370.1997.tb00203.x.

Felder, Urs. 1993. *Wahl aller Kantonsregierungen unter besonderer Berücksichtigung des Wahlsystems*. Fribourg.

Flick Witzig, Martina, and Adrian Vatter. 2018. 'Electoral Institutions, Social Diversity and Fragmentation of Party Systems: A Reassessment'. *Swiss Political Science Review* 24 (1): pp. 1–15. doi: https://doi.org/10.1111/spsr.12285.

Freiburghaus, Rahel, Sean Mueller, and Adrian Vatter. 2021. 'Switzerland: Overnight Centralisation in one of the World's Most Federal Countries'. In *Federalism and the Response to COVID-19. A Comparative Analysis*, edited by Rupak Chattopadhyay, Felix Knüpling, Diana Chebenova, Liam Whittington, and Phillip Gonzalez, pp. 217–228. New York/London: Routledge.

Fuhrer, Corina. 2019. *Die Umsetzung kantonaler Volksinitiativen*. Zürich/St. Gallen: Dike.

Garrone, Pierre. 1991. *L'élection populaire en Suisse. Etude des systèmes électoraux et de leur mise en oeuvre sur le plan fédéral et dans les cantons*. Basel/Frankfurt a.M.: Helbing und Lichtenhahn.

Germann, Raimund E. 1999. 'Die Kantone: Gleichheit und Disparität'. In *Handbuch der Schweizer Politik*, edited by Ulrich Klöti, Peter Knoepfel, Hanspeter Kriesi, Wolf Linder, and Yannis Papadopoulos, pp. 387–419. Zürich: NZZ.

Giger, Nathalie, Jochen Müller, and Marc Debus. 2011. 'Die Bedeutung des regionalen Kontextes für die programmatische Positionierung von Schweizer Kantonalparteien'. *Swiss Political Science Review* 17 (3): pp. 259–285. doi: https://doi.org/10.1111/j.1662-6370.2011.02020.x.

Glaser, Andreas. 2018. *Das Parlamentswahlrecht der Kantone*. Zürich/St. Gallen: Dike.

Gruner, Erich. 1977. *Die Parteien in der Schweiz*. Bern: Francke.

Häfelin, Ulrich, Walter Haller, Helen Keller, and Daniela Thurnherr. 2016. *Schweizerisches Bundesstaatsrecht. Ein Grundriss*, 8th ed. Zürich/Basel/Geneva: Schulthess.

Koller, Christophe. 2013. 'Die kantonalen Verwaltungen'. In *Handbuch der öffentlichen Verwaltung in der Schweiz*, edited by Andreas Ladner, Jean-Loup Chappelet, Yves Emery, Peter Knoepfel, Luzius Mader, Nils Soguel, and Frédéric Varone, pp. 127–148. Zürich: NZZ Libro.

Koller, Christophe, Alexandre H. Hirzel, Anne-Céline Rolland, and Luisella de Martini. 2012. *Staatsatlas. Kartografie des Schweizer Föderalismus / Atlas de l'Etat. Cartographie du fédéralisme suisse*. Zürich: NZZ Libro.

Kriesi, Hanspeter, Romain Lachat, Peter Selb, Simon Bornschier, and Marc Helbling. 2005. *Der Aufstieg der SVP. Acht Kantone im Vergleich*. Zürich: Verlag Neue Zürcher Zeitung.

Ladner, Andreas. 2003. *Kantonale Parteiensysteme im Wandel. Eine Studie mit Daten der Wahlen in den Nationalrat und in die kantonalen Parlamente 1971–2003*. Neuchâtel: BFS.

Ladner, Andreas. 2004. *Stabilität und Wandel von Parteien und Parteiensystemen. Eine vergleichende Analyse von Konfliktlinien, Parteien und Parteiensystemen in den Schweizer Kantonen*. Wiesbaden: VS Verlag für Sozialwissenschaften.

Leuzinger, Lukas, and Claudio Kuster. 2020. *Kantonale politische Systeme.* https://napoleonsnightmare.ch/kantonale-politische-systeme/ (accessed 31 March 2022).

Lijphart, Arend. 2012. *Patterns of Democracy. Government Forms and Performance in Thirty-Six Countries.* New Haven/London: Yale University Press.

Linder, Wolf, and Diego Hättenschwiler. 1990. 'Kantonale Parlamentsreformen 1973-1988'. In *Die Parlamente der schweizerischen Kantone*, edited by Paul Stadlin, pp. 199–207. Zug: Kalt-Zehnder.

Linder, Wolf, and Sean Mueller. 2017. *Schweizerische Demokratie. Institutionen- Prozesse - Perspektiven*, 4th ed. Bern: Haupt.

Mueller, Sean. 2015. *Theorising Decentralisation: Comparative Evidence from Sub-national Switzerland.* Colchester: ECPR Press.

Neidhart, Leonhard. 1986. 'Funktions- und Organisationsprobleme der schweizerischen Parteien'. *Schweizerisches Jahrbuch für Politische Wissenschaft* 26 (1): pp. 21–43.

Schaub, Hans-Peter. 2016. *Landsgemeinde oder Urne–was ist demokratischer? Urnen- und Versammlungsdemokratie in der Schweiz.* Baden-Baden: Nomos.

Sciarini, Pascal, Sibylle Hardmeier, and Adrian Vatter. 2003. *Analysen zu den Schweizer Wahlen 1999. Swiss Electoral Studies Bd. 6.* Bern/Stuttgart: Haupt.

Seiler, Daniel. 1991. 'La Suisse comme "démocratie consociative": essai de déconstruction d'un mythe de science politique'. In *Passé pluriel: en hommage au professeur Roland Ruffieux*, edited by Bernard Prongue, pp. 341–359. Fribourg: Editions Universitaires.

Stadelmann-Steffen, Isabelle, and Lucas Leemann. 2022. 'Direkte Demokratie'. In *Handbuch für Schweizer Politik/Manuel de la politique Suisse*, edited by Yannis Papadopoulos, Pascal Sciarini, Adrian Vatter, Silja Häusermann, Patrick Emmenegger, and Flavia Fossati, pp. 167–186. Basel: NZZ Libro.

Stutzer, Alois. 1999. *Demokratieindizes für die Kantone der Schweiz.* Working Paper No. 23. Zürich: Institute for Empirical Research in Economics.

Trechsel, Alexander. 2000. *Feuerwerk Volksrechte. Die Volksabstimmungen in den schweizerischen Kantonen 1970-1996.* Basel: Helbing und Lichtenhahn.

Vatter, Adrian. 1998a. 'Konstanz und Konkordanz: Die Stabilität kantonaler Regierungen im Vergleich'. *Schweizerische Zeitschrift für Politische Wissenschaft* 4 (1): pp. 1–21. doi: https://doi.org/10.1002/j.1662-6370.1998.tb00230.x.

Vatter, Adrian. 1998b. 'Politische Fragmentierung in den Schweizer Kantonen: Folge sozialer Heterogenität oder institutioneller Hürden?'. *Kölner Zeitschrift für Soziologie und Sozialpsychologie* 50 (4): pp. 660–680.

Vatter, Adrian. 2000. 'Consensus and Direct Democracy: Conceptual and Empirical Linkages'. *European Journal of Political Research* 38 (1): pp. 171–192. doi: https://doi.org/10.1023/A:1007137026336.

Vatter, Adrian. 2002. *Kantonale Demokratien im Vergleich. Entstehungsgründe, Interaktionen und Wirkungen politischer Institutionen in den Schweizer Kantonen.* Opladen: Leske + Budrich.

Vatter, Adrian. 2003. 'Legislative Party Fragmentation in Swiss Cantons. A Function of Cleavage Structures or Electoral Institutions?' *Party Politics* 9 (4): pp. 445–463.

Vatter, Adrian. 2005. 'The Transformation of Access and Veto Points in Swiss Federalism'. *Regional & Federal Studies* 15 (1): pp. 1–18. doi: https://doi.org/10.1080/13597560500083758.

Vatter, Adrian. 2011. *Vom Schächt- zum Minarettverbot. Religiöse Minderheiten in der direkten Demokratie.* Zürich: NZZ Libro.

Vatter, Adrian. 2018. *Swiss Federalism. The Transformation of a Federal Model*. London/New York: Routledge.

Vatter, Adrian. 2020. *Das politische System der Schweiz*, 4th ed. Baden-Baden: Nomos.

Vatter, Adrian, Tobias Arnold, Alexander Arens, Laura-Rosa Vogel, Marc Bühlmann, Hans-Peter Schaub, Oliver Dlabac, and Rolf Wirz. 2020. *Demokratiemuster in den Schweizer Kantonen, 1979–2018. Datensatz*. Bern: Universität Bern, Institut für Politikwissenschaft.

Walter, André, and Patrick Emmenegger. 2019. 'Majority Protection: The Origins of Distorted Proportional Representation'. *Electoral Studies* 59: pp. 64–77. doi: https://doi.org/10.1016/j.electstud.2019.02.002.

Watts, Ronald. 2008. *Comparing Federal Systems*, 3rd ed. Kingston: Institute of Intergovernmental Relations.

Wirz, Rolf. 2018. 'Oberste Gewalt in den Kantonen? Wahl-, Gesetzgebungs- und Kontrollfunktion kantonaler Parlamente'. In *Das Parlament in der Schweiz. Macht und Ohnmacht der Volksvertretung*, edited by Adrian Vatter, pp. 289–314. Zürich: NZZ Libro.

CHAPTER 14

MUNICIPALITIES

ANDREAS LADNER AND NICOLAS KEUFFER

1 INTRODUCTION

MUNICIPALITIES are of great importance in Swiss politics and society. They provide a large part of essential public services and allow voters to have a direct democratic influence on political decisions. Moreover, they are very heterogeneous and there are many different types of communes, as well as a wide variety of organizational forms and practices of which many are completely unaware.

Municipalities are much older than the Confederation and the cantons and have their origins in the communities of the Middle Ages. As the oldest legal entities in Switzerland, they are made up of a group of people linked by a recognized legal structure and owning communal property allocated to the community or to each of its members. The purpose of these communities was to exploit pastures, forests, or watercourses, and to serve collective and individual interests in the best possible way (Stadler 2015). The Helvetic Republic (1798–1803) marked an important step in the development of municipalities, but only after the complete revision of the federal constitution in 1874 did they acquire their modern form, i.e. a public corporation with all citizens having the right to vote and to stand for election.

Depending on the canton, there are different types of municipalities in Switzerland, some of which vary considerably in terms of their composition, status, and tasks (Auer 2016, 134; Ladner 1991, 28). Only the eight cantons of LU, SZ, FR, SH, AR, VD, NE, and GE have nothing other than general-purpose political municipalities in their territory. In addition to political municipalities, the other cantons have special communes with a specific purpose. In half of the cantons, there are still bourgeois communes in which the emphasis is not on territoriality, but on the management of the bourgeoisie's assets, the granting of the right of citizenship, and sometimes the preservation of historic buildings. There are also special communes in the form of school communes (ZH, SG, NW, AI, and TG), which fulfil the tasks assigned to them in the school and education sector. Almost all cantons also recognize church communes, which are responsible for worship—some as bodies under public law, others under private law. In this contribution, however, we limit ourselves to political municipalities.

The specific and important role of municipalities in Switzerland becomes evident when one looks at municipal income and expenditure or the number of people employed by the municipalities. According to the statistics of the Federal Finance Administration (FFA), municipal expenditure amounted to CHF 48.4 billion in 2017 (FFA 2019). Compared to the expenditure of the Confederation and the cantons (excluding duplication), this represents about one-quarter of public expenditure. Even if social spending is included, this share is still 20 per cent.

At the time of the creation of the federal state, municipalities' share of public expenditure was over 45 per cent, which was roughly equal to cantonal expenditure and significantly higher than federal expenditure. Its gradual decline to third place, behind cantonal and federal expenditure, began after World War II and can be explained by the sharp increase in federal tasks and cantonal expenditure (Ladner 2013) as well as by the growing importance of social security. Compared to other European countries, however, the proportion of municipal expenditure is still relatively high (Keuffer and Ladner 2021).

Swiss municipalities have to cover their expenses through their own income, largely through taxes and fees for their services ('fiscal federalism'). Financial transfers from the Confederation and the cantons play a lesser role. This is also confirmed by international comparisons, which show that in other countries, municipalities are often financially supported directly by the central government to a much greater extent.[1] The great disparities between the resources of Swiss municipalities make it necessary to set up a system of vertical and horizontal financial equalization.

Over the years, our various studies have shown not only that there are significant differences between municipalities in the way they perform their tasks but also that some municipalities reach their limits in the execution of certain tasks. These performance limits can be both structural and cyclical. Since the 1990s, social welfare tasks have been one of the areas in which municipalities have reached their limits, while the problems of asylum seekers and the unemployed, for example, are more closely linked to the international and economic situation. The issues of spatial planning and zoning are mainly the result of regulations at higher levels.

While in the early 1990s many municipalities complained about the limitations of their performance in certain areas, the situation improved considerably in the mid-2010s. However, such complaints have increased somewhat recently. It is remarkable that the performance limits of municipalities do not decrease but increase with their size. This means that substantial economies of scale are achieved only in very large municipalities and that it cannot be assumed that mergers will solve the performance problems of municipalities. Overall, however, the differences are rather small when considered in an aggregate manner (see Figure 14.1).

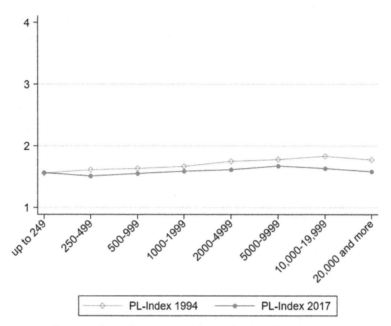

FIGURE 14.1: Performance limits by municipality size (1994 and 2017)
Scale: 1 = no visible performance limits; 4 = performance limits exceeded.
Data source: Surveys of municipal secretaries 1994 (N = 1,952) and 2017 (N = 1,825).

Furthermore, small and medium-sized municipalities are experiencing problems in finding suitable candidates for their executives, since the many positions to be filled are very demanding in terms of time (Freitag et al. 2019, 115) and issues addressed. The shortage of candidates can also lead to an amalgamation with neighbouring municipalities.

2 Legal status and municipal autonomy

The constitutional autonomy of the cantons regarding their internal organization is complete and unlimited: 'In principle, it is up to the cantons to decide whether they wish to divide their territory into municipalities and which tasks and structures they wish to assign to them' (Auer 2016, 125, own translation). There are therefore considerable differences between the cantons in various areas, among others the division of competences or the distribution of tasks within municipalities (Ladner 1991).

As institutions of cantonal law, municipalities fall within the sphere of influence of the cantons. According to the traditional view, matters affecting municipalities would be dealt with by the cantons, which in turn would deal with the national level. The Confederation would not have recourse to the municipalities and would not enter into direct negotiations with them. However, this 'Confederation–cantons' and 'cantons–municipalities' double linkage has become weaker in recent decades, as can be seen by the explicit reference to municipalities in the new federal constitution of 1999 and in certain sectoral policies.

Article 50 of the revised constitution stipulates that municipal autonomy is guaranteed within the limits set by cantonal law and requires the Confederation to consider in its decisions the possible impact on municipalities and the particular situation of towns, agglomerations, and mountain regions. Since then, a large number of new measures have been introduced at the federal level, disrupting the traditional division of competences between the three levels. These include regional transport, ratification of the European Charter of Local Self-Government, agglomeration policy strategies, rural and mountain policies, and integration policy.

A distinction has often been made between the field of delegated tasks and the field of own tasks. However, lawyers and constitutional law experts now regard this distinction as outdated. They consider it more appropriate to speak of general residual competences, according to which municipalities can take on all local tasks that do not fall within the competence of the canton or the federal government (Tanquerel and Bellanger 2007), and of subsidiarity. However, the cantons decide what tasks they assign to municipalities for execution or implementation, and the possibilities for municipalities to refuse delegated tasks are in principle rather limited.

The activities of municipalities are not limited to the execution of cantonal or federal tasks, which are the subject of recurrent complaints because a large part of the expenditure is linked to them. For other tasks, municipalities have more extensive decision-making powers, sometimes in tripartite discussions with the cantons and occasionally with the Confederation.

Particularly relevant for Swiss municipalities is the question of autonomy, which can be defined according to the European Charter of Local Self-Government created by the Council of Europe in 1985, which came into force in Switzerland in 2005. The Charter claims 'the right and the ability of local authorities within the limits of the law, to regulate and manage a substantial share of public affairs under their own responsibility and in the interests of the local population' (Council of Europe 1985, art. 3, para. 1). A large degree of municipal autonomy is therefore considered positive and desirable.

Despite the existence of this European Charter, assessing municipalities and measuring their autonomy are complex undertakings (Keuffer 2016). Municipal autonomy is a multidimensional concept that includes not only the legal anchoring of municipalities in the constitution and their financial autonomy, but also their involvement in the execution of tasks and their organizational autonomy, i.e. the possibility given to municipalities to shape their political system and administration themselves.

Thanks to the bottom-up construction of the Swiss federalist system and the prevailing political culture, the autonomy of Swiss municipalities—despite their small size—is (using the weighted average of the values in the different cantons) very high in comparison with other European countries. According to our Local Autonomy Index, Switzerland is in fact at the top of the ranking, together with the Scandinavian countries (Ladner et al. 2019; Ladner and Keuffer 2021).

But the autonomy of Swiss municipalities varies. An analysis of legislation—in particular cantonal constitutions and municipal laws—and of political, economic, and social factors shows that municipal autonomy is greater in the north-eastern than in the south-western cantons (Keuffer 2019). Figure 14.2 shows the municipal autonomy profiles of four cantons as examples. It clearly illustrates the high legal autonomy of the municipalities in the canton of AR; the strong position of the municipalities in the canton of ZH; the limited latitude of municipalities in the canton of NE to organize their political system; and the low overall level of autonomy of municipalities in the canton of GE, with all facets of municipal autonomy being lower than the national average (CH).

While our research shows that Swiss municipalities enjoy a comparatively high degree of autonomy in an international perspective, Swiss municipal secretaries state that municipalities' autonomy has considerably declined overall. In political discussions, it is often argued that municipalities can no longer determine many things themselves. But perceptions and factual reality do not seem to coincide all the time: studies also show that if municipalities coordinate their activities and proactively use their resources, they can increase their scope for action (Keuffer and Horber-Papazian 2020).

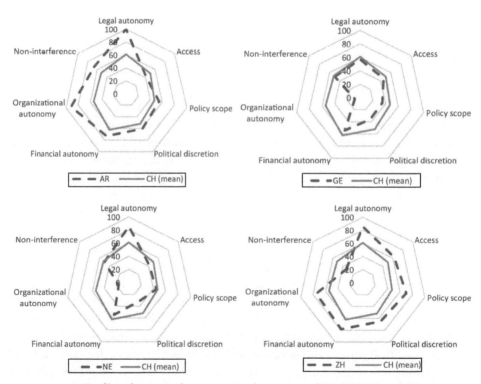

FIGURE 14.2: Profiles of municipal autonomy in the cantons of AR, ZH, NE, and GE

Data source: Keuffer (2020).

3 Diversity of municipalities

From the point of view of public law, all Swiss municipalities are equal. In practice, however, there are major differences between them that have a massive influence on their functioning in almost all areas. The main characteristics of Swiss municipalities are the small size of many of them and, overall, the great differences in size. In addition, there are strong disparities due to their structural and cultural heterogeneity (Horber-Papazian 2006). To meet this challenge, some countries prefer an asymmetric organization in which, for example, cities have more tasks to perform and more decision-making power than rural municipalities. In the case of Switzerland with its symmetric organization, the question is whether diversity should not be better considered in terms of competences. For example, it is difficult to compare the tasks and organization of the city of Zurich (population 400,000) with those of the municipality of Wiesendangen (population 6,500), which is located in the same canton.

3.1 Structural differences

The largest municipality in Switzerland at the end of 2018 (in terms of population) is the city of Zurich, with 415,367 inhabitants, according to the Federal Statistical Office (FSO 2019). In French-speaking Switzerland, the most populous municipality is the city of Geneva, with 201,818 inhabitants. The capital city of Bern had only 133,883. The smallest municipalities had very few inhabitants: eleven in Corippo (TI), twenty-eight in Kammersrohr (SO), and thirty-three in Bister (VS).

With the exception of France, with its 35,000 mostly very sparsely populated municipalities, Switzerland has the smallest municipalities in Europe (Ladner et al. 2019). In 2018, the mean value was 3,845 inhabitants and the median value 1,514 inhabitants, which means that half of the 2,222 Swiss municipalities have less than 1,500 inhabitants (see Table 14.1). The cantons of VD, JU, SH, and UR even have a median number of less than 1,000 inhabitants. Overall, the figures indicate that the Latin cantons have a higher proportion of small municipalities and that in central Switzerland municipalities tend to be larger.

3.2 Cultural differences

The structural differences between Swiss municipalities are combined with cultural and institutional diversity. Almost 30 per cent of municipalities are French-speaking. The French-speaking part of Switzerland is closer to the French idea of a state conceived uniformly from top down, whereas in the German-speaking part of Switzerland the conception of the state strives to find common solutions based on decentralized units. More generally, there is greater 'cantonalization' of the French-speaking municipalities, while

Table 14.1: Resident population in municipalities by canton, 2018

Canton	Average	Median	-499	500-1,999	2,000-4,999	5,000-19,999	20,000-	Population	No. of municipalities
ZH	9,162	4,255	2.4%	28.3%	25.9%	37.3%	6.0%	1,487,969	166
BE	2,983	1,215	23.3%	40.9%	24.2%	10.4%	1.2%	1,026,513	347
LU	4,934	2,635	3.6%	34.9%	37.3%	20.5%	3.6%	403,397	83
UR	1,822	773	35.0%	45.0%	10.0%	10.0%	0.0%	36,145	20
SZ	5,306	3,472	6.7%	26.7%	23.3%	43.3%	0.0%	155,863	30
OW	5,406	5,146	0.0%	0.0%	42.9%	57.1%	0.0%	37,378	7
NW	3,929	3,672	0.0%	18.2%	54.5%	27.3%	0.0%	42,556	11
GL	13,468	12,426	0.0%	0.0%	0.0%	100.0%	0.0%	40,147	3
ZG	11,531	8,868	0.0%	0.0%	27.3%	54.5%	18.2%	123,948	11
FR	2,343	1,257	17.6%	50.7%	22.1%	8.1%	1.5%	311,914	136
SO	2,506	1,438	11.0%	51.4%	23.9%	13.8%	0.0%	269,441	109
BS	64,922	21,339	0.0%	33.3%	0.0%	0.0%	66.7%	193,070	3
BL	3,350	1,296	17.4%	48.8%	11.6%	20.9%	1.2%	285,624	86
SH	3,154	957	23.1%	50.0%	15.4%	7.7%	3.8%	80,769	26
AR	2,762	1,773	0.0%	70.0%	20.0%	10.0%	0.0%	54,954	20
AI	2,691	2,056	0.0%	50.0%	33.3%	16.7%	0.0%	16,003	77
SG	6,593	4,798	0.0%	18.2%	37.7%	40.3%	3.9%	502,552	77
GR	1,837	1,020	27.8%	44.4%	24.1%	2.8%	0.9%	197,550	108
AG	3,199	1,973	8.0%	42.5%	33.0%	15.6%	0.9%	663,462	212
TG	3,456	2,235	2.5%	45.0%	40.0%	10.0%	2.5%	270,709	80

TI	3,073		20.0%		43.5%	25.2%	9.6%	354,375	115
VD	2,586	1,501	35.3%		39.2%	14.6%	9.4%	784,822	309
VS	2,730	847	25.4%		42.9%	18.3%	12.7%	339,176	126
NE	5,705	1,273	19.4%		32.3%	16.1%	25.8%	178,567	31
GE	11,100	1,887	2.2%		33.3%	28.9%	24.4%	489,524	45
JU	1,335	2,501	40.0%		43.6%	10.9%	5.5%	73,122	55
All	3,845	637	17.8%		40.4%	24.0%	15.7%	8,419,550	2,222
		1,514							

Note: Grey cells for categories under 2000 inhabitants correspond to percentages above the national average.
Data source: FSO (2019).

the municipalities in German-speaking Switzerland play a more important role in relation to the canton (Ladner and Desfontaine Mathys 2019, 127).

4 Municipal tasks and their execution

The tasks that municipalities can or must perform have an effect on municipal autonomy. It is important to distinguish between the number and type of tasks on the one hand and municipalities' decision-making powers on the other. The more tasks that municipalities have to perform and the more they can decide on their main modalities and financing, the greater their autonomy (Keuffer 2021).

The principle of subsidiarity, which applies in Switzerland and in many other countries, requires that tasks be performed as close to citizens as possible. However, the extent to which a task can be undertaken independently depends on a municipality's capacity and its task allocation. If the performance of a certain task exceeds the capacity of municipalities or if there are good reasons to perform it in a uniform manner, it is preferable to move it to a higher political level. In the case of municipal tasks for which there is little demand, or which exceed the administrative and financial resources of a municipality, cooperation with neighbouring municipalities or private service providers may be appropriate.

A considerable part of the tasks is carried out by municipalities themselves. These are areas in which municipalities take on tasks of local interest, and for which they have extensive decision-making powers in most cases. However, there are also certain tasks delegated by the cantons and the Confederation for which municipalities have only an executive function. For example, municipalities apply federal law in the areas of water protection, food police, and civil protection, while the school system is governed by cantonal law.

Municipalities' own tasks include the legal regulation of tasks within their sphere of competence. Responsibilities include enforcement, as in the case of delegated tasks, but also the creation and autonomous management of legislation, as well as jurisprudence where appropriate (Steiner and Kaiser 2013, 144). Among municipalities' own tasks, a further distinction can be made between compulsory tasks and those which municipalities have decided to assume on their own. Compulsory tasks are those that must be fulfilled by municipalities under federal or cantonal law, such as local development plans or municipal building regulations. However, it is not always easy to distinguish which tasks belong to which scope of action, as doing so often requires an interpretation of the legal provisions (Grodecki 2007).

Our surveys of municipal secretaries present municipalities' views—as opposed to the provisions of cantonal legislation—on their involvement in the various areas. Table 14.2 shows what tasks, in their view, fall within the sphere of municipalities and in what proportion. The main finding is that almost all municipalities have their own administration and authorities, and that many of them are involved in public works, the granting of building permits, spatial planning and zoning, environmental protection, culture,

Table 14.2: Execution of municipal tasks internally (grouped by percentage of municipalities performing tasks themselves in the specified areas of responsibility)

> 90%	Municipal authorities, municipal administration (residents' registration, financial administration)
60–80%	Public works, granting of building permits, individual transport, spatial planning and zoning, landscape and site protection, environmental protection, culture, sport, and sports facilities
40–60%	Water supply, water treatment and sewage, schools, municipal police
20–40%	Waste management, information technology for the municipal administration, social assistance, youth employment, assistance for asylum seekers, early childhood services, aid and assistance for the elderly, public transport, energy supply, economic promotion, fire services
< 20%	Help and assistance for the unemployed, assistance for drug addicts, homes and medical-social establishments, home care and assistance

Data source: Survey of municipal secretaries 2017 (Nmin = 1,726, Nmax = 1,771).

and sport. Large cities are mainly concerned with the problem of drug abuse, while only a few municipalities manage assistance to the unemployed, old people's homes, and social care centres internally.

When a municipality lacks the financial or administrative resources to take on the tasks assigned to it, it enters into collaboration with one or more neighbouring municipalities or it delegates part of its powers to the supra-municipal structure. This increases the scope of action and allows for economies of scale, but it can also lead to a democratic deficit, as citizens no longer influence decisions directly but only influence them through their elected representatives (Ladner 2005; Steiner et al. 2020).

Intermunicipal cooperation takes various forms under public and private law. Three main forms can be distinguished (Steiner 2016): cooperation in the form of a contract (agreement), cooperation in the form of a legal entity under public law (e.g. an association of municipalities), and cooperation in the form of a legal entity under private law, such as a cooperative society. Approximately one-third of the tasks studied in our survey are carried out through intermunicipal cooperation.

5 THE POLITICAL SYSTEMS OF MUNICIPALITIES

The design of the political system plays a role in the organizational autonomy of municipalities. In this area too, the cantons take different measures. While in some cantons cantonal legislation regulates everything in detail and stipulates, for example, the number of seats that the various communal councils must have, other cantons limit themselves to minimum requirements. In view of their importance, the structure of legislative power and the organization of the executive power of municipalities will be dealt with in this section.

5.1 Legislative power: communal assembly or communal parliament

Probably the most important decision for Swiss municipalities is to determine the structure of legislative power (Ladner 2016). Municipalities can have a communal assembly or a communal parliament. In the first case, voters meet twice or more a year in a communal hall to directly discuss and vote on the most important communal affairs. In the second case, an elected representative body is the intermediary between the executive and the administration on the one hand and voters on the other.

It is not easy to determine the total number of communal parliaments in Switzerland, as there is no up-to-date official list. In the early 1990s, our research identified 493 communal parliaments, which at that time represented 16.3 per cent of municipalities (Ladner 1991, 299). The most recent figures (2019) show 461 communes (about 21 per cent) with a parliament. The increase in the percentage of communes with a parliament is due to the disappearance of small communes with communal assemblies. Only in isolated cases has the transition from the assembly system to the parliamentary system occurred. The absolute number of communes with a parliament has even decreased slightly.[2]

The Latin part of Switzerland prefers communal parliaments. Indeed, even the smallest communes often have a communal council, which can be likened to a communal parliament. This type of legislative body is mandatory in the cantons of NE and GE. At the local level, Latin Switzerland is therefore more inclined to representative democracy than to direct democracy.[3]

Although communal assemblies are often described as the ideal form of direct democracy, participation rates are not very encouraging. The figures on voter turnout clearly indicate that citizens participate less and less in elections as the size of the municipality increases. Moreover, turnouts have been steadily decreasing over the last three decades (see Figure 14.4).

5.2 Executive branch: size and election procedure

Municipal politics is largely shaped by the municipal executive and the person at the head of it: the president, syndic, or mayor (Ladner 1991, 239). This person is responsible for the preparation of matters on which the municipal assembly or parliament deliberates and votes (Häfelin and Müller 2002, 297). In some cases, such as the enactment of police regulations, the municipal executive is also active in the legislative process. In addition, it is responsible for the training and management of administrative services, and communal employees are subordinate to it.

The size of the municipal executive is influenced by at least two factors. Firstly, it must be capable of carrying out the tasks for which it is responsible, and secondly, it must reflect the various segments of the population and differing political sensitivities, in line with the culture of concordance in Switzerland.

The number of seats in communal executives ranges from three to thirty members.[4] The majority of them (56.9 per cent) are composed of five members. Seven-member executives (32.1 per cent) are also relatively common, while other sizes have become much rarer, particularly in recent years. Nearly thirty years ago, executive bodies were larger: 8.2 per cent had nine seats (N = 2,428) and 3.7 per cent had ten seats or more. Today, these figures are 4.2 per cent and 2 per cent respectively.

Over the past few decades, the average size of local executives has decreased from 6.02 to 5.82 seats, according to our 2017 survey (N = 1,777). In other words, one in five municipalities has lost an executive seat, i.e. 450 seats in total have been lost by reducing the size of the executive. However, the total number of executive seats has fallen even more sharply: whereas there were around 18,200 seats in 1988, there were 13,000 at the beginning of 2018 due to the loss of more than 4,500 executive seats through municipal mergers.

Since the larger a municipality is, the more tasks it has, larger municipalities tend to have also larger executive bodies. From a certain size onwards, however, executive work can no longer be carried out on a part-time basis and professionalization takes place (Ladner 1991, 63). As a rule, this leads to a reduction in the number of members of the executive body (see Figure 14.3). With regard to representativeness, it may be advisable, especially for municipalities with a heterogeneous population, to integrate the various parties or sectors of the municipality into the executive by means of larger bodies.

As far as the election process is concerned, the majority of members of the executive are elected by ballot. Only in a little over 10 per cent of municipalities is the election held in the municipal assembly. These are generally small and very small municipalities, mainly in the cantons of BE, GR, and UR. In the canton of NE, the executive is still occasionally elected from the previously elected parliament.

Two different electoral systems are used in Switzerland for the election of the communal executive, but they may be treated differently from canton to canton (Ladner 1991, 69f). These are the proportional system, which is not very widespread, and the majority system, which is used in almost three-quarters of municipalities (73.5 per cent, N = 1,745).

Cantonal legislation prescribes the voting method for the election of communal executives. In some cantons, however, the choice is left to the municipalities. The proportional system is particularly popular in the cantons of TI, VS, and SO. A larger proportion of municipalities also elect their executives by proportional representation in the cantons of BE, FR, JU, and NE. Where there is a choice, then it is mainly the larger municipalities that opt for the proportional representation system.

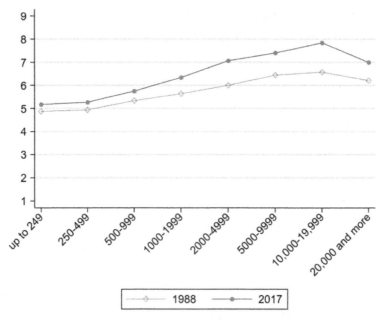

FIGURE 14.3: Average size of the executive branch by size of municipality

Data source: Surveys of municipal secretaries 1988 and 2017 (N = 1,345, municipalities that participated in both surveys).

6 Local Authorities

Almost all Swiss municipalities have their own administration. As a rule, municipal administrations perform a wide range of public tasks and provide many services. For the local population, they are often the first point of contact for matters such as taxes, building permit applications, childcare, financial support, or care of the citizens. In this way, municipal administrations make the Swiss state accessible and tangible for citizens. Municipal administrative structures are as varied as the Swiss municipal landscape.

In 2015, the administrations of Swiss municipalities and cities employed just over 92,000 people. In addition, about 27,000 employees worked in municipal public enterprises. However, municipal administrations have fewer employees than cantonal administrations (190,000), but far more than the federal administration, which has about 36,000 (Ladner 2018, 3). The share of staff in municipal administrations thus represented 1.8 per cent of the total of 5.1 million jobs in 2015.

The central administrations of Swiss municipalities (excluding schools and other decentralized services) have on average more than forty employees. In many municipalities, however, this figure is far from the reality, as the majority of municipalities have very small administrations. In about half of municipalities, five or fewer employees work in the central administration. Often, the administration consists of a municipal secretary and one or two other administrative employees at most (Ladner 2018, 6). In contrast, in cities such as Basel, Geneva, Lausanne, or Zurich, the administrations are highly developed and have several thousand employees. Comparing the language regions, German- and Italian-speaking municipalities have an average of 9.8 and 10.4 employees in the central administration, while French-speaking municipalities have an average of 4.3 employees (Haus 2020, 72).

7 Local politics

Local politics also raises interesting questions: the link between the quality of democracy and the size of the municipality and power structures within municipalities are classic topics to which many studies have been devoted. Research has also been carried out into participation in elections, political actors, the strength of the various political parties, and the representation of women in the municipal executive.

7.1 Local democracy, size of the municipality, and municipal power structures

Surveys of residents have shown that the conditions for effective local democracy tend to be more present in smaller municipalities (Ladner and Bühlmann 2007). Greater media coverage and competition in political affairs, which is more developed in large municipalities, do not, therefore, result in a higher quality of democracy. On the contrary, greater proximity to elected representatives in small municipalities is accompanied by a higher degree of political information and trust, as well as a feeling of being able to influence the affairs of the municipality—conditions conducive to a well-functioning local democracy.

With regard to power structures, members of the executive and presidents are the most influential actors, followed by citizens. This assessment has not changed much since the 1990s. Furthermore, power constellations are pluralistic and three different patterns of influence can be highlighted (Haus and Ladner 2020): while in small municipalities the rural influence model with farmers and long-term residents dominates, in somewhat larger municipalities it is rather the authority-based model (the municipal executive and the president). In densely populated municipalities and cities the model of organized interests prevails, in which collective actors such as business associations, trade unions, and political parties have a decisive influence on local politics.

7.2 Evolution of political parties

Local political parties are not only responsible for recruiting candidates for the many political positions to be filled, but also participate in political decision-making—especially in the larger municipalities.

Switzerland has lively local politics. The first survey of municipal secretaries in 1988 revealed that political groups, i.e. parties as well as locally organized groups and citizens' associations, existed in almost 70 per cent of the municipalities (Ladner 1991). Such a proportion is surprisingly high considering the small size of the municipalities and the organizational weakness of Swiss parties at the national level. The 2003 survey of local parties (Geser et al. 2003) showed that local parties—especially in small communities—were under increasing pressure: they lost members, the number of active people decreased, and they experienced difficulties in reaching young people. This trend was confirmed by the 2017 survey, which found only 61.5 per cent of municipalities with local party branches or other political groups that nominated candidates for political office. There seem to be two types of municipalities: those with 2,000 or more inhabitants, where local parties are the norm, and smaller ones without any organized political actors.

7.3 Voter participation

The turnout rates we collected in 2017 show that voter turnout decreases as the size of municipalities increases (see Figure 14.4). This applies in particular to turnout in elections for the municipal executive, which is the focus of interest here. On average, the turnout in the smallest municipalities (with ballot voting) is around 65 per cent. As

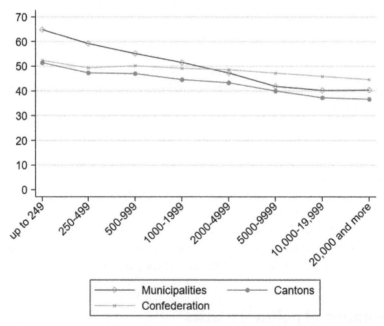

FIGURE 14.4: Average voter turnout for communal, cantonal, and national elections by municipality size (2017).

Data source: Survey of municipal secretaries 2017 (N = 1,212).

the size of the municipalities increases, this figure drops to around 40 per cent. The decline is particularly pronounced in municipalities with fewer than 10,000 inhabitants. Turnout in cantonal elections is always lower, and the great importance of communal elections is also demonstrated by a comparison with national elections, with higher local turnout in the smaller municipalities.

Compared to thirty years ago, participation in municipal elections was much higher in small municipalities (Ladner 2011, 52), and a decrease with increasing municipal size at the cantonal and national levels is not new either. It is at the national level that elections have become comparatively larger in terms of turnout.

7.4 Representation of parties and non-party members in executives

The municipal executive is of particular importance in local politics. Its political representation is therefore also central. It can be argued that local politics, in contrast to politics at higher levels, is much more fact-based, and that party considerations and ideological orientations are less important. Nevertheless, the representation of parties in the executive is a sign of their anchorage in the municipalities and of the political ideas that dominate local politics.

Determining the political affiliation of executive members is not an easy task. Official statistics are only available for cities, and often the political affiliation of a member of the executive cannot be determined because some local parties have no members (Geser et al. 1994, 141) or because a candidate's political affiliation was not an issue in the elections.

In the first national survey of municipal secretaries in 1988, it was found—somewhat surprisingly, given the smallness of Swiss communes—that about three-quarters of the seats in communal executives were held by representatives of the four major parties in the Federal Council, but especially the FDP, CVP, and SVP (Ladner 1991, 218). According to municipal secretaries in 2017, only about half of the seats in the executive were in the hands of the four government parties. The FDP remains the most represented party in the communal executives with about 17 per cent of the seats, followed by the CVP and SVP with about 13 per cent, and the SP with just under 8 per cent of seats on average. However, the largest representation in all communal executives is non-party members, with about 40 per cent of the seats on average.

7.5 Representation of women in the municipal executive

Women are still significantly under-represented in the executive bodies of Swiss municipalities. Less than one in four posts is held by a woman (2,530 out of 10,348 seats in 2017). In the first study conducted at the end of the 1980s, the share of women in municipal executives was well below 10 per cent on average and no woman was represented in more than 60 per cent of executive bodies. In 2017, about 15 per cent of executive bodies were still purely male. The highest growth rates in female representation were in the 1990s, since when growth has tended to level off.

There is no linear relationship between the size of a municipality and the representation of women. In the smallest municipalities, the proportion of women is not lower than in larger ones. In medium-sized municipalities, the proportion of women in executive bodies is slightly lower. In very large municipalities, the proportion is now the highest. To some extent, this is due to the fact that left-wing parties, which send women to political bodies more often, are more strongly represented in cities (Geser et al. 2011).

8 Reforms of the municipal institutional space

Although the Swiss municipal landscape functions relatively well and satisfies residents (Ladner and Bühlmann 2007, Denters et al. 2016), the question is whether more efficient ways of delivering local public services exist. To perform high-quality tasks, a certain degree of professionalization is needed. Moreover, larger-scale institutional or functional spaces have the advantage that the costs incurred are borne by a larger group of people. Autonomy and proximity, on the other hand, also have their advantages, but they become problematic when they effectively allow some municipalities to have their 'right to smallness and independence' financed by others.

This becomes even more problematic when municipalities' space of intervention no longer coincides with the spaces of social life (Klöti 2000), which seems to be frequently the case nowadays. Today, life takes place in metropolitan regions or agglomerations, and services are provided in supra-local and functional spaces, which poses major challenges for traditional municipalities. For example, many people do not vote or pay taxes in the municipality where they work.

Ultimately, the question is whether Switzerland, with its highly fragmented territorial structure and intensive cooperation between the different levels of government, is able to meet current and future challenges. Since the 1990s, municipalities have tried to improve their performance through a wide range of administrative reforms (Keuffer 2018). In this respect, the literature (Kuhlmann and Wollmann 2019) broadly distinguishes between internal reforms, which mainly concern the administration of municipalities, and external reforms, which concern the territorial organization and functional responsibilities of municipalities.

By analogy with the reform of the equalization and division of tasks between the Confederation and the cantons, changes have also been taking place in the division of tasks between municipalities and cantons since the 1990s (Jacot-Descombes 2013). The attempt to allocate tasks optimally between the two levels was based on the same considerations. In many cases, however, tasks were transferred to the cantonal level because many municipalities were too small to fulfil them independently or to bear the costs. The reform also attempted to prevent the municipalities from becoming implementing bodies with no decision-making power.

This implied homogenization is due to a desire not only for greater professionalization and a better distribution of costs, but also for a reduction of differences in the range and the quality of services. It is based on the situation of the small and weak municipalities, which is leading to a decline in the autonomy of all municipalities. The question arises whether asymmetrical solutions should be used, in which tasks remain with municipalities of a certain size and performance capacity while the competences of small municipalities are transferred to the higher level of government.

Since many small municipalities cannot carry out a large number of tasks of the desired quality, merging would allow them to become larger and stronger and to benefit from economies of scale. However, the empirical evidence on the effects of municipal mergers is ambiguous (Vatter 2018, 148). Depending on the size of the new municipality, mergers can lead to a professionalization of the administration and an increase in the quality of services offered. On the other hand, the costs of professionalization may offset efficiency gains. Mergers also have specific political effects, such as a decrease in voter turnout or a greater weight of the municipality at the cantonal level. The results of our survey indicate that positive expectations regarding the administration and the range of services are likely to be fulfilled, while fears regarding identification with the municipality, proximity to citizens, and participation are not necessarily well-founded (Ladner 2018, 179).

Unlike the northern European countries, Switzerland saw no large-scale mergers of municipalities, and the number of municipalities hardly changed between 1874 and the end of the 1990s. Since then, the process of mergers has accelerated and almost a quarter of municipalities have disappeared (3,021 in 1990 and 2,202 in 2020).

Mergers of Swiss municipalities took place mainly in cantons with a large number of small municipalities (see Table 14.3). This phenomenon can be attributed to the limitations of small municipalities, as well as to the proactive commitment of some

Table 14.3: Number of municipalities per canton in 2020 and difference with 1990

	2020	2020–1990		2020	2020–1990		2020	2020–1990		2020	2020–1990
GL	3	–26	UR	20	0	JU	53	–29	TI	115	–132
BS	3	0	AR	20	0	SG	77	–13	VS	126	–37
AI	6	0	SH	26	–8	TG	80	–99	FR	133	–126
OW	7	0	SZ	30	0	LU	82	–25	ZH	162	–9
NW	11	0	NE	31	–31	BL	86	13	AG	210	–22
ZG	11	0	GE	45	0	GR	105	–108	VD	309	–76
						SO	109	–21	BE	342	–70
									Total	2202	–819

Data source: FSO (2020).

cantons through promotional measures and financial incentives (Rühli 2012). However, there are still many small municipalities in cantons promoting mergers, meaning that amalgamations have not been comprehensive. Among cantons with fewer than fifty municipalities in 2020, only the cantons of GL, SH, and NE have experienced mergers, while cantons with very small municipalities, such as TI, FR, and GR, have merged more than 100 municipalities. In cantons such as BE, VD, and AG, the number of municipalities remains very high despite the mergers.

One cannot expect the municipal landscape to be fundamentally altered by simple mergers of neighbouring municipalities. This is one of the reasons why the scope of mergers has widened, and planning has begun in larger areas. In addition to merging municipalities in entire valleys, also regions and agglomerations are envisaged as new territorial spaces for specific tasks (Horber-Papazian and Jacot-Descombes 2013).

It is difficult to predict the direction in which Swiss municipalities will evolve in the coming decades. It can be assumed that there will be no drastic reduction in the number of municipalities—as in Denmark, for example, where the number of municipalities was reduced from 270 to ninety-eight in 2007. The importance of municipalities in Switzerland is too great and they are too strongly protected against direct intervention from the higher level.

In accordance with the country's federal structure, different solutions and development paths will be initiated, and both the municipalities and the cantons will pragmatically choose the form of organization that will improve the current situation.

Although complaints are often made about the complexity of the Swiss structure of local government, in formal terms it is quite simple. Under constitutional law, municipalities are equal, regardless of their size and structure, and the same applies to the cantons. It is likely that the distribution of tasks will be based more on municipalities' actual resources and possibilities for action, and that those with sufficient capacities will be granted more autonomy and competences. This could also lead to asymmetric solutions.

It can also be assumed that specific tasks will play a more important role and that challenges that cross municipal institutional boundaries will be addressed within the boundaries of the municipalities concerned. Single-purpose associations and functional municipalities will complement the traditional multi-purpose municipalities. Finally, cooperation with higher levels will also become more important and roles will have to be more clearly defined if municipalities are not to become implementing bodies.

In our opinion, it is hardly reasonable to reform the Swiss municipal landscape unnecessarily. If, as is the case in many places, municipalities are able to provide services to the satisfaction of their citizens, they make an important contribution to the functioning of Switzerland through their proximity to citizens and the many opportunities they offer for participation in local political life. It is therefore not a question of comprehensive institutional reform, but rather of encouraging political authorities to work within the existing organization in the most efficient way possible.

Notes

1. See https://www.oecd.org/tax/fiscal-decentralisation-database.htm#C_7
2. There are also a few municipalities having both an assembly and a parliament, and some others having neither, but these are rare exceptions.
3. Representative democracy at the local level goes back to the Helvetic Republic. It was only with the Act of Mediation of 1803 that the Swiss-German cantons were able to reintroduce the Landsgemeinde. This historical overview partly explains why representative democracy is more firmly rooted in French- and Italian-speaking Switzerland than in German-speaking Switzerland.
4. As a general rule, executives have an odd number of seats. However, where this is not explicitly prescribed by cantonal legislation, there may be municipalities with an even number of seats.

References

Auer, Andreas. 2016. *Staatsrecht der schweizerischen Kantone*. Bern: Stämpfli Verlag.

Council of Europe. 1985. *European Charter of Local Self-Government*. http://conventions.coe.int/treaty/fr/treaties/html/122.htm (accessed 24 June 2020).

Denters Bas, Andreas Ladner, Poul Erik Mouritzen, and Lary Rose. 2016. 'Reforming Local Governments in Times of Crisis: Values and Expectations of Good Local Governance in Comparative Perspective'. In *Local Public Sector Reforms in Times of Crisis: National Trajectories and International Comparisons*, edited by Sabine Kuhlmann, and Geert Bouckaert, pp. 333–345. Basingstoke/New York: Palgrave Macmillan.

FFA [Federal Finance Administration]. 2019. *Financial Statistics*. Bern. https://www.efv.admin.ch/efv/fr/home/themen/finanzstatistik/daten.html (accessed 24 June 2020).

Freitag, Markus, Pirmin Bundi, and Martina Flick Witzig. 2019. *Milizarbeit in der Schweiz*. Zürich: NZZ Libro.

FSO [Federal Statistical Office]. 2019. *Balance of the Total Permanent Resident Population by Districts and Municipalities*. Neuchâtel. https://www.bfs.admin.ch/bfs/fr/home/statistiques/population/effectif-evolution/repartition-territoriale.html (accessed 24 June 2020).

FSO [Federal Statistical Office]. 2020. *Official Directory of Swiss Municipalities*. Neuchâtel. https://www.bfs.admin.ch/bfs/fr/home/bases-statistiques/agvch.html (accessed 24 June 2020).

Geser, Hans, Andreas Ladner, Urs Meuli, and Roland Schaller. 2003. *Schweizer Lokalparteien im Wandel. Erste Ergebnisse einer Befragung der Präsidentinnen und Präsidenten der Schweizer Lokalparteien 2002/2003*. Zürich: Soziologisches Institut.

Geser, Hans, Andreas Ladner, Roland Schaller, and Th. Huyen Ballmer-Cao. 1994. *Die Schweizer Lokalparteien*. Zürich: Seismo.

Geser, Hans, Urs Meuli, Andreas Ladner, Reto Steiner, and Katia Horber-Papazian. 2011. *Die Exekutivmitglieder in den Schweizer Gemeinden: Ergebnisse einer Befragung*. Glarus: Rüegger.

Grodecki, Stéphane. 2007. 'Les compétences communales: comparaison intercantonale'. In *L'avenir juridique des communes: Journée De Droit Administratif*, edited by Thierry Tanquerel, and François Bellanger, pp. 25–77. Geneva: Schulthess.

Häfelin, Ulrich, and Georg Müller. 2002. *Allgemeines Verwaltungsrecht*. Zürich: Schulthess.

Haus, Alexander. 2020. *Schweizer Stadt- und Gemeindeverwaltungen im Wandel: Public Management Reformen und deren Auswirkungen*. PhD thesis, University of Lausanne.

Haus, Alexander, and Andreas Ladner. 2020. 'Wer hat die Macht in den Gemeinden? Eine Analyse über den Einfluss politischer Akteure auf die lokale Politik in der Schweiz'. *Swiss Yearbook of Administrative Sciences* 11 (1): pp. 66–80.

Horber-Papazian, Katia. 2006. 'Les Communes'. In *Handbuch der Schweizer Politik. Manuel de la politique Suisse*, edited by Klöti, Ulrich, Peter Knoepfel, Hanspeter Kriesi, Wolf Linder, Yannis Papadopoulos, and Pascal Sciarini, pp. 233–258. Zürich: Verlag Neue Zürcher Zeitung.

Horber-Papazian, Katia, and Caroline Jacot-Descombes. 2013. 'Réformes territoriales et gouvernance'. In *Les horizons de la gouvernance territoriale*, edited by Luc Vodoz, Laurent Thevoz, and Prisca Faure, pp. 29–43. Lausanne: PPUR.

Jacot-Descombes, Caroline. 2013. *At the Crossroads of Fiscal and Cooperative Federalism Models: The Results of Cantonal-Municipal Reforms in Switzerland*. PhD thesis, UNIL/IDHEAP.

Keuffer, Nicolas. 2016. 'Local Autonomy, a Multidimensional Concept: How to Define It, How to Measure It and How to Create a Comparative Local Autonomy Index'. *International Journal of Comparative Politics* 23 (4): pp. 443–490.

Keuffer, Nicolas. 2018. 'Does Local Autonomy Facilitate Local Government Reform Initiatives? Evidence from Switzerland'. *International Journal of Public Sector Management* 31 (4): pp. 426–447.

Keuffer, Nicolas. 2019. *L'autonomie locale et ses conséquences dans une perspective internationale, nationale et communale*. PhD thesis, University of Lausanne.

Keuffer, Nicolas. 2020. *L'autonomie communale en Suisse: conceptualisation, classifications empiriques et facteurs explicatifs*. Lausanne: Cahier de l'IDHEAP Nb. 314.

Keuffer, Nicolas. 2021. 'Local Self-Government and the Choice for Local Governance Arrangements in Nine Swiss Municipal Tasks'. In *The Future of Local Self-Government. European Trends in Autonomy, Innovations and Central-Local Relations*, edited by Thomas Bergström, Franzke Jochen, Sabine Kuhlmann, and Ellen Wayenberg, pp. 66–81. Basingstoke/New York: Palgrave Macmillan.

Keuffer, Nicolas, and Katia Horber-Papazian. 2020. 'The Bottom-Up Approach: Essential to an Apprehension of Local Autonomy and Local Governance in the Case of Switzerland'. *Local Government Studies* 46 (2): pp. 306–325.

Keuffer, Nicolas, and Andreas Ladner. 2021. 'Local and Regional Autonomy—Indexes and Trends'. In *Research Agenda for Regional and Local Government*, edited by Mark Callanan, and John Loughlin, pp. 19–34. Cheltenham UK: Edward Elgar.

Klöti, Ulrich. 2000. 'Regieren im verflochtenen dreistufigen Föderalismus'. In *Verwaltung, Regierung und Verfassung im Wandel. Gedächtnisschrift für Raimund E. Germann*, edited by Peter Knoepfel, and Wolf Linder, pp. 17–29. Basel/Genf: Helbing & Lichtenhahn.

Kuhlmann, Sabine, and Hellmut Wollmann. 2019. *Introduction to Comparative Public Administration. Administrative Systems and Reforms in Europe*. Cheltenham UK: Edward Elgar.

Ladner, Andreas. 1991. *Politische Gemeinden, kommunale Parteien und lokale Politik: Eine empirische Untersuchung in den Gemeinden der Schweiz*. Zürich: Seismo Verlag.

Ladner, Andreas. 2005. 'Switzerland: Reforming Small Autonomous Municipalities'. In *Comparing Local Governance: Trends and Developments*, edited by Bas Denters, and Lawrence E. Rose, pp. 139–154. Basingstoke/New York: Palgrave Macmillan.

Ladner, Andreas. 2011. *Wahlen in den Schweizer Gemeinden. Durchführung, Verlauf, Beteiligung und Ergebnisse 1988-2009*. Lausanne: Cahier de l'IDHEAP Nb. 263.

Ladner, Andreas. 2013. 'Der Schweizer Staat, politisches System und Aufgabenerbringung'. In *Handbuch der öffentlichen Verwaltung in der Schweiz*, edited by Andreas Ladner, Jean-Loup

Chappelet, Yves Emery, Peter Knoepfel, Luzius Mader, Nils Soguel, and Frédéric Varone. pp. 23–46. Zürich: NZZ libro.
Ladner, Andreas. 2016. *Gemeindeversammlung und Gemeindeparlament. Überlegungen und empirische Befunde zur Ausgestaltung der Legislativfunktion in den Schweizer Gemeinden.* Lausanne: Cahier de l'IDHEAP Nb. 292.
Ladner, Andreas. 2018. *Der Schweizer Föderalismus im Wandel: Überlegungen und empirische Befunde zur territorialen Gliederung und der Organisation der staatlichen Aufgabenerbringung in der Schweiz.* Lausanne: Cahier de l'IDHEAP Nb. 305.
Ladner, Andreas, and Marc Bühlmann. 2007. *Demokratie in den Gemeinden: Der Einfluss der Gemeindegrösse und anderer Faktoren auf die Qualität der lokalen Demokratie.* Zürich: Rüegger.
Ladner, Andreas, and Laetitia Desfontaine Mathys. 2019. *Le fédéralisme suisse. L'organisation territoriale et l'accomplissement des prestations étatiques en Suisse.* Lausanne: PPUR.
Ladner, Andreas, and Nicolas Keuffer. 2021. 'Creating an Index of Local Autonomy—Theoretical, Conceptual, and Empirical Issues', *Regional & Federal Studies* 31 (2): pp. 209–234.
Ladner, Andreas, Nicolas Keuffer, Harald Baldersheim, Nikos Hlepas, Pawel Swianiewicz, Kristof Steyvers, and Carmen Navarro. 2019. *Patterns of Local Autonomy in Europe.* Basingstoke: Palgrave Macmillan.
Rühli, Lukas. 2012. *Autonomie communale entre illusion et réalité, structures communales et politique structurelle communale des cantons.* Zürich: Avenir Suisse.
Stadler, Hans. 2015. *Communauté. Dictionnaire historique de la Suisse (DHS).* Bern. https://hls-dhs-dss.ch/fr/articles/008970/2015-02-17/ (accessed 24 June 2020).
Steiner, Reto. 2016. 'Interkommunale Zusammenarbeit'. In *Praxishandbuch Public Management*, edited by Andreas Bergmann, David Giauque, Daniel Kettiger, Andreas Lienhard, Erik Nagel, and Adrian Ritz, pp. 897–914. Zürich: Weka.
Steiner, Reto, and Claire Kaiser. 2013. 'Administration communale'. In *Manuel d'administration publique Suisse*, edited by Andreas Ladner, Jean-Loup Chappelet, Yves Emery, Peter Knoepfel, Luzius Madner, Nils Soguel, and Frédéric Varone. pp. 143–160. Lausanne: PPUR.
Steiner, Reto, Andreas Ladner, Claire Kaiser, Alexander Haus, Ada Amsellem, and Nicolas Keuffer. 2020. *Zustand und Entwicklung der Schweizer Gemeinden. Ergebnisse des nationalen Gemeindemonitorings 2017.* Glarus: Somedia Buchverlag.
Tanquerel, Thierry, and François Bellanger. 2007. *L'avenir juridique des communes: Journée de droit administratif.* Zurich: Schulthess.
Vatter, Adrian. 2018. *Swiss Federalism. The Transformation of a Federal Model.* London and New York: Routledge.

CHAPTER 15

METROPOLITAN AREAS

DANIEL KÜBLER

1 Introduction

SWITZERLAND usually evokes the bucolic rural images of Heidi, mountains, and whistling marmots. But according to the latest figures, more than three-quarters of the population (namely 84 per cent) live in cities or metropolitan areas (Bundesamt für Statistik 2014). This chapter focuses on the implications of these new spatial realities for the Swiss political system. It thus addresses the basic question of all space-related social sciences, namely the relationship between spatial organization on the one hand, and the social and political organization on the other hand. The chapter is divided in three parts. The first part (section 2) gives an account of the emergence and the development of metropolitan areas as today's dominant urban systems, as well as the increasing disparities between functional and institutional territories. The second part (section 3) focuses on governance problems that currently result from these disparities. The third part (section 4) discusses strategies aiming at solving these problems. The conclusion summarizes the main aspects of this discussion and points to three fundamental questions that urban policy in Switzerland will need to address in the near future.

2 Urbanized Switzerland

As in other European countries, cities have always been centres of social and political life in Switzerland. However, because of the traditionally decentralized power structure in the old Swiss Confederation, cities have not grown as large as elsewhere. Around the year 1800, Zurich had about 10,500 inhabitants, Berne 12,000, Basel 14,700, Lausanne 8,800, Lucerne 4,300, and Lugano 4,100.[1] London, at that time, had already nearly one million inhabitants, Paris 835,000, Vienna 231,000, and Berlin 172,000.[2] Urbanization in Switzerland set in with industrialization in the nineteenth century. Thanks to coal supplied through the railway, production became independent of traditional energy supplies such as watercourses and forests. In consequence, manufacturing plants settled increasingly in or around cities, the nodal points of the developing railway network. This concentration process and the growth impulses thereof started the process of urbanization of Switzerland.

2.1 Five phases of urbanization

The urbanization process in Switzerland can be divided in five phases (see Rérat 2019; Schuler et al. 2006). The first phase of *urban growth in a narrow sense* extends from approximately 1870 to the First World War. In this phase, the population growth in cities corresponds to the increase in jobs in industry. Workers and their families leave rural areas and move into the city. New factories, new shops, and new dwellings are built, in the proximity of the railway stations.

The second phase, in the years between the two World Wars, is characterized by the *emergence of metropolitan areas*. While further land is made accessible for housing in peripheral areas of the cities, new dwellings are increasingly constructed in adjacent municipalities, whose population begins to grow as well. Metropolitan areas emerge: contiguous areas of settlement, sprawling across the cities' boundaries. This becomes possible by the spatial separation of homes and workplaces. Owing to the further development of transport (mainly tram and railway), employees can commute to their workplace in the core city. Commuting and urban sprawl enforce each other—a mechanism which is the driving force of urbanization in Switzerland to this day.

In the third phase, *suburbanization* (approx. 1945 to 1965), continued economic growth is paralleled by population growth. But because of the lack of space in core cities, growth is increasingly concentrated in surrounding municipalities. Owing to the increasing use of the automobile, formerly rural areas far away from railway connections are made accessible for housing and industry. Still, most jobs are found in the core cities, but their number also increases in the suburban belt.

The fourth phase of *periurbanization* begins in the mid-1960s. The growth of the service sector with its high added value leads to higher prices for land in core cities, but at the same time creates new housing demands due to increased prosperity. The demand for single occupancy houses rises, which leads to development in locations beyond the suburban belt. Contiguity of settlement and population density decrease while commuter entwinement increases. And the population increase in municipalities far away from the cities is contrasted by population decline in the core cities. With middle and upper class families moving out, the cities are left with large segments of low income households.

A fifth dynamic, the so-called *metropolitanization* (Bassand 2005), superimposes the process of periurbanization from the mid-1980s onwards. Metropolitanization is characterized, on the one hand, by a strong internationalization of the urban economy, as well as by the improvement of the traffic infrastructure. Commuter entwinements between metropolitan areas and regional centres intensify. Large urban regions emerge, consisting of a large metropolitan area that entertains strong spatial links to regional centres and smaller metropolitan areas. On the other hand, there is a return to the city: high income households increasingly seek to live in a trendy urban environment. As a consequence, redevelopment of old neighbourhoods or former industrial areas in the core cities takes place and leads to gentrification of these places.

2.2 Metropolitan areas and large urban regions in Switzerland today

Swiss territorial statistics regularly measure the urbanization process, with operational definitions adapted over time to acknowledge the changing dynamics of urbanization. The current definition of the urban space is based on both morphological criteria (i.e. settlement area, as well as population and workplace densities) and functional spatial integration measured through commuter patterns (Bundesamt für Statistik 2014). According to the latest available data for the year 2012, forty-nine metropolitan areas[3] were calculated for Switzerland, which cover 789 municipalities located in Switzerland, as well as, for cross-border metropolitan areas, a substantial number of municipalities in the neighbouring countries. The size of these forty-nine metropolitan areas varies from nearly 1.3 million inhabitants (Zurich) to roughly 30,000 (Delémont) (see Table 15.1).

Table 15.1: The ten largest Swiss metropolitan areas

Metropolitan area	Population	Number of Municipalities	Cantons / Foreign Territories
Zurich	1,280,944	151	Zurich, Aargau, Schwyz, Schaffhausen
Basel	832,112	205	Basel-Stadt, Basel-Land, Solothurn, Aargau, Baden-Wuerttemberg (D), Alsace (F)
Geneva	818,668	200	Geneva, Vaud, Ain (F), Haute Savoie (F)
Berne	398,873	75	Berne, Fribourg
Lausanne	389,614	131	Vaud, Fribourg
Rheintal (CH/A)	334,260	56	St Gallen, Vorarlberg (A)
Como-Chiasso-Mendrisio	229, 438	49	Ticino, Como (I)
Lucerne	220,741	19	Lucerne, Nidwalden
Lugano	175,316	68	Ticino, Varese (I), Como (I)
St Gallen	162,795	23	St Gallen, Appenzell A.Rh.

Data source: Bundesamt für Statistik (2014)

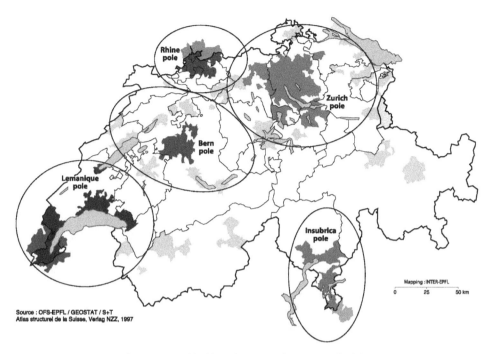

FIGURE 15.1: Large urban regions (dark) and metropolitan areas (light)

Since the 1990 census, large urban regions are delineated as an additional statistical category, based on commuter entwinements between metropolitan areas. There are currently five such large urban regions (Figure 15.1). The top three—Zurich, Geneva–Lausanne, and Basel—are Switzerland's economic powerhouses (Müller-Jentsch 2011). Although they cover only 10 per cent of the country's surface, they generate more than half of the national GDP (Zurich: 29 per cent; Geneva–Lausanne: 14 per cent; Basel: 10 per cent).

2.3 Metropolitan areas and their perception

Traditionally, the Swiss feel strongly attached to their country, as well as to their canton or their municipality. But these institutional entities are not very visible in metropolitan areas: the functional integration of metropolitan areas has led to an increasing emotional attachment to these areas, and to the development of an area-wide orientation. This is particularly strong with people who move around a lot in these metropolitan areas, be it for professional reasons (commuting) or for purposes of leisure time. Metropolitan areas not only exist on a map—they also exist in the minds of their inhabitants. In this sense, there is evidence that ties of political community extend across municipal borders. A closer look at these metropolitan community ties shows, however, important lines of differentiation (see Kübler 2018). The inhabitants of the core cities still feel attached first and foremost to their municipality and much less to their metropolitan area. The reverse is true for the inhabitants of the suburban belt, who feel more attached to the metropolitan area as a whole than to the municipality they live in. Hence, the functional integration of extended urban settlements does not generally lead to a decreasing significance of the municipalities. Rather, their relevance is differentiated according to a centre-periphery pattern. Whereas the inhabitants of the peripheral municipalities more often feel part of a greater metropolitan area, the horizon of the core city population is much more limited to their city.

3 Policy problems in Swiss metropolitan areas

As elsewhere, metropolitan areas in Switzerland spread over the territory of a large number of administrative bodies. In an internationally comparative perspective, Switzerland belongs to the countries with a very high institutional fragmentation of its agglomerations (Table 15.2). In recent years, some metropolitan areas have also spread over cantonal borders—such as Zurich—or have even extended into neighbouring countries—such as the metropolitan areas of Geneva, Basel, or Chiasso–Mendrisio–Como (see also Figure 15.1). There is thus quite a large disparity between functional and institutional territories in Swiss metropolitan areas—a situation that results in a number of policy problems.

3.1 Centrality charges: exploitation of core cities by suburbs

One of those problems is the issue of centrality charges. On the one hand, this issue is driven by the socio-spatial segregation in the wake of suburbanization and periurbanization, leading to a concentration of social problems in core cities driving up social expenditures there. On the other hand, centrality charges are a consequence of uncompensated services which core cities deliver for the whole metropolitan area. The core city still hosts many jobs, and thereby is the target of countless commuters coming from the surrounding municipalities. Core cities are often also the location of public facilities of regional interest, such as hospitals, museums, theatres, etc. Investigations into such *spillover-effects,* based on comparisons of the per capita public expenditures in various policy fields, have consistently shown that core cities face disproportionately higher burdens than suburban municipalities. Such centrality charges are especially present in the fields of policing, culture and leisure, health, transport, and welfare (Table 15.3), where per capita expenditures of core cities are significantly higher than those of suburban municipalities. Of course, core cities do not only bear centrality charges; there

Table 15.2: Institutional fragmentation of major metropolitan areas, international comparison (data for metropolitan areas over 200,000 inhabitants for the year 2000 or near)

Country	Portion of the Core City to the Agglomeration Population in per cent (Average of all Agglomerations)	Number of Municipalities for 100,000 Inhabitants (Average of all Agglomerations)	Fragmentation Index according to Zeigler and Brunn*
Sweden	58	2	0.03
Canada	66	1	0.04
The Netherlands	50	2	0.05
Spain	64	3	0.05
Poland	59	3	0.06
Norway	54	4	0.08
Hungary	75	3	0.17
Czech Republic	70	21	0.3
Germany	31	18	0.63
USA	34	15	0.71
Switzerland	30	21	0.73
France	36	32	1.06

* Zeigler and Brunn's (1980) index of metropolitan geopolitical fragmentation is calculated as the proportion of the core city of overall metropolitan population divided by the number of municipalities per 100,000 inhabitants.

Data source: Hoffmann-Martinot and Sellers (2005).

are also centrality benefits. Among those is a higher income resulting from business tax, as there is usually a higher concentration of businesses in the core cities than in the suburbs. But a look at the municipal tax rates suggests that, in core cities, centrality charges by and large exceed centrality benefits. Indeed, municipal income tax is significantly higher in core cities than in suburbs. In the large metropolitan areas, these differences are particularly high (Table 15.3).

3.2 Entanglement of responsibilities: joint decision systems

Due to institutional fragmentation, intergovernmental cooperation is widespread in Swiss metropolitan areas (see Wittwer 2020). To realize economies of scale or improve supra-local coordination, municipalities often cooperate in public service delivery. Intermunicipal cooperation is most intensive in the fields of culture, supply—i.e. water, gas, and electricity—waste disposal, social policy, security, justice, as well as

Table 15.3: Centrality charges of core cities and surrounding municipalities in Swiss metropolitan areas in 2013, indexed (mean of all municipalities in the same canton [excluding core cities] = 100)

	Large metropolitan areas (Zurich, Bern, Lausanne, Geneva)		Mid-size metropolitan areas (50,000–250,000 inhabitants)	
	Core city	Suburbs	Core city	Suburbs
Police*	331	94	271	81
Culture and leisure*	393	109	437	126
Health*	206	126	168	105
Transport*	186	111	170	101
Social welfare*	207	110	166	107
Tax on an income of 60,000 CHF **	104	96	99	99
Tax on an income of 100,000 CHF **	102	97	99	99

* Net charges per capita (i.e. current expenditures that are not covered by purpose-oriented incomes).
** Mean of taxes of single-earner households with two children with a gross yearly income of 60,000 respectively 100,000 CHF (communal, cantonal, and church taxes).
Data source: Walter and Amacher (2013)

transportation. These cooperation schemes are organized according to an astonishing variety of legal forms: intermunicipal contracts, associations, foundations, joint stock companies, cooperatives. In addition to its horizontal dimension, there is often also a vertical dimension to this intergovernmental cooperation, involving the cantons, and sometimes even the federal government.

Policy-making in metropolitan areas is thus characterized by 'joint decision systems' (Scharpf 1997, 191): although there formally are clearly designated competences for municipalities, cantons, and the Confederation, these state levels are closely tied together in practice. This raises a series of new problems. First, there is the risk of the 'joint decision trap' (Scharpf 1997, 144): due to the unanimity rule, intergovernmental cooperation can stall very easily. Swiss metropolitan areas are replete with examples where cooperation schemes became blocked and therefore proved unable to effectively solve policy problems. Another problem of intergovernmental cooperation is its democratic deficit (Plüss 2015). One issue is municipal autonomy, which is strongly limited by in intermunicipal cooperation. Even if, within single municipalities, citizen participation is extensive, the leeway for municipalities is limited by intermunicipal cooperation, thereby reducing the possibilities of citizens to participate in policy-making. This is even more problematic, as the structures of intermunicipal cooperation do not foresee direct citizen participation. Usually, the management of these cooperation mechanisms is composed of delegates from the involved municipalities, which are elected indirectly at most. Direct-democratic instruments such as initiatives and referendums do exist for some cooperation schemes, but are very rarely used. Citizens can therefore only exert little influence on strategic decisions which are taken in these cooperative schemes. What is more, intermunicipal coordination is often not very transparent, as the high degree of entanglement between the involved authorities makes it difficult to see who is exactly responsible for what.

3.3 Social segregation and political conflicts

Against the background of a highly fragmented institutional landscape, social segregation in metropolitan areas has led to political tensions (Kübler et al. 2013).

In the *core cities*, as a consequence of the sub- and periurbanization leading to an out-migration of wealthier families, the proportion of socially disadvantaged populations grew. Often dependent on social security benefits, political preferences of these groups tend to be on the left. The immigration of wealthy new urbanites in the wake of metropolitanization has not changed this leftward orientation of the core city inhabitants: the traditional (worker-)left has been joined by a new left as well as the greens since the 1990s.

In the *suburban municipalities*, there are large proportions of immigrant workers of the newly settled industrial- and wholesale firms, which has put old-established inhabitants into a minority. Anti-foreign sentiments are complemented by nostalgia of the past, nurtured by the often desolating picture of tiny village centres from ancient times, encircled by apartment buildings, industrial zones, and shopping centres. This provides a fertile ground for national-conservative parties.

The *periurban zone* in turn is mostly a good basis for liberal-conservative parties. People who could afford a singly family house in the country moved there. Economically successful, and mostly bound to a traditional male-breadwinner family model, their political affinities are with economic liberalism and they tend to support liberal-conservative parties.

Political preference structures in Swiss metropolitan areas are therefore characterized by a threefold spatial-political cleavage. Core cities are oriented to the left, suburban municipalities towards national-conservatism, and periurban municipalities towards economic liberalism. This is reflected in the political leaning of local governments. Left-green core city governments are surrounded by municipalities with national-conservative and liberal-conservative majorities. This also leads to increasing divergence between the core cities and their cantons, in whose *hinterland* the political preferences are tendentially to the right. Considering the importance of cooperation and policy-making through joint decision systems, these cleavages are problematic. When tensions intensify, the risk of joint decision traps increases and it becomes more difficult to find appropriate solutions to policy problems.

4 Metropolitan governance: territorial reforms, competition, or cooperation?

Metropolitan areas face numerous challenges: it is here where problems relating to spatial development, transportation, infrastructure, climate change, inequality etc. will be most intense. It is therefore crucial to strengthen governance capacity in metropolitan areas. How can this be achieved? This question is at the core of one of the longest running debates in urban social science: the debate on the appropriate approach to *metropolitan governance*. In this debate, three different models face each other.[4] The oldest, so-called *metropolitan reform* approach holds the view that the institutional fragmentation must be eliminated by territorial reorganization. In contrast to this, the *public choice* approach stresses the beneficial effects of institutional fragmentation, polycentricity, and local autonomy. The third approach, called *new regionalism*, emphasizes the potential of strengthening coordinative ways of policy-making.

4.1 Territorial reforms in Swiss metropolitan areas

The metropolitan reform approach argues that, if problems of metropolitan governance result from institutional fragmentation of the metropolitan area, institutional consolidation is the most promising response.

4.1.1 *City-suburb amalgamations*

One way towards institutional consolidation is the annexation of suburbs by core cities. Substantial such reforms took place in the early twentieth century in Switzerland, when efforts were undertaken to adapt the institutional borders to the sprawling urban settlement area (Table 15.4).

The most significant city-suburb amalgamations took place in the period from 1893 to 1934, when fifty suburbs were merged with core cities. In this period, amalgamations were easy to realize because many suburban municipalities were financially weak and heavily indebted, so the incorporation into the economically flourishing core cities meant a material advantage for them. After the Second World War, however, incorporations only took place sporadically. In the course of the sub- and the periurbanization processes, most suburbs had improved their financial situation, while the core cities ran into difficulties due to the loss of good taxpayers. Suburbs therefore had no strong incentive to agree to amalgamations with the core cities.

At the beginning of the twenty-first century, some cantons have started to promote territorial reforms of their local government structures, leading to a revival of city-suburb amalgamations in some places. Most significant in this respect were the amalgamations in the Lugano and Bellinzona metropolitan areas. Between 2004 and

Table 15.4: City-suburb amalgamations in Swiss metropolitan areas since 1893

Metropolitan area	Year	Number of amalgamated suburbs	Names of amalgamated suburbs
Zurich	1893	11	Aussersihl, Enge, Fluntern, Hirslanden, Hottingen, Oberstrass, Unterstrass, Riesbach, Wiedikon, Wipkingen, Wollishofen
Biel	1900/17/19	4	Bözingen, Madretsch, Mett, Vingelz
Basel	1908	1	Kleinhüningen
Thun	1913/19	2	Goldiwil, Strättlingen
St Gallen	1918	2	Straubenzell, Tablat
Bern	1919	1	Bümpliz
Winterthur	1922	5	Oberwinterthur, Töss, Seen, Veltheim, Wülflingen
Neuchâtel	1930	1	La Coudre
Geneva	1931	3	Les Eaux-Vives, Le Petit-Sacconnex, Plainpalais
Zurich	1934	8	Affoltern, Albisrieden, Altstetten, Höngg, Oerlikon, Schwamendingen, Seebach, Witikon
Schaffhausen	1947/64	2	Buchthalen, Herblingen
Baden	1962	1	Dättwil
Brugg	1970	1	Lauffohr
Lugano	1972	2	Brè-Aldesago, Castagnola
Chiasso	1976	1	Pedrinate
Zofingen	2002	1	Mühlethal
Lugano	2004	8	Breganzona, Cureggia, Gandria, Davesco-Soragno, Pambio Noranco, Pazzallo, Pregassona, Viganello
Mendrisio	2004	1	Salorino
Lugano	2008	3	Villa Luganese, Carabbia, Barbengo
Schaffhausen	2009	1	Hemmental
Lucerne	2010	1	Littau
Brugg	2010	1	Umiken
Aarau	2010	1	Rohr
Wil (SG)	2013	1	Bronschhofen
Lugano	2013	7	Sonvico, Valcolla, Certara, Carona, Cadro, Cimadera, Bogno
Mendrisio	2013	3	Besazio, Meride, Ligornetto
Bellinzona	2017	13	Camorino, Gudo, Gnosca, Gorduno, Giubiasco, Monte Carasso, Moleno, Sementina, Sant'Antonio, Preonzo, Pianezzo, Claro

Note: In metropolitan areas larger than 50,000 inhabitants according to Bundesamt für Statistik (2014).
Data source: Bundesamt für Statistik (2022)

2013, the city of Lugano was merged with eighteen suburbs and its population tripled. Bellinzona's population doubled following the amalgamation with thirteen suburbs in 2017. Together with the amalgamations in the Zurich, Winterthur, St Gallen, and Geneva metropolitan areas, the recent territorial reforms in Lugano and Bellinzona count among the most significant ones since the creation of the modern federal state in 1848. However, they will most probably remain exceptions for the time to come. In most places, indeed, city-suburb amalgamations are met with scepticism, not only from the local political elites but also from the citizens (Strebel 2022). In Lugano, they succeeded because of the good financial situation of the core city and a low municipal tax rate at that time. In addition, the canton of Ticino released a grant ensuring that the municipal tax rate in the newly merged Lugano would remain the same for a few years. In Bellinzona, financial transfers from the cantonal territorial reform programme were also crucial to citizen approval as they curbed fears of tax increases as a consequence of the territorial reform.

4.1.2 *'Mission impossible': mergers of cantons*

As many metropolitan areas have expanded across cantonal borders, the idea of adapting the cantonal boundaries is repeatedly raised. It is highly improbable, however, that a reform of cantonal boundaries or even mergers of cantons will succeed in the near future. The cantons are the cornerstones of the Swiss Confederation and the constitutional hurdles for amalgamations of cantons are so high that they are almost impossible to implement. This is illustrated by the example of the two half-cantons of Basel-Stadt and Basel-Land, separated since 1833.[5] The idea of a re-unification was launched in the early twentieth century, and the will to reunify was confirmed no less than four times in popular votes held in both half-cantons (namely 1936, 1938, 1958, and 1960). Twice, a constitutional assembly was elected and elaborated a constitution for the new reunified canton to be. At the first try, the re-unification of the two half-cantons was rejected by the federal parliament in 1947. The second try came to a halt in 1969, when the electorate of the canton of Basel-Land unexpectedly rejected the re-unification in a popular vote. The most recent attempt stalled in 2014, when a popular initiative to reunify the two cantons was, again, rejected by the citizens of Basel-Land—in Basel-Stadt, a majority of citizens had voted yes.

There was a less painful end, because the process was much shorter, to an attempt to merge the two cantons of Geneva and Vaud. In 2002, the electorate of both cantons rejected a popular initiative suggesting to prepare the merger of the two cantons (77 per cent no in the canton of Vaud, 80 per cent no in the canton of Geneva). This result made it clear that a merger of the two cantons is not a realistic option in the near future.

4.1.3 *Metropolitan governments*

An alternative to reforming existing territories is the creation of a new area-wide institution that would encompass the functional metropolitan area (Lefèvre and Weir 2012). Such a *metropolitan government* would be autonomous with respect to the municipalities and the higher state levels, and would have far-reaching competences and resources in the policy fields that are relevant for urban policy-making. In addition, it should have a strong political legitimacy, e.g. resulting from a direct election of its representatives. Such metropolitan governments can be found in many OECD countries. The most widely known examples are the *Communautés urbaines* in France (created in the 1960s), the *Twin Cities* (Minneapolis–St Paul, created 1967) and *Portland Metro* (1979) in the USA, the *Verband Region Stuttgart* (1994) and the *Region Hannover* (2001) in Germany, and the *Greater London Authority* (2000) in England.

In Switzerland such institutions have been discussed since the early 1990s, but up to now, it is only in the Fribourg metropolitan area, as well as in some regions of the canton of Berne, where they have seen the light of the day. Based on a cantonal law from 1995, the 'Agglomération de Fribourg' was created in 2008, covering the territory of the city of Fribourg and ten surrounding municipalities. It is a new governmental layer situated between the municipalities and the canton, with competences and finances in the areas of spatial planning, transport, environment, economy, tourism, and culture. In the canton of Bern, the constitution and municipal law have made it possible since 2007 for the municipalities to form so-called regional conferences, to which the municipalities cede competences and finances in the areas of transport, spatial development, culture, regional policy, and energy. In the Bern metropolitan area, the 'Regionalkonferenz Bern Mittelland' began its work in 2010. It comprises seventy-seven municipalities with a total population of currently around 415,000. In both Fribourg and Bern, the supreme body of the new institution is an assembly consisting of delegates from the affiliated municipalities, whose voting power is weighted according to population size. In addition, direct-democratic rights ensure that citizens or municipal authorities can demand popular votes on important issues.

4.2 Competition thanks to compensation and disentanglement

The advocates of the second approach, the public choice perspective, strongly oppose territorial reforms or the creation of new governmental institutions in metropolitan areas. Not only do they point out the notorious inefficiencies of large public bureaucracies, but they also emphasize the beneficial effects of decentralization and smallness: competition between the jurisdictions, as well as citizen proximity within them, they argue, leads to better matching of demands and more efficient service delivery. According to this view, metropolitan governance issues are seen to be rooted in distortions in the competition between autonomous municipalities. At the centre of this argumentation is the principle of 'fiscal equivalence' (Olson 1969), according to which the circle of beneficiaries of a public service must correspond to the circle of those who fund this service and decide about it. In order to re-establish fiscal equivalence, it is argued, such external effects need to be internalized. Systems of financial compensation can make a significant contribution in this respect.

4.2.1 Systems of cantonal financial equalization

During the twentieth century, most Swiss cantons developed a system of equalization, ensuring financial redistribution between the richer and the poorer municipalities. During the 1990s, the financial problems of core cities increased—among other things due to increasing centrality charges—and this led on to their initiative to adapt the financial equalization systems in many cantons. Concretely, these reforms consisted of a change in the bases of calculation, where now centrality charges are taken into consideration. To illustrate this, we will briefly discuss the reforms in the cantons of Zurich, Vaud, Lucerne, and Ticino.

In the canton of Zurich, the financial equalization system was revised in 1999 and in 2011. The goal of these revisions was, among others, to improve the compensation of centrality functions assumed by the cities of Zurich and Winterthur by the payment of a yearly lump-sum. In the canton of Vaud, a revision of the equalization system occurred in 2005, featuring the transfer of certain municipal duties to the cantonal level, as well as the introduction of a new equalization fund for transferring payments between municipalities. With respect to the latter, the eligibility of a municipality for a transfer of benefits is determined, among other criteria, by its population size, whereby especially core cities of the Vaud agglomerations are purposefully relieved. In 2002, the canton of Lucerne revised its financial equalization law and introduced a new equalization of charges, which favours municipalities with difficult topographic situations (e.g. mountain municipalities) or with an unfavourable socio-demographic composition when calculating transfer payments. This has led to a clear financial improvement for the city of Lucerne. Something similar happened in the canton of Ticino after a revision of the financial equalization law in 2002, when measures were introduced for the financial discharge of the core cities in the Ticino agglomerations (Bellinzona, Locarno, Lugano).

The organization of financial flows within the cantons is of central importance for spatial equity in Swiss metropolitan areas (Kübler and Rochat 2019). The reorganization of equalization systems in recent years shows that many cantons have addressed the problem of centrality charges and that they helped the core cities of their metropolitan areas through a substantial financial discharge.

4.2.2 Financial equalization at the national level

The national system of financial equalization also contributes compensating centrality charges. In a reform of this system that came into force in 2008, a compensation of special cantonal burdens was introduced. Besides a fund for compensating mountainous regions, a second fund was created to compensate cantons with high centrality charges. These centrality charges are calculated according to socio-demographic characteristics, e.g. the proportion of old, poor, foreigners, unemployed etc. living in a canton, but also according to the part of the population of a canton living in metropolitan areas of national or international importance (Eidgenössisches Finanzdepartement and Konferenz der Kantonsregierungen 2007). This new system benefits, above all, cantons with large urban centres, thereby compensating them for the centrality charges they have to bear.

4.2.3 Disentangling of tasks

In a public choice perspective, the entanglement of municipalities, cantons, and the Confederation with respect to policy-making in metropolitan areas is also viewed as problematic. The disentanglement of tasks between state levels is therefore seen as a further step towards achieving fiscal equivalence.

Following this idea, in some metropolitan areas municipal competencies have been transferred to the next higher state level. This solution is particularly evident in metropolitan areas whose functional territory corresponds more or less to the political-administrative territory of the canton. Such a 'meso level government' (Jouve 2003) is evident, for instance, in the Zurich metropolitan area, where the city of Zurich and the smaller municipalities have transferred tasks and competencies for area-wide policy-making to the cantonal level, which increasingly acts as a metropolitan government, for instance in the field of public transportation (Kübler and Koch 2008). The case of Geneva is similar, as the canton has leadership in many policy fields, basically due to the very weak municipal autonomy (Sager 2002, 193).

Task disentanglement between the cantons and the Confederation was also part of the above mentioned federal reform of 2008. More particularly, the re-ordering of tasks in the fields of transportation (motorways, regional public transport), as well as a new oversight role of the Confederation with respect to intercantonal cooperation in the fields of public transport and cultural amenities, helped strengthen the metropolitan scale of governance (Eidgenössisches Finanzdepartement and Konferenz der Kantonsregierungen 2007).

4.2.4 Functional overlapping competing jurisdictions

However, there are limits to the search for territorial congruence of tasks, competencies, and financial responsibilities of public service provision. Indeed, 'there is no territorial structure that would have the right size for all public services' (Blöchliger 2005, 353).

Two Swiss proponents of the *public choice* approach developed a model to deal with this problem: *Functional Overlapping Competing Jurisdictions (FOCJ)* (Frey and Eichenberger 2001). FOCJ are organizations which provide certain area-wide public services in metropolitan areas (*functional*), which overlap each other (*overlapping*), which are therefore competition-oriented (*competing*), and which are democratically organized (*jurisdictions*), i.e. the clients have their say in strategic decision-making. The geographical area of these organizations is determined by the characteristics of the services they provide; this could be the territory of several municipalities or cantons, but also only parts of these. In this sense, efficiency (minimal size) and spatial criteria (topography, settlement area) are most important. In addition, it is important that the definition of the tasks of a FOCJ is related to a democratic decision-making process, and that there is an 'exit-option', i.e. the possibility to stop the delegation of tasks to an FOCJ. This would increase the pressure on decision makers to allocate public resources in the most adequate and most efficient way.

The FOCJ model certainly has a theoretical elegance. However, examples of concrete inter-communal cooperation that correspond to this model do not currently exist—maybe the Protestant and Catholic church parishes, or the school communities ('*Schulgemeinden*') in some cantons, bear the most similarities to the FOCJ model.

4.3 Metropolitan governance as multi-level cooperation

The third approach—the so-called *new regionalism*—advocates neither institutional consolidation nor inter-jurisdictional competition. Rather, it argues that governance capacity in metropolitan areas lies in voluntary coordination and cooperation between those actors that are relevant to solving concrete policy problems. In this respect, it makes no difference whether these are state agencies, civil society actors, or private businesses—as long as they agree on a common objective and act accordingly.

4.3.1 *The new position of metropolitan areas in the federal state*

In the view of this approach, it is crucial to overcome hurdles and resistance to cooperation. This first and foremost concerns the cooperation between the Confederation, the cantons, and the municipalities in which the traditionally weak position of the cities with respect to the cantons made cooperation across the three state levels particularly difficult (Kübler et al. 2003).

In this respect, things have markedly improved since the beginning of the 1990s. The most salient change has occurred at the national level, where, after years of intensive lobbying, the sensitivity of the federal government to the problems faced by cities and metropolitan areas substantially increased. Indeed, the Swiss Federal Council, in its 1996 report on spatial development, explicitly stated that the country's future depended on the well-being of its cities and metropolitan areas and their international competitiveness. And, based on a new article 50 in the revised federal constitution of 1999, it formulated a new federal policy specifically aimed at metropolitan areas, which was spelled out in two reports released in 1999 and 2001, and reconfirmed and further developed in a report published in 2015. With the approval of the National Roads and Agglomeration Transport Fund Act by the electorate in February 2017, the necessary financial resources were also secured for the longer term.

The federal government's 'metropolitan area policy' ('*Agglomerationspolitik des Bundes*') essentially comprises two thrusts. A first aspect concerns the creation of new coordination structures, with which the federal level tries to influence the behaviour of the actors who are important for metropolitan policy-making. There was first of all the creation of a tripartite conference in 1999, which serves as an exchange platform for representatives of the federal, cantonal, and city municipalities. The aim of this vertical cooperation structure is to bring the respective strategies and sectoral policies, which are relevant for the metropolitan areas, in accordance with each other. Further on, so-called model projects ('*Modellvorhaben*') were started in 2001. Within this programme, the federal government financially supports projects for the improvement of collaboration in metropolitan areas—regardless of whether this involves state agencies, private economic actors, or other civil society organizations.

Apart from the creation of coordination structures, the federal government also provides new funding for metropolitan areas. An important milestone in this regard was the creation of the so-called metropolitan area programmes ('*Agglomerationsprogramme*'), through which the federal government provides substantial financial support for cantons, core cities, and metropolitan municipalities for new metropolitan infrastructure (e.g. in the field of transport), under the condition that certain requirements concerning coordination and spatial planning are fulfilled. Starting in 2007, metropolitan areas were able to submit such programmes and to apply for federal funding every four years. Since then, four generations of these programmes have been realized, involving numerous projects for the expansion of the transport infrastructure. These include not only railway and tram projects (e.g. the Zurich cross-city railway line, the tram Bern West, the Cornavin–Onex–Bernet tram in Geneva, and the Zug urban railway), bus projects, or measures in the area of non-motorized traffic and traffic management, but also new road infrastructure (e.g. bypasses) (see Ecoplan 2016).

All this provides clear evidence for the fact that the relations between the federal, cantonal, and city levels with respect to metropolitan policy problems have changed substantially since the turn of the millennium. Back in the 1990s, scholars found that both the federal and the cantonal level paid too little attention to metropolitan areas and that they limited the room for manoeuvre of cities too strongly (Klöti et al. 1993). In the meantime, the new vertical and horizontal cooperation structures, as well as the financial engagement of the federal government in metropolitan policy-making, have contributed to changing the traditional structure of Swiss cooperative federalism in a way that significantly reduces the risk of joint decision traps. The federal government's new role as an actual political entrepreneur in metropolitan issues should be emphasized. Thanks to financial incentives, it can set substantive accents and thus pre-structure the decisions of the cantons and municipalities. An example of this is the *Spatial Concept for Switzerland*, published in 2012, in which the federal government, the cantons, and the municipalities, after a long consultation process, agreed on the most important goals for the country's future spatial development.

But it is not only vertical cooperation between the federal government, cantons, cities, and municipalities that has improved. Structures for large-scale cooperation have also been established or strengthened at the level of individual metropolitan areas. Such coordination bodies have always been particularly important in the cross-border regions of Geneva ('Conseil du Léman'), Basel ('Trinationaler Eurodistrict Basel'), and in Southern Ticino ('Regio Insubrica'), which ensure cooperation across the national border. But in the other metropolitan areas, municipal and cantonal authorities are also joining forces to foster large-scale cooperation: in Basel with *Metrobasel* (founded in 2008), in Zurich with the *Metropolitan Conference*

(2009), in Bern with the *Capital Region* (2011), and also in the Lake Geneva region, where the cantons of Vaud and Geneva have established the *Métropole lémanique* (in 2011). What all these bodies have in common is a strategic, cross-sectoral ambition. They develop problem analyses and strategy papers to raise awareness of metropolitan problems and to set priorities in the political debate at all levels. Typically, they deal with core issues such as transport, spatial planning, and development, but some also deal with socio-political issues, culture, environmental problems, or economic development. Like other intergovernmental bodies, however, they suffer from a lack of democratic legitimacy, which leads to a limited capacity to act, especially in the fields of regulation and redistribution.

5 Conclusion

More than ever, metropolitan areas are a relevant entity in Switzerland. They are not only a geostatistical analytical category, but they also exist in people's minds and have thus become a social reality. They pose new challenges to the political system of Switzerland. This chapter has shown the nature of these challenges, the responses that were formulated, and the transformations that they portend.

We have seen that the Swiss political system has responded with a whole set of measures. The expansion of metropolitan areas in Switzerland has led to (punctual) adjustments of municipal institutional borders. During a long period, solutions have rather focused on improving the relationships between different jurisdictions—be it through the adaptation of the financial equalization systems, disentanglement of tasks, or the improvement of horizontal and vertical intergovernmental cooperation.

However, these tendencies contain three fundamental problems, for which the Swiss political system must find answers in the medium term. First of all, the 'democratic deficit' raises the question of how citizens can be better included in the search for and implementation of solutions for area-wide policy problems in metropolitan areas. With respect to representative institutions, there seems to be not much room for manoeuvre without the introduction of a fourth level of the state—as e.g. with the metropolitan governments in Fribourg or in Bern. However, direct-democratic instruments (e.g. area-wide initiatives and/or referendums) might offer means by which the citizens could also bring in concrete solutions and decide on them. Contrary to representative institutions, which refer to a fixed area (the constituency), direct-democratic instruments have the advantage that the perimeter can be adapted to the respective problem. The direct-democratic tradition in Switzerland could prove to be an advantage for the improvement of citizen participation in metropolitan governance.

Second, the federal government's new metropolitan area policy points to the fact that cities and metropolitan areas have to find their place in the intergovernmental framework. The cooperation between municipalities, cities, cantons, and the federal government on metropolitan issues will intensify in the near future. This has to be welcomed without doubt. But this development and the associated rising interdependencies change the traditional relations between the three state levels. In particular, it leads to a flattening of hierarchies, which raises the question of whether the cornerstones of Swiss federalism are not undermined in the medium term.

Third, on the level of policy substance, there is the question of the direction that should be given to the development of the Swiss urban system, especially regarding the increasing globalization and the deepening inequalities between the three larger urban regions and the smaller metropolitan areas. Is it appropriate to concentrate mostly on the international competitiveness of the three large regions? What measures are to be taken in order to prevent smaller metropolitan areas losing their connection to the larger ones? And what happens to the rural areas? The Federal Council's comments on the need for 'coherent spatial development' and the coordination of its metropolitan area policy with its policy for rural and mountain areas (Schweizerischer Bundesrat 2015, 14) indicate that the federal government intends to promote the various regions of the country equally. Given the importance of small and secondary centres in the spatial-structural fabric of Switzerland, this certainly seems justified (Meili and Mayer 2017). In the face of increasingly scarce public funds it could turn out that Switzerland cannot afford both of these strategies. The dilemma between international competitiveness and regional solidarity will probably be one of the most important ones that Swiss federalism has to solve in the near future.

Notes

1. Source: Helvetic Census 1798/99: population tables of cantons (federal archives document B0 9001 1090k).
2. Source: Le Galès (2002: 58).
3. The original category in Swiss spatial statistics is 'Agglomeration' in German, 'agglomération' in French, and 'agglomerato' in Italian. As it is conceptually very similar to the statistical Metropolitan Area used by the US census bureau (see Hoffmann-Martinot and Sellers 2005), we use the term 'metropolitan area' in English.
4. In the following, I will not refer to the wide literature for every approach in depth. For an overview of the arguments and of the literature of the respective approaches see Ostrom (1972), Savitch and Vogel (2009), and Lefèvre and Weir (2012).
5. On the following, see *Akte Gemeinsamer Verfassungsrat BL/BS 1960-1969*, Staatsarchiv Basel-Landschaft 2004 (Code VR 3606).

References

Bassand, Michel. 2005. *La métropolisation de la Suisse*. Lausanne: Presses polytechniques et universitaires romandes.
Blöchliger, Hansjörg. 2005. *Baustelle Föderalismus. Metropolitanregionen versus Kantone: Untersuchungen und Vorschläge für eine Revitalisierung der Schweiz*. Zürich: Avenir Suisse/Verlag NZZ.

Bundesamt für Statistik. 2014. *Raum mit städtischem Charakter 2012. Erläuterungsbericht.* Neuchâtel: Bundesamt für Statistik.

Bundesamt für Statistik. 2022. *Amtliches Gemeindeverzeichnis der Schweiz.* https://www.bfs.admin.ch/bfs/de/home/grundlagen/agvch.html (accessed 02 September 2022).

Ecoplan. 2016. *Agglomerationsprogramme: Bilanz und Perspektiven. Erfogreiche Abstimmung zwischen Verkehr und Siedlung.* Bern: Schweizerischer Städteverband.

Eidgenössisches Finanzdepartement and Konferenz der Kantonsregierungen. 2007. *Neugestaltung der Aufgabenteilung zwischen Bund und Kantonen—NFA.* Bern: Eidgenössisches Finanzdepartement.

Frey, Bruno S., and Reiner Eichenberger. 2001. 'Metropolitan Governance for the Future: Functional Overlapping Competing Jurisdictions (FOCJ)'. *Swiss Political Science Review* 7 (3): pp. 124–130.

Hoffmann-Martinot, Vincent, and Jeffrey M. Sellers (eds). 2005. *Metropolitanization and Political Change.* Opladen: Verlag für Sozialwissenschaften.

Jouve, Bernard. 2003. 'Les formes du gouvernement urbain en Europe'. *DISP-The Planning Review* 39 (152): pp. 37–42.

Klöti, Ulrich, Theo Haldemann, and Walter Schenkel. 1993. *Die Stadt im Bundesstaat— Alleingang oder Zusammenarbeit? Umweltschutz und öffentlicher Verkehr in den Agglomerationen Lausanne und Zürich.* Chur: Rüegger.

Kübler, Daniel. 2018. 'Citizenship in the Fragmented Metropolis: An Individual-Level Analysis from Switzerland'. *Journal of Urban Affairs* 40 (1): pp. 63–81.

Kübler, Daniel, and Philippe Koch. 2008. 'Re-scaling Network Governance. The Evolution of Public Transport Management in Two Swiss Agglomerations'. *Flux. International Scientific Quarterly on Networks and Territories* 72–73: pp. 108–119.

Kübler, Daniel, and Philippe E. Rochat. 2019. 'Fragmented Governance and Spatial Equity in Metropolitan Areas: The Role of Intergovernmental Cooperation and Revenue Sharing'. *Urban Affairs Review* 55 (5): pp. 1247–1279.

Kübler, Daniel, Walter Schenkel, and Jean-Philippe Leresche. 2003. 'Bright Lights, Big Cities? Metropolization, Intergovernmental Relations and the New Federal Urban Policy in Switzerland'. *Swiss Political Science Review* 9 (1): pp. 35–60.

Kübler, Daniel, Urs Scheuss, and Philippe Rochat. 2013. 'The Metropolitan Bases of Political Cleavage in Switzerland'. In *The Political Ecology of the Metropolis*, edited by Jefferey Sellers, Daniel Kübler, Melanie Walter-Rogg, and R Alan Walks, pp. 199–226. Essex: ECPR Press.

Le Galès, Patrick. 2002. *European Cities. Social Conflicts and Governance.* Oxford: Oxford University Press.

Lefèvre, Christian, and Margaret Weir. 2012. 'Building Metropolitan Institutions'. In *The Oxford Handbook of Urban Politics*, edited by Karen Mossberger, Susan E. Clarke, and Peter John, pp. 624–641. Oxford: Oxford University Press.

Meili, Rahel, and Heike Mayer. 2017. 'Small and Medium-Sized Towns in Switzerland: Economic Heterogeneity, Socioeconomic Performance and Linkages'. *Erdkunde:* pp. 313–332.

Müller-Jentsch, Daniel. 2011. 'Metropolitanregionen und potenzialarme Räume. Die beiden Pole der regionalen Wirtschaftsentwicklung'. *Die Volkswirtschaft* 2011 (5): pp. 12–15.

Olson, Mancur. 1969. 'The Principle of "Fiscal Equivalence": the Division of Responsibilities Among Different Levels of Government'. *The American Economic Review* 59 (2): pp. 479–487.

Ostrom, Elinor. 1972. 'Metropolitan Reform: Propositions Derived from Two Traditions'. *Social Science Quarterly* 53: pp. 474–493.

Plüss, Larissa. 2015. 'Municipal Councillors in Metropolitan Governance: Assessing the Democratic Deficit of New Regionalism in Switzerland'. *European Urban and Regional Studies* 22 (3): pp. 261–284.

Rérat, Patrick. 2019. 'The Return of Cities: the Trajectory of Swiss Cities from Demographic Loss to Reurbanization'. *European Planning Studies* 27 (2): pp. 355–376.

Sager, Fritz. 2002. *Vom Verwalten des urbanen Raumes*. Bern: P. Haupt.

Savitch, Hank, and Ronald K. Vogel. 2009. 'Regionalism and Urban Politics'. In *Theories of Urban Politics*, edited by Jonathan S. Davies, and David L. Imbroscio, pp. 106–124. 2nd ed. London: Sage.

Scharpf, Fritz. 1997. *Games Real Actors Play. Actor-Centered Institutionalism and Policy Research*. Boulder (Co): Westview.

Schuler, Martin, Pierre Dessemonet, Christophe Jemelin, Alain Jarne, Natacha Pasche, and Werner Haug (eds). 2006. *Atlas des räumlichen Wandels der Schweiz*. Zürich: NZZ Verlag.

Schweizerischer Bundesrat. 2015. 'Agglomerationspolitik des Bundes 2016+'. Bern: Bundesamt für Raumentwicklung.

Strebel, Michael A. 2022. 'Who Supports Metropolitan Integration? Citizens' Perceptions of City—Regional Governance in Western Europe'. *West European Politics* 45 (5): pp. 1081–1106.

Walter, Felix, and Mathias Amacher. 2013. *Zentrums- und Sonderlasten in Agglomerationen. Grundlagenstudie im Rahmen des Monitorings urbaner Raum Schweiz*. Bern: Bundesamt für Raumentwicklung.

Wittwer, Stefan. 2020. 'Voluntary Regional Cooperation in Swiss Polycentric Regions'. *Territory, Politics, Governance*: pp. 1–20.

Zeigler, Don J., and Stanley D. Brunn. 1980. 'Geopolitical Fragmentation and the Pattern of Growth and Need'. *The American Metropolitan System: Present and Future*, edited by Stanley D. Brunn, and James O. Wheeler, pp. 77–92. New York: John Wiley.

PART IV
ACTORS

CHAPTER 16

FEDERAL ADMINISTRATION

FRÉDÉRIC VARONE AND DAVID GIAUQUE

1 INTRODUCTION

PUBLIC administration has a powerful role in policy-making. It contributes to framing collective problems and designing policy solutions in the drafting of legal and regulatory documents. Civil servants benefit from discretionary power in the implementation of public policies and the adaptation of administrative outputs to particular situations in the field. Finally, it has a key intermediary role between interest groups, citizens, and elected politicians. The administration's power and legitimacy are grounded in its ability to provide technical expertise as well as neutrality and commitment to the public interest. It maintains privileged relationships with different policy stakeholders. Furthermore, it often enjoys an advantage in access to specialized information. Thus, the administration enjoys a certain degree of autonomy, enabling its political role while transgressing the classical dichotomy between political responsibility and the technical execution of policies, which normally places it in a subordinate position to that of elected politicians.

Five peculiarities of the Swiss political system must be considered, when assessing the resources and effective power of the federal administration. First, the Federal Assembly (i.e. Swiss parliament) exercises oversight over the federal administration (see art. 160 of the federal constitution) and ensures that federal policies are evaluated regarding their effectiveness (art. 170 of the federal constitution). However, the Federal Assembly is still a *militia* parliament: most elected members of parliament (MPs) are not full-time politicians and have a professional occupation beyond their parliamentary mandate. Therefore, MPs have a limited capacity to control an administration's activities (Pilotti et al. 2019).

Second, even the Federal Council (i.e. Swiss government) portrays weaknesses in steering the federal administration, which has been organized as seven departments since 1848, each of which is headed by a federal councillor (arts 175 and 178 of the federal constitution). This fixed organizational structure has led *de facto* to an overload of the Federal Council as each federal councillor is a member of the government and is concurrently in charge of managing a department. Inter-ministerial coordination is also hindered because federal councillors tend to focus on their department business and furthermore are not bound by a coalition agreement regarding policy priorities.

Third, Switzerland belongs to the liberal version of neo-corporatist states, with weak unions and strong business associations (Katzenstein 1985, 104–105 and 129). Economic peak-level associations have traditionally been considered influential political actors in the context of an underdeveloped central state (due to strong federalism), weak national political parties, and a weakly professionalized parliament. Major economic interest groups have thus exerted a key policy role due to their resources in finances, membership, expertise, and institutional recognition (Eichenberger and Mach 2011). Their advocacy activities, at each stage of the policy-making process, are thus an important counterpower to the federal administration.

Fourth, the internationalization and, specifically, the Europeanization of public policies (Gava and Varone 2014) has moved some decision-making power from the national to the international level. In Europeanized policies, pre-parliamentary negotiations between national neo-corporatist actors are weakened while the policy-making power of the federal administration is strengthened (Mach et al. 2003; Sciarini 2014).

Finally, Switzerland is characterized by 'executive federalism'—the implementation of federal laws by subnational government entities (i.e. cantons or communes). This model of implementation by federal delegation leads not only to divergences across cantons, which have significant manoeuvring space when producing policy outputs and delivering public services, but also to reductions in the expansion of the federal administration. Furthermore, the federal administration has no coercive instruments at its disposal to reduce diversity among cantons. Conversely, it must either tolerate differences in implementation and thus in the effectiveness of federal policies or foster learning processes that enable the diffusion of appropriate implementation practices across cantons.

These five peculiarities raise complex questions about the manner in which the federal bureaucracy both performs its role in policy agenda-setting, decision-making, and implementation and fulfils its purpose as an interface between politicians, interest groups, and citizens. Additionally, one dominant theme of the political discourse concerns the internal functioning of the federal administration per se. For at least the past two decades, the federal government has assumed that the provision of high-quality public services presupposes a greater degree of both managerial and organizational flexibility. In this light, it is not surprising that several reforms of the Swiss federal administration have drawn on the New Public Management (NPM) movement (Schedler 1995; Mastronardi and Schedler 1998; Ritz 2003), such as the use of performance indicators in the management of several offices, the liberalization of public network services (e.g. telecommunications, electricity and gas, railways, or postal services), the levelling of administrative hierarchies, and the loss of civil servants' permanent status.

To detail these changes, the chapter begins with an outline of the federal administration and its evolution over time. Then, attention is drawn to the fundamental aspects of its ministerial structure. Finally, the effects of NPM and the challenges relating to human resource management are identified and discussed.

2 Evolution of the Federal Administration

From a legal standpoint, the 'central' administration consists of the Federal Chancellery and seven federal departments: Federal Department of Foreign Affairs (FDFA), Federal Department of Home Affairs (FDHA), Federal Department of Justice and Police (FDJP), Federal Department of Defence, Civil Protection, and Sport (DDPS), Federal Department of Finance (FDF), Department of Economic Affairs, Education, and Research (EAER), and the Federal Department of the Environment, Transport, Energy, and Communications (DETEC). These federal departments comprise general secretariats, federal offices, and their respective subsidiary units.

The 'decentralized' administration comprises committees with decision-making powers, certain independent authorities, such as the Federal Data Protection Commissioner, Presence Switzerland, the Swiss Agency for Therapeutic Products, and the Office of the Prosecutor General of the Swiss Confederation as well as autonomous firms and organizations.[1] As a result of executive federalism—delegation of the implementation of federal legislation to cantons, which is characteristic of the Swiss political system—the framework of the decentralized administration also includes cantonal administrations and the decentralization of federal agencies such as customs management and border control.

Beyond this formal distinction, the federal administration can be represented by concentric circles with politics dominating the central core. As one moves away from the centre, one observes an increase in the influence of private market forces on the administration. The 'central administration', which performs the roles of leadership, such as formulating and coordinating policies and providing internal management services, comprises the essential core. The general secretariats of the departments, the Federal Office of Justice, and the State Secretariat for Economic Affairs are prime examples of core elements. Within the widest circle, one finds private or special-agreement companies in which the federation is the sole or majority owner. This category includes former monopolistic public companies, including Swiss Federal Railways,[2] Swisscom,[3] and Swiss Post.[4] These public service sectors have gradually been opened to competition (through the liberalization process) and have in some cases been subject to a transformation in their legal and ownership status (through the privatization process).

Table 16.1: Evolution of the workforce (full-time, permanent employees)

Unit/Year	1975	1995	2000	2019
General federal administration	32 355	34 883	31 269	37 000
Post, telephone, and telegraph (PTT)	50 578	58 975	Swiss Post: 42 884 Swisscom SA: 18 155	Swiss Post: 39 700 SwisscomSA:19 300
Swiss Federal railways (SBB)	40 487	32 661	SBB: 28 272	SBB: 32 500

Data source: Varone (2006, 292) from 1975 to 2000 and Federal Finance Administration (2020, 14) for 2019.

To illustrate the evolution of the frontiers of the federal administration, Table 16.1 presents an inventory of the number of full-time permanent employees in various administrative units from 1975 to the present. The general federal administration employs approximately 37,000 civil servants, whereas network industries (i.e. railways, post offices, and telecommunication companies) employ approximately 91,000 persons. If all decentralized units are included, such as the Federal Institutes of Technology (with approximately 18,900 full-time permanent employees), then the federal administration offers approximately 160,000 full-time positions.

3 THE DEPARTMENTS AS MINISTERIAL STRUCTURES

The structure of the seven ministries of the federal administration appears to be as permanent as the *Churfirsten* string of seven mountain peaks in the canton of Saint Gallen (Germann 1996, 34). Since the adoption of the 1848 federal constitution, the number of federal councillors has been seven (see art. 175 of the current federal constitution). Each federal councillor is a member of the government and concurrently the head of a ministry (art.178 of the federal constitution). Switzerland has thus not experienced the kind of restructuring, division, or creation of governmental ministries that has been typical with the arrival of new governments in other Western democracies. Nevertheless, the immutability of the seven departments has been subject to ultimately unsuccessful challenges on several occasions, including the question appearing on ballots in 1900 and 1942. Political opposition to institutional change is not absolute, however, as several reorganizations have been conducted in the distribution of offices across the departments.

The federal offices that are directly under the control of a department represent the real 'spinal cord of the federal administration' (Grisel 1984, 213). Considering the steadfastness of the departments, the evolution of state activities has occurred at this level, following the emergence of the welfare state and according to the respective weights of various public policies.

Thus, distributing offices across departments is no small undertaking. Should the balance of responsibilities be distributed equally across the seven departments and the federal councillors responsible for each department? Alternatively, should the responsibilities be grouped along functional lines, combining complimentary policy fields? From a management perspective, should the primary concern be department governability? These three approaches seem to form the basis of the organization and management of the administration by the Federal Council, which conducts the distribution of 'offices between the departments according to the demands of management, the closeness of the links between administrative tasks, and the political and financial equilibrium'.[5]

Nevertheless, the departments remain unbalanced in the number of employees they occupy and the public expenditures they administer. Table 16.2 illustrates that the DDPS accounts for one-third of the staff resources, while the FDF consumes 25 per cent, the FDFA accounts for 15 per cent, and the other departments account for 7 per cent or less. However, a smaller size does not necessarily translate into less prestige or political weight, especially when one considers the growing importance of the FDJP and the FDFA. Conversely, the DDPS is often a training ground for the most recently elected federal councillor (Germann 1996, 45).

Furthermore, there is not necessarily a linear relationship between the number of employees in a department and the public expenditure it administers. For example, the

Table 16.2: Distribution of employees and expenditure (in billions of Swiss francs) by department, 2018

Department	Workforce (absolute)	Workforce (in per cent)	Expenditure (absolute)	Expenditure (in per cent)
Chancellery	204	0.6	0.079	0.1
Foreign Affairs (FDFA)	5 499	15.6	2.95	4.2
Home Affairs (FDHA)	2 448	6.9	17.84	25.1
Justice and Police (FDJP)	2 529	7.2	2.88	4.1
Defence, Civil Protection and Sport (DDPS)	11 596	32.8	7.06	9.9
Finance (FDF)	8 701	24.6	15.45	21.7
Economic Affairs, Education and Research (EAER)	2 081	5.9	12.24	17.2
Environment, Transport, Energy and Com. (DETEC)	2 242	6.4	12.58	17.7
Total	35 300	100	71.079	100

Data source: Federal Chancellery (2022, 44–75).

FDHA has only 6.9 per cent of total administrative employees but administers 25.1 per cent of federal expenditures. The DDPS has the opposite situation, with one-third of federal employees managing only one tenth of the expenditures.

Additionally, comparing the historical evolution of federal spending by task group is useful. The primary changes in sectoral spending are related to national defence (from 34.7 per cent in 1960 to 8 per cent in 2018) and food and agriculture (from 12.3 to 5 per cent). Those related to social security (from 13.4 to 32 per cent), traffic (from 5.9 to 15 per cent), and education and training (from 3.6 to 11 per cent) have increased, although at different levels.

In addition to the structural inequalities between the departments and areas regulated by the federal state, the governability of the ministries must be critically examined. Limiting the extent of supervisory capacity (in the number of subordinate offices answering to one department head), would seem to be a *sine qua non* condition for efficient management (Gulick and Urwick 1937). In fact, the range of offices that answer to the departments remains high at times. The majority of departments had a large range of responsibilities, which grew primarily in the 1980s (see Table 16.3). The DDPS has been subject to the reverse tendency, despite its significant size, because of office regrouping. In the 1980s, the FDFA, which was by definition a diverse department, was also subject to reforms aimed to improve its governability such as regrouping offices responsible for science and research (which were moved to the EAER).

Table 16.3: Services that have answered directly to department heads, 1928–2018

Year/Department	FDFA	FDHA	FDJP	DDPS	FDF	EAER	DETEC	Total
1928	1	7	6	15	7	6	3	45
1959	4	12	6	11	8	6	6	53
1980	5	14	8	7	13	7	7	61
1991	6	11	11	7	11	8	7	61
2001	5	11	11	7	10	8	9	61
2005	6	11	9	7	11	8	9	61
2011	7	13	11	7	12	11	9	70
2018	8	12	12	8	12	12	9	73

Note: From 2004, the services directly under a department consisted only of the units within the central federal administration (not including general secretariats). The services from the decentralized federal administration, such as decision-making committees and the various autonomous corporations and (regulatory) agencies, were no longer included in the calculations.

Data source: Germann (1996) from 1928 to 1991 and Federal Chancellery (2022)–'The Swiss Confederation–a brief guide' from 2001 to 2018.

4 The New Public Management in Switzerland

Since the 1960s and a political scandal linked to the public procurement of fighter jets (Urio 1972), administrative and governmental reforms have been recurrent issues on the Swiss political agenda. The scope and success of various modernizations of the administrative apparatus differ.

4.1 Strengthening staff

The first phase of these reforms resulted in the adoption of the Federal Act of 19 September 1978 on the Organization and Management of the Federal Council and Federal Administration (LOA). This legislation was based on the work of two expert commissions, which were chaired by the Director of the Central Organization Office, O. Hongler, in 1967, and the Chancellor of the Confederation, K. Huber, in 1971. Four innovations were legally anchored in the law (Germann 1996, 35).

First, the Federal Chancellery was upgraded in 1968 as a consequence of Hongler's report, formally becoming the general staff of the Federal Council. The chancellor is elected by parliament, enjoys the same legitimacy as federal councillors, and has a ministerial rank.

Second, the LOA established two secretaries of state to head the Political Affairs and Foreign Economic Affairs Directorates. Their number was increased to three in 1991 by parliament, with a new secretary of state for education and research being appointed in March 1992. This number increased to four in 2010, with the creation of a secretary of state specifically dedicated to international financial matters, and to five in 2015, with the transformation of the former Federal Office for Migration into a secretary of state position.

Third, each department has a general secretariat. Since 1991, department heads have been free to choose the secretary-general as their closest collaborator, although this person does not enjoy tenure security.

Fourth, a minister may have two personal assistants. Accordingly, a trend is underway in Switzerland: the growing importance of political entourages and their increasing involvement in the decision-making process. These entourages are not comparable to the ministerial cabinets in France or Belgium. However, these personal advisers and political communication specialists are acquiring a status that increasingly places them in the spotlight. It is reasonable to assume that they will occupy a central place in the future as support for members of the government, when they face political, economic, environmental, or health crises.

4.2 Interdepartmental savings measures

The second stage of the reform process involved managerial reform. Faced with deteriorating public finances, parliament passed the Federal Act of 4 October 1974, instituting measures to improve federal finances and prohibiting an increase in federal personnel for three years. The temporary freeze was transformed into a permanent cap in June 1983. This approach proved insufficient, and in autumn 1984, a first reform project (1984–1987) was established with the principal aim of increasing federal administration efficiency. The proposed measures sought to save 3 per cent in permanent positions, 5 per cent in working hours, and 5 per cent in operating expenses. Although these objectives were achieved overall, with 514 jobs cut by the end of 1987, it remained imperative to improve the allocation of tasks between departments and furthermore to determine political priorities.

A second change initiative (1986–1996) focused on interdepartmental measures. Such an exercise appeared ambitious in a collegial system wherein each minister enjoyed significant autonomy and no real head of government could arbitrate interdepartmental conflicts. Ultimately, the premature withdrawal of several measures, which would have involved the transfer of important competencies between departments, demonstrated the inability of the Federal Council to find a consensus on a true transformation of the administration, calling into question the management of federal government businesses.

4.3 Reforms in government and administration

In June 1992, the Federal Council opted for a two-stage reform of the federal state. The Reform of Government and Administration (RGA) consisted of a complete revision of 1978's LOA. However, the government postponed the Reform of the State Management, which was only reactivated in April 1997 within the framework of the revision of the federal constitution and was finally abandoned in autumn 2004. All subsequent attempts to reform the Federal Council also failed. Finally, the RGA could only be based on the new Law on the Organization of Government and Administration (LOGA), which was enacted on 1 October 1997. The two foremost innovations of the LOGA concern the following: first, attribution to the Federal Council regarding its competence to organize the administration (previously a parliamentary prerogative); and second, the potential to manage some groups and offices through performance mandates and the budgetary envelope.

The reforms of the LOA (1964–1978, see section 4.1 in this chapter) and LOGA (1990–1997, current section) were characterized by two common elements (Germann 1996, 257ff). On the one hand, they adopted a technocratic and apolitical approach to governmental problems, emphasizing the Federal Council overload. On the other hand, they enabled a recurrent debate between the Federal Council and parliament about the distribution of competencies related to the power to organize the administration. The compromise reached in 1978 stipulated that only the parliament had the power to create an office, while the Federal Council could assign an office to a department. In 1997, the power to organize the administration was transferred to the executive branch.

Additionally, the Federal Council introduced NPM tools to improve the efficiency and effectiveness of Swiss public administration. In line with NPM principles, the government aimed to clarify the division of tasks between strategic steering by politicians and operational management by public servants. Since 1997, twelve voluntary offices have experimented with NPM tools in a pilot project called 'Management by Performance Mandate and Budget Envelope' (GMEB). In this NPM framework, the Federal Council controls the GMEB offices with a four-year performance mandate by which it defines the tasks and services to be provided by the administrative units according to administrative product groups. These performance mandates are submitted to the relevant parliamentary committees for their opinions. The department concerned provides a concrete form to each mandate in an annual agreement with the GMEB office. In return, the GMEB office has more flexibility in its use of resources, which are allocated as a global budget. The scope of the GMEB pilot project remains limited, as the participating agencies account for only 5 per cent of operating expenses, 1 per cent of revenues, and 7 per cent of jobs.

According to the RGA evaluation report (Federal Chancellery 2000), these objectives were largely achieved: fifteen offices were transferred, merged, dissolved, or created without any redundancies. In accordance with the provisions of the LOGA, the Federal Council presented a report on the GMEB project in December 2001, which was based on an external evaluation (Balthasar et al. 2001). Consequently, the federal government extended the GMEB project to other administrative units: in April 2003, it renewed nine performance mandates from 2004 to 2007, which were standardized and simplified to guarantee further transparency and improved understanding, especially within the *militia* parliament. The government's goal was to expand the scope of the GMEB and allocate a budget for the entire office rather than for separate product groups, thus waiving the savings measures that were initially set at 10 per cent over four years and simplifying the system, whereby GMEB offices submitted reports to political authorities. Another aim was to avoid involving parliament in defining performance mandate goals—the offices' strategic objectives—as recommended by external evaluators and as requested by management and finance committees from both chambers of the parliament.

In May 2011, the Federal Council announced its intention to strengthen the GMEB and coordinated it with financial planning. Accordingly, it mandated the Federal Finance Administration to develop a new management model (NMG) for the federal administration. Implemented on 1 January 2017, the NMG aims to strengthen administrative management and efficiency in all federal administrative units. To ensure the implementation of the 'debt brake', which was enshrined in the Constitution in 2001 and introduced in 2003, and to curb structural budget deficits and debt growth, the NMG has several objectives:

- to improve the Confederation's budget planning by establishing connections between the tasks to be performed and finances as well as between services and resources at all levels (the parliament, the Federal Council, and the administration),
- to promote administrative management and a culture based on management by objectives and results as well as administrative units' accountability and each unit's room for manoeuvres, and
- to achieve greater administrative efficiency and effectiveness.

Management tools and principles through which objectives are to be achieved were also defined as follows:

- a budget with an integrated task and financial plan (PITF) structured by administrative and service groups,
- budgetary envelopes for the domains of all administrative units, with performance groups and objectives included in the budget with the PITF, and
- performance agreements that each department negotiates annually with its offices to coordinate political and operational objectives and define the means necessary to achieve these objectives.

It should be noted that the Finance Administration will evaluate the application and effects of the NMG, and the Federal Council will present the results and possible improvement proposals to parliament by 2022 at the latest. However, the conclusions of this evaluation remain unknown.

4.4 Switzerland: a good student of managerial reforms

In an international comparison, the Swiss federal administration can be considered a good student in defining and implementing NPM reforms. This may be unexpected, as federalist and decentralized countries are generally reluctant to introduce major managerial reforms, which seem to be the prerogative of countries with Anglo-Saxon or Napoleonic traditions (Giauque 2013). To some extent, the Swiss bureaucratic apparatus mirrors Swiss political institutions. Specifically, it is marked by the *militia* character of the Swiss political system. Even if Swiss MPs tend to become authentic, political professionals (Pilotti et al. 2019), the federal bureaucracy remains a major actor in policy-making processes. Its expertise is frequently solicited in the agenda-setting, decision-making, and implementation stages. Those in political and administrative spheres work closely together, as many politicians admit their dependence on those in the administration when developing and managing public policies. Moreover, the Swiss federal administration occasionally assumes a political role because of the overload of the federal executive branch (federal councillors).

This observation is reinforced by the internationalization of politics and public policies, which contributes to strengthening the role of the executive branch and federal administration to the detriment of parliamentary actors in decision-making processes (Kriesi and Trechsel 2008; Sciarini et al. 2015). The paradox is that characteristics of the Swiss political system—which is based on a search for balance and consensus—contribute to institutional inertia, although the bureaucratic apparatus is open to change, adopting NPM management principles and tools from the private sector. Administrative reforms are often described as technically oriented and apolitical, emphasizing the importance of modernizing management principles within the administration. In an international comparison, the Swiss federal administration can be considered to belong to the so-called reformist countries, even if the transformations are more incremental than revolutionary.

5 HUMAN RESOURCES MANAGEMENT

While the Confederation had thus far refrained from introducing lifelong mandates for the federal civil servants, it relied in practice on a system that neared career regulation. According to the federal law of 30 June 1927 regarding the status of civil servants, recruitment was based on a competitive process, with the appointing authority having discretionary power and promotion abilities (thus replacing the concept of career). Civil servants were appointed for an 'administrative period' of four years to assume a function. Although it was opposed to the classical career, the Swiss system of functions (*Aemtersystem* in German) was, nevertheless, close to it in practice (Germann 1996, 114). On the one hand, employment contracts that were theoretically limited to an administrative period were renewed almost automatically. On the other hand, several sets of functions corresponded to true career paths, which is the same as in the diplomatic sector.

The Federal Personnel Law (LPers) of 24 March 2000 abolished the permanent civil service status, granting public employers more latitude to encourage goal-oriented work and reward individual and collective performances. The LPers refers to the abandonment of the public service system, salary scale, and automatic salary progression. By lifting the ban on strikes, this framework law, which replaced a detailed law, simultaneously sought to revitalize the 'social partnership' between unions and managers. Fearing a loss of job security and protection against dismissal as well as the new salary system, the union that represented federal public employees' interests launched a referendum against the LPers, but the law was accepted by 67 per cent of voters on 26 November 2000.

5.1 The end of the civil service

In September 2010, the Federal Council adopted a new personnel strategy to accompany the implementation of the LPers. The Swiss federal civil service has undergone significant reforms in recent decades: the status of civil servants was abrogated with the entry into force of the LPers on 1 January 2002, which maintained public law status but removed lifetime appointments. Accordingly, fixed-term and ad hoc contracts are multiplying within the federal public administration, thus opening the way to the individualization of working conditions. Increasingly, selection is made on the basis of professional competencies according to job specifications rather than on the basis of both general and universal criteria specific to public service. Furthermore, the skills sought are changing. Legal training and associated skills are losing their importance in favour of managerial and project management skills. Career development is no longer based solely on seniority and experience but on an assessment of individual skills and results, therefore becoming less vertical and increasingly horizontal via promotions in other administrative departments or responsibility for specific projects. Financial remuneration is becoming more diversified and individualized, as it also depends on individual performance, albeit still minimally. Finally, the identity of public servants also seems to be evolving, as they increasingly seem to identify with their field of activity (i.e. the public policy sector within which they work) or with their profession and less with a specific body of civil servants (Emery and Giauque 2012).

5.2 The representativeness of the administration

It is also important to know the extent to which the different socio-economic and political groups in Swiss society are represented in the federal administration. Few studies have been devoted to this question in Switzerland. Although such studies exist, they have focused on the senior civil service, which is admittedly at the intersection of administration and politics, and they are dated (Klöti 1972; Urio et al. 1989). A more recent study highlights senior civil servants' characteristics prevailing in 1910, 1937, 1957, 1980, 2000, and 2010. This prosopographical study provides interesting information regarding the composition of the Swiss senior civil service and related changes across time (Emery et al. 2014).

The first finding relates to education. Approximately 97 per cent of Swiss senior officials have a university degree, whereas only 63 per cent had degrees in 1910. Graduates from law and the hard sciences (technical, natural, medical, and mathematical sciences) were the most numerous until the 1980s; however, the number of graduates from economics and humanities has increased significantly in the more recent period. In 1980, 61 per cent of senior civil servants were officers in the Swiss army; they are now a minority (falling to 42 per cent in 2010). Finally, while the majority of senior officials (67 per cent) came from internal administrative positions in 1957, only 45 per cent did so in 2010. These figures underscore the increase in the number of senior officials coming from outside public administration and notably from the private sector (a few come from associative sectors or non-governmental organizations).

Despite these trends, the current top public managers remain primarily academics, who have a background in law and have significant seniority; they have typically made their careers primarily within public administration. Thus, they have benefited from internal promotions, with the majority (with the exception of the 2010 cohort) declaring an officer's rank within the militia. However, this situation is evolving, notably through a progressive 'managerialization' of senior civil servants, a trend that is revealed in the increased number of persons with a university education in the social sciences (particularly in economics) or continuing education courses in economics or business and public management. Additionally, this trend is evidenced by the increase in the number of senior civil servants coming from the business world and private sector.

Since 1 January 2018, the linguistic distribution of federal employees (72 per cent German-speaking, 20 per cent French-speaking, 7 per cent Italian-speaking, and less than 1 per cent Romansh-speaking) has corresponded roughly to that of the Swiss population, which has undergone notable changes over time. Between 1970 and 2018, the proportion of federal employees indicating German (or Swiss German) as their main language was slightly lower (from 66 per cent in 1970 to 62 per cent in 2018). The proportion of employees reporting Italian as their main language decreased from 11 to 8 per cent, and the proportion of employees claiming Romansh as their main language fell from 0.8 to 0.5 per cent. Finally, the proportion of employees who indicated French as their primary language increased from 18 to 23 per cent.

A recent publication (Kübler et al. 2020) demonstrates that linguistic representation differs significantly from one department to another. Yet, some common trends are at work: a downward trend for the German-speaking community, an upward trend for the French-speaking community, a representation of the Italian-speaking community that corresponds to the target of proportional representation, and a slight increase for the Romansh-speaking community. Kübler et al. (2020) conclude overall that 'the representation of the different language communities in the federal administration has come close to the target in recent years' (Kübler et al. 2020, 53). However, the Italian-speaking community is particularly underrepresented in senior positions. Moreover, the study notes that the most common languages spoken in the federal administration are German (or even Swiss German) and English (also used in the recruitment process). The ideal of representativeness is, therefore, confronted with the test of practice, which indicates the use of German within the administration.

Women comprise 44 per cent of the Confederation staff. According to figures from 2020, in the middle range of salaries, women accounted for just over one-third of the employees. The situation was worse in the higher salary grades, in which women accounted for only 23 per cent. The FDFA was the best performer, with 35 per cent of the senior managers being women. This rate dropped to 7 per cent in the DDPS. Another recent finding is that the health crisis caused by the COVID-19 pandemic has highlighted the substantial underrepresentation of female specialists in management. The glass ceiling that has hindered women's careers (Engeli 2011) remains, as does salary inequality between male and female federal employees. Finally, both multilingualism and equal opportunities for everyone have been reaffirmed as political priorities by the Federal Council (Office Fédéral du Personnel 2004a, 2004b).

6 Challenges

In conclusion, four political issues are related to administrative actions and reforms. These represent challenges for both political-administrative authorities and political scientists, as the uncertainties that characterize them remain numerous.

6.1 Reforming the political institutions versus the administration?

Federal authorities frequently distinguish between reforming political institutions and reforming the administration. Moreover, the Federal Council is abandoning the former while increasing the latter, as if these two approaches are either independent or substitutable. Multiplying administrative reforms instead of truly transforming government is telling in this respect. Furthermore, several instruments of the interface between political power and the senior civil service prove to be problematic, as in the controversy surrounding the increase in the number of secretaries of state or even the growing importance and influence of political advisers. The question that arises is whether and how the political-administrative relationship will be changed by the various reforms underway, and more importantly, who will ultimately benefit from the administrative reforms? Several international studies attest to the fact that new 'public service bargains' (Hood 2001) are negotiated between political authorities and senior civil servants. These bargains extend beyond the dichotomy naively postulated by the NPM between, on the one hand, strategic management, for which the political authorities alone are responsible, and on the other hand, operational management, which is the responsibility of administrative services. One can conclude that the over-accountability of administrative services' achievement of policy output indicators, as defined in their performance mandates, cannot replace improvements in governmental capacities for conducting state affairs or the effectiveness of public policies (measured at the level of the effects on citizens and policy outcomes).

6.2 Competencies of the Federal Council versus competencies of the parliament?

The division of powers between the legislative and executive branches of government has been a nagging problem for almost five decades of administrative reform in

Switzerland. Throughout these decades, citizens have witnessed a steady loss of parliamentary power, primarily in organizational matters. However, the recent interventions of the supervisory and legislative commissions of the parliament, particularly regarding NPM, suggest a renewed legislative interest in the concrete steering of administrative actions. Here again, a fundamental question remains as to the effective role that legislative leaders assume in high-level supervision of the executive branch, whether it be the federal government, ministerial administration (departments), or bodies to which public service missions are delegated (e.g. independent regulatory agencies in liberalized network industries). Eventually, this could enhance the value of the Federal Assembly in its functions of aggregating preferences, making decisions, and controlling public action—at the risk, however, of interfering excessively in the operational management of administrative actions.

6.3 Public finance as a single reference point?

Since the mid-1970s, the evolution of public finances and curbing public debt have become priority reference points, if not the sole framework for reforms. Moreover, this concern is dominant following the financial crisis of 2007–2008 and the increasing debt resulting from management of the COVID-19 pandemic. In Switzerland, the FDF is leading the predominant modernization projects, such as NPM, and several reforms are connected to the strategy of consolidating federal finances. Thus, will administrative reforms be aimed solely at reducing public deficits, or will other objectives (such as the timeliness and effectiveness of policies or transparency and proximity to citizens) also be included in the government's agenda? This question is important for the roles assigned to federal departments and offices as well as for future strategies in the face of the state's subordination to private market rules, both internally (e.g. through the introduction of market instruments in the functioning of the administration) and externally (e.g. as a result of the liberalization of monopolistic sectors and privatization of public enterprises).

6.4 Motivation of the Confederation's employees?

The abandonment of the civil servant status and application of new management tools and guidelines encourage administrative units to align themselves with the management modes, principles, and practices used in private companies, which are oriented towards performance and individual results. Concurrently, considerations for the human, cultural, and motivational dimensions of these changes may seem insufficient (Giauque and Emery 2016). Some observers believe that these transformations have detrimentally impacted the values of federal employees and may have reduced the professionalization of the administration (Suleiman 2003). Will successive reforms produce a crisis of professional identity, organizational detachment, and even lower productivity? Conversely, will they lead to the desired effects in increasing federal employees' motivation by financial incentives, as NPM postulates? This is an open question, as research on public servants' motivation in Switzerland (Anderfuhren-Biget et al. 2014) demonstrates that various values, such as civic sense and compassion for the most disadvantaged citizens, are powerful motivating factors. Moreover, introducing financial incentives and performance-related pay (which remains modest in Switzerland) is a risky mechanism. Scholars have established that these practices can have a perverse effect; that is, they can focus employees' expectations primarily on working conditions to the detriment of work content (Frey and Jegen 2001), which is a dangerous gamble from the perspective of human resource management (Ritz 2009; Emery and Giauque 2012).

Eventually, could the current reforms lead to value conflicts (i.e. between serving the public interest and maximizing one's performance and bonuses) among federal employees that result in resignations (Giauque et al. 2012)? Public employees are fatigued from facing, for at least the past thirty years, constant transformations and reforms of the public organizations in which they perform their work. These perpetual transformations have contributed to the development of a feeling of weariness among public employees (Emery and Giauque 2019). Human resource management in the public sector does not perpetually emerge victoriously from reforms that aim to align public management tools and practices with those employed in private sector organizations. However, in view of public administrations' reactions to the crisis caused by the COVID-19 pandemic, most public administrations have demonstrated remarkable organizational flexibility, agility, and resilience. What is certain is that the administrative culture and organizational regulations are being reconfigured, although the contours and effects of this reshaping are difficult to predictively determine.

Notes

1. See arts 6, 7, and 8 as well as the appendix of the Ordinance of 25 November 1998 on the organization of the government and administration (OLOGA, SR 172.010.1).
2. The federal law of 20 March 1998 on the Swiss Federal Railways (LCFF, SR 742.31) transformed the former public corporation into a private company in which the Federation is the sole shareholder.
3. The Swisscom SA corporation was created by the federal law of 30 April 1997 on the structure of the federal telecommunications corporation (LET, SR 784.11).
4. The federal law of 30 April 1997 on the structure of the federal postal corporation (LOP, SR 783.1) created Swiss Post as a legally independent institution with its own legal identity.
5. Art. 43 para. 2 LOGA.

References

Anderfuhren-Biget, Simon, Frédéric Varone, and David Giauque. 2014. 'Policy Environment and Public Service Motivation'. *Public Administration* 92 (4): pp. 807–825.
Balthasar, Andreas, Stefan Rieder, Luzia Lehmann, Norbert Thom, and Adrian Ritz. 2001. *Evaluation FLAG. Gesamtbeurteilung.* Bern: Eidg. Personalamt / Eidg. Finanzdepartement.

Eichenberger, Pierre, and André Mach. 2011. 'Organized Capital and Coordinated Market Economy: Swiss Business Associations Between Socio-Economic Regulation and Political Influence'. In *Switzerland in Europe: Continuity and Change in the Swiss Political Economy*, edited by Christine Trampusch, and André Mach, pp. 61–81. London: Routledge.

Emery, Yves, and David Giauque. 2012. *Motivations et valeurs des agents publics à l'épreuve des réformes*. Québec: Presses de l'Université Laval.

Emery, Yves, and David Giauque. 2019. 'Les paradoxes d'une gouvernance publique à distance par les indicateurs'. In *Manager les paradoxes dans le secteur public*, edited by Ragaigne, Aurélien, Yves Emery, and David Giauque, pp. 9–30. Laval: Presses de l'Université Laval.

Emery, Yves, David Giauque, and Frédéric Rebmann. 2014. 'La lente mutation des élites administratives fédérales suisses'. *Revue Internationale des Sciences Administratives* 80 (4): pp. 725–747.

Engeli, Isabelle. 2011. 'L'évolution de la promotion de l'égalité entre les femmes et les hommes au sein de l'administration: Le cas de l'administration fédérale suisse'. *Politiques et Management Public* 28 (2): pp. 181–200.

Federal Chancellery. 2000. *Réforme du gouvernement et de l'administration: Rapport final de la Direction du projet approuvé par le Conseil Fédéral le 18 octobre 2000*. Bern: Federal Chancellery.

Federal Chancellery. 2022. *The Swiss Confederation – A Brief Guide*. https://www.bk.admin.ch/bk/en/home/dokumentation/the-swiss-confederation--a-brief-guide.html (accessed 28 December 2022).

Federal Finance Administration. 2020. *Report on the Federal Consolidated Financial Statements 2019*. Bern: Federal Publication Sales.

Frey, Bruno S., and Reto Jegen. 2001. 'Motivation Crowding Theory'. *Journal of Economic Surveys* 15 (5): pp. 589–611.

Gava, Roy, and Frédéric Varone. 2014. 'The EU's Footprint in Swiss Policy Change: A Quantitative Assessment of Primary and Secondary Legislation (1999–2012)'. *Swiss Political Science Review* 20 (2): pp. 216–222.

Germann, Raimund E. 1996. *Administration publique en Suisse. L'appareil étatique et le gouvernement*. Bern: Haupt.

Giauque, David. 2013. 'L'administration publique fédérale suisse en comparaison internationale: À la recherche d'une tradition administrative'. In *Manuel d'administration publique suisse*, edited by Andreas Ladner, Jean-Loup Chappelet, Yves Emery, Peter Knoepfel, Luzius Mader, Nils Soguel, and Frédéric Varone, pp. 31–45. Lausanne: Presses polytechniques et universitaires romandes.

Giauque, David, and Yves Emery. 2016. *L'acteur et la bureaucratie au XXIème siècle*. Québec: Presses de l'Université Laval.

Giauque, David, Adrian Ritz, Frédéric Varone, and Simon Anderfuhren-Biget. 2012. 'Resigned But Satisfied: The Negative Impact of Public Service Motivation and Red Tape on Work Satisfaction'. *Public Administration* 90 (1): pp. 175–193.

Grisel, André. 1984. *Traité de droit administratif*. Neuchâtel: Ides et Calendes.

Gulick, Luther H., and Lyndall Urwick. 1937. *Papers on the Science of Administration*. New York: Institute of Public Administration.

Hood, Christopher. 2001. 'Relations entre ministres/politiciens et fonctionnaires: L'ancien et le nouveau marchandage'. In *La gouvernance au XXIe siècle: Revitaliser la fonction publique*, edited by Guy Peters, and Donald J. Savoie, pp. 129–150. Québec: Presses de l'Université Laval.

Katzenstein, Peter J. 1985. *Small States in World Markets*. Ithaca: Cornell University Press.

Klöti, Ulrich. 1972. *Die Chefbeamten der Schweizerischen Bundesverwaltung: Soziologische Querschnitte in den Jahren 1938, 1955 und 1969*. Bern: Francke.

Kriesi, Hanspeter, and Alexander Trechsel. 2008. *The Politics of Switzerland: Continuity and Change in a Consensus Democracy*. Cambridge: Cambridge University Press.

Kübler, Daniel, Emilienne Kobelt, and Roman Zwicky. 2020. *Les langues du pouvoir. Le plurilinguisme dans l'administration fédérale*. Lausanne: Presses polytechniques et universitaires romandes.

Mach, André, Silja Häusermann, and Yannis Papadopoulos. 2003. 'Economic Regulatory Reforms in Switzerland: Adjustment without European Integration or How Rigidities Become Flexible'. *Journal of European Public Policy* 10 (2): pp. 301–318.

Mastronardi, Philippe, and Kuno Schedler. 1998. *New Public Management in Staat und Recht*. Bern: Haupt.

Office fédéral du personnel. 2004a. *Plurilinguisme dans l'administration fédérale. Rapport d'évaluation, 11 novembre 2004*. Bern: Office fédéral du personnel.

Office fédéral du personnel. 2004b. *L'égalité des chances entre femmes et hommes dans l'administration fédérale. Rapport d'évaluation, 11 novembre 2004*. Bern: Office fédéral du personnel.

Pilotti, Andrea, Pascal Sciarini, Frédéric Varone, and Fabio Capelletti. 2019. 'L'Assemblée fédérale: un parlement de milice en voie de professionnalisation'. In *Le système de milice et la professionnalisation politique en Suisse*, edited by Andrea Pilotti, and Oscar Mazzoleni, pp. 53–89. Lausanne: Alphil.

Ritz, Adrian. 2003. *Evaluation von New Public Management*. Bern: Haupt.

Ritz, Adrian 2009. 'Public Service Motivation and Organisational Performance in Swiss Federal Government'. *International Review of Administrative Sciences* 75 (1): pp. 53–78.

Schedler, Kuno. 1995. *Ansätze einer wirkungsorientierten Verwaltungsführung*. Bern: Haupt.

Sciarini, Pascal. 2014. 'Eppure si muove: The Changing Nature of the Swiss Consensus Democracy'. *Journal of European Public Policy* 21 (1): pp. 116–32.

Sciarini, Pascal, Manuel Fischer, and Denise Traber. 2015. *Political Decision-Making in Switzerland: The Consensus Model Under Pressure*. Basingstoke/New York: Palgrave MacMillan.

Suleiman, Erza. 2003. *Dismantling Democratic States*. Princeton: Princeton University Press.

Urio, Paolo. 1972. *L'affaire des Mirages: Décision administrative et contrôle parlementaire*. Lausanne: Médecine et Hygiène.

Urio, Paolo, Gabriella Arigoni, Elisabeth Baumann, and Dominique Joye. 1989. *Sociologie politique de la haute administration publique de la Suisse*. Paris: Economica.

Varone, Frédéric. 2006. 'L'administration fédérale'. In *Manuel de la politique suisse*, edited by Ulrich Klöti, Peter Knoepfel, Hanspeter Kriesi, Yannis Papadopoulos, and Pascal Sciarini, pp. 289–316. Zürich: Verlag Neue Zürcher Zeitung.

CHAPTER 17

PARTIES AND PARTY SYSTEMS

ANDREAS LADNER, DANIEL SCHWARZ,
AND JAN FIVAZ

1 INTRODUCTION

Swiss political parties hold a rather weak position in state and society. They are organized as private associations and until recently, they did not have to fulfil any legal or organizational requirements beyond that. There is no specific party legislation in Switzerland, and parties—unlike business associations and unions—were not even mentioned in the federal constitution until 1999. This reflects the fact that, for a long time, the Swiss parties were hardly perceived as relevant and independent actors within the country's parliamentary-representative institutions; on the contrary, their role was rather ridiculed and seen as dependent on the large associations for financial and other resources.

This chapter describes and explains the origins and development of the Swiss political parties (section 3) and the characteristics of the party system (section 4). Furthermore, the organizational structures of the parties (section 5) and their political orientation (section 6) are outlined. First, however, the chapter addresses in section 2 the role that Switzerland's state structure and peculiar institutions play in the weakness of the parties.

2 IMPACT OF STATE STRUCTURE ON THE ROLE OF PARTIES

The weak position of the parties—both in terms of their organization and political influence—only became apparent after World War II with the expansion of the pre-parliamentary process of law-making into an extensive and formalized consultation procedure. To make new or amended legislation 'referendum-proof' (Neidhart 1986) not only parties but all important organized interests (e.g. cantonal authorities, business associations, NGOs, and other civil society organizations) are asked to comment and to suggest improvement proposals on the preliminary version of the legislation. Further indications of the parties' weak position can be found at the level of their organizations. They are small, have a low-professionalized apparatus, and—since Switzerland has no state funding for political parties—limited financial resources. Due to their bottom-up structure, the Swiss parties are weakly centralized, which is also reflected in a comparatively low level of internal homogeneity.

Admittedly, the situation has changed somewhat since the 1990s. On one hand, due to the internationalization of politics and the heating up of competition between the parties, the influence of organized interests in the pre-parliamentary process has decreased and the role of political parties in the parliamentary process has increased accordingly (Sciarini 2015). On the other hand, party organizations have become more professionalized—at least at the federal level and in the largest cantons. Nevertheless, the main institutional factors which prevent political parties from acquiring a similar role like in many (even similar-sized) European countries remain in place.

A main cause for the weak role of parties is the socio-economic diversity of Switzerland (a strong social and cultural heterogeneity with four language groups and two confessions, large economic differences between rural and urban regions) as well as the distinct small-scale federal structure (26 cantons and 2,200 municipalities for a country with 8.6 million inhabitants). This combination presents the parties with major integration challenges. Furthermore, the small size of the country allows only for a limited pool of personnel for political offices and leads to a system with non- or semi-professional politicians and parties. A large part of political work is done by 'after-work politicians' and therefore remains non-professional for long stretches. On the one hand, this system results in a strong integration of the social, economic, and political subsystems, which leads to more 'down-to-earth' politics (Neidhart 1986, 42). On the other hand, in recent years the semi-professional political system of Switzerland has shown increasing difficulties in coping with modern politics, which has become more demanding and more globally interdependent, with faster policy cycles and increasing complexity.

Both federalism, with subdivided electoral districts, and strong local autonomy make it difficult for centralized party organizations to emerge at the national level. Accordingly, Swiss parties are organized in an equally decentralized pattern with numerous cantonal and local sections. In 2022, one could count ten nationally active parties, organized in about 180 cantonal and 4,500 local party sections besides additional parties with a purely local or regional focus. The parties at the federal level are essentially amalgamations of their cantonal party sections. In a comparison with other federal states, Thorlakson (2009, 167) shows a considerably higher influence of subordinate (cantonal) party sections over the national parties, accompanied by a relatively large autonomy. Moreover, cantonal party sections often address different voter groups depending on the specific settings and circumstances in their cantons. It is therefore often tempting to speak not of one but of twenty-six different party systems in Switzerland. This gives an idea of the coordination effort the national party headquarters are confronted with. However, developments since the 1990s also indicate that the cantonal systems are partly converging (Bochsler et al. 2016; Nicolet and Sciarini 2010, 28–29). The non-centralized party structure also increases flexibility in dealing with local and regional circumstances (Kriesi 1986, 337) and enables broader possibilities for identification. Depending on their needs, party members can identify more strongly with the national party or with their cantonal party, which may differ.

The Swiss system of direct democracy originally contributed to the early emergence of political parties (Gruner 1977, 25–27.). In the long term, however, it led to a weakening of their role, as financially strong interest groups and social movements capable of mobilizing voters outstripped the parties in referendum battles. The introduction of a broad institutionalized pre-parliamentary consultation procedure further weakened the parties. In addition, the importance of elections is relatively low because voters can still correct unpopular decisions of parliament by referendums. On the other hand, studies have also shown that in cantons where initiatives and optional referendums are frequent, the parties are better organized than in other cantons (Ladner and Brändle 1999). Parties are prompted by a greater number of referendum proposals to engage in continuous political activity, which can lead to a more professional organizational structure. Even parties that see themselves as state-bearing and located in the political centre have recognized the instruments of direct democracy as an additional means of exerting influence, internal mobilization, and political agenda-setting.

The consociational system (Lijphart 2012) with its so-called 'magic formula' (fixed allocation of government seats among the major parties) provided stability for decades and granted parties a high degree of certainty of expectation, but it also reduced competition to form the government and led to self-sufficiency in setting electoral goals. For the period between 1959 and 2003, the Swiss government was composed according to a constant party proportional representation. Since the early 1990s, a phase of electoral instability and volatility led to the end of the 'magic formula' and subsequently to several adjustments in the composition of government. Such fixed formulas lead to a kind of a cartel among the governing parties and reduce party competition. The main beneficiaries are the large established parties, while smaller or new parties are denied access to executive mandates. The principle of collegiality associated with the consociational system, according to which the government representatives of the various parties must take important decisions together and defend them in public, makes it difficult for the individual parties to show a clear political profile.

3 Parties: formation and development

3.1 Party formation and cleavage theory

It is characteristic for Swiss parties that they did not emerge top-down from parliamentary factions or election committees, but rather bottom-up directly from citizens' associations and other grassroots organizations (Gruner 1977, 25–27). It is also characteristic that the parties first organized themselves in the cantons and municipalities and only relatively late merged into national party organizations. Thus, with reference to their origins, Swiss parties were described both as 'children of the direct-democratic institutions' (Gruner 1977) and as 'children of the cantons' (Vatter 2002). The precursors of Swiss political parties in the first half of the nineteenth century were little-structured political movements that formed around well-known politicians' ideas (see Gruner 1977 and Vatter 2014, 96–112).

In 1888, the Social Democratic Party of Switzerland (SP) was the first party to be formed at the national level. As a direct consequence, other political movements also began to organize themselves nationally: the liberal Free Democratic Party (FDP) was founded in 1894. Today's 'Die Mitte' was founded in 1912 as the Christian Conservative Party before going through multiple rebranding processes as the Conservative Christian Social People's Party in 1957, the Christian Democratic People's Party (CVP) in 1971, and since January 2021 with the current name 'Die Mitte' (this chapter continues to use CVP as an abbreviation, as the data and the figures in this chapter do not extend beyond 2020). And as the last of the four historically dominant parties, today's Swiss People's Party (SVP) followed in 1936—at that time still as the Swiss Peasants, Trades and Citizens Party (BGB). The party was renamed to its current name in 1971.

In their seminal work, Lipset and Rokkan (1967) identified four political cleavages that played a central role in the formation of European party systems. These four cleavages were also responsible for the formation of the Swiss party system: the centre–periphery cleavage and the state–church cleavage led to conflicts between Catholic-conservative and liberal and radical movements in the first half of the nineteenth century, culminating in a civil war in 1847 ('Sonderbundskrieg'), which resulted in a victory for the liberals, and ultimately led to the founding of the modern Swiss state as a federal democracy in 1848. The conflicts themselves did not end there, however, but manifested themselves in a political-cultural struggle ('Kulturkampf'), which was, among others, responsible for the formation of the Catholic-conservative CVP and the liberal FDP as organized and structured political parties. The labour–capital conflict as the third cleavage led to the formation of the SP, whereas the urban–rural conflict led to the founding of the SVP.

Roughly 100 years later, these traditional cleavages began to lose their power as structuring forces of the party system, while at the same time new conflicts emerged (e.g. materialism/post-materialism, on migration, globalization, or environmental and cultural issues) and led to a restructuring of the party system (Ladner 2004). Because of the increasing importance of environmental issues, the Green Party of Switzerland (GPS) was founded in 1983, and the SVP was able to position itself successfully along the conflict lines of foreign and migration policies in the beginning of the 1990s with distinct anti-European Union and anti-immigration positions.

3.2 Development to a modern multi-party system

From the founding of the federal state in 1848 until far into the twentieth century, Swiss politics was dominated by the liberal FDP, whereas other parties played only minor roles in parliament. Two aspects were decisive for establishing a multi-party system: first, the introduction of a proportional electoral system at national level in 1919, which put an end to the absolute supremacy of the FDP (and related liberal parties) and led to a much more diverse and equal representation of the different political parties in the National Council. Second, the gradual integration of other larger parties into government responsibility. In 1891, the first member of the CVP was elected as one of the seven members of the federal government. Until then, the government had exclusively consisted of liberal members. The CVP gained a second seat in government in 1919, followed by a member of the SVP in 1929, and finally a representative of the SP in 1943. In 1959, the so-called magic formula was established, according to which the three strongest of the four major parties (FDP, CVP, SP) were represented with two seats each, and the SVP with one seat according to their vote shares.

In 2003, due to the massive electoral gains by the SVP since the mid-1990s, the composition of the Federal Council was modified. Contrary to custom, a CVP member of government, who was standing for re-election, was not elected and was replaced by an additional SVP federal councillor. After a turbulent period (by Swiss standards)—with among other things the voting out of the additional SVP federal councillor after only four years, internal power struggles, and a party split within the SVP—a new formula with two representatives from FDP, SVP, and SP and one representative of the smaller CVP was finally established in 2015. However, it seems that due to continuing shifts in voter shares (gains for the green parties and losses by the established major parties), this new formula will have a much shorter lifespan than the old one, which lasted over forty years (see 'The Federal Government' in this volume).

The vote share of the most important parties (Figure 17.1) shows the high stability which led to the consociational system in the 1950s and early 1960s. Even global developments such as the economic growth phase in the post-war period, the Cold War, the 1968 movement, and the recession in the 1970s left hardly any traces in the Swiss party system. However, this began to change from the late 1980s onwards: the emergence of environmental issues, the fall of the Berlin Wall, the issues of European integration and globalization, as well as the economic crisis in the 1990s broke up the hitherto 'frozen' Swiss party system.

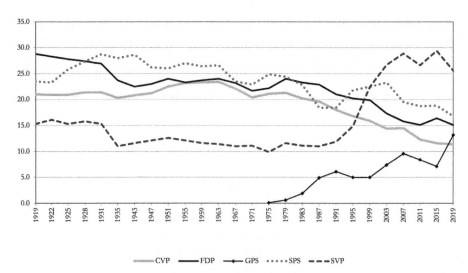

FIGURE 17.1: Voter shares of the five largest parties, 1919–2019 (in per cent)

Data source: Federal Statistical Office (2019).

In the mid-1980s and early 1990s, ecology gains importance. Environmental problems, which have already been emerging since the early 1980s, increasingly shape politics. From the early 1990s to mid-2010s, the conservative backlash and the rise of the SVP fundamentally changed the balance of power. This party takes a defensive stance against European integration and immigration and pursues a clear and successful right-wing course. The political extreme positions are no longer occupied by small parties. Now it is the two largest parties—SP and SVP—that occupy these positions and drive the process of polarization. From 2010 onwards, environmental issues gain in importance once again, which is reflected above all in the strong gains made by the Greens. The Greens even overtook the CVP in the 2019 elections and lag only just two percentage points behind the FDP. Likewise, the Green Liberal Party (GLP), which emerged in 2007 at the national level as a split from the Greens and takes a mix of left and liberal positions (Ladner 2012), reached in the 2019 elections a vote share of 7.8 per cent. This raises the question of whether a new phase in the history of political parties has begun, in which the parties based on the traditional cleavages have lost part of their relevance.

3.3 Nationalization of the party system

For a long time, local and regional (cantonal) party systems have differed significantly from the national party system. Caramani (2004) and Armingeon (2003) show that in Switzerland, more than in other Western European countries, local and regional party systems resisted the trend towards nationalization and retained their own characteristics.

This started to change in the mid-1990s when the SVP gained considerable electoral support in both the small Catholic German-speaking cantons and the French-speaking cantons. In addition, the small Liberal Party (LPS) merged with the FDP in 2009 and disappeared as an independent party. Finally, the green parties (GPS and GLP) managed to break out of the urban centres and gain an electoral basis in rural regions, too. Thus, the cantonal party systems have become much more like the national pattern (Nicolet and Sciarini 2010, 28–29; Bochsler et al. 2016). However, given the persistence of those factors responsible for the strong decentralization of both the Swiss political system and the parties, it is highly unlikely that the cantonal party systems will fully adapt to the national party system.

4 Party system: fragmentation, volatility, and polarization

4.1 Fragmentation

Party system research uses various indicators to describe party systems and compare them internationally (Ladner 2004, 41–43). One of those is the fragmentation of a party system measured with the effective number of parties (Laakso and Taagepera 1979). According to this indicator, the Swiss party system belongs to the most fragmented systems with an average value for the period between 1948 and 2019 of 5.9. Interestingly, that great fragmentation does not necessarily have to go hand in hand with political instability, as will be shown subsequently. This is significant insofar as research has long assumed, based on the examples of the UK and the USA, that party systems with two parties of roughly equal size would be superior to multi-party systems in terms of political stability.

Like in other countries (Ladner 2004, 74), an increase in the number of parties can be observed in Switzerland after the Second World War. This began around the mid-1960s, followed by a decline in the 1970s, and a resurgence in the 1980s. In the aftermath of the 1991 elections, there is a marked decline, which is due to the disappearance of small parties on the left and right extremes of the political spectrum, which were absorbed by the SP and the SVP. Since the 2007 elections this trend reversed. The gains in vote shares by the GPS and the emergence of the GLP cause the fragmentation to rise again. Over the entire period, a trend towards greater fragmentation can be observed. This also applies to the cantonal party systems, whose fragmentation increases almost linearly (Figure 17.2).

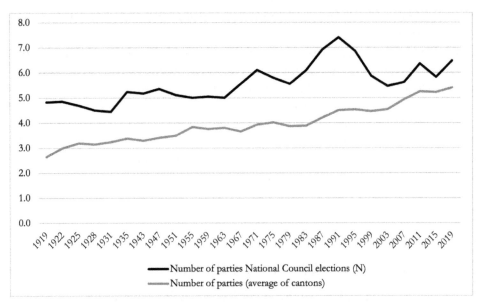

FIGURE 17.2: Effective number of parties at national level and mean value of the effective number of parties in the cantons

Data source: Federal Statistical Office (2019), own calculations.

4.2 Volatility

However, change in party systems can only be captured to a limited extent with the effective number of parties alone. Major shifts in voter shares do not necessarily have to be reflected in the number of parties. Thus, volatility is also helpful to capture party system change.

The stability of a party system is usually measured by Pedersen's (1979) aggregate volatility. It measures the shift in voter shares between two rounds of elections. In Switzerland, the average value of volatility for the period since 1945 is 5.6 per cent, which is very low with other countries having values of over 30 per cent. Volatility in Switzerland was particularly low in the 'quiet' 1950s, which ultimately has also led to the emergence of the 'magic formula' of party representation in government (Figure 17.3). The Swiss party system was more dynamic in the second half of the 1960s. Small parties from the far right, the left-liberal centre, and the far left all benefited from new issues: immigration, the loss of trust in the political elites, and the claims of the 1968 movements. With the onset of the economic crisis in the 1970s, the situation calmed down. It is only with the emergence of the Greens and the 'Car Party' (anti-green group, which in the 1990s dissolved into the SVP) that the competition picked up again. Since then, the fluctuations have been at a slightly higher level. In the 2011 and 2019 elections, volatility reached peaks of 10 per cent, like the peak in the interwar period. As with fragmentation, a long-term trend towards higher volatility is noticeable over the entire period.

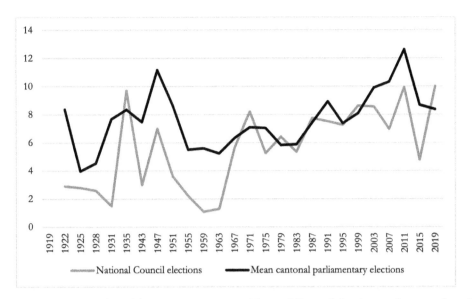

FIGURE 17.3: Volatility of the Swiss party system, National Council elections and mean value of cantonal parliamentary elections (in per cent)

Data source: Federal Statistical Office (2019), own calculations.

The volatility indicator, however, has the problem that it is not sensitive enough to capture all cases of party system change. The developments in the Swiss party system since the mid-1990s caused by the emergence of the SVP are significantly greater than the figure shows in relation to earlier phases. The reason for this is that gains in votes of medium magnitude lasting over several rounds of elections do not drive up the value of volatility but can fundamentally change the party system.

4.3 Polarization

Another indicator for describing party systems that is somewhat less common in the literature is the extent of political polarization, i.e. the degree of divergence among parties regarding important political issues (Bochsler et al. 2015, 476). For a long time, Switzerland was considered as a country with moderate polarization only (Lane and Ersson 1994, 185). However, more recent research shows a completely different picture. In a comparative analysis of thirty European countries based on codings of party programmes as well as interviews with parties and experts, Ladner et al. (2010, 84) showed that Switzerland had the most polarized party system (see also Dalton 2008; Bochsler et al. 2015).

In addition to the high degree of polarization comes the fact that, unlike in most other countries where small parties tend to occupy the extreme positions of the polarization scales, in Switzerland these positions are occupied by the two parties with the strongest electoral support (SP and SVP). Armingeon and Engler (2015) show that the polarization is not driven by pre-existing strong political divisions within the population but rather by strategic decisions of the respective party leaderships. The results of Fivaz and Schwarz (2015) also point in the same direction, showing that candidates who adopt significantly more extreme positions than the respective party voters foster the strong polarization of Swiss politics.

These findings could be read as a contradiction to the Swiss system of consociationalism, which is often confused with a harmonious relationship. In fact, direct democracy—the underlying reason for consociationalism—indirectly favours polarization. Since the Swiss multi-party government reacts very sluggishly to shifts in the electorate and since smaller parties are effectively excluded from the outset, the parties to the left and right of the centre feel less incentive than in other countries to win majorities with moderate positions. In addition, decisions in parliament are made independently of the composition of the government by changing majorities on a case-by-case basis. Three of the four governing parties are sufficient to form a case-wise legislative majority, which means that the defection of one party (usually the SP or SVP) has no consequences. Furthermore, despite being represented in the government, the parties are free to launch popular initiatives whose content deviates from the government line and mobilizes their own core electorate, which also has a polarizing effect on the party system as a whole.

5 Party organizations: members, professionalization, and financial resources

5.1 Membership

To understand party change, it is also necessary to look inside the parties. While Duverger (1954) regarded the mass membership party as the ideal form of organization (Ware 1996, 96), more recent party types such as the catch-all party of Kirchheimer (1965), the professional electoral party of Panebianco (1988), or the cartel party of Katz and Mair (1995) propose counter-models. Voter orientation is gaining in importance at the expense of party membership, and party organizations—according to these models—are becoming increasingly professional, with the ideological component receding into the background. The increasing importance of digital communication and social media is changing the organizational conditions for parties. This gives rise to models that do not rely on formal membership or institutionalized connections to social organizations and associations, but rather on ad hoc committed 'followers' who can be mobilized for specific political projects without any long-term commitment to the party (Gauja 2017). From the 1970s onwards, Swiss parties tried to adapt their organizations to the changing circumstances. At the centre of these efforts, entirely in the spirit of Kirchheimer, were the opening of parties to broader sections of the population, a professionalization and centralization of party organizations, and, by copying grassroots movements, the expansion of intra-party democracy.

Unfortunately, membership figures of the parties in Switzerland are weakly reliable, due to the lack of a clearly defined membership principle which would distinguish between members who pay contributions and those who vote for or merely feel close to the party. The membership principle was implemented relatively late in the case of the centre and right-wing parties and, above all, not consistently. The FDP and CVP, for example, only began to organize themselves with registered members in the 1970s. Until then, parties relied on readers of the party press or party-affiliated newspapers. For the 1970s, Gruner (1977, 218) assumed that about 11 per cent of those eligible to vote were members of a party, which corresponded to about 390,000 party members. In international comparison, this was a clearly above-average figure.

However, if a restrictive definition of membership (paying members) is used to determine the number of members, according to a survey of all cantonal parties carried out in 1998, party members accounted for only 6–7 per cent of those eligible to vote (Ladner and Brändle 2001, 134). This study found only about 300,000 members for 1998 for all Swiss parties combined. Currently, based on preliminary findings of an ongoing research project (Swiss National Science Foundation grant number 182283), a membership rate of 3–4 per cent of eligible voters can be assumed for the year 2021. According to this preliminary data, of roughly 220,000 party members in total, 69,000 belong to the SVP, 59,000 to the FDP, 38,000 to the CVP/die Mitte, 34,000 to the SP, and 13,000 to the GPS. Only the SVP and the Greens can record a gain in members. The FDP, CVP, and SP, on the other hand, have lost large numbers of members, which is particularly noteworthy as the 'recruitment pool' of eligible voters has increased significantly at the same time.

5.2 Professionalization

The success and prospects of parties do not depend solely on the development of their membership figures. The decline in membership can also be a sign that the parties have found a more successful organizational principle with their increased voter orientation. If members are missing, however, parties are dependent on committed activists or professional party staff. Switzerland's tradition of non- or semi-professionalized political structures are of particular importance since Swiss parties have few paid cadres or staff at the cantonal and local levels (Ladner 2001, 134–136). Moreover, state funding is fairly low (albeit increasing, particularly in the form of contributions to parliamentary groups; see next section).

As far as professionalization is concerned, in the mid-1970s the parties in the medium-sized and larger cantons began to staff the party secretariats increasingly on a full-time basis (Fagagnini 1978, 91). A survey of the cantonal parties at the end of the 1990s showed that they had around ninety full-time positions in total (Ladner and Brändle 2001, 206). If one adds to this about fifty positions in the national party organizations, one can assume a total of 140 to 150 positions. Some twenty years later—based on interviews with representatives of the general secretariats in 2020—the eight largest parties have around 100 full-time posts. The CVP, FDP, SP, and SVP alone account for around eighty of these. The cantonal parties have around 130 full-time positions, which amounts to a total number of well over 200 full-time positions. A comparison with other countries of similar size and structures is not easy, also because the reliability of the available international data seems questionable. Data published by the Political Party Database (PPDB) show similar figures for Denmark and Norway, but much higher ones for e.g. Belgium and Sweden (Poguntke et al. 2020).

To assess the quality of professionalization it is crucial to know whether the additional party employees are assigned to purely administrative tasks or also to programmatic or strategic political work. At the end of the 1990s about 72 per cent of the cantonal parties stated that they had become more professional in administrative matters in the last ten years. For 60 per cent, this is also true in terms of programmatic work and policy formulation. Since at that time it was mainly the two most successful parties SP and SVP that claimed to have become more professional in terms of content (Ladner and Brändle 2001, 211), it can be assumed that this also explains part of their success back then.

Fagagnini's observation in the mid-1970s (Fagagnini 1978, 91), according to which parties were organizationally based on non-professionalism, is still valid today in many cases, especially regarding the local and cantonal levels. The number of people professionally involved in politics remains small, especially when one considers that the total number of posts is divided between numerous national and cantonal party organizations. However, several studies are now available, especially for the federal level, which note an increase in the number of people who fulfil other mandates in parliament and policy-related organizations in addition to their party office, and who thus make their living overall from, and not only for, politics (Z'graggen 2009; Bütikofer 2014).

5.3 Financial resources

With respect to their financial resources, parties have a larger budget than in the past, but it is unevenly distributed between them and the state levels. In the second half of the 1990s, the parties at all three levels—estimated and extrapolated based on their own statements—had a budget of between CHF 41 and 44 million in an average non-election year and between CHF 65 and 74 million in an average election year (Ladner and Brändle 2001, 169). The largest budget was available to the cantonal level (in total, not per party).

Looking at the federal level, the budget for the governmental parties FDP, CVP, SVP, and SP at the end of the 1990s was between CHF 2.0 and 3.5 million. The most recent yet-unpublished survey from 2020, for which a complete overview of all parties is not yet available, shows a budget of CHF 3.5 million for the CVP and CHF 5.5 million for the SP for a non-election year. Of the smaller parties, the budget of the GPS is CHF 1.2 million and that of the GLP around CHF 0.7 million. These figures can still be considered modest, not least in international comparison. PPDB data show that at national level the financial resources are comparable to the figures of Denmark and Ireland, while parties in Austria and Sweden enjoy a roughly five times higher budget (Poguntke et al. 2020). If one compares the party budgets with the budgets of Swiss unions, employers' associations, and various Swiss NGOs, which regularly reach double-digit millions, the weakness of the Swiss parties in terms of their financial resources is even more striking. However, these figures do not include money that flows into politics but not into party coffers. The expenses of many committees for referendum and election campaigns as well as for special projects and events (e.g. the annual event of the SVP Zurich 'Albisgüetli Convention' or expensive mailing campaigns to all households) do not run through regular party budgets. A study commissioned by the Federal Department of Justice and Police showed that the parties' recordable advertising expenditure for the 2011 elections amounted to CHF 42 million (Hermann 2012, 23–24).

The lack of transparency in the financing of politics and political parties in Switzerland and the considerable differences between the various actors has recently led to various complaints from NGOs and international bodies such as Transparency International or the Council of Europe's anti-corruption agency (GRECO). However, the situation has begun to change in recent years—albeit very slowly. Some cantons and cities went ahead and enacted transparency rules for party financing, often under pressure from popular initiatives. Most recently the federal level has followed suit and will apply new transparency rules from the 2023 elections on: political parties are to disclose the donations they receive from an amount of CHF 10,000. Likewise, campaign budgets for elections and referendums must be made transparent from a threshold of CHF 50,000 and individual donations from CHF 15,000 must be published. If parties or politicians deliberately violate the new regulations, they face a fine of up to CHF 40,000.

State funding of Swiss parties is only indirect (and to a modest extent by international standards) in that the federal parliament and several cantonal parliaments grant contributions to parliamentary groups. Due to the overall scarcity of parties' financial resources, the parliamentary group contributions nevertheless represent a significant share of the total budget. Since the contributions depend on the status of the parliamentary group and the number of seats, losses of seats often have a noticeable impact on the financial and personnel resources of the party secretariats. The continuing lack of direct state party funding in Switzerland can be cited as a weighty argument that the cartel-party model of Katz and Mair (1995) does not apply to Swiss parties, despite the magic formula of proportional representation in government of the major parties (Ladner 2004, 243–245; Detterbeck 2005, 178). In addition, the still comparatively low level of professionalization speaks at least in part against Panebianco's (1988) model of the professionalized voters' party. The question remains as to Kirchheimer's (1965) assumption that the parties throw their ideological component overboard and move towards each other in the struggle for as many votes as possible. The next section shows that this is not true, especially in recent years.

6 Parties' political orientation

What political goals do the different Swiss parties pursue? Another characteristic peculiarity of the party types described by Kirchheimer (1965), Panebianco (1988), and Katz and Mair (1995) is that they turn away from their original focus on their traditional base (members), adopt an increased voter orientation, and consequently become more moderate. Looking at the political orientation of the Swiss parties, however, shows that the parties keep their positions. There are no signs of a centripetal party competition. The political differences of the parties on the left-right axis have by no means become smaller in recent years. This conclusion is reached based on various studies that have arrived at similar results using different data sources and research methods (Hug and Schulz 2007; Geser et al. 2003). The self-positioning of the cantonal parties clearly reveals that between 2000 and 2020, the SVP shifted to the right and the SP and the Greens to the left, whereas the CVP and FDP moved to the centre.

The fact that the parties still differ clearly from each other in terms of ideology, values, and policy positions can also be seen in their profiles provided by the voting advice application 'smartvote' for every national election since 2003. These profiles are drawn up on a questionnaire of seventy-five questions on policy positions and political values, which are answered by thousands of candidates (85 per cent response rate). The 'smartvote' profiles of the six largest parties based on 2019 election data are shown below in the form of the so-called 'smartspider' graphs (Figure 17.4).

These graphs show the candidates' answers aggregated on party level and assigned to eight political dimensions that shape the Swiss political landscape—formulated as policy goals with which the parties can (dis-) agree to varying degrees: open foreign policy, liberal economy, restrictive financial policy, tough law and order policy, restrictive migration policy, expanded environmental protection, expanded welfare state, and liberal society.

The first profile at the top left represents that of the CVP and shows the party as a typical representative of the political centre. On all dimensions, the CVP takes a middle position. The FDP profile at the top right is most similar to the CVP. Clear differences between these two parties are visible in their attitude towards liberal economy as well as regarding welfare state and environmental protection: overall, the FDP stands for less regulation and a leaner state than the CVP. The SVP's national-conservative profile, which is characterized by strict law and order and restrictive migration policies, clearly differs from the previous ones. It also opposes an open foreign policy and liberal society and an expanded welfare state. The political counterpart to the SVP is formed by the SP and the GPS with a strong emphasis on environmental protection, the welfare state, and a liberal society, as well as their rejection of a tough migration policy, law and order, and a liberal economic and financial policy, respectively. The profiles of the SP and GPS can be classified as typical for the political left and prove to be practically congruent. Finally, the GLP has an independent profile (progressive on societal issues, economically liberal,

PARTIES AND PARTY SYSTEMS 331

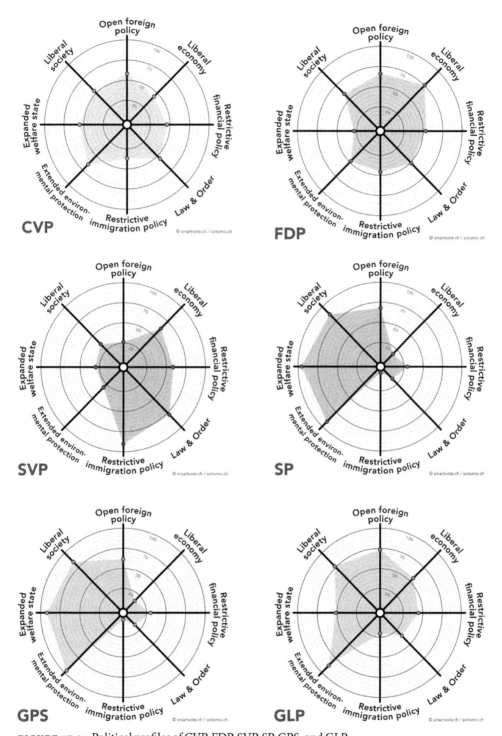

FIGURE 17.4: Political profiles of CVP, FDP, SVP, SP, GPS, and GLP

Source: Reproduced with permission from Smartvote/SOTOMO, www.smartvote.ch

and ecological), positioning itself in the space between the traditional left (SP/GPS) and the economically liberal FDP.

Looking back at the goals pursued by the Swiss parties in the 1970s, it can be stated that they could only be realized in part. Despite increasing professionalization at the federal level, which brought a clear disciplining of the previously heterogeneous bourgeois parties (Schwarz 2018), many parties are still quite undisciplined overall due to the bottom-up structure and the socio-cultural diversity of the country. Not only has Kirchheimer's prediction regarding converging political profiles of the parties not come true in Switzerland, but the country even has one of the most polarized party systems in Europe (Ladner et al. 2010, 82–84). There are still striking and, in some cases, even increasing differences in party positions.

7 Outlook

For decades, Swiss politics and its party system were considered the epitome of political stability. The clearest expression of this at the political level was the 'magic formula', which ensured that the party-political composition of the Swiss government remained unchanged for more than forty years from 1959. This changed abruptly from the 1990s onwards. Within ten years, the SVP rose from a 10 per cent share of the vote to clearly become the strongest party in the country (Kriesi et al. 2005). Although the power-sharing principle inherent in the Swiss political system has prevented the SVP from becoming too powerful, its electoral success has left clear traces. The rise of the SVP has been accompanied by a steady decline of classic people's parties. Christian Democrats, Social Democrats, and Liberals have steadily lost voter shares—albeit somewhat less markedly and more slowly than in other European countries—, a development that in the 2019 parliamentary elections led to the CVP, SP, and FDP achieving their worst results since the introduction of proportional representation in 1919.

These shifts in political power can largely be attributed to the emergence of new issues (e.g. the environment or cultural-identity issues) (Kriesi et al. 2008). But it is not only the substantive-ideological orientations of the parties that have changed. Bartolini and Mair (1990) pointed out that the classical cleavages were also based on a party system structured along denominations and social classes. This socio-demographic structural basis has also collapsed in the past thirty years. The rise of the SVP and the decline of the classic people's parties are the clearest, but by no means the only signs that Swiss parties are undergoing a profound transformation. The party system has become more fragmented and differentiated. Parallel to the rise of the SVP, the Greens also steadily gained strength and were only just behind the CVP in the 2019 elections. In addition, the GLP was able to establish itself as a new centre-left party at the national level and further differentiations of the party system also took place at the cantonal and local levels.

In addition to fragmentation, the volatility and, above all, the polarization of the party system have also increased significantly. Especially regarding polarization and the tendency towards national-conservative and right-wing populist parties, Switzerland has for once anticipated an international development. Today, Switzerland is one of the most polarized countries as regards its partisan landscape (Ladner et al. 2010, Norris 2020). Finally, the parties themselves have also changed. They have become more professional and much more tightly organized. This can be seen, for example, in voting behaviour in parliament, where votes are now taken more along party lines (Dermont 2019).

Quite significantly, this transformation of parties and the party system was—and still is—driven by the changing environment. The advancing economic globalization as well as a constantly increasing social individualization pose greater challenges to parties (e.g. in recruiting new members or organizing public support for political campaigns). The media system and the way the media report on politics have also changed significantly. To survive economically, Swiss media increasingly focus their reporting on simplification, emotionalization, personalization, and the emphasis on conflicts (scandalization), which in turn is reflected in how political parties conduct and communicate politics (Udris et al. 2015).

Finally, digitalization is another key challenge for parties. Search engines, social media, and other digital offerings have fundamentally changed both the amount of information available, and the way voters inform themselves. Specialized platforms such as the online voting tool 'Smartvote' offer individualized voting recommendations based on issue-matching and are now used by roughly 20 per cent of voters. Their use leads to significantly more vote-switching and vote-splitting (Fivaz et al. 2020). With their focus on policy positions, platforms such as Smartvote offer equal opportunities to large and small parties, as well as to known, unknown, or even non-party candidates. Thus, they tend to undermine the importance of candidates' party affiliation and the monopolistic position of parties in the recruitment of political officeholders, since, for example, candidates without large campaign budgets can present themselves to a large number of voters via such platforms. Similarly, e-collecting platforms such as 'WeCollect' enable both established parties and actors with smaller budgets (e.g. citizens' committees) to collect signatures for popular initiatives and referendums.

Overall—especially in comparison to other countries—the digitalization of Swiss democracy and politics is not yet very advanced, as is also noted in a study on the 2019 election campaign, which shows that the parties have integrated the new digital possibilities into their campaigns only very hesitantly and to a limited extent (Gilardi et al. 2020). Nevertheless, the digitalization of political information, communication, and opinion-forming has the fundamental potential to lower the barriers to entry into the political arena and thus also offers smaller parties or other actors the chance to be heard. In recent years, the Swiss parties have repeatedly faced competition from new political actors such as citizens' committees, movements, or 'ad hoc' groups. These are generally characterized by open structures and usually cover only a few topics, which makes them attractive for many politically interested citizens who increasingly want to get involved only in a thematically focused way and for a limited time. Typical is the intensive use of digital channels for communication but also for mobilizing human and financial resources via crowdsourcing and crowdfunding. Especially during the

Corona pandemic, such movements and ad hoc groups became political actors to be taken seriously. While focusing on one or a very few issues allows them to mobilize quickly and greatly, on the other hand, this also gives them only a temporary character. It is therefore questionable whether these organizations can develop into real alternatives to the classic parties in the long term. However, they do put pressure on the parties to become more open, to communicate in a more modern way, and to react more quickly to new issues.

In general, the developments that are emerging in the Swiss party system are very similar to those in many European countries: the departure from a party landscape structured by the classic cleavages on a confessional or class basis, the emergence of new issues and dividing lines, the strengthening of national-conservative and right-wing populist parties, a party system with increasing volatility and fragmentation, and characterized by ever greater polarization. The parties themselves are becoming more centralized and increasingly professionalized. They will also have to become more open and participatory and find new ways to mobilize voters and members and integrate them into party work. The new digital possibilities will play a central role in this.

References

Armingeon, Klaus. 2003. *Das Parteiensystem der Schweiz im internationalen Vergleich. A study with data from the National Council elections 1971–1999*. Neuchâtel: Swiss Federal Statistical Office.

Armingeon, Klaus, and Sarah Engler. 2015. 'Polarisierung als Strategie. Die Polarisierung des Schweizer Parteiensystems im internationalen Vergleich'. In *Wahlen und Wählerschaft in der Schweiz*, edited by Markus Freitag, and Adrian Vatter, pp. 355–379. Zürich: Verlag Neue Zürcher Zeitung.

Bartolini, Stefano, and Peter Mair. 1990. *Identity, Competition, and Electoral Availability. The Stabilisation of European Electorates 1885–1985*. Cambridge: Cambridge University Press.

Bochsler, Daniel, Regula Hänggli, and Silja Häusermann. 2015. 'Introduction: Consensus Lost? Disenchanted Democracy in Switzerland'. *Swiss Political Science Review* 21 (4): pp. 475–490.

Bochsler, Daniel, Sean Müller, and Julian Bernauer. 2016. 'An Ever Closer Union? The Nationalisation of Political Parties in Switzerland, 1991–2015'. *Swiss Political Science Review* 22 (1): pp. 29–40.

Bütikofer, Sarah. 2014. *Das Schweizer Parlament: Eine Institution auf dem Pfad der Moderne*. Baden-Baden: Nomos.

Caramani, Daniele. 2004. *The Nationalization of Politics. The Formation of National Electorates and Party Systems in Western Europe*. Cambridge: Cambridge University Press.

Dalton, Russell J. 2008, 'The Quantity and the Quality of Party Systems. Party System Polarization, its Measurement, and its Consequences'. *Comparative Political Studies* 41 (7): pp. 899–920.

Dermont, Clau. 2019. Aus bipolar wird tripolar: Polarisierung bei Parlamentsabstimmungen. In *Konkordanz im Parlament. Entscheidungsfindung zwischen Kooperation und Konkurrenz*, edited by Marc Bühlmann, Anja Heidelberger, and Hans-Peter Schaub, pp. 317–332. Basel: NZZ Libro.

Detterbeck, Klaus. 2005. 'Cartel Parties in Western Europe'. *Party Politics* 11 (2): pp. 173–191.
Duverger, Maurice. 1954. *Political Parties*. London: Methuen & Co.
Fagagnini, Hans Peter. 1978. 'Die Rolle der Parteien auf kantonaler Ebene'. *Schweizerisches Jahrbuch für politische Wissenschaft*: pp. 75–94.
Federal Statistical Office. 2019. *National Council Elections: Strength of the Parties 1919-2019*. Neuchâtel: Swiss Federal Statistical Office FSO (consulted online on 26 November 2020).
Fivaz, Jan, and Daniel Schwarz. 2015. 'Die smarte Wahlspinne: Politische Positionen von Wählern und Kandidaten im Vergleich'. In *Wahlen und Wählerschaft in der Schweiz* edited by Markus Freitag, and Adrian Vatter, pp. 301-324. Zürich: Verlag Neue Zürcher Zeitung.
Fivaz, Jan, Daniel Schwarz, and Andreas Ladner. 2020. Effects of VAAs on Electoral Decision-Making—Evidence from a Large-Scale Field Experiment. Paper presented at the ECPR Virtual General Conference, 24–28 August 2020.
Gauja, Anika. 2017. *Party Reform. The Causes, Challenges, and Consequences of Organizational Change*. Oxford: Oxford University Press.
Geser, Hans, Andreas Ladner, Urs Meuli, and Roland Schaller. 2003. *Swiss Local Parties in Transition. First Results of a Survey of the Presidents of Swiss Local Parties 2002/2003*. Zürich: Sociological Institute, University of Zürich.
Gilardi, Fabrizio, Clau Dermont, Maël Kubli, and Lucien Baumgartner. 2020. *Selects Medienstudie 2020: Der Wahlkampf 2019 in traditionellen und digitalen Medien*. Zürich: Digital Democracy Lab, Universität Zürich.
Gruner, Erich. 1977. *Die Parteien der Schweiz*. Bern: Francke.
Hermann, Michael. 2012. *Das politische Profil des Geldes*. Zürich: Forschungsstelle sotomo.
Hug, Simon, and Tobias Schulz. 2007. 'Left-Right Positions of Political Parties in Switzerland'. *Party Politics* 13 (3): pp. 305–330.
Katz, Richard S., and Peter Mair. 1995. 'Changing Models of Party Organisation and Party Democracy: The Emergence of the Cartel Party'. *Party Politics* 1 (1): pp. 5–28.
Kirchheimer, Otto. 1965. 'Der Wandel des westeuropäischen Parteiensystems'. *Politische Vierteljahresschrift* 6 (1): pp. 20–41.
Kriesi, Hanspeter. 1986. 'Perspektiven neuer Politik: Parteien und neue soziale Bewegungen'. *Swiss Yearbook of Political Science*: pp. 333–350.
Kriesi, Hanspeter, Romain Lachat, Peter Selb, Simon Bornschier, and Marc Helbling. 2005. *Der Aufstieg der SVP. Acht Kantone im Vergleich*. Zürich: NZZ.
Kriesi, Hanspeter, Edgar Grande, Romain Lachat, Martin Dolezal, Simon Bornschier, and Timotheos Frey. 2008. *West European Politics in the Age of Globalization*. Cambridge: Cambridge University Press.
Laakso, Markku, and Rein Taagepera. 1979. 'Effective Number of Parties. A Measure with Application to West Europe'. *Comparative Political Studies* 12 (1): pp. 3–27.
Ladner, Andreas. 2001. 'Swiss Political Parties—Between Persistence and Change'. *West European Politics* 24 (2): pp. 123–144.
Ladner, Andreas. 2004. *Stabilität und Wandel von Parteien und Parteiensystemen. Eine vergleichende Analyse von Konfliktlinien, Parteien und Parteiensystemen in den Schweizer Kantonen*. Opladen: VS Verlag für Sozialwissenschaften.
Ladner, Andreas. 2012. 'Switzerland's Green Liberal Party: A New Party Model for the Environment?' *Environmental Politics* 21 (3): pp. 510–515.
Ladner, Andreas, and Michael Brändle. 1999. 'Does Direct Democracy Matter for Political Parties?' *Party Politics* 5 (3): pp. 283–302.

Ladner, Andreas, and Michael Brändle. 2001. *Die Schweizer Parteien im Wandel. Von Mitgliederparteien zu professionalisierten Wählerorganisationen?*. Zürich: Seismo.

Ladner, Andreas, Gabriela Felder, Stefani Gerber, and Jan Fivaz. 2010. *Die politische Positionierung der europäischen Parteien im Vergleich. Eine Analyse der politischen Positionen der europäischen Parteien anlässlich der Wahlen des Europäischen Parlaments 2009 mit besonderer Berücksichtigung der Schweizer Parteien. Cahier de l'IDHEAP 252*. Chavannes-près-Renens: IDHEAP, University of Lausanne.

Lane, Jan-Erik, and Svante O. Ersson. 1994. *Politics and Society in Western Europe*. London: Sage.

Lijphart, Arend. 2012. *Patterns of Democracy*. New Haven and London: Yale University Press.

Lipset, Seymour M., and Stein Rokkan. 1967. 'Cleavages Structures, Party Systems and Voter Alignments: An Introduction'. In *Party Systems and Voter Alignments*, edited by Seymour M. Lipset, and Stein Rokkan, pp. 1–64. New York: Free Press.

Neidhart, Leonhard. 1986. 'Funktions- und Organisationsprobleme der schweizerischen Parteien'. *Swiss Yearbook of Political Science*: pp. 17–43.

Nicolet, Sarah, and Pascal Sciarini (eds). 2010. *Le destin électoral de la gauche. Le vote socialiste et vert en Suisse*. Geneva: Georg.

Norris, Pippa. 2020. Measuring Populism Worldwide. *Party Politics* 26 (6): pp. 697–717.

Panebianco, Angelo. 1988. *Political Parties: Organisation and Power*. Cambridge: Cambridge University Press.

Pedersen, Morgens. 1979. 'The Dynamics of European Party Systems: Changing Patterns of Electoral Volatility'. *European Journal of Political Research* 7 (1): pp. 1–26.

Poguntke, Thomas, Susan E. Scarrow, and Paul D. Webb. 2020. PPDB_Round1a_1b_consolidated_v1. Harvard Dataverse: https://dataverse.harvard.edu/dataset.xhtml?persistentId=doi:10.7910/DVN/NBWDFZ (accessed 18 July 2022).

Schwarz, Daniel. 2018. 'Professionalised, Centralised and Disciplined: The Parliamentary Groups of the Federal Assembly'. *Parlament—Parlement—Parlamento* 2: pp. 3–7.

Sciarini, Pascal. 2015. 'From Corporatism to Bureaucratic and Partisan Politics: Changes in Decision-Making Processes Over Time'. In *Political Decision-Making in Switzerland: The Consensus Model under Pressure*, edited by Pascal Sciarini, Manuel Fischer, and Denise Traber, pp. 24–50. Basingstoke and New York: Palgrave Macmillan.

Thorlakson, Lori. 2009. 'Patterns of Party Integration, Influence and Autonomy in Seven Federations'. *Party Politics* 15 (2): pp. 157–177.

Udris, Linards, Jens Lucht, and Jörg Schneider. 2015. 'Contested Elections in Increasingly Commercialized Media. A Diachronic Analysis of Executive and Parliamentary Election News Coverage in Switzerland'. *Swiss Political Science Review* 21 (4): pp. 578–595.

Vatter, Adrian. 2002. *Kantonale Demokratien im Vergleich. Entstehungsgründe, Interaktionen und Wirkungen politischer Institutionen in den Schweizer Kantonen*. Opladen: Leske + Budrich.

Vatter, Adrian. 2014. *Das politische System der Schweiz*. Baden-Baden: Nomos.

Ware, Alan. 1996. *Political Parties and Party Systems*. New York: Oxford University Press.

Z'Graggen, Heidi. 2009. *Die Professionalisierung von Parlamenten im historischen und internationalen Vergleich*. Bern: Haupt.

CHAPTER 18

INTEREST GROUPS

ANDRÉ MACH AND STEVEN EICHENBERGER

1 INTRODUCTION

IN the context of a weak central state and the relative weakness of political parties at the national level, the main interest groups, predominantly economic, organized very early on at the end of the nineteenth century and were closely involved in the federal decision-making process. In general and from a comparative point of view, interest groups are considered central actors in Swiss society, particularly in political life.

Among the many terms used to describe the associative phenomenon (e.g. pressure groups, lobbies, interest groups, and associations), we favour interest groups or interest associations. Indeed, the idea of pressure is closely associated with the pluralist approach of the 1960s. It refers to a hierarchical relationship between the state and interest associations, where the latter would attempt to exert pressure on the state. This approach ignores the possibility of institutionalized relations between political authorities and major interest groups, as highlighted in the neo-corporatist literature. The term lobbying is too vague for our purposes: first, it is limited to the action and influence of groups on the authorities, neglecting an analysis of the collective organization of these groups. Second, lobbying includes not only the activities of interest groups but also those of individual companies, communication agencies, or other actors.

Interest groups cover a wide range of collective organizations, all of which aim to defend and promote the interests of a greater or lesser part of society vis-à-vis the political authorities or public opinion in general. They are distinct from social movements and political parties (see 'Parties and Party Systems in Switzerland' and 'Social Movements' in this volume). Unlike social movements, interest groups have a formal organization and structure that codifies their functioning; moreover, they differ from political parties, as they do not participate directly in elections. Over the decades, scholarly attention to interest groups in Switzerland has varied. After the pioneering work of Gruner (1956) and Meynaud (1963) in the post-war period, followed by the studies of Kriesi (1980) and

Farago (1987) in the 1980s, research on interest groups waned in the 1990s and 2000s; however, over the last decade, it has experienced a certain revival (Mach 2015).

The remainder of this chapter is organized as follows: section 2 is devoted to the different categories of interest groups and the formation of the main ones. Then, section 3 presents the historical development of the traditional model of interaction between interest groups and political actors, while section 4 discusses the various arenas of intervention of interest groups. Next, section 5 discusses the relevance of the concept of neo-corporatism, which is traditionally applied to the Swiss case. Finally, section 6 addresses the recent period (i.e. since the 1990s), which has been marked by profound changes in both the organization of interest groups and their political strategies.

2 Origin and formation of the main interest groups

Various typologies exist for classifying interest groups according to their main characteristics. Five main categories can be identified in the literature: first, business interest associations, which represent companies and their managers; second, trade unions, which organize employees; third, occupational groups, which exclusively group together people who practise the same trade; fourth, public interest groups, which are open to the whole population; and fifth, identity groups, which are generally not open to all (for more details, see Mach 2015). These groups can be differentiated according to their membership (type and number of members), organizational characteristics (financial resources and internal structuring), political activities (inside/outside lobbying), and period of creation. Business associations, trade unions, and occupational groups, emanating from the economic sphere, mainly came into existence during the nineteenth century and at the beginning of the twentieth century. They were the most important categories of the twentieth century, both numerically and politically. Only in the second half of the twentieth century did the last two categories of groups develop and flourish, with some notable exceptions.

The importance of economic interest groups in Switzerland is partly explained by their early creation in the second half of the nineteenth century. They organized relatively early at a national level, unlike the more divided political parties. This was due in particular to the early industrial revolution and the weakness of the central state. In contrast to guilds, which regulated trades and access to professions, modern economic associations are a consequence of the establishment of the principle of freedom of trade and industry in the 1848 federal constitution. The development of peak-level associations occurred during the long period of economic depression between the 1870s and the end of the century.[1] The decisive factors in the creation and consolidation of the first economic associations include the following: the controversial issues of customs tariffs, the Factory Act or the granting of subsidies to certain economic sectors, and more generally the transition from a liberal state (around 1848–1870) to a more interventionist state.

The first peak-level business interest association (BIA) was the Swiss Federation of Commerce and Industry (USCI, since 2000 *economiesuisse*, in this chapter we use the French abbreviations), established in 1870. Until then, trade and industry organizations had organized predominantly at a regional level. In 1878, a permanent secretariat was created, which was later funded through public subsidies (Wehrli 1972). The Swiss Employers' Association (UPS), which represents the same sectors as the USCI, was founded later in 1908 in reaction to numerous strikes and labour conflicts. While the USCI deals with economic and financial policy issues, the UPS deals with industrial relations and social insurance. The organization of the arts and crafts sector is even older. The first National Union of Arts and Crafts was founded in 1849 but was quickly dissolved. It was not until 1879 that the Swiss Union of Crafts and Small and Medium-Sized Enterprises (Swiss Industry and Trade Association, USAM) was founded. The USAM was inspired by the USCI and received federal subsidies to finance its secretariat (Gruner 1956; USAM 1979).

The Swiss Farmers' Union (USP), the main farmers' organization, was founded later in 1897. At that time, more than 40 per cent of the working population was primarily or secondarily employed in agriculture. However, numerous differences within the peasantry delayed the creation of a peak-level association. The prospect of the USP receiving federal subsidies to finance its secretariat also played a critical role in its creation. Shortly after its founding, the USP achieved major successes, both in membership recruitment and political terms (Baumann 1993; Gruner 1956, 55–59). At this time, the so-called 'bourgeois bloc' of the three main Swiss BIAs (the USCI, USAM, and USP) took shape, setting the tone for economic and social policy. The USP played a central role in the development of Swiss politics due to its pivotal position in the cleavage between business and labour (Baumann 1993; Moser 1994; Humair 2004).

Despite early industrialization, the organization of the labour movement was hesitant, late, and decentralized. The existence of religious and linguistic divisions, the decentralization of the industrial fabric, and the relatively low level of urbanization favoured the creation of trade union organizations at a local or regional level; moreover, these factors slowed the formation of a class-consciousness among workers on a national scale. In most industrial sectors, the first real trade union organizations only took shape from the 1870s onwards. In the second half of the nineteenth century, the labour movement was characterized by a large diversity of associations, often stemming from different ideological inspirations (Gruner 1987/89). Founded in 1880, the Swiss Federation of Trade Unions (USS) had extremely difficult early years due to divisions among the numerous workers' associations.[2] For several years, the question of the organization's political neutrality remained a source of major conflict with Catholic workers' organizations. In 1886, the federal government also granted a subsidy to workers' organizations to finance a permanent secretariat responsible for compiling various social statistics. Gradually, the USS established itself as the main trade union organization (see Gruner 1987/89; Fluder et al. 1991; Boillat et al. 2006). Following the inclusion of the principle of class struggle in the programme of the USS, the less radical Christian Social Union was founded in 1907, later becoming the Swiss Federation of Christian Trade Unions. Finally, in 1918 following the general strike, the Swiss Federation of Employees was founded to defend the interests of employees more effectively.

Unlike BIAs and trade unions, occupational groups have retained a logic of professional membership and not of class opposition, as exists between employers and employees. As such, they are the direct descendants of the guilds of the *Ancien Régime* and play a critical role in organizing and defending the interests of the liberal professions. While these organizations are not as well-known as BIAs or trade unions, they have a significant sectoral influence and are often very old. They include the Swiss Medical Association (FMH), which was formally constituted at the federal level in 1901 but already existed long before in the cantons; the Swiss Bar Association, founded in 1898; the Swiss Notary Association, which is still mainly organized at the cantonal level; and the Swiss Society of Engineers and Architects (SIA), founded in 1837. These associations play a central role in the organization and self-regulation of the professions by defining the criteria for access to them (professional examinations) or issuing directives that codify their practice.

Among the organizations that do not directly pertain to the economic sphere, public interest groups defend a cause without seeking primarily to satisfy the material interests of certain social categories. In addition to the 'universal' character of the defended cause, membership of such groups is voluntary and not conditioned on professional status or social attributes. Public interest groups include the various environmental organizations founded in the 1960s and 1970s, such as the Swiss League for Nature Conservation (founded in 1909 and renamed Pro Natura in 1997), the WWF, Greenpeace, and the Association for Transport and the Environment as well as the Swiss Society for Environmental Protection (founded in 1971 and renamed *Equiterre* in 2002). Public interest groups also comprise organizations with charitable or humanitarian aims, such as Caritas, which was founded in 1901 and linked to the Catholic Church; EPER, a Protestant aid organization founded in 1945; the Swiss Labour Assistance (OSEO), which was created in 1936 by trade unions and became *Solidar* in 2012; the Bern Declaration (which became Public Eye in 2016), founded in 1968; as well as human rights organizations such as Amnesty International (1961). Consumer organizations also fall into this category, as each individual represents a potential consumer. Among these public interest groups, there are also organizations with a more explicitly ideological or political character, such as the Association for an Independent and Neutral Switzerland, which was founded in 1986 in the wake of the campaign against Swiss membership in the United Nations; New European Movement Switzerland, which was formed in 1998 from the merger of several pro-European movements; and the Group for a Switzerland without an Army, which was founded in the 1980s.

Finally, identity groups defend the cause of a certain category of the population. Even if their demarcation from public interest groups is not always obvious, they can be distinguished by the fact that they mobilize for a cause that primarily benefits certain sections of the population. Notably, the potential number of members can vary considerably depending on the categories of represented people. Feminist organizations, for example, despite advocating a categorical cause potentially represent half of the population. By contrast, the organization *Pro Infirmis*, which was founded in 1920 and advocates for the disabled, is committed to a more targeted category of people. The defence of the interests of the elderly is characterized by the existence of several associations, which often express divergent political orientations, including *Pro Senectute*, founded in 1917 and subsidized by the Confederation, and *AVIVO*, which was founded in 1943 and is more left-wing. In addition, the Swiss Tenants' Association, Touring Club Suisse (TCS; founded in 1896), and Automobile Club Suisse (ACS; founded in 1898) can potentially count on a large number of members.

3 Institutionalization of Relations with Political Authorities

The end of the nineteenth century was a decisive period for the development of relations between economic associations and the political authorities. In parallel with the creation of the main peak-level associations, the period was characterized by the development of state interventionism in the economic and social spheres. These dynamics led to the establishment of stable and institutionalized relations between the political authorities and organized interests. Furthermore, the early organization of economic circles and the weak administrative resources of the central state gave rise to a particular configuration of relations between the state and economic agents. This configuration, which was to last throughout the twentieth century,[3] combined the self-regulation of economic sectors and the extension of state interventionism.

As early as the 1870s, the demands of trade and industry for enhanced cooperation with the political authorities led, on the one hand, to the subsidization of peak-level associations by the Confederation so that they could take on certain tasks of public interest. On the other hand, the demands also led to the direct involvement of interest groups in the legislative process. At the time, the federal government and its administration were extremely weak as the political elites were reluctant to expand the central bureaucracy (Gruner 1956 and 1964; Zimmermann 1980). Subsidizing the main peak-level associations to perform a number of public tasks (e.g. collecting statistical data and preparing reports on the economic situation) was a much easier solution than enlarging the bureaucracy. Thus, owing to federal subsidies, the leading BIAs were able to set up a permanent secretariat. The consolidation of the BIAs was the result not only of the demands of the business community but also of the strategy of political authorities (see Hauser 1985; Zimmermann 1980).

At the beginning of the twentieth century, the strong conflict between trade unions and employers reached its peak with the general strike of November 1918. However, from the 1930s onwards, the integration of the labour movement into capitalist society took shape both economically (e.g. the labour peace agreements in 1937) and politically (e.g. increasing participation of trade union representatives in parastatal structures and the election of a socialist to the federal government in 1943; see Parri 1987a; Degen 1991). While the 'bourgeois bloc', consisting of the three main BIAs (the USCI, USAM, and USP) and the right-wing parties, had formed at the turn of the century, trade union representatives only participated in the decision-making process on a minority basis from the 1930s and after the Second World War.

In the first half of the twentieth century, periods of war and crisis intensified the connections between organized economic interests and the federal state. In the mid-1930s, under the impetus of the arts and crafts sector, which advocated for a political system based on corporatism, a wide-ranging debate was launched on the revision of the economic articles of the constitution (Gruner 1964; Linder 1983). In 1947, after several years of debate interrupted by the war, the new economic articles of the constitution were adopted, formally recognizing the role of economic associations.[4] The gradual institutionalization of the relations between associations and the state resulted in a particular form of cooperation between public bodies and private associations, which can be described as 'interweaving' (*Verflechtung*) between the public and private spheres. This interpenetration has been defined by some as a '*militia administration*', emphasizing the central role of private experts (Germann et al. 1985), and also as an 'intermediary sector' (Steinmann 1988) or a 'para-state administration' (Hotz 1979).

However, the development of state interventionism did not occur in a social vacuum; in most cases, associations had previously established modes of regulation on a purely private basis for certain public tasks (e.g. social insurance, vocational training, and the regulation of certain professions and markets). The content of legislation and public policies was thus pre-structured by the choices of private actors (see Hotz 1979; Farago 1987; Steinmann 1988). Economic associations have always expressed a strong attachment to the principle of subsidiarity to prevent the federal state from taking too much control. Increased state interventionism has not meant that competences are delegated to public authorities, but rather that there has been only a partial transfer of functions previously assumed by private associations.

Several sectoral case studies have analysed the following forms of public–private cooperation: social policies (Immergut 1992; Leimgruber 2008; Trampusch 2008; Eichenberger 2016); agricultural policy (Sciarini 1994; Wagenmann 2005); vocational education and training (Emmenegger et al. 2020); market regulation and competition policy (Hotz 1979); banking regulation and corporate governance (Mach et al. 2006; Sancey 2015); and foreign labour management (Schmidt 1985; Afonso 2004).

4 Arenas of intervention of interest groups

In close interaction with the authorities, the main interest groups intervene during the various stages of the decision-making process, from setting the political agenda to implementing public policies. These phases also correspond to the three main arenas in which groups intervene to promote their interests. First, there is the administrative arena, where groups attempt to influence the administration in both the drafting of laws and their implementation. Second, interest groups also mobilize towards parliament to promote their interests among elected representatives. Third, the media and the direct-democratic arena represent an opportunity for interest groups to raise awareness of their cause among the public and citizens during referendum vote campaigns. Each of these arenas operates according to specific logics, requiring interest groups to adapt their political strategies. Depending on their characteristics and power resources (e.g. number of members, financial resources, expertise, and public recognition by the authorities), interest groups tend to favour certain arenas over others. For example, large associations with significant resources tend to favour the administrative and parliamentary arenas, whereas public interest groups tend to be more active in the media and direct-democratic arena.

As previously mentioned, from the end of the nineteenth century onwards, the main economic interest groups were directly involved in the preparation of laws in the pre-parliamentary phase. This involvement was through various bodies (expert committees) as well as more or less formalized consultation procedures. Thus, they maintained close and institutionalized relations with the administration. Several authors have emphasized the importance of the pre-parliamentary phase, in which the main interest groups are closely involved, as it has become increasingly crucial in the decision-making process (see Neidhart 1970; Germann et al. 1985). As for the consultation procedure, it serves, among other things, to predict the acceptance of draft legislation among the various stakeholders, who can launch a referendum if they are not satisfied. Traditionally, the broad outlines of a legislative project were already laid down in the pre-parliamentary phase; subsequent amendments by parliament were generally minor in scope. Until the 1990s, parliament was regarded as a mere rubber-stamping body for the compromises worked out in the pre-parliamentary phase; however, this has changed significantly since then (see below).

In the parliamentary arena, interest groups are less directly involved than in the administrative arena. However, not least because of the importance of the *'militia'* principle and the weak professionalization of parliament, many MPs (members of parliament) maintain close ties with interest groups; this is either as paid officials or members of their governing bodies, or as members of company boards (for recent developments, see below as well as David et al. 2009; Erne and Schief 2017; Pilotti 2017).

Although the involvement of interest groups in the media and direct-democratic arena has remained relatively understudied, they play a particularly critical role, especially in referendum campaigns, which require significant financial resources. Furthermore, the use of direct democracy allows a political issue to be put on the agenda, either to challenge a parliamentary decision (optional referendum) or to promote a cause without going through the administrative or parliamentary arena (popular initiative). This demonstrates that direct-democratic tools are mainly used by 'outsider' interest groups that cannot assert their positions in other arenas.

Finally, the associations also have a critical influence in the implementation of public policies. For example, many extra-parliamentary committees, in which representatives of the associations are represented, also have competences in the area of implementation, such as the Competition Committee, the Unemployment Insurance Compensation Fund Committee, and the Agriculture Committee (see Rebmann and Mach 2013).

5 A NEO-CORPORATIST MODEL DOMINATED BY BUSINESS ASSOCIATIONS

Due to their early organization and the weakness of the central state, the main interest associations managed to establish themselves as central players in Swiss political life. This mode of cooperation took shape at the end of the nineteenth century. As Parri (1987b) highlighted, the Confederation was not the architect of this so-called 'neo-corporatist' configuration; rather, the state was penetrated by socio-economic actors. In the academic literature, the Swiss political system has thus traditionally been described as neo-corporatist because of the central role of large economic associations, BIAs, and trade unions in the political process. However, some crucial specificities should be underlined, particularly the dominant position of BIAs and the impact of instruments of direct democracy.

In the mid-1970s, some authors noted the increasing involvement of the main interest associations—particularly trade unions and BIAs—in economic and social policy-making as well as the declining power of parliament (among the first were Schmitter and Lehmbruch 1979). In response, they developed the concept of neo-corporatism to characterize the institutionalized interactions between the state and the organized interests of society. This approach assumes the existence of a centralized structure of large economic associations, each with a monopoly of representation as well as institutionalized relations with the state. Such structures of consultation between private and public actors have developed concomitantly with the extension of state intervention in the economic and social spheres since the 1930s. The neo-corporatist model differs from the pluralist model, which refers to the existence of multiple interest groups competing to influence state decisions. While most authors have emphasized the neo-corporatist character of the Swiss political system, some debate has occurred regarding the qualification of Switzerland.[5] Among these works, Katzenstein's socio-historical analysis seems to be the most accurate.

In his two main books on 'democratic corporatism' in small European states, Katzenstein (1984 and 1985) focused on these countries' processes of adaptation to international economic change. They developed economic strategies that differed from the liberal or statist solutions of large, industrialized states (e.g. few protectionist measures and no massive state interventions to support ailing sectors). The key to their economic success has been their ability to combine economic flexibility with political stability. The similarities between these countries lie both in the flexibility of their adjustment policy to external economic pressure and in the structure of interest representation. According to Katzenstein, small European countries have implemented policies that combine international economic liberalism with domestic compensations, such as generous social, wage, and employment policies. Their dependence on foreign markets favoured the development of neo-corporatist arrangements on the eve or in the aftermath of the Second World War. According to Katzenstein, neo-corporatism is based on the following three characteristics: first, the prevalence of an ideology of social partnership; second, a relatively centralized system of interest representation; and third, voluntary, informal, and continuous consultation between political and economic actors. However, Katzenstein distinguished between a liberal version (Switzerland, the Netherlands, and Belgium) and a social version (Austria, Denmark, and Norway).[6] These two variants differ in terms of the strength and characteristics of BIAs and trade union organizations. The Swiss case represents the more liberal variant, with weak trade unions and a well-organized and largely foreign market-oriented BIAs.

In his analyses of the power structure in the 1970s, Kriesi (1980 and 1982) considered that the Swiss political system contains certain structures equivalent to neo-corporatist arrangements. Without focusing specifically on interest groups, but considering all the important actors involved in federal decision-making processes, Kriesi highlighted the concentration of power in an informal core of individual and collective actors, particularly large economic associations.

While the Swiss political system is indeed characterized by certain neo-corporatist features, several noteworthy elements distinguish it from the neo-corporatist system. The most notable are the sectoral character of the negotiated arrangements, decentralization of industrial relations, dominance of BIAs, and existence of instruments of direct democracy.

In contrast to Austria and Sweden, Switzerland never had a tripartite body responsible for outlining macroeconomic management based on the coordination of fiscal, monetary, and income policies. Cooperation between the state and the main interest groups is primarily sectoral (e.g. health, agriculture, banking, foreign labour, and unemployment insurance). In this respect, it would be more relevant to conceptualize the relationship between interest associations and the state in terms of policy networks, which would more clearly emphasize the sectoral dimension of this relationship.

Another indicator frequently used to measure the degree of corporatism of a political system is income policy, and more precisely the degree of centralization of collective bargaining between trade unions and BIAs. In Switzerland, industrial relations are highly decentralized, as it is not uncommon for negotiations to occur at the company level. Collective labour agreements, negotiated by industry-level trade unions and employer organizations, are the main pillar of the Swiss social partnership; however, they covered only half of private sector employees in the 1990s. Among European countries, only the United Kingdom had a lower rate of private sector coverage by collective agreements (see Mach and Oesch 2003; Oesch 2007).

Both Katzenstein (1984 and 1985) and Kriesi (1980) have emphasized the dominant position of BIAs in relation to trade unions. The latter, together with the political left, appear to be minor partners in bargaining structures, which are dominated by the better-coordinated and well-resourced BIAs. To understand this asymmetry, Culpepper's (2011) general analysis in his book *Quiet Politics and Business Power* is particularly convincing. According to him, business power is greater when it can be exercised in informal governance spaces and when the issues under discussion are not highly salient in the eyes of citizens; conversely, business power is weaker when political debates occur in formal arenas (parliament or even direct democracy) and when the issues are of broad public concern. The Swiss business community developed a deliberate strategy of depoliticizing certain issues, so that they are debated in confidential administrative arenas away from the public and regulated by loose self-regulatory standards. This allowed them, despite the gradual integration of trade unions in certain decision-making bodies from the 1930s onwards, to maintain control over many socio-economic issues; examples include the regulation of the banking sector, corporate governance, or taxation, which remained essentially debated in relatively confidential arenas with a technical character (for more details, see Mach et al. 2021).

It can be hypothesized that the BIAs' high degree of coordination and their strong political commitment are largely due to the existence of direct-democratic instruments, which allow trade unions, but also public interest groups, to bypass neo-corporatist structures and parliament and appeal directly to the people. Indeed, the consolidation of the coordination of business organizations can be interpreted as a reaction to the popular initiatives of the left and trade unions from the 1920s onwards. For all of these initiatives, the business circles deployed large-scale campaigns and successfully opposed them (for more details, see Billeter 1983, ch. 10; Guex 1994). For example, following the business victory against the crisis initiative of the trade unions and a large section of the farming community in 1935, employer circles consolidated their propaganda instrument by founding the Society for the Development of the Swiss Economy (SDES) in 1942 (see Werner 2000).

In sum, the originality of the position of interest groups in Swiss political life can be traced back to the two main possibilities of access to political processes offered by the institutional framework of the Swiss political system: first, the neo-corporatist character of the relationship between the federal state and the main interest groups; and second, the existence of direct-democratic instruments (i.e. referendums and popular initiatives), which offer interest groups possibilities to directly promote their cause. In this context, the Swiss parliament, despite its formal competences, has long remained a secondary actor in the decision-making process. The direct-democratic and administrative arenas, the latter being central to both law-making and implementation, were for a long time at the centre of the decision-making process (see 'Decision-Making Process' in this volume). Well-established and -integrated interest groups tend to favour the administrative arena, which is more confidential and historically less formalized, for making their views prevail. They may occasionally resort to instruments of direct democracy, but they remain a secondary option, as the compromises reached in the pre-parliamentary phase are generally not threatened in parliament. Thus, the selective and elitist character of neo-corporatist structures is counterbalanced by the existence of direct-democratic instruments, which offer opportunities for more marginal actors to have direct recourse to the people.

6 Recent changes: towards pluralization

Since the beginning of the 1990s, the economic, institutional, and political contexts in which interest groups evolve have undergone profound changes. First, increasing international pressure has called into question the selective protectionism that mainly benefited the agricultural sector and certain branches of industry producing for the domestic market (Sciarini 1994; Mach 2006). Second, the revalorization and professionalization of the Federal Assembly has reinforced its role in the legislative process (Sciarini 2014 and see 'Decision-Making Process' in this volume). Finally, the growing importance of post-materialist values in Swiss society has contributed to the strengthening and consolidation of new public interest groups (Eichenberger 2020). Together, these contextual changes have profoundly affected the landscape of interest groups and their strategies. Therefore, this section first reviews how these contextual changes have transformed interest groups (i.e. reorganizations and the emergence of new groups). Then, it reviews how this new context has refined interest groups' political strategies.

6.1 Reconfiguration of the interest group landscape

A first consequence of these contextual changes relates to the weakening of the main peak-level associations. Growing external pressures have accentuated internal divisions and membership heterogeneity. Numerous economic reforms, partly induced by changes in the international environment, have caused tensions between and within BIAs. Examples of such reforms are as follows: agricultural policy reform (Sciarini 1994), the revision of the Cartel Act and measures for liberalizing the internal market (Mach 2006), reform of foreign labour policy (Afonso 2004), liberalization of the electricity market (Afonso et al. 2010), and the questioning of banking secrecy (Eggenberger and

Emmenegger 2015). These reforms are also indicative of the weakening of interest groups that represent sectors producing for the domestic market and who traditionally benefit from protectionist measures, namely the USP, certain economic sectors represented by the USAM, and certain member federations of the USCI.[7] In the 1990s, the largest Swiss multinationals became known for criticizing traditional BIAs and expressing liberal demands, questioning certain policies head-on that benefited the sectors producing for the domestic market. These demands led to the creation of the liberal think-tank *Avenir Suisse* in 1999, which, even though its function differed from that of traditional BIAs, represents a certain competition for them (Eichenberger and Mach 2011).

Over the last twenty years, the major BIAs have undergone large-scale reorganizations. The USCI and the SDES merged into *economiesuisse* in 2000 (Kriesi 2006; Eichenberger and Mach 2011). Similarly, faced with a steady decline in membership, the trade union movement has undergone numerous mergers and reorganizations. The most critical was that in 2004 of the two largest USS federations, namely the SIB (construction industry) and the FTMH (machinery industry, metalworking, and watchmaking) into UNIA. Furthermore, Christian trade unions and associations of the Swiss Federation of Employees merged into *Travail.Suisse* in 2002 (Oesch 2011; Widmer 2007).

In the more competitive context of the 1990s, economic associations redefined their role. On the one hand, the social- and market-regulation activities of interest groups became less important because of economic liberalization measures and the affirmation of the regulatory state (Mach et al. 2006; Oesch 2007).[8] On the other hand, the services provided by associations to their members (legal advice, social insurance administration, and technical certifications) were strengthened to better justify their existence to their constituencies (Wagenmann 2005; Kriesi 2006).

Finally, a growing number of public interest groups has challenged the representativeness of economic associations. Unlike BIAs, trade unions, and occupational groups, public interest groups defend causes that go beyond the restricted circle of their members. These include environmental, human rights, consumer, and feminist groups, which have often emerged from the new social movements of the 1970s. Between 1970 and 2010, the number of public interest groups almost doubled while the number of economic associations remained stable (Mach 2015; Eichenberger 2020).

6.2 Redefinition of political strategies

This changing and more uncertain socio-political context has led to a redirection of lobbying strategies towards parliament, a pluralization of groups participating in decision-making processes, and an increased use of direct democracy. For similar dynamics in other small European countries, such as Denmark and Norway, see the study of Rommetvedt et al. (2013).

Furthermore, heightened tensions within and between the main economic associations have made negotiating compromises in the pre-parliamentary phase more difficult. Political parties, defending less sectoral interests, now play a more critical role in developing compromises (Häusermann et al. 2004).[9] This trend has been accentuated by increased competition from public interest groups, increased media coverage, the formalization of extra-parliamentary committees, and the revaluation of parliament. These developments have made the parliamentary phase increasingly crucial to the detriment of the pre-parliamentary phase[10] and contributed to redirecting economic groups' influence strategies towards parliament or public opinion and direct democracy (Mach et al. 2021).

Reflecting this redirection of lobbying strategies towards parliament is the significant growth of MPs' mandates within interest groups (Gava et al. 2017; Eichenberger 2020). Therefore, the professionalization of the parliamentary mandate has not led to an 'emancipation' of MPs from interest groups. On the contrary, as the parliamentary mandate has become more demanding, both in expertise and time (Pilotti 2017; Sciarini et al. 2017), MPs have had to increasingly rely on the expertise provided by interest groups. They have also increasingly granted accreditations to parliament to interest groups and professional lobbying agencies.

In redirecting their strategies, interest groups focus particularly on legislative committees, which have become the centre of the decision-making process (Eichenberger and Mach 2017; Sciarini 2014). Interest groups 'recruit' MPs to their governing bodies based on their membership in legislative committees. The realignment of influence strategies towards parliament also affects electoral campaigns: most major interest groups publish 'ratings', which assess whether MPs' parliamentary votes are in line with the group's positions.

Moreover, a diversification of the interest groups participating in decision-making processes can also be observed. The share of extra-parliamentary committee seats held by public interest groups has increased since the 1980s. Similarly, the share of MPs' interest ties held by public interest groups has also increased (Eichenberger 2020). More sectoral studies also point to the increased importance of public interest groups (e.g. in the fields of energy policy and the environment; see Ingold 2008).

However, this does not mean that BIAs and public interest groups are now on an equal footing in terms of their participation in public policy-making. If one focuses on the groups with the largest number of seats in extra-parliamentary committees in 2010, BIAs still dominated (Eichenberger 2020). On the other hand, the revaluation of parliament tends to strengthen the position of public interest groups in the decision-making process (Weiler et al. 2019). Nevertheless, Varone et al. (2021) demonstrated that BIAs are still more likely to see the outcome of a decision-making process correspond to their interests.

Finally, in a less consensual context, interest groups focus more heavily on public opinion in their political strategies, investing more heavily in their communication activities. This is especially true for BIAs, which seek a stronger media presence to ensure their legitimacy among their members. Public interest groups, which have greater difficulty in making themselves heard by the administration, have always relied on strategies of indirect influence, appealed to public opinion, or resorted to the instruments of direct democracy. In addition, over the past few decades, public interest groups and trade unions have increased their reliance on popular initiatives (Mach 2015). Although these are rarely successful, probably due to the far greater means of the opponents (see Jaquet et al. 2022 on campaign expenses), they keep certain issues on the agenda and pressure the political authorities. Compared with a neo-corporatist country such as Denmark, which has no direct-democratic instruments, the access of public interest groups to the administrative and parliamentary arena is greater in Switzerland (Christiansen et al. 2018; Weiler and Brändli 2015).

In conclusion, the stronger focus on parliament in the lobbying strategies of interest groups in general, along with the integration of public interest groups into the decision-making process, are not necessarily incompatible with the neo-corporatist model of public policy-making. Armingeon (2011) already raised the possibility of a shift of neo-corporatist negotiations to legislative committees. However, the increased use of direct-democratic instruments by all types of interest groups is more difficult to reconcile with the neo-corporatist notion of the largest associations engaging in compromise negotiations. It also indicates a shift towards a more pluralistic model, encompassing a larger number of groups while maintaining a certain hierarchy among them.

Notes

1. On the creation of peak-level associations, see Gruner (1956, 1964, 1987/88); USAM (1979), Zimmermann (1980); Hauser (1985); Baumann (1993); Moser (1994); Eichenberger and Mach (2011); and Humair et al. (2012); on BIAs, their leaders, and their political strategies, see Mach et al. (2016, chs 6–8).
2. At its foundation, the USS had only 133 individual members and twelve sections (Gruner 1956).
3. On the institutionalization of these relationships, see Gruner (1964); Neidhart (1970, 139ff); Zimmermann (1980); Steinmann (1988); and Humair (2004).
4. Art. 32 para. 3: 'The economic groups concerned shall be consulted during the drafting of the implementing laws and may be called upon to cooperate in the application of the implementing regulations.' This article has been replaced by art. 147 of the new constitution of 2000.
5. See Kriesi (1980, 1982), Katzenstein (1984, 1985), Parri (1987a, 1987b), Piotet (1987), and Sciarini (1994). Mancur Olson's (1983) analysis of the economic consequences of the political mobilization of interest groups has also inspired some studies on the Swiss case: see Lehner (1991) as well as Mach (2015, ch. 5).
6. Sweden is a special case given the presence of strong trade unions and employer organizations.
7. Afonso et al. (2010) demonstrated that the divide between industries producing for the domestic market and those focused on export markets, accentuated by the logics of Europeanization and internationalization, can lead internationalized sectors to make certain concessions to trade unions, as was the case with flanking measures accompanying the extension of the free movement of persons in the framework of bilateral agreements negotiated with the European Union (EU).

8. The adoption of flanking measures to the free movement of persons with the EU is a counter-example to this trend, which has led to a sharp increase in the coverage rate of collective labour agreements in the private sector.
9. However, the progress of the Swiss People's Party (SVP) in parliament makes it more difficult to reach compromises in this arena (Afonso and Papadopoulos 2015).
10. This development may seem paradoxical in the context of increased international pressure, leading, according to some, to a 'de-parliamentarization' of national political systems. However, in the Swiss case, the historical weakness of parliament means that its role has been strengthened in recent times.

References

Afonso, Alexandre. 2004. *Internationalisation, économie et politique migratoire*. Lausanne: IEPI Travaux de science politique.

Afonso, Alexandre, Marie-Christine Fontana, and Yannis Papadopoulos. 2010. 'Does Europeanisation Weaken the Left? Changing Coalitions and Veto Power in Swiss Decision-making Processes'. *Policy & Politics* 38 (4): pp. 565–582.

Afonso, Alexandre, and Yannis Papadopoulos. 2015. 'How the Populist Radical Right Transformed Swiss Welfare Politics: From Compromises to Polarization'. *Swiss Political Science Review* 21 (4): pp. 617–635.

Armingeon, Klaus. 2011. 'A Prematurely Announced Death? Swiss Corporatism in Comparative Perspective'. In *Switzerland in Europe: Continuity and Change in the Swiss Political Economy*, edited by Christine Trampusch, and André Mach, pp. 165–185. London: Routledge.

Baumann, Werner. 1993. *Bauernstand und Bürgerblock*. Zurich: Orell Füssli.

Billeter, Geneviève. 1983. *Le pouvoir patronal: les patrons des grandes entreprises suisses des métaux et des machines (1919-1939)*. Geneva: Droz.

Boillat, Valérie, Bernard Degen, Elisabeth Joris, Stefan Keller, Albert Tanner, and Rolf Zimmermann. 2006. *La valeur du travail. Histoire et histoires des syndicats suisses*. Lausanne: Antipodes.

Christiansen, Peter, André Mach, and Frédéric Varone. 2018. 'How Corporatist Institutions Shape the Access of Citizen Groups to Policy-Makers: Evidence from Denmark and Switzerland'. *Journal of European Public Policy* 25 (4): pp. 526–545.

Culpepper, Pepper. 2011. *Quiet Politics and Business Power: Corporate Control in Europe and Japan*. Cambridge: Cambridge University Press.

David, Thomas, Stéphanie Ginalski, André Mach, and Frédéric Rebmann. 2009. 'Networks of Coordination. Swiss Business Associations as an Intermediary between Business, Politics and Administration during the 20th Century'. *Business and Politics* 11 (4): pp. 1–38.

Degen, Bernhard. 1991. *Abschied vom Klassenkampf*. Basel: Helbing & Lichtenhahn.

Eggenberger, Katrin, and Patrick Emmenegger. 2015. 'Economic Vulnerability and Political Responses to International Pressure: Liechtenstein, Switzerland and the Struggle for Banking Secrecy'. *Swiss Political Science Review* 21 (4): pp. 491–507.

Eichenberger, Pierre. 2016. *Mainmise sur l'Etat social. Mobilisation patronale et caisses de compensation en Suisse (1908-1960)*. Neuchâtel: Alphil.

Eichenberger, Steven. 2020. 'The Rise of Citizen Groups within the Administration and Parliament in Switzerland'. *Swiss Political Science Review* 26 (2): pp. 206–227.

Eichenberger, Pierre, and André Mach. 2011. 'Organized Capital and Coordinated Market Economy: Swiss Business Associations between Socio-Economic Regulation and Political Influence'. In *Switzerland in Europe, Continuity and Change in the Swiss Political Economy*, edited by Christine Trampusch, and André Mach, pp. 63–81. London: Routledge.

Eichenberger, Steven, and André Mach. 2017. 'Formal Ties between Interest Groups and Members of Parliament: Gaining Allies in Legislative Committees'. *Interest Groups & Advocacy* 6 (1): pp. 1–21.

Emmenegger, Patrick, Lukas Graf, and Alexandra Strebel. 2020. 'Social versus Liberal Collective Skill Formation Systems? A Comparative-Historical Analysis of the Role of Trade Unions in German and Swiss VET'. *European Journal of Industrial Relations* 26 (3): pp. 263–278.

Erne, Roland, and Sebastian Schief. 2017. 'Strong Ties between Independent Organizations'. In *Left-of-Centre Parties and Trade Unions in the Twenty-First Century*, edited by Elin Allern, and Time Bale, pp. 226–245. Oxford: Oxford University Press.

Farago, Peter. 1987. *Verbände als Träger öffentlicher Politik*. Grüsch: Rüegger.

Fluder, Robert, Heinz Ruf, Walter Schöni, and Martin Wicki. 1991. *Gewerkschaften und Angestelltenverbände in der schweizerischen Privatwirtschaft*. Zurich: Seismo.

Gava, Roy, Frédéric Varone, André Mach, Steven Eichenberger, Julien Christe, and Corinne Chao-Blanco. 2017. 'Interests Groups in Parliament: Exploring MPs' Interest Affiliations (2000–2011)'. *Swiss Political Science Review* 23 (1): pp. 77–94.

Germann, Raimund, Andreas Frutiger, Monica von Sury, Alain-Valéry Poitry, and Jean-Daniel Müller. 1985. *Experts et commissions de la Confédération*. Lausanne: Presses polytechniques romandes.

Gruner, Erich. 1956. *Die Wirtschaftsverbände in der Demokratie*. Erlenbach: Rentsch Verlag.

Gruner, Erich. 1964. '100 Jahre Wirtschaftspolitik. Etappen des Interventionismus in der Schweiz'. *Revue suisse d'économie politique et de statistique* 100 (I/II): pp. 35–70.

Gruner, Erich. 1987/89. *Arbeiterschaft und Wirtschaft in der Schweiz 1880–1914*. Zurich: Chronos.

Guex, Sébastien. 1994. 'L'initiative socialiste pour une imposition extraordinaire sur la fortune en Suisse (1920-1922)'. *Regards sociologiques* 8: pp. 101–116.

Hauser, Benedikt. 1985. *Wirtschaftsverbände im frühen schweizerischen Bundesstaat (1848-74)*. Basel: Helbing & Lichtenhahn.

Häusermann, Silja, André Mach, and Yannis Papadopoulos. 2004. 'From Corporatism to Partisan Politics: Social Policy Making under Strain in Switzerland'. *Revue suisse de science politique* 10 (2): pp. 33–59.

Hotz, Beat. 1979. *Politik zwischen Staat und Wirtschaft*. Diessenhofen: Rüegger.

Humair, Cédric. 2004. *Développement économique et Etat central (1815-1914): un siècle de politique douanière suisse au service des élites*. Bern: Lang.

Humair, Cédric, Sébastien Guex, André Mach, and Pierre Eichenberger. 2012. 'Les organisations patronales suisses entre coordination économique et influence politique: bilan historiographique et pistes de recherche'. *Vingtième Siècle, Revue d'Histoire* 115 (3): pp. 115–127.

Immergut, Ellen. 1992. *Health Politics. Interests and Institutions in Western Europe*. Cambridge: Cambridge University Press.

Ingold, Karin. 2008. *Les mécanismes de décision: Le cas de la politique climatique suisse*. Zurich: Rüegger Verlag.

Jaquet, Julien, Pascal Sciarini, and Roy Gava. 2022. 'Can't Buy Me Votes? Campaign Spending and the Outcome of Direct Democratic Votes'. *West European Politics* 45 (2): pp. 335–359.

Katzenstein, Peter. 1984. *Corporatism and Change. Austria, Switzerland and the Politics of Change*. Ithaca: Cornell University Press.

Katzenstein, Peter. 1985. *Small States in World Markets*. Ithaca: Cornell University Press.
Kriesi, Hanspeter. 1980. *Entscheidungsstrukturen und Entscheidungsprozesse in der Schweizer Politik*. Francfort: Campus.
Kriesi, Hanspeter. 1982. 'The Structure of the Swiss Political System'. In *Patterns of Corporatist Policy Making*, edited by Gerhard Lehmbruch, and Philippe Schmitter, pp. 133–162. London: Sage.
Kriesi, Hanspeter. 2006. 'Institutional Filters and Path Dependency. The Impact of Europeanization on Swiss Business Associations'. In *Governing Interests. Business Associations Facing Internationalization*, edited by Wolfgang Streeck, Jürgen Grote, Volker Schneider, and Jelle Visser, pp. 49–67. London: Routledge.
Lehner, Franz. 1991. 'The Institutional Control of Organized Interest Intermediation'. In *Political Choice, Institutions, Rules and the Limits of Rationality*, edited by Roland Czada, and Adrienne Heritier, pp. 233–256. Francfort: Campus.
Leimgruber, Matthieu. 2008. *Solidarity Without the State? Business and the Shaping of the Swiss Welfare State, 1890-2000*. Cambridge: Cambridge University Press.
Linder, Wolf. 1983. 'Entwicklungen, Strukturen und Funktionen des Wirtschafts- und Sozialstaates in der Schweiz'. In *Handbuch Politisches System der Schweiz*, edited by Alois Riklin, pp. 255–382. Bern: Haupt.
Mach, André. 2006. *La Suisse entre internationalisation et changements politiques internes. Législation sur les cartels et relations industrielles dans les années 1990*. Zurich: Rüegger.
Mach, André. 2015. *Groupes d'intérêt et pouvoir politique*. Lausanne: PPUR.
Mach, André, and Daniel Oesch. 2003. 'Collective Bargaining between Decentralization and Stability: A Sectoral Model Explaining the Swiss Experience during the 1990s'. *Industrielle Beziehungen* 10 (1): pp. 160–182.
Mach, André, David Thomas, Stéphanie Ginalski, and Felix Bühlmann. 2016. *Les élites économiques suisses au 20e siècle*. Neuchâtel: Alphil.
Mach, André, David Thomas, Stéphanie Ginalski, and Felix Bühlmann. 2021. 'From Quiet Politics to Noisy Politics: Transformations of Swiss Business Elites' Power'. *Politics and Society* 49 (1): pp. 17–41.
Mach, André, David Thomas, Gerhard Schnyder, and Martin Lüpold. 2006. 'Transformations de l'autorégulation et nouvelles régulations publiques en matière de gouvernement d'entreprise en Suisse (1985-2002)'. *Revue suisse de science politique* 12 (1): pp. 1–32.
Meynaud, Jean. 1963. *Les organisations professionnelles en Suisse*. Lausanne: Payot.
Moser, Peter. 1994. *Der Stand der Bauern*. Frauenfeld: Huber.
Neidhart, Leonhard. 1970. *Plebiszit und pluralitäre Demokratie*. Bern: Frank.
Oesch, Daniel. 2007. 'Weniger Koordination, mehr Markt? Kollektive Arbeitsbeziehungen und Neokorporatismus in der Schweiz seit 1990'. *Revue suisse de science politique* 13 (3): pp. 337–368.
Oesch, Daniel. 2011. 'Swiss Trade Unions and Industrial Relations after 1990. A History of Decline and Renewal'. In *Switzerland in Europe, Continuity and Change in the Swiss Political Economy*, edited by Christine Trampusch, and André Mach, pp. 82–102. London: Routledge.
Olson, Mancur. 1983. *Grandeur et décadence des nations. Croissance économique, stagflation et rigidités sociales*. Paris: Bonnel Editions.
Parri, Leonardo. 1987a. 'Staat und Gewerkschaften in der Schweiz: 1873-1981'. *Politische Vierteljahresschrift* 28 (1): pp. 35–58.
Parri, Leonardo. 1987b. 'Neo-corporatist Arrangements, "Konkordanz" and Direct Democracy: the Swiss Experience'. In *Political Stability and Neo-Corporatism*, edited by Ilja Scholten, pp. 70–94. London: Sage.

Pilotti, Andrea. 2017. *Entre démocratisation et professionnalisation: le Parlement suisse et ses membres de 1910 à 2016*. Zurich: Seismo.

Piotet, Georges. 1987. *Restructuration industrielle et corporatisme. Le cas de l'horlogerie suisse 1974-1987*. Lausanne: Imprivite SA.

Rebmann, Frédéric, and André Mach. 2013. 'Les commissions extra-parlementaires'. In *Manuel d'administration publique suisse*, edited by Andreas Ladner, Jean-Loup Chappelet, Yves Emery, Peter Knoepfel, Luzius Mader, Nils Soguel, and Frédéric Varone, pp. 161–176. Lausanne: Presse polytechniques et universitaires romandes.

Rommetvedt, Hilmar, Gunnar Thesen, Peter Christiansen, and Asbjorn Norgaard. 2013. 'Coping with Corporatism in Decline and the Revival of Parliament: Interest Group Lobbyism in Denmark and Norway, 1980–2005'. *Comparative Political Studies* 46 (4): pp. 457–485.

Sancey, Yves. 2015. *Quand les banquiers font la loi*. Lausanne: Antipodes.

Schmidt, Manfred. 1985. *Der Schweizerische Weg zur Vollbeschäftigung*. Frankfurt: Campus Verlag.

Schmitter, Philippe, and Gerhard Lehmbruch. 1979. *Trends Towards Corporatist Intermediation*. London: Sage Publications.

Sciarini, Pascal. 1994. *Le système politique suisse face à la Communauté européenne et au GATT: le cas-test de la politique agricole*. Geneva: Georg.

Sciarini, Pascal. 2014. 'Eppure Si Muove: The Changing Nature of the Swiss Consensus Democracy'. *Journal of European Public Policy* 21 (1): pp. 116–132.

Sciarini, Pascal, Frédéric Varone, Giovanni Ferro-Luzzi, Fabio Cappelletti, Vahan Garibian, and Ismail Muller. 2017. *Étude sur le revenu et les charges des parlementaires fédéraux*. Université de Genève: Services du Parlement.

Steinmann, Walter. 1988. *Zwischen Markt und Staat*. Konstanz: Wisslit.

Trampusch, Christine. 2008. 'Von einem liberalen zu einem post-liberalen Wohlfahrtsstaat: Der Wandel der gewerkschaftlichen Sozialpolitik in der Schweiz'. *Revue suisse de science politique*: 14 (1): pp. 49–84.

USAM. 1979. *Les arts et métiers en Suisse 1879-1979*. Bern: USAM.

Varone, Frédéric, Steven Eichenberger, Roy Gava, Charlotte Jourdain, and André Mach. 2021. 'Business Groups and Advocacy Success: Insights from a Multi-Venue Approach'. *Acta Politica* 56: pp. 477–499.

Wagenmann, Claudius. 2005. 'Private Interest Government are Dead. Long Live Private Interest Governments? Lessons from Swiss Cows'. *Revue suisse de science politique* 11 (3): pp. 1–25.

Wehrli, Bernhard. 1972. *Le Vorort, mythe ou réalité. Histoire de l'Union suisse du commerce et de l'industrie*. Neuchâtel: La Baconnière.

Weiler, Florian, and Matthias Brändli. 2015. 'Inside versus Outside Lobbying: How the Institutional Framework Shapes the Lobbying Behaviour of Interest Groups'. *European Journal of Political Research* 54 (4): pp. 745–766.

Weiler, Florian, Steven Eichenberger, André Mach, and Frédéric Varone. 2019. 'More Equal than Others: Assessing Economic and Citizen Groups' Access across Policymaking Venues'. *Governance* 32 (2): pp. 277–293.

Werner Christian. 2000. *Für Wirtschaft und Vaterland*. Zürich: Chronos.

Widmer, Frédéric. 2007. 'Stratégies syndicales et renouvellement des élites: le syndicat FTMH face à la crise des années 1990'. *Revue suisse de science politique* 13 (3): pp. 395–431.

Zimmermann, Beat. 1980. *Verbands- und Wirtschaftspolitik am Übergang zum Staatsinterventionismus*. Bern/Franckfurt: Lang.

Chapter 19

Social Movements

Marco Giugni

1 Introduction

In the early 1990s, social movement research in Switzerland was characterized as a 'marginal field of research in an underdeveloped social science community' (Kriesi 1991). The first systematic empirical studies of social movements and protest politics in Switzerland were conducted in the late 1970s and early 1980s by a team of researchers at the University of Zurich (Kriesi et al. 1981); such work at the time was still an isolated case. However, research in the field has since progressed considerably (Balsiger 2016), so that we can hardly speak of a marginal field today.

There are several descriptions of social movements, but most authors agree on a definition that identifies informal networks of actors with a collective identity that mobilize around conflicting issues and through different forms of protest (della Porta and Diani 2020). As such, social movements form a specific political arena in which citizens can make their voices heard and try to influence those holding power. Unlike political parties and interest groups, social movements follow a logic of participation rather than representation.

The next section characterizes the context in which movements in Switzerland operate compared to other countries: It describes the structure of political opportunities for the mobilization of social movements in Switzerland. What follows discusses the mobilization of different movements and movement families in Switzerland: traditional movements, new social movements, radical-right movements, global justice movements, and anti-austerity movements. The conclusion summarizes the key aspects discussed in the chapter and aims to dismantle certain stereotypes that claim the Swiss are not very inclined to take to the streets.

2 The context for social movement mobilization in Switzerland

Social movements in Switzerland confront a context of marked institutional openness due to federalism, a strong fragmentation of power, a weak state, and the presence of direct democracy (Kriesi 1995). Indeed, federalism and direct democracy—two core aspects of Switzerland's institutions—play an important role in producing the openness that characterizes the Swiss institutional opportunity structure, which in turn impacts the levels and forms of movement mobilization. In particular, the federal structure of the country, with its multiplication of access points, tends to facilitate the mobilization of social movements (Giugni 1996).

However, perhaps the most important institutional factor in Switzerland is direct democracy, an instrument widely used by social movements in the country (Giugni 2022; Kriesi et al. 1995).[1] The presence of direct-democratic instruments provides an additional channel for the mobilization of social movements in Switzerland; this has led to an increase in their mobilization level, but at the same time has had a moderating effect on their action repertoire (Kriesi 1998). Epple-Gass (1988) warned precisely against the dangers of this moderating effect when he noted the moderating and integrative function of the popular initiative, which in his view transformed the peace movement into an 'initiative movement'. He considered this latent function of the initiative as one of the great limits of protest in Switzerland (Epple-Gass 1991). However, this author arguably neglects the positive and indirect effects of this instrument on the mobilization of social movements, especially the possibility of placing an issue on the political and public agenda (Giugni 1991). Moreover, direct democracy—especially the optional referendum—can also be an instrument used by social movements to block government decisions and public policies (Giugni and Passy 1993).

The institutional openness produced by direct democracy is not homogeneous but varies across both cantons and movements. On the one hand, the entry price to direct democracy—the signatures required and deadlines for signature collection—is lower in German-speaking Switzerland than Latin Switzerland, generally leading to a more radical action repertoire in the latter due to the more frequent use of direct-democratic instruments, especially the popular initiative (Kriesi and Wisler 1996). On the other hand, access to direct-democratic procedures depends on the resources available to the movement, especially for conducting voting campaigns but also concerning strategic choices about the forms of action. In other words, not all movements have the means or the will to use direct democracy. The lack of success of the feminist movement, for example, can be attributed in part to its failure to seize the opportunities offered by the Swiss political system (Banaszak 1991, 1996).

In parallel to the formal openness of the Swiss opportunity structure, political authorities generally opt for an inclusive strategy of negotiation, and the political system leans towards the consensual integration of conflicts. Thus, the political opportunity structure in Switzerland is marked by its openness to contentious groups, offering many both formal and informal opportunities; indeed, Switzerland is characterized by its combination of an open institutional structure with a prevailing inclusive strategy (Kriesi 1998). The result of this double openness is often a high level of mobilization and generally moderate forms of action, at least compared to other countries with a more closed opportunity structure, such as France (Kriesi et al. 1992, 1995).

Alliances and power configurations depend on the movements or movement families involved. For example, Kriesi et al. (1995) emphasize the importance of the configuration of power within the left on the mobilization of new social movements. The possibility of forming political alliances with parties on the left is particularly important for these movements, since it increases the chance their demands will be taken seriously and their goals achieved. More specifically, Kriesi et al. (1995) show that the presence of the socialists in government hinders the mobilization of new social movements, while a left opposition can facilitate mobilization. Obviously, when investigating other movement families, we must consider other types of alliance. For example, far-right parties should be the natural allies of radical-right movements. In this case, it seems that the mere presence of an electorally strong far-right party tends to demobilize the extra-parliamentary radical right, since these two strategic alternatives neutralize each other (Giugni et al. 2005; Koopmans 1996).[2]

3 Social movements and movement families in Switzerland

While, to our knowledge, no clear-cut and definitive typology exists despite various attempts, social movements are often grouped into broader movement families due to sharing salient features, such as the social cleavages that condition their mobilization, their core constituency, and the issues they address. The basic distinction is drawn between traditional movements that rest on traditional cleavages and new social movements based on new 'post-materialist' cleavages and whose core constituency is composed of the so-called 'social-cultural specialists' (Kriesi 1989). These are the first two movement families discussed below. In addition, three other movements are treated separately: radical-right movements may be considered part of the traditional movement families, but they often rest on the new cleavage between the 'winners' and 'losers' of globalization; global justice movements also rest, at least in part, on this cleavage and moreover share some features with both traditional and new social movements; anti-austerity movements, the most recent, also combine some features of more traditional movements—most notably, the focus on economic issues typical of labour movements—with issues originally addressed by the new social movements, such as democratic rights, citizen participation, participatory democracy, and social inequalities.

3.1 Traditional movements

Traditional movements are the expression of the traditional cleavage structures as highlighted by Rokkan (1970). The labour movement is certainly the most important of such movements, if only for its political significance. In Switzerland, however, labour mobilization has generally remained very weak, except under special circumstances. From a Rokkanian perspective, this weakness can be explained by the pacification of the class cleavage in Switzerland and its resultant low salience.[3] Thus, the international comparison conducted by Kriesi et al. (1995) shows that between 1975 and 1989 the Swiss workers' movement mobilized less than its German, French, and Dutch counterparts. The difference with France is particularly marked, especially if we take into account strikes as the preferred form of worker mobilization.

Labour mobilization was very strong at the beginning of the twentieth century and, above all, during the general strike of 1918. At that time, the labour movement was still radical, but its action gradually became more moderate as its main organizations—the trade unions and the Socialist Party—were integrated into the political system. Gradually inserted into the logic of the concordance system—that is, the integration of all major parties into the government—the labour movement resurfaced for the first time after the Second World War and a second time at the end of the 1960s, thanks to the contribution of the New Left, only to become latent again from the mid-1970s after the darkest period of the economic crisis. However, labour mobilization regained some momentum in the new millennium, particularly in relation to the difficult economic situation and the erosion of social gains that took place throughout Europe, and parallel to the emergence of the anti-globalization movement.

Another important mobilization based on traditional cleavages—in this case, the centre-periphery cleavage—has characterized the Swiss social protest sector: the regionalist or autonomist Jura movement (Jenkins 1986). Despite the weakness of this cleavage in Switzerland, the Jura movement was strongly mobilized, especially from the 1950s onwards, and led to the creation of the new canton of Jura in 1979. Of the four countries studied by Kriesi et al. (1995), only France, where the centre-periphery divide has remained prominent, has a higher level of mobilization of regionalist movements compared to Switzerland. A centre-periphery conflict can always occur within one of the units of the federal state due to the presence of minorities, who are politically discriminated against. This was precisely the case in Jura, where the French-speaking Catholic minority of the former canton of Bern fought for a long time for the creation of a separate canton.

The urban–rural divide has, for several reasons, retained a certain capacity for mobilization in Switzerland and is witnessed by the strong presence of farmers' organizations. However, such organizations are closer to interest groups: they follow a logic of representation and act mainly inside the political system and its institutions, in particular within the administrative arena, compared to social movement organizations carrying out protest actions, as is the case in France. The openness of the Swiss political opportunity structure for this type of mobilization is partly responsible.

3.2 New social movements

The beginning of the protest wave of the late 1960s was partly spurred by the student movement; however, student protests in Switzerland never reached the scale of neighbouring countries. In Switzerland, the first wave of new social movement protests was built around the politicization of environmental issues. It was above all the emergence of new social movements that contributed to the large protest wave that took place in Switzerland, as elsewhere in Europe, from the mid-1960s. These movements have been the most important ones in Switzerland in recent decades (Giugni and Passy 1997; Giugni 1995; Hutter and Giugni 2009; Kriesi et al. 1981).

The new social movements differ from traditional movements both in terms of the issues raised and the groups mobilized. These movements have emerged from the process of value change that took place in Europe since the end of the Second World War. They emphasize cultural rights and a better quality of life, criticize the risks of economic growth, reject bureaucratic control of the individual, especially by the state, and advocate more direct forms of citizen participation in political life (Beck 1986; Brand 1985; Raschke 1985). In terms of their social composition, these movements articulate a new cleavage within the new middle class between a socio-cultural and a technocratic component (Kriesi 1989). Among their activists, we find a large proportion of professionals from social and cultural services, although they mobilize wider sectors of the population.

The pacification of traditional cleavages offers space for a significant mobilization of new social movements in Switzerland. Kriesi et al. (1995) showed that, during the period studied (1975–1989), they mobilized far more than other movements; a similar trend applies to the subsequent years, albeit to a lesser extent (Hutter 2014).

Koopmans (1992) has proposed distinguishing between instrumental, subcultural, and countercultural movements, depending on how each reacts to political opportunities. This distinction, based on the more common distinction between strategy and identity (Cohen 1985) that captures the movements' underlying logic of action (whether instrumental or identity-based), adds a further dimension relating to the movements' general orientation (whether internal or external). As such, '[s]ubcultural movements are predominantly internally oriented and identity-based. Instrumental movements are in some way their antithesis since they have an external orientation. Finally, countercultural movements are in between, for they combine their identity basis with a strong external orientation' (Kriesi et al. 1995, 84).[4]

This distinction is then used to explain why certain movements in a given context react differently to the same mix of political opportunities, but here it is used more descriptively to briefly depict the mobilization of new social movements in Switzerland. Following Kriesi et al. (1995), environmental, peace, and solidarity movements can be considered as predominantly instrumental, the women's movement as predominantly subcultural, and the squatters' movement as predominantly countercultural.

Instrumental movements have largely contributed to the mobilization of new social movements in Switzerland. Amongst them, the environmental and anti-nuclear movements have certainly played a key role, especially in the 1970s and 1980s, but, as far as environmental issues are concerned, also more recently. The anti-nuclear movement mobilized strongly in the second half of the 1970s, mainly to protest against plans to build the Kaiseraugst power plant in the northwestern part of the country. Thereafter, anti-nuclear protest declined sharply, with a slight revival following the Chernobyl accident in 1986. Obviously, the success of the initiative for a moratorium on nuclear power plants in 1990 deprived the movement of its main goal, thus contributing to its demobilization. However, this goal came to the fore again in the 2000s, in the context of the end of the moratorium, and the anti-nuclear movement was thus somewhat remobilized, as well as under the impetus of the accident at the Japanese nuclear power plant in Fukushima in March 2011.

Although the climate strikes in recent years have mobilized a large number of people, especially from the youngest generations, the environmental movement has traditionally been characterized more by its important organizational infrastructure and resources than its capacity to mobilize through mass protest actions. The same applies to the solidarity movement.[5] Their strong organizational infrastructure ensures that both movements remain active even over periods of low popular participation. Moreover, several organizations of the environmental and solidarity movements have gained better access to the administrative arena in Switzerland, sometimes becoming privileged interlocutors of the state and cooperating with it in the formulation and implementation of public policies (Giugni and Passy 1998). This shows the strong process of institutionalization these two movements have undergone; however, both have still sometimes been at the origin of unconventional actions.

As far as environmental issues are concerned, the end of the 2010s saw a large protest wave across Europe and even worldwide on the issue of climate change: the so-called 'climate strikes' or 'Fridays for Future'. Initiated by the school strike of the young Swedish girl Greta Thunberg in autumn 2018 and carried out mainly by the younger generation—especially college and university students—this protest wave has affected many countries, including Switzerland. One of the largest protests, if not the largest, in this country took place in Bern on 28 September 2019, with an estimated crowd of 100,000 people.[6] This large wave of protests contrasts with the history of the environmental movement in Switzerland, which has mostly centred around less visible activities carried out by movement organizations. In the context of these new protests around climate change, the organization Extinction Rebellion, which may be considered the more radical branch of the movement and acting primarily through civil disobedience, has also gained some notoriety in Switzerland.

The early 1980s represent the peak of new social movements' mobilization in Switzerland and elsewhere in Europe, although they did continue to mobilize in important ways later on. This peak was mainly due to the action of the peace movement and squatters' movements. At that time, the peace movement mobilized considerably around the issue of nuclear weapons, in contrast to its traditional main target in

Switzerland: national authorities and domestic politics. After a period of sharp demobilization, the peace movement re-emerged in the late 1980s and early 1990s, mainly in relation to the campaign around a popular initiative for a Switzerland without an army and for a global peace policy. Then there was a major mobilization in 2003 to protest, as in other countries, against the American intervention in Iraq.

Moving to subcultural movements, we must emphasize the low level of mobilization of the women's movement, a movement which does not seem to have exploited all the opportunities offered by the Swiss political system (Banaszak 1996) and which, moreover, has gradually become institutionalized since the introduction of universal suffrage in 1971. This should not make us forget that women's issues have sometimes led to important protests, particularly around specific events with a particular symbolic charge, such as International Women's Rights Day or the World March of Women. In this respect, it is worth recalling the women's strike of 14 June 1991 and, more recently, that of 14 June 2019. Moreover, we should mention the Swiss offshoot of the #MeToo movement, which first broke out in the United States following the Weinstein affair and the allegations of sexual assault against him, and then elsewhere in the world. Without mobilizing the masses, this movement had a significant echo in Switzerland. Although it addresses different issues from those traditionally advanced by the women's movement, we can consider it as a recent expression of this movement.

Finally, the most prominent countercultural movement, both in Switzerland and other countries, is arguably the squatters' movement. Squatters were very active in several European countries—most notably in Germany and the Netherlands, but also in Switzerland—in the early 1980s. In Switzerland, the Zurich movement of 1980–1981 is responsible for most of these actions, although squatters were present in several Swiss cities especially during the 1980s, for example in Basel, Bern, Geneva, and Lausanne. After a phase, lasting several years, characterized by a certain latency, the squatters' movement became somewhat more active again in the mid-2000s.

3.3 Radical-right movements

From the perspective of cleavage theory, the new social movements arise from a cleavage within the new middle class between a socio-cultural component and a technocratic component (Kriesi 1989) and, from the point of view of the values underlying their mobilization, they stress 'left-libertarian' values (Kitschelt 1988). By contrast, radical-right movements (and parties) rest on a more recent new cleavage that opposes the 'winners' and 'losers' of globalization or, perhaps more accurately, the process of denationalization (Kriesi et al. 2008, 2012), and advance 'right-authoritarian' values. In a way, radical right-wing actors can be seen as resting on traditional cleavages and thus, when acting as social movements, appear as traditional movements. However, at least today, it is probably more correct to associate these radical right-wing groups with the emergence of this new cleavage, which largely contributes to structuring the contemporary political space in numerous countries (Kriesi et al. 2006), including protest politics (Hutter

2012). Others have referred to the winners–losers cleavage as one between openness and tradition (Brunner and Sciarini 2002) or between a position stressing 'integration' (for example, with respect to the process of European integration) and another favouring 'demarcation'. New radical-right movements and parties—but also actors from the radical fringes of the left—clearly display the latter stance (Kitschelt 1995).

Although the extreme right in Switzerland is characterized by its significant presence in public space as well as its radicalism (Giugni et al. 2005), when examining its protest actions—that is, as a social movement—the Swiss case emerges rather as a case of weak mobilization (Giugni 2019). More generally, while the cleavage that has contributed to the emergence of new social movements is expressed in both the electoral (voting) and non-electoral (social movements) arenas, right-wing extremism and populism largely favour the former (Hutter and Kriesi 2013). This may be due to a fundamental preference for political participation on the left, while the right is more attached to institutional channels (Hutter 2014). At the same time, there are significant variations across countries, which could be partly explained by a 'substitution' hypothesis: the stronger the presence of the radical right in political institutions—especially in government—the less room there is for extra-parliamentary mobilization (Koopmans 1996). In this sense, the strength and presence in the Federal Council of the Swiss People's Party—the main right-wing party—could serve as a sort of 'shock absorber' for right-wing radicalism outside the institutional arenas.

Even though the protest arena, and not only in Switzerland, is dominated by cultural issues and positions associated with the left (Hutter 2014), the radical right in Switzerland has nevertheless produced actions, sometimes violent, such as attacks on asylum centres. Its favourite issues are known immigration and, in part, resistance to integration within or with Europe—and these are also the two central issues of the institutional populist right. Over time, the issue of immigration in particular has become central to the political and public agenda in several European countries, including Switzerland.

A major mobilization phase took place in Switzerland in the early 1990s (Altermatt and Kriesi 1995; Gentile 1998), particularly around the issue of asylum seekers. The mobilization of the radical right was also quite strong in the first half of the 2000s, and mainly linked to the issue of immigration, which has traditionally been a central concern for these actors in Switzerland. More recently, the issue of Islam has come to be superimposed on that of immigration: the issue is cultural in nature and often expressed by right-wing extremist circles as the 'Islamization of Switzerland'. The creation of PEGIDA in Germany is in line with this trend. However, this organization has not met with much popular success in Switzerland. In this respect, we must emphasize that radical right-wing movements are not very mobilizing in the protest arena. Unlike, for example, some new social movements or the global justice movement, there have been no large demonstrations from these movements, at least in Switzerland. Right-wing protest actions often result from the efforts of a handful of activists. Thus, for example, a small group of organizations is responsible for the majority of the actions carried out by the extreme right in the period 1984–1993 (Altermatt and Kriesi 1995). Moreover, most of the events originated from the four parties of this political tendency, which reinforces the idea that the mobilization of the radical right is mainly the preserve of parties rather than social movements. In this sense, one of the characteristics of right-wing movements is that they are polarized along the lines of partisan intervention, on the one hand, and the lines of violence and marginalization (such as skinheads), on the other, whereas the new social movements have developed a large sector of extra-parliamentary demonstrative and non-violent mobilization.

3.4 Global justice movements

In a way, the winners-against-losers-of-globalization cleavage can also be seen as the basis for the emergence and mobilization of another important movement of the past few decades: the global justice movement. The ideological and political stance of this movement is, of course, very different and even opposed to that of the radical right. In both cases, however, we observe a mobilization that relates to the articulation of the national and the transnational.

Global justice movements have mobilized at local and national levels, but above all at the transnational—global—level; they perhaps share common ground in the struggle against neoliberalism as well as promoting democracy on a global scale and emphasizing its participatory and deliberative forms (della Porta 2005). The early 2000s mark the heyday of global justice movements worldwide, after the triggering event of the protest in Seattle in the United States on 30 November 1999 during a meeting of the World Trade Organization (WTO), which took on an important symbolic dimension as the 'Battle of Seattle'.

Switzerland has also witnessed this new wave of contention, even if the movement was perhaps not as strong as elsewhere (Bandler and Giugni 2008; Eggert and Giugni 2007). In fact, the triggering event for the wave of protest in Switzerland even took place before the Seattle events, in May 1998, during a protest against the WTO in Geneva, and that led to violence and confrontations with the police. This event marked a phase of radicalization of the Swiss global justice movement, and from then on there were demonstrations and strong protest actions. These often involved confrontations with the police, especially during the annual meeting of the World Economic Forum, one of the movement's favourite targets along with the WTO, and especially the G8 meetings. Indeed, the G8 meeting in Evian, 2003, was a key moment for the movement, including in terms of media coverage. With an attendance of around 75,000 people, the Geneva demonstration is still one of the largest demonstrations ever organized in Switzerland. The event raised the question of the so-called black bloc, the radical fringe of the movement that has often produced radical actions within or on the sidelines of the movement's demonstrations, especially during those organized at G8 summits.

Although for this form of protest on a global scale one should consider political opportunities beyond the national framework, the characteristics of the global justice movement in Switzerland—and probably in other countries as well—have largely depended on certain aspects of the national context. Thus, while this movement has often made the headlines because of its radicalism and even the violence of its protest actions, the Swiss context has probably seen less radicalism because of the weaker level of repression in the country (even if it has been stronger than that exerted towards other movements). In general, the Swiss global justice movement largely reflected the lines of conflict and traditions of protest that have characterized this country in recent decades, in particular the weakness of the class divide and the strength of new social movements (Eggert and Giugni 2007).

The global justice movement is a heterogeneous movement which in Switzerland has been articulated around two main branches, each with its own strategies and forms of action (Eggert and Giugni 2007). On the one hand, we note a moderate and institutionalized branch, which mainly relies on organizations and activists from the two most important new social movements (the environmental and solidarity movements), but also on institutional actors such as small left-wing parties and trade unions (less present than in other countries, however). On the other hand, there is a more radical and less institutionalized branch that revolves around autonomous, anarchist, and squatters' milieus. On a global scale, this distinction between the two main branches is reflected in the two main modalities of the movement's action: demonstrations, including direct and sometimes violent actions, counter-summits, and social forums.

In the second half of the 2000s, global justice movements seemed to have lost their mobilizing capacity, not only in Switzerland but also worldwide. The Swiss global justice movement continued to be active at least until the end of the 2000s, but popular participation diminished drastically.

Solidarity has recently been given new impetus and connotation by the Black Lives Matter movement and the protests against police abuse and, more generally, racial discrimination against members of the black community in several US cities. These protests, which began in some US cities where police abuses had occurred, later spread to other countries. They have developed into an international movement against racism and racial discrimination, especially connected to law enforcement and political institutions. The movement also had ramifications in Switzerland, sometimes marked by significant protests, such as the demonstrations that took place in June 2020 in several Swiss cities.

3.5 Anti-austerity movements

Anti-austerity movements were an important mobilizing force during the years of the economic crisis that started in 2008. Indeed, the first years of the 2010s were characterized by a deep economic crisis—sometimes referred to as the 'Great Recession', echoing that of the 1920s—that affected several European countries, especially those in the south of the continent such as Greece, Italy, and Spain. These years were also characterized by austerity measures and policies on the part of European institutions and states in response to the economic crisis. The central issues addressed by anti-austerity movements revolved around the fight against austerity measures, but also, more globally, in favour of the reduction of social and economic inequalities as well as a more equitable redistribution of income within society.

The movements gained momentum in those countries most affected by the economic crisis and government austerity measures, but have also mobilized elsewhere. Perhaps the best known are the Spanish '15-M movement'—or *Indignados* movement'—and the Occupy Wall Street (OWS) movement in the US. Both movements burst onto the public scene in 2011, in May and September of that year respectively, and influenced similar actions in other countries, including—albeit on a smaller scale—Switzerland. After 2012, however, anti-austerity protests faded, except perhaps in Greece due to the Tsipras government's conflict with the European institutions and the bailout policy that mobilized the population around the referendum of support announced by the Greek prime minister.

Although Switzerland did not experience an economic crisis of the same intensity as other European countries, there was a downturn in the economy and negative growth in gross domestic product in 2009, as well as an increase in the unemployment rate during the peak years of the crisis. However, no austerity measures were implemented, which could help to explain the weakness of anti-austerity protests: according to some authors (Bermeo and Bartels 2014), during a crisis citizens react more to austerity measures than the crisis itself or its consequences. However, solidarity actions with protests against the budget-cutting policies imposed on several European countries have taken place in Switzerland at times.

Anti-austerity movements have mobilized to protest against the negative effects of the economic crisis, especially against the measures which were imposed by most European governments and which were given strong support by European and international institutions (notably the European Commission, the European Central Bank, and the International Monetary Fund). However, such protests more generally highlighted the issue of democratic rights, citizen participation, participatory democracy, and economic and social inequalities. In this sense, a link can be made between these movements and global justice movements (Giugni and Grasso 2020). Like the latter, and perhaps even more so, they also combined issues typical of the new social movements—of which they are in some respects the heirs—such as participatory democracy, coupled with issues traditionally carried by the labour movement such as economic inequality.

In a way, anti-austerity movements were both preceded and followed by similar protests aimed at protesting against an economic situation deemed unbearable and, above all, against the political elites accused of being responsible for the situation. The so-called Yellow Vests (*gilets jaunes*), which mobilized in France in 2018 and 2019, are perhaps the most recent and important example of this type of protest. It is a very heterogeneous movement, which began as a protest against the introduction of a new tax on energy products and later evolved into a broader citizens' protest movement.

4 Conclusion

Over the last thirty years, a growing body of works has focused on social movements in Switzerland (Balsiger 2016). Moreover, Swiss movements are often studied from a comparative perspective (see for example Giugni and Grasso 2019; Hutter 2014; Kriesi et al. 1995, 2020).[7] Despite their diversity and heterogeneity, the various works on social movements in Switzerland highlight the impact of the context in which they operate. From this perspective, the structure of political opportunities in Switzerland favours the institutionalization of social movements. More specifically, the open institutional structure of the state—in particular, the presence of direct-democratic instruments—and the inclusive prevailing strategies of the political authorities favour the integration of movements and their demands (Giugni and Passy 1997). However, this process also depends on other factors, such as the nature of the issues at stake, the organizational structure of the movements, and their action repertoire. In some cases, incorporation is so pronounced that movements are transformed into interest associations.

Despite this process of integration, and sometimes of institutionalization, the Swiss people often take to the streets. Contrary to some preconceived ideas, the Swiss make extensive use of non-institutional forms of political participation, including street demonstrations (Giugni 2019). Several recent protests attest to the vitality of the social movement sector in Switzerland: the women's strike of 14 June 2019, the youth climate strikes, and most notably the national demonstration of September 2019 in Bern. The surely not huge but still present protests of the Swiss 'Yellow Vests' as well as those of the #MeToo and Black Lives Matter movements all testify to the vitality of Swiss civil society. In this sense, we can say that Switzerland is participating in the protest wave that has characterized the world in recent years.

The key point here is that, despite or thanks to the possibility of launching popular initiatives or optional referendums, the Swiss are no less active than citizens of other countries, at least in terms of levels of mobilization relative to population density. What differs, as Kriesi et al. (1995) and Hutter (2014) have shown, is rather the modalities of their action: social movements in Switzerland are often characterized by their moderation—except in some, often local, exceptions—and this is largely due to the institutional characteristics of the country. Thus, the real difference between Switzerland and other countries is not so much in the quantity or frequency of protests, but rather in their scale—the latter being relative to the size of the country—and especially their modalities.

Another preconceived idea is that the Swiss often agree with the political authorities, with their rulers, and that this demonstrates an uncritical attitude towards their government's decisions and actions. This view overlooks the number of citizens who are critical of the authorities, of some of their decisions, and, more generally, of institutional politics and representative democracy. These are often the very people who engage in social movements or other forms of protest. Even in Switzerland, therefore, large sections of the population prefer to take personal action, thus showing a preference for participatory democracy.

In this sense, the people who take to the streets and, more generally, engage in social movements represent those critical citizens that some authors have spoken of (Dalton 2004; Norris 1999). These citizens are by no means detached from politics, but are driven by a distrust of traditional political institutions and representative democracy and by strong feelings of political efficacy. Moreover, participants in social movements and protest activities are not necessarily alien from institutional politics, whether in Switzerland or elsewhere. Far from being socially isolated and frustrated individuals who adopt the most varied forms of collective behaviour as a reaction to such isolation and frustration, protesters are highly integrated and politically aware, and rationally choose protest politics amongst the means at their disposal. Demonstrators are often keenly engaged in both institutional and non-institutional actions (Giugni and Grasso 2019). Therefore, voting and protest—or ballots and barricades, to borrow McAdam and Tarrow's (2010) apt formulation—are not opposed to each other. Quite the contrary, they are two complementary ways of engaging in and with politics or even two sides of the same coin: that of the political commitment of citizens—in the broadest and noblest sense of the term—which, in the end, can only lead to an expansion of the democratic space, in Switzerland as elsewhere.

Notes

1. The introduction of direct democracy in Switzerland can also be seen as a product of protest action, an impact facilitated by certain conditions connected to the structure of political opportunities, such as federalism, the lack of institutionalization of the state, and a division within political elites (Kriesi and Wisler 1999).
2. Work on collective mobilizations in the field of immigration and ethnic relations politics has maintained that, in addition to institutional opportunities, discursive opportunities must also be taken into account (Giugni and Passy 2004; Koopmans and Statham 1999, 2000; Koopmans et al. 2005). These refer to the chances that collective identities and movement claims gain visibility in the media, resonate with the claims of other collective actors, and gain legitimacy in public discourse. Other works have attempted to apply this approach to the political field of employment and, more specifically, to collective mobilizations dealing with the issue of unemployment (Giugni 2010; Berclaz et al. 2012; Giugni et al. 2014). These works establish a link between the dominant conception of the welfare state and institutional approaches towards unemployment on the one hand, and collective mobilizations dealing with themes related to unemployment, its causes, consequences, and resolution on the other. These two bodies of literature point to the need to define political opportunities specific to a given field (Berclaz and Giugni 2005) and to consider their discursive side as well as their institutional side.
3. In addition to the pacification of the class conflict, the Swiss labour movement was also negatively affected by the presence of important cultural cleavages that divided the movement from the very beginning of its appearance on the political scene, as well as by the early democratization that soon deprived it of its main objective (Bartolini 2000).

4. Of course, this is only an analytical distinction and points to the main feature of different social movements. In reality, all movements include some doses of instrumentality and identity.
5. Following Passy (1998), we may consider the solidarity movement as consisting of four branches: development aid, human rights, asylum, and anti-racism. Development aid and asylum have been the main focus in Switzerland.
6. See de Moor et al. (2020) and Wahlström et al. (2019) for findings of a number of coordinated protest surveys conducted in several countries and covering various climate strike events that took place in 2019.
7. See Passy and Monsch (2020) for a recent work that takes a different comparative approach, not across countries, but across activists from different movement organizations within the same country, notably Switzerland, and shows how a community of engagement develops shared values, identities, and meanings through interaction.

References

Altermatt, Urs, and Hanspeter Kriesi (eds). 1995. *L'extrême droite en Suisse: Organisations et radicalisation au cours des années quatre-vingt et quatre-vingt-dix*. Fribourg: Editions Universitaires Fribourg Suisse.

Balsiger, Philip. 2016. 'The Land of Opportunities? Social Movement Studies in Switzerland'. In *Social Movement Studies in Europe: The State of the Art*, edited by Olivier Fillieule, and Guya Accornero, pp. 102–117. New York and Oxford: Berghahn Books.

Banaszak, Lee Ann. 1991. 'The Influence of the Initiative on the Swiss and American Women's Suffrage Movements'. *Annuaire Suisse de Science Politique* 31: pp. 187–207.

Banaszak, Lee Ann. 1996. *Why Movements Succeed or Fail: Opportunity, Culture, and the Struggle for Woman Suffrage*. Princeton, NJ: Princeton University Press.

Bandler, Marko, and Marco Giugni (eds). 2008. *L'altermondialisme en Suisse*. Paris: L'Harmattan.

Bartolini, Stefano. 2000. *The Political Mobilization of the European Left, 1860–1980: The Class Cleavage*. Cambridge: Cambridge University Press.

Beck, Ulrich. 1986. *Risikogesellschaft: Auf dem Weg in eine andere Moderne*. Frankfurt: Suhrkamp.

Berclaz, Julie, and Marco Giugni. 2005. 'Specifying the Concept of Political Opportunity Structures'. In *Economic and Political Contention in Comparative Perspective*, edited by Maria Kousis, and Charles Tilly, pp. 15–32. Boulder, CO: Paradigm Publishers.

Berclaz, Michel, Katharina Füglister, and Marco Giugni. 2012. 'Political Opportunities and the Mobilization of the Unemployed in Switzerland'. In *The Mobilization of the Unemployed in Europe: From Acquiescence to Protest?*, edited by Didier Chabanet, and Jean Faniel, pp. 221–246. Houndmills: Palgrave.

Bermeo Nancy, and Larry M. Bartels. 2014. 'Mass Politics in Tough Times'. In *Mass Politics in Tough Times: Opinions, Votes and Protest in the Great Recession*, edited by Nancy Bermeo, and Larry M. Bartels, pp. 1–39. Oxford: Oxford University Press.

Brand, Karl-Werner. 1985. 'Vergleichendes Resümee'. In *Neue Soziale Bewegungen in Westeuropa und den USA: Ein internationaler Vergleich*, edited by Karl-Werner Brand, pp. 306-334. Frankfurt: Campus.

Brunner, Matthias, and Pascal Sciarini. 2002. 'L'opposition ouverture-traditions'. In *Changement de valeurs et nouveaux clivages politiques en Suisse*, edited by Simon Hug, and Pascal Sciarini, pp. 29–93. Paris: L'Harmattan.

Cohen, Jean L. 1985. 'Strategy and Identity: New Theoretical Paradigms and Contemporary Social Movements'. *Social Research* 52 (4): pp. 663–716.
Dalton, Russell J. 2004. *Democratic Challenges, Democratic Choices: The Erosion of Political Support in Advanced Industrial Democracies*. Oxford: Oxford University Press.
della Porta, Donatella. 2005. 'Making the Polis: Social Forums and Democracy in the Global Justice Movement'. *Mobilization* 10 (1): pp. 73–94.
della Porta, Donatella, and Mario Diani. 2020. *Social Movements: An Introduction*, 3rd ed. Oxford: Wiley Blackwell.
de Moor, Joost, Katrin Uba, Mattias Wahlström, Magnus Wennerhag, and Michiel De Vydt (eds). 2020. *Protest for a Future II: Composition, Mobilization and Motives of the Participants in Fridays For Future Climate Protests on 20-27 September, 2019, in 19 Cities Around the World*. https://osf.io/asruw/ (accessed 18 September 2022).
Eggert, Nina, and Marco Giugni. 2007. 'The Global Justice Movement in Switzerland: The Heritage of the New Social Movements'. In *The Global Justice Movement: Cross-national and Transnational Perspectives*, edited by Donatella della Porta, pp. 184–209. Boulder, CO: Paradigm.
Epple-Gass, Rudolf. 1988. *Friedensbewegung und Direkte Demokratie in der Schweiz*. Frankfurt: Haag und Herchen.
Epple-Gass, Ruedi. 1991. 'Neue Formen politischer Mobilisierung: (k)eine Herausforderung der schweizerischen Demokratie?'. *Annuaire Suisse de Science Politique* 31: pp. 151–171.
Gentile, Pierre. 1998. 'Radical Right Protest in Switzerland'. In *Acts of Dissent: New Developments in the Study of Protest*, edited by Dieter Rucht, Ruud Koopmans, and Friedhelm Neidhart, pp. 227–252. Berlin: Sigma.
Giugni, Marco. 1991. 'Les impacts de la démocratie directe sur les nouveaux mouvements sociaux'. *Annuaire Suisse de Science Politique* 31: pp. 173–185.
Giugni, Marco. 1995. *Entre stratégie et opportunité: Les nouveaux mouvements sociaux en Suisse*. Zurich: Seismo.
Giugni, Marco. 1996. 'Federalismo e movimenti sociali'. *Rivista Italiana di Scienza Politica* XXVI: pp. 147–170.
Giugni, Marco (ed.). 2010. *The Contentious Politics of Unemployment in Europe: Welfare States and Political Opportunities*. Houndmills: Palgrave.
Giugni, Marco. 2019. *La Suisse dans la rue: Mouvements, manifestations, manifestants*. Lausanne: Presses polytechniques et universitaires romandes.
Giugni, Marco. 2022. 'Vie associative et les mouvements sociaux'. In *Démocraties directes*, edited by Raul Magni-Berton, and Laurence Morel, pp. 351–358. Brussels: Bruylant.
Giugni, Marco, Michel Berclaz, and Katharina Füglister. 2014. *La politique contestataire du chômage en Suisse: Etat-providence, opportunités et revendications politiques*. Zurich: Seismo.
Giugni, Marco, and Maria T. Grasso. 2019. *Street Citizens: Protest Politics and Social Movement Activism in the Age of Globalization*. Cambridge: Cambridge University Press.
Giugni, Marco, and Maria T. Grasso. 2020. 'Nothing Is Lost, Nothing Is Created, Everything Is Tranformed: From Labor Movements to Anti-Austerity Protests'. In *Routledge Handbook of Contemporary European Movements: Protest in Turbulent Times*, edited by Cristina Flesher Fominaya, and Ramón A. Feenstra, pp. 129–141. London: Routledge.
Giugni, Marco, Ruud Koopmans, Florence Passy, and Paul Statham. 2005. 'Institutional and Discursive Opportunities for Extreme-Right Mobilization Five Countries'. *Mobilization* 10 (1): pp. 145–162.

Giugni, Marco, and Florence Passy. 1993. 'Une aporie de la démocratie: le blocage des politiques publiques par les nouveaux mouvements sociaux'. *Annuaire Suisse de Science Politique* 33: pp. 165–183.

Giugni, Marco, and Florence Passy. 1997. *Histoires de mobilisation politique en Suisse: De la Contestation à l'intégration*. Paris: L'Harmattan.

Giugni, Marco, and Florence Passy. 1998. 'Contentious Politics in Complex Societies: New Social Movements between Conflict and Cooperation'. In *From Contention to Democracy*, edited by Marco Giugni, Doug McAdam, and Charles Tilly, pp. 81–107. Boulder, CO: Rowman and Littlefield.

Giugni, Marco, and Florence Passy. 2004. 'Migrant Mobilization between Political Institutions and Citizenship Regimes: A Comparison of France and Switzerland'. *European Journal of Political Research* 43 (1): pp. 51–82.

Hutter, Swen. 2012. 'Restructuring Protest Politics: The Terrain of Cultural Winners'. In *Political Conflict in Western Europe*, edited by Hanspeter Kriesi, Edgar Grande, Martin Dolezal, Marc Helbling, Dominic Höglinger, Swen Hutter, and Bruno Wüest, pp. 151–181. Cambridge: Cambridge University Press.

Hutter, Swen. 2014. *Protesting Culture and Economics in Western Europe: New Cleavages in Left and Right Politics*. Minneapolis: University of Minnesota Press.

Hutter, Swen, and Marco Giugni. 2009. 'Protest Politics in a Changing Political Context: Switzerland, 1975–2005'. *Swiss Political Science Review* 15 (3): pp. 395–430.

Hutter, Swen, and Hanspeter Kriesi. 2013. 'Movements of the Left, Movements of the Right Reconsidered'. In *The Future of Social Movement Research: Dynamics, Mechanisms, and Processes*, edited by Jacquelien van Stekelenburg, Conny M. Roggeband, and Bert Klandermans, pp. 281–298. Minneapolis: University of Minnesota Press.

Jenkins, John R.G. 1986. *Jura Separatism in Switzerland*. Oxford: Clarendon Press.

Kitschelt, Herbert. 1988. 'Left-Libertarian Parties: Explaining Innovation in Competitive Party Systems'. *World Politics* 40 (2): pp. 194–234.

Kitschelt, Herbert. 1995. *The Radical Right in Western Europe: A Comparative Analysis*. Ann Arbor: University of Michigan Press.

Koopmans, Ruud. 1992. *Democracy from Below: New Social Movements and the Political System in West Germany*. Boulder, CO: Westview Press.

Koopmans, Ruud. 1996. 'Explaining the Rise of Racist and Extreme Right Violence in Western Europe: Grievances or Opportunities?'. *European Journal of Political Research* 30 (2): pp. 185–216.

Koopmans, Ruud, and Paul Statham. 1999. 'Challenging the Liberal Nation-State? Postnationalism, and the Collective Claims Making of Migrants and Ethnic Minorities in Britain and Germany'. *American Journal of Sociology* 105 (3): pp. 652–696.

Koopmans, Ruud, and Paul Statham. 2000. 'Migration and Ethnic Relations as a Field of Political Contention: An Opportunity Structure Approach'. In *Challenging Immigration and Ethnic Relations Politics*, edited by Ruud Koopmans, and Paul Statham, pp. 13–56. Oxford: Oxford University Press.

Koopmans, Ruud, Paul Statham, Marco Giugni, and Florence Passy. 2005. *Contested Citizenship: Immigration and Cultural Diversity in Europe*. Minneapolis: University of Minnesota Press.

Kriesi, Hanspeter. 1989. 'New Social Movements and the New Class in the Netherlands'. *American Journal of Sociology* 94 (5): pp. 1078–1116.

Kriesi, Hanspeter. 1991. 'Switzerland: A Marginal Field of Research in an Underdeveloped Social Science Community'. In *Research on Social Movements: The State of the Art in Europe and Western Europe*, edited by Dieter Rucht, pp. 203–229. Frankfurt/Boulder, CO: Campus/Westview.

Kriesi, Hanspeter. 1995. 'The Political Opportunity Structure of New Social Movements: Its Impact on Their Mobilization'. In *The Politics of Social Protest: Comparative Perspectives on States and Social Movements*, edited by J. Craig Jenking, and Bert Klandermans, pp. 167–198. Minneapolis: University of Minnesota Press.

Kriesi, Hanspeter. 1998. *Le système politique suisse*. Paris: Economica.

Kriesi, Hanspeter, Edgar Grande, Martin Dolezal, Marc Helbling, Dominic Höglinger, Swen Hutter, and Bruno Wüest. 2012. *Political Conflict in Western Europe*. Cambridge: Cambridge University Press.

Kriesi, Hanspeter, Edgar Grande, Romain Lachat, Martin Dolezal, Simon Bornschier, and Timotheos Frey. 2006. 'Globalization and the Transformation of the National Political Space: Six European Countries Compared'. *European Journal of Political Research* 45 (6): pp. 921–956.

Kriesi, Hanspeter, Edgar Grande, Romain Lachat, Martin Dolezal, Simon Bornschier, and Timotheos Frey. 2008. *West European Politics in the Age of Globalization*. Cambridge: Cambridge University Press.

Kriesi, Hanspeter, Ruud Koopmans, Jan Willem Duyvendak, and Marco Giugni. 1992. 'New Social Movements and Political Opportunities in Western Europe'. *European Journal of Political Research* 22 (2): pp. 219–244.

Kriesi, Hanspeter, Ruud Koopmans, Jan Willem Duyvendak, and Marco Giugni. 1995. *New Social Movements in Western Europe: A Comparative Analysis*. Minneapolis: University of Minnesota Press.

Kriesi, Hanspeter, René Levy, Gilbert Ganguillet, and Heinz Zwicky (eds). 1981. *Politische Aktivierung in der Schweiz, 1945–1978*. Diessenhofen: Rüegger.

Kriesi, Hanspeter, Jasmine Lorenzini, Bruno Wüest, and Silja Häuserman (eds). 2020. *Contention in Times of Crisis: Recession and Political Protest in Thirty European Countries*. Cambridge: Cambridge University Press.

Kriesi, Hanspeter, and Dominique Wisler. 1996. 'Social Movements and Direct Democracy in Switzerland'. *European Journal of Political Research* 30 (1): pp. 19–40.

Kriesi, Hanspeter, and Dominique Wisler. 1999. 'The Impact of Social Movements on Political Institutions: A Comparison of the Introduction of Direct Legislation in Switzerland and the United States'. In *How Social Movements Matter*, edited by Marco Giugni, Doug McAdam, and Charles Tilly, pp. 42–65. Minneapolis: University of Minnesota Press.

McAdam, Doug, and Sidney Tarrow. 2010. 'Ballots and Barricades: On the Reciprocal Relationship between Elections and Social Movements'. *Perspectives on Politics* 8 (2): pp. 529–542.

Norris, Pippa (ed.). 1999. *Critical Citizens: Global Support for Democratic Government*. Oxford: Oxford University Press.

Passy, Florence. 1998. *L'Action altruiste: Contraintes et opportunités de l'engagement dans les mouvements sociaux*. Genève: Droz.

Passy, Florence, and Gian-Andrea Monsch. 2020. *Contentious Minds: How Talk and Ties Sustain Activism*. Oxford: Oxford University Press.

Raschke, Joachim. 1985. *Soziale Bewegungen: Ein historisch-systematischer Grundriss*. Frankfurt: Campus.

Rokkan, Stein. 1970. *Citizens, Elections, Parties*. Oslo: Universitetsforlaget.

Wahlström, Mattias, Piotr Kocyba, Michiel De Vydt, and Joost de Moor (eds). 2019. *Protest for a Future: Composition, Mobilization and Motives of the Participants in Fridays For Future Climate Protests on 15 March, 2019 in 13 European Cities*. https://protestinstitut.eu/wp-content/uploads/2019/07/20190709_Protest-for-a-future_GCS-Descriptive-Report.pdf (accessed 18 September 2022).

CHAPTER 20

MEDIA AND POLITICAL COMMUNICATION

REGULA HÄNGGLI FRICKER AND
ALEXANDRA FEDDERSEN

1 INTRODUCTION

POLITICAL communication refers to an interactive process of generating, promoting, and disseminating information between political actors, the media, and the population, as well as the effects of this communication on the opinion-formation process and on the behaviour of the actors involved (Norris 2001, 11631). Political communication is central to democracy: the democratic process requires that citizens have an 'enlightened understanding' (Dahl 1989, 112) of the decisions at stake.

Figure 20.1 shows the interactions between the three categories of actors involved in the political communication process: political actors (politicians, parties, and political institutions), media actors (editors, journalists), and citizens (see also Kriesi 2012a).

Through their communication, political actors aim to gain favourable media coverage and to shape citizens' opinions either directly or indirectly through the media. Citizens, in turn, can influence political and media actors through their (mainly indirectly) communicated priorities and preferences. As political communication today is primarily mediatized and most citizens in Switzerland—as elsewhere in Western Europe—get their political information from the news media, media actors play a central role in this process.

In this chapter, we will put the Swiss communication landscape in international perspective, before looking more narrowly into each of the three actors' roles in the political communication process in Switzerland.

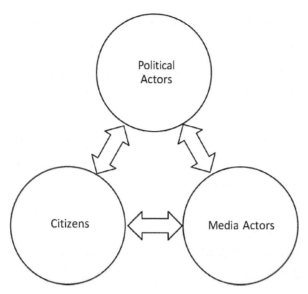

FIGURE 20.1: Actors and interactions in political communication

2 THE SWISS CONTEXT OF POLITICAL COMMUNICATION

The specificities of a country's political and media systems are central to political communication. Switzerland can be classified as a democratic-corporatist system[1] (Hallin and Mancini 2004; Pfetsch 2003; Kriesi et al. 2019) with public service broadcasters financed mainly by compulsory licence fees. It is characterized by a high degree of journalistic professionalism and traditionally displays a comparatively low degree of commercialization and audience-orientation of the mass media. This model grants the media a certain independence vis-à-vis the political actors, and prevents them from being too profit-oriented, which could lead to inadequate or incomplete political reporting.

Furthermore, the Swiss context is characterized by high linguistic diversity and political federalism. On the one hand, linguistic diversity leads to a highly segmented communication landscape (Meier and Schanne 1994) and, on the other hand, to a degree of cultural and political influence from the respective neighbouring countries that speak the same language (Blum 2005). Swiss federalism goes hand in hand with a relatively decentralized communication context, characterized by 'regional publics' (Kriesi et al. 1992). For instance, Twitter communication among politicians and journalists happens mostly within linguistic regions (Rauchfleisch and Metag 2016). In international comparison, the low level of political centralization also leads to a relatively low level of professionalism among Swiss political parties when it comes to communication (Blum 2005).

In recent years, the importance of the platforms of the global tech giants (Facebook, Google, YouTube, etc.) has increased rapidly, leading to major changes in the Swiss communication landscape (FÖG 2019). This is putting (traditional) media under great economic pressure due to a decline in advertising revenue (Puppis et al. 2014; Hofstetter and Schönhagen 2017), resulting in increasing media concentration. In 2019, the three largest publishers owned 82 per cent of the print media market in German-speaking Switzerland, 89 per cent in French-speaking Switzerland, and 68 per cent in Italian-speaking Switzerland (FÖG 2020). Media concentration also means increased centralization of editorial offices, which has a negative effect on regional coverage and content diversity (Eisenegger 2018, 5) and weakens professional information journalism (FÖG 2019). The increasing competition for attention also means that reporting more frequently follows what has been called the media logic (Altheide and Snow 1979). Polarized party actors (Landerer 2014) and especially prominent or flamboyant personalities enjoy more media attention, which can lead to conflicts appearing to be more important than they really are politically.

3 Political actors and their communication activities

In political communication, political actors generally aim to influence the attitudes and behaviours of other political actors and the public—i.e. the voters. To achieve this purpose, they need to gain media coverage. Two types of strategic choices are at the forefront: strategies for mobilizing support (coalition building, action repertoire) and strategies concerning the message (content, style, channel). The production of political communication depends on the basic values and preferences of political actors, their power and resources, and their coalition possibilities (Kriesi et al. 2009; Hänggli and Fossati 2019).

In terms of message, political communication is generally about what content an actor emphasizes (at the issue or frame level) and the style they use to present the content (whether arguments are presented positively or negatively, and how substantive, emotional, or person-oriented their arguments are; see Kriesi et al. 2009), as well as the channel they choose. These decisions are important because they can have specific effects.

Regarding the content of a message, the literature distinguishes between agenda-setting, priming, and framing effects. Agenda setting was first empirically studied by McCombs and Shaw (1972) and was guided by the famous conclusion of an early study that 'the press may not often be successful in telling people what to think but it is remarkably successful in telling its readers what to think about' (Cohen 1963; see also

Kinder 2003, 361ff). By drawing attention to certain issues, political news influences 'the standards by which governments, presidents, policies, and candidates for public office are judged' (Iyengar and Kinder 1987, 63). This is called priming (for a discussion of the priming concept, see Marquis 2015). For Scheufele (2000, 306), priming is the result of agenda setting. Framing studies go beyond agenda setting and priming. They examine not only *what* people talk or think about, but *how* they think and talk about political issues (Pan and Kosicki 1993, 70). Framing analyses are concerned with the way actors understand a political issue and how they try to influence the public's interpretation of it.

Based on an analysis of press releases on the migration issue, Feddersen (2019) shows that Swiss parties are effectively pursuing differentiated content-related communication strategies. She distinguishes between communication strategies in terms of salience of the issue, framing, and position. Although parties' communication on the migration issue strongly depends on ideological preferences (especially when looking at position and framing), their communication strategies are also influenced by the communication behaviour of rival parties (especially the issue owner or the party that public opinion regards as being competent on this issue) and public opinion.

During election campaigns, the question of which issues a political actor chooses to address is crucial. Based on the issue ownership theory (Petrocik 1996), Lanz and Sciarini (2016) show that which party is perceived to be the most competent one to deal with the issue that a voter considers to be the most important in an election campaign is decisive for her vote choice. It is therefore important for parties to build a reputation on an issue (or several issues) and to bring this issue on the public's agenda. In the Swiss direct-democratic system of decision-making, certain parties succeed in doing so by launching direct-democratic initiatives, among other things.

In direct-democratic campaigns, the topic is set and actors thus concentrate on framing. Hänggli (2020, 25) examines this for three direct-democratic campaigns. According to her model, framing occurs in three phases: frame construction, frame promotion, and frame edition. In a direct-democratic vote and in parliamentary debates, political actors are active in the first two and media actors in the third phase. In elections or public debates, media actors are more active in constructing the frames as well. Hänggli (2020, 74) shows that frames that can attract attention and/or with which the speaker can convince voters more easily are chosen over other frames.

Regarding the style of communication, Nai and Sciarini (2018) conclude that negative campaigns in Switzerland are more likely to come from the populist right-wing Swiss People's Party (Schweizerische Volkspartei, SVP), when political actors defend the status quo, lag behind in the polls, or are caught in an especially intensive campaign. In a comparative study of election campaigns, Valli and Nai (2022) show that challengers, extreme, and right-wing candidates are more likely to engage in negative campaigning. While women use this strategy no more or less often than men, the use of negative campaigning is further driven by candidates who are extraverted, competitive or self-centred, and impulsive (Nai et al. 2022).

Swiss direct-democratic campaigns intensify seven to four weeks before the vote (Bernhard 2012, 175; Hänggli 2020, 97 ff, 182), i.e. around and before the time when the official campaign and information material is sent out by the government, and media reporting intensifies. This gives citizens enough time to gather information before they cast their ballot. According to Marquis and Bergman (2009), more intensive campaigns have a positive effect on the level of information among citizens. Furthermore, the authors find a clear increase in the duration of voting campaigns between 1981 and 1999, but not any significant intensification.[2]

In general, there has been a professionalization of party communication. Today, party representatives must be reachable and able to quickly comment on issues. Sciarini et al. (2017) show that media work is indeed a relevant part of parliamentary work. For members of Switzerland's lower chamber of parliament, the National Council, the median time spent on public relations work is 192 hours per year or just under four hours per week. In the upper chamber, the Council of States, it is 120 hours per year or around 2.5 hours per week. Although the level of professionalization depends on the size of the party and parliamentary group, Swiss parties have strengthened their communication departments over the years (Donges et al. 2007) and hire external communication consultants. Unlike the majority of democracies worldwide, Switzerland does not provide public funding to political parties (Puppis et al. 2014), nor are there any transparency requirements regarding parties' finances (e.g. disclosure of donors or the amount of money spent; van Biezen 2010; Puppis et al. 2014). As a result, researchers do not know exactly how much money parties spend on campaigns nor how they are financed. However, due to the lack of public funding, private donations make up a large share of political financing in Switzerland (90 per cent according to Buomberger and Piazza 2022). For the thirty-nine direct-democratic voting campaigns that took place between 2005 and 2011, Hermann and Nowak (2012) estimate the average spending to be around CHF 2.9 million per campaign. For election campaigns, advertising is estimated to have cost approximately CHF 42 million in 2011, while the candidates had a total budget of CHF 47 to 48 million in 2019 (Buomberger and Piazza 2022, 114). These figures might be underestimated given the lack of transparency. It is slightly lower than the national election campaign spending in Germany in 2018 (54 million euro, Bateson and Hallam (2021); although higher when calculated per person) and considerably less than US presidential election spending (US$ 2.6 billion in 2012, US$ 14 billion in 2020; Open Secrets (2013, 2020)). It constitutes a very small share of the Swiss GDP (CHF 641,200 million in 2011 or CHF 727,212 million, Federal Statistical Office (2021)).

Political actors do not rely on different messages on social media than on traditional channels. In that sense, social media has not fundamentally changed campaign practices in Switzerland. The use of social media is part of the media presence (Feddersen 2019) and is used because it creates direct opportunities for interaction with citizens and journalists or helps with mobilization. Facebook, SMS, WhatsApp, email, personal websites, or blogs are at the forefront (Tresch et al. 2018; Klinger and Russmann 2017), with male, populist, and person-centric political mobilization and engagement patterns on Facebook in particular (Maitra and Hänggli 2023).

4 The media

Table 20.1 provides an overview of the Swiss print and online media with the largest readerships in 2022 by linguistic region. It shows that, a priori, different media actors are represented in each language region, but that newspapers are in the hands of relatively few publishers. Therefore, if a topic gets on the media agenda, it gets widely publicized.

Numerous studies on the interdependence between the political agenda and the media agenda have examined whether the media or the political actors drive the

Table 20.1: Most important print and online media by language region, 2022

Print media (daily newspapers)—2022			Online—September 2022		
Publisher	Title	Circulation (in 1000)	Website + application	Unique IDs per day (in 1000)
German-speaking Switzerland				
TX Group / Tamedia	20 Minuten (free)	326	20min.ch	1282
	Tages-Anzeiger	106	tagesanzeiger.ch	272
	BZ / Der Bund	105		
	- Der Bund	32	derbund.ch	37
	- Berner Zeitung	32	bernerzeitung.ch	67
	Basler Zeitung	35	baslerzeitung.ch	57
CH Media	Die Nordwestschweiz	113		
	- Aargauer Zeitung	19	aargauerzeitung.ch	84
	- BZ Basel	19	bzbasel.ch	24
	Luzerner Zeitung	97	luzernerzeitung.ch	84
	- Luzerner Zeitung	56		
	St. Galler Tagblatt	95	tagblatt.ch	70
	- St.Galler Tagblatt	27		
	- Thurgauer Zeitung	23		
			watson.ch	247
Ringier AG	Blick	84	blick.ch	1144
NZZ group	Neue Zürcher Zeitung	85	nzz.ch	-
Somedia Press AG	Die Südostschweiz	65	suedostschweiz.ch	-
	- Bündner Zeitung	24		
Zürcher Oberland Medien AG	Zürcher Oberländer	20	zueriost.ch	-

(continued)

Table 20.1: Continued

		Print media (daily newspapers)—2022	Online—September 2022	
Publisher	Title	Circulation (in 1000)	Website + application	Unique IDs per day (in 1000)
French-speaking Switzerland				
TX Group / Tamedia	20 Minutes (free)	134	20min.ch/fr	340
	24 Heures	41	24heures.ch	63
	Tribune de Genève	26	tdg.ch	58
			leMatin.ch	163
Editions Suisse Holding Médias (Groupe Hersant)	Le Nouvelliste	47	lenouvelliste.ch	57
	ArcInfo	32	arcinfo.ch	29
Imprimerie St.Paul	La Liberté	37	laliberte.ch	-
Fondation Aventinus	Le Temps	35	letemps.ch	-
Ringier SA			blick.ch/fr	43
Italian-speaking Switzerland				
Società editrice del CdT SA	Corriere del Ticino	29	cdt.it	-
TX Group and Regiopress SA	20 Minuti (free)	26	tio.ch	126
Regiopress SA	La Regione Ticino	24	laregione.ch	-

Notes: Information unavailable (-); Common segment of local editions ('Mantelzeitungen') in italic.
Data source: print media (REMP/WEMF 2022); online media (Mediapulse 2022).

choice of issues addressed. While the political agenda determines the topic in direct-democratic votes, research results including Switzerland suggest that in event-driven or symbolic debates with a domestic focus, the media agenda also influences the political agenda (Dalmus et al. 2017; Sciarini and Tresch 2019). When the media has an impact on the political agenda, this affects parliament more than government (e.g. Kingdon 2002, 58) but in a multi-party system like Switzerland, political parties also react to the media agenda (Vliegenthart et al. 2016). A comparison between the Netherlands and Switzerland shows that this effect is stronger in Switzerland, due to the presence of direct democracy and the 'militia' system in politics. On the one hand, direct democracy moderates the power of political parties in general and forces parliamentarians to monitor topics that attract media attention in order to take up demands from society and to minimize the use of popular initiatives. On the other hand, politicians have few resources and thus have to work with journalists to get their message across

(Sciarini et al. 2020). For Switzerland, Landerer (2015) shows that MPs from ideologically polarized parties behave in a more mediatized way than MPs from ideologically moderate centre-right parties.

Political parties tend to address important issues when media attention on that issue is high (Bernhard 2019, 254). Dalmus et al. (2017) show that external events also influence candidates' choices of issues. When it can be used to their own advantage, candidates take action and attempt to enter the media arena by speaking out on an issue, a phenomenon called topic surfing. In a study comparing Switzerland to the Netherlands, Helfer and Van Aelst (2020) find that the size of the constituency also plays a role in whether politicians react to media reports. In the Swiss system with small constituencies, politicians tend to be generalists who deal with (almost) all issues that are relevant for their voters. In the Netherlands the opposite is true, with the relatively large constituencies leading to a division of labour. Dutch MPs build their personal profiles around very specific issues. This issue specialization determines when they react or use media coverage to take political initiative. In general, however, since only a limited number of direct-democratic votes take place every year and the parliament only meets up to five times a year, the direct effect of media on politics is probably more limited in Switzerland compared to other countries (Tresch et al. 2013).

Furthermore, the general quality of reporting on Swiss direct-democratic campaigns can be described as satisfactory. It is substantial, i.e. informative and topic-oriented (Marquis et al. 2011; Marcinkowski and Donk 2012; Hänggli 2020, 170; Hänggli and Kriesi 2010) and relatively balanced (Marquis et al. 2011; Tresch 2012; Marcinkoski and Donk 2012; Jandura and Udris 2019; Hänggli 2020). The main information comes from the political actors, who take the lead in in the communication process during Swiss direct-democratic campaigns (Hänggli 2020, 184). The most frequently mentioned individual actor is the government, the Federal Council, while the most important collective actors are the major political parties. In addition to the commitment of the political actors, formal competencies and the official role of a politician or their power and prominence are the most relevant factors for the selection of news by the media (Sigal 1973; Gans 1979; Wolfsfeld 1997; Tresch 2009; Hänggli 2020, 141). Weak actors find it more difficult to get their arguments into media, especially on unfamiliar topics. These mechanisms depend on the type of debate (Hänggli 2019, 198), but power always seems to play a role. The emphasizing of a message by one's own organization and the importance that opponents and allies attach to a message play a role above all in direct-democratic, parliamentary, and corporatist debates. Compared to other countries, a broader range of political actors makes it into the news in Switzerland (Vos and van Aelst 2018). This is linked to the shared power structure in a federalist multi-party system and the system of direct democracy.

Most reporting is done from around five weeks to two weeks before the vote (Gerth et al. 2012; Marquis et al. 2011; Marcinkowski and Donk 2012). Of course, the media give varying degrees of attention to different referenda. The intensity of reporting is particularly high when a lot of money is spent for political advertising, on referenda on controversial issues, issues related to identity politics (instead of socio-economic issues), and campaigns with a populist spin (Udris et al. 2018; Udris et al. 2016; Marcinkowski and Donk 2012).

Even though it could be expected that the media crisis might lead to a decline in media coverage of direct-democratic campaigns over time, no such general decline can be observed. However, studies indicate that the new economic situation the media find themselves in play a certain role in terms of coverage intensity: there are many reports on issues which stir public interest and sell well, and not primarily on those that are most relevant from a societal perspective.

The role of the media as a third, independent actor in the entire process of political communication is a very important one (Hänggli 2020, 12). The political actors anticipate the actions of the media and adapt their communication accordingly. They proactively discuss opposing arguments in their press releases, while refraining from doing so in the internal channels (e.g. information material to members). The traditional media thus define the rules of the game that decisively and positively shape the opinion-formation process. So far, there is no evidence that social media provide a similarly positive effect informing citizens. On the contrary, the tech platforms skim off a large part of the advertising revenue that used to go to the traditional media (FÖG 2019, 2020), and information journalism thus finds itself in a precarious financial situation. Media concentration has increased, which has negative consequences for media quality. There are fewer regionally different perspectives on national political events and increasingly similar voting recommendations. There are also more opinion-led articles—i.e. more editorials, comments, and reviews (FÖG 2020, 23). In other words, while media professionalism remains stable, diversity and the availability of background information decrease (FÖG 2020, 19).

The transformation of the media landscape and the increasing focus on click rates also has an impact on how journalists perceive and perform their role. A recent study among Swiss newspaper journalists (Raemy et al. 2019) shows that the traditional journalistic roles—watchdog and citizen journalism—are seldom implemented in the reporting. On the contrary, the implementation of an audience-oriented infotainment role is more common. Market-oriented roles have become more popular, especially among younger journalists. Focusing on audience centricity can be an important survival strategy for media in an increasingly competitive environment. Indeed, on online news platforms, entertainment stories generate the largest number of viewers in terms of click rates (Fürst 2017; Hofstetter and Schönhagen 2017). Therefore, there are incentives to write infotainment stories, and if you can scandalize them as well, all the better for business.

5 Citizens

While the Swiss media landscape and journalists' role have evolved in recent years, media use in Switzerland has changed as well. The proportion of citizens who prefer to obtain information online increased by 7 per cent to a quarter of the population from

2009 to 2018 (Eisenegger 2018, 11), and daily newspapers are more frequently read online (Udris and Hauser 2017). This evolution entails two challenges: on the one hand, only free and tabloid media (20 minutes, bluewin, blick) achieve a high reach online. However, the quality of the free newspapers is low (e.g. Rademacher et al. 2012; Hänggli 2020). On the other hand, 40 per cent of users do not access offers from media brands directly (via app or website) but look for news via search engines or social media instead. This makes it more difficult for the media companies to generate their own advertising revenue and it is less controllable where and in what context the content is presented. Citizens are dependent on the algorithms of the search engines and social media platforms without necessarily knowing how they work. For Switzerland as a whole, social media are still less important for citizens' opinion-formation process than traditional media. However, there are differences. In French-speaking Switzerland, social media are used more often than traditional media online offers, at about the same rate to print media (Federal Office of Communications 2020).

In the Swiss direct-democratic context, however, an overwhelming majority of citizens still obtain information about direct-democratic votes via newspaper articles and the official information booklet sent out by the government (see Figure 20.2). Television and radio broadcasting are used by more than two-thirds of voters, while internet news sites and social media are less important but are used by 58 and 25 per cent of voters respectively. In general, there is little evidence that voters are turning their backs on offline sources for political information. Figure 20.2 shows that citizens, although they have increasingly searched for political information online in the last three years, still primarily obtain this information offline.

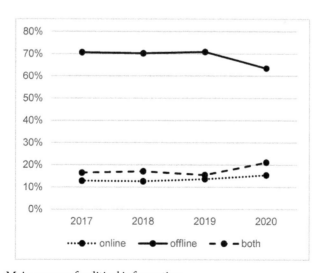

FIGURE 20.2: Main source of political information

Only voters considered. Online sources considered are news sites on the internet; offline sources are newspaper articles, television, and radio broadcasting.

Data source: FORS (2020).

In light of these recent transformations, are the media still facilitating the opinion-formation process and contributing to social cohesion? In order for the opinion-formation process[3] to succeed, i.e. for the individual's voting decision to be coherent with their preferences, it is important to be able to rely on independent, financially stable, and diverse media, as well as the attention of the public. The quality of opinion formation depends, among other things, on the complexity and intensity of political campaigns (Kriesi 2005; Marquis and Bergman 2009). Essentially, the Swiss context of direct democracy offers favourable conditions for the opinion-formation process (e.g. Gruner and Hertig 1983; Bütschi 1993; Kriesi 2005; Milic et al. 2014, 276; Colombo 2018; Hänggli 2020). Depending on the intensity, balance, and diversity of news coverage (Bowler and Donovan 1998; Kriesi 2005; Marcinkowski 2005; Marquis and Bergman 2009; Van Aelst 2014), the media can have a (de-)mobilizing effect, reinforce existing preferences, or change voters' opinions (Kriesi 2012b). Intense campaigns increase mobilization. Challengers tend to prefer high-visibility campaigns because this makes their relatively less-known arguments more visible and tangible (Kriesi 2005; for an overview see Milic et al. 2014, 233–262). In addition, the news media also have the potential to influence mobilization, especially in (intensive) referendum campaigns (Tresch et al. 2018).

Looking at the effects of national election campaigns, Tresch and Feddersen (2019) show that voters are more likely to retain their issue ownership perceptions when the party they identify as the issue owner receives a higher proportion of media coverage in the campaign. Furthermore, Maier et al. (2017) show in a survey experiment that mainstream parties have no advantage over far-right parties in terms of perceived credibility.

It thus seems that while Swiss citizens' media use in general has changed, their information-seeking behaviour in voting and election campaigns has remained largely the same. Even when citizens get information via social media, they mostly read shared information from the news media (Puppis 2017, 77). In that sense, the increasing use of online media is not (yet) especially worrying for the quality of the opinion-formation processes in Switzerland. Furthermore, the new media could play a role in mobilizing younger citizens and organizing social movements (e.g. climate youth).

6 Conclusion

Which issues we debate and how we think about them is defined by political communication, i.e. by the flow of information in which political actors, the media, and citizens are involved. In the Swiss context of direct-democratic votes and elections, voters' preferences are dependent on this information (Disch 2011; Hänggli 2020, 17, 232f.). Public debates are usually led by political actors, but in a context where most citizens get their information via the news, the media are key players. The interplay of actors varies depending not only on the political and media systems but on the power of the actors involved and the arena in which a public debate takes place, as well as, in the Swiss context of direct democracy, the issue addressed in the debate.

Even though political communication in Switzerland can be seen as a latecomer in terms of digitalization, it is undergoing important changes. First, news is increasingly distributed and received digitally. The existing conditions, however, reduce the risk of increased disinformation and hate speech (Humprecht et al. 2021). Secondly, the media concentration has increased in recent years, leading to a reduction of content diversity and journalistic quality. Finally, platformization has led to a drastic deterioration in funding for quality journalism. Despite these changes, traditional news media remain important for Swiss citizens' opinion formation, and traditional news coverage reaches more people than information transmitted by other channels. Looking at the interactions in the process of political communication it becomes apparent that the media and, more recently, the platforms are relevant social actors, which fulfil important functions for society. Together with other institutions, they are supposed to enable the formation of an enlightened public opinion, facilitate social integration and cohesion, contribute to maintaining social order, and observe and report socially relevant events, as well as stimulate change and innovation (McQuail 2013, 37ff; Hänggli et al. 2021). Politicians need to adapt the legislative framework to the new circumstances, as it is crucially important that these functions are maintained.

Notes

1. This places Switzerland in the same category as, e.g. Germany and Austria. In contrast, other neighbouring countries like France or Italy are classified as polarized pluralist systems, while the United Kingdom or the United States qualify as liberal systems.
2. See also 'Direct Democratic Votes' in this volume.
3. Regarding opinion formation, see 'Direct Democratic Votes' and 'National Elections' in this volume.

References

Altheide, David. L., and Robert P. Snow. 1979. *Media Logic*. Beverly Hills, CA: Sage.
Bateson, Ian, and Mark Hallam. 2021. *German Election: Party and Campaign Financing*. Bonn: Deutsche Welle https://www.dw.com/en/german-election-party-and-campaign-financing/a-58807353 (accessed 22 September 2022).
Bernhard, Laurent. 2012. *Campaign Strategy in Direct Democracy*. London: Palgrave Macmillan.
Bernhard, Laurent. 2019. 'Inside the Interaction Context'. In *Debating Unemployment Policy. Political Communication and the Labour Market in Western Europe*, edited by Laurent Bernhard, Flavia Fossati, Regula Hänggli, and Hanspeter Kriesi, pp. 233–256. Cambridge: Cambridge University Press.
Blum, Roger. 2005. 'Bausteine zu einer Theorie der Mediensysteme'. *Medienwissenschaften Schweiz* 2: pp. 5–11.

Buomberger, Peter, and Daniel Piazza. 2022. *Wer finanziert die Schweizer Politik?*. Zürich: NZZ Libro.

Bowler, Shaun, and Todd Donovan. 1998. 'Direct Democracy and Minority Rights: An Extension'. *American Journal of Political Science* 42 (3): pp. 1020–1024.

Bütschi, Danielle. 1993. 'Compétence pratique'. In *Citoyenneté et démocratie directe. Compétence, participation, et décision des citoyens et citoyennes suisses*, edited by Hanspeter Kriesi, pp. 99–119. Zürich: Seismo.

Cohen, Bernard C. 1963. *The Press and Foreign Policy*. Princeton: University Press.

Colombo, Céline. 2018. 'Justifications and Citizen Competence in Direct Democracy: A Multilevel Analysis'. *British Journal of Political Science* 48 (3): pp. 787–806.

Dahl, Robert A. 1989. *Democracy and its Critics*. New Haven: Yale University Press.

Dalmus, Caroline, Regula Hänggli, and Laurent Bernhard. 2017. 'The Charm of Salient Issues? Parties' Strategic Behavior in Press Releases'. In *How Political Actors Use the Media*, edited by Peter Van Aelst, and Stefaan Walgrave, pp. 183–202. Cham: Palgrave Macmillan.

Disch, Lisa. 2011. 'Toward a Mobilization Conception of Democratic Representation'. *American Political Science Review* 105 (1): pp. 100–114.

Donges, Patrick, Otfried Jarren, and Martina Vogel. 2007. 'Immer schneller und jederzeit reagieren. Die Parteien unter medialem Anpassungsdruck'. *Neue Zürcher Zeitung* 225, 28.09.2007: p. 70.

Eisenegger, Mark. 2018. *Qualité des médias: Schweiz – Suisse – Svizzera: annales 2018: principaux constats*. Basel: Schwabe.

Feddersen, Alexandra. 2019. *The Dynamics of Political Parties' Issue Competition: The Case of the Migration Issue in Switzerland*. Genève: Université de Genève.

Federal Statistical Office. 2021. *Bruttoinlandprodukt, lange Serie*. https://www.bfs.admin.ch/bfs/en/home/statistics/national-economy/national-accounts/gross-domestic-product.assetdetail.18584979.html (accessed 22 September 2022).

Federal Office of Communications. 2020. *Media Monitor Switzerland*. https://www.bakom.admin.ch/bakom/en/homepage/ofcom/ofcom-s-information/press-releases-nsb.msg-id-77855.html (accessed 22 September 2022).

FORS. 2020. *VOTO Studies: Standardized Post-Vote Surveys, 2016–2020*. Lausanne: FORS. https://www.swissubase.ch/en/catalogue/studies/13948/16830/overview (accessed 29 January 2021).

FÖG—Forschungsinstitut Öffentlichkeit und Gesellschaft. 2019. *Qualität der Medien*. Basel: Schwabe. doi: 10.5167/uzh-174109.

FÖG—Forschungsinstitut Öffentlichkeit und Gesellschaft. 2020. *Qualität der Medien*. Basel, Schwabe. https://www.foeg.uzh.ch/dam/jcr:13f6efc8-f9c4-45dd-816c-b6a8356edfe6/2020_Gesamtausgabe.pdf (accessed 27 April 2022).

Fürst, Silke. 2017. 'Die Etablierung des Internets als Self-Fulfilling Prophecy? Zur Rolle der öffentlichen Kommunikation bei der Diffusion neuer Medien'. *Medien & Zeit* 32 (2): pp. 43–55.

Gans, Herbert J. 1979. 'Deciding What's News: Story Suitability'. *Society* 16 (3): pp. 65–77.

Gerth, Matthias A., Urs Dahinden, and Gabriele Siegert. 2012. 'Coverage of the Campaigns in the Media'. In *Political Communication in Direct-Democratic Campaigns. Enlightening or Manipulating?*, edited by Hanspeter Kriesi, pp. 108–124. Hampshire: Palgrave Macmillan.

Gruner, Erich, and Hans P. Hertig. 1983. *Der Stimmbürger und die 'neue' Politik. Wie reagiert die Politik auf die Beschleunigung der Zeitgeschichte?* Bern: Haupt.

Hallin, Daniel C., and Paolo Mancini. 2004. *Comparing Media Systems: Three Models of Media and Politics*. Cambridge: Cambridge University Press.

Hänggli, Regula. 2019. 'Framing Strategies – Important Messages in Public Debates'. In *Debating Unemployment Policy*, edited by Laurent Bernhard, Flavia Fossati, Regula Hänggli, and Hanspeter Kriesi, pp. 191–211. Cambridge: Cambridge University Press.

Hänggli, Regula. 2020. *The Origin of Dialogue in the News Media*. London: Palgrave Macmillan.

Hänggli, Regula, and Flavia Fossati. 2019. 'Theoretical Framework: Production of Policy-specific Political Communication'. In *Debating Unemployment Policy. Political Communication and the Labour Market in Western Europe*, edited by Laurent Bernhard, Flavia Fossati, Regula Hänggli, and Hanspeter Kriesi, pp. 29–42. Cambridge: Cambridge University Press.

Hänggli, Regula, and Hanspeter Kriesi. 2010. 'Political Framing Strategies and Their Impact on Media Framing in a Swiss Direct-Democratic Campaign'. *Political Communication* 27 (2): pp. 141–157.

Hänggli, Regula, Evangelos Pouranaras, and Dirk Helbing. 2021. Human-centered Democratic Innovations with Digital and Participatory Elements. Conference Paper. The 22nd Annual International Conference on Digital Government Research (DG.o'21). 7–11 June 2021, Omaha, NE, USA. https://doi.org/10.1145/3463677.3463708.

Helfer, Luzia, and Peter Van Aelst. 2020. 'Why Politicians React to Media Coverage. A Comparative Experiment of Political Agenda-Setting'. *The Agenda Setting Journal* 4 (1): pp. 88–108.

Hermann, Michael, and Mario Nowak. 2012. *Das politische Profil des Geldes. Wahl- und Abstimmungswerbung in der Schweiz*. Zürich: Forschungsstelle Sotomo am Geographischen Institut UZH.

Hofstetter, Brigitte, and Philomen Schönhagen. 2017. 'When Creative Potentials Are Being Under-Mined by Commercial Imperatives. Change and Resistance in Six Cases of Newsroom Re-Organization'. *Digital Journalism* 5 (1): pp. 44–60.

Humprecht, Edda, Frank Esser, Peter Van Aelst, Anna Staender, and Sophie Morosoli. 2021. 'The Sharing of Disinformation in Cross-National Comparison: Analyzing Patterns of Resilience'. *Information, Communication & Society*. DOI: 10.1080/1369118X.2021.2006744.

Iyengar, Shanto, and Donald R. Kinder. 1987. *News That Matters: Television and American Opinion*. Chicago: University of Chicago Press.

Jandura, Olaf, and Linards Udris. 2019. 'Parteigänger oder neutrale Berichterstatter? Die Berichterstattung in Schweizer Printmedien vor den eidgenössischen Abstimmungstagen'. *Zeitschrift für Parteienwissenschaften* 25 (1): pp. 111–120.

Kinder, Donald R. 2003. 'Communication and Politics in the Age of Information'. In *Oxford Handbook of Political Psychology*, edited by David O. Sears, Leonie Huddy, and Robert Jervis, pp. 357–393. Oxford: Oxford University Press.

Kingdon, John W. 2002. *Agendas, Alternatives, and Public Policies*, 2nd ed. New York: Longman.

Klinger, Ulrike, and Uta Russmann. 2017. 'Beer is More Effective Than Social Media. Political Parties and Strategic Communication in Austrian and Swiss National Elections'. *Journal of Information, Technology and Politics* 14 (4): pp. 299–313.

Kriesi, Hanspeter. 2005. *Direct Democratic Choice: The Swiss Experience*. Lanham: Lexington Books.

Kriesi, Hanspeter. 2012a. 'Political Communication: An Integrated Approach'. *Political Communication in Direct-Democratic Campaigns. Enlightening or Manipulating?*, edited by Hanspeter Kriesi, pp. 1–16. London: Palgrave Macmillan.

Kriesi, Hanspeter. 2012b. 'Conclusion'. In *Political Communication in Direct Democratic Campaigns: Enlightening or Manipulating?*, edited by Hanspeter Kriesi, pp. 225–240. London: Palgrave Macmillan.

Kriesi, Hanspeter, Laurent Bernhard, and Regula Hänggli. 2009. 'The Politics of Campaigning – Dimensions of Strategic Action'. In *Politik in der Mediendemokratie*, edited by Frank Marcinkowski, and Barbara Pfetsch, pp. 345–365. Wiesbaden: VS Verlag für Sozialwissenschaften.

Kriesi, Hanspeter, Flavia Fossati, and Laurent Bernhard. 2019. 'The Political Contexts of the National Policy Debates'. In *Debating Unemployment Policy*, edited by Laurent Bernhard, Flavia Fossati, Regula Hänggli, and Hanspeter Kriesi, pp. 32–82. Cambridge: Cambridge University Press.

Kriesi, Hanspeter, Ruud Koopmans, Jan W. Duyvendak, and Marco Giugni. 1992. 'New Social Movements and Political Opportunities in Western Europe'. *European Journal of Political Research* 22 (2): pp. 219–244.

Landerer, Nino. 2015. *Mass Media and Political Decision-Making. Analyzing Mediatization in Switzerland*. Baden-Baden: Nomos.

Landerer, Nino. 2014. 'Opposing the Government but Governing the Audience?' *Journalism Studies* 15 (3): pp. 304–320.

Lanz, Simon, and Pascal Sciarini. 2016. 'The Short-Time Dynamics of Issue Ownership and Its Impact on the Vote'. *Journal of Elections, Public Opinion, and Parties* 26 (2): pp. 212–231.

Maier, Michaela, Adam Silke, and Jürgen Maier. 2017. 'Does the Messenger Matter? A Comparison of the Effects of Eurosceptic Messages Communicated by Mainstream and Radical Right-Wing Parties on Citizens' EU Attitudes'. *Journal of Elections, Public Opinion and Parties* 27 (3): pp. 330–349.

Maitra, Julian, and Regula Hänggli. 2023. 'Who speaks and who is heard on Facebook? Political mobilization and engagement patterns of partisanship and gender in Switzerland's direct democracy'. *Journal of Quantitative Description: Digital Media* 3.

Marcinkowski, Frank. 2005. 'Deliberation. Medienöffentlichkeit und direktdemokratischer Verfassungsentscheid – Der Fall Liechtenstein'. In *Demokratie in Europa und europäische Demokratien. Festschrift für Heidrun Abromeit*, edited by Tanja Hitzel-Cassagnes, and Thomas Schmidt, pp. 1–27. Wiesbaden: VS Verlag für Sozialwissenschaften.

Marcinkowski, Frank, and André Donk. 2012. 'The Deliberative Quality of Referendum Coverage in Direct Democracy: Findings from a Longitudinal Analysis of Swiss Media'. *Javnost—The Public Journal of the European Institute for Communication and Culture* 19 (4): pp. 93–109.

Marquis, Lionel. 2015. 'Priming'. In *The International Encyclopedia of Political Communication*, edited by Gianpietro Mazzoleni, Kevin G. Barnhurst, Ken'ichi Ikeda, Rousiley C. M. Maia, and Hartmut Wessler, pp. 1236–1245. Hoboken: Wiley-Blackwell.

Marquis, Lionel, and Manfred M. Bergman. 2009. 'Development and Consequences of Referendum Campaigns in Switzerland, 1981–1999'. *Swiss Political Science Review* 15 (1): pp. 63–97.

Marquis, Lionel, Hans-Peter Schaub, and Marlène Gerber. 2011. 'The Fairness of Media Coverage in Question: An Analysis of Referendum Campaigns on Welfare State Issues in Switzerland'. *Swiss Political Science Review* 17 (2): pp. 128–163.

McCombs, Maxwell E., and Donald L. Shaw. 1972. 'The Agenda-Setting Function of Mass Media'. *Public Opinion Quarterly* 36 (2): pp. 176–187.

McQuail, Denis. 2013. *Journalism & Society*. London: Sage.

Mediapulse. 2022. *Traffic Data*. https://www.mediapulse.ch/online/mediapulse-online-data/brand-view-daily/ (accessed 14 October 2022).

Meier, Werner A., and Michael Schanne. 1994. *Medien-"Landschaft" Schweiz*. Zürich: Pro Helvetia.

Milic, Thomas, Bianca Rousselot, and Adrian Vatter. 2014. *Handbuch der Abstimmungsforschung*. Zürich: Verlag NZZ.

Nai, Alessandro, and Pascal Sciarini. 2018. 'Why "Going Negative?" Strategic and Situational Determinants of Personal Attacks in Swiss Direct Democratic Votes'. *Journal of Political Marketing* 17 (4): pp. 382–417.

Nai, Alessandro, Anke Tresch, and Jürgen Maier. 2022. 'Hardwired to Attack. Candidates' Personality Traits and Negative Campaigning in Three European Countries'. *Acta Politica* 57: pp. 772–797. https://doi.org/10.1057/s41269-021-00222-7.

Norris, Pippa. 2001. 'Political Communication'. In *International Encyclopedia of the Social & Behavioral Sciences*, edited by Neil J. Smelser, and Paul B. Baltes, pp. 11631–11640. Amsterdam: Elsevier.

Open Secrets. 2013. *2012 Presidential Race*. https://www.opensecrets.org/pres12/ (accessed 22 September 2022).

Open Secrets. 2020. *2020 Election to Cost $14 Billion, Blowing Away Spending Records*. https://www.opensecrets.org/news/2020/10/cost-of-2020-election-14billion-update/ (accessed 22 September 2022).

Pan, Zhongdang, and Gerald M. Kosicki. 1993. 'Framing Analysis: An Approach to News Discourse'. *Political Communication* 10 (1): pp. 55–75.

Petrocik, John R. 1996. 'Issue Ownership in Presidential Elections, with a 1980 Case Study'. *American Journal of Political Science* 40 (3): pp. 825–850.

Pfetsch, Barbara. 2003. *Politische Kommunikationskultur, Politische Sprecher und Journalisten in der Bundesrepublik und den USA im Vergleich*. Wiesbaden: Westdeutscher Verlag.

Puppis, Manuel. 2017. 'Einleitung'. In *Medien und Meinungsmacht*, edited by Manuel Puppis, Michael Schenk, and Brigitte Hofstetter, pp. 73–84. Zürich: vdf Hochschulverlag AG.

Puppis, Manuel, Philomen Schönhagen, Silke Fürst, Brigitte Hofstetter, and Mike Meissner. 2014. *Arbeitsbedingungen und Berichterstattungsfreiheit in journalistischen Organisationen. Beiträge und Studien Medienforschung*. Fribourg: Bundesamt für Kommunikation (BAKOM) and University of Fribourg.

Rademacher, Patrick, Matthias A. Gerth, and Gabriele Siegert. 2012. 'Media Organizations in Direct-Democratic Campaigns'. In *Political Communication in Direct-Democratic Campaigns. Enlightening or Manipulating?*, edited by Hanspeter Kriesi, pp. 93–107. Hampshire: Palgrave Macmillan.

Raemy, Patric, Daniel Beck, and Lea Hellmüller. 2019. 'Swiss Journalists' Role Performance. The Relationship Between Conceptualized, Narrated, and Practiced Roles'. *Journalism Studies* 20 (6): pp. 765–782.

Rauchfleisch, Adrian, and Julia Metag. 2016. 'The Special Case of Switzerland: Swiss Politicians on Twitter'. *New Media & Society* 18 (10): pp. 2413–2431.

REMP/WEMF 2022. *Bulletin des tirages / Auflagebulletin 2022*. https://remp.ch/media/remp.ch/media/remp_bulletin_tirages.pdf?redirect=true (accessed 14 October 2022).

Scheufele, Dietram A. 2000. 'Agenda-Setting, Priming, and Framing Revisited: Another Look at Cognitive Effects of Political Communication'. *Mass Communication and Society* 3 (2–3): pp. 297–316.

Sciarini, Pascal, and Anke Tresch. 2019. 'The Political Agenda-Setting Power of the Media: The Europeanization Nexus'. *Journal of European Public Policy* 56 (5): pp. 734–751.

Sciarini, Pascal, Anke Tresch, and Rens Vliegenthart. 2020. 'Political Agenda-Setting and -Building in Small Consensus Democracies: Relationships Between Media and Parliament in the Netherlands and Switzerland'. *Agenda Setting Journal* 4 (1): pp. 109–134.

Sciarini, Pascal, Frédéric Varone, Giovanni Ferro-Luzzi, Fabio Cappelletti, Vahan Garibian, and Ismail Muller. 2017. *Studie über das Einkommen und den Arbeitsaufwand der Bundesparlamentarierinnen und Bundesparlamentarier*. Genève: Université de Genève et Département de science politique et relations internationales et Institut de recherche appliquée en économie et gestion (IREG).

Sigal, Leon V. 1973. *Reporters and Officials: The Organization and Politics of Newsmaking*. Lexington: DC Heath and Company.

Tresch, Anke. 2009. 'Politicians in the Media: Determinants of Legislators' Presence and Prominence in Swiss Newspapers'. *The International Journal of Press/Politics* 14 (1): pp. 67–90.

Tresch, Anke. 2012. 'The (Partisan) Role of the Press in Direct Democratic Campaigns: Evidence from a Swiss Vote on European Integration'. *Swiss Political Science Review* 18 (3): pp. 287–304.

Tresch, Anke, and Alexandra Feddersen. 2019. 'The (In)Stability of Voters' Perceptions of Competence and Associative Issue Ownership: The Role of Media Campaign Coverage'. *Political Communication* 36 (3): pp. 394–411.

Tresch, Anke, Lukas Lauener, and Laura Scaperrotta. 2018. *VOTO-Studie zur eidgenössischen Volksabstimmung vom 4. März 2018*. Lausanne, Aarau, Luzern: FORS, ZDA, LINK.

Tresch, Anke, Pascal Sciarini, and Frédéric Varone. 2013. 'The Relationship between Media and Political Agendas: Variations across Decision-Making Phases'. *West European Politics* 36 (5): pp. 897–918.

Udris, Linards, Mark Eisenegger, and Jörg Schneider. 2016. 'News Coverage about Direct-Democratic Campaigns in a Period of Structural Crisis'. *Journal of Information Policy* 6 (1): pp. 68–104.

Udris, Linards, Mark Eisenegger, and Jörg Schneider. 2018. 'Medienresonanz von Abstimmungsvorlagen im Vergleich'. In *Schriften zur Demokratieforschung*, edited by Daniel Kübler, pp. 65–88. Zürich: Schulthess.

Udris, Linards, and Lucie Hauser. 2017. *Reuters Institute Digital News Report. Ergebnisse für die Schweiz*. Zürich: FÖG—Forschungsinstitut Öffentlichkeit und Gesellschaft/Universität Zürich.

Valli, Chiara, and Alessandro Nai. 2022. 'Attack Politics from Albania to Zimbabwe. A Large-Scale Comparative Study on the Drivers of Negative Campaigning'. *International Political Science Review* 43 (5): pp. 680–696. https://doi.org/10.1177/01925121209464 10.

Van Aelst, Peter. 2014. 'Media, Political Agendas and Public Policy'. In *Political Communication*, edited by Carsten Reinemann, pp. 231–248. Berlin, Boston: De Gruyter Mouton. doi.org/10.1515/9783110238174.231.

Van Biezen, Ingrid. 2010. 'Campaign and Party Finance'. In *Comparing Democracies 3. Elections and Voting in the 21st Century*, edited by Lawrence LeDuc, Richard G. Niemi, and Pippa Norris, pp. 65–97. Los Angeles/London/New Delhi/Singapore/Washington: Sage.

Vliegenthart, Rens, Stefaan Walgrave, Ruud Wouters, Swen Hutter, Will Jennings, Roy Gava, Anke Tresch, Frédéric Varone, Emiliano Grossman, Christian Breunig, Sylvain Brouard, and Laura Chaques-Bonafort. 2016. 'The Media as a Dual Mediator of the Political Agenda-Setting Effect of Protest. A Longitudinal Study in Six Western European Countries'. *Social Forces* 95 (2): pp. 837–859. doi.org/10.1093/sf/sow075

Vos, Debby, and Peter Van Aelst. 2018. 'Does the Political System Determine Media Visibility of Politicians? A Comparative Analysis of Political Functions in the News in Sixteen Countries'. *Political Communication* 35 (3): pp. 371–392. doi: 10.1080/10584609.2017.1383953.

Wolfsfeld, Gadi. 1997. *Media and Political Conflict: News from the Middle East*. Cambridge: Cambridge University Press.

PART V
ELECTIONS AND VOTES

CHAPTER 21

NATIONAL ELECTIONS

GEORG LUTZ AND ANKE TRESCH

1 INTRODUCTION

ELECTIONS in Switzerland are particular in several ways. Indeed, the electoral system is rather complex and offers manifold possibilities for voters to express their preferences for parties and candidates. Elections to the two chambers of parliament take place simultaneously but under different electoral rules, an issue we return to in section 2. Campaigns are expensive but remain traditional compared to other countries with relatively little use of modern campaigns techniques and social media, as we cover in section 3. This is also due to the large number of candidates and the relative inability of parties to run coordinated campaigns. Turnout is among the lowest for national elections in Western countries, an aspect we discuss in section 4. The electoral system means there are many political parties, but that voting behaviour remains rather stable, as shown in Section 5.

Political scientists have mostly ignored national parliamentary elections as the cornerstone of representative democracy in Switzerland, not least because of pronounced direct-democratic elements, strong federalism, and concordance government. It was not until the beginning of the 1980s that national elections regularly gave rise to representative surveys of the electorate and smaller evaluations within the framework of VOX election analyses (Hertig 1980; Longchamp 1984, 1988; Longchamp and Hardmeier 1992). This changed in 1995 when the Swiss Election Study (Selects) was launched, and data collection became more academically driven[1] (Bühlmann et al. 2006; Giger et al. 2018, 2022; Kriesi et al. 1998; Lutz et al. 2010; Sciarini et al. 2003). Selects conducts a post-election survey supplemented by a panel survey with waves before and after the elections. Since 2007, Selects surveys candidates for the National Council and Council of States elections as part of a 'Comparative Candidate Survey'.

2 Electoral systems for the National Council and the Council of States

Members of both chambers of parliament, the National Council and the Council of States, are elected by the people every four years, whereas the government is elected indirectly by the United Federal Assembly, i.e. the National Council and the Council of States together (see 'The Federal Government' in this volume). The twenty-six cantons and half-cantons form the electoral districts for both the 200-member National Council and the forty-six members of the Council of States. The National Council is elected according to federal law. Regarding the Council of States, the constitution stipulates only that each canton has two representatives in the Council of States (and only one in the case of the six half-cantons of Obwalden, Nidwalden, Basel-Stadt, Basel-Landschaft, and the two Appenzell), but the cantonal legislation decides on the mode of election.

2.1 National Council

The National Council's size has been fixed at 200 seats since 1962. Each legislative term sees the 200 mandates distributed among the cantons in proportion to their population of permanent residents with each canton guaranteed at least one seat. The number of seats varies greatly according to the size of the population, ranging from one seat in six small cantons to thirty-six in the largest canton of Zurich for the 2023 election.

The National Council has been elected in Switzerland according to proportional representation since 1919; before then, Switzerland had a majoritarian system with multi-member constituencies (Lutz 2004). However, the small size of many cantons greatly hinders proportionality and creates de facto quorums (Taagepera and Shugart 1989), making it difficult for small parties to win a seat. Less than 5 per cent of the vote share is sufficient to secure a seat only in the densely populated cantons of Zurich and Bern. Votes are distributed among the lists (or list alliances) according to the so-called Hagenbach-Bischoff procedure,[2] with candidates receiving the most votes on the list being elected. The lists in a canton can be combined to bundle votes for seat distribution, so-called 'apparentements'. While this seems a rather technical detail, it has consequences for the number of parties and candidates. Indeed, in many cantons parties present more than one list. Small parties with little chance of gaining seats run, without completely losing out on votes, through a list alliance ('apparentement') within a party family. In 2019, a record number of 4,645 candidates on 511 lists stood for National Council elections.

The election for the National Council takes place every four years on the second to last weekend in October. All Swiss citizens, who are at least eighteen years old, are eligible to vote. Swiss citizens abroad are also entitled to vote, but must register with the respective embassy to exercise their right and renew their registration in the electoral register every four years. They can choose whether to vote in their last municipality of residence or in their home municipality. Women were granted the right to vote and to stand for election at the national level only in 1971, and in some cantons even later (Lutz and Strohmann 1998). Foreigners cannot vote on the national level. With 25 per cent of the country's residential population not holding citizenship, this excludes a large group from voting. Together with the citizens below eighteen years of age that also do not have voting rights, this amounts to the exclusion of 36 per cent of the resident population.

For a long time, voting took place in person at the ballot box mainly on election weekends. In recent decades, postal voting has been greatly facilitated in all cantons with the aim of increasing voter turnout. Voters receive documents at home three to four weeks before the elections and can return them immediately. Precise statistics on the extent of postal voting are unavailable, but surveys and data from cantons and municipalities indicate that today over 90 per cent of voters cast their ballots by mail (Tresch et al. 2020, 57).

Compared to other countries, Swiss voters have many opportunities to express their views. It is possible to give a candidate two votes (cumulative voting), write candidates from other lists on the ballot paper ('panachage'), and cross off candidates from a list. These possibilities are actively used in Switzerland: in 2019, just under half of voters submitted an unchanged list, while the other half changed the list or filled out a blank one.[3] Open lists with possibilities of awarding preferential votes to candidates mean strong in-party competition between candidates on the same party list: to be elected, a candidate must be on a list that amounts to at least one seat, but above all, they must also generate more preferential votes than the other candidates on the same lists (Lutz 2011).

2.2 Council of States

Elections to the Council of States are based on cantonal legislation. Until the 1970s, some cantons saw their cantonal parliaments elect members of the Council of States. Today, all elections take place by popular vote, even if specific features persist (see Lutz and Strohmann 1998 for a detailed account; Vatter and Ladner 2020). For example, the cantons of Jura and Neuchâtel elect their two representatives by proportional representation, while Appenzell Innerrhoden elects its representative at the 'Landsgemeinde'[4] in April of the election year. In all cantons with elections by majority vote, an absolute majority is required in the first round; a relative majority is then sufficient if a second round is necessary.

Eligibility to vote can vary between elections to the National Council and to the Council of States (Lutz and Strohmann 1998). Before 1991, women in the canton of Appenzell Innerrhoden could vote in National Council elections but not in those for Council of States, since women were not yet granted voting rights in cantonal elections. Similarly, for a long period, some cantons set the voting age at twenty, although the voting age is now eighteen, except for Glarus, where 16-year-olds are already entitled to vote in cantonal matters and therefore in elections to the Council of States. Foreigners, who are long-standing residents in the cantons of Jura and Neuchâtel, are entitled to vote in cantonal matters as well as in elections to the Council of States.

3 ELECTION CAMPAIGNS

Before the early 2000s, election campaigns received scant academic attention in Switzerland. But in response to growing international literature on the professionalization of electoral campaigning (e.g. Farrell and Webb 2000), which identified different stages of campaigning along three dimensions (resources, techniques, and content), Swiss researchers have begun to study election campaigns and their development (Bühlmann et al. 2016; Engeli and Tonka 2010; Hardmeier 2003; Weinmann 2009). The first stage of electoral campaigning was predominant in the US until the 1950s. Aiming at the mobilization of core voters, it relied on decentralized campaign operations run by local party activists and volunteers, combined with communication through the party press, posters, and canvassing. The second stage saw the nationalization of electoral campaigning, the concentration of resources in the central party headquarters, an increased weight of national party leaders, the reliance on professional consultants and marketing specialists, and a focus on a nationwide, standardized campaign message. The third stage started in the late 1980s and saw the arrival of the permanent campaign, the dominance of professional consultants, marketing specialists, and pollsters, as well as the narrowcasting of messages through direct mailing and targeted advertising on TV and the Internet. The rise of social media and big data technologies in the first decade of this century inaugurated a fourth stage of political campaigning, characterized by data-driven micro-targeting and direct, two-way interactions between parties, candidates, and their voters (e.g. Semetko and Tworzecki 2018).

Studies of various aspects of electoral campaigning suggest that Swiss election campaigns remain rather traditional in many respects despite a certain tendency towards greater professionalization, especially where campaign resources and organization are concerned. Swiss election campaigns have long appeared as a series of cantonal and local campaigns due to the large autonomy of cantonal party organizations and the scarce financial resources of national parties, with national parties offering structure and support (Church 1996, 642). Yet, the 2015 national elections saw the seven largest parties put national campaign teams in place, allowing for greater coordination and a degree of nationalization of advertising campaigns, although large differences between parties subsist (Bühlmann et al. 2016). While election campaigns remain short—ad campaigns start around eight to ten weeks before Election Day—campaign spending has sharply increased from an estimated 28 million Swiss francs in the 2003 election to about 50 million in 2015 (Hermann 2012; Longchamp and Jans 2015). Although precise figures were unavailable until recently because of the absence of (national) campaign finance regulation, it can be assumed that per capita campaign spending (circa CHF 10) is in the upper segment in international comparison (Longchamp and Jans 2015). Campaign content and techniques in Switzerland are mostly traditional. The consensus-style of Swiss democracy means that negative campaigning is used sparsely both by parties (Stückelberger 2021) and individual candidates (Nai et al. 2022). Parties' advertising campaigns and the media's campaign coverage place little emphasis on national leader figures (Engeli and Tonka 2010; Kriesi 2011). However, given that the Swiss electoral system incentivizes candidates to attract preference votes and run individualized campaigns (Lutz 2011), a very significant share of campaign ads (ranging from 58 per cent for the SP to 97 per cent for the Green Liberals in the 2015 election) promote only one candidate (Bühlmann et al. 2016). This can be seen as 'decentralized' personalization (Balmas et al. 2014), whereby rank-and-file candidates feature instead of party or executive leaders. Regarding issue management, Swiss parties generally remain strongly focused on traditional core issues rather than strategically adapting to short-term public priorities (Dalmus et al. 2017). With respect to campaign techniques, Swiss parties have only begun to integrate digital campaigning tools since the 2011 elections (Klinger and Russmann 2017). However, traditional means such as door-to-door canvassing, campaign leaflets, posters, and newspaper ads remain important (as Swiss law prohibits political advertisements on TV and radio). In addition, parties use the targeting potential of Facebook ads primarily to reach existing demographic and regional voter strongholds rather than to expand their voter base (Stückelberger and Koedam 2022). Among candidates, almost 60 per cent used Facebook in the 2019 election campaign and roughly a third Twitter, but only a handful of candidates generated a significant following at the national level (Gilardi et al. 2020). Overall, social media seem to play a growing yet limited role in Swiss elections.

4 Turnout

When proportional representation was introduced in the 1919 National Council elections, it initially led to an increase in turnout of around 20 per cent. However, turnout has declined steadily since with few exceptions (Figure 21.1). In 1971, when women gained the right to vote, turnout dropped to below 60 per cent as women initially participated less than men did. In 1979, turnout in National Council elections dipped below 50 per cent for the first time and sunk to an all-time low of 42.2 per cent in 1995. Afterwards, it rose to 48.5 per cent in 2011 and 2015, only to fall again to 45.1 per cent in 2019. Compared to elections, average turnout in popular votes has been lower for longer and below 50 per cent since the 1970s on average. Turnout in election and popular votes has converged in the last few decades and levelled off at an average of 40–45 per cent.

Switzerland therefore ranks among the countries with the lowest turnout internationally.[5] Various institutional factors help explain why (Blais 2014): the stability of the party system and the government is a key element. Indeed, all major parties have been represented in government since 1959 and election outcomes bear no direct consequences on government formation (see 'The Federal Government' in this volume).

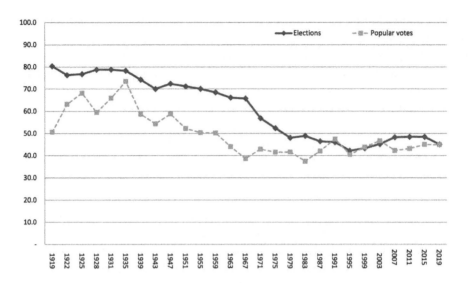

FIGURE 21.1: Turnout in national elections and popular votes, 1919–2019
The indicated turnout for popular votes is the mean value of ballots following the legislative election.
Data source: Federal Statistical Office (2019a, 2022).

The party system is also steady (Chiaramonte and Emanuele 2017), even though the rise of the Swiss People's Party (SVP) led to change in the last three decades. The resulting volatility explains the increase in voter turnout between 1999 and 2015, when the composition of the government changed twice (in 2003 and 2007, an incumbent federal councillor was ousted) and the polarization this led to had a mobilizing effect (Selb and Lachat 2004; Giugni and Sciarini 2009). Yet, the importance of elections in the eyes of the electorate did not increase (Selb and Lachat 2004). The frequency of direct-democratic ballots in Switzerland is another factor: the multiplicity of opportunities to participate entail lower interest in elections and a decreased average turnout per ballot (Blais 2014, 526). The stakes are lower in parliamentary elections than elsewhere because the population can take a separate position on substantive issues several times a year in referenda. Blais (2014) also underlines that elections in Switzerland are perceived as being complex, because in large cantons especially, voters have a great amount of choice and can express preferences for parties as well as for candidates.

At the individual level, the determinants of turnout resemble those of other countries (Gallego 2007). Participation varies strongly according to education levels and income: people with tertiary education and very high incomes participate over 20 percentage points more often than people with compulsory education or low incomes (Tresch et al. 2020). Age is another marker of difference, with the gap between the youngest and oldest age groups amounting to almost 30 percentage points. In contrast to other Western European countries (Gallego 2007), but also to Swiss direct-democratic votes (Fatke 2015), a gender gap persists in electoral turnout: women remain less likely to participate in elections than men, although the difference decreased from 24 percentage points in 1971, when women were entitled to vote for the first time, to about 8 percentage points in 2019. However, this divide manifests mainly among older generations with younger ones displaying no observable differences (Bernhard et al. 2021; Tawfik et al. 2012). In some instances, young women are even more likely to participate than young men,[6] which can be related to late female enfranchisement, inequalities in resources, and social integration as well as, most importantly, the lack of politicization of women (Engeli et al. 2006; Sciarini et al. 2001).

5 Electoral choice and behaviour

5.1 Electoral outcomes

Shortly after the introduction of proportional representation in 1919 for National Council elections, a stable balance of power between the four major parties emerged in Switzerland, lasting for seventy years (Figure 21.2) (see 'Parties and Party Systems in Switzerland' in this volume). The Liberals (FDP), the Christian Democrats (CVP), and the Social Democrats (SP) each received between 20 and 25 per cent of the vote and the SVP between 10 and 15 per cent. From the mid-1990s onwards, however, the rapid rise of the right-wing SVP meant a marked shift had taken place within the electorate and in 1999, the SVP became the party with the highest vote share. The two other conservative parties, CVP and FDP, suffer from a continuous downward trend. For the first time in the post-war period in 1987, the CVP's vote share fell below 20 per cent and neared 10 per cent in the 2019 elections. These losses led the party to merge with the Conservative Democratic Party (BDP), rebranded as 'The Centre' in 2021. The FDP fell under 20 per

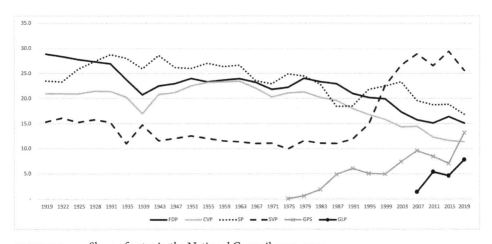

FIGURE 21.2: Share of votes in the National Council, 1919–2019

Data source: Federal Statistical Office (2019b), FDP since 2011 incl. Liberal Party.

cent vote share for the first time in 1999. Despite their 2009 merger with the Liberal Party, the FDP continues to lose ground, gaining only 16 per cent of the vote in the 2019 elections. The fourth governing party, the left-wing SP, lost votes in the 1980s with the rise of environmental issues and in 1987, fell below 20 per cent for the first time since 1919. After some gains, it achieved its worst election result to date in 2019, namely just under 19 per cent.

Major fluctuations have occurred among the small parties overtime. From the 1970s onwards, various smaller left-wing parties emerged, most of which then joined the Green Party (GPS). The GPS, which grew from a loose association to a national party (Baer and Seitz 2008; Nicolet and Sciarini 2010), established itself as the fifth strongest party from 1987 onwards. In the 2019 elections, the GPS succeeded in clearing the symbolic 10 per cent hurdle, thus outperforming the CVP and becoming the fourth largest party. At the turn of the millennium, new parties in the political centre emerged: the Green Liberal Party (GLP) split off from the GPS in 2007, and the BDP broke away from the SVP in 2008. Whereas the BDP suffered heavy losses in the 2019 elections and merged with the CVP to form 'The Centre' in 2021, thereby disappearing, the GLP managed to establish itself in several cantons and enjoyed electoral success in 2019 with almost 8 per cent of the vote.

Although women's suffrage was introduced at the national level only in 1971, the representation of women in the National Council is now at 42 per cent (against 5 per cent in 1971), well above the European average and close to that of the Nordic countries, where the proportion of women in political office was at 44 per cent in 2019.[7] Among newly elected members, women even formed a majority (53 per cent) in the National Council in 2019.

The marked shifts in power between the major parties observed in the National Council since the 1990s are only minimally reflected in the Council of States. This chamber has always been a stronghold of the FDP and CVP, which together continue to hold a majority of seats (Figure 21.3). For decades, the SP was underrepresented in the Council of States compared to its presence in the National Council, but it has significantly increased its representation since the early 2000s. The SVP, by far the largest group in the National Council, remains heavily underrepresented with seven seats currently. Only in exceptional cases do small parties or independent candidates have a chance of winning seats.

One key element helps explain the SVP's weak representation. Since elections to the Council of States (except in the cantons of Jura and Neuchâtel) are majoritarian elections, candidates must be able to win a majority. This is a reality that favours the two moderate bourgeois parties, the FDP and CVP, rather than the SVP, which in many cantons is characterized by a right-wing opposition position that renders it unelectable to FDP and CVP voters.[8] The underrepresentation of the SP in the Council of States is conditioned by the fact that left-wing parties do not have a solid majority in any canton and win seats when no electoral agreements are concluded in the bourgeois camp or when the electorate flouts them. This has increasingly been the case over the last twenty

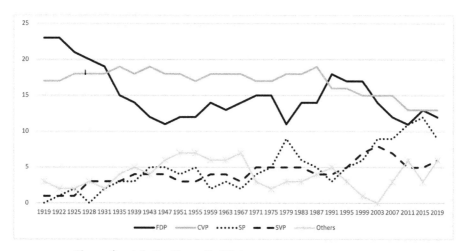

FIGURE 21.3: Share of seats in the Council of States, 1919–2019

Data source: Federal Statistical Office (2019c).

years, whereby the competition between the FDP, CVP, and SVP weakened each other and enabled left-wing gains in many cantons.

5.2 Cleavage-based voting and party identification

The extent to which party choices are structured by social divisions like class or religion is a question that has driven electoral research since its inception (Lazarsfeld et al. 1968; Lipset and Rokkan 1967). While some researchers have reported a general decline of cleavage-based voting in Western countries (e.g. Franklin et al. 1992), others have stressed that they still structure voting behaviour and give rise to many cross-national variations (e.g. Elff 2007). In Switzerland, Nabholz (1998) finds evidence for the declining relevance of traditional conflict lines between 1971 and 1995 such as those between religious denominations, social classes, and rural/urban areas, a trend more recent studies have confirmed. Goldberg (2017, 2020) states that the marked weakening of traditional conflict lines is largely behavioural and only to a limited extent the consequence of changing social structures. Although the relative size of the working class has decreased as a result of de-industrialization, and secularization has meant the proportion of the non-denominational increased, the erosion of class and religious conflict is more likely to be due to behavioural dealignment, meaning a less homogeneous party vote among the members of a given religion or social class. Goldberg (2020) also finds evidence for political dealignment, as expressed by increasing turnout gaps regarding both class and religious cleavage. While the influence of these two cleavages has not disappeared completely (Goldberg 2017; Lachat 2007), the ties between specific social groups and parties are changing, sometimes resulting in new connections between parties and voters ('realignment'). As an example, the SVP, a formerly predominantly Protestant party, was able to gain ground among Catholics between 1995 and 2003, but only among voters who did not or only rarely went to church (Selb and Lachat 2004).

Regarding the class cleavage, many studies note a fundamental transformation of class-based voting since the mid-1990s: in Switzerland, traditional workers in the manufacturing and service sectors now vote SVP disproportionately, while parts of the new middle class have turned to the SP (Bühlmann and Gerber 2015; Kriesi et al. 2005; Nicolet and Sciarini 2010; Oesch 2008; Oesch and Rennwald 2010; Rennwald 2020), and unionized workers continuing to favour the SP (Mosimann et al. 2019).

These new ties are related to the emergence of a new value conflict in the areas of environmental protection, feminism, or democratic rights and a new cultural, openness–closedness cleavage. The structural basis of this new conflict is formed by the winners and losers of the economic and cultural globalization process, which began at the latest at the beginning of the 1990s with the collapse of communist regimes (Kriesi et al. 2006). This political conflict is central to understanding the rise of the SVP, which succeeded in attracting those perceived as the losers of globalization, like unskilled workers and members of the old middle class, added to its traditional base of self-employed workers in agriculture, trade, and commerce (Kriesi et al. 2005). At the same time, the SP and the Greens, and the GLP later, mobilized the educated and high-income middle class from urban zones according to the openness–closedness cleavage (Nicolet and Sciarini 2010). Meanwhile, the centre-right parties can boast continuity in terms of the class affiliation of their core electorate and receive their staunchest support from large employers, liberal professional groups, and managers (Rennwald 2020).

Another traditional factor that explains (stable) voting behaviour is party identification, a type of psychological party membership that figures as a central variable in social psychological models of voting behaviour (Campbell et al. 1960). Despite some fluctuation over the years, party affiliation has declined in Switzerland since 1971, when about 60 per cent of voters identified with a party, to around 31 per cent in 2019. These findings match the results of the international 'dealignment' literature, which asserts a general decline in the binding power of political parties in Western democracies (e.g. Dalton and Wattenberg 2000; Garzia et al. 2022), especially among the younger generation (Önnudóttir and Harðarson 2020). Nevertheless, party identification continues to be relevant to party choice in Switzerland at least up to the 2011 national elections (Ackermann and Kijewski 2015).

5.3 Issue voting

Issues affect voting behaviour in various ways. The two influential approaches of issue voting are the spatial model of vote choice, advanced by Downs (1957) and which assumes that voters cast their ballot for the party that comes closest to their own preferences on political issues, and issue ownership voting, which postulates that voters prefer the party most competent and attentive on the issue that matters most to them (e.g. Petrocik 1996). Both approaches have attracted attention in Swiss electoral research.

When it comes to voters' preferences on policy issues, the initial assumption was that they play only a subordinate role in Swiss parliamentary elections due to the substitution function of direct democracy (Schloeth 1998), but their central importance soon became apparent (Holzer and Linder 2003; Linder 1998). The influence of issues on party choice has increased over time, but it varies greatly between issues and parties (Kriesi and Sciarini 2004; Nicolet and Sciarini 2006). The competitiveness of elections acts to strengthen issue voting while reducing the impact of party identification (Lachat 2011). Issues related to the new cultural openness–closedness cleavage—questions of foreign policy, in particular Swiss-EU relations, as well as immigration and asylum—now exert a stronger influence on voting behaviour than issues related to the traditional socio-economic divide. Although party constituencies have converged over time in their attitudes to the EU (Bühlmann and Gerber 2015, 89–90), these attitudes strongly predicted the vote for/against the SVP and the SP between 1999 to 2007 (Bochsler and Sciarini 2010; Kriesi and Sciarini 2004; Nicolet and Sciarini 2006), respectively for/against the SVP and the GPS in the 2011 elections (Ackermann and Kijewski 2015). Clearly positioned against international integration, the SVP holds a unique spot in the party system and has managed to win over voters distant in terms of economic preferences but close on cultural issues (Kriesi et al. 2005; Kurella and Rosset 2018; Oesch and Rennwald 2010).

Despite the prevalent influence of the openness–closedness cleavage since the mid-1990s, economic issues still matter for electoral decisions. Traditionally, attitudes towards a higher taxation of top earners have polarized voters between the liberal FDP and the SP on the left. More recently, views on social investment policies (i.e. providing continuing education or childcare) have held more sway on party choices than income redistribution has. Interestingly, both dimensions help differentiate party choice within the left: while support for social investment policies is positively linked to vote choice in favour of the Greens and the SP, preferences for redistribution only matter for voting SP (Fossati and Häusermann 2014).

Swiss researchers have recently applied an issue ownership model of voting. In line with issue ownership theory, studies demonstrate that voters' perceptions of issue-handling competences by parties bear a direct effect on vote choice, and that this effect is generally stronger than voters' perceptions of the associative ownership of parties (Lachat 2014; Lutz and Sciarini 2016). This effect is strongest when voters' ownership perceptions are highly accessible (i.e. when voters can quickly attribute ownership to a given party) and when the issue at stake is considered important (Marquis and Tresch 2022). Competence ownership also serves as a stronger predictor of vote choice when party system fragmentation is high (Lanz 2020). Moreover, voters' perceptions of competence and associative ownership moderate the impact of issue distances between voters and parties on voting decisions (Lachat 2014). If a voter deems a party competent on a particular issue, the general alignment of the voter with the party matters less. Conversely, ideological distance has a stronger influence on the vote if a party is seen as the most committed to dealing with the issue.

5.4 Campaign effects

Research on campaign effects began after the 1999 Swiss election, when panel survey data became available. A study using that year's data showed that 25–40 per cent of voters changed their opinion on various political issues within six months before the elections (Kriesi and Sciarini 2004, 734; Sciarini and Kriesi 2003, 445). The likelihood of opinion change depends on the intensity of the issue-specific information flow as measured by newspaper ads during the campaign, while the direction of this change depends on the direction of political campaign messages. Yet, changes of issue preferences during the campaign had only a limited effect on the vote for changing opinions on EU membership. Hence, the authors conclude that the primary effect of election campaigns is less on shaping policy preferences than on linking existing issue preferences to political parties. However, when the issue-specific information flow during the campaign is very one-sided, significant opinion changes can nevertheless occur (Sciarini and Kriesi 2003). Similarly, Lachat (2003, 2007) shows that the reinforcement and activation of predispositions are the main function of campaigns, while conversion is less frequent though not negligible (see Lazarsfeld et al. 1968). More recent research on the 2011 and 2015 elections suggests a low impact from political advertising in the form of newspaper ads overall. Ad campaigns help reinforce vote intentions, but only when voters already identify strongly with a party and when they are exposed to its election advertising over a long period of time (Gerber and Bühlmann 2014). However, the example of the SVP and FDP campaigns in the 2015 elections shows that not all parties are equally apt in reinforcing vote intentions or activating predispositions: this was only observed for the SVP, which suggests that reinforcement effects may occur mainly in relation to highly contentious issues (Zumofen and Gerber 2018).

Several studies have also shown the effects of election campaigns on the perception of party competence ownership. Issue-specific media coverage contributes to maintaining existing ownership evaluations (Tresch and Feddersen 2019), especially when the issue is salient. However, a high volume of political messages in party ads on a given issue tends to change voters' perceptions of competence ownership (Petitpas 2022, 41–83). This instability of issue ownership perceptions also affects the dynamics of party choice: voters who change their issue ownership perceptions during the campaign are more likely to reconsider their party choice (Lanz and Sciarini 2016; Petitpas and Sciarini 2018). A party that gains 'cumulative' ownership of multiple issues is most likely to benefit from vote switching (Petitpas and Sciarini 2020). Shifts in voters' ownership perceptions can account for the choice between two programmatically close parties like the greens and the SP (Petitpas and Sciarini 2022). Delving deeper, Petitpas (2022, 171–212) observed the entire causal chain and demonstrated that party issue emphasis in electoral ads can prompt voters to change their ownership perceptions and, in turn, their voting behaviour.

Studies have also dealt with the influence of campaigns on the electoral success of individual candidates. Individual campaign spending has been shown to have a clear influence on the number of votes cast for candidates (Lutz 2010a, b). Election advertising can greatly increase the name recognition of individual candidates, which is crucial to electoral success. However, Selb (2003) finds that new candidates are those who benefit most from personal advertising, while the election chances of incumbents is not increased through advertising.

6 Conclusion

Research about Swiss national elections has taken off in recent decades in the wake of substantial shifts in the country's political landscape since the mid-1990s. Like other Western European countries, Switzerland has witnessed the rise of a populist radical right and the growing importance of a new, cultural openness–closedness cleavage, leading to the realignment of traditional voter groups and the strengthening of identity politics. While the relevance of party identification and traditional cleavages has declined, situational factors such as (changing) issue priorities or perceptions of party competence have become critical to electoral decisions. Parties have begun to adapt their campaign organization and techniques accordingly to mobilize traditional voters and attract new ones. Swiss electoral research now faces the task of explaining polarization and change rather than stability, and of analysing the impact of new trends like increasing online news consumption or digitalized campaigning on voters' preferences and behaviour.

Notes

1. http://www.selects.ch (FORS 2022).
2. The basis for the distribution are the party votes per list, which consist of the sum of the votes of all candidates as well as empty lines on designated lists. Seats are distributed first to the list alliances and secondly within list alliances.
3. The proportion of changed lists varies greatly from canton to canton and from list to list. In 2019, for example, only 20 per cent of the lists in the canton of Graubünden were unchanged, whereas 69 per cent were unchanged in the canton of Geneva (Federal Statistical Office 2020).

4. The Landsgemeinde is a gathering of all citizens with the right to vote in a canton, and voting takes place mostly through raising hands.
5. Data from https://www.idea.int/data-tools/data/voter-turnout (International IDEA 2022).
6. See the contribution by Sciarini and Stojanović (2019).
7. https://data.ipu.org/women-averages (IPU Parline 2022).
8. This explanation also holds for the weak representation of the SVP in cantonal governments (e.g. Sciarini 2011, 111–116).

References

Ackermann, Maya, and Sara Kijewski. 2015. 'Themen, Köpfe oder Zuneigung? Wer wählt wen und warum?'. In *Wahlen und Wählerschaft in der Schweiz*, edited by Markus Freitag, and Adrian Vatter, pp. 163–185. Zürich: Verlag Neue Zürcher Zeitung.

Baer, Matthias, and Werner Seitz. 2008. *Die Grünen in der Schweiz*. Zürich: Rüegger Verlag.

Balmas, Meital, Gideon Rahat, Tamir Sheafer, and Shaul R. Shenhav. 2014. 'Two Routes to Personalized Politics: Centralized and Decentralized Personalization'. *Party Politics* 20 (1): pp. 37–51.

Bernhard, Laurent, Nathalie Eggenberg, Anke Tresch, and Lukas Lauener. 2021. 'Wählen Frauen anders als Männer?'. *DeFacto*, 8.2.2021. https://www.defacto.expert/2021/02/08/waehlen-frauen-anders-als-maenner/ (accessed 27 September 2022).

Blais, André. 2014. 'Why is Turnout So Low in Switzerland? Comparing the Attitudes of Swiss and German Citizens Towards Electoral Democracy'. *Swiss Political Science Review* 20 (4): pp. 520–528.

Bochsler, Daniel, and Pascal Sciarini. 2010. 'So Close But So Far. Voting Propensity and Party Choice for Left-Wing Parties'. *Swiss Political Science Review* 16 (3): pp. 373–402.

Bühlmann, Marc, and Marlène Gerber. 2015. 'Von der Unterschichtspartei zur Partei des gehobenen Mittelstands? Stabilität und Wandel der Wählerschaften der Sozialdemokraten und anderer grosser Schweizer Parteien zwischen 1971 und 2011'. In *Wahlen und Wählerschaft in der Schweiz*, edited by Markus Freitag, and Adrian Vatter, pp. 71–94. Zürich: Verlag Neue Zürcher Zeitung.

Bühlmann, Marc, Sarah Nicolet, and Peter Selb. 2006. 'National Elections in Switzerland: An Introduction'. *Swiss Political Science Review* 12 (4): pp. 1–12.

Bühlmann, Marc, David Zumbach, and Marlène Gerber. 2016. 'Campaign Strategies in the 2015 Swiss National Elections: Nationalization, Coordination and Personalization'. *Swiss Political Science Review* 22 (1): pp. 15–28.

Campbell, Angus, Philip E. Converse, Warren E. Miller, and Donald E. Stokes. 1960. *The American Voter*. Chicago and London: University of Chicago Press.

Chiaramonte, Alessandro, and Vincenzo Emanuele. 2017. 'Party System Volatility, Regeneration and De-Institutionalization in Western Europe (1945–2015)'. *Party Politics* 23 (4): pp. 376–388.

Church, Clive H. 1996. 'The Swiss Elections of 1995: Real Victors and Real Losers at Last?'. *West European Politics* 3: pp. 641–648.

Dalmus, Caroline, Regula Hänggli, and Laurent Bernhard. 2017. 'The Charm of Salient Issues? Parties' Strategic Behavior in Press Releases'. In *How Political Actors Use the Media. A Functional Analysis of the Media's Role in Politics*, edited by Peter Van Aelst, and Stefaan Walgrave, pp. 187–205. Cham: Palgrave MacMillan.

Dalton, Russell J., and Martin Wattenberg. 2000. *Parties Without Partisans: Political Change in Advanced Industrial Societies*. Cambridge: Oxford University Press.

Downs, Anthony. 1957. *An Economic Theory of Democracy*. New York: Harper & Brothers.

Elff, Martin. 2007. 'Social Structure and Electoral Behavior in Comparative Perspective: The Decline of Social Cleavages in Western Europe Revisited'. *Perspectives on Politics* 5 (2): pp. 277–294.

Engeli, Isabelle, Thanh-Huyen Ballmer-Cao, and Marco Giugni. 2006. 'Gender Gap and Turnout in the 2003 Federal Elections. National Elections in Switzerland: An Introduction'. *Swiss Political Science Review* 12 (4): pp. 217–242.

Engeli, Isabelle, and Luc Tonka. 2010. 'L'évolution des campagnes électorales en Suisse. Un processus de modernisation en demi-teinte'. In *Le destin électoral de la gauche. Le vote socialiste et vert en Suisse*, edited by Sarah Nicolet, and Pascal Sciarini, pp. 397–437. Genève: Georg.

Farrell, David M., and Paul Webb. 2000. 'Political Parties as Campaign Organizations'. In *Parties without partisans: political change in advanced industrial democracies*, edited by Russell J. Dalton, and Martin P. Wattenberg, pp. 102–128. Oxford: Oxford University Press.

Fatke, Matthias. 2015. 'Participation and Political Equality in Direct Democracy: Educative Effect or Social Bias'. *Swiss Political Science Review* 21 (1): pp. 99–118.

Federal Statistical Office. 2019a. *Nationalratswahlen: Wahlbeteiligung*. https://www.bfs.admin.ch/bfs/de/home/statistiken/politik/wahlen/nationalratswahlen/wahlbeteiligung.assetdetail.11048422.html (accessed 27 September 2022).

Federal Statistical Office. 2019b. *Nationalratswahlen: Stärke der Parteien*. https://www.bfs.admin.ch/bfs/de/home/statistiken/politik/wahlen/nationalratswahlen/parteistaerken.assetdetail.11048421.html (accessed 27 September 2022).

Federal Statistical Office. 2019c. *Ständeratswahlen: Mandatsverteilung nach Parteien* https://www.bfs.admin.ch/bfs/de/home/statistiken/politik/wahlen/staenderatswahlen.assetdetail.11048401.htm (accessed 27 September 2022).

Federal Statistical Office. 2020. *Nationalratswahlen: Typen von Wahlzetteln*. https://www.bfs.admin.ch/bfs/de/home/statistiken/kataloge-datenbanken/tabellen.assetdetail.12047666.html (accessed 9 October 2022).

Federal Statistical Office. 2022. *Entwicklung der Stimmbeteiligung bei eidgenössischen Volksabstimmungen*. https://www.bfs.admin.ch/bfs/de/home/statistiken/politik/abstimmungen/stimmbeteiligung.assetdetail.22866699.html (accessed 27 October 2022).

FORS. 2022. *Selects Swiss Election Study*. http://www.selects.ch (accessed 27 September 2022).

Fossati, Flavia, and Silja Häusermann. 2014. 'Social Policy Preferences and Party Choice in the 2011 Swiss Elections'. *Swiss Political Science Review* 20 (4): pp. 590–611.

Franklin, Mark, Mackie, Thomas, and Henry Valen. 1992. *Electoral Change: Responses to Evolving Social and Attitudinal Structures in Western Countries*. New York: Cambridge University Press.

Gallego, Aina. 2007. 'Unequal Political Participation in Europe'. *International Journal of Sociology* 37 (4): pp. 10–25.

Garzia, Diego, Frederico Ferreira da Silva, and Andrea De Angelis. 2022. 'Partisan Dealignment and the Personalization of Politics in West European Parliamentary Democracies, 1961-2016'. *West European Politics* 45 (2): pp. 311–334.

Gerber, Marlène, and Marc Bühlmann. 2014. 'Do Ads Add Up? The Impact of Parties' Advertisements on the Stability of Vote Choice at the Swiss National Elections 2011'. *Swiss Political Science Review* 20 (4): pp. 632–650.

Giger, Nathalie, Line Rennwald, and Anke Tresch. 2018. 'Introduction to the Special Issue "The 2015 Swiss National Elections"'. *Swiss Political Science Review* 24 (4): pp. 371–380.

Giger, Nathalie, Denise Traber, and Anke Tresch. 2022. 'Introduction to the Special Issue "The 2019 Swiss National Elections"'. *Swiss Political Science Review* 28 (2): pp. 157–168.

Gilardi, Fabrizio, Clau Dermont, Maël Kubli, and Lucien Baumgartner. 2020. *Selects Medienstudie 2020: Der Wahlkampf 2019 in traditionellen und digitalen Medien.* Zurich: Digital Democracy Lab.

Giugni, Marco, and Pascal Sciarini. 2009. 'Polarisation et politisation en Suisse'. In *Rapport social 2008. La Suissse mesurée et comparée*, edited by Christian Suter, Silvia Perrenoud, René Levy, Ursina Kuhn, Dominique Joye, and Pascale Gazareth, pp. 222–243. Zürich: Seismo.

Goldberg, Andreas. 2017. *The Impact of Cleavages on Swiss Voting Behavior: A Modern Research Approach.* Cham: Springer.

Goldberg, Andreas. 2020. 'The Evolution of Cleavage Voting in Four Western Countries: Structural, Behavioural or Political Dealignment?'. *European Journal of Political Research* 59: pp. 68–90.

Hardmeier, Sibylle. 2003. 'Amerikanisierung der Wahlkampfkommunikation? Einem Schlagwort auf der Spur'. In *Schweizer Wahlen 1999 – Elections Fédérales 1999*, edited by Pascal Sciarini, Sibylle Hardmeier, and Adrian Vatter, pp. 219–255. Bern/Stuttgart/Wien: Haupt.

Hermann, Michael. 2012. *Das politische Profil des Geldes.* Zürich: Forschungsstelle sotomo.

Hertig, Hanspeter. 1980. *Analyse der Nationalratswahlen 1979.* Bern: Forschungszentrum für Schweizerische Politik.

Holzer, Thomas, and Wolf Linder. 2003. 'Die Wahlentscheidung im Wechselspiel zwischen Parteiidentifikation und Sachfragenorientierung'. In *Schweizer Wahlen 1999 – Elections Fédérales 1999*, edited by Pascal Sciarini, Sibylle Hardmeier, and Adrian Vatter, pp. 85–122. Bern/Stuttgart/Wien: Haupt.

International IDEA. 2022. *Voter Turnout Database.* https://www.idea.int/data-tools/data/voter-turnout (accessed 27 September 2022).

IPU Parline. 2022. *Global and Regional Averages of Women in National Parliaments.* https://data.ipu.org/women-averages (accessed 27 September 2022).

Klinger, Ulrike, and Uta Russmann. 2017. '"Beer is More Efficient Than Social Media" – Political Parties and Strategic Communication in Austrian and Swiss National Elections'. *Journal of Information Technology & Politics* 14 (4): pp. 299–313.

Kriesi, Hanspeter. 2011. 'Personalization of National Election Campaigns'. *Party Politics* 18 (6): pp. 825–844.

Kriesi, Hanspeter, Edgar Grande, Romain Lachat, Martin Dolezal, Simon Bornschier, and Timotheos Frey. 2006. 'Globalization and the Transformation of the National Political Space: Six European Countries Compared'. *European Journal of Political Research* 45 (6): pp. 921–956.

Kriesi, Hanspeter, Romain Lachat, Peter Selb, Simon Bornschier, and Marc Helbling. 2005. *Der Aufstieg der SVP. Acht Kantone im Vergleich.* Zürich: Verlag Neue Zürcher Zeitung.

Kriesi, Hanspeter, Wolf Linder, and Ulrich Klöti. 1998. *Schweizer Wahlen 1995.* Bern/Stuttgart/Wien: Haupt.

Kriesi, Hanspeter, and Pascal Sciarini. 2004. 'The Impact of Issue Preferences on the Voting Choices in the Swiss Federal Elections 1999'. *British Journal of Political Science* 34 (4): pp. 725–759.

Kurella, Anna-Sophie, and Jan Rosset. 2018. 'The Rise of Cultural Issues as an Opportunity for the Right? Insights from the 2015 Swiss Election'. *Swiss Political Science Review* 24 (4): pp. 381–399.

Lachat, Romain. 2003. 'Formation des intentions de vote: effets de conversion et d'activation'. In *Schweizer Wahlen 1999 – Elections Fédérales 1999*, edited by Pascal Sciarini, Sibylle Hardmeier, and Adrian Vatter, pp. 369–393. Bern/Stuttgart/Wien: Haupt.

Lachat, Romain. 2007. *A Heterogeneous Electorate: Political Sophistication, Predisposition Strength, and the Voting Decision Process*. Baden-Baden: Nomos Verlag.

Lachat, Romain. 2011. 'Electoral Competitiveness and Issue Voting'. *Political Behavior* 33 (4): pp. 645–663.

Lachat, Romain. 2014. 'Issue Ownership and the Vote: The Effect of Associative and Competence Ownership on Issue Voting'. *Swiss Political Science Review* 20 (4): pp. 727–740.

Lanz, Simon. 2020. *No Substitute for Competence. On the Origins and Consequences of Issue Ownership*. London/New York: ECPR Press / Rowman & Littlefield International.

Lanz, Simon, and Pascal Sciarini. 2016. 'The Short-Time Dynamics of Issue Ownership and Its Impact on the Vote'. *Journal of Elections, Public Opinion and Parties* 26 (2): pp. 212–231.

Lazarsfeld, Paul F., Bernard Berelson, and Hazel Gaudet. 1968. *The People's Choice. How the Voter Makes Up His Mind in a Presidential Campaign*. New York: Columbia University Press.

Linder, Wolf. 1998. 'Parteien-, Persönlichkeits-, Europa- oder Traditionswahl? Eine systematische Untersuchung des Einflusses der Sachthemen auf den Wahlentscheid'. In *Schweizer Wahlen 1995*, edited by Hanspeter Kriesi, Wolf Linder, and Ulrich Klöti, pp. 131–160. Bern/Stuttgart/Wien: Haupt.

Lipset, Seymour, and Stein Rokkan. 1967. 'Cleavage Structures, Party Systems, and Voter Alignments: An Introduction'. In *Party Systems and Voter Alignments: Cross-National Perspectives*, edited by Seymour Lipset, and Stein Rokkan, pp. 1–64. New York: The Free Press.

Longchamp, Claude. 1984. *Analyse der Nationalratswahlen 1983*. Bern: Forschungszentrum für Schweizerische Politik.

Longchamp, Claude. 1988. *Analyse der Nationalratswahlen 1987*. Bern: Forschungszentrum für Schweizerische Politik.

Longchamp, Claude, and Sibylle Hardmeier. 1992. *Analyse der Nationalratswahlen 1991*. Bern: Forschungszentrum für Schweizerische Politik.

Longchamp, Claude, and Chloé Jans. 2015. 'Wer zahlt, befiehlt? Über den Einfluss von Geld und Kommunikation in den Wahlkämpfen der Schweiz'. In *Wahlen und Wählerschaft in der Schweiz*, edited by Markus Freitag, and Adrian Vatter, pp. 273–300. Zürich: Verlag Neue Zürcher Zeitung.

Lutz, Georg. 2004. 'Switzerland: Introducing Proportional Representation from Below'. In *Handbook of Electoral System Choice*, edited by Josep Colomer, pp. 279–293. Houndsmills/Basingstoke/Hampshire: Palgrave.

Lutz, Georg. 2010a. 'The Electoral Success of Beauties and Beast'. *Swiss Political Science Review* 16 (3): pp. 457–480.

Lutz, Georg 2010b. 'First Come, First Served: The Effect of Ballot Position on Electoral Success in Open List PR Elections'. *Representation* 46 (2): pp. 167–181.

Lutz, Georg. 2011. 'Open Ballot'. In *Personal Representation: The Neglected Dimension of Electoral Systems*, edited by Josep Colomer, pp. 153–174. Colchester: ECPR Press.

Lutz, Georg, and Dirk Strohmann. 1998. *Wahl- und Abstimmungsrecht in den Kantonen*. Bern: Haupt.

Lutz, Georg, Thomas Milic, and Marco Steenbergen. 2010. 'Introduction: The Swiss National Elections 2007'. *Swiss Political Science Review* 16 (3): pp. 335-341.

Lutz, Georg, and Pascal Sciarini. 2016. 'Issue Competence and its Influence on Voting Behavior in the Swiss 2015 Elections'. *Swiss Political Science Review* 22 (1): pp. 5-14.

Marquis, Lionel, and Anke Tresch. 2022. 'The Accessibility and Electoral Consequences of Issue Competence Perceptions: Evidence from the Swiss 2019 Election'. *Swiss Political Science Review* 28 (2): pp. 254-276.

Mosimann, Nadja, Line Rennwald, and Adrian Zimmermann. 2019. 'The Radical Right, the Labour Movement and the Competition for the Workers' Vote'. *Economic and Industrial Democracy* 40 (1): pp. 65-90.

Nabholz, Ruth. 1998. 'Das Wählerverhalten in der Schweiz: Stabilität oder Wandel?'. In *Schweizer Wahlen 1995*, edited by Hanspeter Kriesi, Wolf Linder, and Ulrich Klöti, pp. 17-43. Bern/Stuttgart/Wien: Haupt.

Nai, Alessandro, Anke Tresch, and Jürgen Maier. 2022. 'Tailored Negativity. Campaign Consultants, Candidate Personality, and Attack Politics'. *Swiss Political Science Review* 28 (2): pp. 338-360.

Nicolet, Sarah, and Pascal Sciarini. 2006. 'When Do Issue Opinions Matter, and to Whom? The Determinants of Long-Term Stability and Change in Party Choice in the 2003 Swiss Elections'. *Swiss Political Science Review* 12 (4): pp. 159-190.

Nicolet, Sarah, and Pascal Sciarini. 2010. 'Introduction'. In *Le destin électoral de la gauche. Le vote socialiste et vert en Suisse*, edited by Sarah Nicolet, and Pascal Sciarini, pp. 9-44. Genève: Georg.

Oesch, Daniel. 2008. 'The Changing Shape of Class Voting: an Individual-Level Analysis of Party Support in Britain, Germany and Switzerland'. *European Societies* 10 (3): pp. 329-355.

Oesch, Daniel, and Line Rennwald. 2010. 'The Class Basis of Switzerland's Cleavage between the New Left and the Populist Right'. *Swiss Political Science Review* 16 (3): pp. 343-372.

Önnudóttir, Eva H., and Ólafur Þ. Harðarson. 2020. 'Party Identification and Its Evolution Over Time'. In *Research Handbook on Political Partisanship*, edited by Henrik Oscarsson, and Sören Holmberg, pp. 167-176. Cheltenham, UK/Northampton, MA, USA. Edward Elgar Publishing.

Petitpas, Adrien. 2022. *Party Competence on Issues*. Geneva: University of Geneva, PhD thesis 172.

Petitpas, Adrien, and Pascal Sciarini. 2018. 'Short-Term Dynamics in Issue Ownership and Electoral Choice Formation'. *Swiss Political Science Review* 24 (4): pp. 423-441.

Petitpas, Adrien, and Pascal Sciarini. 2020. 'The More the Better? Cumulative Issue Ownership and Intra-Campaign Party Switching'. *Electoral Studies* 64 (April 2020, 102118): pp. 1-15.

Petitpas, Adrien, and Pascal Sciarini. 2022. 'Competence Issue Ownership, Issue Positions and the Vote for the Greens and the Social Democrats'. *Swiss Political Science Review* 28 (2): pp. 230-253.

Petrocik, John R. 1996. 'Issue Ownership in Presidential Elections, with a 1980 Case Study'. *American Journal of Political Science* 40 (3): pp. 825-850.

Rennwald, Line. 2020. *Social Democratic Parties and the Working Class. New Voting Patterns*. Cham: Palgrave MacMillan.

Schloeth, Daniel. 1998. *Vor die Wahl gestellt. Die eidgenössischen Wahlen 1995 im Blickwinkel dreier konkurrierender Wahltheorien*. Bern: Haupt.

Sciarini, Pascal. 2011. *La politique suisse au fil du temps*. Genève: Georg.

Sciarini, Pascal, Thanh-Huyen Ballmer-Cao, and Romain Lachat. 2001. 'Genre, Age, et Participation Politique: Les Elections Fédérales de 1995 dans le Canton de Genève'. *Revue Suisse de Science Politique* 7 (3): pp. 83-98.

Sciarini, Pascal, Sibylle Hardmeier, and Adrian Vatter. 2003. *Schweizer Wahlen 1999 – Elections Fédérales 1999*. Bern/Stuttgart/Wien: Haupt.

Sciarini, Pascal, and Hanspeter Kriesi. 2003. 'Opinion Stability and Change During an Electoral Campaign: Results from the 1999 Swiss Election Panel Study'. *International Journal of Public Opinion Research* 15 (4): pp. 431–453.

Sciarini, Pascal, and Nenad Stojanović. 2019. *Die ersten Daten zur Wahlbeteiligung bei den eidgenössischen Wahlen leigen vor. Sie zeichnen kein gutes Bild der Jungen – wären da nicht die Frauen.* https://www.nzz.ch/schweiz/wahlbeteiligung-junge-frauen-auf-dem-vormarsch-ld.1521877 (accessed 14 July 2022).

Selb, Peter. 2003. 'Werbeaufwand und Wahlerfolg. Der Effekt von Inserateausgaben auf Wahlchancen und Stimmengewinn Zürcher Kandidierender für den Nationalrat'. In *Schweizer Wahlen 1999 – Elections Fédérales 1999*, edited by Pascal Sciarini, Sibylle Hardmeier, and Adrian Vatter, pp. 257–285. Bern/Stuttgart/Wien: Haupt.

Selb, Peter, and Romain Lachat. 2004. *Wahlen 2003. Die Entwicklung des Wahlverhaltens.* Zürich: Institut für Politikwissenschaft.

Semetko, Holli A., and Hubert Tworzecki. 2018. 'Campaign Strategies, Media, and Voters. the Fourth Era of Political Communication'. In *The Routledge Handbook of Elections, Voting Behavior and Public Opinion*, edited by Justin Fisher, Edward Fieldhouse, Mark Franklin, Rachel Gibson, Marta Cantijoch, and Christoper Wlezien, pp. 293–304. London: Routledge.

Stückelberger, Simon. 2021. 'Mobilizing and Chasing: The Voter Targeting of Negative Campaigning – Lessons from the Swiss Case'. *Party Politics* 27 (2): pp. 341–350.

Stückelberger, Simon, and Jelle Koedam. 2022. 'Parties' Voter Targeting Strategies: What Can Facebook Ads Tell Us?'. *Electoral Studies* 77 (June 2022, 102473): pp. 1–13.

Taagepera, Rein, and Mathew Soberg Shugart. 1989. *Seats and Votes. The Effects and Determinants of Electoral System*. New Haven/New York: Yale University Press.

Tawfik, Amal, Pascal Sciarini, and Eugène Horber. 2012. 'Putting Voter Turnout in a Longitudinal and Contextual Perspective: an Analysis of Actual Participation Data'. *International Political Science Review* 33 (3): pp. 352–371.

Tresch, Anke, and Alexandra Feddersen. 2019. 'The (In)stability of Voters' Perceptions of Competence and Associative Issue Ownership'. *Political Communication* 36 (3): pp. 394–411.

Tresch, Anke, Lukas Lauener, Laurent Bernhard, Georg Lutz, and Laura Scaperotta. 2020. *Eidgenössische Wahlen 2019. Wahlteilnahme und Wahlentscheid*. Lausanne: FORS.

Vatter, Adrian, and Andreas Ladner. 2020. 'Vom Gesandtenkongress zur gewählten Volkskammer. Der Ständerat im Wandel der Zeit'. In *Der Ständerat. Die Zweite Kammer der Schweiz*, edited by Sean Mueller, and Adrian Vatter, pp. 35–70. Basel: NZZ Libro.

Weinmann, Benjamin. 2009. *Die Amerikanisierung der politischen Kommunikation in der Schweiz. Bestandesaufnahme und Experteninterviews vor dem Hintergrund der Eidgenössischen Parlamentswahlen 2007*. Chur: Rüegger.

Zumofen, Guillaume, and Marlène Gerber. 2018. 'Effects of Issue-Specific Political Advertisements in the 2015 Parliamentary Elections of Switzerland'. *Swiss Political Science Review* 24 (4): pp. 442–463.

CHAPTER 22

DIRECT-DEMOCRATIC VOTES

PASCAL SCIARINI AND ANKE TRESCH

1 INTRODUCTION

DIRECT democracy is a distinctive feature of the Swiss political system. Indeed, over the course of the twentieth century, half of the direct-democratic votes held on the national level worldwide took place in Switzerland (Altman 2011). Two fundamental questions must be asked if we are to understand how direct-democratic institutions work (Morel 2018): (i) which actors are entitled to trigger direct-democratic votes? (ii) what is the role of the political elite in the process?

Depending on the top-down versus bottom-up logic of direct-democratic processes and on the extent of governmental and parliamentary involvement in them, Kriesi (2009) identifies three variants of direct democracy: the 'unmediated' (or 'populist'), the 'mediated', and the 'plebiscitary' variant. In the unmediated variant, direct-democratic votes follow a bottom-up logic that results from citizen-sponsored initiatives: if legal requirements are met, the legislature cannot react to the initiative, which is submitted as it is to a popular vote. This 'direct' type of initiative is widespread in many American states, such as California, where they enable interest groups and social movements to circumvent state parliaments (Lupia and Matsusaka 2004). Moreover, legal restrictions in terms of involvement, support, and spending mean that state governments do not actively engage in initiative campaigns. By contrast, in the plebiscitary variant, only the executive can submit a policy proposal to a referendum. According to this top-down logic, the referendum represents a 'unilateral instrument in the hands of the governing elites' (Kriesi, 2009, 80) who play a leading role in the campaign. As a result, such votes tend to translate into a plebiscite for or against the executive, as is typically the case in France.

Swiss direct democracy belongs to the 'mediated' variant, an intermediary category between the other two 'ideal-types'. When it comes to triggering direct-democratic votes, the Swiss system combines bottom-up and top-down elements. Popular initiatives are bottom-up in nature, while compulsory referendums have a top-down character, and optional referendums mix both features as they relate to legislative proposals adopted by the legislature (top-down), but result in a popular vote if opponents gather the required number of signatures (bottom-up). Where the involvement of elites is concerned, governmental intervention is stronger in Switzerland than in the unmediated variant: in Switzerland, initiatives are of the indirect type and go first to the government and then to the legislature, which takes a stance on the initiative and can respond with a counter-proposal. Then, the government actively campaigns for or against a ballot measure to influence the decision of voters.

In this chapter, we begin by describing the use and outcome of direct-democratic institutions, before providing insights into the proceedings of direct-democratic campaigns and the actors behind them. The third and fourth sections address the two questions crucial to research on direct democracy: who votes and how do citizens form their opinion for or against a ballot proposal? This allows us to provide new answers to old questions regarding for example voters' competence or the role money plays for the outcome of direct-democratic votes.

2 Use and outcome of direct-democratic processes

2.1 Use of direct-democratic institutions

Between 1848 and 2020, 653 popular votes took place at the Swiss federal level. As Table 22.1 shows, the number of popular votes rocketed in the 1970s, with two-thirds of all popular votes occurring in the last five decades. One reason for this increase is the economic downturn of the 1970s (oil crisis and resulting redistributive conflicts). Another lies in the problems that arose in the second half of the last century (welfare state, environment, energy, mobility, technological innovation, etc.) and related activities of (new) social movements. Finally, the internationalization of Swiss politics also contributed to this increase, with a growing number of popular votes focusing on foreign and European policy (Sciarini 2017).

Over the entire period 1848–2020, compulsory referendums account for 37 per cent of the total number of votes, optional referendums for 30 per cent, and popular initiatives for 34 per cent. Between the end of the Second World War and the close of the 1980s, compulsory referendums accounted for almost half of all popular votes. Since then, the share of compulsory referendums has declined in favour of optional referendums and, more heavily, in favour of popular initiatives.

The increasing number of direct-democratic votes is a matter of controversy. For a technocratic view, the high number of ballots overloads the political system and should be combated by raising the 'entry price' of direct democracy, i.e. increasing the number of signatures required to trigger a referendum or initiative (see for example Adler and Rübli 2015). However, a study conducted at the cantonal level invalidates the postulated link between the 'entry price' and the use of direct-democratic

Table 22.1: Frequency of direct-democratic votes, 1848–2020

Period	Total Number of votes	Total Accepted	Total Refused	Compulsory referendum Number of votes	Compulsory referendum Accepted	Compulsory referendum Refused	Optional referendum Number of acts	Optional referendum Number of votes	Optional referendum Accepted	Optional referendum Refused	Popular Initiative Qualified for ballot	Popular Initiative Withdrawn	Popular Initiative Number of votes	Popular Initiative Accepted	Popular Initiative Refused
1848–1873	11	2	9	11	2	9	–	–	–	–	–	–	–	–	–
1874–1880	11	5	6	3	2	1	63	8	3	5	–	–	–	–	–
1881–1890	12	5	7	4	3	1	75	8	2	6	–	–	–	–	–
1891–1900	24	10	14	9	6	3	74	10	3	7	5	0	5	1	4
1901–1910	12	8	4	5	4	1	59	4	3	1	4	1	3	1	2
1911–1920	15	12	3	9	8	1	57	3	2	1	9	0	3	2	1
1921–1930	28	11	17	10	8	2	94	5	1	4	8	1	13	2	11
1931–1940	23	10	13	8	8	0	73	9	2	7	21	5	6	0	6
1941–1950	21	9	12	7	4	3	104	7	4	3	11	8	7	1	6
1951–1960	42	18	24	22	14	8	205	11	4	7	23	12	9	0	9
1961–1970	29	16	13	14	12	2	213	8	4	4	16	8	7	0	7
1971–1980	87	47	40	47	36	11	278	18	11	7	40	9	22	0	22
1981–1990	66	27	39	25	18	7	259	12	6	6	45	16	29	3	26
1991–2000	106	55	51	36	28	8	494	36	25	11	54	10	34	2	32
2001–2010	82	40	42	18	11	7	544	28	23	5	43	13	36	6	30
2011–2020	84	32	52	12	10	2	528	26	18	8	67	12	46	4	42
Total	653	307	346	240	174	66	3'120	193	111	82	346	95	220	22	198

Data source: Swissvotes (2022), Sciarini et al. (2020). Status as of 31 December 2020.

instruments (Barankay et al. 2003): neither the number of signatures nor the time limit for collecting them bears a significant impact on the frequency of popular votes, which are hence presumably determined by other factors, like the size and degree of urbanization of the cantons.

As far as federal popular initiatives are concerned, the main element that contributes to their increase is their frequent use by political parties, and by governing parties in particular (Leemann 2015; Braun Binder et al. 2020). While its original function was to offer a say to minority groups not (or poorly) represented in parliament, the initiative is increasingly used by governing parties not for policy-seeking reasons but as part of a vote-seeking strategy. Furthermore, since the late 1960s, the majority of initiatives have no longer addressed economic or social issues along the classic left–right dimension but have focused on issues relating to the progressive–conservative dimension (e.g. Switzerland's international openness or environmental policy) (Leemann 2015).

2.2 Support to federal authorities

Despite its active involvement in referendum and initiative campaigns, the government evidently does not exercise full control over direct-democratic processes. The outcome of a popular vote is always—at least partly—uncertain (Papadopoulos 1994, 118). It can hence be viewed as an indicator of people's support for the authorities.

Figure 22.1 shows the evolution of the success rate of the Swiss government (and parliament), measured by the proportion of popular votes that resulted in a decision

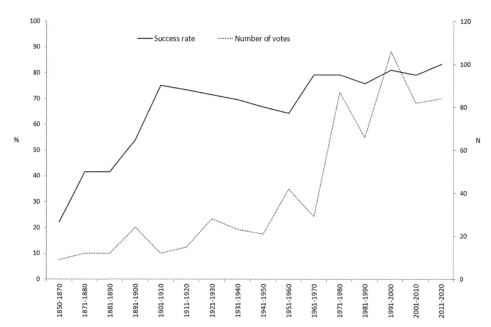

FIGURE 22.1: Success rate of federal authorities and number of direct-democratic votes, 1850–2020

Data source: Swissvotes (2022).

in line with the voting recommendation of the Federal Council. The early days of the federal state saw federal authorities suffer from repeated defeats in popular votes before the tide turned in their favour. Their success rate in direct-democratic votes (only 20 per cent in the first two decades) then rose rapidly to around 70–75 per cent in the first half of the twentieth century. From the 1960s onwards, authorities have been successful in about four out of five ballots, even when the number of popular votes increased significantly (right-hand scale in Figure 22.1). The great convergence of views between the Swiss people and the federal authorities is noteworthy.

Figure 22.2 shows the evolution of the success rate of the authorities since the end of the Second World War for each of the three direct-democratic institutions. The highest figures are for popular initiatives (92 per cent), followed by optional referendums (76 per cent) and mandatory referendums (65 per cent). The success rate of the authorities has increased markedly since the 1970s on matters subjected to optional referendums. Finally, the federal authorities suffered a temporary loss of support in the period 2003–2011 in compulsory referendums and popular initiatives; despite its position as a governing party, the Swiss People's Party succeeded in passing several initiatives that ran counter to the government at the turn of the 2010s (Varone et al. 2014).

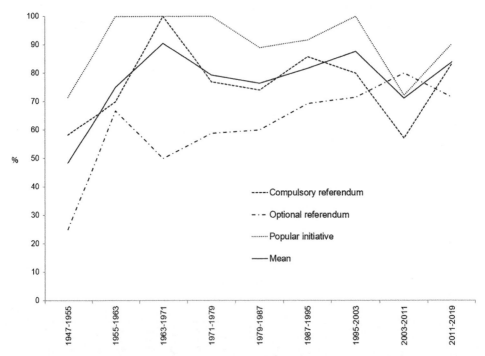

FIGURE 22.2: Success rate of federal authorities by direct-democratic institutions, 1947–2019

Data source: Swissvotes (2022).

3   Campaigns

Prior to the early 2000s, direct-democratic campaigns received scant attention, both in Switzerland and internationally (Bernhard 2012, 3–11). Swiss scholars have since become much more interested in the topic, and efforts have been made to systematically collect data on political actors' advertising campaigns and media campaign reporting in the run-up to federal votes.[1]

3.1   Actors

Although the Federal Council must refrain from any form of propaganda during campaigns and cannot use public funds (von Arx 2002, 207), it nevertheless remains one of the most influential actors in any vote (Kriesi 2009). Federal councillors represent and defend the position of the parliamentary majority in press conferences, at public events, and in the media. Importantly, before each vote, the government publishes a brochure presenting the proposals, as well as the arguments of the authorities and the opponents. This information booklet, sent to each voter, is a critical source of information for the electorate (see Table 22.2).

Political parties engage heavily in campaigns and, depending on their voting recommendations, form 'objective' coalitions in favour or against a proposal. The line-up of coalitions is threefold: left against (moderate and conservative) right, left and moderate right against conservative right, and a grand coalition including all four governing parties. Roughly a third of all federal votes between 1981 and 2007 gave rise to a grand coalition, about 44 per cent were characterized by a left–right conflict, and a minority of about 19 per cent were dominated by a conflict pitching the conservative right against the left and the moderate right (Bernhard and Kriesi 2012, 21). Meanwhile, grand coalitions have become rarer (25 per cent from 2011 to 2019) because of opposition of the Swiss People's Party or the Socialist party (or both).[2] As has been shown, partisan coalitions play a key role in determining the outcome of the vote (Jaquet et al. 2022; Kriesi 2005).

Yet the lack of financial resources means that Swiss parties rely on the financial and logistic support of interest groups to campaign. A wide array of organizations (from employers' organizations and trade unions to religious and environmental groups) become active in the campaign when their core issue is at stake. Ad hoc committees with political parties are formed to coordinate campaign activities.

3.2   Channels and resources

The opposing coalitions make use of two main channels for mobilizing and convincing the public (Bernhard 2012, 27): through the media, by running newspaper advertisements, giving interviews, or attracting news coverage of their activities, or through their own organization, by contacting members and supporters directly (e.g. via direct mailing) or indirectly (e.g. with leaflets and flyers).

On average, data collected between 1990 and 2016 shows that voters used more than five sources of information to make their decision, a number that has remained relatively stable over time, in line with the order of importance of each source (Table 22.2). Given that Swiss law prohibits political advertising on radio and television, the press is of prime importance to campaigners, and is by far the most important source of information for citizens: 84 per cent read newspaper articles to form their views on an upcoming vote, while almost half consult letters to the editor and newspaper ads. Radio and television are also frequently consulted, as is the Federal Council's official information booklet, while the information disseminated by campaign organizations is less used. Since the 2000s, the importance of digital and social media has increased. Yet far from replacing the traditional media, the internet and social media (Facebook and Twitter) have become a complementary source of information for about a quarter of the voters, according to VOTO surveys (not reported here). Some newer, movement-like organizations, like Operation Libero, launched in 2014 to promote an open-minded, multicultural, and forward-looking Switzerland, have seized on these platforms to create digital communication campaigns and also engage in crowdsourcing and crowdfunding activities.[3]

Table 22.2: Voters' sources of information (in per cent)

	1990-2016	1990-1999	2000-2009	2010-2016
Newspaper articles	83.6	84.6	84.6	81.9
TV	73.8	75.1	74.3	72.2
Official information booklet	70.6	66.2	71.1	73.7
Radio	58.2	60.2	58.4	56.4
Readers' letters to the editor	49.1	46.4	53.9	46.5
Newspaper advertising	46.7	45.2	49.4	45.2
Leaflets, brochures, etc.	43.8	38.6	45.6	46.4
Campaign posters in the street	37.2	27.3	41.5	40.8
Opinion polls	36.5	-	37.6	35.7
Direct mailing	19.8	16.2	22.5	19.7
Information on the internet	16.6	3.0	10.8	25.0
Information at work	14.7	18.9	14.1	12.5
Information stands	9.1	8.5	9.9	8.8

Data source: VoxIt (1990-2016)

Some of these campaign channels, like newspaper ads and campaign posters, can only be used by financially strong players (Bernhard 2012, 88), which may explain why a limited number of advertisements are sponsored by political parties (Marquis 2006, 426) that have little funds to spare. Until recently, campaign finance regulations were absent in Switzerland (at least at the federal level[4]). Thus, it is difficult to obtain precise figures on campaign spending. However, the estimated costs of newspaper advertisements and campaign posters suggest a great asymmetry in favour of the political right, with the Swiss People's Party and the peak organization of the employers' associations (*economiesuisse*) being the actors with the greatest financial capacity. Overall, between 2005 and 2011, campaign spending for newspaper ads and street posters reached an estimated average of CHF 2.9 million per voting proposal, with large variations between proposals depending on the expected closeness of the vote; the ten most expensive campaigns alone accounted for 69 per cent of total expenditures, with the SVP outspending the other governing parties by a factor of four (FDP) to nine (SP, CVP) (Hermann and Nowak 2012). Between 2013 and 2018, spending on newspaper ads and street posters were smaller (1.4 million per ballot proposal, on average), presumably because campaigners turned to other media like the internet or social networks.

3.3 Flux and resonance of campaign messages

Advertisements are used by researchers to estimate campaign spending but also provide a measure of the intensity and direction of a campaign. Campaign intensity, as measured by the number and surface of newspaper ads for or against a proposal, generally increases when political actors expect a close vote, when the issue at stake is highly controversial, and when opposition comes from the conservative right (Kriesi 2005), with variation between policy areas (Nai 2014). Campaigns have become longer and more constant, with advertisements distributed evenly throughout the weeks before a popular vote (Marquis and Bergman 2009; Nai 2014). Yes and No campaigns run largely in parallel, although opposition campaigns tend to start earlier (Marquis 2006), and both camps generally focus on a limited number of arguments to promote their positions (e.g. Hänggli et al. 2012; Tresch 2008).

Of all the phases of the policymaking process, the voting campaign phase is the one that attracts most media attention (Tresch et al. 2013), especially when campaign intensity is high and advertising expenditures increase (Udris et al. 2016). Although newspapers often position themselves openly for or against a proposal (Gerth et al. 2012), a study of twenty-four social policy votes between 1995 and 2004 shows that campaign coverage is fairly balanced and neutral (Marquis et al. 2011), with the arguments of political actors faithfully reflected (Hänggli 2012). MPs and the federal councillor in charge of the issue at stake generally receive the greatest media coverage (Gerth et al. 2012; Hänggli 2012), but direct-democratic campaigns also allow weaker actors (including minor parties) to access the media and speak to audiences that far exceed their usual reach (Höglinger 2008; Tresch 2008).

4 Participation

Switzerland is known to have low electoral turnout when compared with other countries (Franklin 2004, 94). This is also true of participation in federal votes: between the end of the Second World War and the end of the 1970s, the increase in the number of direct-democratic votes described above went hand in hand with a steady decline in the turnout rate (from an average of 60 per cent to 40 per cent per legislature). The average turnout has since stabilized at around 45 per cent on average, with large variations across votes.[5] However, the notion of Switzerland as a low-turnout country needs to be qualified. If one takes a dynamic perspective and looks at 'cumulative' participation (Serdült 2013), for example over ten successive federal votes, it turns out that only 20 per cent of the electorate never vote (Heidelberger 2018; Sciarini et al. 2016).[6] Less than 20 per cent always vote, while the remaining 60 per cent participate in one to nine federal votes. The latter category is hence made up of 'selective' or 'occasional' voters who alternate between participation and abstention, depending on factors like the importance of the ballot proposal or their interest in them.

Thus, in contrast to the binary categorization of the 'habitual voting' theory, which divides citizens into voters and abstainers (e.g. Aldrich et al. 2011), Swiss studies have highlighted the relevance of the threefold categorization of citizens in abstentionists, selective voters, and permanent voters (Dermont 2016; Sciarini et al. 2016). While selective or occasional voters are very heterogeneous in socio-demographic terms, their political attitudes in terms of political interest, ideology, or political competence resemble those of abstainers (Sciarini et al. 2016). If selective voters participate at least occasionally, it is therefore because of the characteristics of the issue to be voted on and the related political campaign. Selective voters are particularly sensitive to the intensity of the referendum campaign (Goldberg et al. 2019): the more intense the campaign, the greater the likelihood that selective voters will participate.

4.1 Determinants of participation

Studies that consider individual and contextual factors show that both influence participation in direct-democratic votes, although individual factors have stronger effects (Goldberg and Sciarini 2021; Kriesi 2005). At the individual level, participation increases with age, political interest, education, 'political competence', and, most importantly, with previous frequency of participation. The disappearance of the 'gender gap' in terms of participation in federal votes is another notable element, with women partaking as much as men.

At the contextual level, institutional factors should be mentioned first. The most obvious of which is compulsory voting, which subsists in only one Swiss canton (Schaffhausen). The introduction of simplified postal voting has increased turnout in

Swiss cantons by 3 to 4 percentage points (Luechinger et al. 2007), but e-voting has not yielded the same beneficial effects (Germann and Serdült 2017). While e-voting does not have measurable effects on aggregate turnout, it nevertheless stimulates participation among citizens who usually abstain or rarely vote (Petitpas et al. 2021).

The intensity of the referendum campaign and familiarity of the ballot proposal both increase turnout and a substitution effect exists between the two: the influence of campaign intensity on turnout is low when the issue is very familiar; conversely, campaign intensity can compensate for the demobilizing effects of an unfamiliar proposal (Kriesi 2005). Turnout is also influenced (negatively) by the degree of negativity of the political campaign (Nai 2012) and (positively) by the expected closeness of the outcome (Strijbis et al. 2016).

4.2 Political competence and participation

In direct democracies, citizens enjoy important co-decision rights over legislation. Questions about voter competence are therefore especially important and have been the subject of intense debate. Widespread is the view that ordinary citizens do not possess the required qualifications to make a reasonable choice, which leads to either random or manipulated decisions—a criticism voiced by contemporary scholars (Sartori 1973) but which is as old as democratic thought itself.

In Switzerland, factual knowledge questions asked in survey polls help evaluate voters' level of political competence. However, it is extremely difficult to provide a conclusive answer as to the extent of voters' competence, since results depend heavily on the criteria used (Bütschi 1993; Gruner and Hertig 1983; Kriesi 2005; Sciarini and Tresch 2009). For example, according to Kriesi's (2005) measure, 30 per cent of Swiss voters are not competent, 18 per cent are mildly so, and up to 40 per cent are. These results are, however, based on weak criteria. A more promising research strategy is to investigate the conditions under which citizens are competent. At the individual level, interest in politics, age, and level of education emerge as key factors (Colombo 2018; Kriesi 2005). At the contextual level, the characteristics of the ballot measure and the related campaign play a crucial role (Bernhard 2018; Colombo 2018; Kriesi 2005): the level of competence decreases with the complexity of the ballot proposal and increases with campaign intensity. Competence is also lower when the ballot measure is highly polarising, probably because polarization undermines debate quality and blurs messages.

Citizens' competence, in turn, has a strong influence on the propensity to vote, with weakly competent people prone to abstain. This form of self-censorship reduces the risk of arbitrary voting but raises that of the inequality of participation and therefore of the legitimacy of decisions. However, the (very) small proportion of permanent abstainers and the (very) large proportion of occasional voters highlighted above means abstainers are not always the same, thereby reducing the risk that the opinions of a segment of the population are systematically neglected.

Low turnout does not seem to be consequential for the outcome of direct-democratic votes (Lutz 2007). First, according to post-referendum surveys, a decision varies less between voters and non-voters than between weakly competent and highly competent voters. Secondly, less competent voters tend to favour positions of right-wing parties, but low turnout tends to favour the left. Ultimately, it is difficult to anticipate which camp would benefit from an increase in turnout, as the expected positive effect for the right could be counterbalanced by the parallel increase in overall competence benefiting the left.

In short, if one considers the frequency of votes, turnout in Switzerland is not that low; only a small minority of citizens systematically stay away from the ballot box. Moreover, selective participation both reduces the risk of unequal participation and limits the risk of arbitrary voting. Finally, the importance of the campaign intensity and issue complexity means that elites can influence the level of participation. On the one hand, by actively engaging in voting campaigns, they can increase the amount of information delivered to voters. This, in turn, facilitates voters' decision-making and encourages participation. On the other hand, elites can also help prevent abstention by making complex proposals intelligible to the electorate.

5 Voting decision

Decisions at the ballot are the result of a complex set of factors and have rightly been the subject of increased research interest in Switzerland over the last few decades (Sciarini 2018). Whereas earlier work sought to identify the impact of social cleavages at the aggregate and individual levels, recent studies are concerned with the circumstances under which voters make 'reasoned' or 'correct' choices, and with the influence of the campaign on opinion formation.

5.1 The role of cleavages

Since seminal work by Lipset and Rokkan (1967) in the late 1960s, the study of social cleavages has become a classical paradigm of electoral and voting research. This line of enquiry thrived in Switzerland in the 1970s and 1980s, with renewed interest in the last few decades when researchers used voting outcomes at the regional, district, or communal level to identify entrenched conflict dimensions (e.g. Gilg 1987; Nef 1980), the components of the ideological space (Hermann and Leuthold 2003), or the long-term evolution of traditional cleavages (Linder et al. 2008). The so-called VOX surveys carried out after each federal vote enabled researchers to examine the impact of cleavages on the voting decision at the individual level. Sardi and Widmer (1993) found that traditional cleavages such as class, religion, language, or gender had only a minimal impact on voting behaviour. Importantly, their study was the first to identify an openness–closure cleavage in votes related to labour issues, foreigners, and the army, which serve to form a collective representation of 'Swissness' (see also Christin et al. 2002a). This cleavage often manifests itself in conjunction with linguistic or urban–rural cleavages (Kriesi et al. 1996), with voters from the German-speaking countryside defending the presumed national way of life and voters from French-speaking cities tending towards a more cosmopolitan view. This cleavage is akin to what international scholars have called a 'transnational cleavage', as expressed in the Brexit referendum (Hooghe and Marks 2018).

5.2 Opinion formation

Zaller's (1992) model of opinion formation has often been applied to Swiss direct-democratic votes. The reception of elite communication here depends on a citizen's level of political competence (or 'awareness', Zaller 1992, 42): a person's attentiveness to and knowledge of politics increases his/her likelihood of exposure to a given political message and subsequent understanding of it. Additionally, political predispositions and political competence jointly regulate the acceptance of the information a person receives (Zaller 1992, 44): more competent citizens are more exposed to elite messages, but are also better equipped to assess and select them according to their political predispositions. Zaller (1992) further argues that the reception and acceptance mechanisms operate differently depending on the degree of conflict among the political elite, i.e. depending on whether there is a consensus ('mainstream effect') or a conflict ('polarization effect') (Zaller 1992, 98–102).

Swiss studies provide consistent support for Zaller's model (Bützer and Marquis 2002; Kriesi 2005; Marquis 2006; Marquis and Sciarini 1999; Sciarini et al. 2007; Sciarini and Tresch 2011).[7] For example, our 2011 study of twenty-five direct-democratic votes in foreign, European, and immigration policy confirms that when elites are united, support for government proposals increases with political competence among followers of all parties. Conversely, when parties are divided, the polarization effect kicks in depending on the specific line-up of partisan coalition for or against a ballot proposal.

Other studies rely on panel survey data to study the dynamics of opinion formation in direct-democratic votes. In line with Lazarsfeld et al.'s (1944) claim that campaigns mostly help activate and reinforce predispositions, these studies find that voting intentions converge on pre-campaign partisan orientations over the course of the campaign (Kriesi 2012; Selb et al. 2009). Moreover, ambivalent voters whose initial voting intentions run counter to their partisan predispositions resolve such conflicts in favour of the latter (Selb et al. 2009).

5.3 Heuristics and systematic strategies

An aspect of direct democracy heavily researched internationally relates to whether voters make decisions based on a systematic treatment of information or on heuristics (Lupia 1994). In Switzerland, Kriesi's (2005) study of survey data covering 148 direct-democratic votes between 1981 and 1999 provides evidence on the prevalence of systematic decision-making based on the arguments delivered by elites versus simplifying strategies based on cognitive shortcuts. The study distinguishes four types of heuristics. Abstaining or voting for the status quo, the two simplest ones, are most prevalent among less competent voters (Kriesi 2005; see also Christin et al. 2002b). The two others consist in voting according to trust in the government or voting following the recommendation made by the political party the voter feels closest to. These last two strategies are the most common and they allow voters to make reasonable choices. Yet the study argues that systematic decision-making outweighs heuristics, especially when the campaign is intense and the ballot proposal highly familiar. Nonetheless, these results should be taken with caution as systematic decision-making is difficult to grasp methodologically.

Similarly, measuring the partisan heuristic is challenging and often only possible indirectly. For instance, Kriesi (2005) assumes that a voter who identifies with a party and casts a vote in line with their party's recommendation is actually following the recommendation, although in reality the voter could simply be unaware of the party position. Milic (2020) uses a more direct measure of heuristic voting based on an open-ended survey question which asked voters about the reasons behind their decisions. Voters who explicitly stated they had (exclusively) followed a party's recommendation were considered to have applied the partisan heuristic. In the twenty-one votes at the federal level between September 2016 and November 2018, on average only about 8 per cent of voters exclusively relied on party cues. This figure varies considerably across proposals, but most markedly across voters, with the most motivated and competent relying less on the partisan heuristic. Yet it is very likely that a higher proportion of voters follow the recommendation of their preferred party as a decision-making criterion without making mention of it.

In addition to issues around measurement, another difficulty lies in the fact that party cues can affect the processing of arguments through motivated reasoning. Colombo and Kriesi (2017) show that citizens' vote intentions are determined both by their evaluation of the campaigns' main arguments and party cues. However, over the course of the campaign, voters tend to align their evaluation of the arguments with their preferred party's vote recommendation. In other words, voters process information in a biased way, preferring arguments consistent with their party preference. This finding suggests that voters do not *either* follow cues *or* develop views on arguments; both decision-making modes work in parallel and interact with each other. To better disentangle how party cues and policy information interact, Dermont and Stadelmann-Steffen (2019) relied on a multifactorial survey experiment: based on a vote on energy legislation in 2017, they found that policy information does not fundamentally change voters' policy preferences, unless a certain aspect of the legislation is intensively discussed during the campaign and raises controversy.

5.4 Correct voting and the role of money

A corollary issue is whether voters make 'correct' choices, that is, decisions that reflect their argument-based opinions or political values. Although current studies use slightly different definitions, terminology, measures, and time spans to assess the extent of correct voting in Swiss direct-democratic ballots, they all reach similar conclusions: around 70–75 per cent of voters cast a correct vote (Lanz and Nai 2015; Lauener 2020; Milic 2012; Milic et al. 2014; Nai 2015). However, considerable variation exists across votes and between individuals. On the individual level, voter competence is the most powerful determinant of correct voting (Milic 2012), although Lanz and Nai (2015) find its effect is limited to voters who rejected the ballot proposal. In addition, voters with a higher level of education, a stronger interest in politics, and a party identification are unsurprisingly more likely to cast a vote in line with their underlying political values (Lauener 2020). On the contextual level, intense campaigns are more likely to lead to correct voting, while negative and complex ones have a dampening effect, especially in the case of popular initiatives (Lanz and Nai 2015).

Campaign spending is yet another controversial issue. The question of whether money can 'buy' votes, thereby inhibiting the ability to make decisions consistent with underlying interests and values, has long been a research concern (Lupia and Matsusaka 2004). In an early Swiss study, Hertig (1982) found a statistical correlation between the money spent on campaign propaganda and success in federal votes between 1977 and 1981. Yet studies with more sophisticated methodologies have later arrived at more nuanced conclusions. The most complete and recent analysis was conducted by Jaquet et al. (2022) between 1981 and 2019 (with a disaggregated analysis at the cantonal level for the years 2013–2019). It shows that both government and opposition spending have a statistically significant but small effect on the outcome of the vote, although the effect is usually smaller for the camp in line with the government's position. Importantly, the study highlights the crucial role of the size of the party coalition that rallies behind the government's position: if this coalition is large, the government's camp can influence the outcome of the vote to a large extent and diminish the effect of advertising expenditures. The importance of party coalitions for the outcome of the vote relativizes the idea that a vote can be bought, but it does not rule out the possibility that campaign spending can be decisive when a vote is tight.

In sum, despite methodological limitations, research draws a rather optimistic picture regarding the quality of direct-democratic decision-making in Switzerland: money and propaganda have limited effects on the outcome of the votes, systematic processing of the arguments delivered during the campaign is widespread, and the level of correct voting is relatively high (although probably overestimated). Nevertheless, it must be noted that voters tend to disregard the arguments of parties they dislike, a fact that somewhat qualifies the optimistic view that Swiss citizens weigh up arguments from both sides before casting their votes.

6 Conclusion

In the Swiss 'laboratory' (Kriesi 2005), studies on opinion formation and voting behaviour in direct-democratic votes have flourished in recent decades. At the individual level, studies show that decision-making based on information shortcuts coexists with more systematic strategies that stem from voters reflecting about the messages they receive during campaigns. However, it remains to be clarified whether and under what conditions the latter take precedence over the former or vice versa. Similarly, more work is needed to identify how and to what extent individual and contextual factors interact and influence voters' choice. Finally, open questions subsist as to the dynamics of opinion formation during voting campaigns. Hence, we still know little about the relative importance of party cues and policy-related arguments on information processing, how strong is the partisan-biased processing of policy arguments, and how this in turn influences the stability and change of vote intentions.

Notes

1. Since 2013, the Année Politique Suisse at the University of Bern systematically collects advertising data (https://anneepolitique.swiss/pages/campaign_research). The Research Center for the Public Sphere and Society at the University of Zurich launched a media campaign reporting monitor that same year. (https://www.foeg.uzh.ch/de/forschung/Projekte/Abstimmungsmonitor.html)
2. See 'Decision-Making Process' in this volume.
3. See 'Parties and Party Systems in Switzerland' in this volume.
4. Under the pressure from a popular initiative, the Swiss parliament adopted new transparency rules in June 2021, which came into force in autumn 2022 (see also 'Parties and Party Systems in Switzerland' in this volume).
5. Turnout reached 78 per cent in a vote on 6 December 1992 on Switzerland's accession to the European Economic Area, but it barely exceeded 25 per cent in the vote of 21 May 2006 on the new constitutional article on education.
6. If the analysis is extended to thirty successive votes, the share of chronic abstainers falls to less than 10 per cent; the same applies to the share of permanent voters (Sciarini et al. 2016). Note that these results are based on official turnout data, i.e. not on survey data. Remember further that in Switzerland citizens vote in both elections and direct-democratic votes, and this at the three levels of government (federal, cantonal, and communal).
7. While accepting the basic premise of the model, some scholars criticize its cognitive bias and argue that political predispositions do have a direct impact on political attitudes (Milic et al. 2014; Sciarini et al. 2007; Sciarini and Tresch 2011).

References

Adler, Tibère, and Lukas Rübli. 2015. *L'initiative populaire: Réformer l'indispensable trublion de la politique suisse*. Zurich: Avenir Suisse.

Aldrich, John H., Jacob M. Montgomery, and Wendy Wood. 2011. 'Turnout as Habit'. *Political Behavior* 33 (4): pp. 535–563.

Altman, David. 2011. *Direct Democracy Worldwide*. Cambridge: Cambridge University Press.

Barankay, Yvan, Pascal Sciarini, and Alexander H. Trechsel. 2003. 'Institutional Openness and the Use of Referendums and Popular Initiatives: Evidence from Swiss Cantons'. *Swiss Political Science Review* 9 (1): pp. 169–199.

Bernhard, Laurent. 2012. *Campaign Strategy in Direct Democracy*. Hampshire: Palgrave Macmillan.

Bernhard, Laurent. 2018. 'What Prevents Knowledge Inequalities Among Citizens from Increasing? Evidence from Direct-Democratic Campaigns in Switzerland'. *Studies in Communication Sciences* 18 (1): pp. 103–116.

Bernhard, Laurent, and Hanspeter Kriesi. 2012. 'Coalition Formation'. In *Political Communication in Direct Democratic Campaigns. Enlightening or Manipulating?*, edited by Hanspeter Kriesi, pp. 54–68. Basingstoke/New York: Palgrave Macmillan.

Braun Binder, Nadja, Thomas Milic, and Philippe E. Rochat. 2020. *Volksinitiative als (ausser-)parlamentarisches Instrument. Eine Untersuchung der Parlamentsmitglieder in Initiativkomitees und der Trägerschaft von Volksinitiativen*. Zürich: Schulthess Verlag.

Bütschi, Danièle. 1993. 'Compétence pratique'. In *Citoyenneté et démocratie directe. Compétence, participation et décision des citoyens et citoyennes suisses*, edited by Hanspeter Kriesi, pp. 99–119. Zürich: Seismo.

Bützer, Michael, and Lionel Marquis. 2002. 'Public Opinion Formation in Swiss Federal Referendums'. In *Do Political Campaigns Matter? Campaign Effects in Elections and Referendums*, edited by David Farrell, and Rüdiger Schmitt-Beck, pp. 163–182. London and New York: Routledge.

Christin, Thomas, Simon Hug, and Pascal Sciarini. 2002a. 'La mobilisation des clivages lors des votations populaires'. In *Changements de valeurs et nouveaux clivage politiques en Suisse*, edited by Simon Hug, and Pascal Sciarini, pp. 237–267. Paris: L'Harmattan.

Christin, Thomas, Simon Hug, and Pascal Sciarini. 2002b. 'Interests and Information in Referendum Voting. An Analysis of Swiss Voters'. *European Journal of Political Research* 41 (6): pp. 759–776.

Colombo, Céline. 2018. 'Justifications and Citizen Competence in Direct Democracy: A Multilevel Analysis'. *British Journal of Political Science* 48 (3): pp. 787–806.

Colombo, Céline, and Hanspeter Kriesi. 2017. 'Party, Policy – or Both? Partisan-Biased Processing of Policy Arguments in Direct Democracy'. *Journal of Elections, Public Opinion and Parties* 27 (3): pp. 235–253.

Dermont, Clau. 2016. 'Taking Turns at the Ballot Box: Selective Participation as a New Perspective on Low Turnout'. *Swiss Political Science Review* 22 (2): pp. 213–231.

Dermont, Clau, and Isabelle Stadelmann-Steffen. 2019. 'The Role of Policy and Party Information in Direct-Democratic Campaigns'. *International Journal of Public Opinion Research* 32 (3): pp. 442–466.

Franklin, Mark N. 2004. *Voter Turnout and the Dynamics of Electoral Competition in Established Democracies since 1945*. Cambridge: Cambridge University Press.

Germann, Micha, and Uwe Serdült. 2017. 'Internet Voting and Turnout: Evidence from Switzerland'. *Electoral Studies* 47: pp. 1–12.

Gerth, Matthias A., Dahinden, Urs, and Gabriele Siegert. 2012. 'Coverage of the Campaigns in the Media'. In *Political Communication in Direct Democratic Campaigns. Enlightening or Manipulating?*, edited by Hanspeter Kriesi, pp. 108–124. Basingstoke/New York: Palgrave Macmillan.

Gilg, Peter. 1987. 'Stabilität und Wandel im Spiegel des regionalen Abstimmungsverhaltens'. *Annuaire suisse de science politique* 27: pp. 121–158.

Goldberg, Andreas C., Lanz, Simon, and Pascal Sciarini. 2019. 'Mobilizing Different Types of Voters: The Influence of Campaigns in Direct Democratic Votes'. *Electoral Studies* 57, pp. 196-222.

Goldberg, Andreas C., and Pascal Sciarini. 2021. 'Voter Turnout in Direct Democracy: A Joint Analysis of Individual, Referendum and Community Factors'. *European Journal of Political Research* (early view). doi: 10.1111/1475-6765.12493.

Gruner, Erich, and Hans Peter Hertig. 1983. *Der Stimmbürger und die 'neue' Politik. Le citoyen et la 'nouvelle' politique*. Bern: Haupt.

Hänggli, Regula. 2012. 'Key Factors in Frame Building'. *American Behavioral Scientist* 56 (3): pp. 300–317.

Hänggli, Regula, Laurent Bernhard, and Hanspeter Kriesi. 2012. 'Construction of the Frames'. In *Political Communication in Direct Democratic Campaigns. Enlightening or Manipulating?*, edited by Hanspeter Kriesi, pp. 69–81. Basingstoke/New York: Palgrave Macmillan.

Heidelberger, Anja. 2018. *Die Abstimmungsbeteiligung in der Schweiz. Psychologische und soziale Einflüsse auf die Abstimmungsneigung*. Baden-Baden: Nomos Verlag.

Hermann, Michael, and Heiri Leuthold. 2003. *Atlas der politischen Landschaften. Ein weltanschauliches Porträt der Schweiz*. Zürich: vdf Hochschulverlag AG.

Hermann, Michael, and Mario Nowak. 2012. *Das politische Profil des Geldes. Wahl- und Abstimmungswerbung in der Schweiz*. Zürich: Forschungsstelle Sotomo.

Hertig, Hans Peter. 1982. 'Sind Abstimmungserfolge käuflich? Elemente der Meinungsbildung bei eidgenössischen Abstimmungen'. *Schweizerisches Jahrbuch für Politische Wissenschaft* 22: pp. 35–57.

Höglinger, Dominic. 2008. 'Verschafft die direkte Demokratie den Benachteiligten mehr Gehör? Der Einfluss institutioneller Rahmenbedingungen auf die mediale Präsenz politischer Akteure'. *Schweizerische Zeitschrift für Politikwissenschaft* 14 (2): pp. 207–243.

Hooghe, Liesbet, and Gary Marks. 2018. 'Cleavage Theory Meets Europe's Crises: Lipset, Rokkan, and the Transnational Cleavage'. *Journal of European Public Policy* 25 (1): pp. 109–135.

Jaquet, Julien M., Pascal Sciarini, and Roy Gava. 2022. 'Can't Buy Me Votes? Campaign Spending and the Outcome of Direct Democratic Votes'. *West European Politics* 45 (2): pp. 335–359.

Kriesi, Hanspeter. 2005. *Direct Democratic Choice. The Swiss Experience*. Lanham: Lexington Books.

Kriesi, Hanspeter. 2009. 'The Role of the Federal Government in Direct-Democratic Campaigns'. In *Rediscovering Public Law and Public Administration in Comparative Policy Analysis: a Tribute to Peter Knoepfel*, edited by Stéphane Nahrath, and Frédéric Varone, pp. 79–96. Bern: Haupt.

Kriesi, Hanspeter. 2012. 'The Role of Predispositions'. In *Political Communication in Direct Democratic Campaigns. Enlightening or Manipulating?*, edited by Hanspeter Kriesi, pp. 143–167. Basingstoke/New York: Palgrave Macmillan.

Kriesi, Hanspeter, Boris Wernli, Pascal Sciarini, and Matteo Gianni. 1996. *Le clivage linguistique. Problèmes de compréhension entre les communautés linguistiques en Suisse*. Bern: Bundesamt für Statistik.

Lanz, Simon, and Alessandro Nai. 2015. 'Vote as you Think: Determinants of Consistent Decision Making in Direct Democracy'. *Swiss Political Science Review* 21 (1): pp. 119–139.

Lauener, Lukas. 2020. 'Why do Citizens Vote Against Their Basic Political Values?' *Swiss Political Science Review* 26 (2): pp. 153–180.

Lazarsfeld, Paul F., Bernard Berelson, and Hazel Gaudet. 1944. *The People's Choice*. New York: Columbia University Press.

Leemann, Lucas. 2015. 'Political Conflict and Direct Democracy: Explaining Initiative Use 1920–2011'. *Swiss Political Science Review* 21 (12): pp. 596–616.

Linder, Wolf, Regula Zürcher, and Christian Bolliger. 2008. *Gespaltene Schweiz – geeinte Schweiz. Gesellschaftliche Spaltungen und Konkordanz bei den Volksabstimmungen seit 1874*. Baden: hier + jetzt.

Lipset, Seymour M., and Stein Rokkan. 1967. 'Cleavage Structures, Party Systems, and Voter Alignments: an Introduction'. In *Party Systems and Voter Alignments*, edited by Seymour M. Lipset and Stein Rokkan, pp. 1–64. New York: The Free Press.

Luechinger, Simon, Myra Rosinger, and Alois Stutzer. 2007. 'The Impact of Postal Voting on Participation. Evidence for Switzerland'. *Swiss Political Science Review* 13 (2): pp. 167–202.

Lupia, Arthur. 1994. 'Shortcuts Versus Encyclopedias: Information and Voting Behavior in California Insurance Reform Elections'. *American Political Science Review* 88 (1): pp. 63–76.

Lupia, Arthur, and Matsusaka, John G. 2004. 'Direct Democracy: New Approaches to Old Questions'. *Annual Review of Political Science* 7: pp. 463–482.

Lutz, Georg. 2007. 'Low Turnout in Direct Democracy'. *Electoral Studies* 26 (3): pp. 624–632.

Marquis, Lionel. 2006. *La formation de l'opinion publique en démocratie directe. Les référendums sur la politique extérieure suisse 1981–1995*. Zurich: Seismo.

Marquis, Lionel, and Manfred Max Bergman. 2009. 'Development and Consequences of Referendum Campaigns in Switzerland', 1981–1999. *Swiss Political Science Review* 15 (1): pp. 63–97.

Marquis, Lionel, Hans-Peter Schaub, and Marlène Gerber. 2011. 'The Fairness of Media Coverage in Question: An Analysis of Referendum Campaigns on Welfare State Issues in Switzerland'. *Swiss Political Science Review* 17 (2): pp. 128–163.

Marquis, Lionel, and Pascal Sciarini. 1999. 'Opinion Formation in Foreign Policy: The Swiss Experience'. *Electoral Studies* 18 (4): pp. 453–471.

Milic, Thomas. 2012. 'Correct Voting in Direct Legislation'. *Swiss Political Science Review* 18 (4): pp. 399–427.

Milic, Thomas. 2020. 'The Use of the Endorsement Heuristic on Swiss Popular Votes'. *Swiss Political Science Review* 26 (3): pp. 296–315.

Milic, Thomas, Bianca Rousselot, and Adrian Vatter. 2014. *Handbuch der Abstimmungsforschung*. Zürich: NZZ Verlag.

Morel, Laurence. 2018. 'Types of Referendums: Provisions and Practice at the National Level Worldwide'. In *The Routledge Handbook to Referendums and Direct Democracy*, edited by Laurence Morel, and Matt Qvortrup, pp. 15–59. London: Routledge.

Nai, Alessandro. 2012. 'What Really Matters is Which Camp Goes Dirty: Differential Effects of Negative Campaigning on Turnout During Swiss Federal Ballots'. *European Journal of Political Research* 52 (1): pp. 44–70.

Nai, Alessandro. 2014. *Choisir avec l'esprit, voter avec le cœur. Causes et conséquences des processus cognitifs de formation de l'opinion en Suisse lors des votations fédérales*. Zürich: Seismo.

Nai, Alessandro. 2015. 'The Maze and the Mirror: Voting Correctly in Direct Democracy'. *Social Science Quarterly* 96 (2): pp. 465–486.

Nef, Rolf, 1980. 'Struktur, Kultur und Abstimmungsverhalten. Zur interregionalen Variation von politischen Präferenzen in der Schweiz 1950-1977'. *Schweizerische Zeitschrift für Soziologie* 6 (2): pp. 155–190.

Papadopoulos, Yannis. 1994. 'Les votations fédérales comme indicateur de soutien aux autorités'. In *Elites politiques et peuple en Suisse. Analyse des votations fédérales: 1970–1987*, edited by Yannis Papadopoulos, pp. 113–160. Lausanne: Réalités sociales.

Petitpas, Adrien., Jaquet, Julien M., and Pascal Sciarini. 2021. 'Does E-Voting Matter for Turnout, and to Whom?' *Electoral Studies* 71, 102245.

Sardi, Massimo, and Eric Widmer. 1993. 'L'orientation du vote'. In *Citoyenneté et démocratie directe. Compétence, participation et décision des citoyens et citoyennes suisses*, edited by Hanspeter Kriesi, pp. 191–212. Zürich: Seismo.

Sartori, Giovanni. 1973: *Democratic Theory*. London: Praeger Publishers Inc.

Sciarini, Pascal. 2017. 'Direct Democracy in Switzerland: the Growing Tension Between Domestic Politics and Foreign Politics'. In *Let the People Rule? Direct Democracy in the Twenty-First Century*, edited by Saskia Ruth, Yanina Welp, and Laurence Whitehead, pp. 171–188. London: ECPR Press.

Sciarini, Pascal. 2018. 'Voting Behaviour in Direct Democratic Votes'. In *the Routledge Handbook to Referendums and Direct Democracy*, edited by Laurence Morel, and Matt Qvortrup, pp. 289–306. London: Routledge.

Sciarini, Pascal, Nicholas Bornstein, and Bruno Lanz. 2007. 'The Determinants of Voting Choices on Environmental Issues: A Two-Level Analysis'. In *The Dynamics of Referendum Campaigns. An International Perspective*, edited by Claes H. De Vreese, pp. 234–266. New York: Palgrave Macmillan.

Sciarini, Pascal, Fabio Cappelletti, Andreas C. Goldberg, and Simon Lanz. 2016. 'The Underexplored Species: Selective Participation in Direct Democratic Votes'. *Swiss Political Science Review* 22 (1): pp. 75–94.

Sciarini, Pascal, Roy Gava, and Julien M. Jaquet. 2020. *Swiss Legislative Processes (1987–2019) [LegPro database]*, Department of Political Science and International Relations, University of Geneva, https://legpro.unige.ch/.

Sciarini, Pascal, and Anke Tresch. 2009. 'A Two-Level Analysis of the Determinants of Direct Democratic Choices in European, Immigration and Foreign Policy in Switzerland'. *European Union Politics* 10 (4): pp. 456–481.

Sciarini Pascal, and Anke Tresch. 2011. 'Campaign Effects in Direct-Democratic Votes in Switzerland'. *Journal of Elections, Public Opinion & Parties* 21 (3): pp. 333–357.

Selb, Peter, Hanspeter Kriesi, Regula Hänggli, and Mirko Marr. 2009. 'Partisan Choices in a Direct-Democratic Campaign'. *European Political Science Review* 1 (1): pp. 155–172.

Serdült, Uwe. 2013. 'Partizipation als Norm und Artefakt in der schweizerischen Abstimmungsdemokratie'. In *Direkte Demokratie. Herausforderungen zwischen Politik und Recht Festschrift für Andreas Auer zum 65. Geburtstag*, edited by Andreas Good, and Bettina Platipodis, pp. 41–50. Bern: Stämpfli.

Strijbis, Oliver, Arnesen Sveinung, and Laurent Bernhard. 2016. 'Using Prediction Market Data for Measuring the Expected Closeness in Electoral Research'. *Electoral Studies* 44: pp. 144–150.

Swissvotes. 2022. *Swissvotes – the Database on Swiss Popular Votes: Dataset*. Année Politique Suisse, University of Bern. https://swissvotes.ch/page/dataset (accessed 09 September 2022).

Tresch, Anke. 2008. *Öffentlichkeit und Sprachenvielfalt. Medienvermittelte Kommunikation zur Europapolitik in der Deutsch- und Westschweiz*. Baden-Baden: Nomos.

Tresch, Anke, Pascal Sciarini, and Frédéric Varone. 2013. 'The Relationship between Media and Political Agendas: Variations across Decision-Making Phases'. *West European Politics* 36 (5): pp. 897–918.

Udris, Linards, Mark Eisenegger, and Jörg Schneider. 2016. 'News Coverage about Direct-Democratic Campaigns in a Period of Structural Crisis'. *Journal of Information Policy* 6: pp. 68–104.

Varone, Frédéric, Isabelle Engeli, Pascal Sciarini, and Roy Gava. 2014. 'Agenda Setting and Direct Democracy: The Rise of the Swiss People's Party'. In *Agenda Setting, Policies, and Political Systems. A Comparative Approach*, edited by Christoffer Green-Pedersen, and Stefaan Walgrave, pp. 105–122. Chicago: University of Chicago Press.

Von Arx, Nicolas. 2002. *Ähnlich, aber anders: die Volksinitiative in Kalifornien und in der Schweiz*. Basel: Helbing & Lichtenhahn.

VoxIt. 1981–2016. *Standardisierte Umfragen VoxIt 1981-2016 [Dataset]*. https://doi.org/10.23662/FORS-DS-689-2 (accessed 09 September 2022).

Zaller, John R. 1992. *The Nature and Origins of Mass Opinion*. Cambridge: Cambridge University Press.

CHAPTER 23

DIGITAL DEMOCRACY

FABRIZIO GILARDI[1] AND ALEXANDER H. TRECHSEL

1 INTRODUCTION

THE relationship between digital technology and democracy has received increased attention in recent years, notably after the alleged impact of social media, and Facebook in particular, on the 2016 United States presidential elections.[2] Since then, phrases such as 'fake news' and 'echo chambers' have entered common usage and have spurred significant political and academic discussions, often centred on the dangers that digital technology presents for democracies. As one commentary on the 2016 elections put it: 'Can Democracy Survive the Internet?' (Persily 2017). However, the influence of digital technology goes well beyond social media and spans a wide spectrum covering all parts of democratic processes, including in particular political communication, political participation, and policy-making (Gilardi 2022). While the trend is relevant for all countries, it takes specific forms in Switzerland. The rich set of political institutions, characterized by a strong interplay of representative and participatory forms of democracy at different levels of the federal state, the multitude of organized political actors, a politically active citizenry, and the widespread use of Internet-based technologies throughout society have led to innovative experimentation with online instruments and processes as well as internationally relevant research. The goal of this chapter is to provide an overview of major developments and debates in the Swiss case, with a focus on three main areas: campaigning, opinion formation, and Internet voting.

First, the chapter considers the role of digital technology for political campaigning in Switzerland, that is, how political actors have used digital tools in their efforts to shape political processes and outcomes. Social media is a relevant channel both for elections and for direct-democratic campaigns, but its effects are not as prominent as in other countries. A specificity of the Swiss case is the ongoing efforts to enable the electronic collection of signatures to put referendums or initiatives on the ballot.

Second, opinion formation, with the proliferation of Voting Advice Applications (VAAs) across all levels of government, has been the focus of numerous research contributions over the past two decades. The chapter assesses these platforms' impact on political behaviour before addressing novel research on algorithmic recommendation systems, potentially altering opinion formation during referendum campaigns. Moreover, the chapter considers how different groups can leverage social media to increase the salience of certain issues, as well as the ways in which those issues are perceived or framed.

Third, Switzerland played a pioneering role in the development and implementation of Internet voting. The rich Swiss experience has led to a series of studies focusing on the effects of this channel of voting on outcomes such as patterns of participation, turnout, and electoral choice. As these studies show, Internet voting above all led to a displacement of habitual voters to this new form of casting a ballot, altering turnout for particular segments of the voting population, without affecting turnout in the aggregate.

2 Campaigning

2.1 Social media and politicians

Swiss politicians have not been early adopters of social media. In 2014, only one-third of the members of the national parliament had a Twitter account (Rauchfleisch and Metag 2016). During the 2019 election campaign, most candidates had a social media presence, but by no means all, and to different degrees depending on the platform (Gilardi et al. 2020a). Table 23.1 shows that for the National Council, 56 per cent of candidates had an account on Facebook, 32 per cent on Twitter, and 22 per cent on Instagram. The numbers were higher (but still well below 100 per cent) for candidates to the Council of States, where the election centres more around persons and personalities, and consequently popularity and visibility play a greater role than for the National Council election. Professionalization also plays a role, as illustrated by the comparison between incumbents and challengers, with a significant gap between the two groups in favour of the former. While the difference makes sense in view of professionalization, it is surprising given that social media may give an edge precisely to candidates with fewer resources and who might not receive much attention in the traditional media. However, it is important to note that the sample covers all candidates, most of which had little hope (or even real ambition) to be elected. The gender breakdown is also interesting: the percentage of male candidates with a social media account is larger than that of female candidates across the three platforms.

Beyond mere presence, what matters on social media is visibility and user engagement (e.g. likes and shares), both of which are linked to the number of followers. A study

Table 23.1: Percentage of candidates with social media accounts (2019 national elections)

	Facebook	Twitter	Instagram
National Council	56	32	22
Council of States	85	62	27
Incumbents	83	72	42
Challengers	56	32	21
Women	55	29	21
Men	59	36	22

Data source: Gilardi et al. (2020a).

covering the 2011–2015 period showed that Swiss politicians had, on average, a quite small number of followers: 2,106 on Facebook and 2,533 on Twitter (Keller and Kleinen-von Königslöw 2018). Similar numbers were measured in the 2019 national elections, with very few candidates over the 10,000 threshold (Gilardi et al. 2020a). Apart from just a few outliers, such as the controversial SVP member of parliament Roger Köppel, most politicians achieved a modest number of engagements.

A comparison of election and referendum campaigns showed that politicians were more active on Twitter (that is, posted more tweets) before elections than before referendums (Gilardi et al. 2020b). This finding suggests that many politicians use social media as a tool for their personal election campaign, with limited intensity and possibly limited success, but even less to shape public opinion on substantive issues ahead of a popular vote. To the extent that they do post on those issues, however, they tend to achieve greater engagements than during the election campaign (Gilardi et al. 2020b).

The fact that Swiss politicians are not very present online does not imply that social media does not matter. First, an analysis of candidates in the 2015 national elections revealed a positive correlation between the engagements candidates received on Twitter and the probability of being elected, controlling for media presence, voting list rank, incumbency status, and gender (Kovic et al. 2017). Second, the relevance of social media may be more indirect. To the extent that their messages are amplified by traditional media, social media may enable politicians to influence the debate despite limited direct reach (Gilardi et al. 2022). Third, survey experiments suggest that candidates could increase the appeal of their social media activity if they adopted a stronger policy-oriented communication style (Giger et al. 2021).

2.2 Social media and direct democracy

Social media has become a common element of direct-democratic campaigns in Switzerland. While it has been used by both proponents and opponents of initiatives and referendums, it is especially the former that can benefit the most, particularly compared to other channels that require more resources such as newspaper ads (Fischer and Gilardi 2023). While actors in the challenger camp (supporting the referendums/ initiatives) and government camp (opposing them) publish a similar number of posts on Facebook, challengers tend to achieve more engagements than the government camp, both for initiatives and for referendums, and regardless of the specific composition of the government camp (Fischer and Gilardi 2023). These findings support the view that social media contributes to levelling the playing field in direct-democratic campaigns, offering new opportunities to overcome the structural disadvantages (particularly resources) of actors challenging the status quo.

A Twitter analysis of the referendum campaign on the nuclear withdrawal initiative, held in 2016, demonstrated the relevance of social media for the political discourse in a direct-democratic context (Arlt et al. 2018). In particular, it uncovered a significant degree of interaction not only within communities (identified using the follower network), but also between them. Throughout the campaign, the number of replies was larger between different groups than within them. This finding contrasts with the view that social media inevitably leads to the formation of echo chambers and points to exchanges between users holding different views.

Another study analysed the Twitter discourse for all direct-democratic votes held at the national level in 2022 (three initiatives and seven referendums) (Gilardi et al. 2023). The comparison of several votes showed that the amount of discussion and the degree of polarization of the discourse vary significantly across items in ways that are quite predictable. That is, the votes that attract more attention in the media, and which are generally perceived to be more important or controversial, are those that gain more traction on Twitter, and for which two contrasting communities can be identified more clearly. Moreover, a specificity of the study is that it considers not only tweets that discuss the votes, but also all tweets posted by a large sample of users (over 380,000) who follow Swiss politics or Swiss media, which supplies a denominator to measure the frequency of tweets on direct-democratic votes. That frequency is very low. It fluctuates during the campaign, but is mostly below 0.5 per cent. The percentage of users who post about the votes is also very low, about 2 per cent, of which about half post for every voting period (though not necessarily every item). Therefore, the direct-democratic discourse on Twitter is driven by a very small number of users, not only in absolute terms, but also relative to a sample of users who are in principle interested in news and politics. Finally, the role of bots is very limited: only about 1 per cent of the tweets can be linked to automatized accounts.

2.3 Social media and agenda setting

Social media can play a significant role in agenda setting, due to their potential for users to influence discourse without having to rely on traditional gatekeepers, coupled with the fact that journalists pay close attention to discussions on social media. This idea is supported by evidence from the Swiss case. A survey conducted in 2014 revealed that tweets by politicians are considered important sources by journalists, particularly as a way to generate ideas for news stories as well as to consider a variety of viewpoints (Metag and Rauchfleisch 2017). Moreover, the same survey showed that Swiss journalists consider Twitter in general one of the main sources of breaking news. Although the social media landscape has changed considerably since the study was conducted, its main conclusions are supported by more recent work in the US context (McGregor and Molyneux 2020). Furthermore, a study tracking over 300,000 Swiss Twitter users for three months in 2019 found that, in a sample of the 1,800 tweets that received the most engagements, tweets from private individuals were overrepresented relative to tweets from politicians or organizations (Vogler et al. 2019), particularly for political topics and other kinds of 'hard' news. This finding suggests that private individuals shape the agenda (what social media users care about) to a degree that would be impossible in traditional media, given the barriers to entry set by journalists and publishers. The authors conclude that '[t]he hierarchy of the most influential agenda-setters is thus turned upside down to a certain extent in comparison to the classic, mass-media public sphere' (Vogler et al. 2019, 56, our translation).

Other studies considered more explicitly the connections among different kinds of users as well as between social media and traditional media. An analysis of the 'first wave' of the COVID-19 pandemic (February–August 2020) examined COVID-19 as a general topic as well as of two of the most important policies at the time, namely face masks and the contact-tracing app (Gilardi et al. 2021). Specifically, the study considered the salience of these topics in traditional media (400,000 articles published in seventy-six newspapers) and on Twitter, distinguishing between politicians (68,000 tweets from 696 users), parties (2,200 tweets from sixty-nine accounts), and 'attentive' users following at least five Swiss media (500,000 tweets from over 19,000 users). During that period, the salience of COVID-19 was enormous, between 30 per cent and 60 per cent of all newspaper articles. The salience of COVID-19 in general was largely exogenous, that is, driven neither by parties, nor by politicians, nor by attentive users. On the other hand, specific policies, in particular those requiring face masks, were subject to clearer agenda-setting dynamics linked to social media. In particular, tweets mentioning face masks by attentive users predicted subsequent newspaper articles as well as tweets from politicians on that topic to a larger extent than news articles or tweets from politicians could predict the number of tweets attentive users posted on face masks. In other words, for this specific policy intervention, attentive users played a significant role both for the political and for the media agenda.

A related study examined the salience of four issues (the environment, Europe, gender equality, and immigration) in 2018 and 2019, with a focus on the traditional media agenda (2.8 million news articles) as well as the social media agenda of politicians (6,500 tweets) and parties (210,000 tweets), but not regular or 'attentive' users (Gilardi et al. 2022). The main finding is the large extent of interdependence between the agendas, which both tend to lead and follow each other to comparable degrees, with the exception of the 'environment' topics, for which traditional media are more responsive to the social media agenda of parties than the other way around. Overall, the study confirms the relevance of social media for agenda setting as well as the close interconnection between traditional and social media in the Swiss case.

2.4 E-collecting

Direct democracy is, of course, one of the most important institutions of the Swiss political system. Both referendums and popular initiatives require the collection of handwritten citizen signatures. In this context, 'e-collecting' refers to procedures that would allow citizens to sign electronically. The idea has been discussed for several years. For example, in 2008, a motion in the national parliament requested legislative action to conduct pilot projects,[3] which the Federal Council rejected with arguments linked to technical problems related to the verification of the electronic signatures. The successful 2021 referendum[4] against an electronic identity tool officially recognized by the state, but issued by private providers, further delayed the adoption of e-collecting at the national level, whereas some pilot projects are planned at the cantonal level.

Despite the impossibility to collect electronic signatures, activists have established a platform, called WeCollect,[5] to facilitate the online collection of signatures for referendums and popular initiatives. The project started in 2016 with a focus on the national level, but was later extended to the cantonal and local levels. Figure 23.1 shows that the number of ongoing projects increased over time, from six at the national level in 2016 to about twelve from 2018 on. Projects at the cantonal and local level were introduced later, and their number has steadily increased. To assess the impact of the projects, the key question is the number of signatures that they helped collect. Figure 23.2 shows the distribution over time, keeping in mind that the minimum number of signatures required is 50,000 for referendums and 100,000 for initiatives. Unfortunately, the data does not permit a systematic distinction between referendums and initiatives. However, we see that projects typically collected about 5,000 signatures, with significant variations and some projects well over 10,000 signatures. To interpret these numbers correctly, it is important to note how the platform works in practice. After users sign a project online, they need to download, print, sign, and mail a pre-filled, pre-stamped PDF form for their signature to be valid. This is due to the rules set by the Swiss Federal Chancellery, which does not accept electronic signatures. Due to this friction, the conversion rate of WeCollect is certainly below one, but the specific number is unknown. Therefore, Figure 23.2 shows an upper bound for the number of signatures gained through WeCollect.

Table 23.2 shows the top ten WeCollect projects by number of signatures. We can see that (again, keeping in mind the caveat regarding the conversion rate, which is unknown) some projects made a significant difference for the success of the referendum or initiative. For example, the top project was a referendum against new measures against terrorism, for which WeCollect signatures amounted to up to 30 per cent of the total signatures collected. The second most successful project, supporting an initiative to introduce parental leave for fathers, collected enough signatures to push the referendum

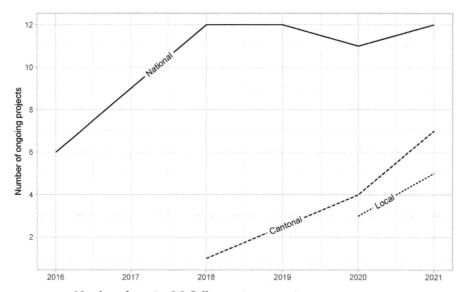

FIGURE 23.1: Number of ongoing WeCollect projects over time

Data source: WeCollect (2022).

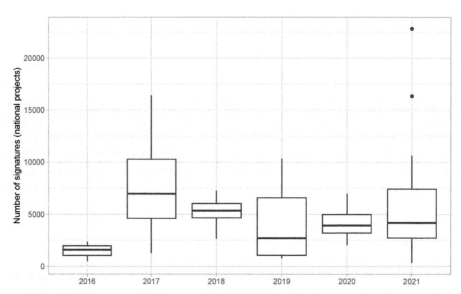

FIGURE 23.2: Number of signatures for national WeCollect projects, over time

Data source: WeCollect (2022).

over the threshold of 100,000 signatures. And the third most successful project, an initiative to make personal taxation independent of marital status, had already received over 16,000 signatures at the time of data collection (March 2022), with several months to go until the deadline for the submission of the signatures. Of course, these examples

Table 23.2: Top ten WeCollect projects by number of signatures

Project	Type	Year	WeCollect signatures	Total signatures	WeCollect (in per cent)
Anti-terrorism law	Referendum	2021	22,826	76,926	29.7
Paternity leave	Initiative	2017	16,411	107,075	15.3
Taxation of married couples*	Initiative	2022	16,353	n/a	n/a
Frontex	Referendum	2021	10,627	54,377	19.5
Intensive livestock farming	Initiative	2019	10,327	106,125	9.7
Nursing	Initiative	2017	8,229	114,078	7.2
Glacier preservation	Initiative	2019	7,534	113,125	6.7
Monitoring of social security beneficiaries	Referendum	2018	7,264	56,026	13.0
Electronic identity	Referendum	2020	6,983	64,933	10.8
Biodiversity	Initiative	2020	6,754	107,885	6.3

Data source: Federal Chancellery (2022); WeCollect (2022).
*Ongoing at the time of writing.

are not representative—they are the most successful ones. However, they demonstrate the potential of WeCollect to influence Swiss politics through established direct-democratic instruments, but leveraging online channels.

These descriptive data can help us assess some claims made regarding the possible consequences of e-collecting. In particular, some scholars have argued that e-collecting could drastically reduce the time needed to collect signatures. Based on the Dutch experience, Bisaz and Serdült (2017) estimated that a popular initiative might succeed as quickly as in one week. Of course, a direct test of this hypothesis is not possible with the existing rules. The current system still requires users to print out, sign, and mail the forms. Moreover, there is no data on the actual number of signatures obtained via WeCollect. The numbers refer to the online step of the signature collection (how many people downloaded a pre-filled form), but not to the conversion rate (how many people signed and mailed the forms, and how many of those forms were validated by the Federal Chancellery). That said, the figures and table above reveal a number of relevant insights. First, the number of national projects has been stable since 2018. Second, with a few exceptions, the number of signatures is low. Third, even for the few projects that generate many signatures, the number makes up for a relatively small share of the total number of signatures. While the process is not fully digitalized, it is important to recognize that the signatures were collected over 100 days (for referendums) or eighteen months (for initiatives), and that they overestimate the actual number of signatures that the Federal Chancellery ultimately declared valid. It is of course difficult to extrapolate these figures to a fully digital collection scenario. However, on balance, the evidence does not suggest that massive amounts of signatures could be obtained very quickly for a typical initiative or referendum.

In sum, e-collecting is likely to be introduced at some point. Despite current limitations, WeCollect has already become a relevant actor for Swiss direct democracy, but its effect has not been disruptive so far.

3 OPINION FORMATION

3.1 Voting Advice Applications

Switzerland has a rich experience with so-called VAAs, which appeared in the early 2000s and have since spread across all levels of the polity. Modern VAAs are Internet-based platforms that use a set of policy statements to map the congruence of political positions of parties and candidates and the positions of voters regarding these statements. Typically, users take a stance on a series of political statements and are matched with the positions taken by parties and/or candidates on the same statements. A matching-algorithm then produces an output that comes in the form of an 'advice', usually consisting of a rank-ordered list or graph. It indicates to what extent the user overlaps with the positions taken by parties and/or candidates, either on a single dimension, or within a multi-dimensional space constituted by various axes of party politics (such as left–right) or political positioning on clusters of issues (such as preferences for law and order or social policy). Thus, the essence of VAAs lies in their customized, personalized, and tailor-made recommendations to their users (Trechsel and Garzia 2019).

In Switzerland, voters have been able to get such advice by using a VAA called 'smartvote' since 2003. Developed by the politically neutral non-profit organization 'Politools', smartvote has been offered in over 200 elections in Switzerland. During the campaign to the last federal elections in 2019, over 1.9 million voting pieces of advice have been computed. Likewise, for cantonal elections, an average share of 16 to 18 per cent of the electorate have used smartvote during electoral campaigns (Benesch et al. 2023). The approach and methodology of smartvote has also been adopted by several other European democracies (e.g. Bulgaria and Luxembourg), and it has inspired a transnational VAA developed uniquely for European Parliament elections—the 'EU Profiler' and its subsequent editions, euandi (Sudulich et al. 2014).

With such large proportions of the electorate using smartvote prior to elections, political science research picked up on its potential effects. An early analysis found that in the 2007 Swiss federal election over 40 per cent of survey respondents indicated that smartvote was decisive or at least slightly relevant for their decision to cast a ballot (Ladner and Pianzola 2010). This initial study estimated that smartvote also had a mobilizing effect on the electorate, in the order of a 0.6 to 1 percentage point turnout increase. Several studies have since been produced to measure the potential impact of *smartvote* on participation rates and came to similarly optimistic conclusions (Dinas et al. 2014; Fivaz and Nadig 2010; Ladner et al. 2012). Particularly among young voters, *smartvote* seems to have a mobilizing effect, as shown by an analysis of the 2011 federal elections (Germann and Gemenis 2019). Most of the early studies on the effects of *smartvote* on political participation relied on observational data, struggling with identifying causal effects. More recently, research using experimental designs could show that (self-reported) turnout rates increased by over 10 per cent for VAA users in Italy (Garzia et al. 2017). For the Swiss case, however, the most recent and comprehensive study concluded that *smartvote* did not affect turnout per se, but instead led voters to more actively select particular candidates from multiple parties by splitting their ballot (Benesch et al. 2023). This finding also speaks to a growing literature looking at more nuanced effects of VAA exposure that go beyond the at best limited impact on participation *tout court*.

Among outcomes of interest beyond turnout, vote intention stands out. A field experiment showed that using the VAA 'strengthened the vote intention for the most preferred party and also increased the number of parties considered as potential vote options' (Pianzola et al. 2019, 883). The mechanisms behind such effects are probably linked to processes of self-learning, echoing earlier work on 'knowledge effects' (Ladner et al. 2009). Such cognitive processes can be understood as a form of 'self-persuasion' (Trechsel and Garzia 2019) that may reinforce pre-existing preferences, nuance the latter, or even change them.

The Swiss literature on VAAs also speaks to normative debates regarding technology and democracy. VAAs such as *smartvote* may foster transparency, accountability, and responsiveness of the electoral process (Fivaz and Schwarz 2015). An early assessment of *smartvote* not only emphasized 'huge opportunities' but also pointed to potential risks (Thurman and Gasser 2009). Among the latter, they mention biases in the survey tool that collects information for *smartvote* as well as 'insufficiently rich data in matching voters to candidates' (Thurman and Gasser 2009, 2). Other biases may arise from uneven usage of VAAs across strata of the electorate, potentially deepening a digital divide in election information (Fivaz and Schwarz 2015). Also, and in particular when combined with Internet voting, the risk of 'instant voting', lacking a serious engagement with political issues and party positions, may arise. So far, however, such a push-button democracy, a term coined by Giovanni Sartori, is unlikely to have materialized. Meanwhile issues surrounding data protection or further integration of social media into VAA developments are on the horizon. For instance, a recent study shows how candidate profiles can be made more dynamic using Twitter data and sentiment analysis (Terán and Mancera 2019). In general, and independently from what platforms will be linked to VAAs, more powerful algorithms may help produce more precise matches between a user's demand and the electoral offer (Romero Moreno et al. 2022).

3.2 Algorithmic recommendation systems

Algorithmic recommendation systems have strongly spread into all areas of society, including politics. The rationale behind ever more precise content personalization through algorithms is to keep and engage users on the respective platforms (Abiteboul and Dowek 2017). This also goes for media platforms that increasingly make use of algorithms that personalize content for their users, thus potentially impacting on opinion formation of the electorate. However, the evidence regarding the potential impact of algorithmic-driven information on public opinion is mixed. For pessimists, algorithms contribute to the development of filter bubbles (Cho et al. 2020), selective avoidance of political news (Thorson 2020), and mechanisms of discrimination (Noble 2018; Obermeyer et al. 2019). For optimists, algorithms may well lead to a boost in political participation (Gil de Zúñiga et al. 2021).

In the Swiss context, the effects of algorithms on politics are still largely under-studied. One of the reasons for this is the difficulty to experimentally manipulate the degree of algorithmic personalization of political content on platforms. As these algorithms are paramount to the business model of platforms, accessing the latter is difficult at best. A recent study innovated in this regard by making use of a custom news feed smartphone application that functions as a media aggregator, pushing content from news portals to its users during a referendum campaign (De Angelis et al. 2022). The study measured the causal impact of personalized news feeds on news consumption, public opinion, voter turnout, and voting behaviour. The authors conducted a pre-registered lab-in-the-field experiment during the June 2021 federal ballot votes. Findings show that algorithmic-driven personalization of political news during a referendum campaign significantly skews the consumption patterns of the latter, and in particular of politically extreme users. Also, personalized news feeds reinforce prior beliefs of users, and in particular lead to a demobilization effect of voters that were unsure about turning out from the outset. More research is needed to fully assert the impact of algorithms on democratic decision-making, potentially leading to a larger debate on the necessity of regulation.

4 Internet voting

We refer to Internet voting as a form of remote voting over the Internet and during a certain time period prior to the closure of the ballot box on voting day (Alvarez et al. 2009). In 2000, the Federal Chancellery launched a pilot project regarding electronic voting over the Internet, i.e. Internet voting. Given the high frequency with which Swiss voters are called to the ballot box, due to direct-democratic practices, and combined with a relatively early adoption of Internet technologies, Switzerland offered a laboratory for testing Internet voting. Add to this federalism, with its multitude of subnational jurisdictions that enabled experimentation. Three cantons came forward and were chosen to run early trials relying on different systems of Internet voting, namely the cantons of Geneva, Zurich, and Neuchâtel.

After a number of trials, studies found that above all a displacement of former postal voters towards Internet voting could be observed (Trechsel et al. 2016). The most promising advantage offered by Internet voting was seen among those voters that potentially had to struggle to vote at all, i.e. Swiss citizens living abroad. As no tangible failures in the trials seemed to appear, the federal government allowed Swiss citizens living abroad to cast their ballots over the Internet in several cantons. Internet voting became particularly useful to Swiss citizens living abroad and became, in the various cantons experimenting with this offer, highly popular (Germann and Serdült 2014).

Despite its success in terms of usage, Internet voting in Switzerland underwent a bumpy ride, mainly due to security concerns and breaches. Thus, the attempt by the federal government to make Internet voting a standard channel for casting ballots failed to reach sufficient levels of consensus. Nevertheless, the government decided to push its Internet voting agenda, preparing a new set of legal bases for redesigning and relaunching trials. In 2022, these legal bases entered into force, and it is expected that new trials will be held in the coming years. Overall, after an initial hype, first successes, and a multiplication of different solutions, technological problems led to a complete, momentary shutdown.

Almost two decades of Internet voting trials in Switzerland led to a strong accumulation of scientific knowledge and data. From a social science perspective, numerous studies have discussed the promises and pitfalls of Internet voting in the Swiss context. The main promise was, from the outset, that Internet voting would enable the electorate to cast a vote in a simple, modern, and less costly effort, thus potentially boosting turnout. Also, the efficiency of the entire voting process, including vote counting, was expected to become maximized. Focusing on the main potential promise—a boost in turnout—the evidence for such an effect to occur is rather slim. Initial survey analyses were optimistic (Auer and Trechsel 2001). A replication of the study concluded that the introduction of Internet voting did not boost participation rates in the canton of Geneva (Sciarini et al. 2013). Predominantly, former postal voters, used to cast their ballots remotely, switched to Internet voting.

The results by Sciarini et al. (2013) are echoed by a more recent study by Germann and Serdült (2017). Exploiting quasi-random variation in communes that were chosen for the trials, they employ difference-in-difference estimations to show that Internet voting did not increase turnout in federal referendums, either in the canton of Geneva or in the canton of Zurich. Also, the authors show that Internet voting above all is a substitute for remote postal voting. Studies focusing on expatriate voters—a category of voters for whom Internet voting is particularly appealing—show that turnout was not boosted due to the introduction of Internet voting (Germann and Serdült 2014), despite its popularity (Germann et al. 2014; Serdült et al. 2015b). A study by Petitpas et al. (2021) leverages individual-level data covering thirty ballots between 2008 and 2016 in the canton of Geneva. Focusing on the differential effects across different types of voters, Petitpas et al. (2021) confirm the findings of Trechsel (2007), i.e. that Internet voting has increased turnout among abstainers and occasional voters, who constitute about 20 per cent of eligible voters. These patterns are further conditioned by age and gender: for younger cohorts and female voters the difference between frequent and rare voters or non-voters is smaller, thus increasing the age and gender gaps in participation.

This finding leads to potential pitfalls in Internet voting and, in particular, to issues of inequality among voters accessing the ballot box. Is Internet voting easing or, to the contrary, worsening existing demographic, socio-economic, and political biases in democratic participation? A meta-analysis by Serdült et al. (2015a) covering studies on the Swiss case show that Internet voters are generally more highly educated, between thirty and forty-nine years old, male, and displaying an above average income. Note, however, that studies employing multivariate models show that covariation between socio-demographic factors and the probability of Internet voting vanishes once measures of Internet usage and attitudes towards digitalization are controlled for. Two studies not included in the meta-analysis come to similar conclusions. The research by Trechsel (2007) shows that in the canton of Geneva, voters tend to replace traditional voting methods with Internet voting mainly due to ICT-related factors (information and communications technology), such as trust in online communication and computer literacy, rather than the effects of age, gender, and education. Similarly, a recent study by Lust (2018) finds that the demographic biases in favour of young, male, and university-educated voters have not only diminished over time in Swiss elections, but more fundamentally have been replaced by a new divide based on computer skills (which are, however, themselves correlated with higher education). The studies by Trechsel (2007), Sciarini et al. (2013), and Lust (2018) also show that Internet voting in the canton of Geneva has been politically neutral. In the September 2004 referendums in the canton of Geneva, no significant political distortions occurred due to the availability of Internet voting (Trechsel 2007). Lust (2018) reports that supporters of different parties are equally likely to vote on- and offline. Replicating the analyses in the context of expatriate voters, two studies find that among Swiss citizens abroad the same socio-demographic factors as well as ICT-factors are associated with using Internet voting (Germann et al. 2014; Germann and Serdült 2014). Estonia's experience with Internet voting is arguably the best documented case. Analyses covering over a decade of Internet voting show that the diffusion of this means of participation only gradually started to homogeneously affect the voting population in this Baltic state (Vassil et al. 2016). Whether Internet voting in Switzerland bears the same potential to bridge societal divisions can only be asserted when—and if—this form of voting has established itself.

Although it would be too early to speculate about any form of Internet voting's 'second spring' in Switzerland, one of the most promising innovations in online voting technologies is block chain-based. First trials have already taken place, such as a test vote in the city of Zug in 2018, and may lead to optimal levels of security (Taş and Tanrıöver 2020). Still, and even if the promise of block chain technology is to overcome the need for trust in intermediaries, the trust of all the political actors in any form of voting system, be it on- or offline, will remain paramount.

5 Conclusion

Switzerland has undergone innovative experimentation with digital instruments and processes as well as having generated internationally relevant research on digital technology and politics. This chapter has discussed some of the most important trends and insights, with a focus on political campaigning, opinion formation, and Internet voting. On this basis, we can identify a few points that are specific to the Swiss case.

First, some of the aspects that have generated the most public attention, such as fake news, have played a limited role in the Swiss context so far. One reason is that while Swiss politics does take place in online spaces to some extent, parties and politicians have not embraced social media to the same degree that can be observed in other countries, particularly those, such as the United States, that receive the most media and research attention. Therefore, one lesson is that international trends cannot be easily extrapolated to the Swiss case.

Second, an innovation specific to Switzerland, the electronic collection of signatures for initiatives and referendums, is linked to the direct-democratic institutions of the country. Moreover, its arrested development, so to speak (signatures still cannot be fully collected electronically), illustrates the bumpy road that many digital democracy projects face in Switzerland, due to a combination of administrative hurdles at the federal level and the lack of coordination among cantons.

Third, public opinion formation during electoral and referendum campaigns has changed over the last two decades. The availability of VAAs at all levels of government regularly attracts large proportions of the electorate. While studies show that their impact on participation rates is limited at best, VAAs do alter political preferences of voters, above all by reinforcing prior preferences and widening the choice-set of electorally available parties and candidates. A particular focus is currently put by political scientists on the potential effects of (social) media algorithmic recommendation systems on public opinion. First studies point at the non-negligible impact of algorithmic news feed personalization on political preferences and mobilization patterns.

Fourth, Switzerland is a pioneering country with respect to Internet voting. The rich experience with this channel of voting has been extensively studied in the literature. Similar to the effects of VAAs, Internet voting does not so much affect turnout rates per se. Rather, and while studies show Internet voting's political neutrality when it comes to vote choice, different segments of the electorate, and in particular expatriates, make disproportionally intensive use of Internet voting when put at their disposal. The ever more sophisticated research designs and findings stemming from studies regarding the Swiss experience may well serve the debate in other contexts, i.e. in countries willing to introduce such modes of voting.

While this chapter covered key aspects of digital democracy in Switzerland, it is by no means exhaustive. In particular, the chapter did not discuss important elements such as the role of digital technology for public administration (e-government), including the controversial issue of algorithmic decision-making, that is, the extent to which automatized tools and artificial intelligence (e.g. for facial recognition) could and should be used by public authorities. Due to space constraints, we leave this important discussion for another project.

We conclude by highlighting the constraints that research on digital technology and politics faces, particularly the challenge of accessing relevant social media data. The problem is amplified in Switzerland due to its multilingual context, its small size, and the fact that it is not part of the European Union, which is the most active actor in the area of platform regulation. Overcoming these challenges will be important to generate more and better evidence on the role of digital technology for Swiss democracy.

Notes

1. Fabrizio Gilardi received funding from the European Research Council (ERC) under the European Union's Horizon 2020 research and innovation programme (grant agreement number 883121).
2. We thank Daniel Graf and Samuel Raymann for kindly sharing WeCollect data, Dr Samuel D. Schmid for valuable research assistance, and Pascal Sciarini for helpful feedback.
3. The Federal Assembly (2022).
4. Federal Council (2022).
5. WeCollect (2022).

References

Abiteboul, Serge, and Gilles Dowek. 2017. *Le Temps Des Algorithmes*. Paris: Éditions Le Pommier.

Alvarez, R. Michael, Thad E. Hall, and Alexander H. Trechsel. 2009. 'Internet Voting in Comparative Perspective: The Case of Estonia'. *PS: Political Science & Politics* 42 (3): pp. 497–505.

Arlt, Dorothee, Adrian Rauchfleisch, and Mike S. Schäfer. 2018. 'Between Fragmentation and Dialogue. Twitter Communities and Political Debate About the Swiss 'Nuclear Withdrawal Initiative'. *Environmental Communication* 13 (4): pp. 440–456.

Auer, Andreas, and Alexander H. Trechsel. 2001. *Voter Par Internet? Le Projet e-Voting Dans Le Canton de Genève Dans Une Perspective Socio-Politique et Juridique*. Basel: Helbing & Lichtenhahn.

Benesch, Christine, Rino Heim, Mark Schelker, and Lukas Schmid. 2023. 'Do Voting Advice Applications Change Political Behavior?'. *Journal of Politics* 85 (2): pp. 684–700.

Bisaz, Corsin, and Uwe Serdült. 2017. 'E-Collecting als Herausforderung für die direkte Demokratie der Schweiz'. *LeGes: Gesetzgebung Evaluation* 28 (3): pp. 531–545.

Cho, Jaeho, Saifuddin Ahmed, Martin Hilbert, Billy Liu, and Jonathan Luu. 2020. 'Do Search Algorithms Endanger Democracy? An Experimental Investigation of Algorithm Effects on Political Polarization'. *Journal of Broadcasting & Electronic Media* 64 (2): pp. 150–172.

De Angelis, Andrea, Alexander H. Trechsel, and Alessandro Vecchiato. 2022. 'How Personalizing Algorithms on Digital Media Platforms Affect News Consumption, Public Opinion and Voting Behavior'. Working paper.

Dinas, Elias, Alexander H. Trechsel, and Kristjan Vassil. 2014. 'A Look into the Mirror: Preferences, Representation and Electoral Participation'. *Electoral Studies* 36: pp. 290–297.

Federal Assembly. 2022. *Stärkung der Demokratie durch E-Collecting*. https://www.parlament.ch/de/ratsbetrieb/suche-curia-vista/geschaeft?AffairId=20083908 (accessed 23 December 2022).

Federal Chancellery. 2022. *Political Rights*. https://www.bk.admin.ch/bk/de/home/politische-rechte.html (accessed 23 December 2022).

Federal Council. 2022. *Federal Act on Electronic Identification Services (e-ID Act)*. https://www.admin.ch/e-id (accessed 23 December 2022).

Fischer, Michaela, and Fabrizio Gilardi. 2023. 'Leveling the Playing Field or Politics as Usual? Equalization vs. Normalization in Swiss Direct Democratic Online Campaigns'. *Media and Communication* 11 (1): pp. 43–55.

Fivaz, Jan, and Giorgio Nadig. 2010. 'Impact of Voting Advice Applications (VAAs) on Voter Turnout and Their Potential Use for Civic Education'. *Policy & Internet* 2 (4): pp. 162–195.

Fivaz, Jan, and Daniel Schwarz. 2015. 'Smart Democracy Für Smart Cities – Online-Wahlhilfen Und Ihr Beitrag Zu Einer Modernen Demokratie'. *HMD Praxis der Wirtschaftsinformatik* 52 (4): pp. 482–501.

Garzia, Diego, Alexander H. Trechsel, and Andrea De Angelis. 2017. 'Voting Advice Applications and Electoral Participation: A Multi-Method Study'. *Political Communication* 34 (3): pp. 424–443.

Germann, Micha, Flurin Conradin, Christoph Wellig, and Uwe Serdült. 2014. 'Five Years of Internet Voting for Swiss Expatriates'. In *CeDEM 14. Conference for E-Democracy and Open Government*, edited by Peter Parycek and Edelmann, Noella. pp. 127–140. Krems: Danube University Krems.

Germann, Micha, and Kostas Gemenis. 2019. 'Getting Out the Vote With Voting Advice Applications'. *Political Communication* 36 (1): pp. 149–170.

Germann, Micha, and Uwe Serdült. 2014. 'Internet Voting for Expatriates: The Swiss Case'. *JeDEM - eJournal of eDemocracy and Open Government* 6 (2): pp. 197–215.

Germann, Micha, and Uwe Serdült. 2017. 'Internet Voting and Turnout: Evidence from Switzerland'. *Electoral Studies* 47: pp. 1–12.

Giger, Nathalie, Stefanie Bailer, Adrian Sutter, and Tomas Turner-Zwinkels. 2021. 'Policy or Person? What Voters Want from Their Representatives on Twitter'. *Electoral Studies* 74: pp. 1–9.

Gil de Zúñiga, Homero, Alberto Ardèvol-Abreu, and Andreu Casero-Ripollés. 2021. 'WhatsApp Political Discussion, Conventional Participation and Activism: Exploring Direct, Indirect and Generational Effects'. *Information, Communication & Society* 24 (2): pp. 201–218.

Gilardi, Fabrizio. 2022. *Digital Technology, Politics, and Policy-Making*. Cambridge: Cambridge University Press.

Gilardi, Fabrizio, Clau Dermont, and Maël Kubli. 2020a. 'Die digitale Transformation der Demokratie'. In *Jahrbuch für direkte Demokratie 2019*, edited by Nadja Braun Binder, Lars P. Feld, Peter M. Huber, Klaus Poier, and Fabian Wittreck, pp. 11–37. Baden-Baden: Nomos Verlagsgesellschaft.

Gilardi, Fabrizio, Clau Dermont, Maël Kubli, and Lucien Baumgartner. 2020b. *Der Wahlkampf 2019 in traditionellen und Digitalen Medien*. Zurich: University of Zurich.

Gilardi, Fabrizio, Theresa Gessler, Maël Kubli, and Stefan Müller. 2021. 'Social Media and Policy Responses to the COVID-19 Pandemic in Switzerland'. *Swiss Political Science Review* 27 (2): pp. 243–256.

Gilardi, Fabrizio, Theresa Gessler, Maël Kubli, and Stefan Müller. 2022. 'Social Media and Political Agenda Setting'. *Political Communication* 39 (1): pp. 39–60.

Gilardi, Fabrizio, Dominik Hangartner, Philip Grech, and Maël Kubli. 2023. 'Social Media During Referendum Campaigns'. Working paper.

Keller, Tobias R., and Katharina Kleinen-von Königslöw. 2018. 'Followers, Spread the Message! Predicting the Success of Swiss Politicians on Facebook and Twitter'. *Social Media + Society* 4 (1): pp. 1–11.

Kovic, Marko, Adrian Rauchfleisch, Julia Metag, Christian Caspar, and Julian Szenogrady. 2017. 'Brute Force Effects of Mass Media Presence and Social Media Activity on Electoral Outcome'. *Journal of Information Technology & Politics* 14 (4): pp. 348–371.

Ladner, Andreas, Jan Fivaz, and Giorgio Nadig. 2009. 'Voting Assistance Applications as Tools to Increase Political Participation and Improve Civic Education'. In *Civic Education and Youth Political Participation*, edited by Murray Print, pp. 43–59. Boston: Brill.

Ladner, Andreas, Jan Fivaz, and Joëlle Pianzola. 2012. 'Voting Advice Applications and Party Choice: Evidence from Smartvote Users in Switzerland'. *International Journal of Electronic Governance* 5 (3/4): pp. 367–387.

Ladner, Andreas, and Joëlle Pianzola. 2010. 'Do Voting Advice Applications Have an Effect on Electoral Participation and Voter Turnout? Evidence from the 2007 Swiss Federal Elections'. In *Electronic Participation*, edited by Efthimios Tambouris, Ann Macintosh, and Olivier Glassey, pp. 211–224. Berlin/Heidelberg: Springer.

Lust, Aleksander. 2018. 'I-Vote, Therefore I Am? Internet Voting in Switzerland and Estonia'. *SAIS Review of International Affairs* 38 (1): pp. 65–79.

McGregor, Shannon C., and Logan Molyneux. 2020. 'Twitter's Influence on News Judgment: An Experiment among Journalists'. *Journalism* 21 (5): pp. 597–613.

Metag, Julia, and Adrian Rauchfleisch. 2017. 'Journalists' Use of Political Tweets'. *Digital Journalism* 5 (9): pp. 1155–1172.

Noble, Safiya Umoja. 2018. *Algorithms of Oppression: How Search Engines Reinforce Racism*. New York: New York University Press.

Obermeyer, Ziad, Brian Powers, Christine Vogeli, and Sendhil Mullainathan. 2019. 'Dissecting Racial Bias in an Algorithm Used to Manage the Health of Populations'. *Science* 366 (6464): pp. 447–453.

Persily, Nathaniel. 2017. 'Can Democracy Survive the Internet?' *Journal of Democracy* 28 (2): pp. 63–76.

Petitpas, Adrien, Julien M. Jaquet, and Pascal Sciarini. 2021. 'Does E-Voting Matter for Turnout, and to Whom?' *Electoral Studies* 71: pp. 1–14.

Pianzola, Joëlle, Alexander H. Trechsel, Kristjan Vassil, Guido Schwerdt, and R. Michael Alvarez. 2019. 'The Impact of Personalized Information on Vote Intention: Evidence from a Randomized Field Experiment'. *The Journal of Politics* 81 (3): pp. 833–847.

Rauchfleisch, Adrian, and Julia Metag. 2016. 'The Special Case of Switzerland: Swiss Politicians on Twitter'. *New Media & Society* 18 (10): pp. 2413–2431.

Romero Moreno, Guillermo, Javier Padilla, and Enrique Chueca. 2022. 'Learning VAA: A New Method for Matching Users to Parties in Voting Advice Applications'. *Journal of Elections, Public Opinion and Parties* 32(2): 339–357.

Sciarini, Pascal, Fabio Cappelletti, Andreas Goldberg, Alessandro Nai, and Amal Tawfik. 2013. *Étude Du Vote Par Internet Dans Le Canton de Genève. Rapport Final*. Geneva: Université de Genève.

Serdült, Uwe, Micha Germann, Maja Harris, Fernando Mendez, Alicia Portenier, and Efthimios Tambouris. 2015a. 'Who Are the Internet Voters?'. In *Electronic Participation*, edited by Efthimios Tambouris, pp. 27–41. Cham: Springer.

Serdült, Uwe, Micha Germann, Fernando Mendez, Alicia Portenier, and Christoph Wellig. 2015b. 'Fifteen Years of Internet Voting in Switzerland [History, Governance and Use]'. In *2015 Second International Conference on eDemocracy & eGovernment (ICEDEG)*, pp. 126–132. Quito, Ecuador: IEEE.

Sudulich, Laura, Diego Garzia, Alexander H. Trechsel, and Kristjan Vassil. 2014. 'Matching Voters with Parties in Supranational Elections: The Case of the EU Profiler'. In *Matching Voters with Parties and Candidates. Voting Advice Applications in Comparative Perspective*, edited by Diego Garzia, and Stefan Marschall, pp. 175–182. Colchester: ECPR Press.

Taş, Ruhi, and Ömer Özgür Tanrıöver. 2020. 'A Systematic Review of Challenges and Opportunities of Blockchain for E-Voting'. *Symmetry* 12 (8): pp. 1–24.

Terán, Luis, and José Mancera. 2019. 'Dynamic Profiles Using Sentiment Analysis and Twitter Data for Voting Advice Applications'. *Government Information Quarterly* 36 (3): pp. 520–535.

Thorson, Kjerstin. 2020. 'Attracting the News: Algorithms, Platforms, and Reframing Incidental Exposure'. *Journalism* 21 (8): pp. 1067–1082.

Thurman, James, and Urs Gasser. 2009. 'Three Case Studies from Switzerland: Smartvote'. *Berkman Center Research Publication No. 2009-03.3*: pp. 1–22.

Trechsel, Alexander H. 2007. 'E-Voting and Electoral Participation'. In *The Dynamics of Referendum Campaigns: An International Perspective*, edited by Claes H. de Vreese, pp. 159–182. London: Palgrave Macmillan UK.

Trechsel, Alexander H., and Diego Garzia. 2019. 'Voting Advice Applications: The Power of Self-Persuasion'. In *The Oxford Handbook of Electoral Persuasion*, edited by Elizabeth Suhay, Bernard Grofman, and Alexander H. Trechsel, pp. 924-945. New York: Oxford University Press.

Trechsel, Alexander H., Vasyl V. Kucherenko, and Frederico Ferreira Da Silva. 2016. *Potential and Challenges of E-Voting in the European Union*. Brüssel: EUDO.

Vassil, Kristjan, Mihkel Solvak, Priit Vinkel, Alexander H. Trechsel, and R. Michael Alvarez. 2016. 'The Diffusion of Internet Voting. Usage Patterns of Internet Voting in Estonia between 2005 and 2015'. *Government Information Quarterly* 33 (3): pp. 453–459.

Vogler, Daniel, Adrian Rauchfleisch, Mark Eisenegger, and Lisa Schwaiger. 2019. 'Agenda-Setting auf Twitter: Welche Rolle spielen Informationsmedien in der Schweizer Twitter-Sphäre?'. In *Qualität der Medien. Schweiz – Suisse – Svizzera. Jahrbuch 2019*, edited by FÖG – Forschungszentrum Öffentlichkeit und Gesellschaft / Universität Zürich, pp. 47–57. Basel: Schwabe.

WeCollect. 2022. *Plattform für direkte Demokratie*. https://wecollect.ch/ (accessed 23 December 2022).

PART VI

DECISION-MAKING PROCESSES

CHAPTER 24

DECISION-MAKING PROCESS

PASCAL SCIARINI

1 Introduction

THE formulation of policy lies at the heart of any political system, and it is the crucial task assigned to decision makers. Analysing problems, identifying possible solutions, bargaining over draft proposals and bills, and—eventually—adopting a legislative act is the routine business of senior officials, interest groups, experts, political parties, and MPs. According to the 'policy cycle model' (Hill and Varone 2021; Knoepfel et al. 2011), policies are developed through a multi-stage process. This chapter focuses on the decision-making (or elaboration) phases, which include the initiation phase (the political recognition of a problem and agenda setting), the preparation (or pre-parliamentary) phase, and the decision phase (parliamentary and referendum phase).[1] In Switzerland, the analysis of decision-making processes first gained momentum in the 1980s (Linder 1987) and again in the second half of the 1990s, in the context of the internationalization and Europeanization of Swiss politics (Fischer 2005; Mach et al. 2003; Papadopoulos 1997, 2008; Sciarini and Nicolet 2005; Sciarini et al. 2002, 2004). This interest has been confirmed in the more recent period, notably under the impetus of studies conducted by the author of this contribution and his team (Fischer and Sciarini 2014; Gava et al. 2021; Jaquet et al. 2019; Sciarini 2014a; Sciarini et al. 2015; Sciarini et al. 2020).

The purpose of this chapter is to present the state of knowledge on Swiss decision-making processes. It starts with a brief description of the institutional set-up of processes and then turns to a finer-grained analysis of each decision-making phase and the links between them. The analysis of these links is all the more important as the multiplication of decision-making arenas—what Ossipow (1994) calls, after Bendor (1985), the 'institutional redundancy'—is characteristic of the Swiss decision-making system. The chapter will also assess the respective weights of the main state and non-state actors participating in the process, highlight how institutions influence actors' strategies, and examine changes in the characteristics of decision-making processes over time. On this basis, it will evaluate the relevance of some claims that one finds in the contemporary literature, such as those regarding the ineffectiveness of the pre-parliamentary procedures, the 'end of consensus', or the slow pace and low innovation capacity of the Swiss decision-making process.

2 INSTITUTIONAL SET-UP AND IMPORTANCE OF DECISION-MAKING PHASES

2.1 Institutional set-up

From a comparative perspective, Swiss decision-making processes display a number of peculiarities worth mentioning.[2] In the initiation phase, several political actors can set the agenda in Switzerland: in addition to federal state actors (parliament, government and administration), Swiss citizens (through constitutional popular initiatives) and cantons (through cantonal initiatives) can also initiate a legislative process. Agenda setting can also arise 'from abroad', namely from an international negotiation. The policy formulation and adoption stage divides into several sub-phases. Once an issue has successfully been set onto the agenda, it first passes through an extensive preparatory phase called the 'pre-parliamentary phase'. In this phase, a preliminary legislative proposal is drafted by state officials, possibly with the help of experts, and is then developed by the federal administration in close collaboration with non-state actors. Representatives of state agencies, interest groups, parties, and cantons meet in extra-parliamentary committees, also called 'expert commissions' (Germann 1985; Rebmann and Mach 2013). In addition, all stakeholders may express their view on a legislative proposal during the consultation procedure (Papadopoulos 1997; Sciarini 2011b). This procedure usually consists of a written consultation in which all the principal political parties and interested organizations, as well as the cantons, are invited to express their opinions with respect to the draft. The outputs of the expert commission and/or consultation procedure pave the way for the final draft of a legislative act by the federal administration. This draft, together with a 'message' that provides information on the aims, content, and financial implications of the legislative act, is submitted to a consultation within the federal administration. Following this last examination, the legislative act and related 'message' are adopted by the Federal Council and then passed to the parliament.

The *parliamentary phase* is very typical of a system of perfect bicameralism. In this phase, a legislative proposal is examined by the specialized committee of the first chamber, before being discussed in the plenary session. This procedure is then repeated in the second chamber. In case of differences between the two chambers, a 'shuttle' (*navette*) procedure takes place, in which the bill goes back and forth between the two chambers. If the chambers still disagree after two rounds, a conciliation committee is set up to resolve the disagreements. The resulting compromise is then submitted to the final vote in both chambers.

Yet, the adoption of a bill by both chambers does not end the decision-making process. In Switzerland, the parliamentary phase is followed by a referendum phase, which gives citizens the opportunity to oppose the bill prepared by parliament. Depending on the normative level of the legislative act, a direct-democratic vote may or must take place. If a referendum is not requested or if the people support the decision of the parliament, the text is definitively adopted and then published in the Federal Gazette. The date on which the law will enter into effect is either decided by the Federal Council or may be fixed in the law itself.

2.2 Importance of decision-making phases

Kriesi's (1980) study on the thirteen most important decision-making processes of the years 1971–1976 has for a long time served as a landmark. According to this study, which was based on interviews with actors who took part in the most important decision-making processes, the pre-parliamentary phase was overall the most important phase, by far (Table 24.1): more than 75 per cent of respondents saw it as the most important phase, compared to just over 20 per cent for the parliamentary phase.[3] Within that phase, the earlier the procedure, the higher its importance: the initial drafting of a proposal was the most important sub-phase; extra-parliamentary committees and consultation procedures came next; and then the adoption of a legislative proposal by the Federal Council. The parliamentary phase was comparatively much less important (Kriesi 1980, 589, 607f). While the parliament was formally decisive, in most cases MPs had their hands tied by the deals struck in the pre-parliamentary phase. This was especially true in social policy and economic policy, which were the realm of 'neo-corporatist' concertation between interest groups.[4]

The results of our study of the eleven most important processes in the period 2001–2006 (Sciarini et al. 2015), based on a research design similar to that of Kriesi's (1980) study, show that the weight of the decision-making phases has changed significantly (Sciarini 2014a; 2015a). While the preparatory phase it still seen as the most important by a majority of respondents (61 per cent), there was a clear shift in favour of the parliamentary phase (39 per cent).

As Table 24.1 shows, the importance of both expert committees and consultation procedures has halved between the early 1970s and the early 2000s. The weakening of the pre-parliamentary phase would be even more acute without the inclusion of the extra consultation of cantons/inter-cantonal conferences, which did not play any role in the 1970s. The only classic sub-phase of the pre-parliamentary phase that has gained some importance across time is the final decision by the Federal Council. The work of the parliamentary committees is now at least as important as the elaboration of the draft proposal—the importance of which has also diminished, especially if one puts international negotiation aside.

Table 24.1: Importance of decision-making phases (percentage of interview partners who mention a specific sub-phase as 'one of the three most important')

Decision-making phase/sub-phase	1971–1976	Total	2001–2006	Total
Pre-parliamentary phase				
Draft proposal	28		21	
(among which international negotiation)	–		(8)	
Extra-parliamentary committee	18		8	
Consultation procedure	15	78	7	61
Extra consultation of cantons	0		9	
Final draft (administration)	7		2	
Final decision—Federal Council	10		14	
Parliamentary phase				
Parliamentary committee	14	22	24	39
Plenum	8		15	
Total	100	100	100	100
(Number of interviews)	(353)	(353)	(309)	(309)

Data source: Kriesi (1980, 316) for 1971–1976; Sciarini (2014a, 122; 2015a, 35) for 2001–2006.

Beyond these general trends, our study shows strong variations in the importance of phases depending on the nature of the decision-making process at stake (Sciarini 2015a). The latter can be grouped into four categories: (1) three directly Europeanized processes, namely the processes related to bilateral agreements with the EU (agreement on the taxation of savings, accession to the Schengen-Dublin agreements, extension of the agreement on the free movement of persons), in which the preparation phase within the administration and negotiations with the EU were crucial; (2) two processes characterized by indirect Europeanization (Foreigners law and Telecommunication Act), i.e. cases where Switzerland was inspired by existing European rules, in which the parliamentary phase was decisive; (3) two processes with a strong federalist component (reform of financial equalization and task distribution, and the new constitutional article on education), in which the arenas for cooperation between the cantons and the Confederation were central, and the parliamentary phase was moderately important; and finally, (4) four other processes relating to domestic issues, in which the parliament (especially the parliamentary committees, but also the plenum) played a very important role.

According to the same study, changes in the importance of decision-making phases went hand in hand with changes in the power relations between political actors. In general, the increased importance of the parliamentary phase—at the expense of the pre-parliamentary phase—went along with the strengthening of governmental parties (the main actors in the parliamentary phase) at the expense of economic interest groups (the main actors in the pre-parliamentary phase) (Sciarini 2014a; 2015b). Or to put it differently, in Switzerland as in other small European countries such as Austria, the Netherlands, or the Scandinavian countries (Christiansen and Rommetvedt 1999; Crepaz 1994; Gerlich 1992; Rommetvedt et al. 2012; Slomp 2002), the weakening of corporatist intermediation in the pre-parliamentary phase coincided with the strengthening of partisan politics in parliament.

Yet, as with the importance of decision-making phases, the power relations between actors vary significantly from one type of decision-making process to another. The government and the administration were predominant in the directly Europeanized processes, mostly at the expense of the governmental parties, while the same two actors (governmental parties and the executive) were both decisive in the indirectly Europeanized processes. In the federalist processes, the government and the administration shared the leadership with the cantonal actors; finally, in the other internal policy processes, power was relatively evenly distributed between state actors, umbrella associations of the economy, and governmental parties.

3 THE INITIATION PHASE

The political actor who initiates a legislative process is likely to leave its mark on the subsequent stages of the public policy formulation process, as well as on the content of the policy in question. A recent empirical study identifies the actors who initiated decision-making processes over the last thirty years (Jaquet et al. 2019). This study covers all acts adopted by parliament and subject to optional or mandatory referendum, or resulting from a popular initiative.

From 1987 to 2015, the Federal Council and its administration initiated about half and the parliament about a quarter of processes. The remaining quarter is divided between the international level and the people (via popular initiatives), whereas cantons play a marginal role. The evolution over time shows a decrease in the weight of the Federal Council and the federal administration in favour of the international level. This development reflects the internationalization of Swiss politics. Policies that were previously defined at the national level are now often negotiated at the international or supranational level through treaties, agreements, or conventions; this is known as direct internationalization (Sciarini et al. 2002; 2004). As a result, the share of international law in the normative production in Switzerland has steadily increased through the second half of the twentieth century (Linder 2014; Linder et al. 1985). Since the mid-1990s, international treaties have begun to outnumber domestic legislation in terms of number of pages or articles.

That said, the Federal Council and its administration still takes the lion's share in the agenda-setting phase, while parliament plays a secondary role. Moreover, the decrease in the share of processes initiated by the executive over time is counterbalanced by the

Table 24.2: Initiation of decision-making processes (in per cent)

	1987–1996	1997–2006	2007–2015	Total
Government and administration	55.8	52.7	38.5	49.5
Parliament	25.9	26.1	28.8	26.9
People	9.9	8.6	10.5	9.6
Cantons	1.0	0.7	0.4	0.7
International	7.4	11.9	21.9	13.3
Total	100	100	100	100
(N)	(514)	(605)	(535)	(1654)

Data source: Jaquet et al. (2019, 224f).

increase in the share of internationally initiated processes, which are usually the output of an action taken by the executive. Finally, while the number of popular initiatives has risen sharply over the past thirty years,[5] Table 24.2 shows that the weight of the people in driving decision-making processes has remained fairly constant.

4 THE PRE-PARLIAMENTARY PHASE

In the pre-parliamentary phase, the federal administration relies on various forms of consultation of—and negotiation with—non-state actors to develop draft bills that are both technically appropriate and politically acceptable (Papadopoulos 1997, 69f). Although the resort to external expertise and the consultation of the main stakeholders in the preparatory phase of legislation also holds in other contexts, they have traditionally played a particularly important role in Switzerland. According to a widespread view, direct democracy accounts for this. The (optional) referendum gives citizens the opportunity to oppose policies adopted by parliament. According to Neidhart's (1970) hypothesis, the risk of failure in a referendum led to the institutionalization, in the first half of the twentieth century, of pre-parliamentary procedures that should help the political elite to find broadly supported bills. The 'referendum threat', so the argument goes, progressively transformed the Swiss majoritarian democracy into a 'negotiation democracy', and also granted powerful interest groups access to the decision-making process and gave them great influence on policy outputs (Germann 1990).

4.1 Extra-parliamentary committees

The reliance on expert committees deviates from Max Weber's bureaucratic model with respect to professionalism and hierarchy, and was therefore labelled—by analogy with military vocabulary—as the 'militia administration' (Germann 1985). This is defined as 'an organization that handles state affairs and that is composed entirely or in part of people for whom this involvement is part-time and incidental to a principal professional activity' (Germann 1996, 80; my translation). In 1979, the Federal Chancellery for the first time published the list of all existing extra-parliamentary committees. At that time, there were 373 committees, with a total of 5,376 seats held by 3,866 experts, of whom 3,105 were not members of the administration.

More recent studies point to several important changes in extra-parliamentary committees (Beetschen and Rebmann 2016; David et al. 2009; Eichenberger 2017, 2020; Rebmann and Mach 2013). First, the total number of committees increased sharply between the 1930s and the 1980s, but has strongly declined since. Secondly, the number of economic associations represented in committees has decreased, whereas the proportion of public interest groups and scientific experts has increased. The resulting pluralization of actors weakened the extra-parliamentary committees as arenas for corporatist intermediation (Beetschen and Rebmann 2016).

4.2 Consultation procedures

To further test the quality and acceptability of a draft bill, the federal administration simulates the reactions of stakeholders in 'consultation procedures' (Papadopoulos 1997, 78). The consultation procedure is rooted in article 147 of the federal constitution, according to which 'the cantons, political parties, and interested parties are invited to comment on important legislative acts and other major projects during the preparatory work, as well as on important international treaties'. The Federal Law on the Consultation Procedure (LCo) sets three objectives to consultation procedures (art. 2 para. 2): make sure that a project is materially correct ('technical quality'), that it is likely to be supported politically ('political acceptability'), and that it can be implemented ('applicability'). Political acceptability—and the related referendum threat—is thus not the only driver of consultation procedures. For example, if the cantons are systematically consulted, it is mostly because they will then be responsible for implementing the legislation.

Christe et al. (2016) reviewed the 946 consultations set up between 2006 and 2014. In more than nine of ten cases, the decision to open a consultation procedure was taken by the executive, in less than one of ten cases by parliament. Two of the seven federal departments alone—Environment, Transport, Energy, and Communications (DETEC) and Justice and Police (FDJP)—initiated almost half of the consultation procedures. Further, more than half of the consultation procedures concerned an ordinance not subject to a referendum, which again demonstrates that the referendum threat is not the only driver of consultation. Finally, interest groups represent almost two-thirds of the actors who participate in consultation procedures (Christe et al. 2016). However, the majority of interest groups participate only very occasionally: 60 per cent participated in only one consultation and 80 per cent in three consultations at most; only a tiny share of interest groups (1 per cent, among which are umbrella organizations) participated in 10 per cent or more of all procedures. It is not surprising that organizations are selective in their participation, since formulating an informed opinion on draft bills requires expertise and may be time-consuming.

4.3 The use and contribution of pre-parliamentary procedures

Table 24.3 presents the share of legislative acts that gave rise to a pre-parliamentary procedure in the early 1970s and from the late 1980s onwards. It shows significant differences between expert committees and consultation procedures. In the early 1970s, more than one in three legislative processes involved an extra-parliamentary committee. This share was more than twice as low in the 1987–2015 period. In contrast, the frequency of consultation procedures has increased almost constantly. Since the early 2000s, more than one in two processes has included a consultation procedure.

Several—complementary—hypotheses may account for these contrasted evolutions (Sciarini 2014b). On the one hand, the lower use of extra-parliamentary committees may for instance be explained by the considerable development of Swiss public administration during the last fifty years, which thus is less dependent than before on external expertise; on the other hand, the increased use of consultation procedures is at least in part due to growing legal obligations.

As already mentioned, the resort to pre-parliamentary procedures should help to find broadly supported policy measures and is, therefore, supposed to ease the acceptance of a bill in the subsequent phases of the decision-making process. This is, in any case, the assumption that underlies Neidhart's (1970) argument about the institutionalization of pre-parliamentary procedures. However, empirical tests tend to question the contribution of pre-parliamentary procedures to conflict resolution (Sciarini et al. 2002, 21f). Bills that gave rise to an extra-parliamentary committee or to a consultation procedure did not display a lower level of conflict in parliament than bills that did not include either procedure; legislative proposals that were highly conflictual

Table 24.3: Percentage of legislative acts that gave rise to a pre-parliamentary procedure

	1971–1976	1987–1995	1995–2003	2003–2011	2011–2015	Total 1987–2015
Expert commission	37	19	20	17	8	17
Consultation procedure	39	41	43	53	53	47
Number of legislative acts	163	389	450	510	288	1637

Data sources: Poitry (1989, 227, 30) for 1971–1976; Sciarini et al. (2020) for 1987–2015.

at the outset of the decision-making process remained so in the parliamentary phase, regardless of whether a pre-parliamentary procedure was held. Similarly, setting up an expert committee or a consultation procedure had no impact on the likelihood of an optional referendum.

4.4 The pre-parliamentary phase and the duration of decision-making processes

Observers of Swiss politics often complain about the slow pace and low innovation capacity of its political decision-making (e.g. Kriesi 1998, 293ff). Table 24.4 provides information on the duration of decision-making processes and their related phases.

During the 1971–1976 period, the average length of decision-making processes was around five years. The corresponding figure was slightly smaller during the 1995–1999 legislature. The median—more appropriate given the strong variations in duration across processes—indicates that half of processes lasted approximately three years. The pre-parliamentary phase is by far the longest part of the process: in the two periods under consideration, it lasted roughly three years, on average, and accounted for two-thirds (1995–1999 legislature) and three-quarters (1971–1976 period) of the total response time.

A more detailed analysis shows that the duration of decision-making processes varies considerably according to whether formal pre-parliamentary procedures are implemented (Sciarini 2014b): setting up an extra-parliamentary committee lengthens the decision-making process by more than one year (fifteen months); setting up a consultation procedure lengthens the decision-making process by more than two years (twenty-six months). As the standard duration of a consultation procedure

Table 24.4: Duration of decision-making processes, in total and by phase (in months)

	1971–76			1995–99		
Phase	Mean	Median	N	Mean	Median	N
Pre-parliamentary	41	28	133	35	18	184
- expert committees	21	11	45	20	14	32
- consultation	3	3	63	3	3	92
Parliamentary	8	7	137	12	9	188
Referendum	8	5	130	4	4	188
Total	57	39	137	51	33	184

Note: This table does not include popular initiatives.
Data source: For 1971–76: data from Poitry (1989); for 1995–99: data-bank Sciarini et al. (2002).

is three months, it is not the procedure itself but rather its management by the administration (preparation, analysis, and synthesis of the consultation results, intra-administration coordination, and preparation of the final bill) which takes so much time. Besides the pre-parliamentary procedures, the duration of decision-making processes also depends on the juridical type and novelty of a bill: for instance, processes are longer for constitutional acts and laws than for urgent federal laws; new legislative acts lead to longer decision-making processes than the revision of legislative acts (Sciarini 2014b).

However, in the absence of comparative data it is difficult to conclude that Swiss decision-making processes are especially lengthy. Similarly, while many observers claim that the multiplicity of institutional veto points in general, and the referendum in particular, affects the innovativeness of the Swiss decision-making system (e.g. Borner et al. 1990; Germann 1994; Kriesi 1998; Linder 1987), the study on the eleven most important decision-making processes of the early 2000s departs from this negative assessment (Fischer 2015). According to the evaluation of decision makers who participated in these processes, policy outputs were fairly to highly innovative in a majority of cases.

5 The parliamentary phase

Law-making is the 'core business' of parliaments in democratic systems (Blondel 1970). In addition to its contribution to the initiation of decision-making processes (section 3), parliament exercises its legislative function by drafting bills or federal decrees that it has itself initiated, by examining and amending draft legislative acts prepared by the executive, and, ultimately, by adopting legislative acts. But how much policy-making power does a legislature really have (Mezey 1979)? The question has animated scholarly debates for a long time. However, knowledge about the extent to which parliaments influence legislation is still scarce, and mainly stems from studies on the US Congress or the British parliament (Saiegh 2014). Even less is known about how this influence is exercised and what determines it: why do parliamentarians amend some bills more than others?

5.1 Parliamentary committees

In Switzerland, it first falls to the specialized committees to study draft legislation and, where appropriate, to propose amendments. It is particularly difficult to evaluate the importance of parliamentary committees in the decision-making process because their debates are not public. Some studies nevertheless provide some insight into the work achieved by these bodies. With the help of a quantitative analysis of all of the bills handled by the commissions of the two chambers between 1990 and 1994, and interviews with members of parliament and the secretaries of the commissions, Lüthi (1996) examined the effects of the 1992 shift from ad hoc to standing committees—a reform that explicitly aimed to reinforce the weight of the Federal Assembly in the decision-making process. According to her 'before–after' study, the institutional reform did achieve its goal. Thus, the number of modifications introduced by the commissions (of the National Council in particular) to proposals submitted by the executive markedly increased after the reform. In addition, in both chambers, these modifications were almost always endorsed by the plenum (Lüthi 1996, 92). On the qualitative side, Lüthi's (1996) analysis reveals that permanent commissions have become a valuable (and critical) interlocutor for the Federal Council and the administration. The very fact that members of the commissions are occupied with the same matters over many years increases their general level of competence. According to Linder and Mueller (2017, 250), the new committee system has strengthened the parliament vis-à-vis both the executive and pre-parliamentary procedures. In that sense, this reform undoubtedly contributed to rebalancing the weight between the pre-parliamentary and parliamentary phases.

5.2 The plenum

The legislative influence of a parliament can be measured by the share of bills it amends and, relatedly, by the degree of change operated by parliament. According to various one-off studies from the 1970s (Zehnder 1988), 1990s (Jegher 1999), 2000s (Schwarz et al. 2011), or 2010s (Vatter 2018), the proportion of legislative acts modified by the Swiss parliament amounts to about 40 per cent, with little change across time. According to these studies, more than half of the legislative acts are therefore adopted by parliament without any amendment. However, while the proportion of modified legislative acts has remained stable over time, the number of acts adopted by parliament has increased significantly. Scholars use this last result to argue that the parliament's influence over legislation has been reinforced over time (e.g. Vatter 2018).

Gava et al. (2021) undertake a more systematic examination of parliamentary amendments to legislative texts using an innovative methodology that electronically compares legislative texts as they enter and leave the parliamentary phase. The resulting dissimilarity index not only helps to distinguish modified from non-modified texts, but also to estimate the degree of change operated by parliament. Over the period from 1999 to 2015 and for the 1,672 legislative acts included in the analysis, the proportion of modified acts amounted to 38 per cent, a share that is very close to the result of the aforementioned studies based on manual coding. The dissimilarity index amounted to 0.22 (median 0.18) on average, which means that parliament amended about one-fifth of each text, a proportion that has remained stable across legislatures. The authors interpret these results as a sign that the Swiss Parliament is fairly active in amending legislation and, therefore, does exert some influence over legislation (Gava et al. 2021).

Gava et al. (2021) further observe that parliament amends more bills subject to direct democracy than simple federal decrees not submitted to it and, within these two broad categories, more domestic bills than decrees relating to an international treaty. The authors also show that the degree of change is higher for more important legislative acts, as well as for acts that receive greater media attention. Furthermore, acts that emanate from a parliamentary initiative are more amended than acts submitted by the Federal Council. Finally, they find that the likelihood that acts are significantly amended increases with the degree of development of the pre-parliamentary phase, which again qualifies the contribution of this phase.

5.3 Perfect bicameralism

In a system of perfect bicameralism, the decision-making capacity of the parliament depends closely on the ability of the two chambers to find common ground. According to the literature, this ability is pronounced in Switzerland and has increased over time (Huber-Hotz 1991, 174f): between 1875 and 1945, 44 per cent of constitutional acts and 38 per cent of federal laws were adopted without resorting to the 'shuttle' procedure, on average; the corresponding figures increased between 1946 and 1972 (49 per cent and 52 per cent, respectively) and even more so between 1972 and 1989 (77 per cent and 55 per cent). Additionally, between 1902 and 1991 it was necessary to resort to a conciliation committee between the two chambers in only seventeen cases.

More recent data does not show a decrease in the agreement between the two chambers (Sciarini et al. 2020): between 1987 and 2019, the share of acts adopted without resorting to the shuttle was somehow lower than before with respect to constitutional amendments (41 per cent), but has remained stable for acts subject to the optional referendum (52 per cent). Further, since the limitation of the shuttle procedure to two rounds in 1992, a conciliation conference has had to be set up 106 times, i.e. about fifteen times per legislature on average (Sciarini et al. 2020). However, this represents only 6 per cent of the total number of legislative acts adopted by the parliament during this period, without any sign of increase over time.

6 THE REFERENDUM PHASE

6.1 Government support in direct-democratic votes

The integration of all major political parties in the governing 'coalition' was supposed to render them co-responsible for—and loyal to—the government's line of action (e.g. Germann 1996; Neidhart 1970). In particular, parties in government were expected to refrain from launching or supporting referendums and popular initiatives. However, Table 24.5 shows that the positive side effects of government participation got lost, which questions the vividness of the Swiss 'consensus' or 'consociational' democracy.

Table 24.5: Percentage of voting recommendations running counter to the Federal Council (number of votes in parenthesis)

	Socialist Party		Swiss People's Party		Socialist Party *or* Swiss People's Party		
	1971–1979	1995–2003	1971–1979	1995–2003	1971–1979	1995–2003	2003–2011	2011–2019
Compulsory referendum	25%	15%	3%	30%	28% (39)	40% (19)	71% (14)	75% (12)
Optional referendum	47%	43%	6%	29%	53% (16)	71% (26)	95% (20)	90% (21)
Popular initiative	52%	65%	0%	18%	52% (34)	83% (60)	100% (18)	66% (41)

Data source: Swissvotes (2022).

The table presents the share of voting recommendations that went against the position of the Federal Council.

In the 1970s, the Socialist Party frequently opposed the Swiss government in direct-democratic votes: it supported almost half of the optional referendums and more than half of popular initiatives. In the late 1990s and early 2000s, its opposition to the Federal Council slightly diminished on acts subject to referendum, but increased on acts arising from popular initiatives. The evolution of the Swiss People's Party is even more interesting. In the 1970s, that party had a highly governmental profile: its voting recommendations almost always coincided with those of the Federal Council. Between 1995 and 2003, however, the Swiss People's Party opposed the government in one case out of three on legislative acts subject to referendum, and in one case out of five on legislative acts arising from a popular initiative. As a result, the number of popular votes where either the Socialist Party *or* the Swiss People's Party opposes a project supported by the Federal Council has starkly increased between the 1970s and the period 1995–2003. The problem worsened further in the period 2003–2011: the Swiss People's Party or the Socialist Party (or both together) opposed the Federal Council on all popular initiatives, on almost all laws put to the direct-democratic vote, and on almost three-quarters of the mandatory referendums.

Although in the most recent period (2011–2019) opposition has slightly reduced, the Federal Council can hardly go to a popular vote without facing opposition from at least one governmental party. On the basis of this indicator, and in light of the 'double game' of government and opposition played by the two largest parties (the Socialist Party and the Swiss People's Party), one is tempted to conclude that consensus no longer exists in Switzerland (Sciarini 2011a, ch. 6).

The outcome of direct-democratic votes also indicates support for the authorities, but this time on the part of citizens. Since the end of the Second World War, such support has remained at a very high level (a success rate of around 75 per cent, more for popular initiatives and slightly less for optional referendums). In Switzerland, the convergence of views between the people and the political elites is thus high and stable, and has hardly been affected by the increase of partisan polarization.[6]

6.2 The influence of parliamentary consensus on the acceptability of acts in the referendum phase

While empirical evidence casts doubt on the contribution of pre-parliamentary procedures to consensus formation (see above) several studies highlight the influence of consensus in parliament on the acceptance of a legislative act in the referendum phase (Lehner 1984; Sciarini and Trechsel 1996; Trechsel and Sciarini 1998). The degree of acceptance of an act in the parliament to a large extent determines the acceptance (or not) of the act in the plebiscitary arena. According to the analysis of all the popular votes held from 1947 to 1995, there is a strong relationship between the degree of support given to an act in the National Council—the chamber that is most representative of the population—and the outcome (Yes or No) of the direct-democratic vote for acts subject to the compulsory referendum and for those arising from a popular initiative (Sciarini and Trechsel 1996; Trechsel and Sciarini 1998): the higher the acceptance rate in the National Council, the higher the likelihood of success for the government and parliament, i.e. the higher the likelihood that the people vote in line with the authorities' voting recommendations. By contrast, there is no such relation for legislative acts submitted to the optional referendum: the probability of a Yes in the direct-democratic vote is 50 per cent when an act is supported by 60 per cent of MPs, and barely exceeds 60 per cent if they support a legislative act unanimously. The latter result is all the more remarkable because there is a strong relationship between the level of consensus in the National Council and the successful use of the optional referendum (Sciarini 2014b, 552; Sciarini and Trechsel 1996, 220): the higher the level of support to a legislative act, the lower the risk that the optional referendum is successfully used.[7]

To account for these contrasting results, Sciarini and Trechsel (1996, 224f; see also Trechsel and Sciarini 1998, 118) point to a lack of consistency within the circle of political elites with respect to acts contested by optional referendum. While the popular vote directly follows the parliamentary vote in the case of the compulsory referendum and the popular initiative, with respect to the optional referendum it is preceded by—and depends on—the successful collection of 50,000 signatures. This may lead part of the parliamentary elite to change its mind and oppose a given legislative act in the referendum campaign, which then weakens the impact of parliamentary consensus on the outcome of the popular vote.

7 CONCLUSION

For analytical purposes, each decision-making phase was examined sequentially in this chapter, notwithstanding the limitations of this approach. As has been shown above, one of the major characteristics of the decision-making process in Switzerland lies in the procedures and strategies elaborated over time to ease the passage of a legislative act from one phase to the next, and ultimately to reduce the risk of failure in a referendum. The pre-parliamentary phase is a central piece of the Swiss decision-making system, and for a long time was considered paramount. By favouring consensus-building, pre-parliamentary procedures were supposed to smooth the adoption of legislative proposals in the subsequent decision-making phases. Empirical records, however, tell a different story. Setting up pre-parliamentary procedures does not seem to reduce conflict in the parliamentary or referendum phases. Moreover, these procedures appear costly in terms of time. While still important, the pre-parliamentary phase has substantially weakened during the last decades. This holds in particular for the two procedures that used to be the centrepieces of corporatist intermediation, the extra-parliamentary committees, and consultation procedures.

With regard to the importance of the parliamentary phase, the results presented in this chapter paint a nuanced picture. On the one hand, for the most important decision-making processes, the reduced importance of the pre-parliamentary phase went hand in hand with the increased importance of the parliamentary phase. On the other hand, the parliament lags far behind the executive in the initiation phase. Moreover, its footprint on legislation through amendment activities is not negligible, but it is not considerable either. Overall, it seems that the parliament focuses its attention primarily on the most important acts, which is in line with the limited resources of a 'militia' parliament that is not composed of professional politicians. Further, the findings reported here also underline the influence of the level of consensus in parliament on the destiny of legislative acts in the referendum phase.

The relative decline of the pre-parliamentary phase and the increased importance of the parliamentary phase also has implications from the perspective of consensus and conflict in Swiss democracy. More specifically, the replacement of corporatist intermediation and consensus-seeking behind closed doors in the pre-parliamentary phase by competitive and confrontational partisan politics in parliament threatens the basis of consensual policy-making, and may move Switzerland further away from the ideal-type of consensus or consociational democracy and closer to a form of 'imperfect' or 'competitive consensus' (Sciarini 2015c).

The opposition to the federal government in direct-democratic votes by governing parties (the Socialist Party and the Swiss People's Party) is arguably the indicator that demonstrates most clearly the decline of consensus. While the integration of the main political parties in the federal government was intended to reduce the risk of opposition in the direct-democratic arena, the cases in which governing parties unanimously support the Federal Council have become the exception. Consensus could survive the opposition of the Socialist Party in the 1970s, but it can hardly survive the joint opposition of the Socialist and Swiss People's Parties.

Notes

1. For the implementation and evaluations phases, see 'The Implementation and Evaluation of Public Policies' in this volume.
2. Legislative acts do not necessarily pass through all stages mentioned in the following overview, which describes a 'standard' process. In particular, urgent federal laws, international treaties, and popular initiatives follow specific procedures.
3. In Kriesi's (1980) study, the referendum phase was not included in this part of the analysis. For the processes of the years 2001–2006, however, the inclusion of the referendum phase hardly changes the results. According to the respondents, this phase played an important role in a limited number of processes (four out of eleven).
4. See 'Interest Groups' in this volume.
5. See 'Direct-Democratic Votes' in this volume.
6. For more details, see 'Direct-Democratic Votes' in this volume.
7. Increasing the likelihood of acceptance of a legislative act in the referendum phase through consensus-building in parliament is nevertheless a demanding strategy, in the sense that

it requires forming 'oversized' legislative coalitions: to reduce the risk of the use of the optional referendum—or the risk of a popular defeat in a compulsory referendum—to less than one out of two, the level of support in the National Council must reach a majority of more than two-thirds of MPs (Trechsel and Sciarini 1998, 110f).

References

Beetschen, Marion, and Frédéric Rebmann. 2016. 'Le néo-corporatisme suisse en déclin? Les commissions extra-parlementaires dans un environnement en mutation (1957–2010)'. *Swiss Political Science Review* 22 (1): pp. 123–144.

Bendor, Jonathan B. 1985. *Parallel Systems: Redundancy in Government*. Berkeley: University of California Press.

Blondel, Jean. 1970. 'Legislative Behaviour: Some Steps Towards a Cross-National Measurement'. *Government and Opposition* 5 (1): pp. 67–85.

Borner, Silvio, Aymo Brunetti, and Thomas Straubhaar. 1990. *Schweiz AG. Vom Sonderfall zum Sanierungsfall?* Zürich: Neue Zürcher Zeitung.

Christe, Julien, Roy Gava, and Frédéric Varone. 2016. 'Consultations et groupes d'intérêt: un aperçu quantitatif'. *Leges – Gesetzgebung & Evaluation* 27 (2): pp. 211–224.

Christiansen, Peter Munk, and Hilmar Rommetvedt. 1999. 'From Corporatism to Lobbyism: Parliaments, Executives, and Organized Interests in Denmark and Norway'. *Scandinavian Political Studies* 22 (3): pp. 195–220.

Crepaz, Markus L. 1994. 'From Semisovereignty to Sovereignty. The Decline of Corporatism and the Rise of Parliament in Austria'. *Comparative Politics* 27 (1): pp. 45–65.

David, Thomas, Stéphanie Ginalski, André Mach, and Frédéric Rebmann. 2009. 'Networks of Coordination: Swiss Business Associations as an Intermediary between Business, Politics and Administration during the 20th Century'. *Business and Politics* 11 (4): 1–38.

Eichenberger, Steven. 2017. *Interest Groups' Access to Policy Venues: The Rise of Citizen Groups in Switzerland?* Lausanne: University of Lausanne.

Eichenberger, Steven. 2020. 'The Rise of Citizen Groups within the Administration and Parliament in Switzerland'. *Swiss Political Science Review* 26 (2): pp. 206–227.

Fischer, Alex. 2005. *Die Auswirkungen der Internationalisierung und Europäisierung auf Schweizer Entscheidungsprozesse. Institutionen, Kräftverhältnisse und Akteursstrategien in Bewegung*. Zürich/Chur: Rüegger.

Fischer, Manuel. 2015. 'Reactive, Slow and ... Innovative? Decision-Making Structures and Policy Outputs'. In *Political Decision-Making in Switzerland: Challenges to Consensus Politics*, edited by Pascal Sciarini, Manuel Fischer, and Denise Traber, pp. 219–237. London: Palgrave/McMillan.

Fischer, Manuel, and Pascal Sciarini. 2014. 'The Europeanization of Swiss Decision-Making Processes'. *Swiss Political Science Review* 20 (2): pp. 239–245.

Gava, Roy, Julien Jaquet, and Pascal Sciarini. 2021. 'Legislating or Rubber-Stamping? the Impact of Parliament on Law-Making'. *European Journal of Political Research* 60 (1): pp. 175–198.

Gerlich, Peter. 1992. 'A Farewell to Corporatism'. In *Politics in Austria. Still a Case of Consociationalism?*, edited by Kurt Richard Luther, and Wolfgang C. Müller, pp. 132–146. West European Politics Special Issue 15, London: Frank Cass.

Germann, Raimund E. 1985. *Experts et commissions de la confédération*. Lausanne: Presses polytechniques romandes.

Germann, Raimund E. 1990. 'Pour une constitution fédérale "Euro-compatible"'. *Revue de droit suisse* 109 (1): pp. 1–16.

Germann, Raimund E. 1994. *Staatsreform. Der Übergang zur Konkurrenzdemokratie.* Berne: Haupt.

Germann, Raimund E. 1996. *Administration publique en Suisse. L'appareil étatique et le gouvernement.* Berne: Haupt.

Hill, Michael, and Frédéric Varone. 2021. *The Public Policy Process*. London: Routledge (8th edition).

Huber-Hotz, Annemarie. 1991. 'Das Zweikammersystem – Anspruch und Wirklichkeit'. In *Das Parlament—'Oberste Gewalt des Bundes'?*, edited by Parlamentsdienste, pp. 165–182. Berne: Haupt.

Jaquet, Julien M., Pascal Sciarini, and Frédéric Varone. 2019. 'Policy-Agenda-Setting: Regierung als Hauptinitiator von Entscheidungsprozessen?' In *Blackbox Exekutive*, edited by Adrian Ritz, Theo Haldemann, and Fritz Sager, pp. 213–233. Zurich: NZZ Libro.

Jegher, Annina. 1999. *Bundesversammlung und Gesetzgebung. Der Einfluss von institutionellen, politischen und inhaltlichen Faktoren auf die Gesetzgebungstätigkeit der Eidgenössischen Räte.* Bern: Haupt.

Knoepfel, Peter, Corinne Larrue, Frédéric Varone, and Michael Hill. 2011. *Public Policy Analysis*. Bristol: The Policy Press.

Kriesi, Hanspeter. 1980. *Entscheidungsstrukturen und Entscheidungsprozesse in der Schweizer Politik.* Frankfurt: Campus Verlag.

Kriesi, Hanspeter. 1998. *Le système politique suisse*, 2nd ed. Paris: Economica.

Lehner, Franz. 1984. 'Consociational Democracy in Switzerland: A Political Economic Explanation and some Empirical Evidence'. *European Journal of Political Research* 12 (1): pp. 25–42.

Linder, Wolf. 1987. *La décision politique en Suisse*. Lausanne: Réalités sociales.

Linder, Wolf. 2014. 'Swiss Legislation in the Era of Globalization: a Quantitative Assessment of Federal Legislation (1983–2007)'. *Swiss Political Science Review* 20 (2): pp. 223–231.

Linder, Wolf, and Sean Mueller. 2017. *Schweizerische Demokratie. Institutionen, Prozesse, Perspektiven*, 4th ed. Bern: Haupt.

Linder, Wolf, Stefan Schwager, and Fabrizio Comandini. 1985. *Inflation législative? Une recherche sur l'évolution quantitative du droit suisse 1948-82.* Lausanne: IDHEAP.

Lüthi, Ruth. 1996. 'Der Einfluss von institutionnelle Reformen auf den politischen Prozess dargestellt am Beispiel der Reform des Kommissionensystem der Schweizerischen Bundesversammlung von 1991'. *Swiss Political Science Review* 2 (2): pp. 81–111.

Mach, André, Silja Häusermann, and Yannis Papadopoulos. 2003. 'Economic Regulatory Reforms in Switzerland: Adjustment without European Integration or How Rigidities Become Flexible'. *Journal of European Public Policy* 10 (2): pp. 302–319.

Mezey, Michael L. 1979. *Comparative Legislatures*. Durham, N.C: Duke University Press.

Neidhart, Leonard. 1970. *Plebiszit und pluralitäre Demokratie, Eine Analyse der Funktionen des schweizerischen Gesetzesreferendum.* Bern: Francke.

Ossipow, William. 1994. 'Le système politique suisse ou l'art de la compensation'. In *Elites politiques et peuple en Suisse. Analyse des votations fédérales: 1970–1987*, edited by Yannis Papadopoulos, pp. 9–55. Lausanne: Réalités sociales.

Papadopoulos, Yannis. 1997. *Les processus de décision fédéraux en Suisse*. Paris: L'Harmattan.

Papadopoulos, Yannis. 2008. 'Europeanization? Two Logics of Change of Policy-Making in Switzerland'. *Journal of Comparative Policy Analysis* 10 (3): pp. 255–278.

Poitry, Alain-Valéry. 1989. *La fonction d'ordre de l'Etat. Analyse des mécanismes et des déterminants sélectifs dans le processus législatif suisse*. Berne: Lang.

Rebmann, Frédéric, and André Mach. 2013. 'Commissions extra-parlementaires fédérales'. In *Manuel de l'administration publique en Suisse*, edited by Andreas Ladner, pp. 161–176. Lausanne: Presses polytechniques et universitaires romandes.

Rommetvedt, Hilmar, Gunnar Thesen, Peter Munk Christiansen, and Soone Norgaard. 2012. 'Coping with Corporatism in Decline and the Revival of Parliament: Interest Groups Lobbyism in Denmark and Norway, 1980–2005'. *Comparative Political Studies* 46 (4): pp. 457–485.

Saiegh, Sebastian M. 2014. 'Lawmaking'. In *The Oxford Handbook of Legislative Studies*, edited by Martin Shane, Thomas Saalfeld, and Kaare W. Strøm, pp. 481–513. Oxford: Oxford University Press.

Schwarz, Daniel, André Bächtiger, and Georg Lutz. 2011. 'Agenda-Setting Power of the Government in a Separation-of-Powers Framework'. In *The Role of Government in Legislative Agenda Setting*, edited by Bjorn Erik Rasch, and George Tsebelis, pp. 127–143. London: Routledge.

Sciarini, Pascal. 2011a. *La politique suisse au fil du temps*. Genève: Georg.

Sciarini, Pascal. 2011b. 'Les effets de la consultation sur les processus de décision au niveau fédéral'. *Leges – Gesetzgebung & Evaluation* 22 (2): pp. 191–228.

Sciarini, Pascal. 2014a. 'Eppure si muove: The Changing Nature of the Swiss Consensus Democracy'. *Journal of European Public Policy* 21 (1): pp. 116–132.

Sciarini, Pascal. 2014b. 'Le processus législatif'. In *Handbuch der Schweizer Politik*, edited by Peter Knoepfel, Yannis Papadopoulos, Pascal Sciarini, Adrian Vatter, and Silja Häusermann, pp. 527–561. Zurich: NZZ Libro.

Sciarini, Pascal. 2015a. 'From Corporatism to Bureaucratic and Partisan Politics: Changes in Decision-Making Processes Over Time'. In *Political Decision-Making in Switzerland: The Consensus Model Under Pressure*, edited by Pascal Sciarini, Manuel Fischer, and Denise Traber, pp. 24–50. Basingstoke/New York: Palgrave/McMillan.

Sciarini, Pascal. 2015b. 'More Power Balance, Less Consensus: Changes in Decision-Making Structures Over Time'. In *Political Decision-Making in Switzerland: The Consensus Model Under Pressure*, edited by Pascal Sciarini, Manuel Fischer, and Denise Traber, pp. 51–77. Basingstoke/New York: Palgrave/McMillan.

Sciarini, Pascal. 2015c. 'Conclusion'. In *Political Decision-Making in Switzerland: The Consensus Model Under Pressure*, edited by Pascal Sciarini, Manuel Fischer, and Denise Traber, pp. 238–259. Basingstoke/New York: Palgrave/McMillan.

Sciarini, Pascal, Alex Fischer, and Sarah Nicolet. 2002. 'L'impact de l'internationalisation sur les processus de décision en Suisse: Une analyse quantitative des actes législatifs 1995–1999'. *Revue suisse de science politique* 8 (3): pp. 1–34.

Sciarini, Pascal, Alex Fischer, and Sarah Nicolet. 2004. 'How Europe Hits Home: Evidence From the Swiss Case'. *Journal of European Public Policy* 11 (3): pp. 353–378.

Sciarini, Pascal, Manuel Fischer, and Denise Traber (eds). 2015. *Political Decision-Making in Switzerland: The Consensus Model Under Pressure*. Basingstoke/New York: Palgrave Macmillan.

Sciarini, Pascal, Roy Gava, and Julien M. Jaquet. 2020. 'Swiss Legislative Processes (1987–2019) [LegPro database]'. https://legpro.unige.ch/data/.

Sciarini, Pascal, and Sarah Nicolet. 2005. 'Internationalization and Domestic Politics: Evidence From the Swiss Case'. In *Contemporary Switzerland: Revisiting the Special Case*, edited by

Hanspeter Kriesi, Peter Farago, Martin Kohli, and Milad Zarin-Nejadan, pp. 221–238. New York: Palgrave/McMillan.

Sciarini, Pascal, and Alexandre Trechsel. 1996. 'Démocratie directe en Suisse: l'élite victime des droits populaires?' *Revue suisse de science politique* 2 (2): pp. 201–232.

Slomp, Hans. 2002. 'The Netherlands in the 1990s: Towards "Flexible Corporatism" in the Polder Model'. In *Policy Concertation and Social Partnership in Western Europe*, edited by Stefan Berger, and Hugh Compston, pp. 235–247. Oxford: Berghahn Books.

Swissvotes. 2022. Swissvotes— the Database of the Swiss Popular Votes. Dataset. www.swissvotes.ch (accessed 15 May 2022).

Trechsel, Alexander H., and Pascal Sciarini. 1998. 'Direct Democracy in Switzerland: Do Elites Matter?' *European Journal of Political Research* 33 (1): pp. 99–124.

Vatter, Adrian. 2018. 'Einleitung und Überblick: Macht und Ohnmacht des Parlaments in der Schweiz'. In *Das Parlament in der Schweiz*, edited by Adrian Vatter, pp. 17–67. Zürich: NZZ Libro.

Zehnder, Ernst. 1988. *Die Gesetzüberprüfung durch die Schweizerische Bundesversammlung. Untersuchung der parlamentarischen Veränderungen von Vorlagen des Bundesrates in der Legislaturperiode 1971 bis 1975*. St. Gallen: Hochschule St. Gallen.

CHAPTER 25

IMPLEMENTATION AND EVALUATION OF PUBLIC POLICIES

ANDREAS BALTHASAR

1 INTRODUCTION: IMPLEMENTATION RESEARCH AND POLICY EVALUATION IN SWITZERLAND

Swiss implementation research in its current state is built on a series of research programmes and case studies which began in the 1970s (Bussmann 2008).[1] Drawing on examples from the fields of agriculture, spatial planning, and environmental protection, a research programme launched in 1976 made clear that, in Switzerland as well as elsewhere, implementation needs to be understood as a social process involving the expectations, ideas, and interests of a variety of different actors (Bussmann et al. 1997; Linder 1987). Implementation research has now become an established part of policy analysis in Switzerland and benefits from strong international links (Leifeld and Ingold 2016). This research is dominated by examinations of the prevailing implementation models in Switzerland (section 2) and their impact on implementation outcomes (section 3).

Over the past thirty years, Swiss evaluation research has developed significantly and become heavily institutionalized (section 4). This was a good basis for meta-research on evaluation (section 5). Section 6 summarizes the key findings and outlines the main challenges facing implementation and evaluation research in Switzerland.

2 PATTERNS OF IMPLEMENTATION IN SWITZERLAND

In Switzerland, policy implementation is determined by the strongly federalist structure of the state. Two factors are decisive. First, bottom-up federalism assigns responsibility to the cantons for all tasks that the constitution does not explicitly allocate to the federal state. This means that the cantons are responsible for designing and implementing key tasks such as education or social welfare. Second, the cantons are also in charge of implementing many policies designed on the federal level, such as agriculture or migration policy. There are only a few areas where the Swiss Confederation has its own executive authorities (e.g. customs or federal tax office for all indirect taxation such as Value Added Tax). These two factors in particular lead to implementation models that may vary greatly from one canton to another. To define this phenomenon, the term 'Vollzugsföderalismus' ('implementation by federal delegation') was coined in Switzerland (Germann 1986, 347). 'Vollzugsföderalismus' means that, within the scope of their powers, the cantons assign responsibilities, set operational targets, and formulate guidelines for implementation.

The Federal Act on the Acquisition of Immovable Property in Switzerland by Foreign Non-Residents serves as an object lesson in this concept (Linder 1987). The aim of this—frequently revised—law was to restrict the sale of Swiss land to foreigners. However, in view of the different interests involved, the cantons interpreted the corresponding federal legislation in different ways: some cantons implemented it in a way that resulted in the restrictive authorization practice envisaged by the law, while others took an approach that involved minimal restrictions for the local construction market, or used the law to promote social housing. Numerous other examples of 'Vollzugsföderalismus' in practice can be found in health, environmental, or agricultural policy.

As a rule, the federal doctrine does not regard 'Vollzugsföderalismus' as problematic. In fact, it tends to be seen as offering the potential for more effective problem-solving than under a standardized national regime. This approach gives the cantons scope to adapt federal specifications to suit the conditions at the local level (Wälti 2001). The cantons can ensure that the adopted cantonal implementation model accounts for local variations in problem pressure, in resources, or even in political styles (cf. Battaglini and Giraud 2003). This does, however, mean that, in this case, the cantons function not just as execution authorities, but as programme authorities too (Rieder et al. 2014). Sometimes, the federal state also uses the cantons as 'federal laboratories' for developing and testing out different solutions to the same problems (Sager and Mavrot 2015). There are a number of examples showing how successful models from other cantons have been recognized and adopted (Kissling-Näf and Wälti 2007). Yet there are also instances where this process has not worked. This is particularly the case when specific cantonal priorities are not sufficiently taken into account (Balthasar 2003).

Political science literature offers varying assessments of the concept of 'Vollzugsföderalismus' (Sager et al. 2017b). The fact that the possibility of adapting the implementation model to canton-specific circumstances increases both acceptance and effectiveness of national policies is seen as positive. The 'federal laboratories' approach also offers the opportunity to identify particularly effective and efficient implementation models. This can encourage decentralized decision-making too, and thus promote democratic participation—something to which Switzerland, with its tradition of direct democracy and the broad participation rights enjoyed by its citizens, attaches a great deal of importance.

Political science literature cites the fact that citizens may be treated very differently depending on where they live as the primary disadvantage of the 'Vollzugsföderalismus' approach. The case of premium reductions in compulsory health insurance offers a particularly clear example of this (Balthasar 2003). Switzerland has a per capita premium system for health insurance. This means that everyone has to pay their own health insurance premiums themselves, but federal law requires the cantons to provide financial support for people living under modest economic circumstances. The federal state itself bears a portion of the costs associated with this. However, it gives the cantons a lot of leeway when it comes to structuring premium reductions. The cantons actively exploit this room for manoeuvre by incorporating their own political priorities into developing and setting the amount of premium reductions. The premium that insured people still have to pay once the reduction has been applied therefore varies considerably depending on where they live and the composition of their household (Ecoplan 2018).

Another disadvantage of the Swiss 'Vollzugsföderalismus' system according to political science experts is the fact that specific cantonal interests are given substantial scope for influencing the implementation process (Kissling-Näf and Wälti 2007): if the political majority in a canton does not share the concerns of the federal government, for example, the canton will usually find opportunities to implement federal requirements for their own benefit. There is evidence of this in the aforementioned example regarding the Federal Act on the Acquisition of Immovable Property in Switzerland by Foreign Non-Residents, in the case of the health insurance premium reductions described above, and in unemployment insurance (Battaglini and Giraud 2003). Even if the federal state disapproves of these differences and believes that the will of the federal legislature is being flouted, it is unwilling to intervene. There are two main reasons for this. Firstly, its options for exerting influence are very limited. While it can invoke its sovereign supervisory powers, it has very few effective tools with which to enforce this. Secondly, it has no suitable executive authorities within the cantons, so it is reliant on the cantons' willingness to cooperate when it comes to implementation. It, therefore, prefers consensual strategies over interventions (Sager et al. 2017b). It is occasionally up to the Federal Supreme Court to urge the cantons to conduct their implementation along federal lines (Flückiger et al. 2000; Byland et al. 2015, cf. also 'The Judicial System' in this volume).

The reason why 'Vollzugsföderalismus' is so prevalent in Switzerland is due to the principle of subsidiarity, which is enshrined in the Swiss federal constitution. According to this principle, the federal state can only act if the constitution expressly gives it the authority to do so. In general, the cantons are reluctant to agree to this delegation of powers. However, as already mentioned there are areas where the responsibility for implementation lies with a national authority—aspects of defence and research policy, for example, or areas relating to Swiss foreign relations. Alternative systems to 'Vollzugsföderalismus' are also in place where the task of fulfilling public functions is entrusted either wholly or partially to nationally organized para-state organizations. For instance, the Swiss state has delegated tasks relating to agricultural, vocational training, and health policy to these kinds of organizations (Ladner 2013).

Different implementation models, such as the decentral, central, or para-state systems described, have a significant impact on the way in which public policies are implemented and the intensity of implementation. Different responsibilities also often mean that different steering mechanisms are used. With regard to the effectiveness of public policies, it makes a difference whether instructions are given or bans imposed, whether respect for political objectives is motivated by financial incentives or whether purely persuasive methods such as information, advice, or education and training are deployed. Sager et al. (2017b) note that the main steering tools used in Switzerland have changed, as they have in the rest of Europe. Originally, the emphasis was on exercising sovereign rights, but, over time, these tools have been supplemented with public service offerings. In parallel with this, regulatory instruments have come into play. The importance of financial incentives increased significantly in the post-war period in particular, while the use of persuasive methods is a more recent development. The Swiss state has also been making greater use of networks involving both public and private actors in its control procedures in recent years. In some cases, agencies have been formed out of these networks, for example, to promote renewable energies or to support innovation (Varone et al. 2019).

3 Differences in implementation: a typically Swiss phenomenon

Different implementation models, responsibilities, and mechanisms are largely responsible for the (in some cases very significant) differences in the implementation of various policies across the Swiss cantons. However, the greatest variations can be seen in cases where the cantons delegate the task of implementation to one of the roughly 2,100 Swiss municipalities. Each of these municipalities manages the responsibilities entrusted to it within the specified parameters in its own way. This is demonstrated by examples relating to local environmental protection (Vatter 1999). Comparative research has shown that, in Switzerland's case, there are four key factors that affect the intensity with which cantons and municipalities implement the tasks assigned to them (Sager et al. 2017b). The first is *political will*. A lack of political will is not conducive to high-intensity implementation. The second factor is *problem pressure*. This is closely linked to political will. Cantons whose inhabitants are more significantly affected by traffic problems or unemployment, for example, will implement federal requirements in these areas with more intensity than other cantons. The third factor is the canton's *resource potential*: intensive implementation is only possible if the authorities have the necessary financial and human resources available for it. The fourth factor affecting implementation intensity is the canton's *geographical and social structure*. If it covers a large area with both urban and rural districts, it is more difficult to implement policies intensely than it is in a smaller canton with a socially homogeneous structure (Sager et al. 2017b).

The interpretation of differences in implementation between territorial entities is also increasingly supported by theory, including in Switzerland. Sager and Huegli (2013), for example, analyse recent measures in regional policy based on a *top-down theory* and the analytical framework developed by Sabatier and Mazmanian (1980). The study clearly shows that not all of the success factors identified by Sabatier and Mazmanian were observed in the implementation of regional policy in Switzerland. For instance, the implementation procedure was executed not by a central coordinating authority but by extremely heterogeneous cantonal actors. Contrary to the assumption made by Sabatier and Mazmanian, however, it is evident that this heterogeneity did not hinder the implementation process and in fact facilitated its success: thanks to the leeway they were given, the cantonal actors were able to respond effectively to the needs of the target groups concerned and thus drive forward the implementation of regional policy in a targeted way.

Top-down theories focus on the decision maker's perspective and analyse the implementation of a law or administrative scheme from this point of view. *Bottom-up theories* take as their starting point the dynamics that influence the actors involved in the implementation process who are in direct contact with the target groups (Hill and Hupe 2021). One example of a Swiss study that adopts a bottom-up perspective is an analysis of the implementation of regulations on the use of medicinal products on animals (Sager et al. 2014). In Switzerland, independent veterinarians often also undertake implementation tasks on behalf of the state. In the example studied, the vets are expected to encourage the farms under their supervision to comply with certain regulations regarding the use of feed to which medicinal products had been added. However, the supervised farmers are also customers of the vets and therefore the vets want to maintain a good relationship with them. The study by Sager et al. (2014) shows that the interaction between vets and farmers could result in the federal requirements not being adequately implemented. Further examples of Swiss studies that examine implementation from the perspective of the 'street-level bureaucrats' (Lipsky 2010) and the target groups involve the receipt of social benefits. These studies found that eligible beneficiaries did not claim their benefits due to a sense of shame, or because they were afraid that doing so would lead to negative consequences (Lucas et al. 2019; Hupe and Buffat 2014).

Another option—'*hybrid approaches*'—could be classed as a third group of theories in implementation research. These incorporate findings from top-down and bottom-up theories into new theoretical models. Hill and Varone (2017) showed that these approaches take into account the fact that the hierarchical nature of traditional state controls is increasingly being superseded by mechanisms that blur the traditional line between state and society ('new modes of governance') (cf. also Benz and Papadopoulos 2006). Examples of this include private organizations taking over state tasks (e.g. the Swisstransplant foundation), negotiations with target groups being favoured over hierarchical governance (e.g. agreements with the industry on climate policy targets), or responsibility for achieving objectives being transferred to target groups (e.g. cost objectives for inpatient or outpatient treatment under compulsory health insurance).

4 Strongly institutionalized evaluation in Switzerland

In Switzerland, direct democracy plays a key role in the legitimation and control of political decision-making. It could be argued that there is no real need for evaluation as another instrument of legitimacy and control. Sager et al. (2017b) clearly demonstrate that the various power-sharing and compromise institutions in Switzerland are designed to ensure a high input legitimacy of political decisions (cf. also Widmer 2009). Evaluations are increasingly supplementing this legitimation process with information concerning the output of political decision-making. As long as comprehensive control powers were assigned to the state, it was sufficient to legitimize state actions primarily on the basis of input-related factors. Deregulation, liberalization, and privatization have changed the state's political steering capacity. Output control has taken its place alongside input control (Beywl 2006). Simply verifying legitimacy is no longer enough to justify state actions. Control tools that show whether public funds are also being used effectively are needed too (Varone 2009). One such tool is evaluation, which provides an additional means of legitimizing political actions in a changing state.

A number of studies show a distinct path towards the institutionalization of evaluation in Switzerland compared with other countries (Furubo et al. 2002; Stockmann et al. 2020). There are two main factors behind this (e.g. Horber-Papazian and Baud-Lavigne 2019).

The first factor is the fact that the evaluation function is *embedded in the constitution*. Since 2000, the Swiss federal constitution has even contained a specific article on evaluation, which states that the Federal Assembly must ensure that federal measures are evaluated with regard to their effectiveness (Mader 2009). The Federal Administration subsequently drafted proposals for implementing this constitutional article which apply not just to the federal offices, but to the federal departments, the Federal Council, and the Federal Audit Office too. To enable it to fulfil its constitutional obligation, the Federal Assembly created an administrative unit, the Parliamentary Control of the Administration, which provides support in monitoring the effectiveness of the administration (Bättig and Schwab 2015). In a similar vein, the Swiss Federal Audit Office set up a team of experts for carrying out evaluations systematically (Crémieux and Sangra 2015). The evaluation task has also been enshrined in numerous federal laws and ordinances in the form of what is referred to as evaluation clauses (Mader 2015).

The second factor that has encouraged the institutionalization of evaluation is the Swiss Evaluation Society (Sager et al. 2021). This organization now has more than 500 members from the fields of public administration, higher education, and the private sector. It runs regular conferences and workshops and maintains permanent working groups that focus on topics such as development cooperation, quality assurance, or evaluation skills. With widely accepted quality standards for carrying out evaluations and a strong commitment to education and research, the Swiss Evaluation Society is instrumental in ensuring the credibility and professionalization of evaluation activities (Friedrich et al. 2017; Horber-Papazian 2015; Widmer 2011).

The distinct institutionalization of evaluations in Switzerland has led to a high number of evaluations being carried out every year. Evaluation activities increased significantly in the period up to 2010, and since then between eighty and a hundred evaluations have been carried out annually at the federal level (Balthasar and Strotz 2017). In recent years, however, this trend has levelled off, but there has been a sharp rise in the number of cantonal evaluations conducted (around seventy to eighty per year). It can therefore be assumed that the overall number of evaluations carried out in Switzerland each year ranges from approximately 150 to 180 (Balthasar 2022).

Over the last few years, evaluations have taken place in virtually all policy areas in Switzerland. In areas where the state exercises sovereign rights, aspects of the judicial system or the police have been evaluated, for example (e.g. Lienhard et al. 2013). Evaluations which focus on the role of the *state as a provider of goods and services* have proved popular. There have also been numerous examples from the fields of health, transport, and science (cf. the federal government's research database, www.aramis.admin.ch). Cantons have been taking a very systematic approach to evaluating their educational offerings in some cases (Balthasar and Rieder 2009). On the other hand, the effectiveness of *regulatory instruments* features comparatively rarely as an evaluation topic, although examples can be found, for instance, in transport and health policy (e.g. Siegrist and Cavegn 2017 or Laubereau et al. 2021). The most common form of evaluation is probably those which deal with the effects of using *financial instruments*. Recent examples involve examining the effectiveness of financial support for businesses and self-employed individuals during the COVID-19 pandemic (EFK 2020). Numerous evaluations have also been conducted that relate to *persuasive policy instruments*, such as information campaigns, advisory services, and training and education schemes. Various studies have highlighted the fact that information campaigns are most effective if they are combined with other measures such as advisory services (Bonfadelli and Friemel 2006). These findings indicate that analyses of the effectiveness of policy instruments no longer focus primarily on the effects of individual instruments. The issue of identifying the optimum *mix of instruments* is of particular concern in this regard (Howlett et al. 2006).

Even if the number of evaluations being carried out is high and the range of measures being evaluated is broad, the intensity of evaluations still varies considerably from one policy area to another. Switzerland therefore cannot be said to have a consistent evaluation culture at the national level (Dolder et al. 2017). Development cooperation, health policy, social policy, economic policy, and research and innovation policy are some of the areas that can boast a stable and comparatively intensive evaluation practice. Widmer (2008) hypothesizes that policies which delegate tasks to third parties are more likely than average to resort to evaluations for control purposes. Balthasar (2007) attributes the varying distribution of evaluations across the policy areas partly to differences in the policies' need for legitimacy. For example, development cooperation in Switzerland has a much greater obligation to justify itself than agricultural policy.

The large number of evaluations carried out in Switzerland compared to other countries in Europe has also created scope for using standard international evaluation procedures and developing them further. One method that is currently particularly popular in Switzerland is *theory-based evaluations,* which are usually centred around an impact model (cf. Chen and Rossi 1980; Haunberger 2018). Using an impact model as a starting point is one of the specifications for evaluations carried out on behalf of the Federal Office of Public Health, for example. However, theory-based evaluations often leave out or pay little attention to *contextual factors.* This is something that the *'realistic evaluation'* approach (Pawson and Tilley 1997) attempts to counter. To date, realistic evaluations have been used in Switzerland to examine issues relating to areas such as transport policy (Sager and Andereggen 2012). One methodological development which has its roots in Switzerland is the *'critical friend approach'* (Balthasar 2011). Following along the lines of *utilization-focused evaluations,* this method combines elements of self-evaluation and external evaluation.

Recently, however, the institutionalization of evaluation has come under some critical scrutiny, including—though not exclusively—in Switzerland. It has been argued, for example, that this institutionalization is also linked to a 'ritualisation of evaluation' (Meyer and Stockmann 2017, 248). It is therefore not surprising that Widmer, in his overview of the history of evaluation in Switzerland, describes its development since 2010 under the heading 'bureaucratization phase': he highlights 'bureaucratic routine' as a distinctive trait of evaluations during this period, aimed primarily at ensuring that investigations are carried out as smoothly and efficiently as possible (Widmer 2017, 61). The institutionalization of evaluation can, therefore, be quite problematic, which makes it all the more important to reflect critically on evaluation activities. We will now take a look at Switzerland's contribution to this.

5 RESEARCH ON EVALUATION

Research on evaluation in Switzerland has gained in prominence over recent years (Widmer et al. 2016; cf. also Hense and Widmer 2013). This development began with investigations into the use of evaluations by the government and administration and, since then, around twenty studies of this kind have been produced in Switzerland (Frey and Ledermann 2017). Frey and Ledermann distinguish between two approaches in this regard: the 'forward tracking' option is used to examine whether the results of individual evaluations have been used by the administration or policymakers and, where applicable, which factors have influenced this use. The second approach takes as its starting point decision-making processes or administrative units that have been the subject of evaluation (e.g. Ledermann 2014). This involves analysing whether and, if applicable, under what conditions government and administrative actions are based on one or more evaluations. This approach is known as 'backward tracking'. There are also studies which combine these two methods (Frey 2012). More recent work on the use of evaluations takes up the concept of evidence-based policy-making, which aims to promote an evidence-based approach to policy development over an ideology-based one (Frey and Ledermann 2010; Balthasar and Müller 2016).

Having examined the studies available, Frey and Ledermann (2017) conclude that evaluations have rarely been drawn upon to prepare legislation. They are more commonly used by the administration to assess the effectiveness of implementation and make improvements where necessary (Frey and Ledermann 2017). The use of evaluations by the Swiss parliament and in referendums was the subject of a comprehensive study conducted as part of the 'Policy Evaluation in the Swiss Political System—Roots and Fruits' research programme carried out at the Universities of Zurich, Geneva, Lausanne, Bern, and Lucerne (Sager et al. 2017a; Widmer 2020). A survey linked with this study involving national and cantonal members of parliament gave the general impression that, while they are aware of evaluation as a tool and appreciate its value, they are more likely to commission evaluations than use them (Eberli and Bundi 2017; Eberli 2020). Therefore, it can reasonably be assumed that Swiss members of parliament are more interested in the processes triggered by evaluations than in the findings from them (Widmer 2020; Varone et al. 2018). The significance of evaluations with regard to direct-democratic decision-making is something that Stucki and Schlaufer (2017) and Schlaufer (2018) looked into by analysing daily newspapers' reports on voting campaigns in the fields of education and health. The result was sobering: evaluation findings played a negligible role in the battle for votes.

This raises a key question about the relationship between the Swiss political system and evaluation activities: what do evaluations contribute to the problem-solving capabilities of the Swiss political system? The answer to this is twofold: on the one hand, evaluations lend a factual basis to the debate on how public policies should be implemented in an impact-oriented way. Nowadays, actors involved in public administration at the federal and cantonal levels regularly use the results of evaluations to support their decisions in a number of policy areas. This applies particularly to health, education, social, economic, environmental, innovation, and development policy. On the other hand, evaluations are used only moderately by parliament or for referendums, which is not very encouraging. Nevertheless, it can be concluded that the greater institutionalization of evaluation in Switzerland compared to other countries has not diminished the role of democratic institutions in decision-making. Parliamentarians seem to be used to dealing with evaluations, and the inclusion of evaluation results can increase the deliberative quality of democratic discussion: democracy and evaluation do seem to be compatible (Sager 2018).

6 Conclusion and outlook

Implementation and evaluation research has helped to develop a better understanding of the peculiarities and dynamics of implementing public policies in Switzerland. Thanks to evaluations, we also know more about the effects of different implementation models. In the final section, we will discuss the state of Swiss implementation and evaluation research in a broader context and highlight the challenges facing future research.

6.1 Findings from the theoretical debate surrounding implementation

The theoretical debate surrounding the differences in implementation that are so typical of the Swiss 'Vollzugsföderalismus' system has generated numerous valuable insights in recent years. For one thing, the top-down perspective has shown that effective policies are reliant on factors such as clear objectives, appropriate implementation actors and a sufficient level of acceptance amongst both the actors involved in the implementation and the target groups (Rüefli 2017). For another, the bottom-down angle has directed attention towards the scope available to implementation actors who are in direct contact with target groups. In many cases, these actors operate within a complex and conflicting environment due to their involvement in both implementation and the market. Finally, hybrid research approaches have highlighted the analytical potential offered by combining both perspectives. The research findings also show that implementation analysis also needs to factor in decisions made during the policy formulation phase. Shortcomings in implementation are caused not only by errors during the policy implementation process (implementation failure) but also by inadequate policy-making (policy failure; Suchman 1967). It is, therefore, essential to analyse the various phases of the policy cycle as a whole. The advocacy coalition framework designed for this (Sabatier 1987) has generated considerable interest, including in Switzerland (cf. Sager et al. 2017b). Examples include studies examining issues relating to climate policy (Ingold and Fischer 2016), drug policy (Wenger et al. 2014), and family policy (Kübler 2007).

6.2 Implementation and evaluation in a political context

In recent years, implementation and evaluation research has focused heavily on analysing administrative processes and their impact. This approach has often pushed the political debate that plays a part in the implementation and evaluation of public policies into the background. Yet, the power play amongst political actors continues to be a crucial factor in implementation and in impact assessment, which are parts of the political debate. For instance, the results of impact analyses do not just facilitate policy improvements. The Federal Assembly often uses evaluations in pursuit of strategic objectives too. Incorporating evaluation clauses into laws can help to forge coalitions and mobilize support for political projects. The fact that evaluations are carried out only very rarely or not at all in a number of policy areas is also a political statement in itself. The significant inconsistency in evaluation activities at the federal level, and between and within the individual cantons, comes as no surprise to those who are familiar with Swiss politics. However, it is neither democratically legitimized nor objectively justified (Widmer 2020, 55).

Evaluators are also faced with the politicization of implementation and evaluation research. It is therefore not surprising that a survey of members of the Swiss Evaluation Society has revealed that the majority of them did not perceive themselves as independent when carrying out evaluations (Pleger et al. 2017). This unwelcome finding coincides with the results of comparable studies from Germany and the United States, underlining the need to step up research into evaluation procedures that ensure that evaluations can be conducted independently. That is the only way to guarantee that evaluations retain their credibility and acceptance (cf. Astbury 2017).

6.3 Challenges

Although some valuable insights have been gained in recent years, Swiss implementation and evaluation research is still facing a number of challenges.

The first challenge is a *methodological* one. So far, neither implementation nor evaluation research in Switzerland has really touched upon the inclusion of large data sets (big data), yet this is playing an increasingly important role in social science (Lemire et al. 2020). There is a great deal of potential here that ought to be harnessed for the purposes of implementation and evaluation research, too. Data generated in administrative processes, for example, could also be used for implementation research in future (Huber 2019; see also opendata.swiss).

The second challenge relates to *reflecting* on evaluation (Stockmann 2017). Switzerland does not currently have a specific academic institute for evaluation research, but a facility of this kind would be important for enabling international methodological and theoretical developments to be continuously fed into Swiss evaluation research too. An institute like this could also be given the task of systematically raising and addressing critical questions regarding the methods and role of evaluation in Switzerland. This is the best way to guarantee that evaluations will continue to be accepted, or even gain more acceptance, both within and outside the political system.

The third challenge arises from the question of how *useful* implementation and evaluation research are in terms of increasing society's capacity for solving problems. It is still unclear whether the government and administration taking evaluation results into account actually leads to more effective and efficient policy-making (Frey and Ledermann 2017). It may transpire that the value of implementation analyses and evaluations lies in showing the limits affecting the steering capacity of a modern state rather than in providing specific, highly effective, and efficient problem-solving strategies. This would be a useful finding that should be factored into future problem-solving strategies. It could also be argued that implementation analysis and evaluation are valuable elements of a democratic society simply because they demonstrate that public authorities make an effort to learn from their mistakes (Dahler-Larsen 2017).

Note

1. Tobias Arnold, Sean Müller, and Frédéric Varone gave me valuable feedback on previous drafts for this article. Roland Blättler edited the bibliography. I would like to thank them all for their help and support.

References

Astbury, Brad. 2017. 'Von der Evaluationstheorie zum Testen von Evaluationstheorien?' In *Die Zukunft der Evaluation: Trends, Herausforderungen, Perspektiven*, edited by Reinhard Stockmann, and Wolfgang Meyer, pp. 223–242. Münster/New York: Waxmann.

Balthasar, Andreas. 2003. 'Die Prämienverbilligung im Krankenversicherungsgesetz: Vollzugsföderalismus und sekundäre Harmonisierung'. *Schweizer Föderalismus in vergleichender Perspektive (= Swiss Political Science Review)* 9 (1) (special issue edited by Adrian Vatter, and Sonja Wälti): pp. 335–354. Zürich: Rüegger.

Balthasar, Andreas. 2007. *Institutionelle Verankerung und Verwendung von Evaluationen: Praxis und Verwendung von Evaluationen in der schweizerischen Bundesverwaltung*. Zürich/Chur: Rüegger.

Balthasar, Andreas. 2011. 'Critical Friend Approach: Policy Evaluation between Methodological Soundness, Practical Relevance, and Transparency of the Evaluation Process'. *German Policy Studies* 7 (3): pp. 187–231.

Balthasar, Andreas. 2022. 'Der Vollzug und die Wirkungen öffentlicher Politiken'. In *Handbuch der Schweizer Politik = Manuel de la politique Suisse*, edited by Yannis Papadopoulos, Pascal Sciarini, Adrian Vatter, Silja Häusermann, Patrick Emmenegger, and Flavia Fossati, pp. 635–673. 7th ed. Zürich: NZZ Libro.

Balthasar, Andreas, and Franziska Müller. 2016. 'Gender Equality and Evidence-Based Policy Making: Experiences from Social Transfer and Tax Policy Reforms'. In *Gender Equality in Context: Policies and Practices in Switzerland*, edited by Brigitte Liebig, Karin Gottschall, and Birgit Sauer, pp. 87–108. Opladen/Berlin/Toronto: Barbara Budrich Publishers.

Balthasar, Andreas, and Stefan Rieder. 2009. 'Wo ist evidenzbasierte Politik möglich? Die Verbreitung von Evaluationen auf kantonaler Ebene'. In *Demokratie als Leidenschaft: Planung, Entscheidung und Vollzug in der schweizerischen Demokratie (Festschrift für Prof. Dr. Wolf Linder)*, edited by Adrian Vatter, Frédéric Varone, and Fritz Sager, pp. 403–429. Bern/Stuttgart/Wien: Haupt.

Balthasar, Andreas, and Chantal Strotz. 2017. 'Verbreitung und Verankerung von Evaluation in der Bundesverwaltung'. In *Evaluation im politischen System der Schweiz—Entwicklung,*

Bedeutung und Wechselwirkungen, edited by Fritz Sager, Thomas Widmer, and Andreas Balthasar, pp. 89–117. Zürich: NZZ Libro,

Battaglini, Monica, and Olivier Giraud. 2003. 'Policy Styles and the Swiss Executive Federalism: Comparing Diverging Styles of Cantonal Implementation of the Federal Law an Unemployment'.*Schweizer Föderalismus in vergleichender Perspektive (= Swiss Political Science Review)* 9 (1) (special issue edited by Adrian Vatter, and Sonja Wälti): pp. 285–308. Zürich: Rüegger.

Bättig Christoph, and Philippe Schwab. 2015. 'La place de l'évaluation dans le cadre du contrôle parlementaire'. In *Regards croisés sur l'évaluation en Suisse*, edited by Katia Horber-Papazian, pp. 1–22. Lausanne: PPUR.

Benz, Arthur, and Yannis Papadopoulos. 2006. *Governance and Democracy: Comparing National, European and International Experiences* (Routledge/ECPR studies in European political science, vol. 44). London: Routledge.

Beywl, Wolfgang. 2006. 'The Role of Evaluation in Democracy: Can it be Strengthened by Evaluation Standards? A European Perspective'. *Journal of MultiDisciplinary Evaluation* 3 (6): pp. 10–29.

Bonfadelli, Heinz, and Thomas Friemel. 2006. *Kommunikationskampagnen im Gesundheitsbereich: Grundlagen und Anwendungen*. Konstanz: UVK Verlagsgesellschaft.

Bussmann, Werner. 2008. 'The Emergence of Evaluation in Switzerland'. *Evaluation* 14 (4): pp. 499–506.

Bussmann, Werner, Ulrich Klöti, and Peter Knoepfel. 1997. *Einführung in die Politikevaluation*. Basel/Frankfurt am Main: Helbing & Lichtenhahn.

Byland, Karin, Roy Gava, and Frédéric Varone. 2015. 'Impacts of Courts on Policy Implementation in a Federal State: Evidence from Disability Insurance in Switzerland'. *Jahrbuch der Schweizerischen Verwaltungswissenschaften* 6: pp. 167–180.

Chen, Huey T., and Peter H. Rossi. 1980. 'The Multi-Goal, Theory-Driven Approach to Evaluation: A Model Linking Basic and Applied Social Science'. *Social Forces* 59 (1): pp. 106–122.

Crémieux, Laurent, and Emmanuel Sangra. 2015. 'La place de l'évaluation dans le cadre du Contrôle fédéral des finances'. In *Regards croisés sur l'évaluation en Suisse*, edited by Katia Horber-Papazian, pp. 37–57. Lausanne: PPUR.

Dahler-Larsen, Peter. 2017. 'Die sich verändernde Rolle der Evaluation in einer sich verändernden Gesellschaft'. In *Die Zukunft der Evaluation: Trends, Herausforderungen, Perspektiven*, edited by Reinhard Stockmann, and Wolfgang Meyer, pp. 21–34. Münster/New York: Waxmann.

Dolder, Olivier, Walter Rohrbach, and Frédéric Varone. 2017. 'Evaluationskultur auf kantonaler Ebene: politikfeld- oder kantonsspezifische Entwicklungspfade?' In *Evaluation im politischen System der Schweiz: Entwicklung, Bedeutung und Wechselwirkungen*, edited by Fritz Sager, Thomas Widmer, and Andreas Balthasar, pp. 119–153. Zürich: NZZ Libro.

Eberli, Daniela. 2020. 'Wissen, was funktioniert: die Nutzung von Politikevaluationen in den Schweizer Parlamenten'. *Parlament: Mitteilungsblatt der Schweizerischen Gesellschaft für Parlamentsfragen* 23 (1): pp. 33–40.

Eberli, Daniela, and Pirmin Bundi. 2017. 'Parlament und Evaluation: Guts Meets Brain'. In *Evaluation im politischen System der Schweiz: Entwicklung, Bedeutung und Wechselwirkungen*, edited by Fritz Sager, Thomas Widmer, and Andreas Balthasar, pp. 243–278. Zürich: NZZ Libro,

Ecoplan. 2018. *Wirksamkeit der Prämienverbilligung—Monitoring 2017: Schlussbericht im Auftrag des Bundesamtes für Gesundheit (BAG)* (Experten-/Forschungsberichte zur Kranken- und Unfallversicherung). Bern: BAG.

EFK—Eidgenössische Finanzkontrolle. 2020. *COVID-19-Prüfungen. Dritter Zwischenbericht. Massnahmen des Bundes, Stand 31. Juli 2020.* Bern: EFK.

Flückiger, Alexandre, Charles-Albert Morand, and Thierry Tanquerel. 2000. *Evaluation du droit de recours des organisations de protection de l'environnement.* Berne: OFEFP Office fédéral de l'environnement, des forêts et du paysage.

Frey, Kathrin. 2012. *Evidenzbasierte Politikformulierung in der Schweiz: Gesetzesrevisionen im Vergleich.* Baden-Baden: Nomos.

Frey, Kathrin, and Simone Ledermann. 2010. 'Evidence-Based Policy: A Concept in Geographical and Substantive Expansion'. *German Policy Studies* 6 (2): pp. 1–15.

Frey, Kathrin, and Simone Ledermann. 2017. 'Nutzung von Evaluationen in Regierung und Verwaltung'. In *Evaluation im politischen System der Schweiz: Entwicklung, Bedeutung und Wechselwirkungen*, edited by Fritz Sager, Thomas Widmer, and Andreas Balthasar, pp. 211–242. Zürich: NZZ Libro,

Friedrich, Verena, Caroline Schlaufer, and Iris Michel. 2017. 'Professionalisierung der Evaluation: Ergebnisse der SEVAL-Mitgliederbefragung'. *LeGes—Gesetzgebung & Evaluation* 28 (2): pp. 347–367.

Furubo, Jan-Eric, Ray C. Rist, and Rolf Sandahl. 2002. *International Atlas of Evaluation.* New Brunswick: Transaction Publishers.

Germann, Raimund E. 1986. 'Die Beziehungen zwischen Bund und Kantonen im Verwaltungsbereich'. In *Handbuch Politisches System der Schweiz, vol. 3: Föderalismus*, edited by Raimund E. Germann, and Ernest Weibel, pp. 343–369. Bern/Stuttgart: Haupt.

Haunberger, Sigrid. 2018. 'Nichts ist praktischer als ein gutes Wirkungsmodell'. *LeGes—Gesetzgebung & Evaluation* 29 (2). https://leges.weblaw.ch/legesissues/2018/2/nichts-ist-praktisch_dbd238c9fb.html (accessed 21 July 2022).

Hense, Jan, and Thomas Widmer. 2013. 'Ein Überblick zum internationalen Stand der Forschung über Evaluation'. In *Forschung über Evaluation: Bedingungen, Prozesse, Wirkungen*, edited by Jan Hense, Stefan Rädiker, Wolfgang Böttcher, and Thomas Widmer, pp. 251–278. Münster: Waxmann.

Hill, Michael, and Peter Hupe. 2021. *Implementing Public Policy. An Introduction to the Study of Operational Governance*, 4th ed. London: Sage.

Hill, Michael, and Frédéric Varone. 2017. *The Public Policy Process*, 7th ed. London: Routledge.

Horber-Papazian, Katia (ed.). 2015. *Regards croisés sur l'évaluation en Suisse.* Lausanne: PPUR.

Horber-Papazian, Katia, and Marion Baud-Lavigne. 2019. 'Factors Contributing to the Strong Institutionalization of Policy Evaluation in Switzerland'. In *Swiss Public Administration: Making the State Work Successfully*, edited by Andreas Ladner, Nils Soguel, Yves Emery, Sophie Weerts, and Stéphane Nahrath, pp. 355–371. New York: Palgrave Macmillan.

Howlett, Michael, Jonathan Kim, and Paul Weaver. 2006. 'Assessing Instrument Mixes through Program- and Agency-Level Data: Methodological Issues in Contemporary Implementation Research'. *Review of Policy Research* 23 (1): pp. 129–151.

Huber, Martin. 2019. 'Politikevaluation profitiert von Datenflut'. *Die Volkswirtschaft* 2019 (10), 7–11.

Hupe, Peter, and Aurélien Buffat. 2014. 'A Public Service Gap: Capturing Contexts in a Comparative Approach of Street-level Bureaucracy'. *Public Management Review* 16 (4): pp. 548–69.

Ingold, Karin, and Manuel Fischer. 2016. 'Belief Conflicts and Coalition Structures Driving Subnational Policy Responses: the Case of Swiss Regulation of Unconventional Gas Development'. In *Policy Debates on Hydraulic Fracturing: Comparing Coalition Politics in North America and Europe*, edited by Christopher M. Weible, Tanya Heikkila, Karin Ingold, and Manuel Fischer, pp. 201–237. New York: Palgrave Macmillan.

Kissling-Näf, Ingrid, and Sonja Wälti. 2007. 'The Implementation of Public Policies'. In *Handbook of Swiss Politics*, edited by Ulrich Klöti, Peter Knoepfel, Wolf Linder, Yannis Papadopoulos, and Pascal Sciarini, pp. 501–524. 2nd ed. Zürich: NZZ Verlag.

Kübler, Daniel. 2007. 'Understanding the Recent Expansion of Swiss Family Policy: An Idea-Centred Approach'. *Journal of Social Policy* 36 (2): pp. 217–237.

Ladner, Andreas. 2013. 'Der Schweizer Staat, politisches System und Aufgabenerbringung'. In *Handbuch der öffentlichen Verwaltung in der Schweiz*, edited by Andreas Ladner, Luzius Mader, Jean-Loup Chappelet, Nils Soguel, Yves Emery, Frédéric Varone, Peter Knoepfel, pp. 23–45. Zürich: NZZ Verlag.

Laubereau, Birgit, Sarah Fässler, Kristin Thorshaug, and Andreas Balthasar. 2021. *Summative Evaluation des Transplantationsgesetzes (1. Etappe). Bericht zuhanden des Bundesamts für Gesundheit*. Luzern & Lausanne: Interface Politikstudien Forschung Beratung.

Ledermann, Simone. 2014. 'Evidenz und Expertise im vorparlamentarischen Gesetzgebungsprozess: Die Rolle von Verwaltung und externen Experten'. *Swiss Political Science Review* 20 (3): pp. 453–485.

Leifeld, Philip, and Karin Ingold. 2016. 'Co-Authorship Networks in Swiss Political Research'. *Swiss Political Science Review* 22 (2): pp. 264–287.

Lemire, Sebastian, Laura R. Peck, and Allan Porowski. 2020. 'The Growth of the Evaluation Tree in the Policy Analysis Forest: Recent Developments in Evaluation'. *PSJ Policy Studies Journal* 48 (Special issue): pp. S47–S70.

Lienhard, Andreas, Stefan Rieder, Martin Kilias, Christof Schwenkel, Sophie Nunweiler, and Andreas Müller. 2013. *Evaluation der Wirksamkeit der neuen Bundesrechtspflege. Schlussbericht zuhanden des Bundesamtes für Justiz*. Bern/Luzern/Zürich: kpm/Interface/Universität Zürich.

Linder, Wolf. 1987. *Politische Entscheidung und Gesetzesvollzug in der Schweiz. Schlussbericht des Nationalen Forschungsprogramms Nr. 6 'Entscheidungsvorgänge in der schweizerischen Demokratie'*. Bern/Stuttgart: Haupt.

Lipsky, Michael. 2010. *Street-Level Bureaucracy: Dilemmas of the Individual in Public Services*. Updated ed. New York: Russell Sage Foundation.

Lucas, Barbara, Catherine Ludwig, Jérôme Chapuis, Jenny Maggi, and Eric Crettaz. 2019. *Le non-recours aux prestations sociales à Genève: quelles adaptations de la protection sociale aux attentes des familles en situation de précarité? Rapport de recherche*. Genève: Haute Ecole de Travail Social and Haute Ecole de Santé (= HES-SO Hautes Ecoles Spécialisées de Suisse Occidentale).

Mader, Luzius. 2009. 'Die institutionelle Einbettung der Evaluationsfunktion in der Schweiz'. In *Evaluation: ein systematisches Handbuch*, edited by Thomas Widmer, Wolfgang Beywl, and Carlo Fabian, pp. 52–63. Wiesbaden: VS Verlag für Sozialwissenschaften.

Mader, Luzius. 2015. 'Le rôle des clauses d'évaluation dans le processus législatif fédéral'. In *Regards croisés sur l'évaluation en Suisse*, edited by Katia Horber-Papazian, pp. 67–78. Lausanne: PPUR.

Meyer, Wolfgang, and Reinhard Stockmann. 2017. 'Gemeinsame Perspektiven für die Institutionalisierung von Evaluation?' In *Die Zukunft der Evaluation: Trends, Herausforderungen, Perspektiven*, edited by Reinhard Stockmann, and Wolfgang Meyer, pp. 243–257. Münster/New York: Waxmann.

Pawson, Ray, and Nick Tilley. 1997. *Realistic Evaluation*. London: Sage.

Pleger, Lyn, Fritz Sager, Michael Morris, Wolfgang Meyer, and Reinhard Stockmann. 2017. 'Are Some Countries more Prone to Pressure Evaluators than Others? Comparing Findings from the United States, United Kingdom, Germany, and Switzerland'. *American Journal of Evaluation* 38 (3): pp. 315–328.

Rieder, Stefan, Andreas Balthasar, and Ingrid Kissling-Näf. 2014. 'Vollzug und Wirkung öffentlicher Politiken'. In *Handbuch der Schweizer Politik = Manuel de la politique suisse*, edited by Peter Knoepfel, Yannis Papadopoulos, Pascal Sciarini, Adrian Vatter, and Silja Häusermann, pp. 563–598. 5th ed. Zürich: NZZ Verlag.

Rüefli, Christian. 2017. 'Ansätze und Instrumente besserer Regulierung—eine Auslegeordnung'. *LeGes—Gesetzgebung & Evaluation* 28 (3): pp. 445–467.

Sabatier, Paul A. 1987. 'Knowledge, Policy-Oriented Learning, and Policy Change: An Advocacy Coalition Framework'. *Knowledge: Creation, Diffusion, Utilization* 8 (4): pp. 649–692.

Sabatier, Paul A., and Daniel Mazmanian. 1980. 'The Implementation of Public Policy: A Framework of Analysis'. *Policy Studies Journal* 8 (4): pp. 538–560.

Sager, Fritz. 2018. 'Policy Evaluation and Democracy: Do They Fit?' *Evaluation and Program Planning* 69 (special issue): pp. 125–129.

Sager, Fritz, and Céline Andereggen. 2012. 'Dealing with Complex Causality in Realist Synthesis: The Promise of Qualitative Comparative Analysis (QCA) '. *American Journal of Evaluation* 33 (1): pp. 60–78.

Sager, Fritz, Susanne Hadorn, Andreas Balthasar, and Céline Mavrot. 2021. *Politikevaluation: eine Einführung*. Wiesbaden: Springer VS.

Sager, Fritz, and Eveline Huegli. 2013. *Evaluation des Mehrjahresprogramms 2008-15 zur Umsetzung der Neuen Regionalpolitik (NRP)*. Bern: Kompetenzzentrum für Public Management der Universität Bern and Büro Vatter AG.

Sager, Fritz, Karin Ingold, and Andreas Balthasar. 2017b. *Policy-Analyse in der Schweiz: Besonderheiten, Theorien, Beispiele*. Zürich: NZZ Libro.

Sager, Fritz, and Céline Mavrot. 2015. 'Les spécifités méthodologiques de l'évaluation en Suisse'. In *L'évaluation à la croisée des regards*, edited by Katia Horber-Papazian, pp. 175–195. Lausanne: PPUR.

Sager, Fritz, Eva Thomann, Christine Zolliger, Nico van der Heiden, and Céline Mavrot. 2014. 'Street-Level Bureaucrats and New Modes of Governance: How Conflicting Roles Affect the Implementation of the Swiss Ordinance on Veterinary Medical Products'. *Public Management Review* 16 (4): pp. 481–502.

Sager, Fritz, Thomas Widmer, and Andreas Balthasar (eds). 2017a. *Evaluation im politischen System der Schweiz: Entwicklung, Bedeutung und Wechselwirkungen*. Zürich: NZZ Libro,

Schlaufer, Caroline. 2018. 'The Contribution of Evaluations to the Discourse Quality of Newspaper Content'. *Evaluation and Program Planning* 69 (special issue): pp. 157–165.

Siegrist, Stefan, and Mario Cavegn. 2017. 'Evaluation SVG und Via sicura—eine Zwischenbilanz'. In *Evaluation, Kriminalpolitik und Strafrechtsreform*, edited by Daniel Fink, Stefan Keller, Madleina Manetsch, and Christian Schwarzenegger, pp. 175-190. Bern: Stämpfli.

Stockmann, Reinhard. 2017. 'Die Zukunft der Evaluation in modernen Wissensgesellschaften'. In *Die Zukunft der Evaluation: Trends, Herausforderungen, Perspektiven*, edited by Reinhard Stockmann, and Wolfgang Meyer, pp. 35-52. Münster/New York: Waxmann.

Stockmann, Reinhard, Wolfgang Meyer, and Lena Taube. 2020. 'The Institutionalisation of Evaluation in Europe: A Synthesis'. In *The Institutionalisation of Evaluation in Europe*, edited by Reinhard Stockmann, Wolfgang Meyer, and Lena Taube, pp. 483-522. Cham: Springer International Publishing.

Stucki, Iris, and Caroline Schlaufer. 2017. 'Die Bedeutung von Evaluationen im direktdemokratischen Diskurs'. In *Evaluation im politischen System der Schweiz: Entwicklung, Bedeutung und Wechselwirkungen*, edited by Fritz Sager, Thomas Widmer, and Andreas Balthasar, pp. 279-310. Zürich: NZZ Libro,

Suchman, Edward A. 1967. *Evaluative Research: Principles and Practice in Public Service and Social Action Programs*. New York: Russell Sage Foundation.

Varone, Frédéric. 2009. 'Nouvelle gestion publique et évaluation: un couplage réussi grâce à la légistique?' In *De l'évaluation à l'action législatives: Actes du colloque en l'honneur du professeur Jean-Daniel Delley*, edited by Ursula Cassani, and Alexandre Flückiger, pp. 27-46. Genève: Université, Centre d'étude, de technique et d'évaluation législatives CETEL.

Varone, Frédéric, Pirmin Bundi, and Roy Gava. 2018. 'Policy Evaluation in Parliament: Interest Groups as Catalysts'. *International Journal of Administrative Sciences* 86 (1): pp. 98-114.

Varone, Frédéric, Karin Ingold, and Manuel Fischer. 2019. 'Policy Networks and the Roles of Public Administrations'. In *Swiss Public Administration: Making the State Work Successfully*, edited by Andreas Ladner, Nils Soguel, Yves Emery, Sophie Weerts, and Stéphane Nahrath, pp. 339-353. Cham/Switzerland: Springer International Publishing.

Vatter, Adrian. 1999. 'Föderaler Politikvollzug am Beispiel des kommunalen Umweltschutzes in der Nordwestschweiz'. *Gesetzgebung heute—LeGes* 10 (1): pp. 107-120.

Wälti, Sonja. 2001. *Le fédéralisme d'exécution sous pression: la mise en œuvre des politiques à incidence spatiale dans le système fédéral suisse*. Genf, Basel, München: Helbing & Lichtenhahn.

Wenger, Jonas, Michael Surber, Nina Lanzi, Fionn Gantenbein, and Daniel Kübler. 2014. *Politikfeldanalyse Sucht: Advocacy-Koalitionen in der Schweizer Alkohol-, Tabak- und Drogenpolitik*: Schlussbericht zuhanden des Bundesamtes für Gesundheit. Zürich: Universität, Institut für Politikwissenschaft, Forschungsbereich Policy-Analyse & Evaluation.

Widmer, Thomas. 2008. 'Evaluationsansätze und ihre Effekte'. In *Wissenschaft unter Beobachtung: Effekte und Defekte von Evaluationen* (= Leviathan Sonderheft 24), edited by Hildegard Matthies, and Dagmar Simon, pp. 267-287. Wiesbaden: VS Verlag für Sozialwissenschaften.

Widmer, Thomas. 2009. 'The Contribution of Evidence-Based Policy to the Output-Oriented Legitimacy of the State'. *Evidence and Policy: a Journal of Research, Debate and Practice* 5 (4): pp. 351-372.

Widmer, Thomas. 2011. 'Zehn Jahre Evaluationsstandards der Schweizerischen Evaluationsgesellschaft (SEVAL-Standards)'. *Schweizerische Zeitschrift für Kriminologie* 10 (2): pp. 23-30.

Widmer, Thomas. 2017. 'Geschichte der Evaluation im schweizerischen politischen System'. In *Evaluation im politischen System der Schweiz: Entwicklung, Bedeutung und Wechselwirkungen*, edited by Fritz Sager, Thomas Widmer, and Andreas Balthasar, pp. 51–66. Zürich: NZZ Libro,

Widmer, Thomas. 2020. 'Wechselwirkungen von Politik und Evaluation: Befunde aus der Schweiz'. *dms—der moderne staat—Zeitschrift für Public Policy, Recht und Management* 13 (1): pp. 44–60.

Widmer, Thomas, Daniela Eberli, Caroline Schlaufer, Felix Strebel, Günter Ackermann, Lars Balzer, Pirmin Bundi, Christian Hirschi, Tanya Kasper, Peter K. Neuenschwander, Björn Neuhaus, and Walter Rohrbach. 2016. 'Forschung über Evaluation in der Schweiz: Stand und Aussichten'. *LeGes—Gesetzgebung & Evaluation* 27 (3): pp. 459–483.

PART VII
PUBLIC POLICIES

CHAPTER 26

FOREIGN POLICY

LAURENT GOETSCHEL

1 INTRODUCTION

FOREIGN policy used to be a policy serving the survival of nations and their balancing against each other. Inter- and transnational exchanges were of limited extent. Small states were considered as weak states because the size of the population and the territory were the paramount factors of military power. Switzerland's foreign policy emerged in the second half of the nineteenth century at a time when larger neighbouring states such as Germany and Italy were struggling for their national unity and when wars were characteristic for the European context. Switzerland was consolidating its structure as a federal state and developing its direct democracy. For both these external and internal reasons, an active foreign policy was barely on the agenda. Neutrality became Switzerland's dominating foreign policy role concept. It reflected the country's priority to remain outside of wars which were fought in its neighbourhood. From an external perspective, this should strengthen its security. From an internal perspective, this would prevent the country from falling apart due to the tendencies of the French- and German-speaking parts of the population to support different war parties. Neutrality allowed for the development of strong direct-democratic control instruments, which also extended into the foreign policy sphere because it promoted a passive foreign policy with few decisions and little need for action.

Changes in international relations and in foreign policy, which occurred after the end of the Cold War, caused considerable challenges for Swiss foreign policy: the heightened frequency of foreign policy decisions, the broadened and deepened content of foreign policy, and the enhanced public debates resulting from them impacted on existing traditions and institutions. This particularly affected the legitimation of foreign policy, as direct democracy gives the public a greater say in foreign policy-making than in any other country of the world. The need to engage more actively on a regional and global level encountered public opposition, which resulted in several referendums disapproving governmental propositions. European politics[1] and neutrality are most crucially affected by direct democracy. Thus, joining the UN in 2002 and becoming a non-permanent member of the UN Security Council in 2023/24 was a landmark in the reorientation of Swiss foreign policy towards a more active stance at the global level.

The chapter first summarizes significant historical developments, second provides information on the constitutional and legal framework, third describes actors and coordination mechanisms, and finally looks at perspectives and upcoming challenges.

2 Historical developments: small state, neutrality, and direct democracy

In contrast to most other countries, foreign policy in Switzerland was historically not seen as a critical policy. Until the end of the nineteenth century, the president of the Federal Council not only ran his own department but at the same time also acted as foreign minister—a kind of secondary office. Reasons for this were Switzerland's role as a small state, its neutrality, direct democracy, and federalism.

Small states can be defined as countries that wield a deficit of power compared to most states in the international community. Power can be divided into positive and negative power. Positive power equals the ability to change or influence things, whereas negative power refers to the ability to resist change or remain autonomous (Goetschel 1998, 14–15). If states had the choice, they would like to increase both their influence and their autonomy. However, this is rarely possible because increased influence tends to be accompanied by loss of autonomy, especially in case of assuming contractual obligations, e.g. by entering into an international organization. In the case of small states, the corresponding trade-off is particularly notable. Hegemons, on the other hand, can leave their stamp on an international association or institution (Goetschel 1998, 17–18). Thus, small states tend to have relatively little influence and autonomy within their spheres. At the same time, this makes the question of whether to seek influence or autonomy with priority a particularly acute issue. Switzerland was historically viewed as a small state as its direct neighbours were geographically and demographically much larger. They were also prepared to use these attributes to achieve their objectives by force, as was shown by the two world wars.

Switzerland's neutrality tradition developed out of this context. This was a right to 'refrain from war' or not to involve itself in the military affairs of third parties (Frei 1969). Neutrality was a survival strategy. Its legal obligations codified into international law are rooted in the so-called Hague Conventions of 1907. Their core is the mandatory abstention from taking sides in wars among third-party states. Neutral states should send neither troops nor arms. Neutrality policy includes all measures a neutral country takes to ensure the credibility of its neutrality. In contrast to neutrality law, no obligations for this exist under international law. Neutrality policy may be adapted to the preferences of any given neutral state. Neutrality has always been seen as a tool of Swiss foreign policy, not an end in itself. It serves to implement foreign policy interests and goals. At the same time, it has become one of the core elements of Switzerland's political identity. This is corroborated by surveys conducted regularly, according to which a large portion of Swiss citizens would wish to preserve the country's neutrality, even if all the functions were no longer valid (Szvircsev Tresch et al. 2020, 129).

After the Cold War ended, Switzerland continuously scaled down the scope of its neutrality policy. Assessing the changing international environment and its foreign policy interests, the country opted for a stronger multilateral involvement. Since 1990, it has regularly taken part in UN economic sanctions. Even if such sanctions occur in a military invention setting, as in the case of the first Gulf War or somewhat later, on the territory of the former Republic of Yugoslavia or in Somalia, they remain compatible with the country's neutral status, according to the Federal Council. This is because the Security Council does not impose such sanctions in conventional wars but as international police measures against lawbreakers. Moreover, it is worth recalling that no collective security organizations existed when the neutrality law was codified at the outset of the last century. Therefore, neutrality policy grants substantial leeway regarding such organizations.

The Kosovo war in 1999 presented a special challenge to Switzerland's neutrality policy through a combination of differing economic sanctions, out of which the UN approved only some. Moreover, a collective military intervention led by NATO was not supported by any UN resolution. Switzerland adopted some, but not all, the economic sanctions decided by the EU in addition to the UN sanctions. It closed its airspace for NATO except for humanitarian flights (Interdepartementale Arbeitsgruppe 2000). In parallel to these international developments, the country prepared for its accession to the UN, which it joined after a successful national plebiscite in 2002. This was a logical step since Switzerland had declared UN sanctions to be compatible with neutrality and given the organization's increased role in international conflicts. Neutrality experienced its most remarkable renaissance since the end of the Cold War when the military invasion of Iraq occurred without a UN resolution: Switzerland declared itself formally neutral (Couchepin 2003). Consequently, the Swiss foreign minister reaffirmed neutrality as a core element in Swiss foreign policy (Calmy-Rey 2004). She saw the concept as a testimony to Switzerland's solidarity with international law that formed the basis of the country's success in activities promoting international peace.

The pendulum swung back in 2014, when Switzerland did not adopt the EU's economic sanctions after Russia's annexation of Crimea but opted for a middle way, ensuring that the country would not benefit economically from staying aloof (Häfliger 2014). At that time, Switzerland also had the chairmanship of the Organization for Security and Co-operation in Europe (OSCE), which might have influenced this decision of the Federal Council. But in 2022, after Russia had launched its military attack against the whole of Ukraine, the government first lingered, communicating a similar position to the one of 2014. A few days later, it nonetheless decided to adopt the same sanctions as the EU (SECO 2022). The price it had to pay for this was the opposition Russia signalled a couple of months later when Ukraine had asked Switzerland to represent the country's interests in Moscow as part of a protecting power mandate (Gafafer 2022). Clearly, for Russia, Switzerland was no longer a neutral country.

Above all, in connection with direct democracy, neutrality supplied its own bastion against more intense Swiss international involvement during the Cold War and even into the 1990s. Political opponents repeatedly defeated plebiscite proposals to open the country's foreign policy and reprimanded their drafters for (presumably) endangering neutrality. Direct democracy served historically as a natural barrier to the supremacy of foreign policy over domestic policy. However, in practice, most foreign policy issues are less subject to public opinion and parliamentary and direct-democratic control than domestic policy topics (Klöti et al. 2005).

In the past, federalism, too, has tended to favour a passive and neutral policy: opposition partisanship in specific regions of the country toward neighbouring states should be avoided. This aspect has become irrelevant these days to the extent that no more hostilities occur in the immediate setting of Switzerland. On the other hand, the altered content of foreign policy affects the cantons ever more. To avoid being degraded to mere implementation authorities on topics of international negotiations that they see as lying within their sphere of competence, the cantons have developed a more substantial interest in foreign policy's decision-making process. This applies particularly to Switzerland's European policy, where the cantons had suffered the experience of the Treaty on the European Economic Area (TEEA), which had been negotiated without their participation. For the same reasons, direct-democratic joint decision-making has gained importance within the foreign policy framework. In contrast to the Cold War era, neutrality issues no longer take centre stage. Instead, more foreign policy debates focus on similar topics as those debated at the national policy-making level, such as in the fields of environmental, transport, or research policies.

Therefore, the unique traits of Switzerland's political system regarding foreign policy have not lost their importance so much as shifted in their relevance: Switzerland, after World War II, was no longer seen as a small state by its neighbours. Nonetheless, the perception of its relative lack of importance remained firmly anchored in its population. This becomes evident given the widespread scepticism now as in the past towards institutional ties for gaining influence in foreign policy. Hence, the danger of systematic understatement exists regarding the importance of one's own actions. It is only a small step toward self-perceived irrelevance and hence to a lack of responsibility. How Swiss officialdom in the mid-1990s reacted to the international debate on dormant accounts provides an enlightening illustration of this (Maissen 2005). The subsequent efforts of the administration to discuss Switzerland's contact with potentates' funds in a preventive sense provided indications that lessons were learned from the experiences. They eventually led to the adoption of specific legislation (SR 196.1), which entered into force in 2016. Its implementation faces many challenges, as examples in the context of the Arab Spring in Egypt and in Tunisia have shown (Bruppacher 2020, 129, 155–159;

Sharman 2017). But Switzerland has come to realize that a so-called small country must also take care of its reputation and behave accordingly, especially if it oversees a significant share of private fortunes globally.

3 GOALS AND LEGAL BASIS

For a long time, the Swiss federal constitution (FC) mentioned the 'assertion of the Fatherland's independence against the outside, [and] handling of domestic peace and order' as overarching goals.[2] In the new federal constitution that took effect on 1 January 2000, the article stating its purpose says: 'The Swiss Confederation shall protect the liberty and the rights of the people, and shall ensure the independence and security of the country' (art. 2, para. 1, FC). The federal constitution specifically assigned the foreign policy of Switzerland to pursue the following goals:

- to strengthen liberty, democracy, independence, and peace in a spirit of solidarity and openness towards the world, conscious of our common achievements and our responsibility towards future generations (FC, preamble),
- to protect the liberty and rights of the people and safeguard the independence and security of the country (art. 2, para. 1, FC),
- to promote the common welfare, sustainable development, internal cohesion, and cultural diversity of the country (art. 2, para. 2, FC), and
- to secure the long-term preservation of natural resources, and to promote a just and peaceful international order (art. 2, para. 4, FC).

In the constitutional section on responsibilities, these statements are transformed into the following goals: 'The Confederation shall strive to preserve the independence of Switzerland and its welfare; it shall, in particular, contribute to alleviate need and poverty in the world and to promote respect for human rights, democracy, the peaceful coexistence of nations, and the preservation of natural resources' (art. 54, para. 2, FC). Foreign trade policy receives special treatment: it is expressly held that the federal government safeguards the interests of the Swiss economy abroad (art. 101, FC). Hence the five essential goals set in the foreign policy report of 1993 (Federal Council 1993, 20–42) were upheld. New are a special mention of business interests and a supplement to the 'supreme goal' of preserving the independence and welfare of Switzerland. Both these updates also appeared in the following foreign policy report (Federal Council 2000, 294).

According to the federal constitution, foreign policy belongs to the federal government's sphere of authority (art. 54, para. 1, FC). At the same time, however, it must take into account the responsibilities of the cantons and protect their interests (art. 54, para. 3, FC). In particular, the cantons can participate in preparing foreign policy decisions that affect their powers or essential interests (art. 55, para. 1, FC). The federal government must inform the cantons in a timely way and consult them. It must also seek their opinions, meaning the cantons have not only the possibility to accept or reject, but they may also bring in their points of view (art. 55, para. 2, FC). The corresponding constitutional law and especially the three elements of information, hearings, and joint decision-making are further specified in the federal law on joint participation of the cantons in the federal foreign policy of 22 December 1999 (SR 138.1). The clause in the constitution integrating joint decision-making is primarily intended to defuse those constellations in which federal authority in foreign policy opposes domestic policies of cantonal authorities. This should counteract a creeping weakening of federalist structures through centralized foreign policy decision-making. These constitutional articles and laws took form at the outset of the 1990s through negotiations on the European Economic Area (EEA). At the time, the cantons felt insufficiently informed on negotiating topics that lay within their domestic authority. They subsequently insisted on institutionalizing a cooperative procedural flow in foreign policy as well. The Conference of Cantonal Governments (CCG), founded in 1993, also served this purpose. It aimed to ensure the coordination of objectives between the cantons and their joint participation in the federal government's decision-making processes (Münger 1994). According to this law, the federal government must justify its decisions if it considers acting contrary to the cantons' opinion. Regarding potential future regulations, particularly concerning the adoption of EU-law by Switzerland, the cantons would like to strengthen their influence further. This concerns both their right to be informed and their possibility to participate in decision-making (KdK 2011).

The parliament also participates in shaping foreign policy. It supervises the executive branch in this area (art. 166, FC). The federal constitution intends to create competing and overlapping responsibilities in the foreign policy sector and thus requires the executive and legislative branches to cooperate and always coordinate (Wildhaber 1992, 132). The parliamentary law from 13 December 2002 (SR 171.10) contains detailed regulations on joint participation in both chambers within the foreign policy sector. A major portion of parliamentary joint involvement occurs in the foreign policy committees. They can provide no binding instructions to the Federal Council, but they are consulted already at the forefront of important negotiations. As a rule, the total membership of parliament only debates a treaty if it qualifies as a document awaiting ratification. However, many treaties never even come to parliament's attention (Klöti et al. 2005).

The electorate is also involved in foreign policy decision-making through the right to participate in direct democracy. Constitutional guidelines on the popular initiative do not differentiate between domestic and foreign policy content. Therefore, the same rules and limitations apply as in domestic politics (100,000 signatures within eighteen months for an initiative to be launched). Generally, an initiative may not violate mandatory international law (art. 139, para. 3, FC). Otherwise, the federal assembly can declare it entirely or partially invalid. The best-known example of a successful foreign policy initiative was the 2002 plebiscite on UN admission. But also, the primarily domestic

1990 policy initiative to protect the Alps had far-reaching and much-discussed foreign policy consequences after its unexpected acceptance in 1994 because it contradicted a recent agreement between Switzerland and the EU on transit across the Alps (Germann 1995). Normal law proposals may also have foreign policy implications. For example, a referendum tried to challenge (without success) the 2001 revision of the military law facilitating Switzerland's participation in military peacekeeping operations.

In contrast to the initiative, special regulations for foreign policy govern the referendum. The criterion here is not the content but the form of enactment: bills that assume the form of an international treaty are subject to referendums (optional or obligatory). A mandatory referendum is required if a bill seeks admission to an organization for collective security or a supranational community (art. 140, para. 1 (b), FC). Supranational communities are defined as organizations possessing bodies of independent people. As another defining criterion, decisions in these communities are based on the majority principle and are immediately binding for individuals (Rhinow 2000, 380). To be accepted, such a provision requires the majority of voters and cantons. So far, its only application occurred in 1986 at the first (unsuccessful) plebiscite on entering the UN. The optional referendum on an international treaty only requires the acceptance of a simple majority of voters. It presents the counterpart for referendums on laws concerning domestic policy and underlies the same formal rules for validity (50,000 signatures within 100 days). International treaties are subject to the optional referendum if they a) are permanent and irrevocable, b) foresee entry into an international organization, or c) lead to a multilateral standardization of law (art. 141, para. 1 (d), FC).

Since its introduction, the optional referendum affecting treaties has only rarely been employed. Supplementing laws covering obligatory and optional referendum on treaties, the Federal Assembly can subject other international agreements to the optional referendum according to its own discretion (art. 141, para. 2, FC). In the past, deviating from the constitutional requirements valid at the time, the federal assembly also subjected treaties to the obligatory referendum if they failed to fulfil the corresponding conditions. Even though the approval of the respective treaties would not have needed such a comprehensive direct-democratic legitimization, the parliament went for it because it attributed a very high political relevance to those agreements. This occurred regarding Switzerland's entry into the League of Nations in 1920 and the Free Trade Agreement with the European Community in 1972. Both were accepted. Viewed objectively, the 1992 plebiscite on the EEA was also such a step, although the discussion, in this case, dodged the involvement of partial constitutional revision in the overall proposal.

Therefore, viewed in its entirety, a broad range of direct-democratic options stand available to the electorate for involvement in shaping foreign policy. Additional interlinkages with foreign and domestic policy increase the electorate's opportunities to participate in decision-making. In this regard, referendum tools on treaties are less often used than the 'ordinary' tools: the initiative and particularly the referendum.

4 Actors and coordination

The 'supreme goal' of foreign policy in the federal constitution and in the 2000 foreign policy report (Interdepartementale Arbeitsgruppe 2000), i.e. the preservation of independence, is deceptive: it cannot hide the fact that foreign policy is mainly about the day-to-day management of mutual dependencies. Horizontal networks of actors (national, international, and private) and several levels of actors (international, national, regional) drive Swiss policy. At the same time, foreign policy has been subdivided into numerous policy fields, including development, European, and peacebuilding policy. Federal laws and decrees regulate the assignment and use of resources for some foreign policy fields. Examples are international development cooperation and humanitarian aid, cooperation with countries in Eastern Europe, and programmes for peacebuilding and strengthening human rights. These sub-spheres of foreign policy are reflected in administration units inside the Federal Department of Foreign Affairs (FDFA) and outside it.

Foreign trade policy is accorded utmost importance. It remains a core component of Swiss foreign relations, which expresses itself institutionally by the fact that a State Secretariat for Economic Affairs (SECO) has been dedicated to it within the Federal Department for Economic Affairs, Education and Research (EAER). The current head of the FDFA, Federal Councillor Ignazio Cassis, reinforced the central importance of foreign trade relations again in its latest position paper (Avis 2019). With the Swiss Agency for Development and Cooperation (SDC), the development cooperation has its own directorate within the FDFA, too. It accounts for more than two-thirds of the department's total budget. The SECO and the SDC must coordinate closely since the shared budget for development cooperation provides about four-fifths to the SDC and a fifth to the SECO. In 2010, the State Secretariat for International Finance (SIF) was newly established in the Federal Department of Finance (FDF) for coordination and as a strategic lead on issues of international finance, currency, and taxes. Since 2013, the Directorate of European Affairs (DEA) has overseen the relations with the EU and European countries.

Having no directorate of its own but 'only' a division (within the Political Directorate), the peace and human rights division focuses on promoting peacebuilding and human rights. It coordinates its activities with the respective services and programmes of the SDC and with the regional services in charge of the respective countries in the Political Directorate (Heiniger 2021).

Finally, the Directorate for International Law (DIL) in the FDFA plays an essential role in critical specialized issues of foreign policy. Neutrality is by far the best known of them. To the extent that, in this case, it involves a concept supported by international law, the DIL enjoys a significant degree of independence in its interpretation. Yet the application of neutrality is essentially subject to political factors. For this reason, a strong need emerges for coordination within the FDFA, yet particularly also with other departments and ultimately within the Federal Council. As an example, the Federal Council's early declaration that the war in Iraq had ended in the spring of 2003 'coincidently' cleared the way for an arms deal with the USA at just that moment (Associated Press 2003). This illustrates how the handling of neutrality is subject to negotiations among different stakeholders and the interests they represent.

The 'five-sided goal' from the two Federal Council reports on Swiss foreign policy quoted above visualizes what in practice has long since become a component of foreign policy—a reality by the emergence of various policy fields. While priorities existed historically, the sides have become more or less equal over time, which makes coordination both necessary and complex.

Besides the cantons, the parliament, and the population (who enjoy constitutionally granted possibilities of participation), further actors have developed stronger interests in foreign policy, particularly the economy and civil society. Economic interests have played a significant role since the early days of Swiss foreign policy. Besides foreign economic relations, these interests have also particularly been present in Swiss European policy (Freiburghaus 2009) and in international cooperation (Federal Council 2020). Economic interests impact both the objectives and the implementation of these policies. In European policy, economic interests enjoy de facto a veto position. But unions, too, became more involved and influential in this field, particularly concerning the free movement of persons. Most recently, this has been shown in the political debates on the institutional agreement with the EU, which eventually were aborted.[3] In addition, international cooperation has increasingly relied on collaboration with economic actors (Federal Council 2020). Under the label 'public-private partnerships', new types of cooperation emerged, following the logic that public funding might pave the way for private investments (Brinkerhoff 2002; Zollinger 2006). Private aid and peacebuilding organizations, both Swiss and international, also participate significantly in the implementation of international cooperation and peacebuilding policies. They contribute at the conceptual level with their thematic and contextual expertise, as well as in implementation through their process experience and their networks, which strengthen the quality and the legitimacy of these policies (Klein and Roth 2007; Heiniger 2021).

This cooperation between state and non-state actors needs coordination and exchange. Examples of this are the consultative commission for international cooperation, which is an extra-parliamentary commission with about a dozen members, or the Swiss Platform for Peacebuilding (KOFF), located with swisspeace and which counts all relevant public and private cooperation and peacebuilding organizations as members. State actors acknowledge the benefit of this intense cooperation and exchange with private and civil society actors (Greminger 2011, 20–21). Private institutions may also enter the field of foreign policy not as implementation partners but as actors to be included in order to achieve specific goals. Private military security companies (PMSC), such as Blackwater in the USA or Aegis and in the UK, are interesting examples. Such firms provide all kinds of services linked to military engagements. They bear the danger of being used to circumvent relevant international humanitarian law (IHL) (Krahmann 2010; Leander 2005). As the depositary state of the Geneva Conventions of 1949, Switzerland was particularly affected and played a major role in supporting the negotiation of a voluntary international code of conduct, which had the objective to make sure that PMSC would also abide by IHL. Eventually, the International Code of Conduct Association (ICoCA) was established in Geneva to encourage and monitor the implementation. Developing international legislation on corporate social responsibility (CSR) and responsible business conduct (RBC) follows a similar pattern. In this field, however, Switzerland has not yet taken the place of a forerunner. This might have been the case had the popular initiative 'For responsible businesses—protecting human rights and the environment' been accepted in November 2020. While the initiative managed to gather the majority of the population (with 50.7 per cent yes-votes), it missed the majority of the cantons.

5 Perspectives and upcoming challenges

Neutrality no longer supplies Switzerland with a strategy for survival these days. However, it remains firmly anchored in the citizenry. It may also provide the basis for an active Swiss policy promoting peace. But its handling in situations of military crises needs clarification. The large-scale military aggression of Russia in Ukraine prompted a political debate in- and outside Switzerland about the political and legal implications of neutrality. At the beginning of the war, only neutrality policy came under pressure, because Switzerland was hesitant about adopting all of the EU sanctions against Russia, which it eventually then did quite rapidly. When during the following months Western states considerably developed their military support, neutrality law and the respective Swiss legislation also came in for critique. The reason was that Switzerland did not allow Swiss arms or ammunition, which had been sold to European states in earlier times, to be re-exported to Ukraine. A policy paper published by the think tank foraus (2022) suggested increasing cooperation with politically like-minded countries and organizations based on a community of values. On the opposite side, the still-leading figure of the Swiss People's Party (SVP), Christoph Blocher, launched a popular initiative, which, if accepted, would prevent Switzerland from adopting any kind of sanctions adopted outside of the UN framework against conflict parties in a war (Kirchner 2022). The government had announced it would publish a new report on neutrality, but in the end it failed to agree on the necessity of such a text. At the same time, Switzerland will, for the first time, be a non-permanent member of the UN Security Council for the years 2023/24. Considering the issues at stake and the forthcoming debates, the country is looking towards major foreign policy discussions in the next years—even beyond the pending issues of its European policy.

Federalism and direct democracy—originally more of a brake pedal on progress to an active foreign policy—today form valuable containers for binding Swiss foreign policy commitments to domestic politics again or for legitimizing it within the political system. The cantons could, in time, conclude that they can only preserve their constitutional authority if they seek additional ways to involve themselves in international decision-making procedures inside and outside the country. To this extent, the foreign policy 'special case' factors remain significant. However, in the future, they must be less of a factor in slowing down an active foreign policy than in supporting a further sustainable opening of Switzerland within domestic politics. In that sense, even larger cities have become involved in an increasing number of international networks at the regional and global level.

Switzerland's historically influenced dilemma of deciding between national autonomy and international influence is one of the crucial points in understanding the direction of its foreign policy. To preserve its neutrality as well as protecting federalism and direct democracy, Switzerland has almost always given priority to preserving autonomy rather than strengthening its influence in the past. Swiss business was not unhappy about this because it enabled it to deal under the shadow of neutrality (Kreis 2005). However, this apolitical phase in foreign policy is over. Since the end of the Cold War, Switzerland itself has gained leeway even if honouring neutral viewpoints. However, as new international regulations and norms have surfaced in many policy fields, hardly any domestic policy sector in Switzerland still operates completely independent of foreign policy linkage. This counts even more for development and foreign trade or international finance policies, which continuously bear in mind the political dimension of their actions.

This raises the twofold issue of whether autonomy is still worth the struggle or achievable at all. There is a danger that the autonomy banner will continue to be waved out of purely parochial motives. However, this may only represent the second-best option or even a strictly fictitious one. European policy provides the most specific example: if Switzerland's autonomy is addressed here, the numerous cases of 'autonomous' implementation are deliberately overlooked (Oesch 2012). The silent adaptations and further developments of bilateral treaties on the EU's continuously developing legal assets are also concealed. Moreover, the Europeanizing effect of Swiss policy occurs largely independent of required integration options. Compared to the possibilities of shared participation in the case of EU membership, bilateral treaties are not favourable to democracy. The options are also limited for the cantons. Though they would enjoy shared EU participation via their formal and informal presence in Brussels, resulting in numerous chances to influence and shape policy, their options to act in case of bilateral treaties are limited to joint decision-making at the end of the negotiating process. Not only in preserving interests in general but particularly in preserving national policy uniqueness, adherence to the European Union might well be the better option.

Where various foreign policy sectors and actors meet with their own goals and interests, conflicting goals are almost unavoidable. The constitution is of little help in this regard since it indeed defines the common goals of safeguarding independence and welfare as a sort of 'supreme goal'. It identifies four special goals: the alleviation of need and poverty, the promotion of the respect for human rights and democracy, the peaceful co-existence of peoples, and the conservation of natural resources. But it establishes no hierarchy. Hence, dealing with cases of conflict is left to the political process. At the same time, one must keep in mind that conflicting goals do not result primarily from incomplete administrative procedures but are the expression of real, tangible opposing interests.

Effectiveness and credibility are foreign policy's main criteria for coherency. However, coherency cannot emerge one-sidedly at the cost of material or idealistic values and interests. Coherency does not mean one-sided dominance but balance and avoidance of contradictions. To be legitimized within domestic policy, foreign policy must reflect the prevailing social consensus on the topics affected (Goetschel et al. 2005, 127–146). The coherency postulate can be considered fulfilled if the activities of government and non-governmental actors do not undermine the policy-specific goals or rob the means earmarked for achieving them in the same or other policy sectors.

Achieving domestic policy legitimacy ranks among the significant challenges of foreign policy—but also the most interesting ones in the immediate future. Debates about differing world views, which characterized the political discussions about Switzerland entering the UN twenty years ago, are joined by more 'grounded' and tangible foreign policy challenges in fields such as health, energy, or research: how to deal with pandemics, how to liberalize the electricity market, or how to manage international research cooperation have become crucial foreign policy matters. The further one peers into the future, the less it will suffice to refer simply to Switzerland's generally upheld international responsibilities. It will become more important to refer to Switzerland's benefits and interests. Thereby, the increasing influence achieved by Switzerland through its international commitment should duly be considered.

In contrast to other policy sectors, evaluating foreign policy is a complex task: treaties can be acknowledged, and international cooperation or peacebuilding projects can be assessed regarding the achievement of their goals. Yet the real impact of foreign policy remains an object of speculation. Consequently, political discussions on foreign relations may tend to increase. In addition, more actors will be involved in the future as the boundary between domestic and foreign policy is becoming increasingly permeable. This will hardly simplify foreign policy-making. On the other hand, we can expect a more vivid presence of foreign relations in policy discussions to be a lasting contribution to its anchorage and legitimacy in domestic policy.

Neutrality, which has gained increased visibility through the recent Russian attack on Ukraine, will most probably continue to serve as a significant foreign policy maxim through which the Swiss population and politicians discuss the international political involvement of the country. But future neutrality discussions do not need to follow old paths. In light of the geopolitical changes and the discussions on new world orders, neutrality could be seen as a progressive framework serving the strengthening of Switzerland's engagement in various policies in the realm of sustainability, peace, and development (Goetschel 2022). While neutrality contains military involvement, it provides at the same time opportunities for problem-oriented contributions in politically sensitive policy areas such as the governance of cyberspace or the protection of the

Arctic. Such involvement would be in line with strengthening the science–policy nexus in the realm of foreign policy—one of the domains in which Switzerland has traditionally been engaged in the North–South realm (KFPE 2010) and where the country has started new programmes at the global level such as the Geneva Science and Diplomacy Anticipator (GESDA) (Federal Council 2022).

Notes

1. See 'Switzerland and the European Union' in this volume.
2. This section is based on explanations in Goetschel et al. (2005, 29–44).
3. See 'Switzerland and the European Union' in this volume.

References

Associated Press. 2003. 'Tiger-Verkauf auf dem Spiel'. *Neue Zürcher Zeitung*, 23 April 2003, 11.

Avis. 2019. *Bericht der Arbeitsgruppe 'Aussenpolitische Vision Schweiz 2028' zuhanden von Bundesrat Ignazio Cassis*. Bern: EDA https://www.eda.admin.ch/avis28 (accessed 03 September 2022).

Brinkerhoff, Jennifer M. 2002. *Partnership for International Development: Rhetoric or Results?* Boulder, CO.: Lynne Rienner.

Bruppacher, Balz. 2020. *Die Schatzkammer der Diktatoren. Der Umgang der Schweiz mit Potentatengeldern*. Zurich: NZZ Libro.

Calmy-Rey, Micheline. 2004. *La neutralité suisse*. Discours prononcé à l'occasion de l'ouverture académique de l'école de hautes études commerciales (HEC), 21 October 2004, Lausanne.

Couchepin, Pascal. 2003. *Ouverture des hostilités en Irak. Discours présenté devant l'Assemblée fédérale à l'occasion de l'ouverture des hostilités en Irak*, 20 March 2003, Berne https://www.admin.ch/ch/d/cf/referate/edi/2003/030320Irak-f.pdf (accessed 03 September 2022).

Federal Council. 1993. *Bericht über die Aussenpolitik der Schweiz in den 90er Jahren (appendix to: Bericht zur Neutralität) of 29 November 1993*. Berne: EDMZ (special issue).

Federal Council. 2000. *Aussenpolitischer Bericht 2000 (Präsenz und Kooperation: Interessenwahrung in einer zusammenwachsenden Welt) vom 15. November 2000*. Bern: EDMZ (special issue).

Federal Council. 2020. *Botschaft zur Strategie der internationalen Zusammenarbeit 2021–2024 (IZA-Strategie 2021–2024)*. https://www.eda.admin.ch/dam/deza/de/documents/aktuell/dossiers/Botschaft-IZA-2021-2024_DE.pdf (accessed 03 September 2022).

Federal Council. 2022. Science Diplomacy: Bundesrat unterstützt die Stiftung GESDA nach erfolgreicher Pilotphase weiter. https://www.admin.ch/gov/de/start/dokumentation/medienmitteilungen.msg-id-87442.html (accessed 03 September 2022).

foraus. 2022. Kooperative Neutralität. Sieben Empfehlungen für ein Update der Schweizer Neutralität. https://www.foraus.ch/wp-content/uploads/2022/08/20220804_Neutralita%CC%88tspolitik_WEB.pdf (accessed 27 October 2022).

Frei, Daniel. 1969. *Dimensionen neutraler Politik: Ein Beitrag zur Theorie der Internationalen Beziehungen*. Geneva: Institut universitaire de hautes études internationales.

Freiburghaus, Dieter. 2009. *Königsweg oder Sackgasse? Sechzig Jahre schweizerische Europapolitik*. Zurich: NZZ Libro.

Gafafer, Tobias. 2022. 'Ukraine-Krieg: Es ist gefährlich, die Guten Dienste der Schweiz zu überhöhen'. NZZ, 19.08.2022. https://www.nzz.ch/meinung/ukraine-krieg-es-ist-gefaehrlich-die-guten-dienste-zu-ueberhoehen-ld.1697682 (accessed 03 September 2022).

Germann, Raimund E. 1995. 'Die bilateralen Verhandlungen mit der EU und die Steuerung der direkten Demokratie'. *Schweizerische Zeitschrift für Politische Wissenschaft* 1 (2–3): pp. 35–60.

Goetschel, Laurent. 1998. 'The Foreign and Security Policy Interests of Small States in Today's Europe'. In *Small States Inside and Outside the European Union: Interests and Policies*, edited by Laurent Goetschel, pp. 13–31. Boston: Kluwer.

Goetschel, Laurent. 2022. 'Neutrality and Geopolitics: Responding to Change'. In *Neutral Beyond the Cold. Neutral States and the Post-Cold War International System*, edited by Pascal Lottaz, Heinz Gärtner, and Herbert R. Reginbogin, pp. 3–18. Lanham: Lexington Books.

Goetschel, Laurent, Bernath, Magdalena, and Daniel Schwarz. 2005. *Swiss Foreign Policy. Foundations and Possibilities*. London and New York: Routledge.

Greminger, Thomas. 2011. *Swiss Civilian Peace Promotion: Assessing Policy and Practice*. Zurich: Center for Security Studies/ETHZ.

Häfliger, Markus. 2014. 'Schweizer Mittelweg in der Krim-Krise'. NZZ, 27.03.2014. https://www.nzz.ch/schweiz/der-schweizer-mittelweg-in-der-krim-krise-ld.647118 (accessed 03 September 2022).

Heiniger, Markus. 2021. *Rückblick für die Zukunft: 30 Jahre Friedensengagement im EDA 1990–2020*. Bern: EDA. https://www.shareweb.ch/site/Conflict-and-Human-Rights/Documents/Broschu%CC%88re%2030%20Jahre%20Friedensengagement%20im%20EDA.pdf (accessed 03 September 2022).

Interdepartementale Arbeitsgruppe. 2000. *Bericht der interdepartementalen Arbeitsgruppe vom 30. August 2000 ('Neutralitätspraxis der Schweiz – aktuelle Aspekte')* (special issue). Bern https://www.eda.admin.ch/dam/eda/de/documents/aussenpolitik/voelkerrecht/bericht-neutralitaetspraxis-kosovo-2000_DE.pdf (accessed 03 September 2022).

KdK – Conference of Cantonal Governments. 2011. *Innerstaatliche Reformen zur Festigung der föderalistischen und demokratischen Staatsorganisation im Rahmen der Europapolitik des Bundes*. Positionsbezug der Kantonsregierungen, 24. Juni 2011, Bern. https://kdk.ch/fileadmin/redaktion/themen/europapolitik/standortbestimmung/2_positionsbezug_vom_24_juni_2011.pdf (accessed 03 September 2022).

KFPE. 2010. *Weshalb mehr Forschungskooperationen mit Ländern des Südens und Ostens? Ein Diskussionspapier der KFPE—Kommission für Forschungspartnerschaften mit Entwicklungsländern*. Bern: Science and Policy Platform of the Swiss Academy of Sciences.

Kirchner, Thomas. 2022. 'Blochers letzte grosse Schlacht'. Süddeutsche Zeitung. 27. Juli 2022. https://www.sueddeutsche.de/politik/schweiz-blocher-neutralitaet-1.5628939 (accessed 03 September 2022).

Klein, Ansgar, and Silke Roth (eds). 2007. *NGOs im Spannungsfeld von Krisenprävention und Sicherheitspolitik*. Wiesbaden: VS Verlag für Sozialwissenschaften.

Klöti, Ulrich, Christian Hirschi, Uwe Serdült, and Thomas Widmer. 2005. *Verkannte Aussenpolitik. Entscheidungsprozesse in der Schweiz*. Zurich and Chur: Verlag Rüegger.

Krahmann, Elke. 2010. *Private Security Companies and the State Monopoly on Violence: A Case of Norm Change?* Frankfurt a.M: Peace Research Institute Frankfurt (PRIF-Reports No. 88).

Kreis, Georg. 2005. *Die Schweiz und Südafrika 1948–1994*. Schlussbericht des im Auftrag des Bundesrates durchgeführten NFP 42+. Bern, Stuttgart, Wien: Haupt.

Leander, Anna. 2005. 'The Market for Force and Public Security: The Destabilizing Consequences of Private Military Companies'. *Journal of Peace Research* 42 (5): pp. 605–622.

Maissen, Thomas. 2005. *Verweigerte Erinnerung. Nachrichtenlose Vermögen und die Schweizer Weltkriegsdebatte 1989–2004*. Zurich: Verlag Neue Zürcher Zeitung.

Münger, Bernhard. 1994. 'Die Konferenz der Kantonsregierungen'. In *Die Kantone und Europa*, edited by Dieter Freiburghaus, pp. 247–263. Bern: Haupt.

Oesch, Matthias. 2012. 'Die Europäisierung des schweizerischen Rechts'. In *Die Europakompatibilität des schweizerischen Wirtschaftsrechts: Konvergenz und Divergenz*, edited by Thomas Cottier, pp. 13–39. Zürich: Schulthess.

Rhinow, René. 2000. *Die Bundesverfassung 2000. Eine Einführung*. Basel: Helbing und Lichtenhahn.

SECO. 2022. 'Massnahmen im Zusammenhang mit der Situation in der Ukraine'. https://www.seco.admin.ch/seco/de/home/Aussenwirtschaftspolitik_Wirtschaftliche_Zusammenarbeit/Wirtschaftsbeziehungen/exportkontrollen-und-sanktionen/sanktionen-embargos/sanktionsmassnahmen/massnahmen-zur-vermeidung-der-umgehung-internationaler-sanktione.html (accessed 03 September 2022).

Sharman, Jason Campbell. 2017. *The Despot's Guide to Wealth Management: On the International Campaign against Grand Corruption*. Ithaca: Cornell University Press.

Szvircsev Tresch, Tibor, Andreas Wenger, Stefano De Roasa, Thomas Ferst, and Jacques Robert. 2020. *Sicherheit 2020. Aussen-, Sicherheits- und Verteidigungspolitische Meinungsbildung im Trend*. Zürich: ETHZ Forschungsstelle für Sicherheitspolitik und Militärakademie.

Wildhaber, Luzius. 1992. 'Aussenpolitische Kompetenzordnung im schweizerischen Bundesstaat'. In *Neues Handbuch der Schweizerischen Aussenpolitik*, edited by Alois Riklin, Hans Haug, and Raymond Probst, pp. 121–149. Berne: Haupt.

Zollinger, Urs. 2006. 'Public Private Partnerships: Das neue Zauberwort?'. In *Die Beziehung zwischen Wirtschaft und Aussenpolitik: eine natürliche Symbiose?*, edited by Laurent Goetschel, and Danielle Lalive d'Epinay, pp. 43–55. Basel: Europainstitut.

CHAPTER 27

SWITZERLAND AND THE EUROPEAN UNION

FABIO WASSERFALLEN

1 INTRODUCTION

As a small and open country in the middle of Europe, Switzerland is socially, culturally, economically, and politically closely intertwined with its neighbours (see 'Switzerland's Position in Europe and the World' in this volume). Institutionally, Switzerland is one of the forty-six members of the Council of Europe, the European guardian of human rights, democracy, and the rule of law—but as far as the European Union (EU), the most extensive project of integration in Europe, is concerned, Switzerland stands apart. Critical for this non-membership was when Swiss voters rejected the accession to the European Economic Area (EEA) in a historic referendum in 1992. Since then, Switzerland and the EU have developed a unique relationship, with more than 120 bilateral agreements. Although Switzerland is not a member of the EU, these bilateral agreements significantly integrate Switzerland into the EU, most notably into parts of the single market and the Schengen and Dublin frameworks. The unique Swiss–EU relationship is the result of a stepwise process over three decades, which has recently come to a standstill. Instead of further developing the Swiss model of integration, the recent developments have induced much uncertainty regarding the resilience and sustainability of Swiss–EU relations.

How and why did the Swiss model of EU integration become so contested? Why is it a possible scenario that Swiss–EU relations will likely further deteriorate instead of consolidating and expanding, given that both sides have established a broad net of cooperation and have a vital interest in realizing further mutual gains with updated and extended agreements? This chapter aims to shed light on these questions by analysing (a) the milestones of Swiss–EU relations over the last thirty years, (b) the EU's politicization in Switzerland in the context of direct democracy, and (c) the EU's transformation into the EU-27. Before exploring these developments, the first part of the chapter discusses several aspects of the history of EU integration that are relevant for Switzerland. Key insights from the history of EU integration are that economic and political integration require one another and that national resistance to political integration is not a genuine Swiss phenomenon. Overall, this part highlights that the Swiss case resonates well with the experience of EU member states, which is an important finding standing in contrast with the Swiss political discourse emphasizing the narrative of Switzerland as a 'Sonderfall' (special case).

A defining moment strengthening this narrative was the Swiss electorate's rejection of EEA membership in 1992, which came as a shock for the Federal Council and most of the political and economic elite. Without a plan B, the Swiss government had to find a model of cooperation with the EU under the context of a highly politicized domestic discourse. Against this backdrop, the Swiss government sought to integrate Switzerland into the single market with minimal political integration. The most important milestone on that path was realized in 1999 with the Bilateral Agreement I, which integrates Switzerland into parts of the single market, including an agreement on the free movement of persons. Five years later, the bilateral relations were extended with the accession to Schengen and Dublin.

Since the EEA's rejection in 1992, fourteen public votes have confirmed and established the Swiss model of integration through bilateral agreements (see 'Direct Democracy' and 'Direct-Democratic Votes' in this volume). The only exception to this continuous support is one initiative against migration in 2014, which aimed at restricting migration to Switzerland, including demands that were in conflict with the agreement on the free movement of persons. Overall, however, direct democracy has shaped Swiss–EU relations and highly legitimized the Swiss model of EU integration (see 'Foreign Policy' in this volume). The public votes also show that a very large domestic coalition has to support integration steps to be successful at the ballot box (Wasserfallen 2021). Forming this large supportive coalition is the key challenge for continuing and further developing Swiss–EU relations.

For a more complete understanding of the history and current state of Swiss–EU relations, one also has to analyse the EU side, particularly because the EU has changed substantially over the last three decades. For example, with the introduction of a common currency in the Eurozone, the EU member states have further pooled sovereignty and deepened European integration to a new level, while terrritorial expansions have extended the EU to Central and Eastern Europe. Last but not least, the United Kingdom (UK) has left the EU. The discussions on Brexit were particularly closely connected to the Swiss model of integration with a strong impact on the current Swiss–EU relations. All of these transformations have consequences for Switzerland. Defending the single market's integrity has become a key principle of the EU-27, which increased concerns about the flexible Swiss model of selective integration into the single market. The EU-27 formulates distinct demands in terms of the legal adoption and enforcement of EU market rules for Switzerland. In sum, developments in the EU and Switzerland have politically alienated both sides, resulting in a deterioration of the joint relationship.

On 26 May 2021, the Federal Council decided—again without having a plan B—to withdraw from the negotiations on an institutional agreement. The main critique in Switzerland against the agreement was related to the free movement of persons and its possible effects on wage protection and the access of EU citizens to welfare benefits. The Swiss government's unilateral withdrawal from negotiations in spring 2021 marks a low point in Swiss–EU relations and questions the resilience and sustainability of the Swiss model of integration. The final part of this contribution formulates several conditions that may be conducive to returning to a successful further development of Swiss–EU cooperation.

2 Lessons from EU integration history

At the most basic level, Switzerland's main goal is to participate in the single market with as little political integration as possible. Although the Swiss debate may suggest that this is the specific Swiss approach towards Europeanization, the complexity and interplay between deeper economic integration and political integration is a defining feature of European integration history. The key insight from several decades of integration is that economic integration cannot be intensified without deeper political integration. Economic and political integration are not a trade-off (De Grauwe 2006). Rather, they are complementary and mutually reinforcing: more economic integration requires a further deepening of political integration.

In the early years of integration, Jean Monnet had already forcefully advocated the idea that economic integration serves as an engine for political integration, and it turned out to be highly successful in the following decades. In the 1950s, Monnet advocated the approach of starting European cooperation by strengthening economic interdependence to pave the way for political integration. In that spirit, France and Germany, together with Italy, Belgium, the Netherlands, and Luxemburg, created the European Coal and Steel Community (ECSC) in 1951. The ECSC's signatory states pooled coal and steel production—the two industries providing the resources for military capacity.

A few years later, in 1957, the same six countries signed the founding document of the European Community, the Treaty of Rome, with an even more ambitious goal. The member states committed themselves to creating a common economic market, which was supposed to provide wealth and prosperity through increased transnational exchange and interdependence. Deeper integration in the form of a common market should not only provide prosperity. Beyond that, the Rome Treaties were supposed to establish and trigger deeper political integration among their signatory states. To that end, the treaty introduced a supranational institutional structure with the European Commission, Council, European Parliament, and European Court of Justice (Gilbert 2012).

The political science scholarship theorized Monnet's European integration approach of starting with economic integration to trigger further political integration as neo-functionalism (Haas 1961). A core premise of neo-functionalism is the spillover concept. The economic version of this idea is that integration in one industry and sector will increase interdependence and lead to higher demand for integration in other economic sectors (Schmitter 1969). The dynamic of sectoral spillovers should automatically lead to an ever more economically integrated union. In addition to this economic dynamic, neo-functional scholars also theorized, in the spirit of Monnet (1976), that economic integration would spill over into deeper political integration.

In the more recent political science literature, political integration is conceptualized as pooling and delegation (Tallberg 2002). 'Pooling' refers to joint decision-making among member states that goes beyond intergovernmental cooperation and the requirement of unanimous decision-making. Member states pool sovereignty by giving up veto power and introducing qualified majority voting, which enhances policy-making capacities. The concept of delegation means that member states transfer authority to supranational institutions. The combination of pooling and delegation makes the EU a truly supranational institution and specifies how deeply the EU is politically integrated with authority transfers from the national to the European level. Pooling and delegation strengthen the political decision-making capacity and the credibility of joint commitments on the supranational level. The more recent term 'strategic autonomy', widely used in Brussels, also captures this idea of strong joint EU action on the global stage through pooled sovereignty.

The history of European integration shows that the development towards such deeper integration was accompanied by conflicts and setbacks in the 1960s, 1970s, and more recent decades. The work of intergovernmentalists stresses national governments' crucial role in this process (Hoffmann 1966; Moravcsik 1998). A critical finding of the intergovernmental literature is that deeper political integration triggers national resistance. In the long run, this resistance, however, could not block the development towards deeper political integration. The following three examples illustrate the patterns of national resistance and integration. First, in the 1960s Charles de Gaulle opposed the planned deepening of integration in agricultural policy by suspending French participation in the European Community's institutions. Second, for the Federal Republic of Germany, the abandonment of the Deutsche mark, a symbol of German stability and recovery in the post-war period, was a painful loss of national autonomy. And third, during the Eurozone crisis, the national room for manoeuvre in fiscal policy was further constrained, fuelling protest and contestation in Greece and other southern member states of the EU.

These examples illustrate that all European countries were (and are) confronted with the basic problem that higher levels of economic integration (in the single market, agricultural policy, or the Eurozone) require further transfers of political authority to the European level in the form of pooling and delegation and that this process triggers national resistance. All member states face specific institutional and political obstacles in this process. As a general pattern, the history of European integration shows that national resistance may cause temporary gridlock but does not block deeper political integration in the medium and long term. Rather, it leads to opt-outs and increased differentiated integration, which essentially means that not all EU countries are, to the same extent, integrated into specific EU policy areas (Schimmelfennig et al. 2015). Denmark, for example, has not joined the Eurozone, and Ireland is not part of Schengen.

In sum, we can draw three lessons from the history of European integration, which are relevant for Switzerland:

1) Economic integration is the main driver of European integration.
2) Economic and political integration are complementary (i.e. deeper levels of economic integration require additional political integration).
3) Political integration triggers national resistance.

A key insight from this historical perspective is that the experience of EU member states is not fundamentally different to that of Switzerland. This stands in contrast to large parts of the Swiss discourse, which centres on Swiss exceptionalism, using the term 'Sonderfall' (special case), which delimits Switzerland from EU member states (Eberle and Imhof 2007). The short discussion above emphasizes that economic integration, which is Switzerland's main motivation to maintain its relation to the EU, was also the main driver of European integration. Moreover, any step in the direction of further political integration is contested in Switzerland—just like integration steps fuel national resistance in EU member states.

From this perspective, the Swiss case resonates well with the experience of EU member states. The understanding that deeper economic integration requires some level of political integration, however, is underdeveloped in Switzerland. The EU's member states have learned this lesson. The Swiss debate still does not acknowledge the complementarity between political and economic integration, which is problematic because this insinuates that deeper levels of economic integration can be achieved without transfers of political autonomy.

The existing bilateral treaties between Switzerland and the EU already include rules on the Swiss adoption of market law, and the Schengen and Dublin association even comes with the obligation of a dynamic updating of EU rules. Swiss legislation is, therefore, highly Europeanized (Jenni 2014). In other words, integration in several EU policy areas is *de facto* already very substantial, while the Swiss discourse still builds on the premise that Switzerland, as a non-member of the EU, stands apart.

Accordingly, a widely held belief is that Switzerland has successfully resisted any form of political integration—despite the existing deep level of integration in respect of the adoption of EU law—and that the Swiss–EU relations could be further deepened without any loss of national political autonomy. The often somewhat self-referential EU discourse in Switzerland on the narrative of the 'Sonderfall' suggests that losing some national autonomy would be a genuine Swiss concern. While the history of European integration documents that this is a constant feature of integration, the extent of the involvement of Swiss voters through direct democracy is special in Switzerland. The following section discusses how direct democracy has shaped Swiss–EU relations since the early 1990s.

3 THE SHOCK OF THE EEA REJECTION AND THE BILATERAL AGREEMENTS

In 1960, Switzerland, Austria, Denmark, Norway, Portugal, Sweden, and the UK founded the European Free Trade Association (EFTA). All EFTA founding members later became members of the EU, except for Norway and Switzerland. A few decades after EFTA was formed, only Switzerland, Norway, Iceland, and Liechtenstein remained as members of this association. Unlike Switzerland, the other three remaining EFTA countries, which did not become members of the EU, joined the EEA. They are thus institutionally integrated into the EU single market.

Joining the EEA was also supposed to be the next integration step for Switzerland. On 6 December 1992, however, 50.3 per cent of the electorate (and eighteen of the twenty-six cantons) rejected the Swiss accession to the EEA. The vote followed a heated political debate with an exceptionally high turnout of 79 per cent. The result came as a shock to the Federal Council and most of the political and economic elite. The vote was also the starting point of a fundamental transformation of the national conservative Swiss People's Party (SVP). Christoph Blocher established himself as the uncontested party leader of the SVP. He vehemently opposed the EEA accession, arguing that Switzerland would lose national autonomy. The narrative of Switzerland as a 'Sonderfall', a country that is not compatible with EEA or EU membership, established itself in the Swiss discourse. Building on the success of the EEA vote, the SVP's resistance against any further integration became a key mission of the party (Kriesi et al. 2005). With this programmatic orientation, the SVP increased its vote share from 11.9 per cent in the 1991 elections to 29.4 per cent in 2015, which is the highest vote share of a Swiss party since the introduction of proportional representation in 1918 (Vatter 2020).

After the rejection of EEA membership in 1992, the Federal Council had to find a new Swiss–EU relationship within the context of a politicized discourse. The SVP's fundamental opposition has shaped Swiss politics ever since. Closer ties to the EU, even in the form of predominantly economic integration, have been framed as problematic because they entail the adoption of foreign rules ('fremde Gesetze') and judicial review by foreign judges ('fremde Richter'). The political debate therefore strongly focuses on the costs of sovereignty losses and Switzerland as a 'Sonderfall'. The contrasting view to this national conservative narrative is that joint European decision-making does not undermine European countries' sovereignty in an interdependent, globalized, and increasingly multi-polar and hostile world. Along these lines, several academics have argued that, for Switzerland, deeper integration into the EU with pooled sovereignty would eventually increase its de facto political capacity to act (Gentinetta and Kohler 2010; Cottier and Holenstein 2021).

Beyond such discussion on sovereignty's role in our times, the main problem in respect to the public discourse in Switzerland is that it largely ignores that deeper integration in the economy and other policy fields can only be achieved by pooling decision-making power. A typical misperception is the widely held belief that completely autonomous self-determination would be compatible with more elaborated forms of cooperation and integration. A substantial part of the Swiss discourse essentially builds on the assumption that the adoption of EU market rules would be voluntary and can be done selectively, which the EU criticizes as 'cherry picking'. Important in that respect is also the distinction between single-market integration and free trade agreements. Any deeper economic integration beyond free trade agreements comes with an inevitable loss of national political autonomy.

Against this political backdrop, the Swiss approach, after the EEA vote, was to maximize economic integration into the EU's single market while minimizing political integration. The Federal Council also officialized its intention of EU accession with the deposition of an EU application request on 26 May 1992. After the EEA vote, the Federal Council started negotiations with the EU for market access in some sectors and gradually developed over two decades a bilateral relationship with the EU. The EU, on its part, was willing to negotiate the sectoral integration of Switzerland because it believed that this would be a transitory stage. The EU assumed that Switzerland was on a path towards EU membership. From the EU's perspective, the bilateral agreements were negotiated on the premise that Swiss accession to the EU was the long-term goal (Müller 2020).

After several years of negotiations, Switzerland and the EU signed seven bilateral agreements on 21 June 1999 (on the free movement of persons, technical barriers to trade, public procurement, agriculture, land transport, air transport, and research). These seven agreements, the so-called Bilateral Agreements I, are legally linked to one another, which means that none of them can be individually suspended (known as the 'guillotine clause'). As far as Swiss politics are concerned, the SVP's support was unusual in the vote on the Bilateral Agreements I. Although Christoph Blocher, the SVP's leader, argued for a rejection of the Bilateral Agreements I at the party meeting, in which the SVP decided on its position, the party delegates narrowly voted in support of them. On 21 May 2000, the Swiss electorate approved the Bilateral Agreements I with 67 per cent of the vote, which is an exceptionally large 'yes' vote for an EU referendum.

The treaty on the free movement of people mutually opened the labour markets. On this question, the support of the trade unions was—and still is—central. With so-called accompanying measures ('flankierende Massnahmen'), the trade unions were able to negotiate regulations and a control system, which protect Swiss wage levels. The Swiss trade unions negotiated wage protection measures in return for their support of the free movement of people. The legacy of this bargain is that the trade unions still expect compensation in the form of worker and employee protection for their continued support for economic integration. In Switzerland, the trade unions are strengthened in EU politics compared to standard domestic politics because their consent is necessary for securing a public majority.

The bilateral path was expanded on 16 October 2004 with the Bilateral Agreements II. In addition to various other treaties, the Bilateral Agreements II include cooperation in the areas of internal security and asylum with the accession to Schengen and

Dublin. The Schengen agreement strengthens police cooperation through the exchange of information and simplifies cross-border mobility. The Dublin agreement coordinates asylum procedures. On 5 June 2005, 55 per cent of the electorate voted in favour of the Bilateral Agreements II. In terms of political cleavages, this vote divided Switzerland along the typical lines of conflict in EU politics, which are similar in EU member states, with divisions between national conservatives and progressives and the rural and urban population. The SVP opposed the Bilateral Agreements II against all other major parties; the rural regions rejected it against the population in the cities; and there was a clear difference between the German- and French-speaking parts of Switzerland, whereby the French-speaking cantons were in favour of the agreement (Engeli and Tresch 2005).

4 The transformation of the EU and its consequences for Switzerland

Since the bilateral agreements were signed two decades ago, the EU has undergone fundamental changes, including its expansion to Central and Eastern Europe. On 1 May 2004, ten new member states joined the EU. Romania and Bulgaria followed on 1 January 2007 and Croatia on 1 July 2013. The bilateral framework between Switzerland and the EU was successfully adapted to the enlarged EU in various votes: on 25 September 2005, 56 per cent of the Swiss electorate supported the extension of the free movement of people to the ten new member states; on 26 November 2006, 53 per cent voted in favour of the payment of CHF 1 billion for economic development in Eastern Europe; and on 8 February 2009, 60 per cent said yes to the extension of the free movement of people to Bulgaria and Romania.

With its expansion to Central and Eastern Europe, the EU became more heterogeneous. Along with the EU's transformation through enlargement, the introduction of the Euro has also changed the EU. When the EU leaders created the Economic and Monetary Union at the Maastricht summit in 1991, they discussed how creating a common currency had to be complemented by further political integration in the form of fiscal, labour-market, and economic integration. The debate is still ongoing, with advocates of strict budget and debt rules conflicting with supporters of more fiscal transfers and burden sharing (Brunnermeier et al. 2016; Lehner and Wasserfallen 2019). Similar conflicts shape the negotiations regarding the EU budget and the economic recovery package NGEU (Next Generation EU), which is a fiscal instrument designed to counter the economic downturn caused by the COVID-19 pandemic. In the NGEU negotiations, the EU member states agreed, for the first time, to finance a vast spending programme by raising joint credits on the financial markets. In essence, this means that they are taking up common debts, which was, as a fiscal integration approach, not a politically feasible option in the Eurozone's reforms, not least because of the opposition of Germany (Wasserfallen 2023). Taking a broader perspective, the basic pattern of the Eurozone's development follows the standard process of integration discussed earlier: deeper economic integration (here in the form of a common currency) leads to further competence shifts to the EU level (despite national resistance).

Finally, Brexit has also transformed the EU. The UK officially left the EU on 31 January 2020. Like the Swiss approach, the UK tried in the Brexit negotiations to obtain access to the single market with substantial exceptions to basic rules, such as the free movement of people. The member states of the EU-27, however, were very united in the Brexit negotiations and rejected any such model of flexible integration in the single market – even though such an agreement may have been economically beneficial for the EU and the UK. As a result, the UK eventually negotiated a free trade agreement with the EU. British goods are subject to customs procedures (such as inspections, controls, and registration). The main consequence of Brexit for Switzerland is that the EU-27 formulated a consolidated and tough stance concerning the single market's integrity: participation in the single market requires the constant adoption of the EU market rules. This basic principle of the EU-27 seriously limits the room for manoeuvre in Swiss–EU relations.

Taken together, the EU has undergone fundamental changes in the last few decades. Today, the EU-27 is an entirely different union than the EU that negotiated bilateral agreements with Switzerland in the late 1990s and early 2000s. The EU is more deeply integrated, has expanded to Eastern and Central Europe, and has lost the UK as a member state. The most direct consequences for Switzerland are that (a) the new member states from Central and Eastern Europe are politically and economically more distant from Switzerland, (b) internal and external challenges dominate the agenda in Brussels, and (c) the single market's integrity has become a consolidated core principle of the EU-27. Policy-wise, Switzerland's main problem is that the EU is not willing to take an accommodative stance on the question of selective economic integration. For the EU-27, the regular updating of market rules and the institutionalized enforcement of these rules are necessary conditions for participation in the single market. This is also expected from the Swiss—and goes beyond the current bilateral framework. From the EU's perspective, the bilateral approach is therefore outdated. The Swiss government does not share this institutional perspective, while, in the Swiss debate, the controversies centre on the question of the free movement of people.

5 Direct democracy and the free movement of people

In 2014, a referendum troubled the relationship between Switzerland and the EU. The initiative 'against mass immigration', launched by the SVP, was approved by 50.3 per cent of the electorate. After several public votes have established the bilateral framework as the Swiss model of integration, the successful initiative 'against mass immigration' called the existing relationship with the EU into question. Central to the initiative's success were the rising numbers of EU citizens coming to Switzerland and the high proportion of cross-border commuters.

Since the introduction of the free movement of people in 2002, the number of incoming EU citizens from the EU, particularly from Germany, had risen steadily until 2008, when 113,000 people moved from the EU to Switzerland (which corresponds to a net migration of 84,000). After this peak, net migration sunk to 36,000 in 2018. As a further consequence of the free movement of people, the number of cross-border commuters, especially from France and Italy, steadily increased. The large share of cross-border commuters is driven by the substantial wage disparities between Switzerland and its neighbouring countries, Italy, France, Germany, and Austria. The already large wage differences have increased further in real terms due to the Euro weakening in relation to the Swiss franc (1 euro was worth 1.60 Swiss francs in 2008; in March 2022, the exchange rate arrived at parity).

Against this backdrop, the consequences of the free movement of people agreement have become a dominant issue in Swiss political debates. The success of the initiative 'against mass immigration' also set a difficult task for the Swiss parliament, as it had to implement the initiative without threatening the agreement on the free movement of people (and the entire Bilateral Agreements I because of the guillotine clause). The parliament opted for a minimalist implementation. The SVP reacted to this by launching the 'limitation initiative', which explicitly requested the suspension of the free movement of people. Swiss voters, however, rejected this more extreme initiative with a vote share of 61.7 per cent on 27 September 2020. Eventually, these public votes on migration did not endanger the free movement of people and the entire Bilateral Agreements I. Still, the success of the initiative 'against mass immigration' amplified the SVP's strong mobilization potential. Moreover, the trade unions' critical role in EU politics was highlighted because of the demonstrated salience of Swiss wage protection in relation to the free movement of people.

Direct democracy shapes EU politics in Switzerland with initiatives, as discussed above, and with referendums called against new treaties signed with the EU or any other new law related to Swiss–EU relations (see 'Foreign Policy' and 'Direct-Democratic Votes' in this volume). As far as new treaties with the EU are concerned, the constitutional question of whether they are subject to a mandatory or an optional referendum is politically very sensitive. In case of an obligatory referendum, a majority of the people *and* of the cantons have to approve the proposal. With the requirement of this double majority, the rural population in small cantons is overrepresented, which increases the threshold for such proposals, given that the rural population is more sceptical about the EU and integration proposals. Approximately a minority of only 46 per cent of the Swiss electorate can achieve a majority in the cantonal vote—and thus block a treaty that a popular and a cantonal majority has to approve (Vatter 2020, 414). In other words, the de facto requirement for support in the popular vote increases from 50 to 54 per cent.

Despite the setbacks in Swiss–EU relations through the votes on the EEA and the initiative 'against mass immigration', the main direct democratic story is the Swiss electorate's strong backing of Swiss–EU relations. Since the EEA's rejection in 1992, fifteen proposals related to Swiss–EU relations have been submitted to the Swiss electorate.

Table 27.1: Votes on EU proposals with the 'yes' percentages for voters

Date	Proposal	Legal Form	Yes-Share	Turnout
06.12.1992	Accession of Switzerland to the European Economic Area	Mandatory referendum	49.7% (7)	78.73%
08.06.1997	'EU membership negotiations before the people!'	Popular initiative	25.9% (0)	35.44%
21.05.2000	Bilateral Agreements I between Switzerland and the European Union	Optional referendum	67.2%	48.30%
04.03.2001	'Yes to Europe!'	Popular initiative	23.2% (0)	55.79%
05.06.2005	Acceptance of the Schengen/Dublin association agreement	Optional referendum	54.6%	56.63%
25.09.2005	Extension of the agreement on the free movement of persons and the revision of the accompanying measures	Optional referendum	56.0%	54.51%
26.11.2006	Federal Act on Cooperation with Eastern Europe	Optional referendum	53.4%	44.98%
08.02.2009	Continuation/extension of the agreement on the free movement of persons	Optional referendum	59.6%	51.44%
17.05.2009	Introduction of the biometric passport (Schengen)	Optional referendum	50.1%	38.77%
09.02.2014	Initiative 'against mass immigration'	Popular initiative	50.3% (14.5)	56.57%
30.11.2014	Stop overpopulation—to safeguard the natural basis of life	Popular initiative	25.9% (0)	49.98%
28.02.2016	Initiative 'for the effective expulsion of foreign criminals'	Popular initiative	41.1% (4.5)	63.73%
25.11.2018	'Self-determination Initiative'	Popular initiative	33.7% (0)	48.41%
19.05.2019	EU firearms directive	Optional referendum	63.7%	43.88%
27.09.2020	'For moderate immigration (Limitation initiative)'	Popular initiative	38.3% (3.5)	59.49%
15.05.2022	Participation in the European border and coast guard Frontex	Optional referendum	71.5%	39.98%

Note: The number in brackets shows the number of cantons supporting an initiative or referendum when the constitutional requirement of a double majority holds (with a total of twenty-three cantonal votes as half-cantons are counted as 0.5).

Data sources: Swissvotes/Année Politique Suisse (2022), Federal Chancellery (2022).

Table 27.1 documents for all these votes the proportion of 'yes' votes of the people and cantons, the turnout, and the legal form (obligatory referendum, initiative, or optional referendum). Over the long run, Swiss integration into the EU, as advocated by the Federal Council and the broad coalition of parties seeking to strengthen Switzerland's relationship with the EU, has been supported in fourteen referendums since the EEA's rejection. The adoption of the SVP initiative 'against mass immigration' in 2014 was the only exception to this pattern. However, it is also evident that the proportion of yes votes was in several votes only slightly above 50 per cent, which shows how divisive EU votes are.

6 THE FAILED INSTITUTIONAL AGREEMENT

The Bilateral Agreements II were signed in 2004. No further milestone in Swiss–EU relations has been achieved since then. The previous sections discussed how the EU has changed fundamentally in the last few decades and how the free movement of people became a hot topic in Swiss politics. Against this backdrop, Switzerland and the EU have tried to consolidate and improve Swiss–EU relations. Although Switzerland wants to conclude further bilateral market access agreements, for example in the electricity sector, the EU defends the single market's integrity and requests a dynamic adoption of Swiss law and an institutional procedure that ensures compliance with EU market law.

After the EU and Switzerland started to negotiate a new framework on 22 May 2014, the two sides supposedly reached a deal at the end of 2018 with the so-called institutional agreement (InstA). The InstA framework should deliver legal certainty for the existing market access agreements and lay the foundation for future market access agreements. As such, the agreement had an exclusive focus on institutional questions, as compared to the Bilateral Agreements I and II, which both included deeper integration in specific policy fields. The InstA entailed, through the institutional approach, more indirect effects instead of extending the material scope of integration to pertinent fields, such as energy, health, or security.

The InstA included a dynamic mechanism of legal adoption of EU market law and a dispute settlement procedure to ensure the uniform application of common market rules. This framework satisfied the EU's insistence on the single market's integrity. According to the InstA, Switzerland would have been able to articulate its concerns in the EU legislative process but then had to adopt new market rules. Disputes would have been settled by an arbitral tribunal, which would submit questions on the interpretation of EU law to the Court of Justice of the European Union (CJEU). If the EU or Switzerland were to implement a decision of the arbitral tribunal insufficiently, the other party could take proportionate compensatory measures. The aim of the InstA was, therefore, to provide legal certainty and to link Swiss legislation more closely to legal developments in the EU single market—with the CJEU taking a central role in disputes.

A majority in the Federal Council did not support the result of the InstA and launched on 7 December 2018 an unusual process to explore the domestic support for the agreement. In this consultation process, the main domestic political actors presented their assessment of the InstA. The consultation was disappointing for the supporters of the agreement, as it became clear that the treaty's content was subject to broad and heavy criticism. The Federal Council (2019) stated that, based on the consultation, there was insufficient political support for the InstA. Whereas the SVP would reject such a framework anyway, the opposition extended well beyond the SVP.

At the core of the concerns were the anticipated effects of the free movement of people. The trade unions with the support of the Social Democrats were concerned that the InstA would weaken wage protection arrangements. The Christian Democrats, among others, wanted to exclude the EU Citizenship Directive from the framework because they feared that the adoption of the InstA would burden the welfare state. And finally, the CJEU's role was heavily contested. The SVP reiterated its established narrative against 'foreign judges'. Although this was not surprising, the more damaging outcome of the consultations was the widely shared fear that an activist CJEU would extend free movement of people rights based on the InstA. The trade unions were concerned that the CJEU would further weaken wage protection arrangements, and centre-right politicians argued that the court would stepwise introduce the EU Citizenship Directive, which would facilitate EU citizens' eligibility to welfare benefits. Surveys of the Swiss electorate showed a similar picture. The InstA attracted the most criticism in the electorate around the question of how the framework would affect wage protection and access to social benefits.[1]

After some back and forth and additional rounds of talks between the EU and Switzerland, the Federal Council decided on 26 May 2021 to withdraw unilaterally from the negotiations on the institutional agreement. This was surprising because the Swiss government had no plan B for Swiss–EU relations—and the InstA resulted from several years of negotiations. Almost ironically, in hindsight, the starting initiative for an institutional agreement came from Switzerland: a conservative member of the Swiss parliament proposed a framework agreement in 2005 attempting to stabilize and extend the bilateral relations with the EU (Müller 2020). This initiative was taken up by both sides and translated in the (eventually unsuccessful) InstA agreement.

7 CONCLUSION AND OUTLOOK

Politics in Switzerland and the EU have changed in the last few decades, with substantial consequences for their joint relationship. On the EU side, the expansion to Eastern and Central Europe has transformed the EU to Switzerland's disadvantage. The new member states are less understanding of the tailored and selective Swiss model of integration, as they had to adopt the EU's full legal framework. Brexit was not helpful for Switzerland either. The EU-27 formulated in the Brexit negotiations a tough stance protecting the single market's integrity, which reduced the flexibility in terms of selective integration and legal compliance. On the Swiss side, the effects of the free movement of people have been politicized, strengthening national conservatives, who emphasize sovereignty concerns, and trade unions, who are concerned with the protection of Swiss wage levels.

Taken together, the developments in the EU and Switzerland have politically alienated the two. The basic principles articulated on both sides are challenging to reconcile. Although Switzerland wants to consolidate the bilateral relations and sign further agreements (e.g. in the electricity sector), the EU is not willing to extend the relationship without an institutional agreement regulating the dynamic updating of rules within the EU's legal framework. Despite these complications, the unifying forces in Swiss–EU relations remain strong: Switzerland and the EU have an enormous interest in comprehensive and deep relations as far as the economic exchange is concerned but also well beyond, for example in energy, climate, education, research, health, digitalization, and security policy.

This contribution sought to stress that deeper levels of integration (in economics and other policy fields) require further political integration, which has consequences. Although deeper political integration constrains national political autonomy, it simultaneously enhances the joint problem-solving capacity, particularly in an interdependent world with global challenges. At the end of the day, integration and cooperation must for Switzerland, like for any other country, enhance the capacity to address public policy problems that it cannot resolve on its own. The discourse in Switzerland could build on this premise if it were to acknowledge more explicitly that further political integration is a necessity to consolidate and intensify the relationship with the EU (and not something to be avoided at any costs). On this basis, a more informed political discussion would be feasible on whether the gains of deeper integration outweigh the costs. This should, in turn, lead to a recalibration of the Swiss integration model. Three points may be particularly conducive to this path.

First, the EU and Switzerland should focus on mutual gains and the set of shared common values. The joint relationship deteriorated to a level where the EU and Switzerland expect the other to compromise over basic principles. Schimmelfennig (2022) rightly concluded that both sides have even taken solidarity measures hostage to improve their respective bargaining positions. For example, Switzerland used its contribution to social cohesion as a bargaining chip, and the EU downgraded Switzerland to a non-associated third country in the Horizon Europe research programme, which is a problematic example of tit-for-tat defection, simply attempting to hit the other side (even at the cost of own losses).

Second, the Swiss debate should move beyond an exclusive economic narrative and a focus on minimizing political integration. Rather, the gains of mutual cooperation regarding market integration and in other policy fields have to become an equally important part of the equation in the search for a new Swiss model of integration. This, however, also implies that the gains from a new joint agreement are tangible. The failed InstA only included an institutional perspective, which has amplified concerns over the political costs. The gains from this integration step were diffuse and indirect. Consequently, the agreement's potential negative effects, in respect of wage protection and welfare access, dominated the Swiss debate. Overall, the InstA's content was too narrow and technical to build the necessary broad support in Switzerland. For the debate and politics to change, tangible cooperative gains, for example in energy and electricity production and supply, must be part of an agreement.

Finally, the political debate in Switzerland should include the advantages, disadvantages, and consequences of all available options in Swiss–EU relations (Oesch 2021; Walter 2021). The status quo means, about twenty years after the Bilateral Treaty II, no further updated cooperation and a slow erosion of the existing framework. This is the perspective if both sides cannot renew their relationship. Besides the failed InstA, three options exist for Swiss integration: (a) Switzerland joins the EU (Schwok 2009), which is a highly unpopular option that will not happen in the foreseeable future; (b) accession to the EEA (Freiburghaus and Kreis 2013), which would meet the EU's demand for institutional integration but is, in light of the Swiss criticism raised against the InstA, even worse (with stricter rules about the dynamic updating and the regulations on the free movement of people); or (c) a free trade agreement, following the model of the UK, which would decrease the current level of integration and restrict the joint relations to economic exchange. Although the Swiss debate has identified the InstA's flaws from the Swiss perspective, the problem is that the alternatives to such an agreement, such as EU or EEA membership, hardly fulfil Switzerland's interests better.

The assessment of various integration options is, of course, politically highly controversial, and, eventually, a new model of Swiss–EU relations must be supported by a large domestic coalition against the SVP's resistance. In this process towards a renewed Swiss–EU relationship, the Federal Council is the key actor connecting the negotiations with the EU and the domestic political arena (see 'Foreign Policy' and 'The Federal Government' in this volume). The Swiss government has the main responsibility to define Switzerland's interests, negotiate a new framework, and form a broad domestic coalition. This requires more leadership and a more systematic interplay between domestic politics and the negotiations with the EU on the Federal Council's part.

Note

1. See a post-poll conducted by LeeWas on the federal referendums of 19 May 2019. Zurich, 20 May 2019.

References

Brunnermeier, Markus K., Harold James, and Jean-Pierre Landau. 2016. *The Euro and the Battle of Ideas*. Princeton: Princeton University Press.
Cottier, Thomas, and André Holenstein. 2021. *Die Souveränität der Schweiz in Europa*. Bern: Stämpfli Verlag.
De Grauwe, Paul. 2006. 'On Monetary and Political Union'. *CESifo Forum* 7 (4): pp. 3–10.
Eberle, Thomas S., and Kurt Imhof. 2007. *Sonderfall Schweiz*. Zurich: Seismo.

Engeli, Isabelle, and Anke Tresch. 2005. 'Analyse der eidgenössischen Volksabstimmungen vom 5. Juni 2005'. *VOX-Analysen eidgenössischer Urnengänge* 87. Bern and Genf: gfs.Bern and University of Geneva.

Federal Chancellery. 2022. *Chronologie Volksabstimmungen*. https://www.bk.admin.ch/ch/d/pore/va/vab_2_2_4_1.html (accessed 07 November 2022).

Federal Council. 2019. *Bericht über die Konsultationen zum institutionellen Abkommen zwischen der Schweiz und der Europäischen Union*. https://www.eda.admin.ch/dam/europa/de/documents/bericht_konsultationen_insta/BR-Bericht-Konsulationen-InstA-190607_de.pdf (accessed 07 November 2022).

Freiburghaus, Dieter, and Georg Kreis. 2013. *Der EWR—verpasste oder noch bestehende Chance?* Zurich: Verlag Neue Zürcher Zeitung.

Gentinetta, Katja, and Georg Kohler. 2010. *Souveränität im Härtetest: Selbstbestimmung unter neuen Vorzeichen*. Zurich: NZZ Libro.

Gilbert, Mark. 2012. *European Integration: A Concise History*. Lanham: Rowman & Littlefield.

Haas, Ernst B. 1961. 'International Integration: The European and the Universal Process'. *International Organization* 15 (3): pp. 366–392. https://doi.org/10.1017/S0020818300002198.

Hoffmann, Stanley. 1966. 'Obstinate or Obsolete? The Fate of the Nation-State and the Case of Western Europe'. *Daedalus* 95 (3): pp. 862–915.

Jenni, Sabine. 2014. 'Europeanization of Swiss Law-Making: Empirics and Rhetoric are Drifting Apart'. *Swiss Political Science Review* 20 (2): pp. 208–215. https://doi.org/10.1111/spsr.12098.

Kriesi, Hanspeter, Peter Selb, Romain Lachat, and Marc Helbling. 2005. *Der Aufstieg der SVP. Acht Kantone im Vergleich*. Zurich: Verlag Neue Zürcher Zeitung.

Lehner, Thomas, and Fabio Wasserfallen. 2019. 'Political Conflict in the Reform of the Eurozone'. *European Union Politics* 20 (1): pp. 45–64. https://doi.org/10.1177%2F1465116518814338.

Monnet, Jean. 1976. *Mémoires*. Paris: Fayard.

Moravcsik, Andrew. 1998. *The Choice for Europe: Social Purpose and State Power from Messina to Maastricht*. London: Routledge.

Müller, Felix E. 2020. *Kleine Geschichte des Rahmenabkommens: Eine Idee, ihre Erfinder und was Brüssel und der Bundesrat daraus machten*. Zurich: NZZ Libro.

Oesch, Matthias. 2021. 'Die schweizerische Europapolitik auf dem Prüfstand'. In *Eine Aussenpolitik für die Schweiz im 21. Jahrhundert*, edited by Thomas Bernauer, Katja Gentinetta, and Joëlle Kuntz, pp. 108–113. Zurich: NZZ Libro.

Schimmelfennig, Frank. 2022. 'Switzerland: Solidarity Taken Hostage'. In *European Solidarity in Action and the Future of Europe*, edited by Michael Keading, Johannes Pollack, and Paul Schmidt, pp. 764–782. Cham: Springer.

Schimmelfennig, Frank, Dirk Leuffen, and Berthold Rittberger. 2015. 'The European Union as a System of Differentiated Integration: Interdependence, Politicization and Differentiation'. *Journal of European Public Policy* 22 (6): pp. 764–782. https://doi.org/10.1080/13501763.2015.1020835.

Schmitter, Philippe C. 1969. 'European Integration and Supranational Governance'. *International Organization* 23 (1): pp. 161–166. https://doi.org/10.1017/S0020818300025601.

Swissvotes / Année politique suisse. 2022. *Abstimmungen*. https://swissvotes.ch/votes (accessed 07 November 2022).

Schwok, René. 2009. *Schweiz – Europäische Union: Beitritt unmöglich?* Zurich: Rüegger Verlag.

Tallberg, Jonas. 2002. 'Delegation to Supranational Institutions: Why, How, and with What Consequences?'. *West European Politics* 25 (1): pp. 23–46. https://doi.org/10.1080/713601584.

Vatter, Adrian. 2020. *Das politische System der Schweiz*, 4th ed. Baden-Baden: Nomos.
Walter, Stefanie. 2021. 'What Swiss Voters Expect to Happen Next, After EU Talks Fail'. *Bruegel blog, 31 May*. https://www.bruegel.org/2021/05/what-swiss-voters-expect-to-happen-next-after-eu-talks-fail/ (accessed 07 November 2022).
Wasserfallen, Fabio. 2021. 'Weshalb war das Rahmenabkommen hochumstritten, wenn es doch von der Schweiz selbst initiiert wurde?'. In *Eine Aussenpolitik für die Schweiz im 21. Jahrhundert*, edited by Thomas Bernauer, Katja Gentinetta, and Joëlle Kuntz, pp. 102–107. Zurich: NZZ Libro.
Wasserfallen, Fabio. 2023. 'The Politics of Fiscal Integration in Eurozone Reforms and Next Generation EU'. In *Cambridge Handbook on European Monetary, Economic, and Financial Market Integration*, edited by Dariusz Adamski, Fabian Amtenbrink, and Jakob de Haan. Cambridge: Cambridge University Press.

CHAPTER 28

SECURITY POLICY AND POLITICS

ANDREAS WENGER

1 INTRODUCTION

As a result of the current economic globalization and geopolitical fragmentation of our environment, Switzerland's security policy has become the joint responsibility of a wide range of government bodies, all of which contribute to the prevention, defence, and management of a multitude of threats, dangers, risks, disasters, and emergencies.[1] Over the past three decades, Swiss security policy—with its three areas of defence, foreign security, and domestic security—has become significantly wider and deeper, both conceptually and in practice. By contrasting today's security policy orientation with that which existed during the Cold War, we can see how the threats once considered relevant by the federal government, the cantons, and the communes have changed, as have the strategic and operational responses to these threats by the state, the economy, and society.

During the Cold War, Swiss security policy was largely determined by a military threat situation that was clearly definable and considered to be permanent; Swiss security policy was therefore shaped in large part by a sense of continuity and by a few basic principles. Following on from historical experience, the Swiss security strategy was based at its core on the state maxims of armed neutrality and the principle of *dissuasion*, which was understood as the prevention of war through defence readiness. This strategy was defensive by nature and found its most lasting expression in Switzerland's autonomous national defence (Spillmann et al. 2001, 27–82). As an element of so-called 'high politics', Swiss security policy was dominated politically and administratively by the Swiss Federal Council and the then Federal Military Department (FMD).[2] In parliament and among the Swiss population, it was exceptional in that it was backed by a solid consensus across political parties.

Today's political answers to the two key issues of security policy—What is threatened and how? And who should protect Switzerland against threats and how?—are fundamentally different from those of the Cold War era. Over the past three decades, the types and geographical sites of the threats and risks that are relevant to Switzerland's security have expanded considerably. In the 1990s, the issues relevant to Swiss security focused on the civil wars in the Balkans. In the following decade, the conflicts in the Middle East and in South-West Asia, and the associated violent cross-border extremism and terrorism, became an additional concern. Since the 2010s, geopolitical tensions between the great powers have also increased: relations between China and the USA have deteriorated in a series of structural power shifts, while the strategic partnership between China and Russia has gradually deepened. Between Russia and Europe, on the other hand, there has been a persistent alienation, brought on by the military annexation of Crimea (2014) and the ongoing invasion of Ukraine (2022).

In today's environment of uncertainty and complexity caused by increased globalization and recent technological developments, the once-protective effect of geographical distances and state sovereignty have at least partially become questionable. In the past thirty years, as the threat situation changed, Switzerland redefined its concept of security along two dimensions. First, in the 1990s, in order to better understand and overcome ongoing crises and conflicts, the Federal Council *widened its concept of security* to allow for the increasing significance of non-military risk factors (Fanzun and Wenger 2000). Second, in the following decade, the federal government and the cantons *deepened the concept of threats* as a reaction to an increase in the number of hybrid, low-intensity threats perpetrated by state actors, semi-state actors, and non-state actors in Switzerland against its population, its infrastructure, and the exercise of the state's authority (Wenger et al. 2010).

The implementation of this widened and deepened security policy concept brought about two new challenges. On the one hand, new interfaces with other policy fields emerged, for example, with infrastructure, digitalization, health, migration, climate, and energy policy. This in turn resulted in complex questions about how the boundaries should be set between the responsibilities of various agents and levels of government. On the other hand, the boundaries became blurred between the exercise of everyday politics, in the form of regulations, and exceptional actions necessitated by emergency law. For security policy, also, soft approaches became more important and impacted regulations, norms, and industry standards. This could be observed, for example, in relation to cybersecurity and critical infrastructure protection.

This chapter provides an in-depth evaluation of the development of Swiss security policy since the end of the Cold War against this broader background. The *first three parts* of the chapter concentrate on the most important Swiss security policy papers, the associated legal foundations, and the responsibilities of the most important actors in the Swiss state, the economy, and society. Thereafter, the *subsequent part* of this chapter takes a deeper look at the current state of the implementation of the new policies in the three sub-fields of Swiss security. The *final part* of this chapter discusses the effects of the war in Ukraine on future developments in Swiss security policy.

2 THE DEVELOPMENT OF SWITZERLAND'S SECURITY POLICY AND ITS AGENTS

The policy papers that the Federal Council submits to parliament at irregular intervals are directional documents on Switzerland's security policy; they contain an evaluation of the security policy situation and of the strategic priorities of any given time period. These policy papers represent a compromise between the Federal Council's top-down directional approach and the administration's bottom-up desire to maintain existing practices. Over time, the strategic terminology in these policy papers became increasingly vague, as Switzerland's security policy concept widened and deepened. Looking back, we can identify three phases in which Swiss security policy developed.

2.1 Phase 1: policy paper 73—security through national defence

Until the late 1980s, Switzerland regarded its security policy as that part of its global policy whose role it was to integrate all means of the state into a general national defence system, which in turn was responsible for countering all dangers that emanated from an environment that was potentially prepared to use military force against the nation. The main aim of Switzerland's security strategy was to preserve the country's independence and to protect its national territory and its citizens. Switzerland's restrictive neutrality policy and its strict separation of politics from the economy meant that the country's security policy also remained largely detached from its foreign policy, both conceptually and administratively. Instead, Switzerland remained true to the paradigm of 'total national defence' (Däniker 1966).

The term 'security policy' was first introduced into the Swiss political landscape in 1973, in Switzerland's first security policy paper (Federal Council 1973). This paper reflected the Federal Council's response to the emerging *détente* between East and West, which in turn led to negotiations on the final Act of the Conference on Security and Cooperation in Europe (CSCE). The 1973 policy paper acknowledged the need to upgrade Switzerland's security policy to include a wider reaching, outwardly active strategic component. However, in practice, the country's foreign (security) policy was limited to heightening international acceptance of Switzerland's neutrality and its good offices (Breitenmoser 2002). However, regarding its defence and armed forces, Switzerland was to remain as autonomous as possible. Consequently, between 1966 and into the 1980s, Switzerland systematically pushed ahead with an upgrade of its armed forces in accordance with its doctrine of military national defence (Spillmann et al. 2001, 117–146; Däniker 1966; Gasteyger 1984).

2.2 Phase 2: the 1990–2000 policy papers—security through international cooperation

In its 1990 policy paper, the Federal Council initiated a change of course from an autonomous security policy to a cooperative security policy (Federal Council 1990). The 1990 security policy status report was, on the one hand, an expression of a strategic upheaval in Switzerland's surroundings, and on the other, a sign of built-up pressure for reform following the public initiative to abolish the armed forces and the so-called 'surveillance scandal' (in German, the *Fichenaffäre*)[3] of 1989. Conceptually, the 1990 policy paper broadened Switzerland's security policy goals to include a contribution to international stability (*Beitrag an die internationale Stabilität*), while the 1993 foreign policy paper broadened Switzerland's foreign policy goals to include the preservation and promotion of security and peace (Federal Council 1993). With these papers, the future course for a conceptual expansion and a differentiation of the tools of Swiss foreign security policy was set in the mid-1990s.

The 2000 policy paper enlarged the field of security policy more comprehensively beyond Switzerland's national defence policy. It laid the conceptual foundation for a more international outlook for the armed forces and for a move towards institutional co-determination by Swiss security policy (Federal Council 1999). Security policy was redefined as a cross-sectional task, and it was to deal with the prevention and management of violence that was of strategic significance. This new formulation clearly expressed Switzerland's wish to strengthen its security by actively engaging in peacebuilding and crisis management through active civilian and military contributions in and with various multilateral security institutions. At the same time, the federal government's security policy confined itself to supra-regional, national, and international potential acts of violence. This left the responsibility for domestic security largely with the individual cantons, rather than with the federal government (Fanzun and Wenger 2000).

The international context in which these security concepts were to be implemented was determined by the consolidation and expansion of an inclusive and liberal European security order (provided by the Organization for Security and Co-operation in Europe [OSCE], the North Atlantic Treaty Organization [NATO], and the European Union [EU]). Through its foreign security policy, Switzerland strengthened its involvement in the former CSCE, renamed OSCE in 1995 (Goetschel 1997). Thus, Switzerland substantially expanded its profile in civilian peacebuilding and in humanitarian arms control policy. When Switzerland joined the United Nations (UN) in 2002 with widespread domestic political support, it established a solid basis for its role as an active bridge builder. However, the change in course of its defence policy was more controversial. The Armed Forces 95 reform—a project in which funding and staffing of the Cold War armed forces were to be restructured—was unable to meet the requirements of Switzerland's new peacebuilding mission. Its successor, Armed Forces XXI, went a step further: military peacebuilding efforts were to become a defining feature of the structure of the armed forces, which were to be oriented towards Europe (Mäder 2001).

2.3 Phase 3: the 2010–2016 policy papers—security through national resilience

During the 2000s, there was a gradual increase of reservations in Swiss political circles about military peacebuilding and about the growing orientation of the armed forces toward a European defence policy framework. On the one hand, Switzerland's signing of the Bilateral Agreements I (1999) and II (2004) with the EU reduced the urgency of Switzerland's earlier strategic goal of joining the EU, and public support for such a move diminished considerably. More decisive from a security policy perspective were the agreements with the EU on police and asylum issues (Schengen and Dublin 2005), which greatly enhanced the focus of Switzerland's domestic security towards Europe (Möckli 2001). On the other hand, following the terrorist attacks of 11 September 2001 and the subsequent military interventions in Afghanistan and Iraq, disagreements within NATO and the EU increased, while the threat of terrorism and violent extremism was emphasized in Switzerland, as well.

As a result of these developments, domestic security increasingly became the focus of attention, including at the federal government level. In 2000, the Federal Office of Police (fedpol) was created. It was to act as the interface between Switzerland and its European partner organizations. Two years later, the Federal Council decided to fill the gaps in security policing, identified by the Federal Department of Justice and Police (FDJP) and the Conference of Cantonal Justice and Police Directors, by expanding the armed forces' domestic tasks (fedpol 2004). The 2010 security policy paper (Federal Council 2010) thus refocused the policy field on domestic security and re-oriented the armed forces away from peacebuilding and back to operations within Switzerland (Wenger et al. 2010).

The conceptually decisive innovations in the 2010 policy paper included the deepening of the concept of security to include everyday violence and the integration of cantonal and communal security efforts into Swiss security policy. Initially, there was controversy surrounding the extent to which the armed forces should be engaged in subsidiary operations for the cantons or, conversely, in classic defence tasks. The main conceptual contribution of the 2016 policy paper was the redefinition of the concept of defence (Wenger and Nünlist 2017). This paper defined the task of defence as the protection of socio-technical systems against a hybrid threat spectrum in which armed attacks could emanate from non-state groups operating within Switzerland (Federal Council 2016). Eventually, with the launch of the Armed Forces Development Programme (WEA), the battles over the future direction of the armed forces subsided in the late 2010s.

3 SECURITY POLICY OBJECTIVES AND LEGISLATION

According to Article 2 of the federal constitution of 18 April 1999 (SR 101), which came into force on 1 January 2000, the Swiss Confederation shall 'protect the liberty and rights of the people and safeguard the independence and security of the country'. It is also committed to a 'just and peaceful international order'.[4] Thus, the constitution's purpose article already refers to security policy (Federal Council 1999). Switzerland's security policy goals are defined in the 2016 security policy paper (Federal Council 2016) as:

- The preservation of Switzerland's ability to act, of its self-determination, and of its integrity;
- The safeguarding of its citizens and of their livelihood;
- The contribution to stability and peace beyond Switzerland's borders.

The revision of the federal constitution and the 2010/2016 security policy papers laid out the objectives of Swiss security policy clearly for the time being. However, the increase in the number of popular initiatives, referendums, government dispatches, and laws around the turn of the millennium shows that questions surrounding the best strategies and agents for achieving these objectives continued to be hotly debated.

Switzerland's system of government is marked by departmentalism and federalism, and as a result, the conceptual systems of domestic security and external security developed separately, to a large extent, as did those of the country's foreign policy and security policy. Many of the difficulties in the operative design of Switzerland's security system can basically be attributed to a lack of integration between three policy areas: while the frame of reference for Swiss foreign (security) policy has become increasingly globalized since 1991, and while the domestic security system has gradually become Europeanized, the frame of reference for Switzerland's defence has oscillated between a focus on Europe and national imperatives.

Regarding Switzerland's defence, the people voted twice against abolishing the armed forces and once against abolishing conscription. Over the years, the people approved a comprehensive reform project (Armed Forces XXI) and associated amendments to Swiss military law. There was also controversy surrounding armaments policy, cost–benefits aspects of the military, and the range of tasks that the armed forces should perform, in particular with regard to foreign deployments of Swiss troops and to the role of domestic subsidiary operations.

Regarding foreign (security) policy, a possible rapprochement between Switzerland and the EU was at the centre of the political debate for a long time. With the signing of Bilateral Agreements I and II, Switzerland, following popular decisions, opted for the bilateral path. The police and asylum agreements with the EU (Schengen and Dublin), which were approved by the electorate in June 2005, were also subject to debate. And on 3 March 2002, Swiss voters approved their country's accession to the UN.

In terms of Switzerland's domestic security, the Federal Department of Defence, Civil Protection, and Sport (DDPS) introduced a comprehensive reform of civilian operational elements with the Civil Protection XXI project (*Bevölkerungsschutz XXI*).[5] The focus of the project was the creation of a network of partner organizations, including police, the fire department, the public health system, civil protection, and technical services.

4 ACTORS AND THEIR RESPONSIBILITIES

As a cross-sectional task, Swiss security policy comprises a large number of actors from the state, society, and the private sector. These actors cooperate with each other on several levels, from communes to international organizations. Security policy is implemented through bundles of agents that affect many different policy areas, including foreign policy, the armed forces, civil protection (for which the cantons are responsible), economic policy, national economic supply, protection of the state and police (for which the cantons are responsible), the customs administration, the civil service, and the intelligence service. Overall, the image that emerges is that of a complex web of actors, responsibilities, and interdependencies.

4.1 Strategic leadership: the Swiss Federal Council and cantonal governments

The Swiss Federal Council plays a prominent role in Switzerland's security policy. In the various security policy papers, the Federal Council defines its objectives and orientation for the coming years and assigns mandates to the various agents. Regarding so-called strategic leadership, the Federal Council coordinates the country's contingency planning, is responsible for the government's crisis response, and, during a crisis, leads the federal government's and the cantons' crisis management. During the Cold War, strategic leadership at the federal level was geared primarily towards military crisis scenarios, in line with Switzerland's general defence concept (Carrel 2004). This changed after 1991: as the threat perception expanded, and as the policy field widened and deepened, the pressure increased to adapt the structures of strategic leadership. Later, these structures were reformed and realigned several times.

In Switzerland, the cantons are responsible for domestic security. The federal government intervenes only in a supportive capacity, i.e. on a subsidiary basis, if the cantons' resources are insufficient and if they request support from the federal level. However, in practice, the distinction between domestic and foreign security has become increasingly difficult to make, given the changing threat spectrum. Consequently, since the 2010s, the cantons have increasingly expressed an interest in having their concerns and efforts taken into account in the federal government's security policy. The Federal Council responded, as mentioned, by deepening its concept of security in its 2010/2016 policy papers. Nevertheless, overall, in the past twenty years, the federal government's role in the Europeanization of Switzerland's police, justice system, national borders, and asylum regulations has increased considerably.

4.2 The Swiss federal administration

The Federal Department of Defence, Civil Protection and Sport (DDPS), the Federal Department of Foreign Affairs (FDFA), the Federal Department of Justice and Police (FDJP), and the Federal Department of Finance (FDF) are the four bodies that deal most intensively with security-related issues. The Federal Military Department (FMD) was reformed from the ground up in various stages as part of the DDPS's administrative reform, and on 1 January 1998, the FMD was renamed the DDPS. The creation of the position of Chief of the Armed Forces as part of the Armed Forces XXI project entailed a separation of the political leadership level from the military leadership level. The coordination and leadership mandate of civil protection is now carried out by the Federal Office for Civil Protection (FOCP), while research and development in the armament sector were incorporated into the Federal Office for Defence Procurement (*armasuisse*).

As Switzerland's foreign security policy was upgraded, it became more important to look at how the DDPS and the FDFA would coordinate their work and ensure consistency in the decision-making process. Of particular importance is the coordination between the DDPS's security policy division (*Bereich Sicherheitspolitik*) and the International Security Division of the FDFA's Directorate of Political Affairs. There are other important interfaces to peacebuilding, namely, on the one hand, with the Peace and Human Rights Division of the FDFA's Directorate of Political Affairs and, on the other, with the Swiss Agency for Development and Cooperation.

As the federal government's security policy deepened and cantonal and communal security efforts were incorporated into Switzerland's security strategy (Federal Council 2010), the role of the FDJP and the FDF in security policy grew significantly. In the area of domestic security, the federal government upgraded the structure of its police services (Federal Criminal Police, Federal Security Service), which are incorporated in fedpol. Fedpol, as the core of Swiss national police work, is responsible for coordinating national and international police activities, and it operates various national information systems and competence centres. From a public security perspective, the State Secretariat for Migration also plays an important role at the interface between Switzerland and various European institutions (Schengen/Dublin).

The Federal Office for Customs and Border Security (FOCBS) in the FDF also deals with border issues. In the Border Guard Corps (BG), the FOCBS maintains an important security authority that has long been an integral part of the Swiss security network. The BG performs a wide range of security tasks at Swiss borders, in rail traffic, and at airports, and it is responsible for the FOCBS's cooperation between partner authorities at home and abroad. The FDF also plays an important role in cybersecurity by hosting both the Digital Transformation and ICT Steering Division and the Federal Office of Information Technology, Systems, and Telecommunication. The creation of the National Cyber Security Centre (NCSC) has further increased the FDF's importance in this area.

4.3 The Swiss parliament

The Swiss parliament's involvement in security policy occurs mainly through the Security Policy Committees of the National Council and the Council of States. These committees are involved in the drafting of legislative proposals and in some cases have a considerable influence on the formulation of these. Parliament is only able to acknowledge security policy papers; it cannot subject them to detailed consideration. However, its budget authority gives it considerable influence over the design of various security policy agents. Only a few years ago, for example, parliament's austerity programmes forced the DDPS to adjust its medium-term plans for the armed forces. In the meantime, the attitudes of the Federal Council and parliament about financing the armed forces have turned around. For several years, both councils have been calling for an increase in the armed forces' annual expenditure ceiling.

Overall, parliament's willingness to participate in security policy has increased significantly. The number of parliamentary procedural requests calling on the Federal Council to become active in security policy has risen markedly, for example, in the area of cybersecurity. For many years, parliament also called for more regular security policy reporting from the national government. The Federal Council only recently took up this request: in its 2021 security policy paper (Federal Council 2021), it commits to submitting a paper every four years.

4.4 The public

A quick look at the annual studies on public opinion on foreign, security, and defence policy shows that the Swiss people generally feel safer today than they have felt in the past thirty years. Their trust in their most important political institutions appears to be robust, as does their approval of the current orientation of the most important security policy agents (Tresch et al. 2020).

This has not always been the case: with the end of the Cold War, the general consensus on security policy issues disintegrated. At the same time, the population's participation in security policy increased, in particular, through such means as referendums and pre-parliamentary consultation procedures. Right-wing circles expressed their fundamental opposition to the principle of 'security through international cooperation' ('*Sicherheit durch internationale Kooperation*'), and the political centre and left-wing circles had trouble developing sustainable visions for a comprehensive security policy (Tresch et al. 2020). Only in recent years has a basic consensus on security policy re-emerged—most recently in view of the Armed Forces Development Programme (WEA).

4.5 The economy and society

Security policy has become considerably more pluralistic in recent years, partly because it is increasingly understood as a joint task of the state, the economy, and society. As far as the armed forces are concerned, national-political and socio-political considerations have always played a central role in their development due to conscription and the nature of Switzerland's conscript armed forces model. Nowadays, private and civil society actors are also making indispensable contributions to security policy in many other areas, such as cybersecurity, critical infrastructure protection, and civil peacebuilding and humanitarian arms control policy.

In order to ensure public security, private security service providers are taking on a rapidly growing role. At the end of 2019, a study that was conducted in the form of a status report on public and private security forces in Switzerland concluded that around 70 per cent of security staff worked in the public sector, and 30 per cent worked in the private sector.[6] There is also a growing market for private cybersecurity companies, without which the security of the omnipresent technical tools used by industry and private individuals could not be guaranteed.

5 THE STATUS OF POLICY IMPLEMENTATION

5.1 Upgrading and activating foreign security policy

Since the early 1990s, with regard to the farther-reaching elements of Swiss security policy, the Federal Council has pursued a much more active policy of co-determining the international environment (Fanzun and Lehman 2000). In so doing, Switzerland has significantly increased its involvement within a multilateral framework, both qualitatively and quantitatively. Of particular note are the two years of Swiss presidency of the OSCE in 1996 and 2014. In those years, Switzerland made a significant contribution to the OSCE's overcoming of its two greatest operational challenges to date, in Bosnia and Ukraine (Goetschel 1997). Switzerland's contributions to the Partnership for Peace in the 1990s and 2000s have also been internationally recognized (Breitenmoser et al. 1998). The same is true for Switzerland's contributions to the UN; these have gained in value and importance since Switzerland joined in 2002.

In substance, the upgrading of Switzerland's contributions to global peace and security focused on two areas. *First*, in the 1990s and 2000s, Switzerland made innovative contributions to the design and implementation of the international Anti-Personnel Mine Ban Convention in cooperation with various research institutions, the Geneva International Centre for Humanitarian Demining, and like-minded other states. With additional contributions in the monitoring of small and medium-sized arms, Switzerland has also been able to position Geneva as an international site for humanitarian, non-classical armaments control (Dahinden 2003; Gerber 2006).

Second, Switzerland has substantially built up its contributions to peacebuilding and peace talks. The FDFA has worked closely with multilateral partner organizations and like-minded states, and it has solidified its upgraded peace policy capacities through targeted partnerships with non-governmental organizations and research institutes. Today, with its long-term commitment and the gradual professionalization of its capacities, Switzerland is well placed to make a sustainable contribution to the mitigation and resolution of violent conflicts and to the construction of functioning states and resilient societies (Wenger 2011; Trachsler 2002, 2003, 2004).

5.2 Solidification of the Armed Forces Development Programme (WEA)

Compared to the reforms in foreign security policy, the restructuring of the armed forces at the end of the Cold War was much more sluggish. The Armed Forces 95 reform was a bottom-up reform project that was determined mainly by financial, demographic, and domestic political factors. Armed Forces XXI, on the other hand, was a top-down reform project, controversial within the armed forces and in politics, not least because of its international orientation and because it sought to strengthen the professional elements of the armed forces (Eberhard and Stahel 2000). Not until the step-by-step development of the WEA between 2014 and 2018, whose implementation will continue until the end of 2022, was a new basic consensus on military policy issues reached in politics and in the armed forces.

The WEA helped to clarify military doctrine and included changes to the armed forces in relation to national politics, society, and finance. In 2013, the clear rejection of the federal popular initiative to abolish conscription ended a period of about ten years during which regular opinion polls had shown how voters' opinions had fluctuated between retaining conscription and establishing a professional army (Tresch et al. 2020). For the societal context, the main point was to make armed forces' service and training more consistent with changes that had occurred in the economy and in education. Now, in the past ten years, there has been some evidence of a trend reversal in the people's attitude toward defence expenditure (Tresch et al. 2020). Consequently, in the debate surrounding the WEA, the National Council and the Council of States have demanded that the Federal Council raise the expenditure ceiling of the armed forces. With the expansion of the concept of defence as discussed above, the central task of the armed forces remains to this day the defence of Switzerland against an armed attack.

5.3 Cybersecurity: from IT security to national security

No issue is better suited than the growing threats in cyberspace to reveal the increasing complexity of the current security policy challenges as these intersect between 'low and high politics', defence, foreign security policy, and domestic security policy, as well as between the state, the economy, and society. In the 1990s, cybersecurity was discussed primarily by technical experts who specialized in IT security issues. However, more recently, cybersecurity has become a core issue in security policy and politics. The main reason why cybersecurity is now seen as one of the most acute security policy challenges is the increasing politicization and militarization of cyber conflicts. With increasing geopolitical tensions, the number of strategically motivated activities by states in cyberspace—including espionage, sabotage, cyber defence, and cyber attacks as part of military operations—have also increased significantly (Wenger and Dunn Cavelty 2020).

For Switzerland, the integration of cybersecurity into its national security efforts took place in three stages. In the first stage, the federal government focused on the one hand on establishing and expanding the Federal IT Steering Unit (FITSU) within the FDF; FITSU is responsible for designing guidelines and strategic programmes on information and communication technologies. On the other hand, the federal government created the Reporting and Analysis Centre for Information Assurance and the Special Task Force for Information Assurance, whose primary task is to support the operators of critical infrastructures.

In a second step, the Federal Council adopted the first National strategy for the protection of Switzerland against cyber risks (NCS).[7] This was preceded by protracted discussions about the increased centralization of responsibilities at the federal level and questions surrounding which department should take the overall lead on cybersecurity. However, the 2012 NCS eventually chose a decentralized approach based on risk and resilience; this approach relied heavily on the principle of self-reliance and defined the protection of Switzerland against cyber risks as a joint task of the state, the economy, and society.

A third step in this development was driven by a series of cyber attacks on the federal administration (Ruag 2014 and Labor Spiez 2018).[8] At this time, parliament, the economy, and society were increasingly calling for more centralization and clearer federal structures in relation to cybersecurity. As a result, the DDPS intensified its internal action plan for strengthening cyber defence (*Aktionsplan zur Stärkung der Cyber-Defense*), which included all of the department's units and offices (the DDPS General Secretariat, the Federal Intelligence Service, the armed forces, armasuisse, and the FOCP). Parallel to this, work intensified on NCS Strategy 2018, which was compiled and developed into an implementation plan in collaboration with the economy, the cantons, and universities.[9]

To strengthen its leadership role in the area of cyber risks, the Federal Council created a cyber committee consisting of the heads of the FDF, the DDPS, and the FDJP. Further, it decided to create the National Cyber Security Center (NCSC) within the FDF. Under the leadership of a federal cyber security delegate, the NCSC was to play a key role in the implementation of NCS 2018. The NCSC was placed directly within the General Secretariat of the FDF. These developments led to significant progress. However, the coordination between these new cyber structures and the general structures of Switzerland's strategic leadership will continue to be demanding. The negotiation processes between the state, the economy, and society in implementing NCS 2018 also remain a challenge.

6 Perspectives and Remaining Questions

In the 2010s, the implementation of Swiss security policy progressed considerably. At the same time, a look back at developments since 1991 reminds us of how fundamentally the security policy environment has changed in only three decades. Looking forward, we can already see future dynamic changes in the internal and external environment of Swiss security policy. The national setting will continue to develop on many levels, in light of digitalization and climate change, and this cannot remain without repercussions for a security policy that is executed as a joint task of the state, the economy, and society. The global and regional environment, in turn, is marked by volatile shifts of power in the economy, politics, institutions, and the military. In particular, from a European perspective, the ongoing war in Ukraine in particular is a wake-up call for defence policy. In Switzerland, as elsewhere, fundamental security policy questions are emerging.

6.1 Consistency and the delimitation of security policy

The conceptual consistency of Swiss security policy and the demarcation of security policy from other policy areas are ongoing challenges to a policy field in which the three areas—defence, foreign security, and domestic security—have developed largely independently. In the foreseeable future, threats, dangers, and risks are likely to continue to arise primarily where defence, foreign security, and domestic security intersect, so in order to ensure the success of Swiss security policy, these three areas need to be better integrated with due regard to their interdependencies. A security policy that is comprehensive and interconnected will be successful if these three areas can be combined into a single overall strategy.

At the same time, it is worth considering the horizontal and vertical delimitation of the policy field more intensely, not least in light of state policy and constitutional law. The more diffuse the strategic terminology, and the less clear the boundaries of security policy become, the greater the chance that issues which are driven by economic and political interests might become 'securitized'. Regarding horizontal expansion,

Swiss security policy has done well with its limited expansion, leaving the primary responsibility for issues such as migration and climate change to other policy areas, while remaining capable of supporting other areas through prevention and in times of emergencies and short-term overloads.

With regard to vertical expansion, a certain lack of clarity has crept in. In essence, cantonal and communal security efforts should be considered an integral part of national security policy when they are directly connected to a potential for strategic violence and/or when the cantons and communes need to call upon the federal government to coordinate their efforts with international security organizations. The 2021 policy paper on Switzerland's security policy addresses this lack of clarity in that it places particular emphasis on the federal government's national duty to ensure that the state as a whole is capable of action (Federal Council 2021).

6.2 Strategic leadership and crisis organization

The downside of a system of government like Switzerland's, which is geared toward consensus, compromise, and a high degree of legitimacy, remains its unwieldiness, which hampers fast, coordinated, and strong reactions to unexpected developments. The most recent and loosely coordinated reforms of Switzerland's crisis response are not the end of the process of reform within the country's strategic leadership. We can already foresee that Switzerland's crisis response will have to be reviewed and adapted once more in years to come.

Where various policy fields intersect with cantonal responsibilities, there is still a lack of clarity about how national security cooperation and civil defence-related incidents should be integrated into the federal government's overall crisis response. This became abundantly clear in the management of the Covid pandemic. The division of responsibilities between the federal government and the cantons, from the normal to the exceptional to the crisis situation, needs to be more clearly defined and simplified. In particular, the role of the Federal Civil Protection Crisis Management Board and its integration into the political-strategic decision-making level must be improved (Wenger et al. 2020).

At the federal level, the question arises as to when and how situation analyses currently undertaken by the Security Core Group will be integrated with the Federal Council's ad hoc crisis unit, and how the latter will cooperate with departmental crisis units in the event of a crisis. Hybrid threats do not primarily affect the armed forces, as argued in the 2016 policy paper (Federal Council 2016). In situations involving state and semi-state disinformation and propaganda, Switzerland must re-examine whether its civil command and control equipment and processes are able to cope with the changed parameters. Switzerland's hesitant and insufficiently coordinated response to the war in Ukraine also underscores how Switzerland's decentralized political system struggles to think in terms of scenarios, to develop an overall strategy, and to deal with conflicting goals.

6.3 The return of a defence policy in Switzerland's security strategy

The war in Ukraine represents a turning point for Switzerland, as it does for other countries. Switzerland must once again adapt to a confrontational European security order. As in all European states, since the Russian invasion began in February 2022, the political will to increase the defence budget significantly by 2030 has gained considerable traction. Essentially, this represents the return of a defence policy for Switzerland's security strategy. Precisely because more money is likely to be available to the armed forces, policymakers need to define the long-term direction of the entire military system more clearly. Finances are driving the current debate on the armed forces too strongly; it focuses too heavily on the short term; and it concentrates too much on individual weapons systems. As of 2024, for each legislative period, parliament is to receive a capability dispatch from the Federal Council that describes the required military capabilities and capital expenditures for the subsequent twelve years.

Policymakers will need to develop a new understanding of what defence might mean in the context of Switzerland's foreseeable threat situation. Long-term planning of armed forces' capabilities should not be geared retrospectively towards a 'classic' defence model that starts at national borders, but forward-looking to an expanded understanding of defence. The state's ability to act might be challenged by terrorist groups operating in the country. Alternatively, states can employ new ways to cross the threshold into potentially violent armed attacks: first, across wider geographic spaces, with long-range weapons, and with covert operations; second, in new operational spaces such as cyberspace and outer space; and third, with hybrid means of coercion in the form of disinformation and political and economic blackmail.

In most conceivable threat scenarios, Switzerland is unlikely to be the sole target of an adversary, and other civil means of coercion are likely to be applied in addition to military means. There are two additional issues regarding the role of the armed forces in a forward-looking security strategy. First, in an environment characterized by rapid technological development and limited finances, the importance of closer collaboration between the parties involved in the country's defence is likely to increase. In future, Switzerland should make better use of the growing scope for pragmatic defence cooperation with NATO and the EU. Second, the armed forces should not be understood as merely a tool that can fight, protect, and help in any given situation. Thanks to their deterrent effect, the armed forces are also a resource that can be utilized in international politics.

Difficult issues will arise in the armed forces, not only regarding the provision of material resources, but also regarding the provision of staff. Switzerland faces complex challenges with regard to its professional military, concerning the members and cadres of its conscript armed forces, and a likely shortage of specialists and civilian staff. To mitigate this, some measures can be taken directly by its Defence Group and armed forces. In other areas, however, politicians face challenges, as is already the case today regarding the considerable transfer from the armed forces to civil service. In the midterm, the (re-)introduction of universal conscription is once more likely to be discussed more intensely in politics and society.

6.4 Adapted neutrality as one foreign security policy tool among many

The war in Ukraine has triggered an intense debate on Switzerland's understanding of its identity in terms of its neutrality policy. Switzerland will remain true to its neutrality because neutrality is an integral part of the country's political identity and because it is not a member of NATO or the EU. Yet the law of neutrality places certain limitations on military cooperation, namely: there can be no joining of alliances, no binding military commitments in peacetime, and no direct support for countries at war. Switzerland has always been flexible in adapting its neutrality to changing environments. But these days, in view of the increasing rivalry between the great powers, Switzerland's neutrality policy guidelines are being questioned with renewed urgency. Ultimately, politicians will need to weigh up the country's best interests when deciding how to deal with sanctions, overflights, and arms exports in specific situations.

Switzerland's law of neutrality dates back to an era when wars of aggression had not yet been prohibited. Initially, it regulated limited combat operations conducted with conventional weapons, and it largely excluded economic and ideological warfare. These days, the UN Charter outlaws war as a means of international conflict resolution. However, conflicts of interest between the great powers are increasingly being fought not only by military means but also in novel ways, such as on the high seas, in outer space, in cyberspace, and with new agents, such as through the political manipulation of asymmetric market power, technological dependence, and institutional dominance. Accordingly, neutrality has become only one means of many through which Switzerland can safeguard its foreign and security policy interests.

In the context of a weakened multilateralism, it is *firstly* of vital importance that Switzerland is seen as consistent within its multi-, mini-, and bilateral environment, in particular by the great powers. Switzerland's candidacy for a non-permanent seat on the UN Security Council (2023–2024) offers the country an opportunity to do this and will place great demands on the Federal Council and the administration, especially with regard to security policy issues. *Second*, Switzerland could act as a bridge builder between peace policy and foreign affairs technology policy (*Technologieaussenpolitik*) (Fischer and Wenger 2019). In the current geopolitical environment, it seems unlikely that the major powers will be willing to make serious progress on the regulation through arms control policy of current and future dual-use technologies. Softer approaches and governance processes that concentrate on the design phase of new technologies and that take effect through scientific diplomacy channels can counter the ongoing politicization of artificial intelligence, 5G networks, and the chip industry where these intersect with 'low and high politics'.

Third, the unpredictability and volatility of the threat environment will lead to more and more frequent questions about which contributions Switzerland can make to support an internationally coordinated response to global supply disruptions, disasters, and emergencies. Technical expertise is located in various Swiss departments, depending on the type of risk, for example, in health, energy, migration, large-scale technology, and natural disasters, and each department maintains its own relationships with its international counterparts. However, the more that nationalism dominates during acute crises, the more important is the support of diplomacy and local embassies in order to guarantee Switzerland's participation in international ad hoc crisis mechanisms and political processes.

6.5 Domestic security as a shared, cross-border responsibility of the federal government and the cantons

In the foreseeable future, the central national security issues will continue to be relevant to both domestic and foreign policy. The cantons are making important contributions to overcoming violent cross-border events in the European environment. At the same time, the federal government is acting as a central coordinator of police security actions in connection with international actors and the private security sector. Both levels of government have cross-border responsibilities that are becoming more and more interwoven in practice. Managing cross-border mobility at domestic borders, national borders, and external borders to Europe will remain a central challenge of modern Swiss security policy. Accordingly, the question arises of how Switzerland should deal with the divergence between state policy and constitutional principles, on the one hand, and the pragmatic adaptation of practical security operations, on the other (Bieri and Wenger 2018).

Notes

1. My thanks go to Oliver Roos for his careful review of this manuscript.
2. Since 1998, the Federal Department of Defence, Civil Protection, and Sport.
3. In the so-called surveillance scandal, the legal mandate on the collection of data of suspects during the Cold War was partially exceeded by the Swiss Federal Police and by the Office of the Attorney General of Switzerland. In 1990, the appointed Parliamentary Investigation Commission (PUK FMD) also discovered the secret P-26 army and the secret P-27 intelligence service during its investigations in connection with the surveillance scandal. In November 1990, the PUK FMD presented its detailed report on these incidents. The surveillance scandal led to a re-organization of the Office of the Attorney General of Switzerland and of the Swiss Federal Police in the 1990s.
4. https://www.fedlex.admin.ch/eli/cc/1999/404/en (accessed 09 September 2022).
5. https://fedlex.data.admin.ch/eli/cc/2003/620 (accessed 20 June 2023).
6. https://www.admin.ch/gov/de/start/dokumentation/medienmitteilungen.msg-id-77492.html (accessed 13 May 2022).

7. National strategy for the protection of Switzerland against cyber risks (NCS), 2012–2017. https://www.isb.admin.ch/isb/de/home/themen/cyber_risiken_ncs/ncs_strategie-2012.html (accessed 27 August 2020).
8. Ruag: https://www.govcert.ch/downloads/whitepapers/Report_Ruag-Espionage-Case.pdf (accessed 20 June 2023). Labor Spiez: https://www.newsd.admin.ch/newsd/message/attachments/56712.pdf (accessed 20 June 2023).
9. National strategy for the protection of Switzerland against cyber risks (NCS), 2018–2022. https://www.isb.admin.ch/isb/de/home/themen/cyber_risiken_ncs/ncs_strategie.html (accessed 27 August 2020).

References

Bieri, Matthias, and Andreas Wenger. 2018. 'Subsidiarität und die Schweizer Sicherheitspolitik'. In *CSS Analysen zur Sicherheitspolitik* 227, edited by Christian Nünlist, pp. 1–4. Zurich: ETH Zurich.

Breitenmoser, Christoph. 2002. 'Strategie ohne Aussenpolitik: Zur Entwicklung der schweizerischen Sicherheitspolitik im Kalten Krieg'. In *Studien zu Zeitgeschichte und Sicherheitspolitik* 10, edited by Kurt R Spillmann, and Andreas Wenger, pp. 1–268. Bern: Peter Lang.

Breitenmoser, Christoph, Jon Fanzun, Patrick Lehmann, Kurt R. Spillmann, and Andreas Wenger. 1998. *Bulletin 1997/98 zur schweizerischen Sicherheitspolitik*, edited by Kurt R. Spillmann. Zürich: ETH Zürich. https://css.ethz.ch/content/dam/ethz/special-interest/gess/cis/center-for-securities-studies/pdfs/Bulletin_1997_98.pdf.

Dahinden, Martin. 2003. 'Die Schweiz und die Ächtung der Personenminen'. In *Bulletin zur schweizerischen Sicherheitspolitik*, edited by Andreas Wenger, pp. 105–127. Zürich: ETH Zürich. https://css.ethz.ch/publikationen/bulletin-zur-schweizerischen-sicherheitspolitik/details.html?id=/d/i/e/s/die_schweiz_und_die_chtung_der_personenm.

Carrel, Laurent F. 2004. *Leadership in Krisen: Ein Handbuch für die Praxis*. Zurich: Neue Zürcher Zeitung.

Däniker, Gustav. 1966. *Strategie des Kleinstaats: Politisch-militärische Möglichkeiten schweizerischer Selbstbehauptung im Atomzeitalter*. Frauenfeld: Huber.

Eberhard, Hans, and Albert A. Stahel (eds). 2000. *Schweizerische Militärpolitik der Zukunft: Sicherheitsgewinn durch stärkeres internationales Engagement*. Zurich: Verlag Neue Zürcher Zeitung.

Fanzun, Jon A., and Patrick Lehmann. 2000. 'Die Schweiz und die Welt: Aussen- und sicherheitspolitische Beiträge der Schweiz zu Frieden, Sicherheit und Stabilität, 1945–2000'. In *Zürcher Beiträge zur Sicherheitspolitik und Konfliktforschung*, 57, edited by Kurt R. Spillmann, and Andreas Wenger, pp. 1–362. Zurich: ETH Zurich.

Fanzun, Jon A., and Andreas Wenger. 2000. 'Schweizer Sicherheitspolitik im Umbruch: Der Bericht 2000 vor dem Hintergrund des Kosovo-Konflikts'. In *Bulletin zur schweizerischen Sicherheitspolitik*, edited by Kurt R. Spillmann, and Andreas Wenger, pp. 9–43. Zürich: ETH Zürich. https://css.ethz.ch/content/dam/ethz/special-interest/gess/cis/center-for-securities-studies/pdfs/Bulletin_2000-Sicherheitspolitik_im_Umbruch.pdf.

Federal Council. 1973. 'Bericht des Bundesrates an die Bundesversammlung über die Sicherheitspolitik der Schweiz: Konzeption der Gesamtverteidigung (27 June 1973)'. *BBL 1973* II (34): pp. 112–153.

Federal Council. 1990. 'Schweizerische Sicherheitspolitik im Wandel: Bericht 90 des Bundesrates an die Bundesversammlung über die Sicherheitspolitik der Schweiz (1 October 1990)'. *BBL 1990* III (46): pp. 847–904.

Federal Council. 1993. 'Bericht über die Aussenpolitik der Schweiz in den 90er Jahren. (29 November 1993)'. *BBL 1994* I (3): pp. 153–242.

Federal Council. 1999. 'Sicherheit durch Kooperation: Bericht des Bundesrates an die Bundesversammlung über die Sicherheitspolitik der Schweiz (SIPOL B 2000) (7 June 1999)'. *BBL 1999* VII (38): pp. 7657–7734.

Federal Council. 2010. 'Bericht des Bundesrates an die Bundesversammlung über die Sicherheitspolitik der Schweiz (SIPOL B 2010) (23 June 2010)'. *BBL 2010* 30: pp. 5133–5222.

Federal Council. 2016. 'Die Sicherheitspolitik der Schweiz (SIPOL B 2016) (24 August 2016)'. *BBl 2016* 61: pp. 7763–7888.

Federal Council. 2021. 'Die Sicherheitspolitik der Schweiz (SIPOL B 2021) (24 November 2021)'. *BBl 2021*. 70, 2895.

Fedpol. 2004. *Sicherheitssystem der Schweiz mit Schengen/Dublin. Vertiefung der Planungsvarianten Kombi und Kantone aus USIS IV*. Bern: Bundesamt für Polizei.

Fischer, Sophie-Charlotte, and Andreas Wenger. 2019. 'Ein neutraler Hub für KI-Forschung'. *CSS Policy Perspectives 7* (2): pp. 1–4. Zurich, ETH Zurich.

Gasteyger, Curt (ed.). 1984. *Die Herausforderung der Zukunft: Zur Sicherheitspolitik der Schweiz*. Basel: BDV Basilius.

Gerber, Marcel. 2006. *Schweizer Aussenpolitik und Internationale Rüstungskontrolle*. Bern: Peter Lang.

Goetschel, Laurent (ed.). 1997. *Vom Statisten zum Hauptdarsteller: Die Schweiz und ihre OSZE-Präsidentschaft*. Bern: Paul Haupt.

Mäder, Markus. 2001. Euro-atlanitischer Streitkräftewandel nach dem Kalten Krieg—wo steht die Schweizer Armee? In *Bulletin zur schweizerischen Sicherheitspolitik*, edited by Kurt R. Spillmann, and Andreas Wenger, pp. 41–68. Zürich: ETH Zürich. https://css.ethz.ch/publikationen/bulletin-zur-schweizerischen-sicherheitspolitik/details.html?id=/e/u/r/o/euroatlantischer_streitkrftewandel_nach_.

Möckli, Daniel. 2001. 'Schengen und Dublin'. In *Bulletin zur schweizerischen Sicherheitspolitik*, edited by Kurt R. Spillmann, and Andreas Wenger, pp. 125–146. Zürich: ETH Zürich. https://css.ethz.ch/publikationen/bulletin-zur-schweizerischen-sicherheitspolitik/details.html?id=/s/c/h/e/schengen_und_dublin.

Spillmann, Kurt R., Andreas Wenger, Christoph Breitenmoser, and Marcel Gerber (eds). 2001. *Schweizer Sicherheitspolitik seit 1945: Zwischen Autonomie und Kooperation*. Zurich: Neue Zürcher Zeitung.

Trachsler, Daniel. 2002. 'Zivile Friedensförderung'. In *Bulletin zur schweizerischen Sicherheitspolitik*, edited by Kurt R. Spillmann, and Andreas Wenger, pp. 63–96. Zürich: ETH Zürich. https://css.ethz.ch/publikationen/bulletin-zur-schweizerischen-sicherheitspolitik/details.html?id=/z/i/v/i/zivile_friedensfrderung.

Trachsler, Daniel. 2003. 'Menschliche Sicherheit'. In *Bulletin zur schweizerischen Sicherheitspolitik*, edited by Andreas Wenger, pp. 69–103. Zürich: ETH Zürich. https://css.ethz.ch/publikationen/bulletin-zur-schweizerischen-sicherheitspolitik/details.html?id=/m/e/n/s/menschliche_sicherheit.

Trachsler, Daniel. 2004. 'Gute Dienste—Mythen, Fakten, Perspektiven'. In *Bulletin zur schweizerischen Sicherheitspolitik*, edited by Andreas Wenger, pp. 33–64. Zürich: ETH

Zürich. https://css.ethz.ch/publikationen/bulletin-zur-schweizerischen-sicherheitspolitik/details.html?id=/g/u/t/e/gute_dienste__mythen_fakten_perspektiven.

Tresch, Tibor Szvircsev, Andreas Wenger, Stefano de Rosa, Thomas Ferst, and Jacques Robert. 2020. *Sicherheit 2020*, edited by Tibor Szvircsev Tresch, and Andreas Wenger. Zürich: ETH Zürich. https://css.ethz.ch/publikationen/studie-sicherheit/details.html?id=/s/i/c/h/sicherheit_2020.

Wenger, Andreas (ed.). 2011. *Zivile Friedensförderung der Schweiz: Bestandsaufnahme und Entwicklungspotential (Zürcher Beiträge zur Sicherheitspolitik 83)*. Zurich: ETH Zurich.

Wenger, Andreas, and Myriam Dunn Cavelty. 2020. 'Cyber Security Meets Security Politics: Complex Technology, Fragmented Politics, and Networked Science'. *Contemporary Security Policy* 41 (1): pp. 5–32.

Wenger, Andreas, Andrin Hauri, Benjamin Scharte, Julian Kamasa, Jan Thiel, Michael Haas, Kevin Kohler, Oliver Thränert, Annabelle Vuille, and Benno Zogg. 2020. *Bulletin zur schweizerischen Sicherheitspolitik*, edited by Oliver Thränert, and Benno Zogg. Zürich: ETH Zürich. https://css.ethz.ch/publikationen/bulletin-zur-schweizerischen-sicherheitspolitik/details.html?id=/b/u/l/l/_bulletin_2020_on_swiss_security_policyb.

Wenger, Andreas, Victor Mauer, and Daniel Möckli. 2010. 'Sicherheitspolitischer Bericht 2010'. In *Bulletin zur schweizerischen Sicherheitspolitik*, edited by Andreas Wenger, Victor Mauer, and Daniel Trachsler, pp. 9–26. Zürich: ETH Zürich. https://css.ethz.ch/publikationen/bulletin-zur-schweizerischen-sicherheitspolitik/details.html?id=/s/i/c/h/sicherheitspolitischer_bericht_2010.

Wenger, Andreas, and Christian Nünlist. 2017. 'SIPOL-B 16: Ein Bedrohungsbericht, keine neue Strategiekonzeption'. *Military Power Review* 1: pp. 6–19.

CHAPTER 29

ECONOMIC POLICY

PATRICK EMMENEGGER

1 Introduction

For the most part, Swiss economic policy is a success story.[1] While Switzerland has the third-highest gross domestic product (GDP) per capita among OECD member states (Organisation for Economic Co-operation and Development) (OECD 2019, 14), it ranks first in the 2021 World Competitiveness Ranking (IMD 2021). These positions reflect the highly competitive nature of the Swiss economy, which has also demonstrated its resilience in the face of the COVID-19 pandemic, already reaching its pre-pandemic GDP in the second quarter of 2021 (OECD 2022a, 15). Should we therefore assume that all is well in the Alpine paradise? And what is the secret behind this success?

Switzerland is not easy to locate in the standard typologies of economic policy models. Moreover, it features some rather unusual characteristics. Mach and Trampusch (2011, 11) emphasize three particularities compared to other Western market economies: the limited room for manoeuvre of the central state,[2] the important role of self-regulation by private actors, and the political dominance of the bourgeois bloc (which is close to the powerful employers' associations). However, the Swiss system described above should by no means be confused with an Anglo-style liberal market economy (Hall and Soskice 2001), although the liberal advantages of its economic model are often invoked in political speeches in Switzerland. On the contrary, Switzerland is characterized by a combination of liberal and interventionist measures that evolved over time. The liberal labour market (Emmenegger 2011), for example, contrasts with a protectionist, closed-off agriculture sector and high levels of product market regulation (OECD 2022a, 36–39). This coexistence of liberal and interventionist policies led Erich Gruner (1964, 63, own translation) to succinctly describe the Swiss economic policy as a 'strange mixture between state socialism and association interventionism along with the occasional homesickness for liberalism'. Similarly, Milton Friedman (1972, 41) criticized the country for its 'extraordinary collection of governmental interventions into imports, exports, cartelized arrangements' and, therefore, considered Switzerland to be far from 'a capitalistic, liberal state'.

Nevertheless, the Swiss model proved successful for most of the twentieth century. Only since the late twentieth century has the model shown clear signs of erosion (Armingeon and Emmenegger 2007), as reflected in persistently low economic growth rates. While GDP continues to increase due to population growth, per capita income and productivity growth have been below average since the 1990s (OECD 2022a, 18). The labour market shows a similarly mixed picture. While the employment rate and the volume of work—starting from an already high level—have continued to increase in recent decades (Siegenthaler 2017), Switzerland now has an unemployment rate that is quite comparable with its neighbours, Austria and Germany (OECD 2019, 17). The country is thus undoubtedly in a good position in terms of economic policy, but it has partially lost its special status. A series of highly symbolic events that have taken place since the 1990s (e.g. Swissair grounding, UBS bailout, abandonment of banking secrecy, collapse of Credit Suisse) have also contributed to bringing Switzerland's economy back to the hard ground of economic realities. Lately, clouds have been gathering over the Alpine paradise.

In response to these economic difficulties, a flurry of reform activity started in the 1990s, which aimed at putting Switzerland back on the path to prosperity (Mach 2006). These reforms, which were implemented in a comparatively conflictual manner (at least for Swiss standards), addressed areas such as antitrust law, technical barriers to trade, public procurement, or agricultural policy. Although these reforms may indeed have triggered relevant growth and modernization impulses, they have ultimately been the exception rather than the rule in Switzerland's 'negotiation democracy' (Lehmbruch 2003) and owed much to the temporary combination of several parallel processes (economic crisis, European integration process, end of the Cold War). By the mid-2000s, having lost much of its momentum, this liberalizing wave suffered heavy defeats at the ballot box. Instead, Switzerland returned to its reliance on inclusive negotiation processes and reforms, which combine liberalizing and compensatory elements (Fill 2019).

Despite the intermezzo of the 1990s, Switzerland has overall remained true to its economic policy approach, which Armingeon (2017, 696) described as 'pragmatic muddling through'. This approach, which is relatively free of ideology and lacks any regulatory consistency, is an emergent trait of its negotiation democracy, which grants all major economic policy interest groups a say in shaping economic policy. As a result, usually being the outcome of protracted negotiations, economic and fiscal policy reforms often have the character of broad compromises (Gruner 1964, 67). Nevertheless, although Switzerland has generally been successful with this approach, it is not without weaknesses. Politically well-connected groups with strong mobilization power are often able to protect their interests, which results in high consumer prices and protectionist economic policies. In addition, Swiss economic policy has proven to be less proactive because of the complex decision-making processes. Necessary reforms are often initiated only in response to emerging or erupting crises and this sometimes with painful consequences, as observed with the conflict over banking secrecy (Emmenegger 2017).

Economic policy is subject to constant change. Although this change is mostly incremental in nature in Switzerland, a historical perspective shows that its economic policy has indeed evolved significantly over time, as the next section shows. Subsequently, the decision-making processes and lines of conflict that shaped these developments are discussed. The last two sections evaluate Switzerland's economic policy performance in recent years and identify the main challenges facing economic policy. These sections show that Switzerland is well equipped to meet the challenges of the knowledge economy despite having shed many of its distinctive features in recent decades.

2 Development and Characteristics

By the end of the nineteenth century, Switzerland was one of the most industrialized countries in the world (Müller and Woitek 2012), which was also reflected in growing export activity and an important position in international merchant trade. This foreign trade orientation was made possible by domestic policy structures that were intended to maintain competitiveness. In particular, the emerging class conflict of the time had to be pacified. Switzerland succeeded exceptionally well in this thanks to the development of a neo-corporatist interest intermediation system (Katzenstein 1985). Most notably, the 1937 'peace agreement' in the metal and machine industries contributed to the spread of collective labour agreements and prohibited industrial action on contractually regulated issues (Trampusch 2008, 65–66). Moreover, the 'economic articles' incorporated into the constitution in 1947 placed the government under an obligation to consult the most important interest groups on all legislative issues as part of a consultation procedure (Eichenberger and Mach 2011, 65).

However, this Swiss-style neo-corporatism was unusual in two respects. On the one hand, this economic policy compromise pitted strong employers' associations against weak trade unions and their respective political allies, which led Katzenstein (1985) to assign Switzerland to the type of 'liberal corporatism'. The political strength of the employers was the result of their comparatively early organizational development relative to the expansion of the central state and the establishment of political parties at the federal level, as well as a close-knitted network of the local economic elites, which grew even more cohesive in the first half of the twentieth century (Emmenegger 2009, 202–209; Eichenberger and Mach 2011, 63–66). This series of developments also contributed to the fact that Switzerland, in international comparison, strongly relied on the self-regulation of private actors and on business associations as vehicles of public policy, and in some cases even actively promoted them as the functional equivalent of an efficient state administration (Hotz 1979; Farago 1987).

On the other hand, Swiss corporatism was never characterized by strongly centralized and coordinated wage negotiations and Keynesian-inspired macroeconomic concertation (Armingeon 2011). This lack of centralization was due in part to the trade unions' organizational weakness, which found it difficult to form effective organizations in the context of Switzerland's decentralized pattern of industrialization, as well as the ideological fragmentation of the labour movement into a social democratic and a Christian democratic camp (Emmenegger 2010, 193–195). In parallel, the Social Democrats remained a junior partner in the bourgeois-dominated government. These unusual features of Swiss corporatism also explain why researchers have often struggled with the Swiss case (Kenworthy 2003).

At the centre of the compromise between capital and labour was the exchange between social peace and a lean state, on the one hand, and full employment and high wages with generous company social benefits on the other. At the same time, however, Swiss economic policy was also shaped by a second compromise, which required its competitive export-oriented economy to be balanced with its non-competitive domestic market-oriented economy (Bonoli and Mach 2000, 132). This second compromise, which originated in the late nineteenth century in the context of political conflicts about trade policies and tariffs, enabled the formation of a united bourgeois bloc against the emerging labour movement (Gruner 1956). It was primarily supported by the large business associations, the Swiss Commerce and Industry Association (founded in 1870), the Swiss Trade Association (founded in 1879), and the Swiss Farmers' Association (founded in 1897).

Various public policies of the centre-right government supported these two compromises. For example, while agriculture was supported by high state subsidies and a protective tariff policy, a highly regulated product market, toothless cartel law, and various state monopolies nipped any competition in the internal market in the bud (Armingeon and Emmenegger 2007). Swiss workers, in turn, benefited from de facto full employment because unemployment was exported to other countries by revoking work permits for foreign guest workers (Emmenegger 2010, 199). In turn, the competitiveness of the Swiss export-oriented industry was greatly facilitated by the state's restraint in imposing taxes and duties, or as in the case of the internationally oriented financial sector, promoted by self-government and a lack of state regulation (Emmenegger 2014).

For most of the post-war period, Switzerland prospered under this this economic policy model, although it also benefited from having been spared two world wars, and the associated destruction of capital. According to OECD figures, the country was still the second richest country in the OECD after Luxembourg in 1990, and had an unemployment rate of less than 1 per cent (see Figures 29.1 and 29.2). However, over time, clear signs of erosion of the traditional Swiss model could be observed. After years of weak economic growth, the economic crisis in the 1990s, which triggered the highest unemployment rates since the 1930s, finally opened a window for more radical changes.

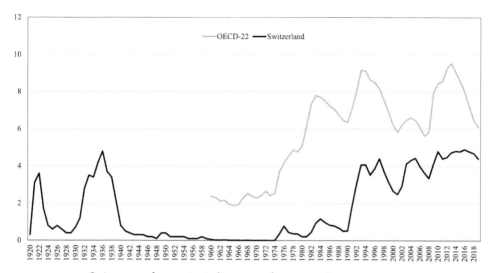

FIGURE 29.1: Swiss unemployment rate (in per cent), 1920–2018

OECD-22 are Australia, Austria, Belgium, Canada, Denmark, Finland, France, Germany, Great Britain, Iceland, Ireland, Italy, Japan, Luxembourg, Netherlands, New Zealand, Norway, Portugal, Spain, Sweden, and the USA.

Data source: 1920–1959: Emmenegger (2009, 214); 1960–2019: Armingeon et al. (2021).

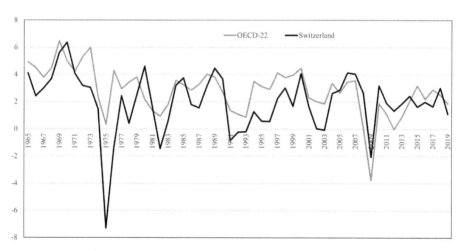

FIGURE 29.2: Real GDP growth (in per cent), 1965–2019

OECD-22 are Australia, Austria, Belgium, Canada, Denmark, Finland, France, Germany, Great Britain, Iceland, Ireland, Italy, Japan, Luxembourg, Netherlands, New Zealand, Norway, Portugal, Spain, Sweden, and the USA.

Data source: Armingeon et al. (2021).

2.1 PERIOD OF LIBERALIZATION

While weak growth was partly the result of a high starting level, global economic developments triggered a recession in the 1990s, which was further exacerbated by an unnecessarily restrictive monetary policy. However, the fundamental problems of the Swiss economy were home-made. In an endogenous evolutionary process, the economic model had gradually eroded its own foundations, thereby making the liberalization push of the 1990s possible in the first place (Armingeon and Emmenegger 2007).

For example, international developments in trade policy and participation in the European single market were becoming increasingly incompatible with the Swiss product market regulation and protectionist agricultural policies (Sciarini 1994). Simultaneously, public monopolies, antitrust law, and trade barriers undermined the competitiveness of the export industry (Mach 2006). While numerous reforms were necessary for Swiss financial service providers to retain access to international financial markets (Mach et al. 2006), reforms in immigration policy—responding to both domestic and foreign political pressures—robbed Switzerland of the opportunity to export unemployment abroad (Afonso 2005). Since the 1990s, the unemployment rate has never shrunk back to its pre-crisis levels. The high level of prosperity also promoted the expansion of social policy (see 'Social Policy' in this volume). However, this increased non-wage labour costs and contributed to a dramatic (by Swiss standards) growth in public debt due to weak growth, especially in the 1990s (see Figure 29.3).

From the mid-1990s onwards, these growing tensions erupted into a crisis discourse that demanded far-reaching liberalization steps (De Pury et al. 1995; SECO 2002). Importantly, this criticism did not come primarily from the most important supporters of the old model, the established business associations, but was carried by a coalition of business leaders, economists, and parts of the federal administration (Armingeon and Emmenegger 2007, 196–198; Eichenberger and Mach 2011, 74–75). The pent-up pressure for reform was unleashed in a liberalizing storm that lasted until the mid-2000s (Fill 2019). For example, from 1992 onwards, Swiss agricultural policy gradually moved

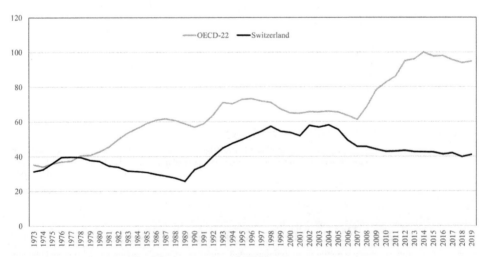

FIGURE 29.3: Swiss public debt (in per cent of GDP), 1973–2019

Data source: Armingeon et al. (2021).

away from product-linked market support, state price and purchase guarantees, and volume quotas (Sciarini 1994; Armingeon and Emmenegger 2007, 179–181). However, the liberalizing storm was short-lived. For instance, although the average share of state support in agricultural revenues fell from 71 per cent in 1990 to 52 per cent in 2020, Switzerland is still well above the European average (OECD 2022b).

Agricultural policy is the most prominent example of a fundamental issue of Swiss economic policy. Despite the wave of liberalization around the millennium, the degree of product market regulation, state intervention, and self-management by private actors remain comparatively high. For example, the Cartel Act was tightened in several steps from 1995 onwards. Prior to that year, there were hardly any barriers to cartels in Switzerland. The infamous 'beer cartel', which from 1935 onwards standardized products, fixed prices, and carved up Switzerland into regions with respective monopoly suppliers, is perhaps the best-known example. Yet, despite these reforms in product market regulation and competition law, Switzerland still retains higher barriers to competition compared to the OECD average (OECD 2019, 45; OECD 2022a, 37) and is characterized by a high number of companies that are state-owned. Although monopoly companies in the infrastructure sector such as railways, postal services, and telecommunication were privatized in the 1990s, the state remains the main owner of the successor companies. Such state interventions are often defended with reference to the need to politically control markets in key areas. However, in the Scandinavian countries, where there is ideological support for the political control of markets, the extent of product market regulation is nevertheless considerably lower (OECD 2018, 8).

Instead, strong product market regulation usually serves the interests of producers already present in a market, while new entrants face market entry barriers and consumers suffer from high prices (Armingeon and Emmenegger 2007, 183–184, 194). Thus, more than twenty years after the privatization of the state telecommunication company, the market share of its successor Swisscom is very high, while prices are still far above the OECD average today (BAKOM 2017; OECD 2018, 9). Accordingly, 'the situation is not at all advantageous for Swiss users' (BAKOM 2017, 16, own translation). This persistent focus on producer interests is also reflected in the continuing high level of self-regulation. Although various new state regulatory authorities, such as the Competition Commission, have been set up, these authorities are not very independent in international comparison, cooperate with private stakeholders in the implementation of regulations, and are partly made up of representatives of the business associations (Maggetti et al. 2011). Thus, although many areas are now explicitly regulated by the state, the effective design of the rules and their monitoring still follow a self-regulatory logic, meaning that it is not so much the content of self-regulation that has changed as its form (Mach et al. 2006). The Swiss case shows that the relationship between state regulation and a liberal market economy is more complex than popular election campaign slogans such as 'more freedom—less state' suggest. In some cases, it is precisely state regulations that make competition possible in the first place, while elsewhere state regulations are the result of the protectionist demands of individual economic sectors (Vogel 2018).

By the mid-2000s, the liberalization wave had lost most of its momentum as reflected in a series of symbolic political defeats in both parliament and direct democratic votes (Fill 2019, 140–143) and in the strengthening of the trade unions (Oesch 2011, 91–98). However, another measure introduced in response to the crisis of the 1990s was more successful. In 2001, Switzerland had introduced a debt brake, which obliged the government to keep revenues and expenditures in balance over the economic cycle. Together with the economic upturn in the 2000s, the debt brake had a resounding effect, as the development of public debt shows (see Figure 29.3).

2.2 Economic policy as crisis management

The year 2008 marked the dawn of a new era in Swiss economic policy. Whereas until then economic policy had been primarily concerned with competitiveness, Switzerland was suddenly confronted with several global policy challenges. First, the country faced a series of global economic crises. The turbulence in the US real estate market that began in 2007 also affected several Swiss financial institutions. In October 2008, UBS, by virtue of it being considered systemically important, had to be rescued from collapse with an unprecedented injection of government money. At the same time, UBS was allowed to outsource large amounts of bad mortgage papers to a fund managed by the Swiss National Bank (SNB). Although this bailout ultimately ended smoothly (both the government and SNB were able to sell their bonds and mortgage securities at a profit), the subsequent global financial crisis posed major challenges for Switzerland. In the search for safe investment opportunities, money flew into the 'Swiss haven' driving up the value of the franc (see Figure 29.4). In January 2015, the SNB was forced to abandon the euro floor of 1.20 francs, which it had furiously defended until then. Nevertheless, it continued to intervene massively in the foreign exchange market (see Figure 29.5) and had to lower the policy interest rate below zero to combat the appreciation of the franc. In turn, these negative interest rates fuelled lending in the mortgage sector, which translated in sharply rising residential property prices and growing private household debt (OECD 2022a, 27, 50).

In 2020, Switzerland was hit by the economic consequences of the COVID-19 pandemic. While GDP dropped by 2.5 per cent, unemployment remained low thanks to effective government interventions, most notably the expansion of short-time work compensation schemes (OECD 2022a, 10). This was facilitated by Switzerland's strong fiscal position (see Figure 29.3). In economic terms, Switzerland weathered both the COVID-19 and the global financial crisis well, which can be largely attributed to effective economic policy-making and a highly competitive export sector. However, as an open economy, Switzerland remains at risk of being affected by trade disruptions, the most recent of which emerged from the Russian aggression against Ukraine.

Parallel to the global economic crises, Switzerland was caught up in a tax evasion scandal that brought down banking secrecy. After initially refusing to cooperate further in tax matters with the American authorities in the wake of a whistle-blower affair, the

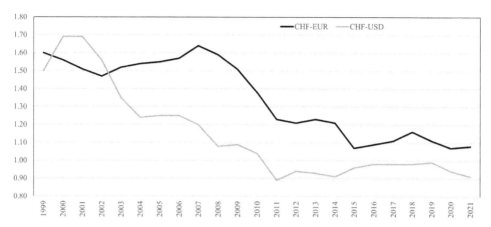

FIGURE 29.4: Currency exchange rates, yearly average, in Swiss francs, 1999–2021

Data source: Statista (2022).

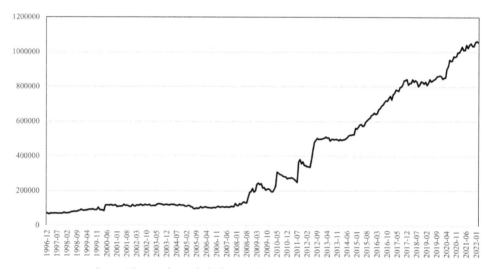

FIGURE 29.5: Swiss National Bank balance sheet (in million CHF), December 1996 to January 2022

Data source: Swiss National Bank (2022).

Swiss government eventually decided to hand over bank client data to the American judicial authorities to prevent UBS from being criminally indicted. Further investigations forced Switzerland to agree to a bilateral exchange of information in tax matters (Emmenegger and Eggenberger 2018). Meanwhile, on the international stage, Swiss authorities were strongly incited to agree to an automatic exchange of information, which could no longer be avoided in view of the developments in the USA (Emmenegger 2017). Moreover, in 2019, under pressure from both the European Union (EU) and the OECD, which criticized the state of its corporate taxes, the country abolished several tax privileges for international companies. However, Switzerland managed to maintain its position in international tax competition with the help of new tax instruments (e.g. patent boxes) and the reduction of corporate taxes at cantonal level (OECD 2022a, 51). Still, recent global developments, such as the proposed global minimum tax for large multinational companies, will certainly challenge Switzerland's position in international tax competition.

Finally, Switzerland has been struggling with its relationship to the EU for three decades now. Economic relations with the EU are of considerable importance for Switzerland. According to a recent analysis, no country benefits more from the European single market (Bertelsmann Stiftung 2019). Furthermore, immigration from the EU area contributes a great deal to combating skilled worker shortages in the Swiss labour market (see 'The Structural Shifts in Switzerland's Economy and Society, 2000–2020' in this volume). At the same time, the relationship with the EU is characterized by a strong asymmetry as Switzerland is more dependent on EU-market access than vice versa. Despite Swiss–EU relations having enjoyed a relatively stable footing with the help of bilateral agreements for more than a decade, this basis was shaken in 2014 by the mass immigration initiative, which called for sovereign control in immigration matters (Emmenegger et al. 2018). In addition, for some time the EU has been calling for an institutional agreement to further develop the Swiss–EU relationship and introduce dispute settlement mechanisms (see 'Switzerland and the European Union' in this volume). With the EU compatible implementation of the mass immigration initiative, a new conflict with the EU could be avoided. In contrast, no agreement could be reached on the demanded institutional agreement. Disagreements primarily concern aspects of the traditional economic model: state aid, wage protection for domestic workers, and access to the Swiss welfare state for immigrant workers.

In sum, the Swiss economy has lost some of its magic in recent years, but Switzerland remains one of the richest countries in the world. Numerous reforms have contributed to the modernization of the economy, although these reform processes—due to Switzerland's negotiation democracy—have been characterized by long-winded negotiations and political compromises. In the process, Switzerland has typically reacted to international developments, rather than shaping reform processes proactively. Still today, a highly competitive export sector stands in contrast to a protected domestic economy, while Swiss citizens benefit from high wages and job security. But the foundations of this model have been further eroded in recent years. The export sector suffers from the strong franc and worries about access to the European market, which increases the pressure on the protected domestic economy and the labour market. For this reason, the idea of an institutional agreement with the EU remains controversial in Switzerland: it addresses the very foundations of this increasingly shaky compromise.

Switzerland's pragmatic and reactive approach to economic policy also explains why the country is difficult to classify in the currently most important typology of market economy systems (Hall and Soskice 2001). As Mach and Trampusch (2011, 12–14) point out, the liberal labour market, rather weak trade unions, and underdeveloped forms of co-determination are typical of liberal market economies, while the strongly developed vocational education and training (VET) system, the inclusion of private intermediary associations in policy formulation and implementation, and the now well-developed welfare state speak for a coordinated market economy. The Swiss 'hybrid' model consequently combines elements of both types. Nevertheless, this hybrid approach proved to be successful for a long time.

3 ACTORS AND DECISION-MAKING

As is the case in other democratic market economies, the conflict between capital and labour structures Swiss economic policy. As mentioned, this conflict was characterized by a certain asymmetry because the trade unions struggled to develop the organizational clout to consistently assert their interests (Katzenstein 1985). However, the employers' side also has to contend with conflicting interests. First, there is the conflict of interest between the export-oriented sectors and the domestic market-oriented economy, which found organizational expression in the opposition between the Swiss Commerce and Industry Association, on the one hand, and the Swiss Trade Association and the Swiss Farmers' Association on the other (Eichenberger and Mach 2011, 69–70). Second, there is the conflict between industry and finance, primarily concerning issues of monetary policy and corporate financing. Accordingly, the Swiss Bankers Association, founded in 1912, remained independent of the main employer confederations until 2000.

Despite these conflicting interests, the leading employers' associations made efforts early on to develop common economic policy positions. Of particular importance for this was the customs issue in the late nineteenth century. In response to the first crisis of globalization, employers' associations were created and soon agreed on a protective tariff policy (Gruner 1956, 32). The government was willing to take the employers' position into account. For example, the government negotiated the 1902 tariff directly with the main employers' associations (Emmenegger and Walter 2022, 595–596), not least because the government lacked the necessary resources and competences for such issues due to the comparatively late centralization and professionalization of Swiss politics (Gruner 1964, 49–50; Emmenegger 2010, 190–193). This protective tariff policy, which favoured producer interests, also led to the final rift between the Farmers' Association and the trade unions, the latter of which favoured consumer interests (Gruner 1988, 1397). The financial industry was initially not part of this compromise but was brought on board in the following years. The increasing focus on asset management, supported by the 1934 Banking Act codifying banking secrecy, partially resolved the remaining conflicts of interest between the financial industry and the other economic sectors. As some sectors of the economy increasingly focused on exports in the course of the twentieth century, these partial openings were compensated for by new product market regulations and subsidies (Bonoli and Mach 2000).

Parallel to this bloc formation in the interest intermediation system, a bourgeois bloc developed in parliament and in government. At the turn of the century, after decades of political conflict, the Catholic Conservatives (renamed the Christian Democratic People's Party in 1970 and The Centre in 2020) finally joined the Free Democrats in government. In 1929, the coalition government also integrated the new Farmers' Party (renamed the Swiss People's Party in 1971). Due to the close ties between the employers' associations and the three main bourgeois parties, the pro-business alliance faced a much weaker social democratic and trade union camp in both arenas (Eichenberger and Mach 2011).

Switzerland's 'conservation interventionism' (Gruner 1964, 47) reached a new dimension during the 1929–1939 Great Depression. While the state intervened massively in the economy, this was always done in consultation with the main employers' associations. Furthermore, in view of the growing class conflict, it also increasingly strived for a balance with the trade unions. The resulting interventionist policy in collaboration with the social partners was given constitutional status in 1947 with the so-called 'economic articles' (Gruner 1964, 63). After 1947, the government was obliged to consult the most important interest groups on all legislative issues within the framework of a consultation procedure. Promoting competition through state intervention to limit the power of associations was not envisaged in this arrangement. Although individuals were to be 'protected against arbitrariness and encroachments by associations', the government explicitly stated that it had no intention to 'prevent or combat cartels' (Federal Council 1937, 850, 889). Compromises reached in the pre-parliamentary phase were generally not changed in parliament (Sciarini et al. 2015, 3–8). This dominance of the pre-parliamentary phase and large associations—especially of employers—in political decision-making remained in place until the 1980s (Kriesi 1980) and was expressed, among other things, by the fact that the director of the Swiss Commerce and Industry Association (since 2000 Economiesuisse) used to be referred to as the eighth member of the Federal Council.

3.1 New actor constellations

In recent years, decision-making processes have changed significantly. The parliamentary phase has experienced an upgrade, which has gone hand in hand with a shift in the opportunities for various actors to exert influence. Actors who mainly focus their activities on the pre-parliamentary phase have lost influence (Häusermann et al. 2004). According to Sciarini et al. (2015, 59), this primarily concerns employer associations and trade unions, while the central actors in the parliamentary phase—political parties—have gained influence. Only Economiesuisse seems to have been able to hold its ground, although in recent years the association has also been confronted with accusations of dwindling assertiveness. These shifts in power also explain why employer associations and trade unions increasingly rely on lobbying to achieve their political goals, and why the number of interest ties of members of the Federal Assembly has increased significantly (Gava et al. 2017). This stronger role of parliament is also reflected in several reforms, most notably the standing commissions created in 1992.

Several factors help explain these changes. As already mentioned, conflicts among employers have become more important. International competition has increased heterogeneity and reduced the room for compromise, which makes it more difficult to put together comprehensive packages that can be carried from the pre-parliamentary to the parliamentary phase (Häusermann et al. 2004). This increasing heterogeneity and the dwindling scope for negotiation are putting pressure on employer associations and trade unions, forcing them to undertake a series of organizational reforms in recent years (Eichenberger and Mach 2011; Oesch 2011).

At the same time, the growing electoral strength of the Swiss People's Party has broken up the old economic policy blocs. Over the years, the party has morphed from a farmers' party into a right-wing populist party that primarily mobilizes with cultural issues (e.g. migration). However, these issues often have significant economic implications, and thus reduce the ability of business-friendly parties to act together, which in turn strengthens the position of the Social Democratic Party. Meanwhile, Switzerland is one of the most polarized countries in Europe on economic and cultural policy issues (Bochsler et al. 2015, 478). The increase in the number of interest groups, especially civil society ones, and the ever-increasing media monitoring of politics also contribute to making it more difficult to find compromises in the pre-parliamentary phase (Häusermann et al. 2004; Gava et al. 2017). When compromises that are agreed upon in the pre-parliamentary phase finally reach parliament, their fate is much less certain than was the case thirty years ago, due to the shift in power away from the political centre (Free Democrats and the Centre) towards the periphery (Social Democratic Party and Swiss People's Party).

3.2 Classification of the Swiss model

There is considerable disagreement in the political science literature on how to assess these new decision-making processes (Armingeon 2011; Mach and Eichenberger 2011). The 'old' model of economic policy decision-making was already peculiar. Although Switzerland was usually assigned to the group of countries with neo-corporatist interest intermediation systems, Kriesi (1980, 689–690) highlighted that Switzerland's decentralized wage bargaining system and the power asymmetry between employers' associations and trade unions were not in line with prototypical neo-corporatist systems. Kriesi's critical assessment, however, is due to a specific understanding of neo-corporatism, which emphasizes organizational features of intermediary associations. In contrast, other approaches emphasize the involvement of intermediary associations in political decision-making processes and their implementation (Lehmbruch 1979; Katzenstein 1985; Streeck and Schmitter 1985). In this respect, Switzerland used to represent an almost ideal case of a neo-corporatist interest intermediation system due to the dominant role of the pre-parliamentary phase and the prominent role of private interest governments.

However, this model of economic policy-making has changed since the 1990s. With the upgrading of the parliamentary phase and the political regulation of policy areas formerly left to self-administration by private actors, a long-overdue normalization of Swiss politics has taken place. Moreover, decision-making is now less organized and more unpredictable because, with the strengthening of the parliamentary phase, other actors have become more influential. In parallel, the formerly dominant bourgeois bloc has partially dissolved.

Despite these changes, research shows that employers' associations continue to be strongly involved in economic policy-making, although their activities are increasingly shifting to the parliamentary phase (Gava et al. 2017). The corporatist pre-parliamentary negotiation system has been joined by a more conflictual lobbying system. Moreover, intermediary associations are still heavily involved in policy implementation. Although the nature of self-government has changed, the influence of intermediary associations remains high (Wagemann 2005; Mach et al. 2006; Maggetti et al. 2011). Finally, Swiss economic policy continues to be characterized by a strong social partnership orientation, which results from Switzerland's negotiation democracy as well as from a distinctly consensus-oriented political culture that endures (Lehmbruch 2003), despite important conflictive elements having accumulated due to party-political polarization (Afonso 2013). All in all, economic policy decision-making in Switzerland—despite these erosive tendencies—must still be assigned to the neo-corporatist interest intermediation system type.

4 Evaluation

Figure 29.2 has already shown that the annual growth of Switzerland's GDP per capita has generally been below the average of the comparison group, although after a long period of weak growth in the mid-2000s, Switzerland has once again come closer to the comparison group (OECD 2022a, 10). In particular, Switzerland has weathered the global financial crisis and the more recent COVID-19 pandemic well, which can be attributed to well-functioning crisis management based on social partnership and a competent administration, a highly trained workforce, and a knowledge-intensive economic structure. Moreover, Switzerland has managed to keep the growth of income inequality below the OECD average in recent years. In terms of income inequality (but not wealth inequality), Switzerland is now one of the most egalitarian countries in the OECD, which is also reflected in the population's high level of satisfaction with their living conditions (OECD 2019, 22–23; OECD 2022a, 17).

A similarly mixed assessment can be made of labour market developments. For many years, Switzerland has had well above-average employment rates for both men and women (see Figure 29.6). Siegenthaler (2017) speaks, not without reason, of a 'job miracle'. On the negative side, however, Switzerland has lost its special position regarding unemployment (see Figure 29.1). While the difference between Switzerland and the OECD in terms of unemployment rates was still over five percentage points at the beginning of the 1990s, this number has fallen steadily in recent years to around

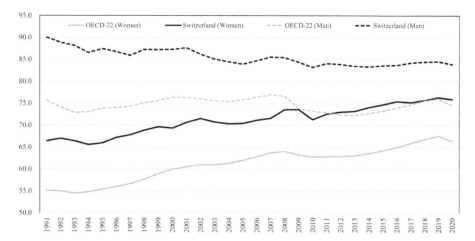

FIGURE 29.6: Employment rate by gender (in per cent of population aged 15-64), 1991–2020

Data source: OECD (2022c).

two percentage points. Furthermore, the above-average employment rate of women in Switzerland hides a very high level of part-time employment. Almost 50 per cent of women work for less than thirty hours a week, which is the second highest share in the OECD behind the Netherlands (OECD 2022a, 8, 77).

In the face of deindustrialization and globalization processes, countries such as Switzerland must increasingly reinvent themselves as knowledge economies. Switzerland has managed this transition well so far. It has a high proportion of knowledge-intensive jobs, especially in the field of information and communication technology (ICT). In addition, the occupational structure has undergone a significant upgrade in recent years, not least because jobs have been created in the highest income brackets (see 'The Structural Shifts in Switzerland's Economy and Society, 2000–2020' in this volume). This development, guided by the needs of the economy, is the result of high private investment activity in the ICT sector, a well-developed public infrastructure, active participation in education and training programmes, and an immigration policy geared towards highly skilled immigrants (OECD 2019, 41–52). However, Switzerland has deficits in the participation of the non-working and the low-skilled working population in education and training programmes (OECD 2022a, 96). These can partly be explained by the lack of alignment between active labour market policies (which cater to the unemployed and non-working population) and the thriving (often private) VET sector (which focuses on the working population). Furthermore, the high quality of Switzerland's ICT infrastructure contrasts with the only average use of this infrastructure in the private sector and public administration (OECD 2019, 42–48).

With good reason, the OECD (2019, 43) speaks of a 'productivity paradox'. While individual sectors and companies invest heavily in research and development, and are among the most productive in the world, the gap with the rest of the Swiss economy is growing (Arvanitis et al. 2017). This duality is also reflected in various rankings where Switzerland is regularly ranked among the most competitive economies (IMD 2021).

However, these rankings focus primarily on export-oriented sectors, which are indeed highly competitive. These sectors continue to contrast with a relatively strongly protected domestic economy (OECD 2022a, 37–41). Admittedly, the domestic economy has been increasingly exposed to competition in recent years. However, other countries have often liberalized to a greater extent during the same period. As a result, regarding product market regulation, Switzerland is still clearly above the OECD average and other highly competitive Western European countries (OECD 2018, 8). Accordingly, foreign trade in Switzerland contributes around 40 per cent to overall economic value added, thus outperforming the self-proclaimed 'export world champion' Germany (Müller 2019, 4). However, the Swiss 'job miracle' (Siegenthaler 2017) is primarily supported by the less productive domestic economy. Due to the continuing strength of the Swiss franc (see Figure 29.4), the pressure to liberalize the domestic economy is therefore likely to continue.

In terms of fiscal policy, Switzerland is in an advantageous position (see Figure 29.3). It has managed to keep public debt low, which is conducive to effective crisis management. However, demographic change and the associated funding gaps in social welfare systems are likely to pose greater challenges for public finances in the future (OECD 2019, 69–124). In addition, current developments in international tax cooperation will severely impact Switzerland, which hosts many internationally active companies and collects taxes on at least part of their profits. Therefore, should new guidelines on the taxation of these companies be issued, Switzerland will certainly be among the losers. In response to such international pressure, some tax privileges for multinationals have already been abolished and have been replaced by expanded possibilities for tax deductions for R&D expenditures as well as lower cantonal corporate tax rates. Further reforms are expected in the next few years (OECD 2022a, 51).

5 Challenges

Weak productivity growth will remain a key challenge for Swiss economic policy in the coming years (OECD 2022a, 18), although several factors put this weakness into perspective somewhat (high starting level, unsuitable measurement methods for knowledge-intensive service industries, high employment rate). Export-oriented industries, such as the financial sector and the pharmaceutical industry, contribute the lion's share to labour productivity growth (Eberli et al. 2015, 88), which once again shows how strongly Switzerland depends on economic openness. Thus, the main reason for weak productivity growth can be primarily located in the rest of the economy, which, in contrast to comparable Western economies, only makes a modest contribution to productivity growth (Eberli et al. 2015, 88; OECD 2019, 43). This once again highlights the duality of the Swiss economy where some parts are at the forefront of the international knowledge economy while digitization, innovation, and competition have only partially arrived in other parts.

Switzerland's most important trading partner remains Europe, which underlines the importance of Switzerland's bilateral agreements with the EU. As mentioned, Switzerland benefits from the European single market, while immigration from the EU area does much to address Switzerland's skills shortages. Being a pragmatic compromise between economic integration and non-membership, the bilateral treaties have proven their worth in recent years. However, for some time now, the EU has been pushing for an institutional agreement that would 'dynamize' the development of their relationship (e.g. adapting Swiss law to the more developed single market law) and introduce a dispute settlement mechanism. There is considerable resistance in Switzerland to such an agreement with the EU, which insists on better access to the Swiss market in return for access to the European single market. Next to populist political groups emphasizing issues such as sovereignty, the most opposition, both on the employers' and the employees' side, comes from economic groups that benefit from the highly protected Swiss domestic market.

There is also potential for improvement in labour market policy. The educational level and employment rate of women have improved significantly in recent years. However, due to widespread part-time employment, there is still a shortage of skilled workers in most professions requiring tertiary education. Skill gaps are met thanks to an immigration policy geared towards highly skilled immigrants, whereas fiscal disincentives and insufficient measures to reconcile work and family life prevent women from exploiting their full labour force potential (see 'Family Policy' in this volume). In addition, age-related pension fund contributions increase employment costs for older workers. Although the employment rate of older people is high by international standards, this population group increasingly suffers from long-term unemployment (OECD 2019, 54, 92). Finally, Switzerland would be well advised to invest in the education and training of the unemployed and low-skilled population. While the principle of lifelong learning is a long-standing phenomenon in Switzerland, it is precisely these groups that have the lowest participation rates in education and training programmes (OECD 2019, 51–52). Better linking active labour market policies with the dynamic, often privately organized VET sector could help increase labour market efficiency.

Notes

1. I thank Klaus Armingeon for helpful comments and Tobias Straumann for pointing me to the Friedman quote.
2. Swiss economic policy is strongly influenced by federalism. Various economic policy measures are within the competence of the cantons and sometimes display considerable differences within Switzerland. For this reason, this chapter is limited to the federal level.

References

Afonso, Alexandre. 2005. 'When the Export of Social Problems is no Longer Possible: Immigration Policies and Unemployment in Switzerland'. *Social Policy & Administration* 39 (6): pp. 653–668.

Afonso, Alexandre. 2013. *Social Concertation in Times of Austerity: European Integration and the Politics of Labour Market Reforms in Austria and Switzerland*. Amsterdam: Amsterdam University Press.

Armingeon, Klaus. 2011. 'A Prematurely Announced Death? Swiss Corporatism in Comparative Perspective'. In *Switzerland in Europe: Continuity and Change in the Swiss Political Economy*, edited by Christine Trampusch, and André Mach, pp. 165–185. London: Routledge.

Armingeon, Klaus. 2017. 'Wirtschafts- und Finanzpolitik'. In *Handbuch der Schweizer Politik*, edited by Peter Knoepfel, Yannis Papadopoulos, Pascal Sciarini, Adrian Vatter, and Silja Häuserman, pp. 695–720. 6th ed. Zürich: NZZ Libro.

Armingeon, Klaus, and Patrick Emmenegger. 2007. 'Wirtschaftspolitik: Die Erosion des schweizerischen Modells'. In *Schweizer Wirtschaft – Ein Sonderfall?*, edited by Hanno Scholtz, and Michael Nollert, pp. 175–207. Zürich: Seismo.

Armingeon, Klaus, Sarah Engler, and Lucas Leemann. 2021. *Comparative Political Data Set 1960-2019*. University of Zurich: Institute of Political Science.

Arvanitis, Spyros, Florian Seliger, Andrin Spescha, Tobias Stucki, and Martin Wörter. 2017. *Die Entwicklung der Innovationsaktivitäten in der Schweizer Wirtschaft 1997-2014*. Bern: SECO.

BAKOM. 2017. *Der Schweizer Fernmeldemarkt im internationalen Vergleich*. Bern: Bundesamt für Kommunikation.

Bertelsmann Stiftung. 2019. *Estimating Economic Benefits of the Single Market for European Countries and Regions*. Gütersloh: Bertelsmann Stiftung.

Bochsler, Daniel, Regula Hänggli, and Silja Häusermann. 2015. 'Consensus Lost? Disenchanted Democracy in Switzerland'. *Swiss Political Science Review* 21 (4): pp. 475–490.

Bonoli, Giuliano, and André Mach. 2000. 'Switzerland: Adjustment Policies within Institutional Constraints'. In *Welfare and Work in the Open Economy: Diverse Responses to Common Challenges*, edited by Fritz W. Scharpf, and Vivien A. Schmidt, pp. 131–174. Oxford: Oxford University Press.

De Pury, David, Heinz Hauser, and Beat Schmidt. 1995. *Mut zum Aufbruch: Eine wirtschaftspolitische Agenda*. Zürich: Orell Füssli.

Eberli, Andreas, Mark Emmenegger, Michael Grass, Natalia Held, and Rebekka Rufer. 2015. *Beitrag branchenspezifischer Effekte zum Wachstum der Schweizer Arbeitsproduktivität*. Bern: SECO.

Eichenberger, Pierre, and André Mach. 2011. 'Organized Capital and Coordinated Market Economy: Swiss Business Interest Associations between Socio-Economic Regulation and Political Influence'. In *Switzerland in Europe: Continuity and Change in the Swiss Political Economy*, edited by Christine Trampusch, and André Mach, pp. 63–81. London: Routledge.

Emmenegger, Patrick. 2009. *Regulatory Social Policy: The Politics of Job Security Regulations*. Bern: Haupt.

Emmenegger, Patrick. 2010. 'Low Statism in Coordinated Market Economies: The Development of Job Security Regulations in Switzerland'. *International Political Science Review* 31 (2): pp. 187–205.

Emmenegger, Patrick. 2011. 'Ever More Liberal? The Regulation of Job Security and Working Time in Switzerland'. In *Switzerland in Europe: Continuity and Change in the Swiss Political Economy*, edited by Christine Trampusch, and André Mach, pp. 124–143. London: Routledge.

Emmenegger, Patrick. 2014. 'The Politics of Financial Intransparency: The Case of Swiss Banking Secrecy'. *Swiss Political Science Review* 20 (1): pp. 146–164.

Emmenegger, Patrick. 2017. 'Swiss Banking Secrecy and the Problem of International Cooperation in Tax Matters: A Nut Too Hard to Crack?' *Regulation and Governance* 11 (1): pp. 24–40.

Emmenegger, Patrick and André Walter. 2022. 'International Trade, the Great War, and the Origins of Taxation: Sister Republics Parting Ways'. *Swiss Political Science Review* 28 (4): pp. 585–603.

Emmenegger, Patrick, and Katrin Eggenberger. 2018. 'State Sovereignty, Economic Interdependence and U.S. Extraterritoriality: The Demise of Swiss Banking Secrecy and the Re-Embedding of International Finance'. *Journal of International Relations and Development* 21 (3): pp. 798–823.

Emmenegger, Patrick, Silja Häusermann, and Stefanie Walter. 2018. 'National Sovereignty vs. International Cooperation: Policy Choices in Trade-Off Situations'. *Swiss Political Science Review* 24 (4): pp. 400–422.

Farago, Peter. 1987. *Verbände als Träger öffentlicher Politik*. Grüsch: Rüegger.

Federal Council. 1937. 'Botschaft des Bundesrates an die Bundesversammlung über eine Partialrevision der Wirtschaftsartikel der Bundesverfassung'. *Bundesblatt* 89 (37): pp. 837–902.

Fill, Anna. 2019. *The Political Economy of De-Liberalization: A Comparative Study on Austria, Germany and Switzerland*. Cham: Springer.

Friedman, Milton. 1972. 'Whatever Happened to Free Enterprise?' Interview by Richard Howe. April 1972. https://miltonfriedman.hoover.org/objects/57765/m-friedman-whatever-happened-to-free-enterprise

Gava, Roy, Frédéric Varone, André Mach, Steven Eichenberger, Julien Christie, and Corinne Chao-Blanco. 2017. 'Interest Groups in Parliament: Exploring MP's Interest Affiliations (2000–2011)'. *Swiss Political Science Review* 23 (1): pp. 77–94.

Gruner, Erich. 1956. *Die Wirtschaftsverbände in der Demokratie*. Zürich: Rentsch.

Gruner, Erich. 1964. '100 Jahre Wirtschaftspolitik: Etappen des Interventionismus in der Schweiz'. *Swiss Journal of Economics and Statistics* 100 (1): pp. 3–70.

Gruner, Erich. 1988. *Arbeiterschaft und Wirtschaft in der Schweiz 1880–1914*. Zürich: Chronos.

Hall, Peter, and David Soskice. 2001. *Varieties of Capitalism: The Institutional Foundations of Comparative Advantage*. Oxford: Oxford University Press.

Häusermann, Silja, André Mach, and Yannis Papadopoulos. 2004. 'From Corporatism to Partisan Politics: Social Policy Making under Strain in Switzerland'. *Swiss Political Science Review* 10 (2): pp. 33–59.

Hotz, Beat. 1979. *Politik zwischen Staat und Wirtschaft*. Diessenhofen: Rüegger.

IMD. 2021. *World Competitiveness Ranking 2021*. International Institute for Management Development (IMD): World Competitiveness Center. 17 June 2021. https://www.imd.org/centers/world-competitiveness-center/rankings/world-competitiveness/

Katzenstein, Peter. 1985. *Small States in World Markets: Industrial Policy in Europe*. Ithaca: Cornell University Press.

Kenworthy, Lane. 2003. 'Quantitative Indicators of Corporatism'. *International Journal of Sociology* 33(3): pp. 10–44.

Kriesi, Hanspeter. 1980. *Entscheidungsstrukturen und Entscheidungsprozesse in der Schweizer Politik*. Frankfurt: Campus.

Lehmbruch, Gerhard. 1979. 'Liberal Corporatism and Party Government'. In *Trends Toward Corporatist Intermediation*, edited by Philippe Schmitter, and Gerhard Lehmbruch, pp. 47–183. London: Sage.

Lehmbruch, Gerhard. 2003. *Verhandlungsdemokratie: Beiträge zur vergleichenden Regierungslehre*. Wiesbaden: Verlag für Sozialwissenschaften.

Mach, André. 2006. *La Suisse entre Internationalisation et Changement Politiques Internes: La Législation sur les Cartels et les Relations Industrielles dans les Années 1990*. Chur: Rüegger.

Mach, André, Gerhard Schnyder, Thomas David, and Martin Lüpold. 2006. 'Transformations de l'Autorégulation et Nouvelles Régulations Publiques en Matière de Gouvernement d'Entreprise en Suisse (1985-2002)'. *Swiss Political Science Review* 12 (1): pp. 1-32.

Mach, André, and Christine Trampusch. 2011. 'The Swiss Political Economy in Comparative Perspective'. In *Switzerland in Europe: Continuity and Change in the Swiss Political Economy*, edited by Christine Trampusch, and André Mach, pp. 11-26. London: Routledge.

Maggetti, Martino, Alexandre Afonso, and Marie-Christine Fontana. 2011. 'The More It Changes, the More It Stays the Same? Swiss Liberalization and Regulatory Policies in Comparative Perspective'. In *Switzerland in Europe: Continuity and Change in the Swiss Political Economy*, edited by Christine Trampusch, and André Mach, pp. 205-223. London: Routledge.

Müller, Larissa. 2019. 'Internationaler Handel als Rückgrat der Schweizer Wirtschaft'. *Die Volkswirtschaft* 8-9: pp. 4-8.

Müller, Margrit, and Ulrich Woitek. 2012. 'Wohlstand, Wachstum und Konjunktur'. In *Wirtschaftsgeschichte der Schweiz im 20 Jahrhundert*, edited by Patrick Halbeisen, Margrit Müller, and Beatrice Veyrasset, pp. 91-222. Basel: Schwabe.

OECD. 2018. *Product Market Regulation*. Paris: OECD.

OECD. 2019. *OECD Economic Surveys: Switzerland*. Paris: OECD.

OECD. 2022a. *OECD Economic Surveys: Switzerland*. Paris: OECD.

OECD. 2022b. *Agricultural Support*. https://data.oecd.org/agrpolicy/agricultural-support.htm, (accessed 4 April 2022).

OECD. 2022c. *OECD.Stat*. https://stats.oecd.org/ (accessed 6 April 2022).

Oesch, Daniel. 2011. 'Swiss Trade Unions and Industrial Relations after 1990: A History of Decline and Renewal'. In *Switzerland in Europe: Continuity and Change in the Swiss Political Economy*, edited by Christine Trampusch, and André Mach, pp. 82-102. London: Routledge.

Sciarini, Pascal. 1994. *La Suisse Face à la Communauté Européenne et au GATT: Le Cas Test de la Politique Agricole*. Geneva: Editions George.

Sciarini, Pascal, Manuel Fischer, and Denise Traber. 2015. *Political Decision-Making in Switzerland: The Consensus Model under Pressure*. Houndmills: Palgrave Macmillan.

SECO. 2002. *Der Wachstumsbericht: Determinanten des Schweizer Wirtschaftswachstums und Ansatzpunkte für eine wachstumsorientierte Wirtschaftspolitik*. Bern: SECO.

Siegenthaler, Michael. 2017. 'Vom Nachkriegsboom zum Jobwunder: Der starke Rückgang der Arbeitszeit in der Schweiz seit 1950'. *Social Change in Switzerland* 9. doi:10.22019/SC-2017-00004.

Statista. 2022. *Statistiken zum Thema Devisen*. https://de.statista.com/themen/1400/devisen/, (accessed 6 April 2022).

Streeck, Wolfgang, and Philippe Schmitter. 1985. *Private Interest Government: Beyond Market and State*. London: Sage.

Swiss National Bank. 2022. *Datenportal der Schweizerischen Nationalbank*. https://data.snb.ch (accessed 6 April 2022).

Trampusch, Christine. 2008. 'Von einem Liberalen zu einem Post-Liberalen Wohlfahrtsstaat: Der Wandel der Gewerkschaftlichen Sozialpolitik in der Schweiz'. *Swiss Political Science Review* 14 (1): pp. 49-84.

Vogel, Steven. 2018. *Marketcraft: How Governments Make Markets Work*. Oxford: Oxford University Press.

Wagemann, Claudius. 2005. 'Private Interest Governments Are Dead: Long Live Private Interest Governments? Lessons from Swiss Cows'. *Swiss Political Science Review* 11 (3): pp. 1-25.

CHAPTER 30

BANKING AND THE SWISS FINANCIAL CENTRE

ROY GAVA

1 INTRODUCTION

THE Swiss financial centre is highly developed and relatively large for the size of the country. This chapter provides an overview of the regulatory framework and the political environment that shape this prominent industry.

Business interests do not always secure their preferred policies (Culpepper 2015). Nevertheless, they are generally well positioned to shape their regulatory environment in capitalist economies. First, economic growth and job creation, common priorities for policymakers, depend on investment decisions. This 'structural power' makes business preferences difficult to ignore when choosing policy options. Second, business interests also tend to be well equipped in terms of 'instrumental power': those advocacy strategies used to persuade policymakers such as lobbying. Third, many business regulatory issues are characterized by technical complexity and low salience on both political and media agendas. In such a 'quiet politics' environment, business positions and expertise are rarely challenged (Culpepper 2011).

Switzerland can be described as a 'coordinated market economy with a business bias' (Mach et al. 2021, 20). A series of interrelated factors further strengthen the advantages of business in policy-making. Both government and parliament have been uninterruptedly dominated by centre-right parties entertaining close ties with business interest associations (BIAs). Moreover, the principles of low state intervention and business self-regulation have repeatedly enjoyed broad support from the majority of the political elite and voters. At the same time, state actors, such as the federal administration, have traditionally relied on relatively small budgets and structures to carry out their activities.

The privileged position of business also seems reinforced when looking at the Swiss financial sector. Indeed, the financial industry has structural prominence in capitalist economies (Young and Park 2013) but it is particularly large in Switzerland. In contrast to policy-making in other economic sectors, the interest group landscape of financial regulation is more densely populated by business interests (Pagliari and Young 2015). BIAs therefore face less competition from groups that frequently promote critical views, such as public interest groups. The Swiss Bankers' Association (SBA) is an umbrella organization that has long been considered the voice of the entire sector. As such, internal differences have traditionally been addressed behind closed doors rather than in the public sphere. The industry has thus often been able to showcase business unity (Busch 2009), a strong predictor of advocacy success (Chalmers 2020).

Against this backdrop, the political power of the Swiss financial industry is put at risk by exogenous shocks such as crises, scandals, or international pressure. The Global Financial Crisis (GFC) that began in 2008 combined all three. The bailout of the largest bank, the repeated revelations on how banks benefited from foreign tax evasion, and the diplomatic clashes with major countries seeking access to information on Swiss bank accounts tainted the reputation of the entire sector. The GFC thus initiated a period of 'noisy politics' that put the industry mainly on the defensive against a wave of regulatory reforms.

This chapter is structured as follows. The second part discusses the economic importance and diversity of market participants active in the industry. In particular, it explores the segmentation and heterogeneity of the banking sector. The third part focuses on the roles and characteristics of those specialized actors that shape the regulatory and political environment, from both public and private sides. The fourth part provides an overview of the regulatory framework, mapping the public and private rules that guide market participants' behaviour. The fifth part deals with policy-making since the GFC and begins with a brief review of the erosion of Swiss banking secrecy for tax matters. This particular issue, which attracted most of the political and media attention, illustrates how exogenous shocks led to major policy changes long resisted by both the industry and centre-right parties. The section closes with a bird's eye view of how political parties have dealt with financial regulation in parliament since the GFC.

2 The Swiss financial centre

In 2021, the Swiss financial sector accounted for 9 per cent of the national GDP. During the 2000s, before the GFC, peaks of around 12 per cent were registered. The relative importance of the financial industry to the national economy is greater in only a handful of small jurisdictions with prominent financial sectors such as Luxembourg, Hong Kong, and Singapore (Figure 30.1). Finance remains of utmost importance to the Swiss economy, despite a slight relative decline since the GFC.

Financial market participants are intermediaries that offer intangible services and products. Their business models are based on activities such as lending, insuring, trading, managing assets, and providing services against a fee.

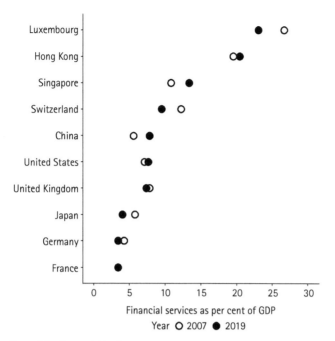

FIGURE 30.1: Size of the financial industry

Data source: OECD (2022).

A banking licence allows firms to engage in diverse business areas, such as deposit-taking, lending, securities dealing, asset management, investment banking, and proprietary trading. The Swiss banking sector is, however, renowned for its niche specialization in offshore wealth management. Private banking or wealth management refers to the provision of portfolio management services to affluent individuals. While its position is increasingly under threat, Switzerland remains the global leader in this specific segment with an estimated quarter of the global market (Boston Consulting Group 2022).

Beyond banks, the Swiss financial centre accounts for 193 insurance companies (FINMA 2022a). Individuals or firms seeking protection from expensive damages transfer risks to insurers in exchange for premiums. Life insurers provide compensation in the event of death or disability. Non-life insurers protect against accidents or damages on persons, property, or assets. Reinsurance companies hedge the risks of other insurers.

The asset management industry, dedicated to handling assets on behalf of investors, is another important segment of the Swiss financial sector. Asset management firms primarily serve institutional clients such as pension funds and insurance companies. This segment of the industry comprehends 356 fund management companies and managers of collective investment schemes (FINMA 2022b). In addition, hundreds of independent wealth managers provide investment services but cater principally to private clients (FINMA 2022c).

Switzerland has a large stock market relative to the size of its economy. In 2020, the market capitalization of domestic listed companies was around 266 per cent of its

GDP (World Bank 2022). While far from the exceptional Hong Kong (1,769 per cent), Switzerland comes ahead of jurisdictions such as the US (194 per cent), Singapore (192 per cent), Japan (133 per cent), the UK (117 per cent), or Germany (59 per cent). The principal stock exchange is SIX Swiss Exchange (the other being BX Swiss). This trading venue resulted from the fusion of the Zurich, Geneva, and Basel exchanges in 1993. In terms of market capitalization, SIX Swiss Exchange is ranked fourteenth in the world and fifth in Europe (World Federation of Exchanges 2022).

In recent decades, the contribution of the different segments of the financial industry to the national economy has evolved (Federal Office of Statistics 2017). The part of banks has been declining from a peak in the 2000s, when they accounted for roughly 60 per cent of the total added value of the financial sector. Since the end of the 2010s, the contribution of banking and insurance has been roughly equal at around 40 per cent each (Federal Office of Statistics 2022). Meanwhile, the part of other financial intermediaries has become increasingly relevant (around 20 per cent).

2.1 The banking sector

Switzerland has a large banking sector when compared to other jurisdictions with a prominent financial industry. Figure 30.2 shows the relative size of banking systems in selected economies (as of 2016). It is not unusual for banking systems to be larger

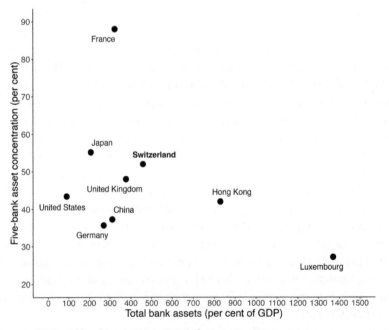

FIGURE 30.2: National banking sectors: size and concentration

Data source: Author's calculations based on data from World Bank (2019) and OECD (2022).

than the economies in which they are embedded. Swiss banks are still especially large, accounting for around five times the size of the national economy (490 per cent in 2020).

The number of banks has continuously declined. Banks have decreased from 375 in 2000 to 320 in 2010 and 243 in 2020 (Swiss National Bank 2022). This consolidation was largely driven by mergers and acquisitions. Figure 30.2 indicates the part of the five largest banks over the total balance sheet across major jurisdictions (2016), a common indicator of market concentration. This metric suggests that the Swiss banking sector is relatively concentrated.[1] In March 2023, the largest bank in the country, UBS, announced the acquisition of Credit Suisse, the second largest bank. This operation was brokered by public authorities to rescue Credit Suisse, which was in financial distress. As of March 2023, the precise details and consequences of the announced takeover remain unknown. Although the takeover is expected to further increase market concentration, it is still too early to assess the impact it will have on the Swiss banking sector.

The international vs. domestic market orientation of banks represents, together with size, a key dimension to understanding the banking landscape in Switzerland. Market orientation refers in this case to both the geographical scope and line of business. While in some cases a substantial part of income comes from Swiss clients, banks with a strong asset and wealth management profile are for the most part oriented towards the international market. In contrast, banks privileging the domestic market compete primarily in the traditional interest business at national, regional, or local levels.

The segmentation of the banking industry in Switzerland can be grasped by the categories retained by official statistics (Swiss National Bank 2022), which have historically relied on size, business focus, geographic scope, and legal structures to distinguish between types of banks. Banks are grouped into (1) big banks, (2) cantonal banks, (3) *Raiffeisen* banks, (4) regional and savings banks, (5) stock-exchange banks, (6) foreign banks, (7) private bankers, and (8) other banking institutions.

Figure 30.3 provides an overview of the size and business profile of the eight different bank categories. When it comes to size, the vertical axis depicts the part of bank categories in the Swiss banking sector according to balance sheets. The business profile of each bank category is captured on the horizontal axis by the importance of interest operations for banks' income. Banks generating a large part of their income from interest operations tend to focus on the domestic lending business. A large part of the Swiss banking sector is based, however, on alternative sources of income. Numerous banks have a more international-oriented business model that privileges income from commission services and trading activities.

Until spring 2023, UBS and Credit Suisse were the two big banks resulting from a series of mergers in the 1990s. These universal banks offered all types of financial services, from investment to retail banking. They combined global activity, particularly prominent in wealth management, with leadership of the domestic market across segments. Both have been designated annually as institutions of global systemic importance (G-SIB) by the Financial Stability Board (2021). Their part in the total balance sheet of the Swiss banking system had progressively increased until reaching a peak before the GFC (69 per cent in 2006). The share of the two big banks has declined since

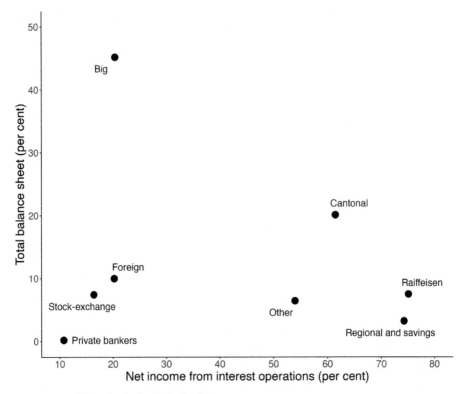

FIGURE 30.3: Diversity in the Swiss banking sector
Data source: Author's calculations based on data from the Swiss National Bank (2022).

then (45 per cent in 2020). UBS took over its rival Credit Suisse in an emergency rescue orchestrated by the Federal Council and regulatory authorities in March 2023 (Morris et al. 2023). Revelations of mismanagement and a series of scandals led to a severe crisis of confidence that pushed Credit Suisse to the brink of collapse.

State-owned banks have played an important role in Switzerland since the nineteenth century. A total of twenty-four cantonal banks are partially or fully owned by the cantonal authorities.[2] Most of their activity takes place within cantonal limits and focuses on retail banking and services for small and medium companies. However, there are considerable differences between institutions in terms of the size and scope of their business activities. The cantonal banks of Zurich and Vaud offer a wide range of services and represent the fourth and fifth largest banks in the country. Cantonal banks also differ when it comes to state guarantees (i.e. none, full, or partial), legal structures (i.e. public law institution or joint-stock company), and share of cantonal ownership (from 50.1 to 100 per cent). The share of the total assets of cantonal banks reached a historical low in 2006 (11 per cent) and has bounced back since then (20 per cent in 2020).

Raiffeisen banks are a network of cooperatives organized under an umbrella organization representing the third largest banking group. These banks have traditionally privileged local development, have a strong presence in rural and semi-urban areas, and have a business profile similar to that of the smaller cantonal banks. Regional and savings banks (fifty-nine in 2020) represent an additional category of small and medium-sized institutions active in the mortgage and saving business and with a narrow geographical focus.

Stock-exchange banks, foreign banks, and private bankers primarily offer asset and wealth management services. Most are predominantly geared towards the international market. Stock-exchange banks (thirty-nine in 2020) tend to cater to both institutional and individual clients; prominent examples include Julius Baer and Pictet. Foreign banks (ninety-four in 2020) include foreign-controlled banks and branches of foreign banks that primarily offer wealth management to offshore private clients. Private bankers (five in 2020) compete in the same business segment. They are simultaneously owners and managers of their institutions, for which they are personally and unlimitedly liable.

Other banking institutions (seventeen as of 2020) include a variety of banks with no common features. The biggest among them is the postal bank *Postfinance*, which is state-owned. This bank, which has a special status, is a major player in the areas of payments and savings.

Five banks have been designated as systemically relevant by the Swiss National Bank (SNB) based on their size, interconnectedness in the financial system, importance for the economy, and substitutability of services in the short-term. Systemically important banks operate under strengthened supervision and supplementary regulatory obligations (e.g. capital requirements, leverage ratios, and risk management). In addition to UBS and Credit Suisse, three banks are of domestic systemic relevance: the Zurich Cantonal Bank (ZKB), *Raiffeisen*, and *Postfinance*.

3 ACTORS

3.1 Public actors

The Federal Department of Finance (FDF) is the ministry in charge of financial markets policy. This includes responsibility for bills the government proposes to parliament as well as the technical regulations (i.e. ordinances) that the latter delegates to the former. The FDF has traditionally been led by federal councillors from centre-right parties.[3]

The State Secretariat for International Financial Matters (SIF) concentrates the expertise of the federal administration on financial regulation. Created within the FDF in 2010, the SIF represents the 'one-stop shop' of the administration for the financial industry and international partners. The SIF is responsible for the elaboration of the regulatory framework and the promotion of the Swiss financial centre. Crucially, the SIF is charged with drafting and revising legislation on behalf of the FDF. The SIF covers banking, financial markets and infrastructure, insurance, and anti-money laundering issues. It also represents Switzerland in bilateral and multilateral negotiations. Taxation topics with an international dimension, such as double taxation agreements and corporate taxation, are also part of its mandate.

The Financial Markets Supervisory Authority (FINMA) is the regulator of the financial industry. It can be considered the gatekeeper of financial markets: it licenses market participants, implements financial regulation, monitors compliance, and enforces supervisory law. FINMA began its operations in 2009 following a major reform of the financial supervisory architecture. The process that led to its creation can be traced back to the early 2000s and was unrelated to the GFC (Gugler 2005).

FINMA is an integrated supervisor with responsibility for individuals and firms active in banking, insurance, and financial markets. FINMA inherited the functions of three predecessors: the Federal Banking Commission (SFBC, established in 1934), tasked with banking and securities supervision; the Federal Office of Private Insurance (FOPI, active since 1881 as the Federal Office of Insurance), in charge of the insurance sector; and the Anti-Money Laundering Control Authority (AMLCA, created in 1998), which focused on anti-money laundering (AML) for non-banking financial intermediaries.

FINMA was conceived with substantial institutional, financial, and operational autonomy from political authorities in accordance with the independent regulatory agency (IRA) model promoted by international organizations (Federal Council 2006; Zulauf and Kuhn 2021, 176–181). FINMA's political independence and managerial autonomy can be considered relatively high when contrasted to those of its predecessors[4] as well as in cross-sectoral and cross-national comparison (Hanretty and Koop 2012, 203; Jordana et al. 2018).

The supervisory board, responsible for FINMA's strategy, is formed by seven to eight part-time members and a full-time chairperson. Experts with an academic or industry background are appointed to this body by the Federal Council. Once appointed, board members lead the agency without receiving orders from other public authorities. The supervisory board delegates the running of the agency's operations to a management board. The management board carries out the strategy defined by the supervisory board and is chaired by a CEO confirmed by the Federal Council. Notably, the supervisory board is not only tasked with management oversight: it approves FINMA's regulations and decides on cases of 'substantial importance'.

The creation of FINMA substantially increased the supervisory competencies and resources on the regulator's side. Regulatory supervision takes place through a 'dual system' (Gugler 2005, 130; Busch 2009, 186–187; Zulauf and Kuhn 2021, 183–185). Before FINMA, the monitoring of compliance by the SFBC was largely indirect and based on reports made by auditing firms paid by the supervised entities. While these external audits are still the basis of supervision, FINMA has gained substantial capacity to carry out direct monitoring, on-site inspections, and investigations on its own. This extension of competencies came with an increase in organizational resources. FINMA is the most important IRA in Switzerland when it comes to resources, with 517 collaborators and a budget of CHF 144 million (2021).[5] The budget is funded through fees and charges levied from supervised entities. The agency has a special status that allows for flexibility in compensation policy to attract staff with industry experience.

FINMA also received an extension of enforcement powers that have been increasingly used (Zulauf and Gava 2019). Except for criminal law, the enforcement of financial regulation is for the most part the task of FINMA. FINMA may sanction supervised entities (i.e. individuals and/or firms) for regulatory breaches. The measures at its disposal include reprimands (i.e. public blames), the restriction or withdrawal of authorizations (e.g. industry bans against individuals), and financial penalties (i.e. disgorgement of illicit gains). In contrast to many of its counterparts in other jurisdictions, FINMA cannot impose fines and only discloses exceptionally the names of sanctioned entities (Gava 2022).

The SNB was founded in 1904 as the country's central bank. In addition to its focus on monetary policy and price stability, the SNB is tasked with the safeguarding of financial stability. This concerns the banking sector and financial infrastructures. When it comes to banking, the SNB is responsible for the soundness of the banking system as a whole through a macroprudential approach. Supervision at the firm level (i.e. microprudential) is the resort of FINMA. In particular, the SNB monitors the banking system, fulfils the role of lender of last resort, and designates the banks of systemic importance. The SNB is also responsible for the oversight of financial market infrastructures (i.e. payment system, securities settlement, and central counterparty) operated by a private firm (SIX Group) owned by banks. The SNB is regularly part of working groups on the elaboration of the regulatory framework at the domestic level and it represents Switzerland in international institutions.

3.2 Interest groups

BIAs representing the industry play an important role in shaping financial regulation in the pre-parliamentary, parliamentary, and implementation phases. These groups mobilize across multiple arenas, seeking to influence policymakers. When lobbying, one of their key assets is technical expertise, which is highly valued by politicians and regulatory authorities. In the context of Swiss financial regulation, BIAs also have a long tradition of participating in the self-regulation of various issues.

The Swiss Bankers' Association (SBA) is, in every aspect, the most important BIA of the financial industry in Switzerland.[6] The vast majority of banks, banking associations, and high-ranked bank professionals come together under this umbrella organization. The SBA's legitimacy stands on its encompassing membership base, which includes almost all banks and thousands of practitioners. The SBA also plays a major role in banking self-regulation with numerous guidelines and recommendations. However, the SBA membership goes beyond banking and includes other types of financial firms and BIAs (e.g. insurance and asset managers). The SBA is therefore generally considered the representative voice of the entire Swiss financial sector (Eichenberger and Mach 2011, 68).

Banking associations that are members of the SBA mirror the segmented nature of the sector. They include the Association of Swiss Cantonal Banks (UBCS), the Association of Foreign Banks in Switzerland (AFBS), the Association of Regional Banks (ABRS), the Association of Swiss Private Banks (ABPS), and the Association of Swiss Asset and Wealth Management Banks (ABG).

Writing before the GFC, Busch (2009, 179) noted that divergences in preferences among different bank categories emerged only occasionally, signalling a 'general consensus on banking policy'. This was not the case in the aftermath of the GFC. In a context of increased competition, reduced margins, and a wave of regulatory initiatives, differences in preferences between banks (e.g. big banks vs. smaller banks; domestic vs. internationally oriented banks) have been frequently publicly voiced (Gava 2014; Eggenberger and Emmenegger 2015). For example, the SBA was openly criticized from within the industry for privileging the position of big banks. Some of these tensions led to the creation of *Inlandbanken*, an association of domestic-oriented banks.[7]

The number and diversity of BIAs widens as non-banking financial intermediaries are taken into consideration. Prominent BIAs with considerable political activity and self-regulatory responsibilities include the Swiss Insurance Association (ASA), the Asset Management Association (AMAS), and the Swiss Association of Wealth Managers (ASG). Groups of non-financial firms but heavily related businesses are also numerous and active in financial regulatory issues. Examples include individuals or firms working in auditing and advisory services (*ExpertSuisse*) or in the fiduciary business (*TreuhandSuisse*). Recent developments, such as the emergence of new financial technologies (FinTech) and the increasing awareness of the role of finance in efforts to combat climate change, have led to the creation of new thematic BIAs (e.g. Swiss Finance and Technology Association and Swiss Sustainable Finance).

Table 30.1 presents a selection of the most important BIAs representing the financial sector. The table combines data from multiple primary sources to portray groups' profile and policy activity. The type of membership hints at a group's organizational resources and scope. The self-regulation column designates groups fulfilling a self-regulatory function recognized by FINMA (e.g. issuing guidelines or recommendations and responsibility for professional self-regulatory organizations). Involvement in policy formulation is indicated through mobilization in consultations and access to policy arenas.

Participation in consultations provides insight into the intensity of BIA's mobilization in the executive and regulatory arenas. However, members of parliament (MPs) are gatekeepers to the parliamentary arena and decide which groups are granted access. Based on different ways that Swiss MPs may give access to groups, Table 30.1 includes a cumulative score of access to the parliamentary arena.

The cumulative score ranges from zero to three and refers to group access during part of the fifty-first legislative term (2019–2022). First, groups gain access when individual MPs agree to occupy leadership positions in interest groups or provide them with access badges to carry out lobbying activities in the parliament building. Second, parliamentary committees may organize hearings when treating bills and invite a restricted number of groups. Third, groups may be trusted with the administration of

Table 30.1: Main BIAs of the Swiss financial sector

Association	Foundation	Self-regulation	Membership Firms	Membership Individuals	Membership BIAs	Consultations 2008–2020 (in per cent)	Parliament Access
Bankers' Association (SBA)	1912	X	253	11 770	10	95	3
Cantonal Banks (UBCS)	1971		24	0	0	55	2
Private Banks (ABPS)	2014		8	0	0	46	2
Asset and Wealth Management Banks (ABG)	1981		23	0	0	36	2
Foreign Banks (AFBS)	1972		86	0	0	32	1
Regional Banks (ABRS)	2018		59	0	0	18	1
Inlandbanken	2013		2	0	2	3	3
Insurance Association (ASA)	1900	X	69	0	0	39	2
Asset Management Association (AMAS)	1992	X	182	0	1	23	2
Wealth Managers (ASG)	1986	X	839	1385	1	36	1
ExpertSuisse	1925	X	996	9814	0	77	2
TreuhandSuisse	1963	X	1833	380	0	17	3

Data source: Author's compilation. Information on foundation and membership compiled from associations' annual reports and websites. Share of participation in consultations based on the manual coding of 135 reports of consultation procedures on laws, ordinances, and circulars between 2008 and 2020. Recognition of self-regulation based on FINMA (2022d). Access to parliament based on various registers (Parliamentary Services 2022a, 2022b, 2022c) and press releases of parliamentary committees (Swiss Parliament 2022).

MPs' cross-party groups in parliament, which promote exchanges between MPs from different parties interested in specific issues. BIAs are given one point for each of the three complementary ways of having privileged access to the parliamentary arena.

As in other countries, non-business groups such as trade unions, consumer, or environmental organizations occasionally mobilize and engage on financial regulatory matters during consultations or parliamentary hearings (Pagliari and Young 2015). One peculiarity is that a few non-governmental organizations (NGOs) have specialized in raising awareness about the negative consequences of certain regulations and practices of the Swiss financial centre for developing countries. Public Eye, founded in 1968 and formerly known as the Bern Declaration, is one of the most active and better resourced among these NGOs. Banks in particular were regularly accused by these NGOs of benefiting from the acceptance of funds from foreign clients that exacerbate capital flight, corruption, and tax evasion in other countries. Finally, activists and public interest groups are increasingly visible on the topic of finance and climate change. By means of protests and public actions, they highlight the role played by financial market participants in investing in businesses responsible for greenhouse gas emissions.

4 REGULATORY FRAMEWORK

The rules that govern the Swiss financial centre are found across three types of regulatory text: laws, ordinances, and circulars. Laws refer to acts of parliament. One level below in the hierarchy of rules, ordinances refer to regulations enacted by the Federal Council or FINMA following a delegation from parliament. They tend to contain technical rules requiring special expertise or frequent updates. Finally, FINMA issues circulars that define how it interprets the law and makes use of its discretion (Zulauf and Kuhn 2021, 19–21).

Narrowly defined, financial services legislation comprises ten financial markets acts designated as such by parliament.[8] Nevertheless, rules targeting or specifically relevant to financial market intermediaries are also present in other laws and ordinances.

Based largely on the scope used by Thévenoz and Zulauf (2022),[9] Figure 30.4 traces the evolution of the stock of financial regulation since the GFC. The left panel focuses on the number of texts while the right panel indicates the corresponding total number of pages at the end of each year. Two points are particularly worth noting. First, a substantial part of policy-making on financial intermediaries and products takes place not in parliament but in the executive and regulatory arenas. Second, the amount of regulation increased considerably in the wave that followed the GFC (Zulauf and Kuhn 2021, 10–12). Growth seems to be particularly important regarding laws and ordinances. The total number of pages expanded from 1,533 pages in 2008 to 2,462 in 2021 (+61 per cent).

New policy proposals usually come from the executive rather than parliament or direct democracy. None of the financial market acts have been challenged by a

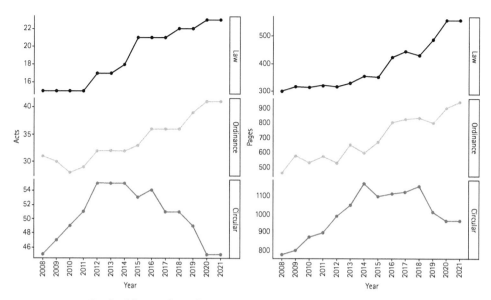

FIGURE 30.4: Stock of financial regulation

Data source: Author's calculations from legislation available at Fedlex (Federal Chancellery 2022) and FINMA (2022a).

referendum. Popular initiatives that specifically target financial regulatory issues have been rare and unsuccessful.[10]

Around three-quarters of voters rejected the two proposals fiercely opposed by the industry and the majority of parliament that made it to the ballot box. First, the Social Democrats launched a popular initiative in the late 1970s as a direct response to revelations about business fraud and activities fostering capital flight at a branch of Credit Suisse, in what became known as the Chiasso scandal (Busch 2009, 190–195; Gava 2014). While most of the attention focused on the proposed relaxation of banking secrecy before tax authorities, the initiative included additional industry restrictions and increased public intervention in the sector. The proposal was eventually defeated with 73 per cent of the popular vote in 1984. Second, the 'Sovereign Money Initiative' aimed to abolishing fractional reserve banking. It was promoted by the Modernizing Money Association, a small group created in the aftermath of the GFC. None of the parties in government supported the initiative, which was also actively opposed by the SNB. The proposal was defeated with 75 per cent of the popular vote in 2018.

Since the 1990s, the impulse for reform has in most cases been a reaction to the development of supranational standards, either at the global or European levels. For example, Switzerland regularly adapts its framework to the soft law of bodies such as the Basel Committee on Banking Supervision (BCBS) on prudential regulation or the Financial Action Task Force (FATF) on anti-money laundering. While Switzerland is not a member of the European Union (EU), changes in EU legislation are a frequent trigger for reforms due to the interconnectedness and importance of this market for the Swiss financial sector.[11]

Once the government decides to proceed with reforms, the federal administration prepares a draft of the new legislation. Before the creation of the SIF in 2010, it was common to entrust this task to ad hoc expert committees with representatives of public authorities, the industry, and academia. The Federal Council eventually proposes a bill to parliament after considering the feedback received during a public consultation.

Financial regulatory issues are treated within parliament by the Economic Affairs and Taxation committees before moving to the plenum. After adoption in parliament, the FDF and FINMA also put the content of eventual new or revised ordinances and circulars to consultation. Ordinances and circulars may be thereafter revised and adapted, if necessary, without further involvement from parliament.

Strong business self-regulation was for a long time considered a distinctive feature of Swiss banking and financial regulation (Busch 2009). While far from its apogee in the twentieth century (Giddey 2019), self-regulation is still alive. In a compilation of legislation and self-regulation relevant for financial market participants, Thévenoz and Zulauf (2022) identified a total of 128 texts from forty-two business organizations.

Business self-regulation is institutionalized (Steinlin and Trampusch 2012a). In particular, two hybrid arrangements mixing private rule-making with FINMA oversight are substantially more important than pure voluntary self-regulation (Zulauf and Kuhn 2021, 186–193). First, FINMA may recognize self-regulation as a minimal standard. Recognized self-regulation is binding and subject to FINMA's supervision and enforcement. As of 2022 FINMA recognizes twenty-two self-regulations, among which are eleven from the SBA and seven from the AMAS. Second, the duty of business organizations to set up self-regulation has been introduced by parliament in areas such as stock exchanges, deposit protection, AML, and independent wealth management. This type of mandatory self-regulation normally requires FINMA approval. In such cases business organizations remain responsible for monitoring and enforcement but can be sanctioned by FINMA for failings.

5 Policy-making since the Global Financial Crisis

The GFC pushed the financial sector into the media and political spotlight in an unprecedented way (Gava 2016). To illustrate the explosion in the media coverage of financial regulatory issues, Figure 30.5 traces references in the press to three key actors: FINMA, SBA, and SIF. The increase in issue saliency that came with the GFC radically and temporarily changed the context in which policy-making took place, moving many financial regulation issues from 'quiet' into 'noisy' politics.

In the case of Switzerland, two particular developments in 2008 shaped debates and contributed to keeping financial regulation among political and media priorities. First, the state had to bail out UBS, Switzerland's biggest bank. This came as a result of massive

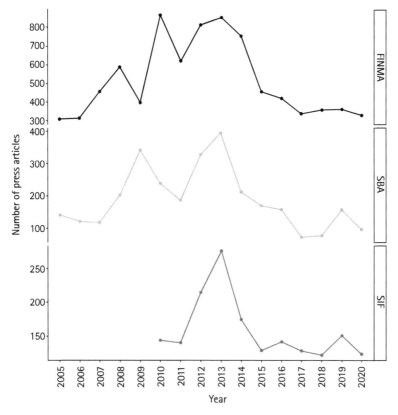

FIGURE 30.5: Media coverage to actors of Swiss financial regulation

Data source: Author's calculations based on Factiva searches. The print and online versions of three quality newspapers are considered (*Neue Zürcher Zeitung*, *Tages Anzeiger*, and *Le Temps*). References to FINMA include articles mentioning its predecessors (SFBC, FOPI, and AMLCA).

losses in the American sub-prime market (Steinlin and Trampusch 2012a, 154–156; Mach et al. 2021, 33–34). The programme, orchestrated by the SNB, required a total of CHF 60 billion. Second, continuous revelations of abusive practices and increasing international pressure led to lifting the, until then, sacrosanct banking secrecy for tax matters. In the context of the GFC, these two developments significantly damaged the reputation of the entire industry.

The most dramatic and resisted policy change of the period was the lifting of Swiss banking secrecy before tax authorities. The possibility of hiding assets from foreign tax authorities had long represented a comparative advantage for Switzerland as an offshore centre specialized in wealth management. Switzerland moved from denying foreign tax authorities access to clients' bank information, using a cumbersome administrative procedure, to automatically sharing these data. This radical policy transformation took place between 2008 and 2015 under extraordinary international pressure (Steinlin and Trampusch 2012b, 2012a; Emmenegger 2014, 2015, 2017; Gava 2014; Eggenberger and Emmenegger 2015).

While the origins of the GFC had little to do with tax havens, the erosion of banking secrecy quickly became one of the priorities of the newly created G20. This was due to a large extent to revelations of massive tax evasion by US residents facilitated by UBS. US criminal proceedings threatened the survival of UBS, which as a bank is dependent on access to the US market (Emmenegger 2015; Verdier 2020). With the largest Swiss bank brought to the brink of collapse and with looming sanctions from OECD partners, the government changed a policy that it had fiercely defended for almost eighty years. The government reluctantly began to erode banking secrecy through a series of incremental concessions from 2009. The breaches opened up by the US were capitalized on by other European states eager to access Swiss bank records to fight against tax evasion. Multilateral cooperation on tax matters accelerated over a short period of time and more demanding international standards became the norm (Emmenegger 2017). The government, centre-right parties, and the banks invested heavily in alternatives to avoid what they considered as the worst possible outcome: the automatic exchange of information. These efforts ultimately failed in late 2012 due to lack of international support. From that point on, it became clear that the automatic exchange of information could not be avoided for a small and open economy like Switzerland. It would eventually be adopted by parliament in 2015.

The lifting of banking secrecy attracted most of the attention and resources in the post-GFC period. Nevertheless, the wave of reforms concerned numerous regulatory issues and the entire sector.[12] The noisy environment around financial regulation became common in the parliamentary arena and the wave of reforms triggered by the GFC was characterized by unprecedented parliamentary conflict and scrutiny. The broad support that government bills used to attract went down as their number went up. Many salient votes dealt with the successive legal changes that eroded banking secrecy for tax matters. However, policy processes such as those focusing on too-big-to-fail banks, investor protection, or adaptations to international AML standards were also contested.

In another indication of the noisy politics surrounding debates on financial regulation, conflict often materialized in the lack of support given to bills from the pole parties of the government coalition: the Swiss People's Party on the conservative right and the Social Democrats on the left. Both parties are known to simultaneously play the double role of government and opposition in Swiss politics when dealing with salient issues. Conflict over bills was particularly observable in the National Council, which is traditionally less consensual that the Council of States, partly due to a stronger presence of the pole parties in government. On many occasions, the Social Democrats found that the reforms did not go far enough in terms of regulatory restrictions. By contrast, the Swiss People's Party blamed the imposition and uncritical adoption of rules from abroad for damaging the competitiveness of (particularly smaller) market participants.

Discrepancies within the centre-right and between the centre-right and representatives of the financial industry became more visible following the GFC. Figure 30.6 compares voting recommendations on financial regulation issued by the SBA before parliamentary sessions and the subsequent voting behaviour of parliamentary groups. There is a congruence between the SBA and parties when a majority of MPs of a given

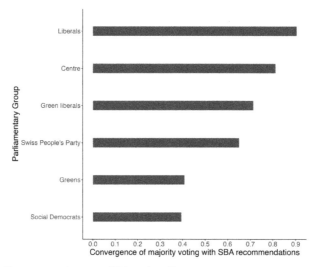

FIGURE 30.6: Congruence between SBA and parliamentary groups, 2017–2021

Data source: Author's calculations based on SBA newsletters and data from Parliamentary Services (2022d). Mean for thirty-six parliamentary proposals dealing with financial regulation based on 132 voting recommendations issued by the SBA. Recommendations on all types of parliamentary votes (e.g. postulates, motions, bill amendments, entire bills) issued for the National Council between the winter sessions of 2017 and 2021 are considered.

group vote in line with the SBA recommendations.[13] Figure 30.6 shows a mean ranging between zero and one. Low values indicate disagreement between parties and the SBA, whereas values closer to one indicate that parties tend to vote in accordance with the SBA preferences.

Figure 30.6 covers a period (2017–2021) during which most of the controversies and reforms of financial regulation triggered by the GFC were already settled. While highly frequent, the alignment of centre-right parties of the government coalition with the SBA is not to be taken for granted. The disagreement between the centre-right parties with traditional ties to the industry is still observable. MPs from the Liberals and Centre remained most of the time aligned with the SBA. By contrast, MPs from the Swiss People's Party followed the SBA recommendations considerably less frequently. The main representative of the financial industry has sometimes failed to secure the support of the largest party of the centre-right government coalition. On certain occasions, the numerous BIAs representing the diverse Swiss financial sector may thus still fail to engage with a single voice before MPs.

6 CONCLUSION

Since the GFC, the financial industry has evolved in a more challenging political environment. While remaining significant in international comparison, the prominence of the banking sector and its big banks has been declining. The whole industry was put into the spotlight and suffered a loss of reputation in the eyes of the public and policymakers. The GFC opened a window of opportunity for reforms that would have been unimaginable before. Many of these policy changes originated or were imposed from abroad, making them harder for the industry to resist.

With the creation of FINMA, the industry also emerged from the GFC facing a more resourceful and determined regulator. Business unity seems to have become harder to obtain and to signal. Market participants from different segments or with contrasting business models do not hesitate to show disagreement before policymakers or to invest resources to have their own specific voices heard.

The financial industry as a whole, or banks in particular, may not be as powerful as they used to be in the recent past and have certainly lost important policy battles. The sector nevertheless retains powerful political actors with vast resources and access to shape their regulatory environment. This capacity will continue to be put to the test as financial regulation remains on political agendas. On the one hand, a new wave of issues, such as sustainable finance and the regulation of Fintech innovations, will likely lead to novel regulatory responses. On the other hand, the government involvement to rescue the too-big-to-fail Credit Suisse in March 2023 resulted in the creation of an even bigger UBS. This major event is set to reignite debates on banking regulation that had gradually subsided since the GFC.

Notes

1. Note that the size of balance sheets is only part of the story when assessing the size of banking institutions. For example, assets under management are not reported in balance sheets. This item is of particular importance in the Swiss context due to the numerous banks specialized in the asset and wealth management business. Data on assets under management are unfortunately difficult to obtain for a large number of banks.
2. Only two cantons no longer have cantonal banks: Appenzell Ausserrhoden (sold to UBS in 1998) and Solothurn (privatized in 1995).
3. Except for the periods 1944–1954 and 1980–1995 during which the FDF was under the Social Democrats.
4. Note that in contrast to the FOPI and AMLCA, the SFBC had a higher level of autonomy from government (Hirszowicz 2003, 245–253; Gugler 2005, 132; Busch 2009, 185–186). The few comparative empirical assessments available of the real independence from both politicians and regulatees have analysed the SFBC and not FINMA (Maggetti 2007, 2012, 75). In particular, they found that the SFBC combined a relatively high independence from politicians with a low independence from industry (Maggetti et al. 2011, 214–215; Maggetti 2014, 286–287).
5. FINMA started operations in 2009 with 333 collaborators. The SFBC had a staff of ninety in 2000 and 161 in 2007.
6. In a tradition that hints at the associations' importance and prestige, a federal councillor traditionally gives a keynote speech every September in the SBA-organized Bankers Day.

7. *Inlandbanken* regroups the cantonal banks (UBCS) and the regional and savings banks (ABRS) as well as Raiffeisen and Migros Bank. Raiffeisen is the only member of Inlandbanken having left the SBA (in 2021).
8. These are defined in the Financial Market Supervision Act (2007) and include the Mortgage Bond Act (1930), Act on Contracts of Insurance (1908), Collective Investment Schemes Act (2006), Banking Act (1934), Financial Institutions Act (2018), Anti-Money Laundering Act (1997), Insurance Supervision Act (2004), Financial Market Infrastructure Act (2015), and the Financial Services Act (2018).
9. Their definition includes for example the National Bank Act (2003), the Federal Act on Intermediary Securities (2008), and the Consumer Credit Act (2001).
10. Note that the financial sector has nevertheless been concerned and mobilized by popular votes dealing with issues affecting multiple industries or the general business environment.
11. One prominent example from the post-GFC period is regulation on investor protection, which was substantially changed following the Markets in Financial Instruments Directive (MiFID).
12. In a comprehensive assessment of the scope of post-crisis banking reforms among OECD countries, Young and Park (2013) ranked Switzerland among the top countries with substantial changes.
13. For a similar approach to identify voting coalitions between parties see Traber (2015, 707–708).

References

Boston Consulting Group. 2022. *Global Wealth 2022.* https://www.bcg.com/publications/2022/standing-still-not-an-option. (accessed 1 October 2022).

Busch, Andreas. 2009. *Banking Regulation and Globalization.* Oxford/New York: Oxford University Press.

Chalmers, Adam William. 2020. 'Unity and Conflict: Explaining Financial Industry Lobbying Success in European Union Public Consultations'. *Regulation & Governance* 14: pp. 391–408. doi:10.1111/rego.12231.

Culpepper, Pepper D. 2011. *Quiet Politics and Business Power.* Cambridge/New York: Cambridge University Press. doi:10.1017/cbo9780511760716.

Culpepper, Pepper D. 2015. 'Structural Power and Political Science in the Post-Crisis Era'. *Business and Politics* 17 (3): pp. 391–409. doi:10.1515/bap-2015-0031.

Eggenberger, Katrin, and Patrick Emmenegger. 2015. 'Economic Vulnerability and Political Responses to International Pressure: Liechtenstein, Switzerland and the Struggle for Banking Secrecy'. *Swiss Political Science Review* 21 (4): pp. 491–507. doi:10.1111/spsr.12181.

Eichenberger, Pierre, and André Mach. 2011. 'Organized Capital and Coordinated Market Economy: Swiss Business Interest Associations between socio-economic regulation and political influence'. In *Switzerland in Europe. Continuity and Change in the Swiss Political Economy*, edited by Christine Trampusch, and André Mach, pp. 63–81. London: Routledge.

Emmenegger, Patrick. 2014. 'The Politics of Financial Intransparency: The Case of Swiss Banking Secrecy'. *Swiss Political Science Review* 20 (1): pp. 146–164. doi:10.1111/spsr.12092.

Emmenegger, Patrick. 2015. 'The Long Arm of Justice: U.S. Structural Power and International Banking'. *Business and Politics* 17 (3): pp. 473–493. doi:10.1515/bap-2014-0046.

Emmenegger, Patrick. 2017. 'Swiss Banking Secrecy and the Problem of International Cooperation in Tax Matters: A Nut Too Hard to Crack?'. *Regulation & Governance* 11 (1): pp. 24–40. doi:10.1111/rego.12106.

Federal Chancellery. 2022. *Fedlex*. https://www.fedlex.admin.ch (accessed 1 October 2022).

Federal Council. 2006. *Message concernant la loi fédérale sur l'Autorité fédérale de surveillance des marchés financiers*. https://www.fedlex.admin.ch/eli/fga/2006/303/fr (accessed 1 October 2022).

Federal Office of Statistics. 2017. 'Analyse du secteur financier au sein des comptes nationaux suisses', *Actualités OFS*, (1731–1700) https://www.bfs.admin.ch/bfsstatic/dam/assets/4946614/master (accessed 1 October 2022).

Federal Office of Statistics. 2022. *Comptes nationaux*. https://www.bfs.admin.ch/bfs/fr/home/statistiques/economie-nationale/comptes-nationaux.html (accessed 1 October 2022).

Financial Stability Board. 2021. 'List of Global Systemically Important banks (G-SIBs)'. https://www.fsb.org/wp-content/uploads/P231121.pdf (accessed 1 October 2022).

FINMA. 2022a. *Insurance Market Report 2021*. https://www.finma.ch/en/~/media/finma/dokumente/dokumentencenter/myfinma/finma-publikationen/versicherungsbericht/20220909-versicherungsmarktbericht-2021.pdf (accessed 1 October 2022).

FINMA. 2022b. *List of Authorised Fund Management Companies, Managers of Collective Assets and Representatives of Foreign Collective Investment Schemes*. https://www.finma.ch/~/media/finma/dokumente/bewilligungstraeger/pdf/flvervt.pdf (accessed 1 October 2022).

FINMA. 2022c. *List of Portfolio Managers and Trustees Licensed by FINMA and Monitored by a Supervisory Organisation*. https://www.finma.ch/~/media/finma/dokumente/bewilligungstraeger/pdf/vvtr.pdf (accessed 1 October 2022).

FINMA. 2022d. *Autorégulations*. https://www.finma.ch/fr/documentation/autoregulation/anerkannte-selbstregulierung/ (accessed 1 October 2022).

Gava, Roy. 2014. *Trusting Bankers: Continuity and Change in Swiss Banking Policy*. PhD thesis. Faculty of Economic and Social Sciences, University of Geneva.

Gava, Roy. 2016. 'Financial Regulation and Agenda Dynamics: Impacts of the Global Financial Crisis'. In *Handbook of Public Policy Agenda Setting*, edited by Nikolaos Zahariadis, pp. 433–456. Cheltenham: Edward Elgar.

Gava, Roy. 2022. 'Challenging the Regulators: Enforcement and Appeals in Financial Regulation'. *Regulation & Governance* 16 (4): pp. 1265–1282. doi:10.1111/rego.12405.

Giddey, Thibaud. 2019. *Histoire de la régulation des banques en Suisse (1914-1972)*. Genève: Droz.

Gugler, Philippe. 2005. 'The Integrated Supervision of Financial Markets: The Case of Switzerland'. *The Geneva Papers on Risk and Insurance – Issues and Practice* 30 (1): pp. 128–143. doi:10.1057/palgrave.gpp.2510001.

Hanretty, Chris, and Christel Koop. 2012. 'Shall the law Set Them Free? The Formal and Actual Independence of Regulatory Agencies'. *Regulation & Governance* 7 (2): pp. 195–214. doi:10.1111/j.1748-5991.2012.01156.x.

Hirszowicz, Christine. 2003. *Schweizerische Bankpolitik*. Bern: Haupt.

Jordana, Jacint, Xavier Fernández-i-Marin, and Andrea C. Bianculli. 2018. 'Agency Proliferation and the Globalization of the Regulatory State: Introducing a Data Set on the Institutional Features of Regulatory Agencies'. *Regulation & Governance* 12 (4): pp. 524–540. doi:10.1111/rego.12189.

Mach, André, Thomas David, Stéphanie Ginalski, and Felix Bühlmann. 2021. 'From Quiet to Noisy Politics: Transformations of Swiss Business Elites' Power'. *Politics & Society* 49 (1): pp. 17–41. doi:10.1177/0032329220985693.

Maggetti, Martino. 2007. 'De facto Independence After Delegation: A Fuzzy-Set Analysis'. *Regulation & Governance* 1 (4): pp. 271–294. doi:10.1111/j.1748-5991.2007.00023.x.

Maggetti, Martino. 2012. *Regulation in Practice. The de facto Independence of Regulatory Agencies.* Colchester: ECPR Press.

Maggetti, Martino. 2014. 'Institutional Change and the Evolution of the Regulatory State: Evidence from the Swiss Case'. *International Review of Administrative Sciences* 80 (2): pp. 276–297. doi:10.1177/0020852313514517.

Maggetti, Martino, Alexandre Afonso, and Marie-Christine Fontana. 2011. 'The More It Changes, the More It Stays the Same? Swiss Liberalization and Regulatory Policies in Comparative Perspective'. In *Switzerland in Europe: Continuity and Change in the Swiss Political Economy*, edited by Christine Trampusch, and André Mach, pp. 205–223. London: Routledge.

Morris, Stephen, James Fontanella-Khan, and Arash Massoudi. 2023. 'How the Swiss 'Trinity' Forced UBS to Save Credit Suisse'. *Financial Times*. https://www.ft.com/content/3080d368-d5aa-4125-a210-714e37087017 (accessed 24 March 2023).

OECD. 2022. *OECD.stat*. https://stats.oecd.org/ (accessed 1 October 2022).

Pagliari, Stefano, and Kevin L. Young. 2015. 'The Interest Ecology of Financial Regulation: Interest Group Plurality in the Design of Financial Regulatory Policies'. *Socio-Economic Review* 14 (2): pp. 309–337. doi:10.1093/ser/mwv024.

Parliamentary Services. 2022a. *Registre des accrédités*. https://www.parlament.ch/centers/documents/de/zutrittsberechtigte-nr.pdf (accessed 1 October 2022).

Parliamentary Services. 2022b. *Registre des intérêts*. https://www.parlament.ch/fr/über-das-parlament/portrait-du-parlement/deputes/statut-juridique-des-deputes/obligation-de-signaler-les-interets (accessed 1 October 2022).

Parliamentary Services. 2022c. *Registre: Intergroupes parlementaires*. https://www.parlament.ch/centers/documents/de/gruppen-der-bundesversammlung.pdf (accessed 1 October 2022).

Parliamentary Services. 2022d. 'Open Data / Services Web'. https://www.parlament.ch/fr/über-das-parlament/faits-donnees-chifrees/open-data-web-services (accessed 1 October 2022).

Steinlin, Simon, and Christine Trampusch. 2012a. 'Increasing Vulnerability: Financial Market Regulation in Switzerland'. In *Crisis and Control: Institutional Change in Financial Market Regulation*, edited by Renate Mayntz, pp. 143–170. Frankfurt: Campus.

Steinlin, Simon, and Christine Trampusch. 2012b. 'Institutional Shrinkage: the Deviant Case of Swiss Banking Secrecy'. *Regulation & Governance* 6 (2): pp. 242–259. doi:10.1111/j.1748-5991.2012.01128.x.

Swiss National Bank. 2022. *Statistique bancaire annuelle*. https://data.snb.ch/fr/publishingSet/BIDS (accessed 1 October 2022).

Swiss Parliament. 2022. *Rechercher dans les actualités*. https://www.parlament.ch/fr/services/suche-news (accessed 1 October 2022).

Thévenoz, Luc, and Urs Zulauf. 2022. *BF 2022: Réglementation et autoréglementation des marchés finaciers en Suisse*. Geneva: Centre de droit bancaire et financier.

Traber, Denise. 2015. 'Disenchanted Swiss Parliament? Electoral Strategies and Coalition Formation'. *Swiss Political Science Review* 21 (4): pp. 702–723. doi:10.1111/spsr.12185.

Verdier, Pierre-Hugues. 2020. *Global Banks on Trial*. New York; London: Oxford University Press. doi:10.1093/oso/9780190675776.001.0001.

World Bank. 2019. *Bank Regulation and Supervision Survey*. https://datacatalog.worldbank.org/search/dataset/0038632 (accessed 1 October 2022).

World Bank. 2022. *Market Capitalization of Listed Domestic Companies.* https://data.worldbank.org/indicator/CM.MKT.LCAP.GD.ZS (accessed 1 October 2022).

World Federation of Exchanges. 2022. *Statistics Portal.* https://statistics.world-exchanges.org/ (accessed 1 October 2022).

Young, Kevin L., and Sung Ho Park. 2013. 'Regulatory Opportunism: Cross-National Patterns in National Banking Regulatory Responses following the Global Financial Crisis'. *Public Administration* 91 (3): pp. 561–581. doi:10.1111/j.1467-9299.2012.02102.x.

Zulauf, Urs, and Roy Gava. 2019. 'FINMA's Enforcement in Court. An Empirical and Legal Assessment of the Court Rulings Regarding the Swiss Financial Markets Supervisory Authority's Financial Regulation Enforcement'. *Swiss Review of Business and Financial Market Law* 19 (2): pp. 99–113.

Zulauf, Urs, and Hans Kuhn. 2021. *Finanzmarktrecht.* Zürich/St. Gallen: Dike.

CHAPTER 31

INFRASTRUCTURE POLICY
Transport and energy

FRITZ SAGER AND DAVID KAUFMANN

1 DEFINITION

THE term 'infrastructure' denotes the material basis needed for the operation of a society and economy to enable connectivity, communication, and exchange (Frey 1985, 201; Graham and Marvin 2001).[1] Infrastructure comprises physical and technical structures and facilities, such as transport networks and power supplies. Infrastructure policy refers to the provision, maintenance, and regulation of these services and facilities. The construction and maintenance of infrastructure is often protracted, complicated, and expensive (Flyvbjerg 2007) and defines the landscape for decades. This underlines the high importance and immediacy of infrastructure policy.

The term 'infrastructure' has only been used since the 1960s in the above mentioned sense and has not been conclusively defined. Basically, there are two definitions of infrastructure that are relevant to political science: firstly, the term in a material sense denotes 'that part of a national economy (...) that forms the physical basis for actual economic activity' (physical infrastructure) (Frey 1985, 201), while secondly, in a broader definition, it also includes the institutional and human-resource basis for any economic activity (intangible infrastructure) (Joachimsen 1966). Whereas the latter understanding seeks to cover the political system as a whole, the first definition proves more analytically helpful for a policy analysis, in that infrastructure is understood not as a systemic feature of the state but as something that the state provides.

There is no unanimity in the literature about infrastructure sectors and categories. What is undisputed is simply that transport and energy are part of the infrastructure sector. In this chapter, we discuss the transport and energy infrastructure sectors. Environmental protection and spatial planning are sometimes also considered as being part of infrastructure policy, yet both fields have established themselves as their own policy fields (see 'Environmental and Spatial Planning Policies' in this volume), though they have important interdependencies with transport and energy infrastructure policy.

We first present the transport and then the energy infrastructure policy sector. The two main parts of this chapter are structured as follows. In a first section, the general developments in Switzerland in the given policy field are considered, and the fundamental problems that this policy branch is intended to solve are identified (sections 2.1 and 3.1). The second section provides a summary of the development and state of the Swiss legislation (sections 2.2 and 3.2). In the third section, the key actors are portrayed (sections 2.3 and 3.3). The fourth section considers the implementation structures and briefly goes into the extent to which policy has been implemented and its effects (sections 2.4 and 3.4). The final part of the chapter considers the two policy fields in the light of current social challenges (section 4).

2 Transport policy

Transport is basically moving people, goods, and information from one location to another. Transport takes place on roads, railways, and waterways, and in the air, involving a variety of carriers in each case, and is offered and used as both a public and private service.

2.1 Starting position and challenges

In 2015, 89 per cent of the population over the age of six participated in some form of transport every day. In 2018, a total of 21 billion passenger kilometres were travelled by rail and 102 billion passenger kilometres by road. By comparison, in 2018, in France about 108 billion passenger kilometres were travelled by rail and 859 billion passenger kilometres by road, while in Germany 98 billion passenger kilometres were travelled by rail and 979 billion passenger kilometres by road (OECD 2022). In 2015, the average person in Switzerland travelled for ninety minutes each day, covering 36.8 km in Switzerland. That year a person thus covered 13,755 km in Switzerland and a further 11,095 km abroad. The largest portion was made up of travel for leisure purposes, comprising 44 per cent of the kilometres covered in Switzerland. Some distance behind in second place came travel to work with 24 per cent and in third place came travel to go shopping with 13 per cent. By far the most popular means of transport is the car: it is used to travel around 65 of every 100 kilometres covered—in contrast, only just under 24 km are travelled using public transport. The typical Swiss resident travels an average of two kilometres a day by bicycle and one kilometre less by motorbike. In total, the Swiss road network covers 71,555 km, while the rail network is 5,177 km in length with 1750 stations (FSO 2017, 2019a). Unsurprisingly, these values are higher for the large neighbouring countries Germany and France. In Germany, the rail network covers a total of around

67,000 km and in France around 28,000 km. The road network for instance in France comprises a total of 1.1 million km in 2018 (OECD 2022). The density of the rail network and road networks is shown in Figures 31.1 and 31.2 for the countries of the Organisation for Economic Co-operation and Development (OECD). In 2018, the rail network in Switzerland had a density of around 10.2 km per hundred square kilometres. In France,

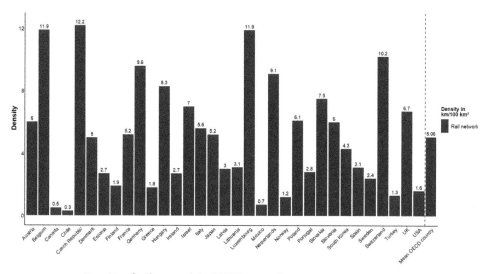

FIGURE 31.1: Density of rail network in OECD countries

Missing Countries: Australia, Colombia, Costa Rica, Iceland, and New Zealand.

Source: OECD (2022).

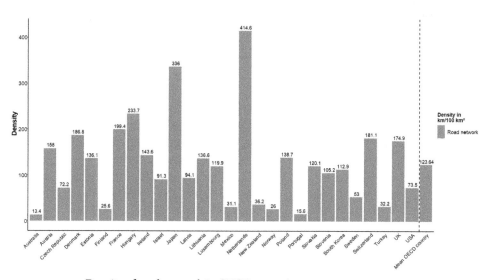

FIGURE 31.2: Density of road network in OECD countries

Missing Countries: Belgium, Canada, Chile, Colombia, Costa Rica, Germany, Greece, Iceland, Italy, and Spain.

Data source: OECD (2022).

this value was 5.2 km and in Germany 9.6 km per hundred square kilometres. In terms of the density of the road network, in 2018, Switzerland had a density of about 181 km per hundred square kilometres. France was slightly above with 199.4 km per hundred square kilometres and Austria below with 158 km of road network per hundred square kilometres (OECD 2022). Comparing network densities, the expansion of the rail network and road network in Switzerland is similar to that of neighbouring countries.

Mobility has experienced a marked rise in significance in Swiss society in recent decades. Goods transport between 1960 and 2018 grew from around 6.5 billion to 27.9 billion tonne-kilometres a year. In passenger transport, movements have almost quintupled over the same period: while in 1960 in Switzerland, a total of 28.5 billion passenger kilometres travelled by road and rail, the number in 2018 was 135.7 billion passenger kilometres. Figure 31.3 shows the distribution of passenger kilometres in Switzerland among the various means of transport and how the situation has changed in the last fifty years. Figure 31.4 presents the shares of rail and road passengers in the total share of all passengers for the year 2018 in OECD countries. In Switzerland, the share of rail passenger transport was about 16.5 per cent and the share of road passenger transport was about 83.5 per cent. In France, the share of rail passenger transport was around 11.2 per cent and the share of road passenger transport around 88.8 per cent. In Germany, the share of rail passenger transport was even lower at 9.1 per cent and the share of road passenger transport correspondingly higher at 90.9 per cent. The share of rail passenger transport in Italy was lower still at only 6.3 per cent, while the share of road passenger transport was 93.7 per cent (OECD 2022). The share of rail passenger transport in Switzerland is therefore relatively high.

Even taking population growth into account, transport traffic has continually increased in recent years. This has been accompanied by a shift in the shares of the individual means of transport in the traffic volume (a 'modal split'). In passenger transport (in passenger kilometres), the share of the railways has fallen from 30 per cent to 20 per cent. In goods transport, rail companies saw a decline in tonne-kilometres between 1960 and 2018 from just under 67 per cent to 37 per cent of the Swiss total. This trend is also reflected in transalpine goods traffic, where the share transported by rail, when measured in tonnes, fell from 93 per cent (1980) to around 70 per cent (2018). On the road, the volume of traffic increased between 1990 and 2017 by 34 per cent. The kilometres covered on national highways in the same period more than doubled (+223 per cent), which means that a large part of the increase in motorized private transport is accounted for by the national highways (FEDRO 2018). This increase in motorized private transport has an above average effect on major urban areas such as Basel, Bern, and Zurich (FEDRO 2019). The growing volume of traffic leads to increasing congestion in the transport system and has negative economic consequences. For example, in 2018, a total of 25,366 hours of congestion were recorded, of which 22,110 alone were due to road traffic congestion (FSO 2019b). It is estimated that the cost of congestion in 2015 amounted to CHF 1.89 billion, which corresponds to 0.3 per cent of GDP. Between 2010 and 2015 alone, congestion costs rose by around 7 per cent (ARE 2019).

INFRASTRUCTURE POLICY   589

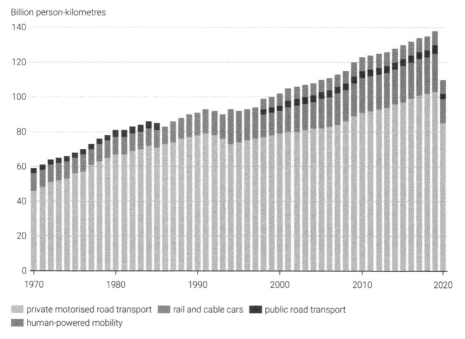

FIGURE 31.3: Movements in Swiss passenger transport, 1970–2018

Data source: Federal Statistical Office (FSO 2021).

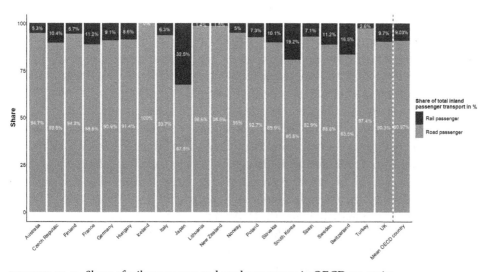

FIGURE 31.4: Share of rail passengers and road passengers in OECD countries

Missing Countries: Austria, Belgium, Canada, Chile, Colombia, Costa Rica, Denmark, Estonia, Greece, Ireland, Israel, Latvia, Luxembourg, Mexico, Netherlands, Portugal, Slovenia, and USA.

Data source: OECD (2022).

Transport policy encompasses numerous fields of activity. These can be grouped as follows: first, road traffic for persons and goods; second, public overland transport, including national and international passenger transport, goods transport, and rail infrastructure; third, shipping; and fourth, civil aviation. The subsequent presentation follows this order, while other carriers such as cableways and funicular railways are not considered. Shipping and civil aviation are not discussed separately.

2.2 Developments leading to the current legislation

Until the 1970s, transport policy was structured in sectors. The two main areas of legislation related to road construction and the railways.

Road construction was characterized in the post-war years by faith in planning and economic growth, reflected in articles 36 and 37 of the constitution, adopted in 1958, and in the Federal Decree on the National Road Network (the 'Network Decree') of 1960,[2] which have formed the basis for the construction of national highways to this day. The roads are funded primarily through the tax levied on motor fuel, which, because of being tied to this purpose, has in fact become the 'driving force for building roads' (Merki 1994, 322).

The railway system has been the responsibility of the federal government since 1874 (art. 8 of the federal constitution 1874). The railways are run by Swiss Federal Railways (SBB) and by the private rail companies that form part of the general transport system.

In 1978, a commission appointed by the Federal Council submitted a report on achieving improved coordination between the various transport sectors. The resultant constitutional basis for a coordinated transport policy (CTP) was, however, rejected by the people and cantons in a popular vote in 1988. Despite this, the CTP may be regarded as the starting point for current transport policy. Many of its ideas, such as stricter environmental protection and improved cooperation between the Confederation and cantons (Federal Council 1988), have become part of the current transport policy.

In the area of road transport, two new transport taxes introduced in 1984, the motorway vignette (a flat tax of CHF 40) and the heavy goods vehicle tax, consolidated the spirit of the CTP by strengthening the polluter-pays principle. Heavy goods transport underwent particular changes in the course of European integration. In 1994, both the continuation of the flat-rate heavy goods vehicle charge and the constitutional basis for the introduction of a new mileage-related heavy goods vehicle charge (HGVC)[3] met with clear approval at the ballot box. The HGVC has been levied since 2001 and has been increased several times since. The HGVC has made it possible to stabilize the volume of heavy goods traffic crossing the Alps, which had been rising sharply since the 1980s (DEA 2019). With the Alpine Initiative adopted in 1994, the people and the cantons obliged the Confederation to shift all transalpine freight traffic from border to border from road to rail (art. 84 of the federal constitution). Under this pressure, elements of the HGVC and an Alpine transit tax were included in the national transport dossier for the bilateral negotiations with the EU in December 1998. In 1999, Switzerland ratified the

Alpine Convention, an international treaty between the Alpine countries, signing the related transport protocol the following year. In 2016, voters approved a revision of the Federal Act on Road Transit Traffic in the Alpine Region, paving the way for the construction of a second road tunnel at the Gotthard. Finally, the National Highways and Agglomeration Traffic Fund (NAF), which was approved by the people and the cantons, was created in 2017 to ensure the long-term financing of the national road network. This open-ended fund is intended to help cope with the steadily increasing volume of traffic, especially in cities and urban areas. In addition, the construction of the second Gotthard tube will also be financed from it. The NAF itself is financed in part by the mineral oil tax surcharge and the motorway vignette as well as a levy on e-vehicles. The Strategic Development Programme for National Highways, adopted by parliament in 2019, is an important steering instrument in the road sector at federal level. This provides for the gradual expansion of motorway sections at particularly congested locations—especially in urban areas—in the period to 2040.

In the area of public overland transport, a large-scale expansion of rail network capacity was approved in 1987 with the adoption of the Rail 2000 Strategy,[4] which had become increasingly needed since the introduction of the clock-face scheduling in 1981. The Federal Decree on the Construction of the New Transalpine Rail Link (NRLA)[5] was introduced in 1992 and with it the construction of the three new base tunnels, Lötschberg, Gotthard, and Ceneri, as the new Swiss north–south transit axis was adopted. The NRLA represents the largest infrastructure project in Swiss history to date. With the adoption of the Federal Decree on the Construction and Financing of Public Transport Infrastructure Projects in 1998, the financial basis for the NRLA and other major rail projects was secured. With the strategy for the future development of the railway infrastructure and the associated federal act,[6] parliament established a successor programme for Rail 2000 in 2009. One year later, the Goods Traffic Transfer Act[7] came into force. It formulates specific shift targets to fulfil the Alpine protection article. To guarantee the efficiency of the railway system in the long term, the decree on financing and expanding the railway infrastructure (FABI[8]) was drawn up. Approved by the people and the cantons in 2014, FABI includes the open-ended Rail Infrastructure Fund (RIF), which aims to secure the long-term financing of the entire rail infrastructure. FABI also includes the Strategic Rail Infrastructure Development Programme. This provides for the gradual expansion of the railway infrastructure network. Expansion Phase 2025 was adopted in 2014 and provides CHF 6.4 billion in funding for the expansion of capacity at major railway hubs such as Geneva, Bern, and Basel. Expansion Phase 2035 was approved by parliament in 2019 and earmarks CHF 12.89 billion for investments in the expansion of the railway infrastructure by 2035. Both phases will be financed by the RIF.

2.3 Actors

Numerous actors have an influence over the design, construction, and development of transport infrastructure in Switzerland. Coordination and intermediation between these actors is often a major challenge. At a national level, the Federal Department of the Environment, Transport, Energy, and Communications (DETEC) is the government department responsible for transport policy—a task borne by several of its offices. The Federal Roads Office (FEDRO) has oversight over the construction, maintenance, and operation of the national highways. Public transport and the transport of freight by rail fall within the remit of the Federal Office of Transport (FOT). Among the FOT's responsibilities are the maintenance and expansion of the rail network, and it supervises, coordinates, and manages the implementation of major railway expansion projects. In addition, it is the supervisory authority for public transport, which includes not only the railways, buses, and ships but also cableways. To improve transport coordination and spatial planning, the Federal Office for Spatial Development (ARE) was established in the year 2000 as the federal government's specialist centre for all matters relating to spatial development, mobility policy, and sustainable development. ARE devises basic concepts and plans and coordinates projects that involve both spatial planning and transport. The Federal Office of Civil Aviation oversees aircraft, airfields, and the airspace. The Federal Office for the Environment (FOEN) is also important to transport policy, as it is responsible for noise protection and air pollution control.

At the cantonal level, the departments of economic affairs are usually responsible for public transport and the building departments for road construction and spatial planning. Transport safety and security aspects are usually covered by the cantonal police departments.

The transport companies are important players in transport policy. In the rail sector, the SBB is the most important provider of transport services, but great importance is also attached to the so-called 'private railways' that form part of the general transport system, the majority of which, despite their name, are publicly owned. The most important interest group is the Public Transport Union, which represents the interests of the railways at a political level. In the roads sector, the interests of freight transport carriers are represented by the Swiss Road Transport Association (ASTAG). Since 2020, the industry organization Alliance SwissPass has also represented transport companies and transport associations.

The interests of motorists are represented by the Touring Club of Switzerland (TCS) and the Automobile Club of Switzerland (ACS), which have joined forces with ASTAG to form the Road Transport Federation as an umbrella organization. The Swiss Association for Transport and the Environment is another representative of interests in the road sector. It focuses on environmental and climate policy issues in transport.

Practically all the Swiss political parties have a keen interest in transport policy. At a parliamentary level, the Transport and Telecommunications Committees of the National Council and Council of States play an important role in shaping Swiss transport policy.

Finally, the actors at a European level play a significant role in Swiss transport policy, particularly the EU Commission, the transport ministries of neighbouring countries, the Conference of European Ministers of Transport, and interest groups, such as the

International Road Transport Union, the International Union of Railways, Community of European Railway and Infrastructure Companies, and the environmental umbrella organization Transport & Environment, which are well connected to their Swiss counterparts.

2.4 Implementation structures, current status, and impact

When compared with other policy areas, the federal government has relatively far-reaching competences in transport policy in that it is responsible for constructing railway infrastructure and for the supervision of the railways. Today, one-third of the maintenance, modernization, and expansion of the railway infrastructure is financed by the track access charges that the railway companies have to pay to the federal government for using the rail network. The remaining two-thirds are covered by the federal government through the RIF.

Construction of the NRLA began in 2000. The Lötschberg Base Tunnel came into operation in 2007. The Gotthard Base Tunnel—the longest railway tunnel in Europe at 57 km—was completed in 2016. The NRLA, Switzerland's project of the century, was completed in 2020 when the Ceneri Base Tunnel came into service. NRLA, HGVC, and other railway reforms have helped to shift transalpine traffic from road to rail (Federal Council 2019, 6). The number of transalpine truck journeys has fallen from 1.4 million in 2000 to around 940,000 in 2019 (FOT 2019, 4). Nevertheless, the target of a maximum of 650,000 journeys per year set out in the Goods Traffic Transfer Act has yet to be achieved (Federal Council 2019, 5–6).

In the road sector, the federal government, cantons, and communes share responsibilities. The cantons are solely responsible for the main road network and receive lump sums from the federal treasury to finance this task. The federal government is solely responsible for the construction, operation, and maintenance of the national highway network and finances these roads entirely from federal funds (except for the cost of completing the current network). In 2018, the national highway network comprised 1858.9 km. Historically a joint task, the completion of the national highway network is the responsibility of the cantons, in which work is being carried out, while the federal government has oversight and bears most of the costs via the NAF.

3 ENERGY POLICY

As a country with few natural resources, the issue of energy supply is an important one in Switzerland. Gross energy consumption has increased exponentially since the 1950s, generating an enormous demand for more efficient and new energy sources.

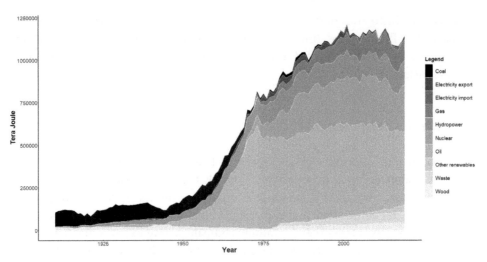

FIGURE 31.5: Gross energy consumption 1910–2019 (SFOE 2019a)

Data for energy from waste was collected for the first time in 1978. The data collection methodology for energy from wood changed in 1990. The category 'Other renewables' includes sun, wind, natural gas, biogenic fuel, and environmental heat. This data was collected for the first time in 1990.

Data source: SFOE (2019a).

3.1 Starting position and challenges

Over the last thirty years, the overall energy consumption of the resident population has increased by only 5 per cent, despite population growth of 27 per cent (see Figure 31.5). This development is due to increasing energy efficiency, which has led to a decrease in energy consumption per person of 18 per cent (FSO 2020). The energy price surges resulting from the two oil price crises of 1973 and 1979 highlighted Switzerland's dependence on imported resources for energy production. Currently, 75 per cent of energy resources are imported (FSO 2020). In addition, Switzerland's energy policy is shaped by general international conditions, especially those that apply in the European Union.

In the longer term, dependence on fossil fuels from abroad, the reduction of CO_2 emissions, ecological awareness, and thus the fight against global warming will shape Swiss energy policy and the accompanying discussions on encouraging the use of independent, efficient, and renewable energy sources.

3.2 Development of the current legislation

The Confederation remained in the background of Swiss energy policy until the 1970s; energy legislation consisted essentially of the Federal Act on Electrical Weak and Heavy Current Installations[9] and the Federal Act on the Use of Hydraulic Power.[10] The federal government's tasks were limited to oversight and safety regulations, and the electricity industry and the cantons enjoyed a great deal of freedom. Only in the nuclear sector did the federal government take the lead from the outset and had certain powers based on the Atomic Energy Act (1959). Overall, however, the federal government lacked the constitutional basis to pursue a coordinated energy policy.

In the wake of the oil crisis, efforts were increased to find alternatives to fossil fuels. The electricity industry promoted nuclear power, which initially met with general acceptance (Jegen 2003, 76). Switzerland built five nuclear power plants by the end of the 1960s. However, after permission to build a new nuclear power plant was granted in 1969, opposition to nuclear power began to form.

The reactor accident at Chernobyl in 1986 gave new impetus to Swiss energy policy. In 1987, two more anti-nuclear popular initiatives (a moratorium and a phase-out) were submitted, and in 1989, the federal government finally decided not to build a new power plant after all. The year 1990 was a landmark for Swiss energy policy. The electorate simultaneously adopted the energy article and the moratorium initiative. This meant that no new building permits for nuclear power plants could be issued for the next ten years.

Since the turn of the millennium, the core of Swiss energy policy has essentially consisted of the Nuclear Energy Act, the CO_2 Act, the Electricity Supply Act, and the Energy Act. The revisions made to these four acts reflect the strategic orientation of Swiss energy policy.

First, the Nuclear Energy Act (NEA) has the aim to regulate the peaceful use of nuclear energy. As early as the 1990s, ecological sustainability and the question of radioactive waste disposal were the focus of the political debate. The storage of radioactive waste met with great resistance in the communities where the federal government had carried out exploratory work. The NEA made the construction of new nuclear facilities subject to an optional referendum and created a new option for appeals to a court that was independent of the administration. The new NEA was passed by parliament in March 2003. To solve the hitherto unresolved problem of radioactive waste disposal, the Deep Geological Repositories Sectoral Plan was adopted in 2008, which formed the basis for a transparent and clearly regulated selection procedure (SFOE 2021a).

Second, the fundamental goal of the CO_2 Act is to reduce CO_2 emissions. The CO_2 Act remains the centrepiece of Swiss climate policy to this day (Ingold 2008, 70). After Switzerland committed itself to reducing six greenhouse gases (mainly CO_2) by 8 per cent by signing the Kyoto Protocol in 1997, parliament passed the two-stage CO_2 Act[11] in 1999 (see 'Environmental and Spatial Planning Policies' in this volume). The aim of this first CO_2 Act was to reduce CO_2 emissions by 10 per cent compared to 1990 levels by 2010, with emissions from the use of fossil fuels for energy being reduced by 15 per cent and those from fossil fuels by 8 per cent. The CO_2 Act provides for the introduction of a CO_2 incentive tax, but only as a subsidiary measure if voluntary measures failed to achieve the reduction targets. Since it soon became apparent that the targets would not be met, in 2005, the Federal Council submitted a CO_2 ordinance[12] to parliament, seeking to introduce a levy on fossil fuels of CHF 35 per tonne of CO_2. The amendment of the Mineral Oil Tax Act[13] has lowered the tax on natural, liquid, and biogas used as fuel but increased the tax on petrol. This is intended to increase the demand for environmentally friendly fuels and thus reduce CO_2 emissions.

At the beginning of 2014, the Federal Office for the Environment (FOEN) announced that Switzerland had not only achieved the CO_2 reduction targets that were set by the Kyoto Protocol and the first CO_2 Act but had slightly exceeded them (FOEN 2014). In a second commitment period under the Kyoto Protocol, from 2013–2020, a totally revised CO_2 Act[14] came into force at the beginning of 2013, defining new targets and measures. It provided for a reduction in greenhouse gas emissions of 20 per cent by 2020 compared to 1990, which was primarily to be achieved domestically. In the measures required, the Confederation relied on continuity: the CO_2 incentive tax was set at CHF 37 per tonne and could be increased to up to CHF 120 if necessary; the Emissions Trading Scheme was further expanded and made more comprehensive; the buildings programme introduced in 2010 was continued and given more financial support. The incentive tax was gradually increased due to insufficient emission reductions and currently amounts to CHF 96 per tonne of CO_2 (as of 2018).

According to the latest figures from the FOEN (as of 2020), the current indications are that the target values will not be achieved. In 2017, Switzerland also ratified the Paris Climate Agreement and thus undertook to halve its greenhouse gas emissions by 2030 (compared to 1990 levels). Reacting to new scientific findings and widespread climate change demonstrations, the Federal Council, in August 2019, additionally announced 'net zero emissions' by 2050 as a new climate target.

Third, the Electricity Supply Act (ESA) aims to regulate the prerequisites for a secure electricity supply and for a competitive electricity market. After the bill for an Electricity Market Act, and thus the gradual opening of the Swiss electricity market, failed to pass a referendum in 2002, the liberalization of the electricity market did not take place until 2007 within the framework of the first ESA.[15] The introduction of the ESA also led to the amendment of the Energy Act (EnA) in 2009, introducing feed-in remuneration at cost for renewable energies. As a consequence, grid operators were required to accept electricity from solar power, wind energy, biomass, or geothermal energy produced in new plants at cost-covering prices.

Fourth, the Swiss Federal Office of Energy (SFOE) published a synthesis report entitled 'Energy Perspectives 2035' in 2007 (SFOE 2007). Due to the expiry of operating licences for some nuclear power plants and of electricity supply contracts from 2018 onwards, it is apparent from all scenarios that, without an expansion of capacities, electricity supply will no longer be able to meet demand. With the prospect of electricity shortages, the construction of gas-fired combined cycle power plants has once again become a topic in the debate about the form and scope of electricity production. However, these power plants emit relatively large amounts of CO_2, which would create a conflict of objectives between CO_2 reduction and energy supply security (SFOE 2021b).

Based on Energy Perspectives 2035, the Federal Council adopted its energy strategy in 2007 (SFOE 2021b). This was based on the following four pillars: energy efficiency, renewable energies, large-scale power plants (gas-fired combined cycle power plants as a transitional solution and the replacement of existing nuclear power plants or construction of new plants), and foreign energy policy. The strategic goals were specified in two action plans. The 'Renewable Energies' action plan envisaged increasing the share of renewable energies in total energy consumption by 50 per cent by 2020. The 'Energy Efficiency' action plan aimed to reduce the consumption of fossil energy by 20 per cent by 2020.

However, following the reactor catastrophe at Fukushima in 2011, the Federal Council decided to phase out nuclear energy. Energy Strategy 2050 has the overriding goal of ensuring the most autonomous and secure electricity supply possible. The four priorities are: reducing energy consumption, increasing energy efficiency, promoting renewable energies, and banning the construction of new nuclear power plants. This energy strategy has far-reaching consequences for Switzerland's energy policy and its legislation. As part of the first package of measures, parliament decided in 2016 on the total revision of the EnA.[16] In a referendum on 21 May 2017, the electorate approved the new EnA, which came into force in January 2018. The new EnA comprises seventy-six articles and thus introduces many new regulations and has a knock-on effect for other acts and ordinances, which will have to be amended in the near future.

Further packages of measures are planned for coming years. However, Swiss voters rejected the total revision of the existing CO_2 Act[17] in June 2021, which brought the political debate on the reduction of greenhouse gas emissions back to square one. A new revision of the ESA, which aims to fully open the electricity market and thus improve the integration of decentrally produced electricity, is currently being planned by DETEC. The Russian invasion of Ukraine in February 2022 and the consequences for the supply of fossil fuels from Russia has relaunched the debate about nuclear energy and national energy independence beyond the climate change debate.

3.3 Actors

The most important actors in Swiss energy policy can be divided into three groups: the federal government, the energy industry, and the environmental organizations. The SFOE is the central actor at federal level. It is responsible for drafting and implementing energy policy laws and programmes and deals with energy industry and technical issues. The FOEN is responsible for water protection, accident prevention, air quality, and overseeing CO_2 policy. Since energy is a key issue for both domestic and foreign trade, the State Secretariat for Economic Affairs (SECO) is also involved in energy policy. Finally, it is the task of the Federal Office for National Economic Supply to ensure that the population is supplied with energy in times of crisis. At the cantonal level, the relevant offices ensure that the federal legislation is implemented and are also responsible for cantonal promotion programmes within the framework of the national policy programme EnergieSchweiz.

The National Co-operative for the Disposal of Radioactive Waste was founded in 1972 by the nuclear power plant companies and the federal government with the joint mandate to prepare for and carry out the disposal of all categories of radioactive waste. The international conventions on nuclear safety require an independent supervisory authority in the field of nuclear safety. Based on the Federal Nuclear Safety Inspectorate

Act, the Swiss Federal Nuclear Safety Inspectorate[18] commenced its activities at the beginning of 2009.

The energy industry is organized around the various energy sources. The numerous companies in the fragmented electricity sector are intertwined horizontally and vertically through countless shareholdings. These include large interconnected utilities—such as Alpiq Holding AG, BKW Energie AG, and Axpo Holding AG (known as NOK until 2009), which cover all areas from production to distribution—as well as around thirty cantonal and around 900 commune-specific utilities.

The major customers from industry represent their interests mainly through the Interest Group for Energy Intensive Industries. Until now, the most influential representatives of nuclear energy interests have included the 'Campaign for Sensible Energy Policy Switzerland' (AVES), established in 1979, and the Swiss Nuclear Forum. However, because of international reactor accidents, they visibly lost influence and in 2018, the umbrella organization AVES was dissolved. The interests of fossil energy companies are represented at a political level by the Swiss Petroleum Association. Companies in the natural gas industry have joined forces to form the Swiss Gas Industry Association. In the field of renewable energies, there are various smaller associations for almost every single energy source such as the Swiss Solar Energy Society and Geothermal Energy Switzerland. The umbrella organization for the renewable energy and energy efficiency industry (AEE Suisse) represents the interests of thirty-two industry associations and 15,000 companies and energy providers in the renewable energy and energy efficiency sectors.

The third group of actors comprises various environmental organizations. Especially in the 1970s, numerous local groups emerged to oppose nuclear power plant construction and mobilize the general public. The Swiss Energy Foundation, which was involved in all the anti-nuclear initiatives, also came into being at this time. In addition, there are several other actors such as WWF, Greenpeace, Pro Natura, and many other regional or issue-specific organizations.

3.4 Implementation structures, current status, and impact

The energy article in the federal constitution describes the enforcement structures of Swiss energy policy as follows: 'Within the scope of their powers, the Confederation and the cantons shall endeavour to ensure a sufficient, diverse, safe, economic, and environmentally sustainable energy supply as well as the economical and efficient consumption of energy' (art. 89 para. 1 of the federal constitution).

The implementation of energy policy in Switzerland is strongly influenced by federalism. The Federal Council has oversight and thus monitors the basic thrust, political goals, and the energy policy dialogue. The advisory steering body is a strategy group composed of representatives of the Confederation, cantons, business, and environmental associations. The Confederation draws up framework laws and programmes and, for example, issues requirements for the energy consumption of appliances and systems. However, their implementation is mainly the responsibility of the cantons. The cantons are primarily responsible for legislation and enforcement in the buildings sector. In addition, they are responsible for promotion programmes under the EnA. The communes also play an important role in enforcing the cantonal and federal laws. Various tasks have been transferred to private organizations partly founded by business associations to promote alternative energies in industry.

The impact of the programmes and measures is diverse and influenced by other factors in addition to energy policy. The SFOE is actively evaluating its programmes. The reactor disaster in Fukushima has significantly changed Switzerland's energy policy (Fischer 2015). The policy reorientation within the framework of the Energy Strategy 2050 and the EnergieSchweiz promotion programme have contributed significantly to the progressive change in energy production structures. For example, electricity production from renewable energy sources has more than tripled since 2010 (SFOE 2019a). Overall, renewable energies now cover around 25 per cent of energy consumption. The debate on renewable energies received new momentum when Russia invaded Ukraine in February 2022 and Russian gas supplies became a major international bone of contention.

4 Prospects for Swiss Infrastructure Policy

Infrastructure policy is characterized by long planning horizons, complex technologies, and the involvement of different actors with diverging interests in decision-making processes and implementation (Flyvbjerg 2007, 579). Due to these characteristics, infrastructure projects tend to have performance shortfalls and cost overruns. Forward-looking infrastructure planning is therefore crucial, but future developments are difficult to anticipate and subject to great uncertainties.

Nevertheless, politicians and authorities must plan infrastructure expansion and maintenance for the long term. In terms of future scenarios, Swiss authorities, like their counterparts worldwide, are often guided by emerging global transformations such as climate change, population growth, urbanization, or digitalization. The departmental strategy of DETEC, for example, describes three overarching challenges for Switzerland's infrastructure policy: reduction of energy and resource consumption, coordination of transport and spatial development, and digitalization (DETEC 2016). Similarly, the Swiss Federal Office of Energy (SFOE) defines urbanization, digitalization, and climate protection as cross-cutting issues of high relevance for all energy planning (SFOE 2019b). Thus, these global transformations lie at the heart of the problems that the infrastructure policy has to address.

These global transformations are often interdependent. In transport planning, a substantial increase in volumes of traffic is forecast by 2040 because of population and economic growth (DETEC 2017). Traffic congestion is accentuated in densely populated urban areas, which is why the coordination of transport and spatial planning is particularly necessary for managing urban traffic (Sager 2002, 29). Traffic management measures, for example by means of mobility pricing, are therefore well suited for urban areas (Chevreuil 2014), but the political acceptance of mobility pricing in Switzerland is very low (Wicki et al. 2020). The growth in traffic, which nevertheless continues, is to be largely cushioned by the expansion of resource-saving transport options. The electrification of the transport sector, for example, as well as a reduction in the volume of traffic, is necessary to fight climate change (Creutzig et al. 2015). The decarbonization of transport is also in line with the general thrust of current energy policy worldwide. In addition, digitalization is expected to encourage the interconnection of intermodal and resource-efficient transport options into integrated mobility services (Canzler and Knie 2016; Guidon et al. 2020).

In the long term, Swiss energy policy will be shaped by the transformation to more sustainable energy sources, the reduction of CO_2 emissions, and the decision to phase out nuclear energy. The need to move in this direction became ever clearer with the Russian invasion of Ukraine in 2022, which suddenly made energy independence a major priority. The political management of the energy consequences of the Russian war in Ukraine has only started and was ongoing at the time of writing (August 2022). As in transport policy, these changes will have to be implemented in the face of a steadily increasing demand for energy due to population growth and higher individual energy consumption. In contrast to transport policy, however, this demand can be compensated a little more easily with efficiency gains through technological innovations (Schmidt and Sewerin 2017).

This brief discussion of the prospects for Swiss infrastructure policy suggests that careful consideration should be given to the way in which these global changes are dependent on each other. These global trends and transformations will be most clearly visible in their speed, intensity, and relentlessness in dense urban areas (Kaufmann and Sidney 2020). Innovative policy measures, such as climate-positive infrastructure projects or experimentation with car-free neighbourhoods, are therefore often developed and implemented in urban areas. The search for appropriate policy measures for such transformation processes should not only focus on technological and evidence-based solutions; it is also important to explore the acceptance, feasibility, and evaluation of infrastructure policies (Sager et al. 2020). Often, (local) resistance to changes to and developments in infrastructure arises (Wicki and Kaufmann 2022), which in Switzerland can lead to the termination of infrastructure projects using direct-democratic instruments.

Given that Swiss infrastructure policy is strongly influenced by the ongoing changes around the globe, many policy developments and debates related to Swiss infrastructure policy can be compared with those in other countries, especially democratic countries that have highly developed infrastructure systems integrated into dense settlement structures and that also experience high population and economic growth rates. Maybe the most important future topic in Swiss infrastructure policy will be balancing environmental and social sustainability, such as realizing ambitious environmental goals, while not amplifying social inequalities. The increasing scarcity of land and other resources and the urgent need to slow down climate change will likely make debates and negotiations on infrastructure policy more important and salient as well as potentially more conflict-ridden.

Notes

1. The authors would like to thank Deborah Fritzsche, Mala Walz, Leroy Ramseier, and Fiona Kauer for their support in writing this chapter and Kenneth R. MacKenzie for the translation from German.
2. Federal Decree of 21 June 1960 on the National Highways Network, SR 725.113.11.
3. Federal Act of 19 December 1997 on a Mileage-related Heavy Goods Vehicle Charge (Heavy Goods Vehicle Charge Act, HVCA), SR 641.81.
4. Federal Act of 19 December 1986 on the Rail 2000 Strategy, SR 742.100.
5. Federal Decree of 4 October 1991 on the Construction of the Swiss Transalpine Rail Link, SR 742.104.
6. Federal Act of 20 March 2009 on the Future Development of Railways Infrastructure, SR 742.140.2.
7. Federal Act of 19 December 2008 on the Transfer of Transalpine Heavy Goods Traffic from Road to Rail, SR 740.1.
8. Memorandum of 18 January 2012 on the popular initiative 'For public transport' and on the direct counter-proposal, SR 12.016.
9. Federal Act of 24 June 1902 on Low and High Voltage Electrical Installations, ElecA, SR 734.0.
10. Federal Act of 22 December 1916 on the Use of Hydraulic Power, Water Rights Act, WRA, SR 721.80.
11. Federal Act of 8 October 1999 on the Reduction of CO_2 Emissions, SR 641.71.
12. Ordinance of 8 June 2007 on the CO_2 levy, CO_2 Ordinance, SR 641.712.
13. Mineral Oil Tax Act of 21 June 1996, MinOTA, SR 641.61.
14. Federal Act of 23 December 2011 on the Reduction of CO_2 emissions, SR 641.71.
15. Federal Act of 23 March 2007 on the Supply of Electricity, ESA, SR 734.7.
16. Energy Act of 30 September 2016, EnA, SR 730.0.
17. Federal Act on the Reduction of Greenhouse Gas Emissions (CO_2 Act) (draft).
18. Federal Act of 22 June 2007on the Swiss Federal Nuclear Safety Inspectorate, ENSIA, SR 732.2.

References

ARE (Federal Office for Spatial Development). 2019. *Staukosten Schweiz 2015 – Schlussbericht*. Bern.
Canzler, Weert, and Andreas Knie. 2016. 'Mobility in the Age of Digital Modernity: Why the Private Car is Losing Its Significance, Intermodal Transport is Winning and Why Digitalisation is the Key'. *Applied Mobilities* 1 (1): pp. 56–67.
Chevreuil, Martial. 2014. 'Tolling, Mobility Pricing'. In *Encyclopedia of Automotive Engineering*, edited by David Crolla, David E. Foster, Toshio Kobayashi, and Nicholas Vaughan. Chichester: John Wiley & Sons, Ltd. https://doi.org/10.1002/9781118354179.auto185

Creutzig, Felix, Patrick Jochem, Oreane Y. Edelenbosch, Linus Mattauch, Detlef P. van Vuuren, David McCollum, and Jan Minx. 2015. 'Transport: A Roadblock to Climate Change Mitigation?'. *Science* 350 (6263): pp. 911–912.

DEA (Directorate for European Affairs). 2019. *Landverkehr*. Bern.

DETEC (Federal Department of the Environment, Transport, Energy, and Communications). 2016. *Departementsstrategie UVEK 2016*. Bern.

DETEC (Federal Department of the Environment, Transport, Energy, and Communications). 2017. *Zukunft Mobilität Schweiz: UVEK-Orientierungsrahmen 2040. UVEK 2017*. Bern.

Federal Council. 1988. *Volksabstimmung vom 12. Juni 1988. Erläuterungen des Bundesrates*. Bern.

Federal Council. 2019. *Bericht des Bundesrats. Bericht über die Verkehrsverlagerung vom November 2019. Verlagerungsbericht Juli 2017 – Juni 2019*. Bern.

FEDRO (Federal Roads Office). 2018. *Verkehrsentwicklung und Verfügbarkeit der Nationalstrassen. Jahresbericht 2018*. Bern.

FEDRO (Federal Roads Office). 2019. *Strassen und Verkehr 2019 - Entwicklungen, Zahlen, Fakten: Jährliche Publikation des Bundesamtes für Strassen*. Bern.

Fischer, Manuel. 2015. 'Collaboration Patterns, External Shocks and Uncertainty: Swiss Nuclear Energy Politics before and after Fukushima'. *Energy Policy* 86: pp. 520–528.

Flyvbjerg, Bent. 2007. 'Policy and Planning for Large-Infrastructure Projects: Problems, Causes, Cures'. *Environment and Planning B: Planning and Design* 34 (4): pp. 578–597.

FOEN (Federal Office for the Environment). 2014. *Faktenblatt 1. Schweizer Kyoto-Bilanz 2008 bis 2012*. Bern.

FOT (Federal Office of Transport). 2019. *Schweizer Verkehrspolitik von A bis Z*. Bern.

Frey, René L. 1985. 'Infrastruktur'. In *Handwörterbuch der Wirtschaftswissenschaft*, edited by Willi Albers, Karl Erich Born, Ernst Dürr, Helmut Hesse, Alfons Kraft, Heinz Lampert, Klaus Rose, Hans-Heinrich Rupp, Harald Scherf, Kurt Schmidt, and Waldemar Wittmann, pp. 200–215. 4th ed. Stuttgart/New York: Fischer, Mohr, Vandenbeck & Ruprecht.

FSO (Federal Statistical Office). 2017. *Verkehrsverhalten der Bevölkerung 2015*. Neuchâtel.

FSO (Federal Statistical Office). 2019a. *Leistungen im Personenverkehr*. https://www.bfs.admin.ch/bfs/de/home/statistiken/mobilitaet-verkehr/personenverkehr/leistungen.html (accessed 23 May 2022).

FSO (Federal Statistical Office). 2019b. *Stau*. https://www.bfs.admin.ch/bfs/de/home/statistiken/mobilitaet-verkehr/verkehrsinfrastruktur-fahrzeuge/schweiz-strassenverkehrszaehlung/stau.html (accessed 23 May 2022).

FSO (Federal Statistical Office). 2020. *Energie: Panorama 2020*. https://www.bfs.admin.ch/bfs/de/home/statistiken/energie.assetdetail.13695300.html (accessed 23 May 2022).

FSO (Federal Statistical Office). 2021. *Passenger Transport Performance*. https://www.bfs.admin.ch/bfs/en/home/statistics/mobility-transport/passenger-transport/performance.assetdetail.19904746.html (accessed 31 October 2022).

Graham, Stephen, and Simon Marvin. 2001. *Splintering Urbanism: Networked Infrastructure*. London: Routledge.

Guidon, Sergio, Michael Wicki, Thomas Bernauer, and Kay Axhausen. 2020. 'Transportation Service Bundling – For Whose Benefit? Consumer Valuation of Pure Bundling in the Passenger Transportation Market'. *Transportation Research Part A: Policy and Practice* 131: pp. 91–106.

Ingold, Karin. 2008. *Analyse des mécanismes de décision: Le cas de la politique climatique suisse*. Zürich/Chur: Rüegger Verlag.

Jegen, Maya. 2003. *Energiepolitische Vernetzung in der Schweiz: Analyse der Kooperationsnetzwerke und Ideensysteme der energiepolitischen Entscheidungsträger*. Basel: Helbing und Lichtenhahn.

Joachimsen, Reimut. 1966. *Theorie der Infrastruktur. Grundlagen der marktwirtschaftlichen Entwicklung*. Tübingen: Mohr.

Kaufmann, David, and Mara Sidney. 2020. 'Toward an Urban Policy Analysis: Incorporating Participation, Multilevel Governance, and "Seeing Like a City"'. *Political Science & Politics* 53 (1): pp. 1–5.

Merki, Christoph Maria. 1994. 'Der Treibstoffzoll aus historischer Sicht: Von der Finanzquelle des Bundes zum Motor des Strassenbaus'. In *Das 1950er Syndrom. Der Weg in die Konsumgesellschaft*, edited by Christian Pfister, pp. 311–332. Bern: Haupt.

OECD. 2022. *ITF Transport Statistics*. https://www.oecd-ilibrary.org/transport/data/itf-transport-statistics_trsprt-data-en (accessed 28 June 2022).

Sager, Fritz. 2002. *Vom Verwalten des urbanen Raums. Institutionelle Bedingungen von Politikkoordination am Beispiel der Raum- und Verkehrsplanung in städtischen Gebieten*. Bern: Haupt.

Sager, Fritz, Céline Mavrot, Markus Hinterleitner, David Kaufmann, Martin Grosjean, and Thomas F. Stocker. 2020. 'Utilization-Focused Scientific Policy Advice: A Six-Point Checklist'. *Climate Policy* 20 (10): pp. 1336–1343.

Schmidt, Tobias, and Sebastian Sewerin. 2017. 'Technology as a Driver of Climate and Energy Politics'. *Nature Energy* 2 (6): pp. 1–8.

SFOE (Swiss Federal Office of Energy). 2007. *Die Energieperspektiven 2035 – Band 1 Synthese*. Bern.

SFOE (Swiss Federal Office of Energy). 2019a. *Swiss General Energy Statistics 2019*. Bern.

SFOE (Swiss Federal Office of Energy). 2019b. *Programmstrategie EnergieSchweiz 2021 bis 2030*. Bern.

SFOE (Swiss Federal Office of Energy). 2021a. *Sachplan geologische Tiefenlager*. https://www.bfe.admin.ch/bfe/en/home/supply/nuclear-energy/radioactive-waste/deep-geological-repositories-sectoral-plan.html (accessed 23 May 2022).

SFOE (Swiss Federal Office of Energy). 2021b. *Energiestrategie 2050*. https://www.bfe.admin.ch/bfe/en/home/policy/energy-strategy-2050.html (accessed 23 May 2022).

Wicki, Michael, Robert Alexander Huber, and Thomas Bernauer. 2020. 'Can Policy-Packaging Increase Public Support for Costly Policies? Insights from a Choice Experiment on Policies Against Vehicle Emissions'. *Journal of Public Policy* 40 (4): pp. 599–625.

Wicki, Michael, and David Kaufmann. 2022. 'Accepting and Resisting Densification: The Importance of Project-Related Factors and the Contextualizing Role of Neighbourhoods'. *Landscape and Urban Planning* 220 (104350): pp. 1–11.

CHAPTER 32

EDUCATION POLICY

ANJA GIUDICI AND PATRICK EMMENEGGER

1 INTRODUCTION

THE institutionalization and enforcement of compulsory schooling in the mid-nineteenth century transformed formal education into a powerful instrument to mould society in Switzerland and across the world. In the twentieth century, like other countries, Switzerland expanded compulsory education for up to sixteen and sometimes eighteen year olds. Kindergarten, early childhood education, after-school programmes, adult education, and lifelong learning policies further increased the presence of formal education in individuals' lives. They also extended its social and political relevance. Since World War II, education has grown to become a core public policy task. For parties, education constitutes 'the archetypal crowd-pleaser' (Ansell 2010, 136). Among the public, education spending is highly popular (Busemeyer et al. 2020), despite education systems already requisitioning significant shares of public funds.

Education policy serves different aims. Following Fend (2008), we distinguish three historically dominant aims: skill production, redistribution, and enculturation. Generating the skills needed for the industrial age was a major motive behind the institutionalization of modern education in the nineteenth century (Gellner 1983; Green 2013). Skill formation has not lost its importance as an educational goal, as evidenced by current discussions on education's role in upskilling populations for the knowledge economy (Iversen and Soskice 2019; Carstensen and Emmenegger 2023). Rhetorically, this goal is particularly present in Switzerland. As the leading economic think tank, Avenir Suisse, put it: 'A well-educated population is a must in a country like Switzerland that is poor in raw materials' (Schellenbauer 2012).

The production of skills as a collective good, however, comes with strong redistributive implications. On the one hand, education reform affects the status and career perspectives of a large body of professionals, from teachers to administrators, to experts, and to textbook producers. On the other hand, it also shapes the opportunities of the population at large. Less stratified education systems (Van de Werfhorst and Mijs 2010), as well as systems that prioritize primary and state-led schooling (Ansell 2010), produce more redistribution than systems characterized by early tracking and investments in schools with higher upper-class representation. And educational redistribution does not only matter for class disparities as testified by discussions on affirmative action and single-sex schooling. Parties' distributive preferences vary accordingly (Ansell 2010; Gingrich 2011; Giudici et al. 2023).

Finally, education is also a means for enculturation. Education systems have long served as the key means to transform localized populations into unified 'nation-states' (Weber 1976). The educational marginalization (or worse) of cultural minorities has always been a source of conflict. Increased recognition of liberal and cultural rights since World War II has further fuelled the question of whose values and cultures education systems should convey to the next generations (Giudici 2019; Gutmann 1999). Struggles fought first on battlefields, and now in parliaments and in school boards, touch on fundamental cultural issues: should schools convey religious or political views, and if yes, whose views should be given institutional representation? Should children of different genders or ethnicities receive the same education?

The economic, redistributive, and cultural character of education puts governance and decision-making at the centre of education politics. In liberal societies, these dimensions are bound to be controversial. Since no consensus can arise on the content and structure of education, the establishment of legitimate decision-making procedures and power distribution becomes crucial (Gutmann 1999).

Switzerland is a case in point. No educational issue has been more contested since the establishment of the Swiss federal state in 1848 than the distribution of authority, vertically, between the different levels of the political system (municipalities, cantons, Confederation), and horizontally, between educational stakeholders (public authorities, teachers, churches, schools, employers' organizations, experts, and parents). These discussions have shaped the peculiar blend of federalism and centralization that characterizes Swiss education policy to date—a blend that differs substantially between different parts of the education system, particularly between vocational and general education.

This chapter first offers a comparative characterization of Swiss education (see section 2 in this chapter). Building on this analytical description, we show that the different orientations of vocational and general education—with the former being oriented primarily towards upskilling, and the latter being perceived more in redistributive and enculturation terms—have produced distinctive cleavages and coalitions, thus leading to different developments in terms of governance (see section 3 in this chapter), institutional reconfigurations (see section 4 in this chapter), and future challenges (see section 5 in this chapter).

2 AIMS AND CHARACTERISTIC FEATURES

Contemporary education systems stem from three pre-modern institutions: elite schooling, common schooling, and vocational training (Criblez et al. 1998; Green 2013).

In agrarian states, these were parallel systems characterized by specific tasks, governance, and target groups. Eighteenth century Swiss territories had comparatively well-developed common schooling systems, organized by churches and communes and dedicated primarily to conveying basic skills and religious values to the lower classes (Messerli and Chartier 2000). No connection existed between these school and the private institutes and embryonic universities dedicated to shaping the future elite. Such elite organizations were again separate from vocational education and training (VET), which was largely organized by guilds (Gonon and Maurer 2012).

Liberal movements and the transition to industrial societies were among the drivers leading to the integration of these separate institutions into one interconnected system (Ansell and Lindvall 2021; Green 2013). In Switzerland, common schools merged with lower-level elite schools to form primary education, an institution that aimed at conveying basic education to an entire age cohort (ISCED level 1, typically ages 6–12). Pre-primary education (ISCED level 02, typically ages 3–5) and lower-secondary schooling (ISCED level 2, typically ages 13–16) acquired similar roles during the twentieth century. At the upper-secondary level, the traditional divisions remain more visible. Switzerland maintains a rather clear separation between general (ISCED level 34) and vocational (ISCED level 35) upper-secondary education—the latter of which includes both fully school-based and combined school- and firm-based training (apprenticeships). In 2019, just below 30 per cent of all students completing their upper-secondary schooling obtained a general education degree whereas the remaining approximately 70 per cent obtained a VET degree (Emmenegger et al. 2023).

Traditionally, only general education awarded baccalaureates granting access to higher education, and attendance was limited to a narrow academic elite. Recent reforms and in particular the introduction of the vocational baccalaureate in 1994 have weakened this steep hierarchy. Since then, the share of the population that is awarded baccalaureates granting access to higher education is rapidly growing. However, this growth is mainly due to more students acquiring a vocational baccalaureate, which provides holders of federal VET diplomas with a more general education and access to tertiary-level education. In 2019, 40 per cent of all awarded baccalaureates were vocational ones (Emmenegger et al. 2023).

With recent reforms, Swiss tertiary education has also acquired a dual structure. Universities, following the tradition of elite education, combine research with theory-focused education. In the 1990s, they were complemented by universities of applied sciences. The latter have a more practical orientation and primarily recruit their students among holders of vocational baccalaureates. In 2019, almost half of all tertiary-level students were enrolled in universities of applied sciences (Emmenegger et al. 2023). With the integration of Switzerland into the European higher education area in the 2000s, the two institutions acquired the same structure. They now award bachelor degrees and short higher vocational certificates (ISCED 6) as well as master degrees and long higher vocational certificates (ISCED 7), but only universities can award PhDs (ISCED 8).

Finally, Switzerland features a large post-secondary VET sector. In 2019, roughly 40 per cent of all VET graduates successfully pursued an additional VET degree at the post-secondary level (Emmenegger et al. 2023).

How does this structure compare internationally? To answer this question, we typify the Swiss system with regard to the three dimensions of institutional variation the political and educational literature considers most influential in determining educational and political outcomes: centralization, standardization, and stratification (Allmendinger 1989).

2.1 Centralization

Centralization describes the allocation of control over human resources, access, finances, and the curriculum (Ansell and Lindvall 2021; Hega 2000). On these dimensions, Switzerland is often considered a case of extreme localism. The empirical situation, however, is slightly more complex. Depending on the perspective taken, Switzerland qualifies either as a comparatively decentralized or as a comparatively centralized country.

On the one hand, Switzerland concentrates comparatively little power at the central (federal) level. When joining the Swiss Confederation in 1848, the cantons renounced some of their autonomy—especially regarding infrastructure and defence. However, cantonal representatives vigorously defended their control over education, in particular general education. Propositions aimed at establishing federal universities and teacher training stood no chance, in both the 1848 constitutional deliberations and later debates (Criblez 2008). Until very recently, attempts to impose national curriculum regulations and supervision for mandatory schooling were also repealed, and there was no education ministry at the federal level. Despite recent reforms (see section 3 in this chapter), Swiss federal authorities still continue to play a comparatively minor and subsidiary role in education (Dardanelli and Mueller 2019). The federal state currently covers 10 per cent of public spending on education, while 27 per cent of the sum is borne by communes and 63 per cent is covered by the cantons (FSO 2020).

On the other hand, schools, the most localized institutional actor in education, also have comparatively little power. Across the Western World, in the last four decades, reformers have introduced market principles in education by combining increased state monitoring with parental choice and school autonomy (Gingrich 2011). Switzerland has followed this trend only in part. Since the 1990s, schools have acquired some autonomy in setting their budgets or when it comes to participation in educational projects (Imlig and Ender 2018). From a comparative perspective, however, these reforms are very limited in scope. Among OECD countries, an average 34 per cent of decisions are made at the school level. In Switzerland, the share is at 8 per cent (OECD 2019, 147).

While cantons play the main role in governing general education, governance structures in vocational education are more varied. The Swiss VET system is governed by strict federal regulations, which typically aim at the strategic development of the system. Cantons are tasked with implementing these regulations. They provide school-based training, organize examinations and vocational counselling, and monitor firms' training activities. Finally, private actors are involved in the governance of VET through professional training organizations (called organizations of the world of work, an umbrella term for all non-governmental organizations involved).

Professional training associations have two central functions. First, many of them, usually employer-based associations, are recognized by the federal state as representatives for a training occupation. As a result, they are typically organized along occupational, not sectoral, lines. In this function, they define the content of national training regulations and framework curriculums. Moreover, these organizations are in regular contact with training firms. Second, they are involved in the strategic development of the VET system at the federal level. Peak-level organizations representing employers and employees meet regulary with representatives of the cantons and the federal state to discuss the strategic development of Swiss VET (Emmenegger et al. 2020).

Due to the important role of employer organizations, the academic literature classifies the Swiss VET system—alongside the Austrian, Danish, Dutch, and German ones—as a collective skill formation system. Four features distinguish collective skill systems from more state-driven (e.g. France) or market-driven (e.g. UK) models. First, they are based on dual training combining school-based and work-based learning. Second, employers and their associations are involved in the financing and administration of training, meaning that collective skill formation regimes presuppose inter-firm cooperation and employers willing to engage in collective action. Third, intermediary organizations, including trade unions, play an important role in these systems' administration and development. Finally, collective systems lead to certified and standardized occupational skills that are portable between firms (Busemeyer and Trampusch 2012).

2.2 Standardization

The standardization of education systems is linked to their centralization. Countries without strong central governments typically lack the means to enforce common curriculums as well as hiring, testing, and budgets policies. Such lack of standardization often leads to more inequality (Chetty et al. 2014). Due to its peculiar governance system, the standardization of Swiss education is, again, a matter of perspective.

From a federal perspective, the Swiss education system is not standardized. Despite recent harmonization efforts (see section 3 in this chapter), the cantons still have different timetables, mandatory schooling periods, salary scales, and structures (e.g. tracking). From a cantonal perspective, however, formal education is comparatively standardized. Communes do play a role in supervision and hiring policies, especially in German-speaking Switzerland (Hega 2000). However, their scope is limited, as since the nineteenth century, cantonal governments have developed powerful educational bureaucracies and regulations to tackle regional educational disparities across their territories. Within each canton, financing is standardized as are salaries and requirements regarding teacher–pupil ratios and infrastructure. Cantonal authorities also regulate educational content via official syllabuses, timetables, and textbook lists (Criblez 2008; Criblez et al. 2023). As a result, the public considers schools to be largely equal. Proposals aimed at introducing school choice or rankings—common in countries such as the UK—are deeply unpopular (Braun 2019).

The second factor contributing to a high degree of standardization within the cantons is the comparably low share of private schooling. Swiss private boarding institutes feature among the most expensive institutions in the world and educate international elites and royalties. However, private schools play little role in educating the local population. In 2019, 5 per cent of primary school pupils attended a private school—the OECD average is of 12 per cent (OECD 2021). Swiss private schools only receive state funding in exceptional cases, so costs must be borne entirely by students and their families (Nikolai 2019).

This policy has strong political support. Proposals to introduce charter schools, vouchers, or state funding for private schools have been repeatedly rebuffed in parliaments or popular referendums—e.g. in Bern (1982), Ticino (2001), Basel-Landschaft (2008), and Thurgovia (2010). This support for state schools might also result from the public's perception of them as offering better quality. Indeed, controlling for resources and pupils' socio-economic background, Swiss state schools perform better than private schools in international attainment tests (OECD 2014).

2.3 Stratification

A third crucial feature of education systems is their stratification (Allmendinger 1989). Systems characterized by a high degree of stratification allot children to different specialized paths early, mostly after they complete primary school at the age of 10 to 12. Typically, high stratification goes hand in hand with strong selectivity. In stratified systems, such as those in place in the German states, children are allocated to different schools based on their academic performance rather than choice, as is partly the case of the less stratified UK or US.

Stratification matters for both skill production and redistribution. In systems characterized by a higher degree of stratification, educational certificates correspond more directly to positions in the labour market, whereas in less stratified systems the correspondence is looser, and job changes are more frequent (Allmendinger 1989). No empirical links have been established between stratification and the overall academic or economic performance of education systems. However, a vast literature suggests that stratification increases the impact of pupils' background on their academic performance and social mobility (Van de Werfhorst and Mijs 2010). Children from more privileged backgrounds are more likely to be selected into tracks leading to prestigious positions because they dispose of the kind of knowledge and attitudes schools reward, and because they are able to invest in longer educational paths (the literature calls these primary and secondary socialization effects, Jackson 2013). These effects are not neutralized by selective allocation mechanisms. Research shows that, with equal academic performance, children from higher strata are still more likely to be recommended for more demanding tracks. This also occurs because their parents can more effectively pressure teachers to issue such recommendations (Dumont et al. 2019).

The Swiss cantons show different degrees of stratification. Comprehensive schooling reforms, which swept Europe in the 1960s and 1970s (Giudici et al. 2023), only suceeded in some French- and Italian-speaking cantons (EDK 2019). Like the German states, most German-speaking cantons stream children into tracks with different curriculums and certificates based on either testing or previous grades at the age of twelve, after six years of primary schooling. The hierarchy across tracks has been recently softened by reforms aligning the curriculum across tracks and facilitating transfers. A few cantons have also introduced cooperative models, with individual schools offering multiple tracks and teaching some subjects to all pupils together (SCCRE 2023).

Selective allocation mechanisms are also used to regulate access to upper-secondary vocational and academic tracks. In turn, an academic baccalaurate grants access to all university courses (with very few exceptions, such as medicine). This means that Swiss universities cannot select their undergraduates, but must accept everyone holding a recognized upper-secondary certificate. Holders of vocational baccalaureats have automatic access to selected courses at universities of applied sciences, but must pass an additional exam to access university. The share of students with access to tertiary education varies across cantons. In Geneva, in 2020, more than half of the student cohort acquired either a vocational or a general baccalaureate. A third (36 per cent) did so in Schaffhausen, and a quarter (27 per cent) in Uri—both of which are characterized by higher degrees of stratification (FOS 2022).

Data on the overall performance of cantonal systems is lacking (SCCRE 2023). However, like international studies, comparisons within Switzerland evidence that it is more difficult for pupils from less privileged backgrounds to acquire higher certificates in cantons with higher stratification (Bauer and Riphahn 2006; Kost 2018). At the same time, students in cantons with higher shares of baccalaureate holders are more likely to fail at university (Wolter et al. 2014). More developed vocational education is also shown to loosen the link between wages and types of degree (Busemeyer 2015), meaning that vocational and school-based certificates of the same level provide access to similar opportunities and salaries with some differences across genders (Korber and Oesch 2019).

Despite cantonal variation, these developments highlight the impact of reforms aimed, on the one hand, at expanding the academic tracks, including in formerly underserved rural populations and among girls, and, on the other hand, at increasing the quality and opportunities offered by non-academic and vocational schooling. Taken together, these reforms have transformed tertiary education from an elite institution involving 2 or 3 per cent of a cohort to a more diversified offer, catering to students with a broader set of interests and backgrounds.

3 THE POLITICS OF EDUCATION

Since the establishment of the Swiss federal state in 1848, Swiss education has been federalized. The degree and specifics of Swiss educational federalism, however, are highly contentious and vary considerably between different types of education. Vocational education, originally governed by guilds and employers, is primarily oriented towards skill production. Its structure and content are therefore meant to integrate the needs of the labour market (Busemeyer and Trampusch 2012). Therefore, the main point of contestation has been the extent to which the state should intervene to solve collective action problems and coordinate diverging regional or economic interests.

3.1 Historical educational cleavages: religion and federalism

General education has traditionally aimed at enculturating citizens rather than forming professionals. As a result, struggles over the control of schools and universities have more closely mirrored dominant societal cleavages, opposing urban and rural elites, liberals and conservatives, church and state (Ansell and Lindvall 2021). These struggles were foundational for the emergence of modern party systems (Lipset and Rokkan 1967) and remain visible in current parties' approaches to education (Ansell 2010; Busemeyer 2015; Giudici et al. 2023).

The religious cleavage dominated Swiss politics in the nineteenth century. The struggles over the control of schooling largely saw nascent liberal movements opposing conservatives and the Protestant and Catholic churches. Within the cantons, depriving churches of educational power was a key liberal priority (Criblez et al. 1998). Until recently, the centralization of educational control thus varied according to local political majorities. Whereas, in 1846, liberals in Italian-speaking Ticino forcefully seized control of all secondary schools from Catholic orders and expropriated church buildings, in conservative-dominated Fribourg, teacher training and upper-secondary schools remained under religious management until the mid-twentieth century (Giudici 2019).

These differences disappeared together with the religious struggles in the 1960s, and today, religious providers play little role in Swiss schooling. However, some variation continues to exist between German-speaking cantons, most of which are characterized by less centralized governance systems, including, for instance, locally elected school officials, and the more centralized and professionalized administrations of French- and Italian-speaking cantons (Hega 2000).

Historically, across cantons these different political and cultural sensibilities resulted in a largely pillarized education landscape. Mobility across language regions has always been relatively common among Swiss elites, but the same does not apply to denominational regions. Until the 1960s, Catholics and Protestants tended to remain within their respective education networks. Despite the 1874 constitution trying to ease the religious conflict by requiring state schools to be neutral, both religious groups shaped their own education systems, underpinning them with specific didactics and philosophies (Giudici 2019). The Catholic minority completed this project in 1899 with the establishment of the Catholic University of Fribourg—an institution explicitly dedicated to the formation of a Catholic Swiss elite.

At the federal level, these differences translated into distinct educational preferences. The Liberal Party—and its Protestant constituencies in particular—supported more centralization. For the Catholic Conservatives, who controlled several cantonal governments but constituted a minority at the national level, centralization meant losing control over the enculturation of their populations. Despite being a minority, the latter largely succeeded in preventing the federal state from acquiring powers over general primary, secondary, and tertiary education. In their opposition, they were aided by other groups struggling to retain educational power, including the linguistic minorities and some liberal cantonal representatives (Criblez 2008; Giudici 2019). This coalition achieved a path-shaping victory in 1882, when it won a popular referendum that blocked the federal authorities from being granted the means to control that cantons were actually organizing 'enough primary schooling' under 'state control' as required by the 1874 constitution (art. 27). Liberals refrained from any centralization effort in the following few decades (Criblez 2008).

As a result, until very recently, the role of the federal authorities in general education was limited to a few tasks considered essential for economic and defence-related reasons. The federal authorities ran the Swiss Federal Institute of Technology (ETH) in Zurich, established in 1855 for technical upskilling. They issued curriculums for gymnastics teaching, because boys' fitness was considered important for military purposes and regulated access to universities by formulating standards for admission to medicine studies (Criblez 2008). The latter intervention was needed to solve a coordination problem that affected all cantons and denominations. Until 1960, only nine universities existed on the Swiss territory: the universities of Basel (established in its modern form in 1818), Zurich (1833), Bern (1834), Geneva (1873), Fribourg (1889), Lausanne (1890), and Neuchâtel (1909), as well as the ETH (1855, also in Zurich) and the Business Academy of St Gallen (1898, turned into a university in 1939). The remaining cantons needed to ensure that their students could access these institutes, whereas the cantons maintaining these institutes needed criteria to regulate admissions (Criblez 2008).

However, the politics of general education are not only structured by partisan cleavages. Actors specifically involved in this policy field, i.e. teachers and administrators, also play powerful roles (Cibulka 2001; Moe and Wiborg 2017). In Switzerland, these actors' vested interests in federalism mean they have largely opposed the centralization of educational control.

Cantonal administrations constitute the traditional centres of educational power. They therefore have traditionally resisted attempts to shift power to their federal counterparts—including in cantons dominated by the centralization-friendly Liberal Party (Giudici 2019). The literature disagrees on whether the cantons can be considered veto players in Swiss politics based on their institutional means of influence (second parliamentary chamber and majority requirements for referendums; see 'Federalism' in this volume). When it comes to education, however, cantonal ministries are directly involved in decision-making processes through pre-parliamentary hearings and negotiations (Fischer et al. 2010). To further increase their influence, since 1895, the cantonal ministries have constituted a body to represent their collective interests, the Swiss Conference of Cantonal Ministers of Education (known under the German acronym

EDK). Studies show that their cooperation and channels of influence have allowed cantons to shape federal educational policy-making—even in situations of perceived crisis such as the World Wars or the Europeanization process—(Fischer et al. 2010; Giudici 2021). At the same time, intercantonal collaboration also constitutes a channel of cross-cantonal policy dissemination and alignment.

Teachers play a somewhat similar role. Swiss teachers' organizations largely reflect the structure of the Swiss polity. Each canton had, and still has, its own teacher organization(s). Disposing of formal and informal influence at the cantonal level, these organizations have regularly mobilized to oppose centralization attempts (Giudici 2019; Criblez et al. 2023). At the same time, teachers are connected across Switzerland. Traditionally, cantonal organizations convened in umbrella organizations representing either men or women, Catholics or Protestants, or French- or German-speakers. However, as common interests increased, these groups consolidated into broader, language-based organizations. While opposing centralization as such, through their publications, meetings, and other communication channels, these umbrella organizations provide networks that have facilitated the diffusion of policies and pedagogy across Switzerland, thus contributing to the harmonization of Swiss education from the bottom up (Fontaine 2015).

3.2 Post-War Developments: centralization vs cooperation

In the second post-war period, economic developments (lack of skills and increasing interregional mobility), social movements, growing student numbers, and the consolidation of the European economic and higher education areas have challenged the federal organization of Swiss education. Both national and international actors have questioned the performance and equity of this decentralized mode of educational control and of the resulting educational fragmentation (Criblez 2008). Differences in the concentration of vested interests in federalism explain the diverging reactions to this pressure across levels.

In tertiary education, this pressure has led to an unprecedented reform momentum. Cantons hosting universities needed financial help to cater to the growing number of students, whereas cantons without universities needed to secure their students' access to tertiary education. Both favoured the recognition of certificates across Switzerland and between Switzerland and Europe to secure the skills their economies needed. As a result, starting in the 1990s, a series of reforms has revolutionized Swiss higher education. This has led to the establishment of two new types of tertiary education (universities of applied sciences and universities for teacher education), several new universities, and the vocational baccalaureate, as well as the granting of mutual recognition of diplomas and certificates across Switzerland, and then across Europe with the implementation of the Bologna system (Criblez 2008; Gonon and Maurer 2012). Finally, a constitutional amendment passed in 2006 (art. 62 of the federal constitution) and the Higher Education Act (2011) formally established the federal authorities—which, in 1969, acquired a second tertiary institute, the École Polytechnique Fédérale de Lausanne—as an equal partner in the governance of tertiary education.

Compulsory education was confronted with similar problems. In the post-WWII period, moves across cantons became more frequent. Parents and teachers therefore started to perceive the fact that some cantons started the school year in autumn and others in spring and that all had different curriculums and foreign language teaching systems as a problem. Cantonal variations in the curriculum, graduation rates, and schooling periods were also increasingly deemed unjust and considered potential drivers of inequality. By the late 1960s, a consensus emerged on the need to harmonize the structures of compulsory education (Giudici 2019). However, teachers' and administrators' vested interests in educational federalism were stronger at the primary and secondary levels, which have therefore not experienced the same level of centralization as tertiary education.

To avoid federal interventions, the cantons strengthened intercantonal cooperation. At the regional level, they formed bodies tasked with coordinating textbook and curriculum policies (Hofstetter et al. 2015; Criblez et al. 2023). At the Swiss level, cantons strengthened inter-ministerial cooperation. Their joint body, the EDK, began issuing agreements with which cantons could voluntarily commit themselves to implementing common policies (Criblez 2008). Several educational areas are now regulated by such inter-ministerial agreements, including school structures, scholarships, and special needs education.

The passage of the 2006 constitutional amendment changed the nature of these agreements. In what some analysts have called a 'change of paradigm' (Sciarini and Bochsler 2006, 277), the surprisingly uncontroversial amendment institutionalized the principle of cooperative federalism in Swiss education politics. For the first time, the amendment acknowledged the existence of a 'Swiss education area', declaring both cantons and the Confederation responsible for its quality and permeability (art. 61a of the federal constitution). The amendment also mandates the Confederation to regulate school entry age, compulsory schooling, duration, and goals of compulsory education levels as well as transitions and certificates if no harmonization is reached via coordination (art. 62 of the 1999 Federal Constitution). The cantons agreed on benchmarks in these areas in the 2007 Intercantonal Agreement on the Harmonization of Compulsory Schooling (HarmoS)—which federal authorities can now declare binding to ensure compliance.

Not all cantons have aligned their system to the HarmoS requirements. Whether this means federal authorities should now intervene remains controversial. This debate testifies to three key changes in Swiss education politics in the last decade. First, partisan alignments have changed. With the depoliticization of the religious cleavage in the 1970s, the Swiss Christian Democrats (CVP, now The Centre) joined other parties in demanding more coordination and centralization in Swiss education. Since then, the far-right Swiss People's Party has assumed the role as main educational opposition, elaborating a detailed programme for education reform and launching several initiatives, including proposals aimed at banning veils from classrooms, preventing the introduction of compulsory pre-schooling, and opposing the teaching of foreign languages in primary schools, and of high German—as opposed to local dialects—in kindergarten. Some of these initiatives have been successful.

Second, the depoliticization of religion has been accompanied by a politicization of the language cleavage (Giudici 2019). Official linguistic minorities have long benefitted from education federalism, at least in places where they form a majority at the cantonal level and can use the education system to protect their language and identity. At the same time, however, they have often relied on the federal state for protection. Their resolute mobilization in defence of education federalism in the last few decades as well as the emergence of language-specific policies and curriculums have raised concerns about whether Switzerland is developing towards a more ethnic form of federalism (Erk 2008).

Third and most crucially, the discussions on the harmonization of compulsory education testify to a centralization not only of educational institutions but also of their politics. Despite education still largely constituting a cantonal matter, federal parties now issue statements and programmes on education, and sometimes launch parallel education initiatives across cantons. Educational institutions are cantonal, but their politics are increasingly less so, and they often involve several cantons at once. With the concentration of education-related tasks within the Federal Department of Economic Affairs, Education, and Research, Switzerland also has established an office akin to that of an education ministry, which can represent the country at the international level.

Centralization processes can also be observed in vocational education. However, these developments have taken place under different auspices, as party-political conflicts in VET tend to be of secondary importance (Thelen 2004). Instead, reforms and debates primarily concern the distribution of competences between the federal government, the cantons, and professional training organizations. In vocational education, the federal government has developed from an absent party (before 1884) to a passive provider of subsidies and to an increasingly influential player (Gonon and Maurer 2012). The 2002 VET act has cemented this new governance structure. It has increased the degree of national standardization of training and processes, extending its scope to occupational groups previously covered by separate regulations (e.g. nursing professionals and agriculture), while augmenting federal contributions to overall spending.

4 Implementation and Current State

The criteria typically used to evaluate education policy are equality, academic performance, and labour market outcomes. Given the longstanding debate on the equality and performance implications of its educational federalism, in Switzerland, the harmonization of educational structures and outcomes constitutes an additional criterion.

In terms of academic performance, the OECD's Programme for International Student Assessment (PISA) finds Swiss students to perform comparatively well or average in the tested subjects. Perceived instances of underperformance, for instance an increase in the number of students with low reading skills noted in 2018, are quickly addressed with targeted programmes (Konsortium PISA.ch 2019).

In terms of skill production, the Swiss system is also found to perform well. Swiss universities are highly recognized—as evidenced by international rankings and the decision of a number of international firms (e.g. Google) to operate from Switzerland. The vocational education system is also often hailed as a success, not least due to Switzerland's consistently low levels of youth unemployment, which experts link to the close employer involvement in content definition and training (Busemeyer 2015). There have been numerous international attempts to adopt elements of the Swiss (or German) skill formation system in both developed and developing countries. However, the transfer of collective skill formation systems has often proven to be challenging because such systems have manifold prerequisites (Maurer and Gonon 2014).

In terms of equality, the diagnosis is less positive. According to the OECD (2018, 2) 'in Switzerland, social background is more closely linked to success at school than it is in many other countries'. Quantitative analysis drawing on PISA 2015 shows that, in Switzerland, social background explains around 16 per cent of the variation in students' science performance. Student background thus plays a much larger role in determining academic success here than in countries such as Estonia and Norway (both 8 per cent) (OECD 2018). The Swiss system seems to specifically fail some groups of pupils. Research shows that boys, and children who do not speak the local language at home, show worse academic performance and are over-represented in programmes dedicated to pupils with special needs (Kronig 2007).

The cross-cantonal harmonization of Swiss education through intercantonal agreements has also only been a partial success. Intercantonal agreements are treaties negotiated by cantonal authorities, which must be ratified by parliaments and voters—who might reject, and have repeatedly rejected, specific agreements or the included reforms. The 2006 constitutional amendment allows federal authorities to intervene to harmonize selected structural features such as the duration of compulsory education. However, whether such intervention is needed—and therefore, whether harmonization has been achieved—remains a political decision.

In its most recent report, the EDK states that 'the harmonization of the structures of compulsory schooling is largely implemented' (EDK 2019, 3), and that federal interventions are therefore unnecessary. From a historical perspective, this conclusion appears legitimate. Today, cantonal educational structures look much more similar than they did fifteen years ago. In all cantons but one, pupils transfer from primary to secondary schooling after grade six. Seventeen cantons out of twenty-six have also implemented two years of mandatory kindergarten, while the others have either extended mandatory provision or attendance requirements (EDK 2019).

Still, substantial intercantonal variation continues to exist in terms of institutions and outcomes. In pre-primary education, attendance rates among three-to-five-year-old children vary between 39 per cent in rural regions in central Switzerland and 86 per cent in Italian-speaking regions in the south (OECD 2019). Differences also persist in terms of educational spending (SCCRE 2023), mandatory education requirements (not all cantons have two years of mandatory kindergarten, and one canton, Geneva, has recently extended the mandatory education period up to the age of eighteen), and the hours children spend in schools. A typical primary school pupil in the Canton of Aargau spends 673 hours in school per year, whereas a pupil schooled in Geneva receives 834 hours of instruction (EDK 2022). Finally, common curriculum frameworks have been introduced in the three main language regions (German, French, and Italian)—leading to more regional alignment in terms of educational content. However, the monitoring system implemented to assess the effect of these policies is more fragmented than originally planned (Imlig and Ender 2018; SCCRE 2023). Some cantons and regions have established their own testing systems and have little interest in expanding the national testing programme on which cantons without their own assessment policies rely. One canton has halted its participation entirely. The results of these assessments are mixed, showing a rather high degree of harmonization in student performances in language subjects, but 'considerable' variation in mathematics (EDK 2019, 18).

5 Perspectives and future challenges

In the last few decades, Swiss education policy has changed substantially. In the 1970s, the cantonal sovereignty over (general) education was largely set in stone. Today, the Confederation is allowed to intervene in what the constitution explicitly labels the 'Swiss education space' in order to harmonize its structures. In 1990, cantonal authorities agreed to the OECD conducting the very first Swiss-wide evaluation of the education system. Today, Switzerland regularly participates in international surveys and has implemented its own assessment system. Diploma and certificates—and the courses awarding them—have been significantly standardized and granted mutual recognition not only within Switzerland but also across Europe. Still, current developments pose new challenges for Swiss education. This conclusion highlights three that are particularly crucial.

First, Switzerland is adapting to new economic developments. In the era of knowledge economies, education has become a key determinant in the international competition for knowledge and skills. To attract internationally mobile firms and skilled individuals, states need well-performing and attractive education and research sectors, whose quality is authenticated by international testing and rankings.

Adapting to this fast-moving situation is challenging for Swiss education with its characteristic decentralization and wide inclusion of stakeholders. Addressing global dynamics such as the 'digital revolution' (BAKOM 2018) requires fundamental reforms across the entire system, and therefore a strong vertical coordination between cantons, federal authorities, and other education providers, as well as horizontal coordination between parliaments, governments, and educational stakeholders. The lack of formally institutionalized cooperation mechanisms between these actors, as well as of a forum for the public to discuss the direction of education politics at the Swiss level, renders reform processes slower, more complex, and less transparent.

Vocational education faces similar challenges as increasingly knowledge-intensive and specialized production processes put employers' ability to act collectively to the test (Bonoli and Emmenegger 2022). Moreover, although the Swiss VET system continues to function well, the system's capacity to include weaker students has come under pressure in recent years. This is reflected not least in the increase in primarily state-funded measures to increase the integration capacity of the VET system through so-called interim solutions and bridging offers (Bonoli and Emmenegger 2021).

A second challenge the Swiss education systems continues to face is equality. In the 1960s, the figure of the 'Catholic rural working-class girl' was used to condense the main group-specific educational disadvantages existing in Switzerland (Rieger 2001, 62). Due to both reforms and social change, today, denomination and rural–urban differences play only a minor role in determining educational success, and formal gender-based educational differentiation has been eliminated (Giudici and Manz 2018).

However, this structural change has not translated into equal access to prestigious certificates. While today, on paper, girls are achieving better qualifications than boys are, this qualification structure is the result of gender-based imbalances in educational choices across sectors, with girls being more likely to enrol in newly tertiarized and less prestigious courses such as teaching and health, and men instead opting for vocational education. Biases can also be found within vocational and academic education. In both sectors, many disciplines are dominated by either women (nursing) or men (engineering) with the latter often leading to better income opportunities (SCCRE 2023).

Gender differences are but one source of educational inequality. As mentioned earlier, the Swiss education system systematically disadvantages pupils from less privileged backgrounds and children whose families do not speak the local languages. While several policy initiatives have been launched to address this discrimination, including the expansion of pre-schooling, teacher sensibilization, and pedagogical interventions, new causes of concern have recently arisen. The emergence and growth of shadow education, a result of parents' increased reliance on private tutoring to increase their children's chances of academic success, is particularly worrying from an equality perspective (SCCRE 2023).

Finally, across the Western World, the politicization of culture and identities—race in the US, religion in the UK or France—poses new questions for how education deals with diversity. Historically, schools were often used to assimilate minorities and create unified national collectives (Green 2013). The affirmation of individual and cultural rights has triggered a debate as to whether education systems should continue to strive towards producing more unified societies or whether they should instead valorize cultural and social diversity in curriculums, assessments, admissions, and hiring.

Swiss schools have traditionally served the enculturation into local identities. To date, some cantons strictly limit any teaching in languages other than the local one (Giudici 2019). Still, in recent decades, a consensus has emerged between left and centre-right parties on the need to either recognize cultural diversity in schools or, at least, to tackle the most glaring forms of cultural discrimination. Programmes for intercultural learning, heritage language teaching, and inter-denominational religious instruction all represent attempts to acknowledge pupils' diverse identities and backgrounds. Such initiatives, however, have also produced a backlash. Regularly resurfacing debates on the banning of non-local religious symbols from classrooms, on replacing the teaching of literary German with local dialects in kindergartens, and on mandating the singing of Christmas carols and hymns illustrate that some believe that schools should reacquire a more integrative function.

These debates show that education continues to constitute an important arena for negotiating cultural values and discussing our future as a society. Protecting this function is a crucial task faced by education systems across the world, including in Switzerland, especially in a context characterized by an increasing fragmentation, internationalization, and marketization of education systems.

REFERENCES

Allmendinger, Jutta. 1989. 'Educational Systems and Labor Market Outcomes'. *European Sociological Review* 5 (3): pp. 231–250.

Ansell, Ben. 2010. *From the Ballot to the Blackboard. The Redistributive Political Economy of Education*. Cambridge: Cambridge University Press.

Ansell, Ben, and Johannes Lindvall. 2021. *Inward Conquest. The Political Origins of Modern Public Services*. Cambridge: Cambridge University Press.

BAKOM. 2018. *Strategie Digitale Schweiz*. Biel: Geschäftsstelle Digitale Schweiz des Bundes.

Bauer, Philipp, and Regina T. Riphahn. 2006. 'Timing of School Tracking as a Determinant of Intergenerational Transmission of Education'. *Economics Letters* 91: pp. 90–97.

Bonoli, Giuliano, and Patrick Emmenegger. 2021. 'The Limits of Decentralised Cooperation: The Promotion of Inclusiveness in Collective Skill Formation Systems?'. *Journal of European Public Policy* 28 (2): pp. 229–247.

Bonoli, Giuliani, and Emmenegger, Patrick. 2022. *Collective Skill Formation in the Knowledge Economy*. Oxford: Oxford University Press.

Braun, Roger. 2019. 'Wir wollen keine Ranking-Kultur wie in den USA'. *Neue Zürcher Zeitung*. 2.5.2019.

Busemeyer, Marius. 2015. *Skills and Inequality*. Cambridge: Cambridge University Press.

Busemeyer, Marius, Julian Garritzmann, and Erik Neimanns. 2020. *A Loud, but Noisy Signal? Public Opinion and Education Reform in Western Europe*. Cambridge: Cambridge University Press.

Busemeyer, Marius, and Christine Trampusch. 2012. *The Political Economy of Collective Skill Formation*. Oxford: Oxford University Press.

Carstensen, Martin B., and Patrick Emmenegger. 2023. 'Education as Social Policy: New Tensions in Maturing Knowledge Economies'. *Social Policy and Administration* 57 (2): pp. 109–21.

Chetty, Raj, Nathaniel Hendren, Patrick Kline, Emmanuel Saez, and Nicholas Turner. 2014. 'Is the United States Still a Land of Opportunity? Recent Trends in Intergenerational Mobility'. *American Economic Review* 104 (5): pp. 141–147.

Cibulka, James G. 2001. 'The Changing Role of Interest Groups in Education: Nationalizing and the New Politics of Education Productivity'. *Educational Policy* 15 (1): pp. 12–40.

Criblez, Lucien. 2008. *Bildungsraum Schweiz. Historische Entwicklungen und aktuelle Herausforderungen*. Bern: Haupt.

Criblez, Lucien, Carlo Jenzer, Rita Hofstetter, and Charles Magnin. 1998. *Eine Schule für die Demokratie*. Bern: Lang.

Criblez, Lucien, Anja Giudici, Rita Hofstetter, Karin Manz, and Bernhard Schneuwly. 2023. *Die schulische Wissensordnung im Wandel. Schulfächer, Lehrpläne, Lehrmittel*. Zürich: Chronos.

Dardanelli, Paolo, and Sean Mueller. 2019. 'Dynamic De/centralization in Switzerland, 1848–2010'. *Publius* 49 (1): pp. 138–165.

Dumont, Hanna, Denise Klinge, and Kai Maaz. 2019. 'The Many (Subtle) Ways Parents Game the System: Mixed-method Evidence on the Transition into Secondary-school Tracks in Germany'. *Sociology of Education* 92 (2): pp. 199–228.

EDK. 2019. *Bilanz 2019*. Bern: EDK.

EDK. 2022. *EDK-Kantonsumfrage. Unterrichtsdauer: Wochenlektionen, Lektionsdauer, Schulwochen*. https://www.edk.ch/de/bildungssystem/kantonale-schulorganisation/kantonsumfrage/a-2-unterrichtsdauer (accessed 10 October 2022).

Emmenegger, Patrick, Lukas Graf, and Alexandra Strebel. 2020. 'Social versus Liberal Collective Skill Formation Systems? A Comparative-historical Analysis of the Role of Trade Unions in German and Swiss VET'. *European Journal of Industrial Relations* 26 (3): pp. 263–278.

Emmenegger, Patrick, Scherwin Bajka, and Cecilia Ivardi (forthcoming). 'How Coordinated Capitalism Adapts to the Knowledge Economy: Different Upskilling Strategies in Germany and Switzerland'. *Swiss Political Science Review*. Doi: https://doi.org/10.1111/spsr.12569.

Erk, Jan. 2008. *Explaining Federalism*. London: Routledge.

Fend, Helmut. 2008. *Neue Theorie der Schule*, 2nd ed. Wiesbaden: VS Verlag für Sozialwissenschaften.

Fischer, Manuel, Pascal Sciarini, and Denise Traber. 2010. 'The Silent Reform of Swiss Federalism: The New Constitutional Article on Education'. *Swiss Political Science Review* 16 (4): pp. 747–771.

Fontaine, Alexandre. 2015. *Aux Heures Suisses de l'École Républicaine*. Paris: Demopolis.

FSO. 2020. *Öffentliche Bildungsausgaben*. https://www.bfs.admin.ch/bfs/de/home/statistiken/bildung-wissenschaft/bildungsfinanzen/oeffentliche-bildungsausgaben.html (accessed 10 October 2022).

FSO. 2022. *Maturitätsquote nach Wohnkanton, 2020*. https://www.bfs.admin.ch/bfs/de/home/statistiken/bildung-wissenschaft/bildungsindikatoren/indicators/maturitaetsquote.html (accessed 18 August 2023).

Gellner, Ernest. 1983. *Nations and Nationalism*. Malden: Blackwell.

Gingrich, Jane R. 2011. *Making Markets in the Welfare State*. New York: Cambridge University Press.

Giudici, Anja. 2019. 'Explaining Swiss Language Education Policy'. *PhD Dissertation*, University of Zurich, Faculty of Arts, Zürich. https://www.zora.uzh.ch/id/eprint/166199/ (accessed 10 October 2022).

Giudici, Anja. 2021. 'Teacher Politics Bottom-up: Theorising the Impact of Micro-politics on Policy Generation'. *Journal of Education Policy* 36 (6): pp. 801–821.

Giudici, Anja, and Karin Manz. 2018. 'Knabenlernzeiten – Mädchenlernzeiten: gleich, gleicher, ungleich?'. *Swiss Journal of Educational Research* 40 (3): pp. 603–620.

Giudici, Anja, Jane Gingrich, Tom Chevalier, and Matthias Haslberger. 2023. 'Center-right Parties and Post-War Secondary Education'. *Comparative Politics* 55(2): pp. 193–218.

Gonon, Philipp, and Markus Maurer. 2012. 'Educational Policy Actors as Stakeholders in the Development of the Collective Skill System: The Case of Switzerland'. In *The Political Economy of Collective Skill Formation*, edited by Markus Busemeyer, and Christine Trampusch, pp. 126–149. Oxford: Oxford University Press.

Green, Andy. 2013. *Education and State Formation*. Basingstoke: Palgrave Macmillan.

Gutmann, Amy. 1999. *Democratic Education*. Princeton: Princeton University Press.

Hega, Gunther M. 2000. 'Federalism, Subsidiarity and Education Policy in Switzerland'. *Regional & Federal Studies* 10 (1): pp. 1–35.

Hofstetter, Rita, Josianne Thévoz, Liliane Palandella, Grégory Durand, and Georges Pasquier. 2015. *Les Bâtisseurs de l'École Romande*. Chêne-Bourg: Georg.

Imlig, Flavian, and Susanne Ender. 2018. 'Towards a National Assessment Policy in Switzerland'. *Assessment in Education* 25 (3): pp. 272–290.

Iversen, Torben, and David Soskice. 2019. *Democracy and Prosperity. Reinventing Capitalism through a Turbulent Century*. Princeton: Princeton University Press.

Jackson, Michelle V. 2013. *Determined to Succeed? Performance versus Choice in Educational Attainment*. Stanford: Stanford University Press.

Konsortium PISA.ch. 2019. *PISA 2018: Schülerinnen und Schüler der Schweiz im internationalen Vergleich*. Bern: SBFI/EDK und Konsortium PISA.ch.

Korber, Maïlys, and Daniel Oesch. 2019. 'Vocational versus General Education: Employment and Earnings over the Life Course in Switzerland'. *Advances in Lifecycle Research* 40: pp. 1–13.

Kost, Jakob. 2018. *Erreichte und verpasste Anschlüsse – Zur Durchlässigkeit der Schweizer Sekundarstufe II*. Bielefeld: Bertelsmann.

Kronig, Winfried. 2007. *Die systematische Zufälligkeit des Bildungserfolgs*. Bern: Haupt.

Lipset, Seymour M., and Stein Rokkan. 1967. *Party Systems and Voter Alignment*. New York: Free Press.

Maurer, Markus, and Philipp Gonon. 2014. *The Challenges of Policy Transfer in Vocational Skills Development*. Bern: Peter Lang.

Messerli, Alfred, and Roger Chartier. 2000. *Lesen und Schreiben in Europa 1500-1900*. Basel: Schwabe.

Moe, Terry M., and Susanne Wiborg. 2017. *The Comparative Politics of Education*. Cambridge: Harvard University Press.

Nikolai, Rita. 2019. 'Staatliche Subventionen für Privatschulen: Politiken der Privatschulfinanzierung in Australien und der Schweiz'. *Swiss Journal of Educational Research* 41 (3): pp. 559–575.

OECD. 2014. *Education at a Glance 2014*. Paris: OECD.

OECD. 2018. *Equity in Education: Breaking Down Barriers to Social Mobility, PISA*. Paris: OECD.

OECD. 2019. *Education at a Glance 2019*. Paris: OECD.

OECD. 2021. *Education at a Glance 2021*. Paris: OECD.

Rieger, Andreas. 2001. 'Bildungsexpansion und gleiche Bildungspartizipation am Beispiel der Mittelschulen im Kanton Zürich, 1830 bis 1980'. *Swiss Journal of Educational Research* 23 (1): pp. 41–72.

Schellenbauer, Patrik. 2012. 'Warum Bildung für alle wichtig ist'. avenir suisse. https://www.avenir-suisse.ch/warum-bildung-fur-alle-wichtig-ist (accessed 10 October 2022).

Sciarini, Pascal, and Daniel Bochsler. 2006. 'Réforme du fédéralisme suisse: contributions, promesses et limites de la collaboration intercantonale'. In *Contributions à l'action publique*, edited by Jean-Loup Chappelet, pp. 267–286. Lausanne: Presses polytechniques et universitaires romandes.

SCCRE. 2023. *Education Report Switzerland 2023*. Aarau: Swiss Coordination Centre for Research in Education.

Thelen, Kathleen. 2004. *How Institutions Evolve*. Cambridge: Cambridge University Press.

Van de Werfhorst, Herman G., and Jonathan J.B. Mijs. 2010. 'Achivement Inequality and the Institutional Structure of Educational Systems: A Comparative Perspective'. *Annual Review of Sociology* 36: pp. 407–428.

Weber, Eugen. 1976. *Peasants into Frenchmen*. Stanford: Stanford University Press.

Wolter, Stefan C., Andreas Diem, and Dolores Messer. 2014. 'Drop-outs from Swiss Universities: An Empirical Analysis of Data on all Students between 1975 and 2008'. *European Journal of Education* 49 (4): pp. 471–483.

CHAPTER 33

RESEARCH, TECHNOLOGY, AND INNOVATION POLICIES

LUKAS BASCHUNG AND
JEAN-PHILIPPE LERESCHE

1 INTRODUCTION

For a long time, national authorities have been in control of research, technology, and innovation policies in Europe. The European Union's (EU) increasing role has changed this since the launch of the first Joint European Programme. Due to the EU, national authorities and regions in member countries are more and more entangled in developing research, technology, and innovation policies both in a complementary and in a competing way (Kuhlmann 2001). To understand developments in this policy field, a multi-level governance perspective is needed as a horizontal and vertical coordination problem with a multiplicity of actors. This is not different for Switzerland even though it is not an EU member. Similar to other public policies, research, technology, and innovation policies in Switzerland can only be understood through discussing the relationships among the federal state, the traditionally strong regional authorities—i.e. the cantons—and the EU. The stronger role of the federal government and the EU as well as the growing internationalization has implications for Swiss federalism, which has become more cooperative both horizontally and vertically (Gingras 2002; Leresche et al. 2009). In addition, for a small country such as Switzerland, the impressively high number of actors present in the research and innovation (R&I) system also reinforces the need for coordination. Despite this complex governance (or perhaps due to it), the Swiss R&I system is one of the most performant in the world. That said, Switzerland and its R&I policy is also a good example of how fragile multi-level governance can be, especially for non-EU members. Indeed, due to its very weak political links with the EU, the Swiss R&I system's performance is increasingly and seriously threatened, as seen when regarding the Horizon programmes from which Switzerland was excluded.

Research policy seeks to encourage the production of knowledge and its practical use. Technology policy is a subcategory of research policy. It concentrates on the transformation of specific technological knowledge into production processes. Finally, as in most other countries, Swiss innovation policy became relevant at the beginning of the 2000s and has become a reference for research and technology policies. Since the federal government's Education, Research, and Technology Strategy for the years 2004–2007, the priority has been given to a research policy that favours the creation and application of structures conducive to innovation. Meanwhile, the term 'innovation' replaced the term 'technology'. The Federal Act on the Promotion of Research and Innovation (RIPA) of 2012 defines the 'science-based innovation' as 'the development of new products, methods, processes, and services in industry and society through research, particularly applied research, and the exploitation of its results' (art. 2 lit. b RIPA).

In the case of Switzerland, R&I policies strongly relate to higher education policy (Hotz-Hart and Kissling-Näf 2013). Three elements explain this link. First, due to Switzerland's federal structure, most publicly funded research is carried out by universities (UNI), federal institutes of technology (FIT), and increasingly by universities of applied sciences (UAS) and universities of teacher education (UTE). This institutional feature distinguishes Switzerland from many other countries, such as France and Germany, where a large part of publicly funded research is carried out in non-university research institutes. Thus, Swiss higher education policy can be considered as a research policy. Second, higher education policy even became a technology and innovation policy through the growth of applied research activities at the UAS and the increasing collaboration of private enterprises and higher education institutions (HEI) regarding technological developments. Third, HEI are where future researchers, for both the academic and the private sector, are educated. Indeed, doctoral graduates, whose number doubled between 1990 and 2020 (FSO 2022a), and masters and bachelor graduates are an important source for Swiss innovation due to their knowledge and skills. Lehnert et al. (2020) show that enterprises, situated closely to UAS, increased the size of their research and development (R&D) groups.

As in most other countries, Swiss R&I policies are increasingly related to the development of other public policy fields, such as health (e.g. personalized medicine or COVID-19, see 'Health Policy' in this volume), climate and environment ('Green Deal', see 'Environment and Spatial Planning Policy' in this volume), and digital transition and the economy ('knowledge society', see 'Economic Policy' in this volume). Hence, Swiss R&I policies are also an instrument to achieve other goals. Consequently, the choice of scientific fields within which research is carried out is not neutral. It is the result of the private enterprises' economic strategies, the federal government's political choices, cantonal initiatives, and HEI strategies.

This chapter aims to answer five questions. First, how is the Swiss R&I system organized in the context of federalism and what are its main evolutions regarding policies? Second, what are the roles and strategies of the various actors in the Swiss R&I system? Third, what type of governance rules the R&I system? Fourth, how has this sector progressively become Europeanized in a non-EU state and can it become de-Europeanized? In other words, as for the UK, this raises the question of temporalities and the reversibility of the Europeanization processes. Fifth, how performant is the Swiss R&I system?

2 The late but continuous development of research, technology, and innovation policies

Given Switzerland's liberal and federal characteristics, the federal government had very few legal competences in the field of R&I policies until the 1960s (Joye-Cagnard 2010; Benninghoff and Braun 2010). The task of research promotion has been largely attributed to the Swiss National Science Foundation (SNSF), founded in 1952, and to the cantonally regulated universities, whereas decisions about technology development have been taking place directly within private enterprises.

However, the federal government's role gradually developed due to legal and institutional modifications, which are briefly summarized hereafter:

- 1968: Through the 'federal act on financial assistance to universities', the federal government started intervening in the (co-)funding of universities.
- 1969: The Polytechnic School of the University of Lausanne became the Federal Institute of Technology Lausanne (EPFL), thus it became the second Federal Institute of Technology after the one in Zurich (ETHZ), which has existed since 1855.
- 1973: The introduction of a new article in the federal constitution allowed the federal government, among others, to promote scientific research, to relate research funding to appropriate coordination, to create its own research institutes, and to take over existing institutions.
- 1983: The 'federal research act' was created, which aimed at developing a global vision of the research promotion.
- 1995: Seven UAS were created through the 'federal act on UAS', in the fields of technology, architecture, economy, and design.
- 1995: The Commission for the promotion of scientific research, founded in 1944, became the Commission for Technology and Innovation, and the funding body for the UAS applied research activities (renamed Innosuisse in 2017).
- 1999: The 'federal act on financial assistance to universities' was replaced through a new 'federal act on financial assistance to universities'; a common political body of the federal government and the cantons was created to reinforce the national coordination and the performance of the higher education and research system (e.g. through a new funding formula).

- 1999: The 'federal research act' was revised, introducing National Centres of Competence in Research, which the SNSF managed with the objective of supporting the analysis and exploitation of research results.
- 2002 and 2004: Bilateral agreements were signed concerning participation in the Research Framework Programmes and the European Research Area.
- 2004: The 'federal act on UAS' was revised and the fields of health, social work, and arts were integrated in the UAS perimeter and the tertiary Swiss education system (see 'Education Policy' in this volume).
- 2011: The 'federal act on financial assistance to universities' was replaced through the 'federal act on funding and coordination of the Swiss higher education sector'; the federal government sought to better articulate higher education and R&I policies and to increase the competition between HEI in the field of research; HEI need institutional accreditation to get federal funding.
- 2012: The 'federal research act' was revised towards the 'federal act on the promotion of research and innovation'.

The Swiss federal government's R&I policies are essentially based on an incentive system, comprising the principles of competition, 'bottom-up', spontaneous entrepreneurial initiatives, and coordination, especially in the framework of the competitive funding system that the SNSF and Innosuisse manage (SERI 2020a). Nevertheless, issues related to physical and digital infrastructure became increasingly central. Therefore, several political initiatives focusing on infrastructure emerged at the federal and cantonal levels.

The State Secretariat for Education, Research, and Innovation (SERI) mandated swissuniversities, the umbrella organization of the Swiss universities, to elaborate a national open access strategy with the help of the SNSF. The goal consists of proposing free access to all publicly funded scientific publications by 2024, at the latest. In the same vein, and similar to European initiatives, swissuniversities and the two FIT also developed an Open Research Data strategy. Besides financial and knowledge democratization aspects related to the open access issue, all these reflections must also be seen in the context of the digitalization of the society and economy. Indeed, in its strategy 'Digital Switzerland', adopted in 2018 and updated in 2020, the Federal Council attributes an important role to research and HEI in developing a digital society and economy, and, therefore, expressed its preference for Swiss participation in international programmes related to digitalization in the field of research and innovation (OFCOM 2020).

A physical infrastructure project started emerging in 2016. The Federal Council, together with the cantonal ministers in charge of economy, organized a call for candidate sites, which would become part of the Swiss Innovation Park. Finally, six sites were included. This public-private partnership, supported by the public authorities (federal government and cantons), the scientific community, and the private economy, aims at attracting R&D units of Swiss and foreign enterprises and putting them into contact with Swiss HEI to foster innovation (Federal Council 2015). Although effective infrastructure, such as new buildings, developed with varying paces depending on the different sites, a certain repartition regarding scientific topics seems to have been carried out among the sites. However, most topics have a technological character.

Although the establishment of a national innovation park is new, other 'incubators', techno parks, and innovation parks were already developed several decades ago through public-private partnerships at the cantonal level (Thierstein and Willhelm 2001). Numerous cantons also support start-ups and innovative small and medium-sized enterprises by consulting offers and especially by direct financial aid. Even municipalities launched initiatives promoting innovation (SSIC 2015a) and some identified economic innovation as a strategic objective in their legislative programmes' framework. Thus, in the case of innovation policy, the multi-level governance approach must also consider the local level.

Finally, several cantons also decide about important infrastructure projects, which impacts research. For instance, the Canton of Vaud supported the construction of a new building dedicated to cancer research by allowing the use of an important land reserve. The canton of Bern has similar intentions to support the development of knowledge transfer from research to industry in the field of medicine (Regierungsrat Bern 2019).

In summary, since the end of the 1960s, R&I has become an increasingly important aspect on the policy agendas, especially at the federal level, where an increasing number of initiatives aimed at R&I development have been materialized. Consequently, the need for coordination between the federal and cantonal levels also increased.

3 A LARGE NUMBER OF ACTORS AND DIFFERENT STRATEGIES

A further detailed description of the key actors in the field of R&I and their respective strategies is necessary to understand concrete policies and initiatives regarding coordination problems. These key actors can be presented by distinguishing the federal, national, and cantonal level.

At the federal level, an important change took place in 2013, when all federal competences relative to R&I were concentrated within the Department of Economic Affairs, Education, and Research (EAER) and more precisely its State Secretariat for Education, Research, and Innovation (SERI). Previously, the Department of Home Affairs oversaw UNI, FIT, and the SNSF, whereas the former Department of Economic Affairs' competences were limited to vocational education, UAS, and the Commission for Technology and Innovation (CTI). Through this concentration of competences, SERI became a central actor concerning the coordination of policies in the field of education, research, and innovation at the national and international levels.

The Swiss Science Council was founded in 1965 as a consultant body of the Federal Council in the field of science and its mission remained quite stable over time. It issues recommendations, leads evaluations on mandates of the Federal Council or the SERI, and establishes reports about issues related to science policy.

In 2017, Innosuisse—the Swiss Innovation Agency—became more independent of the Department of Economic Affairs after it obtained the status of a public law institution. Innosuisse essentially took over the CTI's activities, that is, co-funding R&D projects that researchers and enterprises commonly submit. Such common bottom-up initiatives should assure coordinated identification of relevant innovations. Besides R&D projects, Innosuisse also sustains the creation of start-ups and entrepreneurships as well as knowledge and technology transfer. Since the beginning of the 2000s, Innosuisse's budget more than doubled from about half a billion to about one billion Swiss francs (for a four-year period).

At the federal level, the FIT Council is another important actor because it constitutes the strategic management and supervisory body of the two federal institutes of technology (i.e. ETHZ and EPFL) and the four research institutes (i.e. the Paul Scherrer Institute, WSL (forest, snow, and landscape research), EMPA (Materials Science and Technology), and EAWAG (aquatic research)). ETHZ and EPFL occupy a particular position within the Swiss higher education landscape because the federal government funds them, not the cantons. Together with the four research institutes, they receive about two-fifths of the federal budget dedicated to education, research, and innovation, that is almost 11 billion Swiss francs for a four-year period (Federal Council 2020).

At the national level, six other actors occupy intermediary and influential positions relative to R&I policies. The Swiss Higher Education Institution Conference is the national coordinating body of HEI policy. Among others, coordination happens at its presidency level: the federal councillor in charge of the EAER is the designated president, whereas two cantonal ministers in charge of higher education are vice-presidents. Its main missions concern education and HEI accreditation, as well as research to the extent that it has the competences to coordinate HEI policies at the national level, to decide about the repartition of tasks in particularly expensive fields, and to make contributions related to projects (art. 12 Higher Education Act).

The umbrella organization of Swiss HEI, swissuniversities, represents all three types of Swiss universities, that is, UNI and FIT, UAS, and UTE. Despite this common organization, these three types still have a separate chamber within swissuniversities.

The Swiss Accreditation Council also plays a role regarding research to the extent that research is one out of five fields within which quality standards are examined in the institutional accreditation procedure of HEI.

Another important actor, situated between the political sphere and the research system, is the SNSF, whose focus is essentially on basic research. Its initial mission consisted of making progress and promoting the attractiveness of the quality of free research in Switzerland (Fleury and Joye 2002). Later, the federal government expanded its portfolio of research promotion activities with politically oriented research. Concretely, the Federal Council regularly determines politically relevant topics and researchers can answer to the given calls by suggesting research projects within these topics. The SNSF is a private foundation that scientific organizations and the academic community support. Its financial resources are entirely federal and the federal parliament validates them every four years. In 2020, its annual budget was about CHF 1.11 billion (SNSF 2021). The federal government traditionally exerts some influence on the SNSF, essentially through appointing several members of the latter's foundation board, whose tasks consist of approving annual reports and authorizing big projects.

Although less directly involved in R&I governance, the four academies of arts and sciences are the connecting points between the scientific community and the public.

Finally, the cantons play a central role for all HEI (except the two FIT) regarding regulation and funding. Each canton within which a UNI, UAS, and/or UTE is situated holds its own act(s). In the case of multi-cantonal UAS, inter-cantonal regulations complement the legal framework. Therefore, the governance of individual HEI and wage scales of research and teaching staff vary according to the canton. Regarding direct subsidies, the cantons are the most important funder for 'their' HEI (own calculations, based on data of FSO 2022b).

These different actors, completed by the target of R&I policies, that is, HEI and private enterprises, can be positioned regarding two dimensions to understand their respective roles in the R&I system: first, concerning the dimension 'basic research versus applied research' and second, in respect of the dimension 'politics versus science and innovation' (the former having a purely political, the latter having an operational orientation). These two dimensions should be understood as a continuum.

Figure 33.1 does not express all interests and strategies of the different actors who participate in research policy. For instance, SERI certainly has strategic objectives for all of Switzerland (such as struggling for Switzerland's place in European research projects). Yet, it also elaborates the federal government's budget regarding R&I, which decides, for instance, about the repartition of resources between 'its' research organizations

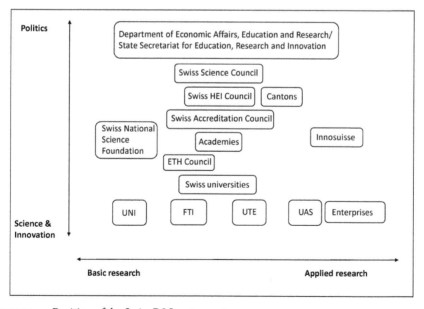

FIGURE 33.1: Position of the Swiss R&I system actors

belonging to the FIT domain and the cantonal universities. Among others, available resources within the different HEI have an effect on the professors' salaries, which is a central element for the HEI's competitiveness in the academic market.

Obviously, the individual cantons' financial capacity also has an effect on the competitiveness of 'their' HEI. In addition, legislative programmes, strategic plans, and performance agreements decided on between cantonal governments and HEI express political preferences for certain scientific domains and topics, often related to ambitions regarding economic development.

For the past few years, HEI and their rectorates have also become more strategic actors, thinking about their place or niche in the national and international higher education and research landscape (Fumasoli and Lepori 2011). Indeed, such strategic reflections are necessary because research and HEI must answer to the double request of 'international excellence' and useful contributions at the regional and national levels.

The various HEI types' interest to collaborate with each other also affects the innovation chain's performance. Indeed, UNI are principally in charge of basic research, whereas UAS take care of applied research and transfer their knowledge to enterprises. Therefore, collaboration between UNI and UAS, on the one side, and between UAS and enterprises, on the other, determines innovation. However, this ideal-typical innovation chain does not always happen in such a linear way. Certain UNI, especially the FIT, also directly transfer their knowledge to enterprises, whereas certain scientific fields of UAS have less direct access to enterprises. Indeed, in the past, the main public funder of HEI regarding innovation—Innosuisse—understood innovation mostly as technological innovation. This changed in more recent strategies of the Federal Council, for example, concerning the period 2018–2020, where the government requested Innosuisse 'to support more often innovation projects in non-technological fields with a major interest for the economy (for instance, social sciences projects in fields such as health or mobility; projects related to the development of new business models in the service sector or data management)' (Federal Council 2017, 7525). Most Innosuisse projects must be realized in collaboration with enterprises. Thus, obtaining and realizing innovation projects within certain scientific fields rather than in others also depends on the enterprises' interests and strategies. Finally, the cantons also try to become involved by putting into place initiatives aimed at promoting innovation.

These various interests, which must be understood in a nationally and internationally competitive context, may constitute centrifugal forces within a national R&I system.

4 A GOVERNANCE TYPE THAT MULTIPLE COORDINATION MECHANISMS SHAPE

Given the above mentioned potentially centrifugal forces of the various actors and as in other federal countries such as Germany, the issue of national and international coordination is at the epicentre of the Swiss R&I system's governance (Griessen and Braun 2010). At the federal level, the government privileged an 'external coordination mode' until 2012, with a distribution of competences regarding R&I and tertiary education on two federal departments and several administrative units (Braun et al. 2007). Since the concentration of all competences within the EAER, an 'internal coordination mode' prevails in the federal administration. However, the competition between policy fields did not disappear. Being external before 2012, it simply became internal starting in 2013. Therefore, it survives through trade-offs and compromises within the Department of Economic Affairs, Education, and Research and between it and the cantons. Yet, it may be facilitated at the international level in discussions with the European Union and through Switzerland's representation in international education and research organizations such as OECD, UNESCO, CERN, and EMBO (Strasser and Joye 2005).

Because the Swiss government and the cantons share political competence regarding higher education and research and because of the strong autonomy of HEI, Swiss research policy is probably more limited than any other policy area is in its possibilities for hierarchical and regulatory influence. This is the case even though it concerns such sensitive and important topics as artificial intelligence, genetically modified organisms, stem cell manipulation, and human research in general. Yet, in fact, research policy cannot be implemented without the support of its addressees, that is, scientists and their organizations. Therefore, indirect and flexible forms of management are widely used. Similar to other countries, the funding instrument is central in Switzerland, that is, the distributive policy with which the choice of research topics is guided. Other possible instruments include indirect management through performance contracts, strategic coordination, and evaluation. These instruments are used in different ways depending on who uses them.

First, the main steering instrument, mentioned in the Federal Institutes of Technology Act, is the performance contract or mandate that sets out the overall objectives and which, since 2013, has been negotiated with the State Secretariat for Education, Research, and Innovation for a four-year period. The parliament must approve these agreements. On this basis, the FIT Council concludes performance contracts with the two FIT and the four research institutes of the FIT Domain. At the end of the four-year period, an evaluation is carried out according to the contract's requirements, which the parliament must approve. Although there is a performance contract, the FIT Council controls the core strategic competencies, which is why this Council has relatively strong autonomy.

Second, the UAS are also familiar with the performance contract instrument, which, according to the institution, is used in a more or less binding way.

Third, contractualization is also a management instrument between the federal government and the Swiss National Science Foundation (a performance agreement). Similar to the FIT Council, the SNSF must discuss its financial needs and goals with the federal department. Formulating strategic objectives is also an important task of the SNSF. However, according to the law, the Federal Council can mandate the SNSF to conduct special research programmes 'of national interest' (NRP) (art. 6 para. 2 RIPA), as it did urgently in March 2020 with the 'special' NRP COVID-19. In addition, the federal government can also exert influence through its representatives on the SNSF Foundation Board.

Fourth, the Federal Council has more direct and hierarchical influence through research institutes within the federal administration (such as Agroscope in agricultural research, which is part of the Federal Office for Agriculture). Thus, the Federal Council decides on research interests and determines the distribution of resources.

Fifth, under article 15 of the Federal Act on the Promotion of Research and Innovation, non-university institutes are 'research institutions of national importance' ('research institutions' such as the Swiss Tropical and Public Health Institute, 'research infrastructures' such as the Jean Monnet Foundation for Europe, or 'technological competence centres' such as the Swiss Center for Musculoskeletal Biobanking and Imaging and Clinical Movement Analysis). They are controlled in the sense that they are subject to regular evaluations (which the Swiss Science Council often manages). Performance contracts also exist in some cases but are not generalized. Another of the federal government's means of influence is its power to dissolve institutes, if it no longer considers the research carried out within them to be necessary, or to reorganize them, for example by integrating them into the universities (cf. the integration of the Swiss Institute for Cancer Research into the EPFL in 2008 and its integration into the wider Agora cancer research cluster in 2018).

Sixth, the federal government has various funding instruments through which higher education research can be influenced, starting with the SNSF through its competence to select research topics; the same applies to the Innosuisse programmes, which are primarily oriented towards UAS. The federal government can also exert a certain influence by stipulating the conditions for subsidies under the federal act on funding and coordination of the Swiss higher education sector. Over the past two decades, subsidies have been increasingly linked to performance criteria. Finally, the Federal Council can assign tasks or mandates that address specific concerns and that university researchers are to conduct. In addition to the research of the federal administration, this type of promotion, even if it is decreasing (Lepori 2007), is the most direct possibility for the federal government to influence research. Although scientific institutions used to rely on federal and cantonal subsidies, a trend has emerged over the last twenty years, whereby third-party funds (especially through the SNSF) increasingly support universities.

Seventh, finally, as in other European countries (Paradeise et al. 2009), evaluations are increasingly used as a management tool in the research system. The transition to 'new public management' instruments in the field of research not only determines the formulation of research (and teaching) goals to be pursued, but also the monitoring of compliance with these goals. The procedure of calling in international experts is not the only one used here; accreditation agencies (mainly the Swiss Accreditation Agency since 2015) are also consulted.

From this overview, it is possible to identify a series of management instruments in R&I policies: there is a desire to bring about strategic coordination of the entire national system, the objectives of which are realized through financial incentives as well as performance contracts and research institution evaluations. However, note that the coordination of research and innovation depends not only on the management instruments of the main political players but, above all, on the willingness and ability of the players in the 'field', that is, researchers at universities and in business, to coordinate and cooperate.

5 FROM EUROPEANIZATION TO DE-EUROPEANIZATION?

In contrast to the national level, the governance's complexity between Switzerland and the EU is not due to a high number of actors and limited regulatory power, but to the nature of Switzerland's status within the EU. Since the end of the Second World War and in the context of an intergovernmental cooperation, Switzerland has participated in major international and European science and technology organizations, such as CERN (European Organization for Nuclear Research), EMBO (European Molecular Biology Organization), or ESA (European Spatial Agency) (Strasser and Joye 2005), and in European scientific and technological programmes, such as Euratom, COST (European Cooperation in Science and Technology), and Eureka, even without being a member of the EU. Switzerland is a member of most international scientific institutions but with respect to its membership status regarding the European Research Area, its status varies between an associated or third country (Leresche and Baschung 2022).

As a small country situated in the heart of Europe, Switzerland's coordination at the international level has become a crucial element for the field of R&I and its performance. For instance, this may be illustrated in financial terms. Similar to other European countries, such as Austria, France, and the Netherlands, the share of international programmes in public project funding has strongly increased since 1985, and by 2002, achieved more than a quarter of all public project funding (Lepori et al. 2007). The EU research policies' governance, based on intergovernmental coordination through policy networks rather than supranational legislation, seemed to offer particularly good framework conditions for integrating non-EU members, also because it followed scientific rather than political imperatives. In the case of Switzerland, the highly performant R&I system reinforced the mutual interest of both Switzerland and the EU for collaboration (Lavenex 2009). Consequently, Switzerland became a fully associated member of the European Research Area and has been very successful in obtaining European funding. As a direct process of Europeanization in a non-EU member state, bilateral agreements approved in 2002 and 2004 have allowed participation in the Research Framework Programmes and the European Research Area. However, they must be renewed at the end of each period, which, each time, introduces uncertainty for a non-EU member state.

The situation changed following the vote on 9 February 2014 on the Swiss People's Party's initiative 'Against mass immigration', which 50.3 per cent of the Swiss population approved. Accusing Switzerland of contravening the free movement agreements through this vote, the European Commission took various measures against Switzerland: exclusion from the Erasmus mobility programme and from two calls for European Research Council grants, and 'partial' and 'provisional' relegation from Horizon 2020 between 2014 and 2016. Since 2017, due to the decision to continue the free movement with the EU and its extension to Croatia, Switzerland participates as a fully associated member in the Horizon 2020 programme (period 2014–2020). Yet, after the Federal Council broke off negotiations on the institutional agreement with the EU on 26 May 2021, Switzerland's status was reduced to a non-associated third country in the Horizon Europe framework programme. Concretely, this means that Swiss researchers can no longer lead European research projects and obtain European funding. Even though the Swiss federal government elaborated 'parallel' programmes that allow obtaining equivalent funding, Swiss researchers cannot use the label 'European funding', which means they cannot benefit from the positive reputational effects. Therefore, fewer projects are submitted, and some high-profile researchers quit working in Switzerland. The fact that Switzerland, similar to Great Britain, is no longer associated with the Horizon Europe programme led to a 16 per cent decrease in spending on R&D activities between 2019 and 2021 (FSO 2022c).

In the future, Switzerland's participation in Horizon Europe (period 2021–2027) and programmes of the next generation may depend on a 'global' or 'institutional' agreement between Switzerland and the EU. By agreeing in autumn 2021 to pay a further CHF 1 billion in EU cohesion funding, Switzerland hoped in vain to unlock its association with the Horizon Europe programme. Switzerland's participation in the Erasmus+ programme is also under discussion. Thus, Swiss R&I policy at the European level is highly dependent on more cross-cutting public policies and, above all, on the relations that the EU will want to develop with Switzerland in the future. In other words, EU R&I policy is no longer only following scientific considerations but, in the case of Switzerland and the UK, is subordinate to higher level politics (Matthews 2022). It is a paradox that a public policy field that has never been the source of this conflict suffers from these difficulties.

Meanwhile, the Swiss government aims to intensify bilateral cooperation with countries such as the US, the UK, Brazil, and Israel. The future will show whether Swiss R&I policy will be more globalized instead of Europeanized. The case of Norway shows that one does not exclude the other (Smeby and Trondal 2005).

Members of the European scientific community launched the Stick to Science initiative in February 2022 (Stick to Science 2022). The initiative's signatories called on the EU, the UK, and Switzerland to find quickly an association agreement on research. They asked them to separate research issues from global political and institutional negotiations. They mentioned that the participation of the UK and Switzerland would bring more than 18 billion euros to the EU research budget of the Horizon Europe programme over the period 2021–2027, which stands at 95.5 billion euros.

6 A HIGHLY PERFORMING R&I SYSTEM WITH ROOM FOR IMPROVEMENT

Over the past few decades, Swiss R&I spending has grown significantly, which illustrates the crucial role that R&I plays for Switzerland. Total R&D spending, that is, spending by private and public sectors together, also indicates research intensity. The higher the spending, the higher the research intensity. Regarding expenditure on R&D, Switzerland ranks seventh in an international comparison: 3.15 per cent of Gross Domestic Product was allocated to R&D in 2019 (FSO 2021) (see Figure 33.2). In 2015 and 2017, it was in third place.

This relatively high level of spending is not exclusively the result of the political authorities' endowment of the R&D domain. It can be largely attributed to private company spending (although this part has declined since 2000 from 74 to 67.5 per cent of intramural R&D spending). The public share of spending has fluctuated since the Second World War between 17 per cent and 30 per cent, one of the lowest rates among OECD countries. However, between 2008 and 2017, total federal and cantonal spending on education, research, and innovation increased from CHF 32.9 billion to CHF 39.6 billion (SERI 2020b). More specifically, in absolute terms, intramural expenditure on research and development more than doubled between 2000 and 2019 (see Table 33.1). The particularly high growth of universities' R&D spending (from CHF 2.44 billion in 2000 to CHF 6.606 billion in 2019) illustrates the increasing

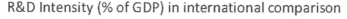

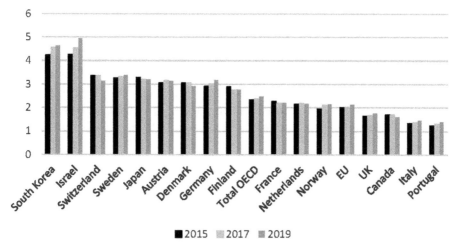

FIGURE 33.2: R&D Intensity (per cent of Gross Domestic Product) in international comparison

Data source: OCDE—Data basis PIST, Division STI—EAS, Paris, 2021; FSO—Research and development (R&D) Swiss synthesis.

Table 33.1: *Intramuros* research and development expenditures (in billion CHF) in Switzerland according to the activity sector, 2000–2019

Sector/Year	2000	2004	2008	2012	2015	2017	2019
Private enterprises	7,890	9,660	11,980	12,820	13,960	14,120	15,454
Federal government	140	140	120	140	194	184	214
HEI	2,440	3,000	3,940	5,210	5,885	6,217	6,606
Private non-profit organizations	205	300	260	340	524	526	610
Total	10,675	13,100	16,300	18,500	20,560	21,050	22,884

Data source: FSO (2021)—Research and development (R&D) Swiss synthesis.

importance political authorities give to the R&D field within the education, research, and innovation domain and to universities as the main public actor within research and innovation.

As developed earlier, the number of actors active in R&I at the policy and 'operational' levels is greater than ever. This wide variety of actors makes it difficult to assess the performance of different policies separately. That said, research and innovation in Switzerland is monitored by a working group of external and internal experts at the State Secretariat for Education, Research, and Innovation, which produces a report every four years to assess the education, research, and innovation system's performance (SERI 2020a). Therefore, trends can be identified for the different policies combined and in an international comparison.

In general, the authors of the previously mentioned report conclude that Switzerland is among the best performing systems in the world. Switzerland is at the top or among the top regarding framework conditions for the development of R&I activities, R&D expenditure (see Figure 33.2), human capital, and the number of scientific publications and international patent applications per capita. This high performance is also visible in the international university rankings, which are heavily based on the universities' research activities (and criticized for their methodology), and within which Swiss UNI rank very highly compared to other European countries. Indeed, seven out of eleven ranked UNI appear among the 200 best universities of the Shanghai and Times rankings (see Table 33.2).

In contrast, Switzerland's R&I system has potential for improvement in e-governance, number of researchers, cyber security, entrepreneurship, and number of new products commercialized. Other points of attention concern the decline of small and medium-sized enterprises engaged in R&D activities and the share of innovative companies. Finally, recruiting foreign researchers, technicians, and staff supporting R&D activities remains a key factor and therefore, a permanent challenge due to its higher degree of complexity (SERI 2020a).

Table 33.2: Swiss universities' places in international rankings

University/Ranking	Shanghai Ranking 2019	QS Ranking 2021	Times Ranking 2020	Leiden Ranking 2019
EPFL	78	14	38	16
ETHZ	19	6	13	14
Basel	87	149	94	53
Bern	101–150	114	113	181
Fribourg	401–500	601–650	301–350	
Geneva	58	106	144	71
Lausanne	151–200	169	198	116
Lugano	501–600	273	301–350	
Neuchâtel	901–1000		501–600	
St Gallen		428	401–500	
Zurich	61	69	90	60

Data source: The State Secretariat for Education, Research, and Innovation (SERI 2020c).

For the time being, the multiplication of policy initiatives related to R&I thus seems to benefit the Swiss economy and society. At the same time, while the growing interest in this field is notable, the need for coordination and coherence is stronger than ever if redundancies or overcapacities, for example, in technology parks, are to be avoided, and if Switzerland is to achieve international leadership (Bassin 2020).

Finally, the potentially positive effect of an innovation should not be limited to the economic dimension because the quality of life also depends on other factors, such as health, which R&I also influences. Therefore, the orientation of research topics, whether by the political authorities or the actors in the field, also has an important effect on such other dimensions. Non-technological areas are receiving more attention from the federal authorities, but the potential of social innovations is still under-exploited (SSIC 2015b).

7 Conclusion: A competitive system under pressure

Since the end of the 1960s, research and innovation have been taking a steadily increasing place in the Swiss political agenda at all institutional levels. A growing number of actors must coordinate at political and operational levels to use the growing budgets in an effective and efficient way. In this multi-level governance perspective, this coordination cannot be done in a hierarchical way but by a series of institutionalized coordination bodies, which assure integrating the main actors in policy formation and indirect management instruments. Considering the high performance of the Swiss R&I system, this coordination within Switzerland seems to work rather well. However, the coordination with the European Union represents a true sword of Damocles hanging on the Swiss R&I system and its competitiveness due to higher level politics and its conflict potential in the Swiss political system. Over the last twenty years, Swiss R&I policy has been an example of the Europeanization of a sectoral policy in a non-EU member state before illustrating a risk of de-Europeanization. Similar to the UK after Brexit, Switzerland must also develop a strategy to participate in the European Research Area. It is too early to know whether the Stick to Science initiative will produce the expected political effects, in particular to strengthen European research. The situation regarding the relationship with the EU is even trickier because most challenges for research and innovation have a European or even international dimension. Given Switzerland's potential contribution to solving these challenges, it is even more striking to observe that the EU uses these policies to exercise pressure on Switzerland, although other policies form the core of the European Union's dissatisfaction with Switzerland's role in Europe.

Over the past ten years, the challenges of innovation, and subsequently the ecological and digital transitions, have profoundly affected the research and innovation policy agendas. Within Swiss universities and the Swiss research and innovation system, issues of evaluation, intellectual property, scientific infrastructure, Big Data processing/storage (SSIC 2015c), and funding of research publications as well as ethical issues of sustainability in general and of research institutions and activities in particular (SSIC 2016) are becoming increasingly important. This is a profound change that questions the balance between basic and applied research within the innovation paradigm and the place of science in society and politics.

Policy changes at the system level also affect the functioning of the scientific community. Many Swiss research and higher education institutions signed the San Francisco Declaration on Research Assessment (DORA) in December 2017. They have adopted the theme of 'open access' as a priority within the framework of an institutional policy. The challenge will be to apply all the considerations that will have consequences for the world of scientific publishing and the hierarchies established between publication media and disciplines. In addition to the issues of integrity control, the questions of content quality control criteria, sources of funding, and the types of research to be developed remain open.

Applying the main principles of transparency and accountability may be accelerated by the awareness that the COVID-19 tragedy raised, particularly regarding the need for greater international scientific collaboration when addressing global threats (a pandemic, natural disasters, climate change, etc.). In the follow-up to the pandemic, the media and politicians called upon scientists to advise elected representatives and even to legitimize political decisions on health crisis management through task forces or scientific councils. Similar to the role played in raising awareness of climate change (work of the Intergovernmental Panel on Climate Change), science has regained the power to guide politics and society. In the future, how can this new power be managed without being subject to political injunctions, without weakening basic research, and without giving in to market pressures? Some even fear a 'covidization of research' ('towards pandemic-focused science') that 'distorts' usual priorities, funding, and protocols and wonder whether this evolution would be 'at the expense of other disciplines' (Adam 2020, 381).

Answers to these challenges and questions are not easy and need coordination between the various actors present within national R&I systems and international political and science communities. For the moment, apart from the critical issue of Europe, these internal coordination problems have not prevented the Swiss research system's excellent performance.

References

Adam, David, 2020. 'Scientists Fear That "Covidization" is Distorting Research'. *Nature* 588: pp. 381–382.
Bassin, Aline. 2020. 'L'inflation des centres de recherche'. *Le Temps*. 26.11.2020.
Benninghoff, Martin, and Dietmar Braun. 2010. 'Research Funding. Authority Relations and Scientific Production in Switzerland'. In *Reconfiguring Knowledge Production: Changing Authority Relations in the Sciences and their Consequences for intellectual Innovation*, edited by Richard Whitley, Jochen Gläser, and Lars Engwall, pp. 81–109. Oxford: Oxford University Press.
Braun, Dietmar, Thomas Griessen, Lukas Baschung, Martin Benninghoff, and Jean-Philippe Leresche. 2007. 'Zusammenlegung aller Bundeskompetenzen für Bildung, Forschung und Innovation in einem Departement'. *Les Cahiers de l'Observatoire* 16: pp. 1–104.
Federal Council. 2015. Message sur l'organisation et le soutien du Parc suisse d'innovation. https://www.sbfi.admin.ch/sbfi/fr/home/recherche-et-innovation/la-recherche-et-linnovation-en-suisse/parc-suisse-d_innovation.html (accessed 2 November 2022).
Federal Council. 2017. 'Objectifs stratégiques du Conseil fédéral pour l'Agence suisse pour l'encouragement de l'innovation (Innosuisse) pendant les années 2018 à 2020'. Bern.
Federal Council. 2020. 'Message relatif à l'encouragement de la formation, de la recherche et l'innovation pendant les années 2021 à 2024'. https://www.sbfi.admin.ch/sbfi/fr/home/politique-fri/fri-2021-2024.html (accessed 2 November 2022).
OFCOM (Federal Office of Communications). 2020. 'Digital Switzerland Strategy'. Biel/Bienne.
FSO (Federal Statistical Office). 2021. 'Dépenses de recherche et développement (R-D)'. https://www.bfs.admin.ch/bfs/fr/home/statistiques/themes-transversaux/mesure-bien-etre/tous-indicateurs/economie/depenses-r-et-d.assetdetail.19384459.html (accessed 5 April 2022).
FSO (Federal Statistical Office). 2022a. 'Titres délivrés dans les hautes écoles universitaires'. www.bfs.admin.ch (accessed 7 November 2022).
FSO (Federal Statistical Office). 2022b. 'Finances et coûts des hautes écoles'. https://www.bfs.admin.ch/bfs/fr/home/statistiques/education-science/finances-systeme/hautes-ecoles.html (accessed 6 April 2022).
FSO (Federal Statistical Office). 2022c. 'Decrease in Confederation Research and Development Expenditure in 2021'. *Press Release 27.6.2022*. https://dam-api.bfs.admin.ch/hub/api/dam/assets/22644568/master (accessed 11 October 2022).

Fleury, Antoine, and Frédéric Joye. 2002. *Les débuts de la politique de recherche en Suisse. Histoire de la création du FNS (1934-1952)*. Genève: Droz.

Fumasoli, Tatiana, and Benedetto Lepori. 2011. 'Patterns of Strategies in Swiss Higher Education Institutions'. *Higher Education* 61: pp. 157–178.

Gingras, Yves. 2002. 'Les formes spécifiques du champ international'. *Actes de la recherche en sciences sociales*, 2 (141): pp. 31–45.

Griessen, Thomas, and Dietmar Braun. 2010. 'Hochschulföderalismus zwischen Kooperationszwang und Blockadegefahr: Deutschland und die Schweiz im Vergleich'. *Swiss Political Science Review*, 16 (4): pp. 715–746.

Hotz-Hart, Beat, and Ingrid Kissling-Näf. 2013. 'Structures politico-administrative de la politique de la formation, de recherche et d'innovation'. In *Manuel d'administration publique suisse*, edited by Ladner, Andreas, Jean-Loup Chappelet, Yves Emery, Peter Knoepfel, Luzius Mader, Nils Soguel, and Frédéric Varone, pp. 789–810. Lausanne: PPUR.

Joye-Cagnard, Frédéric. 2010. *La construction de la politique de la science en Suisse. Enjeux scientifiques, stratégiques et politiques (1944-1974)*. Neuchâtel: Editions Alphil-Presses universitaires suisses.

Kuhlmann, Stefan. 2001. 'Future Governance of Innovation Policy in Europe – Three Scenarios'. *Research Policy* 30: pp. 953–976.

Lavenex, Sandra. 2009. 'Switzerland in the European Research Area: Integration Without Legislation'. *Swiss Political Science Review* 15 (4): pp. 629–51.

Lehnert, Patrick, Curdin Pfister, and Uschi Backes-Gellner. 2020. 'Employment of R&D Personnel After an Educational Supply Shock: Effects of the Introduction of Universities of Applied Sciences in Switzerland'. *Labour Economics* 66. doi: 10.1016/j.labeco.2020.101883.

Leresche, Jean-Philippe, Philippe Larédo, and Karl Weber. 2009. *Recherche et enseignement supérieur face à l'internationalisation. France, Suisse et Union européenne*. Lausanne: PPUR.

Leresche, Jean-Philippe, Lukas Baschung. 2022. 'Politique de la recherche, de la technologie et de l'innovation'. In *Manuel de la politique suisse*, edited by Yannis Papadopoulos, Pascal Sciarini, Adrian Vatter, Silja Häusermann, Patrick Emmenegger, and Flavia Fossati, pp. 811–834. Zurich: NZZ Libro.

Lepori, Benedetto. 2007. *La politique de la recherche en Suisse. Institutions, acteurs et dynamique historique*. Bern: Paul Haupt.

Lepori, Benedetto, Peter van den Besselaar, Michael Dinges, Bianca Potì, Emanuela Reale, Emanuela, Stig Slipersaeter, Jean Thèves, and Barend van der Meulen. 2007. 'Comparing the Evolution of National Research Policies: What Patterns of Change?' *Science and Public Policy* 34 (6): pp. 372–388.

Paradeise, Catherine, Emanuela Reale, Ivar Bleiklie, and Ewan Ferlie. 2009. *University Governance, Western European Comparative Perspectives*. Berlin: Springer.

Regierungsrat Bern. 2019. 'Engagement 2030. Regierungsrichtlinien der Regierungspolitik 2019-2022'. Bern.

Matthews, David. 2022. 'How UK and Swiss Researchers Are Coping without Association to Horizon Europe'. *Science/Business*. 31 March. https://sciencebusiness.net/news/how-uk-and-swiss-researchers-are-coping-without-association-horizon-europe (accessed 31 October 2022).

SERI (State Secretariat for Education, Research, and Innovation). 2020a. 'Research and Innovation in Switzerland 2020'. Bern: SERI.

SERI (State Secretariat for Education, Research, and Innovation). 2020b. 'Financement de la formation, de la recherche et de l'innovation par les cantons et la Confédération'. Bern: SERI.

SERI (State Secretariat for Education, Research, and Innovation). 2020c. 'Classements internationaux des hautes écoles universitaires suisses'. Bern: SERI.

Smeby, Jens-Christian, and Jarle Trondal. 2005. 'Globalisation or Europeanisation? International Contact Among University Staff'. *Higher Education* 49: pp. 449–466.

SNSF (Swiss National Science Foundation). 2021. 'Financial Statement'. https://www.snf.ch/media/en/1pMl5vwQAbWF6xoc/jahresrechnung_kurzversion_en.pdf (accessed 5 April 2022).

SSIC (Swiss Science and Innovation Council). 2015a. 'Inventar der schweizerischen Innovationspolitik. Eine Analyse der Förderinitiativen von Bund, Kantonen und ausgewählten Städten'. Bern: SWIR.

SSIC (Swiss Science and Innovation Council). 2015b. 'Innovation und staatliche Innovationsförderung'. Bern: SWIR.

SSIC (Swiss Science and Innovation Council). 2015c. 'Evaluation de l'encouragement stratégique des infrastructures de recherche et des disciplines au Fonds national suisse'. Bern: CSSI.

SSIC (Swiss Science and Innovation Council). 2016. 'Exigences pour un système durable d'enseignement supérieur et de recherche'. Bern: CSSI.

Strasser, Bruno, and Frédéric Joye. 2005. 'Neutralité politique, neutralité scientifique: la coopération scientifique internationale dans la politique étrangère de la Suisse au temps de la Guerre froide'. *Relations internationales* 121: pp. 59–72.

Stick to Science. 2022. 'An Online Signature Campaign for an Open and Inclusive European Research Area'. https://stick-to-science.eu (accessed 7 November 2022).

Thierstein, Alain, and Beate Willhelm. 2001. 'Incubator, Technology, and Innovation Centres in Switzerland: Features and Policy Implications'. *Entrepreneurship & Regional Development* 13 (4): pp. 315–331.

CHAPTER 34

ENVIRONMENTAL AND SPATIAL PLANNING POLICIES

KARIN INGOLD AND STÉPHANE NAHRATH

1 INTRODUCTION

THIS chapter deals with two related and specific policy areas: environment and spatial planning. In Switzerland, as in many other countries, what are usually defined as environmental policies are a set of different sectoral policies that address the main negative externalities generated by human activities on the environment. The areas of intervention are water management and hydrology, forestry, landscape and biodiversity, air protection and chemicals, waste and raw materials management, noise and non-ionizing radiation control, soil and contaminated site remediation, biotechnology, hazard prevention, and climate change. In federalist Switzerland, many competences to regulate the environment are driven by national policies. Still, the protection of most natural resources lays in the hands of the canton. And different than many might think, Swiss environmental performance does not for many issues, such as climate change, biodiversity, or species protection, rank highest and would need serious improvement to become exemplary.

Also spatial planning policy is conceived as a cross-cutting policy and stands for the coordination of the many competing uses of space in general and of land (in its quantitative dimension) in particular. Its function is to coordinate a large number of different public policies as long as they have spatial effects. In Switzerland, like in most European countries, spatial planning policy is rather decentralized: only the main principles and objectives as well as the main categories of spatial planning instruments are defined at federal level. Their implementation is the responsibility of the cantons and municipalities. This results in great disparities in the implementation of the instruments and in the achievement of the policy objectives, particularly those of a measured use of land and a limitation of urban sprawl.

Whereas environmental policies are often much focused on protecting people and ecosystems from pollution and combating the overexploitation and destruction of natural resource systems, spatial planning policy pursues more heterogeneous and sometimes even contradictory objectives. Spatial planning not only aims to protect resource systems in general and to ensure economical and efficient use of land in particular but is also responsible for making these resources available and exploiting them for the benefit of various socio-economic sectors.

2 Main Features and Historical Development of Environmental and Spatial Planning Policies

We can distinguish four characteristics of environmental problems and related policies that make them a particularly interesting policy field to study (Ingold et al. 2016): first, uncertainty about the origin of problems and/or the pace and severity of their effects; second, fragmentation across different decision-making levels (local, regional, national, and international); third, fragmentation across sectors; and fourth, tensions between short-term objectives and long-term solutions. Overall, these characteristics constitute a major challenge for all states and, in particular, for the Swiss federalist system characterized by its instruments of direct democracy and consensual decision-making. Thus, solving the increasingly complex and interdependent environmental problems requires the development of new environmental governance arrangements that combine multi-level, cross-sectoral, and cross-territorial approaches (Driessen et al. 2012; Varone et al. 2013; Ingold et al. 2018).

Spatial planning policy shares three of the four characteristics of environmental policies, namely characteristics two, three, and four above. However, they are distinguished by the central role played by property rights holders, primarily landowners, in their formulation and especially in their implementation (Nahrath 2003; Varone and Nahrath 2014).

From a historical perspective, the two policy areas have partially developed in parallel; however, their development also took different pathways, as outlined hereafter. After a slow emergence since the end of the nineteenth century, their constitution into autonomous subsystems proceeded in parallel throughout the 1960s (political recognition of public problems and the first cantonal and federal legislation), the 1970s (constitutional articles), the 1980s (federal legal bases), and the 1990s (implementation in the cantons) (Knoepfel et al. 2010; Ingold et al. 2016). However, their respective development pathways thereafter are quite different.

The regulation and steering modalities of environmental policies underwent significant and steady development in the form of increasing specialization in many areas and of different programmes during the 1980s and 1990s. Spatial planning policy, on the other hand, developed and was implemented much more slowly and laboriously between the 1980s and 2000 (Nahrath 2003; Varone and Nahrath 2014). It was not until the turn of the 2010s that this public policy underwent significant new developments, notably through a major revision of the Federal Act on Spatial Planning (SPA) in 2012. This difference is mainly explained by the fact that environmental policies have experienced at their emergence political conditions that were not as conflicting as those of land use planning.

2.1 The history and development of environmental policies

Looking at the history of Swiss environmental policy and politics, we can distinguish between three main stages of development and maturation.

2.1.1 *Stage 1: ad hoc regulation of certain natural resources (1874–1950)*

In this first stage, key tasks were assigned to the Confederation mainly in the areas of mountain forest management (largely overexploited) and flood control (dyking of rivers). However, this stage does not yet correspond to the emergence of a coherent environmental policy subsystem.

2.1.2 *Stage 2: empowerment and institutionalization (1950–1990)*

The empowerment of environmental policy as a specific subsystem began in the 1950s, particularly following the revision of article 24 of the constitution in 1953, which gave the Confederation the responsibility of protecting surface water and groundwater. This process of empowerment was reinforced by the development of a nature and landscape protection policy in 1966. Following the clear adoption of a constitutional article on environmental protection by the Swiss people (92.7 per cent) in 1971, the Federal Act on the Protection of the Environment (EPA) was introduced in 1983. The creation of the Federal Office for Environmental Protection (FOEP) in 1971 and the establishment of the main principles of environmental law (notably prevention and polluter pays) as well as the main procedural rules (right of appeal for environmental protection organizations and environmental impact assessment (EIA)) contributed to the institutionalization of environmental policies and strengthened the weight of environmental interests in the political arena.

The second half of the 1980s was characterized by a very important development of environmental policies, both in terms of policy and polity. On the one hand, the implementation of the EPA implied the adoption of a large number of ordinances and cantonal implementing legislation as well as the creation of numerous administrative services (federal, cantonal, and communal) requiring a significant increase in the public budgets allocated to the environmental field. On the other hand, the 1980s were characterized by a series of 'external shocks' that changed the political power balance in favour of the environment: The debate on the 'death of the forests', conflicts over the construction of nuclear power plants, the chemical accident in *Schweizerhalle* (industry site near Basel) in 1986, and the adoption in 1987 of the popular initiative '*Rothenturm*' for the protection of wetlands are key examples thereof. The last two events had consequences for the environment. *Schweizerhalle* led to the introduction of the Ordinance on Protection Against Major Accidents (MAO) (1991) and *Rothenturm* led to the inclusion of a constitutional article on the protection of wetlands (1987) as well as the adoption in 1996 of the Federal Ordinance on the Protection of Wetlands of Special Beauty and National Importance.

2.1.3 Stage 3: consolidation and internationalization (1990–2020)

This third stage is marked by three processes: first, the impact of international conventions and the United Nations (UN) regime on Swiss environmental policies; second, the increasing complexity and 'cross-sectoral spill over' of these same policies; and third, the rise of economic and strategic planning instruments.

The World Summit on Environment and Development in Rio de Janeiro in 1992 was the main vehicle for the internationalization of Swiss environmental policies over the past thirty years, particularly through the dissemination of the concept of sustainable development (Böhlen and Clémençon 1992). In the case of Switzerland, this summit was above all the trigger for the policy to combat climate change as well as a factor in putting biodiversity conservation on the agenda. However, despite the great enthusiasm after the Rio Summit, the CO_2 Act only came into force in the year 2000 and the biodiversity strategy only in 2012. To date, Switzerland is not meeting the national and international targets set for these two areas.

Evaluations of the environmental policy programmes in the 1990s show both the successes and the limitations of the highly sectoralized and regulatory approach introduced and adopted during the 1980s (for an overview, see Ingold et al. 2016, ch. 4). They further highlight the cross-sectoral, cross-territorial, and multi-level nature of many environmental problems and thus a further need for cross-sectoral activity and integration. This observation led to the reformatting of certain fields of intervention, which became more cross-cutting (landscape, climate, biodiversity, and biotechnologies) or integrated (water, air, soil, forest, and waste). Environmental mainstreaming of non-environmental sectors began in the 1990s: notably, agriculture and food, energy, transport, infrastructure, urbanization, housing, and industry experienced some 'greening'.

Moreover, the choice of instruments in environmental policies further evolved and is characterized by a strong growth in economic incentives (taxes and subsidies) and market-based instruments (tradable emission certificates) as well as by the multiplication of strategic action plans (landscape, national territory, climate, and biodiversity).

In sum, this three-stage chronological approach makes it possible to show: first, that the development of environmental policies was initially dominated by the objectives of protecting crucial natural resources (water, forests, and landscapes)—as well as protecting populations against natural disasters (floods)—before undergoing empowerment and institutionalization in the context of the dissemination of ecosystem approaches and the generalization of the paradigm of the generalized limitation of (polluting) emissions; second, that the development of different policies took diverse pathways: climate and biodiversity were late-comers, whereas other sectoral policies developed in regular and steady development pathways (e.g. water); and third, that the way of perceiving environmental problems today is increasingly inter-sectoral, trans-territorial, and multi-scalar (climate, biodiversity, and biotechnologies).

2.2 The history and development of spatial planning policy

The development of spatial planning policy is broadly similar to that of environmental policies but with a more chaotic rhythm that follows five stages, the dominant historical dynamic of which is 'bottom up'.

2.2.1 Stage 1: land law, local planning, and protection of agricultural land (1912–1950)

One of the founding elements of the regulation of land use in Switzerland is the anchoring—in the Swiss Civil Code of 1907—of the legal definition of ownership in general and by extension of land and property ownership in particular. This (private law) definition of 'exclusive' ownership, which was further strengthened by the introduction of the principle of guarantee of ownership in the federal constitution in 1969, has had a fundamental impact on the development of spatial planning policy to this day as it has contributed to the empowerment of landowners vis-à-vis the planning authorities. From the 1930s onwards, cities developed the first urban planning instruments in the form of street and district level 'alignment plans'. Later on, in the context of the Second World War and the strengthening of the country's capacity for self-sufficiency, the first federal legal bases were put in place to protect agricultural land.

2.2.2 Stage 2: first cantonal laws and indirect demarcation of building zones (1950–1970)

From the 1950s onwards, some cantons adopted the first laws on building and land use, primarily with the aim of protecting agricultural land, vineyards, and lakeshores from the first forms of urban and landscape sprawls. The municipalities, concerned to rationalize urbanization, also began using the channelling plans to informally delimit their buildable areas.

2.2.3 Stage 3: formulation of the federal spatial planning policy (SPA) (1970–1980)

During the quite long and conflicting policy programming phase (1960s and 1970s), two opposing political projects clashed. The left-wing political organizations (Swiss Socialist Party (SP)), trade unions and the far-left party of Labour, environmental non-governmental organizations (NGOs), certain interest groups (tenants and families), and the evangelical churches defended the option of a reform of land law (strengthening of pre-emption and expropriation rights in favour of the state and resocialization of land value gains) as well as the implementation of an ambitious federal land policy. In response to various popular initiatives launched during the 1960s by the SP and the Swiss Trade Union against land speculation, the Federal Council, with the support of the right-wing parties, proposed the introduction of a federal spatial planning policy based on zoning (Federal Council 1966). The political solution that the federal government eventually succeeded in imposing was the inclusion in 1969 in the federal constitution of a political compromise (called *Bodenrechtartikel*) that introduced a federal spatial planning policy in return for the constitutional recognition of the guarantee of private property.

The conflicts that marked the process of drafting the SPA in the 1970s centred on two main issues: first, the division of competences between the Confederation and the cantons; and second, the inclusion in the law of a series of land law instruments such as the right of pre-emption and the tax on added land value. The latter instrument was the centrepiece of the system—it was supposed to separate the financial issues of the land market from the supposedly technical work of zoning. The first version of the SPA thus included both these instruments as well as assigning significant planning powers to the Confederation. Opponents of the spatial planning policy found this draft unacceptable and launched a referendum, which they surprisingly won in June 1976 after a fierce battle.

The second version of the law finally accepted in 1979 no longer included these land instruments and preserved a large part of the cantons' autonomy. In the face of the threat posed by landowners' claims for compensation for material expropriation, and in the absence of the financial means that the tax on added land value was supposed to provide to finance these compensations, the rescue of spatial planning policy came through the judicialization of its implementation (Nahrath 2003). In particular, the intervention of the federal judges tightening, in their jurisprudence, the conditions for granting compensation for material expropriation proved to be crucial for the reduction of financial risks for local planning authorities (Moor 2002).

2.2.4 *Stage 4: implementation of the SPA in the cantons and municipalities (1980–2000)*

The 1980s and 1990s were dedicated to the implementation of the SPA in the cantons, which legislated and developed their master plans, and in the municipalities, which implemented their land use plans.

2.2.5 *Stage 5: revisions of the SPA (2000–2020)*

Since its entry into force on 1 January 1980, the SPA has undergone four partial revisions and a major revision in 2012. This last—and most substantive—revision[1] pursues four objectives—densification, reduction of oversized building zones, introduction of a compensation mechanism for land value gains and losses (i.e. the tax rejected in 1976 on added land value), and combating the hoarding of building land—and provides new instruments for strengthening federal spatial planning policy.

As these five stages show, the development of spatial planning policy initially involved the regulation of land uses through private law; a genuine public policy was later developed, first at cantonal and then at federal level (Varone and Nahrath 2014). In terms of policy instruments, note the reintroduction in 2012 of the tax on added land value, almost forty years after its removal from the 1979 law.

3 The main governance modes of environmental and spatial planning policies

3.1 Steering and regulation of environmental policies

Environmental policies are based on the following three main principles:

- First, the 'causality principle' (or 'polluter pays' principle), which requires the internalization of the negative externalities generated by producers and/or consumers of polluting products.
- Second, the 'principle of prevention', which 'aims to prevent damage that is scientifically proven to be causally related to the event causing the damage' (Flückiger 2005, 112).
- Third, the 'principle of weighing interests', which implies, in the context of any decision, whether administrative or judicial, the balancing of the interests of the different parties involved. On the one hand, the interests of the users or operators of the environment (i.e. the 'polluters') and, on the other, those of the victims of negative environmental externalities and/or the protectors of the environment (Morand 1996) are taken into consideration. This implies the use of the proportionality principle, mainly known in legal contexts or disputes.

To achieve the objectives set in the legal bases, various instruments (substantive and procedural) have been put in place. Table 34.1 presents and exemplifies the main categories of substantive instruments available to political-administrative authorities. The following are the main procedural instruments:

- The Environmental Impact Assessment (EIA) is based on the principle that any developer, public or private, whose project to build new infrastructure or to modify or expand an existing industrial or infrastructure facility is likely to affect the environment, is required to produce—at its own expense—an environmental impact report.
- The right of appeal for environmental protection organizations is, in international comparison, a very unique instrument for environmental protection. It comprises a right of appeal against decisions taken by public authorities concerning the planning, construction, modification, or operation of facilities that may adversely

Table 34.1: The different categories of substantive environmental policy instruments

Instrument categories	Examples
Regulatory	Prohibitions and emission permits, operating permits, emission limit values (e.g. water, air, soil, and noise), and national emission quotas (e.g. CO_2)
Fiscal and economic incentives	Taxes and charges (e.g. VOCs, CO_2, and rubbish bags), fines, subsidies (e.g. solar panels), tax rebates (e.g. building insulation), and market instruments (e.g. tradable CO_2 certificates)
Persuasive	Information campaigns, monitoring, and research & development
Self-regulation	Self-reporting of emissions by emitters

Note: 'Emission limit values' refers to the maximum permissible intensity of pollutant emissions per emitter during a given period (concentration and flow).

Data source: The authors.

affect the environment, nature, or landscape. This right has been granted to organizations for the protection of nature, the environment, and the cultural and built heritage that have been in existence for more than ten years, are active nationwide, and are non-profit-oriented.

3.2 Regulatory modes in spatial planning policy

Spatial planning policy is based on two main principles:

First, the principle of 'judicious and measured land use' implies a clear separation of building and non-building areas to avoid the dispersal of buildings and the sprawl of the landscape, the long-term preservation of soil fertility, and the reduction of arable land losses.

Second, the principle of 'rational land use' means improving the distribution of land uses, optimizing the use of building zones (proportionate to the needs of the next fifteen years and sustainable densification), and harmoniously developing the whole territory (decentralized concentration of urbanization and maintenance of regional balance).

The following are the main policy instruments provided in the SPA:

- The Confederation's sectoral concepts and plans are the two most important direct planning instruments of the Confederation for the coordination of federal sectoral tasks with spatial implications.
- Zoning plans—distinguishing between buildable and non-buildable areas (agricultural and protected areas)—is the main spatial planning instrument for regulating land uses. These plans are drawn up at different planning levels: cantonal, regional, and municipal. They do not have the same objectives or the same legal scope depending on the planning scale chosen:

- The cantonal master plan (CMP) is the most important instrument for the management and coordination of (cantonal) spatial planning. Based on a detailed description of the state of coordination of federal, cantonal, and municipal spatial activities, it provides an overview of the spatial development objectives. In doing so, it serves as an instrument for guiding and approving municipal land use plans. CMPs are submitted to the relevant federal authority, the Federal Office for Spatial Development (ARE), for approval. They are binding on the public authorities but not on property owners.
- The communal land use plan (CLUP) defines, in a legally binding manner for all property owners, the possible uses of the various parts of the communal territory. It strictly separates buildable and non-buildable areas. In so doing, CLUPs determine for each landowner the manner and limits of economic exploitation of his or her property. The CLUP is drawn up by the municipality in a democratic procedure and must comply with the CMP and the federal sectoral plans. To give concrete form to the CLUP, special land use plans regulating the development of more limited areas (neighbourhood or housing estate) are also possible. These plans are approved by the cantonal authorities and serve as the basis for issuing building permits.
- The building permit is the concretization of the right to build conferred by the CLUP. It depends on compliance with the following principles: the obligation to equip the land, the conformity of land uses with zoning regulations, and the obligation to obtain an exemption in the opposite case (e.g. constructions outside the building zone).

The revision of 15 June 2012 introduced the following new instruments: first, the compulsory tax on added land value (by at least 20 per cent) resulting from development measures; second, the development of a federal method (compulsory for the cantons) for calculating the size of communal building zones according to the fifteen-year development needs criterion; third, the obligation to reduce oversized building zones; fourth, the possibility for cantonal and communal authorities to impose land improvement measures or an imperative deadline for the construction of strategic land plots; and fifth, the introduction of densification and urban requalification objectives within CMPs.

4 The actors and their coordination

In Switzerland, as probably in any consensual democracy, the inclusion of the different public and private actors into policy-making starts very early in the policy design process. This is not least reinforced through the fact that the referendum, and thus the vote at the ballot by the people, hangs like Damocles' sword over any elite or government decision. Thus, different interests are taken into account through the whole process and these include, besides the political parties and the leading and non-leading administrative agencies, the cantons, the peak associations from industry and civil society, trade unions, NGOs, sciences, and sector/non-sector specific regulators.

Both sets of policies, environmental and spatial planning, are distinguished by politically and economically very powerful target groups able to provide strong resistance throughout the policy cycle. This is why, in order to counterbalance these powerful target groups, the legislator has endowed environmental NGOs with a strong right of appeal that is supposed to guarantee the effective implementation of environmental law and the achievement of policy objectives.

5 Current implementation status

5.1 Implementation of environmental policies

Providing a comprehensive overview of the current state of implementation and the effectiveness (beneficial or otherwise) of the various sectoral environmental policies is not easy. Based on the latest Federal Council report on the state of the environment in Switzerland (Federal Council 2018), the following general findings are obtained (Table 34.2), which give us some indication of the 'performance' of the various sectoral environmental policies.

The following lessons can be learned from this summary table. First, although Swiss environmental policies seem to achieve high environmental performance in international comparison,[2] some policy areas such as biodiversity protection, waste reduction, implementation of minimum flow rates, and reduction of greenhouse gas emissions have significantly lower performance. Second, the degree to which environmental problems are solved significantly varies between different environmental policy areas. Third, classical (i.e. sectoral emission limitation-based) policies that address more specific and limited problems and whose interventions are based on clearly identified technical devices (chemicals, contaminated sites, waste, and, to a lesser extent, air, water, soil quality protection, and noise) seem to perform better than more cross-cutting and ecosystem-based policies (biodiversity, landscape, and climate). This makes Switzerland for instance a forerunner in water quality management (Metz and Ingold 2014), but not so in climate change mitigation performance for example where the UK or also Denmark rank among the highest and much above Switzerland (Burck et al. 2018). Typically, climate policy has not yet achieved the urgently needed targets for reducing greenhouse gas emissions (Ingold and Pflieger 2016), which explains the many and frequent revisions of the CO_2 Act. Fourth, resource management policies in the traditional sectors of water and forestry are likely to come under increasing pressure because of global warming. Thus, successes of these classical policies do not seem to be able to guarantee a truly sustainable management (i.e. one that respects planetary limits) of the resource systems concerned. Fifth, in areas such as climate change adaptation and biodiversity conservation, the Confederation chose to introduce not laws but two strategies in 2012, supplemented in 2017 (biodiversity) and 2020 (climate change adaptation) by action plans. This choice makes clear that these issues do not have top regulatory priority and that this also involves a significant delegation of implementation to the cantons (Widmer 2018).

Table 34.2: Current status (2018) of implementation of key environmental policies

	Contributions	Limits
Climate	10 per cent reduction in GHG emissions between 1990 and 2016. Targets achieved for the construction and industry sectors. Strategy and action plan for adaptation to climate change.	2020 targets (20 per cent reduction) difficult to achieve, with unmet targets mainly in the transport sector. International civil aviation and agriculture not taken into account. Warming in Switzerland is above global average. Compliance with Paris Agreement not ensured after rejection of revised CO_2 Act at the ballot in 2021.
Air	Clear decrease in air pollution from 1988 to 2017, which is good compared with Europe.	Regular exceedance of target limits for fine particles (PM10), nitrogen dioxide (NO_2), and ozone (O_3).
Water	Continuous decrease (since the 1970s) of phosphorus and nitrogen pollution (nutrients) in surface waters, in particular following the obligation to connect to waste water treatment plants.	Frequent exceedance of emission limits for nitrates in groundwater. Persistent pollution of small rivers by nutrients and pesticides. Micropollutants from households and industries in watercourses. Partial implementation of minimum flow rates. Increase in average river temperatures.
Biodiversity	Development of an action plan in the framework of the Swiss Biodiversity Strategy (2017).	Continued reduction and degradation of high quality natural areas. Half of the native species are threatened or potentially threatened.
Forests	Steadily increasing forest area and species diversity. Stability or even increase in the volume of wood produced. Targets for creation of forest reserves achieved.	Increasing impacts of global warming (drought and new pests). Air pollution and soil acidification.
Soils	Decrease in the rate of growth of sealing. Tendency to reduce soil erosion. Development of a national soil strategy (2017).	Continued increase of sealed surfaces (+29 per cent since 1979), covering 4.7 per cent of the country's surface in 2009. Increased chemical pollution of soils (zinc, copper, and nitrogen).

Landscapes	Increase in the size of protected areas. Creation of sixteen regional nature parks since 2007.	Continued sprawl and fragmentation of landscapes (e.g. transport).
Noise	Reduction of certain noise nuisances (road, rail, and air traffic) through measures to reduce noise emissions at source.	Noise abatement targets only partially met (population growth, increased road traffic, and urbanization). More people exposed to noise levels exceeding target limits than in 1987.
Municipal waste	Generalization of the causality principle (polluter pays). Reduction of environmental impact and increase of thermal recovery capacity through incineration plants modernization. Doubling the recycling rate between 2000 and 2020.	Increase in the amount of waste per capita. End-of-pipe strategy. Difficult to implement circular economy and close material flow loops. Little eco-design measures for products and very low reuse rate.
Polluted sites	By 2025, all polluted sites to be investigated should have been investigated (two out of three investigated so far). All contaminated sites should be remediated through OCRCS compensation by 2040 (one out of four remediated so far).	Three thousand contaminated sites still need to be cleaned up.
Chemical products	Applying international conventions and the precautionary principle. Market and company control. National Chemical Strategy and Action Plan for Plant Protection Products.	Presence of residues of phytosanitary products in water. Insufficient scientific knowledge about their effect on soils and biodiversity.

Data source: Knoepfel et al. (2010) and Federal Council (2018).

5.2 Implementation of spatial planning policy

Following the entry into force of the SPA in 1980, the Federal Council conducted several evaluations of its effects (e.g. ARE 2005; Federal Council 2017). These various reports, as well as the results of several scientific studies on spatial development and social, economic, and ecological land use (Häberli et al. 1991), all point to the identification of the main contributions and shortcomings of the SPA.

The SPA has made it possible to generalize the principle of separation between buildable and non-buildable areas. In doing so, it has reduced the scale of speculation, limited the spread of construction, and improved the protection of agricultural land and sensitive natural areas. However, the preparation and implementation of the cantonal and municipal plans proved to be more complicated than expected.

Numerous implementation problems remain. These include the recurrent oversizing of building zones and their difficult resizing (because of material expropriation risks); the continued urban sprawl and sprawl of the landscape (and fragmentation of ecosystems); the poor compensation of gains and losses resulting from planning measures owing to the very late introduction (2014) of a tax on added land value; the difficulty for municipalities to meet their obligation to provide facilities in these same building zones (because of their oversizing); the hoarding strategies of (small) landowners preventing coherent urbanization; the overly liberal practice of granting exceptional building permits outside the building zone; and the institutional fragmentation that makes coherent planning at the scale of functional spaces (particularly in the case of agglomerations) very difficult (Jeannerat 2012).

According to the joint report of the European Environment Agency and the Swiss Federal Office for the Environment (EEA and FOEN 2016) comparing the urban sprawl index of the twenty-eight EU and four EFTA Countries, Switzerland has a higher urban sprawl index than the average of the thirty-two countries.

6 Conclusion and Outlook

As is probably the case for any emerging field of public policy, the emergence and maturation of environmental and spatial planning policies initially consisted of the establishment of the main institutional arrangements (constitutional articles, legal bases, and administrative departments). Interestingly, these arrangements have not fundamentally changed to date. After an intense phase of substantial and legal development from the mid-twentieth century until the 1990s, the last thirty years have been marked above all by a trend towards the internationalization of national policy programmes (stronger in the case of the environment than in that of spatial planning) as well as by more or less significant revisions of existing laws and ordinances. All this seems 'business as usual' in many policy fields. But two cornerstones of the policy fields discussed here are clearly the most recent revision of the SPA in 2012 and the ongoing revision of the CO_2 Act since its introduction in 2000. The updated CO_2 Act was rejected by the people at the ballot in June 2021, which threw Switzerland further back in its international climate commitments.[3]

Meanwhile, the ongoing energy transition mainly gives some economic sectors and actors potential for innovation and promotion, which fosters new alliances between business and pro-ecology actors that might push Swiss climate policy further. At the same time, new conflicts also arise: the Russian military intervention in Ukraine has even more strongly emphasized the Swiss energy dependence on foreign countries as well as the need to reduce fossil energy consumption and enhance renewable energy production. Renewables and storage options can, however, have spatial planning or biodiversity implications that some of the cantons, regions, municipalities, and also green NGOs are not willing to accept. Therefore, further challenges to balance energy, environment, and spatial planning priorities remain.

Finally, new public issues arrive on the Swiss environmental policy agenda such as food and plastic waste (Lauwerier et al. 2021). In both cases, Switzerland is currently relying on self-regulation (Brunner 2004) and measures taken by individuals, households, and companies within the different economic sectors. Thus, whereas the 1990s–2020 seem to have been marked by a strong development of regulations, notably with the help of market instruments, we may now be witnessing the genesis of a new and fourth stage that would be characterized by (a return of) self-regulation under the increased pressure and control of a more strongly mobilized civil society.

The joint analysis of environmental and spatial planning policies makes it possible to identify three main challenges for their future development.

First, the sectoral organization of environmental policies raises the question of coherence between environmental policies themselves as well as with economic and infrastructural (e.g. renewable energies) policies. Although the first generation of environmental policies encountered major coordination and 'problem shifting' issues (Knoepfel et al. 2010), improvements seem to have been made from the 1990s onwards, particularly owing to improved legislative procedures and the development of more cross- cutting programmes and action plans (landscape, biodiversity, floods, climate, and agglomerations). However, the very strong development of environmental regulations during this same period seems to have been more rapid and important than that of coordination mechanisms, with the growing risk of blocking policy integration dynamics, the consequence of which is the falling into 'institutional complexity traps' (Bolognesi and Nahrath 2020).

Second, the development of the 'ecological transition' discourse conveys a double critique of contemporary environmental and spatial planning policies. On the one hand, the critique of the 'weak' conception of sustainability and the call for strict respect of 'planet boundaries' implies a paradigm shift of these policies towards sustainable resource management. On the other hand, it calls for a broadening of the scope of environmental policies through the greening of a number of non-environmental policies, such as agricultural, transport, energy, housing, industrial development, and spatial planning policies.

Third, environmental and spatial planning failures highlight the tensions that exist in Switzerland between public policy objectives and instruments, on the one hand, and private property protection regime on the other hand. It is indeed quite usual to see the implementation of policy instruments limited, or even blocked, by the target groups holding property or use rights on the resources that are supposed to be protected by environmental policies or by spatial planning policy. Such blockages, which sometimes lead to the judicialization of environmental and spatial planning policies, invite reflection on the opportunity to redefine the property regime so as to reduce the contradictions between public and private law (Aubin and Nahrath 2015).

Taking these three issues into account to achieve national and international sustainability objectives will undoubtedly require in-depth reflection and reorganization of Swiss environmental and spatial planning policies in the future.

Notes

1. Accepted by the Federal Parliament on 15 June, 2012, this revision was attacked in a referendum, notably by the Swiss Union of Arts and Crafts (USAM). The referendum was rejected by 69.2 per cent of voters on 3 March 2013.
2. Switzerland is ranked ninth in the 2022 Environmental Performance Index (EPI) developed by the Yale Centre for Environmental Law & Policy (EPI 2022).
3. On 18 June, 2023, a majority of the Swiss people finally voted in favour of the revised CO_2 act. This act contained less stringent policy instruments that the previous one, but still should help Switzerland reach its commitments made under the Paris agreement.

References

ARE. 2005. *Rapport 2005 sur le développement territorial*. Bern: ARE.
Aubin, David, and Stéphane Nahrath. 2015. 'De la plura dominia à la propriété privative: l'émergence de la conception occidentale de la propriété et ses conséquences pour la régulation des rapports sociaux à l'égard de l'environnement et du foncier'. In *Les conceptions de la propriété foncière à l'épreuve des revendications autochtones: Possession, propriété et leurs avatars*, edited by Céline Travési, and Maïa Ponsonnet, pp. 51–78. Marseille: Pacific-Credo Publications.
Böhlen, Bruno, and Raymond Clémençon. 1992. 'Die internationale Umweltschutzpolitik der Schweiz'. In *Neues Handbuch der schweizerischen Aussenpolitik*, edited by Alois Riklin, Hans Haug, and Raymond Probst, pp. 1015–1026. Bern: Haupt Verlag.
Bolognesi, Thomas, and Stéphane Nahrath. 2020. 'Environmental Governance Dynamics: Some Micro Foundations of Macro Failures'. *Ecological Economics* 170: pp. 1–13. doi: 10.1016/j.ecolecon.2019.106555.
Brunner, Ursula. 2004. 'Regulierung, Deregulierung und Selbstregulierung im Umweltrecht'. *Zeitschrift für Schweizerisches Recht* 123 (3): pp. 307–370.
Burck, Jan, Franziska Marten, and Christoph Bals. 2018. *Climate Change Performance Index – Results 2017*. Berlin: Germanwatch.
Driessen, Peter P.J., Carel Dieperink, Frank van Laerhoven, Hens A.C. Runhaar, and Walter J.V. Vermeulen. 2012. 'Towards a Conceptual Framework for the Study of Shifts in Modes of Environmental Governance: Experiences from the Netherlands'. *Environmental Policy and Governance* 22 (3): pp. 143–160.

EEA, and FOEN. 2016. *Urban Sprawl in Europe. Joint EEA-FOEN Report*. Luxembourg: Publications Office of the European Union.

EPI. 2022. 'About the EPI'. https://epi.yale.edu/ (accessed 7 November 2022).

Federal Council. 1966. 'Rapport du Conseil fédéral à l'Assemblée fédérale sur l'initiative populaire contre la spéculation foncière (du 31 mai 1966)'. *Feuille Fédérale* 1966: pp. 898–927.

Federal Council. 2017. 'Évaluation de la planification sectorielle de la Confédération'. *Federal Council Report*. Bern: ARE.

Federal Council. 2018. 'Environnement Suisse 2018'. *Federal Council Report*. Bern: FOEN.

Flückiger, Alexandre. 2005. 'La preuve juridique à l'épreuve du principe de précaution'. *Revue européenne des sciences sociales* XLI-128: pp. 107–127.

Häberli, Rudolf, Claude Lüscher, Brigitte Praplan Chastonay, and Christian Wyss. 1991. 'L'affaire sol. Pour une politique raisonnée de l'utilisation du sol'. *FNRS – rapport final du programme national de recherche (PNR 22) 'Utilisation du sol en Suisse'*. Geneva: Georg.

Ingold, Karin, Peter P.J. Driessen, Hens A.C. Runhaar, and Alexander Widmer. 2018. 'On the Necessity of Connectivity: Linking Key Characteristics of Environmental Problems with Governance Modes'. *Journal of Environmental Planning and Management* 62 (11): pp. 1821–1844.

Ingold, Karin, Eva Lieberherr, Isabelle Schläpfer, Kathrin Steinmann, and Willi Zimmermann. 2016. *Umweltpolitik der Schweiz – ein Lehrbuch*. Zürich/St. Gallen: Dike Verlag.

Ingold, Karin, and Géraldine Pflieger. 2016. 'Two Levels, Two Strategies: Explaining the Gap Between Swiss National and International Responses Toward Climate Change'. *European Policy Analysis* 2 (1): pp. 20–38.

Jeannerat, Eloi. 2012. 'La planification dans les espaces fonctionnels'. *Territoire & Environnement* 1 (6): pp. 2–31.

Knoepfel, Peter, Stéphane Nahrath, Jérôme Savary, and Frédéric Varone. 2010. *Analyse des politiques suisses de l'environnement*. Zürich/Chur: Ruegger Verlag.

Lauwerier, Ewoud, Laura Gatto, Dunia Brunner, Stéphane Nahrath, and Pirmin Bundi. 2021. *Comparing European and Swiss Strategies for the Regulation of Plastic*. Lausanne: Cahier de l'IDHEAP; Bern: OFEV.

Metz, Florence, and Karin Ingold. 2014. 'Sustainable Wastewater Management: Is It Possible to Regulate Micropollution in the Future by Learning From the Past? A Policy Analysis'. *Sustainability* 6 (4): pp. 1992–2012.

Moor, Pierre. 2002. 'L'expropriation matérielle'. In *Droit administratif II*, edited by Pierre Moor, and Etienne Poltier, pp. 741–755. Bern: Stämpfli.

Morand, Charles-Albert. 1996. *La pesée globale des intérêts: droit de l'environnement et de l'aménagement du territoire*. Basel: Helbing & Lichtenhahn.

Nahrath, Stéphane. 2003. *La mise en place du régime institutionnel de l'aménagement du territoire en Suisse entre 1960 et 1990*. Doctoral thesis, IDHEAP – Université de Lausanne. https://doc.rero.ch/record/501/files/these_Nahrath.pdf (accessed 7 November 2022).

Varone, Frédéric, and Stéphane Nahrath. 2014. 'Regulating the Use of Natural Resources: When Policy Instruments Meet Property Rights'. In *L'instrumentation de l'action publique. Controverses, résistances, effets*, edited by Charlotte Halpern, Pierre Lascoumes, and Patrick Le Galès, pp. 237–264. Paris: Presses de Sciences Po.

Varone, Frédéric, Stéphane Nahrath, David Aubin, and Jean-David Gerber. 2013. 'Functional Regulatory Spaces'. *Policy Sciences* 46 (4): pp. 311–333. doi: 10.1007/s11077-013-9174-1.

Widmer, Alexander. 2018. 'Mainstreaming Climate Adaptation in Switzerland: How the National Adaptation Strategy is Implemented Differently Across Sectors'. *Environmental Science & Policy* 82: pp. 71–78.

CHAPTER 35

MIGRATION POLICY

SANDRA LAVENEX

1 INTRODUCTION

MORE than a third of the resident population of Switzerland has a migration background and almost a third of the resident population was born abroad.[1][2] In quantitative terms, Switzerland's immigration reality hence certainly compares with that of the classic immigration countries Australia, Canada, or the USA (Piguet 2004, 11; cf. Figure 35.1). However, this is not the case when it comes to the national self-image or immigration policy. In stark contrast with classic immigration countries, Switzerland was for a long time a prime example of the continental European guest worker country with an active recruitment of temporary economic migrants and at the same time restrictive integration and naturalization practices (see 'Integration Policy' in this volume). In the field of asylum, the country prides itself on a long humanitarian tradition, yet few policy areas have seen as many restrictive reforms as Swiss asylum law. In Switzerland like in other European countries, immigration has become deeply politicized and anti-immigrant rhetoric has been a major factor fuelling the rise of Switzerland's largest political group, the right-wing populist Swiss People's Party (Kriesi et al. 2005 and 2012; see also 'Parties and Party Systems in Switzerland' in this volume).

Traditionally treated as one of the core state powers deeply tied to notions of sovereignty, Swiss asylum and immigration policies have gradually expanded from the field of domestic politics into the realms of European and foreign policy. Participation in the European Union's (EU) regional scheme of free movement of persons has profoundly reshaped Switzerland's highly regulated immigration policy and has become a central bone of contention in both Swiss domestic politics and Swiss–EU relations (Schwok 2020). From the mid-1960s up to the Agreement on the Free Movement of Persons (AFMP) with the EU in 2002, the Swiss immigration policy was based on a system of annual quotas for labour migrants, who were distributed via a dense web of corporatist ties benefiting, in particular, employers in labour-intensive industries. The AFMP replaced this system of controlled economic immigration with a free market for citizens from the EU and EFTA (European Free Trade Association). From then on, the system

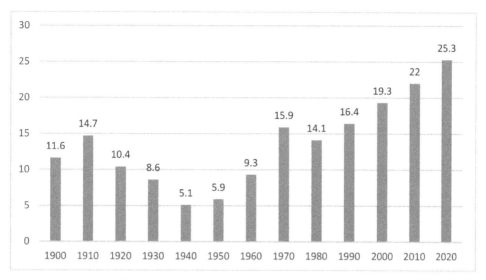

FIGURE 35.1: Share of foreigners in the total permanent resident population since the end of December 1900 (in per cent)

Data source: FSO 2022a.

of controlled immigration only applies to so-called 'third-country nationals' from non-EU/EFTA countries, whose immigration has been restricted to the highly skilled.

Cooperation with the EU in the area of irregular migration and asylum via association to the so-called Dublin and Schengen frameworks has been less controversial as it shields Switzerland from the main migratory routes.

Beyond this partial Europeanization of its domestic asylum and immigration policy, Switzerland has also developed an active role in bilateral and multilateral cooperation in the field of migration. In line with the humanitarian orientation of its foreign policy, it has sought to play a leading role in intergovernmental consultations on migration including the negotiations leading to the 2018 United Nations (UN) Compact on international migration. Like the AFMP, however, this cooperation has also faced harsh popular backlash. As a result, and notwithstanding its leading role in the process, Switzerland has hitherto not been able to sign the UN Compact.

In this chapter, we first introduce the legislative developments, the actors, and conflict lines surrounding domestic immigration and asylum policies in Switzerland. We then turn to their European dimension, before addressing the Swiss government's role in international initiatives.

2 Immigration policy

Migration policy distinguishes between immigration policy, which refers to primarily voluntary migration, and asylum and refugee policy, which regulates involuntary migration. Immigration policy encompasses the management of the economically motivated influx of labour, the socially motivated reunification of family members of foreigners, who have already entered the country, and the control of irregular migration. While states are fundamentally sovereign in deciding whether to admit foreign persons to their territory, the right to family reunification (and refugee protection, see section 3 in this chapter) is protected under constitutional and international law. As the legal status of foreign workers in Switzerland has improved, family immigration has steadily increased.

Along with labour, family reunification has become one of the most important reasons for immigration (see Figure 35.2). Since the introduction of the free movement of persons with the EU/EFTA in 2002, Switzerland has had a dual immigration system. The free movement of persons for EU and EFTA citizens establishes a liberal policy for the European area, which is contrasted by a restrictive admission policy for citizens from all other so-called 'third countries'. In some way, the current solution can be seen as a compromise between the two most important domestic factors influencing immigration policy: the continuing demand of the economy for foreign labour on the one hand and xenophobic tendencies in the public on the other.

However, this compromise is not necessarily stable as shown by recurring popular initiatives against the free movement of persons, especially by the Swiss People's Party (see section 2.2 in this chapter). These ambivalences are reflected not least in the legislative development of immigration policy.

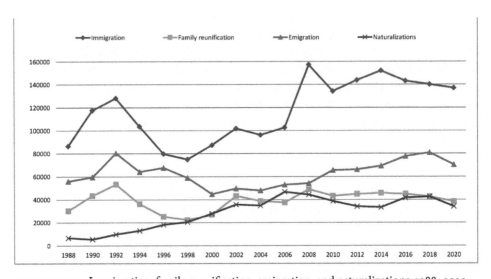

FIGURE 35.2: Immigration, family reunification, emigration, and naturalizations, 1988–2020

Family reunification is part of the total number of immigrants from 2002, including family reunification of Swiss nationals and foreign nationals with a Swiss spouse.

Data source: FSO 2022b. Balance sheet of the permanent foreign population since the end of December 1988.

2.1 Legislative development and instruments

Swiss immigration policy can be roughly divided into eight phases (see Piguet 2004; Wicker et al. 2003). The first Federal Act on the Residence and Settlement of Foreigners (ANAG), enacted in 1931, has remained untouched legislatively for more than seventy years, and saw its first legislative reform only in 2005. This is also the case with the provision in article 16 according to which 'In their decisions, the granting authorities shall take into account the intellectual and economic interests as well as the degree of foreign infiltration (*Überfremdung*) of the country' (own translation).[3] During this period, immigration has been a prime site of executive policy-making (see Table 35.1). The use of administrative ordinances and directives allowed for a dense web of corporatist ties to develop between employers in labour-intensive, less competitive industries (agriculture, construction, and hospitality) and cantonal authorities responsible for the allocation of immigrant quotas. The result were continuously high numbers of immigrants—notwithstanding the anti-immigrant tenets in the law (ANAG) and in public opinion (Spescha 1999). According to Dhima (1991, 172, own translation) there was 'a tacit understanding that aliens policy is regulated by the associations and executive authorities, while the parliament and political parties do not intervene'. The isolation of this sensitive policy field from the legislative arena has channelled the mounting popular opposition into the direct-democratic arena, contributing to the extraordinary frequency of anti-immigration direct-democratic initiatives from the 1960s until today (see Table 35.2). The AFMP with the EU, concluded in 1999 and implemented in 2002, was the decisive factor paving the way to the fundamental legislative reform of 2005 (Lavenex 2004). This reform ended the xenophobic framing of the Alien's Law and the corporatist system of labour immigration. Instead, it introduced a free market for EU/EFTA citizens and restrictive provisions for the admission of so-called 'third-country nationals', whose immigration would be limited to highly skilled professionals. In the following, we briefly summarize the eight phases of Swiss immigration policy:

1. Liberalism and industrialization (1850–1914): The influx of labour began in the second half of the nineteenth century. In 1890, the number of immigrants exceeded that of emigrants for the first time. To a certain extent, as a harbinger of today's AFMP with the EU, Switzerland concluded settlement treaties with a total of twenty-one countries during this period, which put their citizens on an equal footing with Swiss citizens, with the exception of political rights. In 1914, foreigners already accounted for more than 15 per cent of the population.
2. Closure (1915–1947): With the First World War, all European states introduced immigration controls. It is in these years that the notion of 'foreign infiltration' (*Überfremdung*) took shape. In 1925, a legal basis for a federal policy on foreigners was included in the federal constitution; until then, this had been the responsibility of the cantons. In 1931, the first Alien's Law, the ANAG, was enacted with a view to avoid an expansive immigration like in the late eighteenth century and

to keep the rights of newcomers strictly limited in order to preclude them from settling down (Spescha 1999, 32). Accordingly, a federal mandate for the integration of immigrants was not provided by the law before the end of the 1990s (Niederberger 2001). This initiated a period of restrictive admission policies that would last until the end of World War II. By the end of the war, the share of the immigrant population had returned to pre-1880 levels (Arlettaz and Arlettaz 2004).

3. The guest worker era (1948–1962): The end of World War II ushered in a period of active recruitment to rebuild the national economy. Recruitment agreements were signed with Italy (1948) and Spain (1961). During this phase, the political model of the 'guest worker' was coined with a temporary residence status as a seasonal worker. In opposition to the liberal policy of the pre-World War I period, this status was intended to strictly avoid the settlement of foreigners in Switzerland while allowing the economy to benefit from a flexible rotating labour force. Seasonal workers were allowed to work in Switzerland only for a period of up to nine months and then they were obliged to return to their countries. Bringing in family members was possible only after having worked for three consecutive years in Switzerland (Mahnig and Piguet 2003). While strongly restricting the rights of migrants, the federal government opted for a 'laisser-faire' attitude with regards to their numbers, giving companies and associations a free hand in active recruitment (Arlettaz and Arlettaz 2004).

4. First attempts at limitation (1963–1973): Facing rapidly increasing immigration numbers in 1963 and 1965, the federal government introduced ceiling measures that sought to limit the number of persons employed in a company and the total number of foreigners. Partly in contradiction with this goal, the second recruitment agreement with Italy was concluded in 1964. Responding to Italian requests in an increasingly competitive European market for labour recruitment, this agreement decisively improved the legal status of Italian nationals. Around the same time, the first xenophobic initiatives emerged (see Table 35.2). In response, the global ceiling was introduced, which set annual admission quotas.

5. The end of the first immigration wave (1974–1984): As in other European countries, the first oil crisis initiated a restrictive turn in immigration policy. When about 10 per cent of all Swiss jobs were eliminated in the wake of the recession, it was the foreigners who were the first to be laid off and often forced to leave.

6. The second wave of immigration (1985–1992): In the early 1980s, the economic demand for immigration increased again. The main recruitment countries were now Portugal and Yugoslavia. Immigration policy followed the system of annual quotas introduced in the early 1970s (see section 2.2 in this chapter). At the same time, residence conditions for Italian, Spanish, and Portuguese immigrants were improved during the 1980s, allowing them to enjoy permanent residence permits and the right to family reunification more quickly.

7. Internationalization and reorientation (1993–2004): In the 1990s, it became clear that a large proportion of the guest workers and their families, who had been called to work in agriculture, in the tunnels, and on the motorways, would stay.

This was particularly evident during the recession, when many immigrants became unemployed and, unlike in the 1970s, did not leave the country. The improvement in the legal rights of guest workers, such as the right to social security and unemployment insurance (see 'Social Policy' in this volume) and the influx of their families, which was also guaranteed by the European Convention on Human Rights, meant that the established system of immigration policy lost much of its flexibility and grip. In addition, the wars in the former Yugoslavia brought asylum numbers to a head. Against this background, the idea of the so-called 'three-circle model' emerged. In anticipation of the European Economic Area (EEA), this model allowed immigration from countries beyond the first circle (EU/EFTA) and the second circle (North America/Australia/possibly Central Europe) only in exceptional cases (Federal Council 1991). However, following the identitarian tenets of *'Überfremdung'* enshrined in the 1931 Alien's Law, this attempt to privilege migrants from culturally closer countries over the 'rest of the world' no longer fitted into the normative environment of the 1990s. Established in the context of Switzerland's ratification of the UN Convention on the Elimination of Racial Discrimination, the Federal Commission against Racism put a definitive end to the 'three-circle model' and sharply criticized it as 'fundamentally racist' (Eidgenössische Kommission gegen Rassismus 1996, 7).

With the conclusion of the 1999 Bilateral Agreements with the EU, the concept of the two circles was realized. The first circle introduced freedom of movement for the EU/EFTA countries. All other European and non-European countries henceforth constitute the second circle with strict immigration regulations (see Koch and Lavenex 2006; Lavenex and Manatschal 2022).

8. Selective admission with intensified integration support (2005–today): With the consolidation of the two-circle model, immigration from EU/EFTA countries enjoying freedom of movement intensified. For labour migration from non-EU/EFTA countries, however, the new Federal Act on Foreign Nationals (AuG), passed in 2005, brought tighter restrictions. It stipulates that only well-qualified or specialized workers are admitted from these countries—and only if no comparably suitable workers can be found in Switzerland and in the EU/EFTA (cf. art. 2 AuG). In addition, the AuG replaced the precarious seasonal worker status with a short-term residence permit of a maximum of one year, extendable to a maximum of two years (art. 32 AuG). In contrast, the situation of lawfully and permanently present foreigners improved with the new law: changes of profession and place of residence as well as family reunification were facilitated (art. 37 and chapter 7 AuG). The federal government significantly increased its efforts around integration, especially at the cantonal level. Following the motto of simultaneous promotion and demand, the integration logic found legal expression in the newly named Foreign Nationals and Integration Act (AIG) and the reform of citizenship law of 2019. All these developments are accompanied by a continuing and, in some cases, even intensifying politicization of the migration process in Switzerland.

Table 35.1: Development of the right of residence and right of establishment

SR 142.20	Federal Act of 26 March 1931 on the Residence and Settlement of Foreign Nationals (ANAG)
SR 142.201	Enforcement Ordinance of 1 March 1949 on the Federal Act on the Residence and Settlement of Foreign Nationals (ANAV)
SR 142.261	Ordinance of 19 January 1965 on the Assurance of Residence Permit to Take up Employment
SR 142.212	Ordinance of 20 January 1971 on the Notification of Departing Foreigners
SR 142.202	Ordinance of 20 April 1983 on the Consent Procedure in Aliens Law
SR 142.241	Ordinance of 20 May 1987 on Fees for the Federal Act on the Residence and Settlement of Foreign Nationals (Fees Ordinance ANAG)
SR 142.215	Ordinance of 23 November 1994 on the Central Register of Foreigners, ZAR Ordinance
SR 142.211	Ordinance of 14 January 1998 on the Entry and Registration of Foreign Nationals (VEA)
SR 142.281	Ordinance of 11 August 1999 on the Enforcement of Removals and Expulsions of Foreign Nationals (VVWA)
SR 143.5	Ordinance of 11 August 1999 on the Delivery of Travel Documents to Foreign Persons
SR 142.205	Ordinance of 13 September 2000 on the Integration of Foreign Nationals (VIntA)
SR 142.203	Ordinance of 22 May 2002 on the gradual establishment of the free movement of persons between the Swiss Confederation and the European Community and its Member States and among the Member States of the European Free Trade Association
SR 142.51	Federal Act of 20 July 2003 on the Information System on Foreign Nationals and Asylum (BGIAA)
SR 142.20	Federal Act of 16 December 2005 on Foreign Nationals (Foreign Nationals Act, AuG, replaces ANAG)
SR 142.513	Ordinance of 12 April 2006 on the Central Migration Information System (ZEMIS Ordinance)
SR 142.201	Ordinance of 24 October 2007 on Admission, Residence and Gainful Employment (VZAE)
SR 142. 209	Ordinance of 24 October 2007 on Fees under the Federal Act on Foreign Nationals (Fees Ordinance AuG)
SR 142.204	Ordinance of 22 October 2008 on Entry and the Issuance of Visas (VEV)
SR 143.5	Ordinance of 20 January 2010 on the Issuance of Travel Documents for Foreign Nationals (RDV)
SR 142.512	Ordinance of 6 July 2011 on the Central Visa Information System (Visa Information System Ordinance, VISV)
SR 141.0	Revised Federal Act of 20 June 2014 on Swiss Citizenship (Citizenship Act, BüG)
SR 142.20	Federal Act of 16 December 2005 on Foreign Nationals and Integration (Foreign Nationals and Integration Act, AIG, replaces AuG on 1 January 2019)
SR 141.01	Revised Ordinance on Swiss Citizenship of 17 June 2016 (Ordinance on Swiss Citizenship, BüV)

Data source: SEM (2022) and the collection of legal documents from the Federal Council (2022).

In its basic features, Switzerland's immigration policy is comparable to that of other European immigration countries: the extensive freedom of movement within the EU/EFTA area contrasts with the highly selective admission of third-country national migrants, which is geared to the needs of the labour market. Unlike other countries, however, Switzerland does not have a special programme for the immigration of highly skilled workers such as the blue card introduced at the EU level. Rather, Switzerland regulates this form of immigration through cantonally allocated admission quotas (see Sandoz 2019).

Although a cornerstone of Swiss migration policy, the AFMP with the EU is continuously under political fire. The 'mass immigration initiative' (2014), which was narrowly adopted, and the 'limitation initiative', which was rejected in autumn 2020, put the AFMP into question. These popular initiatives demanded that Switzerland return to an 'independent' management of immigration, i.e. without restrictions under international law. Article 121a of the federal constitution, which was added because of the mass immigration initiative, was implemented by means of rather minor amendments to the AuG, which are compatible with the AFMP and aim to better exploit the domestic labour potential. This is to be realized with the introduction of a job notification requirement in sectors with high unemployment, which will give job seekers resident in Switzerland an advantage over foreign competitors. Since the initiators felt that the implementation of the mass immigration initiative did not go far enough, the Swiss People's Party called for the termination of the AFMP (new art. 121b and implementing provisions) with its limitation initiative. However, this initiative was rejected by the people on 27 September 2020.

2.2 Actors and lines of conflict

The enforcement of the law on foreigners is primarily the responsibility of the cantons. In the distribution of the quotas for immigration from third countries to which they are entitled each year, the cantons have broad discretionary powers regarding the interpretation of federal laws (Spescha 1999, 41). As evidenced in the repeatedly documented differences between cantonal admission practices, the cantons make extensive use of this leeway and, thus, have an important influence on policy-making (Wichmann et al. 2011, ch. 6; Probst et al. 2019, ch. 7).

The political science literature describes the Swiss system of immigration policy as a corporatist web until the reforms of the late 1990s. Three groups of actors were central in it: the Federal Office for Industry, Trade, and Labour (BIGA), which was responsible until 1998; the cantonal immigration authorities; and the employers' organizations of labour-intensive sectors (Dhima 1991; Lavenex 2004). In particular, seasonal status has long served sectors with high demand for low-skilled labour, such as domestically oriented sectors like construction or hospitality, as a kind of cyclical buffer through which labour could be flexibly brought in and removed.

With the liberalization of intra-European migration and subsequent reforms, the field of actors has also begun to move. At the federal level, the merger of the former BIGA with the Federal Office for Foreign Trade (BAWI) in 1998 and their joint transfer to the newly founded State Secretariat for Economic Affairs (SECO) in 1999 should be mentioned. This weakened the position of the associations of domestically oriented sectors. Most aspects of the free movement of persons with the EU/EFTA were removed from the area of Alien's Law and now fall under the competence of the SECO (Koch and Lavenex 2006). The Federal Department of Justice and Police is now responsible for Alien's Law. The relevant departments of the BIGA were transferred to the Federal Office for Foreigners' Affairs, which, after merging with the Federal Office for Refugees (BFF) (see section 3 in this chapter), was first renamed the Federal Office for Migration (BFM) in 2005 and finally the State Secretariat for Migration (SEM) in 2015.

This reorganization illustrates the strengthening of the position of export-oriented associations with their demand for higher-skilled labour vis-à-vis structurally weak sectors as well as the increased political importance of the policy field.

This development went hand in hand with the increasing shift of legal adjustments to foreigners' legislation into the legislative arena and, as already mentioned above, an increased politicization of the immigration issue. This is reflected not least in the frequency and outcome of direct-democratic votes on the topic (see Table 35.2). While earlier popular initiatives critical of foreigners failed at the ballot box, proposals such as the minaret initiative in 2009, the deportation initiative in 2010, or the mass immigration initiative of 2014 found a majority. Thus, maintaining and shaping the free movement of persons with the EU has become an ongoing political issue.

Table 35.2: Federal popular initiatives around migration policy since 1968

Year	Initiative	Yes-votes in per cent
1968	First initiative against Überfremdung ('foreign infiltration') (withdrawn)	
1970	Second initiative against Überfremdung (Schwarzenbachinitiative)	46.0
1974	Third initiative against the 'foreign infiltration and overpopulation of Switzerland'	34.2
1977	Fourth initiative against Überfremdung	29.5
	'For a restriction of naturalizations'	33.8
1981	'Together-initiative for a new policy on foreigners'	16.2
1984	'Against the sell-out of the homeland'	48.9
1987	Fifth initiative against 'foreign infiltration' (failed at the collection stage)	
1988	'For a limitation of immigration'	32.7
1988	'For a limit on the admission of asylum seekers' (failed at the collection stage)	
1991	'Against the mass immigration of foreigners and asylum seekers' (failed at the collection stage)	
1996	'For a sensible asylum policy' (declared invalid by parliament)	

Table 35.2: Continued

Year	Initiative	Yes-votes in per cent
1996	'Against illegal immigration'	46.3
1997	'Moderation in immigration' (failed at the collection stage)	
2000	'For a regulation of immigration'	36.2
2002	'Against the abuse of the asylum law'	49.9
2004	'For limiting immigration from non-EU countries' (failed at the collection stage)	
2008	'For democratic naturalizations'	36.2
2009	'Against the construction of minarets (minaret initiative)'	57.5
2010	'For the deportation of criminal foreigners (deportation initiative)'	52.3
2014	'Against mass immigration'	50.3
2014	'Stop overpopulation - to safeguard the natural basis of life (ECOPOP)'	25.9
2015	'Breaking the deadlock. Renounce the reintroduction of immigration quotas' (withdrawn)	
2016	'On the enforcement of the deportation of criminal foreigners (enforcement initiative)'	41.0
2020	'For moderate immigration (limitation initiative)'	38.3
2021	'Yes to a ban on full facial coverings'	51.2

Data source: Swiss Federal Chancellery (2022).

3 REFUGEES AND ASYLUM POLICY

Apart from its inglorious policies before and during the Second World War, Switzerland prides itself on a long tradition as a country of asylum, firmly anchored in its political self-image (Parini 1997). This self-image shaped asylum practice during the Cold War period, when Switzerland granted asylum to numerous Hungarian (1956), Tibetan (1963), Czechoslovak (1968), and other Asian and African refugees.

Asylum seekers are granted a right of presence in Switzerland for the duration of the procedure. Refugees are persons to whom the SEM ultimately grants asylum under the 1951 UN Convention relating to the Status of Refugees and Swiss asylum law, or who enjoy protection in Switzerland on other humanitarian grounds.

Like elsewhere in Western liberal democracies, the tide began to turn in the 1980s as the causes and origins of asylum migration multiplied. The dissociation of refugee movements from the context of East–West antagonism also removed a key ideological element that had underpinned generous admission practices. At the same time, recognition rates for refugees began to decline and the possible abuse of the asylum system became an increasing topic of discussion. The first Asylum Act has been partially or

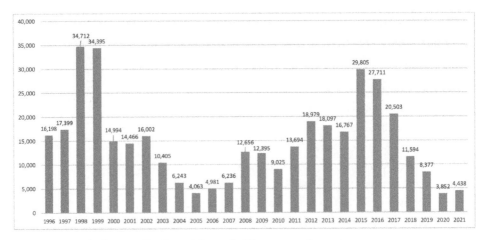

FIGURE 35.3: Asylum applications at the end of the year, 1996–2019

Data source: FSO 2022b.

totally revised no less than nine times between 1981 and the present. In addition, external influences (wars in the former Yugoslavia in the 1990s, the 'Arab Spring' and the war in Syria since the end of December 2010) have repeatedly put pressure on the asylum system (see Figure 35.3). In this way, the right to asylum has become a bone of contention in politics and a highly sensitive issue in public votes and elections. This was also the case during the humanitarian crisis of 2015–2016, even though Switzerland saw less dramatic surges of asylum seekers than other European countries (Gessler and Hunger 2022, 531). In the wake of the Russian war against Ukraine in 2022, Switzerland has aligned its response to that of the EU and has granted, in an unbureaucratic manner, humanitarian protection to persons fleeing Ukraine. Similar to the 'temporary protection' Directive activated by the EU, a special status was activated for the first time, which gives the right to residence, work, reunite with the family, and obtain social benefits for an initial duration of one year. By the time of writing (July 2022), some 60,000 Ukrainians had received temporary protection in Switzerland—thereby exceeding the average number of annual asylum seekers by far (see Figure 35.3). Like in other European countries, however, Ukrainian refugees have been admitted with great solidarity and have at least so far not been subject to the usual political controversies concerning asylum seekers in Switzerland.

3.1 Legislative development and instruments

The first asylum law was enacted in 1981. The main objective of this law was to formalize the already existing asylum practice, which had previously been based on a single article of the Federal Act on the Residence and Settlement of Foreigners (ANAG) of 1931. Influenced by the liberal asylum practice of the post-war period, the new law was soon confronted with the growing politicization of the asylum issue. The numerous revisions of the last four decades were primarily aimed at tightening up asylum law, in particular by speeding up procedures, combating abuse, and providing more consistent enforcement of legally binding expulsion decisions. At the same time, subsidiary, less comprehensive, and temporary forms of humanitarian protection have been expanded.

In 1984, the first partial revision classified certain applications as 'manifestly unfounded', abolished the possibility of appeal to the Federal Council, and imposed restrictions on the granting of work permits to asylum seekers. A second reform followed in 1988, expanding the categories of 'manifestly unfounded applications' and giving the Federal Council the authority to limit the number of asylum seekers to be admitted, even in peacetime, in the event of an exceptionally high influx. Asylum seekers were distributed among the cantons in proportion to the population. The possibility of deciding on files without a personal hearing by the deciding authority was introduced, as well as a detention period pending deportation for up to thirty days for foreigners who do not leave the country voluntarily. Furthermore, the cantons were allowed to ban asylum seekers from working for the first three months. Just two years later (1990), Switzerland adopted its third partial revision of the asylum law with which it introduced, as the first country in Europe, the safe country provision: applications for asylum from countries classified as 'safe' by the Federal Council were no longer considered. As further restrictions, the cantonal aliens police were no longer allowed to issue residence permits (e.g. for 'humanitarian reasons' to long-term asylum seekers) during the asylum procedure and a general ban was introduced on the right to work for the first three months with the possibility of extension. The 1995 Federal Act on Coercive Measures in the Law on Foreign Nationals extended the possibility of three months' detention pending deportation to nine months' detention and restricted the right to mobility of asylum seekers. In the same year, the fourth partial revision of the asylum law and the Federal Decree on Savings Measures in the Area of Asylum and Foreigners introduced a special charge for asylum seekers in gainful employment by which they contribute to the costs of the asylum procedure. Three years later, the 1998 fifth partial revision introduced new grounds for non-admission via the urgent federal decree on asylum. The sixth total revision of the Asylum Act of 1999 diversified the refugee status by introducing the status of persons in need of protection. This replaced the prior practice of collective temporary admission and was targeted at people fleeing a situation of general violence without individual proceedings. The revision also called for better consideration of women-specific reasons for fleeing. Reacting to the long duration of asylum procedures, the revision also provided that if an asylum procedure lasted longer than four years, provisional admission could be ordered if there is a serious personal emergency. New restrictions were introduced in 2004 as part of the austerity programme: the appeal period for decisions not to grant asylum was shortened; detention pending deportation was extended; and social assistance was abolished in cases of refusal (the so-called 'welfare stop' or *Fürsorgestopp*). Again, only two years later, the 2006 seventh partial revision of the Asylum Act tightened the third-country regulation, but at the same time widened the grounds for recognition as a refugee by recognizing non-governmental persecution. Temporary admission was replaced by humanitarian admission (civil war refugees and hardship cases) and provisional admission (for rejected asylum seekers, who cannot be expelled through no fault of their own). The eighth partial revision occurred in 2012. Its core points were the simplification and acceleration of procedures as well as the abolition of embassy asylum. The so-far last, ninth total revision of the Asylum Act took place in 2019 and primarily aimed at accelerating procedures. From then on, asylum seekers are first sent to one of the six federal asylum centres maintained by the State Secretariat for Migration for a maximum of 140 days, where their application is processed ('accelerated procedure'). If no decision can be reached within this period (positive decision, negative decision, or determination of the responsibility of another state within the meaning of the Dublin Convention), asylum seekers are assigned to the cantons within the framework of the 'extended procedure'. For the entire accelerated procedure, asylum seekers receive free counselling and legal representation.

3.2 Actors and lines of conflict

The asylum procedure is regulated at federal level. After 1990, the first-instance asylum procedure was the responsibility of the then newly created BFF, which has been affiliated to the BFM since 2005 and to the SEM since 2015. At the same time, the Asylum Appeals Commission (ARK) was created as a special court in asylum matters that is independent of the administration and is responsible for reviewing the asylum decisions of the Federal Office. On 1 January 2007, the ARK was transferred to the new Federal Administrative Court.

While the decision-making competence on asylum applications lies with the federal government, the cantonal authorities are responsible for many practical aspects, such as in particular the enforcement of expulsions of rejected asylum seekers and Dublin transfers. Within the framework of the extended procedure (no decision possible within the first 140 days), asylum seekers are distributed among the cantons according to a key, including persons entitled to protection. In these cases, the cantons are henceforth responsible for accommodation, integration measures, and the payment of social assistance. The tightening of asylum law up to the ninth revision had increased the financial burden on the cantons, which further intensified the politicization of the issue. The federal government and the cantons now hope that the accelerated procedures will reduce costs in the long term. The 'Integration Agenda for Asylum' launched jointly by the Confederation and the cantons in 2018 is also intended to help reduce social assistance costs. This pursues the goal of early integration support for the purpose of rapid labour market participation of recognized refugees and provisionally admitted persons. In addition to other subsidies, the Confederation pays the cantons so-called integration lump sums in this area (art. 58 para. 2 AIG).

In addition to state actors, humanitarian aid organizations and civil society traditionally play an important role in refugee policy. The presence of representatives of an aid organization during the asylum hearing was abolished with the last revision of the law and replaced by the new legal protection principle: the Confederation now commissions four private and non-profit relief organizations—Caritas Switzerland, *Hilfswerk der Evangelischen Kirchen Schweiz, Berner Rechtsberatungsstelle für Menschen in Not*, and *Schweizer Arbeiterhilfswerk*—to provide counselling and legal representation for asylum seekers during the accelerated procedure. Since the 1990s, some cantons have transferred accommodation, social counselling, and integration work with refugees to private and profit-oriented actors such as the *Organisation für Regie und Spezialaufträge* or to public-law bodies such as the Asyl Organisation Zurich or the *Etablissement vaudois d'accueil des migrants*. This move towards market-based mechanisms and instruments of new public management in the asylum sector, which can be observed at both federal and cantonal level, is sometimes viewed critically by NGOs as they fear a decline in attention towards humanitarian priorities.

While the issue of economic immigration was able to build on a relatively strong party-political consensus for a long time, the issue of asylum/refugee policy has been polarizing since the early 1980s. The asylum issue is also a central motive behind the rise of the Swiss People's Party and, coupled with criticism of the EU, has decisively contributed to the shift in the party landscape (Kriesi et al. 2005; Manatschal and Rapp 2015). The direct-democratic arena plays a central role in this (see also Table 35.2).

In addition to domestic controversies, refugee policy is also strongly influenced by external actors. At the international level, the United Nations High Commissioner for Refugees (UNHCR) monitors the implementation of the International Refugee Convention. Developments in the EU have also shaped Swiss asylum policy. This applies first and foremost to the ambition to participate in the Dublin Convention system, which the Swiss government has pursued since the early 1990s (Brochmann and Lavenex 2002; Lavenex et al. 2022). The next sections address this European and international dimension of Swiss asylum and immigration policy.

4 THE FOREIGN POLICY DIMENSION

Switzerland's asylum and immigration policy is heavily influenced by the European Union. Apart from the above-mentioned bilateral agreement extending freedom of movement for EU/EFTA nationals to Switzerland, Switzerland participates in the EU's policy on immigration control towards third-country nationals and asylum by associating itself with the Schengen and Dublin frameworks.

The 1990 Schengen Agreement, which was subsequently incorporated into EU legislation, includes, next to abolishing controls at the internal borders of the Schengen countries, also a common visa policy, cooperation on external border controls, and internal security. Switzerland joined the Schengen area in 2004 as part of the Bilateral Agreements II. Unlike most other bilateral agreements with the EU, this agreement also binds Switzerland to the further development of EU rules. In return, it opens up opportunities for Switzerland to participate directly in the EU Council of Ministers and its various bodies. Switzerland can thus be actively involved in the further development of the Schengen acquis. Switzerland is also an associate member of the European Border Management Agency FRONTEX and supports it both financially and by contributing experts and border guards.

By joining the Schengen area in 2004, Switzerland also became associated with the Dublin Regulation determining the state responsible for carrying out asylum procedures in the Schengen area. As a country surrounded by EU member states, Switzerland benefits from this regulation, which allocates responsibility to the member state whose territory an asylum seeker first enters.

Switzerland has also sought close cooperation with the EU's external policies on migration and participates in several EU programmes and dialogues with third countries (Lavenex et al. 2022). The priority of cooperation with countries of origin and transit of asylum seekers and migrants transpires also in Switzerland's development cooperation. In recent years, more aid has been allocated to measures tackling the causes of forced migration and countries producing large numbers of refugees and migrants—thereby changing some of the geographic and thematic priorities of development aid.

In addition to its European and bilateral foreign policies, Switzerland is also strongly committed to multilateral cooperation in the area of migration. The most important international institutions in this field, the International Labour Organization (ILO), the International Organization for Migration (IOM), and the UNHCR, all have their seat in Geneva. While these organizations date from the inter-war and post-World War II period, Switzerland has shown strong commitment to revived efforts at strengthening international governance from the 1990s onwards. In 1990, the BFF launched an intergovernmental dialogue, the so-called 'Berne Initiative'. This aimed to introduce a process of continued consultation between all states affected by migration—countries of origin, transit, and destination—with a view to developing efficient cooperation mechanisms on a non-binding basis. As a result of these efforts, the International Agenda for Migration Management (IAMM) was adopted, which includes a common basis for understanding as well as practices that are widely considered to be effective in dealing with migration. Switzerland has also supported efforts within the UN in the framework of the 2006 High Level Dialogue on Migration and Development leading to the establishment of a new platform: the Global Forum for Migration and Development (GFMD), where Switzerland has a seat on the steering committee. In the light of the challenges presented by climate change, Switzerland launched, together with Norway, the so-called Nansen Initiative in 2012. The aim of this initiative was to provide better protection to refugees, who have had to leave their countries of origin due to environmental hazards. Led by the Bernese law professor Walter Kälin, the Nansen Initiative brought together innovative approaches and examples of good practice from affected states and formulated a comprehensive Protection Agenda on disaster preparedness, adaptation to climate change, and humanitarian aid. A total of 109 states adopted the legally non-binding Protection Agenda in Geneva in October 2015. The Platform on Disaster Displacement, which is also based in Geneva, was set up to implement the Agenda. The culmination of Switzerland's multilateral engagement in migration issues to date came with its engagement, from 2016 onwards, for a multilateral 'compact' on migration in the framework of the UN. Together with the Mexican ambassador to the UN, the Swiss UN ambassador Jürg Lauber acted as 'co-facilitator' planning and coordinating the consultation and negotiation process that led to the adoption of the UN Migration Compact in December 2018. According to a 2018 report by the Federal Council, Switzerland was striving to achieve 'an ambitious, politically binding GCM (Global Compact for Migration) that sets out globally recognized principles, guidelines, and targets for dealing with migratory movements based on international obligations, follows a human rights approach, and helps to ensure that the potential of migration is more effectively exploited in the interests of all stakeholders' (Federal Council 2018, 2798). The agreement, which was negotiated over two years, sets out twenty-three goals that aim to do justice to the complexity of the challenge. It refers to the human rights of migrants both during the migration process and in host countries and calls upon states to facilitate legal immigration channels. However, it also calls for international cooperation against irregular migration and human trafficking and addresses the relationship between development and migration. Although the migration Compact's final draft was adopted by consensus in the summer of 2018 by all negotiating delegations—except those of the USA and Hungary—the draft met with strong domestic political headwind in a number of countries. In Switzerland too, a deep gulf opened up between the country's foreign policy ambitions and its domestic scope for action. Conservative political parties and numerous members of the National Council refused to support the Compact. After a heated political debate, Switzerland's formal accession to the GCM was suspended until further notice, with the result that the Compact was finally adopted by 152 states—but not by one of its main sponsors—in December 2018.

5 Outlook

Immigration policy in Switzerland has evolved from an issue narrowly dealt with from the prerogatives of the 'foreigner's police' to a highly politicized issue touching upon virtually all aspects of domestic and foreign policy. Domestically, the country has remained split between a (mostly) vibrant economy demanding foreign labour and strong anti-immigrant politics. While benefiting economic needs, the free movement regime with the EU/EFTA has remained hotly contested and has continued to compromise Swiss–EU relations. Like the negative referendum on joining the European Economic Area in 1992, the Swiss government's decision to dismiss an overarching Institutional Agreement with the EU in 2021 is mainly attributed to concerns with freedom of movement. While anti-immigrant parties have maintained their opposition, leftist groups, in particular trade unions, have shifted towards Eurosceptic positions for fears over negative implications of EU rules for wages and labour conditions in Switzerland. Relentless politicization of immigration has, however, not only hampered Swiss foreign relations with the EU. The failure to sign the Global Compact on Migration, the first ever UN agreement to foster international cooperation on the matter, negotiated under the lead of Swiss UN diplomats, is another witness of the divisive power of the subject. Navigating between economic, humanitarian, and diplomatic demand on the one hand, and popular backlash on the other hand, migration policy in Switzerland is likely to remain a delicate issue. This notwithstanding, hosting one of the largest shares of non-national population in the world, Switzerland has clearly evolved towards a country of immigration.

Notes

1. This chapter draws partly on Lavenex and Manatschal (2022). Support by the Swiss National Science Foundation NCCR on the move (grant 51NF40-182897) is gratefully acknowledged.
2. Source: FSO 2022c. Statistics by migration status refer to the permanent resident population over fifteen years of age (SAKE, see FSO 2022d), those by country of birth to the total permanent resident population (STATPOP, see FSO 2022e).
3. The original wording in German is 'Die Bewilligungsbehörden haben bei ihren Entscheidungen die geistigen und wirtschaftlichen Interessen sowie den Grad der Überfremdung des Landes zu berücksichtigen'.

References

Arlettaz, Gérald, and Silvia Arlettaz. 2004. *La Suisse et les étrangers: immigration et formation nationale (1848-1933)*, Lausanne: Antipodes.
Brochmann, Grete, and Sandra Lavenex 2002. 'Neither In nor Out: The Impact of EU Asylum and Immigration Policies on Norway and Switzerland'. In *Migration and the Externalities of European Integration*, edited by Sandra Lavenex, and Emek M. Uçarer, pp. 55–74. Lanham: Lexington Books.
Dhima, Giorgio. 1991. *Politische Ökonomie der schweizerischen Ausländerregelung: eine empirische Untersuchung über die schweizerische Migrationspolitik und Vorschläge für ihre künftige Gestaltung*. Chur/Zürich: Rüegger.
Eidgenössische Kommission gegen Rassismus. 1996. *Stellungnahme der Eidg. Kommission gegen Rassismus zum Drei-Kreise-Modell des Bundesrats über die schweizerische Ausländerpolitik*. Bern.
Federal Council. 1991. *Bericht des Bundesrates zur Ausländer- und Flüchtlingspolitik*. Bern.
Federal Council. 2018. *Bericht des Bundesrates über die Aktivitäten der schweizerischen Migrationsaussenpolitik 2017*. Bern.
Federal Council. 2022. *Der Bundesrat. Das Portal der Schweizer Regierung*. https://www.admin.ch (accessed 29 November 2022).
FSO (Federal Statistical Office). 2022a. *Ausländische Bevölkerung*. https://www.bfs.admin.ch/bfs/de/home/statistiken/bevoelkerung/migration-integration/auslaendische-bevoelkerung.html (accessed 29 November 2022).
FSO (Federal Statistical Office). 2022b. *Asylstatistik*. https://www.sem.admin.ch/sem/de/home/publiservice/statistik/asylstatistik.html (accessed 29 November 2022).
FSO. 2022c. *Bundesamt für Statistik*. https://www.bfs.admin.ch (accessed 30 November 2022).

FSO. 2022d. *Schweizerische Arbeitskräfteerhebung (SAKE)*. https://www.bfs.admin.ch/bfs/de/home/statistiken/arbeit-erwerb/erhebungen/sake.html (accessed 30 November 2022).

FSO. 2022e. *Statistik der Bevölkerung und der Haushalte*. https://www.bfs.admin.ch/bfs/de/home/statistiken/bevoelkerung/erhebungen/statpop.html (accessed 30 November 2022).

Gessler, Theresa, and Sophia Hunger. 2022. 'How the Refugee Crisis and Radical Right Parties Shape Party Competition on Immigration'. *Political Science Research and Methods* 10 (3): pp. 524–544.

Koch, Philippe, and Sandra Lavenex. 2006. 'The (Contentious) Human Face of Europeanization: Free Movement and Immigration'. In *Switzerland and the European Union*, edited by Clive Church, pp. 148–166, London: Routledge.

Kriesi Hanspeter, Edgar Grande, Martin Dolezal, Marc Helbling, Dominic Höglinger, Swen Hutter, and Bruno Wueest. 2012. *Political Conflict in Western Europe*. Cambridge: Cambridge University Press.

Kriesi, Hanspeter, Romain Lachat, Peter Selb, Simon Bornschier, and Marc Helbling (eds). 2005. *Der Aufstieg der SVP: acht Kantone im Vergleich*. Zürich: Verlag Neue Zürcher Zeitung.

Lavenex, Sandra. 2004. 'Whither the Liberal Democratic Model? Immigration Politics in Switzerland and Japan'. *Schweizerische Zeitschrift für Politikwissenschaft* 10 (3): pp. 179–209.

Lavenex, Sandra, Paula Hoffmeyer-Zlotnik, and Philipp Lutz. 2022. 'Chapter 10: Migration'. In *A Swiss Foreign Policy for the 21st Century*, edited by Thomas Bernauer, Katja Gentinetta, and Joelle Kuntz, pp. 857–882. Zürich: NZZ libro.

Lavenex, Sandra, and Anita Manatschal. 2022. 'Migrationspolitik'. In *Handbuch der Schweizer Politik*, edited by Yannis Papadopoulos, Pascal Sciarini, Adrian Vatter und Silja Häusermann, Patrick Emmenegger, and Flavia Fossati, pp. 857–882. Zürich: NZZ Verlag.

Mahnig, Hans, and Etienne Piguet. 2003. 'Die Immigrationspolitik der Schweiz von 1948 bis 1998: Entwicklung und Auswirkungen'. In *Migration und die Schweiz: Ergebnisse des Nationalen Forschungsprogramms 'Migration und interkulturelle Beziehungen'*, edited by Hans-Rudolf Wicker, Rosita Fibbi, and Werner Haug, pp. 63–103. Zürich, Seismo.

Manatschal, Anita, and Carolin Rapp. 2015. 'Welche Schweizer wählen die SVP und warum? Die SVP-Wählerschaft im Wandel'. In *Wahlen und Wählerschaft in der Schweiz. Analysen anlässlich der eidgenössischen Wahlen 2015*, edited by Markus Freitag, and Adrian Vatter, pp. 187–216. Zürich: NZZ Verlag.

Niederberger, Josef Martin. 2001. 'Von der "Wiederentfernung" zur Integration – der Entwurf zu einem neuen Ausländergesetz'. *Swiss Political Science Review* 7 (1): pp. 18–24.

Parini, Lorena 1997. *La politique d'asile en Suisse: une perspective systémique*. Paris: L'Harmattan.

Piguet, Etienne. 2004. *L'immigration en Suisse: 50 ans d'entrouverture*. Lausanne: Presses polytechniques et universitaires romandes.

Probst, Johanna, Gianni D'Amato, Samantha Dunning, Denise Efionayi-Mäder, Joelle Fehlmann, Andreas Perret, Didier Ruedin, and Irina Sille. 2019. *Kantonale Spielräume im Wandel: Migrationspolitik in der Schweiz*. SFM Studies #73d. Neuchâtel: Swiss Forum for Migration and Population Studies.

Sandoz, Laure. 2019. *Mobilities of the Highly Skilled towards Switzerland: The Role of Intermediaries in Defining 'Wanted Immigrants'*. Cham: Springer.

Schwok, René. 2020. 'Switzerland-EU relations: The bilateral way in a fragilized position'. *European foreign affairs review* 25 (2): pp. 159–176.

Spescha, Marc. 1999. *Handbuch zum Ausländerrecht*. Bern: Verlag Paul Haupt.

SEM (State Secretariat for Migration). 2022. *Staatssekretariat für Migration SEM*. www.sem.admin.ch (accessed 29 November 2022).

Swiss Federal Chancellery. 2022. *Bundeskanzlei BK*. https://www.bk.admin.ch/bk/en/home.html (accessed 29 November 2022).

Wichmann, Nicole, Michael Hermann, Gianni D'Amato, Denise Efionayi-Mäder, Rosita Fibbi, Joanna Menet, and Didier Ruedin. 2011. *Gestaltungsspielräume im Föderalismus: die Migrationspolitik in den Kantonen*. Bern: Eidgenössische Migrationskommission EKM.

Wicker, Hans-Rudolf, Rosita Fibbi, and Werner Haug (eds). 2003. *Migration und die Schweiz*. Zürich: Seismo.

CHAPTER 36

INTEGRATION POLICY

ANITA MANATSCHAL

1 THE SWISS CASE IN INTERNATIONAL PERSPECTIVE

More than one-third of people residing in Switzerland have a migrant background and one-quarter are foreign nationals (BFS 2019; Piguet 2013). From a quantitative perspective, the country thus resembles classic settler states such as Canada, the United States, or Australia (Piguet 2013). In contrast to these former settler states, however, this immigration reality is not reflected in Switzerland's national identity, because, for a long time, the country did not perceive itself as a country of immigration. In the post-World War II era, Switzerland was a prime example of a continental European guest-worker country. Like other Germanic countries, such as Austria and Germany, that had guest-worker programmes in the post-war era (Ellermann 2013), Switzerland actively recruited foreign workers. All the while, the country maintained a restrictive position regarding naturalization and immigrant integration. Increasing critique in the 1980s led to the abolishment of the guest-worker programme, and Swiss immigration policy was completely reformed after the introduction of the free movement of labour in the European Union in 2002. Yet, history left its marks. Despite the fact that a significant proportion of the population has a migrant background or holds a foreign passport, the country generally has an assimilationist understanding of immigrant integration, prioritizing cultural assimilation over concessions towards cultural-religious diversity, while holding on to high formal hurdles that must be overcome to acquire citizenship, compared to other nations (Koopmans et al. 2012; Banting and Kymlicka 2013; Manatschal 2015).

1.1 An assimilationist integration regime

At the turn of the millennium, Robinson (1998, 167) described integration as a 'chaotic concept: a word used by many but understood differently by most'. The fact that it often bears strong normative connotations in public and political discourse has not facilitated consensus in defining the term. In Switzerland, the State Secretariat for Migration (SEM) or legislation such as the Foreign Nationals and Integration Act (AIG) describe integration as a mutual process involving immigrants and natives alike, yet its success or failure is typically 'measured' exclusively against immigrants' actions. Immigrants are considered integrated when they have equal opportunities or are on an equal footing with natives, e.g. in the socio-economic, cultural, and political realms of society (Ager and Strang 2008; Harder et al. 2018).

As scientific concepts, the notions of integration and integration policy reflect the gradual expansion of non-citizens' rights over time. Whereas in the eighteenth century a *citoyen* was primarily defined in terms of his civil rights (note e.g. that Switzerland only introduced women's suffrage in 1971), the contemporary understanding of citizenship goes beyond individual political and social rights (see Marshall 1950) and also encompasses rights that pertain to gender equality and the cultural diversity of certain groups (Castles and Davidson 2000, 105). Consequently, various conceptions of integration are reflected in scholarly accounts of integration policies. Most accounts, however, agree on three principal policy dimensions (Manatschal et al. 2020; Koopmans et al. 2012; Boswell 2003): first, civic-political policies govern immigrants' political rights, e.g. in terms of non-citizen voting rights or access to citizenship; second, cultural-religious policies address questions of cultural assimilation or adaptation, e.g. language acquisition, and diversity, e.g. religious minority rights, often also referred to as 'multiculturalist policies' (Bloemraad and Wright 2014); and third, socio-economic integration policies regulate aspects such as immigrants' access to the labour market or social benefits. All three policy dimensions can have inclusive or exclusive orientations. Inclusive examples encompass policies that facilitate access to social benefits, Swiss citizenship, or non-citizen voting rights, whereas the absence or limitation of these rights, such as regulations that restrict access to citizenship, represent exclusive policies. In the cultural domain, inclusive policies typically accommodate diversity, e.g. via state sponsoring of cultural-religious organizations, while exclusive policies focus on assimilation, e.g. by demanding a certain level of language proficiency to access social benefits.

In line with this gradual expansion of rights, traditional accounts that classify different national integration approaches primarily focus on policies regulating immigrants' political rights, in particular access to citizenship (Brubaker 1992; Favell 2001). These categorizations distinguish between countries that grant citizenship based on the restrictive *jus sanguinis* principle and those that use the more inclusive *jus soli* principle. Under *jus sanguinis*, access to citizenship is tied to the bloodline, and hurdles to citizenship for foreign nationals of a 'different blood' are relatively high as is the case in Switzerland. *Jus soli* citizenship, commonly illustrated with the case of the United States, is automatically granted to children of non-citizens born on the country's soil, even if their parents have an undocumented legal status.

Since political discourses on what it means to be a citizen of a country are also tied to cultural understandings of national identity, subsequent studies on approaches to granting citizenship have expanded their view to include questions regarding immigrants' cultural rights and obligations, drawing a distinction between assimilationist and multiculturalist approaches to integration (Banting and Kymlicka 2013; Koopmans et al. 2012). So far, however, research on national integration policies has neglected the aspect of socio-economic integration. Two factors may explain this (but see Lafleur and Vintilla 2020). First, official policy debates in the socio-economic integration domain focus on immigrants' access to the labour market, which depends on non-citizens' legal status in a country. This issue is closely tied to questions surrounding immigrant selection, such as who is allowed to enter and work in the country, and under which conditions. Labour market access is thus frequently discussed in the context of immigrant selection, i.e. immigration policy, and not integration policy (see 'Migration Policy' in this volume). Second, spatial rescaling of social policy from the national level to subnational regions has been ongoing since the mid-1970s (Keating 2013; Kleider 2018; Vampa 2016). The implication of this policy devolution is that subnational regions, rather than nations, preside over the socio-economic issues most relevant to immigrants' everyday lives, including, for instance, access to social benefits (Manatschal et al. 2020).

Consequently, classic typologies of integration policy regimes still focus on the two policy dimensions regulating immigrants' access to political and cultural-religious rights and obligations, resulting in four different types of integration policy, as shown in Figure 36.1. According to this typology, Switzerland is still classified as assimilationist, characterized by a restrictive access to citizenship and a cultural notion of integration that prioritizes assimilation over concessions towards cultural diversity (D'Amato 2010; Manatschal 2015; Giugni and Passy 2004).

International policy indices corroborate Switzerland's restrictive position on these two policy dimensions. Access to Swiss citizenship is limited by the country's adherence to the *jus sanguinis* principle and a relatively long period of ten years of residence,

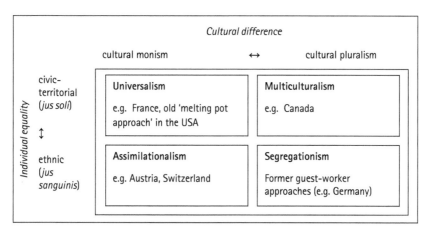

FIGURE 36.1: Two-dimensional typology of immigrant integration policy regimes
Data source: adapted from Manatschal (2013, 57), based on Koopmans et al. (2005) and the Migrant Integration Policy Index (Niessen et al. 2007).

which are required to apply for naturalization in the ordinary procedure (see section 3 in this chapter for a more detailed discussion). As the left plot in Figure 36.2 shows, Switzerland has some of the harshest naturalization requirements in Western Europe, as indicated by its low naturalization policy scores on the Migrant Integration Policy Index MIPEX (Solano and Huddleston 2020). Countries with easier access to citizenship, such as Sweden or Portugal, require only five years of residence for their standard application procedures.

With regard to the second policy dimension, the Multiculturalism Policy Index MCP (Wallace et al. 2021) confirms the country's minimal cultural concessions towards ethno-religious minority groups (see the right plot in Figure 36.2). Of the eight policy components of the MCP, which includes, among other things, state funding to support cultural activities of ethnic minority groups or for bilingual or mother-tongue education, affirmative action, and the inclusion of ethnic minority representation in the mandate of public media or media licensing, Switzerland scores only in the category 'dual citizenship', which has been allowed since 1992 (Wallace et al. 2021). At regular intervals, popular votes on cultural-religious minority rights have confirmed Switzerland's restrictive stance: in 2009, the Swiss people accepted a federal popular initiative against the construction of minarets on Swiss soil, and in 2021, another popular vote resulted in a prohibition on the wearing of full-face coverings, including religious veils, in Switzerland (see Table 36.1 below). Switzerland's assimilationist orientation thus stands in a stark contrast with states such as Sweden and Finland, which have the most inclusive multiculturalist provisions in Europe.

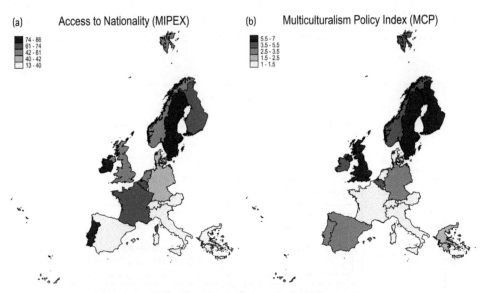

FIGURE 36.2: Integration policies in Western Europe

Data source: Own illustration based on the Migrant Integration Policy Index MIPEX from 2020 (Solano and Huddleston 2020) in the left plot, and the Multiculturalism Policy Index MCP (Wallace et al. 2021) in the right plot. Policies range from exclusive (low scale values and brightly marked countries) to inclusive (high scale values and darkly marked countries).

1.2 The impact of Swiss federalism

At the level of political institutions, two structural principles shape the making and implementation of Swiss integration policy, namely the country's pronounced federalism and the principle of subsidiarity. The latter is defined in article 3 of the federal constitution, stating that Swiss cantons are responsible for all policy areas which are not regulated at the federal level. Similar to other federal republics, including Germany or the USA, but also to quasi-federal states, such as Italy or Spain, there is much more regional policy-making activity in the field of immigrant integration, whereas the regulation of immigration flows remains largely the prerogative of the national level (Manatschal et al. 2020; Tränhardt 2001). This separation of tasks across state levels can be attributed to the different regulatory logic underlying each of the two policy fields. On the one hand, immigration policies regulate who can enter the country and under which conditions. The demarcating lines for these policies are—mainly national—borders, with immigration policies assuming the role of gatekeepers presiding over entry and exit. Immigration policies are thus primarily a national prerogative. If subnational states can define their own immigration policies, as is the case in Canada, for example, this represents the exception rather than the rule, which can be explained by the particular immigration approach in the relevant country (Paquet and Xhardez 2020). Immigrant integration policies, on the other hand, regulate the inclusion of resident immigrants into a country's society, economy, and polity, after foreign nationals have crossed national borders and settled in a local context. Given that individual integration processes are strongly embedded in a particular place, the predominantly local and regional policy-making activity in this policy field is hardly surprising.

Swiss federalism provides several channels, through which cantons can influence integration policy-making, including autonomous policy-making, policy implementation of federal law, bicameralism, and symbolic politics. First, Swiss cantons act autonomously when they are designated as the main regulatory actors in a given policy area, as is the case with non-citizen voting rights or the official recognition of minority religions (Christmann 2010; Piccoli 2021; Manatschal 2011). Other policy domains, such as citizenship policy, are co-regulated by different tiers of government. This means that not only the Swiss Citizenship Act (BüG) but also one of twenty-six cantonal citizenship laws and local regulations determine non-citizens' access to citizenship. Second, the principle of executive federalism, defined in article 46 of the federal constitution, stipulates that the cantons are responsible for the implementation of federal law, which often gives them some leeway in policy implementation (Linder 2012; Vatter and Wälti 2003). The fact that certain national legal provisions are formulated in a facultative way means that cantons have de facto liberty in policy-making. One example is the restrictive policy instrument of the 'integration agreement' (Kurt 2020), which allows cantons to tie the granting of residence permits to a certain degree of integration, for instance, language proficiency or economic self-sufficiency.[1] Third, cantons may influence the national integration policy debate via the second parliamentary chamber (*Ständerat*).

Especially direct democracy (including *Ständemehr* or majority of cantonal votes and *Standesinitiative* or cantonal initiative) offers the cantons comprehensive opportunities to be heard in decision-making processes at the federal level (see 'The Cantons' in this volume). Finally, the instruments of direct democracy also offer very fertile ground for symbolic party politics in Switzerland: ever since the post-World War II era, right-wing populist parties have been using these instruments, often by taking up local or regional debates, to restrict national legislation in the fields of immigration, asylum, and immigrant rights (Niederberger 2004; Skenderovic 2009). Successes at the polls of federal popular initiatives launched by the right-wing populist Swiss People's Party (SVP), such as the 2009 initiative against the construction of minarets and the 2014 initiative against mass immigration, demonstrated that direct democracy continues to provide powerful instruments for (right-wing) populist mobilization against immigration and its effects (cf. Giugni and Passy 2006, 21).

The following sections provide a detailed account of how these mechanisms shaped the historical and legal evolution of the field of integration policy over time and shed light on the rich variety of official and civil society actors, who are involved in or influence policy-making at different levels of Swiss government. Since integration and citizenship are different legal fields in Switzerland, the two policy areas are treated in separate sections.

2 Integration policy

Due to the bottom-up nature of immigrant integration processes, Switzerland's guest-worker legacy, and the country's pronounced federal structure, integration policy is a relatively recent policy field at the federal level. For a long time, questions of immigrant integration were left up to social institutions, i.e. schools, businesses, and associations or clubs, for instance, religious organizations such as the Aid Agency of the Protestant Churches of Switzerland (HEKS) or Caritas. This resulted in the development of a multitude of integration approaches across communes and cantons that is difficult to grasp fully (Cattacin and Kaya 2005; Manatschal 2011). Only by the mid-1990s had integration policy finally reached the federal level in connection with problems that were emerging in cities.

According to the law, integration ought to enable foreigners, who legally reside in Switzerland in the longer term, to take part in Swiss society's economic, social, and cultural life (art. 4 para. 2 AIG). The focus is thus placed on foreigners adapting to Swiss society through societal, economic, and cultural integration rather than on concessions made in areas such as political or cultural minority rights. However, behind this restrictive official understanding of integration based on *jus sanguinis* citizenship and cultural assimilation, there are also marked regional differences. Whereas German-speaking cantons often draft more restrictive integration policies, French-speaking Switzerland in particular is usually more inclusive, as for instance the widespread prevalence of voting rights for foreign residents in French-speaking cantons indicates. Five out of six French-speaking cantons grant non-citizen voting rights at the local (Fribourg, Geneva, and Vaud) and occasionally even at the cantonal (Neuchâtel and Jura) level, whereas only three among the remaining nineteen German-speaking cantons plus Ticino provide some limited form of non-citizen voting rights at the local level, namely Grisons, Basel City, and Appenzell Outer-Rhodes (Arrighi de Casanova and Piccoli 2018; Manatschal 2011).

2.1 Historical evolution of Swiss integration policy

The integration of foreign residents as a federal task first found its way into legislation only in the 1980s. Enacted in 1986, the revision of the Federal Act on the Residence and Establishment of Foreigners of 1931 (SR 142.20) introduced a funding provision that allowed the Confederation to provide financial support for the social integration of foreigners. Based on this provision, the Federal Council passed the ordinance of 13 September 2000 on the Integration of Foreign Nationals (VIntA), in which the goals of integration were defined for the first time. The ordinance conceives of integration as a cross-sectional task, so it also regulates issues of oversight as well as financial aspects. It maintains that integration primarily takes place within societal structures, namely schools, workplaces, and social welfare and healthcare institutions, and that financial support from the government ought to be merely complementary (art. 2 VIntA).

The position of integration gained a stronger foothold in legislation with the further revision as well as renaming of the Federal Act of 1931: in 2008 it became the Foreign Nationals Act (AuG), and since 2019 it is the Foreign Nationals and Integration Act (AIG). The Tripartite Process to Further Develop Swiss Integration Policy launched in 2009 played a central role in this concretization of a national integration policy. To gather input and debate issues around immigrant integration through this process, a range of experts was pooled from all levels of government, peak-level organizations of employers and employees, and members of the foreign national population as well as other civil society groups. Subsequent changes in the legislation were strongly oriented towards the *Fördern und Fordern* principle (see chapter 8 AIG), which has been a cornerstone of Swiss integration policy since the Federal Council's 2010 integration report (Bundesrat 2010). According to this principle, the government actively supports integration (*Fördern*) while, simultaneously, certain demands are made of immigrants in terms of furthering their integration themselves (*Fordern*). Political developments since these changes in legislation have tended to place much more emphasis on the demands side of the equation. This is reflected, for example, in the constitutional amendment that followed the adoption of the 2014 Swiss immigration initiative: a newly introduced article mentions working foreigners' 'ability to integrate' as one of the 'decisive criteria for granting residence permits' (art. 121a para. 3 of the federal constitution). The AIG has, however, also been used to implement the other side of the principle: also in 2014, the Confederation and the cantons used it as a basis to create the Cantonal Integration

Programmes (KIP) that provide financial support for individual integration processes (art. 55 and art. 58 para. 3 AIG). These programmes aim to foster immigrant integration at the arrival stage (information and counselling) and in everyday life (education and work), and to support communication (language courses) and social exchange. After a first round of these programmes (2014–2017) proved successful, all cantons implemented a second round of integration programmes (2018–2021) co-financed by the Confederation.

Although the 2009 Tripartite Process to Further Develop Swiss Integration Policy was unsuccessful in its initial aim to establish a separate integration law, the country has been working towards a uniform conception of integration with concrete targets within the framework of existing legislation, particularly AIG, over the last decade. The current legal situation thus reflects the position taken by the Federal Council in its report concluding this Tripartite Process, in which it stated that integration must be anchored in legislation primarily by amending existing laws (Bundesrat 2010, 2).

2.2 Actors and political lines of conflict

Swiss law, subsequent to these changes, defines integration as an overarching and cross-sectional task that must be taken on by the federal, cantonal, and communal authorities together with non-governmental organizations, including those that make up the social partnership between employers and workers as well as organizations for foreigners (art. 53 para. 4 AIG and art. 2 para. 2 VIntA). Therefore, beyond financial integration support from the government, social institutions in relevant areas of society, such as healthcare and education, are central players in everyday integration activities. Despite progress being made towards the goal of achieving a common conception of integration at the federal level, each of the bodies involved continues to hold their own view of what integration is, especially regarding which side of the *Fördern und Fordern* principle is emphasized more, and how each of the two sides is implemented.

As detailed in section 1.2, the cantons take on a central role in this context (Cattacin and Kaya 2005; Manatschal 2011; Wichmann et al. 2011; Probst et al. 2019). With the revisions that resulted in the AuG, the cantons' role was further reinforced. Since 2008, each canton has had its own integration delegate, who serves as a direct point of contact for the State Secretariat for Migration (SEM). These experts have a central coordinating body known as the Conference of Cantonal, Communal, and Regional Integration Delegates (KID). In this context, the Confederation plays a primarily strategic role by financially supporting cantonal and communal integration programmes. In addition to cantons, cities are also important players in this policy field, not least because a higher number of foreign residents in urban areas leads to more integration challenges. At the same time, however, it falls under the remit of cantonal law to define cities' authority within the realm of integration (TAK 2005, 26).

Since various aspects of integration were written into federal law at a relatively late stage, the topic of integrating immigrants was not politicized significantly at a national

Table 36.1: Federal popular initiatives in the field of integration and citizenship policy since 1968

Date	Initiative	Yes-votes in per cent
1968	(Withdrawn on 20/03) First initiative against 'foreign infiltration' (*Gegen Überfremdung*)	
07/06/1970	Second initiative against 'foreign infiltration' (*Schwarzenbachinitiative*)	46.0
20/10/1974	Third initiative against the 'foreign infiltration' and overpopulation of Switzerland	34.2
13/03/1977	Fourth initiative against 'foreign infiltration'	29.5
13/03/1977	Initiative for a restriction of naturalizations	33.8
05/04/1981	'Together' initiative for a new policy on foreigners	16.2
1987	(Failed on 04/08 at the collection stage) Fifth initiative against 'foreign infiltration'	
01/06/2008	Initiative for democratic naturalization decisions	36.2
29/11/2009	Initiative against the construction of minarets (minaret initiative)	57.5
28/11/2010	Initiative for the deportation of criminal foreigners (deportation initiative)	52.3
28/02/2016	Initiative on the enforcement of the deportation of criminal foreigners (enforcement initiative)	41.0
07/03/2021	Initiative 'Yes to a ban on full facial coverings'	51.2

Note: Listed are popular initiatives (no referendums) in the policy fields of integration and citizenship. Initiatives in the related field of immigration policy (e.g. initiative against mass immigration from 2014) are excluded, unless they refer to the cultural aspect of integration (e.g. initiatives against 'foreign infiltration').
Data source: Swiss Federal Chancellery (2022).

level for some time. Though here, too, direct democracy has proven to be a powerful tool for advancing right-wing populist causes in the twenty-first century. This was particularly evident in the adoption of the SVP's federal popular initiative against the construction of minarets in 2009, which resulted in a ban on new structures of this type on Swiss soil (see Table 36.1). The Swiss electorate's scepticism towards religious minority rights is in accord with the assimilative conception of what it means to be a member of Swiss society: immigrants' adaptation is valued more highly than the recognition of cultural diversity (Skenderovic 2009, 48). Both parties to the left and the centre or centre-right avoided the topic of integration for a long time, because a sceptical position towards immigration was already occupied by right-wing populists while a decidedly pro-immigration stance would have garnered no votes (Manatschal 2015). Parties from the left to centre-right did, however, become more active in the early 2000s: motions from the Social Democratic Party (SP) and the Liberal Democratic Party (FDP) provided the basis for the aforementioned 2009 Tripartite Process to Further Develop Swiss Integration Policy.

Beyond the various non-governmental organizations and governmental bodies that have already been introduced, the Federal Commission on Migration (EKM), the Conference of Cantonal Governments, and the Tripartite Conference also bear mentioning for their role in taking on integration as an overarching and cross-sectional task. They have all been instrumental in advancing Swiss integration policy over recent decades.

3 Citizenship policy

The tension between immigration as an everyday reality and its political incarnation in the nation-state is most evident in naturalization policy. The high proportion of foreign nationals in the Swiss population has come up again and again in so-called *Überfremdungsinitiativen* (literally: initiatives against 'foreign infiltration'), which call for limiting or even reducing the number of foreign residents to avoid the perceived cultural threat of the nation being inundated or overrun by immigrants (see Table 36.1). An example from the related field of immigration policy is the initiative for moderation in immigration from September 2020, also known as the 'limitation initiative', a federal popular initiative aimed at limiting influx by decoupling Swiss immigration law from European Union freedom of movement provisions. These political disputes illustrate the strong symbolic value that statistics on foreigners can carry. The fact that the high number of foreign nationals in Switzerland is indeed a result of the country's comparatively strict naturalization policies, which limit access to citizenship, is often overlooked.

At the same time, social and economic rights are increasingly detached from formal citizenship, as is exemplified by facilitated labour market access for certain non-citizen groups such as EU citizens or provisionally admitted individuals in the asylum domain (Jacobson 1996; Joppke 2007). Coupled with this evolution has been a paradigm shift, away from the image of the migrant worker to the image of the fellow member of the citizenry, although these individuals still face significant hurdles before they can acquire formal citizenship.

3.1 Historical evolution of Swiss citizenship law

Nationality law in Switzerland is a product of the country's federalist system. Before the Swiss federal state was founded in 1848, only cantons could grant citizenship. In 1874, the Confederation obtained oversight of naturalization and the authority to determine the minimum requirements for acquisition and loss of citizenship. One could make the claim that federal policy almost exclusively focused on granting residence permits until the mid-1990s, whereas citizenship largely remained within the purview of municipalities and cantons. Today, the regular, non-facilitated procedure for acquiring citizenship in Switzerland still involves all three levels of government: federal, cantonal, and communal (Helbling 2008). Communal authorities are the primary decision-makers, whereas cantons and the Confederation determine binding minimum requirements for naturalization (see Arrighi de Casanova and Piccoli 2018).

Until 1 January 2018, citizenship was based on the 1952 Federal Act on Acquisition and Loss of Swiss Citizenship, at which point it was replaced by the Swiss Citizenship Act of 20 June 2014 (BüG; SR 141.0). Similar to the field of integration policy, attempts to restrict Swiss citizenship law or to keep decision-making power in the hands of 'the people' were typically launched in a bottom-up manner via popular initiatives (see Table 36.1). Proposals that sought to introduce easier access, e.g. via facilitated naturalization or automatic citizenship for descendants of immigrants, were in turn often proposed via referendums but generally failed to obtain a popular majority at the polls. One of the first referendums that aimed at facilitating naturalization for young foreign nationals, who grew up in Switzerland, was rejected in 1983. Two years earlier, the *Mitenand* or 'together' initiative, a uniquely xenophile federal popular initiative in Swiss history, had also been rejected at the ballot box (see Table 36.1). Originating from trade union circles in 1977, this initiative called for foreigners resident in Switzerland to be considered broadly equal with Swiss citizens.

A second referendum on facilitated naturalization took place in 1994. The majority of voters backed the measure, but it failed to achieve the double majority required via yes-votes from a majority of cantons (*Ständemehr*). Some cantons in which a majority of voters accepted the proposal thus decided to act within their own sphere of influence to facilitate naturalization for young foreign nationals who had grown up or been born in Switzerland. In 2004, a comprehensive revision of constitutional tenets, that would permit facilitated naturalization of young second-generation foreign nationals and automatic acquisition of Swiss citizenship at birth for third-generation children, was once again rejected, this time by the Swiss people and the cantons. Finally, on 12 February 2017, both 60.4 per cent of voters and a majority of cantons voted yes in a referendum vote on the Federal Decree on the Simplified Naturalization of Third-Generation Immigrants. From this point onwards, grandchildren of immigrants benefited from simplified procedures, which only spouses of Swiss nationals had enjoyed thus far.

According to article 9 of the BüG, the formal requirements for naturalization are at least ten years of residency—of which the years spent living in Switzerland between the ages of eight and eighteen count double—as well as possession of a permanent residence permit. Besides this national residency requirement, a canton may require between two and eight years of continuous residency in the canton. At the level of material requirements, the BüG (art. 11) also exacts proof of an applicant's successful integration and their familiarity with the Swiss way of life. An applicant should also not pose any threat to the internal or external security of Switzerland. Article 12 of the BüG and the new Ordinance on Swiss Citizenship (BüV; SR 141.01) further specify how particularly the criterion of successful integration ought to be construed. The focus is on language skills, participation in economic life, and respect for the values enshrined in the constitution. Although certain provisions have been made more stringent, the reform also relaxed some points, as can be seen in a call for consideration of special circumstances when evaluating integration criteria (art. 12 para. 2 BüG).

The Confederation must first grant an applicant a naturalization licence before the process can continue at the communal and cantonal levels. Additional naturalization requirements come into play here (e.g. duration of residency, material requirements, and fees), and they may differ from place to place, despite national efforts to improve consistency through the aforementioned changes to the legislation. Cantons and communes still command considerable decision-making powers, which they have successfully defended against harmonization efforts at the national level for a long time. One of the first steps towards more consistent federal alignment was a Federal Supreme Court decision of 1 January 2006 according to which cantons and communes could levy only administrative fees in the naturalization process. Since 2018, general standards for the naturalization process have been formalized in both the new BüG and an ordinance designed for this purpose in particular. These measures have provided applicants with more certainty in terms of their rights and given Swiss citizenship law a solid push in the direction of harmonization. Compared to other nations, however, the hurdles to acquiring citizenship remain significant, especially given the rigid adherence to the *jus sanguinis* principle.

3.2 Actors and political lines of conflict

Differences between communes' and cantons' terms for acquiring citizenship are not only formal but also institutional in nature. In many communes, whether an applicant is granted citizenship is decided by a naturalization commission, while in other places this decision is the responsibility of the cantonal or communal executive, or in a few communes also of the legislature. The fact that in some instances the legislature (local parliament) and, until 2003, potentially all citizens of a municipality could co-determine who does or does not become a Swiss citizen gives this process a political rather than a purely administrative character. Even if an applicant meets all formal requirements, the applicant may still have no legal claim to citizenship; this is a fundamental difference in the law between Switzerland and most other constitutional democracies (Helbling 2008). The potentially discriminatory effect of votes cast for or against a citizenship application was recognized in two rulings by the Federal Supreme Court in the summer of 2003. Naturalization by ballot was thus declared principally unconstitutional, allowing for appeals based on the violation of anti-discrimination rules to be made to the Court (BGE 129 I 232 and BGE 129 I 217 of 9 July 2003; see also Helbling and Kriesi 2004; Hainmueller and Hangartner 2013). Opposition to these efforts to make the naturalization process more objective mostly came from the far-right fringes of the political spectrum, namely the SVP and the Campaign for an Independent and Neutral Switzerland (AUNS). The SVP subsequently launched a federal popular initiative against the ban on naturalization by ballot in 2008 (Initiative for democratic naturalization decisions, see Table 36.1). It was also these two groups and their campaigning efforts in the previously discussed 2004 referendum regarding facilitated naturalization and automatic citizenship that had a large hand in the resulting clear rejection of this federal vote (see section 3.1 in this chapter). In contrast to the SVP, the other three parties in government at the time—the Social Democratic Party (SP), the Christian Democratic People's Party (CVP), and the Liberal Democratic Party (FDP)—had indeed campaigned for the yes-vote in this third attempt at getting facilitated naturalization to pass, but after the referendum they were criticized for not publicly advocating for their position enough.

Beyond the narrower circle of government bodies that are directly involved in the naturalization process and the political parties, who have an ideological interest in this question, there are other important national players such as the Federal Commission against Racism (EKR). The EKR was established after Switzerland acceded to the 1965 International Convention on the Elimination of All Forms of Racial Discrimination (ICERD) in the mid-1990s. This United Nations Convention requires its signatories not only to criminalize racist acts and prohibit racist propaganda, but also to actively formulate policies against discrimination and guarantee equal treatment for all people regardless of their ethnic identity, nationality, race, or religion. The EKR got involved in naturalization policy in 2007 through the publication of its report on discriminatory practices in the naturalization process at the communal level. The EKR also collaborates with the EKM, mentioned previously, to fulfil a coordinating role between state authorities, non-governmental organizations, and international bodies (Niederberger 2004, 142).

4 Conclusion

Taken together, the current regulatory situation in the field of Swiss integration policy, which regulates immigrants' socio-economic, civic-political, and cultural-religious rights and obligations, can be read as the result of three interacting factors (Manatschal 2014). The first factor is the country's former guest-worker approach to immigration, which incorrectly assumed that guest workers would eventually return to their country of origin. Consequently, questions about immigrant integration were neglected at the federal level for many years. The second factor concerns the bottom-up nature of locally embedded processes of immigrant integration. The third point relates to Switzerland's pronounced federalism, which implied that lower-level authorities, mainly cities and cantons, were the first to start actively regulating these local and regional questions of immigrant integration in Switzerland. It was only via this communal and cantonal policy-making that immigrant integration found its way into the federal political arena. Federalism also left its imprint on the country's nationality law, as Swiss citizenship continues to be granted via a worldwide unique three-tiered system, requiring communal, cantonal, and federal approval.

From a historical perspective, the development of a national integration policy coincided with a gradual improvement in the social and economic rights of permanent resident foreigners in Switzerland. This development was fostered by the processes of globalization and European integration as well as by the liberal values of Switzerland's legal system. The most important achievement in this context was the introduction of the Agreement on Free Movement of Persons between Switzerland and EU/EFTA countries in 2002, which facilitated EU citizens' access to the Swiss labour market. A liberalizing trend can also be observed in areas that were traditionally exempt from integration measures such as the asylum domain. Based on the observation that provisionally admitted asylum-related migrants often stay in Switzerland for a long time, if not forever, a reform of Swiss asylum law implemented between 2006 and 2008 facilitated labour market integration, family reunification, and participation in integration programmes (e.g. language courses) for this particular migrant group (Pecoraro et al. 2022). This reform clearly reflects a change in perspective and recognition of the fact that early integration support for migrants, who will most likely stay in Switzerland for the long term, is beneficial for everyone.

National resistance to the decreasing formal difference between Swiss citizens and resident foreign nationals is concentrated in naturalization law—and thus in the field of political rights—as well as in the field of cultural-religious diversity. Liberalizing trends in the naturalization domain remain modest. A facilitated naturalization procedure for descendants of migrants in the third generation, meaning the grandchildren of former migrants, was accepted via referendum only in 2017, after numerous unsuccessful attempts. More far-reaching reforms that aim, for instance, to introduce *jus soli* elements into Swiss citizenship law are neither seriously discussed nor do they appear realistic in Switzerland. This despite the fact that Germany, with its very similar *jus sanguinis* citizenship tradition and guest-worker legacy, had already enacted such a reform in 1999 (Avitabile et al. 2013).

This resistance is also evident in the domain of cultural-religious minority rights. From an institutional perspective, Swiss federalism and the country's frequent use of direct democracy at all levels of government can partly explain this restrictive status quo in the fields of immigrants' political and cultural-religious rights. Taken together, both institutions guarantee a very strong say for the popular will, i.e. the enfranchised majority population, in these policy areas. In this context, direct democracy has aptly been described as a brake for the expansion of religious minority rights in Switzerland (Vatter 2011; see also Vatter and Danaci 2010). Exemplary for this restrictive interplay between federalism and direct democracy is the national initiative for the ban on full facial coverings that was accepted by popular vote in 2021 (see Table 36.1). Before the nationwide acceptance of this federal initiative, two cantons, Ticino in 2013 and St Gall in 2018, had already accepted a 'burka ban' via direct democratic votes, prohibiting the wearing of this garment in these cantonal territories.

Political actors, such as the right-wing populist SVP, clearly profited from Switzerland's political institutions to make their anti-immigrant agenda heard. In the late 1990s, Swiss federalism allowed the party to carry its restrictive agenda from the canton of Zurich to the federal level (Kriesi et al. 2005). Once the party established its anti-immigrant agenda at the national level, it successfully launched various federal initiatives from the early 2000s onwards, aiming at a restriction of Swiss migration policy (see Table 36.1). This increased use of direct democratic instruments over the first two decades of the twenty-first century, not only in the integration realm but also in the related field of immigration policy (see 'Migration Policy' in this volume), also points to an increased politicization of Swiss migration policy.

Overall, the country thus represents a paradigmatic example of international trends according to which direct democratic and federal states formulate more restrictive integration policies (Manatschal and Bernauer 2016). At the same time, these institutional constraints do not impede the country from exhibiting spontaneous solidarity with immigrants, as witnessed by the quick adoption of a protection status (S permit) in the spring 2022 Ukrainian humanitarian migration crisis. The fact that this protection status was not enacted earlier, for example, during the 2015 humanitarian migration crisis in the aftermath of the Arab spring, is no Swiss idiosyncrasy. Rather, it is illustrative of double standards and ethnic hierarchies more generally (Krause 2021) that shape the way countries in the Global North regulate their migration policies.

Note

1. See in particular art. 58b of the Foreign Nationals and Integration Act (AIG) and art. 5 of the Ordinance on the Integration of Foreign Nationals (VIntA).

References

Ager, Alastair, and Alison Strang. 2008. 'Understanding Integration: A Conceptual Framework'. *Journal of Refugee Studies* 21 (2): pp. 166–191.

Arrighi de Casanova, Jean-Thomas, and Lorenzo Piccoli. 2018. 'SWISSCIT Index on Citizenship Law in Swiss Cantons: Conceptualisation, Measurement, Aggregation'. *NCCR working paper #18*.

Avitabile, Ciro, Irma Clots-Figueras, and Paolo Masella. 2013. 'The Effect of Birthright Citizenship on Parental Integration Outcomes'. *Journal of Law and Economics* 56 (3): pp. 777–810.

Banting, Keith, and Will Kymlicka. 2013. 'Is There Really a Retreat from Multiculturalism Policies? New Evidence from the Multiculturalism Policy Index'. *Comparative European Politics* 11 (5): pp. 577–598.

BFS. 2019. 'Vielfalt und Sichtbarkeit'. *Demos 1/2019*. Neuchâtel: Bundesamt für Statistik.

Bloemraad, Irene, and Matthew Wright. 2014. '"Utter Failure" or Unity out of Diversity? Debating and Evaluating Policies of Multiculturalism'. *International Migration Review* 48 (1): pp. 292–334.

Boswell, Christina. 2003. *European Migration in Flux. Changing Patterns of Inclusion and Exclusion*. Oxford: Blackwell publishing.

Brubaker, Rogers. 1992. *Citizenship and Nationhood in France and Germany*. Cambridge, MA etc.: Harvard University Press.
Bundesrat. 2010. 'Bericht zur Weiterentwicklung der Integrationspolitik des Bundes'. Bern.
Castles, Stephen, and Alastair Davidson. 2000. *Citizenship and Migration. Globalization and the Politics of Belonging*. New York: Routledge.
Cattacin, Sandro, and Bülent Kaya. 2005. 'Le développement des mesures d'intégration de la population migrante sur le plan local en Suisse'. In *Histoire de la politique de migration, d'asile et d'intégration en Suisse depuis 1948*, edited by Hans Mahnig, pp. 288–320. Zürich: Seismo.
Christmann, Anna. 2010. 'Damoklesschwert Referendum? Die indirekte Wirkung ausgebauter Volksrechte auf die Rechte religiöser Minderheiten'. *Swiss Political Science Review* 16(1): 1–41.
D'Amato, Gianni. 2010. 'Switzerland: A Multicultural Country without Multicultural Policies?'. In *The Multiculturalism Backlash. European Discourses, Policies and Practices*, edited by Steven Vertovec, and Susanne Wessendorf, pp. 130–151. London/New York: Routledge.
Ellermann, Antje. 2013. 'When Can Liberal States Avoid Unwanted Immigration? Self-Limited Sovereignty and Guest Worker Recruitment in Switzerland and Germany'. *World Politics* 65 (3): pp. 491–538.
Favell, Adrian. 2001. 'Multicultural Nation-Building: Integration as Public Philosophy and Research Paradigm in Western Europe'. *Swiss Political Science Review* 7 (2): pp. 116–124.
Giugni, Marco, and Florence Passy. 2004. 'Migrant mobilization between political institutions and citizenship regimes: A comparison of France and Switzerland'. *European Journal of Political Research* 43 (1): pp. 51–82.
Giugni, Marco, and Florence Passy. 2006. *Dialogues on Migration Policy*. Lanham: Lexington Books.
Hainmueller, Jens, and Dominik Hangartner. 2013. 'Who Gets a Swiss Passport? A Natural Experiment in Immigrant Discrimination'. *American Political Science Review* 107 (1): pp. 159–187.
Harder, Niklas, Lucila Figueroa, Rachel M. Gillum, Dominik Hangartner, David. D. Laitin, and Jens Hainmueller. 2018. 'Multidimensional Measure of Immigrant Integration'. *Proceedings of the National Academy of Sciences* 115 (45): pp. 11483–11488.
Helbling, Marc. 2008. *Practising Citizenship and Heterogeneous Nationhood. Naturalisations in Swiss Municipalities*. Amsterdam: Amsterdam University Press.
Helbling, Marc, and Hans-Peter Kriesi. 2004. 'Staatsbürgerverständnis und politische Mobilisierung: Einbürgerungen in Schweizer Gemeinden'. *Swiss Political Science Review* 10(4): pp. 33–58.
Jacobson, David. 1996. *Rights across Borders: Immigration and the Decline of Citizenship*. Baltimore: Johns Hopkins University Press.
Joppke, Christian. 2007. 'Transformation of Citizenship: Status, Rights, Identity'. *Citizenship Studies* 11 (1): pp. 37–48.
Keating, Michael. 2013. *Rescaling the European State. The Making of Territory and the Rise of the Meso*. Oxford: Oxford University Press.
Kleider, Hanna. 2018. 'Redistributive Policies in Decentralised Systems: The Effect of Decentralisation on Subnational Social Spending'. *European Journal of Political Research* 57 (2): pp. 355–377.
Koopmans, Ruud, Ines Michalowski, and Stine Waibel. 2012. 'Citizenship Rights for Immigrants: National Political Processes and Cross-National Convergence in Western Europe, 1980-2008'. *American Journal of Sociology* 117 (4): pp. 1202–1245.

Koopmans, Ruud, Paul Statham, Marco Giugni, and Florence Passy. 2005. *Contested Citizenship. Immigration and Cultural Diversity in Europe*. Minneapolis/London: University of Minnesota Press.

Krause, Ulrike. 2021. 'Colonial Roots of the 1951 Refugee Convention and its Effects on the Global Refugee Regime'. *Journal of International Relations and Development* 24: pp. 599–626.

Kriesi, Hanspeter, Romain Lachat, Peter Selb, Simon Bornschier, and Marc Helbling. 2005. *Der Aufstieg der SVP. Acht Kantone im Vergleich*. Zürich: NZZ Verlag.

Kurt, Stefanie. 2020. 'Verrechtlichung des Integrationsbegriffs: Wo bleiben die inklusiven Ansätze?'. *terra cognita* 36: pp. 70–72.

Lafleur, Michel, and Daniela Vintilla. 2020. *Migration and Social Protection in Europe and Beyond (Volume 1)*. Cham: Springer.

Linder, Wolf. 2012. *Schweizerische Demokratie. Institutionen, Prozesse, Perspektiven*. Bern: Haupt Verlag.

Manatschal, Anita. 2011. 'Taking Cantonal Variations of Integration Policy Seriously – or How to Validate International Concepts at the Subnational Comparative Level'. *Swiss Political Science Review* 17 (3): pp. 336–357.

Manatschal, Anita. 2013. *Kantonale Integrationspolitik im Vergleich. Eine Untersuchung der Determinanten und Auswirkungen subnationaler Politikvielfalt*. Baden-Baden: Nomos.

Manatschal, Anita. 2014. 'Swiss Immigration Federalism'. In *Immigration Regulation in Federal States: Challenges and Responses in Comparative Perspective*, edited by Sasha Baglay, and Delphine Nakache, pp. 179–198. Dordrecht etc.: Springer.

Manatschal, Anita. 2015. 'Switzerland – Really Europe's Heart of Darkness?'. *Swiss Political Science Review* 21 (1): pp. 23–35.

Manatschal, Anita, and Julian Bernauer. 2016. 'Consenting to Exclude? Empirical Patterns of Democracy and Immigrant Integration Policy'. *West European Politics* 39 (2): pp. 183–204.

Manatschal, Anita, Verena Wisthaler, and Christina Zuber. 2020. 'Making Regional Citizens? The Political Drivers and Effects of Subnational Immigrant Integration Policies in Europe and North America'. *Regional Studies* 54 (11): pp. 1475–1485.

Marshall, Thomas Humphrey. 1950. *Citizenship and Social Class and Other Essays*. Cambridge: Cambridge University Press.

Niederberger, Josef Martin. 2004. *Ausgrenzen, assimilieren, integrieren. Die Entwicklung einer schweizerischen Integrationspolitik*. Zürich: Seismo.

Niessen, Jan, Thomas Huddleston, Laura Citron, Andrew Geddes, and Dirk Jacobs. 2007. 'Migrant Integration Policy Index – Second edition'. British Council and Migration Policy Group.

Paquet, Mireille, and Catherine Xhardez. 2020. 'Immigrant Integration Policies When Regions Decide "Who Comes In": The Case of Canadian Provinces'. *Regional Studies* 54 (11): pp. 1519–1534.

Pecoraro, Marco, Anita Manatschal, Eva G. T. Green, and Philippe Wanner. 2022. 'How Effective Are Integration Policy Reforms? The Case of Asylum-Related Migrants'. *International Migration* 60 (6): pp. 95–110.

Piccoli, Lorenzo. 2022. 'Multilevel Strategies of Political Inclusion: The Contestation of Voting Rights for Foreign Residents by Regional Assemblies in Europe'. *Regional & Federal Studies* 32 (3): pp. 331–352.

Piguet, Etienne. 2013. *L'immigration en Suisse. 50 ans d'entrouverture*. Lausanne: Presses polytechniques et universitaires romandes.

Probst, Johanna, Gianni D'Amato, Samantha Dunning, Denise Efionayi-Mäder, Joëlle Fehlmann, Andreas Perret, Didier Ruedin, and Irina Sille. 2019. 'Marges de manœuvre cantonales en mutation. Politique migratoire en Suisse'. Neuchâtel: Swiss Forum for Migration and Population Studies SFM.

Robinson, Vaughan. 'Defining and Measuring Succesful Refugee Integration'. In Proceedings of ECRE International Conference on Integration and Refugees in Europe, Antwerp, November 1998, Brussels. ECRE.

Skenderovic, Damir. 2009. *The Radical Right in Switzerland: Continuity and Change, 1945–2000.* New York: Berghahn Books.

Solano, Giacomo, and Thomas Huddleston. 2020. 'Migrant Integration Policy Index 2020'. Barcelona/Brussels: CIDOB and MPG.

Swiss Federal Chancellery. 2022. *Bundeskanzlei BK.* https://www.bk.admin.ch/bk/en/home.html (accessed 30 November 2022).

TAK—Tripartite Agglomeration Conference. 2005. 'Rechtliche Integrationshemmnisse. Auslegeordnung und Lösungsansätze'. Bern: Tripartite Agglomerationskonferenz.

Tränhardt, Dietrich. 2001. 'Zuwanderungs- und Integrationspolitik in föderalistischen Ländern'. In *Integrationspolitik in föderalistischen Systemen*, edited by Lale Akgün, and Dietrich Tränhardt, pp. 15–33. Münster: Lit.

Vampa, Davide. 2016. *The Regional Politics of Welfare in Italy, Spain and Great Britain.* Palgrave Macmillan.

Vatter, Adrian. 2011. *Vom Schächt- zum Minarettverbot. Religiöse Minderheiten in der direkten Demokratie.* Zürich: NZZ Verlag.

Vatter, Adrian, and Deniz Danaci. 2010. 'Mehrheitstyrannei durch Volksentscheide? Zum Spannungsverhältnis zwischen direkter Demokratie und Minderheitenschutz'. *Politische Vierteljahresschrift* 51 (2): pp. 205–222.

Vatter, Adrian, and Sonja Wälti. 2003. 'Schweizer Föderalismus in vergleichender Perspektive – Der Umgang mit Reformhindernissen'. *Swiss Political Science Review* 9 (1): pp. 1–15.

Wallace, Rebecca, Erin Tolley, and Madison Vonk. 2021. 'Multiculturalism Policy Index: Immigrant Minority Policies'. Kingston: Queen's University.

Wichmann, Nicole, Michael Hermann, Gianni D'Amato, Denise Efionayi-Mäder, Rosita Fibbi, Joanna Menet, and Didier Ruedin. 2011. 'Gestaltungsräume im Föderalismus: Die Migrationspolitik in den Kantonen'. Bern-Wabern: Eidgenössische Komission für Migrationsfragen EKM.

CHAPTER 37

SOCIAL POLICY

GIULIANO BONOLI AND FLAVIA FOSSATI

1 Introduction

The notion of 'social policy' is widely used and has become part of everyday language. However, it is not easy to give a precise definition of the term. In general, this notion refers to any public action that aims to ensure the well-being of the population, reduce social inequalities, and combat poverty. Sometimes an attempt is made to delimit the scope of social policy by listing the public policies that are part of it: social insurance, health services, social assistance, support for reintegration into the labour market, childcare services, housing support, etc. However, such a definition is not conceptually satisfactory. An interesting alternative refers to the notion of decommodification: in this view, the aim of social policy is to reduce the dependence of individuals on market exchanges in general and in particular on their participation in the labour market (Esping-Andersen 1990).

Regardless of the definition chosen, social policy is a central task of the state. This can be seen by comparing the combined budget of the various social insurance schemes of approximately CHF 166 billion in 2019 to the budget of the federal government (which does not include social insurance) of CHF 71 billion in the same year. To this must be added the social expenditure at the level of the subnational entities (i.e. cantons and municipalities), which can be very substantial in the area of social assistance and other social services. This financial importance is accompanied by a fundamental role in the economy. Social policy is not just about transferring money. It can change economic incentives, encourage or discourage work or savings, attract some people to the country, and cause others to move abroad. In short, today, social policy is arguably one of the state's activities that has the greatest impact on the functioning or malfunctioning of a country's political economy.

Equally important to this economic centrality is the politics of social policy. Over the past thirty years, almost all major social insurance reforms have been challenged in referendums and many of them did not survive the popular vote. Governments have been trying to reform some areas, such as pensions, for over two decades (Häusermann et al. 2019). Unsurprisingly, all the main political actors have become cautious in the field of social policy to avoid rejection by voters, which explains the difficulty that the government has in reforming the welfare state.

This difficulty is compounded by the rather favourable economic situation of the country, which makes it hard to adopt reforms that reduce especially traditional social benefits. Undeniably, it is difficult to explain to the population why the retirement age should be raised, when the federal government has been running a budget surplus for several years, especially since the COVID-19 crisis did not put too great a strain on public finances in this country (see 'Economic Policy' in this volume). However, in the past, especially during the economic crisis of the 1990s, the Swiss political system has shown a good capacity to reform the welfare state (Armingeon 2003; Bonoli 1999). Thus, at present, the prevailing picture is one of a system that has stalled in terms of major reforms but is still able to move forward, albeit in small steps.

Today, Switzerland has one of the most comprehensive and costly welfare states among the members of the Organisation for Economic Co-operation and Development (OECD). The most important financial area is, as in most ageing democracies, pension expenditures (see Figure 37.1). In 2017, Switzerland spent 11 per cent of gross domestic product (GDP) on this function, significantly more than the averages of other OECD countries. For a long time, the Swiss welfare state was seen as a largely passive welfare state: that is, a state that focused on income replacement benefits and was relatively

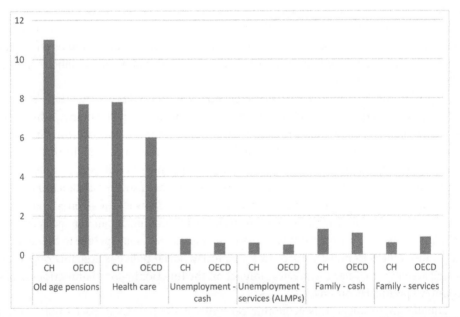

FIGURE 37.1: Compulsory private and public social expenditure in Switzerland and OECD average as a percentage of GDP, 2017

Data source: OECD (2022).

inactive in reintegrating people into the labour market and promoting labour force participation. However, this has changed and since the mid-2010s, Switzerland spends more than the OECD average on labour market reintegration, despite having one of the lowest unemployment rates.

The Swiss welfare state is the product of its history, its political institutions, and its actors. Political institutions—in particular, federalism, and direct democracy—still have a decisive impact on collective social policy choices. Within the framework set by these institutions, political actors with different interests clash and produce change (Bonoli and Häusermann 2011).

In this contribution, we discuss two of the main factors that affect social policy in Switzerland: institutions and political actors. First, we will discuss the historical development of the Swiss welfare state. Second, we present the positions and roles of the main actors in this policy field. Subsequently, we examine the issue of social policy coordination across the different levels of the federal state. Finally, the last two parts of this chapter are devoted to an evaluation of the Swiss welfare state and its future perspectives.

2 THE DEVELOPMENT OF SOCIAL POLICY IN SWITZERLAND

The welfare states in Western Europe were mainly built during the so-called 'trente glorieuses' (1945–1975), a period characterized by strong and continuous economic growth, full (male) employment, and a high degree of stability in family and labour market structures. Switzerland, however, is an exception as the construction of the welfare state was not completed until the mid-1980s (Armingeon 2001; Bonoli 2001). There were delays at every stage during the construction of the welfare state, which can be largely explained by the country's political institutions: direct democracy, federalism, and the interaction between the two (Armingeon 2001; Bonoli 2001; Obinger 1998). The option of a referendum has repeatedly allowed opponents of social policies to challenge and often also to prevent them. Federalism, in combination with direct democracy, has also contributed to delaying the development of a centralized welfare state because cantons retained control of many policies for a long time (Gilliand 1993; Armingeon 2001).The assignment of residual competences to the cantons in the federal constitution meant that every new federal social law had to be preceded by a constitutional amendment, forcing the authorities to pass the referendum process not once, but twice for each subject. While direct democracy and federalism together have thus delayed the construction of the welfare state in Switzerland to a considerable extent, they have also influenced its form (Armingeon 2001). In fact, the lack of economic security led to the construction of a parallel, private welfare system, for example in the field of occupational pensions (pension funds) or health insurance (Bonoli 2007). This private system had to be integrated into the welfare state as it developed and has determined its shape to this day (Leimgruber 2008).

The development of the Swiss welfare state can be divided into four periods. The first, from the end of the nineteenth century to the Second World War, was characterized mainly by the failure of attempts to introduce social protection schemes. The second phase, after the war, saw the adoption of the structures that carried the Swiss welfare state forward, such as the basic old-age pension and disability insurance. The third phase began in the early 1970s and saw the realization of a complete welfare state, comparable to those of other European countries, with the definitive adoption of compulsory unemployment insurance (1982) and the entry of occupational pensions into law in 1985. The fourth phase, from the early 1990s to present day, is characterized by a shift towards an active welfare state that pays more attention to new social risks and includes an important role for family policy (Bonoli and Häusermann 2011).

2.1 First attempts and failures

Inspired by the German example, the Federal Council considered amending the constitution to give the federal state a mandate to legislate the field of social insurance in the late nineteenth century. Abandoning old-age and disability insurance for financial reasons and because of the perceived risks involved in operating a large social insurance system, the Federal Council proposed in its communication to parliament of 28 November 1889 that article 34bis be included in the constitution, covering only health and accident insurance (see Table 37.1 and 'Health Policy' in this volume). This constitutional amendment was accepted by voters in 1890 after parliament had partially modified the Federal Council's proposal.

The radical National Councillor Ludwig Forrer (who was later elected to the Federal Council) was given the mandate to prepare a health and accident insurance bill, which passed through parliament in 1899. A referendum was launched by a heterogeneous coalition of health insurance companies, doctors' representatives, trade unions, and right-wing parties, all of whom had different motives: protecting the status quo, economic freedom for doctors and ideological anti-statism and. Their combined effort resulted in the rejection of the bill the following year. This failure undoubtedly marked a halt in the development of the Swiss welfare state. It was not until 1911 that parliament passed a new law introducing health and accident insurance. However, this law was much less ambitious than the bill previously rejected in 1900 and only provided for subsidies to health insurance funds and the establishment of a national insurance fund for accidents.

The initial steps for pensions followed a similar path. A national old-age insurance scheme was one of the demands of the 1918 general strike, which prompted the Federal Council to present a proposal in 1919 that provided for the introduction of an old-age and disability insurance scheme. Following numerous parliamentary debates, a proposal to amend the federal constitution by adopting article 34^{quater} (now art. 112) was submitted to the people and accepted in 1925. The Confederation was thus given the mandate to set up an old-age and survivors' insurance scheme and was also authorized to introduce a disability insurance. However, as with the Forrer Act of 1900, legislation needed to implement, following the incorporation of article 34^{quater} into the constitution (the Schulthess Act), failed to pass the popular vote in 1931. Thus, a national pension policy would have to wait for more favourable times.

2.2 The post-war period

As in other European countries, the Second World War considerably strengthened the sense of national unity, which was particularly conducive for adopting comprehensive social policies (Obinger and Schmitt 2020). Additionally, in 1939, the Federal Council set up a system of compensation funds, which guaranteed a replacement income for active soldiers. At the end of the war, this measure, which was regarded highly by the population, formed the basis for a national pension system. In 1944, the Federal Council set up a commission of experts, which quickly submitted its report. The government proposal and the parliamentary work were carried out swiftly, and they were implemented following popular acceptance (with more than 80 per cent of favourable votes) of a federal old-age and survivors' insurance in 1947, which came into force on 1 January 1948.

The post-war period saw further important achievements in social policy. In response to a popular initiative calling for federal family allowances, a counterproposal granting the Confederation the power to legislate these allowances was adopted at the end of 1945 but was exercised only in favour of farmers. A new article, which authorized the Confederation to set up an unemployment insurance scheme, was ratified by voters in 1947. Finally, disability insurance, which came into effect in 1960, was also the indirect result of a popular initiative. This time by the Socialist Party and the Labour Party, which pushed the federal authorities to fulfil the constitutional mandate that had been in force since 1925.

2.3 The 1970s and 1980s and the completion of the welfare state

At the end of the *trente glorieuses*, the Swiss welfare state was still underdeveloped compared to other European countries in several areas, particularly regarding the absence of compulsory unemployment insurance and pension coverage beyond the subsistence minimum provided by the basic pension old-age and survivors' insurance (OASI). The first gap was closed in response to the economic crisis of the mid-1970s by means of an urgent federal decree. The constitution was then amended to allow the Confederation to declare membership of unemployment insurance compulsory. The corresponding law would only come into force in 1984, but a provisional regime guaranteed coverage against the risk of unemployment in the interim.

The 1970s also saw the emergence of the three-pillar system in the area of pensions. In 1969, a popular initiative by the *Parti du Travail* called for the transformation of

Table 37.1: Political institutions and delay in the adoption of the main social laws

Policy field	Modification of the Constitution	Entry into force	Time lag (in years)	Law currently in force
Compulsory health insurance	1890	1996	106	Federal Law of 18 March 1994 on health insurance, SR 832.10
Accident insurance	1890	1918	28	Federal Law of 20 March 1981 on accident insurance, SR 832.20
Old-age insurance	1925	1948	23	Federal Law of 20 December 1946 on old-age and survivors' insurance (OASI), SR 831.10
Invalidity insurance	1925	1960	35	Federal Law of 19 June 1959 on invalidity insurance, SR 831.20
Family allowances	1945	1953/ 2009*	8/ 64	Federal Law on Family Allowances, SR 836.2
Maternity insurance	1945	2005	60	Federal Law of 25 September 1952 on allowances for loss of earnings in the event of service and maternity, SR 834.1
Occupational pension insurance	1972	1985	13	Federal Law of 25 June 1982 on occupational retirement, survivors' and invalidity pensions, SR 831.40
Compulsory unemployment insurance	1976	1984	8	Federal Law of 25 June 1982 on compulsory unemployment insurance and compensation in the event of insolvency, SR 837.0

* For farmers only, entered into force in 1953 for all others in 2009.

Data source: adapted from Armingeon 2001 and Gilliand 1993.

the OASI from a basic pension to a full pension scheme, ensuring the replacement of 60 per cent of wages. In response, a bourgeois committee, later joined by the Socialist Party, proposed making membership of a pension fund compulsory for every employee. This second solution was adopted by voters and led, in 1972, to the introduction of the three-pillar concept in the constitution. The second pillar (occupational pension), which is compulsory, is intended to enable pensioners to keep their standard of living in retirement, while the third pillar, which is voluntary, is intended to enable everyone to adapt their pension coverage to their personal requirements. The introduction of compulsory pension-fund membership was a difficult task, because many workers already had this type of coverage and feared changing insurance conditions. Thus, it was not until 1982 that an Occupational Pension Act was passed, which came into force in 1985.

In parallel with these developments at federal level, the cantons instituted social policy schemes mainly in the areas of family policy and social assistance. The latter is the safety net for any resident who does not have access to an adequate income. The federal constitution obliges the cantons to provide this last-resort assistance, but federal law is not very restrictive in terms of the form this assistance should take. The result is a fragmented system with significant differences from canton to canton (Federal Council 2015).

Consequently, the process of building an industrial welfare state was completed in Switzerland by the mid-1980s, two or three decades later than in other Western European countries. However, some anomalies remained: the absence of compulsory health insurance and maternity insurance (see 'Health Policy' and 'Family Policy' in this volume). In fact, these two gaps were only filled in 1996 and 2005, respectively. However, Swiss social policy remains influenced by the federal structure of the state. Thus, several areas remain within the competence of the cantons and even the municipalities. These include family policy, social assistance, and to some extent education policy (see 'Education Policy' in this volume).

Finally, another area of social policy also remains underdeveloped compared to other OECD countries. This is housing policy, even though access to housing is problematic for low-income people in many urban areas. Since the 1970s, the federal government has developed a policy to encourage the construction of low-cost rental housing. This policy has mainly taken the form of soft loans to non-profit organizations, such as housing cooperatives, which rent at affordable prices. Some cantons provide additional funds to make the option more attractive (Cuennet et al. 2002). Overall, however, the federal government's involvement in housing policy is limited. As in many other areas of social policy, housing is mainly a matter for the cantons. According to an inventory of the different forms of support available in the country, nineteen cantons (out of twenty-six) provide housing support to low-income households. A common form of this assistance is a subsidy to the owner (usually a non-profit organization), who rents the accommodations at a lower price. In some cases, such housing is provided on a means-tested basis (Bonoli and Bertozzi 2007). A small number of cantons have introduced a housing allowance for people whose housing costs (also determined by household size) exceed a certain proportion of their income.

These interventions have a limited impact and affect only a small proportion of the population. Financial support for housing is mainly provided by the three main means-tested programmes of the Swiss welfare state: social assistance, supplementary benefits to OASI, and disability insurance.

2.4 The reorientation towards an active welfare state

From the mid-1990s onwards, Switzerland began a process of reorientation of its welfare state aiming at strengthening labour market integration and promoting participation in the labour market, a reorientation that in the past was rather marginal. This trend followed a significant increase in the number of unemployed people as well as in the number of people receiving disability insurance and social assistance from the early 1990s. Between 1990 and 2000, the number of disability insurance beneficiaries increased by 39 per cent, the number of social assistance beneficiaries by 104 per cent, and the number of unemployed by a factor of four (Champion 2011).

In response to these developments, several reforms were adopted. First, unemployment insurance was fundamentally reformed in 1995 (Giriens and Stauffer 1999; Bonoli and Mach 2000). The maximum duration of benefit receipt was limited to eighteen months for most unemployed people, but at the same time, new instruments were introduced to facilitate the labour market integration of the unemployed. These included the creation of regional placement offices and the expansion of the range of measures for labour market integration. A few years later, it was the turn of disability insurance. The fifth revision of disability insurance, adopted in 2007, essentially pursued the same objective: to strengthen the active dimension of occupational integration and to make it possible to access a disability pension only if reintegration measures have failed or cannot reasonably be applied (Champion 2011: 130; OECD 2006).

For cantonal social assistance, the reorientation process is more mixed. Indeed, some cantons and cities have moved faster than others have and are trying to reorient themselves in different ways. In French-speaking Switzerland (especially Vaud, Fribourg, and Geneva), social assistance services are being encouraged to work with employment services and regional employment offices and provide labour market integration services. On the other hand, in the German-speaking part of Switzerland, the combination of social assistance and employment services is concentrated more in the large cities, where social services are little by little acquiring competence in labour market integration and are thus increasingly able to make it available to target groups (Bonoli and Champion 2013).

By reorienting its welfare state towards labour market integration and even more towards promoting the labour market participation of disadvantaged groups, Switzerland is fully in line with a European and even global trend that sees a 'social investment' policy as a solution to the various problems faced by welfare states (Morel et al. 2012; Hemerijck 2017). The notion of social investment refers precisely to social policies that help people in need not with cash benefits but by investing in their human capital to enable them to achieve financial autonomy through labour market participation.

As of the early 2020s, the Swiss welfare state could be regarded as a welfare state in transition, moving from a classical Bismarckian model to a more modern one, oriented towards social investment and the promotion of equal opportunities. This reorientation, however, has not been without difficulty. On the one hand, the general public is still strongly attached to the achievements of the *trente glorieuses*, particularly pension policy. On the other hand, the institutional and political obstacles that characterized the expansion of the Swiss welfare state are still present and slow down the adoption of new social policies.

3 THE MAIN CONFLICTS IN SOCIAL POLICY, THE ACTORS, AND THEIR POSITIONS

The key actors in Swiss social policy are political parties, trade unions, employers' associations, federal departments, cantons, and municipalities. In the following, we present the political positions of these main actors in social policy.

3.1 The position of the actors: economic and cultural conflicts

The main political conflicts that characterize the party systems of Western European countries are the economic dimension (also called left–right) and the cultural dimension. Although these two conflicts have played an important role in the development of public policy in Switzerland, issues relating to the welfare state have mainly revolved around the economic dimension. Thus, in general, left-wing political actors, i.e. the Socialist Party, other left-wing parties, and the trade unions, have favoured an expansion of the welfare state. These actors generally favour policies that allow for wage replacement in the event of traditional social risks, including old age, illness, disability, and unemployment. Historically, they have supported instruments such as generous social insurance schemes, minimum wage regulations, or, more generally, generous redistributive policies (Esping-Andersen 1990).

While left-wing actors call for higher and more comprehensive social benefits to protect workers, right-wing actors advocate for other principles and favour targeted support to meet situations of need. Thus, right-wing parties and employers' organizations adhere to values such as subsidiarity, individualism, and individual initiative, and support minimum and means-tested benefits. For example, the Liberal-Radical Party has successfully opposed the extension of benefits by taking advantage of direct democracy where citizens are reluctant to accept tax increases to finance social spending (Armingeon 2001). In other words, these actors were oriented towards a market logic (Esping-Andersen 1990). In the scientific literature, indicators of the preferred level of social spending, of the degree of state intervention in the economy, or of the need to reduce inequalities in a society are used to capture this conflict dimension (Fossati and Häusermann 2014).

While the expansion phase of the welfare state is dominated by the economic dimension (left–right axis), the cultural dimension is also gaining in importance with the emergence of a multicultural society (Häusermann 2010; Fossati and Häusermann 2014). Thus, today, we are witnessing in Switzerland (and elsewhere in Europe) a new divide between, on the one hand, advocates of a strong welfare state that excludes immigrant populations ('welfare chauvinism') and, on the other hand, a vision close to the active welfare state that invests in the human capital of disadvantaged publics (Häusermann

2012). This vision is also seen as a response to the emergence of a multicultural society, with the idea that an investment-oriented welfare state favours the integration of immigrant populations, who are often over-represented among the beneficiaries of social schemes (Bonoli 2020). This divide, which corresponds to the cultural divide between conservatives and progressives, has little correlation with the economic divide. For example, populist actors, who want a welfare state that is not very open to immigrants, may nevertheless be in favour of high welfare benefits for citizens (Afonso and Rennwald 2018). In Switzerland, this cultural divide is represented by the opposition between the Swiss Popole's Party, which sometimes defends chauvinist positions on social policy, and the Greens, a party that is open to a multicultural society and favours social investment (Afonso and Papadopoulos 2015).

3.2 The political position of interest organizations: trade unions and employers

At the beginning of the welfare state building process, Swiss political parties were not very developed, and the main political actors were in fact the interest groups, in particular the trade unions and employers' associations. Their influence remains important to this day. Traditionally, trade unions represent workers and lobby for increased protection of workers' rights by supporting the introduction and expansion of different social policies (Rueda 2005). The main instruments through which trade unions—in alliance with left-wing parties—try to achieve this protection in Europe are decommodification measures, i.e. cash benefits that replace wages in case of need (Esping-Andersen 1990) as well as a statutory minimum wage (never achieved in Switzerland) and effective legislation for dismissal protection, which is comparatively weak in international terms.

Switzerland, however, is a peculiar welfare state. It started, as is the case in liberal systems, with highly fragmented protection, mainly organized at the municipal and cantonal level. It evolved only very late into a more comprehensive system with a centralized and state-run welfare regime (Armingeon 2001). This can be explained, as previously mentioned, by a highly decentralized and fragmented political and institutional framework, as well as by the nature of the initial social partnership, where agreements between employers and trade unions were settled in a decentralized way, either at regional or sectoral levels, and where the principles of subsidiarity and self-regulation were predominant (Ebbinghaus and Fluder 2000). In addition, trade unions have played an important role for private social insurance organizations. In fact, until the 1970s, they lobbied to run insurances themselves rather than advocating a centralized, state-run scheme. They were also sceptical about social protection through collective agreements. This attitude is illustrated by the fact that they severely criticized the Lex Forrer, which aimed to establish a national health insurance system, and by the fact that they were suspicious of state-run pension schemes (Trampusch 2008, 2010; Leimgruber 2008). It was only after the 1970s, i.e. in the light of the process of deindustrialization and its consequences in terms of their declining mobilization capacity, that trade unions in most countries in Europe began to support state interventions and to join left-wing parties to target the political rather than the economic arena (Trampusch 2010). For example, during the economic crisis of the 1970s, they lobbied for a mandatory federal unemployment scheme (Armingeon 2001; Trampusch 2008, 2010).

Employers in Switzerland have always held a particularly influential position within the corporatist system, which has allowed for very close formal and informal collaboration with the trade unions on the one hand and the state on the other. For example, the employers' associations were more cohesive and therefore more effective in their ability to mobilize than the trade unions, which were divided between socialist and Christian-democratic organizations (Oesch 2011; Eichenberger and Leimgruber 2020). Their political positions have always been clearly opposed to the expansion of redistributive and federal social policies. Instead, they have supported fiscally conservative measures as well as limited, subsidiary, private, and occupational social insurance schemes (Leimgruber 2008; Eichenberger and Leimgruber 2020). Moreover, they clearly adhere to the liberal credo of minimizing state intervention to avoid creating disincentives for entrepreneurship and individual responsibility (Eichenberger and Leimgruber 2020). In Switzerland, for example, they support employer-based social protection systems such as occupational pension schemes. These still exist in the context of the second pillar (Leimgruber 2008). In summary, employers generally support measures that promote individual responsibility and subsidiarity, a view shared by other actors who are ideologically on the right.

4 ORGANIZATION AND COORDINATION IN THE FIELD OF SOCIAL POLICY

The Swiss welfare state is a product of the country's history and institutions, in particular the federal structure of the state. In addition, the Swiss welfare state delegates an important part of its functions to the private sector. This is the case for health insurance, pension's second pillar, and in labour market integration (organizers of active labour market policy measures). The result of this process is a fragmented welfare state with several coordination problems. For reasons of space, we will limit ourselves to examining, as an example, the coordination of social policies for people of working age, which also represent an important share of the overall social policy budget. However, coordination problems between public and private actors, between the Confederation and the cantons, exist in many areas such as family policy and in the health sector (see 'Health Policy' and 'Family Policy' in this volume).

4.1 Coordination of social policies for people of working age population

The problem of coordinating social policies targeting people of working age emerged in the early 1990s. This was due to the economic crisis that hit Switzerland during those years (see 'Economic Policy' in this volume). More or less simultaneously, all social security schemes came under pressure due to a large increase in the number of beneficiaries and thus expenditures. This development made the previous, mainly informal, collaboration more difficult. It made institutions more 'selfish' in the sense that, under pressure, they prioritized the protection of their budget rather than the general interest, when the latter implies devoting resources to beneficiaries covered by other social schemes. In practice, the lack of coordination gives rise to three different problems.

The first problem identified is the carousel effect, i.e. when beneficiaries apply to one institution, they are referred to another, sometimes several times, and end up excluded from the social protection system. A typical example is a person who is unemployed and has health problems. The unemployment insurance may, because of the health problems, not recognize the person as fit for work and therefore exclude him or her from its benefits. Since the decisions of the unemployment insurance are not coordinated with those of the disability insurance, the same person may be considered capable of work by the latter and thus be excluded from its benefits (Champion 2008).

Second, following the reorientation of all social schemes towards reintegration into the labour market, managers of the various institutions are finding that they lack certain capabilities. For example, the social services do not have know-how in terms of labour market placement and vocational reintegration, which is not the case with unemployment insurance. On the other hand, the latter are not at all specialized in caring for unemployed people with health problems, a competence which is found within the disability insurance offices. As a result, it soon became clear that the pooling of all these competences was essential for successfully meeting the challenge of labour market integration (Champion 2008; Egger et al. 2010).

Finally, all actors develop strategies for cost shifting. Faced with the difficulty of containing the increased number of beneficiaries and reintegrating them into the labour market, all actors involved tried to transfer them to other social schemes. This practice, known in the literature as 'cost shifting' (Øverbye et al. 2010; Bonoli and Trein 2016), is achieved in different ways. For example, for federal unemployment insurance, reforms have made it more difficult to access benefits such as by extending the minimum period during which contributions must be paid to be entitled to unemployment benefits.

These restrictions on access to unemployment insurance are likely to have led to a cost shift to cantonal and municipal social assistance, although this burden shift is difficult to quantify. An attempt was made in a study concerning the latest of these reforms (fourth revision of unemployment insurance in 2011). It concluded that the 2011 reform was responsible for an increase in the number of social assistance caseloads of between 5 and 15 per cent in fifteen cities (Salzgeber 2012: 64).

During the same period, cantons and municipalities also practiced a cost shifting strategy aimed at shifting part of the burden of social assistance to federal social insurance. For example, until 2009, the canton of Geneva had a job guarantee system for unemployed people who could not return to the labour market during the eighteen-month unemployment insurance compensation period. The duration of the job offered was twelve months, i.e. the period of contribution required to obtain a federal unemployment benefit. This allowed unemployed people to re-gain entitlement to a new eighteen-month compensation period financed by federal unemployment insurance (Flückiger et al. 2002). Other cantons have implemented similar, but generally less generous and less visible programmes. Neuchâtel, for example, rather than guaranteeing a twelve-month period of employment, has developed a system of job guarantees limited to six months, but renewable once (Bonoli et al. 2011).

Although there is no systematic overview of the extent of these practices, it is certain that many other cantons and municipalities have used the strategy of cost shifting to avoid the financial responsibility of the long-term unemployed. It is difficult to estimate the impact of these practices on the overall system. In 2008, the Federal Council estimated their cost to the unemployment insurance system at CHF 90 million per year, or 2.2 per cent of the expenditure on cash unemployment benefits (Federal Council 2008: 7046).

While it is difficult to precisely put a price tag on the cost of lacking coordination, the problem is a constant source of frustration among policymakers and practitioners. In less favourable economic conditions, lack of coordination may result in substantial extra costs and tensions in the provision of social welfare.

5 AN EVALUATION OF THE SWISS WELFARE STATE

Overall, the Swiss welfare state enjoys a fairly good reputation among experts. This is partly due to its pension system, which in the early 2000s was described by World Bank researchers as a 'triumph of common sense' and used by the Bank as a model for other countries (Queisser and Vittas 2000). The OECD, in its 2019 report on Switzerland, also gives a rather positive assessment of the country's social situation. It notes that inequality has increased less than in other countries but warns Switzerland about the capacity of its pension system to cope with demographic ageing and the risk of exclusion from the labour market for low-skilled profiles and older unemployed people (OECD 2019).

The quality of a social protection system can be assessed in different ways. An important element is undoubtedly its capacity to combat poverty. In Switzerland, the at-risk-of-poverty rate (calculated according to the European Union (EU) method, i.e. the share of the population living in households with a disposable income of less than 60 per cent of the median income) has been around 15 per cent in recent years and thus slightly

Table 37.2: Statistics on relative poverty (per cent) in Switzerland compared to the EU average

At risk-of-poverty rate (whole population)*	2010	2015	2017	2018	2019
Switzerland	15.0	15.6	15.5	14.6	15.4
Unweighted average EU	16.5	17.3	16.9	17.1	17.1

* 'At-risk-of-poverty rate' = share of the population living in households with a disposable income below 60 per cent of the national average.
Data source: OFS (2022a), Eurostat–EU-SILC 2020 (Version of 21.12.2021).

below the EU average (see Table 37.2). Thus, relative poverty indicators indicate that Switzerland is in the average of continental European countries, i.e. it has higher rates than the Scandinavian countries, but lower rates than the southern European countries (Bonoli and Trein 2018).

If, instead of using an indicator of relative poverty, an indicator of material deprivation is used, Switzerland performs best in Europe, with a material deprivation rate of 4.3 per cent in 2020 (against an EU average of 13.8 per cent). This means that most Swiss residents possess what are considered basic items (car, washing machine, telephone, or television), live in a neighbourhood without excessive criminality or noise, and can afford expenditures such as eating meat twice a week, heating their apartment, or paying an unforeseen expenditure of around CHF 2,000. Such a material deprivation indicator reflects a notion of absolute rather than relative poverty, and therefore gives a somewhat different picture of the social situation in Switzerland. Despite not being poor in absolute terms, there are around 15 per cent of people who, compared to the standard of living of other Swiss residents, are considerably worse off. Thus, the relative poverty indicator reflects the extent of poverty on the one hand but also the level of inequality in a country overall.

The ability of a social protection system to combat poverty varies within a population. In general, single parents, large families, immigrants (see 'Integration Policy' in this volume) and the elderly are among the groups most at risk of poverty. In Switzerland in 2021, the at-risk-of-poverty rate rises significantly for single-parent households (26.2 per cent compared to 14.6 per cent for the population as a whole), for couples with three or more children (20.6 per cent), for immigrants (21.7 per cent) and for people aged 65 or more (21.7 per cent) (FSO, 2022). The latter figure is relatively high and may be surprising given that it is well above the EU average (at 19.1 per cent for women and 12.8 per cent for men in 2018). It is believed that this bad performance is at least partly due to the habit of retired individuals in Switzerland of withdrawing all or part of their second pillar pension in the form of a lump sum, which makes many pensioners appear poor in terms of their income, but nevertheless have substantial assets, in particular owner-occupied dwellings (Bonoli 2017; Wanner 2008). This is consistent with the observation that the material deprivation rate of people aged 65 and over in Switzerland is very low (2.1 per cent in 2020) and among the lowest in Europe (EU average: 11.5 per cent).[1]

Overall, the Swiss social protection system can therefore be considered rather effective in protecting the general population from the risk of poverty, although some groups, in particular single-parent households, clearly suffer from an increased risk. This does not mean that the Swiss welfare state will not face several challenges in the coming years.

6 CHALLENGES AND PROSPECTS

The reform of the pension system and its adaptation to the demographic ageing process is undoubtedly the main challenge facing the Swiss political system (OECD 2019). The financial health of the basic pension is strongly dependent on the ratio between contributors and pensioners. With demographic ageing, this ratio will continue to deteriorate rapidly until around 2035 (OFS 2020). Demographic ageing also poses a problem for the financing of second pillar pensions. The increase in life expectancy means that a given capital will have to be used to finance benefits for an increasingly longer period.

These problems have been known for some twenty years and have given rise to several attempts at reform, most of which have failed, either in parliament or in referendums. The ambitious reform known as 'Pension provision 2020', which was intended to ensure the financial sustainability of the two main pillars of the Swiss pension system, was rejected by voters in 2017. Since then, the Federal Council and the main political parties have been reluctant to embark on structural reforms and are currently implementing limited changes. In 2019, however, in a rather spectacular 'political bargain', the left succeeded in having additional funding for the basic pension of up to CHF 2 billion per year included in a corporate tax reform. However, these additional funds will not be able to finance all the additional costs due to ageing.

The second major challenge that the Swiss welfare state will have to face in the coming years concerns the coordination between the different policies at the federal level. As aforementioned, the institutional fragmentation of the welfare state has been a serious obstacle for the reorientation towards labour market integration in the past. In a favourable economic situation, the Swiss welfare state could probably afford the inefficiencies created by fragmentation. However, as we saw during the crisis of the 1990s, in a difficult context of high unemployment, these coordination problems encourage opportunistic reactions rather than the pursuit of a common social policy goal of labour market integration.

Third, family policy in Switzerland remains underdeveloped. In contrast to EU member states, Switzerland does not have parental leave. Maternity insurance provides a paid leave of fourteen weeks and for fathers paid leave lasts two weeks (introduced in 2021). Moreover, childcare services remain insufficient and are generally financially very onerous for parents (see 'Family Policy' in this volume). This situation has several negative consequences, among them a great difficulty in reconciling work and family life, leaving many women working only part-time, and a high poverty rate for single-parent and large families.

As previously mentioned, the development of the Swiss welfare state has been slower than in most other European countries. This was due to the country's political institutions. Today, these same institutions are slowing down the process of reform and reorientation of the welfare state. Nevertheless, this process is underway, and the Swiss welfare state is slowly filling in the gaps and adapting to the socio-demographic changes. The favourable economic situation, in which the country found itself from the 2000s onwards, subsequently contributed to decelerating the adoption of unpopular reforms, such as that of the pension system. However, a turnaround in the economic situation could accelerate the pace of reform—as was the case in the 1990s due to the difficult economic situation, when the Swiss political system proved capable of adopting necessary reforms with unusual speed.

Note

1. All figures are for 2020 (OFS 2022b).

References

Afonso, Alexandre, and Ioannis Papadopoulos. 2015. 'How the Populist Radical Right Transformed Swiss Welfare Politics: From Compromises to Polarization'. *Swiss Political Science Review* 21 (4): pp. 617–635.

Afonso, Alexandre, and Line Rennwald. 2018. 'Social Class and the Changing Welfare State Agenda of Radical Right Parties in Europe'. In *Welfare Democracies and Party Politics: Explaining Electoral Dynamics in Times of Changing Welfare Capitalism*, edited by Philip Manow, Bruno Palier, and Hanna Schwander, pp. 171–194. Oxford: University Press.

Armingeon, Klaus. 2001. 'Institutionalising the Swiss Welfare State'. *West European Politics* 24 (2): pp. 145–168.

Armingeon, Klaus. 2003. 'Renegotiating the Swiss Welfare State'. In *Renegotiating the Welfare State*, edited by Gerhard Lehmbruch, and Frans van Waarden, pp. 169–188. London: Routledge and Kegan Paul.

Bonoli, Giuliano. 1999. 'La réforme de l'Etat social Suisse: Contraintes institutionnelles et opportunités de changement'. *Swiss Political Science Review* 5 (3): pp. 57–77.

Bonoli, Giuliano. 2001. 'Political Institutions, Veto Points, and the Process of Welfare State Adaptation'. In *The New Politics of the Welfare State*, edited by Paul Pierson, pp. 238–264. Oxford: Oxford University Press.

Bonoli, Giuliano. 2007. 'Switzerland: The Impact of Direct Democracy on a Multipillar System'. In *Oxford Handbook of West European Pension Politics*, edited by Ellen M. Immergut, Karen M. Anderson, and Isabelle Schulze, pp. 203–247. Oxford: Oxford University Press.

Bonoli, Giuliano. 2017. *ESPN Thematic Report: Assessment of Pension Adequacy in Switzerland*. Brussels: European Commission.

Bonoli, Giuliano. 2020. 'Immigrant Integration and Social Investment'. *Journal of European Social Policy* 30 (5): pp. 616–627.

Bonoli, Giuliano, and Fabio Bertozzi. 2007. *Aides cantonales au logement et aux chômeurs. Critères de délimitation pour la statistique de l'aide sociale et l'inventaire des prestations sociales liées aux besoins.* Neuchâtel: Office fédéral de la statistique (OFS).

Bonoli, Giuliano, and Cyrielle Champion. 2013. *La réinsertion professionnelle des bénéficiaires de l'aide sociale en Suisse et en Allemagne.* Lausanne: IDHEAP, Cahier de l'IDHEAP.

Bonoli, Giuliano, Cyrielle Champion, and Regula Schlanser. 2011. *Evaluation des mesures de réinsertion professionnelle dans le Canton de Neuchâtel.* Lausanne: IDHEAP.

Bonoli, Giuliano, and Silja Häusermann. 2011. 'Swiss Welfare Reforms in a Comparative European Perspective: Between Retrenchment an Activation'. In *Switzerland in Europe. Continuity and Change in the Swiss Political Economy*, edited by André Mach, and Christine Trampusch, pp. 186–204. Abingdon/New York: Routledge.

Bonoli, Giuliano, and André Mach. 2000. 'Switzerland: Adjustment Politics Within Institutional Constraints'. In *Welfare and Work in the Open Economy, Vol. 2 – Diverse Responses to Common Challenges*, edited by Fritz W. Scharpf, and Vivien Schmid, pp. 131–174. Oxford: Oxford University Press.

Bonoli, Giuliano, and Philipp Trein. 2016. 'Cost-Shifting in Multitiered Welfare States: Responding to Rising Welfare Caseloads in Germany and Switzerland'. *Publius: The Journal of Federalism* 4 (46): pp. 596–622.

Bonoli, Giuliano, and Philipp Trein. 2018. *ESPN Country Profile: Switzerland.* Brussels: European Commission.

Champion, Céline. 2008. 'Davantage collaborer, afin d'éviter l'effet carrousel: les premières expériences MAMAC sont prometteuses'. *Sécurité sociale* 3: pp. 152–156.

Champion, Cyrielle. 2011. 'Switzerland: A Latecomer Catching Up?'. In *Regulating the Risk of Unemployment: National Adaptation to Post-Industrial Labour Markets in Europe*, edited by Jochen Clasen, and Daniel Clegg, pp. 121–141. Oxford: Oxford University Press.

Cuennet, Stéphane, Philippe Faverger, and Philippe Thalmann. 2002. *La politique du logement.* Lausanne: Presses polytechniques et universitaires romandes (PPUR).

Ebbinghaus, Bernhard, and Robert Fluder. 2000. 'Switzerland'. In *Trade Unions in Western Europe since 1945*, edited by Bernhard Ebbinghaus, and Jelle Visser, pp. 657–703. London: Macmillan.

Eurostat (2023) *The risk of poverty among older people*, online: https://ec.europa.eu/eurostat/statistics-explained/index.php?title=Ageing_Europe_-_statistics_on_pensions,_income_and_expenditure&oldid=500271#The_risk_of_poverty_among_older_people, consulted 17.6.2023.

Egger, Marcel, Véronique Merckx, and Adrian Wütrich. 2010. *Evaluation du projet national CII-MAMAC.* Berne: OFAS, Rapport de recherche 9/10.

Eichenberger, Pierre, and Matthieu Leimgruber. 2020. 'Business Interests and the Development of the Public-Private Welfare Mix in Switzerland, 1880–1990'. In *Business Interests and the Development of the Modern Welfare State*, edited by Dennie O. Nijhuis, pp. 84–107. London/New York: Routledge Taylor and Francis Group.

Esping-Andersen, Gøsta. 1990. *Three Worlds of Welfare State Capitalism.* Princeton: Princeton University Press.

Federal Council. 2008. *Message relatif à la modification de la loi sur l'assurance-chômage du 3 septembre 2008.* Berne.

Federal Council. 2015. *Aménagement de l'aide sociale et des prestations cantonales sous condition de ressources. Besoins et possibilités d'intervention. Report du Conseil fédéral.* https://www.

bsv.admin.ch/bsv/fr/home/politique-sociale/soziale-absicherung/amenagement-aide-sociale.html (accessed 12 October 2022).

Federal Statistical Office (FSO). 2022. *Risque de pauvreté, selon différentes caractéristiques sociodémographiques*, online: https://www.bfs.admin.ch/asset/fr/je-f-20.03.02.02.01 (accessed 17 June 2023).

Flückiger, Yves, Augustin de Coulon, and Anatoli Vassiliev. 2002. *Les raisons de la différence entre les taux de chômage genevois et suisse*. Genève: Université de Genève, Cahier du LEA n° 24.

Fossati, Flavia, and Silja Häusermann. 2014. 'Social Policy Preferences and Party Choice in the 2011 Swiss Elections'. *Swiss Political Science Review* 20 (4): pp. 590–611.

Gilliand, Pierre. 1993. 'Politique sociale'. In *Handbuch Politisches System der Schweiz. Band 4. Politikbereiche*, edited by Gerhard Schmidt, pp. 111–223. Bern: Haupt.

Giriens, Pierre-Yves, and Julien Stauffer. 1999. 'Deuxième révision de l'assurance chômage: genèse d'un compromis'. In *Globalisation, néo-libéralisme et politiques publiques dans la Suisse des années 1990*, edited André Mach, pp. 105–144. Zurich: Seismo.

Häusermann, Silja. 2010. *The Politics of Welfare State Reform in Continental Europe. Modernization in Hard Times*. Cambridge: Cambridge University Press.

Häusermann, Silja. 2012. 'The Politics of New and Old Social Risks'. In *The Politics of the New Welfare State*, edited by Giuliano Bonoli, and David Natali, pp. 111–134, Oxford: Oxford University Press.

Häusermann, Silja, Thomas Kurer, and Denise Traber. 2019. 'The Politics of Trade Offs: Studying the Dynamics of Welfare State Reform with Conjoint Experiments'. *Comparative Political Studies* 52 (7): pp. 1059–1095. doi: 10.1177/0010414018797943.

Hemerijck, Anton. 2017. 'Social Investment and Its Critics'. In *The Uses of Social Investment*, edited by Anton Hemerijck, pp. 3–42. Oxford: Oxford University Press.

Leimgruber, Matthieu. 2008. *Solidarity without the State? Business and the Shaping of the Swiss Welfare State, 1890–2000*. Cambridge, UK/New York: Cambridge University Press.

Morel, Nathalie, Bruno Palier, and Joakim Palme (eds). 2012. *Towards a Social Investment Welfare State?: Ideas, Policies and Challenges*. Bristol: The Policy Press.

Obinger, Herbert. 1998. *Politische Institutionen und Sozialpolitik in der Schweiz*. Bern: Peter Lang.

Obinger, Herbert, and Carina Schmitt. 2020. 'World War and Welfare Legislation in Western Countries'. *Journal of European Social Policy* 30 (3): pp. 261–274.

OECD. 2006. *Sickness, Disability and Work. Breaking the Barriers, Norway, Poland and Switzerland*. Paris: OECD.

OECD. 2019. *OECD Economic Surveys: Switzerland*. Paris: OECD Publishing.

OECD. 2022. *Welcome to OECD.Stat*. https://stats.oecd.org/ (accessed 22 April 2022).

OFS. 2020. *Les scénarios de l'évolution de la population de la Suisse et des cantons, de 2020 à 2050*. Neuchâtel: Office fédéral de la statistique, Actualité OFS.

OFS. 2022a. *Armutsgefährdung*. https://www.bfs.admin.ch/bfs/de/home/statistiken/wirtschaftliche-soziale-situation-bevoelkerung/soziale-situation-wohlbefinden-und-armut/armut-und-materielle-entbehrungen/armutsgefaehrdung.html (accessed 13 December 2022).

OFS. 2022b. *Situation sociale, bien-être et pauvreté*. https://www.bfs.admin.ch/bfs/fr/home/statistiques/situation-economique-sociale-population/bien-etre-pauvrete.html (accessed 22 April 2022).

Oesch, Daniel. 2011. 'Swiss Trade Unions and Industrial Relations After 1990: A History of Decline and Renewal'. In *Switzerland in Europe. Continuity and Change in the Swiss Political Economy*, edited by Christine Trampusch, and André Mach, pp. 82–102. London: Routledge.

Øverbye, Einar, Rahel Strohmeier Navarro Smith, Vappu Karjalainen, and Jürgen Stremlow. 2010. 'The Coordination Challenge'. In *Rescaling Social Policies Towards Multilevel Governance*, edited by Yuri Kazepov, pp. 389–413. Farnham: Ashgate.

Queisser, Monika, and Dimitri Vittas. 2000. *The Swiss Multi-Pillar Pension System. Triumph of Common Sense?*. Washington: The World Bank.

Rueda, David. 2005. 'Insider–Outsider Politics in Industrialized Democracies: The Challenge to Social Democratic Parties'. *American Political Science Review* 99 (1): pp. 61–74.

Salzgeber, Renate. 2012. 'Auswirkungen der 4. AVIG-Revision auf die Sozialhilfe'. *Die Volkswirtschaft. Das Magazin für die Wirtschaftspolitik* 9: pp. 62–66.

Trampusch, Christine. 2008. 'Von einem liberalen zu einem post-liberalen Wohlfahrtsstaat: der Wandel der gewerkschaftlichen Sozialpolitik in der Schweiz'. *Swiss Political Science Review* 14 (1): pp. 49–84.

Trampusch, Christine. 2010. 'The Welfare State and Trade Unions in Switzerland: An Historical Reconstruction of the Shift from a Liberal to a Post-Liberal Welfare Regime'. *Journal of European Social Policy* 20 (1): pp. 58–73.

Wanner, Philippe. 2008. *La situation économique des actifs et des retraités, Rapport de recherche no 1/08*. Berne: OFAS.

CHAPTER 38

HEALTH POLICY

PHILIPP TREIN, CHRISTIAN RÜEFLI, AND ADRIAN VATTER

1 INTRODUCTION

HEALTH policy entails the regulation, financing, and provision of a wide range of medical and non-medical services to prevent and cure diseases.[1] This complex task makes it one of the most multifaceted and expensive fields of policy-making in modern states. Strong professional interests, expensive treatments, equality of access, and quality concerns render policy-making challenging. In Switzerland, most of the population is satisfied with the country's health care system (FOPH 2020). From a comparative point of view, Switzerland has a high life expectancy at birth (83.2 years in 2020), low median childhood mortality (3.3 deaths per 1,000 live births in 2019), low rates of preventable mortality (83 per 100,000 in 2018), and rather low cancer death rates (167.1 per 100,000 in 2017) (OECD 2020). The main challenges for Switzerland are rising costs for health and long-term care and the distribution of these costs. In 2019, Switzerland spent 12.2 per cent of its GDP on health care and related expenses, (considerably) more than other European countries (Figure 38.1).

Out-of-pocket expenses for health care are comparatively high in Switzerland as well. The sum individuals and families must pay amounts to more than 25 per cent of national health expenditure (Figure 38.1). The system is financed by different sources: between 2011 and 2020 (average), compulsory insurance—paid by private individuals—and other social insurers covered 43.3 per cent of the total health expenditure, and private households 25.1 per cent (out of pocket). The state financed 19 per cent (cantons: 16.4 per cent). Additional payers are private supplementary insurers (7.1 per cent) and other public (4 per cent) and private sources (1.6 per cent) (FSO 2022a). This distribution of costs indicates the important role of non-state actors, such as health insurers and private financing. The rising costs are a burden for the population, as health insurance premiums continually increase and a considerable share of the population relies on cantonal subsidies to pay them (Trein et al. 2022).

Switzerland differs from other European countries regarding its public health policies which aim to prevent diseases by addressing health hazards (Trein 2018b). Public health

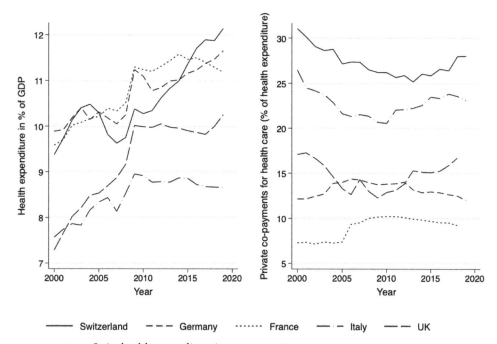

FIGURE 38.1: Swiss health expenditure in a comparative perspective

Data source: OEDC (2020).

policies often entail a regulatory approach where the national government limits economic or individual freedoms, for example regarding the sale and consumption of tobacco. A comparison of Switzerland with other European countries reveals that the federal government is much more reluctant to implement restrictive public health policies. Switzerland has also differed from other European countries concerning its response to the COVID-19 pandemic. Switzerland's restrictions were far more liberal compared to its neighbouring countries, even more so than other liberal economies such as the United Kingdom, as Figure 38.2 shows.

These two examples (Figure 38.1 and Figure 38.2) illustrate some of the basic principles. Firstly, Swiss health policy-making has historically been dominated by the liberal values of individual responsibility, private entrepreneurship, and market mechanisms over public service provision and state regulation (Okma et al. 2010; Achtermann and Berset 2006). Secondly, Switzerland has a decentralized health system, which is in some ways an accumulation of twenty-six subnational (cantonal) systems. Historically, health policy was primarily a domain of cantonal responsibility. The federal government only intervenes in areas where competencies are explicitly delegated. Thirdly, and related to the first two principles, subsidiarity has always played a crucial role in Swiss health policy. Subsidiarity entails that health policy issues should primarily be the concern of private organizations or of the local or cantonal level whenever possible (De Pietro et al. 2015; Trein et al. 2022).

Therefore, health policy-making in Switzerland requires the coordination of a variety of diverse actors. Interest groups play an important role in the policy process, notably

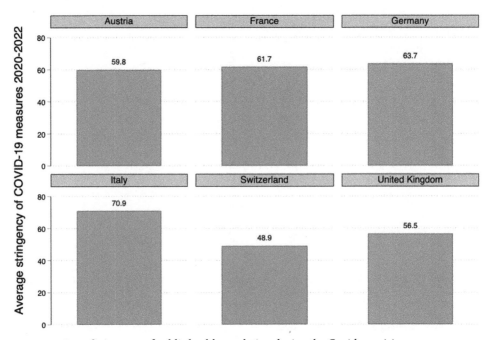

FIGURE 38.2: Stringency of public health regulation during the Covid-19 crisis

Data source: Hale et al. (2021).

in neo-corporatist settings where providers and health insurers negotiate prices. In addition, citizens are crucial in the political process of policy-making. Federal, cantonal, and sometimes even municipal health policy projects often require approval in a popular vote (Vatter 2020).

This section has introduced the reader to the landscape of Swiss health policy structures and actors to provide insights into the political challenges emerging from this context. The chapter now proceeds according to the following steps: section 2 will present the key actors in Swiss health policy. Section 3 will provide the reader with a historical overview of the development of the Swiss health system. Section 4 will argue that strong interest groups and direct democracy shape health policy and that cantonal autonomy influences dynamics in health policy-making. Conclusions and outlook make up the final section.

2 Actors in Swiss health policy

2.1 State actors: division of tasks between the Confederation and the cantons

In international comparison, the landscape of actors in the Swiss health system is fragmented because varieties of public and private actors play important roles.[2]

In contrast to countries with a centralized national health service, such as the United Kingdom, Denmark, or Sweden, Switzerland has twenty-six cantonal health systems, each with its own legislation and competencies regarding the implementation of policies.

The Confederation's competencies include legislation and supervision in areas such as social insurance (health insurance and accident insurance, amongst others), pharmaceuticals, academic training of doctors and pharmacists, education and training of all non-university health professions, reproductive and transplantation medicine, medical research, and genetic engineering. In addition, federal authorities are responsible for areas of public health policy (health protection and prevention), for example in relation to addictive substances and communicable diseases, regulation of narcotics, radiation protection, toxic substances, and food safety. The federal government's legislation is often complemented by cantonal laws (Achtermann and Berset 2006, 34–36; Kocher 2010; Trein 2018b).

Apart from implementing the Confederation's health policies, the cantons are responsible for planning and financing inpatient services (hospitals), ensuring outpatient health and long-term care services, supervising professional licensing, and sanitation policing. In addition, the cantons oversee educational institutions, and are thus responsible for the training of medical and other health professions, and they subsidize health insurance premiums for households with low incomes. They also hold competencies regarding public health and prevention including measures against infectious diseases. However, in the case of an epidemic, a national law authorizes the federal government to centralize the policy responses (Rüefli and Zenger 2018; Sager and Mavrot 2020). Finally, municipalities have a complementary function and are responsible for inpatient care, hospital and nursing homes, and nursing care at home (*Spitex*).

This decentralized organization and the heterogeneity among cantons regarding size, population, and economic structures results in cantonal differences in health care and public health policies, structure of services, expenditure, and costs of insurance premiums. The latter are lower in Central and Eastern Switzerland and rural cantons compared to Western Switzerland and urban cantons (Braendle and Colombier 2016; Crivelli et al. 2006; De Pietro and Crivelli 2015; Rüefli and Vatter 2001; Vatter and Rüefli 2003; Trein 2018a).

Cooperation between the cantons has a long tradition in health policy. As early as 1919, the Conference of Cantonal Directors of Public Health (GDK) was founded as one of the first inter-cantonal government conferences. The organization serves as a platform to coordinate between the cantons and to jointly represent cantonal interests vis-à-vis the federal government (Achtermann and Berset 2006, 94–98; Rüefli et al. 2015, 119f.). In addition, there are other inter-cantonal and regional coordination bodies related to health (Füglister 2012).

2.2 Private actors: self-organization, competition, and personal responsibility

As in other policy areas, subsidiarity and delegation of tasks to private actors are fundamental values of the Swiss health system (Vatter 2003). Comparative analyses show that it is highly market-oriented (Paris et al. 2010). Accordingly, Switzerland has the highest per capita expenditure on health care for private households in an OECD comparison (OECD 2022).

Private actors perform central tasks in health policy: the delivery of outpatient care, the qualification of health professionals, health promotion, and prevention services (Rüefli et al. 2015, 121f.). The subsidiarity principle also shapes the field of health promotion and prevention. At the cantonal and local level, both are provided by civil society organizations, such as health leagues that are committed to the prevention of specific diseases or of tobacco, alcohol, or drug abuse.

Due to their central role in providing health care and prevention services, private actors and their interest groups are influential political actors and play a crucial role in regulating health care. One cornerstone of Switzerland's liberal, subsidiarity-based system is tariff autonomy (Sager et al. 2010, 22): service provider associations and health insurers jointly negotiate tariff agreements and quality requirements according to a logic of corporatist self-governance. State authorities only approve the results of these negotiations. The subsidiarity system also leads to an institutional entanglement of political and private actors in the exercise of state regulatory competencies at the federal and cantonal levels. One example are health insurance companies. They are private companies but not allowed to make profit with compulsory basic insurance while profits with complementary health insurances are legal. Another example of subsidiarity is that private companies certify the approval of medical devices (Maggetti et al. 2017).

From the perspective of health care users, free choice of insurers and doctors are central elements of Swiss health policy. However, against a background of continuously rising insurance premiums, residents have increasingly turned to cheaper models where the insurance restricts the choice of doctor in exchange for lower premiums (De Pietro et al. 2015, 99). At the same time, voters have frequently rejected public policies restricting the choice of insurance or providers (Rüefli 2021).

Individuals retain a large responsibility for financing their health care services, regardless of their income. Switzerland does not have income-related health insurance rates, but rather per capita premiums depending on the insurance plan offered by the insurance company.[3] Consequently, there are no direct redistribution mechanisms from high to low incomes here. In addition, compulsory insurance demands a contribution by the insured (10 per cent deductible, selectable annual deductibles of up to CHF 2,500 per year for adults). Dental care is 95 per cent financed by private households. This payment system results in the comparatively high proportion of out-of-pocket contributions in Swiss health care financing compared to other OECD countries (cf. above). Historically, it builds on individual liberty and choice. The National Health Insurance Law of 1994 created a national obligation for all residents to have health insurance, but with no employer contribution and no adjustment of premiums according to salary (there is separate workplace accident insurance). Households with low incomes can apply for cantonal subsidies for the premiums. In 2020, the share of insured persons who received a premium reduction was 27.6 per cent (FSO 2022b).

3 Historical Overview of Health Policy

3.1 Slow transfer of competencies from the cantons to the federal government

Table 38.1 provides a historical overview of changes in Swiss health policy.[4] Historically, it was a local matter where towns and religious fraternities funded and provided health care services. By the late nineteenth century, as medical practice advanced and churches and charity organizations could no longer guarantee funding, most hospitals were taken over by municipalities and later by cantons, and the latter began regulating sanitary affairs and medical practices (Achtermann and Berset 2006). Hospital policy, including planning and the running of nursing care institutions, has since been the responsibility of the cantons. Outpatient care has always been left to private, self-employed professionals. Until the late nineteenth century, each canton decided autonomously whether and how it would regulate medical practice; some did not even require a licence. When the Swiss Confederation was established in 1848, it was given the constitutional prerogative to control epidemics. The first test case in this field was a typhus epidemic in 1866, which led to a federal law for epidemic control in 1886 and the establishment of what is today's Federal Office for Public Health in 1893. In 1877, a federal law stipulating examination requirements for doctors, veterinarians, and pharmacists set minimum standards for the provision of medical services in the cantons (Federal Council 2004, 182). Apart from this law, which remained unchanged until 2000, there was no federal regulation of medical practice; licensing and supervision of medical practice remained responsibilities of the cantons. Further laws of 2013 and 2016 gave the federal government the competencies to regulate the education, vocational training, and professional practice of psychological professions and of non-academic health care professions. Another example of the transfer of competencies to the federal government is the federal law on pharmaceuticals which entered into force in 2000 and replaced a patchwork of cantonal, inter-cantonal, and federal regulations.

3.2 Introduction of public and private health insurance

Health insurance was originally a private matter. Sickness funds were set up in the early nineteenth century by entrepreneurs, trade unions, or religious organizations to provide financial support to workers and their families in case of illness, disability, or death (Kocher and Oggier 2001, 108). Later, they were transformed into insurance funds reimbursing the cost of medical treatment. Historically, there has been great

Table 38.1: Main reforms regarding health insurance and public health in Switzerland

Year	Event	Provisions
Reforms related to health insurance		
1899	'Lex Forrer'	Introduced health and accident insurance; rejected by referendum
1911	Law on Health and Accident Insurance	Stipulated regulation and subsidies for voluntary sickness insurance funds
1964	Partial Revision of Law on Health and Accident Insurance	Increased subsidies to voluntary sickness insurance funds and limited differences in premiums charged based on gender
1987	Partial Revision of Law on Health and Accident Insurance	Introduced maternity insurance and cost-containment measures; rejected by referendum
1991	Decrees on Risk Adjustment and Cost Control	Introduced new measures for risk adjustment between health insurers, subsidies for low-income groups, limitations of insurance premiums, and co-payments
1994	National Health Insurance Law (KVG)	Established a national health insurance regulation; insurance became mandatory
2000	Partial revision of the KVG	Introduced minimum standards to improve the efficacy of the system and to strengthen solidarity, revised some administrative and technical aspects
2003	Partial revision of the KVG	Linked premium subsidies to income; intended to lift contracting obligation for insurers with all providers; option to increase co-payments; rejected by referendum
2007	Partial revision of the KVG	Substantial reform of hospital financing
2008	Partial revision of the KVG	Reform of financing of long-term care-arrangements
2019	Partial revision of the KVG	Strengthened quality and cost-effectiveness
Reforms related to public health and prevention		
1887	National Law on Epidemics	Health protection and policing related to public health
1970	Revision of the National Law on Epidemics	Definition of tasks for the federal government and cantons in case of a pandemic (generalization of the existing law dealing with tuberculosis)
1984	National law on prevention	Failed attempt for a national prevention law (beyond epidemics)
1993	Popular initiative on public health	Popular initiative to ban alcohol and tobacco advertising failed (*Zwillingsinitiativen*)
2012	Federal smoking ban	Smoking ban in public buildings where individuals work
2012	National law of prevention	Failed attempt to create a national law for prevention with the goal to create a legal basis for preventative health policy
2013	Revision of the National Law on Epidemics	Adaption of the national epidemic laws; strengthened the federal government's role

Data source: Rüefli (2021); Trein (2018).

organizational variety, with private and public (municipal) funds, federal and regional funds, and for-profit or non-profit funds open to everybody or limited to a specific community or occupation. An 1890 constitutional amendment authorized the Confederation to establish a health and accident insurance scheme. A first law to implement this scheme and to introduce a compulsory insurance was blocked by a referendum challenge in 1899. In 1911, the citizens accepted the Federal Law on Health and Accident Insurance in a popular referendum. The law defined the minimum requirements to be met by voluntary health insurance funds to receive public subsidies (Federal Council 1991, 99). Later attempts to introduce a compulsory insurance repeatedly encountered political opposition. Consequently, the 1911 law on subsidies to voluntary sickness funds remained unchanged until 1964 (Federal Council 1991, 106–107). From 1969, due to ever-increasing premiums, health insurance was the subject of many different reform projects initiated by the federal government or by popular initiatives. However, all of them failed due to lack of consensus on two issues: whether insurance should become compulsory or remain voluntary and whether financing should be based on per capita or income-related premiums (Federal Council 1991; Linder et al. 2010). For the most part, left-wing parties and trade unions favoured compulsory insurance and income-related premiums, whereas more conservative and right-wing parties, business associations, and (part of) the medical profession opposed them.

3.3 Cost increase and health insurance reform

In the early 1990s, the Federal Council enacted emergency legislation to tackle the rise in health insurance premiums (Laubscher 2006, 173). In 1991, it eventually presented the proposal for a new law as a counterproposal to the Social Democrats' 1986 popular initiative 'for a healthy health insurance'. The parliamentary process, lasting from 1992 to 1994, was highly conflictual. A coalition between the centrist Christian Democrats (CVP/*Die Mitte*), Liberal Democrats (FDP), and the centre-left Social Democrats (SP) supported the law. Policy formulation resulted in a compromise where the FDP and CVP insisted on maintaining privately organized health insurance, while the Social Democrats were successful in establishing a compulsory insurance. In a referendum in 1994, the electorate eventually supported the parliamentary bill with a majority of 52 per cent (Braun and Uhlmann 2009; Uhlmann and Braun 2011; Linder et al. 2010, 528–529).

The new law on health insurance (*Krankenversicherungsgesetz*; KVG) entered into force on 1 January 1996. The law is the single most important reform in Swiss health care policy in the last few decades. A cornerstone of this legislation was the introduction of an insurance system with a clear separation of compulsory basic and voluntary supplementary insurances. Basic insurance with identical services became mandatory for all residents. Over time, the federal government has continuously expanded these mandatory services. Furthermore, insurance premiums for basic health insurance can no longer vary according to gender and health status.

3.4 Market competition and state planning co-exist in health insurance policy

The new KVG did not replace the Swiss system of private health insurance with public bodies. Rather, the reform made some important adjustments to how insurers are organized (cf. previous section). Since the reform, the system is based on the concept of regulated competition (De Pietro et al. 2015). This concept also applies to health care provision, as regulation of tariffs and quality is left to service providers and health insurers. However, the latter are obliged to execute contracts with all service providers eligible to practice within the system. This limits competition between doctors. Concerning inpatient care, the KVG obliges cantons to conduct hospital planning and to define the types of services that may be billed to insurers ('hospital lists') (Rüefli 2005).

3.5 Further partial reforms of health insurance

The KVG did not slow down the increase in health care costs. Ongoing pressure for cost containment led to a series of reform proposals (cf. Table 38.1, and Rüefli 2021 for details). A first reform in 2000 introduced minimum standards for the cantons' insurance premium subsidies. In 2002, the Federal Council empowered the cantons to limit the admission of outpatient service providers (Rüefli and Monaco 2004; Fuino et al. 2022). Following parliament's rejection of a large project to reform health insurance in 2003, the federal government pursued a strategy to adopt various reforms in small steps (Furrer 2006, 191–192). Some of them were implemented, for example concerning the overall strategy of health insurance policy, risk equalization between patient groups, new admission regulations for doctors, premium reductions, and hospital financing. The hospital financing reform of 2009 increased the Confederation's role in defining the conditions of inpatient care delivery and had a major impact on the hospital sector (De Pietro et al. 2015, 210; Rüefli 2021, 670): it strengthened the competition among hospitals by introducing a new financing system, by harmonizing the previously different regulations of public and private hospitals, and by changing the modalities of cantonal hospital planning. Another reform concerned the financing of long-term care involving health insurers, insured persons, cantons, municipalities, and other branches of social insurance. This reform was approved by parliament in 2008 but only came into force in 2011 after intense debates between the federal government and the cantons. In 2014, a new law on supervision of health insurance was passed delegating new supervisory powers to the Confederation. Due to intense political conflicts, it took until 2021 for the regulations on quality assurance in the KVG to be modified (Federal Council 2022; Haenni 2022).

Other reforms failed. For example, in 2012, a reform proposal aiming to make managed care insurance plans the default option for everyone failed in a referendum. In 2014, citizens rejected a popular initiative aiming to introduce a unitary public health insurance at the federal level at the ballot vote. At the time of writing (September 2022), different reforms of the health care system are in discussion and subject to intense political debate. Since 2018, the federal government has proposed two reform packages aiming at reducing health care cost that combine a variety of measures (cf. Heidelberger 2022a, b). Furthermore, two popular initiatives related to cost containment are pending. One aims to ensure that households do not spend more than 10 per cent of their income on health costs. A second one demands a constitutional rule for cost containment. After a certain level of cost increase, the federal government would be required to impose containment measures.

3.6 Newer reforms related to prevention and public health

In the post-World War II period, the creation of capacities for financing and delivering health care services was the focus of policymakers. One exception was the federal law to combat tuberculosis. It passed both chambers of parliament but was nevertheless rejected in a referendum in 1949 (Immergut 1992, 158–161.). Only in the mid-1970s did the focus of health policy change towards reform proposals emphasizing general medicine, prevention, and public health as well as home care options. For example, in 1972 the reform of the Federal Narcotics Act introduced stricter penalties for drug use. At the same time, a public debate on assisted suicide for elderly and sick individuals resulted in demands by individual cantons (e.g. Basel-Stadt, Zurich) for a federal law on the matter. Today, assisted suicide is legal and widely accepted in Switzerland.

Since the 1980s, prevention and health protection have received more political attention. These issues (re)appeared on the political agenda against the background of increasing case numbers of non-communicable diseases, such as cancer and diabetes, but also due to new infectious diseases, notably HIV/AIDS (Trein 2018b). In the early 1980s, a policy proposal by the Federal Council failed during the consultation process, as the cantons insisted on maintaining their competency on the matter. In 2009, the federal government proposed a new law on prevention and health promotion aiming to define the competencies of the Confederation and the cantons, establishing governance systems and financing and coordination mechanisms, and creating a new Swiss Institute for Prevention and Health Promotion. Although supported by a broad coalition of public health actors, the law was eventually blocked in parliament. The parties associated with economic associations feared restrictions of economic freedoms and a paternalism of citizens through state regulations (APS 2009, 201). Due to the lack of explicit legal competencies in the domain of prevention and health promotion, the Confederation responded with several national strategies, e.g. concerning HIV, addiction, non-communicable diseases, cancer etc., which are implemented in cooperation with the cantons and NGOs active in specific policy areas.

Prevention issues were also subject to popular initiatives. In 1993, with a large majority, voters rejected a popular initiative demanding national bans on alcohol and tobacco advertising, after strong resistance by the federal government, parliament, and interest groups. The defeat of these 'twin initiatives' curbed efforts by the federal administration to push for federal tobacco control and other public health policies. Consequently, advertising restrictions and smoking bans were implemented at the cantonal level (Mavrot and Sager 2018; Trein 2017). The Federal Council and parliament drew up a federal law on protection from passive smoking in a lengthy and sometimes controversial process, which entered into force in 2012. In 2022, voters accepted a popular initiative demanding restrictions on tobacco advertisements for minors. Since the mid-1990s, different cantons have also modernized their legal foundations for health protection and prevention (Trein 2018b).

In 1993, the Federal Council created a framework for the controlled distribution of 'hard' drugs. Initial trials of medically controlled supplies of illicit drugs to addicts showed positive results, so the Federal Council decided to extend the trials (APS 1992–1994). During the same period, a referendum approved the medically prescribed distribution of heroin, confirming the Federal Council's consensus course on drug policy (APS 1996–1998). At the same time, various popular initiatives dealt with drug policy issues. At the end of the 1990s, popular initiatives demanding both a more restrictive and a more liberal drug policy failed at the ballot box.

The agenda to change drug policy from a restrictive prohibition-oriented approach to a policy of harm reduction and social reintegration of addicts was based on experiences with the AIDS epidemic (Kübler 2001). From the late 1980s, federal, cantonal, and municipal authorities took action to prevent HIV infections, coupled with a debate about 'taboo subjects such as sexuality, addiction, and death' (Neuenschwander et al. 2005, 35). The developments in AIDS policy led to a change in drug policy, which started to focus not only on penalties but also on socio-political measures. In 2008, the Federal Narcotics Act was revised to create a legal foundation for the so-called four-pillar concept (prevention including protection of minors, therapy, harm reduction—for example through medically controlled heroin distribution—, and repression). Recent efforts to decriminalize cannabis, such as the creation of a legal basis for conducting scientific studies on cannabis use, represent a continuation of this approach.

In 1970, in the wake of a typhus outbreak in the canton of Valais, the federal government and parliament revised the National Law on Epidemics. The new law contained regulations on the obligation to report communicable diseases and obliged the cantons to delegate the management of measures against infectious diseases to cantonal medical officers (SR 818.101, 327). In 2013, due to more recent pandemics such as the lung disease SARS and the H1N1 flu wave of 2009, the Federal Council undertook a revision of the National Law on Epidemics, which was approved in a referendum. A major change was the creation of the legal basis for a temporary centralization of decision-making powers in the hands of the Federal Council (Trein 2015; Rüefli and Zenger 2018). This played an important role in the policy response to the COVID-19 pandemic in spring 2020, as it allowed the federal government to impose a coherent national response during the first months of the pandemic. Nevertheless, the law did not work in the way as intended, especially regarding the coordination of measures between the national government and the cantons (Freiburghaus et al. 2021; Schnabel et al. 2022).

4 POLITICAL FACTORS AFFECTING HEALTH POLICY REFORMS

The presentation above of actors and reforms in health policy reveals some central dynamics regarding the political factors influencing health policy in Switzerland.[5] From an institutional perspective, parliament, direct democracy, and federalism play crucial roles in the policy process. Many health policy reforms—especially those related to the reform of health insurance-related matters at the federal level—are strongly contested in parliament and need to be approved by a popular vote. Against this background, interest groups and voters are important veto players. Due to the central role of federalism and subsidiarity, subnational—especially cantonal—actors play a key role in Swiss health policy.

4.1 Voters and interest groups as veto players

In health policy, interest groups—doctors, insurers, service providers, and other industries—are decisive veto players in decision-making and in the implementation of reform projects. These actors usually mobilize their influence on policy outcomes in the parliamentary process and in referendum campaigns (Immergut 1992; Trein 2018b; Uhlmann and Braun 2011; Vatter 2003).

The stakeholder interests of all the different players in the health care system—service providers, health insurers, patient organizations, and health leagues—are well-represented in the federal parliament. This makes it difficult for parliament to reach a consensus on reforms and cost-reducing measures in the health insurance system. The lengthy duration of debates on reform proposals and the rejection of some of them illustrate this. Parliament frequently modifies projects presented by the federal government.

Between 1848 and 2022, voters had to decide on a total of sixty-two health policy proposals in the broader sense (including regulations on alcohol, tobacco, organ transplantation, abortion, food hygiene, research, and assisted reproduction). The frequency of these proposals has increased significantly since the 1980s. Traditionally, popular initiatives[6] related to health policy rarely received the necessary support from a majority of voters and cantons, and new transfers of competencies to the federal government often failed due to voter resistance (Vatter 2020). Historical examples of this are the rejection of the first federal epidemic law in 1882 and the first health insurance law ('Lex Forrer') in 1900. In addition, various reforms of the National Health Insurance Law failed in popular votes from the 1970s to the 1990s. Since 2000, five popular initiatives demanding more redistribution in the health system have been rejected. Similarly, referendums and popular initiatives related to public health and prevention regularly failed (a notable exception is a popular initiative banning tobacco advertising targeting minors in early 2022). Nevertheless, voters approved of the pandemic measures taken by the federal government against COVID-19. The law on Switzerland's COVID-19 measures—which put into law the policies taken by the federal government such as financial support for businesses, contact tracing, and vaccination certificates—was approved by voters twice in 2021.

4.2 Cantonal autonomy and implementation of national health policies

Due to the division of tasks between the Confederation and the cantons (cf. section 2), cantons have important autonomy in designing their own health policies including tax-financed measures (Costa-Font and Greer 2013). At the same time, cantons are responsible for the implementation of federal legislation. Research on policy implementation in Switzerland (Sager et al. 2017) has shown that cantons often take certain liberties in the implementation of federal laws and policies. They often pursue their own goals, especially in the allocation of subsidies, and instrumentalize federal laws for other purposes.

This problem is visible, for example, in the considerable differences concerning the design of the system for the reduction of health insurance premiums, especially the definition of eligible groups (Balthasar 2001). Another example is the obligation for cantonal hospital planning, integrated into the KVG. This provision intended to authorize cantons to reduce overcapacities in hospitals to curb costs. However, the instrument only had a very indirect effect on costs but augmented political conflicts within cantons between governments on the one hand and providers and the population on the other (Rüefli 2005). The same holds for the competency to restrict the admission of outpatient service providers (Rüefli and Monaco 2004; Sager et al. 2019; Fuino et al. 2022). If cantonal authorities cannot be convinced of the benefits of federal regulations, or if they use their independent programming and regulatory powers in the context of implementation, there is a risk of implementation gaps (Sager and Rüefli 2001; Sager and Rüefli 2005). This leads to regional policy inequalities and limited ability to harmonize Swiss health policy.

While federalism can lead to a heterogeneous implementation of national policies, cantonal autonomy offers the possibility to lead the way in addressing policy issues that are blocked at the federal level. The effective blocking of framework legislation around health protection and prevention since the 1980s led several cantons to revise their legislation in this area. For example, in tobacco advertising regulation, some cantons took the lead and implemented corresponding advertising restrictions that went further than existing measures at the federal level (Mavrot and Sager 2018; Trein 2017). In the area of protection against passive smoking, the differences between cantonal regulations contributed to the Federal Council and parliament defining uniform minimum standards (Benteli and Rohrer 2020).

5 Outlook and challenges for Swiss health policy

In an international comparison, the Swiss health system appears to be very successful in terms of its policy performance.[7] Due to compulsory health and long-term care insurance, the entire resident population has access to high-quality health care with a comprehensive catalogue of services. Correspondingly, the population's health and quality of life are good, and patient satisfaction is high. In terms of policy, weaknesses of the system are the lack of transparency regarding the quality and efficiency of medical care, the high costs, and the increasing financing pressure (De Pietro et al. 2015; Trein 2019). Politically, complex governance structures (strong interest groups, coalition government, federalism, and direct democracy) impede rapid and sweeping reforms. The complexity of the political process in Switzerland is beneficial for democratic legitimacy and local 'implementability' of reforms (e.g. Vatter 2020). It requires, however, a constant effort to revise and resubmit policy proposals. In looking ahead, there are two main challenges for Swiss health policy: rising expenditure and a growing strategic role of the federal government.

5.1 Rising health care expenditure

Since the mid-1980s, cost containment has been the main task for policymakers. Public and private health expenditure in Switzerland is higher than in most other OECD member states, especially out-of-pocket expenses for private households (see Figure 38.1). For citizens, health insurance premiums rose by an average of 3.4 per cent per year between 2000 and 2019, which is higher than GDP or average income rises (FSO 2021). Most of the federal government's reform projects, parliamentary initiatives, and popular initiatives on health issues are concerned with the following overarching goals: to change the incentive structures and mechanisms of health care management, to improve efficiency, or to curb costs. Since 2003, the Federal Council has presented numerous reform projects, some of which have been adopted and implemented. However, against the background of powerful interest groups, cantonal involvement, and direct democracy, cost saving reforms proceed slowly. Some reform proposals failed at the ballot box (see section 3, and Rüefli 2021). In 2019 and 2021, the federal government presented two packages with various cost-containment measures to parliament. They entail, for example, changes regarding the pricing of drugs and outpatient care. The parliament adopted some of these measures in 2021, while the debate on the others is pending (cf. Heidelberger 2022a, b). It appears likely that health care costs will remain on the political agenda in the near future. At the cantonal level, efforts to make hospital care more efficient are an important trigger for health policy initiatives.

5.2 A growing strategic role of the federal government

In recent years, the role of the federal government has grown ever more important. On the one hand, the Federal Council has resorted to emergency legislation to address urgent problems, for example concerning health expenditure when interest groups and voters blocked quick and comprehensive reforms. In times of crisis, such as the COVID-19 pandemic, the federal government is entitled to come up with a national policy solution. In new areas, such as electronic health records, the federal government takes a leading role in providing framework legislation.

On the other hand, the cantons and federal government have increasingly sought a coordinated approach to health policy. One example of this is the National Health Policy Dialogue (Achtermann and Berset 2006, 161–162). This is primarily an exchange and coordination platform between federal and cantonal authorities on topics that are of mutual importance. Yet, private actors are involved only selectively. In addition, the federal government has begun to develop strategic frameworks for its health policy. In January 2013, the Federal Council presented the strategy paper 'Health2020', which outlines health policy priorities, goals, and measures. In 2019, the revised strategy 'Health2030' followed (Federal Council 2019). The renewed strategy reacts to four main challenges: technological and digital change, demographic and social trends, preserving high-quality and financially sustainable health care provision, and positively influencing the determinants of health.

Overall, at the beginning of the twenty-first century, the Swiss health system is evolving in the path of historically developed structures. Decentralized federalism (where cantons have important fiscal, legislative, and administrative autonomy from the national government), the strong role of direct democracy, and powerful interest groups are likely to limit change to small steps instead of fundamental reforms in health policy in the future.

Notes

1. This section is partially based on Rüefli (2021) and Trein (2019).
2. This section is based on Trein et al. (2022).
3. Several attempts to change the system, i.e. to introduce income-related premiums or to introduce one unitary public health insurance, were rejected by the electorate (Rüefli 2021).
4. This section is based on Rüefli (2021) and Trein et al. (2022).
5. This section is based on Trein et al. (2022).
6. These ballot initiatives emerge from a committee of citizens, parties, and/or interest groups. They are different from referendums, which are votes on laws initiated by the federal government.
7. This section is based on Trein et al. (2022).

References

Achtermann, Wally, and Christel Berset. 2006. *Gesundheitspolitiken in der Schweiz—Potential für eine nationale Gesundheitspolitik*. Bern: Bundesamt für Gesundheit.

APS. 1966–2020. *Année politique suisse 1966–2020. Sozialpolitik; Gesundheit, Sozialhilfe, Sport.* Bern: Année Politique Suisse, Institut für Politikwissenschaft, Universität Bern.

Balthasar, Andreas. 2001. *Evaluation des Vollzugs der Prämienverbilligung, Wirkungsanalyse KVG.* Bern: Bundesamt für Sozialversicherungen.

Benteli, Marianne, and Linda Rohrer. 2020. *Ausgewählte Beiträge zur Schweizer Politik: Kantonale Rauchverbote vor der bundesrechtlichen Lösung, 2005–2008.* Bern: Année Politique Suisse, Institut für Politikwissenschaft, Universität Bern.

Braendle, Thomas, and Carsten Colombier. 2016. 'What Drives Public Health Care Expenditure Growth? Evidence from Swiss Cantons, 1970–2012'. *Health Policy* 120 (9): pp. 1051–1060. doi: https://doi.org/10.1016/j.healthpol.2016.07.009.

Braun, Dietmar, and Björn Uhlmann. 2009. 'Explaining Policy Stability and Change in Swiss Health Care Reforms'. *Swiss Political Science Review* 15 (2): pp. 205–240.

Costa-Font, Joan, and Scott Greer, eds. 2013. *Federalism and Decentralization in European Health and Social Care.* Basingstoke: Palgrave Macmillan.

Crivelli, Luca, Massimo Filippini, and Ilaria Mosca. 2006. 'Federalism and Regional Health Care Expenditures: An Empirical Analysis for the Swiss Cantons'. *Health Economics* 15 (5): pp. 535–541. doi: https://doi.org/10.1002/hec.1072.

De Pietro, Carlo, Paul Camenzind, Isabelle Sturny, Luca Crivelli, Suzsanne Edwards-Garavoglia, Anne Spranger, Friedrich Wittenbecher, and Quentin Wilm. 2015. 'Switzerland: Health System Review'. *Health Systems in Transition* 17 (4): pp. 1–288. doi: https://apps.who.int/iris/handle/10665/330252.

De Pietro, Carlo, and Luca Crivelli. 2015. 'Swiss Popular Initiative for a Single Health Insurer. . . Once Again!'. *Health Policy* 119 (7): pp. 851–855. doi: https://doi.org/10.1016/j.healthpol.2015.05.004.

Federal Council. 1991. *Botschaft über die Revision der Krankenversicherung vom 6. November 1991.* BBl 1992 I 93.

Federal Council. 2004. *Botschaft zum Bundesgesetz über die universitären Medizinalberufe (Medizinalberufegesetz, MedBG) vom 3. Dezember 2004.* BBl 2005 173.

Federal Council. 2019. *Health 2030—The Federal Council's Health Policy Strategy for the Period 2020–2030.* Bern: Bundesamt für Gesundheit.

Federal Council. 2022. *Strategie zur Qualitätsentwicklung in der Krankenversicherung (Qualitätsstrategie). Sicherung und Förderung der Qualität der Leistungen im Rahmen der obligatorischen Krankenpflegeversicherung.* Bern: Bundesamt für Gesundheit.

FOPH—Federal Office for Public Health. 2020. *Die Wohnbevölkerung der Schweiz ist zufrieden mit der Gesundheitsversorgung.* https://www.admin.ch/gov/de/start/dokumentation/medienmitteilungen.msg-id-81536.html (accessed 20 April 2020).

Freiburghaus, Rahel, Sean Mueller, and Adrian Vatter. 2021. 'Switzerland: Overnight Centralization in One of the World's Most Federal Countries'. In *Federalism and the Response to COVID-19. A Comparative Analysis*, edited by Rupak Chattopadhyay, Felix Knüpling, Diana Chebenova, Liam Whittington, and Phillip Gonzalez, pp. 217–228. New York: Routledge.

FSO—Federal Statistical Office. 2021. *Krankenversicherungsprämien.* https://www.bfs.admin.ch/bfs/de/home/statistiken/preise/krankenversicherungspraemien.html (accessed 10 August 2022).

FSO—Federal Statistical Office. 2022a. *Gesundheitskosten, Finanzierung nach Finanzierungsregime.* https://www.bfs.admin.ch/bfs/de/home/statistiken/gesundheit/kosten-finanzierung/finanzierung.html (accessed 06 May 2022).

FSO—Federal Statistical Office. 2022b. *Obligatorische Krankenpflegeversicherung (OKPV). Kennzahlen zur Prämienverbilligung.* https://www.bfs.admin.ch/asset/de/je-d-13.04.03.03 (accessed 06 May 2022).

Füglister, Katharina. 2012. 'Where Does Learning Take Place? the Role of Intergovernmental Cooperation in Policy Diffusion'. *European Journal of Political Research* 51 (3): pp. 316–349. doi: https://doi.org/10.1111/j.1475-6765.2011.02000.x.

Fuino, Michel, Philipp Trein, and Joël Wagner. 2022. 'How Does Regulating Doctors' Admissions Affect Health Expenditures? Evidence from Switzerland'. *BMC Health Services Research* 22 (1): pp. 1–13. doi: https://doi.org/10.1186/s12913-022-07735-7.

Furrer, Marie-Thérèse. 2006. 'Die KVG Revisionen: wo stehen wir heute?'. *Soziale Sicherheit CHSS* 4: pp. 191–195.

Haenni, Miriam. 2022. *Spitalplanung Schweiz. Interkantonale Kooperation im Spannungsfeld von nationalen und föderalen Interessen.* Zürich: Seismo.

Hale, Thomas, Noam Angrist, Rafael Goldszmidt, Beatriz Kira, Anna Petherick, Toby Phillips, Samuel Webster, Emily Cameron-Blake, Laura Hallas, Saptarshi Majumdar, and Helen Tatlow. 2021. 'A Global Panel Database of Pandemic Policies (Oxford COVID-19 Government Response Tracker)'. *Nature Human Behaviour* 5 (4): pp. 529–538. doi: https://doi.org/10.1038/s41562-021-01079-8.

Heidelberger, Anja. 2022a. *Ausgewählte Beiträge zur Schweizer Politik: Erstes Massnahmenpaket zur Kostendämpfung im Gesundheitswesen (BRG 19.046), 2018–2022.* Bern: Année Politique Suisse, Institut für Politikwissenschaft, Universität Bern. https://anneepolitique.swiss/proze sse/59690-erstes-massnahmenpaket-zur-kostendampfung-im-gesundheitswesen-brg-19-046 (accessed 11 November 2022).

Heidelberger, Anja 2022b. *Ausgewählte Beiträge zur Schweizer Politik: Dossier: Anstieg der Krankenkassenprämien dämpfen (seit 2020), 2018–2022.* Bern: Année Politique Suisse, Institut für Politikwissenschaft, Universität Bern. https://anneepolitique.swiss/dossi ers/879-dossier-anstieg-der-krankenkassenpramien-dampfen-seit-2020 (accessed 11 November 2022).

Immergut, Ellen M. 1992. *Health Politics: Interests and Institutions in Western Europe.* Cambridge: Cambridge University Press.

Kocher, Gerhard. 2010. 'Kompetenz- und Aufgabenverteilung Bund – Kantone – Gemeinden'. In *Gesundheitswesen Schweiz 2010–2013. Eine aktuelle Übersicht*, edited by Gerhard Kocher, and Willy Oggier, pp. 133–144. Bern: Verlag Hans Huber.

Kocher, Gerhard, and Willy Oggier (eds). 2001. *Gesundheitswesen Schweiz 2001/2002. Ein aktueller Überblick.* Solothurn: Konkordat der Schweizerischen Krankenversicherer.

Kübler, Daniel. 2001. 'Understanding Policy Change with the Advocacy Coalition Framework: an Application to Swiss Drug Policy'. *Journal of European Public Policy* 8 (4): pp. 623–641. doi: https://doi.org/10.1080/13501760110064429.

Laubscher, Theodor. 2006. 'Was hat das KVG an Neuem und an Veränderungen gebracht?'. *Soziale Sicherheit CHSS* 4: pp. 173–178.

Linder, Wolf, Christian Bolliger, and Yvan Rielle (eds). 2010. *Handbuch der eidgenössischen Volksabstimmungen 1878–2007.* Bern/Stuttgart/Vienna: Haupt.

Maggetti, Martino, Christian Ewert, and Philipp Trein. 2017. 'Not Quite the Same: Regulatory Intermediaries in the Governance of Pharmaceuticals and Medical Devices'. *The Annals of the American Academy of Political and Social Science* 670 (1): pp. 152–169. doi: https://doi.org/10.1177%2F0002716217691240.

Mavrot, Céline, and Fritz Sager. 2018. 'Vertical Epistemic Communities in Multilevel Governance'. *Policy & Politics* 46 (3): pp. 391–407. doi: https://doi.org/10.1332/030557316X14788733118252.

Neuenschwander, Peter, Karin Frey, and Daniel Kübler. 2005. *Die Zukunft der HIV/Aids-Prävention in der Schweiz im Zeitalter der Normalisierung: die Situation auf Bundesebene und in sieben Kantonen (Vol. 5)*. Zürich: Institut für Politikwissenschaft, Universität Zürich.

OECD. 2020. *OECD Health Data*. https://stats.oecd.org/Index.aspx?ThemeTreeId=9 (accessed 25 March 2021).

OECD. 2022. *OECD Health Statistics*. https://stats.oecd.org/Index.aspx?ThemeTreeId=9, (accessed 21 April 2022).

Okma, Kieke G. H., Tsung-mei Cheng, David Chinitz, Luca Crivelli, Meng-kin Lim, Hans Maarse, and Maria Eliana Labra. 2010. 'Six Countries, Six Health Reform Models? Health Care Reform in Chile, Israel, Singapore, Switzerland, Taiwan and the Netherlands'. *Journal of Comparative Policy Analysis* 12 (1–2): pp. 75–113. doi: https://doi.org/10.1080/13876980903076237.

Paris, Valérie, Marion Devaux, and Lihan Wei. 2010. 'Health Systems Institutional Characteristics: A Survey of 29 OECD Countries'. *OECD Health Working Papers No. 50*. Paris: OECD Publishing.

Rüefli, Christian. 2005. *Wirkungsanalyse der kantonalen Spitalplanungen. Forschungsprogramm KVG*. Bern: Bundesamt für Gesundheit.

Rüefli, Christian. 2021. 'Switzerland'. In *Health Politics in Europe: A Handbook*, edited by Ellen M. Immergut, Karen M. Anderson, Camilla Devitt, and Tamara Popic, pp. 652–676. Oxford: Oxford University Press.

Rüefli, Christian, Margreet Duetz, Michael Jordi, and Stefan Spycher. 2015. 'Gesundheitspolitik'. In *Gesundheitswesen Schweiz 2015–2017*, edited by Willy Oggier, pp. 117–136. Bern: hogrefe.

Rüefli, Christian, and Gianna Monaco. 2004. *Wirkungsanalyse Bedarfsabhängige Zulassungsbeschränkung für neue Leistungserbringer (Art. 55a KVG)*. Bern: Bundesamt für Sozialversicherung.

Rüefli, Christian, and Adrian Vatter. 2001. *Kostendifferenzen im Gesundheitswesen zwischen den Kantonen*. Bern: Bundesamt für Sozialversicherung.

Rüefli, Christian, and Christoph A. Zenger. 2018. *Analyse besondere Lage gemäss EpG: Aufgaben, Zuständigkeiten und Kompetenzen des Bundes*. Bern: Büro Vatter, Politikforschung & -beratung.

Sager, Fritz, Karin Ingold, and Andreas Balthasar. 2017. *Policy-Analyse in der Schweiz—Besonderheiten, Theorien, Beispiele*. Zürich: NZZ Libro.

Sager, Fritz, and Céline Mavrot. 2020. 'Switzerland's COVID-19 Policy Response: Consociational Crisis Management and Neo-Corporatist Reopening'. *European Policy Analysis* 6 (2): pp. 293–304. doi: https://doi.org/10.1002/epa2.1094.

Sager, Fritz, and Christian Rüefli. 2001. *Die Auswirkungen der Aufnahme präventivmedizinischer Leistungen in den Pflichtleistungskatalog*. Bern: Bundesamt für Sozialversicherung.

Sager, Fritz, and Christian Rüefli. 2005. 'Die Evaluation öffentlicher Politiken mit föderalistischen Vollzugsarrangements. Eine konzeptionelle Erweiterung des Stufenmodells und eine praktische Anwendung'. *Swiss Political Science Review* 11 (2): pp. 101–129. doi: https://doi.org/10.1002/j.1662-6370.2005.tb00357.x.

Sager, Fritz, Christian Rüefli, and Eva Thomann. 2019. 'Fixing Federal Faults. Complementary Member State Policies in Swiss Health Care Policy'. *International Review of Public Policy* 1 (2): pp. 147–172. doi: http://doi.org/10.4000/irpp.426.

Sager, Fritz, Christian Rüefli, and Marina Wälti. 2010. *Schnittstellen zwischen ambulanter und stationärer Versorgung. Möglichkeiten der Steuerung durch die Kantone. (Obsan Dossier 10)*. Neuchâtel: Schweizerisches Gesundheitsobservatorium.

Schnabel, Johanna, Rahel Freiburghaus, and Yvonne Hegele. 2022. 'Crisis Management in Federal States: The Role of Peak Intergovernmental Councils in Germany and Switzerland During the COVID-19 Pandemic'. *dms—der moderne staat* 15 (1): pp. 42–61. doi: https://doi.org/10.3224/dms.v15i1.10.

Trein, Philipp. 2015. *Implementation of revised bill on Epidemics in Switzerland. ESPN (European Social Policy Network)—Flash Report 2015/46*. Brussels: European Commission.

Trein, Philipp. 2017. 'Europeanisation Beyond the European Union: Tobacco Advertisement Restrictions in Swiss Cantons'. *Journal of Public Policy* 37 (2): pp. 113–142. doi: https://doi.org/10.1017/S0143814X16000167.

Trein, Philipp. 2018a. *ESPN Thematic Report on Inequalities to Access in Health Care – Switzerland*. Brussels: European Commission.

Trein, Philipp. 2018b. *Healthy or Sick? Coevolution of Health Care and Public Health in a Comparative Perspective*. Cambridge: Cambridge University Press.

Trein, Philipp. 2019. 'Health Policy'. In *Swiss Public Administration: Making the State Work successfully*, edited by Andreas Ladner, Yves Emery, Nils Soguel, Sophie Weerts, and Stefan Nahrath, pp. 323–338. Basingstoke: Palgrave Macmillan.

Trein, Philipp, Adrian Vatter, and Christian Rüefli. 2022. 'Gesundheitspolitik'. In *Handbuch der Schweizer Politik*, edited by Yannis Papadopoulos, Pascal Sciarini, Adrian Vatter, Silja Häusermann, Patrick Emmenegger, and Flavia Fossati, pp. 903–930. Zürich: NZZ Verlag.

Uhlmann, Björn, and Dietmar Braun. 2011. *Die schweizerische Krankenversicherungspolitik zwischen Veränderung und Stillstand*. Chur: Rüegger Verlag.

Vatter, Adrian. 2003. 'Strukturen, Prozesse und Inhalte der schweizerischen Gesundheitspolitik'. In *Management im Gesundheitswesen und in der Gesundheitspolitik*. edited by Andreas Zenger, and Tarzis Jung, pp. 155–165. Bern/Göttingen: Verlag Hans Huber.

Vatter, Adrian. 2020. *Das politische System der Schweiz*. Baden-Baden: Nomos.

Vatter, Adrian, and Christian Rüefli. 2003. 'Do Political Factors Matter for Health Care Expenditure? A Comparative Study of Swiss Cantons'. *Journal of Public Policy* 23 (3): pp. 301–323. doi: doi:10.1017/S0143814X03003143.

CHAPTER 39

FAMILY POLICY

SILJA HÄUSERMANN AND RETO BÜRGISSER

1 INTRODUCTION

FAMILY policy comprises all the various programmes and measures, whose purpose is to promote and enhance the wellbeing of families, particularly through financial benefits and support services (Valarino 2020).[1] State support for families through financial benefits and services has become an increasingly important policy field in Switzerland since the mid-1990s, mobilizing both the electorate and the political elite and polarizing them in various ways. A few examples serve to illustrate this political significance. In September 2020, the Swiss electorate decided to introduce a two-week paid paternity leave in Switzerland. By a clear majority (60.3 per cent in favour), they accepted the counterproposal to a popular initiative, which had demanded four weeks of paid leave for fathers. That same Sunday, however, voters clearly rejected an across-the-board increase in tax deductions for children, with 63 per cent of votes against the proposal. Two aspects make these votes particularly indicative of the changing significance of family policy in Switzerland. First, with a popular initiative, a counterproposal, and a legislative referendum at stake on the same day, they show the extent to which family policy has become a salient policy field in Swiss politics after the 2000s (Häusermann and Zollinger 2014). Second, the political coalitions of supporters and opponents of the initiatives were aligned quite differently across the proposals. The issue of paternity leave rallied an encompassing political coalition including the Left/Green camp and the Centre Party (formerly Christian Democratic People's Party, CVP) as well as no fewer than nine dissenting cantonal branches of the Free Democratic Party (FDP). The increase in child tax deductions, by contrast, divided the parties along more traditional distributional conflict lines, opposing the Left and the centre-right. These differences illustrate the multidimensionality and complexity of family policy initiatives in Switzerland today. In this chapter, we describe and explain these two developments—the increasing significance and salience and the multidimensionality of the political space. On that basis, we then construct a framework for analysing more recent developments in this policy field.

The late development and politicization of family policy in Switzerland must be understood in the context of the overall development of the Swiss welfare state. Given political and institutional obstacles to social policy expansion (see 'Social Policy' in this volume; see also Armingeon 2001), it was only in the 1970s and 1980s that the main social insurance schemes (old-age pensions, unemployment insurance, and health) were adopted. This implies that the focus in Swiss social policy reform until the late 1990s lay on 'Bismarckian' income insurance and transfers. It is only after the 2000s that the reorientation of the Swiss welfare state towards activation and social investment—in the fields of labour market policy, education, and family policy—increased in importance and pace (Häusermann 2010).

This reorientation can be attributed to a mix of structural challenges, limited resources, and polarized attitudes (Bonoli 2005). Demographic, social, and economic developments created mounting social and economic pressure, affecting not only Switzerland but also all Western democracies (Hemerijck 2013; Morel et al. 2012). In this context, international organizations, such as the Organisation for Economic Co-operation and Development (OECD) and the European Union (EU), started pushing for a rapid expansion of social investment policies sustaining employment rates and 'fostering, preserving and mobilizing human capital and capabilities' (Garritzmann et al. 2022). In the field of family policy, this push implied a stronger emphasis on state support for working families and female labour market participation (cf. the OECD's 'Babies and Bosses' studies, particularly OECD 2004, 2007, 2011; and the EU's Lisbon Strategy and the European Pillar of Social Rights, particularly European Council 2000, 2017). This expansion of social investment policies, however, came up against the limits of fiscal constraints and, particularly in Switzerland, has been opposed by strengthened national-conservative forces that reject state intervention in family matters for fiscal and/or cultural reasons (see 'The Ideological Space in Swiss Politics: Voters, Parties, and Realignment' in this volume).

This chapter focuses on the political response to these challenges in Switzerland. As we will show, the development of Swiss family policy is heterogeneous across policy subfields and between cantons. The reason is that family policy is an inherently multi-dimensional policy field (Häusermann and Kübler 2010; Häusermann 2018) and can be framed as social policy, education policy, labour market policy, integration policy, or gender equality policy. Depending on the framing and objective, different family policy instruments are placed front and centre. From a social policy perspective, for example, financial benefits for low-income families are central, whereas from a labour market policy perspective, instruments to reconcile employment and childcare are important. From an education policy view, by contrast, the quality of childcare services is at the forefront. Despite this functional differentiation, the objectives and instruments overlap, such that discussions about the development of family policy are always characterized by (at least potential) multiple framing and overlapping lines of conflict. Due to this multiple framing, policy development becomes difficult to steer, fragmented, and sometimes incoherent in terms of objectives. These inherent difficulties of the policy field are exacerbated in the federalist system of Switzerland, as the dimension of the distribution of competences is added to the conflict lines over the substance of family policy (Bonoli and Häusermann 2011). In this web of objectives, conflict lines, and distribution of competences, a somewhat paradoxical picture of policy development in Switzerland emerges. On the one hand, Switzerland has undergone profound reforms in the last twenty-five to thirty years, which clearly contradict the image of a Switzerland incapable of reform and immobilized by veto players. On the other hand, government spending on family policy in Switzerland remains low by international standards and the high net costs of supplementary childcare lead to a strong income-based stratification in the uptake of these services.

In this chapter, we examine this paradoxical development in three steps. First, we analyse the profile of Swiss family policy in an international comparison. Second, we describe the current state of Swiss family policy and its heterogeneity across cantons and municipalities. Third, we provide explanations for these far-reaching but heterogeneous developments by focusing on political actors and reform dynamics. We argue that family policy reforms in Switzerland are fragile mainly because successful policy changes are only possible with (at least partial) support from market-liberal and conservative forces. However, such support is always limited and piecemeal due to the increasingly polarized party landscape in Switzerland (Häusermann 2006; Kübler 2007). Thus, family policy is characterized by unstable majorities, which make finding coherent responses to structural problems more difficult, although not impossible.

2 Financial transfers and reconciliation policies: an international comparison

In social policy, a distinction is made between a) financial transfers vs. welfare services and b) strong vs. moderate government intervention in the market economy (Beramendi et al. 2015). Traditionally, Switzerland is notable for its liberal-conservative family policy model (Esping-Andersen 1999; Dafflon and Abatti 2003): liberal in the sense that it envisages limited government intervention and spending; conservative in that it places strong emphasis on financial transfers to families (child allowances), contrasting with weak service provision (childcare for pre-school and school-age children and parental leave), and tax deductions. The emphasis on financial transfers is therefore described as conservative because it aims to partially compensate for parents' (generally mothers') loss of income instead of promoting a model in which both parents work.

Figure 39.1 illustrates this liberal-conservative profile in public spending on families in Switzerland. Together with Anglo-Saxon and southern European countries, Switzerland still provides below-average state support for families, although it has moved closer to

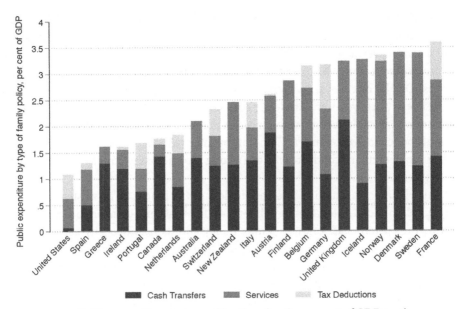

FIGURE 39.1: Public expenditure by type of family policy (in per cent of GDP 2017)

Data source: OECD (2021).

the European average in the last ten years. Financial transfers account for more than half this spending in Switzerland.

However, aggregated spending data can produce a distorted picture of the generosity of family policies because they also depend on families' needs (particularly the distribution of income) and the level of the denominator (gross domestic product, GDP). Figure 39.2 therefore illustrates the generosity of Swiss child allowances in an international comparison, shown as a percentage of the average income of a family with one parent in full-time and one parent in part-time employment (the most common empirically observed model in Switzerland). Here, we see that when it comes to these traditional financial transfers, Switzerland lies precisely in the middle. As child allowances in Switzerland are set at cantonal level, the value for Zurich is shown here as an example, which has been slightly below the Swiss average since the harmonization of child allowances in 2007. In terms of financial transfers to families, Switzerland is thus part of a large group of European countries that pay allowances for two children between 4 and 7 per cent of the average wage.

Figure 39.1 has already shown that financial transfers are the main instrument of family policy in Switzerland. By contrast, investments in family services remain comparatively low. This conservative family policy paradigm, which is based on and promotes the traditional male-breadwinner model (Lewis 1992), has come under significant pressure due to several structural developments in recent years. First, the average fertility rate in continental and southern European countries fell to approximately 1.5 children per woman, a figure which is not only too low to stabilize the working population but is increasingly at odds with most families' preference for two

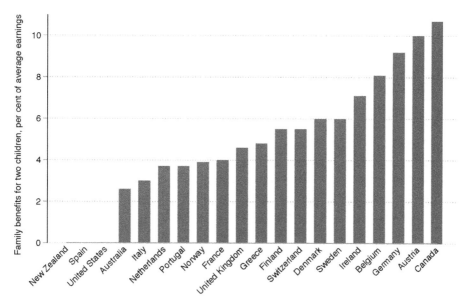

FIGURE 39.2: Total family benefits for two children (aged 6 and 9) as a per cent of average full-time earnings, 2018

Child allowances as such do not exist in the United States. In Spain and New Zealand, there are only 'means-tested' child allowances, where households with two wage earners and average earnings do not qualify for these benefits.

Data source: OECD (2021).

children, which has remained stable over time (Hemerijck 2013, 64; Esping-Andersen 2015). Alongside this demographic challenge, changing family models and gender values are transforming demands about the type of support that should be provided to families, particularly in the area of reconciliation policies (Esping-Andersen 1999). And finally, while the female employment rate in Switzerland has continuously increased, it remains a predominantly part-time employment model. This low rate of full-time or higher-percentage female employment is increasingly recognized as an economic problem (see 'The Structural Shifts in Switzerland's Economy and Society, 2000–2020' in this volume). Considering all these challenges, family policy reforms have become a key issue across continental and southern Europe (Bradshaw and Finch 2010; Häusermann 2018; Bürgisser 2022).

In Switzerland, too, debates about family policy have greatly intensified since the 1990s. All the family policy measures, such as financial transfers, reconciliation policies, and tax deductions, have increasingly featured on the political agenda in the last thirty years compared to the decades after the Second World War. The vast majority of initiatives were submitted in the last thirty years, whereas family policy had hardly been an issue at the federal level between 1945 and 1990 (see the data on the development of the initiatives in Häusermann and Zollinger 2014). Indeed, prior to 1991, not a single policy initiative on early childhood education or day-care structures was tabled in the Swiss parliament.

Despite this growing significance of family policy in Switzerland, family policy services remain low compared to other countries. This applies particularly to policies to reconcile work and family life, which we illustrate here with reference to the length of paid leave for women after giving birth, spending on childcare, and childcare costs. When measured against all three indicators, Switzerland stands out for its strongly liberal-conservative position.

Figure 39.3 shows the number of weeks of paid leave to which women are entitled after giving birth (although payment levels vary). The OECD average is approximately forty weeks and has increased to fifty weeks between 1995 and 2018. Switzerland did not have legally guaranteed maternity leave in 1995. There were provisions on protection from dismissal and continued payment of wages in various collective agreements, and many employers granted their female employees maternity leave on a voluntary basis. However, at the legal level, all that existed was a prohibition on working for eight weeks after giving birth, with no guarantees for wage replacement. In 2004, after several failed attempts, a statutory maternity insurance scheme[2] was introduced following a referendum. It is funded under the Income Compensation Ordinance (*Erwerbsersatzordnung*) and guarantees working mothers 80 per cent of their salary for a period of fourteen weeks. Compared with other countries, this fourteen-week period is clearly at the lower end of the spectrum. Thus, Switzerland ranks in the group of liberal Anglo-Saxon and southern European countries, while statutory maternity leave in most other continental and northern European countries exceeds nine months.

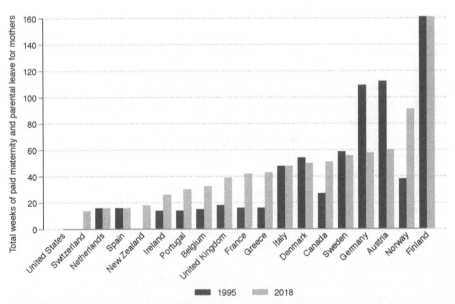

FIGURE 39.3: Length of statutory paid maternity and parental leave for women after birth (in weeks)

The United States still does not provide paid maternity leave. New Zealand and Switzerland did not introduce paid maternity leave until the 2000s.

Data source: OECD (2021).

A direct interpretation of this relatively short maternity leave as a conservative, liberal, or even progressive policy does not stand up to scrutiny, however. The OECD (2007) points out that long leave periods can weaken women's position in the labour market and set negative incentives for employment. Germany and Austria have therefore drastically reduced their respective periods of leave, which used to last more than two years. At first glance, the OECD study suggests that maternity leave in Switzerland is designed to be more labour market oriented. This impression is misleading, however, as very little early childhood care is available that would support or enable young mothers to work after the fourteen weeks of maternity leave. The contrast between the short leave period and the lack of childcare facilities perfectly illustrates the fragmented nature of Switzerland's reluctant approach to family policy and the incentives for female part-time work.

Data on the availability of public childcare are difficult to collect because the boundary between state and non-state provision is often blurred and responsibility for these services is spread across different levels of government. The data provided in Figure 39.4 must therefore be read as approximate rather than precise figures. They show public expenditure on childcare for pre-school children (generally 0–5 years) across all levels of government in the OECD countries.

It is striking that almost all countries have substantially increased their spending on childcare (apart from Sweden and Denmark, which, historically, have offered an extensive range of childcare services, Bonoli 2005). Switzerland also substantially increased its spending between 1990 and 2015, from around 0.1 per cent to more than 0.4 per cent

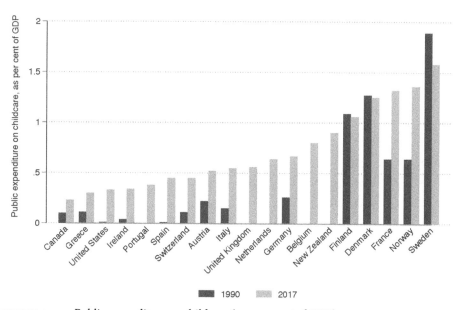

FIGURE 39.4: Public expenditure on childcare (as a per cent of GDP)

No data available for 1990 for the Netherlands.

Data source: OECD (2020).

of GDP. Despite this increase, however, Switzerland remains well below the OECD average of 0.8 per cent of GDP. What's more, roughly half the expenditure in Switzerland goes towards pre-school (kindergarten) facilities, not towards early childcare. Although these data should be viewed as illustrative, they paint a clear picture: the Swiss state's commitment to childcare provision is far less than in most other OECD countries. In fact, data from Eurostat (2020) for the year 2018 show that the uptake of childcare in Switzerland is also low. The average weekly time spent in childcare for children under three is five hours (European average: ten hours) and it is ten hours for children aged three to compulsory school age (European average: twenty-seven hours). Whether this low uptake is due to lack of demand or lack of supply cannot be determined conclusively from these figures. However, demand strongly depends on childcare costs. Here, Switzerland stands out yet again as the country where state support to families is very low compared to other OECD countries.

Figure 39.5 shows how much a family of four with an average household income (generally consisting of one full-time and one part-time wage) would have to spend on full-time childcare for two children. In Switzerland, the costs vary considerably between cantons and providers, and comparative figures are available solely for Zurich. The figures show the costs after deduction of subsidies and other support. With an average monthly household income of around CHF 10,000, the childcare costs that would have to be covered privately amount to more than CHF 3,400 per month. Despite

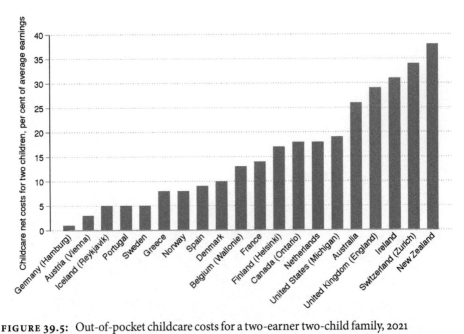

FIGURE 39.5: Out-of-pocket childcare costs for a two-earner two-child family, 2021

Net childcare costs for a two-earner two-child (aged 2 and 3) couple family with earnings at 100 + 67 per cent of average earnings, as a per cent of their earnings.

Data source: OECD (2021).

considerable state subsidies, net childcare costs are still extremely high compared with other countries. The parental share of childcare costs in Switzerland is, on average, at least twice as high as in the rest of the OECD. Only in England, Ireland, and New Zealand are costs at a comparable level.

The continued strong emphasis in Swiss family policy on financial transfers, as opposed to services, also has significant distributional implications. Due to the low availability and high net costs of childcare, there is considerable inequality in parental uptake of childcare services. In Switzerland, these services are utilized to a disproportionate extent by higher-income families (see also Abrassart and Bonoli 2015). Table 39.1 shows the formal childcare rates both as a total and broken down by income tercile. The final column calculates stratified uptake, i.e. the ratio between the lowest and the highest income tercile. Values close to one mean that children from the different income groups attend childcare with equal frequency. Values below one indicate that the services are mainly used by higher-income groups.

In Switzerland, just under 20 per cent of infants from the lowest income tercile attend formal childcare, compared with more than 50 per cent from the highest income tercile. This means that Switzerland, along with Ireland, France, Belgium, and the United

Table 39.1: Participation rates in formal childcare rates (0 to 2 year olds) by income (2019)

	Total	1st tercile	2nd tercile	3rd tercile	Ratio: 1st/3rd tercile
Sweden	51.8	51.3	53.6	49.3	1.04
Norway	50.2	47.0	54.0	48.1	0.98
Portugal	53.4	53.9	46.7	58.8	0.92
Denmark	67.6	62.5	66.5	75.8	0.83
Austria	24.2	21.2	25.8	26.0	0.82
Spain	57.7	52.1	58.8	63.3	0.82
Germany	44.5	34.2	48.0	48.0	0.71
Finland	36.1	29.1	39.6	42.8	0.68
Greece	35.3	27.0	32.1	45.8	0.59
Italy	27.8	20.2	27.3	34.4	0.59
Netherlands	65.5	45.6	67.6	80.9	0.56
United Kingdom	45.1	31.9	41.1	59.3	0.54
Belgium	58.1	35.5	61.9	73.4	0.48
Switzerland	38.9	21.8	36.9	55.1	0.40
France	60.4	29.0	71.4	76.1	0.38
Ireland	42.9	17.9	39.1	68.9	0.26
Average	47.5	36.3	48.2	56.6	0.66

Data source: OECD (2021), based on estimates with EU-SILC data.

Kingdom, has one of the highest levels of stratification in the uptake of formal childcare. The expansion of these services in Switzerland—at least in the initial phase—therefore mainly benefits middle- and higher-income groups, unless such services are specifically designed to target lower income groups. Garritzmann et al. (2022) have theorized how social investment policies can have either inclusive, stratifying, or targeting distributive effects, depending on their institutional policy design. Given the high cost and voluntary nature of childcare services in Switzerland, the country represents a prototypical example of stratifying social investment. As the financial transfers (child allowances and tax relief) have either proportional or regressive redistributive effects (i.e. families benefit according to their income or, indeed, higher-income households benefit disproportionately), the redistributive profile of Swiss family policy overall is clearly stratifying, i.e. it reinforces social stratification.

This brief overview of the structure of Swiss family policy in an international comparison makes it clear that Switzerland lies mid-field in the OECD solely in relation to financial transfers. When it comes to reconciliation policies, it is a clear outlier in Western Europe. What is surprising about this finding is not so much the contrast between Switzerland and the Scandinavian countries, which have undergone a different historical development and have a different balance of political forces; rather, it is the fact that Switzerland differs so strongly from comparable continental European countries (Leitner 2019). Although there has been an expansion of family policy in Switzerland since the 1990s, it remains underdeveloped and features high levels of social stratification.

3 Development and state of family policy in Switzerland

This review of Swiss family policy in an international comparison may seem to suggest stagnation or even a lack of reform capacity. This impression is deceptive, however. Since the late 1990s, Switzerland has experienced genuine reform momentum in the various family policy fields. In this context, it should be noted that this review was produced during a period of major change. The data in this section should therefore be seen as providing a snapshot of current trends. Moreover, after a constitutional amendment to centralize efforts to improve childcare provision was rejected at the ballot box in March 2013, the geographical expansion of childcare provision has been characterized by a high degree of heterogeneity.

In the following, we look at child allowances, maternity/paternity leave, and childcare structures to show which significant changes have occurred, and how much heterogeneity exists in family policy in Switzerland. While centralization and a move towards uniformity can be observed in relation to child allowances and maternity insurance, there has been little harmonization in the provision, costs, and funding of childcare services.

In 2006, the Swiss electorate approved a harmonization of cantonal child allowances at a monthly minimum of CHF 200 per child.[3] As a result, eighteen cantons were required to increase the allowances, although it should be noted that all cantons were already granting child allowances of at least CHF 150 prior to 2006 (Stadelmann-Steffen 2007; Bundesamt für Sozialversicherungen 2022). Following the harmonization, Basel-Stadt, Freiburg, Geneva, Jura, Waadt, Wallis, and Zug still grant higher monthly allowances exceeding CHF 250 per child.

Similar centralization and harmonization occurred in 2005 with the introduction of a statutory maternity insurance scheme. As mentioned above, various attempts to move in this direction had previously failed. This turning point for maternity insurance came about because the FDP and the employers' associations (Swiss Trade Association and Swiss Employers Confederation) agreed to an uniform insurance-based solution after the initiative was limited to benefits for working mothers and provided only a short duration of fourteen weeks of maternity leave with payments equivalent to 80 per cent of the last salary (Häusermann and Kübler 2010). However, individual industries or employers are free to grant more comprehensive benefits. Furthermore, Swiss voters approved the introduction of two weeks of paid paternity leave in September 2020, with 60.3 per cent of votes in favour. Various more far-reaching proposals for longer maternity leave or for genuine parental leave are currently pending in parliament. In particular, various green–liberal and green–social democratic alliances are calling for models of parental leave ranging from twenty-eight to fifty-two weeks. In this area, then, it seems likely that Swiss family policy will remain in a state of flux over the coming years.

While Switzerland thus seems to have become more homogeneous in relation to child allowances and maternity leave over the past two decades, there is much more heterogeneity in the field of childcare services. A study by the Federal Social Insurance Office (Bundesamt für Sozialversicherungen 2018) investigated the ratio of full-time childcare places to the total number of pre-school children in the cantons (= coverage rate). Figure 39.6 shows that, as a national average, a full-time childcare place is available for just 15 per cent of pre-school children. The effective number of pre-school children attending childcare (care rate) is higher than the identified coverage rate, however, as most children do not attend childcare on a full-time basis. Assuming that, on average, a child attends formal childcare two or three days a week, this means that childcare places are available for just under one-third of all pre-school children in Switzerland. A comparison with data from 2010 shows that the coverage rate has almost doubled in less than ten years.

This national average, however, conceals strong geographical disparities. The coverage rate is highest in the French-speaking cantons of Geneva (29 per cent), Neuchâtel (27 per cent), and Vaud (26 per cent). In German-speaking Switzerland, the cantons of Basel-Stadt (24 per cent), Zug (23 per cent), and Zurich (21 per cent) stand out. There is a very low coverage rate in the canton of St Gallen (7 per cent) and in the small, rural German-speaking cantons of Glarus (8 per cent), Nidwalden (7 per cent), Uri (4 per cent), and Appenzell-Innerrhoden (3 per cent).

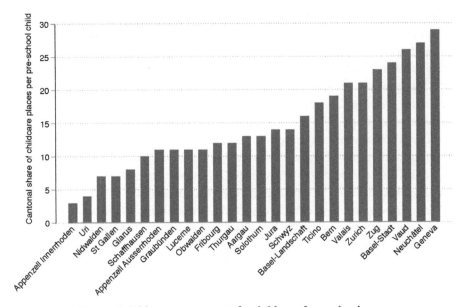

FIGURE 39.6: Cantonal childcare coverage rate for children of pre-school age, 2015–2017
Numbers show the share of childcare places per pre-school child.
Data source: Bundesamt für Sozialversicherungen (2018).

The central role of urban municipalities is also apparent from the fact that the coverage rate in the twenty largest Swiss municipalities averages 34 per cent, with the cities of Zurich, Bern, Lausanne, and Geneva having the highest coverage (40–50 per cent). In small, rural municipalities, the average coverage rate is below 15 per cent. Alongside such formal childcare providers, day-care families play an important role mostly in more rural municipalities. An estimate from 2015 shows that Switzerland had approximately 9,000 day-care families looking after around 24,000 children (Bundesamt für Sozialversicherungen 2018).

In the political debate, a particularly contentious issue is to what extent there is unmet demand, i.e. whether there is a lack of childcare places or whether Swiss families do not want to use formal childcare services. Estimating demand is difficult, but a study by Iten et al. (2005) shows that around 47 per cent of all surveyed households indicated unmet demand for affordable childcare in 2004, with the preferred period of care averaging two days a week. In other words, the supply existing at that time covered just 40 per cent of the estimated aggregate demand. As both supply and demand are likely to have increased since then, it seems likely that in Switzerland, demand for affordable childcare still exceeds supply.

This excess demand has also been recognized at the political level. In 2002, the Swiss parliament passed legislation enabling newly established childcare centres to benefit from 'start-up financing' during their first years in operation[4] (Ballestri and Bonoli 2003). This programme was subsequently extended several times and has been very successful: until the year 2000, it has contributed a total of CHF 394 million to the creation of almost 63,000 new childcare places (Bundesamt für Sozialversicherungen 2020). However, an evaluation of this start-up financing, conducted in 2018 (Bundesamt für Sozialversicherungen 2018), shows that approximately 20 per cent of pre-school children are still not receiving the required childcare to an adequate extent.

There are strong indications that the gap between demand and supply is partly caused by the costs of childcare, which are very high in Switzerland compared with other countries (see Figure 39.5), and by a shortage of means-tested subsidized childcare places. A survey of parents in 2017 showed that 43 per cent of parents rely on alternative forms of care (e.g. informal or by grandparents) because childcare is unaffordable (Bundesamt für Sozialversicherungen 2018). The level, type, and availability of means-tested subsidies that parents can claim vary considerably between cantons and especially between municipalities. A 2011 survey (Preisüberwachung 2011) showed that, in most cantons, the unsubsidized full costs of a childcare place amount to CHF 100–130 per day. The substantial differences between minimum and maximum charges are striking. For childcare places that are subsidized to the maximum amount, parents pay between CHF 5 and CHF 40 per day (depending on municipality), i.e. no more than one-third of the full costs. It should be noted, however, that the subsidies are strongly progressive. This means that for middle-income households with several children, whose demand for childcare is particularly price-elastic (Iten et al. 2005), childcare costs absorb a large amount of household income.

The high costs are partly cushioned by tax measures, albeit to a highly varying extent. In 2011, a new federal law came into force,[5] which requires cantons to grant general tax relief for external childcare via a deductibility of effective costs up to an amount of no less than CHF 5,600 per child per year.[6] Since then, almost all cantons have increased the maximum tax deductions for childcare costs. This is an example of the rapid and substantial shift in reconciliation policy in Switzerland, but it also illustrates how measures are targeted towards middle- and upper-income families. Nevertheless, the costs to families remain high, given that CHF 6,000 is roughly equivalent to the average annual full costs of just one day of formal childcare per week.[7] In practice, this means that the high costs act as a powerful brake on the expansion of childcare provision in Switzerland. Various studies (Ecoplan 2008; Prognos 2009) have identified labour costs as by far the most important cost factors, with rent, food, and administrative costs being less significant.

These findings point to the dilemma that characterizes the debate on childcare policy in Switzerland: lower costs for parents and hence a better match between supply and demand are achievable either through more generous public subsidies or through lowering quality standards (the ratio of caregivers to children). As a result, even advocates of public childcare expansion are divided over how this goal should be achieved. Due to this multidimensionality, complex lines of conflict have emerged among advocates and opponents of family policy in Switzerland. In a final step, we will therefore discuss how these diverse conflict lines have occasionally enabled far-reaching reforms of Swiss family policy without, however, leading to a stable, coherent expansion.

4 Actors and reform dynamics

Besides the governments and administrations at the various state levels, the key actors in Swiss family policy are the political parties. In addition, there are specialized stakeholders such as Pro Familia, the Swiss Childcare Association, and the Federal Commission for the Coordination of Family Affairs (COFF) at national level, as well as the OECD at international level, all of which provide expertise in support of family policy and thus contribute to the debate, but whose political influence is limited. Family policy has also become a key policy field for economic interest groups, trade unions, and particularly employers' associations, in the last two decades.

This expansion of relevant actors must be understood in the context of the changing significance of family policy, as briefly discussed at the beginning of this chapter. Häusermann and Kübler (2010) emphasize, in this context, the importance of framing, i.e. how family policy goals and functions are interpreted. Having been a social policy field first and foremost, family policy has increasingly acquired economic policy relevance. In other words, family policy measures can be supported or rejected depending on the interpretative frames that are used: alongside the social and equality policy frames, the labour market policy frame is central here, whereas integration and education policy arguments have played a less significant role in Switzerland's family policy debate so far.

The emphasis on the multidimensionality of family policy is key to understanding the reform momentum in Swiss family policy since the late 1990s.[8] In fact, the positions of the Left in particular (Social Democratic Party of Switzerland (SP) and trade unions) and family organizations have remained largely unchanged since the 1980s (Häusermann and Zollinger 2014). These actors have consistently supported an expansive and progressive social policy programme in relation to maternity insurance, parental leave, reconciliation policies, and child allowances, and in some cases have themselves placed corresponding demands on the political agenda. However, on their own, they were always too weak to push these demands through the political process.

By contrast, what has changed since the 1980s—on a case-specific basis and with variation over time—are the positions of the centre-right parties, i.e. Centre Party (formerly CVP) and FDP, and the employers' associations (Kübler 2007). Both the maternity insurance scheme in 2004 and the introduction of federal subsidies for childcare centres and paternity leave at national level were successful solely because some groups of employers and factions within the centre-right parties supported them. Palier (2005) coined the term 'ambiguous agreements' for these heterogeneous reform coalitions, whose notable feature is that the various actors within the coalition support a reform for entirely different reasons. In other words, they agree solely on specific reforms, but do not necessarily reach a more far-reaching consensus on the purpose and objective of family policy as a whole. The reform capacity and the substantive direction of family policy reforms in Switzerland therefore crucially depend on the positions of centre-right parties and employer organizations, and on whether they are divided among themselves or not. In Swiss politics, we broadly observe two models of coalition-formation, which allow for reform support to extend into the centre-right camp: labour market policy arguments on the one hand, and broader arguments about societal change on the other hand.

From a labour market policy perspective, it should be emphasized that the mobilization of women into the labour market has gained in importance for employers and centre-right parties due to the growing skills shortage. Reforms, which include incentives to increase the female employment rate, increase the retention of women in the labour market during the family phase, and improve employers' ability to attract skilled female workers, thus have a chance of securing political support from the centre-right parties and employers' associations. There are many examples to illustrate this point. Compulsory maternity insurance, for example, was only approved in the referendum once the benefits for stay-at-home mothers had been removed from the proposal. The start-up funding for childcare centres in 2003 and its numerous extensions were also supported by employers' groups and centre-right parties. At the cantonal and municipal level, too, there are numerous examples of these 'social-liberal' reform coalitions. In the city of Lucerne, for example, there was a fundamental policy shift between 2004 and 2014 towards improving childcare provision, funded inter alia by subsidized childcare vouchers (for a case study, see Häusermann and Zollinger 2014). This policy shift was made possible by a heterogeneous reform coalition, pursuing objectives related to gender equality and the social integration of children as well as the increased participation of well-educated women in the labour market.

Arguments referring to broader societal change can also lead to heterogeneous expansive reform coalitions. Recently, this dynamic was observed in the referendum campaign on the introduction of paternity leave at national level. This proposal can be traced back to a popular initiative, which was launched successfully by an alliance of trade unions, women's organizations, men's organizations, and family organizations calling for four weeks of paid paternity leave. The Federal Council and parliament put forward a counterproposal for two weeks of paternity leave, whereupon the original initiative was withdrawn. This moderate version of the proposal was put to a popular vote and was supported not only by the left-wing parties, Greens, and Green Liberals but also by the Centre Party (formerly CVP). The FDP and employers were internally split over the issue. The arguments in favour of the proposal in the centre-right camp were framed mostly in terms of gender equality policy.

This variance of actor configurations in Swiss family policy has two consequences. First, it implies that reform capacity is weak and fragile. The opportunities for shifting alliances strongly depend on the dynamics of the party system at the national, cantonal, or even municipal level in question, the timing of the reform processes relative to the electoral cycles, and the economic conditions. In particular, the ongoing polarization of the Swiss party system contributes to a political environment in which it will probably become more difficult to implement family policy reforms. The second consequence is that the reforms tend to be substantively incoherent, because support coalitions are situational and come at the price of compensations, which can put the reforms themselves at risk. A recent example is the failure of efforts to increase child tax relief in September 2020. A coalition advocating for reconciliation policies was keen to ensure that this tax deduction would be available solely to working parents or be applicable only to formal childcare. Conservative groups, by contrast, extended the deductions to all parents, resulting not only in a fiscally regressive policy proposal but also in a proposal void of its initial labour market significance and function. As a result, it was ultimately opposed by left-wing and some employers' groups and failed. These examples illustrate the instability of political coalitions for modernizing family policy in Switzerland.

5 Outlook: family policy as a litmus test

As in most European countries, family policy in Switzerland has become an increasingly important and controversial policy field since the 1990s. In this chapter, we have shown that financial transfers to families and reconciliation policies (maternity/paternity leave and childcare policy) have undergone far-reaching changes, which were previously unable to secure a majority in the political process. These reforms became possible because family policy was no longer framed solely as social policy but was also defined and recognized as labour market policy and hence as economically relevant. This multiple framing of family policy made it possible for reforms to be supported by heterogeneous coalitions. The success of these reform coalitions is fragile, however, and depends strongly on the specific policy design. Despite these reforms, family policy in Switzerland continues to be a major work in progress in both functional and political terms: the supply of childcare is (still) insufficient to meet demand, and political advances and controversies still characterize this policy field at all three levels of government. Not least, it is noticeable that Swiss family policy has fallen far behind developments in most other continental European countries.

So why is the modernization of family policy progressing more slowly in Switzerland than in other countries? The most important factor is probably the coordination issues associated with decentralized distribution of competences in this policy field. All three levels of government are involved in policy development, which means that policy debates often focus on institutional competences and the allocation of funding rather than on substantive goals. In the literature, this reform-dampening effect of federalism is illustrated by an image of a revolving door, with the various government levels each passing the responsibility to another (Bonoli and Häusermann 2011). The large number of veto points reinforces this revolving door effect as reform opponents have several instruments available with which they can obstruct family policy initiatives at multiple government levels.

However, the decentralized structure cannot explain these reform difficulties alone, as other countries with federal systems, such as Germany, have adopted even more far-reaching reforms. Two additional factors seem to matter as well: supranational reform pressure on the one hand, and party-political polarization on the other hand. First, the European Union has developed a very active policy to encourage the development of childcare infrastructure, such as setting targets for its member states—e.g. the specific objective of providing childcare for at least 33 per cent of children under three years of age (European Council 2008). This impetus has generated reform pressure at the level of member states that was not present in the same way in Switzerland (Ahrens et al. 2010). Even though the OECD recommendations for Switzerland regularly highlight the patchy coverage with childcare services, this reform pressure is not comparable with the concrete policy goals set by the EU for its member states. Second, the political polarization of the Swiss party system towards an increasingly powerful radical right faction acts as a brake on the expansion of family policy by making it more difficult to forge heterogeneous coalitions between progressive and market-liberal forces.

Given the clear and unequivocal social and economic pressure in favour of family policy expansion on the one hand, and the genuinely political and institutional obstacles that go against such an expansion on the other hand, the adaptation of family policy to changing social and economic needs can be regarded as the litmus test of the Swiss welfare state's capacity to reform. The political balance of power and the experiences of the past three decades suggest that the expansion of formal childcare provision is likely to have good chances of success, at least in the (growing) urban centres and specifically for educated middle-income families. However, this is likely to further reinforce the strongly stratifying effect of these policies. Far-reaching reforms, such as those observed in most other European countries, including generous parental leave, parents' right to work part-time, and the right to a childcare place for pre-school children, are unlikely to garner a broad political majority.

Notes

1. In a broader sense, it can also include legislation that defines the legal framework for the family (Valarino 2020). This article focuses on the social policy dimension of family policy.
2. Federal Act of 25 September 1952 on Compensation for Service Providers' Earnings Loss and Maternity (SR 834.1), version: 22 March 2005.
3. The new Federal Act of 24 March 2006 on Family Allowances (SR 836.2) was a counter-proposal to a popular initiative by the Christian National Trade Union Confederation of Switzerland, which called for child allowances of CHF 450/month.
4. Federal Act of 4 October 2002 on Financial Support for Childcare (SR 861).
5. Federal Act of 25 September 2009 on Tax Relief for Families with Children (SR 642.11).
6. Tax deductions may be claimed for children who have not yet reached the age of fourteen and only if the costs are directly and causally related to the parents' employment, training, or incapacity.
7. This figure is derived from the full costs calculated by Prognos (2009, 11) of around CHF 120 per child per day in the cantons of Zurich and Vaud.
8. The following federal-level reforms should be mentioned in particular: the introduction of maternity insurance in 2005, the harmonization of child allowances in 2007,

the introduction of start-up funding for childcare providers in 2003 (extended several times), the Federal Act on Tax Relief for Families with Children in 2009, the Intercantonal Agreement on Harmonization of Compulsory Education (Harmos) 2009, and the introduction of two weeks of paid paternity leave in 2022.

References

Abrassart, Aurélien, and Giuliano Bonoli. 2015. 'Availability, Cost or Culture? Obstacles to Childcare Services for Low-Income Families'. *Journal of Social Policy* 44 (4): pp. 787–806.

Ahrens, Regina, Sonja Blum, and Irene Gerlach. 2010. 'Introduction: Family Policies in the German-Speaking Countries – Reforms and Explanations'. *German Policy Studies* 6 (3): pp. 1–12.

Armingeon, Klaus. 2001. 'Institutionalising the Swiss Welfare State'. *West European Politics* 24 (2): pp. 145–168.

Ballestri, Yuri, and Giuliano Bonoli. 2003. 'L'Etat social suisse face aux nouveaux risques sociaux: Genèse et déterminants de l'adoption du programme d'impulsion pour les structures de garde pour enfants en bas âge'. *Revue Suisse de Science Politique* 9 (3): pp. 35–58.

Beramendi, Pablo, Silja Häusermann, Herbert Kitschelt, and Hanspeter Kriesi. 2015. *The Politics of Advanced Capitalism*. Cambridge: Cambridge University Press.

Bonoli, Giuliano. 2005. 'The Politics of the New Social Policies: Providing Coverage Against New Social Risks in Mature Welfare States'. *Policy & Politics* 33 (3): pp. 431–449.

Bonoli, Giuliano, and Silja Häusermann. 2011. 'The Swiss Welfare State Between Retrenchment and Expansion'. In *Switzerland in Europe: Continuity and Change in the Swiss Political Economy*, edited by Christine Trampusch, and André Mach, pp. 186–204. London: Routledge.

Bradshaw, Jonathan, and Naomi Finch. 2010. 'Family Benefits and Services'. In *The Oxford Handbook of the Welfare State*, edited by Francis G. Castles, Stephan Leibfried, Jane Lewis, Herbert Obinger, and Christopher Pierson, pp. 462–478. Oxford: Oxford University Press.

Bundesamt für Sozialversicherungen. 2018. *Evaluation Anstossfinanzierung: Entspricht das bestehende Angebot an familienergänzender Kinderbetreuung der Nachfrage?*. https://www.bsv.admin.ch/bsv/de/home/finanzhilfen/kinderbetreuung/publikationen/evaluationen.html (accessed June 21st 2023).

Bundesamt für Sozialversicherungen. 2020. *Finanzhilfen für die Schaffung von familienergänzenden Betreuungsplätzen für Kinder: Bilanz nach 17 Jahren*. https://www.bsv.admin.ch/bsv/de/home/finanzhilfen/kinderbetreuung.html (accessed June 21st 2023).

Bundesamt für Sozialversicherungen. 2022. *Arten und Ansätze der Familienzulagen (Archiv)*. https://www.bsv.admin.ch/bsv/de/home/sozialversicherungen/famz/grundlagen-und-gesetze/ansaetze.html (accessed June 21st 2023).

Bürgisser, Reto. 2022. 'The Partisan Politics of Family and Labor Market Reforms in Southern Europe'. In *The World Politics of Social Investment Volume II*, edited by Julian Garritzmann, Silja Häusermann, and Bruno Palier, pp. 86–107. Oxford: Oxford University Press.

Dafflon, Bernard, and Roberto Abatti. 2003. *La Politique Familiale en Suisse, Enjeux et Défis*. Lausanne: Réalités sociales.

Ecoplan. 2008. *Kosten Kindertagesstätten. Erhebung der effektiven Kosten der ASIV-Kindertagesstätten und Vergleich mit den Normkosten*. Bern: Sozialamt des Kantons Bern.

Esping-Andersen, Gøsta. 1999. *The Social Foundations of Post-industrial Economies*. Oxford: Oxford University Press.

Esping-Andersen, Gøsta. 2015. 'The Return of the Family'. In *The Politics of Advanced Capitalism*, edited by Pablo Beramendi, Silja Häusermann, Herbert Kitschelt, and Hanspeter Kriesi, pp. 157–177. Cambridge: Cambridge University Press.

European Council. 2000. *Presidency Conclusions. Lisbon European Council. 23 and 24 March 2000*. http://www.consilium.europa.eu/uedocs/cms_data/docs/pressdata/en/ec/00100-r1.en0.htm (accessed June 21st 2023).

European Council. 2008. *Implementation of the Barcelona Objectives Concerning Childcare Facilities for Pre-School-Age Children*. https://data.consilium.europa.eu/doc/document/ST-13978-2008-INIT/en/pdf (accessed June 21st 2023).

European Council. 2017. *The European Pillar of Social Rights*. https://op.europa.eu/s/0LMZ (accessed June 21st 2023).

Eurostat. 2020. *EU-SILC: Durchschnittliche wöchentliche Nutzung formaler Kinderbetreuung nach Altersklassen – Kinder mit und ohne Nutzung formaler Kinderbetreuung*. https://data.europa.eu/data/datasets/jl5ritnpovji7d7z92gtg?locale=de (accessed June 21st 2023).

Garritzmann, Julian, Silja Häusermann, and Bruno Palier. 2022. *The World Politics of Social Investment I: Welfare States in the Knowledge Economy*. Oxford: Oxford University Press.

Häusermann, Silja. 2006. 'Changing Coalitions in Social Policy Reforms: The Politics of New Social Needs and Demands'. *Journal of European Social Policy* 16 (1): pp. 5–21.

Häusermann, Silja. 2010. 'Reform Opportunities in a Bismarckian Latecomer: Restructuring the Swiss Welfare State'. In *A Long Goodbye to Bismarck*, edited by Bruno Palier, pp. 207–231. Amsterdam: Amsterdam University Press.

Häusermann, Silja. 2018. 'The Multidimensional Politics of Social Investment in Conservative Welfare Regimes: Family Policy Reform Between Social Transfers and Social Investment'. *Journal of European Public Policy* 25 (6): pp. 862–877.

Häusermann, Silja, and Daniel Kübler. 2010. 'Policy Frames and Coalition Dynamics in the Recent Reforms of Swiss Family Policy'. *German Policy Studies* 6 (3): pp. 163–194.

Häusermann, Silja, and Christine Zollinger. 2014. 'Familienpolitik'. In *Handbuch der Schweizer Politik, 6. Ausgabe*, edited by Peter Knoepfel, Yannis Papadopoulos, Pascal Sciarini, Adrian Vatter, and Silja Häusermann, pp. 911–934. Zürich: NZZ Libro.

Hemerijck, Anton. 2013. *Changing Welfare States*. Oxford: Oxford University Press.

Iten, Rolf, Susanne Stern, Sarah Menegale, Massimo Filippini, Silvia Banfi, Daniela Pioro, Mehdi Farsi, Sergio Tassinari, and Rita Schrottmann. 2005. *Familienergänzende Kinderbetreuung in der Schweiz: Aktuelle und zukünftige Nachfragepotenziale*. Zürich: Infras. https://edudoc.ch/record/24070/usage?ln=en (accessed 21 June 2023).

Kübler, Daniel. 2007. 'Understanding the Recent Expansion of Swiss Family Policy: An Idea-Centered Approach'. *Journal of Social Policy* 36 (2): pp. 217–237.

Leitner, Sigrid. 2019. 'Familienpolitik'. In *Handbuch Sozialpolitik*, edited by Herbert Obinger, and Manfred Schmidt, pp. 739–760. Wiesbaden: Springer VS.

Lewis, Jane. 1992. 'Gender and the Development of Welfare Regimes'. *Journal of European Social Policy* 2 (3): pp. 159–173.

Morel, Nathalie, Bruno Palier, and Joakim Palme. 2012. *Towards a Social Investment Welfare State? Ideas, Policies, and Challenges*. Bristol: Policy Press.

OECD. 2004. *Babies and Bosses – Reconciling Work and Family Life. New Zealand, Portugal and Switzerland*. Paris: OECD.

OECD. 2007. *Babies and Bosses – Reconciling Work and Family Life: A Synthesis of Findings for OECD Countries*. Paris: OECD.

OECD. 2011. *Doing Better for Families*. Paris: OECD.

OECD. 2020. *OECD Social Expenditure Database.* https://stats.oecd.org/Index.aspx?DataSetCode=SOCX_AGG (accessed June 21st 2023).

OECD. 2021. *OECD Family Database.* http://www.oecd.org/els/family/database.htm (accessed June 21st 2023).

Palier, Bruno. 2005. 'Ambiguous Agreement, Cumulative Change: French Social Policy in the 1990s'. In *Beyond Continuity. Institutional Change in Advanced Political Economies*, edited by Wolfgang Streeck, and Kathleen Thelen, pp. 127–144. Oxford: Oxford University Press.

Preisüberwachung. 2011. *Maximaltarife in Kindertagesstätten.* https://www.preisueberwacher.admin.ch/pue/de/home/dokumentation/publikationen/studien---analysen/2011.html (accessed June 21st 2023).

Prognos. 2009. *Analyse und Vergleich der Kosten von Krippenplätzen anhand einer Vollkostenrechnung: Schlussbericht.* https://edudoc.ch/record/33083?ln=de (accessed June 21st 2023).

Stadelmann-Steffen, Isabelle. 2007. *Policies, Frauen und der Arbeitsmarkt. Die Frauenerwerbstätigkeit in der Schweiz im internationalen und interkantonalen Vergleich.* Wien: LIT.

Valarino, Isabel. 2020. 'Familienpolitik'. In *Wörterbuch der Schweizer Sozialpolitik*, edited by Jean-Michel Bonvin, Pascal Maeder, Carlo Knöpfel, Valérie Hugentobler, and Ueli Tecklenburg, pp. 162–164. Zürich: Seismo.

CHAPTER 40

GENDER AND EQUALITY+ POLICY

ISABELLE ENGELI

1 Incremental steps towards equality+ in Switzerland

Switzerland is widely known for being a laggard in granting women the right to vote only in 1971 at the federal level. Since then, Switzerland has made progress towards gender+ equality through the introduction of the principle of gender equality in the federal constitution in 1981 and the Gender Equality Act in 1996. The trajectory of the Swiss gender equality policy is embedded in global action towards equality, which was enshrined in United Nations conferences on women (notably the 1995 Beijing Conference), the 1979 Convention on the Elimination of All Forms of Discrimination Against Women (CEDAW), and the growing emphasis on gender mainstreaming. While Switzerland only granted access to same-sex marriage in 2022, it has already begun to catch up through criminalizing homophobia in 2020, opening up assisted reproductive technology (ART) to same-sex couples, and allowing the changing of gender and legal name in legal documents by self-declaration.

This chapter first traces the trajectory of the gender+ equality policy and the institutional advocacy network towards equality, and then reviews the gains and limitations of the promotion of equality across the three core policy domains of education, the family, and the labour market. Pivotal steps have been taken to move the equality agenda forward under the oversight of the CEDAW. Switzerland has nevertheless shied away from adopting a far-reaching agenda regarding gender+ equality. Instead, the Swiss approach is best characterized as a politics of small steps that has been circumscribed by federalism and direct democracy. More recently, the influence of the far right has also left its conservative footprint on the equality+ agenda.

As a result, Swiss equality policy remains far from having achieved real equality. The institutional family model remains predominantly heteronormative, pink ghettos persist in education and in the labour market, and pay discrimination remains. There is still a long road ahead towards the achievement of equality for the LBGT+ community. In the absence of a comprehensive legal framework, discrimination and homophobic and transphobic violence has risen to record levels (Eisner and Hässler 2021). These limitations raise scepticism about the capability of the existing legal framework to achieve substantive equality and transformative change of gender relations.

2 THE FEDERAL LEGAL FRAMEWORK FOR GENDER EQUALITY

2.1 The 1981 federal provision for equal rights before the law

The addition in 1981 of the provision for equal rights between men and women to the federal constitution has been instrumental in launching the promotion of gender equality in Switzerland. Article 8 paragraph 3 of the Swiss constitution was approved by 60 per cent of the voters in a referendum on 14 June 1981. It established a broad federal provision for equality before the law and its third paragraph provides that men and women have equal rights. As such, it has set the federal mandate to ensure equality in the law and in practice—most specifically in the family, in education, and in the workplace—and it enshrines the right to equal pay for work of equal value. Indeed, the 1981 amendment has laid the foundation for the institutional promotion of equality by establishing two actionable principles. First, it prohibits discrimination based on sex. Second, it makes a critical distinction between formal equality and substantive equality. Formal equality aims at guaranteeing equal treatment of men and women before the law, whereas substantive equality aims at putting equality into practice, notably in providing equal opportunities in education and professional career trajectories. This key turning point was confirmed when the Federal Supreme Court of Switzerland declared unconstitutional differential treatment of individuals according to their sex (CFQF 1998).

2.2 The 1996 Gender Equality Act

While the 1986 equality provision marked the beginning of the legislative overhaul to eliminate sex-based discrimination in the law, severe inequalities in the workplace remained. Cases of wage discrimination, primarily from the public sector, were regularly brought before the courts. This heightened attention to persisting workplace inequalities incited the federal government to further build the legal framework for equality through the Federal Gender Equality Act (GEA) that specifically targets the promotion of equality in the workplace. The GEA was a major turning point for Swiss equality policy. From the focus on eliminating legal discrimination that characterized the constitutional amendment, the goal shifted to policies aimed at promoting equality on the ground.

The GEA bans all sex-based discrimination in the workplace and its policy instruments are equally applicable to the public and private sectors. Among the main innovations, the act bans sexual harassment and extends the legal provision for equal pay to work of equal value, even if the job title is different. The act has also facilitated litigation. The burden of proof has been shifted to the employers who have to demonstrate that they had not discriminated against the claimant, while the latter only needs to demonstrate that the discrimination was likely. In addition, the act has instigated no legal cost to the claimant for bringing an action before the courts and has opened the possibility of collective action suits to reduce the burden on individual plaintiffs.

2.3 The evolution of Swiss gender equality policy since 1996

2.3.1 *The 1997 ratification of CEDAW*

The introduction of the GEA allowed Switzerland to eventually ratify the CEDAW in 1997. Its ratification constitutes a cornerstone in the development of Swiss equality policy because of its constraining character and its global visibility. In addition, the CEDAW mandates signatory states to submit regular reports detailing advances across areas that are not included in the Swiss legal framework per se, such as political life and health. This reporting requirement clearly propelled the federal government to include equality between women and men in its legislative objectives from 1999 onwards and to launch the federal strategy for equality in 2021. The ratification of the CEDAW, in combination with the upsurge of feminist activism and, notably, the Women's Strike of 14 June 2019, turned up the pressure on institutions and was instrumental in maintaining equality on the political agenda. In 2018, Switzerland also ratified the Istanbul Convention on the prevention of and fight against violence towards women and domestic violence. This convention also contained a similar mechanism to monitor and report on the implementation.

2.3.2 *The 1999 adoption of gender mainstreaming*

Adopted in 1999, the 'Equality between Women and Men' action plan was the first federal gender equality action plan of its kind. One of the main features is the adoption of the gender mainstreaming approach across the whole range of policies and actions undertaken by public authorities. Gender mainstreaming is defined as the transversal and systematic analysis of the gender impact in all legislative, administrative, and judicial decisions. The 1999 action plan underlines the governmental commitment to make tangible progress towards the realization of substantive equality by recommending fifteen priorities broken down into more than 300 measures across twelve policy areas. Notwithstanding the ambition of the stated goals, the plan has suffered from the obvious lack of compulsory mandates. For example, although the government has maintained its engagement towards gender mainstreaming by promoting policy impact analyses, it has always refused to adopt gender budgeting, which applies gender mainstreaming to budgetary decisions (Federal Council 2018, 2020).

2.3.3 The 2020 revision of the Gender Equality Act

The persistence of wage inequalities in both the public and private sectors sheds light on the limitations of the GEA in its 1996 version. The voluntary approach that heavily relied on companies had not produced the expected results. The GEA was indeed poorly understood and infrequently used, and pressure mounted towards a reform (Stutz et al. 2005; Sattiva Spring 2019). Adopted by parliament in 2018, the revision of the GEA came into effect in 2020. The revision only partially addressed the concerns of equality advocates and the parliamentary left. It is mainly a compromise in response to the strong opposition from a large share of the right-wing parties. Even if modest, it nonetheless represents a significant change in the scale of policy action. Whereas the 1996 version of the GEA placed the burden on women to fight against wage discrimination, the 2020 revision placed the emphasis on the role of employers—whether public or private sector—in the promotion of wage equality in the labour market.

Companies of more than 100 employees must carry out a wage equality analysis every four years. This analysis must be verified by an independent third party and the results communicated to the employees. This wage disparity audit must be included in shareholder reporting for publicly listed companies or publicly released for the public sector. To assist employers in their gender equality duty, the Federal Office for Gender Equality (FOGE) has developed tools for performing the wage analysis (Federal Council 2020). However, the GEA has remained toothless regarding the absence of sanctions. The revised GEA of 2020 still rests upon the emulation of good practices among employers and the provision of information to employees (Sattiva Spring 2019). Limited to a term of twelve years, the act will be evaluated after nine.

2.3.4 The 2020 criminalization of homophobia

The transformation of equality between men and women into one that is inclusive of gender identity and sexual orientation is far from being achieved in Switzerland. LGBT+ mobilization against discrimination and persecution took off in the 1970s (Walser 2013) before being redirected in the fight against AIDS in cooperation with the authorities (Roca i Escoda 2019).

Almost eighty years after the decriminalization of homosexuality in Switzerland in the Swiss Criminal Code of 1942, there is still no legal framework driving the promotion of LBGT+ equality and systematically tackling sexual orientation- and gender identity-based discrimination. Neither sexual orientation nor gender identity figure explicitly in the constitutional provision on equality. If legal doctrine has established that sexual orientation is included in the lifestyle criteria in article 8, paragraph 2 of the constitution, it rests on a ban on discrimination rather than on a proactive mandate to achieve substantive equality (Kälin and Locher 2015). Neither is there a federal act against LGBT+ discrimination. Part of legal doctrine had shown itself to be favourable to the inclusion of discrimination based on sexual orientation within the scope of the GEA. However, in 2019, the Federal Supreme Court ruled in favour of the restrictive notion of 'sex' as being entirely biological, despite the counter-position of the FOGE (Sattiva Spring 2019).

The main institutional innovation in the fight against discrimination based on sexual orientation is the extension of the provision against racial discrimination in the Swiss Criminal Code to include homophobia, which came into effect in 2020 (article 226bis). This amendment marks an important step in filling in the institutional void regarding discrimination based on sexual orientation. However, LGBT+ equality is still far from receiving a similar level of political attention as for sex-based equality. Indeed, the latest report of the European Commission Against Racism and Intolerance bears a harsh judgement against the lack of concrete engagement by the federal government (ECRI 2020). The criminalization of homophobia does not represent a proactive policy against discrimination and towards the realization of equality of opportunities. There is neither a comprehensive legal framework nor an action plan directed at achieving LGBT+ equality. Nor has any specific institutional structure been put into place.

The absence of a comprehensive framework raises several challenges in the fight on the ground at school and in the workplace against discrimination based on sexual orientation and/or gender identity. Furthermore, trans* and intersex* people remain without legal protection despite the repeated demands of the LBGT+ movement. Finally, violence towards the LBGT+ community is not fully monitored and recorded, despite the significant number of homophobic, trans*phobic, and intersex*phobic acts (LGBT+ Helpline 2018). Cantons such as Fribourg and cities such as Zurich have played a leading role with the creation of a census of hate acts towards the LGBT+ community (ILGA-Europe 2021).

Even if the criminalization of homophobia was just a first step, it was nevertheless a step that was complicated to bring to institutional fruition. Switzerland was on the radar of the international community, notably the European Commission Against Racism and Intolerance, for its lack of concrete action against discrimination linked to sexual orientation and gender identity (ECRI 2014). In 2013, the parliamentary initiative 'Fighting against Discriminations based on Sexual Orientation' launched the parliamentary process to extend the criminal provision against racial discrimination to include homophobia. Submitted by the Social Democrat Mathias Reynard, the initiative was favourably received by the Legal Affairs Committee of the National Council, the lower chamber of the Swiss parliament. Under the impetus from the Social Democrats and the Greens, discrimination against gender identity was added in the draft provision. This important addition received large support during the public consultation process, notably from the Swiss cantons (except for Schwyz). The Swiss Conference of Gender Equality Delegates (CSDE) had argued in favour of the integration of additional sex-based criteria beyond gender identity but was not heeded.

Despite this broad support during the public consultation, the concept of gender identity was viewed by the federal government, the Swiss People's Party, and part of the Liberals as being underdefined and was even painted among its fiercest opponents as 'an atomic bomb in the legal arsenal'.[1] To reach a parliamentary compromise, the extension of criminal provision to include discrimination against gender identity was withdrawn in the parliamentary process after its rejection by the Council of States. Alas, this compromise was insufficient to prevent the successful launch of the referendum by a minor Christian party, the Federal Democratic Union of Switzerland (EDU). The referendum entitled 'No to Censorship' was supported by a large part of the Swiss People's Party. The umbrella associations Pink Cross and Lesbenorganisation der Schweiz (LOS) strategized a referendum campaign based on data and real cases of discrimination. The referendum committee for its part adopted a rhetoric of censorship, freedom of speech, and the free market, themes which are often found in anti-LGBT+ campaigns in Europe and North America. Despite the heated campaign, the Swiss people cast a clear choice in the ballot; the amendment to the Swiss Criminal Code was approved by 63.1 per cent of the electorate on 9 February 2020.

3 THE ADVOCACY NETWORK TOWARDS EQUALITY

The promotion of equality has undergone a growing diversification in its goals and policy instruments. At first focused on the establishment of formal equality, the legal framework has progressively been upscaled to a more transversal approach that covers all areas of policy action. However, a striking variation remains across the range of instruments and the actors in charge of the implementation. If the network of institutional actors and structures in favour of equality between women and men is relatively well developed, there is no structure at the federal level specifically dedicated to LGBT+ rights and the achievement of equality.

3.1 Institutional advocacy for equality between women and men

At the federal level, state feminism is embedded through two main actors, the Federal Commission for Women's Issues (FCWI) and the FOGE, which have played a critical role in the promotion of equality since the end of the 1970s. Appointed in 1976 by the Swiss Federal Government, the FCWI is an extra-parliamentary permanent commission of twenty members representing women's organizations, trade unions, umbrella organizations of employers, and experts. Poorly funded, the FCWI is an advisory body to the Swiss state and publishes positions and recommendations concerning equality. The FCWI has often been a vocal critic of actions of the Swiss Confederation and regularly positions itself in favour of a more ambitious and proactive equality policy, notably in the areas of family law and labour law as well as women in politics. Due to its representativeness, FCWI is instrumental in fostering cooperation among the different stakeholders and securing their buy-in to take the promotion of equality forward. The FOGE's mandate is set out in the constitutional provision for gender equality and the GEA. Sitting within the Federal Department of Home Affairs, the FOGE provides pivotal support for the implementation of the GEA. As such, it has access to considerably more financial and administrative resources than the FCWI, even if it remains vulnerable to budget cuts, such as those implemented in 2014 (Federal Council 2016). Its main activities include supporting the drafting of legislation and delivering opinions, leading information campaigns on equality, promoting coordination across stakeholders, and providing advice to the federal administration and private sector alike. The FOGE has been instrumental in the promotion of the equal pay provision through opinions to the Federal Supreme Court, financial support for gender equality projects, and knowledge transfer activities towards the employers.

The state level is pivotal in the implementation of the federal equality framework in Switzerland. The CSDE brings together all the services and offices of the Confederation, the cantons, and municipalities that are tasked with the promotion of equality. The CSDE supports and coordinates activities at the national level and leads equality information campaigns, notably in the area of domestic violence and women's access to education fields that have been traditionally male-dominated.

The canton of Jura was the first canton to open a cantonal office for gender equality in 1979. It was rapidly followed by several other leading cantons, including Bern, Zurich, Basel-City, and Geneva. By 2020, fifteen cantons and five large cities had an administrative structure dedicated to equality (Bern, Geneva, Lausanne, Zurich, and Winterthur with a Diversity Unit). The cantonal gender equality offices differ as much in their financial resources (often quite modest) as in their mandate. Political pressure is sometimes exerted, and the offices often have to make the business case for their added value, as was recently the case for the office of the canton of Bern and the office of the city of Zurich. The cantonal office in Obwalden was even recently closed and that of Aargau integrated into services for the elderly (Federal Council 2020). In Obwalden, the justification given for the closure was the unsubstantiated assertion that 'The Council of State and the cantonal administration implement equality in their everyday activities' (Federal Council 2020, 10). Despite the unfavourable environment, some cantonal offices show leadership in pioneering initiatives that go far beyond the federal mandate. For example, the cantons of Bern and Basel-City have launched pilot projects on gender controlling that strengthened the evaluation of the implementation of equality policy. Others have launched cantonal action plans for equality. With the revision of the GEA, the offices of the cantons of Bern and Vaud have seen their mandate extended to the oversight of equal pay auditing in public procurement (Federal Council 2020) and the Valais office was tasked with responsibility for the coordination of prevention against domestic violence (Federal Council 2020). This said, other offices, for example the offices of Fribourg, Neuchâtel, and Valais, still focus on more traditional sectors such as family policy.

3.2 The absence of institutional advocacy towards LGBT+ equality

In sharp contrast to the institutional advocacy for equality between men and women, there is no structure at the federal level in charge of the promotion of LGBT+ equality. Despite repeated demands from LGBT+ movements and strong encouragement from the ECRI, the Swiss Government (Federal Council 2016, 18) has until now refused to consider the creation of a dedicated office, arguing notably that 'the financial situation hardly encourages the creation of new institutions'. Even if the FOGE provides financial support to LGBT+ projects—for example, the Trans-Fair project—its formal mandate remains delimited by the GEA and has not been extended to LGBT+ discrimination. If the FOGE has demonstrated commitment to LGBT+ issues, it has not made them yet a priority as adequate supplemental resources are still lacking (Grohsmann et al. 2014). Indeed, LGBT+ issues do not figure in the prioritization list for financial aid for the period 2020–2024 (Federal Council 2020).

The cantonal gender equality offices tend not to anchor LGBT+ issues at the core of their mandate either, or, alternatively, lack the resources to fully embrace the LGBT+ equality agenda (Grohsmann et al. 2014). Among the pioneers is the office of the canton of Geneva, which has adopted an inclusive definition of equality that brings together biological sex, sexual orientation, and gender identity. One of its three consultative commissions is dedicated to themes related to sexual orientation and sexual identity. Initiatives have been launched across the Swiss main cities (ILGA-Europe 2021; ECRI 2020): Zurich has embedded measures towards trans*equality into its equality action plan, Bienne has targeted measures against trans*phobia, while Berne and Geneva have both opened a post in charge of LGBT+ issues. The Swiss Centre for Expertise in Human Rights was put in place in 2011 through a university network (mandated by the Confederation) to support the realization of human rights. It has produced very helpful studies on LGBT+ rights.

The bulk of the promotion of LGBT+ rights is still led forcefully by LGBT+ organizations such as LOS—the umbrella organization for lesbian, bisexual, and queer women*, Pink Cross—the national umbrella organization of gay and bisexual men*, Transgender Network Switzerland, and InterAction—the umbrella organization for intersex* people. Platforms for action also make a significant contribution to the promotion of LGBT+ equality, such as the LGBT+ Helpline that was launched in 2016 to gather reporting of homophobic and trans*phobic violence in response to the repeated refusal of the Swiss authorities to record such data. In response to this institutional inertia, LGBT+ associations seem to have more recently identified a new ally in the form of the business community. Corporate charters and an LGBTI label to endorse companies that promote LGBT+ rights have been developed to incentivize corporate initiatives towards equality+. To give a few examples only, the airline Swiss at Zurich Airport and the Swiss lift manufacturer Schindler have obtained the endorsement while the two leading national chains of supermarkets have adopted a charter that explicitly forbid discrimination based on sexual orientation. Large companies such as Credit Suisse and the major telecommunications provider Swisscom have supported projects such as Trans-Fair through financial resources and workforce.

4 Unequal progress towards equality across education, the family, and the workplace

The promotion of equality in Switzerland has accelerated since attention shifted from removing the legal barriers to equality to the achievement of equality on the ground. If most forms of legal discrimination have been eliminated, real equality remains a long-term goal. A general assessment of the implementation of the promotion of equality in Switzerland is yet to be done and exceeds the scope of this chapter. The few studies done to date align on the marked disparities in implementation largely due to the Swiss model of federalism based on the delegation of the execution to the cantons, as well as the limited resources at the federal and cantonal level devoted to the promotion of equality. The second half of this chapter comes back to the main progress, pitfalls, and challenges for Swiss policy action towards equality in the policy domains highlighted in the GEA: education, the family, and the workplace.

4.1 Education

Federal policy action towards equality in education has mainly focused on incentives towards vocational and continuous training, as well as programmes to support women's access to the university professoriate.

4.1.1 *The gendered educational pathway*

Equality has just about been achieved with regards to access to higher education if generational effects and the integration of health-related training into higher education are considered. In 1980, men were three times more likely than women to gain a higher education level qualification. This trend has been inverted: in 2018, 53.7 per cent of women between the ages of twenty-five and thirty-four held a higher education qualification compared to 48.8 per cent of men (FSO 2019). However, women's access to entry-level vocational training still lags. This educational segregation was already apparent forty years ago, and only seems to be disappearing very slowly. Despite the different projects supported by the Swiss Confederation to increase the participation of women in STEM subjects, gender segregation in the choice of higher education programmes has still not been eliminated. Segregation in education is in turn reproduced in the workplace

(FSO 2019). Men have remained overrepresented in the sectors of architecture, construction, engineering, and Information Technology (IT). If the feminization of male bastions in education is progressing, the masculinization of female bastions has ground to a halt. There is only a handful of exceptions where there the demographic makeup up of the student body is gender balanced (Conseil federal 2020). Women are even more predominant in unskilled occupations than before. This one-way trend is reflective of an educational strategy that has largely focused on the promotion of women in traditional male-dominated subjects (e.g. STEM) but which has barely challenged gender stereotypes related to subjects that have seen an historical concentration of women.

4.1.2 *The slow feminization of university professors*

The composition of the education workforce is strongly gendered. Women have been historically concentrated in nursery and primary teaching, and have largely remained underrepresented in higher education, especially at the professorial level. The Confederation and swissuniversities—the umbrella organization of Swiss universities—have launched equality programmes to catalyse the feminization of the professoriate. The Swiss National Science Foundation has also developed programmes to promote women in research, and, more recently, the PRIMA programme aimed at the professoriate. Even if there have been an ever-growing number of initiatives, equality in university leadership remains a long way off. Women in upper academic management positions are still the exception in the Swiss university landscape, which remains characterized by a leaky pipeline that sees the presence of women progressively diminish up the academic ladders.

4.1.3 *Homophobia and trans*phobia at school*

There is no comprehensive evaluation of the situation of young LGBT+ people in the education environment across Switzerland although this community is at high risk of social exclusion, of mockery and rejection, of discrimination and sexual violence, and of psychological harassment, which can lead to severe well-being issues and to a higher-than-average suicide rate, particularly during the coming-out stage (Häusermann 2014). Support programmes are generally only offered by LGBT+ associations and only a few cantons have put in place action plans against discrimination in schools, like the programme for the Prevention of the Rejection of Sexual Minorities in the canton of Valais. If the promotion of Gender Studies has been supported in Swiss universities and more recently in primary and secondary education, school programmes still rarely make mention of homosexuality and of the LGBT+ movement other than in sex education classes.

4.2 The family

While the elimination of legal discrimination towards women has been effective, the realization of equality within the family has been much less so. Policy to support working women has remained limited. Marriage has continued to feature as the centrepiece of family law, which has in turn contributed to perpetuating the unequal treatment of unmarried couples and, until July 2022, same-sex couples (Engeli and Roca 2012). Approved by popular referendum in September 2021, the opening up of marriage marks a giant step in the legal recognition of same-sex couples in Switzerland.

4.2.1 *The heteronormativity in marriage, divorce, and civil status*

The overhaul of family law began in the 1970s. From 1978 onwards, women have had parental authority over their children on equal footing with men. The revision of the legal framework for marriage in 1988 eliminated the predominant rights of the husband. Since this reform, married women can henceforth sign contracts, open a bank account, or take a job without the agreement of their spouse. The reform also introduced the notion of community property within marriage. A revision of the legal framework took place in 2000 with the introduction of divorce by mutual agreement and the equal division of pension accumulations between the two members of the couple. These revisions have had controversial financial effects on women. The fact that the courts have started to grant shorter and lower child support payments has brought a risk of poverty for divorced women (Freivogel 2007). In practice, the division of pension benefits has also proved to remain highly unequal in most divorces (Baumann and Lauterburg 2007). This was only partially rectified by amendment in 2017 and the gap between men's and women's retirement pensions still persists.

With regard to civil status, the revision of the Civil Code in 2013 has eliminated a significant direct discrimination in family law; each member of a family can now retain their surname and their cantonal and communal right of residence, with children able to take the unmarried name of either of the partners. Finally, in 2020, the Swiss parliament approved a revision to the Civil Code allowing legal gender recognition and the change of first name on the civil registry based on self-determination (article 30b), which entered into force in 2022. Prior to that, requirements for sterilization, sexual organ reconstruction, and medical examination were only officially abandoned in 2012. Despite demands from LGBT+ associations that were supported by the left-wing parties, the Swiss parliament decided against including other categories than male and female in the 2020 revision. It also refused to replace the term 'sex' with 'gender' in response to the strong opposition of the Swiss People's Party.

4.2.2 *Unpaid care work*

The realization of equality within the family exhibits major limitations. The reconciliation between private and professional life still largely depends on the resources of individual families. Care responsibilities remain overwhelmingly with women, even though the gender gap for unpaid care work is narrowing (FSO 2019). The stereotype of the 'negligent working mother' is still present in Switzerland, even if it is steadily declining: 26.9 per cent of women and 37 per cent of men still consider that a pre-school child suffers if the mother works (FSO 2019).

This imbalance in care responsibilities was not, for a long time, counterbalanced by proactive policy to transform gender roles within the family. To the contrary, the institutional architecture around the family has remained largely based on the heteronormative model of the traditional family, even if there has been some improvement. Maternity leave, only introduced in 2002, prominently features among the most restrictive provisions in Europe. The paternity leave that was introduced in 2021 is hardly likely to upset the apple cart, in view of its short duration (two weeks). Parental leave with a fixed number of non-transferable weeks is markedly absent. Parental leave to look after a sick or injured child, which came into effect in 2021, is a step in the right direction but the duration of the leave is not particularly generous in comparison to other countries. Moreover, it is likely that women will have a higher take-up rate than men.

4.2.3 *The legal recognition of same-sex couples and rainbow families*

The legal recognition of same-sex couples came late onto the political agenda and was principally approached through the lens of AIDS policy (Roca i Escoda 2019). The petition 'the same rights for same-sex couples' was filed by the umbrella gay and lesbian organizations in 1995. It triggered a backlash steered by the evangelical conservative right and the filing of a second petition to protect the traditional family model.

During the public consultation on the legal status of same-sex couples in 1999, a majority of cantons and political parties showed support for a legislative change, except for Thurgau and the Christian fundamentalist party EDU. Things became more complicated with regards to the exact form that legal recognition should take. The Swiss People's Party supported limited change to the law only, the Christian Democrats clung to a distinct status and range of legal rights for those who were married, the Liberals and a majority of cantons were in favour of a partnership with similar status to marriage, whereas the Social Democrats and the Greens were strong supporters of opening up marriage to same-sex couples. The focus on the family and marriage as heteronormative institutions weighed heavily on the legislative process with regards to the legal recognition of same-sex couples (Engeli and Roca 2012). It explains in large part the limited character of the legal recognition for same-sex couples enshrined in the Federal Same-Sex Partnership Act, which entered into force in 2007. The same-sex partnership was embedded not in family law but in a special act. It afforded relatively similar rights in the areas of social insurance, the household, the division of property, and the acquisition of citizenship through the entering of a same-sex partnership with a Swiss citizen. However, it did not grant the right to adoption of the children of a partner until 2018, and still to date withholds the right to adopt as a couple and prohibits access to ART.

The consultation on the amendment to the Swiss Civil Code to open up marriage to same-sex couples in 2019 showed that the tension with regards to the family still existed but that the balance of political power had significantly shifted. The cantons and the main political parties largely supported the extension of marriage to same-sex couples, with the exception of four cantons, the Swiss People's Party, the EDU, and the Swiss Evangelical People's Party. The extension of joint adoption and ART received a lukewarm reception. The majority of the cantons and the Christian Democrats were in favour of separating this discussion from that of marriage, while the Swiss People's Party was strongly opposed to both. It was under pressure from the Social Democrats, the green parties, and the Liberals that joint adoption and ART were eventually added to the amendment that was adopted by parliament in 2020. Launched by an interparty committee composed of members of the EDU, the Swiss People's Party, and two members from the Christian Democrats, the referendum was submitted in April 2021. The amendment was clearly upheld by popular vote in September 2021.

4.3 The labour market

Inequality in the labour market has been a long-lasting battleground since the adoption of the constitutional provision for gender equality in 1981. The concept of 'pink ghetto' refers to the high representation of women in part-time and low wage jobs. LGBT+ related discrimination towards LGBT+ communities has remained severe, although few data have been collected to quantify it.

4.3.1 *Persisting glass ceiling and glass walls*

The percentage of women between fifteen and sixty-four years old in the labour market went up from 70.3 per cent in 2004 to 79.7 per cent in 2021 (FSO 2022a). However, this increase has hidden the persistent segregation of women in part-time employment, which remains considerably above the European average. Although in decline, the glass ceiling effect that slows down the career progression of women, even among the most highly educated, is still felt in Switzerland. The proportion of women in leadership positions has gone up; in 1996, 29.4 per cent of managing positions were held by women, rising to 36.6 per cent in 2019. The proportion of women on the boards of Swiss companies listed on the Swiss Infrastructure and Exchange SIX went up from 9.5 per cent in 2012 to 24.9 per cent in 2019, and women in management positions in these companies represented 33.5 per cent in 2019 (OECD 2021). The 2022 Schilling Report arrived at a similar estimate relying on a different sample of companies: 26 per cent of women on supervisory boards and 17 per cent of women on the management boards. In 2021, a mandatory quota for listed companies of 30 per cent of women on the supervisory board and of 20 per cent on management board (Code of Obligation, art. 734f) came into effect. If the threshold is not reached, companies will be required to provide a justification for failing to do so and put in place remedial measures (comply-or-explain mechanism). It is highly likely that this modest quota will be reached by most companies by the end of the transition period. This was a quota that was set to be easily achieved.

Women also run up against glass walls. Occupational segregation has remained pronounced in Switzerland (FSO 2022a). There are still high proportions of women in jobs linked to health and social welfare, as well as sales and tourism. Men are more represented in directorial and managerial positions and in skilled labour.

4.3.2 *Wage discrimination*

The principle of equal pay for work of equal value is one of the cornerstones of the Swiss gender equality policy. The revision of GEA has reinforced the importance of the principle of equal pay by placing the burden of proof upon the employer. The average wage gap was 19.5 per cent in 2020 in the private sector and 15.1 per cent in the public sector (FSO 2022b). Wage discrimination persists; 20 per cent of women respondents to the National Equality Barometer (2018) reported having been a victim of wage discrimination. In 2020, women represented 60.1 per cent of those earning less than CHF 4,000 a month (FSO 2022b). Men represented 78.5 per cent of those earning more than CHF 16,000. The wage gap is the highest in three of the highest-earning industries, such as financial and insurance services (FSO 2022b).

The wage gap between women and men is partially explained by the underrepresentation of the former in leadership positions and in the sectors and occupations that pay the most, as well as by a more punctuated employment trajectory due to career breaks, part-time, and/or fixed term employment. These are the so-called 'objective' factors (even if they are the product of historical structural discrimination). However, the gap is also partly triggered by direct discrimination on the basis of sex. This discriminatory part of the gap is normally calculated as being the unexplained wage difference that remains once the effects of all the 'objective' factors have been taken into account. The Federal Statistical Office has produced an estimate of the size of the direct discriminatory portion of the wage gap (FSO 2022b). In 2020, it was 45.3 per cent for the private sector and 46.7 per cent for the public sector.

4.3.3 *Homophobia in the workplace*

No federal law offers specific protection against workplace discrimination rooted in sexual orientation or gender identity. In spite of international models and the emergence of a sympathetic doctrine, the Swiss Federal Supreme Court took a restrictive stand and decided that the criteria of sex in the GEA was not applicable to sexual orientation. Unfortunately, employment law does not offer the same level of protection as that afforded by GIA for sex-based discrimination (Kälin and Locher 2015). Trans* persons are left in a vulnerable position regarding legal protection (Kälin and Locher 2015). Neither trans* nor intersex* persons or even gender identity are explicitly referenced in Swiss law. This said, the interdiction of discrimination based on lifestyle in article 8 line 2 of the federal constitution has been interpreted as covering sexual orientation and same-sex couples (Kälin and Locher 2015). Article 328 of the Code of Obligations confers on the employer a duty of care towards its employees. Employment law also enjoins the employer to safeguard the integrity of the employees. The understanding is that this legal protection begins at the moment of the job interview and covers the entirety of contractual relations, including post-employment relations. In most cases, it is illegal, for example, to ask interview questions about lifestyle, sexual orientation, and gender identity or to include this information in a reference or a performance evaluation. However, as noted by Kälin and Locher (2015, 21), jurisprudence in this area remains too limited to be able to evaluate its real-world effects.

Based on a voluntary survey of 1,097 people in the LBGT+ community in 2014, the study by Parini (2015) has lifted the veil on the workplace discrimination encountered by the LGBT+ community. Close to 70 per cent of the respondents have witnessed discriminatory practices in the last three years in the form of obscene gestures or comments, comments about masculinity, femininity, or sexual orientation, questioning of professional competence, exclusion from events and professional activities, outing, and sexual harassment. Trans* persons are even more exposed to harsher forms of discrimination. The fear of identification and the homophobic/trans*phobic environment can lead to a feeling of vulnerability, anxiety and well-being issues, and suicidal thoughts. The few respondents who have reported in the survey to have complained did so directly to employers rather than to the court. Their efforts do not appear to have achieved great success. Trans* people are confronted by additional barriers in the workplace. According to a Trans-Fair study (TNS 2015), 20 per cent of trans* people were unemployed in 2012 and 30 per cent of those who lost their job did so for reasons related to their gender identity. Thirty per cent preferred not to come out in their workplace for fear of losing their job. Trans-Fair (TNS 2015) estimates that 25 per cent of those who came out in the workplace suffered from adverse reactions ranging from psychological harassment to discrimination leading to a change in the job or firing. Sixteen per cent of companies said that they are reluctant to hire trans* people.

5 The unfinished business of equality+ in Switzerland

The portrait of the Swiss equality landscape leaves the feeling of incompletion. The formal elimination of direct discrimination towards women has been mostly achieved. The gap in the entry of women into the workforce and in higher education has mostly disappeared. The Swiss equality policy has been behind both accomplishments. It has contributed to raising public awareness about the urgency of taking action in favour of gender equality among both public and private stakeholders. It has also provided a series of legal safeguards that encompass gender relations in the workplace, education, and the family. However, Switzerland is still way off from an inclusive and transformative equality. The persistence of the heterosexist model in the legal framework, the resilience of pink ghettos in education and the labour market, the ever unequal division of labour within the family, and the gender pay gap attest to the limitations of the Swiss gender equality policy. It is largely devoid of affirmative action or mandates acting directly upon the elimination of real barriers between women and men. Slowed down by federalist inefficiency and the strong opposition of the far right to the gender+ equality agenda, the Swiss agenda towards equality+ has been making up ground in small steps without building a proactive strategy of institutional innovation.

There is still a long road ahead towards achieving LGBT+ equality. The fight against discrimination towards LGBT+ communities has been largely isolated from the dedicated gender equality framework and has mostly been relegated to the criminalization of homophobia without real enforcement teeth. Discrimination in the workplace is frequent and remains largely unaccounted for. Homophobic and trans*phobic violence is worrisome and still has not been fully documented by public authorities.

These limitations leave the observer sceptical, for now, about the capacity of the existing legal framework to achieve real equality. Gender equality policy remains cloistered and hierarchized. Sexual orientation is placed at the same level as racism with regard to hate crime but is excluded from the definition of sex-based discrimination. Gender identity does not appear anywhere across the legal framework in an explicit fashion. Gender equality is still anchored in the binary construction of gender and a homogenization of the category of 'women' that prevents equality being thought of in terms of the profound transformation of social relations.

Note

1. National Councillor Nidegger, Official Bulletin of the National Council, 2018, p. 1585. https://www.parlament.ch/fr/ratsbetrieb/amtliches-bulletin/amtliches-bulletin-die-verhandlungen?SubjectId=44369#votum8.

References

Baumann, Katernina, and Margareta Lauterburg. 2007. *Scheidung, Pensionskasse, AHV/IV—Das müssen Sie wissen*. Bern: Conférence suisse des délégué-e-s à l'égalité.

CFQF – Commission fédérale pour les questions féminines. 1998. *Femmes. Pouvoir. Histoire. Événements de l'histoire des femmes et de l'égalité des sexes en Suisse, 1948–1998*. Bern: Commission fédérale pour les questions féminines.

ECRI – Commission européenne contre le racisme et l'intolérance. 2014. *Rapport de l'ECRI sur la Suisse (5ème cycle de monitoring)*. Strasbourg: Conseil de l'Europe.

ECRI – Commission européenne contre le racisme et l'intolérance. 2020. *Rapport de l'ECRI sur la Suisse (6ème cycle de monitoring)*. Strasbourg: Conseil de l'Europe.

Eisner, Léïla, and Tabea Hässler. 2021. Panel Suisse LGBTIQ+ – Rapport de Synthèse 2021. https://swiss-lgbtiq-panel.ch/wp-content/uploads/2021/12/LGBTIQ_Report_2021_Francais-1.pdf (accessed 18 December 2021).

Engeli, Isabelle, and Marta Roca. 2012. 'La reconnaissance limitée des couples de même sexe en Suisse'. *Politique et Sociétés* 31 (2): pp. 51–66.

Federal Council. 2016. *Le droit à la protection contre la discrimination*. Rapport du Conseil fédéral en réponse au postulat Naef 12.3543 du 14 juin 2012. Bern.

Federal Council. 2018. *Rapport intermédiaire de la Suisse sur la mise en œuvre des recommandations du comité CEDEF*. Bern.

Federal Council. 2020. *Sixième rapport de la Suisse sur la mise en œuvre de la Convention sur l'élimination de toutes les formes de discrimination à l'égard des femmes.* Bern.

Freivogel, Elisabeth. 2007. *Contribution d'entretien après le divorce – soutien financier par des proches parents – aide sociale.* Bern: Commission fédérale pour les questions féminines.

FSO – Federal Statistical Office. 2019. *Enquête sur les familles et les générations. Premiers résultats.* https://www.bfs.admin.ch/bfsstatic/dam/assets/10467789/master (accessed 22 February 2021).

FSO – Federal Statistical Office. 2022a. *Le taux d'activité des 55 à 64 ans a fortement augmenté en 10 ans.* https://www.bfs.admin.ch/bfs/fr/home/actualites/quoi-de-neuf.assetdetail.22504573.html (accessed 18 December 2022).

FSO – Federal Statistical Office. 2022b. *En 2020, l'écart salarial global entre les sexes a diminué.* https://dam-api.bfs.admin.ch/hub/api/dam/assets/23546994/master (accessed 18 December 2022).

Grohsmann, Irene, Christina Hausamman, and Olga Vinogradova. 2014. *Ancrage institutionnel des thématiques LGBTI en Suisse.* Bern: Centre suisse de compétence pour les droits humains.

Häusermann, Michael. 2014. 'L'impact de l'hétérosexisme et de l'homophobie sur la santé et la qualité de vie des jeunes gays, lesbiennes et bisexuel-les en Suisse'. In *Le droit de l'enfant et de l'adolescent à son orientation sexuelle et à son identité de genre*, edited by Philippe D. Jaffé, Bernard Lévy, Zoe Moody, and Jean Zermatten, pp. 92–106. Sion: Institut Universitaire Kurt Bösch.

ILGA-Europe. 2021. *Annual Review on the Human Rights Situation of Lesbian, Gay, Bisexual, Trans and Intersex People in Europe and Central Asia.* Brussels: ILGA-Europe.

Kälin, Walter, and Reto Locher. 2015. *Accès à la justice en cas de discrimination. Rapport de synthèse.* Bern: Centre Suisse de compétence pour les droits humains.

LGBT-Helpline. 2018. *Hate Crimes an Lesben, Schwulen, Bisexuellen und Transmenschen in der Schweiz.* https://www.tgns.ch/wp-content/uploads/2018/05/LGBTI-Hate-Crime-Bericht-2018.pdf (accessed 22 February 2021).

OECD – Organization for Economic Co-operation and Development. 2021. *OECD Corporate Governance Factbook 2021.* https://www.oecd.org/corporate/OECD-Corporate-Governance-Factbook.pdf (accessed 18 December 2022).

Parini, Lorena. 2015. *Être LGBT au travail.* Geneva: Institut des Études Genre.

Roca i Escoda, Marta. 2019. 'From Indicting the Law to Conquering Rights'. In *Everyday Resistance*, edited by Bruno Frère, and Marc Jacquemain, pp. 45–73. London: Palgrave.

Sattiva Spring, Christine. 2019. 'Le TF verrouille la porte d'entrée de la LEg aux homosexuels—Commentaire de l'arrêt du Tribunal fédéral 8C-594/2018'. *Newsletter DroitDuTravail.ch.* https://publications-droit.ch/files/analyses/droitdutravail/2-19-juil-commentaire-8c-594-2018.pdf (accessed 07 February 2023).

Schillingreport. 2022. *Transparency at the Top—The Management Boards of Switzerland's Private and Public Sectors.* Zurich: Guido Schilling ag.

Stutz, Heidi, Marianne Schär, and Elisabeth Freivogel. 2005. *Evaluation sur l'efficacité de la loi sur l'égalité.* Bern: BASS.

TNS – Transgender Network Switzerland. 2015. *Projet Trans-Fair.* Fiche d'information.

Walser, Erasmus. 2013. 'Homosexualité'. In *Dictionnaire historique de la Suisse.* https://hls-dhs-dss.ch/fr/articles/016560/2013-12-04/ (accessed 15 January 2020).

PART VIII

EPILOGUE

CHAPTER 41

SWITZERLAND, *QUO VADIS?*

Current challenges and potential solutions for Swiss politics

RAHEL FREIBURGHAUS AND SEAN MUELLER

1 INTRODUCTION

ALTHOUGH Switzerland is often portrayed as a paradise of political stability, peaceful accommodation, and economic prosperity, many of the challenges currently confronting liberal democracies worldwide are no strangers in this land either. Some of these challenges come in the form of fierce debates over whether and how to act in certain policy areas. How can we solve the greatest problems of our time, such as climate change or economic crises, in a way that is broadly acceptable, given the consensual nature of Swiss politics and the significant obstacles to change that this entails (e.g. Vatter 2018; Freiburghaus and Vatter 2019; Linder and Mueller 2021)? Other challenges are more structural and institutional in essence, such as the increasing socio-economic heterogeneity between the country's twenty-six constituent units (cantons), all of which continue to enjoy perfectly equal rights and obligations under the country's symmetric federal architecture. A third type of challenge relates to the political actors and processes that characterize Switzerland's semi-direct democracy. Notably, the polarization of political parties, (non-)participation in elections and referendums, and a glaring lack of transparency about campaign donations, as well as the influence of vested interests over policy-making, have given cause for concern in recent decades (see 'The Ideological Space in Swiss Politics: Voters, Parties, and Realignment', 'Parties and Party Systems in Switzerland', and 'Direct-Democratic Votes' in this volume).

In this chapter, we focus on five developments that potentially call into question the very functioning of Swiss democracy, namely alienation, centralization, digitalization, internationalization/Europeanization, and polarization. These five were chosen because to a greater or lesser extent they have all affected liberal democracies worldwide.

There is thus a broad and varied literature upon which to build. This is not to say that these challenges are the only ones causing problems, nor that they are necessarily always clearly separable from one another. Yet they undoubtedly figure among the most pressing concerns. Moreover, each also poses *particular* challenges for a Swiss political system built upon the premises of 'amicable agreement' (Steiner 1974), non-competition (Lijphart 1968), non-centralization, and neutrality.

The first part of this chapter thus spells out the precise nature and extent of each challenge in general and identifies the kind of problem it potentially poses for Switzerland in particular. The second part of the chapter then reflects on possible solutions and specific reform options. In doing so, we draw on an original online survey conducted among all of the roughly 450 members of the Swiss Political Science Association in January 2022 (see Neidhart 1975 for a similar approach). Our survey gauged their support for different kinds of solutions in the domains of *polity* and *politics*, while also including a short section on *policy* changes. Eighty-three political scientists eventually completed the online survey; they broadly reflect the Swiss political-science community in terms of gender, age, status, linguistic region, and sub-discipline. We will first discuss the five challenges in alphabetical order, before proceeding to the expert evaluation.

2 Challenges for Swiss politics

2.1 Alienation

Alienation encompasses a set of individual attitudes of estrangement from the political system. Typical manifestations of alienation include the progressive loss of political efficacy, a sense of political meaninglessness, discontentment, rejection, and/or voter apathy (Fatke and Freitag 2015). Seen from an international and comparative perspective, alienation is often said to constitute a key dimension in the crisis of representative democracy (e.g. Merkel 2014; Urbinati 2019). Some have gone so far as to state that voters do not actually want to be too heavily involved in decision-making (Hibbing and Theiss-Morse 2002; Brennan 2016). While already problematic for ordinary representative democracies, widespread alienation could be devastating for a political system such as that of Switzerland, with its twenty-six cantons and over 2,000 municipalities, where both general elections and issue-specific referendums take place frequently at all three levels of government. What is more, it is not only necessary for voters to regularly vote in referendums and elect representatives, but given the prevalence of semi-professional structures, especially at the subnational level, many citizens must also be willing—and financially able—to assume a political mandate without adequate compensation (Freitag et al. 2019; Mueller 2015).

At first sight, though, things do not seem to be as bad in Switzerland as elsewhere. Overall turnout in elections and referendums at the national level has remained stable and even increased a little since the 1990s (see 'National Elections' and 'Direct-Democratic Votes' in this volume). Switzerland also continues to dominate international rankings of trust in the federal government and satisfaction with national democracy (Bauer et al. 2019). Even many abstainers are satisfied enough with how things are currently going (Fatke and Freitag 2015).

Yet as regards both passive and active participation, voter apathy is felt particularly strongly at the subnational level. The inability to find enough candidates for local mandates is one of the main reasons for the stark increase in 'voluntary' municipal mergers across Switzerland (Steiner et al. 2021; FSO 2023; see 'Swiss Municipalities' in this volume). The cantons, too, while not lacking interested candidates, have seen participation in their parliamentary elections decline drastically over the past fifty years, from 55 per cent on average to just over 40 per cent (Figure 41.1).

Another indicator of growing alienation from representative democracy is the increase in non-traditional forms of participation, such as demonstrations, strikes, and sit-ins—sometimes combined with, or boosted by, online activism. Two of the most noteworthy developments of the past decade are the Women's Strikes and the gradual uptake of 'Fridays for Future' demonstrations. Both sets of social groups, i.e. women and the youth, have become increasingly vocal and organized in highlighting the insufficient attention paid to gender equality and climate change (see 'Social Movements' in this volume). Yet pressure from the street seems to be directed *at* representatives, not necessarily against them. The data presented in Figure 41.1 point in the same direction: in

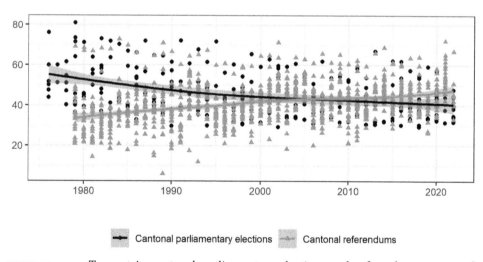

FIGURE 41.1: Turnout in cantonal parliamentary elections and referendums, 1976 and 1978—March 2022 (in per cent)

LOESS lines = annual average with 95 per cent confidence intervals. Each dot represents a cantonal parliamentary election or the annual mean for referendum participation in a canton. No data is available for elections in Appenzell Inner-Rhodes and Grisons and referendums in Appenzell Inner-Rhodes and Glarus, respectively.

Data source: Authors' graph with data from Vatter et al. (2020), BFS (2022), C2D (2022).

parallel to decreasing interest in cantonal elections, average participation in cantonal referendums increased from 35 per cent in the 1980s to almost 50 per cent by early 2022.

2.2 Centralization

Centralization describes the process through which legislative, administrative, and/or fiscal powers originally vested in the cantons are shifted upwards to the national level (Dardanelli and Mueller 2019). Since 1848, Switzerland has experienced centralization in all three dimensions captured by the 'De/Centralisation project' (Dardanelli et al. 2019), although this development has occurred to different degrees (Figure 41.2). This is good news for the cantons, as they remain important players on the level of both implementation and, especially, finances. All direct taxes, for instance, are collected by the cantons, of which they retain the lion's share. However, this development is also bad news for the subnational level, as more and more obligations accrue at the federal level without the cantons having had an adequate say over the details, or even just the existence, of these rules. For although Swiss federalism has over time evolved from a dual-federalism model into a German-style administrative model, it lacks the corresponding archetype of regional shared rule, i.e. a *Bundesrat* where *Länder* executives are directly represented (Mueller and Fenna 2022).

More generally, there are two main problems with the ever-greater centralization of Swiss politics in the legislative sphere. The first relates to a possible disconnect between new or existing state-wide rules and their implementation on the ground. The lack of a regional voice or shared rule could translate into an unwillingness on the part

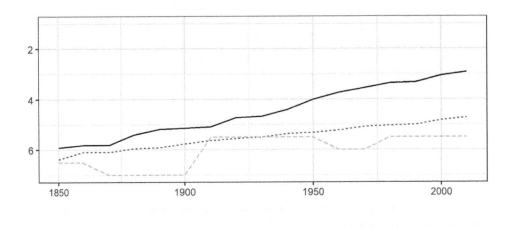

FIGURE 41.2: Development of (de-)centralization in Switzerland, 1850–2010
7 = total cantonal autonomy (de-/non-centralization); 1 = total federal power (centralization).
Data source: Authors' graph with data from Dardanelli and Mueller (2019).

of the cantons to adequately apply what the federal legislator—i.e. parliament and/or the people of the country as a whole (through popular votes)—has decided. Historically, this tension has always been there (see 'The Implementation and Evaluation of Public Policies' in this volume), but the greater the gap between legislative and administrative centralization, the greater the likelihood of such incongruence. The 2004/2008 federal reform recognized this problem, but only partially remedied it through the disentanglement of federal and cantonal powers, on the one hand, and more flexible vertical co-operation mechanisms, on the other (e.g. Ladner 2018; Vatter 2018; Freiburghaus 2023). The fact that they are not directly represented at the federal level also provides cantonal governments with an easy scapegoat if things go awry.

A second problem is a lack of transparency and the violation of the principle of fiscal equivalence, according to which decisions should be made by those who pay for and benefit from public service (Olson 1969). Dividing these overlapping circles potentially creates yet another set of issues, namely legislative encroachment by the federal government into regional domains—in the worst case without adequate compensation (e.g. Bednar 2009)—and greater inequality among the cantons when it comes to acting with their own resources and political will, even in formally federal domains. Moreover, top-down payments in the form of (unconditional) revenue sharing and cantonal discretion in implementation were often granted in exchange for legislative centralization. The cantons are thus often in charge of (implementing) federal policies, while at the same time not being in charge (in the sense of deciding).

2.3 Digitalization

In Switzerland, as elsewhere in the world, the impact of digital technologies on virtually every aspect of life has accelerated tremendously. For the Swiss economy, digitalization can be viewed as a 'supply shock' that affects everything from productivity to labour shares and profits. It also forces employees to transform themselves into a high-skilled digital workforce capable of managing 'frontier technologies' (e.g. artificial intelligence, big data, blockchain, robotics). The Swiss people, in turn, hope that digitalization will expand opportunities and improve welfare. Ambitious e-government projects, in turn, should set 'binding, nationally applicable regulations for the digital transformation' (Digitale Verwaltung Schweiz 2023) to increase the efficiency and accountability of service delivery. According to the 'UN Readiness for Frontier Technologies Index' (UNCTAD 2021), Switzerland ranks second out of 158 countries—only the US is better prepared (Figure 41.3).

Although the 'Industrial Revolution 4.0' is transforming the social, economic, and political realms, we restrict the term 'digitalization' to the increasing use of information and communication technology, as well as of CivicTech, in governance processes (Gilardi 2022). Even on the level of political communication, political participation, and policy-making, the challenges are manifold and multifaceted. Due to its semi-professional politics, weak political parties, and 'federalist' fragmentation, Switzerland is, for instance,

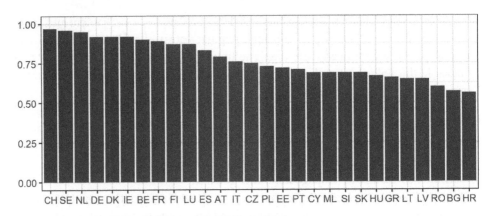

FIGURE 41.3: Readiness for 'Frontier Technologies' Index, 2021

Data source: Authors' graph with data from UNCTAD (2021).

seen as 'the least-likely critical case' for the usage of Twitter for (online) political communication (Rauchfleisch and Metag 2016). And even *if* social media are adopted as a mobilization strategy ahead of direct-democratic votes and/or as a microblogging channel, sender and consumer profiles are heavily skewed by the 'digital divide'.

This divide also manifests itself in modes and practices of, as well as preferences for, political participation. Young people are particularly fond of voting-advice apps, e-collecting, 'hashtivism', and digital-democratic innovations, such as online participatory budgeting. (Cyber-)security issues, lack of transparency, and only partially fulfilled hopes for higher and more equal turnout in internet voting (e.g. Germann and Serdült 2017; Petitpas et al. 2021) pose another challenge for attempts to move beyond Switzerland's 'paper-and-pencil' democracy. There are also fears that through digitalization an already demanding political agenda—with popular votes and elections occurring regularly at all three levels of governance—will become even more burdensome. Finally, as regards policy-making, there is some evidence that social media undermines Swiss policymakers' capacity to craft compromises, as platform users can 'bypass' or even torpedo traditional gatekeepers, such as party elites and the mainstream media (Gilardi et al. 2021).

2.4 Internationalization and Europeanization

Switzerland's position in the world and the domestic consequences of its integration into global governance arrangements pose two separate, yet strongly interdependent challenges: internationalization refers to the increasing importance of global trade, international relations, treaties, and alliances for Swiss politics and policy-making (Sciarini et al. 2015), while Europeanization relates more specifically to the process through which the EU's legal, political, and economic dynamics are felt domestically (Sciarini et al. 2004, 353).

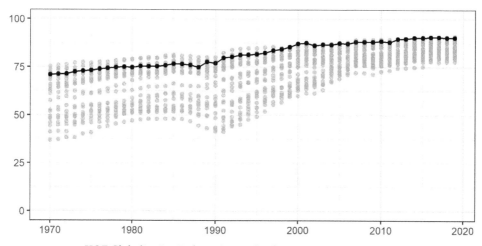

FIGURE 41.4: KOF Globalisation Index—Switzerland vs. EU-27, 1970–2021

Black line = Switzerland; dots = EU-27. The overall 'KOF Globalisation Index' combines *de facto* and *de jure* globalization. Overall indices for each of the eight aggregation levels (i.e. economic, trade, financial, social, interpersonal, informational, cultural, and political globalization) are calculated by averaging the respective *de facto* and *de jure* indices.

Data source: Authors' calculations and figure based on KOF (2022).

Both trends are accentuated by Switzerland's geographic location and social make-up: located in the heart of Western Europe, its population, like its different rivers, branches out and entertains dense relations with neighbouring countries—including important EU founding member states, such as Germany, France, and Italy, with which large swaths of the country share a language, culture, and functional spaces. Given its small size, Switzerland has always been particularly vulnerable in the global economy (Katzenstein 1985). Like other small states, it has strongly benefited from a rules-based international economic order. Aggressive expansion into international markets, with strong, sustained increases in exports and direct investments, have supported a process of intense globalization. According to the 'KOF Globalisation Index', since 1970 Switzerland has always ranked among the top-five most globalized countries. As of 2021, it is even the most globalized in the world (Figure 41.4).

Switzerland's *political* integration into global governance frameworks has, by contrast, been much more reluctant (see 'Switzerland's Position in Europe and the World' and 'Switzerland and the European Union' in this volume). When the UN was founded, the Swiss government ruled out membership, declaring the organization's goals to be incompatible with neutrality. A first attempt failed in a referendum in 1987, resulting in Switzerland only joining in 2002. For the EU, too, Switzerland is a tricky customer. In 1992, Swiss voters rejected accession to the European Economic Area. Swiss–EU relations then developed by means of an ever-tightening web of more than fifteen sectoral or 'bilateral' agreements (Dardanelli and Mazzoleni 2021). Yet, European affairs have remained a highly controversial issue, with several episodes of domestic backlash. In 2021, the Swiss government even unilaterally broke off negotiations on a framework agreement with the EU. While Switzerland thus stays formally aloof from supranational organizations (or takes a long time to apply for membership), in the case of the EU it has reached a level of integration that can be characterized as 'customised quasi-membership' (Jenni 2014).

Both internationalization and Europeanization have spurred decisive changes in the logic of Swiss decision-making and power configurations. In 'directly' Europeanized or internationalized processes where there is a formal transmission mechanism specified by binding law, the centre of gravity has shifted away from the domestic level. The discretionary power of the Federal Council has been strongly enhanced at the expense of both parliament and interest groups. It is, after all, the government that negotiates treaties, drawing upon its (almost) exclusive powers in external affairs. Parliament, in turn, merely 'rubber-stamps' what the executive branch has agreed. Formal domestic consultation procedures also tend to be replaced by more informal and less inclusive mechanisms.

Such power shifts are visible in 'indirectly' Europeanized or internationalized areas, too. Even in the absence of formal treaties, Switzerland often unilaterally adopts rules set by global governance, a process known as 'autonomous adaption' (Sciarini et al. 2004; Jenni 2014). Both 'directly' and 'indirectly' Europeanized or internationalized decision-making processes have strongly contributed to the redefinition of the cleavage structure and to changes in electoral competition and the party system. On the one hand, Europeanization and internationalization foster a pragmatic 'take-it-or-leave-it' domestic consensus of pro-integration forces. On the other hand, they have opened political space for Eurosceptic, anti-globalist, and right-wing populists, as well as for radical-alternative left parties capitalizing on (and polarizing along) such issues. The rise of the Swiss People's Party (SVP), for instance, is intimately tied to the politicization of Swiss–EU relations (Kriesi 2007).

2.5 Polarization

Polarization comes in many different forms (e.g. Sartori 2005 [1976]; Dalton 2008). Its two most prominent manifestations are the increasing ideological distance between extreme positions and the disappearance of centrist voters and parties (e.g. Bochsler et al. 2015). A third, less often discussed manifestation of polarization is the increasing superposition of multiple issue dimensions on just one, typically the left–right, axis (Baldassari and Gelman 2008, 409). At the elite level, the Swiss party system has experienced all three types of polarization: the mainstream left has moved more and more to the left, and the mainstream right more and more to the right; centrist parties have been steadily losing ground since the late 1980s; and ever more issues—e.g. globalization, Europeanization, moral politics, gender equality, climate change, etc.—have been subsumed into the dominant left–right cleavage. Today, the tripolar Swiss party system, consisting of left, centre-right, and radical-right poles, resembles the political space found throughout Western European democracies (Oesch and Rennwald 2018).

To illustrate the disappearance of the centre, Figure 41.5 plots the combined seat share of pole parties across five federal institutions: the National Council (lower house), where since 1919 seats have been distributed proportionally to population; the Council of States (upper house), where each canton has two seats (with the exception of Obwalden, Nidwalden, Basel-Stadt, Basel-Landschaft, Appenzell Ausserrhoden, and Appenzell Innerrhoden, which each have one); the United Federal Assembly, i.e. the joint session of the two houses of parliament; the Federal Council, i.e. the Swiss government elected by this body; and the Federal Supreme Court. The 50 per cent threshold was surpassed in the National Council in 1991, in the joint session in 1999, and in the executive and judiciary in the early 2000s. Only the Council of States, elected mostly using majority/plurality rules, continues to have strong representation from centrist parties.

This is not to say that the left and the right often agree on policy—on the contrary, according to Smartmonitor (2022), since 1996 alliances between the SP and the SVP have fluctuated between representing just 0.5 and 3 per cent of all closing votes every year in the National Council. In any case, the impact of the growing importance of actors at both ends of the left–right scale is probably more subtle: it forces the centrist parties (namely the Liberals and former Christian Democrats, whose party is now aptly called 'The Centre') to seek partners on either side of the hemicycle and often pulls them apart too. The share of parliamentary votes in which all four governing parties agree

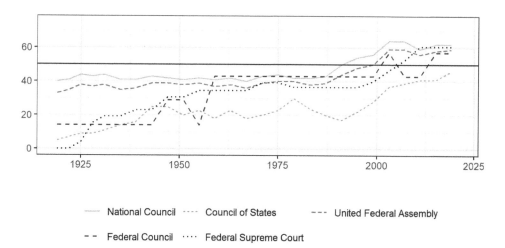

FIGURE 41.5: Combined seat share of pole parties across key federal institutions, 1919–2021 (in per cent)

Pole parties on the left: the Social Democrats (SP), the radical and alternative left, and the Greens. On the right: the SVP (and its predecessors: the BGB and DP), small radical-right parties, and regionalist parties from Geneva (MCG) and Ticino (Lega). Shown are seat shares at the end of the election year (parliament) and at the beginning of the next calendar year (government).

Data source: Authors' calculations using data from FSO (2022).

has correspondingly declined steadily over the past few decades. In parallel, there seems to be increasing discord not only within the two chambers but also between them: the number of conciliation committees, which are instituted if the two chambers of parliament continue to disagree after three readings on each side, has risen from a mere seven instances in the 1991–1995 legislature to more than twenty in every four-year period since 2007 (Freiburghaus 2018).

Although polarization represents a general trend engulfing liberal democracies worldwide, it is particularly challenging for Switzerland, because the entire political system rests on finding compromise solutions. These are not only more difficult to arrive at in a polarized context, but also more easily defeated in the direct-democratic arena. The growth of both the left- and right-wing poles has enabled them to win more easily, both in debates and electorally. For instance, optional referendums, by means of which any group able to gather 50,000 signatures within 100 days of the publication of an act of parliament can force a popular vote, have been used with increasing frequency since the 1990s, rising from an average of just once a year to three times annually (Swissvotes 2022).[1] To these are added an average of six popular initiatives to change the federal constitution every year (ibid.). Here, party polarization intersects with direct democracy to create a unique vicious circle: as each side tries to lock in its (by nature quite radical) demands at the central level and/or uses the direct-democratic arena for mobilization and issue-ownership purposes, this leads to even more polarizing issues being added to the agenda on top of existing levels of polarization.

3 Potential solutions and reform options

To what extent is there broader expert agreement that the five trends just identified do indeed constitute challenges? And what would potential solutions look like? We will now present the results of our survey of Swiss politics experts administered in January 2022.

3.1 What is the problem?

We asked for expert opinions on the most pressing challenges in two different ways. First, we posed a very open initial question: 'Thinking about Swiss politics in very general terms, what are for you the most pressing current challenges? Name at least one and a maximum of three.' We then grouped the replies into six categories, plus two residual ones (Figure 41.6). Europeanization and internationalization were mentioned the most often at all three levels of urgency, followed at a great distance by polarization and centralization. Among 'other policy challenges', climate change, environmental protection, and sustainable development together represented half of the issues mentioned as most urgent.

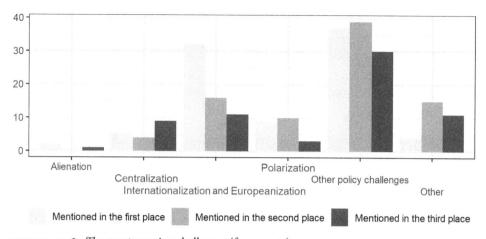

FIGURE 41.6: The most pressing challenges (for experts)

N = 244 challenges mentioned by experts. 'Other policy challenges' include policy fields other than 'Europeanization and Internationalization' and 'digitalization'.

Data source: Authors' data.

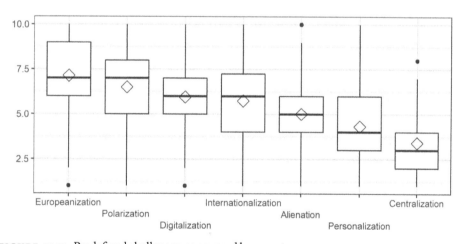

FIGURE 41.7: Predefined challenges, as assessed by experts

Scale ranging from 1 = not at all challenging to 10 = the most challenging; horizontal line in the boxes = median; diamonds = mean values.

Data source: Authors' data.

We then asked the experts to rank several predefined developments on a scale from 1 to 10, based on how challenging they thought they were for Swiss politics. To separate general globalization and internationalization issues from relations with the EU, we created two distinct scales. We also added personalization as a potentially distinct challenge. The results are shown in Figure 41.7, confirming the pattern just identified: Europeanization and polarization are seen as the most pressing challenges, while centralization and personalization are seen as the least pressing challenges. This aligns with the literature, where Switzerland's integration into global governance is prominently discussed. Geographical proximity and extremely close trade partnerships obviously make themselves felt: the EU 'is by far the most important market for the export-oriented Swiss industry' (FDFA 2022).

3.2 Reform options for the five challenges

What do experts think could be done to tackle these challenges? Beginning with Europeanization and internationalization, they point towards two levels of action. The first is mainly discursive: traditional discourse frameworks are still fairly prevalent that portray Switzerland as an 'exceptional country' whose economy is more prosperous and whose political system is more (direct-)democratic than those of most other states (Church 2016). Those in charge often invoke this *Sonderfall* rhetoric, just like citizens opposed to integration, to justify why the Swiss should pursue a 'third way'. Rather than simply following suit, Switzerland should preserve its alleged exceptionalism by negotiating close, but not too close, ties tailored to Swiss needs. According to the survey, some experts believe that political and/or economic leaders should bring an end to this '*Sonderfall* rhetoric'. They should establish a new narrative that emphasizes the opportunities offered by deep(er) (political) integration into global governance over the risks.

The second remedy is situated at the policy level: most experts who mentioned *Europeanization and internationalization* suggest transforming Swiss–EU relations into a 'framework agreement' and/or concluding a modified, 'updated' version of such an agreement that would ensure the further development of the existing sectoral treaties. Some 20 per cent mention EU membership as a way forward, roughly equivalent to the share of the general public (gfs.bern 2021a). Hardly any expert advocates polity reforms that would return power to domestic actors. If they do so at all, their calls concern the further empowerment of the Federal Council in foreign affairs.

Turning to *polarization*, two radically different remedies are proposed: some experts advocate a narrow 'pan-democratic alliance' that excludes the SVP from government, a coalition type that amounts to a form of political rather than purely arithmetic consociationalism but still differs from a classic 'government–opposition system'. The other remedy proposed is to broaden the government's foundation through a 'dialogue with all societal groups', 'political leadership [and] incentives for transparent and honest communication by political elites'. This would not only 'uphold consociationalism', but also force 'parties and politicians to go for consensus [again]'. Both remedies have, in fact, been tried to some extent in the past: first, the SVP's federal executive presence was doubled from one to two seats in 2003 to realign executive representation with popular preferences; second, the SVP departed more or less voluntarily from the government in 2008 (Church and Vatter 2009). Other proposals relate to more transparency and support for local media.

Digitalization is something of the 'odd man out'. When the experts were asked to rate it on a predefined scale, it was seen to be as pressing as internationalization and slightly less pressing than polarization (Figure 41.7). Yet when invited to brainstorm freely about current challenges, only a very small minority of the experts even mentioned digitalization and/or related aspects (Figure 41.6). Only one respondent identified digitalization as *the* most urgent issue, while three others placed it in the top two or three. Since evidence is still scarce (and often inconsistent), even experts may have struggled to grasp the meaning and scope of the challenges for Swiss politics evoked by the rise of digital technologies. Consequently, they also had a hard time coming up with remedies. 'There is no easy solution', as one respondent put it. Another respondent emphasized the need for a transformation of mindset ('rethinking the world in "digital first"') and was supported by a third respondent who stated that successful management of the 'digital revolution' necessitated, in the first instance, massive investment in (centralized) data-collecting, data-processing, and open, crowd-sourced, data-sharing infrastructure. Digitalization might thus be seen more as an administrative and technical problem than as a political challenge.

Alienation was mentioned even less often than digitalization in the open question: only two experts mentioned it in first place and nobody in second or third (Figure 41.6). Of these, only one offered a potential remedy in the form of a 'neutral organization fighting fake news (and not only on traditional media channels) [and] deliberative mini-publics'.

The fifth and final of the specific challenges we identified, *centralization*, was deemed the least urgent when specifically asked about (Figure 41.7). The only reason it was mentioned as often as polarization is that many experts in fact want to see *more* of it. The problems identified most often under this heading are simply '[the functioning of] federalism' and the need for a reform of federalism: i.e. the over-representation of rural interests at the expense of urban ones and the 'veto power of small cantons'; an inadequate vertical division of labour and ensuing coordination problems; and the problematic interplay between federal and (direct-)democratic structures. The solutions proposed are equally varied: five experts suggest institutional reforms involving the weakening of the Council of States and/or the abolition (or 'rethinking') of the double-majority requirement for constitutional change; four would give the central level more power; three demand a reform of the vertical allocation of powers—along with one who would like to see a proper steering committee composed of federal and cantonal representatives in times of crisis; and three others want the cities to have more institutionalized influence. None of the experts called for more decentralization or greater cantonal autonomy.

3.3 Reform options for the Swiss polity and Swiss politics

We also investigated the need for and perceived urgency of reforming specific Swiss institutions (the polity) and decision-making processes (politics). In line with the

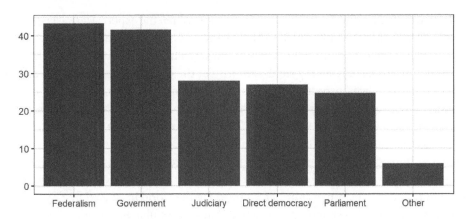

FIGURE 41.8: Swiss institutions that experts regard as most in need of reform (weighted)

Experts were asked to choose up to five institutions (plus a residual 'other' category) and rank them in order of their need for reform. Shown are the total scores arrived at by multiplying the number of times an institution was chosen by its priority (1st place = 1, 2nd place = 0.8, 3rd place = 0.6, 4th place = 0.4, and anything from 5th place onwards = 0.2).

Data source: Authors' data.

previous section, Figure 41.8 illustrates that federalism and the federal government are the two political institutions experts regard as the most in need of some type of reform, followed by the federal judicial and legislative branches. Direct democracy is ranked fourth—nonetheless, roughly every fifth respondent thinks that something should be done to cure the 'world champion of direct democracy' (Altman 2011, 49).

When it comes to Swiss federalism, the experts once again primarily call for a reduction of cantonal veto power in federal policy-making. Adjusting the two-seat guarantee in the Council of States (upper house) for small, rural cantons or changing (if not abolishing) the 'double majority' required to amend the federal constitution are cases in point. While the 2004/2008 landmark reform of the fiscal equalization scheme, along with the division of tasks, affected the *process* of Swiss federalism, the experts obviously believe that it is about time to tackle the so far largely untouched federal institutions. Finally, the experts are quite open to territorial reforms, whereas for the public, territorial integrity remains a 'sacred cow', with all previous attempts to reduce the number of cantons fiercely rejected (Ladner 2018; Vatter 2018).

While the institutional architecture of the national government has remained essentially unchanged since 1848, the workload that the seven federal councillors must come to terms with has increased massively (Vatter 2020). What is more, tasks, duties, and government responsibilities are quite unevenly distributed across the seven federal ministries, which consist of between four and nine federal offices with the number of full-time equivalents ranging from roughly 2,200 to 12,2000 (as of 2020; see 'Federal Administration' in this volume). In terms of possible solutions, the experts think that increasing the number of federal councillors from seven to nine (or even to eleven), in order to lessen the burden for individual ministers, is the most necessary reform proposal. In addition to increasing the size of the cabinet, extending the Swiss president's term of office beyond its current one-year limit is another possible solution popular with experts that would require a constitutional amendment. Reshuffling policy tasks from one department to another would, for its part, be much easier to implement. Generally, the experts favour retaining the unique Swiss 'assembly-independent regime' (Shugart and Carey 1992). Pushing the Swiss governmental system closer to parliamentarism (e.g. by forcing federal councillors to sign a coalition agreement) or switching completely to this form of government are seen as neither urgent nor promising solutions.

Figure 41.9 provides a clear picture of the politics-related aspects that the experts think are the most in need of being reformed. Almost half of all respondents mention transparency of funding in campaigns. This is a finding worth emphasizing. For a long time, Switzerland was the only country in the Council of Europe without such regulations. However, in late 2021 (hence, before the expert survey was conducted), the federal parliament—under pressure from a popular initiative and confronted with political-transparency laws in several cantons—approved legislation obliging political parties to declare all donations above CHF 15,000 ($16,700), and organizers of federal election or referendum campaigns to declare all expenses above CHF 50,000 ($54,000). Experts believe that the idea of transparency should be even more strongly prioritized over donors' privacy. They are less afraid that donors would be more reluctant to open their purse strings if their involvement were to become public knowledge.

On average, fewer than half of all registered Swiss voters participate in federal elections and referendums (and even fewer than that in cantonal votes: Figure 41.1). This is significantly lower than global voter turnout, which oscillates around 66 per cent (Solijonov 2016, 23). While international observers often worry about low voter turnout in Switzerland, only every fifth expert regards abstentionism as the biggest 'political challenge'. Indeed, the share of permanent abstainers barely reaches 10 per cent (Sciarini

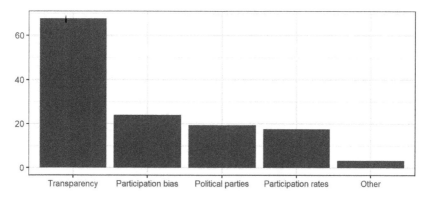

FIGURE 41.9: Swiss actors and processes that experts regard as most in need of reform (weighted)

Experts were asked to choose up to four areas (plus a residual 'other' category) and rank them in order of their need for reform. Shown are the total scores arrived at by multiplying the number of times an actor or process was chosen by its priority (see Figure 41.8 for information on how the data were weighted).

Data source: Authors' data.

et al. 2016). The same holds true for participation biases, such as the over-representation of the elderly. The experts thus seem convinced that the many opportunity structures that the Swiss political system offers to voters (namely parliamentary and, at the subnational level, also governmental elections, as well as popular votes at all three levels) evoke feelings of 'too much, too often', leading eligible voters to participate *selectively* (see 'Direct-Democratic Votes' in this volume).

When asked to rank potential reform options in terms of their necessity, the largest share of experts endorsed legislation that would force political parties to publish their budgets in full. Providing for state funding is fairly popular as well. Whereas some form of state funding is common in many, if not most, established democracies, as well as in many new democracies (van Biezen and Kopecký 2007), such a move would be revolutionary in Switzerland. Here, political parties are traditionally believed to belong to the private domain rather than the public one. Since they aggregate and articulate the preferences of individual citizens, they are correspondingly financed out of *their* pockets too.

Finally, Figure 41.10 plots which national policies our experts think would need to be reformed most urgently. In line with what has been said above regarding the five major challenges, foreign and EU policy tops the list. Policies that address climate change and/or ensure environmental protection, as well as those that tackle demographic imbalances, i.e. health and welfare policy, come next. Culture and language, media, and security and military policy, as well as economic and financial policy, fall at the other end of the range.[2]

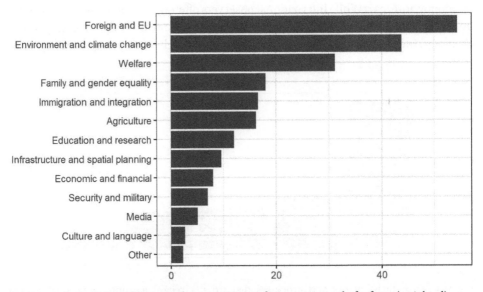

FIGURE 41.10: Swiss policy areas that experts regard as most in need of reform (weighted)

Experts were asked to pick up to 12 policy areas (plus a residual 'other' category) and rank them in order of their need for reform. Shown are the total scores arrived at by multiplying the number of times a policy area was chosen by its priority (see Figure 41.8 for information on how data were weighted).

Data source: Authors' data.

4 CONCLUSION

The nature of Switzerland's consensual, direct-democratic, and profoundly federalized political system makes it simultaneously more immune from and more vulnerable to contemporary challenges. It is more immune because the multiple levels of government and the various phases of decision-making act as safeguards against each other's failure. For instance, the cantons can act autonomously if decision-making at the federal level is stalled, or the people can decide in a referendum whether a bill proposed by parliament is either too radical or too little, too late. But the system is also more vulnerable because this elaborate clockwork depends on each piece playing its part. If parties refuse to even entertain a compromise solution, if fewer and fewer citizens volunteer for office at the local level, or if digitalization overburdens an already loaded political agenda, the system reaches its limits in terms of both legitimacy and problem-solving capacity.

In this chapter, we have focused on five distinct challenges by drawing on the existing literature and comparative data, on the one hand, and a comprehensive expert survey of Swiss political scientists, on the other. This combination of 'objective' accounts with subjective assessments allows for a holistic perspective, i.e. one that is not limited to and/or biased by the excessively narrow boundaries of highly specialized subfields. Indeed, when assessing the five challenges through our experts' answers, a nuanced picture emerges. Europeanization and polarization figure prominently in existing scholarly contributions *and* are widely agreed by experts to represent serious threats to Swiss politics. Digitalization, for its part, is often mentioned as one of the big 'meta-challenges'— big but also vague, and still hardly researched. Hence even experts have a hard time grasping the scope and meaning of this challenge for Swiss politics.

Finally, centralization is an issue that worries scholars of federalism who fear federal dysfunctionality and instability, whereas other experts are more relaxed and even conceive of the empowerment of the federation at the expense of the cantons as a solution rather than a problem, insofar as it helps to overcome policy gridlocks caused by the cantons' federal veto power (e.g. Mueller 2022). Accordingly, the possible solutions and reform options put forth in the expert survey vary widely, from mere discursive strategies (e.g. building new narratives) to redesigning core institutional features, such as the seven-member federal government (Federal Council) or the Senate-style second chamber (Council of States). A complete overhaul remains fairly unpopular among both the experts surveyed and the general public, which overwhelmingly takes pride in the existing Swiss political system. Even in late 2021, amidst the global COVID-19 pandemic, 90 per cent reported being satisfied with how it works (gfs.bern 2021b, 34).

Switzerland, *quo vadis?* In answering the pivotal question posed in this chapter's title, the preferred path forward is thus to *accommodate* the current challenges *within* the current system rather than setting up a new (or radically reformed) polity specifically designed to tackle them. There are basically two conceptually distinct yet inherently linked ways of doing so: changing political actors' behaviour or changing institutional frameworks and the incentives they produce. Consociationalism is dependent not only on power-sharing institutions but also on the political elites' willingness to engage in cooperative compromise—something that is nowadays severely undermined by high levels of conflict fuelled by one of the most polarized party systems in Europe (Bochsler et al. 2015; Freiburghaus and Vatter 2019; Vatter et al. 2020). Behavioural change would require that (party-)political elites once again abide by the values of non-competition and compromise, that the media report favourably on such a change, and that voters reward such newfound consensual strategies electorally and approve its results in popular votes.

While the structural challenges of being a 'small stat[e] in world markets' (Katzenstein 1985), as well as the rise of digital technology, would, of course, be far from being eradicated, reverting back to good, old Swiss-style 'amicable agreement' (Steiner 1974) would help enormously to address them via adequate policy responses. As long as there is no encompassing domestic consensus whatsoever (as is currently the case), Switzerland's bargaining position in relation to the EU and other external powers is seriously weakened. As the Swiss are currently most worried by the lack of ability of the political system to come up with solutions for the major problems of our times (gfs.bern 2021b, 50), breaking with party political wrangling and/or the vicious circle of polarization would certainly also help to strengthen citizens' identification with the representative side of democracy again—and hence lessen alienation.

The second option to accommodate the above mentioned challenges within the current system is to change institutional incentives through minor reform. Slightly reformed political institutions might incentivize actors to behave differently. If, for example, the Federal Council consisted of nine rather than seven members (or was elected by closed-list proportional representation rather than individually and sequentially under majoritarian rules), the breadth of popular political preferences could be accommodated even better. An even more ideologically diverse government could, in turn, better draft and defend broadly acceptable bills. The different groups and political parties would be encouraged to cooperatively feed their demands into the cabinet rather than resort to polarizing direct-democratic campaigns ex ante (through popular initiatives) or ex post (through optional referendums). Or if, to give another example, the number of signatures required to trigger a referendum was increased and e-collecting allowed, politically marginalized groups such as the youth might turn out more regularly, fostering long-term inclusion and political efficacy instead of abstention and (selective) alienation.

Whatever path is chosen, be it institutional reforms or modifying political behaviour (or both), one thing is clear: given the many veto players in Swiss politics, the challenges described here can be tackled only through a broad consensus. The key, as always, is to harness the multitude of political views and interests held and advocated by political parties, interest groups, social movements, and subnational governments. In this sense, it does not even matter *which* of the challenges is tackled first—be it centralization, through yet another federal reform, or Europeanization, through a new agreement with the EU—as long as it serves as an impetus to bring actors together again.

Notes

1. Relatively speaking, the share of acts of parliament challenged through that instrument has remained stable, but because the workload of parliament has grown, absolute numbers have too.
2. Note that the expert survey was fielded in January and February 2022, ahead of the 2022 Russian invasion of Ukraine.

References

Altman, David. 2011. *Direct Democracy Worldwide*. New York: Cambridge University Press.

Baldassarri, Delia, and Andrew Gelman. 2008. 'Partisans without Constraint: Political Polarization and Trends in American Public Opinion'. *American Journal of Sociology* 114 (2): pp. 408–446. doi: 10.2139/ssrn.1010098.

Bauer, Paul C., Markus Freitag, and Pascal Sciarini. 2019. 'Political Trust in Switzerland: Again a Special Case?'. In *Identities, Trust, and Cohesion in Federal Systems: Public Perspectives*, edited by Jack Jedwab, and John Kincaid, pp. 115–145. Montreal/Kingston: McGill-Queen's University Press.

Bednar, Jenna. 2009. *The Robust Federation: Principles of Design*. Cambridge: Cambridge University Press.

Bochsler, Daniel, Regula Hänggli, and Silja Häusermann. 2015. 'Introduction: Consensus Lost? Disenchanted Democracy in Switzerland'. *Swiss Political Science Review* 21 (4): pp. 475–490. doi: 10.1111/spsr.12191.

Brennan, Jason. 2016. *Against Democracy*. Princeton, NJ: Princeton University Press.C2D – Centre for Research on Direct Democracy. 2022. *Data*. https://c2d.ch/ (accessed 30 September 2022).

Church, Clive H. 2016. *Political Change in Switzerland: From Stability to Uncertainty*. London: Routledge.

Church, Clive H., and Adrian Vatter. 2009. 'Opposition in Consensual Switzerland: A Short but Significant Experiment'. *Government & Opposition* 44 (4): pp. 412–437. doi: 10.1111/j.1477-7053.2009.01295.x.

Dalton, Russell J. 2008. 'The Quantity and the Quality of Party Systems: Party System Polarization, Its Measurement, and Its Consequences'. *Comparative Political Studies* 41 (7): pp. 899–920. doi: 10.1177/0010414008315860.

Dardanelli, Paolo, and Oscar Mazzoleni (eds). 2021. *Switzerland-EU Relations: Lessons for the UK after Brexit?* London/New York: Routledge.

Dardanelli, Paolo, and Sean Mueller. 2019. 'Dynamic De/Centralization in Switzerland, 1848–2010'. *Publius: The Journal of Federalism* 49 (1): pp. 138–165. doi: 10.1093/publius/pjx056.

Dardanelli, Paolo, John Kincaid, Alan Fenna, Andé Kaiser, André Lecours, and Ajay K. Singh. 2019. 'Conceptualizing, Measuring, and Theorizing Dynamic De/Centralization in Federations'. *Publius: The Journal of Federalism* 49 (1): pp. 1–29. doi: 10.1093/publius/pjy036.

Digitale Verwaltung Schweiz. 2023. *eGovernment Implementation Plan*. https://www.digital-public-services-switzerland.ch/en/implementation/egovernment-implementation-plan (accessed 30 June 2023).

Fatke, Matthias, and Markus Freitag. 2015. 'Wollen sie nicht, können sie nicht, oder werden sie nicht gefragt? Nichtwählertypen in der Schweiz'. In *Wahlen und Wählerschaft in der Schweiz*, edited by Markus Freitag, and Adrian Vatter, pp. 95–119. Zurich: NZZ Libro.

FDFA – Federal Department of Foreign Affairs. 2022. *Economy and Trade: an Essential Partnership*. https://www.eda.admin.ch/missions/mission-eu-brussels/en/home/key-issues/economy-finance.html (accessed 18 April 2022).

Freiburghaus, Rahel. 2018. 'Ein grosser Scherbenhaufen? Einigungskonferenzen im schweizerischen Zweikammersystem'. In *Das Parlament in der Schweiz: Macht und Ohnmacht der Volksvertretung*, edited by Adrian Vatter, pp. 197–232. Zurich: NZZ Libro.

Freiburghaus, Rahel. 2023. *Lobbyierende Kantone: Subnationale Interessenvertretung im Schweizer Föderalismus*. Baden-Baden: Nomos.

Freiburghaus, Rahel, and Adrian Vatter. 2019. 'The Political Side of Consociationalism Reconsidered: Switzerland between a Polarized Parliament and Delicate Government Collegiality'. *Swiss Political Science Review* 25 (4): pp. 357–380. doi: 10.1111/spsr.12359.

Freitag, Markus, Pirmin Bundi, and Martina Flick Witzig. 2019. *Milizarbeit in der Schweiz: Zahlen und Fakten zum politischen Leben in der Gemeinde*. Basel: NZZ Libro.FSO – Federal Statistical Office. 2023. *Wahlen*. https://www.bfs.admin.ch/bfs/de/home/statistiken/politik/wahlen.html (accessed 30 September 2022).

Germann, Micha, and Uwe Serdült. 2017. 'Internet Voting and Turnout: Evidence from Switzerland'. *Electoral Studies* 47: pp. 1–12. doi: 10.1016/j.electstud.2017.03.001.

gfs.bern. 2021a. *Institutionelles Abkommen: mehrheitlich akzeptiert, allerdings nicht als Königsweg*. https://www.gfsbern.ch/wp-content/uploads/2021/05/standort-schweiz_europafragen_kurzbericht.pdf (accessed 30 September 2022).

gfs.bern. 2021b. *Bürger:innenteilhabe als Motor für Systemzufriedenheit*. https://www.gfsbern.ch/wp-content/uploads/2021/11/212039_demokratie-eu_schlussbericht_def-1.pdf (accessed 30 September 2022).

Gilardi, Fabrizio. 2022. *Digital Technology, Politics, and Policy-Making*. Cambridge: Cambridge University Press.

Gilardi, Fabrizio, Theresa Gessler, Maël Kubli, and Stefan Müller. 2021. 'Social Media and Policy Responses to the COVID-19 Pandemic in Switzerland'. *Swiss Political Science Review* 27 (2): pp. 243–256. doi: 10.1111/spsr.12458.

KOF – Konjunkturforschungsstelle. 2022. *KOF Globalisation Index*. https://kof.ethz.ch/en/forecasts-and-indicators/indicators/kof-globalisation-index.html (accessed 30 September 2022).

Hibbing, John R., and Elizabeth Theiss-Morse. 2002. *Stealth Democracy: Americans' Beliefs About How Government Should Work*. Cambridge: Cambridge University Press.

Jenni, Sabine. 2014. 'Europeanization of Swiss Law-Making: Empirics and Rhetoric are Drifting Apart'. *Swiss Political Science Review* 20 (2): pp. 208–215. doi: 10.1111/spsr.12098.

Katzenstein, Peter J. 1985. *Small States in World Markets: Industrial Policy in Europe*. London: Cornell University Press.

Kriesi, Hanspeter. 2007. 'The Role of the European Union in National Election Campaigns'. *European Union Politics* 8 (1): pp. 83–108. doi: 10.1177/1465116507073288.

Ladner, Andreas. 2018. *Der Schweizer Föderalismus im Wandel: Überlegungen und empirische Befunde zur territorialen Gliederung und der Organisation der staatlichen Aufgabenerbringung in der Schweiz*. Lausanne: IDHEAP.

Lijphart, Arend. 1968. *The Politics of Accommodation: Pluralism and Democracy in the Netherlands*. Berkeley/Los Angeles: University of California Press.

Linder, Wolf, and Sean Mueller. 2021. *Swiss Democracy: Possible Solutions to Conflict in Multicultural Societies*. Basingstoke: Palgrave.

Merkel, Wolfgang. 2014. 'Is There a Crisis of Democracy?' *Democratic Theory* 1 (2): pp. 11–25. doi: 10.3167/dt.2014.010202.

Mueller, Sean. 2015. *Theorising Decentralisation: Comparative Evidence from Sub-national Switzerland*. Colchester: ECPR Press.

Mueller, Sean. 2022. 'Agreeing to Disagree: Federal Veto Powers in Switzerland'. In *Defensive Federalism: Protecting Territorial Minorities from the 'Tyranny of the Majority'*, edited by Ferran Requejo, and Marc Sanjaume-Calvet, pp. 131–152. London: Routledge.

Mueller, Sean, and Alan Fenna. 2022. 'Dual versus Administrative Federalism: Origins and Evolution of Two Models'. *Publius: The Journal of Federalism* 52 (4): pp. 525–552. doi: 10.1093/publius/pjac008.

Neidhart, Leonhard. 1975. *Föderalismus in der Schweiz: Zusammenfassender Bericht über die Föderalismus-Hearings der Stiftung für eidgenössische Zusammenarbeit in Solothurn*. Zurich: Benziger.

Oesch, Daniel, and Line Rennwald. 2018. 'Electoral Competition in Europe's New Tripolar Political Space: Class Voting for the Left, Centre-Right and Radical Right'. *European Journal of Political Research* 57 (4): pp. 783–807. doi: 10.1111/1475-6765.12259.

Olson, Mancur. 1969. 'The Principle of "Fiscal Equivalence": The Division of Responsibilities among Different Levels of Government'. *The American Economic Review* 59 (2): pp. 479–487.

Petitpas, Adrien, Julien M. Jaquet, and Pascal Sciarini. 2021. 'Does E-Voting Matter for Turnout and to Whom?' *Electoral Studies* 71: pp. 102–245. doi: 10.1016/j.electstud.2020.102245.

Rauchfleisch, Adrian, and Julia Metag. 2016. 'The Special Case of Switzerland: Swiss Politicians on Twitter'. *New Media & Society* 18 (10): pp. 2413–2431. doi: 10.1177/1461444815586982.

Sartori, Giovanni. 2005 [1976]. *Parties and Party Systems: A Framework for Analysis*. Cambridge: Cambridge University Press.

Sciarini, Pascal, Fabio Cappelletti, Andreas C. Goldberg, and Simon Lanz. 2016. 'The Underexplored Species: Selective Participation in Direct Democratic Votes'. *Swiss Political Science Review* 22 (1): pp. 75–94. doi: 10.1111/spsr.12178.

Sciarini, Pascal, Alex Fischer, and Sarah Nicolet. 2004. 'How Europe Hits Home: Evidence from the Swiss Case'. *Journal of European Public Policy* 11 (3): pp. 353–378. doi: 10.1080/13501760410001694228.

Sciarini, Pascal, Manuel Fischer, and Denise Traber (eds). 2015. *Political Decision-Making in Switzerland: The Consensus Model under Pressure*. Basingstoke: Palgrave Macmillan.

Shugart, Matthew S., and John M. Carey. 1992. *Presidents and Assemblies: Constitutional Design and Electoral Dynamics*. Cambridge: Cambridge University Press.

Smartmonitor. 2022. *Data: Analysen*. https://www.smartmonitor.ch/de/analyses (accessed 30 September 2022).

Solijonov, Abdurashid. 2016. *Voter Turnout Trends around the World*. Stockholm: IDEA.

Steiner, Jürg. 1974. *Amicable Agreement versus Majority Rule: Conflict Resolution in Switzerland*. Chapel Hill: University of North Carolina Press.

Steiner, Reto, Claire Kaiser, Alexander Haus, Ada Amsellem, Nicolas Keuffer, and Andreas Ladner. 2021. *Zustand und Entwicklung der Schweizer Gemeinden: Ergebnisse des nationalen Gemeindemonitorings 2017*. Glarus: Somedia.

Swissvotes. 2022. *Data: Swissvotes*. https://swissvotes.ch/page/dataset (accessed 30 September 2022).

UNCTAD – United Nations Conference on Trade and Development. 2021. *Technology and Innovation Report 2021*. New York: UN.

Urbinati, Nadia. 2019. *Me the People: How Populism Transforms Democracy*. Cambridge: Harvard University Press.
van Biezen, Ingrid, and Petr Kopecký. 2007. 'The State and the Parties: Public Funding, Public Regulation and Rent-Seeking in Contemporary Democracies'. *Party Politics* 13 (2): pp. 235–254. doi: 10.1177/1354068807073875.
Vatter, Adrian. 2018. *Swiss Federalism: The Transformation of a Federal Model*. London/New York: Routledge.
Vatter, Adrian. 2020. *Das politische System der Schweiz*. Baden-Baden: Nomos.
Vatter, Adrian, Rahel Freiburghaus, and Alexander Arens. 2020. 'Coming a Long Way: Switzerland's Transformation from a Majoritarian to a Consensus Democracy (1848–2018)'. *Democratization* 27 (6): pp. 970–989. doi: 10.1080/13510347.2020.1755264.
Vatter, Adrian, Tobias Arnold, Alexander Arens, Laura R. Vogel, Marc Bühlmann, Hans-Peter Schaub, Oliver Dlabač, and Rolf Wirz. 2020. *Data: Patterns of Democracy in the Swiss Cantons, 1979–2018*. https://www.ipw.unibe.ch/about_us/people/vatter/pdsk/datasets/patterns_of_democracy_in_the_swiss_cantons_dataset/index_eng.html (accessed 30 September 2022).

CHAPTER 42

AN OUTSIDE PERSPECTIVE ON SWISS POLITICS. HOW SUCCESSFUL IS SWITZERLAND'S POLITICAL SYSTEM?

HERBERT OBINGER

> It is rather for us to be here dedicated to the great task remaining before us—... that government of the people, by the people, for the people, shall not perish from the earth.

1 INTRODUCTION

As rightly emphasized in the introduction to this *Handbook*, the Swiss political system is unique in many respects, which makes it a highly interesting object of research in comparative political science.[1] The contributions to this *Handbook* have impressively summarized the current state of research on political institutions and actors, decision-making processes, foreign relations, and public policies in Switzerland.

This concluding essay looks at Switzerland from the outside. From a comparative perspective, it focuses on the performance and, closely related to this, the legitimacy of the political system. The starting point and normative yardstick for this exercise is the above-quoted closing sentence of a famous speech delivered by US President Abraham Lincoln during the American Civil War at the military cemetery in Gettysburg in November 1863. I argue that Switzerland, more than almost any other country in the world, has realized Lincoln's ideal of 'government by the people and for the people'. Nowhere else do citizens have such extensive opportunities to participate in the political decision-making process, and there are very few countries that have a similarly strong track record as Switzerland across all policy areas. The unique rights of citizens to participate in policy-making and the excellent performance of the political system are closely related. In conjunction with consensus democracy, they generate an extraordinarily high degree of input and output legitimacy, which is the root cause for political stability and peaceful coexistence in a multi-dimensionally fragmented society. Both aspects—government by the people and government for the people—structure this chapter, which is rounded off by a brief conclusion.

2 Government by the People

Exactly sixteen years before Lincoln's speech, Switzerland was also shaken by a brief civil war that was to remain the last military conflict on the soil of the Confederation to this day. The result of the so-called *Sonderbundkrieg* between the Catholic-conservative and the liberal Protestant cantons was the adoption of the federal constitution of 1848, which replaced the loose confederation of twenty-five cantons with a democratic federal state. With it, Switzerland became a liberal and democratic outpost on the European continent dominated by authoritarian monarchies. The new constitution, pushed by the victorious liberal forces, borrowed institutional elements from the US political system (majority rule, federalism, and symmetrical bicameralism with the senate principle) as well as from the revolutionary French directorial government. Federalism, with its initially very limited powers of the central state, guaranteed autonomy and minority protection for the defeated Catholic-conservative cantons. In addition, the directorial system of government, with its principle of collegiality and rotation in the executive, not only impeded personality politics but also anchored a strict separation of powers between the legislative and executive branches through the absence of a vote of no confidence. With the newly introduced obligatory referendum, the (male) people became the supreme constitutional authority,[2] whereby the double majority required for a constitutional amendment protected the Catholic minority from a tyranny of the majority. Universal conscription and the militia principle in politics[3] and the army created a symbiosis of state and army constitution (Hintze 1906), but ensured the dominance of men in politics and society longer than elsewhere through personal and positional networks (Tanner 2015, 26). The federal constitution of 1848 also created a unified economic area. Together with liberal rights, political stability, and favourable geographic conditions—Switzerland is located in the middle of the highly dynamic mega-region of the 'Blue Banana' (Roger Brunet), characterized by traditional trade networks along the Rhine—this promoted the country's rapid industrial development. As early as 1870, Switzerland's gross domestic product per capita exceeded that of all neighbouring countries (Maddison 1995, 194–96). In the first forty years after the founding of the federal state, the hegemonic liberal (radical) forces further expanded the direct-democratic instruments at the federal level. In 1874, in the course of a total revision of the federal constitution, the optional referendum was introduced, and in 1891—albeit against opposition from the Liberals—the popular initiative for a partial revision of the federal constitution. Finally, in 1921, the treaty referendum followed. At the cantonal level, too, there was a continuous expansion of direct-democratic rights after the founding of the federal state, which today are more extensive than at the federal level in that all cantons have introduced the financial referendum and the legislative initiative. This continues at the municipal level, where citizens must approve the municipal budget.

In no other country in the world are the people's rights as extensive as in Switzerland and, accordingly, Switzerland is the country with the most referendums held worldwide (Qvortrup 2018; 'Direct Democracy' in this volume). Nowhere else, therefore, is the 'government by the people' realized to a greater extent than in the Swiss Confederation,[4] even though the vast majority of legislation in Switzerland is debated and passed by representative bodies. Since the people's representatives are of course also elected at all levels of government, this, together with direct democracy, opens up a wide range of opportunities for citizens to participate in the political decision-making process at all three levels of government. All this provides the political system with an enormously high degree of input legitimacy. Empirically, this can be seen from the fact that agreement with the question of whether citizens have a say in policy-making is highest in Switzerland in comparative perspective (Figure 42.1).

However, in the long run, the direct-democratic instruments at the federal level, and above all the veto potential of the optional referendum introduced in 1874, had a transformative impact on the political system as political groups with potential veto power were gradually integrated into the federal government (Neidhart 1970; Linder 1994). Together with the introduction of proportional representation after the First World War, this co-optation gradually replaced the majoritarian democracy dominated by the

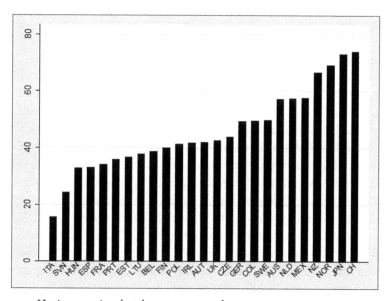

FIGURE 42.1: Having a say in what the government does, ca. 2018

Data source: OECD (2021).

Liberals with a consensus democracy (Lijphart 2012). This process was completed with the integration of the Social Democrats into the federal government in 1943. Based on the so-called magic formula, the distribution of cabinet seats between the four major parties in the Federal Council remained unchanged between 1959 and 2003. Consensus democracy with its high degree of vertical and horizontal power-sharing not only guaranteed the protection and representation of minorities, but was also effective in preventing an optional referendum through broad-based compromises. However, the inclusion of relevant interest groups in the pre-parliamentary decision-making process, the vertical division of power, and the necessity to reach an agreement within the all-party government spanning the entire ideological spectrum usually led, in line with the veto player theory (Tsebelis 2002), to political compromises close to the status quo. Radical proposals could therefore only be put on the political agenda at the federal level by means of popular initiatives. With few exceptions, however, such initiatives were either rejected or defused by more moderate counterproposals from the representative bodies. The result of such lengthy decision-making processes is typically incremental policy change, which some observers have derisively described as 'Swiss slowness' (cf. Abromeit and Pommerehne 1992). Did these institutional constraints inherent in the political system affect the innovative capacity and performance of the political system in terms of policy outputs and outcomes? As the next section shows, this question must be clearly answered in the negative.

3 Government for the People

First, using the example of social policy as by far the largest policy field in fiscal terms, the question of whether the veto-ridden political system has impaired the speed of the decision-making process and the ability to solve problems will be examined, before the performance of the political system is then scrutinized across several policy fields.

With regard to the adoption of social insurance and especially with regard to old-age pensions, 'the single most important welfare-state program' (Esping-Andersen 1990, 77), Switzerland is indeed a latecomer in international comparison, a position which has been attributed not least to federalism and direct democracy (Obinger 1998). The first attempt to introduce public pensions in 1931 ('Lex Schulthess') failed in a referendum. In addition to lacking financial resources, private and occupational pension provision, which was already widespread in Switzerland at the time, played a key role here and gained even more importance after the Lex Schulthess was rejected (Leimgruber 2008). As a result, the private welfare sector reached a critical size over time that made it impossible for the government to replace private provision with public pensions. The solution was to harmonize the historically grown private and occupational forms of social security and the public old-age pensions introduced in 1946 in laborious compromises. This ultimately led to a three-pillar system consisting of public insurance with universal coverage, occupational pensions that secure the standard of living, and tax-privileged self-provision, which was finally enshrined in the federal constitution in 1972 (Armingeon 2018). Thus, in a pragmatic way, a system emerged that the World Bank more than twenty years later adopted as the guiding model for solving the 'old-age crisis' (World Bank 1994) and that served as a blueprint for pension reform in Western democracies in the years that followed (Anderson 2019). The crucial point is that the Swiss three-pillar system is not the result of an intended grand plan but a retrospective and negotiation-based systematization of historically grown structures shaped by direct democracy and federalism. Former Federal Councillor Hans-Peter Tschudi, who was responsible for social security, stated in retrospect that the

> three-pillar system of old-age provision is not an invention of the legislator or theorists, but that it has been created by social practice .... Undoubtedly, no one would propose the three-pillar system if old-age provision in our country needs to be newly enacted. But the given circumstances had to be taken into account. A different arrangement would probably have come into question if Switzerland had followed Bismarck's example of pension insurance without delay in the last century. Also, the second pillar would probably not have developed so strongly if the voters had accepted the first old-age and survivors' insurance bill (Lex Schulthess) in 1931. (Tschudi 1987, 4, my translation)

This example illustrates that veto points such as the optional referendum can indeed delay the pace of reform. However, the associated necessity to negotiate and to find a compromise did not diminish the innovative capacity of the political system and even led to an internationally exemplary solution. This is also shown by Switzerland's track record in other policy areas.

To assess the general performance of Switzerland's semi-direct consensus democracy, a comparative perspective is inevitably necessary. Moreover, this analysis must, for reasons of space, be limited to present policy outcomes and inevitably remain selective. To examine Swiss performance in comparative perspective, I use well-known country rankings on freedom in politics and the media, on the quality and stability of political institutions, and on the general quality of life, as well as on policy outcomes in the most important policy fields such as social and homeland security, migration, health, economic policy, environment, education, and science. Some indices make a global comparison, others refer only to advanced democracies. In concrete terms, nineteen indicators are used, with some indices covering several policy fields.

Switzerland's position in these rankings speaks for itself: with two exceptions, Switzerland is always among the top ten countries with the best performance and eight times even among the top five (Table 42.1). Switzerland's top position in terms of gender equality is particularly remarkable given the very late introduction of female suffrage. We find the same pattern here as with old-age pensions, i.e. a strong contemporary performance despite late policy adoption. The two exceptions concern issues of social justice and the integration of migrants. With regard to social justice, Switzerland is criticized for an education system that discriminates at all levels against students from

Table 42.1: An international comparative look at Switzerland

Index	Description	Ranking
QUALITY AND STABILITY OF DEMOCRACY		
Robust Democracy Index, Sustainable Governance Indicators (SGI), Bertelsmann Stiftung (2020) https://www.sgi-network.org/2020/Robust_Democracy/Quality_of_Democracy	Based on qualitative expert reports. Looks at forty-one EU and OECD countries. Asks: Are democratic institutions and practices robust?	1. Sweden 2. Finland 3. Norway 4. Denmark **5. Switzerland**
Global Freedom Score, Freedom House (2020) https://freedomhouse.org/countries/freedom-world/scores?sort=desc&order=Total%20Score%20and%20Status	Rates people's access to political rights and civil liberties in 210 countries and territories through its annual Freedom in the World report. Individual freedoms—ranging from the right to vote to freedom of expression and equality before the law—can be affected by state or nonstate actors.	1. Sweden (100) 2. Finland (100) 3. Norway(100) 4. New Zealand (99) 5. Uruguay (97) 6. Ireland (97) 7. Denmark (97) **8. Switzerland (96)**
World Press Freedom Index, Reporters without Borders. (2021) https://rsf.org/en/index?year=2021	The degree of freedom available to journalists in 180 countries is determined by pooling the responses of experts to a questionnaire devised by Reporters without Borders.	8. New Zealand 9. Portugal **10. Switzerland**
Corruption Perceptions Index, Transparency International (2021) https://www.transparency.org/en/cpi/2021/index/che	Ranks 180 countries and territories around the world by their perceived levels of public sector corruption. The results are given on a scale of 0 (highly corrupt) to 100 (very clean).	4. Singapore 4. Sweden **7. Switzerland** 8. Netherlands
Good Governance Index (SGI), Bertelsmann Stiftung (2020) https://www.sgi-network.org/2020/Good_Governance	Based on qualitative expert reports. Forty-one EU and OECD countries Asks: Do institutional arrangements enhance the public sector's capacity to act? Can citizens, NGOs, and other organizations hold the government accountable for its actions?	6. Germany 7. Canada **8. Switzerland** 9. Luxembourg
Sustainable Policies Index (SGI), Bertelsmann Stiftung (2020) https://www.sgi-network.org/2020/Sustainable_Policies	Based on qualitative expert reports. Looks at forty-one EU- and OECD countries. Asks: Does the government cultivate the economic, social, and environmental conditions that generate well-being and empowerment? Is the provision of global public goods fostered?	2. Denmark 3. Norway **4. Switzerland** 5. Finland 6. Luxembourg

Table 42.1: Continued

Index	Description	Ranking
WELL-BEING AND QUALITY OF LIFE (combined indicators)		
Human Development Index United Nations (2020) http://hdr.undp.org/en/content/latest-human-development-index-ranking	The Human Development Index (HDI) is a summary measure of average achievement in key dimensions of human development: a long and healthy life, being knowledgeable, and having a decent standard of living. The HDI is the geometric mean of normalized indices for each of the three dimensions. Consists of the life expectancy index, the education index, and the Gross National Income index.	1. Norway 2. **Switzerland** and Ireland 4. Hong Kong 5. Iceland
Better Life Index OECD (2020) https://www.oecdbetterlifeindex.org/#/11111111111	Looks at forty countries and several topics of well-being: 1. Housing: housing conditions and spending (e.g. property pricing) 2. Income: household income (after taxes and transfers) and net financial wealth 3. Jobs: earnings, job security, and unemployment; Community: quality of social support network; Education: education and what one gets out of it; Environment: quality of environment (e.g. environmental health); Governance: involvement in democracy 4. Health; Life Satisfaction: level of happiness; Safety: murder, and assault rates; Work–life balance	4. Canada 5. Denmark 6. **Switzerland** 7. Finland
Quality of City Ranking Mercer (2019) https://mobilityexchange.mercer.com/insights/quality-of-living-rankings	Mercer evaluates local living conditions in more than 450 cities surveyed worldwide. Living conditions are analysed according to thirty-nine factors, grouped in ten categories: Political and social environment; Economic environment; Socio-cultural environment; Medical and health considerations; Schools and education; Public services and transportation; Recreation; Consumer goods; Housing; Natural environment.	**Switzerland** scores highest as four Swiss cities can be found in the top fifteen cities worldwide

(continued)

Table 42.1: Continued

Index	Description	Ranking
POLICY OUTCOMES		
Potential years of life lost (PYLL, 2019) OECD (2022), 'Potential years of life lost' (indicator), https://doi.org/10.1787/193a2829-en (accessed on 01 March 2022).	This indicator is a summary measure of premature mortality, providing an explicit way of weighting deaths occurring at younger ages, which may be preventable. The calculation of the PYLL involves summing up deaths occurring at each age and multiplying this with the number of remaining years to live up to a selected age limit (age seventy-five is used in OECD Health Statistics). In order to assure cross-country and trend comparison, the PYLL are standardized for each country and each year. It is measured in years lost per 100,000 inhabitants, aged zero to sixty-nine.	1. Luxembourg 2. **Switzerland** 3. Japan Sweden
Environmental Performance Index Yale Center for Environmental Law & Policy (2020) https://epi.yale.edu/	Provides a data-driven summary of the state of sustainability around the world. Using thirty-two performance indicators across eleven issue categories, the Environmental Performance Index ranks 180 countries on environmental health and ecosystem vitality.	1. Denmark 2. Luxembourg 3. **Switzerland** 4. UK
Social Justice Index, Bertelsmann Stiftung (2019) https://www.sgi-network.org/docs/publications/Social_Jutice_in_the_EU_2019.pdf	Investigates opportunities for social participation in the forty-one EU and OECD countries on the basis of forty-six quantitative and qualitative criteria. The index examines six dimensions of social justice: poverty, education, the labour market, intergenerational justice, health, and social inclusion and non-discrimination.	1. Iceland 2. Norway 3. Denmark 4. Finland **14. Switzerland** 15. France
Global Social Mobility Index, World Economic Forum (2020) https://www3.weforum.org/docs/Global_Social_Mobility_Report.pdf	Looks at eighty-two countries. Provides an assessment of the current state of the paths to social mobility around the world. The Report features the Global Social Mobility Index, which assesses those policies, practices, and institutions that collectively determine the extent to which everyone in society has a fair chance to fulfil their potential.	5. Iceland 6. Netherlands 7. **Switzerland** 8. Belgium

Table 42.1: Continued

Index	Description	Ranking
Gender Inequality Index (GII), United Nations (also included in the HDI) (2019) https://hdr.undp.org/sites/default/files/2020_statistical_annex_table_5.pdf	Measures gender inequality in 162 countries by looking at maternal mortality, adolescent birth rate, share of seats in parliament, population with at least some secondary education, and labour force participation.	1. **Switzerland** 2. Denmark 3. Sweden
Migrant Integration Policy Index (2020) https://mipex.eu/key-findings	Looks at fifty-six countries. Identifies three key dimensions that underlie all areas of a country's integration policy: 1. Basic rights: Can immigrants enjoy comparable rights to nationals (e.g. equal rights to work, training, health, and non-discrimination)? 2. Equal opportunities: Can immigrants receive support to enjoy comparable opportunities to nationals (e.g. targeted support in education, health, and political participation)? 3. Secure future: Can immigrants settle long-term and feel secure about their future in the country (e.g. family reunification, permanent residence, and access to nationality)?	1. Sweden 2. Finland 25. **Switzerland**
Educational attainment of young adults (2018), OECD https://doi.org/10.1787/888934082860	Share of people aged twenty-five to thirty-four with at least an upper secondary education OECD countries	1. Korea 2. Poland 3. Slovenia 4. Canada 5. Czech R 6. Lithuania 7. **Switzerland** 8. Ireland
Nobel Prizes in hard sciences https://stats.areppim.com/stats/stats_nobelhierarchy_percapita.htm	Nobel Prizes in hard sciences per capita (1901–2021)	1. **Switzerland** 2. Sweden 3. Denmark
Homicide United Nations Office of Drugs and Crime (2018) https://dataunodc.un.org/content/Country-profile?country=Switzerland	Number of victims of intentional homicide per 100,000 population.	*World average: 5.8* Norway: 0.5 **Switzerland: 0.6** Germany: 0.9 Austria: 1.0 Denmark: 1.0

(continued)

Table 42.1: Continued

Index	Description	Ranking
Misery Index Compiled by economist Steve H. Hanke https://www.nationalreview.com/2021/04/hankes-2020-misery-index-whos-miserable-and-whos-happy/	The misery index is the sum of the unemployment, inflation, and bank-lending rates, minus the percentage change in real GDP per capita. 156 countries	1. Guyana 2. Taiwan 3. Qatar 4. Japan 5. China 6. South Korea 7. **Switzerland**

low social status. The relatively high poverty rate of senior citizens and migrants also earns criticism (Hellmann et al. 2020, 193–94). With regard to migration and integration (Migrant Integration Policy Index), Switzerland scores particularly low in terms of policies which provide immigrants with a secure future in the country (i.e. issues of naturalization and permanent residence as well as anti-discrimination legislation). These policies also negatively affect Switzerland's ranking in the Global Freedom Index compiled by Freedom House. Here, Switzerland is criticized for its discrimination of Muslims (e.g. burqa bans, ban on building minarets).

Overall, however, it can be seen that Switzerland occupies top positions both across many policy fields and in terms of the quality and effectiveness of state institutions, which the country mostly shares with other small states in northern and continental Europe. An OECD study of the prosperity and quality of life in the member states (OECD 2020) also underlines the high standard of living in Switzerland. As in other small countries in the top group, this success has been achieved together with relatively low inequality: 'Generally speaking, people in the Nordic countries, the Netherlands, New Zealand, and Switzerland enjoy both comparatively higher levels of current well-being *and* lower inequalities' (OECD 2020, 30, my emphasis).

Indeed, Switzerland has been comparatively successful in balancing the inherent tensions between democracy and capitalism. Before the coronavirus pandemic, the Gini coefficient after taxes and transfers was below average in a comparison of twenty long-term OECD member states and only marginally higher than in Germany, France, or Sweden, the much-vaunted model country of the social-democratic welfare state. The poverty rate in the total population, i.e. the share of people with an income of less than half the median income, was also below average in 2018 at 9.1 per cent and even lower than in Sweden (9.3 per cent).[5]

What is remarkable from a comparative perspective is above all the way in which this relatively good performance record was achieved in the area of poverty reduction and the containment of inequality. Switzerland's path here deviates fundamentally from that of most other high-performing countries in continental and northern Europe. Whereas the northern and continental European countries relied on an extensive intervention state and correspondingly high tax rates to contain social inequality, Switzerland achieved a similar performance with a dramatically lower tax rate and thus a much leaner intervention state and a lower number of civil servants (Figure 42.2). However, the Swiss path also deviates from the profile of liberal welfare states or liberal market economies in the English-speaking world with their sometimes enormous degree of inequality. Despite a similarly low tax ratio as in the US, income inequality is significantly lower in Switzerland. As is so often the case, Switzerland does not fit into any family of nations with regard to public policy (Castles 1998; Castles and Obinger 2008) or well-known typologies of comparative public policy research (e.g. Esping-Andersen 1990).

Three factors shaped this pattern of public policy. First, political institutions played an important role. From the beginning, federalism and direct democracy constrained the growth of the interventionist state. A 'politics against markets' (Esping-Andersen 1985) as in the Nordic states was hardly possible for institutional reasons alone. Second, neutral Switzerland was not involved in the two world wars which contributed significantly to the rise of big government and crowded-out markets on the war-torn European continent. Finally, the political balance of power must be pointed out. After the Liberals had ruled alone between 1848 and 1891, only bourgeois parties were in power at the federal level until 1943. This structural majority to the right of centre and the high institutional hurdles to state intervention paved the way for a 'politics with markets'. This applied above all to foreign trade and led early on to a high degree of world market integration and the emergence of a competitive export economy in sectors such as chemicals, food, watches, and mechanical engineering. Low taxes, political stability (and thus trust), as well as advantageous regulations, also favoured the rise of the banking and insurance sectors. Switzerland was thus quick to take advantage of the opportunities offered by the international division of labour, especially for small states, through specialization and strategic regulation. The latter included low tax rates and business-friendly regulations with a view to attracting capital and companies at the expense of other states.[6] All this ensured extremely high employment rates and very low unemployment, which was virtually non-existent in Switzerland in the post-war decades. Despite low tax rates, high wealth concentration, and comparatively low redistribution through taxes and social transfers (cf. OECD 2021, 211), poverty and income inequality in Switzerland remained within moderate limits due to high employment rates and concomitant low unemployment. This supply-side-oriented policy trajectory with its focus on growth, low taxation, and full employment is vehemently defended by large parts of the economic and political elites, so that efforts for stronger redistribution such as the attempt to introduce an inheritance tax for the super-rich failed spectacularly in a referendum (cf. Emmenegger and Marx 2019).

In view of this performance record, it is not surprising that the Swiss place the greatest trust in their government (Figure 42.3). Trust in the state and government is almost twice as high as the OECD average and shows that the population is highly satisfied with the output of the political system. This is reinforced by the remarkably high efficiency of government activities, especially since the excellent performance is achieved with a comparatively low tax burden on citizens and companies as well as very low government debt (Figure 42.2). In other words, the political system generates an extraordinarily high

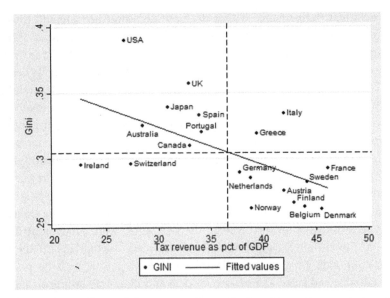

FIGURE 42.2: Gini coefficient (after taxes and transfers) and tax ratio 2017 in twenty OECD countries

The dashed lines denote the means, the solid line is the regression line.

Data source: OECD (2022a, tax revenue); OECD (2022b, Gini index).

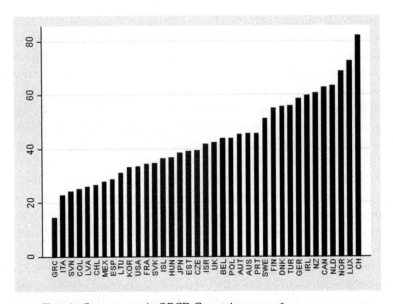

FIGURE 42.3: Trust in Government in OECD Countries, ca. 2018

Share of the population responding 'yes' to a question about confidence in the national government (in per cent).

Data source: Data from OECD (2020).

degree of output legitimacy. Together with the high level of input legitimacy, this forms the basis for the high cohesiveness of a heterogeneous society and ultimately for the stability of the political system.

4 Conclusion

Switzerland is a country where government by the people and government for the people in Lincoln's sense is realized in a way that is unique in the world. In terms of direct-democratic rights, the Swiss people can decide on all political issues. Therefore, radical proposals such as the abolition of the army as well as petty matters such as the reintroduction of carrier pigeons in the armed forces[7] or subsidizing the keeping of farm animals with horns can be put to the vote. It is true that usually only some citizens make use of these direct-democratic rights, while well-organized and financially strong interest groups try to influence referendums in their favour. However, this is no different in purely representative democracies. It was also direct democracy that paved the way to consensus democracy, whose overall track record clearly confirms Lijphart's thesis that 'consensus democracy tends to be the "kinder, gentler" form of democracy' (Lijphart 2012, 274). Although incremental and lengthy decision-making processes dominate in view of the many institutional veto points, this does not diminish the innovative capacity of the political system. Illustrated by the example of federalism as a constitutive core element of consensus democracy, the vertical division of power was undoubtedly a powerful barrier against unitarization and centralization, but federalism also ensured the protection of minorities and offered an arena for experiments and policy-making in line with local or cantonal preferences. Federalism is not only a barrier to big government, but also a laboratory of democracy (Pierson 1995), where innovative solutions can be developed and tried out which later may diffuse horizontally and vertically.[8]

Of course, not all that glitters is gold in Switzerland either. In conclusion, I would like to address three closely related challenges where even the otherwise effective political system is reaching the limits of its problem-solving capacity. The first challenge is the still unresolved relationship between Switzerland and the European Union. As a small open economy in the middle of Europe, Switzerland greatly benefits economically from the European single market, while the EU increasingly attaches conditions to Switzerland's participation in the common market. However, a high degree of political integration or even EU membership would undercut Swiss autonomy and sovereignty. It is difficult to find a solution here, especially since—and this is the second challenge— the strongest party in government is a right-wing populist party which sees itself as the defender of a self-determined, direct-democratic, and federal Switzerland and, in addition, mobilizes against mass immigration (including from the EU) with direct-democratic instruments. However, majority vote—and this is the third challenge—is a sharp weapon against structural minorities (Vatter 2011) and therefore tends to favour restrictive naturalization provisions, leaving a significant part of the resident population excluded from political participation.

The fact that Switzerland is an attractive destination for migration at all is due not least to the excellent track record of the political system. In this respect, Switzerland today is further remote from the Hobbesian state of nature with its 'bellum omnium contra omnes' (cf. Hobbes 1985 [1651], 185–186) than almost any other country in the world: life in Switzerland is (very) long and worth living, for there is hardly any danger of premature or even violent death. And while in the Hobbesian state of nature neither economic activities nor trade come into being and science, art, and literature are at a standstill, international trade, culture, and science are flourishing in the Swiss Confederation. However, this did not require an all-powerful Leviathan but it unfolded in a political system that embodies the antithesis of the Hobbesian idea of the state: a system of government that has no clear centre of power, effectively curtails personality politics, and where direct democracy and federalism secure freedom and at the same time constrain the growth of the Leviathan more than elsewhere in continental Europe. This system is not only capable of performing state functions effectively and efficiently, but has also been able to realize the main concern of Thomas Hobbes, the establishment of internal and external peace, over the past 175 years. In view of the return of the horrors of interstate war to Europe, this achievement of the political system alone cannot be sufficiently appreciated.

Notes

1. I thank Patrick Emmenegger for valuable comments and Emma Gasster and Lea Burmeister for assistance with data research.
2. Given the people's supreme authority in constitutional matters, federal legislation is not subject to judicial review by the Federal Court.
3. The militia principle is another bulwark against personality politics especially since taking on a political office part-time does not make one rich (Tanner 2015, 25). In addition, civil society expertise is brought into the political system, thus making it more difficult for political elites to alienate themselves from social realities. However, the militia principle has lost importance. The overwhelming majority of MPs at the federal level today are professional politicians.
4. This is also accompanied by a high level of citizen involvement in civil society: the more developed direct democracy instruments are at the cantonal level, the greater the civic involvement in associations (Freitag and Schniewind 2007).
5. OECD (2020), 'Poverty rate (indicator)', doi: 10.1787/0fe1315d-en (accessed on 20 May 2020). While child poverty and poverty within the working population is very low, the poverty rate among the elderly is considerably higher. This is also criticized in the Social Justice Index.
6. It is telling that Ireland has a similar profile to Switzerland (see Figure 42.2). Both countries are highly globalized economies that attract firms and capital on a large scale as tax havens. In contrast to Switzerland, Ireland only embarked on this course in the 1990s.
7. However, this referendum did not take place due to insufficient signatures.

8. One example is the internationally exemplary worker protection legislation (Federal Factory Act 1877), which was largely based on cantonal models (e.g. the canton of Glarus).

REFERENCES

Abromeit, Heidrun, and Werner W. Pommerehne. 1992. *Staatstätigkeit in der Schweiz*. Bern: Haupt.

Anderson, Karen M. 2019. 'Old-Age Pensions'. In *Handbuch Sozialpolitik*, edited by Herbert Obinger, and Manfred G. Schmidt, pp. 585–603. Wiesbaden: Springer.

Armingeon, Klaus. 2018. 'Die Entwicklung der schweizerischen Altersvorsorge'. *Swiss Political Science Review* 24 (1): pp. 43–52.

Castles, Francis G. 1998. *Comparative Public Policy. Patterns of Post-War Transformation*. Cheltenham: E. Elgar.

Castles, Francis G., and Herbert Obinger. 2008. 'Worlds, Families, Regimes: Country Clusters in European and OECD Area Public Policy'. *West European Politics* 31 (1–2): pp. 321–344.

Emmenegger, Patrick, and Paul Marx. 2019. 'The Politics of Inequality as Organised Spectacle: Why the Swiss Do Not Want to Tax the Rich'. *New Political Economy* 24 (1): pp. 103–124.

Esping-Andersen, Gösta. 1985. *Politics Against Markets. The Social Democratic Road to Power*. Princeton: Princeton University Press.

Esping-Andersen, Gösta. 1990. *The Three Worlds of Welfare Capitalism*. Cambridge: Polity.

Freitag, Markus, and Aline Schniewind. 2007. 'Direktdemokratie und Sozialkapital. Der Einfluss der Volksrechte auf das Vereinsengagement'. In *Direkte Demokratie. Bestandsaufnahmen und Wirkungen im internationalen Vergleich*, edited by Markus Freitag, and Uwe Wagschal, pp. 251–275. Berlin: LIT.

Hellmann, Thorsten, Pia Schmidt, and Sascha Matthias Heller. 2020. *Social Justice in EU and OECD. Index Report 2019*. Gütersloh: Bertelsmann Stiftung.

Hintze, Otto. 1906. *Staatsverfassung und Heeresverfassung*. Dresden: Zahn & Jaensch.

Hobbes, Thomas. 1985 [1651]. *Leviathan*. London: Penguin Classics.

Leimgruber, Matthieu. 2008. *Solidarity without the State? Business and the Shaping of the Swiss Welfare State, 1890–2000*. Cambridge: Cambridge University Press.

Lijphart, Arend. 2012. *Patterns of Democracy. Government Forms and Performance in Thirty-Six Countries*. New Haven, London: Yale University Press.

Linder, Wolf. 1994. *Swiss Democracy. Possible Solutions to Conflict in Multicultural Societies*. Houndmills, Basingstoke: MacMillan.

Maddison, Angus. 1995. *Monitoring the World Economy*. Paris: OECD.

Neidhart, Leonhard. 1970. *Plebiszit und pluralitäre Demokratie. Eine Analyse der Funktion des schweizerischen Gesetzesreferendums*. Bern: Francke.

Obinger, Herbert. 1998. 'Federalism, Direct Democracy, and Welfare State Development in Switzerland'. *Journal of Public Policy* 18 (3): pp: 241–263.

OECD. 2020. *How's Life? 2020: Measuring Well-being*. Paris: OECD Publishing. doi: https://doi.org/10.1787/9870c393-en.

OECD. 2021. *Governance at a Glance 2021*. Paris: OECD Publishing Paris. doi: https://doi.org/10.1787/1c258f55-en.

OECD. 2022a. *Revenue Statistics: Comparative tables, OECD Tax Statistics* (database) https://doi.org/10.1787/data-00262-en.

OECD. 2022b. *Income inequality (indicator)*. https://doi.org/10.1787/459aa7f1-en.

Pierson, Paul. 1995. 'Fragmented Welfare States: Federal Institutions and the Development of Social Policy'. *Governance* 8 (4): pp. 449–478.

Qvortrup, Matt (ed.). 2018. *Referendums Around the World*. Cham: Palgrave.

Tanner, Jakob. 2015. *Geschichte der Schweiz im 20. Jahrhundert*. München: C.H. Beck.

Tschudi, Hans-Peter. 1987. 'Das Drei-Säulen-Prinzip'. *Schweizerische Zeitschrift für Sozialversicherung und berufliche Vorsorge* 31 (1): pp. 1–20.

Tsebelis, George. 2002. *Veto Players. How Political Institutions Work*. Princeton: Princeton University Press.

Vatter, Adrian (ed.). 2011. *Vom Schächt- zum Minarettverbot. Religiöse Minderheiten in der direkten Demokratie*. Zürich: Verlag der Neuen Zürcher Zeitung.

World Bank. 1994. *Averting the Old Age Crisis*. Washington, D.C.

CHAPTER 43

CHOCOLATE DEMOCRACY

DANIEL BOCHSLER

1 INTRODUCTION

Swiss citizens take pride in their export industry.[1] Although chocolate figures among those products that the global public most frequently associates with its export industry, Switzerland also stands out thanks to the unique features of its model of democracy. Swiss citizens take pride in their democracy, and externally, the Swiss political institutions are widely considered as contributing to the country's exceptional political stability, despite the historically deep splits between cultural and political communities. However, there is very limited knowledge about the diffusion of the Swiss model of democracy in the world. Democracy promotion finds overwhelming support among Swiss citizens; a 90 per cent majority believe that Switzerland shall promote democracy abroad.[2] This is mirrored by scholarly claims that Swiss democracy could offer 'possible solutions to conflict in multicultural societies' (Linder and Mueller 2021). Among others, 'Presence Switzerland', a governmental PR agency tasked with promoting Swiss interests abroad, also supports initiatives to popularize Direct Democracy, a particular feature of Swiss democracy, in the world.

Prominent scholars of Swiss politics identify in the selective pillars of Swiss democracy—direct democracy, the consociational model, and federalism—advantages that beg imitation abroad: Kriesi and Trechsel (2008, 16) praise the Swiss system as 'an ideal model of "unity in diversity" for European integration', Cheneval and Ferrín (2018) see in the three (municipal, cantonal, and federal) layers of Swiss citizenship a solution for EU citizenship, and Stojanović (2022) recommends direct democracy as a cure against populism. In response to separatist challenges, Linder and Mueller (2021, 95) refer to the bargained cascade of 'sovereignty referendums' that were central to settling the Jura conflict. This academic narrative is mirrored in the claims of political elites, who stress that there are important lessons to learn from the Swiss case: 'Based on the largely positive experience with democracy [...] and the strong popular support for such policies, one would expect Switzerland to be at the forefront of global democracy promotion' (Geissbühler forthcoming). Furthermore, due to its neutral foreign policy status, Switzerland indeed sees itself as having a particular responsibility to contribute to peacebuilding globally (Goetschel 2011). As of 2002, the promotion of democracy abroad has been part of the Swiss foreign policy strategy.

However, how are the four main pillars of Swiss democracy—direct democracy, its consensual executive, the consociational democracy model, and federalism—received abroad, and reflected in the literature on comparative politics?

While the diffusion of institutional innovations among the Swiss cantons has become a classic theme in the literature on Swiss federalism (Walter and Emmenegger 2019; Williams 1914), scholars are more reserved as to whether the historically grown and partly idiosyncratic institutions of Swiss democracy can be used as a template for foreign constitutions (Linder and Mueller 2021, 275). Scholarship on cross-national learning from the Swiss case is scarce, in spite of the praise heaped on its unique institutional models.

The contribution of this chapter is threefold. First, capitalizing on the work assembled in this *Handbook*, this chapter reviews the showcases from the Swiss political system, and juxtaposes this work from a 'Swiss politics' perspective with the view of Swiss democracy in the comparative politics literature. Second, it asks where Swiss citizens see the strengths of Swiss democracy, and third, it asks whether and how the promotion of Swiss democracy builds on these supposed strengths of Swiss democracy.

The next section analyses Swiss citizens' self-view in a comparative perspective. The further sections follow four important institutional features (or 'selling points') of the Swiss model, direct democracy, the consensus model, consociational democracy, and federalism, followed by concluding remarks.

2 CONSTITUTIONAL PATRIOTISM 2.0? THE SELF-VIEW

First, I turn to the self-view by the citizens and residents of Switzerland. Freitag and Zumbrunn (in this volume) report that the Swiss citizens express an extraordinarily high satisfaction with their democracy. However, due to the subjective understanding citizens associate with democracy, the normative model of democracy shared by Swiss respondents may be of greater interest. In the European Social Survey in 2012–13, respondents were asked about their expectations of democracy. Four (out of fifteen) survey items highlight a remarkably different understanding of democracy among Swiss citizens and residents compared to their European counterparts. Empirically, these understandings fall along two dimensions, pertaining to *representative democracy* (the importance of clearly distinct parties and of a critical opposition) and *deliberative and direct democracy* (the importance of debate among voters preceding political decisions, and whether citizens should have a final say in referendums).

Figure 43.1 displays the (average) expectation of citizens by country (analytical weights included). Referendums and deliberations play an important role in the Swiss understanding of democracy. Swiss respondents rate the importance of having binding and final referendums as being equally important as having free elections. As best illustrated by the Landsgemeinde, Swiss respondents have a notion of 'Demokratie' that relies heavily on referendums and initiatives, and on deliberation in the course of referendum campaigns, while other democracies are incomplete. My use of the German term 'Demokratie' is deliberate, because German-speakers of Switzerland have much more pronounced views on this, while the Swiss-French and -Italian meaning of democracy is closer to the common European understanding (sample size: 271 and forty-six). Vice versa, Swiss respondents, especially German-speakers, systematically and strongly de-emphasize the importance of conventional mechanisms and institutions of representative democracy, such as alternation between governments and oppositions, and checks and balances on power.

The Swiss often serve as prime example of *constitutional patriots*: they are tied together not by a common language or religion, but by their political history and the practice of democracy (Kriesi 1999). Stutzer and Frey (2000) claim that direct democracy makes the Swiss happier. One might be tempted to call this glorification of Swiss democracy as the real essence of *constitutional patriotism*.

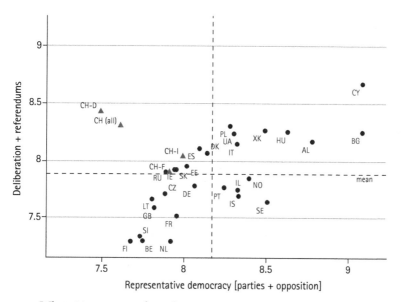

FIGURE 43.1: What citizens expect from democracy

Data source: European Social Survey (2012–13).

3 SWISS INSIGHTS ON DIRECT DEMOCRACY

Switzerland is the global champion in the use of direct democracy, and there is an impressive body of research building on this: empirical evidence from the Swiss cantons shows that frequent referendum and initiative votes boost Swiss citizens' satisfaction with their democracy (Stadelmann-Steffen and Vatter 2012). Meanwhile, non-Swiss political elites and scholars of comparative politics often associate direct democracy with undesirable outcomes: the fears relate to minority rights under majority rule (Gamble 1997), the unpredictability of politics and changing policies (Dibiasi et al. 2018), or the tendency to increase public spending. Direct democracy supposedly offers mobilization advantages either for privileged groups, or for populists and demagogues, while voters decide on issues without being adequately informed. It also supposedly impairs the ability of governments to pursue coherent policies (Schmidt 2002). Accordingly, comparative work finds the most staunch supporters of direct democracy to be citizens with populist attitudes (Mohrenberg et al. 2021).

Research on direct-democratic institutions and practice in Switzerland has debunked many of these concerns. Comparative evidence from Swiss cantons shows that direct democracy does not systematically lead to undesirable policy outcomes, such as increased public spending, and referendums may even have a restrictive effect on spending (Emmenegger et al. 2022). Further, the direct and indirect effects of direct-democratic institutions lead to an improvement of the quality of democracy (e.g. Leemann and Stadelmann-Steffen 2022; Leemann and Wasserfallen 2016), as they help avoid '[a gap] developing between the political elite and ordinary citizens' (Linder and Mueller 2021, 5).

However, moving policies closer to the (median) voter preference also translates into a 'tyranny of the majority' (Gamble 1997), which neglects the rights of political and social minorities. The history of Swiss direct democracy offers numerous examples thereof, from the ban on kosher butchering in 1893, to the rejection of female suffrage in 1959, up to municipal referendums and assembly votes on citizenship issues (Helbling and Kriesi 2004; Vatter et al. 2014). While the cultural rights of domestic linguistic minorities are regularly approved in referendums (Stojanović 2006), rejections of minority rights cover a wide array of structural minorities, including both non-enfranchised groups and other disadvantaged groups: for example, twice, the Swiss people voted against the interests of disabled people (pension reforms in 1995 and 2007), and maternity leave was also twice rejected (in 1987 and 1999), before a more pared-back form was accepted in 2004 (Frey and Goette 1998; Vatter et al. 2014).

For a few vocal Swiss scholars, journalists, and/or activists, the advantages of direct democracy prevail. They translate their enthusiasm into a global agenda: '[Most] places in the world suffer from an absence of, or severe weaknesses in the ability of citizens to be directly involved in policy and decision-making' (Kaufmann et al. 2010, 108). Thereby, Kaufmann et al. (2010, 108) advises against occasional referendums, scheduled top-down by the government, or turnout quorums, as they 'wreak serious harm on the basic idea of direct democracy'. In less emotional language, Cheneval and El-Wakil (2018) recommend mechanisms that allow citizens to trigger referendums, and Linder and Mueller (2021, 5) see in the 'abundance [of direct-democratic votes] not an obstacle, but key to success' of Swiss democracy. Swiss scholars see referendums as the beating heart of the Swiss political culture of compromise (Fleiner and Basta Fleiner 2004, 386), a means to fight populism (Stojanović 2022), or a solution for secessionist conflicts. According to Fleiner, a cascade of sovereignty referendums that were used to settle the Jura conflict could have been applied in the Serbia-Kosovo conflict, and they should become the international standard for secessionist conflicts.[3]

It is nobody less than the Swiss Minister of Foreign Affairs, Micheline Calmy-Rey, and the Swiss President, Doris Leuthard, who have signed two of the most important English-language manuals of direct democracy, the IDEA Handbook of Direct Democracy (Beramendi et al. 2008) and IRI's Guidebook to Direct Democracy. The president's praise appeared under the headline 'No fair and decent globalisation without direct democracy', in a volume that was co-financed by the Swiss ministry of Foreign Affairs and 'Presence Switzerland' (Kaufmann et al. 2010).

Certainly, there is no lack of curiosity around the globe about Switzerland's direct democracy. However, the number of imitators remains limited. Uruguay borrowed elements pertaining to consensus/consociational features (see section 5) and the direct-democratic model in constitutional reforms in 1917, 1934, and 1967 (Altman 2011). In 2012, the president of Mongolia published a five-year-plan 'to reduce centralization through direct democracy and citizens' participation', inspired and advised by Swiss experts, and co-financed by the Swiss Agency for Development and Corporation (2012, 16). In several semi-democratic or authoritarian regimes, referendums have offered a way to paint a democratic facade onto controversial amendments to the constitution. Venezuela's president, Hugo Chavez, relied on advice from Fleiner's group in designing direct-democratic instruments in his plan for '21st century socialism'.[4] Azerbaijan and Russia held referendums in 2009 and 2020 which altered term limit rules for the incumbent president or abolished them altogether. In Venezuela and Bolivia, similar attempts failed (Durán-Martínez 2012).

In European democracies, bottom-up direct-democratic rights at the national level are usually related to high hurdles, impeding the frequent use of these rights (Qvortrup 2017). At the subnational level in Germany, we find more accessible direct-democratic institutions. Furthermore, the Bundesland Baden-Württemberg engages in regular dialogue with the Swiss canton of Aargau about direct-democratic practices (Auer and Holzinger 2013). The country whose direct-democratic institutions bear the closest resemblance to Switzerland is arguably Slovenia with its bottom-up direct-democratic rights.[5]

4 CONSENSUS OR DISSENT?

With its all-party governing coalition and the rotating presidency, the Swiss political system has many exceptional features. However, non-majoritarian democracies, and institutions for power diffusion, are widespread elsewhere: on the European continent, they are the most common type of democracy. It is believed that non-majoritarian democracies are 'kinder and gentler' than their majoritarian counterparts, as they provide for a stronger welfare state, protect human rights better, are less repressive, produce more sustainable policies, and lead to broadly accepted decisions (but see Armingeon 2002; Lijphart 1999, 275–276, 293–300).

The Swiss institutional order represents an alternative to unconstrained rule by the majority. However, scholars do not agree what type of cure it actually constitutes. Language is an issue here. The term used in Swiss politics, also in the French-German edition of this *Handbook*, is 'concordance' (F) or 'Konkordanz' (D). Its English translation is ambivalent, either translated as 'consensus democracy' or 'consociational democracy', both of which were coined by the same author, Arend Lijphart. However, these two English terms do not mean the same, which makes it somewhat surprising that Lijphart uses Switzerland as a prime example of both of these concepts (Lijphart 1969, 1999). For the literature on Swiss politics, and exemplified also by this *Handbook*, the term 'consensus democracy' is central: it is cited fifteen times more often than consociational democracy. The consensus type refers to a set of rules about elections and government formation, large party systems and strong economic interest groups (corporatism), regularly resulting in multi-party coalition governments (Lijphart 1999, 31–41).[6] In contrast, my count of the English-language literature citing Switzerland (via Google Scholar[7]), reveals that references to the 'consociational democracy' type is much more frequent than the consensus democracy type. Consociational democracy, also often referred to as 'power-sharing', is a regime type for societies with persistent identity-based divides, e.g. ethnically divided societies. It is about a culture of inclusion, cooperation, and decision-making by compromise. Formal or informal institutions conducive to consociational rule are governments that include all politically relevant groups, strong group autonomy (e.g. federalism), and veto rights for minorities (Lijphart 1969). There are considerable overlaps with the consensus type, and in many aspects Lijphart's work does not clearly distinguish between his two types of non-majoritarian rule (Andeweg 2000; Bogaards 2000, 4113).

Conceptual rigour matters if Switzerland is to be analysed with a comparative agenda: the institutional features of consociational democracy are in the focus for analyses where Switzerland is studied as a possible solution for heterogeneous societies, while the consensus democracy framework may be more appropriate to analyse the executive party coalition or economic policies. The two theoretical frameworks also differ widely in their implications for the quality of democracy.

Switzerland stands out of from the family of consensus democracies due to the exceptional position of its executive vis-à-vis the legislative, the weak checks by its Federal Court, and its 'magic formula'.

First, the long-living government formula ('magic formula') relieves governments from their electoral accountability to voters. Even single seats have changed party only in exceptional circumstances, so that the voters have little or no chance to unseat the incumbent. The Swiss case thus nourishes the widespread belief that coalition governments are only weakly accountable to their voters, because incumbents can always bypass the disapproval of their voters by finding new coalition partners (Bartolini 1999; Kaiser et al. 2002, 326). Systematic empirical scrutiny reveals this supposed immunity of incumbents in consensus democracies against electoral losses to be a myth (Lundell 2011). However, Switzerland does deviate from this pattern, upholding the myth, due to the informal agreement on the all-party-coalition government. However, this also implies that stability and lack of electoral accountability is a consequence of all-party-coalitions, which are particularly associated with consociational democracies. Possibly, all-party coalitions as in Switzerland should be considered as a very different type from two- or three-party majority coalitions that are much more common in consensus democracies (Lijphart 1999, 91–96, 103–104).

Second, Switzerland differs from the conventional consensus model due to its lack of judicial review in constitutional matters, or even with regards to federal laws. This shifts the balance of power between the judiciary and the legislature towards the legislature. The lack of constitutional review avoids conflicts between the highest court and the people as a legislator (see 'The Judicial System' in this volume), and it is attached to some early predecessors of consociational democracy in Switzerland. By minimizing checks by actors outside the party coalition, the parties retain a maximum degree of autonomy to engage in bargaining. In 1848, the constitution-makers opted for this model in order to uphold segmental autonomy, and thus the possibility for each confessional group governing with minimal federal interference (Bochsler and Juon 2021, 417–418).

Third, both the lack of strong judicial power to intervene in the legislative process, as well as the weak electoral control that voters have over the government, is to be understood in the context of the strong direct-democratic institutions. The weak electoral accountability of the government to voters is substituted by a strong (direct-democratic) control which citizens have over policies. Additionally, if the government composition no longer matches the voters' preferences, referendums might lead to political blockages and thereby push for a change in the composition of the coalition.

Despite the exceptional stability of the informal coalition agreement and the institutional context, the polarization of party politics over recent decades alters the functioning of political institutions and their output, and this has preoccupied scholars of Swiss politics.

There are different readings of the recent changes. More pessimist interpretations argue that the political space to reach joint solutions on major reforms is vanishing. This renders 'policy outputs [...] less predictable' (Sciarini et al. 2015, 21) and has even resulted in political gridlock, not only in Swiss–EU relations (Kriesi 2015, 737), but also in policy fields as diverse as pension reform, climate change mitigation, or tax reform (Afonso and Papadopoulos 2015; Bochsler et al. 2015, 484; Vatter 2016).

A different reading points to more dynamic and inclusive decision-making processes. All-party coalitions in parliament have become less frequent, and parliamentary decision-making has become more conflictual (Traber 2015), but they have been replaced by issue-specific coalitions, 'at variable geometry' (Sciarini et al. 2015, 254). This also represents gains for the quality of democracy: as 'parties have gained power and importance in Swiss politics' (Traber 2015, 705; see also 'Swiss Parliament' in this volume), political power has become more pluralized and the decision-making process more transparent (Bochsler et al. 2015).

This change is echoed by calls for a major reform of the system of government, moving towards a three-party coalition model, with proper coalition agreements on programmatic grounds—a proposal that is also termed the 'small concordance' (Sciarini 2011, 216–217). In this scenario, Switzerland would become a conventional consensus democracy.

The Swiss consensus model, with its institutional specificity ('magic formula') which sets it apart from all other consensus democracies, represents a poor paradigmatic case for scholars of comparative politics. Also, the question of polarized party systems is only rarely pointed to in the comparative politics literature on consensus democracies (e.g. Lowell 1896, 70, 73–74). However, there are some isolated cases globally with similar elements: Uruguay has built a political system with important similarities to Switzerland. In Northern Ireland, the Swiss 'magic formula' regulating government coalitions became a constitutional rule, and is calculated after every election based on the D'Hondt formula. As such, both Uruguay and Northern Ireland would fit the consociational democracy type best (see next section).

5 A MODEL DEMOCRACY FOR MULTICULTURAL SOCIETIES?

Two recent books by Swiss scholars Wolf Linder, Sean Mueller (2021), and Nenad Stojanović (2021) propagate the idea of the Swiss model as a solution to divided societies. Both build in different ways on the consociational features of Swiss democracy. Switzerland is one of the four 'classical' cases of 'consociational democracy', yet today scholars of Swiss politics have been questioning to what degree contemporary Switzerland can still be considered as such.

Three objections to the classification of Switzerland as a consociational democracy have been put forward. The first pertains to Switzerland's cultural divides: there is doubt whether Switzerland has any 'ethnic groups' or a deep cultural divide, usually considered a basis for consociational democracies. Political scientists employ different terms to describe cultural divides in Switzerland, such as 'strongly segmented subcultures' (Steiner 1974), 'multicultural society' (Linder and Mueller 2021), or 'multilingual society' (Stojanović 2021), thereby addressing different dimensions of cultural divides. The Swiss federal state and the liberal elites that founded it have constructed 'a national myth of the civic, republican type to shape the national identity of the populations of all the cantons' (Kriesi and Trechsel 2008, 16). Andreas Wimmer (2011, 719) characterizes Swiss identity as a 'multiethnic nationhood, where the nation is defined as comprising several subnational [...] ethno-linguistic communities', with no aspiration to become a nation. Neither the Catholics nor the Protestants, the two groups related to the historical divide ('Kulturkampf'), see themselves as 'nations' (Wimmer 2011, 726), and there was never a larger movement to recognize neighbouring states as 'cultural homelands' in either of the linguistic communities. The definition of 'Swissness' as a multicultural identity, based on civic nationalism, and political inclusion and compromise as the mode of government was the only possible response which would embrace the multiple lines of diversity in Switzerland (Neidhart 1970; Wimmer 2011). Whether Switzerland was, and still is, a consociational democracy depends on the definition of the politically relevant cultural divides, and the political inclusion of groups along these divides.

Second, of the four 'classical' cases, Austria and the Netherlands are no longer consociational, because their socio-cultural divides have declined. In Belgium, the old cultural conflict has been replaced by more recent conflict between linguistic communities. Political institutions have been reformed, and as of the 1970s, Belgian federalism has been aligned along the linguistic divides (Bogaards et al. 2019). As for the fourth case, Switzerland, assessing whether it is still consociational and why, requires a more nuanced approach. The interpretations related to the classification of contemporary Switzerland in the comparative politics and in the Swiss politics literature differ. Swiss political scientists emphasize the importance of the historical Catholic–Protestant and conservative–liberal divide for the emergence of the constitutional institutions. The federal constitution of 1848, with its bicameral parliament and double-majority rules, offered the Catholic-conservative minority an indirect veto right. The first historical extension of the executive coalition in 1891 was preceded by an elite confrontation in parliament and in the direct-democratic arena (Bolliger and Zürcher 2004, 70–74). It came in reaction to a growing threat from the neighbouring states, where the idea of nations was gaining political ground, with fears that this could spill over to the Swiss linguistic communities (Wimmer 2011, 730–731). Further extensions of the coalition in 1919 and 1943 came after periods of contention and after the establishment of a corporatist arrangement in the economic sphere (see 'The Historical and Institutional Formation of Swiss Political Culture' in this volume), but these extensions were unrelated to cultural divides. In the early twenty-first century, the same four-party-coalition persists, as well as the constitutional rules that were introduced as a reaction to the confessional divide. However, the cultural (and liberal-conservative) divide has become largely irrelevant.

Third, the linguistic divide, which is still subject to some degree of power-sharing, does not even come close in its salience to the historical cultural conflict. The linguistic divide draws attention at times, for example in the context of the debate about international cooperation and European integration in the 1990s, but is limited to a few issues. Some regionalist or local movements in Ticino, Geneva, and the regional party splits in Jura/Jura Bernois could be interpreted as parties along linguistic and cultural divides,[8] but they remain marginal at the national level.

The linguistic divides are, however, the most important basis for characterizing Switzerland as a persistent case of a consociational democracy,[9] as scholars of comparative politics do (Bogaards et al. 2019, 350; Helms et al. 2019). More importantly, a recent branch of this literature in comparative politics has identified Switzerland (at the federal level) as the archetype of the 'liberal' consociational subtype, defined as follows: 'Liberal consociation rewards whatever salient political identities emerge in democratic elections, whether these are based on ethnic or religious groups, or on subgroup or transgroup identities' (McCulloch 2014, 502). The Swiss institutional order of 1848 introduced protections for the Catholic minority, though by indirect means. Thus, the same constitutional rules (double-majority rule for constitutional referendums and the bicameral parliament) that once constituted a veto card for the Catholic-majority cantons can, in contemporary Switzerland, serve other political minorities, or allow alliances across multiple conflict lines to exert a veto. This sets Switzerland, and a few other liberal constitutions, such as Nigeria or Iraq, apart from the 'corporate' consociational type, represented by Belgium. In the latter type, constitutional guarantees of political inclusion and veto rights are either directly codified as the rights of specific ethnic groups, or with federal units designed to separate these groups, and are thus only relevant for these specific groups. In Belgium, political reforms of the 1970s created a federal state, with the linguistic communities as the de facto constituent parts.

Despite the prominence of Switzerland in this typology, the Swiss politics literature has not engaged with this argument. A closer look at the Swiss archetype casts doubt on the argument that liberal consociational rules can accommodate different divides (Stojanović 2020, 33). An excellent case for this is the very limited relevance of Swiss consociational institutions for the linguistic divide: linguistic communities gain extensive autonomy through the federal organization of the state. However, as Stadelmann-Steffen and Leemann (in this volume) show, the key mechanisms that used to provide for confessional power-sharing (bicameral system, double-majority rules) disfavour the linguistic minorities, as cantons of linguistic minorities are under-weighted in relation to their voting population. Instead, the double-majority rules play in favour of rural areas and the conservative-nationalist pole.[10] For linguistic minorities, there is a new, but weak and unspecific constitutional rule concerning government inclusion (Giudici and Stojanović 2016), replacing an earlier informal rule (Wimmer 2011). Weak quotas (aka: 'goals') aim for inclusion of linguistic minorities in the public administration (Kübler et al. 2020). Finally, rigid protections of linguistic minorities exist only at the cantonal level (Bern: special representation rights for the Bernese Jura in parliament and the executive; Valais, indirect rules via territorial quotas).

Novel cultural divides are tangential to the institutional rules, or the rules in vigour may even prevent these divides from becoming manifest in Swiss political institution, as many residents with a migration background are excluded from the franchise.

Ironically, the double-majority rule, introduced to protect political minorities, was pivotal in the landmark constitutional referendum of 1994, and was the reason why citizenship was not liberalized (see 'Federalism' in this volume).

The decline of the relevance of consociational institutions has done no harm to the external view of Switzerland as a successful application thereof, and especially as one avoiding quota rules (Lanz 2021, 66–69), and Switzerland can capitalize on this as a credible mediator for institutional engineering in post-conflict societies.

Recent work has started to investigate the origins of consociational rule globally, and external actors and learning effects from abroad both play a role here: Wucherpfennig and co-authors show that consociational rule emerges in particular in former British colonies, with a tradition of indirect rule (2016). Juon and Bochsler (2022) analyse whether countries introduce liberal or corporate types of constitutional rules. The institutional design is affected by the diffusion of constitutional rules among neighbours, and after civil wars also by the institutions of the external countries active as mediators in the peace process. Thus, the comparative politics literature highlights the importance of external peacebuilding experts in the constitution-making process.

The promotion of peace has become one of the pillars of Swiss foreign policy since the end of the Cold War, with an emphasis on civil/political instruments. Through Swisspeace, the government also sustains a research and policy institute for peacebuilding. Swiss mediators took part in the negotiation of constitutional orders after conflicts involving Burundi, Nepal (Comprehensive Peace Agreement of 2006, following a Maoist insurgency), Macedonia, and Sudan (Greminger 2011, 18–19). However, Swiss scholars are sceptical about the idea of a 'direct export of institutions': a constitution must be grown and adjusted to the respective political, social, and historical context (Linder and Mueller 2021, 275). In practice, the mediation efforts of Swiss experts appear to have occurred with hardly any reference to the idea of institutional learning from the Swiss experience with power-sharing itself. None of the four highlighted cases bears significant similarities to the Swiss power-sharing model. Moreover senior diplomats describe the function of Swiss peacebuilding professionals as using their expertise to support the host states in order to find constitutional solutions suited to their specific political and social context (Baechler and Frieden 2006; Greminger 2011, 18–19). Reports by Swisspeace experts on power-sharing refer primarily to comparative expertise and evidence from post-war societies (e.g. Lanz et al. 2019; Raffoul 2019) and much less to the Swiss case (Iff and Töpperwien 2008).

The most relevant case of imitation of some of the consociational pillars from the Swiss model is Uruguay. It has an inclusive executive with a rotating presidency and an extensive system of quotas in the public administration and publicly owned companies. These institutions serve to provide a balance and power rotation between the two main political identities, the blancos and colorados (Altman 2011). However, Uruguay is neither federal, nor are there strong institutions to provide groups political autonomy or veto rights. The second parliamentary chamber is elected in a single nationwide constituency, offering no indirect advantages to territorial groups.

6 Federalism: Autonomy as an Illusion?

Switzerland belongs to a small group of countries with very strong federal institutions: with Switzerland ranked among the top three federations worldwide when it comes to levels of subnational government revenue and tax autonomy (Filippov et al. 1999, 6–7). However, Swiss federalism is also peculiar because of the combination of federalism with a strong direct democracy (Mueller 2021) and because of the small size of the country and the cantons. Figure 43.2 maps federal democracies and democracies with regional autonomies according to the strength of their institutions of federalism or regional autonomy and in relation to the population size of the countries and the first-level federal units. The institutional degree of autonomy/federalism is measured using the Regional Authority Index (Hooghe et al. 2016).[11] Democracies with strong federal/autonomous institutions are represented by triangles. Switzerland appears as an extreme case on this map. On the X-axis (country population), it is among the three smallest countries that have strong federal institutions, alongside Bosnia and Herzegovina and Austria. The Y-axis (average population size of the segment-states) shows that the Swiss cantons are the smallest regional units worldwide which possess strong levels of autonomy. The only rivals in this group are Portugal and Finland, marked by circles, because both are unitary states featuring island regions which possess strong regional autonomy (FIN: Aland, PRT: Azores, Madeira).

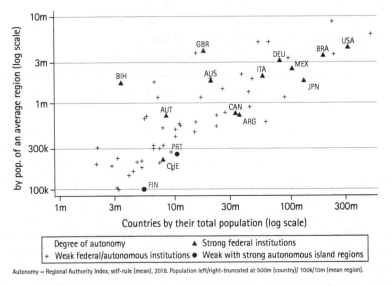

FIGURE 43.2: The size of federal countries and their (median) autonomous units, global comparison

Data source: Regional Authority Index.

Despite institutional stability, the character of Swiss federalism has changed. In the founding period, the cantons had an important function on the input-side of democracy, as they accommodated for the largely territorial political divides, but they no longer play this role. A direct measure for the territoriality of the political splits, available for the largest period of the modern Swiss state, are the results of the federal referendums and popular initiatives by canton: in the late nineteenth century, referendum results varied considerably between the cantons, but by the 1980s this between-cantonal variance had declined to just a third. This systematic assessment, based on salient political issues, corroborates the results reported in the previous section about the historical cultural cleavage: we find the main political divides are no longer related to the federal structure (Bochsler 2017).

Furthermore, the function of cantons on the output-side of democracy, in the provision of public policies, has declined. While cantons have largely been able to retain their policy competences, they are increasingly cooperating with each other in the provision of these policies, especially in domains with territorial interdependencies, e.g. public transportation in metropolitan areas, or in dealing with ecological problems that do not stop at cantonal borders (Bochsler 2009; Bolleyer 2006). Joint state services include, for instance, pooled IT services, intercantonal state universities, hospitals, or police training institutions. To alleviate the consequences of fiscal autonomy and tax competition, cantons and the federal state have set up a complex system of redistribution of tax revenue ('fiscal perequation'), which requires periodic adjustment. This periodic negotiation process also has an impact on tax competition itself—the more the cantons cooperate, the less they compete for the best tax payers (Gilardi and Wasserfallen 2016; Wasserfallen 2015). Thus, while cantons have resisted centralization, an intercantonal system of institutions of 'shared rule' has hollowed out their political and fiscal autonomy (see 'Federalism' in this volume). However, these intercantonal institutions have multiple democratic deficits, due to weak institutions, unanimity rule for decision-making, and only indirect controls by cantonal parliaments and citizens (Bochsler 2009; but see Wasserfallen 2015). A territorial reform, which might reconcile political boundaries with socially and economically relevant geographical spaces and create units that are large enough to function autonomously, is politically unfeasible. In the twenty-first century, attempts to merge cantons have failed in both the Léman and the Basel region (see 'Metropolitan Areas' in this volume).

Despite these symptoms of fatigue, scholars and practitioners still consider federalism a key institutional feature of the Swiss system suited for the promotion of democracy abroad. Two legal scholars, Fleiner and Basta Fleiner (2004, 634), see in the Swiss federal institutions the basis for a culture of compromise in a multicultural democracy. They recommend federalism as the guiding principle of state organization in other multicultural states in order to ensure the protection of minorities (Fleiner and Basta Fleiner 2004, 654–655). The political scientists Linder and Mueller emphasize that Swiss federalism, 'rather than just focusing on autonomy and differences, also allows for participation and coming-together for the purpose of joint problem-solving' (Linder and Mueller 2021, 4). For institutional engineers, they offer a handy checklist for determining whether federalism might be successful, based on lessons learned from the Swiss case: among others, minorities should be effective political minorities in a subnational unit, and a perfect geographical separation of ethno-cultural groups into federal units is to be avoided.

Turning to the four post-conflict countries where Switzerland was particularly engaged in engineering political institutions, results have been mixed (see section 5). Nepal was officially renamed the 'Federal Democratic Republic of Nepal', and Sudan became a 'decentralized state', with an autonomous South Sudanese region, but according to the RAI index, effective regional self-rule is minimal in both cases. Macedonia has been decentralized by creating strong municipalities, but it avoids references to federalism. Whether Swiss peacebuilders have contributed to these reforms must be relegated to further research.

7 Concluding reflections

Shops in many countries worldwide sell Swiss chocolate and, along with watches, it is one of the top two best-known Swiss exports. Meanwhile, Switzerland is not popularly known as a major exporter of democracy. Some are aware that Uruguay's political order follows in substantial parts the Swiss model, with direct-democratic rights. Beyond that, there are no other equally clear-cut cases of institutional learning from the Swiss democratic institutions. However, the degree to which Switzerland has an impact on the establishment of democratic constitutions worldwide depends on the dimension of its political institutions under analysis.

Comparative research shows that institutional learning—or the 'export of democratic institutions'—is not uncommon. For instance, electoral systems (Bol et al. 2015) or (after conflicts) power-sharing institutions are subject to institutional diffusion (Cederman et al. 2018). However, we know much less about the actors and mechanisms that facilitate this institutional learning, e.g. comparative research has only recently started to investigate the role of international actors and mediators after conflicts (McCulloch and McEvoy 2018). This chapter looks at the Swiss case and discusses the domestic view (citizens' and academic), on the assets that Swiss democracy offers for potential imitators, and the external view (in the comparative politics literature), as well as some of the footprints that Swiss democracy promotion has left worldwide (cf. Bochsler and Juon forthcoming).

While the Swiss masses see in direct democracy and consensus government the essence of democracy, these two pillars are not among the most successful pillars of the Swiss democracy promotion activities abroad: consensus democracy is the most common model of democracy in Europe, but its historically grown Swiss version is possibly too antiquated to find imitators today. In contrast, the elites' and activists' call for more direct democracy in the world is echoed primarily by authoritarian or hybrid regimes. Elites in democratic countries and scholars of comparative politics doubt whether complex political issues should be decided by supposedly badly informed citizens. In particular, they warn that strong direct-democratic institutions would increase spending and hurt minorities, although evidence from the Swiss practice dismisses these concerns.

The Swiss power-sharing institutions, also termed consociational democracy, are most relevant for the comparative politics literature, practitioners of democracy promotion, and political peacebuilding. Switzerland is active as a mediator after conflicts. Even though Swiss peacebuilding experts benefit from the Swiss experience with institutions of consociational democracy, they rely not specifically on the Swiss constitutional order but on a broader set of consociational solutions (Bochsler and Juon forthcoming). There is no evident footprint of Swiss constitutional rules being applied in cases where Switzerland was actively mediating. Rather, Swiss peacebuilding experts emphasize that political institutions need to take into consideration the specific political and historical contexts in the countries where they are introduced.

Consociational democracy in Switzerland itself is a prime example of how context matters for constitutional rules. The consociational democracy of Switzerland, which inspired the Swiss democracy promotion and peacebuilding agenda, dates back to the nineteenth and twentieth centuries. However, the cultural divide that was the basis for the Swiss consociational model is no longer relevant. For today's minorities—linguistic minorities and Swiss residents with migration backgrounds—the same institutions offer far less or no minority protection at all. This does no harm for its exports: chocolate companies promote their long history of production in marketing, and similarly, the Swiss promotion of democracy relies on Switzerland's past. Political history has no expiration date.

Notes

1. I am grateful to the editors and to Alexandre Raffoul for helpful comments.
2. According to a survey conducted in 2021 (Geissbühler forthcoming).
3. Fleiner, Thomas. 2012. 'Kreativer Minderheitenschutz', Neue Zürcher Zeitung, 27 March 2012.
4. Gmür, Heidi. 2007. 'Der Berater von Hugo Chávez'. Neue Zürcher Zeitung, 19 August 2007.
5. The Italian referendum rules, which also entail strong bottom-up instruments, rely primarily on the abrogative referendum, which can also be used against existing laws, deviating from the Swiss practice (Qvortrup 2017).
6. A second dimension thereof relates to multiple mechanisms of power diffusion, such as federalism and constitutional courts.
7. In work published as of 2000: 2,660 times 'consensus democracy', 3,010 'consociational democracy', and 16,300 'power-sharing'. This Handbook (German/French language version) almost only refers to consensus (seventy-three times), as opposed to four mentions of consociational, and one of power-sharing. The German/French terms 'Konkordanz'/'concordance' are used ambivalently. Some of the authors select different concepts, depending on whether they analyse decision-making processes in Swiss politics (e.g. Sciarini et al. 2015), or Switzerland in a comparative perspective (Hug and Sciarini 1995).

8. Stojanovic (2021) further refers to the organization of national parties in multilingual cantons.
9. The main comparative datasets used to measure power-sharing either consider linguistic groups as the politically relevant communities (Vogt et al. 2015) or complement them with the larger communities of migrants (Birnir et al. 2018).
10. Bochsler, Daniel. 2013. 'Die CVP verliert das Wallis und das Ständemehr'. *Neue Zürcher Zeitung*, 5 March, 9.
11. The data refers to the year 2018. The figure displays all countries whose units have an average self-rule index of thirteen or above, as those with strong autonomy. The Swiss cantons have a self-rule index of eighteen.

REFERENCES

Afonso, Alexandre, and Yannis Papadopoulos. 2015. 'How the Populist Radical Right Transformed Swiss Welfare Politics: From Compromises to Polarization'. *Swiss Political Science Review* 21 (4): pp. 617–635.

Altman, David. 2011. 'Collegiate Executives and Direct Democracy in Switzerland and Uruguay: Similar Institutions, Opposite Political Goals, Distinct Results'. *Swiss Political Science Review* 14 (3): pp. 483–520.

Andeweg, Rudy B. 2000. 'Consociational Democracy'. *Annual Review of Political Science* 3: pp. 509–536.

Armingeon, Klaus. 2002. 'The Effects of Negotiation Democracy: A Comparative Analysis'. *European Journal of Political Research* 41 (1): pp. 81–105.

Auer, Andreas, and Katharina Holzinger (eds). 2013. *Gegenseitige Blicke über die Grenze: Bürgerbeteiligung und direkte Demokratie in Deutschland und der Schweiz*. Baden-Baden: Nomos.

Baechler, Günther, and Jörg Frieden. 2006. 'Nepal—Entwicklungszusammenarbeit und Konflikttransformation'. *Schweizerisches Jahrbuch für Entwicklungspolitik* 254 (2): pp. 189–209.

Bartolini, Stefano. 1999. 'Collusion, Competition and Democracy: Part I'. *Journal of Theoretical Politics* 11 (4): pp. 435–470.

Beramendi, Virginia, Andrew Ellis, Bruno Kaufman, Miriam Kornblith, Larry LeDuc, Paddy McGuire, Theo Schiller, and Palle Svensson (eds). 2008. *Direct Democracy*. Stockholm: IDEA.

Birnir, Jóhanna K., David D. Laitin, Jonathan Wilkenfeld, David M. Waguespack, Agatha S. Hultquist, and Ted Robert Gurr. 2018. 'Introducing the AMAR (All Minorities at Risk) Data'. *Journal of Conflict Resolution* 62 (1): pp. 203–226.

Bochsler, Daniel. 2009. 'Neighbours or Friends? When Swiss Cantonal Governments Co-Operate with Each Other'. *Regional and Federal Studies* 19 (3): pp. 349–370.

Bochsler, Daniel. 2017. 'Lo stemperamento dei contorni politici dei Cantoni svizzeri'. In *Il federalismo svizzero. Attori, strutture e processi*, edited by Sean Mueller, and Anja Giudici, pp. 63–91. Locarno: Dadò.

Bochsler, Daniel, Regula Hänggli, and Silja Häusermann. 2015. 'Consensus Lost? Disenchanted Democracy in Switzerland'. *Swiss Political Science Review* 21 (4): pp. 475–490.

Bochsler, Daniel, and Andreas Juon. 2021. 'Power-Sharing and the Quality of Democracy'. *European Political Science Review* 13 (4): pp. 411–430.

Bochsler, Daniel, and Andreas Juon. forthcoming. 'Democracy Promotion through Power-Sharing: The Role of Mediators' Constitutional Templates'. In *Democracy and Democracy Promotion in a Fractured World. Challenges, Resilience, Innovation*, edited by Simon Geissbühler. Berlin/Zürich: LIT Verlag.

Bogaards, Matthijs. 2000. 'The Uneasy Relationship Between Empirical and Normative Types in Consociational Theory'. *Journal of Theoretical Politics* 12 (4): pp. 395–423.

Bogaards, Matthijs, Ludger Helms, and Arend Lijphart. 2019. 'The Importance of Consociationalism for Twenty-First Century Politics and Political Science'. *Swiss Political Science Review* 25 (4): pp. 341–356.

Bol, Damien, Jean-Benoit Pilet, and Pedro Riera. 2015. 'The International Diffusion of Electoral Systems: The Spread of Mechanisms Tempering Proportional Representation across Europe'. *European Journal of Political Research* 54 (2): pp. 384–410.

Bolleyer, Nicole. 2006. 'Intergovernmental Arrangements in Spanish and Swiss Federalism: the Impact of Power-Concentrating and Power-Sharing Executives on Intergovernmental Institutionalization'. *Regional and Federal Studies* 16 (4): pp. 385–408.

Bolliger, Christian, and Regula Zürcher. 2004. 'Deblockierung durch Kooptation? Eine Fallstudie zur Aufnahme der Katholisch-Konservativen in die schweizerische Landesregierung 1891'. *Swiss Political Science Review* 10 (4): pp. 59–92.

Cederman, Lars-Erik, Kristian Skrede Gleditsch, and Julian Wucherpfennig. 2018. 'The Diffusion of Inclusion: An Open-Polity Model of Ethnic Power Sharing'. *Comparative Political Studies* 51 (10): pp. 1279–1313.

Cheneval, Francis, and Alice el-Wakil. 2018. 'The Institutional Design of Referendums: Bottom-Up and Binding'. *Swiss Political Science Review* 24 (3): pp. 294–304.

Cheneval, Francis, and Mónica Ferrín. 2018. 'Switzerland as a Model for the EU'. In *Citizenship in Segmented Societies*, edited by Francis Cheneval, and Mónica Ferrín, pp. 10–39. Cheltenham, UK: Edward Elgar.

Dibiasi, Andreas, Klaus Abberger, Michael Siegenthaler, and Jan-Egbert Sturm. 2018. 'The Effects of Policy Uncertainty on Investment: Evidence from the Unexpected Acceptance of a Far-Reaching Referendum in Switzerland'. *European Economic Review* 104: pp. 38–67.

Durán-Martínez, Angélica. 2012. 'Presidents, Parties, and Referenda in Latin America'. *Comparative Political Studies* 45 (9): pp. 1159–1187.

Emmenegger, Patrick, Lucas Leemann, and André Walter. 2022. 'Direct Democracy, Coalition Size and Public Spending'. *Journal of Public Policy* 42 (2): pp. 224–246.

Filippov, Mikhail, Peter C. Ordeshook, and Olga Shvetsova. 1999. *Designing Federalism. A Theory of Self-Sustainable Federal Institutions*. Cambridge: Cambridge University Press.

Fleiner, Thomas, and Lidija R. Basta Fleiner. 2004. *Allgemeine Staatslehre*, 3rd ed. Berlin: Springer.

Frey, Bruno S., and Lorenz Goette. 1998. 'Does the Popular Vote Destroy Civil Rights?'. *American Journal of Political Science* 42 (4): pp. 1343–1348.

Gamble, Barbara S. 1997. 'Putting Civil Rights to a Popular Vote'. *American Journal of Political Science* 41 (1): pp. 245–269.

Geissbühler, Simon. forthcoming. 'Towards an Action-Oriented Democracy Diplomacy Agenda'. In *Democracy and Democracy Promotion in a Fractured World. Challenges, Resilience, Innovation*, edited by Simon Geissbühler. Berlin/Zürich: LIT Verlag.

Gilardi, Fabrizio, and Fabio Wasserfallen. 2016. 'How Socialization Attenuates Tax Competition'. *British Journal of Political Science* 46 (1): pp. 45–65.

Giudici, Anja, and Nenad Stojanović. 2016. 'Die Zusammensetzung des Schweizerischen Bundesrates nach Partei, Region, Sprache und Religion, 1848–2015'. *Swiss Political Science Review* 22 (2): pp. 288–307.

Goetschel, Laurent. 2011. 'Neutrals as Brokers of Peacebuilding Ideas?' *Cooperation and Conflict* 46 (3): pp. 312–333.

Greminger, Thomas. 2011. *Swiss Civilian Peace Promotion: Assessing Policy and Practice*. Zürich: Center for Security Studies (CSS).

Helbling, Marc, and Hanspeter Kriesi. 2004. 'Staatsbürgerverständnis und politische Mobilisierung. Einbürgerungen in Schweizer Gemeinden'. *Swiss Political Science Review* 10 (4): pp. 33–58.

Helms, Ludger, Marcelo Jenny, and David M. Willumsen. 2019. 'Alpine Troubles: Trajectories of De-Consociationalisation in Austria and Switzerland Compared'. *Swiss Political Science Review* 25 (4): pp. 381–407.

Hooghe, Liesbet, Gary Marks, Schakel Arjan H., Sandra Chapman Osterkatz, Sarah Niedzwiecki, and Sarah Shair-Rosenfield. 2016. *Measuring Regional Authority: A Postfunctionalist Theory of Governance*. Oxford: Oxford University Press.

Hug, Simon, and Pascal Sciarini. 1995. 'Switzerland—Still a Paradigmatic Case?' In *Towards a New Europe*, edited by Gerald Schneider, Patricia A. Weitsman, and Thomas Bernauer, pp. 55–74. Westport: Praeger.

Iff, Andrea, and Nicole Töpperwien. 2008. 'Power Sharing. The Swiss Experience'. *Politorbis. Zeitschrift zur Aussenpolitik* 45 (2/2008): pp. 1–83.

Juon, Andreas, and Daniel Bochsler. 2022. 'The Two Faces of Power-Sharing'. *Journal of Peace Research* 59 (4): pp. 526–542.

Kaiser, André, Matthias Lehnert, Bernhard Miller, and Ulrich Sieberer. 2002. 'The Democratic Quality of Institutional Regimes: A Conceptual Framework'. *Political Studies* 50 (2): pp. 313–331.

Kaufmann, Bruno, Rolf Büchi, and Nadja Braun. 2010. *Guidebook to Direct Democracy in Switzerland and Beyond*. Marburg/Brussels: IRI Europe.

Kriesi, Hanspeter. 1999. 'Introduction: State Formation and Nation Building in the Swiss Case'. In *Nation and National Identity: The European Experience in Perspective*, edited by Hanspeter Kriesi, Klaus Armingeon, Hannes Siegrist, and Andreas Wimmer, pp. 13–28. Chur: Rüegger.

Kriesi, Hanspeter. 2015. 'Conclusion: The Political Consequences of the Polarization of Swiss Politics'. *Swiss Political Science Review* 21 (4): pp. 724–739.

Kriesi, Hanspeter, and Alexander H. Trechsel. 2008. *The Politics of Switzerland. Continuity and Change in a Consensus Democracy*. Cambridge: Cambridge University Press.

Kübler, Daniel, Emilienne Kobelt, and Roman Zwicky. 2020. *Les langues du pouvoir. Le plurilinguisme dans l'administration fédérale*. Lausanne: Presses polytechniques et universitaires romandes.

Lanz, David. 2021. 'The Deep Roots of Swiss Conflict Prevention'. In *New Paths and Policies Towards Conflict Prevention*, edited by Courtney J. Fung, Björn Gehrmann, Rachel F. Madenyika, and Jason G. Tower, pp. 65–73. Abingdon: Routledge.

Lanz, David, Laurie Nathan, and Alexandre Raffoul. 2019. 'Negotiations, Continued: Ensuring the Positive Performance of Power-Sharing Arrangements'. In *Special Report* 455: pp. 1–16.

Leemann, Lucas, and Isabelle Stadelmann-Steffen. 2022. 'Satisfaction With Democracy: When Government by the People Brings Electoral Losers and Winners Together'. *Comparative Political Studies* 55 (1): pp. 93–121.

Leemann, Lucas, and Fabio Wasserfallen. 2016. 'The Democratic Effect of Direct Democracy'. *American Political Science Review* 110 (4): pp. 750–762.

Lijphart, Arend. 1969. 'Consociational Democracy'. *World Politics* 21 (2): pp. 207–225.

Lijphart, Arend. 1999. *Patterns of Democracy. Government Forms and Performance in Thirty-Six Countries*. New Haven: Yale University Press.

Linder, Wolf, and Sean Mueller. 2021. *Swiss Democracy. Possible Solutions to Conflict in Multicultural Societies*. Cham: Palgrave.

Lowell, A. Lawrence. 1896. *Government and Parties in Continental Europe*. Boston: Houghton Mifflin.

Lundell, Krister. 2011. 'Accountability and Patterns of Alternation in Pluralitarian, Majoritarian and Consensus Democracies'. *Government and Opposition* 46 (2): pp. 145–167.

McCulloch, Allison. 2014. 'Consociational Settlements in Deeply Divided Societies: The Liberal-Corporate Distinction'. *Democratization* 21 (3): pp. 501–518.

McCulloch, Allison, and Joanne McEvoy. 2018. 'The International Mediation of Power-Sharing Settlements'. *Cooperation and Conflict* 53 (4): pp. 467–485.

Mohrenberg, Steffen, Robert A. Huber, and Tina Freyburg. 2021. 'Love at First Sight? Populist Attitudes and Support for Direct Democracy'. *Party Politics* 27 (3): pp. 528–539.

Mueller, Sean. 2021. 'Federalism and Direct Democracy in Switzerland: Competing or Complementary'. In *Federal Democracies at Work*, edited by Arthur Benz, and Jared Sonnicksen, pp. 99–121. Toronto: University of Toronto Press.

Neidhart, Leonhard. 1970. *Plebiszit und pluralitäre Demokratie. Eine Analyse der Funktion des schweizerischen Gesetzesreferendums*. Bern: Francke.

Qvortrup, Matt. 2017. 'The Rise of Referendums. Demystifying Direct Democracy'. *Journal of Democracy* 28 (3): pp. 141–152.

Raffoul, Alexandre W. 2019. *Tackling the Power-Sharing Dilemma? The Role of Mediation*. Bern: swisspeace.

Schmidt, Manfred G. 2002. 'Political Performance and Types of Democracy: Findings from Comparative Studies'. *European Journal of Political Research* 41 (1): pp. 147–163.

Sciarini, Pascal. 2011. *La Politique Suisse au Fil du Temps*. Genève: Georg.

Sciarini, Pascal, Manuel Fischer, and Denise Traber. 2015. *Political Decision-Making in Switzerland. The Consensus Model under Pressure*. Houndmills: Palgrave.

Stadelmann-Steffen, Isabelle, and Adrian Vatter. 2012. 'Does Satisfaction with Democracy Really Increase Happiness? Direct Democracy and Individual Satisfaction in Switzerland'. *Political Behavior* 34 (3): pp. 535–559.

Steiner, Jürg. 1974. *Amicable Agreement Versus Majority Rule. Conflict Resolution in Switzerland*. Chappel Hill: University of North Carolina Press.

Stojanović, Nenad. 2006. 'Direct Democracy: A Risk or an Opportunity for Multicultural Societies? The Experience of the Four Swiss Multilingual Cantons'. *International Journal on Multicultural Societies* 8 (2): pp. 183–202.

Stojanović, Nenad. 2020. 'Democracy, Ethnocracy and Consociational Democracy'. *International Political Science Review* 41 (1): pp. 30–43.

Stojanović, Nenad. 2021. *Multilingual Democracy: Switzerland and Beyond*. London & New York: ECPR Press / Rowman & Littlefield.

Stojanović, Nenad. 2022. 'A Non-Populist Direct Democracy for Belgium'. In *Sovereignty, Civic Participation, and Constitutional Law: The People versus the Nation in Belgium*, edited by Brecht Deseure, Raf Geenens, and Stefan Sottiaux, pp. 236–251. Abingdon: Routledge.

Stutzer, Alois, and Bruno S. Frey. 2000. 'Stärkere Volksrechte—zufriedene Bürger: eine mikroökonomische Untersuchung für die Schweiz'. *Swiss Political Science Review* 6 (3): pp. 1–30.

Swiss Agency for Development and Cooperation. 2012.*Annual Report 2012 Mongolia.* Ulaanbaatar: SDC.

Traber, Denise. 2015. 'Disenchanted Swiss Parliament? Electoral Strategies and Coalition Formation'. *Swiss Political Science Review* 21 (4): pp. 702–723.

Vatter, Adrian. 2016. 'Switzerland on the Road from a Consociational to a Centrifugal Democracy?' *Swiss Political Science Review* 22 (1): pp. 59–74.

Vatter, Adrian, Isabelle Stadelmann-Steffen, and Deniz Danaci. 2014. 'Who Supports Minority Rights in Popular Votes? Empirical Evidence from Switzerland'. *Electoral Studies* 36: pp. 1–14.

Vogt, Manuel, Nils-Christian Bormann, Seraina Rüegger, Lars-Erik Cederman, Philipp Hunziker, and Luc Girardin. 2015. 'Integrating Data on Ethnicity, Geography, and Conflict: The Ethnic Power Relations Dataset Family'. *Journal of Conflict Resolution* 59 (7): pp. 1327–1342.

Walter, André, and Patrick Emmenegger. 2019. 'Majority Protection: the Origins of Distorted Proportional Representation'. *Electoral Studies* 59: pp. 64–77.

Wasserfallen, Fabio. 2015. 'The Cooperative Capacity of Swiss Federalism'. *Swiss Political Science Review* 21 (4): pp. 538–555.

Williams, J. Fischer. 1914. 'Recent Developments of Proportional Representation'. *Political Science Quarterly* 29 (1): pp. 111–122.

Wimmer, Andreas. 2011. 'A Swiss Anomaly? A Relational Account of National Boundary-Making'. *Nations and Nationalism* 17 (4): pp. 718–737.

Wucherpfennig, Julian, Philipp Hunziker, and Lars-Erik Cederman. 2016. 'Who Inherits the State? Colonial Rule and Postcolonial Conflict'. *American Journal of Political Science* 60 (4): pp. 882–898.

Index

For the benefit of digital users, indexed terms that span two pages (e.g., 52–53) may, on occasion, appear on only one of those pages.

Tables and figures are indicated by *t* and *f* following the paragraph number

A
administrative law claims process (chart) 216
algorithmic recommendation systems 440
alienation, challenges arising from 773–76, 782–84, 785
amendment of Federal Constitution *see* Federal Constitution
anti-austerity movements 364–65
anti-nuclear movement 360
area planning *see* spatial planning
armed forces *see* national security policy
assimilation *see* integration policy
associations *see* interest groups
asylum *see* migration
autonomy
    balancing of national autonomy and international influence 501–2
    cantonal autonomy 726
    federalism and 822–24
    municipal autonomy 256–58

B
banking and finance
    actors involved in 569–74
    authors' analytical approach to 563, 564
    business interest groups 571–74
    decline in prominence of 579–80
    Federal Department of Finance (FDF) 569
    Federal regulatory bodies 569–74
    Financial Markets Supervisory Authority (FINMA) 570–71, 580
    policy-making since Global Financial Crisis 576–80
    power and status of 563–64, 579–80
    regulatory framework 574–76
    size and sophistication of 563
    State Secretariat for International Financial Matters (SIF) 569–70
    Swiss financial centre 563, 564–69
    Swiss National Bank (SNB) 571
bicameralism 142–43
Brexit, impact of 514
building control *see* spatial planning
business associations *see* interest groups

C
cantonal referendum 146
cantons
    cantonal double majority voting system on constitutional amendments 143–45
    cantonal empowerment (1803–1847) 36–38
    cantonal governments 238–40
    cantonal implementation of federal bills 147–49
    cantonal initiative 145–46
    cantonal parliaments, description of 240–41
    cantonal parliaments, weak status of 237, 240–41
    cantonal referendum 146
    cantons in pre-parliamentary decision-making process 146–47
    cantonal sectoral and policy-specific conferences 151
    confederate and cantonal political structures compared 236–37
    Conference of Cantonal Government (KdK) 150–51

cantons (cont.)
  current challenges for 246–47
  'democratic deficit,' and 823
  differences between political systems of 238
  direct democracy, description of 242–46
  direct democracy, strength and success of 237
  direct popular election of executive 236–37
  education systems, harmonization of 616–17
  environment see environment
  family policy see family policy
  greater homogeneity of party-political relationships 237
  institutional differences from Federal government 236
  intercantonal (horizontal) cooperation 149
  intercantonal agreements ('Konkordate') 149–50, 151
  intercantonal conferences 150–51
  intercantonal conferences of experts 151
  international perspective as to direct democracy 167
  legal systems 235
  liberalization and 245
  metropolitan areas see metropolitan areas
  municipal origins of 254
  municipalities see municipalities
  national security policy, and 529–30
  overview of political institutions (appendix) 248
  political institutions 238–46
  political party systems 241–42
  political representation 199
  public health see public health
  representation in Federal Government 199
  no second parliamentary chamber 237
  self-rule rather than shared rule 247
  size of, limitations as to 246–47
  size ratio between smallest and largest canton 247
  spatial planning see spatial planning
  status within Swiss federation 235–36
  strong status of government 236–37
  structural challenges for 246
  Catholicism see religion

centralization, challenges arising from 773–74, 776–77, 782–84, 785, 789
childcare see family policy
chocolate democracy see democracy
Christianity see religion
cities see metropolitan areas
citizenship
  citizen empowerment (1798–1891) 38–40
  direct democracy, and 814
  European Union, and 518, 811–12
  gender policies, and 764
  historical evolution of 686–88
  jus sanguinis 682–83, 690
  jus soli 690
  law reform 663
  multiculturalism, and 820–21
  non-citizen population 392–93
  policy 686–89
  political conflicts as to 688–89
  social integration, and 677–80, 681–83
  three-tier system 689, 811
citizenship policy described 686–89
civil rights see political culture
civil service see Federal administration
civil society representation see interest groups; political representation
civil status see family policy
class structure see social structure
cleavage, concept of 320–21
communications, political see political communications
competition see liberalism, liberalization
'concordance' see consociationalism
Conference of Cantonal Government (KdK) 150–51
consensus government as pillar of democracy 791, 816–18
consociationalism ('Konkordanzdemokratie' or 'concordance') 197–98, 789–90, 811–12, 825
Constitution (Federal) see Federal Constitution
constitutional review see judicial system
consumer prices see economic structure
Council of Europe, membership of 506
Council of States see Federal Assembly
countercultural movements 359, 361

INDEX 833

Covid-19 pandemic *see* public health
crisis response *see* national security policy
culture, political *see* political culture
culture, social *see* social structure
currency exchange rates *see* economic structure
current challenges, issues, and solutions
   alienation 773–76, 782–84, 785
   authors' analytical approach to 773–74, 789
   behavioural change as solution 789–90
   cantons 246–47
   centralization 773–74, 776–77, 782–84, 785, 789
   consensus ('amicable agreement') approach to solution 790
   consociationalism approach to solution 789–90
   democracy-related challenges 773–74
   digitalization 773–74, 777–78, 782–84, 785, 789
   economic policy 544, 558–59
   education system 617–19
   energy policy 594
   environment 654–56
   EU relationship 518–20
   Europeanization 773–74, 778–80, 782–84, 789
   evaluation research on Federal governance and policy implementation 481–82
   family policy 748–49
   Federal administration 312
   federalism 152
   foreign policy and relations 500–3
   gender equality policies 753–54, 767–68
   infrastructure policy 586–90, 594
   institutional reform options 785–88
   internationalization 773–74, 778–80, 782–84
   kinds of challenges 773
   limited-reform approach to solution 790
   migration 673–74
   national security policy 535
   polarization 773–74, 780–84, 789
   political challenges, identification of 776–77
   political challenges, list of 774–82
   political challenges, reform options for 784–85
   political system 1, 807
   political system's susceptibility to challenges 789
   polity (institutional) and political reform options 785–88
   public health 714, 727–28
   research, technology, and innovation (R&I) 637–39
   social policy 709–10
   solution within current system as preferred path 789–90
   '*Sonderfall* rhetoric' 784
   spatial planning 654–56
   transport policy 586–90
cybersecurity *see* national security policy

D

decision-making
   authors' analytical approach to 451
   authors' research findings and explanations 465–66
   bicameral system of 462
   consultation procedures 452, 457–58, 465
   decision-making phases, importance of 453
   duration of decision-making processes 459–60, 465
   economic policy 553–56
   education system 605
   expert commissions 452
   extra-parliamentary committees 456–57, 465
   government support in direct-democratic votes 462–64
   initiation phase 455–56
   institutional framework for 452–53
   parliamentary committees 460–61
   parliamentary phase 460–62, 465
   parliamentary phase, description of 452–53
   parliamentary phase, importance of 466
   perfect bicameralism 462
   phases of decision-making process 452–53
   plenum 461–62
   policy formulation generally 451
   pre-parliamentary phase 452, 456–60, 465
   pre-parliamentary procedures, importance of 458–59, 466
   referendum phase 453, 462–65

decision-making (*cont.*)
  referendum phase, influence of parliamentary consensus on acceptability of acts 464–65
  'shuttle' (*navette*) procedure 452–53
  see also governance (Federal public policy)
defence policy *see* national security policy
degree-level education *see* universities
democracy
  chocolate democracy
  consensus government as pillar of 791, 816–18
  consociational democracy 825
  consociationalism as pillar of 811–12
  democracy-related challenges 773–74
  democratic innovation within political system 5–6
  diffusion of Swiss model worldwide 811, 824
  digital democracy *see* digital democracy
  direct democracy *see* direct democracy
  Federal administration as pillar of 812
  federalism as pillar of 811–12
  local democracy *see* metropolitan areas; municipalities
  multiculturalism and 818–21
  national identity, and 8
  pillars of 811–12, 824–25
  pride in democratic system 811
  support for promotion of 811
'democratic deficit'
  cantons 823
  direct democracy as solution 166–67
  metropolitan areas 287–88, 292
  problem of 5
development assistance to poorer countries 100
development stage 3: formulation of Federal Spatial Planning Policy (SPA) (1970–1980) 646–47
digital democracy
  agenda setting and social media 433–35
  algorithmic recommendation systems 440
  authors' analytical approach to 430–31
  authors' research findings and explanations 443–44
  constraint factors for research on 444
  democracy and digital technology in relation 430
  digital technology and democracy in relation 430
  direct democracy and social media in relation 432–33
  e-collecting of voter signatures, development of 435–38, 443
  further research, areas for 443–44
  innovation in 443
  Internet voting 431, 440–42, 443
  opinion formation 431, 438–40, 443
  political campaigns 430, 431–38
  politicians and social media 431–32, 443
  Voting Advice Applications (VAAs) 438–39
  WeCollect platform, development of 435–38
digitalization
  challenges arising from 773–74, 777–78, 782–84, 785, 789
  direct democracy institutions 169
  economic growth, and 76
  federalism and 148
  political communications 333–34, 383
  political parties, and 333–34
DIL *see* Directorate for International Law
direct democracy
  actors involved in 415
  authors' analytical approach to 410–11
  authors' research findings and explanations 168–69
  campaign message effectiveness 417, 423, 424
  campaign process 415
  campaign spending, effect on vote results 423
  cantons *see* cantons
  channels for 415–17
  citizenship, and 814
  cleavage, concept of 420–21
  consociationalism 197
  'correct' choices by voters 423
  'democratic deficit', and 166–67
  development of use of direct-democratic instruments 159–60
  'different' democracy, as 168
  digitalization of 169

direct effects of 161–62
distinctiveness of 410
effects in general of 161
EU and 514–17
facultative referendums 157–58
Federal Constitution *see* Federal Constitution
further research, areas for 424
heuristics basis for voter decisions 421–22
historical development of 163–64, 168
indirect effects of 162–63
insights on 814–15
institution of 5
institutional framework of 157–63
international perspective at national level of 166–67
international perspective at sub-national level of 167
international perspective generally on 165–67
mandatory referendums 157–58
'mediated' version 410–11
national-level institutions of 157–60
opinion formation 421
optional referendums 158–59
participation decision factors 418–19
participation level 418–20
participation rights and competence 419–20
pillar of democracy, as 811–12, 824–25
'plebiscitary' version 410
political culture, and 33
previous research on 424
representative system and framework of 156–57
resources for 415–17
support to federal authorities for implementation of 413–14
types of 410
'unmediated' ('populist') version 410
use of direct-democratic institutions 411–13
voter decision factors 420–23
voter decisions, heuristics basis for 421–22
voters' systematic analyses of political arguments and information 421–22
see also democracy
Directorate for International Law (DIL) 498–99

diversity *see* gender equality policies; social integration; social structure
divorce law *see* family policy
domestic security *see* national security policy

E

economic policy
 actors involved in 553–56
 authors' analytical approach to 545
 characteristics of 545–46
 classification of model of 543–44, 554–55
 consistency of 544–45
 constant change, and 545
 crisis management view of 550–53
 current challenges for 544, 558–59
 decision-making procedures 553–56
 distinctiveness of 543–44
 employment *see* employment
 EU trade relations, importance of 559
 evaluation of 556–58
 historical development of 545–46
 liberalization and 105–6, 245, 348, 547–53
 new actors involved in 554–55
 productivity growth, weakness of 558
 reform of 544
 success of 543, 544
 trade liberalization 105–6
economic structure
 authors' research findings and explanations 90–91
 business interests, power of 563–64
 'coordinated market economy with a business bias' 563
 data collection for study of 74
 digitalization and 76
 economic equality 74–76, 87–89
 economic growth 543
 economic growth factors 73–74, 90–91
 education and economic growth 73, 80–82
 education policy and 617–18
 employment *see* employment
 GDP growth 74, 543
 Global Financial Crisis, and *see* banking and finance
 ideology and economic change 116–17
 industrialization, distinctiveness of historical development of 22

economic structure (*cont.*)
   international comparisons *see* international position (economic and political)
   international trade policy 498
   labour *see* employment
   links with political system 2, 5, 6–7
   migration and *see* migration
   national security policy, and 532
   political conflict, and 6–7
   population growth, and 73, 76–77
   public finances, and 90
   socio-economic transformational shifts, 2000–2020 73
   superior political and economic reasonableness, sense of 47
   Swiss National Bank, regulatory role 571
   transition from class conflict to socio-economic integration 24–25
   work, workers *see* employment
education system
   academic performance, evaluation of 615–16
   aims of 604, 605–10
   authors' analytical approach to 605
   centralization of 607–8
   characteristics of education system 605–10
   cleavages arising from religion and federalism 611–13
   cross-cantonal harmonization 616–17
   current challenges for 617–19
   decision-making processes, importance of 605
   distribution of governance and oversight powers 605
   diversity challenges for 618–19
   economic challenges for 617–18
   economic growth, and 73, 80–82
   enculturation aspect of 605
   equality challenges for 618
   equality evaluation 616
   equality policies 761
   evaluation criteria 615
   federalism and 610–11
   gender challenges for 618–19
   gendered educational pathway 761–62
   historical development after 1945 613–15
   historical development of 604
   homophobia and transphobia in schools 762
   implementation of policy 615–17
   politics of 610–11
   pre-primary (nursery) sector 606, 762
   pre-primary sector 616–17
   primary sector 17, 604–5, 606, 609–10, 612, 614–15, 616–17, 762
   redistributive implications of 604–5
   research, technology, and innovation, and 624
   secondary sector 17, 80, 121, 606–7, 609–10, 611, 612, 614, 616, 762
   skill production, evaluation of 616
   standardization of 608–9
   stratification of 609–10
   tertiary education *see* universities
   tertiary sector 79–80, 82, 90, 118–19, 121, 396–97, 404, 606–7, 610, 612, 613–14, 630–31
   vocational sector (VET) 22–23, 80–82, 118–19, 342, 552–53, 605–6, 607–8, 610–11, 613–14, 615, 616, 618, 627, 706, 719, 761–62
EEA (European Economic Area) *see* European Union
EFTA (European Free Trade Association), membership of 511
elections
   campaigns 394–95
   Council of States 392, 393–94
   direct popular election of executive 236–37
   effectiveness of campaigns 402–3, 417, 423, 424
   Federal Assembly key officeholders 177
   municipal executives 264–65
   National Council 392–93
   national elections 391
   outcomes 397–99
   previous research on parliamentary elections 391
   results 397–99
   voter behaviour and choice 397–403
   voter turnout 395–97
emigration *see* migration
employers *see* employment

employment
  economic equality, and 87–89
  economic growth, and 73
  economic growth, benefits of 90
  equality policies 765
  Federal administration, in *see* Federal administration
  glass ceiling and glass walls 765
  homophobia in the workplace 766–67
  human resources management 309–12
  labour movement 358
  occupational structure changes 84–87, 91
  potential for policy improvements 559
  sectoral changes in 82–84
  skills production, education system evaluation and 616
  social assistance, social insurance *see* social policy
  wage discrimination 766
  welfare state, and *see* social policy
  women 73
empowerment, political *see* political culture
energy *see* infrastructure policy
environment
  actors involved in 650–51
  areas of intervention 642
  cantonal responsibility for 642
  'causality ('polluter pays') principle' 648
  characteristics of problems and policies 643
  current challenges for 654–56
  development stage 1: ad hoc regulation of certain natural resources (1874–1950) 644
  development stage 2: empowerment and institutionalization (1950–1990) 644–45
  development stage 3: consolidation and internationalization (1990–2020) 645–46
  Environmental Impact Assessment (EIA) 648
  environmental movement 360
  environmental performance level 642
  environmental policies defined 642
  governance and legislative framework 648–49
  historical development of 643–46
  implementation of policy 651
  international comparisons 98
  part of infrastructure policy, as part 585–86
  policy objectives 643
  policy principles 648
  'prevention principle' 648
  right of appeal for environmental protection organizations 648–49
  'weighing interests' principle 648
equality policies
  economic equality, and 74–76, 87–89
  education policy and 604–5, 616, 618
  liberalization and 22–23
  see also gender equality policies
ethnicity *see* social integration
Europe
  challenges from Europeanization 773–74, 778–80, 782–84, 789
  close links with 506
  Council of Europe membership 506
  European Free Trade Association (EFTA) membership 511
  foreign policy and relations
  judicial system and European integration 223–25
  European Economic Area (EEA) *see* European Union
  European Free Trade Association (EFTA), membership of 511
European Union
  bilateral agreements with 506, 507, 512–13
  challenges from Europeanization 773–74, 778–80, 782–84
  change, impact of 513–14
  citizenship, and 518, 811–12
  current challenges for relationship with 518–20
  direct democracy and 514–17
  EU integration history, lessons from 508–10
  EU perspective on relationship 507
  European Economic Area (EEA), rejection of 506, 507, 511–12
  expansion to Central and Eastern Europe 513–14
  free movement of persons, migration policy and 514–17, 658–59, 671–72

European Union (*cont.*)
  improvement in relationship, possible initiatives for 519–20
  initiative 'against mass immigration', and 514–17
  institutional-agreement negotiations, withdrawal from 508, 517–18
  non-membership of 506
  political integration, and 4–5
  research, technology, and innovation (R&I) and 623, 633–34
  trade relations, importance of 559
  UK Brexit withdrawal from 514
  uncertain future relationship with 506–7
exchange rates *see* economic structure

F

facultative referendums 157–58
family policy
  actors involved in 746–48
  authors' analytical approach to 734–35
  conflicts of policy interests 734–35
  current challenges for 748–49
  development of 742–45
  equality policies 762–63
  family reunification *see* migration
  financial transfers policy, international comparison 735–42
  heteronormativity in marriage, divorce, and civil status 763
  historical development of 734
  importance of 733
  increase in welfare state interventionism 734
  legal recognition of same-sex couples and rainbow families 764–65
  multidimensionality of 734–35
  politicization of 734
  reconciliation policy, international comparison 735–42
  reform of 746–48
  scope of 733
  uneven development of 734–35
  unpaid care work 763–64
  welfare state, and 734
family reunification *see* migration
farmers' organizations 358

far-right politics *see* political parties
Federal administration
  administrative and political reform in balance 312
  authors' analytical approach to 301
  civil service reforms 310
  current challenges for 312
  decision-making *see* decision-making
  departmental structure of 299–300, 301, 302–4
  deregulation and 476
  development of 301–2
  employee motivation 313–14
  Europeanization effect on 300
  'executive federalism' 300
  Federal Assembly oversight of 299
  Federal Council and Federal Assembly competencies in balance 312–13
  Federal Council national security responsibilities 529
  Federal Council shortcomings as to 299–300
  governance issues generally 300
  government for the people 798–807
  governmental/administrative reforms 306–8
  human resources management 309–12
  interdepartmental savings measures 306
  internationalization effect on 300
  liberal neo-corporatist approach to 300
  liberalization and 300, 301, 313, 476
  managerial reform successes 308–9
  national security policy, and 530–31
  New Public Management (NPM), and 300, 305
  pillar of democracy, as 812
  policy implementation, liberalization and 476
  policy-making and public administration in relation 299
  privatization 313, 476
  public finance as sole reference point 313
  public health *see* public health
  representativeness of 310–12
  spatial planning *see* spatial planning
  staffing-related reforms 305

Federal Assembly
  areas of activity 176
  authors' analytical approach to 174
  authors' research findings and
    explanations 188–89
  chambers 142–43, 175–76, 178–83
  committees 182–83
  control and oversight functions 177–78
  Council of States 142–43, 175–76, 179
  Council of States election system 392, 393–94
  Covid-19 pandemic, and 174
  crisis/emergency measures by 174
  decision-making *see* decision-making
  elections of key officeholders 177
  Federal administration, and *see* Federal administration
  interest group influence and involvement 187–88, 189
  legislative function 176–77
  National Council 142–43, 175–76, 178
  National Council election system 392–93
  national security policy, and 531
  parliamentary party groups 179–80
  parliamentary services 182
  party system shifts 179
  power and influence generally of 188
  powers of 183–85
  professionalization level 185–86, 189
  representativeness enhancement, authors' proposals for 188
  representativeness of 181–82, 188
  sessions 182
  supremacy of 175–78
  trust in 61–64
  voting in 180–81
Federal Constitution
  adoption of 1798 Helvetic Republic Constitution 35
  adoption of 1802 Helvetic Republic Constitution 35–36
  adoption of 1803 Napoleonic Constitution 36, 164
  adoption of 1848 Constitution 16–17, 27, 38, 139–40
  amendment in 1891 40
  annual popular vote on amendment proposals 15, 33, 157–58
  cantons, provisions for 26, 140–41, 146, 150
  constitutional patriotism 812–13
  direct democracy provisions 156–59, 163–64
  Federal Government provisions 143, 148–49, 175–78
  foreign policy provisions 495–97
  referendum provisions 106, 146
  revision of 1866 39
  revision of 1874 17, 39–40, 41
  revision of 1999 55–57, 106, 146
Federal Council *see* Federal administration
Federal Government (institution)
  authors' analytical approach to 195
  authors' research findings and explanations 206–7
  cantonal representation 199
  Christian confessional/denominational representation 199–200
  collegiality 195, 196, 202–4, 208
  consociationalism ('Konkordanzdemokratie' or 'concordance') 197–98
  departmental and delegation principles 204–5
  electoral history 198–99
  electoral system 196–97
  eligibility of candidates 200
  Federal Council 195
  gender representation 199–200
  governmental system 196–200
  institutional differences from cantons 236
  internal organization 202–6
  limitations to effectiveness of 206–7, 208–9
  longevity of ruling coalition 195, 208
  organizational principles 202
  organizational processes 205–6
  personal reputational profiles of members, changes in 200
  position within federal political system 200–2
  proposals for reform of 207–8
  prospects for reform of 209
  public finances, growth in 90
  stability 195, 208
  trust in 61–64
Federal Parliament *see* Federal Assembly

federalism (political regime and concept of)
  autonomy and 822–24
  basic principles of 140–42
  bicameral system of 142–43
  cantonal double majority voting system on constitutional amendments 143–45
  cantonal implementation of federal bills 147–49
  cantonal initiative 145–46
  cantonal referendum 146
  cantonal sectoral and policy-specific conferences 151
  cantons in pre-parliamentary decision-making process 146–47
  Conference of Cantonal Government (KdK) 150–51
  consociationalism 197
  constitutional patriotism 812–13
  Council of States 142–43
  current challenges for 152
  digitalization and 148
  education system and 610–11
  education system cleavages arising from 611–13
  Federal Assembly chambers 142–43
  federal state empowerment (1847–1891) 38–40
  foreign policy and relations, and 494, 500–1
  historical origins of 139–40
  horizontal institutions of 149–51
  institutional framework of 142–51
  intercantonal (horizontal) cooperation 149
  intercantonal agreements ('Konkordate') 149–50, 151
  intercantonal conferences 150–51
  intercantonal conferences of experts 151
  National Council 142–43
  pillar of democracy, as 811–12
  political integration, and 28
  vertical institutions of 142–49
  see also Swiss Federation
finances, public see economic structure; Federal Government
financial markets and regulation see banking and finance
foreign currency exchange rates see economic structure
foreign policy and relations
  areas of 498
  authors' analytical approach to 492
  balancing of national autonomy and international influence 501–2
  coherency of 502
  continuity and change 100–8
  cooperation between state and non-state actors 499–500
  current challenges for 500–3
  direct democracy, and 494, 500–1
  Directorate for International Law (DIL) 498–99
  domestic policy legitimacy of 502
  evaluation of 502
  federalism and 494, 500–1
  goals of 495–97
  historical origins of 491, 492–95
  human rights 498
  institutional framework of 498–500
  legal basis of 495–97
  migration and see migration
  neutrality 491, 492–94, 500, 501, 502–3
  peacebuilding 498
  political integration, and 4–5
  post-Cold War changes in 491–92
  public opinion on 494–95, 500
  small-state identity 491, 492, 494–95
  tension between globalization and sovereignty 4–5
  trade policy 498
  UN membership 491–92, 500
  see also Europe; European Union
foreign policy and relations
foreign security see national security policy
free movement of people see European Union
French rule (Revolutionary & Napoleonic) 35–36

G

GDP see economic structure
gender equality policies
  advocacy network for 758
  authors' analytical approach to 753
  CEDAW ratification 1997 755
  citizenship, and 764
  criminalization of homophobia 2020 756–58

current challenges for 753–54, 767–68
developments since 1996 Act 755–58
education policy and 618–19
education system and *see* education system
employment and *see* employment
equality+ 753, 760–61, 767–68
family policy and *see* family policy
Federal provision 1981 for equal rights before the law 754
Gender Equality Act 1996 754–55
Gender Equality Act 1996, 2020 revision 756
gender equality principle 753
gender mainstreaming adoption 1999 755–56
gender representation in Federal Government 199–200
institutional advocacy for equality between women and men 758–59
institutional advocacy for LGBT+ equality, absence of 760–61
slow progress in 753
speedier progress in 753
uneven development of 761
women's employment *see* employment
Global Financial Crisis *see* banking and finance
global justice movements 363–64
global relations *see* foreign policy and relations; international position (economic and political)
governance (cantonal) *see* cantons
governance (Federal public policy)
 authors' research findings and explanations 480–82
 decision-making processes 451
 education system 605
 evaluation, institutionalized approach to 476–78
 evaluation, political context 480–81
 evaluation research 471, 478–79
 evaluation research, current challenges for 481–82
 implementation, distinct features of 474–76
 implementation, federalist structure of 471–74

implementation, political context 480–81
implementation, theoretical debate on 480
implementation research 471
implementation research, current challenges for 481–82
liberalization and 635–37
governance (local) *see* metropolitan areas; municipalities
government *see* Federal Government
graduate-level education *see* universities
Green Party, rise of 7
gross domestic product (GDP) *see* economic structure

H
health *see* public health
Helvetic Republic *see* French rule (Revolutionary & Napoleonic)
historical aspects
 beginnings of political integration 27
 democracy 3–4
 industrialization, distinctiveness of historical development of 22
 national identity 2–3
 Sonderbund civil war (1847–1848), political consequences of 3–4, 15–16
 transition from class conflict to socio-economic integration 24–25
 working class political structure, late development of 22–24
homophobia, equality policies against *see* education system; employment; family policy; gender equality policies
human resources *see* employment
human rights
 foreign policy and relations 498
 minority rights (cultural and religious), integration policy and 690

I
ideology
 comparative perspective 116
 constitutional patriotism 812–13
 distrust of 'outsiders' sense of responsibility 47
 economic structural change, and 116–17
 electorate structure changes, and 118–25

INDEX 841

ideology (*cont.*)
   individual responsibility and restraint, sense of 47
   liberalization and 116–17, 127–28
   new ideological space in swiss politics 129–31
   party electorate changes, and 120–22
   personal responsibility for public health 717–18
   political party competition changes 126–29
   political structural change, and 116–18
   radical-right movements 361–63
   relative salience of sociocultural issues 125
   right-wing politics 361–63
   self-organization as to public health 717–18
   superior political and economic reasonableness, sense of 47
   voter polarization over sociocultural issues 122–25
immigration *see* migration
income, national *see* economic structure
income, personal *see* employment
individual responsibility, sense of *see* ideology
industry *see* economic structure
information, political *see* political communications
infrastructure policy
   authors' analytical approach to 586
   definition of 'infrastructure' 585
   definition of 'infrastructure policy' 585
   diversity of definitions of 585–86
   energy policy actors 597–98
   energy policy, description and current challenges 594
   energy policy implementation 598–99
   energy policy, importance of 593
   energy policy legislation 594–97
   energy policy liberalization 347–48, 596
   environment as part of 585–86
   future prospects for 599–601
   infrastructure, elements of 585
   liberalization and 300, 301, 347–48, 596
   spatial planning as part of 585–86
   transport policy actors 591–93
   transport policy, description and current challenges 586–90
   transport policy implementation 593
   transport policy legislation 590–91
   use of 'infrastructure' as term 585
innovation *see* research, technology, and innovation
institutions *see* democracy; Federal Government; federalism; judicial system; Parliament (Federal)
instrumental movements 359–60
integration, political *see* political integration
integration, social *see* multiculturalism; social integration
integration policy
   actors involved in 684–86, 690–91
   assimilationist approach to 45–46, 677–80, 682–83
   bottom-up locally embedded processes of 682, 687, 689
   citizenship policy actors and conflicts of political interests 688–89
   citizenship policy described 686–89
   citizenship policy historical development 686–88
   conflicts of political interests 684–86
   contradictory approaches to 691
   current regulatory factors 689
   description of 682–86
   direct democracy, and 690–91
   EU free movement of persons, and 677, 690
   federalism and 681–82, 689, 690–91
   guest-worker approach to immigration 689, 690
   historical development of 683–84, 690
   international perspective of 677
   jus sanguinis and 678, 684, 690
   jus soli and 678, 679–80, 688, 690
   liberalization of 690
   minority rights (cultural and religious), and 690
   naturalization law 690
   politicization of 690–91
   restrictive approach to 691
   right-wing politics, and 681–82, 684–86, 688–89, 690–91
   see also integration, social; multiculturalism
intercantonal agreements ('Konkordate') 149–50, 151
intercantonal conferences of experts 151

interest groups
  areas of political involvement 343–44
  authors' analytical approach to 338
  business associations, dominance
      of 344–47
  business interest groups 571–74
  contextual changes (economic,
      institutional, and political)
      for 347–48
  historical development of 338–41
  institutionalization of relations with
      political authorities 341–42
  neo-corporatist model of 344–47
  pluralization trends within 347
  power and influence of 337
  previous research on 337–38
  public health, and 725–26
  redefinition of political strategies 348–50
  social policy, and 704–5
  terminological aspect of 337
  variety of 337–38
international position (economic and
    political)
  authors' analytical approach to 94
  challenges from internationalization 773–
      74, 778–80, 782–84
  defence policy 99
  development assistance to poorer
      countries 100
  diffusion of Swiss model of democracy
      worldwide 811, 824
  economic freedom 95–96
  economic output 96–98
  environmental protection 98
  EU relationship 109–10
  foreign policy continuity and change 100–8
  foreign policy in practice 106–7
  foreign policy strategy continuity and
      change 104–6
  future prospects for 110–12
  geopolitical change factors 94
  global justice movements 363–64
  globalization and sovereignty in
      balance 101–3
  international perspective generally 95–100
  international perspective generally on
      direct democracy 165–67
  international perspective on national level
      of direct democracy 166–67
  international perspective on sub-national
      level of direct democracy 167
  international view of political system 795
  judicial system 223–25
  liberalization and 105–6
  metropolitan areas and international
      competitiveness 293
  migration and *see* migration
  political freedom 95–96
  public opinion on 107–8
international relations *see* foreign policy and
    relations
Internet voting 440–42, 443
interventionism *see* Federal Government

J
judicial system
  authors' analytical approach to 215
  authors' research findings and
      explanations 225–26
  comparative research on 214
  constitutional review, limits on 217–20,
      225–26
  European integration, and 223–25
  internationalization effects on 223–25
  judicialization and politicization 217–25, 226
  paradoxical nature of 225–26
  political nature of judicial
      appointments 220–23
  power and influence generally of 225–26
  previous research on 214–15
  structure and organization of 215–17
jus sanguinis 678, 682–83, 684, 690
jus soli 678, 679–80, 688, 690

K
'Konkordanzdemokratie' ('concordance') *see*
    consociationalism
'Konkordate' *see* intercantonal agreements

L
labour, labour movement *see* employment
land planning *see* spatial planning
language/linguistic divisions, political
    integration and 15–16, 19–22

legal system
    cantonal systems 235
    international law, and 223–25
    liberal values of 690
    monism 224
    reform of 221–22
    trust in 61–64
LGBT+ equality *see* education system; employment; family policy; gender equality policies
Liberal Party, in government 15
liberalism, liberalization
    cantons and 245
    economic policy and 105–6, 245, 348, 547–53
    equality policies and 22–23
    Federal administration and 300, 301, 313, 476
    governance (Federal public policy) and 635–37
    ideology and 116–17, 127–28
    infrastructure policy and 300, 301, 347–48, 596
    of integration policy 690
    international position (economic and political) and 105–6
    liberal neo-corporatist approach to Federal administration 300
    Liberal Party in government 15
    liberal values of legal system 690
    market competition within public health 717–18
    migration and 666
    policy implementation and 476
    political integration and 22–23, 25
    social policy and 116–17, 127–28
local authorities *see* municipalities
local democracy *see* municipalities
local planning *see* spatial planning
local politics *see* municipalities

M

mandatory referendums 157–58
market competition *see* liberalism, liberalization
marriage law *see* family policy
maternity *see* family policy

media *see* political communications
metropolitan areas
    authors' analytical approach to 276
    authors' research findings and explanations 292–93
    cantonal boundary reform possibilities 286
    centrality charges 280–81
    city/suburban government amalgamations 284–86
    city/suburbs conflict 280–81
    current status in Federal state 290–92
    'democratic deficit', and 282–83, 292
    disentangling of governmental tasks at municipal, cantonal and federal levels 289, 292–93
    financial equalization at cantonal level 288
    financial equalization at national level 288–89
    Functional Overlapping Competing Jurisdictions (FOCJ) 289–90
    governance issues 284, 292
    governance reform measures 292
    international competitiveness as priority for 293
    'joint decision systems' for policy-making 281–83
    metropolitan governments 286–87
    multi-level cooperative governance 290–92
    policy issues for 280
    policy-making through 'joint decision systems' 281–83
    political conflicts in 283
    population share living in 276
    present day 278–79
    problems for reform 292
    public choice approach to reform 287–88
    public perceptions of 279–80
    social segregation in 283
    territorial approach to reform 284
    urbanization and urban areas 276–80
    urbanization phases 277–78
migration
    asylum legislation 668–70
    asylum policy 667–71
    asylum policy actors 670–71
    asylum policy conflict areas 670–71
    authors' analytical approach to 659

current challenges for 673–74
economic growth, and 73, 91
EU free movement of persons, and 514–17, 658–59, 671–72
foreign policy and relations, and 659, 671–73
highly skilled immigration, increase in 77–80, 91
immigration legislation 661–65
immigration policy 659–66
immigration policy actors 665–66
immigration policy conflict areas 665–66
immigration policy development phases 661–63
initiative 'against mass immigration' 514–17
international cooperation on 659, 672–73
levels of emigration and immigration 73
liberalization and 666
migrant share of population 658
national attitude to 658
national identity, and 8
politicization of 658
refugee policy 667–71
restrictive approach to 658
social structure, and 73
military forces *see* national security policy
minority rights *see* human rights
monism 224
multiculturalism
  citizenship, and 820–21
  multicultural 'nation of will' basis of political system 2–4
  national identity, and 8
  see also integration, social; political integration
multilingualism *see* language
municipalities
  autonomy of 256–58
  communal assembly or communal parliament system 264
  cultural differences 259–62
  diversity of 259
  executive branch election procedure 264–65
  executive branch size 264–65
  executive representation of political parties and non-party members 269

executive representation of women 269–70
important role of 254
institutional reform 270–72
legal status of 256–58
legislative power systems 264
local authorities 266–67
local democracy 267
local politics 267
oldest legal entities, as 254
origins of cantons in 254
political parties, evolution of 267–68
political systems of 263–64
public expenditure share of 255
shortage of executive candidates 256
spatial planning 642
structural differences 259
task performance and limitations on performance 255, 262–63
types of 254–55
voter participation 268–69
women's executive representation 269–70

N
Napoleonic rule *see* French rule (Revolutionary & Napoleonic)
'nation of will,' concept of 2–4
National Bank *see* economic structure
National Council *see* Federal Assembly
national elections *see* elections
national empowerment *see* political culture
national identity
  democracy, and 8
  existence of 8
  'La Suisse n'existe pas' 8
  migration, and 8
  multicultural 'nation of will' basis of 2–4
  multiculturalism, and 8
  non-ethnic concept of nation-state 28
  political integration, and 8, 27
  political system, and 8
national pride *see* ideology
national security policy 525
  actors involved in 529
  areas of 523
  Armed Forces Development Programme (WEA) 533
  armed neutrality 523

national security policy (*cont.*)
　authors' analytical approach to 524
　cantonal governments, and 529–30
　Cold War 523
　consistency in 535
　crisis response, shortcomings in 536
　current challenges for 535
　cybersecurity 534–35
　defence policy 99, 523, 537–38
　delimitation of 535–36
　departmental responsibilities 530–31
　development phases via key policy
　　papers 525
　dissuasion principle 523
　distributed responsibility for 523
　domestic security, area of 523
　domestic security, shared responsibility
　　for 523
　expansion of concept of 524
　Federal administration, and 530–31
　Federal Assembly, and 531
　Federal Council, and 529
　Federal Military Department (FMD) 523
　foreign security, area of 523
　foreign security, enhancement of 532–33
　foreign security, neutrality principle
　　and 538–39
　goals 528
　implementation of 532
　legislation 528–29
　neutrality policy 523, 538–39
　non-governmental involvement 532
　objectives 528–29
　party political consensus, lack of 523
　policy paper 73: security through national
　　defence (development phase 1) 525
　policy papers 1990–2000: security
　　through international cooperations
　　(development phase 2) 526–27
　policy papers 2010–2016: security
　　through international cooperations
　　(development phase 3) 527
　post-Cold War changes in 524
　private security service providers 532
　public opinion on 531–32
　socio-economic aspects 532
　strategic leadership, shortcomings in 536

nationalist politics *see* political parties
naturalization *see* integration policy;
　migration
neutrality *see* foreign policy and relations;
　national security policy
New Public Management (NPM) *see* Federal
　administration
new social movements 359–61
non-governmental organizations (NGOs) *see*
　political representation
nursery education *see* education system

O

occupations *see* employment
optional referendums 158–59
outdated/preconceived analyses and
　understandings
　alternative understanding of political
　　culture 51
　contribution of current book to correction of 1
　environmental concerns 124
　formation of political culture 47
　international perspective of direct
　　democracy 165–66
　judicial system 214–15
　municipalities' task differentiation 257
　people's criticism of government, level
　　of 366–67
　people's propensity for political
　　activism 366
　people's propensity for protest 366
overseas direct investment to poorer
　countries 100

P

parent support *see* family policy
Parliament (Federal) *see* Federal Assembly
patriotism *see* ideology
peacebuilding *see* foreign policy and relations
personal responsibility *see* ideology
planning, spatial *see* environment
polarization, challenges arising from 773–74,
　780–84, 789
policy, defence and security *see* national
　security policy
policy, economic and financial *see* banking
　and finance; economic policy

policy, foreign *see* foreign policy and relations; international position (economic and political)
political challenges and solutions
political communications
  actors involved in 372
  authors' analytical approach to 372
  authors' research findings and explanations 382-83
  citizen involvement in 380-82
  context (economic, institutional, and political) of 373-74
  definition of 'political communication' 372
  digitalization of 333-34, 383
  direct democracy, and 415-17
  important role of 382-83
  mediatization of 372, 377-80
  process of 372
political culture
  academic research on, limitations of previous 50-51
  author's analytical approach to 34
  authors' analytical approach to 51-52, 68
  authors' research findings and explanations 68-69
  cantonal empowerment (1803-1847) 36-38
  Catholic community's integration into (1891-1918) 41-43
  citizen empowerment (1798-1891) 34-40
  cleavage, concept of 320-21
  comparative perspective on 55-66
  concept of 52-54
  conceptual and definitional difficulties as to 50
  data collection for study of 54-55
  direct democracy 33
  distrust of 'outsiders", sense of responsibility 47
  economic poverty and prosperity, and 47
  extensiveness of democratic rights 33
  federal state empowerment (1847-1891) 38-40
  historical development 33-47
  ideological change *see* ideology
  individual responsibility and restraint, sense of 47
  integration phase (1891-1991) 40-47
  integration policy, politicization of 690-91
  judicial appointments, political nature of 220-23
  judicialization and politicization of judicial system 217-25, 226
  'left-wing' analysis of 34
  'left-wing' integration into (1918-1959) 43-44
  majority system 41-43
  measurement of 54-55
  media and *see* political communications
  national empowerment during Helvetic Republic (1798-1802) 35-36
  proportional system 43-44
  public opinion *see* public opinion
  superior political and economic reasonableness, sense of 47
  theoretical approaches to 33-34
  trust in Federal institutions 61-64
  'ultra-moderate' use of institutional tools 34
  understanding of 50-52
  universal integration (1959-1992) 45-47
political information *see* political communications
political integration
  1891-1991 40-47
  authors' analytical approach to 15, 16
  citizenship, and *see* citizenship
  European Union, and 4-5
  federalism, and 28
  historical beginnings of 27
  'left-wing' integration into political culture (1918-1959) 43-44
  lessons from Swiss experience 28-29
  liberalization and 22-23, 25
  linguistic divisions, and 15-16, 19-22
  national identity, and 8, 27
  political Catholicism, and 16-19
  political parties, and 15
  power-sharing [All refs here] 27-28
  proportional representation (proportionality rule), and 26-27
  religion, and 15-19
  social class structure, and 22-25
  superior political and economic reasonableness, sense of 47

political integration (*cont.*)
  Switzerland as 'paradigmatic case' of 3–4, 16
  Switzerland as paradigmatic case of 3–4
  transition from class conflict to socio-economic integration 24–25
  universal integration (1959–1992) 45–47
  working class political structure, late development of 22–24
  see also multiculturalism
political parties
  authors' analytical approach to 317
  cantons *see* cantons
  cleavages in creation of 320–21
  constitutional status of 317
  creation and development of 320–23
  development of modern multi-party system 321–22
  digitalization and 333–34
  electoral history 198–99
  financial resources 328–29
  fragmentation 323
  functional aspects
  Green Party, rise of 7
  ideological aspects
  ideological change *see* ideology
  legal status of 317
  Liberal Party, in government 15
  longevity of Federal Government ruling coalition 195, 208
  membership 326–27
  municipalities *see* municipalities
  nationalist parties, rise of 7
  nationalization of party system 322–23
  new party politics, political system and 6–8
  objectives and orientation 330–32
  parliamentary party groups 179–80
  party electorate changes 120–22
  party system shifts in Federal Assembly 179
  polarization 325–26
  political integration, and 15
  populism and polarization, rise of 6–8
  professionalization 327–28
  prospects for 332–34
  state structure impact on 317–19
  Swiss People's Party, rise of 7
  volatility 324–25

weak position of 317–18
see also ideology
political representation
  authors' analytical approach to 391
  cantons *see* cantons
  choice of consensus or dissent 816–18
  Christian confessional/denominational representation 199–200
  consensus government as pillar of democracy 791
  consociationalism 197
  contextual changes (economic, institutional, and political) for 403
  Council of States election system 392, 393–94
  digital democracy
  digital democracy *see* digital democracy
  direct democracy *see* direct democracy
  distinctiveness of electoral system 391
  effectiveness of election campaigns 402–3, 417, 423, 424
  election campaigns 394–95
  election outcomes 397–99
  election turnout 395–97
  environmental protection organizations, right of appeal for 648–49
  federal system and institutions *see* federalism
  gender representation 199–200
  government by the people 796–98, 807
  interest group influence and involvement 187–88
  interest group influence and involvement in Federal Assembly 189
  interest groups *see* interest groups
  issue voting 400–2
  municipalities *see* municipalities
  National Council election system 392–93
  national elections 391
  national security policy, and 532
  party identification, voters' 399–400
  previous research on 403
  previous research on parliamentary elections 391
  proportional representation (proportionality rule) 26–27, 197
  public health and voter veto of reforms 725–26

representativeness enhancement in Federal Assembly, authors' proposals for 188
representativeness of Federal Assembly 188
results of elections 397–99
see also digital democracy; direct democracy
voter behaviour and choice 397–403
voter turnout 395–97
see also current challenges, issues, and solutions
political system
authors' conclusions as to 825
cantons *see* cantons
comparative perspective of 795–96
core features of 2–8
current book's contribution to research on 1–2
current challenges *see* current challenges, issues, and solutions
democratic innovation 5–6
diminution of *Sonderfall* (special case) status 1, 6–7
distinctiveness of 795
electoral system *see* electorate; political representation
electorate structure changes 120–25
federal system and institutions *see* Federal Government; federalism
global and European relationships, and 4–5
government by the people 796–98, 807
government for the people 798–807
ideological change *see* ideology
international politics *see* international position (economic and political)
links with economic structure 2, 5, 6–7
multicultural 'nation of will' basis of 2–4
municipalities *see* municipalities
national identity, and 8
new party politics, and 6–8
outdated perceptions of, need for correction of 1
proportional representation (proportionality rule) as to power-sharing 26–27
proportionality rule as to power-sharing 26–28
reasons for current book's study of 2–8

Sonderbund civil war (1847–8), consequences for 3–4, 15–16
structure of current book 9–10
success of 795, 808
tension between globalization and sovereignty 4–5
uniqueness of 1
population *see* social structure
populism *see* political parties
power-sharing *see* political integration
pre-primary education *see* education system
prices, consumer *see* economic structure
pride, national *see* ideology
primary education *see* education system
private associations *see* interest groups
private security service providers 532
productivity growth *see* economic policy
professionalization
Federal Assembly 185–86, 189
political parties 327–28
proportional representation *see* political representation
proportionality rule *see* political integration
protest movements 358
Protestantism *see* religion
public finances *see* economic structure; Federal Government
public health
actors involved in 716–18
cantonal autonomy 726
cost increases 721, 727
cost levels 714
current challenges for 714, 727–28
Federal implementation 726
Federal strategic management 728
Federal/cantonal division of tasks 716–17
financing of 714
first-stage health insurance reform 721
historical development of 719–24
interest groups and 725–26
key performance statistics 714
market competition within 717–18, 722
personal responsibility for 717–18
policy priorities 714–15
political factors as to policy reforms 725–26
preventative health reforms 723–24
private sector involvement 717–18

public health (*cont.*)
    public and private health insurance, introduction of 719–21
    public and private sector involvement 722
    public opinion on 714
    scope of 714
    second-stage partial health insurance reform 722
    self-organization approach 717–18
    slow transfer of competencies from cantons to Federal government 719
    voters and interest groups as veto players 725–26
public health insurance *see* public health
public opinion
    choice of consensus or dissent 816–18
    digital democracy and opinion formation 431, 438–40, 443
    direct democracy and opinion formation 421
    foreign policy 494–95, 500
    international position (economic and political) 107–8
    national security policy 531–32
    pride in democratic system 811
    public health 714
    support for promotion of democracy 811
public policy *see* governance (Federal public policy)

R
R&I *see* research, technology, and innovation
race *see* social integration
radical-right movements 361–63
railways *see* infrastructure policy
redistribution, social *see* equality policies
referendums *see* decision-making; direct democracy; Federal Constitution
refugees *see* migration
religion
    Catholic community's integration into political culture (1891–1918) 41–43
    confessional/denominational representation in Federal Government 199–200
    education system cleavages arising from 611–13
    minority rights (cultural and religious), integration policy and 690
    political Catholicism, political integration and 16–19
    Protestant/Catholic division, political integration and 15–19
research, technology, and innovation (R&I)
    actors involved in 627–30, 636
    aims of 624
    authors' analytical approach to 624–25
    current challenges for 637–39
    cybersecurity 534–35
    development of policy 625–27
    education policy and 624
    EU and 623, 633–34
    improvement in, scope for 636–37
    multi-level governance of 623, 630–33
    national control of 623
    other public policy areas in relation 624
    policy variation 627–30
    political innovation *see* political system
    R&I development landmarks 625–26
    R&I spending growth 635–36
    see also universities
responsibility, sense of *see* ideology
rights, civil *see* political culture
right-wing politics *see* political parties
road transport *see* infrastructure policy
Roman Catholicism *see* religion

S
Schmidt, Manfred G. 6
science *see* research, technology, and innovation
secondary education *see* education system
security policy *see* national security policy
small-state, identity as *see* foreign policy and relations
social assistance, social insurance *see* social policy
social integration
    non-ethnic concept of nation-state 28
    transition from class conflict to socio-economic integration 24–25
    see also citizenship
social movements
    anti-austerity movements 364–65

anti-nuclear movement 360
authors' analytical approach to 355
authors' research findings and
    explanations 366–67
comparative aspects 366
context (economic, institutional, and
    political) for arising of 356–57
countercultural movements 359, 361
criticism of government, level of 366–67
environmental movement 360
farmers' organizations 358
global justice movements 363–64
instrumental movements 359–60
labour movement 358
new social movements 359–61
people's criticism of government, level
    of 366–67
people's propensity for political
    activism 366
people's propensity for protest 366
previous research on 355, 366
protest movements 358
radical-right movements 361–63
squatters' movement 361
subcultural movements 359, 361
traditional movements 358
typology of 357–65
women's movement 361
social policy
    actors involved in 703–5
    authors' analytical approach to 697
    cautious approach to 695–96
    centrality of 695
    completion welfare state (1970s and
        1980s) 699–701
    concept of 695
    conflicts of cultural and economic
        interests 703–4
    coordination of 706–7
    current challenges for 709–10
    early attempts and failures
        (1889–1931) 698–99
    economic policy and 696
    employers and 704–5
    evaluation of 707–9
    expenditure 695, 696–97
    historical development of 697–702

increase in welfare state
    interventionism 701–2
interest organizations and 704–5
liberalization and 116–17, 127–28
organization of 705–7
origins of welfare state 697
politics of 695–96
post-1945 developments 699
public and private sector involvement 705
trade unions and 704–5
social structure
    class structure, political integration and 22–25
    core divisions in 16
    economic equality 74, 87–89
    economic growth, benefits of 90
    education and enculturation 605
    integration policy and see integration policy
    migration and see migration
    multiculturalism and democracy 818–21
    national security policy, and 532
    occupational structure changes 84–87, 91
    political representation see political
        representation
    population growth 73, 76–77
    population structure changes 90
    relative salience of sociocultural issues 125
    social movements see social movements
    socio-economic transformational shifts,
        2000–2020 73
    working class political structure, late
        development of 22–24
    see also employment
Sonderbund civil war (1847-8), political
    consequences 1–10
'*Sonderfall* rhetoric' 784
spatial planning
    actors involved in 650–51
    building permits 650
    cantonal master plans (CMPs) 650
    cantonal responsibility for 642
    characteristics of problems and policies 643
    communal land use plans (CLUPs) 650
    current challenges for 654–56
    decentralization of 642
    development stage 1: land law, local
        planning, and protection of
        agricultural land (1912–1950) 646

spatial planning (*cont.*)
   development stage 2: first cantonal laws and indirect demarcation of building zones (1950–1970) 646
   development stage 3: formulation of Federal Spatial Planning Policy (SPA) (1970–1980) 646–47
   development stage 4: cantonal and municipal SPA implementation (1980–2000) 647
   development stage 5: SPA revision (2000–2020) 647–48
   Federal sectoral and area plans 649
   function of 642
   governance and legislative framework 649–50
   historical development of 643–44, 646–48
   implementation of policy 642, 654
   'judicious and measured land use' principle 649
   municipality-level 642
   objectives 642
   part of infrastructure policy, as part 585–86
   policy objectives 642
   policy principles 649
   'rational land use' principle 649
   spatial planning policy defined 642
   zoning plans 649
squatters' movement 361
state interventionism *see* Federal Government
subcultural movements 359, 361
suburban areas *see* metropolitan areas
success of political system *see* political system
'*La Suisse n'existe pas*' *see* national identity
Swiss Federation
   core features of 140–41
   creation (1848) 140, 152, 158, 195, 235, 247
   old Confederation ('Orte'), and 235
   see also federalism
Swiss National Bank *see* economic structure
Swiss People's Party, rise of 7

T

taxation *see* Federal administration
technology *see* research, technology, and innovation
tertiary education *see* education system
town and country planning *see* spatial planning
towns *see* metropolitan areas
trade policy *see* economic structure
trade unions *see* employment; social policy
transphobia, equality policies against *see* education system; employment; family policy; gender equality policies
transport *see* infrastructure policy
trust *see* ideology

U

unemployment *see* employment; social policy
United Kingdom (UK), Brexit withdrawal from EU 514
United Nations (UN), membership of *see* foreign policy and relations
universities
   access to 610, 612, 613–14
   adults with degrees 80, 90, 118–19
   applied sciences, of 606, 613–14, 624, 628
   cantonal financing of 613–14, 823
   civil servants with degrees 310–11
   control of 611
   digital democracy, and 442
   environmental activism by students 360
   European rankings 97–98
   expansion of university education 80–82, 90, 613–14
   federal financing of 823
   federal universities, proposals for 607
   Gender Studies 762
   historical development of 605–6
   human rights, and 760
   immigrants with degrees 73, 79–80, 90
   international rankings 616, 618
   judges with degrees 221
   national cyber-security, and 534
   number of 612
   research and innovation by 624, 625–26, 628, 629–30, 632–33, 635–36, 638
   student (un-)success 610
   swissuniversities (umbrella organization) 626, 628, 762
   teacher education, of 613–14, 624, 628
   women graduates, contribution to economic growth 73

women university professors, slow increase in 762
urbanization and urban areas *see* metropolitan areas

V

vocational education and training (VET) *see* education system
voter, voting *see* digital democracy
voters, voting *see* direct democracy; elections; political representation

W

WEA (Armed Forces Development Programme) *see* national security policy
wealth *see* economic structure
WeCollect *see* direct democracy

welfare state *see* family policy; social policy
women (specific mentions)
    discrimination and equality *see* education system; employment; family policy; gender equality policies
    economic growth, and 73
    employment 73
    municipal executive representation of 269–70
    representation in Federal Government 199–200
    women's movement 361
work, workers *see* employment
working class *see* social structure

Z

zonal planning *see* spatial planning